SIXTH EDITION
Elementary and Middle School Mathematics
Teaching Developmentally

John A. Van de Walle
Virginia Commonwealth University

PEARSON

Boston   New York   San Francisco
Mexico City   Montreal   Toronto   London   Madrid   Munich   Paris
Hong Kong   Singapore   Tokyo   Cape Town   Sydney

Executive Editor: Stephen D. Dragin
Series Editor: Traci Mueller
Development Editor: Sonny Regelman
Editorial Assistant: Angela Pickard
Executive Marketing Manager: Krista Clark
Supplements Editor: Adam Whitehurst
Editorial–Production Service: Omegatype Typography, Inc.
Composition Buyer: Linda Cox
Manufacturing Buyer: Megan Cochran
Electronic Composition: Omegatype Typography, Inc.
Interior Design: Carol Somberg
Cover Administrator: Linda Knowles

For related titles and support materials, visit our online catalog at www.ablongman.com.

Between the time website information is gathered and then published, it is not unusual for some sites to have closed. Also, the transcription of URLs can result in typographical errors. The publisher would appreciate notification where these errors occur so that they may be corrected in subsequent editions.

Library of Congress Cataloging-in-Publication Data

Van de Walle, John A.
    Elementary and middle school mathematics : teaching developmentally / John A. Van de Walle.—6th ed.
        p.   cm.
    Includes bibliographical references and index.
    ISBN 0-205-48392-5
    1. Mathematics—Study and teaching (Elementary) 2. Mathematics—Study and teaching (Middle school) I. Title.

QA135.6 V36 2007
510.71'2—dc22   2005057485

Printed in the United States of America

10 9 8 7 6 5 4 3 2 1   RRD OH   11 10 09 08 07 06

Brief Contents

DETAILED CONTENTS   v

TO STUDENTS AND INSTRUCTORS FROM THE AUTHOR   xvii

TO THE INSTRUCTOR FROM THE AUTHOR   xxiii

SECTION I
Teaching Mathematics: Foundations and Perspectives 1

chapter **1**
Teaching Mathematics in the Era of the NCTM *Standards*   1

chapter **2**
Exploring What It Means to Do Mathematics   12

chapter **3**
Developing Understanding in Mathematics   22

chapter **4**
Teaching Through Problem Solving   37

chapter **5**
Planning in the Problem-Based Classroom   61

chapter **6**
Building Assessment into Instruction   78

chapter **7**
Teaching Mathematics Equitably to All Children   95

chapter **8**
Technology and School Mathematics   107

SECTION II
Development of Mathematical Concepts and Procedures 120

chapter **9**
Developing Early Number Concepts and Number Sense   120

chapter **10**
Developing Meanings for the Operations   143

chapter **11**
Helping Children Master the Basic Facts   165

chapter **12**
Whole-Number Place-Value Development   187

chapter **13**
Strategies for Whole-Number
Computation   216

chapter **14**
Computational Estimation with
Whole Numbers   245

chapter **15**
Algebraic Thinking: Generalizations,
Patterns, and Functions   259

chapter **16**
Developing Fraction Concepts   293

chapter **17**
Computation with Fractions   316

chapter **18**
Decimal and Percent Concepts and
Decimal Computation   333

chapter **19**
Proportional Reasoning   353

chapter **20**
Developing Measurement Concepts   374

chapter **21**
Geometric Thinking and
Geometric Concepts   407

chapter **22**
Concepts of Data
Analysis   452

chapter **23**
Exploring Concepts
of Probability   475

chapter **24**
Developing Concepts of Exponents,
Integers, and Real Numbers   492

appendix **A**
Principles and Standards
for School Mathematics:
Content Standards and Grade
Level Expectations   A-1

appendix **B**
Professional Standards
for Teaching Mathematics:
Teaching Standards   B-1

appendix **C**
Guide to Blackline Masters   C-1

REFERENCES   R-1

INDEX   I-1

Detailed Contents

TO STUDENTS AND INSTRUCTORS FROM THE AUTHOR xvii

TO THE INSTRUCTOR FROM THE AUTHOR xxiii

SECTION I

Teaching Mathematics: Foundations and Perspectives 1

The fundamental core of effective teaching of mathematics combines an understanding of how children learn, how to promote that learning by teaching through problem solving, and how to plan for and assess that learning on a daily basis. Introductory chapters in this section provide perspectives on trends in mathematics education and the process of doing mathematics and develop the core ideas of learning, teaching, planning, and assessment. Additional perspectives on mathematics for special children and the role of technology are also discussed.

chapter 1
Teaching Mathematics in the Era of the NCTM *Standards* 1

The Leadership of NCTM 1

Principles and Standards for School Mathematics 2
The Six Principles 2

A Pre-K-to-12 Perspective 3
The Five Content Standards 4
The Five Process Standards 4

The *Professional Standards for Teaching Mathematics* 5
Five Shifts in Classroom Environment 5
The Teaching Standards 6

The *Assessment Standards for School Mathematics* 6

Influences and Pressures on Reform 6
National and International Studies 6
State Standards 7
Curriculum 8

An Invitation to Learn and Grow 8

REFLECTIONS ON CHAPTER 1 9
Writing to Learn 9
For Discussion and Exploration 9
Recommendations for Further Reading 9

Standards-Based Curricula 10
Online Resources 10

chapter 2
Exploring What It Means to Do Mathematics 12

Contrasting Perceptions of School Mathematics 12
Traditional Views of Mathematics 12
Mathematics as a Science of Pattern and Order 13

What Does It Mean to Do Mathematics? 13
The Verbs of Doing Mathematics 13
What Is Basic in Mathematics? 14
An Environment for Doing Mathematics 14

An Invitation to Do Mathematics 14
Let's Do Some Mathematics! 14
No Answer Book 19
Some More Explorations 19

Helping Students Do Mathematics 20

REFLECTIONS ON CHAPTER 2 20
Writing to Learn 20
For Discussion and Exploration 21
Recommendations for Further Reading 21
Online Resources 21

chapter 3
Developing Understanding in Mathematics   22

A Constructivist View of Learning   22
  The Construction of Ideas   22
  Understanding   24
  Examples of Understanding   25
  Benefits of Relational Understanding   26
Concepts and Procedures   28
  Conceptual and Procedural Knowledge   28
  Interaction of Conceptual and Procedural
    Knowledge   28
Classroom Influences on Learning   28
  Reflective Thought   29
  Students Learning from Others   29
  The Role of Models in Developing
    Understanding   30
Teaching Developmentally   34
REFLECTIONS ON CHAPTER 3   34
  Writing to Learn   34
  For Discussion and Exploration   35
  Recommendations for Further Reading   35
  Online Resources   35

chapter 4
Teaching Through Problem Solving   37

**Problem Solving as a Principal Instructional
  Strategy**   37
  Problems and Tasks for Learning
    Mathematics   37
  An Illustration   38
  A Shift in Thinking About Mathematics
    Instruction   38
  The Value of Teaching with Problems   39
Examples of Problem-Based Tasks   39
  Conceptual Mathematics   39
  Procedures and Processes   40
A Three-Part Lesson Format   41
  The *Before* Phase of a Lesson   41
  Teacher Actions in the *Before* Phase   42
  The *During* Phase for a Lesson   44
  Teacher Actions in the *During* Phase   45
  The *After* Phase of a Lesson   46
  Teacher Actions in the *After* Phase   46
Designing and Selecting Effective Tasks   48
  Your Textbook   48
  Good Problems Have Multiple Entry Points   51
  Children's Literature   51

  Other Resources   52
  A Task Selection Guide   52
The Importance of Student Writing   53
Teaching Tips and Questions   53
  Let Students Do the Talking   53
  How Much to Tell and Not to Tell   54
  Frequently Asked Questions   56
Teaching About Problem Solving   57
  Strategies and Processes   57
Developing Problem-Solving Strategies   57
  Metacognition   58
  Disposition   58
REFLECTIONS ON CHAPTER 4   59
  Writing to Learn   59
  For Discussion and Exploration   59
  Recommendations for Further Reading   59
  Online Resources   60

chapter 5
Planning in the Problem-Based Classroom   61

Planning a Problem-Based Lesson   61
  Sample Lessons   63
  Variations of the Three-Part Lesson   63
Dealing with Diversity   64
  Plan for Multiple Entry Points   64
  Plan Differentiated Tasks   65
  Use Heterogeneous Groupings   65
  Make Accommodations and Modifications   65
  Listen Carefully to Students   66
**Planning Considerations for English Language
  Learners**   67
Drill or Practice?   67
  New Definitions of Drill and Practice   67
  What Drill Provides   67
  What Practice Provides   69
  When Is Drill Appropriate?   69
  Kids Who Don't Get It   69
Homework   70
  Practice as Homework   70
  Drill as Homework   70
The Role of the Textbook   70
  How Are Textbooks Developed?   70
  Teacher's Editions   71
  Two-Page Lesson Format   71
  Suggestions for Textbook Use   71

■ **EXPANDED LESSON:** Fixed Areas   72

■ **EXPANDED LESSON:** Two More Than/
  Two Less Than   74

REFLECTIONS ON CHAPTER 5   76

Writing to Learn   76

For Discussion and Exploration   76

Recommendations for Further Reading   76

Online Resources   77

chapter **6**

Building Assessment into Instruction   **78**

Blurring the Line Between Instruction and Assessment   78
   What Is Assessment?   78
   The Assessment Standards   78
   Purposes of Assessment   79

What Should Be Assessed?   80
   Concepts and Procedures   80
   Mathematical Processes   80
   Disposition   80

Assessment Tasks Are Learning Tasks   80
   Examples of Assessment Tasks   81
   Thoughts About Assessment Tasks   82

Rubrics and Performance Indicators: Scoring—Not Grading   82
   Simple Rubrics   82
   Performance Indicators   83
   Student Involvement with Rubrics   84

Using Observation in Assessment   84
   Anecdotal Notes   85
   An Observation Rubric   85
   Checklists or Forms for Individuals   85
   Checklists for Full Classes   86

Writing and Journals   86
   The Value of Writing   86
   Journals   87
   Writing Prompts and Ideas   87
   Journals for Early Learners   88
   Student Self-Assessment   89

Tests   90

Improving Performance on High-Stakes Tests   90
   Avoid Teaching to the Test   91
   Teach Fundamental Concepts and Processes   91
   Test-Taking Strategies   92

Grading   92
   Confronting the Myth   92
   Grading Issues   92

REFLECTIONS ON CHAPTER 6   93

Writing to Learn   93

For Discussion and Exploration   94

Recommendations for Further Reading   94

Online Resources   94

chapter **7**

Teaching Mathematics Equitably to All Children   **95**

Mathematics for All Children   95
   Diversity in Today's Classroom   95
   The Goal of Equitable Instruction   96
   Negative Effects of Tracking and Homogeneous Grouping   96
   Instructional Principles for Diverse Learners   96

Specific Learning Disabilities   96
   A Perspective on Learning Disabilities   97
   Adaptations for Specific Learning Disabilities   97

Intellectual Disabilities   98
   Modifications in Instruction   98
   Modifications in Curriculum   99

Culturally and Linguistically Diverse Students   99
   Culturally Relevant Mathematics Instruction   99
   Ethnomathematics   100
   English Language Learners (ELLs)   100
   Specific Strategies for Teaching Mathematics to English Language Learners   101

From Gender Bias to Gender Equity   102
   Possible Causes of Gender Inequity   102
   Working Toward Gender Equity: What Can Be Done?   103

Providing for the Mathematically Promising   103
   Identification of Mathematically Promising Students   103
   Acceleration, Enrichment, and Depth   104

REFLECTIONS ON CHAPTER 7   105

Writing to Learn   105

For Discussion and Exploration   105

Recommendations for Further Reading   105

Online Resources   106

chapter **8**

Technology and School Mathematics   **107**

Calculators in the Mathematics Classroom   107
   Benefits of Calculator Use   107
   Addressing Myths and Fears About Using Calculators   108
   Calculators for Every Student, Every Day   109

Graphing Calculators   109
  What the Graphing Calculator Offers   109
  Electronic Data Collection   110

The Computer as a Tool in Mathematics   111
  Electronic Manipulatives for Numeration   111
  Geometry Tools   112
  Probability and Data Analysis Tools   113
  Function Graphers   114

Instructional Software   114
  Concept Instruction   114
  Problem Solving   114
  Drill   115

Guidelines for Selecting and Using Software   115
  How to Select Software   115
  Guidelines for Using Software   116

**Mathematics Education Resources
  on the Internet**   116

REFLECTIONS ON CHAPTER 8   117
  Writing to Learn   117
  For Discussion and Exploration   117
  Recommendations for Further Reading   117
  Online Resources   118

SECTION II

Development of Mathematical Concepts and Procedures   120

This section serves as the application of the core ideas of Section I. Here you will find chapters on every major area of content in the K–8 mathematics curriculum. Numerous problem-based activities to engage students are interwoven with a discussion of the mathematical content and how children develop their understanding of that content. At the outset of each chapter, you will find a listing of "Big Ideas," the mathematical umbrella for the chapter. Also included are ideas for incorporating children's literature, technology, and assessment. These chapters are designed to help you develop pedagogical strategies and to serve as a resource for your teaching.

chapter **9**

**Developing Early
Number Concepts and
Number Sense**   120

▼ **BIG IDEAS**   120

▲ **MATHEMATICS CONTENT**
△▲ **CONNECTIONS**   120

**Number Development in Pre-K and
  Kindergarten**   121
  The Relationships of More, Less, and Same   121
  Early Counting   122
  Numeral Writing and Recognition   122
  Counting On and Counting Back   123

Early Number Sense   124

Relationships Among Numbers 1 Through 10   124
  A Collection of Number Relationships   125
  Spatial Relationships: Patterned Set
    Recognition   125

One and Two More, One and Two Less   126
Anchoring Numbers to 5 and 10   127
Part-Part-Whole Relationships   129
Dot Card Activities   133

■ **INVESTIGATIONS IN NUMBER, DATA, AND
  SPACE:** Grade K, *How Many in All?*   135

Relationships for Numbers 10 to 20   135
  A Pre-Place-Value Relationship with 10   136
  Extending More and Less Relationships   136
  Double and Near-Double Relationships   136

Number Sense and the Real World   137
  Estimation and Measurement   137
  More Connections   137
  Graphs   138

■ **LITERATURE CONNECTIONS**   138
  Anno's Counting House   139
  The Very Hungry Caterpillar   139
  Two Ways to Count to Ten   139

Extensions to Early Mental Mathematics   140

REFLECTIONS ON CHAPTER 9   141

Writing to Learn   141

For Discussion and Exploration   141

Recommendations for Further Reading   141

Online Resources   142

chapter **10**
Developing Meanings for the Operations   143

▼ **BIG IDEAS**   143

▲ **MATHEMATICS CONTENT CONNECTIONS**   143

Addition and Subtraction Problem Structures   144

Examples of Problems for Each Structure   144

Reflections on the Four Structures   145

Teaching Addition and Subtraction   146

Using Contextual Problems   146

Using Model-Based Problems   147

Comparison Models   149

The Order Property and the Zero Property   149

■ **INVESTIGATIONS IN NUMBER, DATA, AND SPACE:** Grade 2, *Coins, Coupons, and Combinations*   151

Problem Structures for Multiplication and Division   152

Examples of Problems for Each Structure   152

Reflections on the Multiplicative Structures   153

Teaching Multiplication and Division   154

Using Contextual Problems   154

Remainders   154

Using Models-Based Problems   155

Multiplication and Division Activities   155

Useful Multiplication and Division Properties   157

Strategies for Solving Contextual Problems   158

Analyzing Context Problems   158

Two-Step Problems   160

Two Additional Concepts of Multiplication   161

Combinations Problems   161

Product-of-Measures Problems   161

■ **LITERATURE CONNECTIONS**   162

How Many Snails?   162

More Than One   162

Each Orange Had 8 Slices   162

REFLECTIONS ON CHAPTER 10   163

Writing to Learn   163

For Discussion and Exploration   163

Recommendations for Further Reading   163

Online Resources   164

chapter **11**
Helping Children Master the Basic Facts   165

▼ **BIG IDEAS**   165

▲ **MATHEMATICS CONTENT CONNECTIONS**   165

Approaches to Fact Mastery   165

Pros and Cons of Each Approach   166

Guiding Strategy Development   166

Drill of Efficient Methods   167

Strategies for Addition Facts   168

One-More-Than and Two-More-Than Facts   168

Facts with Zero   169

Doubles   169

Near-Doubles   170

Make-Ten Facts   170

A Generic Task   172

Other Strategies and the Last Six Facts   172

Strategies for Subtraction Facts   174

Subtraction as Think-Addition   174

Subtraction Facts with Sums to 10   174

The 36 "Hard" Subtraction Facts: Sums Greater Than 10   174

Strategies for Multiplication Facts   177

Doubles   177

Fives Facts   178

Zeros and Ones   178

Nifty Nines   178

Helping Facts   179

Division Facts and "Near Facts"   181

■ **INVESTIGATIONS IN NUMBER, DATA, AND SPACE:** Grade 3, *Things That Come in Groups*   182

Effective Drill   183

When and How to Drill   183

What About Timed Tests?   183

Fact Remediation with Upper-Grade Students   184

Facts: No Barrier to Good Mathematics   185

REFLECTIONS ON CHAPTER 11   185

Writing to Learn   185

For Discussion and Exploration   185

Recommendations for Further Reading   186

Online Resources   186

chapter **12**
Whole-Number Place-Value Development   187

▼ **BIG IDEAS**   187

▲▲ **MATHEMATICS CONTENT CONNECTIONS**   187

Pre-Base-Ten Concepts   188
Children's Pre-Base-Ten View of Number   188
Quantity Tied to Counts by Ones   188

Basic Ideas of Place Value   188
Integration with Base-Ten Groupings with Counts by Ones   188
The Role of Counting in Constructing Base-Ten Ideas   189
Integration of Groupings with Words   189
Integration of Groupings with Place-Value Notation   190

Models for Place Value   191
Base-Ten Models and the Ten-Makes-One Relationship   191
Groupable Models   191
Pregrouped or Trading Models   192

Developing Base-Ten Concepts   192
Grouping Activities   193
The Strangeness of *Ones, Tens,* and *Hundreds*   195
Grouping Tens to Make 100   195

■ **INVESTIGATIONS IN NUMBER, DATA, AND SPACE:** Grade 1, *Number Games and Story Problems*   196
Equivalent Representations   197

Oral and Written Names for Numbers   198
Two-Digit Number Names   198
Three-Digit Number Names   199
Written Symbols   199

Patterns and Relationships with Multidigit Numbers   201
The Hundreds Chart   201
Relationships with Landmark Numbers   204
Number Relationships for Addition and Subtraction   206
Connections to Real-World Ideas   209

Helping Children Work with Money   209
Coin Recognition and Values   209
Using Coin Values   210
Making Change   210

Numbers Beyond 1000   211
Extending the Place-Value System   211
Conceptualizing Large Numbers   212

■ **LITERATURE CONNECTIONS**   213
Moira's Birthday   213
How to Count Like a Martian   213
The King's Commissioners   213
A Million Fish . . . More or Less   213

REFLECTIONS ON CHAPTER 12   214
Writing to Learn   214
For Discussion and Exploration   214
Recommendations for Further Reading   214
Online Resources   215

chapter **13**
Strategies for Whole-Number Computation   216

▼ **BIG IDEAS**   216

▲▲ **MATHEMATICS CONTENT CONNECTIONS**   216

Toward Computational Fluency   217
Direct Modeling   217
Invented Strategies   218
Contrasts with Traditional Algorithms   218
Benefits of Invented Strategies   219
Mental Computation   219
Traditional Algorithms   220

Development of Student-Invented Strategies   220
Integrate Computation with Place Value and Fact Development   221
Use Story Problems Frequently   221
Use the Three-Part Lesson Format   221
Record Students' Progress   221

Invented Strategies for Addition and Subtraction   222
Adding and Subtracting Single Digits   222
Adding and Subtracting Tens and Hundreds   223
Adding Two-Digit Numbers   223
Subtracting by Counting Up   223
Take-Away Subtraction   225
Extensions and Challenges   226

Traditional Algorithms for Addition and Subtraction   226
The Addition Algorithm   226
The Subtraction Algorithm   227

Invented Strategies for Multiplication   228
Useful Representations   229
Multiplication by a Single-Digit Multiplier   230
Using Multiples of 10 and 100   231
Two-Digit Multipliers   231

■ **INVESTIGATIONS IN NUMBER, DATA, AND SPACE:** Grade 4, *Packages and Groups*   233

The Traditional Algorithm for Multiplication 234
  One-Digit Multipliers 234
  Two-Digit Multipliers 235

Invented Strategies for Division 236
  Missing-Factor Strategies 237
  Cluster Problems 238

The Traditional Algorithm for Division 238
  One-Digit Divisors 238
  Two-Digit Divisors 239

■ LITERATURE CONNECTIONS 241
  Cookies 242
  Is a Blue Whale the Biggest Thing There Is? 242

REFLECTIONS ON CHAPTER 13 242
  Writing to Learn 242
  For Discussion and Exploration 243
  Recommendations for Further Reading 243
  Online Resources 244

chapter **14**
Computational Estimation with Whole Numbers 245

▼ BIG IDEAS 245

▲ MATHEMATICS CONTENT
▲▲ CONNECTIONS 245

Introducing Computational Estimation 245
  Understanding Computational Estimation 246
  Choosing a Form of Computation 246
  Suggestions for Estimation Instruction 246
  Estimation Without Estimates 247

Estimations from Invented Strategies 248
  Stop Before the Details 248
  Cluster Problems 249

■ INVESTIGATIONS IN NUMBER, DATA, AND
  SPACE: Grade 5, *Building on Numbers You Know* 250

Computational Estimation Strategies 250
  Front-End Methods 251
  Rounding Methods 251
  Using Compatible Numbers 253

Estimation Exercises 254
  Calculator Activities 254
  More Estimation Activities 256

Estimating with Fractions, Decimals, and Percents 256

■ LITERATURE CONNECTIONS 257
  The Twelve Circus Rings 257
  The 329th Friend 257

REFLECTIONS ON CHAPTER 14 257
  Writing to Learn 257
  For Discussion and Exploration 258
  Recommendations for Further Reading 258
  Online Resources 258

chapter **15**
Algebraic Thinking: Generalizations, Patterns, and Functions 259

▼ BIG IDEAS 259

▲ MATHEMATICS CONTENT
▲▲ CONNECTIONS 259

Algebraic Thinking 260

Generalization in Number and Operations 260
  The Meaning of the Equal Sign 260
  Variables in Equations 262

**Making Structure in the Number System
  Explicit** 266
  Making Conjectures 266
  "Proving" Conjectures 266
  Odd and Even Relationships 267

Repeating Patterns 268

Charts and Other Number Patterns 270
  Patterns and the Hundreds Chart 270
  Number Patterns 270

Growing Patterns—A First Look at Functions 271
  Searching for Relationships 272
  General Function Statements from Patterns 273
  Graphing the Patterns 274

Function Concepts and Representations 275
  Five Representations of Functions 275

■ INVESTIGATIONS IN NUMBER, DATA, AND
  SPACE: Grade 5, *Patterns of Change* 276
  Connect Different Representations 280
  Use Technology 280

Explorations with Functional Relationships 281
  Relationships Found in the Real World 281
  Proportional Situations 282

■ CONNECTED MATHEMATICS: Grade 7, *Variables
  and Patterns* 283
  Functions and Measurement 284
  Maximum/Minimum Problems 284
  Functions from Scatter Plot Data 285
  Fun Experiments 286

Generalizations About Functions 287
  Analysis of Rate of Change 287
  Linear Functions 288

Mathematical Modeling   290

■ LITERATURE CONNECTIONS   290

Pattern   290
Anno's Mysterious Multiplying Jar   290
Anno's Magic Seeds   290

REFLECTIONS ON CHAPTER 15   291
Writing to Learn   291
For Discussion and Exploration   291
Recommendations for Further Reading   291
Online Resources   292

chapter **16**
Developing Fraction Concepts   293

▼ BIG IDEAS   293

▲ MATHEMATICS CONTENT CONNECTIONS   293

Sharing and the Concept of Fractional Parts   294
Sharing Tasks   294
Sharing Tasks and Fraction Language   295

Models for Fractions   295
Region or Area Models   295
Length or Measurement Models   295
Set Models   297

From Fractional Parts to Fraction Symbols   297
Fractional Parts and Words   297
Understanding Fraction Symbols   298

Fraction Number Sense   303
Benchmarks of Zero, One-Half, and One   303
Thinking About Which Is More?   304
Estimation   306

■ INVESTIGATIONS IN NUMBER, DATA, AND SPACE: Grade 4, *Different Shapes, Equal Pieces*   307

Equivalent-Fraction Concepts   308
Concepts Versus Rules   308
Equivalent-Fraction Concepts   309
Developing an Equivalent-Fraction Algorithm   311

■ LITERATURE CONNECTIONS   313

The Doorbell Rang   313
Gator Pie   313
The Man Who Counted: A Collection of Mathematical Adventures   313

REFLECTIONS ON CHAPTER 16   313
Writing to Learn   313
For Discussion and Exploration   314

Recommendations for Further Reading   314
Online Resources   315

chapter **17**
Computation with Fractions   316

▼ BIG IDEAS   316

▲ MATHEMATICS CONTENT CONNECTIONS   316

Number Sense and Fraction Algorithms   316
The Dangerous Rush to Rules   317
A Problem-Based, Number Sense Approach   317

Addition and Subtraction   317
Informal Exploration   317
The Myth of Common Denominators   319
Developing the Algorithm   319
Estimation and Simple Methods   321

■ CONNECTED MATHEMATICS: Grade 6, *Bits and Pieces II: Investigation 4*   322

Multiplication   322
Informal Exploration   322
Developing the Algorithm   324
Mental Techniques and Estimation   326

Division   326
Informal Exploration: Partition Concept   326
Informal Exploration: Measurement Concept   328
Developing the Algorithms   329

REFLECTIONS ON CHAPTER 17   331
Writing to Learn   331
For Discussion and Exploration   332
Recommendations for Further Reading   332
Online Resources   332

chapter **18**
Decimal and Percent Concepts and Decimal Computation   333

▼ BIG IDEAS   333

▲ MATHEMATICS CONTENT CONNECTIONS   333

Connecting Two Different Representational Systems   333
Base-Ten Fractions   334
Extending the Place-Value System   335
Making the Fraction–Decimal Connection   337

Developing Decimal Number Sense   338
Familiar Fractions Connected to Decimals   338
Approximation with a Nice Fraction   340

Ordering Decimal Numbers   341
Other Fraction–Decimal Equivalents   342

Introducing Percents   343
A Third Operator System   343
Realistic Percent Problems   344

Computation with Decimals   346
The Role of Estimation   346
Addition and Subtraction   347
Multiplication   348
Division   348

■ LITERATURE CONNECTIONS   349

The Phantom Tollbooth   350

■ **CONNECTED MATHEMATICS:** Grade 6, *Bits and Pieces II: Investigation 6*   350

REFLECTIONS ON CHAPTER 18   351
Writing to Learn   351
For Discussion and Exploration   351
Recommendations for Further Reading   351
Online Resources   352

chapter **19**
Proportional Reasoning   353

▼ BIG IDEAS   353

▲ **MATHEMATICS CONTENT CONNECTIONS**   353

Ratios, Proportions, and Proportional Reasoning   353
Examples of Ratios in Different Contexts   354
Proportions   354
Proportional Reasoning   355
Additive Versus Multiplicative Situations   355

Informal Activities to Develop Proportional Reasoning   357
Identifying Multiplicative Relationships   357
Equivalent-Ratio Selections   358
Comparing Ratios   359
Scaling with Ratio Tables   361
Construction and Measurement Activities   363

■ **CONNECTED MATHEMATICS:** Grade 7, *Comparing and Scaling*   366

Solving Proportions   366
Within and Between Ratios   366
An Informal Approach   367
The Cross-Product Algorithm   368
Activities That Require Proportions   369

Percent Problems as Proportions   370
Equivalent Fractions as Proportions   370

■ LITERATURE CONNECTIONS   371

If You Hopped Like a Frog   371
Counting on Frank   372
The Borrowers   372

REFLECTIONS ON CHAPTER 19   372
Writing to Learn   372
For Discussion and Exploration   373
Recommendations for Further Reading   373
Online Resources   373

chapter **20**
Developing Measurement Concepts   374

▼ BIG IDEAS   374

▲ **MATHEMATICS CONTENT CONNECTIONS**   374

The Meaning and Process of Measuring   375
Developing Measurement Concepts and Skills   376
A General Plan of Instruction   376
Informal Units and Standard Units: Reasons for Using Each   377
The Role of Estimation in Learning Measurement   378
The Approximate Nature of Measurement   378

Measuring Length   378
Comparison Activities   378
Using Units of Length   379
Two Units and Fractional Parts of Units   380
Making and Using Rulers   381

Measuring Area   382
Comparison Activities   382

■ **INVESTIGATIONS IN NUMBER, DATA, AND SPACE:** Grade 3, *From Paces to Feet*   383

Using Units of Area   384
Using Grids   386
Area and Perimeter   386

Measuring Volume and Capacity   387
Comparison Activities   387
Using Units of Volume and Capacity   388
Making and Using Measuring Cups   389

Measuring Weight and Mass   389
Making Comparisons   389
Using Units of Weight or Mass   390
Making and Using a Scale   390

Measuring Time   390
Comparison of Durations   390
Clock Reading   390

Related Concepts   391
Elapsed Time   392

Measuring Angles   392
Comparing Angles   392
Using Units of Angular Measure   392
Making a Protractor   393

Introducing Standard Units   394
Instructional Goals   394
Important Standard Units and Relationships   396

Estimating Measures   397
Techniques of Measurement Estimation   397
Tips for Teaching Estimation   398
Measurement Estimation Activities   398

Developing Formulas for Area and Volume   398
Common Difficulties   399
The Area of Rectangles, Parallelograms, Triangles, and Trapezoids   399
Circle Formulas   402
Volumes of Common Solid Shapes   402
Reviewing the Formulas   404

■ **LITERATURE CONNECTIONS**   404

How Big Is a Foot?   404
Jim and the Beanstalk   404
Counting on Frank   404
Inchworm and a Half   405
8,000 Stones   405

REFLECTIONS ON CHAPTER 20   405
Writing to Learn   405
For Discussion and Exploration   405
Recommendations for Further Reading   406
Online Resources   406

chapter **21**
Geometric Thinking and Geometric Concepts   407

▼ **BIG IDEAS**   407

▲▲▲ **MATHEMATICS CONTENT CONNECTIONS**   407

Geometry Goals for Students   408
Spatial Sense and Geometric Reasoning   408
Geometric Content   408

The Development of Geometric Thinking   408
The van Hiele Levels of Geometric Thought   409
Characteristics of the van Hiele Levels   412
Implications for Instruction   413
Task Selection and Levels of Thought   414

Learning About Shapes and Properties   414
Shapes and Properties for Level-0 Thinkers   414

■ **INVESTIGATIONS IN NUMBER, DATA, AND SPACE:** Grade 1, *Quilt Squares and Block Towns*   417
Shapes and Properties for Level-1 Thinkers   420
Shapes and Properties for Level-2 Thinkers   427

Learning About Transformations   431
Transformations for Level-0 Thinkers   431
Transformations for Level-1 Thinkers   433
Transformations for Level-2 Thinkers   435

Learning About Location   437
Location for Level-0 Thinkers   437

■ **CONNECTED MATHEMATICS:** Grade 8, *Kaleidoscopes, Hubcaps, and Mirrors*   439

Location for Level-1 Thinkers   440
Location for Level-2 Thinkers   442

Learning About Visualization   443
Visualization for Level-0 Thinkers   443
Visualization for Level-1 Thinkers   445
Visualization for Level-2 Thinkers   447

Assessment of Geometric Goals   449
Clarifying Your Geometry Objectives   449

REFLECTIONS ON CHAPTER 21   450
Writing to Learn   450
For Discussion and Exploration   450
Recommendations for Further Reading   450
Online Resources   451

chapter **22**
Concepts of Data Analysis   452

▼ **BIG IDEAS**   452

▲▲▲ **MATHEMATICS CONTENT CONNECTIONS**   452

Gathering Data to Answer Questions   453
Ideas for Questions and Data   453
Other Sources of Information   454

Classification and Data Analysis   454
Attribute Materials   454

■ **INVESTIGATIONS IN NUMBER, DATA, AND SPACE:** Grade 5, *Data: Kids, Cats, and Ads*   455

Activities with Attribute Materials   455

The Shape of Data   458

Graphical Representations   458
Cluster Graphs   459
Bar Graphs and Tally Charts   459
Stem-and-Leaf Plots   460
Continuous Data Graphs   461
Circle Graphs   463

Descriptive Statistics   464
   Averages   464
      Understanding the Mean: Two Concepts   464

Distribution of Data: Box-and-Whisker Plots   467

Scatter Plots and Relationships   469
   Scatter Plots   469
   Best-Fit Lines   470
      Thinking About Functional Relationships   471

Technology or By-Hand Methods   471

■ LITERATURE CONNECTIONS   472

   The Phantom Tollbooth   472
   The Best Vacation Ever   472
   Frog and Toad Are Friends   472
   Incredible Comparisons   472

REFLECTIONS ON CHAPTER 22   473
   Writing to Learn   473
   For Discussion and Exploration   473
   Recommendations for Further Reading   473
   Online Resources   474

chapter **23**
Exploring Concepts of Probability   475

▼ BIG IDEAS   475

▲ MATHEMATICS CONTENT CONNECTIONS   475

Probability on a Continuum   476
   The Probability Continuum   478

Theoretical Versus Experimental Probability   479
   Theoretical Probability   480
   Experimental Probability   480
   The Law of Large Numbers   481
   Implications for Instruction   483

Sample Spaces and Computing Theoretical Probabilities   483
   Independent Events   484
   Theoretical Probabilities with an Area Model   485
   Dependent Events   486

Simulations   486

■ LITERATURE CONNECTIONS   489

   Do You Wanna Bet? Your Chance to Find Out About Probability   489
   My Little Sister Ate One Hare   490
   Lotteries: Who Wins, Who Loses   490

REFLECTIONS ON CHAPTER 23   490
   Writing to Learn   490
   For Discussion and Exploration   490

Recommendations for Further Reading   491
Online Resources   491

chapter **24**
Developing Concepts of Exponents, Integers, and Real Numbers   492

▼ BIG IDEAS   492

▲ MATHEMATICS CONTENT CONNECTIONS   492

Large Numbers, Small Numbers, and Exponents   492
   Exponents   492
   Calculators and Notation   493
   Very Large Numbers   494
   Representation of Large Numbers: Scientific Notation   494
   Negative Exponents   495

■ CONNECTED MATHEMATICS: Grade 8, *Growing, Growing, Growing: Exponential Relationships*   496

   Very Small Numbers   497

Integer Concepts   497
   Intuitive Models of Signed Quantities   497
   Mathematical Definition of Negative Numbers   498

Operations with Integers   498
   Two Models for Integer Operations   498
   Which Model to Use   499

A Problem-Solving Approach for Integers   499
   Addition and Subtraction   499
   Multiplication and Division   502
   Absolute Value   503

Rational Numbers   504
   Fractions as Indicated Division   504
   Fractions as Rational Numbers   504

Real Numbers   505
   Introducing the Concept of Roots   505
   Discussing Real Numbers   506

■ LITERATURE CONNECTIONS   507

   The Number Devil   507
   The Phantom Tollbooth   507
   In the Next Three Seconds   507
   Math Curse   508

REFLECTIONS ON CHAPTER 24   508
   Writing to Learn   508
   For Discussion and Exploration   508
   Recommendations for Further Reading   508
   Online Resources   509

appendix **A**
**Principles and Standards
for School Mathematics:
Content Standards and
Grade Level Expectations** **A-1**

appendix **B**
**Professional Standards for
Teaching Mathematics:
Teaching Standards** **B-1**

appendix **C**
**Guide to Blackline
Masters** **C-1**

REFERENCES **R-1**

INDEX **I-1**

To Students and Instructors from the Author

Learning is not the result of development; learning is development. It requires invention and self-organization on the part of the learner. Thus teachers need to allow learners to raise their own questions, generate their own hypotheses and models as possibilities, and test them for viability.

—*Fosnot (1996, p. 29)*

What is basic in mathematics is as simple as this: Math makes sense! Every child in his or her own way can come to believe this simple truth. More important, every child can come to believe that he or she is capable of making sense of mathematics. Every child should leave school confident in his or her ability to understand and do mathematics.

This is the goal of *Elementary and Middle School Mathematics*—to help both you and your students come to believe that math makes sense and that you are capable of making sense of it yourself. As the quotation from Catherine Fosnot suggests, students will have to develop this understanding themselves. Their understanding and, thus, their confidence will grow as a result of being engaged in the doing of mathematics. The subtitle of this book, *Teaching Developmentally*, refers to engaging students where you find them so that they can create or develop new ideas that they can use and understand—so they can see that math makes sense through their own eyes and can believe it because they can do it.

Research in mathematics education has consistently found that understanding and skills are best developed when students are allowed to wrestle with new ideas, to create and defend solutions to problems, and to participate in a mathematical community of learners. This student-centered, problem-based approach to learning is a central theme of this book.

You may be surprised to find that your instructor does not "cover" much more than half of the book. In fact, no course can completely prepare you for all you need to know to help children learn mathematics. However, this book has always been more than a textbook. It is a guide for your ongoing learning as you continue your work with children. For each strand of the mathematics curriculum, you will find a discussion of how children develop that mathematics along with tasks and activities for helping students learn. Integrated with this discussion you will find a development of the mathematics content you need to be an effective teacher.

Learning how best to help children believe that mathematics makes sense and that they themselves can make sense of mathematics is an exciting endeavor and a lifelong process. It requires the knowledge gained from research, the wisdom shared by professional colleagues, and the insightful ideas that come from your own daily experiences with students. I hope that this book will assist you on this fantastic journey.

Believe in kids! Allow them to think, to struggle, and to reason with new ideas as together you find the excitement that happens when mathematics makes sense.

John Van de Walle

What You Will Find in This Book

If you look at the table of contents, you will see that the chapters are separated into two distinct sections. The first section of eight chapters deals with important ideas that cross the boundaries of specific areas of content. The second section of 16 chapters offers teaching suggestions for every major topic in the K–8 curriculum. Chapters 3 and 4 are the most important. There you will learn about a constructivist view of learning, how that is applied to learning mathematics, and what it means to teach through problem solving. Chapter 5 will help you translate these ideas of how children best learn mathematics into the lessons you will be teaching. Here you will find practical perspective on planning effective lessons for all children, on the value of drill and practice, and other issues. Sample lesson plans are found at the end of this chapter. Chapter 6 explores the integration of assessment with instruction to best assist student learning.

Surrounding these central ideas are four chapters offering perspective on the challenging task of helping children learn mathematics. It is important to know where mathematics is going and why so that you will know how to play a professional role in that endeavor. It is also important to have a feel for the discipline of mathematics—

to know what it means to "do mathematics." The first two chapters address these issues.

In Chapter 7, you will read about working with children whose needs are special, whether they are English language learners or gifted or have learning disabilities.

Chapter 8 provides perspectives on the issues surrounding technology in the teaching of mathematics. A strong case is made for the use of calculators at all grade levels. Guidance is offered for the selection and use of computer software, and suggestions are made to help you find valuable resources on the Internet.

Each chapter of Section II provides a perspective of the mathematical content, how children best learn that content, and numerous suggestions for problem-based activities to engage children in the development of good mathematics. The problem-based tasks for students are integrated with the text; they are not added on. Reflecting on the activities as you read can help you think about the mathematics from the perspective of the child. Read them along with the text, not as an aside. Like children, become actively engaged in *your* learning *about children learning* mathematics.

Some Special Features of This Text

By just flipping through the book you will notice lots of section headings, lots of figures, and various icons and special features. All are there to make the book more useful as both a textbook and as a resource. Here are a few things to look for.

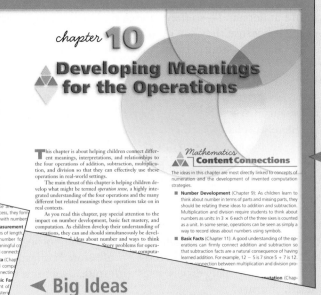

Mathematics Content Connections

Following the Big Ideas lists are brief descriptions of other content areas in mathematics that are related to the content of the current chapter. It is offered to help you be more aware of the potential interaction of content as you plan lessons, diagnose students' difficulties, and learn more yourself about the mathematics you are teaching.

◄ Big Ideas

Much of the literature espousing a student-centered approach suggests that teachers plan their instruction around "big ideas" rather than tiny skills or concepts. Near the start of each chapter in Section II you will find a list of the key mathematical ideas associated with the chapter. Teachers find these lists helpful for quickly getting a picture of the mathematics they are teaching.

Activities ➤

The numerous activities found in every chapter of Section II have always been an integral part of the book. Most of these are clearly framed in a box with a title. Other ideas are described directly in the text or in the illustrations. Every activity is a problem-based task as described in Chapter 4. Each one is designed to engage students in doing mathematics.

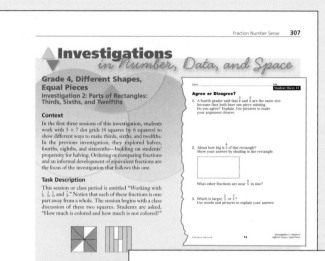

◀ Investigations in Number, Data, and Space and Connected Mathematics Features

In almost every chapter of Section II you will find a feature describing an activity from the standards-based curriculum *Investigations in Number, Data, and Space* (an elementary curriculum) or *Connected Mathematics* (a middle school curriculum). The page includes a description of an activity in the program as well as the context of the unit in which it is found. The main purpose of this feature is to acquaint you with these materials and to demonstrate how the spirit of the NCTM *Standards* and the constructivist theory espoused in this book have been translated into existing commercial curricula.

Assessment Notes ➤

Assessment should be an integral part of instruction. Similarly, it makes sense to think about what to be listening for (assessing) as you read about different areas of content development. Throughout the content chapters, you will see assessment icons indicating a short description of things to be looking for as you teach this material. Reading these assessment notes as you read the text can also help you understand how best to help your students.

◄ Literature Connections

Most of the chapters in Section II contain a Literature Connections section. In each of these sections, children's literature titles are suggested with a brief description of how the mathematics of the chapter can be profitably built on the stories. Though certainly not a comprehensive listing of potential literature, these sections will get you started using this exciting vehicle for teaching mathematics.

◄ NCTM Correlations

Throughout nearly every chapter, you will see an icon indicating a reference to NCTM's *Principles and Standards for School Mathematics*. The notes typically consist of a quotation from the *Standards* and/or a summary of what the *Standards* say about a particular topic. These notes point explicitly to the alignment of this book with the *Standards* and I hope will encourage you to read more about what the authors of that important document have to say.

Technology Notes ➤

When appropriate, a technology icon marks a section discussing how computers can be used profitably to help with the content just discussed. Descriptions are provided of specific software titles and interactive applets available on the Internet. You should not think of these sections as a compendium of available software but as a pointer to the most useful types of computer resources that are available. Inclusion of any title in these notes should not be seen as an endorsement.

The technology icon will also be found with certain activities to indicate the use of computer technology. Similarly, a calculator icon appears with activities that incorporate calculator use.

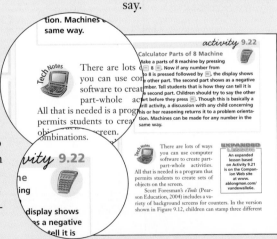

◄ Chapter End Matter

There are four headings at the end of every chapter.

Writing to Learn

To help you focus on the important pedagogical ideas, a list of focusing questions is found at the end of every chapter under the heading "Reflections on Chapter N: Writing to Learn." These study questions are designed to help you reflect on the main points of the chapter. Actually writing out the answers to these questions in your own words is one of the best ways for you to develop your understanding of each chapter's main ideas.

For Discussion and Exploration

These questions ask you to explore an issue, reflect on observations in a classroom, compare text ideas with those found in traditional curriculum materials, or perhaps take a position on a controversial issue. There are no "right" answers to these questions, but I hope that they will stimulate thought and cause spirited conversations.

Recommendations for Further Reading

Under this heading you will find a short annotated list of articles and books to augment the information found in the chapter. Usually these are taken from NCTM journals and books, and from other professional resources designed for the classroom teacher. (Note that all sources cited within the text proper appear in the References at the end of the book.)

A much more complete listing of books and articles related to each chapter of the book can be found on the Companion Web site at www.ablongman.com/vandewalle6e.

◄ Online Resources

Suggested Applets and Web Links. Today there are many mathematics-learning resources available free on the Internet. Most are in the form of interactive applets that allow students to explore a specific mathematics concept or skill. After each chapter in Section II, you will find an annotated list of some of the best of these resources along with their URLs. Exploring these applets will be a learning experience for you as well as a way to learn of a valuable resource for students. At the end of Chapter 8 is a list of the broader sites where these and other Web-based resources can be found.

An easy method of accessing these sites is to visit the Companion Web site for this book (www.ablongman.com/vandewalle6e). There each Web-based resource and applet can be accessed with a simple click of the mouse.

NCTM Standards Appendixes ➤

NCTM's *Principles and Standards for School Mathematics* is described in depth in Chapter 1, pointed out periodically by the NCTM Correlations icon, and reflected in spirit throughout the book. In Appendix A, you will find a copy of the appendix to that document, listing all of the content standards and goals for each of the grade bands: pre-K–2, 3–5, 6–8, and 9–12.

Appendix B contains the six Standards for Teaching Mathematics from *Professional Standards for Teaching Mathematics*.

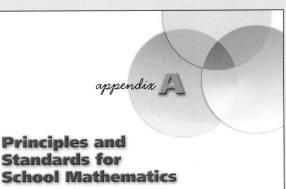

appendix **A**

Principles and Standards for School Mathematics

Content Standards and Grade Level Expectations

appendix **B**

Professional Standards for Teaching Mathematics

Teaching Standards

appendix **C**

Guide to Blackline Masters

This Appendix contains images of all of the Blackline Masters that are listed below. The actual masters can be found in either of two places:

- In hard copy at the end of the Fie[ld]
- On the Compa[nion]

Geoboard recording
Tan[...]

Number and Operations

STANDARD	Pre-K–2	Grades 3–5
Instructional programs from prekindergarten through grade 12 should enable all students to—	**Expectations** In prekindergarten through grade 2 all students should—	**Expectations** In grades 3–5 all students should—
Understand numbers, ways of representing numbers, relationships among numbers, and number systems	• count with understanding and recognize "how many" in sets of objects; • use multiple models to develop initial understandings of place value and the base-ten number system; • develop understanding of the relative position and magnitude of whole numbers and of ordinal and cardinal numbers and their connections; • develop a sense of whole numbers and represent and use them in flexible ways, including relating, composing, and decomposing numbers; • connect number words and numerals to the quantities they represent, using various physical models and representations; • understand and represent commonly used fractions, such as 1/4, 1/3, and 1/2.	• understand the place-value structure of the base-ten number system and be able to represent and compare whole numbers and decimals; • recognize equivalent representations for the same number and generate them by decomposing and composing numbers; • develop understanding of fractions as parts of unit wholes, as parts of a collection, as locations on number lines, and as divisions of whole numbers; • use models, benchmarks, and equivalent forms to judge the size of fractions; • recognize and generate equivalent forms of commonly used fractions, decimals, and percents; • explore numbers less than 0 by extending the number line and through familiar applications; • describe classes of numbers according to characteristics such as the nature of their factors.
Understand meanings of operations and how they relate to one another	• understand various meanings of addition and subtraction of whole numbers and the relationship between the two operations; • understand the effects of adding and subtracting whole numbers; • understand situations that entail multiplication and division, such as equal groupings of objects and sharing equally.	• understand various meanings of multiplication and division; • understand the effects of multiplying and dividing whole numbers; • identify and use relationships between operations, such as division as the inverse of multiplication, to solve problems; • understand and use properties of operations, such as the distributivity of multiplication over addition.
Compute fluently and make reasonable estimates	• develop and use strategies for whole-number computations, with a focus on addition and subtraction; • develop fluency with basic number combinations for addition and subtraction; • use a variety of methods and [tools to compute, including] mental comp[utation...]	• develop fluency with basic [...] and div[...]

Expanded Lessons ➤

Two detailed lesson plans can be found at the end of Chapter 5 on planning problem-based lessons. In addition to these two Expanded Lessons, one activity in each content chapter of the text has been converted to a similar Expanded Lesson that can be found on the Companion Web site (www.ablongman.com/vandewalle6e). These activities are marked with an icon for easy identification. The Expanded Lessons follow the lesson structure described in Chapter 5 and include mathematical goals, notes on preparation, specific student expectations, notes for assessment, and Blackline Masters when needed. They provide a model for converting an activity description into a real lesson plan and indicate the kind of thinking that is required in doing so. Additional Expanded Lessons can be found in the *Field Experience Guide*.

EXPANDED LESSON

An expanded lesson based on Activity 12.23 is on the Companion Web site at www. ablongman.com/ vandewalle6e.

EXPANDED LESSON

Two More Than/Two Less Than *Based on Activity 9.11, p. 126*

Grade Level: Late Kindergarten or early first grade.

Mathematics Goals
- To help students develop the paired relationships of two more than and two less than for numbers to 12.
- To provide continued domino-type dot patterns with the goal of instant recognition.

Thinking About the Students
Students must be able to count a set accurately and understand that counting tells how many. They may or may not be able to recognize patterned sets or be able to count on and count back from a given number. For those students still having difficulty matching the correct numeral and set, the written component of the activity can be omitted.

Materials and Preparation
- This will be a station activity. (Alternatively, students can do the activity at their seats.) Each student doing the activity at the same time will need the materials described.
- Place four dot cards, showing three to ten dots each, in a plastic bag.
- Each bag should also have at least 12 counters and a crayon or pencil.

- Make one two-sided recording sheet for each student as shown here. The backside of the sheet is the same as the front except that it says "2 Less Than" at the top.

Name _____

2 More Than

LESSON

Before
The Task
- For each dot card, the task is to make a set that has two more counters than dots on the card. Similarly, students will make sets that have two fewer counters than dots on the card. The task is completed with the counters.

Establish Expectations
- Show the class (or a small group) a bag of cards and counters. Empty the counters and select one card. Have a student count the dots on the card. Have a second student use counters on the overhead (or on the carpet, if in a circle setting). Say: *Make a set that has two more counters than dots on this card.*
- Discuss with the students how they can decide if the set is actually two more. Accept students' ideas and try them. For example, they might say: *Count each set. Set a counter aside for each dot. Make the counters into a pattern that is the same as on the dot card.*
- Show students the recording sheet. Point out the titles "2 More Than" and "2 Less Than" on the top. Explain that they will record their two-more-than sets on the 2 More Than side. Demonstrate how to first draw the same number of dots as are on the dot card. Next show

EXPANDED LESSON

To the Instructor from the Author

It is my distinct pleasure to offer to you this sixth edition of *Elementary and Middle School Mathematics*. With the preparation of each edition I am amazed at how much new there is to learn about helping children make sense of mathematics—learning from published research and from my ongoing work with both teachers and children. Each edition has contained a few big changes and lots of little ones as I make every effort to keep the book as up to date as possible.

I believe that no other book offers your students as much as this one does. Most important, it develops a strong theoretical perspective of children learning mathematics—not a casual overview. That perspective is reflected consistently throughout the book. Second, no other book of this type develops so clearly the strong position articulated by Hiebert et al. (1996, 1997) that the best approach to teaching mathematics is to teach with problem-based tasks. Third, teachers find the book to be a valuable resource that almost all carry into the classroom rather than sell back to the bookstore. It has become a standard reference for K–8 teachers. Teachers and supervisors continually tell me how readable and valuable they find the book.

It is a large book! It is not a book to "cover" but a book to use. I would not expect you to teach the content of the entire book in a single semester. I've come to believe that fewer topics discussed in class but with time to develop the spirit of Chapters 3 and 4 is the best approach. As you explore the content topics you do select, allow your class to be a model of the instruction you want for all topics. Teaching with problem-based tasks and classroom discourse is a complete shift from the experiences of most teachers.

By providing your students with the detail and information found in this book, you send with them into the classroom the specifics you were unable to cover in class. And you can be assured that the spirit of what you do cover will also be evident in those chapters you skipped.

I wish you and your teachers much success and excitement as you explore good mathematics. Help your teachers to believe in kids. Let them experience what it means to make sense of mathematics.

John Van de Walle

Changes in This Edition

I like to think of this book as being in a constant state of flux—morphing, as it were, from one edition to the next. Some changes are more drastic; for others you have to look closely. No chapter was left untouched.

All features from the fifth edition remain, although some have been altered a bit in format. Assessment notes are now shorter, more focused, and found throughout the content chapters rather than in a section at the end. The technology notes are now indicated only with an icon rather than a full heading to make them more integral to the text. The chapter end matter now contains annotated Web resources. But these are not fundamental changes worthy of a new edition. Let me highlight the larger changes you want to be aware of before you write your syllabus.

Reorganization of Chapters

Three major shifts in chapters were made to keep the book as up-to-date as possible.

Planning for Instruction   The planning and assessment chapters have been reversed in order. Chapter 5, *Planning in the Problem-Based Classroom*, now immediately follows the description of teaching from a student-centered, problem-based perspective.

This chapter has several important additions. First, the lesson-plan model is implemented with two complete lesson plans found at the end of the chapter. One is a full-class lesson, the other is for learning stations in a kindergarten or first grade. Second, greater attention has been given to the issue of planning for a diverse classroom. A distinction is made between *accommodating* the learner and *modifying* a lesson so that all can reach the same goal. Finally, a completely new section addresses planning in a classroom where there are English language learners.

Algebraic Thinking   Perhaps the most important change in this edition is the treatment of algebraic thinking. Chapter 15, *Algebraic Thinking: Generalizations, Patterns, and Functions*, replaces the two chapters previously found near the end of the text. The change more appropriately positions algebra with those chapters dealing with whole numbers. For this revision I was guided by the definition of algebraic thinking developed by the late James Kaput. His description includes five components: generalization, the use of symbolism, the study of structure, patterns and functions, and mathematical modeling. The book *Thinking Mathematically* (Carpenter, Franke, & Levi, 2003) was another major influence. I believe the issue of algebraic thinking is now addressed with a more complete and developmental perspective than in any other book.

Data Analysis and Probability   Data analysis and probability are now developed in separate chapters—Chapters 22 and 23. With this separation, the discussion of probability received the most significant changes. There are new, more accurate definitions of probability, experimental probability, and theoretical probability. More important, there are numerous new activities designed especially for younger students to help them view chance as occurring along a continuum while avoiding the comparison of outcome ratios in experiments with different numbers of trials.

Diversity

In addition to Chapter 5, Chapter 7, *Teaching Mathematics Equitably to All Children*, also attends to ELL concerns. Here they are included in a broader discussion of teaching culturally and linguistically diverse (CLD) students. The focus, as reflected in the new chapter title, is equitable instruction for all students. Six suggestions are listed for teaching second language learners.

Geometry

With the fifth edition, geometry content was expanded and reorganized to reflect the four substrands of geometry found in *Principles and Standards*. In this edition, in order to help your students see these strands more clearly, I organized the chapter around those four strands. Now each of the three van Hiele levels is reflected *within* each strand (shapes and properties, location, transformations, and visualization). The development of the van Hiele theory is highlighted by three activities from the shapes and properties strand. These are now prominently located at the beginning of the chapter.

Other Changes

Although every chapter saw some change, a few specific areas may be worth noting.

- Chapter 3 now includes a section on social constructivism and the basic concept of the *zone of proximal development* as described by Vygotsky.
- Chapter 4, *Teaching Through Problem Solving*, was somewhat rewritten so that the teaching agenda for each of the *before*, *during*, and *after* sections of a lesson are now more clearly articulated and better reflected in the suggested teaching actions. More attention is given to the development of a mathematical community of learners.
- Chapter 12, *Whole-Number Place-Value Development*, now has a significant section indicating how students' understanding of place value can profitably be developed at the same time as an exploration of computation. Exploratory activities that were in the computation chapter are now found here, along with several new activities.

Acknowledgments

Many talented people have contributed to the success of this book, and I am deeply grateful to all those who have assisted me along the way. Without the success of the first edition, there would certainly not have been a second, much less six editions. I will always be most sincerely indebted to Warren Crown (Rutgers), John Dossey (Illinois State University), Bob Gilbert (Florida International University), and Steven Willoughby (University of Arizona), who gave time and great care in offering detailed comments on the original manuscript. Few mathematics educators of their stature would take the time and effort that they gave to that endeavor.

In preparing this sixth edition, I have received thoughtful input from the following educators who offered comments on the fifth edition and/or on the manuscript for the sixth:

Cengiz Alacaci, Florida International University

Shuhua An, California State University–Long Beach

June Chang, Lesley University

Linda S. Dasy, Lesley University

Dana Pomykal Franz, Mississippi State University

Carol H. Geller, Radford University

Stacy Gross, Lesley University

Sandra McCune, Stephen F. Austin State University

Rita McKinley, Lesley University

Marilyn Nash, Indiana University–South Bend

Barbara D. O'Donell, Southern Illinois University–Edwardsville

Christine F. G. Perlo, Lesley University

Dorothy M. Singleton, Winston-Salem State University

Sandra Trotman, Nova Southern University

Frederick L. Uy, California State University–Los Angeles

Each review challenged me to think through important issues. Many specific suggestions have found their way into this book. These professionals each have my thanks.

Special thanks goes to Jennifer Bay-Williams (Kansas State University) and Karen Karp (University of Louisville). In addition to commenting on some new material, these two collaborated to provide both manuscript and advice in bringing a needed ELL perspective to the planning chapter and the equity chapter. I am also indebted to the work of Jon Wray of Howard County Public Schools (Maryland), who reviewed every tech reference in the fifth edition and found the Web resources now at the end of each content chapter.

As in the past, I have received superb help and advice from my friends at Allyn & Bacon. To Sonny Regelman, my development editor through five books, a special word of thanks for her friendly prodding, professional insights, and gentle corrections. While I wish her well in her new position, I will sorely miss her. Thanks go to my editor, Traci Mueller, for being the guiding light for this project. I also extend my sincere appreciation to all of the production and editing people at Omegatype.

A Personal Note

As the sole author of this book, I rely heavily on the research and writings of many leading mathematics educators. It is my hope that the book is a faithful representation of the best and most current thinking in the field. My wife, Sharon, is not a mathematics educator. She is an elementary school psychologist of whom I am most proud. Her contribution to this book, however, is as real as the mathematics educators who guide the content. She is my constant support, my closest friend. She is a part of all that I do. I am truly blessed to be able to share my life with her. I love you, Sharon.

On June 3, 2003, our third granddaughter was born to our daughter, Bridget. Her smiles and hugs add daily to our joy. Gracie, this one's for you!

John Van de Walle

A Note from the Publisher on Supplements

Qualified college adopters can contact their Allyn & Bacon sales representatives for information on ordering any of the supplements below.

Instructor Supplements

Instructor's Manual   The Instructor's Manual for the sixth edition includes a wealth of resources designed to help instructors teach the course, including chapter notes, activity suggestions, suggested essay test questions, and instructor transparency masters.

Computerized Test Bank   The Computerized Test Bank contains hundreds of challenging questions in fill-in-the-blank, multiple-choice, true/false, and essay formats, along with an answer key. Instructors can choose from these questions and write their own to create custom exams.

PowerPoint™ Presentation   Ideal for instructors to use for lecture presentations or student handouts, the PowerPoint presentation provides dozens of ready-to-use graphic and text images tied to the text. Also included are the transparency masters from the Instructor's Manual.

Dale Seymour Developing Mathematical Ideas Video Series: "Numbers and Operations," Part 1 and Part 2   Available upon adoption of the sixth edition to qualified adopters, these professional development videos help preservice and in-service teachers think critically and get to the core of how children approach and understand mathematics.

Student Supplements

Companion Web Site   Think of the Companion Web site (www.ablongman.com/vandewalle6e) as an extension of the text. For each chapter you will find a chapter overview, an online study guide, practice test questions, an extensive listing of related books and articles, and links to useful Web sites on the Internet. Each of the 59 Blackline Masters mentioned in the book can be downloaded as a PDF file. For each content chapter you will also find a detailed lesson plan based on an activity in the book.

Field Experience Guide   This guidebook for both practicum experiences and student teaching at the elementary and middle school levels has been newly written for the sixth edition. The author, Jennifer Bay-Williams, has developed this guide to directly address the new NCATE accreditation requirements. It contains numerous field-based assignments. Each includes reproducible forms to record your experiences to turn in to your instructor. The forms can also be downloaded from the Companion Web site so that you can fill them in on your computer. The guide also includes additional activities for students, full-size versions of all of the Blackline Masters in the text, and 24 additional Expanded Lesson plans that guide students from planning to implementing student-centered lessons.

MyLabSchool   MyLabSchool is a collection of online tools designed to help prepare students for success in this course as well as in their teaching careers.

Visit www.mylabschool.com to access the following:

- Video footage of real-life classrooms
- Help with research papers using Research Navigator
- Help with lesson planning and building digital portfolios
- Professional resources, including study guides for licensure preparation

chapter 1

Teaching Mathematics in the Era of the NCTM *Standards*

In this changing world, those who understand and can do mathematics will have significantly enhanced opportunities and options for shaping their futures. Mathematical competence opens doors to productive futures. A lack of mathematical competence keeps those doors closed. . . . All students should have the opportunity and the support necessary to learn significant mathematics with depth and understanding. There is no conflict between equity and excellence.

NCTM (2000, p. 50)

Someday soon you will find yourself in front of a class of students, or perhaps you are already teaching. What general ideas will guide the way you will teach mathematics? This book will help you become comfortable with the mathematics of the K–8 curriculum. You will also learn about research-based strategies for helping children come to know mathematics and be confident in their ability to do mathematics. These two things—your knowledge of mathematics and how students learn mathematics—are the most important tools you can acquire to be an effective teacher of mathematics. However, outside forces will impact the mathematics teaching in your classroom as well.

For at least two decades, mathematics education has been undergoing slow but steady changes. The impetus for these changes, in both the content of school mathematics and the way mathematics is best taught, can be traced to a variety of sources, including knowledge gained from research. One significant factor in this change has been the professional leadership of the National Council of Teachers of Mathematics (NCTM), an organization of teachers and mathematics educators. Another factor is the significant public or political pressure for change in mathematics education due largely to less-than-stellar U.S. student performance in various international studies. In reaction, state standards and the No Child Left Behind Act (NCLB) press for higher levels of achievement, more testing, and increased teacher accountability. The reform agendas of NCTM and those of the political sector often seem to press teachers in different directions. Although high expectations for students are important, testing alone is not an appropriate answer to improved student learning. NCTM believes that "Learning mathematics is maximized when teachers focus on mathematical thinking and reasoning" (www.nctm.org). The views of NCTM are clearly reflected in the ideas you will read about in this book.

As you prepare to help children learn mathematics, it is important to have some perspective on the forces that influence change in the mathematics classroom. This chapter addresses the leadership that NCTM provides for mathematics education and also the major pressures on mathematics education from outside of NCTM.

Ultimately, it is you, the teacher, who will shape mathematics for the children you teach. Your beliefs about what it means to know and do mathematics and about how children come to make sense of mathematics will have a significant impact on how you approach the teaching of mathematics. These beliefs will undoubtedly be affected, directly or indirectly, by the strong influences on mathematics education that you will read about in this chapter.

The Leadership of NCTM

In April 2000, the National Council of Teachers of Mathematics (NCTM) released *Principles and Standards for School Mathematics*, an update of its original standards document released 11 years earlier in 1989. With this most important document, the council continues to guide a revolutionary reform movement in mathematics education, not just in the United States and Canada but also throughout the world.

The momentum for reform in mathematics education began in the early 1980s. Educators were responding to a "back to basics" movement. As a result, problem solving became an important strand in the mathematics curriculum. The work of Piaget and other developmental psychologists helped to focus research on how children can best learn mathematics.

This momentum came to a head in 1989, when NCTM published *Curriculum and Evaluation Standards for School Mathematics* and the standards movement or reform era in mathematics began. It continues today. No other document has ever had such an enormous effect on school mathematics or on any other area of the curriculum. In 1991, NCTM published *Professional Standards for Teaching Mathematics*. The *Professional Standards* articulates a vision of teaching mathematics and builds on the notion found in the *Curriculum Standards* that good and significant mathematics is a vision for all children, not just a few. NCTM completed the package with the *Assessment Standards for School Mathematics* in 1995. The *Assessment Standards* shows clearly the necessity of integrating assessment with instruction and indicates the key role that assessment plays in implementing change. From 1989 to 2000, these three documents have guided the reform movement in mathematics education. *Principles and Standards for School Mathematics* is an update of all three original standards documents.

Now that we are well into the twenty-first century, it must be admitted that the vision of the 1989 *Curriculum Standards* has still not been realized although much progress has been made. Change is visible, albeit slow and incremental. The political pressures of accountability are often counterproductive. But despite the slow pace of change in long-held beliefs about school mathematics, the revolution continues. This is not a pendulum that will swing backward.

Principles and Standards for School Mathematics

Principles and Standards for School Mathematics is designed to provide guidance and direction for teachers and other leaders in mathematics education from pre-K to grade 12. Figure 1.1 outlines the general structure of *Principles and Standards*. While it is important that teachers read and reflect on the *Standards* document, the next few pages will provide you some idea of what you will find there.

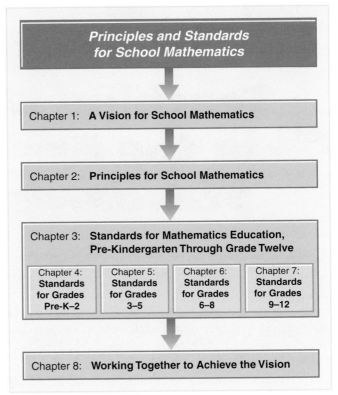

FIGURE 1.1 The structure of *Principles and Standards for School Mathematics* emphasizes the continuity of mathematics across all 14 years of school.

The Six Principles

One of the most important features of *Principles and Standards for School Mathematics* is the articulation of six principles fundamental to high-quality mathematics education:

- Equity
- Curriculum
- Teaching
- Learning
- Assessment
- Technology

According to *Principles and Standards*, these principles must be "deeply intertwined with school mathematics programs" (NCTM, 2000, p. 12). The principles make it clear that excellence in mathematics education involves much more than simply listing content objectives.

The Equity Principle

Excellence in mathematics education requires equity—high expectations and strong support for all students. (NCTM, 2000, p. 12)

The strong message of the Equity Principle is high expectations for all students. All students must have the opportunity and adequate support to learn mathematics "regardless of personal characteristics, backgrounds, or physical challenges" (p. 12). The message of high expectations for all is intertwined with every other principle and the document as a whole.

The Curriculum Principle

A curriculum is more than a collection of activities: it must be coherent, focused on important mathematics, and well articulated across the grades. (NCTM, 2000, p. 14)

Coherence speaks to the importance of building instruction around "big ideas" both in the curriculum and in daily classroom instruction. Students must be helped to see that mathematics is an integrated whole, not a list of isolated bits and pieces.

Mathematical ideas are "important" if they are useful in the development of other ideas, link ideas one to another, or serve to illustrate the discipline of mathematics as a human endeavor.

The Teaching Principle

Effective mathematics teaching requires understanding what students know and need to learn and then challenging and supporting them to learn it well. (NCTM, 2000, p. 16)

What students learn almost entirely depends on the experiences that teachers provide every day in the classroom. To provide high-quality mathematics education, teachers must (1) understand deeply the mathematics they are teaching; (2) understand how children learn mathematics, including a keen awareness of the individual mathematical development of their own students; and (3) select instructional tasks and strategies that will enhance learning. "Teachers' actions are what encourage students to think, question, solve problems, and discuss their ideas, strategies, and solutions" (p. 18).

The Learning Principle

Students must learn mathematics with understanding, actively building new knowledge from experience and prior knowledge. (NCTM, 2000, p. 20)

This principle is based on two fundamental ideas. First, learning mathematics with understanding is essential. Mathematics today requires not only computational skills but also the ability to think and reason mathematically in order to solve the new problems and learn the new ideas that students will face in the future.

Second, the principle states quite clearly that students *can* learn mathematics with understanding. Learning is enhanced in classrooms where students are required to evaluate their own ideas and those of others, are encouraged to make mathematical conjectures and test them, and develop their reasoning skills.

The Assessment Principle

Assessment should support the learning of important mathematics and furnish useful information to both teachers and students. (NCTM, 2000, p. 22)

In the authors' words, "Assessment should not merely be done *to* students, rather, it should also be done *for* students, to guide and enhance their learning" (p. 22). Ongoing assessment conveys to students what mathematics is important. Assessment that includes ongoing observation and student interaction encourages students to articulate and, thus, clarify their ideas. Feedback from daily assessment helps students establish goals and become more independent learners.

Assessment should also be a major factor in making instructional decisions. By continuously gathering information about student growth and understanding, teachers can better make the daily decisions that support student learning. For assessment to be effective, teachers must use a variety of assessment techniques, understand their mathematical goals deeply, and have a good idea of how their students may be thinking about the mathematics that is being developed.

The Technology Principle

Technology is essential in teaching and learning mathematics; it influences the mathematics that is taught and enhances students' learning. (NCTM, 2000, p. 24)

Calculators and computers should be seen as essential tools for doing and learning mathematics in the classroom. Technology permits students to focus on mathematical ideas, to reason, and to solve problems in ways that are often impossible without these tools. Technology enhances the learning of mathematics by allowing for increased exploration and enhanced representation of ideas. It extends the range of problems that can be accessed. It also allows students with special needs to bypass less important procedures so that important mathematics can be considered.

A Pre-K-to-12 Perspective

The structure of *Principles and Standards* emphasizes the continuous growth of mathematics across all grades, pre-K to 12. The largest portion of *Principles and Standards* is built around ten standards: five content standards and five process standards. Chapter 3 of the document helps the reader understand each of these standards from the perspective of the full pre-K–12 curriculum. This broad perspective is followed by chapters that take a closer look at each standard within each of four grade bands: pre-K–2, 3–5, 6–8, and 9–12.

The Five Content Standards

Principles and Standards describes five content standards or strands of mathematics:

- Number and Operations
- Algebra
- Geometry
- Measurement
- Data Analysis and Probability

Each content standard includes a small collection of goals that is applicable to all grade bands. Each grade-band chapter provides specific expectations for what students should know. These grade-band expectations are also concisely listed in the appendix to the *Standards* and in Appendix A of this book.

 pause and reflect

Pause now and turn to Appendix A. Spend a few minutes with these expectations for the grade band in which you are most interested. How do these expectations compare with the mathematics you experienced in school?

Although the same five content standards apply across all grades, you should not infer that each strand has equal weight or emphasis in every grade band. Number and Operations is the largest strand from pre-K to grade 5 and continues to be important in the middle grades but has a lesser emphasis in grades 9–12. That emphasis is reflected in this book, with Chapters 9 to 14 and 16 to 19 addressing content found in the Number and Operations standard.

Algebra is clearly intended as a strand for all grades. This was almost certainly not the case when you were in school. Today, most states and provinces include algebra objectives at every grade level. In this book, Chapter 15 addresses this strand.

Note that Geometry and Measurement are separate strands, suggesting the unique importance of each of these two areas to the elementary and middle grades curriculum.

The Five Process Standards

Following the five content standards, *Principles and Standards* lists five process standards:

- Problem Solving
- Reasoning and Proof
- Communication
- Connections
- Representation

The process standards refer to the mathematical process through which students should acquire and use mathematical knowledge. The statement of the five process standards can be found in Table 1.1.

TABLE 1.1

The Five Process Standards from *Principles and Standards for School Mathematics*

Problem Solving Standard Instructional programs from prekindergarten through grade 12 should enable all students to—	• Build new mathematical knowledge through problem solving • Solve problems that arise in mathematics and in other contexts • Apply and adapt a variety of appropriate strategies to solve problems • Monitor and reflect on the process of mathematical problem solving
Reasoning and Proof Standard Instructional programs from prekindergarten through grade 12 should enable all students to—	• Recognize reasoning and proof as fundamental aspects of mathematics • Make and investigate mathematical conjectures • Develop and evaluate mathematical arguments and proofs • Select and use various types of reasoning and methods of proof
Communication Standard Instructional programs from prekindergarten through grade 12 should enable all students to—	• Organize and consolidate their mathematical thinking through communication • Communicate their mathematical thinking coherently and clearly to peers, teachers, and others • Analyze and evaluate the mathematical thinking and strategies of others • Use the language of mathematics to express mathematical ideas precisely
Connections Standard Instructional programs from prekindergarten through grade 12 should enable all students to—	• Recognize and use connections among mathematical ideas • Understand how mathematical ideas interconnect and build on one another to produce a coherent whole • Recognize and apply mathematics in contexts outside of mathematics
Representation Standard Instructional programs from prekindergarten through grade 12 should enable all students to—	• Create and use representations to organize, record, and communicate mathematical ideas • Select, apply, and translate among mathematical representations to solve problems • Use representations to model and interpret physical, social, and mathematical phenomena

These five processes should not be regarded as separate content or strands in the mathematics curriculum. Rather, they direct the methods or processes of doing all mathematics and, therefore, should be seen as integral components of all mathematics learning and teaching.

To teach in a way that reflects these process standards is one of the best definitions of what it means to teach "according to the *Standards.*"

Problem Solving

The Problem Solving standard says that all students should "build new mathematical knowledge through problem solving" (NCTM, 2000, p. 52). This statement clearly indicates that problem solving is to be viewed as the vehicle through which children develop mathematical ideas. Learning and doing mathematics *as you solve problems* is probably the most significant difference in what the *Standards* indicate and the way you most likely experienced mathematics. Problem-based learning is a major theme of this book.

Reasoning and Proof

If problem solving is the focus of mathematics, reasoning is the logical thinking that helps us decide if and why our answers make sense. Students need to develop the habit of providing an argument or a rationale as an integral part of every answer. Justifying answers is a process that enhances conceptual understanding. The habit of providing reasons can begin in kindergarten. However, it is never too late for students to learn the value of defending ideas through logical argument.

Communication

The Communication standard points to the importance of being able to talk about, write about, describe, and explain mathematical ideas. Learning to communicate in mathematics fosters interaction and exploration of ideas in the classroom as students learn in an active, verbal environment. No better way exists for wrestling with an idea than to attempt to articulate it to others.

Connections

The Connections standard has two separate thrusts. First, the standard refers to connections within and among mathematical ideas. For example, fractional parts of a whole are connected to concepts of decimals and percents. Students should be helped to see how mathematical ideas build on one another in a useful network of connected ideas.

Second, mathematics should be connected to the real world and to other disciplines. Children should see that mathematics plays a significant role in art, science, and social studies. This suggests that mathematics should frequently be integrated with other discipline areas and that

applications of mathematics in the real world should be explored.

Representation

Symbols, charts, graphs, and diagrams are powerful methods of expressing mathematical ideas and relationships. Symbolism in mathematics, along with visual aids such as charts and graphs, should be understood by students as ways of communicating mathematical ideas to other people. Symbols, graphs, and charts, as well as physical manipulatives are also powerful learning tools. Moving from one representation to another is an important way to add understanding to an idea.

 Throughout this book, this icon will alert you to specific information in *Principles and Standards* relative to the information you are reading. However, these notes and the brief descriptions you have just read should not be a substitute for reading the *Standards*. Members of NCTM have access online to the complete *Standards* document as well as the previous three standards documents. For nonmembers, quite a bit of information remains available on the NCTM Web site (www.nctm.org). The site provides a description of each of the principles as well as a shortened version of each of the ten standards including the expectations for each grade (as found in the Appendix to this book.) The Web site also contains a number of applets—interactive tools for learning about mathematical concepts. The applets are referred to as "e-examples." These are available to everyone and many are referenced throughout this book. For other related information, see "Suggested Applets and Web Links" at the end of each chapter of this book.

The *Professional Standards for Teaching Mathematics*

Although *Principles and Standards* incorporates principles of teaching and assessment, the emphasis is on curriculum. In contrast, the *Professional Standards for Teaching Mathematics* focuses on teaching and is as important today as when it was released in 1991. The *Professional Standards* asserts that teachers must shift from a teacher-centered to a child-centered approach in their instruction. Through extended vignettes of real teachers, the document articulates the careful reflective work that must go into teaching.

Five Shifts in Classroom Environment

The introduction to the *Professional Standards* lists five major shifts in the environment of the mathematics classroom that are necessary to allow students to develop mathematical power. Teachers need to shift

- Toward classrooms as mathematics communities and away from classrooms as simply a collection of individuals
- Toward logic and mathematical evidence as verification and away from the teacher as the sole authority for right answers
- Toward mathematical reasoning and away from mere memorizing procedures
- Toward conjecturing, inventing, and problem solving and away from an emphasis on the mechanistic finding of answers
- Toward connecting mathematics, its ideas, and its applications and away from treating mathematics as a body of isolated concepts and procedures

The Teaching Standards

The *Professional Standards for Teaching Mathematics* contains chapters on teaching, the evaluation of teaching, professional development, and necessary support for teaching. The teaching section is extraordinarily useful. It offers six standards for the teaching of mathematics. These standards talk about the selection of tasks for learning and the nature of an interactive classroom atmosphere in which students are engaged in the process of making sense of mathematics. This mathematical environment, in which students work as a community of learners on mathematical tasks, is an integral component of the approach to teaching mathematics described in this book. Reading the *Teaching Standards* is an excellent way to help you understand what this mathematical atmosphere is like.

 *pause and reflect*

The six teaching standards are located in Appendix B of this book. Take a moment now to look over this one-page listing. Select one or two of the standards that seem especially significant to you. Put a sticky note on the page to remind you to return to these important ideas from time to time as you work through this book.

The *Assessment Standards for School Mathematics*

The *Assessment Standards for School Mathematics* was published in 1995, rounding out the trio of NCTM standards documents. The *Assessment Standards* is not a how-to guide but a statement of philosophy and purpose, a book to provide guidance without prescription. It consists of six standards for assessment and describes in some detail four purposes of assessment: to monitor the progress of students, to help make instructional decisions, to evaluate students' achievement, and to evaluate programs.

The inescapable message of the *Assessment Standards* is that assessment and instruction are not separate activities but are intimately intertwined in improving the learning of mathematics. Chapter 6 of this book describes the six assessment standards and discusses the four purposes. There you will find suggestions for making assessment an integral component of instruction, an absolutely essential factor in being a *Standards*-oriented teacher.

Influences and Pressures on Reform

NCTM has provided the major leadership and vision for reform in mathematics education. However, no single factor controls the direction of change. National and international comparisons of student performances continue to make headlines, provoke public opinion, and pressure legislatures to call for tougher standards backed by testing. The pressures of testing policies exerted on schools and ultimately on teachers often have an impact on instruction that is different than the vision of the NCTM *Standards*. In addition to these pressures, there is also the strong influence of the textbook or curriculum materials that are provided to teachers, which are often not well aligned with state standards.

National and International Studies

Large studies that tell the American public how the nation's children are doing in mathematics receive a lot of attention. They influence political decisions as well as provide useful data for mathematics education researchers.

The National Assessment of Educational Progress

Since 1969, the National Assessment of Educational Progress (NAEP), a congressionally mandated program, has been assessing what students know and can do in various curriculum areas. Assessments are based on samples of students 9, 13, and 17 years of age or in grades 4, 8, and 12. The results are often published as "The Nation's Report Card." NAEP is a criterion-referenced study, telling us what percentages of American students know various mathematics concepts and skills. Much of the test is designed to reflect current curriculum. At this writing, the most recent data come from the 2003 test.

On a small core of items that has been used consistently since 1973 to produce trend data, U.S. students do things somewhat better now than in 1973 (Kloosterman &

Lester, 2004). There are those who contend that current mathematics reform produces students who don't know "good old basic mathematics." Since the trend test items focus on traditional computation, the consistently improving scores on the core test clearly negate that view.

Scores on the broader main NAEP tests show much greater gains from 1990 to 2003 than on the core test mentioned earlier. However, that performance remains less than stellar. In 2003, only 32 percent of fourth-grade students and 29 percent of eighth-grade students performed at or above the proficient level (NCTM, 2004). In contrast, the No Child Left Behind legislation expects that all students will be at or above the proficient level by 2014. NAEP data suggest that goal is likely unattainable. Twenty-three percent of fourth-grade students and 32 percent of eighth-grade students remain below the basic level.

The Third International Mathematics and Science Study

In 1995 and 1996, 41 nations participated in the Third International Mathematics and Science Study (TIMSS), the largest study of mathematics and science education ever conducted. Data were gathered in grades 4, 8, and 12 from 500,000 students and from teachers. In 1999, a repeat study (TIMSS-R) was done at the eighth grade. The most widely reported results are that U.S. fourth-grade students are above the average of the TIMSS countries, below the international average at the eighth grade, and significantly below average at the twelfth grade (U.S. Department of Education, 1997a).

Even though the rank ordering for fourth grade places the United States above the average for 26 countries, seven countries (Singapore, Korea, Japan, Hong Kong, Netherlands, Czech Republic, and Austria) had significantly higher scores. Only 9 percent of U.S. fourth graders would fall in the top 10 percent of all students in the TIMSS study. This is in stark contrast with Japan (32 percent) and Singapore (39 percent) (U.S. Department of Education, 1997c).

A major finding of the TIMSS curriculum analysis is that U.S. curriculum is unfocused, contains many more topics than most countries, and involves much more repetition than is found in most countries. We attempt to do everything and as a consequence rarely do it in depth, making reteaching all too common (Schmidt, McKnight, & Raizen, 1996).

Many who advocate a return to "basics" point to the disappointing performance of American students. However, curriculum and instructional approaches in the United States are "less in line with cross-national commonalties than are the demanding curricula and classroom practices found in many high-achieving countries" (Babcock, 1998, p. 6). Furthermore, TIMSS does not support a number of other popular "basics" demands: more homework (U.S. students do more than students in most countries), less TV watching (Japanese students watch as much), and more time spent on mathematics (U.S. students have more hours of mathematics instruction than students in Japan or Germany). Tracking prior to high school, common in the United States, is not practiced in most TIMSS nations.

One of the most interesting components of the TIMSS-R is the eighth-grade video study that was conducted in the United States, Australia, and five of the highest-achieving countries. The results indicate that teaching is a cultural activity; it is quite different in almost every country although there are also many similarities. In all countries problems or tasks are often used to begin a lesson. However, once a lesson progresses, the way these problems are handled in the United States is in stark contrast to the high achieving countries. In the Czech Republic, Hong Kong, and Japan lessons that began with a conceptual problem-solving spirit continued in that spirit from 46 to 52 percent of the time. In the United States, nearly all such lessons (more than 99.5 percent) revert to the teacher showing students how to solve the problem (Hiebert et al., 2003). At least in U.S. eighth-grade classrooms, it is safe to say that the focus is on having students follow directions and rules. In high-achieving countries, there is a much greater focus on conceptual understanding and true problem solving. Teaching in high-achieving countries more closely resembles the recommendations of the NCTM *Standards* than does the teaching in the United States.

State Standards

The term *standards* was popularized by NCTM in 1989. Today it is used by nearly every state in the nation to refer to a grade-by-grade listing of very specific mathematics objectives. These state standards or objectives vary considerably from state to state. Even the grade level at which basic facts for each of the operations are expected to be mastered varies by as much as three grade levels. Although the NCTM *Standards* document lists goals for each of four grade bands, it is not a national curriculum. The United States and Canada are the only industrialized countries in the world without a national curriculum.

Associated with every set of state standards is some form of testing program. Publicly reported test scores place pressure on superintendents, then on principals, and ultimately on teachers. Teachers feel enormous pressure to raise test scores at all costs (Schmidt et al., 1996). For a teacher who has little or no experience with the spirit of the *Standards*, it is very difficult to adopt the student-centered approach to mathematics and the teaching of mathematics espoused by reformers. Unfortunately for children, this often results in excessive drill, review, and practice tests.

Are state standards incompatible with reform? In general, the answer is no. Reform is about helping children understand mathematics and become confident in their abilities to do mathematics and solve problems. There are many wonderful examples of teaching in the spirit of reform. Children in these classrooms achieve quite well, even on the most traditional of standardized tests. These stories need better publicity, and teachers need much more support than is often available.

Curriculum

In most classrooms, the textbook is the single most influential factor in determining what actually gets taught and how. What is becoming increasingly complicated is how teachers and school systems attempt to blend the textbook or other curriculum materials with the mandated state standards. As textbook companies attempt to create books that address the needs of all 50 states, the result is an inordinate amount of repetition and the inclusion of far more topics per grade level than are found in other countries.

Though possibly an oversimplification, mathematics curriculum materials that are used in K–8 classrooms can be categorized as either traditional or standards-based—meaning reflecting the spirit of the NCTM *Standards*. Traditional texts are usually developed by large commercial publishers. Standards-based programs have been developed with funding from the National Science Foundation (NSF) and other outside sources by teams of teachers, educational researchers, and mathematicians.

Traditional Curricula

The publishers of traditional textbooks employ author teams that always include excellent mathematics researchers and educators as well as teachers and supervisors. The tendency is to produce very large textbooks so that they can attend to the wide variety of state and professional agendas (Schmidt et al., 1996). Often publisher statements of compliance with NCTM standards are misleading. NCTM does not approve or sanction any commercial products, so publishers are free to make whatever claims they feel they can support. You should remember that by its very nature, the publishing industry is market driven. The market—the individuals who make the decisions concerning which programs to purchase for the school systems—is composed largely of experienced teachers. Teachers are enormously pressured by state tests. Most of these decision makers have only a cursory understanding of the NCTM *Standards*. The result is that the market requires publishers to stick fairly close to the show-and-explain approach to teaching. Traditional books currently account for well over 80 percent of the textbooks used in schools.

Standards-Based Curricula

At present, there are three elementary and five middle school programs commonly recognized as standards-based curricula.* Originally developed with NSF funds, each is now commercially available. A hallmark of these standards-based or alternative programs is student engagement. Children are challenged to make sense of new mathematical ideas through explorations and projects, often in real contexts. Written and oral communication is strongly encouraged. Teacher training is generally seen as important if not essential for districtwide implementation, a fact that adds to the already high cost of most standards-based programs.

Data concerning the effectiveness of standards-based curricula as measured by traditional testing programs continue to be gathered. It is safe to say that students in standards-based programs perform much better on problem-solving measures and at least as well on traditional skills as students in traditional programs (ARC Center, 2002; Bell, 1998; Boaler, 1998; Fuson, Carroll, & Drueck, 2000; Hiebert, 2003; Reys, Robinson, Sconiers, & Mark, 1999; Riordin & Noyce, 2001; Stein, Grover, & Henningsen, 1996; Stein & Lane, 1996; Wood & Sellers, 1996, 1997).

Comparing any of these with a corresponding traditional textbook would be an effective way to understand what reform or standards-based mathematics is all about.

In each chapter of Section 2 you will find features describing activities from *Investigations in Number, Data, and Space* or *Connected Mathematics*. These features are included to offer you some insight into these nontraditional programs as well as to offer good ideas for instruction.

An Invitation to Learn and Grow

The mathematics education described in the *Standards* is almost certainly not the same as the mathematics and the mathematics teaching you experienced in grades K through 8. Along the way, you may have had some excellent teachers who really did reflect the current reform spirit. Examples of good standards-based curriculum have been around since the early 1990s, and you may have benefited from one of those. But for the most part, with the reform movement nearing the end of its second decade, its goals have yet to be realized in the large majority of school districts in North America.

As a practicing or prospective teacher facing the challenge of the *Standards*, this book may require you to confront some of your personal beliefs—about what it means

---

*A listing of the eight standards-based curricula—the developers, publishers, and Internet contacts—can be found at the end of this chapter.

to *do mathematics*, how one goes about *learning mathematics*, how to *teach mathematics through problem solving*, and what it means to *assess mathematics* integrated with instruction. The next five chapters of this book help you develop these foundational ideas for teaching. Chapters 7 and 8 discuss other topics that influence mathematics teaching across all strands and grade levels: the equitable teaching of all children in mathematics and the role of technology.

Section 2 of the book examines the teaching and learning of specific topics in mathematics. The chapters in the second section are designed not only as text material but also as a source of instructional tasks for your future or current teaching.

Teaching mathematics can be an exciting adventure. Perhaps the most exciting part is that you will grow and learn along with your students. Enjoy the journey!

Reflections on Chapter 1

Writing to Learn

At the end of each chapter of this book, you will find a series of questions under this same heading. The questions are designed to help you reflect on the most important ideas of the chapter. Writing (or talking aloud with a peer) is an excellent way to explore new ideas and incorporate them into your own knowledge base. The writing (or discussion) will help make the ideas your own. After you have written your responses in your own words, return to the book to compare what you have written with the book. Make changes, if necessary, or discuss differences with your instructor.

1. Give a brief description of each of the six principles in *Principles and Standards* (Equity, Curriculum, Teaching, Learning, Assessment, and Technology). Explain the importance of each principle to the teaching and learning of mathematics.
2. What are the five content strands (standards) defined by *Principles and Standards*?
3. What is meant by a *process* as referred to in the *Principles and Standards* process standards? Give a brief description of each of the five process standards.
4. Among the ideas in the *Professional Standards* are five shifts in the classroom environment, from traditional approaches to a *Standards*-oriented approach. Examine these five shifts, and describe in a few sentences what aspects of each shift seem most significant to you.
5. Describe two results derived from NAEP data. What are the implications?
6. Describe two results derived from TIMSS data. What are the implications?
7. Describe the influences of state-level standards on classroom mathematics education.
8. Discuss the difference between traditional textbooks and standards-based curricula.

For Discussion and Exploration

1. In recent years, the outcry for "basics" was again being heard from a loud and very political minority. The debate over reform or the basics is both important and interesting. For an engaging discussion of the reform movement in light of the "back to basics" outcry, read one or more of the first five articles in the February 1999 edition of the *Phi Delta Kappan*. Where do you stand on the issue of reform versus the basics?
2. Examine a traditional textbook at any grade level of your choice. If possible, use a teacher's edition. Page through any chapter and look for signs of the five process standards. To what extent are children who are being taught from this book likely to be doing and learning mathematics in ways described by those processes? What would you have to do to change the general approach to this text?
3. Examine a unit from any one of the eight nontraditional curriculum programs and see how it reflects the NCTM vision of reform, especially the five process standards. How do these curriculum programs differ from traditional textbook programs?

Recommendations for Further Reading

Ferrini-Mundy, J. (2000). The standards movement in mathematics education: Reflections and hopes. In M. J. Burke (Ed.), *Learning mathematics for a new century* (pp. 37–50). Reston, VA: National Council of Teachers of Mathematics.

    Joan Ferrini-Mundy chaired the writing group of *Principles and Standards*. In this article, written before the *Standards* was released, she shares her unique and very well-informed view of this important publication, how it came to be, the impact of the earlier document, the political climate in which the *Standards* was released, and the intentions that the council had for the document. Of particular interest is the discussion of tensions between opposing yet reasoned viewpoints that the authors of the *Standards* had to wrestle with. This article will provide an understanding of the *Standards* that is impossible to get from the document itself.

Hiebert, J. (2003). What research says about the NCTM standards. In J. Kilpatrick, W. G. Martin, & D. Schifter (Eds.), *A research companion to Principles and Standards for School Mathematics* (pp. 5–23). Reston, VA: National Council of Teachers of Mathematics.

    The writings of James Hiebert are always enlightening and interesting. Hiebert is probably the researcher who most influences the broad perspectives found in this book. Although this chapter is found in a book of research papers, it provides one of the best perspectives on what we have learned since the *Standards* was released. It also offers some perspective into typical U.S. classrooms and offers contrasts between traditional mathematics programs and those called "standards based."

National Research Council. (1989). *Everybody counts: A report to the nation on the future of mathematics education.* Washington, DC: National Academy Press.

This little booklet, readable in a single evening, remains a "must read" more than 15 years since its publication. It provides a compelling rationale for reform in both the mathematics we teach and how it is taught. Here you will find the description of mathematics as "the science of pattern and order" used throughout this book. Myths concerning the nature of mathematics, how it is learned, and by whom are challenged from an angle that is difficult to dispute.

National Research Council. (2001). *Adding it up: Helping children learn mathematics.* J. Kilpatrick, J. Swafford, & B. Findell (Eds.). Mathematics Learning Study Committee, Center for Education, Division of Behavioral and Social Sciences and Education. Washington, DC: National Academy Press.

Perhaps the most important book since *Principles and Standards*, this work is the effort of a select committee representing mathematics educators, mathematicians, school administrators, and industry. The authors represent a balanced view of mathematics education in the United States. The book carefully describes the state of mathematics education and makes very specific recommendations about how to improve it. A hallmark of this book is the formulation of five strands of "mathematical proficiency": conceptual understanding, procedural fluency, strategic competence, adaptive reasoning, and productive disposition. Educators and policy makers will cite this book for many years to come.

Teppo, A. R. (Ed.). (1999). *Reflecting on practice in elementary school mathematics: Readings from NCTM's school-based journals and other publications.* Reston, VA: National Council of Teachers of Mathematics.

Frequently, NCTM publishes books of selected readings from its journals. In this instance, the more than 60 articles provide perspective on the reform movement both in general and organized according to major areas of the curriculum. For a teacher wanting to establish a beginning resource of short, easily read articles on a wide variety of topics, this is an excellent book with which to begin.

Standards-Based Curricula

Elementary Programs

Information about the elementary programs can be obtained from the ARC Center:

    E-mail: arccenter@mail.comap.com
    URL: www.arccenter.comap.com

UCSMP Elementary: Everyday Mathematics (K–6)
Developer: University of Chicago School Mathematics Project
Publisher: Everyday Learning

E-mail: aisaacs@midway.uchicago.edu
URL: http://everydaymath.uchicago.edu

Investigations in Number, Data, and Space (K–5)
Developer: TERC
Publisher: Scott Foresman
URL: http://investigations.terc.edu

Math Trailblazers: A Mathematical Journey Using Science and Language Arts (K–5)
Developer: Institute for Math and Science Education, University of Illinois, Chicago
Publisher: Kendall/Hunt
URL: www.math.uic.edu/IMSE

Middle School Programs

Information about the middle school programs can be obtained from the Show-Me Center:

    E-mail: Center@showme.missouri.edu
    URL: www.showmecenter.missouri.edu

Connected Mathematics (CMP) (6–8)
Developer: Michigan State University
Publisher: Prentice Hall
URL: www.math.msu.edu/cmp

Mathematics in Context (MIC) (5–8)
Developer: University of Wisconsin—Madison
Publisher: Encyclopaedia Britannica
URL: mic.brittanica.com

MathScape (6–8)
Developer: Educational Development Center
Publisher: Creative Publications
URL: www.edc.org/mathscape

Middle School Mathematics Through Applications Project (MMAP) (6–8)
Developer: Institute for Research on Learning
Publisher: WestEd
URL: http://mmap.wested.org

Middle Grades Math Thematics (STEM) (6–8)
Developer: University of Montana
Publisher: McDougal/Littell
URL: www.mlmath.com

Online Resources

Suggested Applets and Web Links

Illuminations
www.illuminations.nctm.org
    A companion Web site to NCTM sponsored by NCTM and Marcopolo. Provides lessons, interactive applets, and links to Web sites for learning and teaching mathematics.

Key Issues in Math
www.mathforum.org/social/index.html
    Part of the Math Forum at Drexel University, this page lists numerous questions concerning issues in mathematics education with answers supplied by experts in short articles or excerpts.

NAEP (National Assessment of Educational Progress, "The Nation's Report Card")

http://nces.ed.gov/nationsreportcard/mathematics/

Past and current data and reports related to NAEP assessments.

National Council of Teachers of Mathematics

www.nctm.org

Here you can find all about NCTM, its belief statements, and positions on important topics. Also find an overview of *Principles and Standards* and free access to interactive applets (see Standards—Electronic), membership and conference information, publications catalog, links to related

sites, and much more. Members have access to even more information.

TIMSS (Third International Mathematics and Science Study)

http://nces.ed.gov/timss

Access articles and data from TIMSS.

 An additional list of books and articles related to the ideas in this chapter can be found on the Companion Web site at **www.ablongman.com/vandewalle6e.**

chapter 2

Exploring What It Means to Do Mathematics

As a practical matter, mathematics is a science of pattern and order. Its domain is not molecules or cells, but numbers, chance, form, algorithms, and change. As a science of abstract objects, mathematics relies on logic rather than on observation as its standard of truth, yet employs observation, simulation, and even experimentation as means of discovering truth.

Mathematical Sciences Education Board (1989, p. 31)

How would you describe what you are doing when you are *doing mathematics?* Stop for a moment and write a few sentences about what it means to know and do mathematics, based on your own experiences. Then put your paper aside until you have finished this chapter.

The description of doing mathematics you will read about here may not match your personal experiences. That's okay! It is okay to come to this point with whatever beliefs were developed in your previous mathematics experiences. However, it is *not* okay to accept outdated ideas about mathematics and expect to be a quality teacher. Your obligation and your challenge as you read this chapter and this book are to reconceptualize your own understanding of what it means to know and do mathematics so that the children with whom you work will have an exciting and accurate vision of mathematics.

Contrasting Perceptions of School Mathematics

Much change has taken place since 1989 when NCTM set a vision for change in mathematics classrooms. More teachers are beginning to use what might be called a "*Standards* approach": more cooperative learning, more emphasis on concepts and problem solving, and a greater tolerance for and use of calculators. Often these changes are superficial and are not really changing the nature of what children do and how they think in the mathematics classroom. Furthermore, as noted in Chapter 1, the pressures of state test scores have a tendency to bring out "drill-and-kill" approaches even though such methods have consistently proved ineffective. Fortunately, wonderful exceptions are to be found everywhere.

Traditional Views of Mathematics

Most adults will acknowledge that mathematics is an important subject, but few understand what the discipline is about. For many, mathematics is a collection of rules to be mastered, arithmetic computations, mysterious algebraic equations, and geometric proofs. This perception is in stark contrast to a view of mathematics that involves making sense of mathematical objects such as data, form, change, or patterns. A substantial number of adults are almost proud to proclaim, "I was never any good at mathematics." How has this debilitating perspective of mathematics as a collection of arcane procedures and rules become so prevalent in our society? The best answer can be found in the traditional approaches to teaching mathematics. Traditional teaching, still the predominant instructional pattern, typically begins with an explanation of whatever idea is on the current page of the text followed by showing children how to do the assigned exercises. Even with a hands-on activity, the traditional teacher is guiding students, telling them exactly how to use the materials in a prescribed manner. The focus of the lesson is primarily on getting answers. Students rely on the teacher to determine if their answers are correct. Children emerge from these experiences with a view that mathematics is a series of arbitrary rules, handed down by the teacher, who in turn got them from some very smart source.

This follow-the-rules, computation-dominated, answer-oriented view of mathematics is a gross distortion of what mathematics is really about. It cannot be very exciting. A few children are good at learning rules and thrive on the ensuing good grades. But these are not necessarily the best thinkers in the room. The traditional system rewards the learning of rules but offers little opportunity actually to do mathematics.

Mathematics as a Science of Pattern and Order

Mathematics is the science of pattern and order. This wonderfully simple description of mathematics is found in the thought-provoking publication *Everybody Counts* (MSEB, 1989; see also Schoenfeld, 1992). This definition challenges the popular social view of mathematics as a discipline dominated by computation and rules without reasons. Science is a process of figuring things out or making sense of things. It begins with problem-based situations. Although you may never have thought of it in quite this way, mathematics is a science of things that have a pattern of regularity and logical order. Finding and exploring this regularity or order and then making sense of it is what doing mathematics is all about.

Even the youngest schoolchildren can and should be involved in the science of pattern and order. Have you ever noticed that 6 + 7 is the same as 5 + 8 and 4 + 9? What is the pattern? What are the relationships? When two odd numbers are multiplied, the result is also odd, but if the same numbers are added or subtracted, the result is even. There is a logic behind simple results such as these, an order, a pattern.

Consider the study of algebra. One can learn to graph the equation of a parabola by simply following rules and plotting points. Now calculators are readily available to do that with a speed and precision we could never hope to achieve. But understanding why certain forms of equations always produce parabolic graphs involves a search for patterns in the way numbers behave. Discovering what types of real-world relationships are represented by parabolic graphs (for example, a pendulum swing related to the length of the pendulum) is even more interesting and scientific—and infinitely more valuable—than the ability to plot the curve when someone else provides the equation.

And pattern is not just in numbers and equations but also in everything around us. The world is full of pattern and order: in nature, in art, in buildings, in music. Pattern and order are found in commerce, science, medicine, manufacturing, and sociology. Mathematics discovers this order, makes sense of it, and uses it in a multitude of fascinating ways, improving our lives and expanding our knowledge. School must begin to help children with this process of discovery.

What Does It Mean to Do Mathematics?

Engaging in the science of pattern and order—in doing mathematics—is effortful and often takes time. There are lots of ideas to learn. Often these ideas show up on lists of "basic skills." For example, children should be able to count accurately, know their basic facts for addition and multiplication, have efficient methods of computing whole numbers, fractions, and decimals, know measurement facts such as the number of inches in a foot or quarts in a gallon, know the names of geometric shapes, and so on. But to master these bits and pieces is no more doing mathematics than playing scales on the piano is making music.

NCTM Standards The *Principles and Standards* document makes it very clear that there is a time and a place for drill but that drill should *never* come before understanding. Repetitive drill of the bits and pieces is not doing mathematics and will never result in understanding. Drill may produce short-term results on traditional tests, but the long-term effects have produced a nation of citizens happy to admit they can't do mathematics.

The Verbs of Doing Mathematics

Envision for a moment an elementary mathematics class where students are doing mathematics. What verbs would you use to describe the activity in this classroom? Stop for a moment and make a short list before reading further.

Children in traditional mathematics classes often describe mathematics as "work" or "getting answers." They talk about "plussing" and "doing times" (multiplication). In contrast, the following collection of verbs can be found in most of the literature describing the reform in mathematics education, and all are used in *Principles and Standards*:

explore	represent	explain
investigate	formulate	predict
conjecture	discover	develop
solve	construct	describe
justify	verify	use

These are science verbs indicating the process of "making sense" and "figuring out." When children are engaged in the kinds of activities suggested by this list, it is virtually impossible for them to be passive observers. They will necessarily be actively thinking about the mathematical ideas that are involved.

In classrooms where doing mathematics this way is a daily occurrence, the students are getting an empowering message: "You are capable of making sense of this—you are capable of *doing mathematics!*"

What Is Basic in Mathematics?

In a climate where "basics" are once again a matter of public discussion and there is an unrelenting pressure on teachers to raise test scores, it is useful to ask, "What is basic in mathematics?" The position of this text is as follows:

> The most basic idea in mathematics is that *mathematics makes sense!*
>
> ■ Every day students must experience that mathematics makes sense.
>
> ■ Students must come to believe that they are capable of making sense of mathematics.
>
> ■ Teachers must stop teaching by telling and start letting students make sense of the mathematics they are learning.
>
> ■ To this end, teachers must believe in their students—all of them!

Every idea introduced in the mathematics classroom can and should be completely understood by *every* child. *There are no exceptions!* There is absolutely no excuse for children learning any aspect of mathematics without completely understanding it. All children are capable of learning all of the mathematics we want them to learn, and they can learn it in a meaningful manner in a way that makes sense to them.

An Environment for Doing Mathematics

Look again at the verbs of doing mathematics. They are action verbs. They require reaching out, taking risks, placing ideas out where others can see. Contrast these with the verbs that might reflect the traditional mathematics classroom: *listen, copy, memorize, drill*. These are passive activities. They involve no risks and little initiative. Doing mathematics takes effort and initiative.

Though thinking, reasoning, and sense making can be fun, it can nevertheless be a bit frightening to stick out your neck when no one tells you exactly what to do. The classroom must be an environment where doing mathematics is not threatening and where every student is respected for his or her ideas. Students should feel comfortable taking risks, knowing that they will not be ridiculed if they are wrong.

The teacher's role is to create this spirit of inquiry, trust, and expectation. Within that environment, students are invited to do mathematics. Problems are posed; students wrestle toward solutions. The focus is on students actively figuring things out, testing ideas and making conjectures, developing reasons and offering explanations. Students work in groups, in pairs, or individually, but they are always sharing and discussing. Reasoning is celebrated as students defend their methods and justify their solutions.

An Invitation to Do Mathematics

If you are to create a classroom environment where children are truly doing mathematics, it is important that you have a personal feel for doing mathematics in this manner. It is likely that your experiences in mathematics classes have been quite different. The purpose of this portion of the chapter is to provide you with opportunities to engage in the science of pattern and order—to do some mathematics. Although the tasks or problems are appropriate for students in the intermediate and middle grades, you should not be at all concerned now with how children might approach these problems. Rather, get personally involved in the problems as an adult and discover as much as you can in the process. If possible, find one or two friends to work with you. Get some paper to scribble ideas on. Try not to be shy about your ideas. Respect and listen to the ideas of your friends. You can and should challenge their ideas, but don't belittle them.

The book will provide hints and suggestions in a poor substitution for the interaction of a teacher. Don't read too much at once. Stop and do as much as you can until you and your group are stuck—really stuck; then read a bit more.

Let's Do Some Mathematics!

We will explore four different problems. Each is independent of the others. None requires any sophisticated mathematics, not even algebra. Don't be passive! Try your ideas out. Have fun!

**START AND JUMP NUMBERS:
SEARCHING FOR PATTERNS**

You will need to make a list of numbers that begin with a "start number" and increase by a fixed amount we will call the "jump number." First try 3 as the start number and 5 as the jump number. Write the start number at the top of your list, then 8, 13, and so on, "jumping" by 5 each time until your list extends to about 130.

Your task is to examine this list of numbers and find as many patterns as you possibly can. Share your ideas with the group, and write down every pattern you agree really is a pattern.

Get to work before reading further. Keep looking for patterns until you simply cannot think of any more.

A Few Ideas. Here are some kinds of things you may already have thought of:

- There is at least one alternating pattern.
- Have you looked at odd and even numbers?
- What can you say about the number in the tens place?
- How did you think about the first two numbers with no tens-place digits?
- What happens when the numbers reach above 100? (There are two ways to think about that.)
- Have you tried doing any adding of numbers? Numbers in the list? Digits in the numbers?

 _____

If there is an idea in this list you haven't tried, try that now.

_____

Don't forget to think about what happens to your patterns after the numbers go over 100. How are you thinking about 113? One way is as 1 hundred, 1 ten, and 3 ones. But, of course, it could also be "eleventy-three," where the tens digit has gone from 9 to 10 to 11. How do these different perspectives affect your patterns? What would happen after 999?

When you added the *digits* in the numbers, the sums are 3, 8, 4, 9, 5, 10, 6, 11, 7, 12, 8, ... Did you look at every other number in this string? And what is the sum for 113? Is it 5 or is it 14? (There is no "right" answer here. But it is interesting to consider different possibilities.)

Next Steps. Sometimes when you have discovered some patterns in mathematics, it is a good idea to make some changes and see how the changes affect the patterns. What changes might you make in this problem?

 _____

Try some ideas now before going on.

_____

Your changes may be even more interesting than the following suggestions. But here are some ideas that seem a bit more obvious than others:

- Change the start number but keep the jump number equal to 5. What is the same and what is different?
- Try keeping the start number the same and examine different jump numbers. You will find out that changing jump numbers really "messes things up" a lot compared to changing the start numbers.
- If you have patterns for several different jump numbers, what can you figure out about how a jump number affects the patterns? For example, when the jump number was 5, the ones-digit pattern repeated every two numbers—it had a "pattern length" of two. But when the jump number is 3, the length of the ones-digit pattern is ten! Do other jump numbers create different pattern lengths?
- For a jump number of 3, how is the ones-digit pattern related to the circle of numbers in Figure 2.1? Are

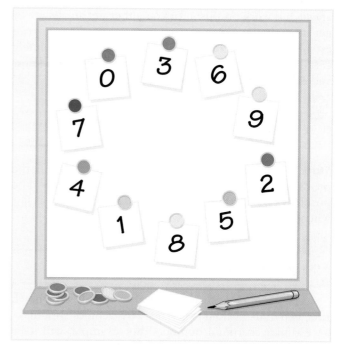

FIGURE 2.1 For jumps of 3, this cycle of digits will occur in the ones place. The start number determines where the cycle begins.

there other circles of numbers for other jump numbers?

- Using the circle of numbers for 3, find the pattern for jumps of multiples of 3, that is, jumps of 6, 9, or 12.

Looking Back. You may want to explore this idea even further—or perhaps you've had enough of jump numbers. There are more ideas than are suggested here.

A calculator can be used to make the list generation easy for young children or to work with big jump numbers, such as 25 or 36. Most simple calculators have an automatic constant feature that will add the same number successively. For example, if you press 3 $\boxed{+}$ 5 $\boxed{=}$ and then keep pressing $\boxed{=}$, you will get the first sequence of numbers you wrote. (The calculator "stores" the last operation of +5 and repeats the operation on the display for each press of $\boxed{=}$. This also works for the other three operations.)

TWO MACHINES, ONE JOB

Ron's Recycle Shop was started when Ron bought a used paper-shredding machine. Business was good, so Ron bought a new shredding machine. The old machine could shred a truckload of paper in 4 hours. The new machine could shred the same truckload in only 2 hours. How long will it take to shred a truckload of paper if Ron runs both shredders at the same time?

Get Started. Sometimes you just have to jump in and do something. Before reading any of the ideas that follow, go ahead and work on this until you either get an answer or get stuck. If you get an answer, try to decide how you can establish that it is correct. If you get stuck, be absolutely certain you are stuck. Write down everything you know and examine every idea you have had.

Work before reading on.

Stuck? Are you overlooking any assumptions made in the problem? Do the machines run simultaneously? The problem says "at the same time." Do they run just as fast when working together as when they work alone?

If this gives you an idea, pursue it before reading more.

Have you tried to predict approximately how much time you think it should take the two machines? Just make an estimate in round numbers. For example, will it be closer to 1 hour or closer to 4 hours? What causes you to answer as you have? Can you tell if your "guestimate" makes sense or is at least in the ballpark? Checking a guess in this way sometimes leads to a new insight.

Some people draw pictures to solve problems. Others like to use something they can move or change. For example, you might draw a rectangle or a line segment to stand for the truckload of paper, or you might get some counters (chips, plastic cubes, pennies) and make a collection that stands for the truckload.

Go back and try some more.

Consider Solutions of Others. Here are solutions of three elementary school teachers who worked on this problem. (The examples are adapted from Schifter & Fosnot, 1993, pp. 24–27.) Betsy teaches sixth grade. Here is Betsy's solution:

> Betsy holds up a bar of plastic cubes. "Let's say these 16 cubes are the truckload of paper. In 1 hour, the new machine shreds 8 cubes and the old machine 4 cubes." Betsy breaks off 8 cubes and then 4 cubes. "That leaves these 4 cubes. If the new machine did 8 cubes' worth in 1 hour, it can do 2 cubes' worth in 15 minutes. The old machine does half as much, or 1 cube." As she says this, she breaks off 3 more cubes. "That is 1 hour and 15 minutes, and we still have 1 cube left." Long pause. "Well, the new machine did 2 cubes in 15 minutes, so it will do this cube in $7\frac{1}{2}$ minutes. Add that onto the 1 hour and 15 minutes. The total time will be 1 hour $22\frac{1}{2}$ minutes." (See Figure 2.2.)

Cora teaches fourth grade. She disagrees with Betsy. Here is Cora's proposal:

> "This rectangle [see Figure 2.3] stands for the whole truckload. In 1 hour, the new machine will do half of this." The rectangle is divided in half. "In 1 hour, the old machine could do $\frac{1}{4}$ of the paper." The rectangle is divided accordingly. "So in 1 hour, the two machines have done $\frac{3}{4}$ of the truck, and there is $\frac{1}{4}$ left. What is left is one-third as much as what they already did, so it should take the two machines one-third as long to do that part as it took to do

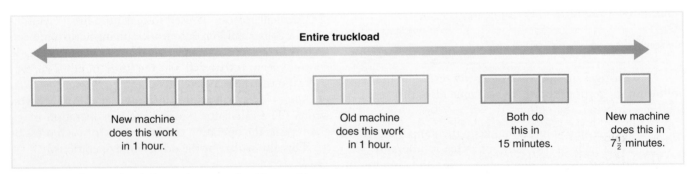

FIGURE 2.2 Betsy's solution to the paper-shredding problem.

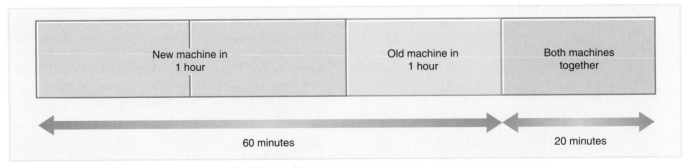

FIGURE 2.3 Cora's solution to the paper-shredding problem.

the first part. One-third of an hour is 20 minutes. That means it takes 1 hour and 20 minutes to do it all."

Sylvia teaches third grade. She and her partner have these thoughts:

At first, we solved the problem by averaging. We decided that it would take 3 hours because that's the average. Then Deborah asked how we knew to average. We thought we had a reason, but then Deborah asked how Ron would feel if his two machines together took longer than just the new one that could do the job in only 2 hours. So we can see that 3 hours doesn't make sense. So we still don't know whether it's 1 hour and 20 minutes or 1 hour and $22\frac{1}{2}$ minutes.

At the SummerMath institute where these teachers were participants, they were not told the solution to this problem. That in itself caused some disturbance. But there is little value in seeing a solution from a book or from a teacher. You end up feeling that the teacher is very smart and you are not so smart. No solution is provided here either.

If you have a solution, a good thing to do is see first why you think you are correct and try to articulate that. Then see if you can find a different way to solve the problem than the way you did it the first time. (What would be the value of two different solutions that both lead to the same answer?)

ONE UP, ONE DOWN

When you add 7 to itself, you get 14. When you make the first number 1 more and the second number 1 less, you get the same answer:

⇑ ⇓

7 + 7 = 14 is the same as 8 + 6 = 14

It works for 5 + 5 too:

⇑ ⇓

5 + 5 = 10 is the same as 6 + 4 = 10

What can you find out about this?

For children in the primary grades, this is a more challenging exploration then you may think. Your task here, however, is to examine *what happens when you change addition to multiplication in this exploration.* Start with 7 × 7. Make one factor go up and the other down. 7 × 7 = 49 and 8 × 6 = 48. *What other products should you examine?* What can you find out about changing factors in opposite directions?

Explore until you have developed some ideas. Write down whatever ideas you discover.

Try Using a Physical Model. You have probably found some interesting patterns. Can you tell why these patterns work? In the case of addition, it is fairly easy to see that

when you take from one number and give to the other, the total stays the same. That is not exactly the way multiplication works. One way to explore this is to make rectangles for each product and see how they change when you adjust one factor up and the other down (see Figure 2.4a).

You may prefer to think of multiplication as equal sets. For example, 7 × 7 means seven sets with seven things in each. You increase the number of sets and decrease the number in each set (or the other way around; see Figure 2.4b).

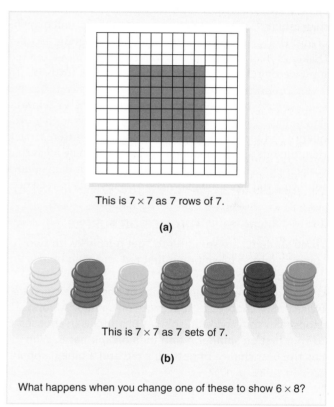

This is 7 × 7 as 7 rows of 7.

(a)

This is 7 × 7 as 7 sets of 7.

(b)

What happens when you change one of these to show 6 × 8?

FIGURE 2.4 Two physical ways to think about multiplication that might help in the exploration.

Work with one or both of these approaches to see if you get any insights.

Things to Examine

There are a few different ways to go with this exploration. Here are a couple of suggestions. You may be pursuing something a bit different than these ideas. That is fine! The idea in this problem is to conduct your own exploration—to see what you can find out.

- Have you looked at how the first two numbers are related? For example, 7 × 7, 5 × 5, and 9 × 9 are all products with like factors. How do those results differ when the two factors are 1 apart (8 × 7 or 13 × 12)? What about when the factors differ by 2 or by 3?

- Maybe you have adjusted the factors up and down by 1. What if you go from 7×7 to 9×5? Try making adjustments by other numbers.
- Does it make any difference in the results if you use big numbers instead of small ones?
- What if *both* factors increase?

This exploration has lots of answers, but the questions to answer are the ones *you* ask. When the problem is really yours and it is not clear that the teacher already knows the answer, students feel more ownership and interest. Rather than asking "What do you want me to do?" problem ownership shifts the situation to "I think I am going to . . ." (Baker & Baker, 1990). The suggested questions offered here were presented as a list because this is a textbook. In a classroom, the teacher can select challenges and make suggestions when necessary. The teacher can also help students make their own conjectures and observations. Frequently, children will pursue a completely different tack than the one anticipated. Scientists explore new ideas that strike them as interesting and promising rather than blindly following the direction of others. Mathematics is a science.

THE BEST CHANCE OF PURPLE

Three students are spinning to "get purple" with two spinners (either by spinning first red and then blue or first blue and then red; see Figure 2.5). They may choose to spin each spinner once or one of the spinners twice. Mary chooses to spin twice on spinner A; John chooses to spin twice on spinner B; and Susan chooses to spin first on spinner A and then on spinner B. Who has the best chance of getting a red and a blue (Lappan & Even, 1989, p. 17)?

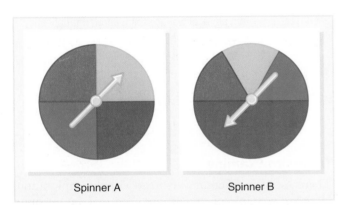

Spinner A   Spinner B

FIGURE 2.5 You may spin A twice, B twice, or A then B. Which option gives you the best chance of spinning a red and a blue?

As with the other problems, first think about the problem and what you know and then try something that gives you some help. Before reading the suggestions, see what you can come up with.

Try It Out

Sometimes it is tough to get a feel for problems that seem too abstract to think about. In situations involving chance find a way to create the chance and see what happens. For this problem, you can easily make spinners using a free-hand drawing on paper, a paper clip, and a pencil. Put your pencil point through the loop of the clip and on the center of your spinner. Now you can flip the paper clip "pointer." Try at least 20 pairs of spins for each choice and keep track of what happens.

- For Susan's choice (A then B), would it matter if she spun B first and then A? Why or why not?
- Explain why you think purple is more or less likely in one of the three cases compared to the other two. It sometimes helps to talk through what you have observed to come up with a way to apply some more precise reasoning.

Try these suggestions before reading on.

Try Tree Diagrams

On spinner A, the four colors each have the same chance of coming up. You could make a tree diagram for A with four branches, and all the branches would have the same chance (see Figure 2.6). On spinner B, what is the relationship between the blue region and each of the others? How could you make a tree diagram for B with each branch having the same chance?

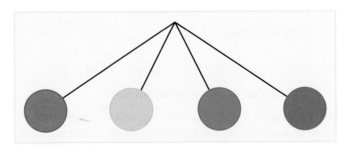

FIGURE 2.6 A tree diagram for spinner A in Figure 2.5.

How can you add to the diagram for spinner A so that it represents spinning A twice in succession? Why does your tree diagram make sense? What branches on your diagram represent getting purple?

How could you make tree diagrams for John's and Susan's choices? Why do they make sense?

Whatever idea you come up with on paper should be tested by actually spinning the spinner or spinners.

Tree diagrams are only one way to approach this. You may have a different way. As long as your way seems to be getting you somewhere, stick with that way. There is one more suggestion to follow, but don't read further if you have an idea to work on.

Using Grids

Suppose that you had a square that represented all the possible outcomes for spinner A and a similar square for spinner B. Although there are many ways to divide a square in four equal parts, if you use lines going all in the same direction, you can make comparisons of all the outcomes of one event (one whole square) with the outcomes of another event (drawn on a different square). When the second event (here the second spin) follows the first event, make the lines on the second square go the opposite way from the lines on the first. Make a tracing of one square in Figure 2.7 and place it on the other. You end up with 24 little sections.

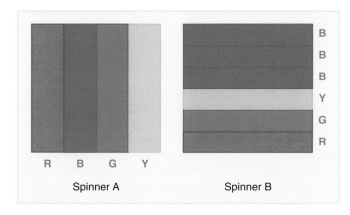

FIGURE 2.7 A square shows the chance of obtaining each color for the spinners in Figure 2.5.

Why are there six subdivisions for the spinner B square? What does each of the 24 little rectangles stand for? What sections would represent purple? In any other method you have been trying, did 24 come into play when you were looking at spinner A followed by B?

No Answer Book

If you have worked hard on any or all of the four tasks just presented, you still may not have answers or found all of the patterns and ideas that someone else found. If you really gave it some effort and took some risks in sharing whatever ideas you had, you are on the right track. The science of pattern and order sometimes takes a little time and nearly always requires effort.

No answers or solutions are given in this text. How do you feel about that? What about the "right" answers? Are your answers correct? What makes the solution to any investigation "correct"?

In the classroom, the ready availability of the answer book or the teacher's providing the solution or verifying that an answer is correct sends a clear message to children about doing mathematics: "Your job is to find the answers that the teacher already has." In the real world of problem solving outside the classroom, there are no teachers with answers and no answer books. Doing mathematics includes deciding if an answer is correct and why. It also includes being able to justify your reasoning to others.

Some More Explorations

Here are four more explorations. For these tasks, there are no hints or discussions, only the problems. The first two you could try with fourth- or fifth-grade children. All four would be useful in the middle grades. The main purpose of presenting them here is to give you an opportunity to do some more mathematics and to begin to experience what that means and feels like.

FOUR CONSECUTIVE NUMBERS

Some people say that to add four consecutive numbers, you add the first and the last numbers and multiply by 2. What can you find out about that?

Here is an example: 4, 5, 6, and 7 are four consecutive numbers. The sum is 22. Also $4 + 7 = 11$ and $11 \times 2 = 22$. The problem is taken from *Natural Learning and Mathematics* (Stoessiger & Edmunds, 1992). The authors use this task to provide a wonderful illustration of how 11- and 12-year-olds can generate ideas and make them grow. The book is highly recommended.

ACROBATS, GRANDMAS, AND IVAN

The problem is to use the information given to figure out who will win the third round of tug-of-war.

> **Round 1:** On one side are four acrobats, each of equal strength. On the other side are five neighborhood grandmas, each of equal strength. The result is dead even.
>
> **Round 2:** On one side is Ivan, a dog. Ivan is pitted against two of the grandmas and one acrobat. Again, it's a draw.
>
> **Round 3:** Ivan and three of the grandmas are on one side, and the four acrobats are on the other.
>
> **Who will win the third round?**

This problem was originally called "A Mathematical Tug-of-War" and is found in *Math for Smarty Pants* by Marilyn Burns (1982). For a discussion of how fifth graders approached the problem, see *50 Problem-Solving Lessons: Grades 1–6* (Burns, 1996). Silver, Smith, and Nelson (1995) discuss solutions offered by eighth graders.

PIZZAS: SMALL, MEDIUM, AND LARGE

Pizzas are often sold in small, medium, and large sizes—usually measured by the diameter of the circular pie. Of course, the prices are different for the three sizes. Is a large pizza usually the best buy?

The Sole D'Italia Pizzeria sells small, medium, and large pies. The small pie is 9 inches in diameter, the medium pie is 12 inches in diameter, and the large pie is 15 inches in diameter. For a plain cheese small pizza, Sole D'Italia charges $6; for a medium pizza, it charges $9; for a large pizza, it charges $12. Are these fair prices?

- **Which measures should be most closely related to the prices charged—circumference, area, radius, or diameter? Why?**
- **Use your results to write a report on the fairness of Sole D'Italia's pizza prices.**

This problem (Lappan & Briars, 1995, p. 139) has a number of characteristics worth noting. First, it is contextual; it is a very realistic problem that might interest middle grade students. Second, the teacher can predict with some certainty what mathematics students will encounter in this problem (measurement and relationships in the geometry of circles). There are lots of ideas about circle measurement involved. This would be a good problem to use *before* the children have developed a collection of formulas. Students have many ways to get at the circle measures, including measuring some actual circles. Formulas are not necessary. There is also a nice opportunity to discuss rate as a type of ratio in this problem.

TRAPEZOIDS

A trapezoid is a four-sided figure with one pair of opposite sides parallel. Draw a trapezoid that has an area of 36.

If a teacher or a text gives you a formula for the area of a trapezoid, this is not a very interesting task. But there are some nice possibilities for discovering patterns and learning about area and perhaps even developing a formula that can come from this problem. One suggestion is to get some grid paper and draw some trapezoids.

Helping Students Do Mathematics

Assuming that you have worked on some of the problems in this chapter, you have most likely been trying to make sense of the situations or tasks that you confronted. You were involved in the science of pattern and order. You were *doing mathematics.*

In the best of situations, you did this science, this mathematics, with others. Perhaps you shared your ideas, right or wrong, and tried to defend them. You listened to your peers and tried to make sense of their ideas. Together you tried to come up with a solution. And then you had to decide if your answer was correct without looking in an answer book or asking the teacher.

When students do mathematics like this on a daily basis in an environment that encourages risk and expects participation, it becomes an exciting endeavor. Individuals who are uncomfortable in an answer-oriented, teacher-directed environment begin to develop confidence. Students talk more, share more ideas, offer suggestions, and challenge or defend the solutions of others.

Being the teacher responsible for creating this environment may sound overwhelming. You may have envisioned teaching mathematics as relatively easy—just demonstrate the rules and manage practice. Creating a classroom culture and environment in which children are doing mathematics is not easy. There is no reason to believe that you will be an expert from the start.

So that you can create this mathematical community, you next need to understand how children develop mathematical ideas. That is what you will encounter in Chapter 3. In Chapter 4, we will build on the vision of what it means to do mathematics and an understanding of how children learn. There you will find strategies for teaching with tasks or problems. It is an exciting venture!

Reflections on Chapter 2

Writing to Learn

1. Explain what is meant by "Mathematics is a science of pattern and order." Contrast this view with traditional school mathematics.
2. How would you describe what it means to "do mathematics"?
3. Why is doing pencil-and-paper computation not "doing mathematics"?
4. What features of a classroom environment are important for students to be engaged in doing mathematics?
5. How can students come to believe that they are capable of making sense of mathematics?

For Discussion and Exploration

1. Explore the teacher's edition of any current basal textbook series for any grade level of your interest. Pick one chapter and identify lessons or activities that promote doing mathematics as a science of pattern and order. In general, would you say that the flavor of the chapter you selected is in the spirit of mathematics as a science of pattern and order? Examine any of the standards-based curricula (see listing on p. 10). Is the approach there any closer to doing mathematics?

2. In the *Professional Standards*, read the first vignette (pp. 11–15), in which a sixth-grade teacher who has taught for 5 years confronts her own realization that she needs to change. In reaction to this vignette you might
   a. Try her lesson with fifth- to seventh-grade children
   b. Design a lesson on a topic of your own choice that would serve the same purpose of getting children actively involved in real mathematics
   c. Take a lesson out of a fifth- to seventh-grade book and discuss how this teacher might now decide to teach the lesson

Recommendations for Further Reading

Lampert, M. (1990). When the problem is not the question and the solution is not the answer: Mathematical knowing and teaching. *American Educational Research Journal, 27,* 29–63.*
Magdelene Lampert is one of mathematics education's most articulate voices for making shifts toward classrooms as communities where children do mathematics. In this article, she clearly articulates the spirit of the traditional classroom and how it adversely affects the concept of mathematics held by children and teachers.

Malloy, C. E. (1999). Developing mathematical reasoning in the middle grades. In L. V. Stiff (Ed.), *Developing mathematical reasoning in grades K–12* (pp. 13–21). Reston, VA: National Council of Teachers of Mathematics.

Russell, S. J. (1999). Mathematical reasoning in the elementary grades. In L. V. Stiff (Ed.), *Developing mathematical reasoning in grades K–12* (pp. 1–12). Reston, VA: National Council of Teachers of Mathematics.
These two articles are the lead chapters in the 1999 NCTM yearbook on reasoning. Both authors provide excellent perspectives on the importance of helping children engage in the logical solution of problems. Russell's chapter begins by stating: "Mathematical reasoning must stand at the center of mathematics learning." Malloy makes the point that even in a diverse classroom different reasoning styles can be engaged to make learning happen.

Mokros, J., Russell, S. J., & Economopoulos, K. (1995). *Beyond arithmetic: Changing mathematics in the elementary classroom.* Palo Alto, CA: Dale Seymour Publications.

---

*Also reprinted in Carpenter, T. P., Dossey, J. A., & Koehler, J. L. (Eds.). (2004). *Classics in Mathematics Education Research.* Reston, VA: NCTM.

These three author/researchers from TERC use numerous examples from the elementary classroom to develop a realistic image of teaching mathematics from a problem-solving perspective. In looking at teaching, curriculum, and assessment, the importance of problem solving as a way of learning mathematics is quite clear. For a realistic look at reform mathematics and children solving problems, consider this useful, easily read book.

Schifter, D., & Fosnot, C. T. (1993). *Reconstructing mathematics education: Stories of teachers meeting the challenge of reform.* New York: Teachers College Press.
The authors describe teachers who confront their own concept of mathematics by doing real mathematics themselves. There are also many insights into the classrooms to which these teachers return. Here Betsy and Cora solve the paper-shredder problem (the context was changed). If you feel a bit threatened by the call for change, this is a book that can give you some company.

Online Resources

Suggested Applets and Web Links

A Maths Dictionary for Kids
www.teachers.ash.org.au/jeather/maths/dictionary.html
An extensive dictionary with each word illustrated by way of a small interactive explanation.

Classic Problems in Math
www.mathforum.org/dr.math/faq/faq.classic.problems.html
A nice collection of well-known problems (Train A leaves the station at . . .) along with discussion, solutions, and extensions.

Circle 21
http://nlvm.usu.edu/en/nav/frames_asid_188_g_2_t_1.html
An applet in which the goal is to insert numbers into overlapping circles so that the sum in each circle is 21. *Circle 0, Circle 3,* and *Circle 99* are similar applets involving integers.

Fibonacci Numbers and the Golden Section
www.mcs.surrey.ac.uk/Personal/R. Knott/Fibonacci/
Perhaps the most extensive collection of information about this well-known ratio.

Figure This
www.figurethis.org/index.html
A collection of 80 different challenges designed to engage middle grades students and their families.

How High
http://nlvm.usu.edu/en/nav/category_g_3_t_3.html
An applet in which two containers are shown with dimensions. The user determines the height the liquid in the first container will reach if poured into the second.

An additional list of books and articles related to the ideas in this chapter can be found on the Companion Web site at **www.ablongman.com/vandewalle6e.**

chapter 3

Developing Understanding in Mathematics

If the creation of the conceptual networks that constitute each individual's map of reality—including her mathematical understanding—is the product of constructive and interpretive activity, then it follows that no matter how lucidly and patiently teachers explain to their students, they cannot understand for their students.

Schifter and Fosnot (1993, p. 9)

It is a commonly accepted goal among mathematics educators that students should understand mathematics (Hiebert & Carpenter, 1992). The most widely accepted theory, known as *constructivism*, suggests that children must be active participants in the development of their own understanding. Constructivism provides us with insights concerning how children learn mathematics and guides us to use instructional strategies that begin with children rather than with ourselves.

A Constructivist View of Learning

Constructivism is firmly rooted in the cognitive school of psychology and the theories of Piaget dating back at least as far as 1960. Constructivism rejects the notion that children are blank slates. They do not absorb ideas as teachers present them. Rather, children are creators of their own knowledge.

The Construction of Ideas

The basic tenet of constructivism is simply this: *Children construct their own knowledge*. In fact, not just children, but all people, all of the time, construct or give meaning to things they perceive or think about. As you read these words, you are giving meaning to them. You are constructing ideas.

To construct or build something in the physical world requires tools, materials, and effort. How we construct ideas can be viewed in an analogous manner. The tools we use to build understanding are our existing ideas, the knowledge that we already possess. The materials we act on to build understanding may be things we see, hear, or touch—elements of our physical surroundings. Sometimes the materials are our own thoughts and ideas. The effort that must be supplied is active and reflective thought. If minds are not actively thinking, nothing happens.

The diagram in Figure 3.1 is meant as a metaphor for the construction of ideas. Consider the picture to be a small section of our cognitive makeup. The blue dots represent existing ideas. The lines joining the ideas represent our logical connections or relationships that have developed between and among ideas. The red dot is an emerging idea, one that is being constructed. Whatever existing ideas (dots) are used in the construction will necessarily be connected to the new idea because those were the ideas that gave meaning to it. If a potentially relevant idea that would add better meaning to the new idea is either not present in the learner's mind or is not actively engaged, then that potential connection to the new idea simply will not be made. Obviously, learners will vary in the number of connections between a new idea and existing ideas. Different learners will use different ideas to give meaning to the same new idea. What is significant is that the construction of an idea is almost certainly going to be different for every learner, even within the same environment or classroom.

Constructing knowledge is an extremely active endeavor on the part of the learner (Baroody, 1987; Cobb, 1988; Fosnot, 1996; von Glasersfeld, 1990, 1996). To construct and understand a new idea requires actively thinking about it. "How does this fit with what I already know?"

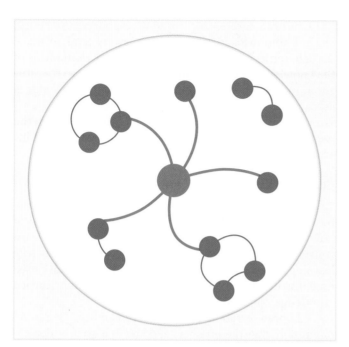

FIGURE 3.1 We use the ideas we already have (blue dots) to construct a new idea (red dot), developing in the process a network of connections between ideas. The more ideas used and the more connections made, the better we understand.

"How can I understand this in the face of my current understanding of this idea?" Mathematical ideas cannot be "poured into" a passive learner. Children must be mentally active for learning to take place. In classrooms, children must be encouraged to wrestle with new ideas, to work at fitting them into existing networks, and to challenge their own ideas and those of others. Put simply, constructing knowledge requires *reflective thought*, actively thinking about or mentally working on an idea. Reflective thought means sifting through existing ideas to find those that seem to be the most useful in giving meaning to the new idea.

Integrated networks, or *cognitive schemas*, are both the product of constructing knowledge and the tools with which additional new knowledge can be constructed. As learning occurs, the networks are rearranged, added to, or otherwise modified. When there is active, reflective thought, schemas are constantly being modified or changed so that ideas fit better with what is known.

The general principles of constructivism are based largely on Piaget's processes of assimilation and accommodation. *Assimilation* refers to the use of existing schemas to give meaning to experiences. *Accommodation* is the process of altering existing ways of viewing things or ideas that contradict or do not fit into existing schemas. Through reflective or purposeful thought, people may modify their existing schemas to accommodate these ideas (Fosnot, 1996).

Examples of Constructed Learning

Consider the solution methods of two fourth-grade children who had been taught the meanings of the operations and had developed a good understanding of place-value concepts, some of the "dots" the children had at their disposal. Both children were from predominantly urban schools where a highly constructivist approach to mathematics had been in place for several years. They were asked to solve the following problem: "Four children had 3 bags of M&Ms. They decided to open all 3 bags of candy and share the M&Ms fairly. There were 52 M&M candies in each bag. How many M&M candies did each child get?" (Campbell & Johnson, 1995, pp. 35–36). Their solutions are shown in Figure 3.2.

Both children were able to determine the product 3×52 mentally. The two children used different cognitive tools to solve the problem of $156 \div 4$. Marlena interpreted the task as "How many sets of 4 can be made from

FIGURE 3.2 Two fourth-grade children construct unique solutions to a computation.

Source: Reprinted with permission from P. F. Campbell and M. L. Johnson, "How Primary Students Think and Learn," in I. M. Carl (Ed.), *Prospects for School Mathematics* (pp. 21–42), copyright © 1995 by the National Council of Teachers of Mathematics.

156?" She first used facts that were either easy or available to her: 10 × 4 and 4 × 4. These totals she subtracted from 156 until she got to 100. This seemed to cue her to use 25 fours. Marlena made no hesitation in adding the number of sets of 4 that she found in 156 and knew the answer was 39 candies for each child.

Darrell's approach was more directly related to the sharing context of the problem. He formed four columns and distributed amounts to each, accumulating the amounts mentally and orally as he wrote the numbers. Like Marlena, Darrell used numbers that were either easy or available to him; first 20 to each, then 5, then 10, and then a series of ones. He added one of the columns without hesitation (Rowan, 1995).

If computational speed and proficiency were your goal, you might be tempted to argue that the children need further instruction. But both children clearly constructed ideas about the computation that had meaning to them. They demonstrated confidence, understanding, and a belief that they could solve the problem.

In contrast to these two children, consider a third-grade child in a traditional classroom. She has made a quite common error in subtraction, as shown in Figure 3.3. The problem appearing on a mathematics worksheet was subtraction, and the class had been doing subtraction with borrowing. This context narrowed the choices of ways to give meaning to the situation (the "dots" she would likely use). But this problem was a little different from the child's existing ideas about borrowing. The next column contained a 0. How could she take 1 from the 0? That part was different, creating a situation that for her was problem based. The child decided that "the next column" must mean the next one that has something in it. She, therefore, borrowed from the 6 and ignored the 0. This child used her existing ideas and gave her own meaning to the rule "borrow from the next column."

FIGURE 3.3 Children sometimes invent incorrect meanings by extending poorly understood rules.

Children rarely give random responses (Ginsburg, 1977; Labinowicz, 1985). Their answers tend to make sense in terms of their personal perspective or in terms of the knowledge they are using to give meaning to the situation. In many instances, children's existing knowledge is incomplete or inaccurate, or perhaps the knowledge we assume to be there simply is not. In such situations, as in the present example, new knowledge may be constructed inaccurately.

Construction in Rote Learning

Constructivism is a theory about how we learn. If it is correct, then that is how *all* learning takes place, regardless of how we teach. We cannot choose to have children learn constructively on some days and not others. Even rote learning is a construction. But what tools or ideas are used for construction in rote learning? To what is rotely learned knowledge connected?

Children searching for a way to remember 7 × 8 = 56 might note that the numbers 5, 6 and 7, 8 go in order. Or they may connect the number 56 to that "hard fact" since 56 is unique in the multiplication table (but then so is 54). Repetition of a routine procedure may be connected to some mantra-type recitation of the rule, as in "Divide, multiply, subtract, and bring down." This sequence has even been related to the mnemonic "Dirty monkeys smell bad." New ideas learned like this are connected to things that can hardly be called mathematical. Nor are they part of networks of ideas. Each newly learned bit is essentially isolated. Rote knowledge will almost never contribute to a useful network of ideas. Rote learning can be thought of as a "weak construction" (Noddings, 1993).

When mathematical ideas are used to create new mathematical ideas, useful cognitive networks are formed. Returning to 7 × 8, imagine a class where children discuss and share clever ways to figure out the product. One child might think of 5 eights and then 2 more eights. Another may have learned 7 × 7 and noted that this is just one more seven. Still another might look at a list of 8 sevens and take half of them (4 × 7) and double that. This may lead to the notion that double 7 is 14, and double that is 28, and double that is 56. Not every child will construct 7 × 8 using all of these approaches. However, the class discussion brings to the fore a wide range of useful mathematical "dots" so that the potential is there for profitable constructions.

Understanding

It is possible to say that we know something or we do not. That is, an idea is something that we either have or don't have. Understanding is another matter. For example, most students in grade 4 or 5 know something about fractions. Given the fraction $\frac{6}{8}$, nearly all students at this level will be able to read the fraction correctly and identify the 6 and 8 as the numerator and denominator, respectively. They may or may not be able to explain what the 6 and the 8 tell us about the fraction. Many students will know that this fraction is more than $\frac{1}{2}$. Some will think that it is a "big" fraction because the numbers are both somewhat big compared to the numbers in $\frac{1}{2}$ or $\frac{2}{3}$. That the fraction is equivalent to $\frac{3}{4}$ is also a reasonably common connection for fifth-grade students to make. However, different students may have different understandings of what it means to be equivalent. They may know that $\frac{6}{8}$ can be reduced to $\frac{3}{4}$ but not understand that $\frac{3}{4}$ and $\frac{6}{8}$ are identical numbers; it may be more difficult for them to see the equivalence of $\frac{6}{8}$ to $\frac{9}{12}$. Some may think that reducing $\frac{6}{8}$ makes it a smaller number. Those with a better understanding will be able to explain using a variety of models that equivalent fractions represent the same quantity. You could easily expand on the range of ideas that students often connect to their individualized concept of fractions—some ideas are correct, others are not. Each student brings a different set of dots to his or her knowledge of fractions. Each "understands" fractions in a different way.

Understanding can be defined as a measure of the quality and quantity of connections that an idea has with existing ideas. Understanding is never an all-or-nothing proposition. It depends on the existence of appropriate ideas and on the creation of new connections (Backhouse, Haggarty, Pirie, & Stratton, 1992; Davis, 1986; Hiebert & Carpenter, 1992; Janvier, 1987; Schroeder & Lester, 1989).

One way that we can think about an individual's understanding is that it exists along a continuum (see Figure 3.4). At one extreme is a very rich set of connections. The understood idea is associated with many other existing ideas in a meaningful network of concepts and procedures. Hiebert and Carpenter (1992) refer to "webs" of interrelated ideas. The two ends of this continuum were named by Richard Skemp (1978) as *relational understanding*—the rich interconnected web of ideas—and *instrumental understanding*—ideas that are isolated and, thus, essentially without meaning. Note that knowledge learned by rote is

at the isolated end of the continuum; it is instrumental knowledge that is learned without meaning.

Examples of Understanding

If we accept the notion that understanding has both qualitative and quantitative differences, the question "Does she know it?" must be replaced with "How does she understand it? What ideas does she connect with it?" In the following examples, you will see how different children may well develop different ideas about the same knowledge and, thus, have different understandings.

Understanding Computation

Computational procedures provide a good opportunity to see how understanding can differ from one child to another. For addition and subtraction with two- or three-digit numbers, a flexible and rich understanding of numbers and place value is very helpful. How might different children approach the task of finding the sum of 37 and 28? For children whose understanding of 37 is based only on counting, the use of counters and a count-all procedure is likely. (See Figure 3.5a.) A student who has learned something about tens and ones but with limited understanding may use the traditional algorithm, lining up the digits and beginning by adding 7 and 8. Some may write 15 for this sum and end up with an answer of 515. (See Figure 3.5b.) The understanding of place value these children possess is limited. It allows them to name the digit in the tens place, but this knowledge is not related to the actual size of the numbers, or the result would most likely be startling. Those who correctly use the algorithm may or may not be able to explain why it works.

Now consider children who understand that numbers can be broken apart in many different ways, who realize that from 38 to 40 is the same as from 8 to 10, or who notice that the sum of two numbers remains the same if you add something to one and subtract it from the other. These students can add in flexible ways. They may add 30

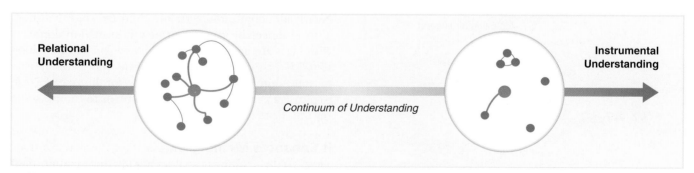

Relational Understanding

Continuum of Understanding

Instrumental Understanding

FIGURE 3.4 Understanding is a measure of the quality and quantity of connections that a new idea has with existing ideas. The greater the number of connections to a network of ideas, the better the understanding.

and 20 and then combine that with the sum of 8 and 7. They may think about 37 and 30 and take 2 away. Students with less flexible thinking might start with 38 and count on by tens and then ones: 38 then 48, 58 then 59, 60, 61, 62, 63, 64, 65. (See Figure 3.5c and d.)

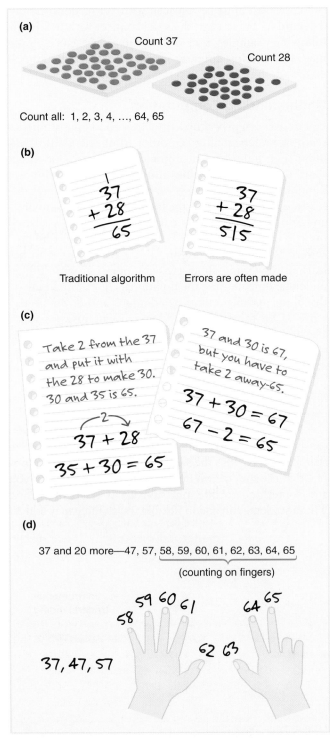

FIGURE 3.5 A range of computational examples showing different levels of understanding.

Connections with Early Number Concepts

Consider the concept of "seven" as constructed by a child in the first grade. Seven for a first grader is most likely connected to the counting procedure and the construct of "more than" and is probably understood as less than 10 and more than 2. What else will this child eventually connect to the concept of seven as it now exists? Seven is 1 more than 6; it is 2 less than 9; it is the combination of 3 and 4 or 2 and 5; it is odd; it is small compared to 73 and large compared to one-tenth; it is the number of days in a week; it is "lucky"; it is prime; and on and on. The web of potential ideas connected to a number can grow large and involved.

A Web of Ideas Involving Ratio

A clear example of the potential for rich relational understanding is found in the many ideas that can be associated with the concept of "ratio" (see Figure 3.6). Unfortunately, many children learn only meaningless rules connected with ratio, such as "given one ratio, how do you find an equivalent ratio?"

Of course, we cannot "see" a child's understanding. We can only make inferences about what it may be. The assumption in the preceding examples is that students use the ideas that they have in order to solve the tasks they are given. In the case of traditional computational rules, the risk is that some students actually learn the rules correctly but have very limited or no understanding of why these rules work.

Benefits of Relational Understanding

To teach for a rich or relational understanding requires a lot of work and effort. Concepts and connections develop over time, not in a day. Tasks must be selected. Instructional materials must be made. The classroom must be organized for group work and maximum interaction with and among the children. The important benefits to be derived from relational understanding make the effort not only worthwhile but also essential.

It Is Intrinsically Rewarding

Nearly all people, and certainly children, enjoy learning. This is especially true when new information connects with ideas already possessed. The new knowledge makes sense; it fits; it feels good. Children who learn by rote must be motivated by external means: for the sake of a test, to please a parent, from fear of failure, or to receive some reward. Rote learning is distasteful.

It Enhances Memory

Memory is a process of retrieving information. When mathematics is learned relationally, there is much less chance that the information will deteriorate; connected information is simply more likely than disconnected information to be

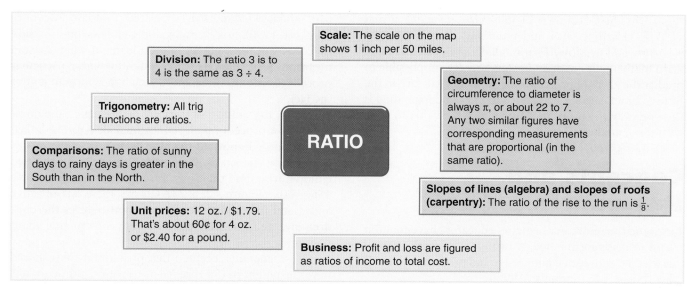

FIGURE 3.6 Potential web of associations that could contribute to the understanding of "ratio."

retained over time. Retrieval of the information is also easier. Connected information provides an entire web of ideas to reach for. If what you need to recall seems distant, reflecting on ideas that are related can usually lead you to the desired idea eventually. Retrieving disconnected information is more like finding a needle in a haystack.

There Is Less to Remember

Traditional approaches have tended to fragment mathematics into seemingly endless lists of isolated skills, concepts, rules, and symbols that often overwhelm teachers and students. Constructivists talk about teaching "big ideas" (Brooks & Brooks, 1993; Hiebert et al., 1996; Schifter & Fosnot, 1993). Big ideas are really just large networks of interrelated concepts. Frequently, the network is so well constructed that whole chunks of information are stored and retrieved as single entities rather than isolated bits. For example, knowledge of place value subsumes rules about lining up decimal points, ordering decimal numbers, moving decimal points to the right or left in decimal–percent conversions, rounding and estimating, and a host of other ideas.

It Helps with Learning New Concepts and Procedures

An idea fully understood in mathematics is more easily extended to learn a new idea. Number concepts and relationships help in the mastery of basic facts, fraction knowledge and place-value knowledge come together to make decimal learning easier, and decimal concepts directly enhance an understanding of percentage concepts and procedures.

Without these and many other connections, children will need to learn each new piece of information they encounter as a separate, unrelated idea.

It Improves Problem-Solving Abilities

The solution of novel problems requires transferring ideas learned in one context to new situations. When concepts are embedded in a rich network, transferability is significantly enhanced and, thus, so is problem solving (Schoenfeld, 1992). NAEP data from 1990 to 2003 indicate significant growth in the number of students who were at or above the basic and proficient levels in mathematics in the United States, especially between 2000 and 2003 (Kloosterman & Lester, 2003; NCTM, 2004). This growth may reflect an increased emphasis on understanding that has been seen in schools over that same period.

It Is Self-Generative

"Inventions that operate on understandings can generate new understandings, suggesting a kind of snowball effect. As networks grow and become more structured, they increase the potential for invention" (Hiebert & Carpenter, 1992, p. 74). Skemp (1978) noted that when gaining knowledge is found to be pleasurable, people who have had that experience of pleasure are likely to seek or invent new ideas on their own, especially when confronting problem-based situations.

It Improves Attitudes and Beliefs

Relational understanding has an affective effect as well as a cognitive effect. When ideas are well understood and make sense, the learner tends to develop a positive self-concept about his or her ability to learn and understand mathematics. There is a definite feeling of "I can do this! I understand!" There is no reason to fear or to be in awe of knowledge learned relationally. At the other end of the continuum, instrumental understanding has the potential of producing mathematics anxiety, a real phenomenon that involves fear and avoidance behavior.

The Learning Principle makes it very clear that learning with understanding is both essential and possible. That is, all children can and must learn mathematics with understanding. It is impossible to predict the kinds of problems that students will face in the future. The Learning Principle says that understanding is the only way to ensure that students will be able to cope with these unknown problems in the future.

Concepts and Procedures

For some time now, mathematics educators have found it useful to distinguish between two types of mathematical knowledge: conceptual knowledge and procedural knowledge (Hiebert & Lindquist, 1990).

Conceptual and Procedural Knowledge

Conceptual knowledge is knowledge that consists of rich relationships or webs of ideas (Hiebert & Lefevre, 1986). In terms of the dot metaphor shown in Figure 3.1, conceptual knowledge is an integrated collection of dots and the relationships between them. It is more than a singular idea. As Hiebert and Carpenter succinctly put it, conceptual knowledge is "knowledge that is understood" (1992, p. 78).

Procedural knowledge of mathematics is knowledge of the rules and the procedures used in carrying out routine mathematical tasks and also the symbolism used to represent mathematics. Procedural knowledge includes knowing the step-by-step procedures for performing a task such as multiplying 47×68. For example, "To add two three-digit numbers, first add the numbers in the right-hand column. If the answer is 10 or more, put the 1 above the second column, and write the other digit under the first column. Proceed in a similar manner for the next two columns in order." We can say that someone who can accomplish a task such as this has knowledge of that procedure. Knowledge of symbolism such as $(9 - 5) \times 2 = 8$, π, $\leq$, and $\neq$ is also part of procedural knowledge of mathematics.

Interaction of Conceptual and Procedural Knowledge

Procedural knowledge of mathematics does have a very important role both in learning and in doing mathematics. Algorithmic procedures help us do routine tasks easily and, thus, free our minds to concentrate on more important tasks. Symbolism is a powerful mechanism for conveying mathematical ideas to others and for "doodling around" with an idea as we do mathematics. But even the most skillful use of a procedure will not help develop conceptual knowledge that is related to that procedure (Hiebert, 1990). For example, doing endless long-division exercises will not help a child understand what division means. In fact, students who are skillful with a particular procedure are very reluctant to attach meanings to it after the fact.

From the vantage of learning mathematics, the question of how procedures and conceptual ideas can be linked is much more important than the usefulness of the procedure itself (Hiebert & Carpenter, 1992). Recall the two children who used their own invented procedure to solve $156 \div 4$ (see Figure 3.2, p. 23). Clearly, there was an active and useful interaction between the procedures the children invented and the ideas they were constructing about division.

It is generally accepted that procedural rules should never be taught in the absence of concepts, although, unfortunately, that happens far too often. These procedures without a conceptual base are the rules without reasons that lead to errors and a dislike of mathematics. All mathematics procedures can and should be connected to the conceptual ideas that explain why they work. As you will experience throughout this book, procedures for doing mathematics, symbolism, and definitions are always preceded by a strong conceptual development. Conceptually developed procedures are often indistinguishable as being conceptual or procedural knowledge. It is this complete connection and integration of concepts and procedures that should be a primary goal.

Classroom Influences on Learning

The theory of constructivism suggests that teaching is not a matter of transferring information to students and that learning is not a matter of passively absorbing information from a book or teacher. Effective teachers must help students construct their own ideas using ideas they already have. This does not mean that we simply let students play around and hope that they will magically discover new mathematical ideas. On the contrary, the manner in which a class is conducted, the social climate that is established within the classroom, and the materials available for students to work with all have an enormous impact on what is learned and how well it is understood. The following three factors influencing classroom learning are worth discussing:

- Student reflective thinking
- Social interaction with other students and with the teacher
- Use of models or tools for learning (manipulatives, symbolism, computer tools, drawings, and oral language)

Each factor impacts what and how well students learn. Each one is significantly influenced by you, the classroom teacher.

Reflective Thought

It is one thing to say, "I want my students to be reflective" and quite another to articulate just what that means. To begin with, *reflective thought* certainly involves some form of mental activity. It is an active, not a passive, endeavor. It involves figuring something out or trying to connect ideas that seem to be related. It happens when students try to make sense of the explanations of others, when they ask questions, and when they make explanations for or justify their own ideas. If you were to stop now and try to come up with your explanation of reflective thought, that process itself would undoubtedly involve reflective thinking.

If we assume that constructivist theory is correct, then we want students to be reflective about the ideas they learn. For a new idea you are teaching to be interconnected in a rich web of interrelated ideas, children must be mentally engaged. They must find the relevant ideas they possess and bring them to bear on the development of the new idea. In terms of the dots in Figure 3.1, we want to activate every blue dot students have that is related to the new red dot we want them to learn. The more relevant blue dots used—the more reflective thinking—the better the new ideas will be constructed and understood.

But we can't just hold up a big THINK sign and expect children to ponder the new thought. The challenge is to get them to be mentally engaged. As you will see later in Chapter 4 and throughout this book, a significant key to getting students to be reflective is to engage them in problems that force them to use their ideas as they search for solutions and create new ideas in the process. The problem-solving approach requires not just answers but also explanations and justifications for solutions. Students should be required to make these explanations both in discussions with their classmates and through writing and drawing.

Students Learning from Others

Reflective thought and, hence, learning are enhanced when the learner is engaged with others working on the same ideas. Students reside in classrooms. An interactive, thoughtful atmosphere in a classroom can provide some of the best opportunities for learning.

A worthwhile goal is to transform your classroom into what might be termed a "mathematical community of learners," or an environment in which students interact with each other and with the teacher. In such an environment students share ideas and results, compare and evaluate strategies, challenge results, determine the validity of answers, and negotiate ideas on which all can agree. The rich interaction in such a classroom significantly raises the chances that productive reflective thinking about relevant mathematical ideas will happen.

Vygotsky's Sociocultural Theory of Learning

Piaget helped us to focus on the cognitive activity of the child and to begin to understand how an individual uses ideas in a reflective manner to construct new knowledge and understanding. Vygotsky focused on social interaction as a key component in the development of knowledge. He believed that mental processes exist between people in social learning settings, and that from these social settings the learner moves ideas into his or her own psychological realm. This transfer of ideas from those that are external to the individual—ideas exchanged in the social setting—to those that are internal, personal constructs, Vygotsky referred to as *internalization*. Internalization only occurs within each learner's *zone of proximal development* (ZPD). "[T]he ZPD is not a physical space, but a symbolic space created through the interaction of learners with more knowledgeable others and the culture that precedes them" (Goos, 2004, p. 262).

To better understand the concept of the ZPD, consider that Vygotsky viewed the ideas that exist in the classroom, in books, and those shared by teachers and other authorities as distinct from the ideas constructed by the child. The well-formulated ideas that are external to the child he called *scientific concepts*, whereas those developed by the child (in the manner described by Piaget) he called *spontaneous concepts*.

Vygotsky talked about these two types of concepts as working in opposite directions, as illustrated in Figure 3.7. The scientific concepts work downward from external authority. As such, they impose their logic on the child. The spontaneous concepts bubble upward as a result of

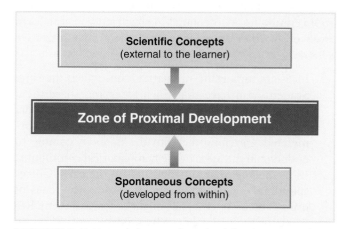

FIGURE 3.7 Vygotsky's zone of proximal development is the place where new external ideas are accessible to the learner with those ideas already developed.

reflective activity. In Vygotsky's ZPD, the child is able to meaningfully work with the scientific concepts from outside including those from classroom discussions. Here the child's own conceptual understanding is sufficiently advanced to begin to take in the ideas from "above."

It is not necessary to choose between a social constructivist theory that favors the views of Vygotsky and a cognitive constructivism that is built on the theories of Piaget (Cobb, 1996). In a classroom mathematical community of learners, students' learning is enhanced by the reflective thought that social interaction promotes. At the same time, the value of the interaction for individual students is determined to a large extent by the ideas that each individual brings to the discussions. When the conversation of the classroom is within any given child's ZPD, the best social learning will occur. Classroom discussion based on students' own ideas and solutions to problems is absolutely "foundational to children's learning" (Wood & Turner-Vorbeck, 2001, p. 186).

Goos (2004) points out that early interpretations of Vygotsky's ZPD led to the notion of *scaffolding* in which teachers and tutors assisted students in the solution of problems that they may not have solved on their own. This scaffolding concept, still popular today, tends to suggest more of a transfer-of-knowledge approach to learning rather than Vygotsky's understanding of internalization. Both Cobb and Goos suggest that in a more current view of the ZPD, knowledge is not transmitted. Rather, in a true mathematical community of learners there is something of a common ZPD that emerges across learners as well as the ZPDs of individual learners. Learning, even as seen with a constructivist viewpoint, occurs and is enhanced when students engage in the social culture of a mathematical community of learners.

Mathematical Communities of Learners

In the wonderful book *Making Sense* (Hiebert et al., 1997), the authors describe four features of a productive classroom culture for mathematics in which students can learn from each other as well as from their own reflective activity.

1. Ideas are important, no matter whose ideas they are. Students can have their own ideas and share them with others. Similarly, they need to understand that they can also learn from the ideas that others have formulated. Learning mathematics is about coming to understand the ideas of the mathematical community.
2. Ideas must be shared with others in the class. Correspondingly, each student must respect the ideas of others and try to evaluate and make sense of them. Respect for the ideas shared by others is critical if real discussion is to take place.
3. Trust must be established with an understanding that it is okay to make mistakes. Students must come to realize that errors are an opportunity for growth as they

are uncovered and explained. All students must trust that their ideas will be met with the same level of respect whether they are right or wrong. Without this trust, many ideas will never be shared.

4. Students must come to understand that mathematics makes sense. As a result of this simple truth, the correctness or validity of results resides in the mathematics itself. There is no need for the teacher or other authority to provide judgment of student answers. In fact, when teachers routinely respond with "Yes, that's correct," or "No, that's wrong," students will stop trying to make sense of ideas in the classroom and discussion and learning will be curtailed.

Classrooms with these characteristics do not just happen. The teacher is responsible for creating this climate. It happens over time in two ways. First, there must be some direct discussion of the ground rules for classroom discussions. Second, teachers can model the type of questioning and interaction that they would like to see from their students. More information on creating a community of learners is found in Chapter 4.

The Role of Models in Developing Understanding

It has become a cliché that good teachers use a "hands-on approach" to teach mathematics. Manipulatives, or physical materials to model mathematical concepts, are certainly important tools for helping children learn mathematics. But they are not the panacea that some educators seem to believe them to be. It is important that you have a good perspective on how manipulatives can help or fail to help children construct ideas.

Logico-Mathematical Concepts

Conceptual knowledge of mathematics consists of logical relationships constructed internally and existing in the mind as a part of a network of ideas. It is the type of knowledge Piaget referred to as logico-mathematical knowledge (Kamii, 1985, 1989; Labinowicz, 1985). By its very nature, mathematical conceptual knowledge is knowledge that is understood, as described earlier. Ideas such as seven, rectangle, ones/tens/hundreds (as in place value), sum, product, equivalent, ratio, and negative are all examples of mathematical relationships or concepts.

Figure 3.8 shows three blocks commonly used to represent ones, tens, and hundreds. By the middle of second grade, most children have seen pictures of these or have used the actual blocks. It is quite common for these children to be able to identify the rod as the "ten" piece and the large square block as the "hundred" piece. Does this mean that they have constructed the concepts of ten and hundred? All that is known for sure is that they have learned the names for these objects, the conventional names of the blocks. The mathematical concept of a ten is

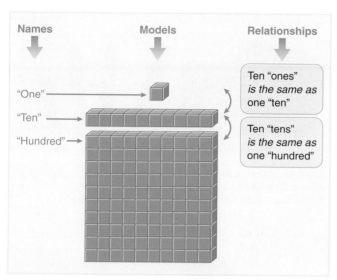

FIGURE 3.8 Objects and names of objects are not the same as relationships between objects.

that *a ten is the same as ten ones.* Ten is not a rod. The concept is the relationship between the rod and the small cube. It is not the rod or a bundle of ten sticks or any other model of a ten. This relationship called "ten" must be created by children in their own minds.

In Figure 3.9, the shape labeled A is a rectangle. But if we call shape B "one" or a "whole," then we might refer to shape A as "one-half." The idea of "half" is the *relationship* between shapes A and B, a relationship that must be constructed in our mind. It is not in either rectangle. In fact, if we decide to call shape C the whole, shape A becomes "one-fourth." The physical rectangle did not change in any way. The concepts of "half" and "fourth" are not in rectangle A; we construct them in our mind. The rectangles help us "see" the relationships, but what we see are rectangles, not concepts.

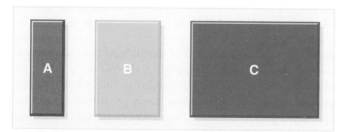

FIGURE 3.9 Three shapes, different relationships.

Models for Mathematical Concepts

A *model for a mathematical concept* refers to any object, picture, or drawing that represents the concept or onto which the relationship for that concept can be imposed. In this sense, any group of 100 objects can be a model of the con-

cept "hundred" because we can impose the 100-to-1 relationship on the group and a single element of the group.

It is incorrect to say that a model "illustrates" a concept. To illustrate implies showing. That would mean that when you looked at the model, you would see an example of the concept. Technically, all that you actually see with your eyes is the physical object; only your mind can impose the mathematical relationship on the object (Thompson, 1994). For a person who does not yet have the relationship, the model does not illustrate the concept *for that person.*

Examples of Models

As noted, physical materials have become enormously popular as tools for teaching mathematics. They can run the gamut from common objects such as lima beans for counters to commercially produced materials such as wooden rods or plastic geometric shapes. Figure 3.10 shows six common examples of models for six different concepts.

Ⅱ *pause and reflect* ——————

Consider each of the concepts and the corresponding model. Try to separate the physical model from the relationship that you must impose on the model in order to "see" the concept. Try this before reading further.

For the examples in Figure 3.10:

(a) The concept of "six" is a relationship between sets that can be matched to the words *one, two, three, four, five, six.* Changing a set of counters by adding one changes the relationship. The difference between the set of 6 and the set of 7 is the relationship "one more than."

(b) The concept of "measure of length" is a comparison of the length attribute of different objects. The length measure of an object is a comparison relationship of the length of the object to the length of the unit.

(c) The concept of "rectangle" includes both spatial and length relationships. The opposite sides are of equal length and parallel and the adjacent sides meet at right angles.

(d) The concept of "hundred" is not in the larger square but in the relationship of that square to the strip ("ten") and to the little square ("one").

(e) "Chance" is a relationship between the frequency of an event's happening compared with all possible outcomes. The spinner can be used to create relative frequencies. These can be predicted by observing relationships of sectors of the spinner.

(f) The concept of a "negative integer" is based on the relationships of "magnitude" and "is the opposite of." Negative quantities exist only in relation to positive quantities. Arrows on the number line model the opposite of relationship in terms of direction and size or magnitude relationship in terms of length.

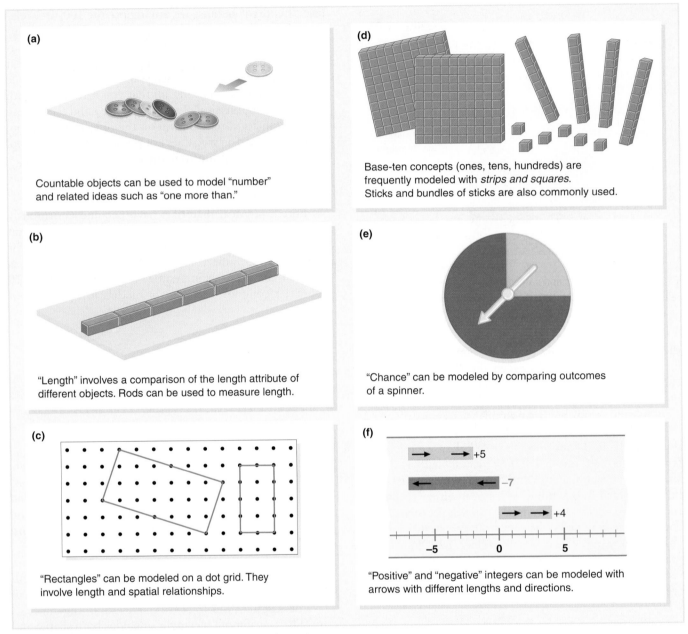

(a)

Countable objects can be used to model "number" and related ideas such as "one more than."

(b)

"Length" involves a comparison of the length attribute of different objects. Rods can be used to measure length.

(c)

"Rectangles" can be modeled on a dot grid. They involve length and spatial relationships.

(d)

Base-ten concepts (ones, tens, hundreds) are frequently modeled with *strips and squares*. Sticks and bundles of sticks are also commonly used.

(e)

"Chance" can be modeled by comparing outcomes of a spinner.

(f)

"Positive" and "negative" integers can be modeled with arrows with different lengths and directions.

FIGURE 3.10 Examples of models to illustrate mathematics concepts.

Staying with integers for a moment, this concept is often modeled with counters in two colors, perhaps red for negative quantities and yellow for positive. The "opposite" aspect of integers can be imposed on the two colors. The "magnitude" aspect is found in the quantities of red and yellow counters. Although colored counters and arrows are physically very different, the same relationships can be imposed on each. Children must construct relationships in order to "see" positive and negative integers in either model.

It is important to include calculators in any list of common models. The calculator models a wide variety of numeric relationships by quickly and easily demonstrating the effects of these ideas. For example, if the calculator is made to count by increments of 0.01 (press ⊞ 0.01 ⊟), the relationship of one-hundredth to one whole is illustrated. Press 3 ⊞ 0.01. How many presses of ⊟ are required to get from 3 to 4? Doing the required 100 presses and observing how the display changes along the way is quite impressive. Especially note what happens after 3.19, 3.29, and so on.

Models and Constructing Mathematics

To "see" a concept in a model, you must have some relationship in your mind to impose on the model. This is precisely why models are often more meaningful to the teacher than to students. The teacher already has the correct mathematical concept and can see it in the model. A student without the concept sees only the physical object or perhaps an incorrect concept.

Thus, it seems that a child would need to know the relationship before imposing it on the model. If the concept does not come *from* the model—and it does not—how does the model help the child get it? The answer lies in the notion of an evolving idea.

Mathematical concepts that children are in the process of constructing are not the well-formed ideas conceived by adults. New ideas are formulated little by little over time. As children actively reflect on their new ideas, they test them out through as many different avenues as we might provide. For example, this is a significant value of student discussion. Talking through an idea, arguing for a viewpoint, listening to others, and describing and explaining are all mentally active ways of testing an emerging idea against external reality. As this testing process goes on, the developing idea gets modified and elaborated and further integrated with existing ideas. When there is a good fit with external reality, the likelihood of forming a correct concept is good.

Models can play this same role, that of a testing ground for emerging ideas. Models can be thought of as "thinker toys," "tester toys," and "talker toys."* It is difficult for students (of all ages) to talk about and test out abstract relationships using words alone. Models give learners something to think about, explore with, talk about, and reason with.

Models should always be accessible for students to select and use freely. A variety of models should be available to help with an important idea. Students should be encouraged to select and use materials to help them work through a problem or explain an idea to their group. They should select models that make sense to them. Do not force students to use a particular model.

You will undoubtedly encounter situations in which you use a model that you think clearly illustrates an idea but the students just don't get it. Remember that you already possess the well-formed concept, so you are able to impose it on the model. The students, however, are in the process of creating the concept and are using the model to test an emerging idea. Your job is to get children to think with models, to work actively at the test-revise-test-revise process until the new concept fits with the physical model you have offered.

---

*The term *thinker toy* is taken from Seymour Papert's book *Mindstorms* (1980), in which the inventor of the Logo computer language describes the computer as a powerful and flexible device that encourages learners to play with ideas and work through problems. "Tester toys" and "talker toys" were suggested in the current context by Laura Domalik, a first-grade teacher.

Expanding the Idea of a Model

Lesh, Post, and Behr (1987) talk about five "representations" for concepts, two of which are manipulative models and pictures (see Figure 3.11). In their research, they also consider written symbolism, oral language, and real-world situations to be representations or models of concepts. Their research has found that children who have difficulty translating a concept from one representation to another are the same children who have difficulty solving problems and understanding computations. Strengthening the ability to move between and among these representations improves the growth of children's concepts.

The five representations illustrated in Figure 3.11 are simply an expansion of the model concept. The more ways that children are given to think about and test out an emerging idea, the better chance they have of correctly forming and integrating the idea into a rich web of ideas and relational understanding.

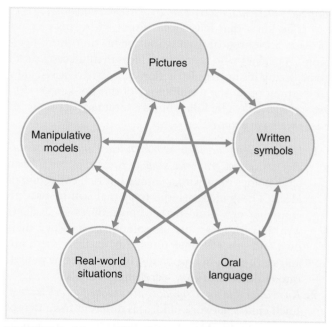

FIGURE 3.11 Five different representations of mathematical ideas. Translations between and within each can help develop new concepts.

Incorrect Use of Models

The most widespread misuse of manipulative materials occurs when the teacher tells students, "Do as I do." There is a natural temptation to get out the materials and show children exactly how to use them. Children will blindly follow the teacher's directions, and it may even look as if they understand. It is just as possible to get students to move blocks around mindlessly as it is to teach them to "invert and multiply" mindlessly. Neither promotes thinking or aids in the development of concepts (Ball, 1992; Clements & Battista, 1990).

A natural result of overly directing the use of models is that children begin to use them as answer-getting devices rather than as thinker toys. For example, if you have carefully shown and explained to children how to get an answer with a set of base-ten blocks, then students may simply follow your directions without any understanding. A mindless procedure with a good manipulative is still just a mindless procedure.

Teaching Developmentally

Teaching involves decision making. Decisions are made as you plan lessons. *What is the best task to propose tomorrow? Considering what happened today, what will move the children forward?* And decisions are made minute to minute in the classroom. *How should I respond? Should they struggle some more, or should I intervene? Is progress being made? How can I help Suzy move in the correct direction without discouraging her?*

The ideas that have been discussed in this chapter provide a theoretical foundation for making those decisions. A teacher who keeps these ideas in mind can be said to be basing his or her instruction on a constructivist view of learning or, in the terminology of this book, a *developmental approach*. The following is a summary of the major ideas we have explored.

1. *Children construct their own knowledge and understanding; we cannot transmit ideas to passive learners.* Each child comes to us with a unique but rich collection of ideas. These ideas are the tools that will be used to construct new concepts and procedures as students wrestle with ideas, discuss solutions, challenge their own and others' conjectures, explain their methods, and solve engaging problems. Ideas cannot be poured into children as if they were empty vessels.
2. *Knowledge and understanding are unique for each learner.* Each child's network of ideas is different from that of the next child. As new ideas are formed, they will be integrated into that web of ideas in a unique way as well. We should not try to make all children the same.
3. *Reflective thinking is the single most important ingredient for effective learning.* For children to create new ideas and to connect them in a rich web of interrelated ideas, children must be mentally engaged. They must find the relevant ideas they possess and bring them to bear on the development of new ideas and the solutions to new problems. Only by being mentally engaged with the task at hand can a true understanding of new ideas ever develop. "Passive learning" is an oxymoron!
4. *The sociocultural environment of a mathematical community of learners interacts with and enhances students' development of mathematical ideas.* Although learning is a reflective, internal process, students can test, explore, modify, and thus develop new ideas through interaction with other students and the teacher. An interactive community of students working together to make sense of mathematics can pull students into their zone of proximal development and contribute significantly to the development of understanding.
5. *Models for mathematical ideas help students explore and talk about mathematical ideas.* Logico-mathematical concepts are relationships rather than physical realities. Physical models and drawings only represent mathematical concepts to the extent that the desired mathematical relationship can be imposed on them. Models represent an external reality against which a child can test an emerging idea. Models are an important instructional tool but are not substitutes for lessons that promote reflective thinking.
6. *Effective teaching is a student-centered activity.* In a constructivist classroom, the emphasis is on learning rather than teaching. Students are given the task of learning. The role of the teacher is to engage the students by posing good problems and creating a classroom atmosphere of exploration and sense making. The source of mathematical truth is found in the reasoning carried out by the class. The teacher is not the arbiter of what is mathematically correct.

Reflections on Chapter 3

Writing to Learn

1. Describe in your own words what it means to say *we construct our own knowledge* as opposed to *we absorb knowledge.*
2. Explain why we should assume that each child's knowledge and understanding of an idea are unique for that child.
3. Contrast knowing an idea with understanding an idea. What does it mean to say that understanding exists on a continuum from relational to instrumental? Give an example of an idea, and explain how it might be learned by rote or with understanding.
4. Examine the seven benefits of relational understanding. Select the ones that you think are most important. Describe each benefit and why you personally believe it is significant.
5. Describe conceptual knowledge of mathematics and procedural knowledge of mathematics. Provide examples of each.

6. Explain the difference between knowing a procedure without a conceptual basis and knowing the same procedure with a conceptual basis. Which should come first?

7. What is reflective thought? Why is reflective thinking so important in the development of conceptual ideas in mathematics?

8. Describe Vygotsky's sociocultural view of learning. What is the zone of proximal development?

9. How can a social view of learning in which ideas come from the classroom be consistent with a constructivist view of learning in which ideas are constructed within the learner?

10. Explain why a *model* for a mathematical idea is not really an *example* of the idea. If it is not an example of the concept, what does it mean to say we "see" the concept when we look at the model?

11. Models were described as "thinker toys," "tester toys," and "talker toys." These refer to the ways that models can help students develop concepts. Explain how models can help a child develop a concept.

12. How can a teacher use models incorrectly?

For Discussion and Exploration

1. Discuss the meaning and validity of the following statement from Labinowicz (1985): "We see what we understand rather than understand what we see" (p. 7).

2. Consider your most recent classroom experience when mathematics was being taught. Would you say that the teaching reflected a constructivist view of learning? Why or why not? Did the teaching reflect a sociocultural view of learning?

3. Not every educator believes in constructivism. A common argument goes something like this: There is not enough time to let kids discover everything. Basic facts and ideas are more efficiently taught through careful, well-planned, and meaningful explanations. Students should not have to "reinvent the wheel." How would you respond to someone with this perception of school and learning?

Recommendations for Further Reading

Ball, D. L. (1997). From the general to the particular: Knowing our own students as learners of mathematics. *Mathematics Teacher, 90,* 732–737.

Don't be fooled because this article is in *Mathematics Teacher.* Deborah Ball, one of the leading advocates for classroom discourse and listening to children, offers a thought-provoking example of third-grade thinking about fractions while raising our awareness of how difficult it is to see into the minds of children. She makes the point that understanding is not an all-or-nothing idea. Trying to know what students know is not an easy task. Ball provides us with useful food for thought.

Brandy, T. (1999). *"So what?" Teaching children what matters in math.* Portsmouth, NH: Heinemann.

In the Introduction to this little book, the author reflects on how he knew how to respond to a child: "I knew because I knew the child. I recognized the process she was attempting to apply. I knew of other children who had been stuck in a similar place and how they had worked their way out of it." Brandy shares anecdotes, student work, and many of his insights gained after 20 years of teaching. This is a fun and informative book showing the inside of a truly student-centered classroom.

Buschman, L. (2003). Children who enjoy problem solving. *Teaching Children Mathematics, 9,* 539–544.

Although about children solving problems, this article is really about the enjoyment that students achieve when they are making sense of mathematics themselves rather than following rules. If you have any doubts about the value of students constructing their own ideas, this article should convince you otherwise.

Lampert, M. (1990). When the problem is not the question and the solution is not the answer: Mathematical knowing and teaching. *American Educational Research Journal, 27,* 29–63. Reprinted in T. P. Carpenter, J. A. Dossey, & J. L. Koehler (Eds.), *Classics in mathematics education research* (pp. 152–171). Reston, VA: National Council of Teachers of Mathematics.

If you are unable to access Lampert's book described next, this classic article is another good choice.

Lampert, M. (2001). *Teaching problems and the problems of teaching.* New Haven, CT: Yale University Press.

Lampert has a long-standing reputation as both a researcher and a teacher. In this large book she reflects on her personal experiences in teaching fifth grade and shares with us her perspectives on the many issues and complexities of teaching. It is wonderfully written and easily accessed at any point in the book. Stigler says it "is one of the most important books about education to appear in a decade." Yackle says that it should be required reading "for teachers who wish to develop into reflective practitioners." A great book to study or to keep by your bedside.

Schifter, D. (Ed.). (1996). *What's happening in math class? Envisioning new practices through teacher narratives* (Vol. 1). New York: Teachers College Press.

In each of the five chapters of this book, three or four teachers share their personal struggles at becoming more of a constructivist teacher. The last articles in each chapter are written by noted mathematics educators who offer their personal perspectives on what the teachers have so candidly shared. This is a book about constructivism in practice. The teacher-authors each work in quite different schools and represent a range of grades. However, the common threads among all of them help us understand why constructivism is such a popular theory in education today.

Online Resources

Suggested Applets and Web Links

Association for Supervision and Curriculum Development (ASCD)
www.ascd.org/portal/site/ascd/index.jsp
The ASCD Web site includes articles, information about its publications, plus articles and other publications related to learning.

Constructivism
http://carbon.cudenver.edu/~mryder/itc_data/
constructivism.html

Based at the University of Colorado, Denver, this site lists definitions and numerous papers on constructivist theories from Dewey to von Glasersfeld and Vygotsky.

Mathematics Education: Constructivism in the Classroom
http://mathforum.org/mathed/constructivism.html

Provided by the Math Forum, this page contains links to numerous sites concerning constructivism as well as articles written by researchers.

Mathematically Sane: Analysis
http://mathematicallysane.com/analysis.asp

Articles by authors who have analyzed issues in mathematics education.

An additional list of books and articles related to the ideas in this chapter can be found on the Companion Web site at **www.ablongman.com/vandewalle6e.**

chapter 4

Teaching Through Problem Solving

Allowing the subject to be problematic means allowing students to wonder why things are, to inquire, to search for solutions, and to resolve incongruities. It means that both the curriculum and instruction should begin with problems, dilemmas, and questions for students.

Hiebert et al. (1996, p. 12)

For nearly two decades since publication of the original NCTM *Standards* document (1989), evidence has continued to mount that problem solving is a powerful and effective vehicle for learning.

> Solving problems is not only a goal of learning mathematics but also a major means of doing so. . . . Problem solving is an integral part of all mathematics learning, and so it should not be an isolated part of the mathematics program. Problem solving in mathematics should involve all the five content areas described in these Standards. . . . Good problems will integrate multiple topics and will involve significant mathematics. (NCTM, 2000, p. 52)

That is, students solve problems not to apply mathematics but to learn new mathematics. When students engage in well-chosen problem-based tasks and focus on the solution methods, what results is new understanding of the mathematics embedded in the task. When students are actively looking for relationships, analyzing patterns, finding out which methods work and which don't, justifying results, or evaluating and challenging the thoughts of others, they are necessarily and optimally engaging in reflective thought about the ideas involved. Learning through problem solving is the topic of this chapter and a theme of this book.

Problem Solving as a Principal Instructional Strategy

The following statement is a major thesis of this chapter. It is a clear reflection of the *Principles and Standards* document as just noted and represents the current thinking of a wide segment of mathematics education researchers.

> **Most, if not all, important mathematics concepts and procedures can best be taught through problem solving.**

Tasks or problems can and should be posed that engage students in thinking about and developing the important mathematics they need to learn. This proposition may strike some as extreme or unrealistic. Rather than accept it blindly or reject it, let's first consider why it may make sense.

Problems and Tasks for Learning Mathematics

A *problem* is defined here as any task or activity for which the students have no prescribed or memorized rules or methods, nor is there a perception by students that there is a specific "correct" solution method (Hiebert et al., 1997).

A problem for learning mathematics also has these features:

* *It must begin where the students are.* The design or selection of the task must take into consideration the current understanding of the students. They should

have the appropriate ideas to engage and solve the problem and yet still find it challenging and interesting. They should see the task as something to make sense of.

- *The problematic or engaging aspect of the problem must be due to the mathematics that the students are to learn.* In solving the problem or doing the activity, students should be concerned primarily with making sense of the mathematics involved and thereby developing their understanding of those ideas. Although it is acceptable and even desirable to have contexts for problems that make them interesting, these aspects should not be the focus of the activity. Nor should nonmathematical activity (cutting and pasting, coloring graphs, etc.) detract from the mathematics involved.

- *It must require justifications and explanations for answers and methods.* Students should understand that the responsibility for determining if answers are correct and why they are correct rests with them. Justification should be an integral part of their solutions.

It is important to understand that mathematics is to be taught *through* problem solving. That is, problem-based tasks or activities are the vehicle by which the desired curriculum is developed. The learning is an outcome of the problem-solving process.

An Illustration

Teaching with problem-based tasks is student centered rather than teacher centered. It begins with and builds on the ideas that children have available—their "blue dots," their understandings. It is a process that requires faith in children—a belief that all children can create meaningful ideas about mathematics.

Suppose that you are teaching fifth grade and the topic is comparison of fractions—given two fractions, tell which is greater. The teach-by-telling approach provides a rule: Get common denominators, and compare the numerators. You accompany the rule with a conceptual explanation and pictures so that students will see the concept. However, students are aware of the exercises to come and how to do them. The explanation is of little value since the rule is all that is necessary to get through the day. As your students find the common denominators and complete the exercises, they are doing little more than third-grade multiplication. They are not thinking about fraction concepts at all.

In contrast, at the 1999 NCTM annual conference, Marilyn Burns shared these two solutions given by fifth graders who were asked to compare $\frac{6}{8}$ and $\frac{4}{5}$. No rules or procedures had been provided.

I know that $\frac{4}{5}$ is the same as $\frac{8}{10}$ and $\frac{8}{10}$ is two-tenths away from a whole. I know that $\frac{6}{8}$ is two-eighths away from a

whole. And since tenths are smaller than eighths, $\frac{8}{10}$ must be closer to the whole and so $\frac{4}{5}$ is larger.

I know that $\frac{6}{8}$ is the same as $\frac{12}{16}$ and $\frac{4}{5}$ is the same as $\frac{12}{15}$. Since fifteenths are bigger than sixteenths, $\frac{4}{5}$ must be larger.

 pause and reflect ——————————

What ideas about fractions were these students using? Did the two students use different ideas? If they had been told, "To compare two fractions first find a common denominator and then choose the fraction with the larger new numerator," how would their thinking have been different?

———————————————————

These students were concentrating on the meaning of fractions and the size of fractional parts. The second student actually used a common *numerator* approach that is never taught in schools but is completely reasonable. These students and the others in their class almost certainly learned more than had they blindly followed rules. (In Chapter 16, you will learn more about ways students can compare fractions without recourse to rules.)

A Shift in Thinking About Mathematics Instruction

Traditionally, the teacher taught the mathematics, the students practiced it for a while, and then they were expected to use the new skills or ideas in solving problems. This approach, strongly engrained in our culture, has rarely worked well. First, it assumes that all children at that time possess the ideas required (the blue dots) to make sense of the explanation in the manner the teacher thinks is best. This means that there is only one way for each student to "get it." It's the teacher's way or no way. However, it is unrealistic to expect the existence of a singular set of ideas across any typical class. Although a show-and-tell approach sometimes succeeds with some children, showing and telling depends on passive absorption of ideas and leaves most students believing that mathematics is mysterious and beyond understanding.

The second difficulty with the teach-then-solve paradigm is that problem solving is separated from the learning process. Children who have come to expect the teacher to tell them the rules are unlikely to solve problems for which solution methods have not been provided. By separating teaching from problem solving and struggling with ideas, learning mathematics is separated from doing mathematics. This simply does not make sense.

Effective lessons begin where the students are, not where teachers are. That is, teaching should begin with the ideas that children already have, the ideas they will use to create new ones. To engage students requires tasks or activities that are problem based and require thought. Students learn mathematics as a *result* of solving problems. Mathematical ideas are the *outcomes* of the problem-solving experience rather than elements that must be taught before problem solving (Hiebert et al., 1996, 1997). Furthermore, the process of solving problems is now completely interwoven with the learning; children are *learning* mathematics by *doing* mathematics!

The Value of Teaching with Problems

There is no doubt that teaching with problems is difficult. Tasks must be designed or selected each day, taking into consideration the current understanding of the students and the needs of the curriculum. It is often difficult to plan more than a few days in advance. If you have a traditional textbook, modifications will need to be made. There are good reasons to go to this effort.

- *Problem solving places the focus of the students' attention on ideas and sense making.* When solving problems, students are necessarily reflecting on the ideas that are inherent in the problems. Emerging ideas are more likely to be integrated with existing ones, thereby improving understanding. By contrast, no matter how skillfully a teacher provides explanations and directions, students will attend to the directions but rarely to the ideas.

- *Problem solving develops the belief in students that they are capable of doing mathematics and that mathematics makes sense.* Every time you pose a problem-based task and expect a solution, you say to students, "I believe you can do this." Every time the class solves a problem and students develop their understanding, confidence and self-worth are enhanced.

- *Problem solving provides ongoing assessment data that can be used to make instructional decisions, help students succeed, and inform parents.* As students discuss ideas, draw pictures or use manipulatives, defend their solutions and evaluate those of others, and write reports or explanations, they provide you with a steady stream of valuable information for planning the next lesson, helping individual students, evaluating their progress, and communicating with parents.

- *Problem solving allows an entry point for a wide range of students.* Good problem-based tasks have multiple paths to the solution. Students may solve 42 − 26 by counting out a set of 42 counters and removing 26; by adding onto 26 in various ways; by subtracting 20 from 40 leaving 22, and then taking off 6 more; by counting forward (or backward) on a hundreds chart; or by using a standard computational method. Each student gets to make sense of the task using his or her own ideas. Furthermore, students expand on these ideas and grow in their understanding as they hear and reflect on the solution strategies of others. In contrast,

the teacher-directed approach ignores diversity to the detriment of most students.

- *A problem-based approach engages students so that there are fewer discipline problems.* Many discipline issues in a classroom are the result of students becoming bored, not understanding the teacher directions, or simply finding following directions to be tedious. Most students who are permitted to solve problems in ways that make sense to them find the process intrinsically rewarding. There is less reason to act out or to cause trouble. The task of learning is engaging.

- *Problem solving develops "mathematical power."* Students solving problems in class will be engaged in all five of the process standards described by the *Principles and Standards* document: problem solving, reasoning, communication, connections, and representation. These are the processes of doing mathematics.

- *It is a lot of fun!* Teachers who teach in this manner never return to a teach-by-telling mode. The excitement of students' developing understanding through their own reasoning is worth all the effort. And, of course, it is fun for the students.

Examples of Problem-Based Tasks

In Chapter 3, you saw that mathematical ideas could be categorized as conceptual or procedural. Students can learn both types of mathematics through problem-based activities. Here are some examples in each category.

Conceptual Mathematics

The following problem may be used for different purposes, depending on the students.

Think about the number 6 broken into two different amounts. Draw a picture to show a way that six things can be broken in two parts. Think up a story to go with your picture.

At the kindergarten or first-grade level, the teacher may want students simply to think about different parts of 6 and to connect these ideas into a context. In first or second grade, the teacher may challenge children to find all of the combinations rather than focus on the story or context. There is a nice relationship and pattern to be constructed. In a class discussion following work on the task, students are likely to develop an orderly process for listing all of the combinations: As one part grows from 0 to 6, the other part begins at 6 and shrinks by ones to 0. There are seven combinations for 6.

The following task might be used in grades 3–6 as part of the development of fraction concepts.

Place an X on the number line about where $\frac{11}{8}$ would be. Explain why you put your X where you did. Perhaps you will want to draw and label other points on the line to help explain your answer.

0   2

Note that the task includes a suggestion for how to respond but does not specify exactly what must be done. Students are able to use their own level of reasoning and understanding to justify their answers. In the follow-up discussion, the teacher may well expect to see a variety of justifications from which to help the class refine ideas about fractions that are greater than 1.

I used two identical shapes to make a rectangle. What might they have been? (Baker & Baker, 1991)

This task, appropriate for grades 3–8, is very open-ended. There is a good potential for students to learn about congruent shapes and rotations. (When two congruent shapes form a rectangle, one can be rotated around the center point of the rectangle to match the other.) With this problem, everyone will be able to contribute some ideas and will be ready to reflect on the ideas of others.

Use your graphing calculator to find the intersection of the lines for $y = 3x - 6$ and $y = -2x + 4$. What do the coordinates of the point of intersection have to do with the two equations? Explain.

Students in an eighth-grade algebra class can use a variety of methods to find the point of intersection (graphing calculator, tables, graphs sketched on paper). They will find that the coordinates of the intersection point are solutions to both equations. This problem is a good example of how students can discover a significant relationship by figuring it out on their own, rather than by having it presented as a fact and explained to them.

Procedures and Processes

Critics of the problem-solving approach often point to the need for students to learn basic skills, saying that these must be taught through direct instruction. In reality, students can develop procedures via a problem-solving approach. Imagine a class of second graders who had never been taught to add two-digit numbers in the conventional

manner. They are challenged to find the sum of 48 and 25. In one second-grade classroom, at least seven different solution methods were offered by the students. Two children employed two different counting techniques using a hundreds chart for assistance. Here are solutions of some of the others:

$4\boxed{8} + 2\boxed{5}$ (Boxed digits help "hold" them.)
$40 + 20 = 60$
$8 + 2 = 10$ $\boxed{3}$ (The 3 is left from the 5.)
$60 + 10 = 70$
$70 + 3 = 73$

$40 + 20 = 60$
$60 + 8 = 68$
$68 + 5 = 73$

$48 + 20 = 68$
$68 + 2 \ (\textit{"from the 5"}) = 70$
"Then I still have that 3 from the 5."
$70 + 3 = 73$

$25 + 25 = 50$ $\boxed{23}$
$50 + 23 = 73$
Teacher: Where does the 23 come from?
"It's sort of from the 48."
How did you split up the 48?
"20 and 20 and I split the 8 into 5 and 3."

$48 - 3 = 45$ $\boxed{3}$
$45 + 25 = 70$
$70 + 3 = 73$

In this class (reported by Russell, 1997), the students show a variety of levels of thinking and many interesting techniques. They had learned from each other the trick of placing numbers in "hold boxes," although not everyone used it. The children who are counting on the hundreds chart are showing that they may not yet have developed adequate place-value tools to understand these more sophisticated methods. Or the class discussion may help them activate those ideas or "dots" they simply had not considered. One question is this: Are these invented methods efficient or adequate? Regardless of how you feel about that, these children are at least minimally prepared to consider a variety of methods because they are developing meaningful ideas about the process. One option is to offer students an efficient way of adding two-digit numbers and asking the students to figure out why it works and to decide if it will work every time.

Imagine for yourself what might happen if fifth-grade students were asked to add 3.72 + 1.6 before having been told about lining up decimal points. Many students will do it incorrectly, perhaps aligning the 2 and 6 or the 3 and 1. The decimal may be placed in various places. But students attempting to defend their solutions will need to confront the size of the answer and the meaning of the digits in each position. A class of practiced problem solvers will soon develop a solid approach for adding decimals.

Gary Tsuruda is a middle school teacher. His classes frequently work in small groups to solve problems. Figure 4.1 shows one example. Notice that the initial questions bring the requisite ideas needed for the task to the students' conscious level. Next they are asked to do some exploration and look for patterns. From these explorations the group must come up with a formula, test it, describe how it was developed, and illustrate its use.

TRAPEZOID AREA

GOAL: *Find an easy way to determine the area of any trapezoid.*

Be sure that you understand the answers to each of these questions:

1. What does "area" mean?
2. What is a trapezoid?
3. How do you find the area of other polygons? Show as many different ways as you can.

Now see if your group can find an easy way to determine the area of any trapezoid.

HINTS:

1. Draw several trapezoids on dot paper and find their areas. Look for patterns.
2. Consider how you find the area of other polygons. Are any of the key ideas similar?
3. You might try cutting out trapezoids and piecing them together.
4. If you find a way to determine the area, make sure it is as easy as you can make it and that it works for *any* trapezoid.

WRITE-UP:

1. Explain your answers to the first three questions in detail. Tell how your group reached agreement on the answers.
2. Tell what you did to get your formula for the area of any trapezoid. Did you use any of the hints? How did they help you?
3. Show your formula and give an illustration of how it works.

FIGURE 4.1 A middle school example in which students are required to construct a formula.

Source: From *Putting It Together: Middle School Math in Transition* (p. 7), by G. Tsuruda, 1994 Portsmouth, NH: Heinemann, a division of Reed Elsevier Inc. Reprinted by permission of Gary Tsuruda.

Tsuruda (1994) reports that every group was able to produce a formula. "Not all the formulas looked like the typical textbook formula, but they were all correct, and more important, each formula made sense according to the way the students in that group had constructed the knowledge from the data they themselves had generated" (p. 6).

In all of these examples, the students are very much engaged in the processes of doing mathematics—figuring out procedures, not accepting them blindly. What is abundantly clear is that the more problem solving that students do, the more willing they are to solve problems and the more methods they develop for attacking future problems (Boaler, 1998, 2002; Boaler & Humphries, 2005; Buschman, 2003 a,b; Campbell, 1996; Rowan & Bourne, 1994; Silver, Smith, & Nelson, 1995; Silver & Stein, 1996; Wood, Cobb, Yackel, & Dillon, 1993).

A Three-Part Lesson Format

U.S. teachers typically spend a small portion of a lesson explaining or reviewing an idea and then go into "production mode," where students wade through a set of exercises. Lessons organized in this explain-then-practice pattern condition students to focus on procedures so that they can finish the exercises. Teachers find themselves going from desk to desk reteaching and explaining to individuals. This is in significant contrast to a lesson built around a single problem, the typical approach for student-centered problem-based lessons.

It is useful to think of a lesson consisting of three simple parts, *before*, *during*, and *after*. (See Figure 4.2.) For most lessons, these three lesson parts are built around a single problem or task for the students. If time is allotted for each segment, it is quite easy to devote approximately one hour or a full class to one problem. There are times when a task may not merit a full lesson; a mental mathematics activity is a good example. Even here, it is useful to keep the same three components of a lesson in mind.

Each part of the lesson has a specific agenda or objective. How you attend to these agendas in each portion of the lesson may vary depending on the class, the problem itself, and the purpose of the lesson.

The *Before* Phase of a Lesson

There are three related agendas for the *before* phase of a lesson:

1. Be sure that students understand the problem so that you will not need to clarify or explain to individuals later in the lesson.
2. Clarify your expectations to students before they begin working on the problem. This includes both how

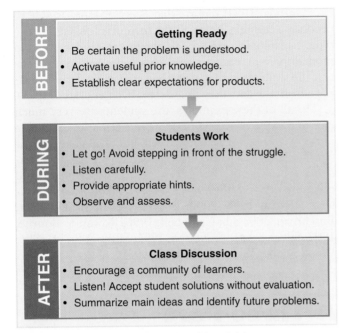

FIGURE 4.2 Teaching through problem solving suggests a simple three-part structure for lessons.

they will be working (individually or in pairs or small groups) and what product you expect in addition to an answer.

3. Get students mentally prepared to work on the problem and think about the previous knowledge they have that will be most helpful.

These *before-phase* agendas need not be addressed in the order listed. For example, for some lessons you will do a short activity to activate students' prior knowledge for the problem and then present the problem and clarify expectations. Other lessons may begin with a statement of the problem and may or may not have a readiness activity.

Teacher Actions in the *Before* Phase

The kinds of things you do in the *before* portion of a lesson will vary with the task. Some tasks you can begin with immediately. For example, if your students are used to solving story problems and know they are expected to use words, pictures, and numbers to explain their solutions in writing, all that may be required is to read through the problem with them and be sure all understand it. The actual presentation of the task or problem may occur at the beginning or at the end of your *before* actions.

Be Sure the Task Is Understood

This action is not optional! You must always be sure that students understand the problem before setting them to work. Remember that their perspective is different from yours.

Consider the task of mastering the multiplication facts. The most difficult facts can each be connected or related to an easier fact already learned.

Use a multiplication fact you already know to help you solve each of these facts: 4 × 6, 6 × 8, 7 × 6, 3 × 8.

For this task, it is essential that students understand the idea of using a helping fact. They have most likely used helping facts in addition. You can build on this by asking, "When you were learning addition facts, how could knowing 6 + 6 help you figure out 6 + 7?" You may also need to help students understand what is meant by a fact they know—one they have mastered and know without counting.

When using a word problem, it is useful in the lower grades to ask a series of direct questions that can be answered just by looking at the problem.

The local candy store purchased candy in cartons holding 12 boxes per carton. The price paid for one carton was $42.50. Each box contained 8 candy bars that the store planned to sell individually. What was the candy store's cost for each candy bar?

"What did the candy store do? What is in a carton? What is in a box? What is the price of one carton? What does that mean when it says 'each box'?" The last question here is to identify vocabulary that may be misunderstood. It is also useful to be sure students can explain to you what the problem is asking. Rereading a problem does little good, but having students restate the problem in their own words forces them to think about what the problem is asking.

Establish Expectations

There are two components to this agenda: how students are to work and what products they are to prepare for the discussion in the third part of the lesson. Each of these is essential; they cannot be skipped.

Whether or not you have students work in groups, it is always a good idea for students to have some opportunity to discuss their ideas with one or more classmates prior to sharing their thoughts in the *after* phase of the lesson. When students work alone, they have no one to look to for an idea or a way to get started if they are stuck. On the other hand, when students work in groups, there is always the possibility of students not contributing or of a dominating student being overly leading. A good compromise is a *think-pair-share* approach in which students first work alone, then pair and exchange ideas with a partner. The sharing is done during the class discussion.

Buschman (2003) suggests *think-write-pair-share*, adding that students should first write their solutions to the problem before pairing with a partner. With written work to share, the two students have something to talk about. Although appropriate for all students, the think-write-pair-share method is especially helpful for K–1 students who often do not know how to go about discussing a solution or even how to work together.

Teaching with problems requires that students change their focus from getting answers to the processes and reasoning behind how they got the answers. Students need to be clearly told what is expected of them beyond an answer so that they will be ready for the discussion portion of the lesson. It is always a good idea to have students write out an explanation for their solution. By preparing a written report, all students are ready for the discussion that will follow. On those few occasions when you do not require something in writing, it remains important that you make clear to students what they will be expected to discuss when they have solved the problem. Written explanations may be in a journal or on a separate sheet of paper. Sometimes a group report can be prepared on a large sheet of newsprint. Even kindergarten children can use drawings and numbers. Figure 4.3 shows one student's solution for ways to make 5. In fourth to eighth grade, you may select students in the *during* phase of the lesson to prepare their report on acetate for sharing using the overhead projector.

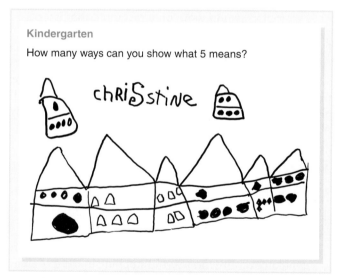

Kindergarten

How many ways can you show what 5 means?

FIGURE 4.3 A kindergarten student shows her thinking about ways to make 5.

Regardless of the method of reporting that you select, specific directions for explaining their solutions should be made clear to students. They should see the explanation as an integral part of the problem-solving process. More will be said later concerning the importance of writing in mathematics class.

Prepare Students Mentally for the Task

Many teachers like to begin their lessons with a short mental math activity or oral drill, regardless of the lesson that will follow. This can be a good idea but it does require extra time that may be needed for a good full lesson including a discussion. The agenda item here is to activate specific prior knowledge related to today's problem. What form this preparation activity might take will vary with the problem or task; in fact, many times, no pretask or activity is required at all. For example, a simple story problem may require nothing more than being sure it is understood and clarification of expectations. At other times, the problem may require a brief review or other action that gets students prepared. Following are some options to consider along with examples.

Begin with a Simple Version of the Task. Suppose that you are interested in developing some ideas about area and perimeter in the fourth or fifth grade. This is the task you plan to present (Lappan & Even, 1989).

Assume that the edge of a square is 1 unit. Add squares to this shape so that it has a perimeter of 18.

Instead of beginning your lesson with this problem, you might consider activating prior useful knowledge.

- Draw a 3-by-5 rectangle of squares on the board and ask students what they know about the shape. (It's a rectangle. It has squares. There are 15 squares. There are three rows of five.) If no one mentions the words *area* and *perimeter*, you could write those words on the board and ask if those words can be used in talking about this figure.
- Provide students with some square tiles or grid paper. "I want everyone to make a shape that has a perimeter of 12 units. After you make your shape, find out what its area is." After a short time, have several students share their shapes.

Each of these "warm-ups" gets the vocabulary you will need for your problem-solving task out in the open. The second activity suggests the tiles as a possible model that students may choose to use. It has the added benefit of hinting that there are different figures with the same perimeter.

Dad says it is 503 miles to the beach. When we stopped for gas, we had gone 267 miles. How much farther do we have to drive?

This problem is designed to help children develop an add-on method of subtraction. Before presenting this problem, have students get mentally ready by asking them to supply the missing part of 100 after you give one part. Try numbers like 80 or 30 at first; then try 47 or 62. When you present the actual task, you might ask students if the answer to the problem is more or less than 300 miles.

Brainstorm Solutions. The following problem for middle school students is designed to address the ideas of ratio and proportion as well as data analysis. Since this is not a straightforward task, brainstorming will likely produce a variety of approaches, resulting in more profitable solutions by more students.

Enrollment data for the school provide information about the students and their families from one class as compared to the whole school:

	School	Class
Siblings		
None	36	5
One	89	4
Two	134	17
More than two	93	3
Race		
African American	49	11
Asian American	12	0
White	219	15
Travel-to-school method		
Walk	157	10
Bus	182	19
Other	13	0

If someone asked you how typical the class was of the rest of the school, how would you answer? Write an explanation of your answer. Include one or more charts or graphs that you think would support your conclusion.

Estimate or Use Mental Computation. When the task is aimed at the development of a computational procedure, a useful *before* action is to have students actually do the computation mentally or suggest an estimated answer. Then list these "pre-answers" on the board. You may even have students explain their reasoning. Again, this process will not spoil the problem for the class.

This technique would be useful with the earlier problem concerning how many more miles to go to the beach.

The following task is another example in which preliminary estimates or mental computations would activate useful prior knowledge.

How many small unit squares will fit in a rectangle that is 54 units long and 36 units wide? Use base-ten pieces to help you with your solution.

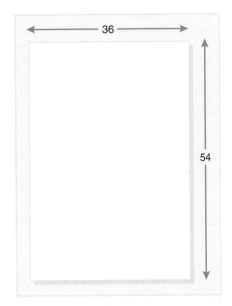

Make a plan for figuring out the total number of squares without doing too much counting. Explain how your plan would work on a rectangle that is 27 units by 42 units.

Prior to estimation or mental computation for this problem, beginning with several simpler problems will also help. For example, rectangles such as 30 by 8 or 40 by 60 could be explored.

The *During* Phase of a Lesson

Although this is the portion of the lesson when students work alone or with partners, there are clear agendas that you will want to attend to:

1. Let go! Give students a chance to work without your guidance or direction. Avoid stepping in front of their struggle.
2. Listen actively to your students. Take this time to find out how different students are thinking, what ideas they are using, and how they are approaching the problem. This is a time for observation and assessment—not teaching!
3. Cautiously provide appropriate hints—but only hints based on students' ideas and students' ways of thinking. Be very careful not to imply that you have the *correct* method of solving the problem.

4. Provide profitable activity for students who finish quickly.

Teacher Actions in the *During* Phase

With the exception of preparing for early finishers, these agendas are difficult to plan for. This does not mean that there are no important things for you to do.

Let Go!

Once your students are ready to work on the task, it is time to let go. Demonstrate confidence and respect for your students' abilities. Set them to work with the expectation that *they will* solve the problem. You *must* let go! Many teachers are tempted to walk around and help students, "stepping in front of the struggle," and promoting learned helplessness. Have faith in your students! Let them solve the problem. This may be very hard for you. You probably went into teaching to help students. Now you need to let them struggle.

Letting go also means allowing students to make mistakes. When you observe an error or incorrect thinking, do not correct it. Students must learn from the very beginning that their mistakes can be profitable (Boaler & Humphries, 2005). The best discussions occur when students disagree. If you correct all faulty thinking, you will have less disagreement, diminish students' security in their own thinking, and have fewer ideas for a profitable discussion.

Listen Actively

This is one of two opportunities you will get in the lesson (the other is in the discussion portion of the lesson) to find out what your students know, how they think, and how they are approaching the task you have given them. You might sit down with a group and simply listen for a while, have the students explain what they are doing, or take notes. If you want further information, try saying, "Tell me what you are doing," or "I see you have started to multiply these numbers. Can you tell me why you are multiplying?" You want to convey a genuine interest in what students are doing and thinking. This is *not* the time to evaluate or to tell students how to solve the problem.

"It's easy. Let me help you." These two simple sentences send two disastrous messages to the student who hears them. For the student who asks for help, it is *not* easy! Rather, the student's reaction—kept silent, of course—is more likely to be, "If it's easy and I can't get it, I must be stupid." The second sentence is equally damaging. It says to the student, "You are not capable of doing this on your own. I have to help you."

Try to avoid those two sentences no matter how much you want to help your students and make it easy for them. Instead, your first reaction should be to listen. Listening

actively includes asking questions, such as the following, and showing an interest in students' ideas.

* What do you think this problem is asking?
* What ideas have you tried so far?
* Do you have an idea of about what the answer might be? Why do you think so?

By asking questions you find out where students are and show that you value their ideas. Many insecure students have very good ideas but lack the confidence to pursue them. When a student's thoughts show some promise, regardless how vague or primitive, you can say, "Why don't you work on that approach? I think that might get you somewhere."

Provide Prompts and Suggestions Cautiously

If a group or student is searching for a place to begin, a hint may be appropriate. You might suggest that the students try using a particular manipulative, draw a picture, or make a table if one of these ideas seems appropriate.

In Fern's Furniture Store, Fern has priced all of her furniture at 20 percent over wholesale. In preparation for a sale, she tells her staff to cut all prices by 10 percent. Will Fern be making 10 percent profit, less than 10 percent profit, or more than 10 percent profit? Explain your answer.

For this problem, consider the following hints:

* Try drawing a picture or a diagram of something that shows what 10 percent off means.
* Try drawing a picture or a diagram that shows what 20 percent more means.
* Maybe you could pick a sample price of something and see what happens when you add 20 percent and then reduce 10 percent.
* Let's try a simpler problem. Suppose that you had 8 blocks and got 25 percent more. Then you lost 25 percent of the new collection.

Notice that these suggestions are not directive but, rather, they serve as starters. Even here, the choice of a hint is best made after listening carefully to what the student has been trying or thinking. After offering a hint, walk away. Don't hover or the student is apt to wait for even further direction without any personal effort.

Encourage Testing of Ideas

Students will look to you for approval of their results or ideas. Avoid being the source of "truth" or of right and wrong. When asked if a result or method is correct, respond by saying, "How can you decide?" or "Why do you think that might be right?" or "I see what you have done. How can you check that somehow?" Even if not asked for an opinion, asking "How can we tell if that makes sense?" reminds students that answers without reasons are not acceptable.

Provide for Students Who Finish Quickly

Some students will always finish well before others. These students need to be profitably engaged so that they do not become troublemakers, but it should not appear to others that there is a reward of a fun activity for finishing quickly. Early finishers can often be challenged in some manner connected to the problem just solved. Alternatively, on-going extended projects should be used as another part of your mathematics program. Students finishing early can use this time to work on their projects.

Lots of good problems are simple on the surface. It is the extensions that are challenging. The area and perimeter task is a case in point. Many students will quickly come up with one or two solutions. "I see you found one way to do this. Are there any other solutions? Are any of the solutions different or more interesting than others? Which of the shapes you found with a perimeter of 18 is the largest and which the smallest? Does the perimeter always change when you add another tile?"

Questions that begin "What if you tried . . . ?" or "Would that same idea work for . . . ?" are also ways to suggest different extensions. For example, "Suppose you tried to find all the shapes possible with a perimeter of 18. What could you find out about the areas?"

The value of students' solving a problem in more than one way cannot be overestimated. It shifts the value system in the classroom from answers to processes and thinking. It is a good way for students to make new and different connections.

For example, consider this sixth-grade problem.

The dress was originally priced at $90. If the sale price is 25 percent off, how much will it cost on sale?

This is an example of a straightforward problem with a single answer. Many students will solve it by multiplying by 0.25 and subtracting the result from $90. The suggestion to find another way may be all that is necessary. Others may require specific directions: "How would you do it with fractions instead of decimals?" "Draw me a diagram that explains what you did." "How could this be done in just one step?" "Think of a way that you could do this mentally."

Second graders will frequently solve the next problem by counting or using addition.

Maxine had saved up $9. The next day she received her allowance. Now she has $12. How much allowance did she get?

"How would you do that on a calculator?" and "Can you write an equation that tells what you did?" are ways of encouraging children to connect 9 plus ? = 12 with 12 − 9.

The *After* Phase of a Lesson

In the *after* phase of the lesson, your students will work as a community of learners, discussing, justifying, and challenging various solutions to the problem all have just worked on. Here is where much of the learning will occur as students reflect individually and collectively on the ideas they have been struggling with. The easiest error to make is failure to plan sufficient time for a discussion or to allow the *during* portion to go on too long. The agendas for the *after* phase are easily stated but perhaps more difficult to achieve:

1. Engage the class in productive discussion, helping students work together as a community of learners.
2. Listen actively without evaluation. Take this second major opportunity to find out how students are thinking—how they are approaching the problem. Evaluating methods and solutions is the duty of your students.
3. Summarize main ideas and identify problems for future exploration.

Teacher Actions in the *After* Phase

Be certain to plan ample time for this portion of the lesson and then be certain to *save* the time. Twenty minutes or more is not at all unreasonable for a good class discussion and sharing of ideas. It is not necessary for every student to have finished. This is not a time to check answers but for the class to share ideas.

Over time, you will develop your class into a mathematical community of learners, where students feel comfortable taking risks and sharing ideas, where students and the teacher respect one another's ideas even when they disagree, where ideas are defended and challenged respectfully, and where logical or mathematical reasoning is valued above all. This atmosphere will not develop easily or quickly. You must teach your students about your expectations for this time and how to interact with their peers.

Promote a Mathematical Community of Learners That Includes All Children

NCTM in its *Standards* documents is very clear in expressing the belief that all children can learn the mathematics of the regular curriculum. This view is supported by a number of prominent mathematics educators who have worked extensively with at-risk populations (Campbell, 1996; NCTM, 1989, 1991; Silver & Stein, 1996; Trafton & Claus, 1994).

Because the needs and abilities of children are different, it requires skill and practice to conduct a large group discussion that is balanced and includes all children. Rowan and Bourne (1994) offer excellent suggestions based on their work in an urban, multiethnic, low-socioeconomic school district. They emphasize that the most important factor is to be clear about the purpose of group discussion—that is, to share and explore the variety of strategies, ideas, and solutions generated by the class and to learn to communicate these ideas in a rich mathematical discourse. Every class has a handful of students who are always ready to respond. Other children learn to be passive or do not participate. So rule number one is that having the discussion is more important than hearing an answer.

Considerable research into how mathematical communities develop and operate provides us with additional insight for developing effective classroom discourse (e.g., see Rasmussen, Yackel, & King, 2003; Stephan & Whitenack, 2003; Yackel & Cobb, 1996). Suggestions from this research include the following:

- Encourage student–student dialogue rather than student–teacher conversations that exclude the class. "Juanita, can you answer Lora's question?" "Devon, can you explain that so that LaToya and José can understand what you are saying?" When students have differing solutions, have students work these ideas out as a class. "George, I noticed that you got a different answer than Tomeka. What do you think about her explanation?"
- Request explanations to accompany *all* answers. Soon the request for an explanation will not signal an incorrect response, as children will initially believe. Correct answers may not represent the conceptual thinking you assumed. Incorrect answers may only be the result of an easily corrected error. By requiring explanations, students learn that reasoning in mathematics is important and useful.
- Call on students for their ideas, often calling first on the children who tend to be shy or lack the ability to express themselves well. When asked to participate early and given sufficient time to formulate their thoughts, these reticent children can more easily participate and thus be valued. Asking, "Who wants to explain their solution?" will result in the same three or four eager students raising their hands. Other students tend to accept that these students are generally correct and may be reluctant to offer ideas that are different from the well-known leaders. Use the *during* portion of a lesson to identify interesting solutions that will add to your discussion—including those that are incorrect. All students should be prepared to share as part of their everyday expectations.
- Encourage students to ask questions. "Pete, did you understand how they did that? Do you want to ask Antonio a question?"
- Be certain that your students also understand what you understand. Your knowledge of the topic may cause you to accept a less than clear explanation because you hear what the student means to say. Select important points in a student's explanation and express your own "confusion." "Carlos, I don't quite get why you subtracted 9 here in this step. Can you tell us why you did that?" Demonstrate to students that it is okay to be confused and that asking clarifying questions is appropriate. A goal is for students to ask these questions without your input.
- Occasionally ask those who understand to offer explanations for others. "Thandie, perhaps you can explain this idea in your own words so that some of the rest of us can understand better." Don't assume that a student who says he or she understands really does.
- Move students to more conceptually based explanations when appropriate. For example, if a student says that he knows 4.17 is more than 4.1638, you can ask him (or another student) to explain why this is so. Another technique is to use a "fooler." With pretend confusion, ask, "How can this be? It seems like the longer decimal ought to be a larger number." Similarly, move students away from simply listing steps in their solutions. "I see *what* you did but I think some of us are confused about *why* you did it that way and why you think that will give us the correct solution."

Listen Actively—Do Not Evaluate

By being a facilitator and not an evaluator, students will be more willing to share their ideas during discussions. This is your window to their thinking. Listen carefully to the discussion without too much interference. You can use this information to plan for tomorrow's lesson and in general to decide on the direction you wish to take in your current unit.

Try to take a neutral position with respect to *all* responses. Resist the temptation to judge the correctness of an answer. You can ask questions to help clarify a response—both right and wrong. But when you say, "That's correct, Dewain," there is no longer a reason for students to evaluate his response. Had students disagreed with an affirmed response, they will not venture forth to challenge it since you've said it was correct. Instead, they will sheepishly hide their ideas and you will not have the chance to hear and learn from them. You can support student thinking without evaluation. "Does someone have a different idea or want to comment on what Daniel just said?"

Use praise cautiously. Praise offered for correct solutions or excitement over interesting ideas suggests that the students did something unusual or unexpected. This can be negative feedback for those who do not get praise. Comments such as "Good job!" and "Super work!" roll off the tongue easily. However, there is evidence to suggest that we should be careful with expressions of praise, especially with respect to student products and solutions (Kohn, 1993; Schwartz, 1996). Praise not only supports students' feelings but also evaluates. "Good job!" says, "Yes, you did that correctly."

In place of praise that is judgmental, Schwartz (1996) suggests comments of interest and extension: "I wonder what would happen if you tried . . ." or "Please tell me how you figured that out." Notice that these phrases express interest and value the child's thinking. They also can and should be used regardless of the validity of the responses.

There will be times when a student will get stuck in the middle of an explanation or when a response is simply not forthcoming. Be sensitive about calling on someone else to "help out." You may be communicating that the child is not capable on his or her own. Always allow ample time. You can sometimes suggest taking additional time to get thoughts together and promise to return to the student later—and then be *certain* to hear what the student figured out.

Summarize Main Ideas and Identify Hypotheses

When you are satisfied with the discussion around the answer and the solution to the problem, summarize the main points of the discussion and make sure that all students understand. Try to use the terminology that was used by the students. When ideas have been well developed, introduce appropriate terms, definitions, or symbolism. Labels come after ideas have been established, not before.

If a problem involves creating a procedure such as a method of computing, a strategy for basic facts, or a formula in measurement, record useful methods on the board. These can be labeled with the student's name and an example. These strategies are then available in future lessons for students to try. However, do not force your methods or those of other students on the class.

Often someone will make a generalization or an observation that he or she strongly believes in but cannot completely justify. These ideas should always be listened to with interest, even if they are incorrect. Untested ideas can be written up on the board as "Andrew's Hypothesis." Explain the meaning of *hypothesis* as an idea that may or may not be true. Testing the hypothesis may become the problem for another day, or the hypothesis may simply be kept on the board until additional evidence comes up that either supports or disproves it. For example, when comparing fractions, suppose that a group makes this generalization and you write it on the board: *When deciding which fraction is larger, the fraction in which the bottom number is closer to the top number is the larger fraction. Example: $\frac{4}{7}$ is not as big as $\frac{7}{8}$ because 7 is only 1 from 8 but 4 is 3 away from 7.* This is not an unusual conclusion, but it is not correct in all instances. A problem for a subsequent day would be to decide if the hypothesis is always right or to find fractions for which it is not right (counterexamples).

Even when students have not suggested hypotheses, discussions will often turn up interesting questions that can profitably be used for tasks to help clarify an emerging idea.

Designing and Selecting Effective Tasks

A key element in teaching with problems is the selection of appropriate problems or tasks. A task is effective when it helps students learn the ideas you want them to learn. It must be the mathematics in the task that makes it problematic for the students so that it is the mathematical ideas that are their primary concern. Therefore, the first and most important consideration for selecting any task for your class must be the mathematics. That said, where do you look for tasks?

Your Textbook

Most teachers find their textbook to be the main guide to their day-to-day curriculum. However, when teachers let the text determine the next lesson, they assume that children learned from each page what was intended. Avoid the "myth of coverage": If we covered it, they must have learned it. Good teachers use their text as a resource and as a basic guide to their curriculum. In the face of the current pressures from state-level standards and the No Child Left Behind law, the state curriculum guide is also an important consideration.

Using Traditional Textbooks

Many traditional textbooks are designed to be teacher directed, a contrast to the approach you have been reading about. But they should not be discarded. Much thought went into the content and the pedagogical ideas. Your book can still be used as a prime resource if you think about translating units and lessons to a problem-oriented approach.

Adopt a *unit perspective.* Avoid the idea that every lesson and idea in the unit requires attention. Examine a chapter or unit from beginning to end, and identify the two to four *big ideas,* the essential mathematics in the chapter. (Big ideas are listed at the start of each chapter in Section 2 of this book. These may be helpful as a reference.) Temporarily ignore the smaller subideas that often take up a full lesson.

With the big ideas of the unit in mind, you can now do two things: (1) adapt the best or most important lessons in the chapter to a problem-solving format and (2) create or find tasks in the text's teacher notes and other resources that address the big ideas. The combination will almost certainly provide you with an ample supply of tasks.

Adapting a Traditional Textbook Lesson

Figure 4.4 shows a page from a first-grade textbook. The lesson addresses an important idea: the connection of addition and subtraction. The approach on this page is fine: A picture of two sets of counters is used to suggest an addition and a subtraction equation, thus connecting these concepts. However, as is typical of traditional K–2 texts, there are blanks to be filled in with very specific correct answers. Student attention turns almost immediately to how

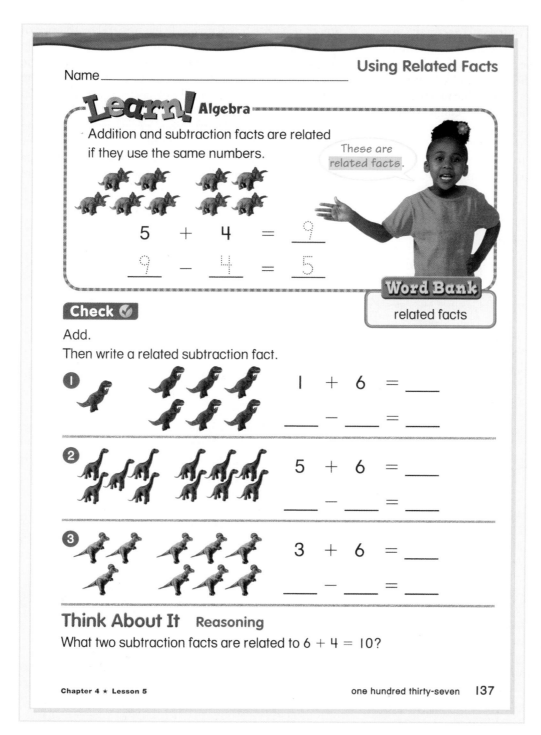

FIGURE 4.4 A first-grade lesson from a traditional textbook.

Source: From *Scott Foresman– Addison Wesley Math: Grade 1* (p. 137), by R. I. Charles et al., 2004, Glenview, IL: Scott Foresman–Addison Wesley. Copyright 2004 by Scott Foresman–Addison Wesley. Reprinted with permission.

to get the right numbers in the blanks. Imagine for a moment how you might help students complete this page correctly. It is easy to slip into a how-to mode that focuses more on the blanks than on addition and subtraction. Let's convert this lesson to a problem-oriented task. How can children be challenged to wrestle with this idea? You might want to try this before reading on.

One thought is to provide a set of perhaps eight counters and have students separate the set into two parts. The students' task is to write addition and subtraction equations that tell how they separated the counters. They should draw a picture to show the two parts of the set. Children can be challenged to see how many different ways they can separate the eight counters.

Another idea is to create a scenario in which there are two amounts, such as toy cars, on two different shelves. *In the toy store, there were 11 cars, 4 on the top shelf and 7 on the next shelf.* Have the students create two story problems about the 11 cars, one that is an addition story and another that is a subtraction story.

In the first modification, the page was translated directly to a task. In the second, a similar task was designed that did not look the same but addressed exactly the same mathematics. In each case, the students will do only one or two examples rather than the eight that are on this page and on the other side. But in the *during* and *after* portions of either modified lesson, there will be a much greater opportunity for students to develop the connection between addition and subtraction. That concept will be the focus of the discussion, not filling in the blanks.

Figure 4.5 is the second page of a geometry lesson from a sixth-grade book. The content involves classifica-

tion of triangles by relative side lengths and by the size of the angles, but notice how much of the lesson is simply providing definitions. Here the question at the top of the page (How can you draw and classify triangles?) is the essence of a good problem-based task. Consider what *you* might do before reading on.

To make this a classification *task*, students need some triangles in all six categories, with two or three triangles per category. You might prepare a set of triangles, reproduce them, and have students cut them out, or geoboards could

FIGURE 4.5 A page from a sixth-grade lesson from a traditional textbook.

Source: From *Scott Foresman–Addison Wesley Math: Grade 6* (p. 497), by R. I. Charles et al., 2004, Glenview, IL: Scott Foresman–Addison Wesley. Copyright 2004 by Scott Foresman–Addison Wesley. Reprinted with permission.

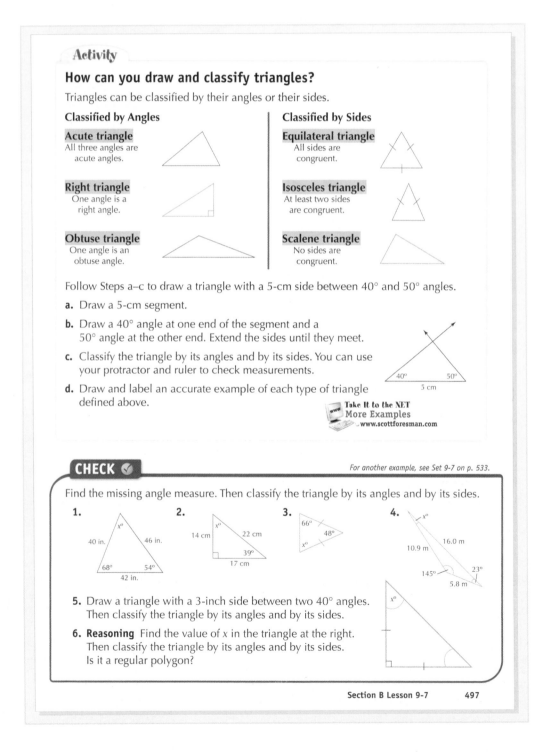

be used if they are available. (These and other ideas are discussed in Chapter 21 and an appropriate Blackline Master is provided.) Given the set of triangles, the task is to find two ways to sort the triangles into three separate piles. You could specify doing this first with a rule about sides and then a rule about angles, or let students develop their own classification schemes. In the *during* portion, you can provide hints that will help assure that some students create the categories you want. After students have created the categories, you can provide the appropriate vocabulary.

Using Standards-Based Programs

If your school is using a "standards-based" textbook series (see p. 10), then you will likely find that most of the lessons are already geared to a problem-solving mode. This is especially true of the *Investigations in Number, Data, and Space* curriculum. Your main difficulty may be assuring yourself that all of the skills and concepts of your local curriculum are appropriately emphasized. Some units may need additional activities or modifications based on the needs of your students, and others you may decide to skip.

Good Problems Have Multiple Entry Points

One of the advantages of a problem-based approach is that it can help accommodate the diversity of learners in every classroom. A problem-based approach does not dictate how a child must think about a problem in order to solve it. When a task is posed, students are told, in essence, "Use the ideas *you* own to solve this problem." Because of the range of students' mental tools, concepts, and ideas, many students in a class will have different ideas about the best way to complete a task. Thus, access to the problem by all students demands that there be multiple entry points—different places to "get on the ramp"—to reach solutions.

Once we stop thinking that there is only one way to solve a problem, it is not quite as difficult to develop good "ramp problems" or problems with multiple entry points. Although most problems have singular correct answers, there are often many ways to get there. The problems presented in this chapter nearly all have multiple entry points. Here are two more examples.

(For third or fourth grade) Find the area of the cover of your math book. That is, how many square tiles will fit on the cover of the book?

(For fifth or sixth grade) Clara has two whole pizzas and $\frac{1}{3}$ of another. All of the pizzas are the same size. If each of her friends will want to eat $\frac{1}{4}$ of a pizza, how many friends will she be able to feed with the $2\frac{1}{3}$ pizzas?

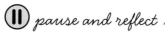 *pause and reflect* ———————

For these two problems or tasks, see if you can think of more than one path to the solution. Try to think of an approach that is near the bottom of the "ramp" (less sophisticated) and another that is closer to the middle or the top of the "ramp." Do this now before reading further.

The area problem can be solved with materials that directly attack the meaning of the problem. The cover of the book can be completely covered with tiles and then counted one at a time. Moving slightly up the ramp, a child may cover the book with tiles but count only the length of the row and the number of rows, multiplying to get the total. Another child may place tiles only along the edges of the book and multiply. Yet another child may use a ruler to measure the book edges, noting that the tiles are 1 inch on each side.

For the pizza task a direct approach is also possible. Plastic circular fraction pieces (or a drawing) can be used to represent $2\frac{1}{3}$ pizzas, and $\frac{1}{4}$ pieces can be placed on top of these until no more will fit. Another child may know that four fourths make a whole; therefore, two of the pizzas will feed eight friends. Children may or may not know how many fourths they can get from the $\frac{1}{3}$ piece and will have to tackle that part accordingly. A guess-and-check approach is possible, starting with perhaps six children, then seven, and so on until the pizza is gone. A few children may have learned a computational method for dividing $2\frac{1}{3}$ by $\frac{1}{4}$.

Having thought about these possible entry points, the teacher will be better prepared to suggest a hint that is appropriate for students who are "stuck" but who are likely different in what they bring to the task.

 The Equity Principle challenges teachers to believe that every student brings something of value to the tasks that they pose to their classes. The Teaching Principle calls for teachers to select tasks that "can be solved in more than one way, such as using an arithmetic counting approach, drawing a geometric diagram and enumerating possibilities, or using algebraic equations [so that tasks are] accessible to students with varied prior knowledge and experience" (p. 19).

Children's Literature

The use of children's literature is sufficiently important as a source of problems that it deserves some separate attention. Children's stories can be used in numerous ways to create reflective tasks at all grade levels, and there are many excellent books to help you in this area (Bay-Williams & Martinie, 2004; Bresser, 1995; Burns, 1992; Sheffield, 1995; Theissen, Matthias, & Smith, 1998; Welchman-Tischler, 1992; Whitin & Whitin, 2004; Whitin & Wilde, 1992, 1995).

By way of example, a very popular children's book, *The Doorbell Rang* (Hutchins, 1986), can be used to explore different concepts at various grade levels. The story is a sequential tale of children sharing 12 cookies. On each page, more children come to the kitchen, and the 12 cookies must be redistributed. This simple yet engaging story can lead to exploring ways to make equal parts of almost any number for children at the K–2 level. It is a springboard for multiplication and division at the 3–4 level. It can also be used to explore fraction concepts at the 4–6 level.

Most of the chapters in Section 2 of this text include a section titled "Literature Connection" that suggests a few ideas for using literature to explore the mathematics of that chapter. Literature ideas are often found in the articles of NCTM's journals. It is an exciting approach to creating problem-solving scenarios.

Other Resources

You will never compile a perfect set of tasks for your class; every class is different. As already noted, your textbook is a good place to begin, and children's literature should always be considered. Here are some additional options to consider:

- Read the NCTM journals regularly: *Teaching Children Mathematics* (for grades K–6) or *Mathematics Teaching in the Middle School* (for grades 5–8) and plan ahead. Copy and file tasks to go with each chapter in your text or each section of your curriculum.
- Begin to develop your personal professional library of resource books. The NCTM *Navigation Series* books are an excellent place to begin, but NCTM's catalog has lots of resources. Don't forget the book in your hands as a first resource. A number of commercial publishers and distributors specialize in materials for teaching mathematics, including resource books for teachers and activity books and manipulatives for students.
- Check out the standards-based curricula at your grade level, even if you don't use them regularly. Buy a single module to get your feet wet. Check out these implementation centers on the Web: for elementary school, Alternatives for Rebuilding Curricula at www.comap.com/arc; for middle school, Show-Me Center at http://showmecenter.missouri.edu.
- Surf the Web. There are lots of Web sites designed to offer help and teaching ideas for teachers. Many include complete lesson plans. One caution: Just because it's on the Web doesn't mean it's of high quality. Good Web sites to get you started are noted in Chapter 8.

NCTM Standards "By analyzing and adapting a problem, anticipating the mathematical ideas that can be brought out by working on the problem, and anticipating students' questions, teachers can decide if particular problems will help to further their mathematical goals for the class" (p. 53).

A Task Selection Guide

Throughout this book, in every student textbook, and in every article you read or in-service workshop you attend, you will hear and read about suggestions for activities, problems, tasks, or explorations that someone believes are effective in helping children learn some aspect of mathematics. Selecting activities or tasks is, as Lappan and Briars (1995) contend, the most significant decision affecting your students' learning. The box below shows a four-step guide you can use when considering a new activity for your students.

Activity Evaluation and Selection Guide

STEP 1: How Is the Activity Done?

Actually do the activity. Try to get "inside" the task or activity to see how it is done and what thinking might go on.

How would *children* do the activity or solve the problem? (They don't know what you do!)

- What materials are needed?
- What is written down or recorded?
- What misconceptions may emerge?

STEP 2: What Is the Purpose of the Activity?

What *mathematical ideas* will the activity develop?

- Are the ideas concepts or procedural skills?
- Will there be connections to other related ideas?

STEP 3: Will the Activity Accomplish Its Purpose?

What is *problematic* about the activity? Is the problematic aspect related to the mathematics you identified in the purpose?

What *must* children reflect on or think about to complete the activity? (Don't rely on wishful thinking.)

Is it possible to complete the activity without much reflective thought? If so, can it be modified so that students will be required to think about the mathematics?

STEP 4: What Must You Do?

What will you need to do in the *before* portion of your lesson?

- How will you activate students' prior knowledge?
- What will the students be expected to produce?

What difficulties might you anticipate seeing in the *during* portion of your lesson?

What will you want to focus on in the *after* portion of your lesson?

The third step is the most important point in determining if an activity will or will not accomplish its purpose.

What is problematic about the activity? What will improve the chances that the children will be mentally active, reflecting on and constructing the ideas you identified in step 2? Try to predict what students will do with the activity. Think about how students might have difficulty with the task. Difficulties are usually the best opportunities for learning, but you would like to anticipate them if possible.

Practice using this Activity Evaluation and Selection Guide with activities throughout this book. Work toward thinking about tasks or activities from the view of what is likely to happen inside children's minds, not just what they are doing with their hands. Good tasks are minds-on activities, not just hands-on activities.

 *pause and reflect* ——————————

Suppose that your goal was for students to learn some of the harder multiplication facts that they had not yet mastered (grade 3 or 4). You pose the task on page 42 about finding a helping fact. Think about the questions in step 3 of the Activity Evaluation and Selection Guide. Do you think this will be an effective activity for your students? Why? Can you make it better? How?

The Importance of Student Writing

As stated earlier, it is often useful to have students write an explanation of their solution process as part of solving the problem. This is so important that it is worth clarifying the value of student writing. There are a number of advantages, regardless of the grade level of the students:

* The act of writing is a reflective process. As students make an effort to explain their thinking and defend their answers, they will spend more focused time thinking about the ideas involved.
* A written report is a rehearsal for the discussion period. It is difficult for students to explain how they solved a problem 15 minutes after they have done so. Students can always refer to a written report when asked to share. Even a kindergarten child can show a picture and talk about it. When every student has written about his or her solution, you need not ask for volunteers to share ideas.
* A written report is also a written record that remains when the lesson is finished. The reports can be collected and looked at later. The information can be used for planning, for finding out who needs help or opportunities to extend their knowledge, and for evaluation and teacher conferences.

It is important to help students understand what they are trying to accomplish in their written report. There is

a significant difference between "Show how you got your answer" and "Explain why you think your answer is correct." With the former direction, students may simply record their steps ("First we did . . . , and then we . . .") or present their work as self-evident. In Figure 4.6 the work of two students illustrates the contrast.

To help elicit better explanations, here are two possible types of directions you might consider:

* Have students begin their report this way: "I (We) think the answer is ____. We think this because ____."
* "Use words, pictures, and numbers to explain how you got your answer and why you think your answer makes sense and is correct."

Figure 4.7 shows the work of two first-grade students who solved a problem more difficult than students typically are asked to do in first grade. Most students used physical materials to solve the problems and then they wrote about their solutions. There is a clear difference between the two solutions and the students' understanding of two-digit numbers. Polly is using groups of ten. DeAustin most likely counted each number by ones.

For young students to copy the problem as these children did can take a lot of time. Printing four or five copies of the problem, copying, and cutting into strips can save the time. Students paste or staple the strip with the problem to the top of the page in their journals. Some teachers provide the printed problem on a separate paper with room for the solution.

Teaching Tips and Questions

The ideas expressed here have been gathered from elementary and middle school teachers who have been working hard at developing a problem-solving approach in their classrooms and from the research literature on teaching via problem solving.

Let Students Do the Talking

Much has already been said about developing a mathematical community in the classroom. However, the value of classroom discussion of ideas cannot be overemphasized. As students describe and evaluate solutions to tasks, share approaches, and make conjectures as members of a community of learners, learning will occur in ways that are impossible otherwise. Students begin to take ownership of ideas and develop a sense of power in making sense of mathematics.

Students should understand when given a task that one of their responsibilities is to prepare for discussion that will occur after they have had an opportunity to work on the problem. One fourth-grade teacher discovered that

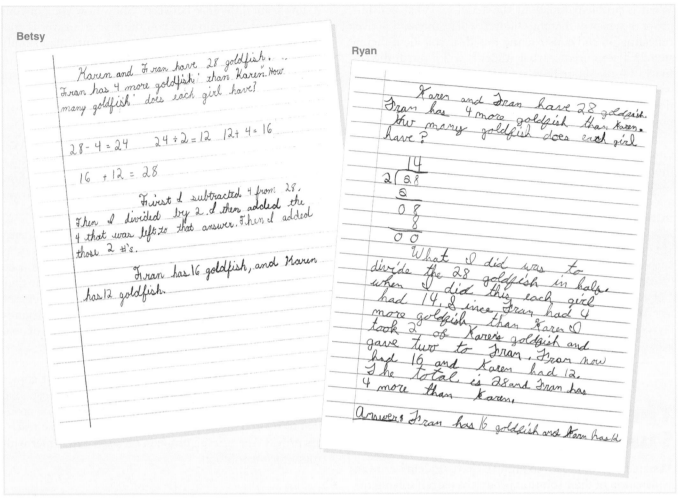

Betsy

Karen and Fran have 28 goldfish. Fran has 4 more goldfish than Karen. How many goldfish does each girl have?

28 - 4 = 24   24 ÷ 2 = 12   12 + 4 = 16

16 + 12 = 28

First I subtracted 4 from 28. Then I divided by 2. I then added the 4 that was left to that answer. Then I added those 2 #'s.

Fran has 16 goldfish, and Karen has 12 goldfish.

Ryan

Karen and Fran have 28 goldfish. Fran has 4 more goldfish than Karen. How many goldfish does each girl have?

What I did was to divide the 28 goldfish in half. when I did this each girl had 14. Since Fran had 4 more goldfish than Karen I took 2 of Karen's goldfish and gave two to Fran. Fran now had 16 and Karen had 12. The total is 28 and Fran has 4 more than Karen.

Answer: Fran has 16 goldfish and Karen has 12.

FIGURE 4.6 Betsy tells each step in her solution but provides no explanation. In contrast, Ryan's work includes reasons for his steps.

she was too involved in her class discussions. The students tended to wait for her questions rather than tell about their solutions. To help her students be more personally responsible, she devised three posters, inscribed as follows:

How did you solve the problem?

Why did you solve it this way?

Why do you think your solution is correct and makes sense?

In the beginning, students referred to the posters as they made presentations to the class, but soon that was not necessary. They continued to refer to the posters as they wrote up the solutions to problems in the *during* portion of lessons. Students began to prompt presenters: "You didn't answer the second question on the poster." One of the best results of these posters was that they helped remove the teacher from the content of the discussions. She was no longer in a position of asking questions that made it seem to students that she had a single "best" answer in mind.

Regardless of the exact structure or time frame for a lesson, an opportunity for discourse should always be built in. After students have played a game, worked in a learning center, completed a challenging worksheet, or engaged in a mental math activity with a full class, they can still discuss their activity: *What strategies worked well in the game? What did you find out in the learning center? What are different ways to do this exercise?*

How Much to Tell and Not to Tell

When teaching through problem solving, one of the most perplexing dilemmas is how much to tell. On one hand, telling diminishes student reflection. Students who sense that the teacher has a preferred method or approach are extremely reluctant to use their own strategies. Nor will students develop self-confidence and problem-solving abilities by watching the teacher do the thinking. On the other hand, to tell too little can sometimes leave students floundering and waste precious class time.

While noting that there will never be a simple solution to this dilemma, researchers connected with four different

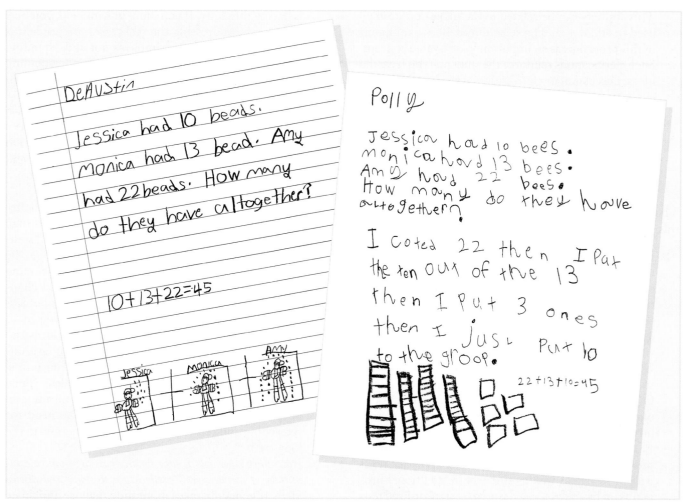

FIGURE 4.7 The work of two first-grade students solving 10 + 13 + 22 indicates a difference in how the children are thinking about two-digit numbers.

constructivist programs offer the following guidance: Teachers should feel free to share relevant information as long as the mathematics in the task remains problematic for the students (Hiebert et al., 1997). That is, "information can and should be shared as long as it does not solve the problem [and] does not take away the need for students to reflect on the situation and develop solution methods they understand" (p. 36).

They go on to suggest three types of information that teachers should provide to their students:

- *Mathematical conventions.* The social conventions of symbolism and terminology that are important in mathematics will never be developed through reflective thought. For example, representing "three and five equals eight" as "3 + 5 = 8" is a convention. Definitions and labels are also conventions. What is important is to offer these symbols and words only when students need them or will find them useful. As a rule of thumb, symbolism and terminology should only

be introduced *after* concepts have been developed and then specifically as a means of expressing or labeling ideas. They should rarely be presented initially or solely as things to be memorized.

- *Alternative methods.* You can, with care, suggest to students an alternative method or approach for consideration. You may also suggest more efficient recording procedures for student-invented computational methods. A teacher must be cautious in not conveying to students that their ideas are second best. Nor should students ever be forced to adopt a teacher's suggestion over their own approach. The rule of thumb here is that the value of a procedure should always be left to the judgment of the students, not the dictates of the teacher. In this spirit, students can learn to consider a teacher's suggestion without feeling obligated to use it.

- *Clarification of students' methods.* You should help students clarify or interpret their ideas and perhaps point out related ideas. A student may add 38 and 5 by noting that 38 and 2 more is 40 with 3 more making 43.

This strategy can be related to the make-ten strategy used to add 8 + 3. The selection of 40 as a midpoint in this procedure is an important place-value concept. Such clarifications reinforce the students who have the ideas. Discussion or clarification of students' ideas focuses attention on ideas you want the class to learn. Teacher attention to one method should not be done in such a way as to suggest that it is the preferred approach.

Frequently Asked Questions

The following are questions teachers have asked about this problem-based approach to teaching mathematics.

1. *How can I teach all the basic skills I have to teach?* Many teachers, especially those feeling the pressures of state testing programs, resort to rote drill and practice to teach "basic skills." There is a tendency to believe that mastery of the basics is incompatible with a problem-based approach. However, the evidence strongly suggests otherwise. First, drill-oriented approaches in U.S. classrooms have consistently produced poor results (Battista, 1999; Kamii & Dominick, 1998; O'Brien, 1999). Short-term gains on low-level skills may possibly result from drill, but even state testing programs require more.

   Second, research data indicate that students in programs based on a problem-solving approach do as well or nearly as well as students in traditional programs on basic skills as measured by standardized tests (Campbell, 1995; Carpenter, Franke, Jacobs, Fennema, & Empson, 1998; Hiebert, 2003; Hiebert & Wearne, 1996; Silver & Stein, 1996; Riordan & Noyce, 2001). Any deficit in skill development is more than outweighed by strength in concepts and problem solving.

   Finally, traditional skills such as basic fact mastery and computation can be effectively taught in a problem-solving approach (for example, see Campbell, Rowan, & Suarez, 1998; Huinker, 1998).

2. *Why is it okay for students to "tell" or "explain" but not for me?* First, students will question their peers when an explanation does not make sense to them, whereas explanations from the teacher are usually accepted without scrutiny (and, hence, without understanding). Second, when students are responsible for explaining, the class members develop a sense of pride and confidence that *they* can figure things out and make sense of mathematics. *They* have power and ability.

3. *Is it okay to help students who have difficulty solving a problem?* Of course, you will want to help students who are struggling. However, as Buschman (2003) suggests, rather than suggest how to solve a problem, a better approach is to try to find out *why* the student is having difficulty. If you jump in with help, you may not even be addressing the real reason the student is struggling. It may be as simple as not understanding the problem or as complex as a lack of understanding of a fundamental concept. "Tell me what you are thinking" is a good beginning.

   Recall the disastrous consequences of these two simple sentences: *It's easy! Let me help you.* (See p. 45.) Rather, try to build on the student's knowledge. Do not rob students of the feeling of accomplishment and the true growth in understanding that come from solving a problem themselves.

4. *Where can I find the time to cover everything?* Mathematics is much more connected and integrated than the itemized objectives found on many state "standards" lists would suggest. To deal with coverage, the first suggestion is to teach with a goal of developing the "big ideas," the main concepts in a unit or chapter. Most of the skills and ideas on your list of objectives will be addressed as you progress. If you focus separately on each item on the list, then big ideas and connections, the essence of understanding, are unlikely to develop. Second, we spend far too much time reteaching because students don't retain ideas. Time spent up front to help students develop meaningful networks of ideas drastically reduces the need for reteaching and remediation, thus creating time in the long term.

5. *How much time does it take for students to become a community of learners and really begin to share and discuss ideas?* It generally takes more time than we anticipate and discussions may seem strained or nonproductive at first. Students in the primary grades will adapt much more quickly than students in the upper grades, as they have not yet developed a firm belief that mathematics class is about sitting quietly and following the rules. You might expect it to take as much as six weeks before students begin to assume responsibility for making sense of mathematics.

6. *Can I use a combination of student-oriented, problem-based teaching with a teacher-directed approach?* No. By switching methods, students become confused as to what is expected of them. More importantly, students will come to believe that their own ideas do not really matter because the teacher will eventually tell them the "right" way to do it (Mokros, Russell, & Economopoulos, 1995). In order for students to become invested in a problem-based approach they must deeply believe that their ideas are important. If they believe that the teacher is later going to show them a preferred method, why should they stick their necks out and risk being wrong?

7. *Is there any place for drill and practice?* Absolutely! The tragic error is to believe that drill is a method of de-

veloping ideas. Drill is only appropriate when (a) the desired concepts have been meaningfully developed, (b) flexible and useful procedures have been developed, *and* (c) speed and accuracy are needed. Watch children drilling basic facts who are counting on their fingers or using some other inefficient method. What they may be improving is their ability to count quickly. They are not learning their facts. Too many children are still counting in middle school because drill has not helped them develop efficient strategies. When you accept that drill does not produce understanding, you find there are really not many topics aside from basic fact mastery that should ever require drill.

8. *What do I do when a task bombs?* It will happen, although not as often as you think, that students just do not know what to do with a problem you pose no matter how many hints and suggestions you offer. Do not give in to the temptation to "tell 'em." Set it aside for the moment. Ask yourself why it didn't work well. Did the students have the prior knowledge they needed? Was the task too advanced? Often we need to regroup and offer students a simpler related task that gets them prepared for the one that proved too difficult. When you sense that a task is not going anywhere, regroup! Don't spend days just hoping that something wonderful might happen. If you listen to your students, you will know where to go next.

Teaching About Problem Solving

The integration of problem solving and mathematics has obviously been a thrust of this chapter. But the standard on problem solving in *Principles and Standards* also speaks to the need to develop problem-solving *strategies and processes*, *metacognitive habits* of monitoring and regulating problem-solving activity, and a *positive disposition* toward mathematical problem solving. Each area suggests objectives or goals for the development of good problem solvers.

Strategies and Processes

Strategies for solving problems are identifiable methods of approaching a task that are completely independent of the specific topic or subject matter. Strategy goals play a part in all phases of problem solving: understanding the problem, solving the problem, and reflecting on the answer and solution.

Strategy and Process Goals

- *Develop problem analysis skills*—to improve students' ability to analyze an unfamiliar problem, identify wanted and needed information, ignore nonessential

information, and clearly state the goal of the problem or task
- *Develop and select strategies*—to help students acquire a collection of problem-solving strategies that are useful in a variety of problem-solving settings and to select and use those strategies appropriately
- *Justify solutions*—to improve students' ability to assess the validity of answers
- *Extend or generalize problems*—to help students learn to go beyond the solution to problems; to consider results or processes applied in other situations or used to form rules or general procedures

Developing Problem-Solving Strategies

When important or especially useful strategies crop up, they should be identified, highlighted, and discussed. Labeling a strategy provides a useful means for students to talk about their methods and for you to provide hints and suggestions. Hints or suggestions about a particular strategy may be appropriate in the *before* or *during* phases of your lesson.

The following strategies are most likely to appear in lessons where mathematical content is the main objective.

- *Draw a picture, act it out, use a model.* This is the strategy of using models as "thinker toys" as described in Chapter 3. "Act it out" extends models to a real interpretation of the problem situation.
- *Look for a pattern.* Pattern searching is at the heart of many problem-based tasks, especially in the algebraic reasoning strand. Patterns in number and in operations play a huge role in helping students learn about and master basic facts and continues to be a major factor into the middle and high school years.
- *Make a table or chart.* Charts of data, function tables, tables for operations, and tables involving ratios or measurements are a major form of analysis and communication. The use of a chart is often combined with pattern searching as a means of solving problems or constructing new ideas.
- *Try a simpler form of the problem.* Here the general idea is to modify or simplify the quantities in a problem so that the resulting task is easier to understand and analyze. By solving the easier problem, the hope is to gain insights that can then be used to solve the original, more complex problem.
- *Guess and check.* This might be called "try and see what you can find out." A good way to work on a task that has you stumped is to *try something*. Make an attempt! Reflection even on a failed attempt can lead to a better idea.

- *Make an organized list.* This strategy involves systematically accounting for all possible outcomes in a situation, either to find out how many possibilities there are or to be sure that all possible outcomes have been accounted for. One area where organized lists are essential is in probability.

Metacognition

Metacognition refers to conscious monitoring (being aware of how and why you are doing something) and regulation (choosing to do something or deciding to make changes) of your own thought process. Good problem solvers monitor their thinking regularly and automatically. They recognize when they are stuck or do not fully understand. They make conscious decisions to switch strategies, rethink the problem, search for related content knowledge that may help, or simply start afresh (Schoenfeld, 1992).

There is evidence that metacognitive behavior can be learned (Campione, Brown, & Connell, 1989; Garofalo, 1987; Lester, 1989). Furthermore, students who learn to monitor and regulate their own problem-solving behaviors do show improvement in problem solving.

Metacognitive Goal

- *Monitor and regulate actions*—to help students develop the habit and ability to monitor and regulate their strategies and progress as they solve problems

We know that it is important to help students learn to monitor and control their own progress in problem solving. A simple formula that can be employed consists of three questions: *What* are you doing? *Why* are you doing it? *How* does it help you?

Though the exact form of the three questions is not significant, the idea is to be persistent with this reflective questioning as students work through problems or explorations. You can ask the questions as you sit down to listen to any group. By joining the group, you model questioning that you want the students eventually to do on their own. In the upper grades, each group will soon be able to designate a member to be the monitor. The monitor's job is to be the reflective questioner in the same way you have modeled when working with the group.

Students can also be helped in developing self-monitoring habits after their problem-solving activity is over. A brief discussion after a problem is over can focus on what types of things were done in solving the problem. "What did you do that helped you understand the problem? Did you find any numbers or information you didn't need? How did you decide what to do? Did you think about your answer after you got it? How did you decide your answer was right?"

Questioning similar to this tells students that all of these things are important. If they know you are going to

be asking such questions, students will think about them ahead of time.

Disposition

Disposition refers to the attitudes and beliefs that students possess about mathematics. Students' beliefs concerning their abilities to do mathematics and to understand the nature of mathematics have a significant effect on how they approach problems and ultimately on how well they succeed.

Students' attitudes (likes, dislikes, and preferences) about mathematics are as important as their beliefs. Children who enjoy solving problems and feel satisfaction or pleasure at conquering a perplexing problem are much more likely to persevere, make second and third attempts, and even search out new problems. Negative attitudes have just the opposite effect.

Attitudinal Goals

- *Gain confidence and belief in abilities*—to develop students' confidence in their ability to do mathematics and to confront unfamiliar tasks
- *Be willing to take risks and to persevere*—to improve students' willingness to attempt unfamiliar problems and to develop their perseverance in solving problems without being discouraged by initial setbacks
- *Enjoy doing mathematics*—to help students learn to enjoy and sense personal reward in the process of thinking, searching for patterns, and solving problems

A classroom environment built on high expectations for all students and respect for each student's thoughts will go a long way toward achieving the attitudinal goals. Here are some additional ideas to help with these goals for all students.

- *Build in success.* In the beginning of the year, plan problems that you are confident your students can solve. Avoid creating a false success that depends on your showing the way at every step and barrier.
- *Praise efforts and risk taking.* Students need to hear frequently that they are "good thinkers" capable of good, productive thought. When students volunteer ideas, listen carefully and actively to each idea, and give credit for the thinking and the risk that children take by venturing to speak out. Be careful to focus praise on the risk or effort and not the products of that effort, regardless of the quality of the ideas.
- *Listen to all students.* Avoid ending a discussion with the first correct answer. As you make nonevaluative responses, you will find many children repeating the same idea. Were they just copying a known leader? Perhaps, but more likely they were busy thinking and did not even hear what had already been said by those

who were a bit faster. Don't forget the suggestion made earlier to call on less secure students early in a discussion so that the most obvious ideas are not taken by the more assertive students.

- *Provide special successes for special children.* Not all children will develop the same problem-solving abilities, but all have abilities and can contribute. This must be something you truly believe because it is difficult to fake. One way to provide success for students who are slower or not as strong is to involve them in groups with strong and supportive children or ask easier ques-

tions early in discussions. In group settings, all children can be made to feel the success of the group work.

NCTM Standards The first two goals of the problem-solving standard concern teaching through problem solving. The third and fourth goals refer to students learning problem-solving strategies and monitoring and reflecting on their own processes (metacognition). It would be beneficial to check these goals for the grade band that interests you most.

Reflections on Chapter 4

Writing to Learn

1. Explain the difference between teacher-centered instruction and student-centered instruction. What does it mean for teaching to begin where the students are?
2. Discuss each of the benefits of teaching with problems.
3. Describe what is meant by tasks or problems that can be used for teaching mathematics. Be sure to include the three important features that are required to make this method effective.
4. What is the teacher's purpose or agenda in each of the three parts of a lesson—*before*, *during*, and *after?*
5. Describe the kinds of actions or things that a teacher should be doing in each of the three parts of a lesson. (Note that not all of these would be done in every lesson.) Which actions should you use almost all of the time?
6. Select an activity from any chapter in Section 2 of this text. How can the activity be used as a problem or task for the purpose of instruction as described in this chapter? If you were using this activity in the classroom, what specifically would you do during the *before* section of the lesson?
7. What are some of the benefits of having students write in mathematics class? When should the writing take place? How can very young students "write"?
8. Describe in your own words what is meant by a "mathematical community of learners."
9. Discuss helping a student who is having difficulty solving a problem. Why is saying, "It's easy! Let me help you" not a good idea?
10. Examine the frequently asked questions on pp. 56–57. Give answers to these questions in your own words.
11. Goals for the development of good problem solving were separated under the headings of "Strategies and Processes," "Metacognition," and "Disposition." Describe what is meant by each of these types of goals.
12. For each category of problem-solving goals, describe how a teacher can help students develop these goals in the *before*, *during*, and *after* phases of a lesson.

For Discussion and Exploration

1. If you were to begin teaching a class of students who had never experienced learning mathematics in a problem-solving environment, they are likely not to know how to work at solving problems, work with a partner, or engage in a classroom discussion. How would you begin to deal with these and similar challenges so that students would develop an understanding of their role in such a classroom?
2. Find a traditional basal textbook for any grade level. Look through a chapter and find at least one lesson that you could convert to a problem-solving lesson without drastically altering the lesson as it was written. Is there any content in the chapter, other than conventions, that you do not feel you could teach through problem solving?
3. Examine a lesson from one of the standards-based curricula. (See Chapter 1 for a list.) How does the general structure of the lesson you selected compare to the problem-solving approach to teaching described in this chapter?

Recommendations for Further Reading

Boaler, J., & Humphreys, C. (2005). *Connecting mathematical ideas: Middle school video cases to support teaching and learning.* Portsmouth, NH: Heinemann.
Cathy Humphreys teaches seventh grade. Jo Boaler is a respected researcher who is interested in the impact of different teaching approaches. This book looks directly into Cathy's classroom in the form of cases based on different content areas and issues in teaching. Cathy writes about the cases in the first person. Each case is followed by Jo's commentary and expert perspective. Accompanying the book are two CDs that provide videos of the cases being discussed. Taping took place throughout the entire year. Although set in the seventh grade, this book will provide insights to any teacher who is interested in developing problem-based instruction in the classroom.

Buschman, L. (2003). *Share and compare: A teacher's story about helping children become problem solvers in mathematics.* Reston, VA: National Council of Teachers of Mathematics.

Larry Buschman is an experienced elementary teacher who has taught with a problem-based approach for many years. In this book he describes in detail how he makes this work in his classroom. Many of the examples come from the first and second grades although Larry has used his techniques from kindergarten to grade 4 and knows other teachers who have applied his methods at higher grades. Much of the book is written as if a teacher were interviewing Larry as he answers the kinds of questions you will undoubtedly have as you begin to teach. You can read the entire book in an evening but you will want to return to it again and again. A must-have on every teacher's shelf!

Buschman, L. (2003). Children who enjoy problem solving. *Teaching Children Mathematics, 9,* 539–544.

If you cannot get a copy of *Share and Compare* (see above), this *TCM* article is a good second best. Buschman is also the author of several other *TCM* articles.

Hiebert, J., Carpenter, T. P., Fennema, E., Fuson, K., Wearne, D., Murray, H., Olivier, A., & Human, P. (1997). *Making sense: Teaching and learning mathematics with understanding.* Portsmouth, NH: Heinemann.

The authors of this highly readable and significant book are each connected to one of four problem-based, long-term research projects. They make one of the best cases currently in print for developing mathematics via problem-based tasks. After discussing features of the general approach and the supporting theory, a vignette from each project is discussed. *Making Sense* and the companion article by the same authors in the *Educational Researcher* (Vol. 25, May 1996) have guided the writing of Chapter 4 of this book. This short book is important reading for every teacher.

Lester, F. K., & Charles, R. I. (Eds.). (2003). *Teaching mathematics through problem solving: Pre-K to 6.* Reston, VA: National Council of Teachers of Mathematics.

This is an important and valuable publication from the council. Topics include "Mathematics as Sense Making," "Designing and Selecting Tasks," "How to Problematize the Curriculum," "Listening to Children," "Problem Solving with Technology," and "Problem Posing." The 17 chapters, all written by top authors in the field, provide an in-depth examination of using a problem-based approach to teaching for understanding. The chapter on social and sociomathematical norms was used extensively in preparing this chapter. The voices of teachers are also included in short reflections by those who have worked to make teaching through problem solving a success in their classrooms. (There is also a grade 6–12 volume.)

Mokros, J., Russell, S. J., & Economopoulos, K. (1995). *Beyond arithmetic: Changing mathematics in the elementary classroom.* White Plains, NY: Cuisenaire—Dale Seymour.

Mokros, Russell, and Economopoulos are lead authors of the *Investigations in Number, Data, and Space* curriculum and this 131-page book was written for those who are thinking about adopting *Investigations* or at least want to consider a standards-based approach to teaching. They provide a teacher-language description of teaching with problems including

answers to many practical questions. This book rounds out a trio of books that everyone who wants to be a problem-based, student-centered teacher should have and read. (The other two books are *Making Sense* and *Share and Compare.* See above.)

Reinhart, S. C. (2000). Never say anything a kid can say! *Mathematics Teaching in the Middle School, 5,* 478–483.

The author is an experienced middle school teacher who questioned his own "masterpiece" lessons after realizing that his students were often confused. The article is the result of the realization that he was doing the talking and explaining, and that was causing the confusion. Reinhart's suggestions for questioning techniques and involving students are superb!

Rowan, T. E., & Bourne, B. (1994). *Thinking like mathematicians: Putting the K–4 Standards into practice.* Portsmouth, NH: Heinemann.

A must read for any teacher in the K–5 range. Rowan and Bourne describe in 132 pages the spirit of the *Standards* as carried out by teachers in urban, multiethnic Montgomery County, Maryland, schools. The schools described were part of a project to explore the effectiveness of a constructivist approach. The book contains practical suggestions and inspiring stories from teachers and from the classroom.

Online Resources

Suggested Applets and Web Links

Annenberg/CPB
www.learner.org/index.html
A unit of the Annenberg Foundation, Annenberg/CPB offers professional development information and useful information for teachers who want to learn about and teach mathematics.

ARC Center
www.comap.com/elementary/projects/arc
Here you can get information about each of the three elementary standards-based curricula and see sample lessons.

ENC Online (Eisenhower National Clearinghouse)
www.enc.org
Click on Digital Dozen, Lessons and Activities, or Web Links. The ENC site is full of useful information for teachers who are planning lessons.

Show-Me Center
http://showmecenter.missouri.edu/
This site contains information for each of the middle school standards-based curricula including links to each site.

Writing and Communication in Mathematics
http://mathforum.org/library/ed_topics/writing_in_math/
This Math Forum page lists numerous articles and Web links concerning the value of writing in mathematics at all levels.

An additional list of books and articles related to the ideas in this chapter can be found on the Companion Web site at **www.ablongman.com/vandewalle6e.**

Planning in the Problem-Based Classroom

Natural learning . . . doesn't happen on a time schedule and often requires more time than schools are organized to provide. Problem-solving experiences take time. It's essential that teachers provide the time that's needed for children to work through activities on their own and that teachers not slip into teaching-by-telling for the sake of efficiency.

Burns (1992, p. 30)

The three-part lesson format described in Chapter 4 provided a basic structure for problem-based lessons. That basic framework resulted from the need for students to be engaged in problems followed by time for discussion and reflection. However, many of the practical details of working with students in this environment are not clear from this general paradigm for a lesson.

This chapter begins with a step-by-step guide for planning problem-based lessons. Also explored here are some variations of the three-part structure, tips for dealing with diversity in the classroom, issues of drill and practice, homework, textbooks, and grading. In short, this chapter discusses the "nuts and bolts" of effective teaching.

Planning a Problem-Based Lesson

Regardless of your experience, it is crucial that you give adequate thought to the planning of your lessons. There is no such thing as a "teacher-proof" curriculum—where you can simply teach every lesson as it is planned and in the order it appears. Every class is different. Choices of tasks and how they are presented to students must be made daily to best fit the needs of your students and the objectives you are hired to teach. The outline in Figure 5.1 il-lustrates the suggested steps for planning a lesson. The first four steps are the most crucial. Decisions made here will define the content and the task that your students will work on. The next four steps are necessary to make sure that the lesson runs smoothly. Finally, you can write a concise lesson plan, knowing that you have thought it through thoroughly. Each step is discussed briefly next.

Step 1: Begin with the Math! Articulate clearly the *ideas* you want students to learn as a result of the lesson. Think in terms of mathematical concepts, not skills. Describe the mathematics, not the student behavior.

But what if a skill is the intended outcome? Perhaps you want students to master their subtraction facts or work on developing a method of multiplying two-digit numbers. For every skill there are underlying concepts and relationships. Identify these concepts at this step of your planning. The best tasks will get at skills through concepts.

Step 2: Consider Your Students. What do your students know or understand about this topic? Are they ready to tackle this bit of mathematics or are there some background ideas that they have not yet developed? Perhaps they already have some ideas that you have been working on and this lesson is aimed at expanding or refining these.

Be sure that the mathematics you identified in step 1 includes something new or at least slightly unfamiliar to your students. At the same time, be certain that your objectives are not out of reach. There is no sense in repeating old ideas. Nor is there any value in posing tasks that students cannot access without clear guidance from you. For real learning to take place, there must be some challenge, some new ideas—even if it is simply seeing an old idea in a new format or with a different model. Keep new ideas within the grasp of your students. If necessary, now is the time to revisit step 1 and make adjustments in your goals.

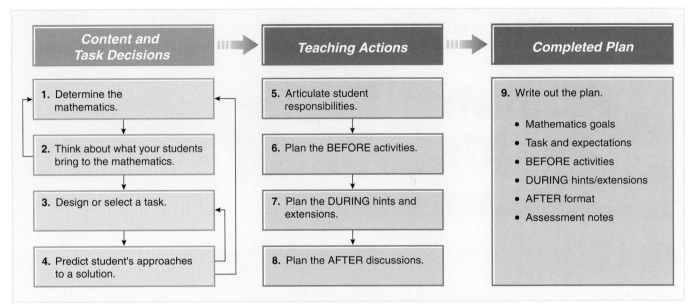

FIGURE 5.1 Planning steps for thinking through a problem-based lesson.

Step 3: Decide on a Task. Keep it simple! Good tasks need not be elaborate. Often a simple story problem is all that is necessary as long as the solution involves children in the intended mathematics.

Chapter 4 gave examples of tasks and suggestions for creating or selecting them. This book is full of tasks. The more experience you have with the content in step 1 and the longer you have had to build a repertoire of task ideas from journals, resource books, conferences, and in-service, the easier this important step in planning will become.

Step 4: Predict What Will Happen. You have made hypotheses about what your students know. Now use that information and think about *all* of the things your students are likely to do with this task. If you catch yourself saying, "Well, I hope that they will . . . ," then *stop*. Predict, don't hope!

Does every student in your class have a chance of engaging in this problem? Although students may each tackle the task differently, don't leave your struggling students to flounder. Perhaps you want to make modifications in the task for different students or provide accommodations that make the task accessible to those with special needs. (See the section on diversity later in this chapter.) This is also a good time to think about whether your students will work alone, in pairs, or in groups. Group work may be an assist to students in need of some extra help.

If your predictions are beginning to make you uneasy about your task, this is the time to revisit the task. Maybe it needs to be modified, or perhaps it is simply too easy or too difficult.

These first four decisions define the heart of your lesson. The next four decisions define how you will carry the plan out in your classroom.

Step 5: Articulate Student Responsibilities. You always want more than answers. For nearly every task, you want students to be able to tell you

- What they did to get the answer
- Why they did it that way
- Why they think the solution is correct

Decide how you want students to supply this information. If responding in writing, will students write individually or prepare a group presentation? Will they write in their journals, on paper to be turned in, on a worksheet, on chart paper to present to the class, or on acetate to use on the overhead?

You may choose to have students simply report or discuss their ideas without writing. Although this option is sometimes adequate, some form of written work that goes beyond the answer is strongly recommended. Remember, writing is a form of rehearsal for discussions.

Step 6: Plan the *Before* Portion of the Lesson. Sometimes you can simply begin with the task and articulation of students' responsibilities. But, in many instances, you will want to prepare students by working quickly through an easier related task or some related warm-up exercise that orients students' thinking. After presenting the task, will you "let go" or do you want students to brainstorm solutions or estimate answers? (See Chapter 4, Teacher Actions in the *Before* Phase.)

Consider how you will present the task. Options include having it written on paper, taken from their texts, shown on the overhead, or written on the board or on chart paper. And don't forget to tell the students about their responsibilities (step 5).

Step 7: Think About the *During* Portion of the Lesson. Look back at your predictions. What hints or assists can you plan in advance for students who may be stuck or who may need accommodations? Are there particular groups or individual students you wish to specially observe or assess in this lesson? Make a note to do so. Think of extensions or challenges you can pose to students who finish quickly.

Estimate how much time you think students should be given for the task. It is useful to tell students in advance. Some teachers set a timer that all students can see. Plan to be somewhat flexible, but do not use up your discussion period.

Step 8: Think About the *After* Portion of the Lesson. How will you begin your discussion? One option is to simply list all of the different answers from groups or individuals, doing so without comment, and then returning to students or groups to explain their solutions and justify their answers. You may also begin with full explanations from each group or student before you get all the answers. If you accept oral reports, think about how you will record on the board what is being said.

Plan an adequate amount of time for your discussion. Five minutes is almost never sufficient. Aim for 20 minutes at least for rich problems. A good average is about 15 to 20 minutes.

Step 9: Write Your Lesson Plan. If you have thought through these steps, a plan is simply a listing of the critical decisions you have already made. The outline shown here is a possible format:

- The mathematics or goals
- The task and expectations
- Materials needed and necessary preparation
- The *before* activities
- The *during* hints and extensions for early finishers
- The *after*-lesson discussion format
- Assessment notes (whom you want to assess and how)

Sample Lessons

Attention to the first two steps in the guide, the mathematics in your curriculum and the particular needs of your students relative to the mathematics, is critical to a successful lesson. Therefore, to plan a lesson without a real class in mind is somewhat artificial. However, two sample lessons, called Expanded Lessons, can be found at the end of this chapter to illustrate the thinking involved.

The first of these sample lessons is designed as a full-class lesson for fourth or fifth grade. The second lesson illustrates the three-part model in a station-based activity for kindergarten or first grade. The tasks in each lesson are taken from activities in the book. In addition to these two lessons, the Companion Web site has an Expanded Lesson related to one activity from each chapter in Section 2. Look for this icon **EXPANDED LESSON** indicating that a lesson is on the Web related to that activity.

Variations of the Three-Part Lesson

The basic lesson structure we have been discussing assumes that a class will be given a task or problem, allowed to work on it, and end with a discussion. Certainly, not every lesson is developed around a task given to a full class. However, the basic concept of tasks and discussions can be adapted to most any problem-based lesson.

Minilessons

Many tasks do not require the full period. The three-part format can be compressed to as little as 10 minutes. You might plan two or three cycles in a single lesson. For example, consider these tasks:

Grades K–1: Make up two questions that we can answer using the information in our graph.

Grade 2–3: Suppose you did not know the answer to problem 14. How could you start to figure it out?

Grades 4–5: On your geoboard, make a figure that has line symmetry but not rotational symmetry. Make a second figure that has rotational symmetry but not line symmetry.

Grades 6–7: Margie has this drawing of the first floor of her house. (Pass out drawing.) She wants to reduce it on the photocopy machine so that it will have a scale of 1 cm to the foot. By what percentage should she reduce it?

These are worthwhile tasks but probably would not require a full period to do and discuss.

A profitable strategy for short tasks is *think-pair-share*. Students are first directed to spend a minute developing their own thoughts and ideas on how to approach the task or even what they think may be a good solution. Then they pair with a classmate and discuss each other's ideas. This provides an opportunity to test out ideas and to practice articulating them. The last step is to share the idea with the rest of the class. The pair may actually have two ideas or can be told to come to a single decision. The entire process, including some discussion, may take less than 15 minutes.

Workstations and Games

It is often useful for students to work at different tasks or games at various locations around the room. Stations are a good way to manage materials without the need to distribute and collect them. They also help when it is unreasonable or impossible for all students to have access to the required materials for an activity. Good computer tasks do exist, especially applets found on the Web. Computer stations make sense for these activities. Stations also allow you to differentiate tasks when your students are at different stages in developing the current concept.

You may want students to work at stations in small groups or individually. Therefore, for a given topic you might prepare from four to eight different activities. Not every station has to be different. Materials required for the activity or game, including any special recording sheets, are placed in a tub or folder to be quickly positioned at different locations in the classroom.

A good idea for younger children or for games and computer activities is to explain or teach the activity to the full class ahead of time. In this way students should not waste time when they get to the station and you will not have to run around the room explaining what to do. The second sample lesson at the end of the chapter is an example of using stations.

Many station activities can be profitably repeated several times. For example, students might be replacing missing numbers on a hundreds chart or playing a "game" where one student covers part of a known number of counters and the other student names the covered part. The game "Fraction Track" in the NCTM *e-Standards* (E-example 5.1) can be played profitably several times.

A game or other repeatable activity may not look like a problem, but it can nonetheless be problem based. The determining factor is this: Does the activity cause students to be reflective about new or developing mathematical relationships? Remember that it is reflective thought that causes growth. If the activity merely has students repeating a procedure without wrestling with an emerging idea, then it is not a problem-based experience. However, the few examples just mentioned and many others do have children thinking through ideas that they have not yet formulated well. In this sense, they fit the definition of a problem-based task.

The time during which students are working at stations is analogous to the *during* portion of a lesson. What kinds of things could you do for the *after* portion of the lesson? Discussions with students who have been working on a task are just as important for games and stations. However, these discussions will generally take place in small groups. You might sit down with students at a station and ask about what they have been doing, what strategies they have discovered, or how they have been going about the activity in general. Try to get at the reasoning behind what they are doing. Another possibility is to wait until all in the class have worked at the same game or station. Now you can have a full group discussion about the learning that came from that activity.

Just as with any task, some form of recording or writing should be included with stations whenever possible. Students solving a problem on a computer can write up what they did and explain what they learned. Students playing a game can keep records and then tell about how they played the game—what thinking or strategies they used.

Dealing with Diversity

Perhaps one of the most difficult challenges for teachers today is to reach all of the students in their increasingly diverse classrooms. Every teacher faces this dilemma because every classroom contains a range of student abilities and backgrounds. English language learners (ELLs) are now found in nearly every classroom and pose unique challenges.

Interestingly and perhaps surprisingly to some, the problem-based approach to teaching is the best way to teach mathematics and attend to the range of students. In the problem-based classroom, children are making sense of the mathematics in *their* way, bringing to the problems only the skills and ideas that they own. In contrast, in a traditional, highly directed lesson, it is assumed that all students will understand and use the same approach and the same ideas. Students not ready to understand the ideas presented must focus their attention on following the teacher rules or directions in an instrumental manner. This, of course, leads to endless difficulties and leaves many students behind or in need of serious remediation.

In addition to using a problem-based approach, there are specific things you can do to help attend to the diversity of learners in your classroom.

- Be sure that problems have multiple entry points.
- Plan differentiated tasks.
- Use heterogeneous groupings.
- Make accommodations and modifications for English language learners.
- Listen carefully to students.

Plan for Multiple Entry Points

As suggested in the planning guidelines, when selecting a task it is important to think about how all of the students in the class are likely to approach it. Many tasks can be solved with a range of methods. This is especially true of computational tasks in classes where student-invented methods are encouraged and valued. (See Chapter 13.) For many tasks, the use or nonuse of manipulative models is all that is necessary to vary the entry point. Students should generally be permitted to use models with which they are familiar whenever they feel the need for them. Other students can be challenged to devise rules or to use methods that are less dependent on manipulatives or drawings.

Plan Differentiated Tasks

The idea here is to plan a task with multiple versions; some less difficult, others more so. There are several ways that you can make this happen.

For many problems involving computations, you can insert multiple sets of numbers. In the following problem students are permitted to select the first, second, or third number in each bracket.

Eduardo had {12, 60, 121} marbles. He gave Erica {5, 15, 46} marbles. How many marbles does Eduardo have now?

Students tend to select the numbers that provide them with the greatest challenge without being too difficult. In the discussions, all children benefit and feel as though they worked on the same task.

Another way to differentiate a task is to present a situation with related but different questions that can be asked. The situation might be data in a chart or graph, a measurement task, or a geometry task. Here is an example:

Students are given a collection of parallelograms including squares and rectangles as well as nonrectangular parallelograms. These questions can be posed:

- ■ **Select a shape and draw at least three new shapes that are like it in some way. Tell how your new shapes are both similar to and different from the shape you selected.**
- ■ **Draw diagonals in these shapes and measure them. See what relationships you can discover about the diagonals.**
- ■ **Make a list of all of the properties that you can think of that every parallelogram in this set has.**

For this fifth- to eighth-grade task there is a challenge to engage nearly every student.

Still another method of differentiating the tasks in your classroom is by using workstations as described in the previous section. For example, if a fourth-grade class is working on equivalent fractions, a variety of equivalent fraction tasks can be designed all for the same concept. As you will experience in Chapter 16, not all such tasks are equally difficult. They are differentiated both by the kinds of materials that are used and the numbers involved. Stations can be assigned to students to best fit their needs and yet all will be working on the same concept.

Use Heterogeneous Groupings

Avoid ability grouping! Trying to split a class into ability groups is futile; every group will still have diversity. It is demeaning to those students not in the top groups. Students in the lower group will not experience the thinking and language of the top group, and top students will not hear the often unconventional but interesting approaches to tasks in the lower group. Furthermore, having two or more groups means that you must diminish the time you can spend with each group.

It is much more profitable to *capitalize* on the diversity in your room by using pairs or cooperative groups that are heterogeneous. Some teachers like to use random pairings or allow students to select the students they want to work with. These techniques may be fun occasionally, but it is advisable to think through carefully how you group your students. Try to pair students in need of help with capable students but also students who will be compatible and willing to assist. What all students will find is that everyone has ideas to contribute.

Make Accommodations and Modifications

There are two paths to making a given task accessible to all students: *accommodation* and *modification*. An *accommodation* is a provision of a different environment or circumstance made with particular students in mind. For example, you might write down instructions instead of just saying them orally. Accommodations do not alter the task. A *modification* refers to a change in the problem or task itself. For example, suppose the task begins with finding the area of a compound shape as shown here.

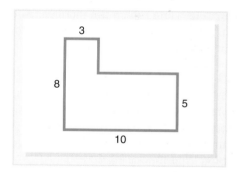

If you decide instead to focus on simple rectangular regions, then that is a modification. However, if you decide to begin with rectangular regions and build to connected compound shapes composed of rectangles, you have *scaffolded* the lesson in a way to ramp up to the original task. Scaffolding a task in this manner is an accommodation. In planning accommodations and modifications the goal is to enable each child to successfully reach your learning objectives, not to change the objectives. This is how equity is achieved in the classroom.

Teaching for Equity

Consideration of your students, step 2 in the planning guide, means consideration for *all* students, which is the foundation of equitable teaching. The Equity Principle in *Principles and Standards* refers to "high expectations and strong support for all students" (p. 12). Note that equity is not the same as equality. As Thomas Jefferson said, "There is nothing so unequal than the equal treatment of unequal people." Commonly used strategies for equality include calling on students by drawing name sticks and randomly assigning groups or jobs. Although encouraging equal participation is important, it cannot be the only strategy we use to create equitable classrooms. We must create accommodations that will help each child be successful.

Return to the example of drawing name sticks. Students who struggle with mathematics or with language may not respond well to being called on unexpectedly or they may not be able to come up with a verbal response on the spot. English language learners in particular need nonthreatening opportunities to mentally compose their ideas before they speak. As one strategy, you might first ask each child to write down his or her idea. Then you can work with students who may not understand the question and rephrase it or illustrate it pictorially or with gestures. Another approach is *think-pair-share*, where students first share their ideas with a partner, giving them a nonthreatening environment to speak in. This allows students to put together a response while clearing up misconceptions they might have. Then they are ready to be called on to explain their answer.

How you assess students is another opportunity to be equitable in your instruction. Equity-minded teachers may have assessments in which some students show what they know in writing while others use pictures. Allowing responses that use words, pictures, numbers, or models accommodates a variety of learners.

High Expectations with Strong Support

In the NCTM Equity Principle, the two phrases "high expectations" and "strong support" are one idea, not two. In the following example, the teacher uses several techniques that provide support for her English language learners while keeping expectations high.

Ms. Steimer is working on a third-grade lesson that involves the concepts of estimating length (in inches) and measuring to the nearest half inch. The task asks students to use estimation to find three objects that are about 6 inches long, three objects that are about 1 foot long, and three objects that are about 2 feet long. Once identified, students are to measure the nine objects to the nearest half inch and compare the measurements with their estimates. Ms. Steimer has a child from Korea who knows only a little English, and she has a child from Mexico who speaks English well but is new to U.S. schools. These two students are not familiar with feet or inches, so they will likely struggle in trying to estimate or measure in inches.

Ms. Steimer takes time to address the language and the increments on the ruler to the entire class. Because the

word *foot* has two meanings, Ms. Steimer decides to address that explicitly before launching into the lesson. She begins by asking students what a "foot" is. She allows time for them to discuss the word with a partner and then share their answers with the class. She explains that today they are going to be using the measuring unit of a foot (while holding up the ruler). She asks students what other units can be used to measure. In particular, she asks her English language learners to share what units they use in their countries of origin. She asks students to study the ruler and compare the centimeter to the inch by posing these questions: "Can you estimate about how many centimeters are in an inch? In 6 inches? In a foot?"

Moving to the lesson objectives, Ms. Steimer asks students to compare how the halfway points are marked for the inches and the centimeters. Then she asks students to tear a piece of paper, without using a ruler, that they think is about one-half of a foot long. Students then measure their paper strips to see how close their strips are to 6 inches. Now she has them ready to begin estimating and measuring.

 pause and reflect

Review Ms. Steimer's lesson. What specific strategies to support English language learners can you identify?

Discussion of the word *foot* using the think-pair-share technique recognized the potential language confusion and allowed students the chance to talk about it before becoming confused by the task. The efforts to use visuals and concrete models (the ruler and the torn paper strip) and to build on students' prior experience (use of the metric system in Korea and Mexico) provide support so that the ELLs can succeed in this task. Most importantly, Ms. Steimer did not diminish the challenge of the task with these strategies. If she had altered the task, for example, not expecting the ELLs to estimate since they don't know the inch very well, she would have lowered her expectations. Conversely, if she had simply posed the problem without taking time to study the ruler or to provide visuals, she may have kept her expectations high but failed to provide the support that would enable her students to succeed. Finally, by making a connection for all students to the metric system, she showed respect for the students' cultures and broadened the horizons of other students to measurement in other countries.

Listen Carefully to Students

Regardless of the classroom, it is always important to listen to your students. Try to find out how they are thinking, what ideas they have, how they are approaching problems causing difficulty, and in general develop as accurate a hypothesis about the ideas they have on the current topic as possible. Listening to children was mentioned as a strategy for effective teaching in Chapter 3. It is also an effective means of assessing students. This is an important idea as you strive to help all children in your classroom. Every child is capable. By listening carefully you will be in a better position to put into practice the other suggestions in this section.

Planning Considerations for English Language Learners

We have already seen some strategies that promote equity for all students. To be an equitable teacher, you must keep your eye on the mathematical goals for your lessons and at the same time attend to the specific learning needs of each child. Attention to the needs of the English language learner must be considered at each step of the nine-step planning guide as detailed in Table 5.1.

Examine the two Expanded Lessons at the end of the chapter. Look for evidence within the lesson that there is already support for the ELL. What additional opportunities can you find in the lessons to provide support for the ELL?

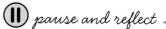 *pause and reflect* ───────

Check these lessons now. The area and perimeter lesson already has good modeling of the ideas and scaffolding suggestions that are helpful. Refer to Table 5.1 for ideas that are not explicitly mentioned in the lessons if there are ELLs in the classroom.

───────

Additional information for working with ELLs in mathematics can be found in Chapter 7.

Drill or Practice?

Drill and practice, if not a hallmark of American instructional methods in mathematics, is a strategy used regularly in nearly every classroom. Most lessons in traditional textbooks end with a section consisting of exercises, usually of a similar nature and always completely in line with the ideas that were just taught in the beginning of the lesson. This repetitive procedural work is supposed to cement the ideas just learned. On the surface, this idea seems to make sense. In addition to this common textbook approach, drill-and-practice workbooks and computer drill programs abound.

A question worth asking is, "What has all of this drill gotten us?" It has been an ever-present component of mathematics classes for decades and yet the adult population is replete with those who almost proudly proclaim "I was never any good at mathematics" and who understand little more about the subject than arithmetic. This section offers a different perspective.

New Definitions of Drill and Practice

The phrase "drill and practice" slips off the tongue so rapidly that the two words "drill" and "practice" appear to be synonyms—and, for the most part, they have been. In the interest of developing a new or different perspective on drill and practice, consider definitions that differentiate between these terms as different types of activities rather than link them together.

> *Practice* refers to different problem-based tasks or experiences, spread over numerous class periods, each addressing the same basic ideas.
>
> *Drill* refers to repetitive, *non*-problem-based exercises designed to improve skills or procedures already acquired.

 *pause and reflect* ───────

How are these two definitions different? Which is more in keeping with the view of drill and practice (as a singular term) with which you are familiar? The drill definition requires that skills are already acquired before they are drilled. What do you think about that?

───────

Using these definitions as a point of departure, it is now useful to examine what benefits we can get from each and when each is appropriate.

What Drill Provides

Drill can provide students with the following:

- An increased facility with a strategy but *only* with a strategy already learned
- A focus on a singular method and an exclusion of flexible alternatives
- A false appearance of understanding
- A rule-oriented view of what mathematics is about

The popular belief is that somehow students learn through drill. In reality, drill can only help students get faster at what they already know. Students who count on their fingers to answer basic fact questions only get very good at counting on their fingers. Drill is not a reflective activity. The nature of drill asks students to do what they already know how to do, even if they just learned it. The focus of drill is on procedural skill.

TABLE 5.1

Considerations in Planning for All Students		
Planning Steps	**Considerations for Any Lesson**	**Additional Considerations for English Language Learners**
1. Begin with the mathematics	• Identify the mathematical concepts. • Align with state and district standards.	• Establish language objectives (reading, writing, speaking, and listening) in the lesson plan. • Write and post content and language objectives, using kid-friendly words.
2. Consider your students	• Relate concepts to previously learned concepts and experiences. • The mathematics should be challenging but within reach of all students.	• Build background by linking to students' social/cultural background and to previous learned content and vocabulary.
3. Decide on a task	• Select a task that will enable students to explore the concept(s) selected in step 1.	• Use visuals and real objects. • Incorporate real-life problem solving, surveys, simulations, modeling, and data.
4. Predict what will happen	• Provide accommodations and modifications for students who may struggle with the task.	• Analyze the task for language pitfalls. Identify words that need to be discussed and eliminate terms that are difficult and not necessary to the lesson. • Watch for homonyms, homophones, and words that have special meanings in math (e.g., mean, similar, product). There are many of these.
5. Articulate students' responsibilities	• Communicate reporting expectations. Include how they solved it, why they picked that strategy, and how they know their answer is correct.	• Consider using a graphic organizer. Ideas include sentence starters ("I solved the problem by . . ."), recording tables, and concept maps. • Maximize language use in nonthreatening ways. Consider pair-share (speak, listen) and collaborative groups; record their strategies and solutions (write). • Encourage students to record in their native language if necessary.
6. Plan the *before* phase	• Determine how you will introduce the task. • Consider warm-ups that orient student thinking.	• Build background! Link task to prior learning and to familiar contexts. • Incorporate review of key vocabulary for the lesson in warm-up. • Set task in written and oral format. Discuss key vocabulary. • Ask students to pair-share what they are supposed to do. • Use translators, if needed. • Provide visuals and real objects.
7. Plan the *during* phase	• Think about hints or assists you might give as students work. • Consider extensions or challenges.	• Group students for both language and academic peer assistance. • Use demonstrations, hands-on activities, modeling, etc. • Maximize language. Ask students to explain and defend. • Encourage students to draw pictures and/or model with objects.
8. Plan the *after* phase	• How will students report their findings? • Determine how you will format the discussion of the task. • What questions will you ask?	• Encourage use of visuals in reports. • Give advance notice that students will be speaking, so they can plan. • Encourage students to choose the language they wish to use, using a translator if possible.
9. Write the lesson plan	• Objectives • The task • Three-step plan • Materials and preparation • Assessment	• List use of key vocabulary. • Build in opportunities to review vocabulary and key concepts in each of the three steps of the lesson. • Build in questions to diagnose understanding. Use translators if needed. • Assessment: distinguish language and content issues.

For most school-level mathematics, including computation, there are numerous ways of doing things. For example, how many different mental methods can you think of to add 48 + 35? To find 25 percent of $84 you can divide by 4 and subtract rather than multiply by 0.25. What approach would you use to find 17 percent of $84? Similar examples of the value of flexible thinking are easily found. Drill has a tendency to narrow one's thinking rather than promote flexibility.

When students successfully complete a page of routine exercises, teachers (and even students) often believe that this is an indication that they've "got it." In fact, what they most often have is a very temporary ability to reproduce a procedure recently shown to them. The short-term memory required of a student to complete the exercises at the end of the traditional lesson is no indication of understanding. Superficially learned procedures are easily and quickly forgotten and confused.

When drill is such a prevalent component of the mathematics classroom, it is no wonder that so many students and adults dislike mathematics. Real mathematics is about sense making and reasoning—it is a science of pattern and order. Students cannot possibly obtain this view of the discipline when constantly being asked to repeat procedural skills over and over.

What is most important to understand is this: Drill will *not* help with conceptual understanding. Drill will *not* provide any new skills or strategies. Drill focuses only on what is already known.

What Practice Provides

In essence, practice is what this book is about—providing students with ample and varied opportunities to reflect on or create new ideas through problem-based tasks. The following list of outcomes of practice should not be surprising:

- An increased opportunity to develop conceptual ideas and more elaborate and useful connections
- An opportunity to develop alternative and flexible strategies
- A greater chance for all students to understand, not just a few
- A clear message that mathematics is about figuring things out and making sense

Each of the preceding benefits has been explored in this or previous chapters and should require no further discussion. However, it is important to point out that practice can and does develop skills. The fear that without extensive drill students will not master "basic skills" is not supported by recent research on standards-based curriculum or practices (see Chapter 1). These programs include lots of practice as defined here and most include very minimal amounts of drill. Students in these programs perform about as well as students in traditional programs on computational skills and much better on nearly every other measure.

When Is Drill Appropriate?

Yes, there is a place for drill in mathematics but it need not occur nearly as frequently as most seem to believe. Consider these two proposed criteria for the profitable use of drill:

- An efficient strategy for the skill to be drilled is already in place.
- Automaticity with the skill or strategy is a desired outcome.

Is it possible to have a skill and still need to perfect it or to drill it? Clearly this happens outside of mathematics all the time with sports and music as good examples. We learn how to dribble a soccer ball or play the chords shown on a sheet of music. At the outset of instruction, we are given the necessary bits of information to perform these skills. Initially, the skills are weak and unperfected. They must be repeated in order to hone them to a state of efficiency. However, if the skill is not there to begin with, no amount of drill will create it.

Automaticity means that the skill can be performed quickly and mindlessly. Most adults have automaticity with basic facts and simple computation. They perform long division without thinking about the meaning behind the steps.

 *pause and reflect*

Stop and make a mental list of the things in K–8 mathematics with which you think students should have automaticity.

Probably your list includes how to count, read, and write numbers. It should include mastery of basic facts (e.g., $3 + 9$ or 8×6). If you are like most people, you may have computation with whole numbers and even with fractions and decimals on your list. What may surprise you is that automaticity with computational skills is not nearly as important as it used to be. Certainly we want skills in computation but not necessarily with a singular or inflexible method. There are more items that are candidates for the list of desired automaticity but generally these will be small bits of mathematics, not big ideas. In fact, the list of things for which automaticity is truly required is actually quite short.

Kids Who Don't Get It

As discussed earlier, the diversity in classrooms is a challenge for all teachers. For those students who don't pick up new ideas as quickly as most in the class, there is an overwhelming temptation to give in and "just drill 'em." Before committing to this solution, ask yourself these two questions: *Has it worked before? What is this telling the child?* The child who has difficulties has certainly been drilled in the past. It is naive to believe that the drill you provide will be more beneficial than the endless drills this child has undoubtedly endured in the past. Although drill may provide some very short-term success, an honest reflection will suggest that it probably will have little effect in the long run. What these children learn from more drill is simple: "I'm no good at math. I don't like math. Math is rules."

The earlier section of this chapter, Dealing with Diversity, suggests strongly that a conceptual approach is the best way to help students who struggle. Drill is simply not the answer.

Homework

Data from the TIMSS suggest that U.S. fourth graders are assigned about as much homework as students in most other countries (U.S. Dept. of Education, 1997c). U.S. eighth graders are assigned more homework and spend more time in class talking about homework than do Japanese students who significantly outperform the U.S. students (U.S. Dept of Education, 1996). The real value of homework is unclear. Many parents expect to see homework and most teachers do assign homework.

But what should homework consist of? How do you deal with homework once it has been assigned? The distinction between drill and practice as described in the previous section provides a useful lens for looking at homework.

Practice as Homework

Homework is a perfectly appropriate way to engage students in problem-based activities—in practice. A problem-based task similar to those described in Chapter 4 can profitably be assigned for homework provided that the difficulty of the task is within reach of most of the students. The difference is that, when at home, students will be working alone rather than with a partner or group.

On the day following a practice or problem-based homework assignment, begin immediately with a discussion of the task—the *after* portion of a lesson. The *before* portion would have occurred at the time of assigning the task. Some form of written work must be required so that students are held responsible for the task and are prepared for the class discussion.

Homework of this nature communicates to parents the problem-based or sense-making nature of your classroom and can help them see the value in this approach. Parents want to see homework but few will have any concept of the type of instruction you have been reading about.

Drill as Homework

Never assign drill for homework as a substitute for practice or before the requisite concepts have been developed. If you do assign drill for homework, here are some things to think about:

- Keep it short. Students don't like homework to begin with and drill is not particularly fun.
- Provide an answer key. At grade 3 and above, students are capable of checking their own work. They should not change their answers but should repeat the missed exercises and/or write a short note indicating where they had difficulty and what they do not understand. If you respond to these notes with assistance, students will begin to understand that homework drills are a way for them to receive help.
- Never grade homework based on correctness. Instead, grade only that it was or was not completed. Rather than penalize wrong answers, use wrong answers as an opportunity to assist students and promote growth. This suggestion applies equally well to practice homework.
- Do not waste valuable classroom time going over drill homework. Especially if the last two suggestions are followed, simply observing that it is complete is all that is required.

The Role of the Textbook

The textbook remains the most significant factor influencing instruction in the elementary and middle school classroom. To make decisions about the use of a textbook, it is good to have an objective view of textbooks and the role they can serve in instruction.

How Are Textbooks Developed?

It is worthwhile to remember that publishing textbooks is a business. If the very best ideas from mathematics educators were incorporated into a textbook that did not sell, those excellent books sitting in warehouses would be of no value to students and would cost the publisher millions of dollars.

Most publishers enlist as authors mathematics educators and teachers who are quite knowledgeable about teaching mathematics. They also do extensive market research to determine what will sell and what teachers think they want in a book. There is frequently a significant gap between what the authors think would be good and what the publisher determines will sell. Compromise between author and market becomes the rule. As a consequence, there is frequently a significant time lapse between state-of-the-art mathematics education and what appears in textbooks.

With exceptions found in occasional lessons, most traditional textbooks remain very close to a "teach by telling" model. Most teachers have not yet adapted the teaching-through-problem-solving approach described in this book. For most of the market, the textbook is expected to teach, not simply pose tasks. The mainstream textbook is designed for a teacher who believes that the best teaching is done by following the text and who values a high proportion of drill.

The standards-based curricula described in Chapter 1 are very different from traditional texts. The development was funded primarily by the National Science Foundation so that publishers did not have that expense. Authors were not bound by the market concerns. To use these texts, teachers must invest a significant amount of time reading the teacher material provided for them. Lessons are problem oriented and often involve extended explorations by students. Extensive drill is not a feature. The market for these programs is growing slowly; it is currently only around 20 percent at the K–5 level and less than that at the middle and high school levels. Traditional textbooks maintain a dominant presence in most classrooms.

Teacher's Editions

The teacher's editions give authors considerably more freedom. The teacher's editions nearly always suggest alternative or additional activities completely separate from those presented on the student pages. Teachers should take advantage of this information. Too many teachers interpret the textbook curriculum as "getting students through the student pages" when in fact the real objectives require the much broader scope presented in the teacher's editions. Pupil pages are just one tool for instruction. Pupil pages are not the objective, nor are they the curriculum.

Two-Page Lesson Format

The typical textbook lesson in the pupil book is presented on two pages or, in the upper grades, occasionally four pages. An observable pattern to these lessons can be seen in almost all popular textbook series. A portion of the first page consists of pictures and illustrations that depict the concepts for that lesson. The teacher is to use this section of the page to discuss the concepts with the students. Next are well-explained examples for the students to follow or an exercise guided by the text. Finally, the lesson has a series of exercises or drill activities usually referred to as practice. Thus, many lessons move almost immediately from conceptual development to symbolic or procedural activities.

This three-part characterization of a textbook lesson is unfairly oversimplified. At the K–2 level, where the children write directly in consumable workbooks, what the student writes for all or most of the two pages may be closely tied to meaningful pictures or even simple hands-on models. The clear adherence to the two-page lesson is not always evident in seventh- and eighth-grade texts.

The two-page format sends a clear message to students that the pictures, concepts, and discussion part of a lesson can be ignored. They begin to tune out until the teacher explains how to do the exercises. Following page by page and assigning procedural exercises from every lesson can easily negate all other efforts to communicate the importance of reasoning, of making and testing conjectures, of justifying results—in short, of doing mathematics. Until the market (this includes you) demands a different approach, the show-and-tell method will dominate mainstream textbooks.

Suggestions for Textbook Use

Our task as teachers is to help children construct relationships and ideas, not to get them to "do pages." We should look on the textbook as simply one of a variety of teaching resources available in the classroom. The textbook is not the object of instruction.

If one considers the limitations of the print medium and understands that the authors and publishers had to make compromises, the textbook can be a source of ideas for designing lessons rather than prescriptions for what each lesson will be. Here are some suggestions:

- Teach to the big ideas or concepts, not the pages. Consider chapter objectives rather than lesson activities. The chapter or unit viewpoint will help focus on the big ideas rather than the activity required to complete a page.
- Consider the conceptual portions of lessons as ideas or inspirations for planning more problem-based activities. The students do not actually have to do the page. Nor do they have to open the book if that will help present the task. (Chapter 4 provides two examples.)
- Let the pace of your lessons through a unit be determined by student performance and understanding rather than the artificial norm of two pages per day.
- Use the ideas in the teacher's edition.
- Remember that there is no law saying every page must be done or every exercise completed. Select activities that suit your instructional goals rather than designing instruction to suit the text. Feel free to omit pages and activities you believe to be inappropriate for the needs of your students and your instructional goals.

The text is usually a good general guide for scope and sequence. There is no reason that you as a teacher should be required to be a curriculum designer. If tasks and activities are adapted from pages covering the objective you are teaching, you can be reasonably sure that they have been designed to work well for that objective. It is not easy to make up good tasks for every lesson. Take advantage of the text.

Textbooks and other supplementary materials (ancillaries) supplied by publishers usually include evaluation instruments that may be of use for diagnosis, for guiding the pace of your instruction, or for evaluation. At present, such tests are more likely to assess computational skills than conceptual understanding, problem solving, or other process objectives. However, there is a definite effort on the part of publishers to develop better assessments for these higher-order skills.

EXPANDED LESSON

Fixed Areas *Based on Activity 20.12, p. 385*

Grade Level: Fourth or fifth grade.

Mathematics Goals

- To help contrast the concepts of area and perimeter.
- To develop the relationship between area and perimeter of different shapes when the area is fixed.
- To compare and contrast the units used to measure perimeter and those used to measure area.

Thinking About the Students

Students have worked with the ideas of area and perimeter. Some if not the majority of students can find the area and perimeter of given figures and may even be able to state the formulas for finding the perimeter and area of a rectangle. However, they often become confused as to which formula to use.

Materials and Preparation

- Each student will need 36 square tiles such as Color Tiles, at least two sheets of centimeter or half-centimeter grid paper, and a recording sheet with columns for recording Rectangle Dimensions, Area, and Perimeter. Make a transparency of this as well.
- This activity can be done in pairs. If students are paired, still provide each student with 36 square tiles, as each student needs to explore how the rectangles can be constructed.
- Overhead tiles and a transparency of the grid paper and recording chart will be helpful to introduce the activity as well as to share students' ideas afterward. If overhead tiles are not available, the Color Tiles will suffice, although they will be opaque and it will be more difficult for students to see the individual tiles.

LESSON

Before

Begin with a simpler version of the task:

- Have students build a rectangle using 12 tiles at their desks. Explain that the rectangle should be filled in, not just a border. After eliciting some ideas, ask a student to come to the overhead and make a rectangle that has been described.
- Model sketching the rectangle on the grid transparency. Record the dimensions of the rectangle in the recording chart, for example, "2 by 6."
- Ask: *What do we mean by perimeter? How do we measure perimeter?* After helping students define perimeter and describe how it is measured, ask students for the perimeter of this rectangle. Ask a student to come to the overhead to measure the perimeter of the rectangle. (Use either the rectangle made from tiles or the one sketched on grid paper.) Emphasize that the units used to measure perimeter are one dimensional, or linear, and that perimeter is just the distance around an object. Record the perimeter in the chart.
- Ask: *What do we mean by area? How do we measure area?* After helping students define area and describe how it is measured, ask for the area of this rectangle. Here you want to make explicit that the units used to measure area are two dimensional and, therefore, cover a region. After counting the tiles, record the area in the chart.
- Have students make a different rectangle using 12 tiles at their desks and record the perimeter and area as before. Students will need to decide what "different" means. Is a 2 by 6 rectangle different than a 6 by 2 rectangle? Although these are congruent, students may wish to consider these as being different. That is okay for this activity.

The Task

See how many different rectangles can be made with 36 tiles. Determine and record the perimeter and area for each rectangle.

Establish Expectations

Write the directions on the board:

- Find a rectangle using *all* 36 tiles.
- Sketch the rectangle on the grid paper.
- Measure and record the perimeter and area of the rectangle on the recording chart.
- Find a new rectangle using *all* 36 tiles and repeat steps 2–4.

During

- Question students to be sure they understand the task and the meaning of *area* and *perimeter*. Look for students who are confusing these terms.
- Be sure students are both drawing the rectangles and recording them appropriately in the chart.

After

- Ask students what they have found out about perimeter and area. Ask: *Did the perimeter stay the same? Is that what you expected? When is the perimeter big and when is it small?*
- Ask students how they can be sure they have all of the possible rectangles. As a class, decide on a systematic method of recording rectangles on the recording chart. For example, start with a side of 1, then 2, and so on. After everyone has had time to consider the information in the chart, have students describe what happens to the perimeter as the length and width change. (The perimeter gets shorter as the rectangle gets fatter. The square has the shortest perimeter.)

NEXT STEPS

Assessment Notes

- Are students confusing perimeter and area?
- As students form new rectangles, are they aware that the area is not changing because they are using the same number of tiles each time? These students may not know what area is, or they may be confusing it with perimeter.
- Are students looking for patterns in how the perimeter changes before you guide them toward that idea?

Two More Than/Two Less Than *Based on Activity 9.11, p. 126*

Grade Level: Late Kindergarten or early first grade.

Mathematics Goals

- To help students develop the paired relationships of two more than and two less than for numbers to 12.
- To provide continued domino-type dot patterns with the goal of instant recognition.

Thinking About the Students

Students must be able to count a set accurately and understand that counting tells how many. They may or may not be able to recognize patterned sets or be able to count on and count back from a given number. For those students still having difficulty matching the correct numeral and set, the written component of the activity can be omitted.

Materials and Preparation

- This will be a station activity. (Alternatively, students can do the activity at their seats.) Each student doing the activity at the same time will need the materials described.
- Place four dot cards, showing three to ten dots each, in a plastic bag.
- Each bag should also have at least 12 counters and a crayon or pencil.

- Make one two-sided recording sheet for each student as shown here. The backside of the sheet is the same as the front except that it says "2 Less Than" at the top.

Name _____

2 More Than

LESSON

Before

The Task

- For each dot card, the task is to make a set that has two more counters than dots on the card. Similarly, students will make sets that have two fewer counters than dots on the card. The task is completed with the counters.

Establish Expectations

- Show the class (or a small group) a bag of cards and counters. Empty the counters and select one card. Have a student count the dots on the card. Have a second student use counters on the overhead (or on the carpet, if in a circle setting). Say: *Make a set that has two more counters than dots on this card.*
- Discuss with the students how they can decide if the set is actually two more. Accept students' ideas and try them. For example, they might say: *Count each set. Set a counter aside for each dot. Make the counters into a pattern that is the same as on the dot card.*
- Show students the recording sheet. Point out the titles "2 More Than" and "2 Less Than" on the top. Explain that they will record their two-more-than sets on the 2 More Than side. Demonstrate how to first draw the same number of dots as are on the dot card. Next show

how to draw dots in the oval to show the number of counters that they made for their two-more-than set. Beside each set they should write the corresponding number.

- If students are ready, have them tell how they think the 2 Less Than side should be completed. (You may choose to do only one side of the sheet at a time.)
- Explain that bags with counters and dots will be at stations. (Or pass out bags at this time to each student.) Bags will be different, so each student's paper will also be different.

During

- Observe the methods that students use to count the dots on the cards and to create their sets.
- Challenge students to explain how they know their set is correct. Focus on the actual counters and dot cards rather than on the recording sheet because that is less important.
- Challenge task for capable students: Make sets and record numbers for sets that are 10 more than the given sets. Look for understanding of the teen numbers.

After (when all students have completed the station)

- Show students a sheet of paper with six dots in a patterned arrangement. Ask: *How many dots? How can we tell how many are two more than this?* Students' suggestions should be tied to the methods they used in the activity. Some students may know immediately that 8 is two more than 6. Begin with students who are likely to be still developing this idea. Have different students explain how they did the activity.

NEXT STEPS

Assessment Notes

- How do students count or know how many dots are on the cards? Do they recognize patterned sets or do they count each dot? Which patterns do they know?
- How do students create their two-more-than sets? Is there an indication of the two-more-than relationship developing or being already developed? If students are working on both sides of the paper, look for similar two-less-than concepts.
- Look for ease or difficulty in recording. Do students correctly write numerals with sets?

Reflections on Chapter 5

Writing to Learn

1. Review the steps for planning a lesson. For each of the first eight steps, describe in your own words the decisions that must be made.
2. Not every lesson will be built around a single task. What are other ways to structure problem-based activities in the class?
3. How can a game be considered a problem-based task?
4. How do you do the *after* portion of a lesson when students are working at stations?
5. Why is a problem-based approach a good way to reach all students in a diverse classroom?
6. Discuss what is meant by (a) tasks with multiple entry points and (b) differentiated tasks.
7. What sort of grouping should be used in a diverse classroom? Why?
8. What is the difference between making an accommodation for students and making a modification in a lesson? Explain why this distinction is important.
9. When planning a lesson for a class that includes English language learners, there are many points you might consider at each stage of the planning process. Summarize some of the key ideas for English language learners described in Table 5.1.
10. This chapter suggests a possible distinction between drill and practice. Explain the difference and what each can provide.
11. When is it appropriate to use drill? Explain.
12. Is it ever appropriate to assign problem-based tasks for homework? Explain.
13. Describe the suggestions offered for drill homework.
14. What is the major difference between the instructional method described in this book and the predominant approach found in most mainstream textbooks? Describe briefly what is meant by the "two-page lesson format" that is often adhered to in traditional basal textbooks. What is a serious drawback of this form?

For Discussion and Exploration

1. Examine a textbook for any grade level. Look at a topic for a whole chapter, and determine the two or three main objectives or big ideas covered in the chapter. Restrict yourself to no more than three, and be sure that nearly all topics in the chapter can be built into these big ideas. Now look at the individual lessons. Are the lessons really aimed at the big ideas you have identified? Will the lessons effectively develop the big ideas for this chapter? Try to find two or three tasks or explorations related to the big ideas you have described. If students work on these explorations, how many of the individual lesson objectives will be met?
2. Select a lesson or a short series of lessons from a traditional textbook. Using the ideas on the student pages, go through the nine steps of planning a lesson. This will include designing or selecting a problem or task. Try to modify the instruction on the student page(s) or the ideas in the teacher notes to create a task. Were you able to create a full-period lesson (about 45 to 55 minutes) from a single task? Did your lesson adequately address the mathematics you described in step one?
3. What homework would you assign for the lessons you described in question 2? What is the purpose of the homework? What would you do with this homework on the following day when it was due?

Recommendations for Further Reading

Burns, M., & Silbey, R. (2000). *So you have to teach math? Sound advice for K–6 teachers.* Sausalito, CA: Math Solutions Publications.

This is a must read for new teachers and also for veteran teachers who are switching grades. Burns and Silbey offer practical advice on leading class discussions, using manipulatives, incorporating writing into your classroom, dealing with homework, dealing with parents, and more. Each topical chapter is organized by questions teachers typically ask. Almost certainly, your questions will be there also. Filled with practical tips, this will be a resource to come back to often.

Edwards, L. D. (2003). Collaborative problem solving in mixed-language groups. *Teaching Children Mathematics, 9,* 534–538.

This is a short article that sheds some light on the value of having English language learners solve problems in cooperative groups. A small research study done collaboratively with classroom teachers gives some credence to the notion that working collaboratively in mixed groupings is an advantage for those who are not English proficient.

Litton, N. (1998). *Getting your math message out to parents: A K–6 resource.* Sausalito, CA: Math Solutions Publications.

Well-meaning parents who remember mathematics to be dominated by memorization and work sheets often challenge a constructivist, student-oriented approach to teaching. Litton is a classroom teacher who has practical suggestions for communicating with parents. The book includes chapters on parent conferences, newsletters, homework, and family math night.

Reeves, C. A., & Reeves, R. (2003). Encouraging students to think about how they think! *Mathematics Teaching in the Middle School, 8,* 374–377.

When students (and also adults) get into a habit of mind—or in this case, a pattern for solving a problem—they often continue to use this pattern even when much easier methods are available. The authors explore this idea with some simple tasks that you can try. The point is that too much drill with little variability may have negative effects.

Online Resources

Suggested Applets and Web Links

Association for Supervision and Curriculum Development (ASCD)
www.ascd.org/portal/site/ascd/index.jsp
The ASCD Web site includes articles and information concerning its publications that address the issues of diverse learners.

Illuminations
www.illuminations.nctm.org
Click on Web resources. A list of Web sites is available for each of the five content standards and each of the five process standards. These are further categorized by grade band. A great resource.

National Council of Teachers of Mathematics
www.nctm.org
This site is constantly changing, so check it periodically to see what's new. Check the table of contents of current journals and look for publications that address issues of planning.

The Math Forum: Internet Mathematics Library
http://mathforum.org/library
Here you will find links to all sorts of information that will be useful in both planning and assessment.

An additional list of books and articles related to the ideas in this chapter can be found on the Companion Web site at **www.ablongman.com/vandewalle6e.**

chapter 6

Building Assessment into Instruction

Assessment should be the servant of teaching and learning. Without information about their students' skills, understanding, and individual approaches to mathematics, teachers have nothing to guide their work.

Mokros, Russell, and Economopoulos (1995, p. 84)

What ideas about assessment come to mind from your personal experiences? Tests? Pop quizzes? Grades? Studying? Anxiety? Getting the correct answers? All of these are typical. Now suppose that you are told that assessment in the classroom should be designed to help students learn and to help teachers teach. How can assessment do those things?

Blurring the Line Between Instruction and Assessment

The Assessment Principle in *Principles and Standards* stresses two main ideas: (1) Assessment should enhance students' learning, and (2) assessment is a valuable tool for making instructional decisions. If your concept of assessment is found primarily in weekly quizzes, chapter-end tests, the nine-week test, or the standardized test that is used in your state or province, then it is time to rethink your ideas about assessment.

What Is Assessment?

The term *assessment* is defined in the *Assessment Standards* as "the process of gathering evidence about a student's knowledge of, ability to use, and disposition toward mathematics and of making inferences from that evidence for a variety of purposes" (NCTM, 1995, p. 3). It is important to note that "gathering evidence" is not the same as giving a test or quiz. Assessment can and should happen every day as an integral part of instruction. If you restrict your view of assessment to tests and quizzes, you will miss seeing how assessment can help students grow and inform instruction.

The *Assessment Standards*

Traditional testing has focused on what students *do not know* (how many wrong answers). In the 1989 *Curriculum Standards* the authors called for a shift toward assessing what students *do know* (what ideas they bring to a task, how they reason, what processes they use). This shift to finding out more about students is also a theme of the *Assessment Standards for School Mathematics* published by NCTM in 1995. The *Assessment Standards* contains six standards for assessment that are deserving of some reflection.

The Mathematics Standard

Assessment should reflect the mathematics that all students need to know and be able to do. (p. 11)

In nearly every school district, state or local standards will define in measurable terms the mathematical content students are to master. The danger is to focus on the tests and low-level skills. The Mathematics Standard indicates that assessment should reflect the mathematics that students *should* know, not just skills found on tests.

The Learning Standard

Assessment should enhance mathematics learning. (p. 13)

The Learning Standard speaks most clearly to the notion that assessment must be an integral part of instruction and not an interruption or a singular event at the end. Regular classroom instruction guides students' learning by informing them about what is important and what is valued.

Assessment also aids students by aiding teachers in the design of instruction. Without listening thoughtfully to your students (assessing) on a daily basis, tomorrow's lesson can be based only on a guess at their needs.

The Equity Standard

Assessment should promote equity. (p. 15)

The Equity Standard mandates that assessments respect the unique qualities, experiences, and expertise of every student. The Equity Principle in *Principles and Standards* echoes this standard when it calls for high expectations for all students while recognizing their individual needs.

The Openness Standard

Assessment should be an open process. (p. 17)

The Openness Standard reminds us that students need to know what is expected of them and how they can demonstrate what they know. As we shift attention from answers to processes, we are telling students that their approach is valued and their reasoning will be listened to. Without this focus, students will learn that there is little more to mathematics than getting the answers by following rules.

The Inferences Standard

Assessment should promote valid inferences about mathematics learning. (p. 19)

In a system of ongoing, integrated assessment, the conclusions we draw are not as objective as when we simply count the number wrong and compute a percentage. The Inferences Standard requires that teachers reflect seriously and honestly on what students are revealing about what they know.

The Coherence Standard

Assessment should be a coherent process. (p. 21)

Finally, the Coherence Standard reminds us that our assessment techniques must reflect both the objectives of instruction as well as the methods of instruction. Students should be evaluated using the same methods, materials, and approaches they used for instruction. This will also ensure that assessments are a reflection of the content you want students to learn.

Purposes of Assessment

Even a cursory glance at the six assessment standards suggests a complete integration of assessment and instruction. The *Assessment Standards* outlines four specific purposes of assessment as depicted in Figure 6.1. With each purpose, an arrow points to a corresponding result on the outside ring.

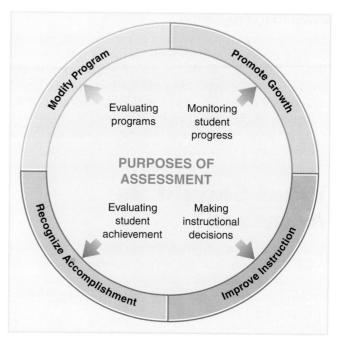

FIGURE 6.1 Four purposes of assessment and their results.
Source: Adapted from NCTM (1995, p. 25). Used with permission.

Monitoring Student Progress

Assessment should provide both teacher and students with ongoing feedback concerning progress toward those goals. Assessment during instruction should inform each individual student and the teacher about growth toward mathematical power and problem-solving ability, not just mastery of procedural skills.

Making Instructional Decisions

Teachers planning tasks each day to develop student understanding must have daily information about how students are thinking and what ideas they are using and developing. Daily problem solving and discussion provide a much richer and more useful array of data than can ever be gathered from a chapter test. It comes at a time when you can formulate plans to help students develop ideas rather than remediate after the fact.

Evaluating Student Achievement

Evaluation is "the process of determining the worth of, or assigning a value to, something on the basis of careful examination and judgment" (NCTM, 1995, p. 3). Evaluation involves a teacher's judgment. It may include test data but should take into account a wide variety of sources and types of information gathered during the course of instruction. Most important, evaluation should reflect performance criteria about what students know and understand; it should not be used to compare one student with another.

Evaluating Programs

Assessment data should be used as one component in answering the question "How well did this program work to achieve my goals?" In this context, *program* refers to any organized unit of study and need not be restricted to decisions such as which textbook should be adopted. For the classroom teacher, program includes such things as self-designed units of instruction or a chapter from a resource book or text.

What Should Be Assessed?

The broader view of assessment promoted here and by NCTM requires that appropriate assessment reflect the full range of mathematics: concepts and procedures, mathematical processes, and even students' disposition to mathematics.

Concepts and Procedures

A good assessment strategy will provide opportunity for students to demonstrate how they themselves understand the concepts under discussion. The traditional test generally targets only one way to know an idea, that determined by the test designer. If you collect information from students as they complete an activity, while it is being discussed, as results are justified—in short, while students are doing mathematics—you will gain information that provides insight into the nature of the students' understanding of that idea.

Procedural knowledge, including skill proficiency, should be included, although it should not be considered as more important than conceptual understanding. If a student can compute with fractions yet has no idea of why he needs a common denominator for addition but not for multiplication, then the rules that have been "mastered" are poorly connected to meaning. This would indicate only the tenuous presence of a skill. Whereas a routine skill can easily be checked with a traditional test, the desired conceptual connections require assessment of a different nature.

Mathematical Processes

Guidelines for defining the specifics of mathematical power can be found in the five process standards of *Principles and Standards*. Now, it is not reasonable to try to assess all of these processes, and certainly not every day. For each grade band, *Principles and Standards* describes what the process standards might look like at that level. Use these descriptions to craft statements about doing mathematics that your students can understand. Here are a few examples, but you should write your own or use those provided by your school system.

Problem Solving

* Works at understanding a problem before beginning work
* Uses drawings, graphs, and physical models to help solve problems
* Has and uses appropriate strategies for solving problems
* Assesses the validity of answers

Reasoning

* Justifies solution methods and results
* Makes conjectures based on reasoning
* Observes and uses patterns in mathematics

Communication

* Explains ideas in writing
* Communicates ideas clearly in class discussions

These statements should be discussed with your students to help clarify them and to let students know that these are values to you. Periodically, use the statements to rate students' mathematical processes based on their individual work, group work, and participation in class discussions. If you use portfolios, work developed and collected over time, process assessment should almost certainly be considered. Processes must also be used in your grading or evaluation scheme, or students will not take them seriously.

Disposition

It is important to make occasional efforts to collect data on students' confidence and beliefs in their own mathematical abilities as well as their likes and dislikes about mathematics. This information is most easily obtained with self-reported checklists and journal writing. Information on perseverance and willingness to attempt problems is available to you every day in a problem-solving approach.

 "Assessment should not merely be done to students; rather, it should also be done for students" (p. 22). "Assessment should become a routine part of the ongoing classroom activity rather than an interruption" (p. 23).

Assessment Tasks Are Learning Tasks

Recall from Chapter 4 that a problem was any task or activity for which the students have no prescribed or memorized rules or specific correct solution method. The same definition should be used for assessment tasks. Perhaps you have heard about *performance assessment tasks* or *alternative assessments*. These terms seem to refer to tasks that are in some way different from those used in instruction. There is no reason for them to be different! A good problem-based task designed to promote learning is also the best type of task for assessment.

Good tasks should permit every student in the class, regardless of mathematical prowess, to demonstrate some knowledge, skill, or understanding. Lower-ability students should be encouraged to use the ideas they do possess to work on a problem even if these are not the same skills or strategies used by others in the room.

Often what are promoted as "alternative assessments" focus on the real-world or authentic contexts of the problems. Although contextual situations are often nice, how a student completes a task and justifies the solution should inform us about his or her understanding of the mathematics. That agenda should not be overshadowed because of difficulties that may arise from context.

The justifications for results, even those given orally, will almost certainly provide more information than the answers alone. Perhaps no better method exists for getting at student understanding.

Examples of Assessment Tasks

Each of the following tasks provides ample opportunity for students to learn. At the same time, each will provide data for the teacher to use in assessment. Notice that these are not elaborate tasks and yet along with a discussion, each could engage students for most of a period. What mathematical ideas are required to successfully respond to each of these tasks? Will the task help you understand how well students understand these ideas?

SHARES (GRADES K–3)

Leila has 6 gumdrops, Darlene has 2, and Melissa has 4. They want to share them equally. How will they do it? Draw a picture to help explain your answer.

At second or third grade, the numbers in Shares would probably be larger. What additional concepts would be involved if the problem were about cookies and the total number of cookies were 14?

SUBTRACTION (GRADES 1–2)

If you did not know the answer to 12 − 7, what are some ways you could find the answer?

HOW MUCH? (GRADES 1–2)

Gustavo has saved $15 to buy a game that he wants. The game costs $23. How much money does Gustavo still need? Explain how you got your answer.

These two problems are similar in that they involve subtraction and allow the teacher to see what strategies a student might use. In the second problem, the context increases the chances that students will use an "add-on" approach (15 and how much more to make 23?). Without context, you get a better chance to see what strategies students are using most regularly. Contrast these tasks with simply giving the corresponding computations.

BROKEN KEYS (GRADES 2–4)

If the ⑤ key on your calculator were broken, how could you do this problem: 458 + 548 + 354? Is there more than one way? Which way do you like the best? Why?

Broken Keys is a good example of a task with many solutions. As students are working, you will be able to assess how easily students arrive at different approaches.

THE WHOLE SET (GRADES 3–5)

Mary counted 15 cupcakes left from the whole batch that Mother made for the picnic. "We've already eaten two-fifths," she noted. How many cupcakes did Mother bake?

This last problem could easily have been posed without any context. What is the value of context in tasks such as these?

In the following task, students are asked to judge the performance of other students. Analysis of student performance is a good way to create tasks.

DECIMALS (GRADES 4–6)

Alan tried to make a decimal number as close to 50 as he could using the digits 1, 4, 5, and 9. He arranged them in this order: 51.49. Jerry thinks he can arrange the same digits to get a number that is even closer to 50. Do you agree or disagree? Explain.

MENTAL MATH (GRADES 4–8)

Explain two different ways to multiply 4 × 276 in your head. Which way is easier to use? Would you use a different way to multiply 5 × 98? Explain why you would use the same or different methods.

Mental computation tasks should be done frequently at all grade levels beginning around grade 2. Other students pick up the methods that students share. The explanations also offer a lot of information about students' concepts and the types of strategies that they have already acquired. This information can be recorded with a variety of simple methods over time.

TWO TRIANGLES (GRADES 4–8)

Tell everything you can about these two triangles.

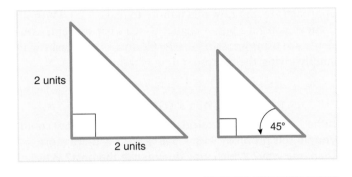

This task is a good example of a very open-ended assessment. Consider how much more valuable this task is than asking for the angle measure in the left-hand triangle.

ALGEBRA: GRAPHING (GRADES 7–8)

Does the graph of $y = x^2$ ever intersect the graph of $y = x^2 + 2$? What are some ways that you could test your idea?

Even with a graphing calculator, to prove that these two graphs will not intersect requires reasoning and an understanding of how graphs are related to equations and tables.

Thoughts About Assessment Tasks

In some instances, the real value of the task or what can be learned about students will come only in the discussion that follows. For others, the information will be in the written report. In many of Marilyn Burns's books, you will see the phrase "We think the answer is . . . We think this because . . . ." Students must develop the habit of adding and listening to justifications. If explanations are not a regular practice in your room, do not expect students to offer good explanations in assessments, either written or oral.

Many activities have no written component and no "answer" or result. For example, students may be playing a game in which dice or dominoes are being used. A teacher who sits in on the game will see great differences in how children use numbers. Some will count every dot on the card or domino. Others will use a counting-on strategy. Some will recognize certain patterns without counting. Others may be unsure if 13 beats 11. This information significantly differentiates students relative to their understanding of number concepts. Data gathered from listening to a pair of children work on a simple ac-

tivity or an extended project provide significantly greater insight into students' thinking than almost any written test we could devise. Data from student conversations and observations of student behavior can be recorded and used for the same purposes that written data can, including evaluation and grading. Especially in the case of grading, it is important to keep dated written notes that can be referred to later.

Rubrics and Performance Indicators: Scoring—Not Grading

Problem-based tasks may tell us a lot about what students know, but how do we handle this information? Often there is only one problem for students to work on in a given period. There is no way to simply count the percent correct and put a mark in the grade book. We used to think of grade-book entries as grades, and often these were averaged at the end of each reporting period. It may be helpful to make a distinction between *scoring* and *grading*. "*Scoring* is comparing students' work to criteria or rubrics that describe what we expect the work to be. *Grading* is the result of accumulating scores and other information about a student's work for the purpose of summarizing and communicating to others" (Stenmark & Bush, 2001, p. 118). The scores can be used (or perhaps not used) along with other information to create a grade. A valuable tool for scoring is a rubric.

A *rubric* is a framework that can be designed or adapted by the teacher for a particular group of students or a particular mathematical task (Kulm, 1994). A rubric consists of a scale of three to six points that is used as a rating of performance rather than a count of how many items are correct or incorrect. The rating or score is applied by examining total performance on a task as opposed to counting the number of items correct.

Note that a rubric is a scale to judge performance on a single task, not a series of exercises.

Simple Rubrics

The following simple four-point rubric was developed by the New Standards Project.

4 Excellent: Full Accomplishment

3 Proficient: Substantial Accomplishment

2 Marginal: Partial Accomplishment

1 Unsatisfactory: Little Accomplishment

This simple rubric allows a teacher to score performances using a double-sort technique as illustrated in Figure 6.2. The broad categories of the first sort are relatively easy to

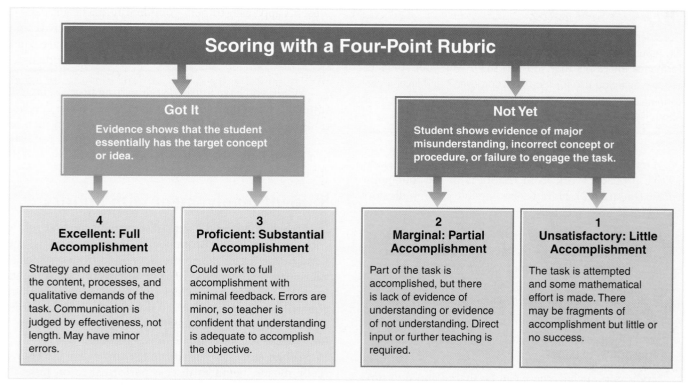

FIGURE 6.2 With a four-point rubric, performances are first sorted into two categories. Each performance is then considered again and assigned to a point on the scale.

discern. The scale then allows you to separate each category into two levels as shown. A rating of 0 is given for no response or effort or for responses that are completely off task.

The advantage of the four-point scale is the relatively easy double sort that can be made. Others prefer a three-point rubric such as the following example:

3 Above and beyond—uses exemplary methods, shows creativity, goes beyond the requirements of the problem

2 On target—completes the task with no more than minor errors, uses expected approaches

1 Not there yet—makes significant errors or omissions, uses inappropriate approaches

These relatively simple scales are *general* rubrics. They label general categories of performance but do not define the specific criteria for a particular task. For any given task or process, it is usually helpful to create performance indicators for each level.

Performance Indicators

Performance indicators are task-specific statements that describe what performance looks like at each level of the rubric and in so doing establish criteria for acceptable performance (Ann Arbor Public Schools, 1993).

A rubric and its performance indicators should focus you and your students on your goals and away from the self-limiting question "How many can you miss and still get an A?" Like athletes who continually strive for better performances rather than "good enough," students should always see the possibility to excel. When you take into account the total performance (processes, answers, justifications, extension, and so on), it is always possible to "go beyond."

What performance at different levels of your rubric will or should look like may be difficult to predict. Much depends on your experience with children at that grade level, your past experiences with students working on the same task, and your insights about the task itself and the ideas that it embodies or that children may use as they work on it.

If possible, it is good to write out indicators of "proficient" or "on target" performances before you use the task in class. This is an excellent self-check to be sure that the task is likely to accomplish the purpose you selected it for in the first place. Think about how children are likely to approach the activity.

Remember that rubrics are applied to performance on a single task, although the task may have multiple components. If you find yourself writing performance indicators in terms of number of correct responses, you are most likely looking at drill exercises and not tasks for which a rubric is appropriate.

pause and reflect

Consider the fraction problem titled "The Whole Set" on page 81. Assume you are teaching fourth grade and wish to write performance indicators that you can share with your students. What would you use for indicators for level-3 and level-4 performances? Start with a level-3 performance, and then think about level 4. Try this before reading further.

Determining performance indicators is always a subjective process. Work from the ideas in the four-point rubric (Figure 6.2). Here is one possible set of indicators for "The Whole Set" task:

3   Determines the correct answer or uses an approach that would give a correct answer if not for minor errors. Reasons are either missing or incorrect. A correct result for the number eaten but not the total baked is also a level-3 performance.

4   Determines the total number baked and uses words and pictures to explain and justify the result and how it was obtained.

Indicators such as these can be shared ahead of time with students. Sharing indicators before working on a task clearly conveys what is valued. If you show students the indicators when you return papers, try including the correct answers and some examples of drawings. This will help students understand how they may have done better. Often it is useful to show work from classmates (anonymously) or from a prior class. Students need to see models of what a top performance looks like.

What about level-1 and level-2 performances? Here are suggestions for the same task:

2   Uses some aspect of fractions appropriately (e.g., divides the 15 into 5 groups instead of 3) but fails to illustrate an understanding of how to determine the whole. The meanings of numerator and denominator are incorrect or confused.

1   Shows some effort but little or no understanding of a fractional part relative to the whole.

It does not seem necessary to share indicators for level-1 and level-2 performances unless students or parents request further explanation. However, you often will be aided in your work if you articulate the differences between these performances.

Unexpected methods and solutions happen. Don't box students into demonstrating their understanding only as you thought or hoped they would when there is evidence that they are accomplishing your objectives in different ways.

Even if you have not written a performance indicator ahead of time, the double-sorting strategy described earlier (two categories, each then separated into two piles) is a useful approach to help you identify on-target performance. There will almost always be differences across your class, although you should make no attempt to have equal piles, and some categories may even have no students in them.

When you have finished your sorting process, use the results to write indicators for the task. Keep the descriptions as general as possible. These indicators can then be shared with students when you return the papers and kept in a file with the task for future use.

Student Involvement with Rubrics

In the beginning of the year, discuss your general rubric with the class. Post it prominently. Many teachers use the same rubric for all subjects; others prefer to use a special rubric for mathematics. In your discussion, let students know that as they do activities and solve problems in class, you will look at their work and listen to their explanations and provide them with feedback in terms of the rubric, rather than as a letter grade or a percentage.

When students start to understand what the rubric really means, begin to discuss performance on tasks in terms of the general rubric. You might have students rate their own work according to the general rubric and explain their reasons for the rating. Older students can do this in written form, and you can respond in writing. For all students, you can have class discussions about a task that has been done and what might constitute good and exceptional performance.

Using Observation in Assessment

All teachers learn useful bits of information about their students every day. When the three-part lesson format suggested in Chapter 4 is used, the flow of data increases dramatically, especially in the *during* and *after* portions of lessons. If you have a systematic plan for gathering this information while observing and listening to students, at least two very valuable things occur. First, you will likely gather a lot more information. Information that may have gone unnoticed is suddenly visible and important. Second, observation data gathered systematically can be added to other data and used in planning lessons, providing feedback to students, conducting parent conferences, and determining grades.

Depending on what information you may be trying to gather, a single observation scheme may require several days to two weeks before it has been observed. Long-term goals can be observed over a full marking period. Shorter periods of observation will focus on a particular cluster of concepts or skills. Over longer periods, you can note growth in mathematical processes, such as problem solving, representation, reasoning, or communication. To use observation effectively as a means of gathering assessment data from performance tasks, you should take seriously the following maxim: *Do not attempt to observe every student in a single class period.*

No single observation recording format will serve all purposes. Further, formats and methods of gathering observation data are going to be influenced by your individual teaching style and habits. Observation methods also vary with the purposes for which they are used.

Anecdotal Notes

A simple system for recording observations is to write short notes either during or immediately after a lesson in a brief narrative style. One possibility is to have a card for each student. Some teachers keep the cards on a clipboard with each taped at the top edge (see Figure 6.3). Each card can

then be accessed quickly. Another option is to select cards for about five students a day, focusing your observations on those five. On another day, different students are selected. The students selected may be members of one or two cooperative groups. An alternative to cards is the use of large peel-off file labels, possibly preprinted with student names on your computer. The label notes are then moved to a more permanent notebook page for each student.

An Observation Rubric

Another possibility is to use your three- or four-point general rubric on a reusable form as in Figure 6.4. Include space for content-specific descriptors and another space to jot down names of students. A quick note or comment may be amended to a name when appropriate. This method is especially useful for planning purposes.

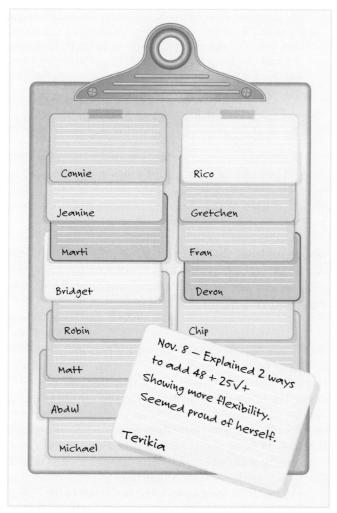

FIGURE 6.3 Cards for observation notes can be taped to a clipboard or folder for quick access.

Making Whole Given Fraction Part (3/17)	
Super Clear understanding. Communicates concept in multiple representations. Shows evidence of using idea without prompting. *Fraction whole made from part in rods and in sets. Explains easily.*	Sally ✓ Latania ✓+ Greg Zal
On Target Understands or is developing well. Uses designated models. *Can make whole in either rod or set format (note). Hesitant. Needs prompt to get unit fraction.*	Lavant Tanisha Julie Lee George J.B. Maria John H.
Not Yet Some confusion or misunderstands. Only models idea with help. *Needs help to do activity. No confidence.*	John S. Mary

FIGURE 6.4 Record names in a rubric during an activity or for a single topic over several days.

Checklists or Forms for Individuals

To cut down on writing and to help focus your attention, a small form with several specific processes or content areas of interest can be devised and duplicated for each student (see Figure 6.5). Some teachers have found methods of printing these on their computer, perhaps on sticky labels. Once a computer format is worked out, it is easy to change the items on the checklist without retyping all the student names. Regardless of the checklist form, a place for comments should be included.

NAME: *Sharon V.*

FRACTIONS	NOT YET	OK	SUPER	COMMENTS
Understands numerator/ denominator		✓		
Area models		✓		
Set models	✓			
Uses fractions in real contexts	✓			
Estimates fraction quantities		✓		*getting better*
PROBLEM SOLVING				
Understands problem before beginning work		✓		*this is good*
Is willing to take risks	✓			*problem area*
Justifies results				

FIGURE 6.5 A focused checklist and rubric can be printed for each student with the help of a computer.

Checklists for Full Classes

Another format involves listing all students in a class on a single page or not more than three pages (see Figure 6.6). Across the top of the page are specific things to look for. Pluses and minuses, checks, or codes corresponding to your general rubric can be entered in the grid. A space left for comments is useful. A full-class checklist is more likely to be used for long-term objectives. Topics that might be appropriate for this format include problem-solving processes, communication skills, and such skills as basic facts or estimation. Dating entries or noting specific activities observed is also helpful.

Writing and Journals

We have been emphasizing that instruction and assessment should overlap. No place is this more evident than in students' writing. Writing is both a learning and an assessment opportunity. Though some students initially have difficulty writing in mathematics, persistence pays off and students come to see writing as a natural part of the mathematics class.

The Value of Writing

When students write, they express their own ideas and use their own words and language. It is personal. In contrast, oral communication in the classroom is very public. Ideas "pop out" without editing or revision. Meaning is negotiated or elaborated on by the class as a whole. The individual reflective quality of writing as compared to classroom discourse is an important factor in considering the value of writing in mathematics.

> The process of writing requires gathering, organizing, and clarifying thoughts. It demands finding out what you know and don't know. It calls for thinking clearly. Similarly, doing mathematics depends on gathering, organizing, and clarifying thoughts, finding out what you know and don't know, and thinking clearly. Although the final representation of a mathematical pursuit looks very different from the final product of a writing effort, the mental journey is, at its base, the same—making sense of an idea and presenting it effectively. (Burns, 1995b, p. 3)

When students write, they are able to stop first and think. They can incorporate drawings and symbolism to help convey their ideas. They can research an idea or look back on related work to help put ideas together. All of this is very powerful and deliberate reflective thinking.

As an assessment tool writing provides a unique window to students' thoughts and the way a student is thinking about an idea. Even a kindergarten child can express ideas in drawings or other markings on paper and begin to explain what he or she is thinking.

Oral communication, valuable as it may be, is gone at the end of the day. When you are able to sit down with students' writing, you can reflect on each person individually as well as on the class as a whole. You can use writing to target feedback and design special work for individual students. Written work helps you assess the progress you are making with the current unit. Finally, student writing is an excellent form of communication with parents during conferences. Writing shows students' thinking to their parents, telling them much more than any grade or test score.

When students write about their solutions to a task prior to the class discussion—that is, as part of the *during* portion of the lesson—the writing serves as a rehearsal for the discussion. Students who otherwise have difficulty thinking on their feet now have a script, so to speak, from

Topic: Mental Computation + of 2 – dig. nos. Names	Not Yet *Can't do mentally*	On Target *Has at least one strategy*	Wow! *Uses different methods with different numbers*	Comments
Lalie		✓ *3-18 -21*		
Pete	✓ *3-20*			*Needs place value help*
Sid			✓ + *3-20*	*Super*
Lakeshia		✓		*Good*
George		✓		
Pam	✓			*Close – getting a tens first idea*
Maria		✓ *3-24*		*Finally!*

FIGURE 6.6 A full-class observation checklist can be used for longer-term objectives or for several days to cover a short-term objective.

which they can talk. This avoids having the few verbal students providing all of the input for the discussion. Call on these more reluctant talkers first so that their ideas are heard and valued. If they have written ahead of time, they will be ready to contribute.

Journals

Writing can, of course, be done on a single sheet of paper and turned in separately, but the use of a journal has real value. A journal may take the form of a composition booklet or, for K–1 children, folded writing paper stapled within a construction-paper cover. Binders and spiral notebooks are other options, but teachers find these bulky, and students are more likely to remove unwanted pages.

Journals are a way to make written communication a regular part of doing mathematics. Journals help you abandon the mistaken, counterproductive myth "If they write it, I must grade it." Journals are a place for students to write about such things as

- Their conceptual understandings and problem solving, including descriptions of ideas, solutions, and justifications of problems, graphs, charts, and observations
- Their questions concerning the current topic, an idea that they may need help with, or an area they don't quite understand
- Their feelings about aspects of mathematics, their confidence in their understanding, or their fears of being wrong

Even if you have students write in their journals nearly every day, be sure that these journals are special places for writing about mathematics. Drill, for example, should not be done in a journal. Lengthy projects done over several days should be separate from journals and given a special presentation. A performance task you plan to use primarily for evaluation purposes should probably not be in a journal. But the work for many of your performance tasks can and should go in the journal, communicating that the work is important and you do want to see it but you are not going to grade it.

To grade journal writing defeats its purpose. Graded journals would communicate that there is a specific "right" response you are seeking. It is essential, however, that you read and respond to journal writing. One form of response for a performance task would be to use the classroom's general rubric along with a helpful comment. This is another way to distinguish between rubrics and grades and still provide feedback.

On a regular basis, it is manageable to read and respond to about five journals a night. Following an especially interesting lesson, you might want to read the journal entry of every student in the class. Allow students to flag entries for which they want your special attention or response. If you do not read and respond to journals, students will quickly come to regard them as busywork and conclude that you do not value their efforts. Teachers whose students have learned to communicate honestly through their journals find them a key element in their assessment program, prized above all other sources of information to improve learning and instruction.

Writing Prompts and Ideas

Students should always have a clear, well-defined purpose for writing in their journals. They need to know exactly what to write about and who the audience is (you, an imaginary friend, a student in a lower grade, an adult, a Martian), and they should be given a definite time frame within which to write. Journal writing that is completely open-ended without goal or purpose will be a waste of time. Here are some suggestions for prompts to get you thinking; however, the possibilities are endless.

Concepts and Problem Solving

- "I think the answer is. . . . I think this because. . . ." (The journal can be used to solve and explain any problem. Always be sure to include the problem. Some teachers duplicate the problem and have students tape it into the journal to save time and effort.)
- Write an explanation for other students (or for students in a lower grade) of why 4×7 is the same as 7×4 and why this works for 6×49 and 49×6.
- Explain to a student in grade X (or who was absent today) what you learned about decimals today.
- What about the work we did today was easy? What was hard? What do you still have questions about?
- If you got stuck today in solving a problem, where did you get stuck? Why do you think you had trouble there? If you did not get stuck, what idea helped you solve the problem?
- After you got the answer to today's problem, what did you do so that you were convinced your answer was correct? How sure are you that you got the correct answer?
- Write a story problem that goes with this picture (this graph, this diagram, this equation).

Affective Ideas

- "What I like most (or least) about mathematics is. . . ."
- Write a mathematics autobiography. Tell about your experiences in mathematics outside of school and how you feel about the subject.
- "Mathematics is like a . . . because. . . ."
- Write to an imaginary friend who is the same age as you, telling how you feel about what we did in mathematics this week.

Journals for Early Learners

If you are interested in working with K–1 children, the writing suggestions presented may have sounded discouraging because it is difficult for prewriters and beginning writers to express ideas like those suggested. There are specific techniques for journals in kindergarten and first grade that have been used successfully.

The Giant Journal

To begin the development of the writing-in-mathematics process, one kindergarten teacher uses a language experience approach. After an activity, she writes the heading "Giant Journal" and a topic or prompt on a large flipchart. Students respond to the prompt, and she writes their ideas, adding the contributor's name and even drawings when appropriate, as in Figure 6.7.

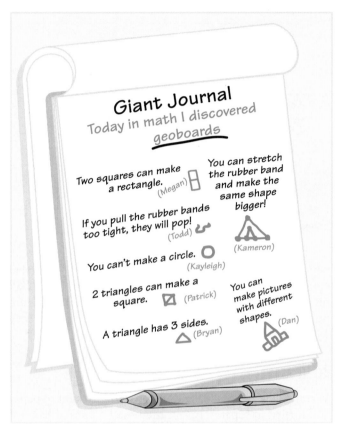

FIGURE 6.7 A journal in kindergarten may be a class product on a flipchart.

Drawings and Early Writing

All students can draw pictures of some sort to describe what they have done. Dots can represent counters or blocks. Shapes and special figures can be cut out from duplicated sheets and pasted onto the journal page.

It is important for the "writing" to be a record of something the student has just done and is comfortable with. Figure 6.8 shows problems solved in first and second grade. Do not be concerned about invented spellings to communicate ideas. Have students read their papers to you.

Brainstorming

Young children have difficulty translating what they say and think into written form. One way to help is to use discussion time to help children think about their journal entries. Record ideas on the board as they are contributed

Grade 1

Read the problem. Think and use "stuff" to help you solve it.

There were 7 owls. They found some mice in the woods to eat. Each owl got 5 mice. How many mice did they find? How do you know? Use pictures and words to show how you solved the problem.

It is 35. I counted by 5s.

Grade 2

The farmer saw five cows and four chickens. How many legs and tails in all did he see?

Shanna Cally

Cout 4 couters out. then take 5 grops Then take 4 grops out of two. Then cout the legs then cout the tails in all? 31.

FIGURE 6.8 Journal entries of children in grades 1 and 2.

by students. For kindergartners and first graders, use very simple abbreviated versions of what they say. For children in grades 2 and 3, you may limit your recording to key phrases and special words. In this manner, the ideas that have been generated are now recorded for students to assemble into their own writing. When a student says, "I don't know what to write," have him tell you about his task or idea. Then have him write what he just told you.

Student Self-Assessment

Stenmark (1989) notes that "the capability and willingness to assess their own progress and learning is one of the greatest gifts students can develop. . . . Mathematical power comes with knowing how much we know and what to do to learn more" (p. 26).

In a self-assessment, students may tell you

- How well they think they understand a piece of content
- What they believe or how they feel about some aspect of mathematics, perhaps what you are covering right now

It is important to see that this is not your measure of their learning or disposition, but rather a record of how *they perceive* these things.

As you plan for a self-assessment, consider how you want the assessment to help you as a teacher. Tell your students why you are having them do this activity. Encourage them to be honest and candid. Though it may seem like fun to collect class information early in the year on a topic such as "Why I like mathematics," do not assign a self-assessment activity just to make yourself feel good about your students.

You can gather self-assessment data in several ways. A common method is to use some form of a questionnaire to which students respond. These can have open-ended questions, response choices (e.g., *seldom, sometimes, often; disagree, don't care, agree*), mind maps, drawings, and so on. Many such instruments appear in the literature, and many textbook publishers provide examples. Whenever you use a form or questionnaire that someone else has devised, be certain that it serves the purpose you intend. Often these forms are too long or include questions in which you have little interest. Modify them to suit your purposes. The fact that a form was professionally prepared or accompanies your text does not necessarily make it appropriate or useful to you.

An open-ended writing prompt such as was suggested for journals is another method of getting self-assessment data:

- How well do you think you understand the work we have been doing the last few days on fractions? If there is something that is causing you difficulty with fractions, please tell me what it is.
- Write one thing you liked and one thing you did not like about math class today (or this week).

You may find that a simple prompt can become familiar to students if you use it on a regular basis. For example, midway through a unit is a good time to listen to what students regard as things they know and do not know. As students learn that you will react in some way that is helpful to them, they will be more apt to provide you with candid, useful information.

Students may find it difficult to write about attitudes and beliefs. An inventory where they can respond "yes," "maybe," or "no" to a series of statements is another approach. Encourage students to add comments under an item if they wish. Here are some items you could use to build such an inventory:

- I feel sure of myself when I get an answer to a problem.
- I sometimes just put down anything so I can get it over with.
- I like to work on really hard math problems.
- Math class makes me feel nervous.
- If I get stuck, I usually just quit or go to another problem.
- I am not as good in math as most of the other students in this class.
- Mathematics is my favorite subject.
- I do not like to work at problems that are hard to understand.
- Memorizing rules is the only way I know to learn mathematics.
- I will work a long time at a problem until I think I've solved it.

Another technique is to ask students to write a sentence at the end of any work they do in mathematics class saying how that activity made them feel. Young children can draw a face on each page to tell you about their feelings.

Tests

Tests will always be a part of assessment and evaluation no matter how adept we become at blending assessment with instruction. However, a test need not be a collection of low-level skill exercises. Although simple tests of computational skills may have some role in your classroom, the use of such tests should be limited. Like all other forms of assessment, tests should reflect the goals of your instruction. Tests can be designed to find out what concepts students have and how their ideas are connected. Tests of procedural knowledge should go beyond just knowing how to perform an algorithm and should allow and require the student to demonstrate a conceptual basis for the process. The following examples will illustrate these ideas.

1. Write a multiplication problem that has an answer between the answers to these two problems:

$$\begin{array}{cc} 49 & 45 \\ \times\, 25 & \times\, 30 \end{array}$$

2. **a.** In this division exercise, what number tells how many tens were shared among the 6 sets?

   b. Instead of writing the remainder as "R 2," Elaine writes "$\frac{1}{3}$." Explain the difference between these two ways of handling the leftover part.

   $$\begin{array}{cc} 49\,R2 & 49\frac{1}{3} \\ 6)\overline{296} & 6)\overline{296} \end{array}$$

3. On the grid, draw two figures with the same area but different perimeters. List the area and perimeter of each.

4. For each subtraction fact, write an addition fact that helps you think of the answer to the subtraction.

   $$\begin{array}{cccc} 12 & 9 & 9 & 14 \\ -\,3 & +\,3 & -\,4 & -\,7 \\ \hline 9 & 12 & & \end{array}$$

5. Draw pictures of arrows to show why $^-3 + ^-4$ is the same as $^-3 - ^+4$.

If a test is well constructed, much more information can be found than simply the number of correct or incorrect answers. Here are some things to think about when constructing a test:

1. *Permit calculators all the time.* Except for tests of computational skills, the calculator allows students to focus on what you really want to test. It also communicates a positive attitude about calculator use to your students.

2. *Use manipulatives and drawings.* Students can use appropriate models to work on test questions when those same models have been used to develop concepts. (Note the use of drawings in Example 5 above.) Simple drawings can be used to represent counters, base-ten pieces, fraction pieces, and the like (see Figure 6.9). Be sure to provide examples in class of how to draw the models before you ask students to draw on a test.

3. *Include opportunities for explanations.*

4. *Avoid always using "preanswered" tests.* These are tests in which questions have only one correct answer, whether it is a calculation, a multiple-choice, or a fill-in-the-blank question. Tests of this type tend to fragment what children have learned and hide most of what they know. Rather, construct tests that allow students the opportunity to show what they know.

Improving Performance on High-Stakes Tests

The No Child Left Behind Act mandates that every state test children in mathematics at every grade beginning with grade 3. The method of testing and even the objectives to be tested are left up to the states. Many districts test their students at every grade level.

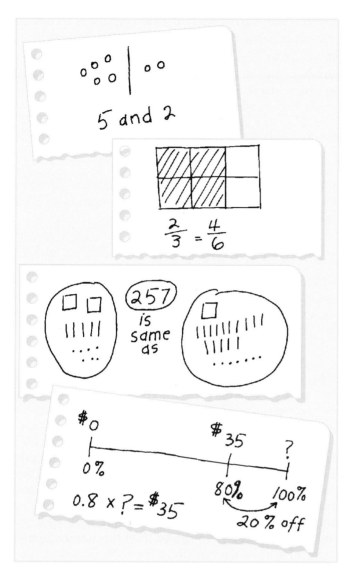

FIGURE 6.9 Students can use drawings to illustrate concepts on tests.

Whatever the details of the testing program are in your particular state, these external tests (originating external to the classroom) impose significant pressures on school districts, which in turn put pressure on principals, who finally place pressures on teachers.

External testing that has consequences for students and teachers is typically referred to as "high-stakes testing." High stakes make the pressures of testing significant for both students (Will I pass? Will I have to go to summer school? Will my parents be upset?) and teachers (Will my class do as well as Mrs. Jones's next door? My scores have been below passing—I've got to get them up.). The pressures almost certainly have an effect on instruction.

You will not be able to avoid the pressures of high-stakes testing. The question is, "How will you respond?"

Avoid Teaching to the Test

The advocates of high-stakes testing argue that teachers should simply teach the content that is in the standards and that, by so doing, students will do well on the tests. The difficulty with this argument is that typical state standards are not in the form of a curriculum. Rather, they are lists of objectives, usually stated in measurable (i.e., behavioral) terms. The result is that teachers work their way through a list of skills, often without attending to the underlying concepts that would connect one skill to another and make the skills meaningful. Students, especially those who have difficulty developing concepts on their own or with minimal assistance, begin to see mathematics as a collection of rules to be mastered. Inevitably, these rules become confused or forgotten. Teaching to the test, even if it means teaching to the required list of standards or objectives, is not in the best interest of students.

In many schools, especially where the scores have been consistently lower than acceptable, teachers are asked or required to give a series of practice tests. Those who advocate practice tests believe that teachers can use the test data to fill gaps in achievement and that the tests will prepare students for the real thing. Although an occasional test is important for a teacher to know where his or her students are, endless testing needlessly saps valuable time away from learning opportunities and can be defeating to students. You may not have control over such zealous approaches by those above you but, if possible, resist this approach to improving scores.

Teach Fundamental Concepts and Processes

Regardless of the state standards, the nature of the tests, or the consequences, the best advice is to teach to the big ideas in the mathematics curriculum. Students who have learned conceptual ideas in a relational manner and who have learned the processes of doing mathematics will always perform well on tests, regardless of the format or specific objectives.

This does not mean that you should ignore the standards you are under contract to teach. Rather, examine these lists of skills and objectives and identify the broader conceptual foundations on which they depend. Be certain that students have an opportunity to learn the content in the standards. At the start of each chapter of Section 2 of this book, you will find a short list of Big Ideas followed by a section called Mathematics Content Connections. These will help you identify the broader ideas behind the objectives that you need to teach and help students deepen their understanding of connecting ideas and strands.

As pointed out in Chapter 1, there is ample evidence that students in the "standards-based" programs developed with NSF funding are doing well on standardized tests. In most cases these students significantly outperform comparable students in traditional programs on measures of problem solving, concepts, and reasoning. On measures of computational skills—what traditional programs teach best—the students in the standards-based program tend to do as well or nearly as well as their counterparts in traditional programs. All of the standards-based programs have in common a focus on conceptual development, problem solving, reasoning, and classroom discussion. In short, a student-oriented, problem-based approach is the best course for raising scores.

Test-Taking Strategies

Another popular approach to raising test scores is to teach students to be test savvy—to teach them specific noncontent strategies useful for taking tests. With a healthy dose of caution, this approach may help some students. The cautions are these: First, if the students have not developed the concepts, the test strategies will be completely useless. Second, time teaching test strategies is best spent shortly before a test. Here are a few strategies that may have some positive effect.

- *Provide experience with different question formats.* If you have information about the types of formats the standardized test will employ, be sure to use these question formats regularly (not exclusively) in class.
- *Teach test-taking strategies.* Students are often not very efficient test takers, so helping them learn to take tests can have some benefits. Here are some teachable strategies:
  - Read questions carefully. Practice identifying what questions are asking and what information is given to get the answer.
  - Estimate the answer before spending time with computation. On multiple-choice tests, estimation and good number sense are often all that are needed to select the correct answer.
  - Eliminate choices. Look at the available options. Some will almost certainly be unreasonable. Does a choice make sense? Can looking at the ones digit eliminate answers?
  - Work backward from an answer.

Remember! Test-taking strategies require good concepts, skills, and number sense. Without good understanding, test strategies will do little good.

Grading

Myth: A grade is an average of a series of scores on tests and quizzes. The accuracy of the grade is dependent primarily on the accuracy of the computational technique used to calculate the final numeric grade.

Reality: A grade is a statistic that is used to communicate to others the achievement level that a student has attained in a particular area of study. The accuracy or validity of the grade is dependent on the information that is used in preparing the grade, the professional judgment of the teacher, and the alignment of the assessments with the true goals and objectives of the course. Look again at the definition of grading on p. 82. Notice that it says scores are used along with "other information about a student's work" to determine a grade. There is no mention of averaging scores.

Confronting the Myth

Most experienced teachers will tell you that they know a great deal about their students in terms of what the students know, how they perform in different situations, their attitudes and beliefs, and their various levels of skill attainment. Good teachers have always been engaged in ongoing performance assessment, albeit informal and usually with no recording. However, even good teachers have relied on test scores to determine grades, essentially forcing themselves to ignore a wealth of information that reflected a truer picture of their students.

The myth of grading by statistical number crunching is so firmly ingrained in schooling at all levels that you may find it hard to abandon. If one thing is clear from the discussions in this chapter, it should be that it is quite possible to gather a wide variety of rich information about students' understanding, problem-solving processes, and attitudes and beliefs. To ignore all of this information in favor of a handful of numbers based on tests, tests that usually focus on low-level skills, is unfair to students, to parents, and to you as the teacher.

Grading Issues

For effective use of the assessment information gathered from problems, tasks, and other appropriate methods to assign grades, some hard decisions are inevitable. Some are philosophical, some require school or district agreements about grades, and all require us to examine what we value and the objectives we communicate to students and parents.

What Gets Graded Gets Valued

In contrast to the many myths of grading, one thing is undeniably true: *What gets graded is what gets valued.* Using rubric scores to provide feedback and to encourage a pursuit of excellence must also relate to grades. However, "converting four out of five to 80 percent or three out of four to a grade of C can destroy the entire purpose of alternative assessment and the use of scoring rubrics" (Kulm, 1994, p. 99). Kulm explains that directly translating rubrics to grades focuses attention on grades and away from the purpose of every good problem-solving activity, to strive for an excellent performance. The difference is between giving students an informative score for their work and assigning a grade. When papers are returned with less than top ratings, the purpose is to help students know what is necessary to achieve at a higher level. Early on, there should be opportunities to improve based on feedback. When a grade of 75 percent or a C– is returned, all the student knows is that he or she did poorly. If, for example, a student's ability to justify her own answers and solutions has improved, should she be penalized in the averaging of numbers by a weaker performance early in the marking period?

What this means is that grading must be based on the performance tasks and other activities for which you assigned rubric ratings; otherwise, students will soon realize that these are not important scores. At the same time, they need not be added or averaged in any numeric manner. The grade at the end of the marking period should reflect a holistic view of where the student is now relative to your goals and your value system. That value system should be clearly reflected in your framework for rating tasks.

Alignment with Objectives

The grades you assign should reflect all of your objectives. Procedural skills remain important but should be weighted in proportion to other goals in keeping with your value system. If you are restricted to assigning a single grade for mathematics, different factors probably have different weights or values in making up the grade. Student X may be fantastic at reasoning and truly love mathematics yet be weak in traditional skills. Student Y may be mediocre in problem solving but possess good communication skills. How much weight should you give to cooperation in groups, to written versus oral reports, to computational skills? There are no simple answers to these questions. However, they should be addressed at the beginning of the grading period and not the night you set out to assign grades.

A multidimensional reporting system is a big help. If you can assign several grades for mathematics and not just one, your report to parents is more meaningful. Even if the school's report card does not permit multiple grades, you can devise a supplement indicating several ratings for different objectives. A place for comments is also helpful. This form can be shared with students periodically during a grading period and can easily accompany a report card.

You can always involve students and parents in a discussion of a multidimensional approach to determining a grade based on rubric ratings for different components of your goals. Traditional test averaging has always done this. Not every test covers the same thing, and various scores (quizzes, homework, exams) are often assigned different weights. These are subjective, teacher-made decisions. The same subjective approach can be used with rubric scores without computing numeric averages.

Writing to Learn

1. How is assessment different from testing or evaluation?
2. The six assessment standards concern *mathematics, learning, equity, openness, inferences,* and *coherence.* For each, describe in your own words what the standard says and its importance for you as a teacher.
3. Describe the four purposes of assessment as outlined by the *Assessment Standards.* How do these purposes relate to you as a teacher?
4. In looking at procedural knowledge, what should be assesssed in addition to skill proficiency? Why?
5. How can a learning task or problem be an assessment task? Why should these be the same thing?
6. What is the difference between scoring and grading? What is the purpose of a score if it is not a grade?

7. Describe the essential features of a rubric. What are performance indicators? What is the difference between a rubric and a performance indicator?
8. How can students be involved in understanding and using rubrics to help with their learning?
9. How can you incorporate observational assessments into your daily lessons? What is at least one method of getting observations recorded? Do you have to observe every student?
10. Journals take many forms. What in your opinion is the best use of journals and the corresponding best *format* for journals?
11. How can children with limited writing skills "write" in mathematics?
12. Why do you think teaching to the test is not a good method of raising scores on high-stakes tests? What is the best way to raise scores?

13. Why does a grade not have to be the average of a collection of scores? Explain.

For Discussion and Exploration

1. Examine a few chapter-end tests in various textbooks. How well do the tests reflect what is important in the chapter? Concepts and understanding? Mathematical processes?

2. Go on your state's department of education Web site and find a few released test items used by your state to determine NCLB requirements of annual yearly progress (AYP). For the released test items, first decide if you think they are good problem-based assessments that would help you find out about student understanding of the concepts involved. Then, if necessary, try to improve the item so that it becomes a problem-based assessment that would be useful in the classroom. To assist in this process, read Judy Zawojewski's *Teaching Children Mathematics* article, "Polishing a Data Task: Seeking Better Assessment," (Vol. 2 (6), Feb. 1996).

3. The literature is full of excellent books with examples of mathematics performance assessments. For example, see the NCTM *Mathematics Assessment Handbooks* listed in the annotated readings sections that follows. Consult your instructor for other possibilities. Use one or more of these assessments with a class of students for which the topic is appropriate. Examine the results. Were the students prepared for this sort of assessment? If so, what made them prepared? If not, why not?

4. How are teachers in your area responding to the pressures of state testing programs? Do you think that what they are doing is in the best interest of students? Is what they are doing the best thing to do in order to raise scores?

Recommendations for Further Reading

Glanfield, F., Bush, W. S., & Stenmark, J. K. (Eds.). (2003). *Mathematics assessment: A practical handbook for grades K–2.* Reston, VA: National Council of Teachers of Mathematics.

Stenmark, J. K., & Bush, W. S. (Eds.). (2001). *Mathematics assessment: A practical handbook for grades 3–5.* Reston, VA: National Council of Teachers of Mathematics.

Bush, W. S., & Leinwand, S. (Eds.) (2000). *Mathematics assessment: A practical handbook for grades 6–8.* Reston, VA: National Council of Teachers of Mathematics.

These three NCTM books are part of a K–12 series on assessment. The handbooks are each authored by experts in the assessment field and offer practical advice for classroom teachers that is considerably beyond the scope of this chapter. The four chapters in each book essentially cover getting started with assessment, the kinds of assessment options that are best used, practical guidelines for implementing a quality assessment program in your classroom, and suggestions for dealing with the assessment data once gathered. The handbook for your grade band is highly recommended as a resource for your personal library.

Kitchen, R., Cherrington, A., Gates, J., Hitchings, J., Majka, M., Merk, M., & Trubow, G. (2002). Supporting reform through performance assessment. *Mathematics Teaching in the Middle School, 8,* 24–30.

Six of the seven authors are middle school teachers working together in the same school. As part of implementing a standards-based curriculum in a school that had recently dropped tracking, these teachers wrote and refined assessments that they believed would help to promote higher-order thinking. Student performance on the rubric scores did improve over three years. The article includes interesting examples and provides useful and inspiring information that is applicable across the grades.

Lambdin, D. V., Kehle, P. E., & Preston, R. V. (Eds.). (1996). *Emphasis on assessment: Readings from NCTM's school-based journals.* Reston, VA: National Council of Teachers of Mathematics.

An assembly of 30 articles on assessment taken from NCTM's various journals and organized in four categories: rationale for change, testing and grading, alternative assessment options, and evaluation of teacher effectiveness. At the end of the book are three annotated bibliographies for elementary and middle school teachers, secondary teachers, and a third from the *Journal for Research in Mathematics Education.*

Leatham, K. R., Lawrence, K., & Mewborn, D. (2005). Getting started with open-ended assessment. *Teaching Children Mathematics, 11,* 413–419.

In this article, the definition of an open-ended assessment item includes the potential for a range of responses and a balance between too much and too little information given. Examples are included. The teacher-author (Lawrence) talks personally about getting started in her third–fourth grade class of "culturally and economically diverse" students and the values that accrued for both her and her class. Among the many articles appearing nearly every year, this is one that is worth reading and keeping.

Online Resources

Suggested Applets and Web Links

The Math Forum: Internet Mathematics Library—Assessment
http://mathforum.org/library/ed_topics/assessment
Here you will find links to all sorts of information that will be useful in both planning and assessment.

PBS Teacher Source: Article Archive—Assessment
www.pbs.org/teachersource/whats_new/math/archives.shtm#a
A listing of downloadable articles on assessment issues.

TERC Educational Resources on Assessment
http://ra.terc.edu/resources/assessment/assessment.html
TERC offers a list of valuable articles and information as well as links to other assessment resources.

Companion Website

An additional list of books and articles related to the ideas in this chapter can be found on the Companion Web site at **www.ablongman.com/vandewalle6e.**

chapter 7

Teaching Mathematics Equitably to All Children

A society can claim success in eradicating the malady of mathematics illiteracy if and only if all its progeny are able to develop to their fullest potential. If its offspring can become employable workers, wisely choosing consumers, and autonomously thinking citizens who can be contributors in the super symbolic quantitative world they will inherit, then society can say, "Victory is ours!"

Elliott and Garnett (1994, p. 15)

NCTM views the education of every child as its most compelling objective. Its "Every Child" statement says:

> By "every child," we mean every child—no exception.
> We are particularly concerned about students who have been denied access to education opportunities for any reason, such as language, ethnicity, physical impairment, gender, socioeconomic status, and so on. We emphasize that "every child" includes:
>
> - learners of English as a second language and speakers of English as a first language
> - members of underrepresented ethnic groups and members of well-represented groups
> - students who are physically challenged and those who are not
> - females and males
> - students who live in poverty and those who do not
> - students who have not been successful and those who have been successful in school and in mathematics (www.nctm.org/about/every_child.htm)

Mathematics for All Children

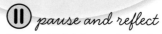 **pause and reflect** ——————

Stop and think for a minute. Do you personally believe the "Every Child" statement? Children with disabilities, children from impoverished homes, minority children, English language learners—can all of these children learn to think mathematically?

It is the responsibility of all who are concerned with children's mathematical learning to make that vision a reality. Most teachers, particularly new teachers, are committed to supporting each of the children in their classrooms. It is critical to equip yourself with a large collection of strategies you can use with children. One strategy may work for one child but be completely ineffective with another, even for a child with the same exceptionality.

Diversity in Today's Classroom

The range of abilities, disabilities, and socioeconomic circumstances in the regular classroom poses significant challenges to teachers. Addressing the needs of *all* children means providing opportunity for any or all of the following:

- *Students who are identified as having a specific learning disability*
- *Students with intellectual disabilities*
- *Students from different cultural backgrounds*
- *Students who do not speak English*
- *Students who are female*
- *Students who are mathematically promising*

In this chapter we will examine issues of diversity in the mathematics classroom and approaches that might be successful in reducing these identified differences. You may think, "I do not need to read the section on culturally and linguistically diverse (CLD) students because I plan on working in a place that doesn't have any immigrants." Did you know that the number of Hispanics registered in schools rose from 6 percent in 1972 to 19 percent in 2003? During the same period, the number of whites registered in school has decreased from 78 percent of the population to 58 percent (U.S. Department of Education, 2005). You may think, "I can skip the section on mathematically promising students because they will be pulled out for math enrichment." Gifted children need to be challenged in regular instruction, not just when they are pulled out for a gifted program.

Recall that issues of equity and English language learners were addressed in Chapter 5 as they relate to planning effective lessons. As you read each section in this chapter, you will discover ways to create more equitable classrooms and you will find the means of helping all students become more mathematically literate.

The Goal of Equitable Instruction

The goal of equity is to offer all students access to important mathematics. Yet, inequities exist, even if unintentionally. For example, if a teacher does not build in opportunities for student-to-student interaction in a lesson, he or she may not be addressing the needs of girls, who are often social learners, or English language learners, who need opportunities to talk, listen, and write in small-group situations. It takes more than just wanting to be fair or equitable; it takes knowing the strategies that accommodate each type of learner and making every effort to incorporate those strategies into your teaching. Although all students should have equal chances to learn grade-level curriculum, equal instruction is not a goal.

Negative Effects of Tracking and Homogeneous Grouping

Tracking students is a significant culprit in creating differential expectations of students. Once students are placed in a lower-level track or in a "slow" class, expectations decline accordingly. Students in low tracks are frequently denied access to challenging material, high-quality mathematics, and the best teachers (Silver, Smith, & Nelson, 1995; Tomlinson, 1999). The mathematics for the lower tracks or classes is almost totally oriented toward remedial drill with minimal success and little excitement (Oakes, 1985a). Teachers' low expectations are reinforced because students are not encouraged to think, nor are they engaged in activities and interactions that encourage problem solving and reasoning.

Similarly, gains made by students in the highest groups have been found to be minimal when compared to similar students in heterogeneous classes. At the same time, low-achieving groups are deprived of quality instruction. Nor can support for tracking or grouping of students at the K–8 level be found in international comparisons. This is particularly true in Asian countries. Among major industrialized countries, only the United States and Canada seem to maintain an interest in tracking (NRC, 2001).

In heterogeneous classes, expectations are often turned upside down as children once perceived as less able come to understand and work meaningfully with concepts to which they would never be exposed in a low-track class. Exposing all students to higher-level thinking and quality mathematics avoids compounding differences from year to year caused by low-track expectations.

Instructional Principles for Diverse Learners

Across the wonderful and myriad diversities of our students, all children essentially learn in the same way (Fuson, 2003). The authors of *Adding It Up* (NRC, 2001) conclude that all children are best served when attention is given to the following three principles:

1. Learning with understanding is based on connecting and organizing knowledge around big conceptual ideas.
2. Learning builds on what students already know.
3. Instruction in school should take advantage of the children's informal knowledge of mathematics.

These principles should come as no surprise. The tenets of constructivism described in Chapter 3 apply to all learners, not just the middle of a so-called typical classroom.

Having said this, it is worth revisiting two ideas from Chapter 5: accommodation and modification. (See p. 65.) An accommodation is a response to the needs of the environment or the learner but does not alter the task. A modification changes the task, making it more accessible to the student. When modifications result in an easier or less demanding task, expectations are lowered. Modifications should be made to lead to the original task, providing scaffolding or support for learners who may need it.

This chapter is about accommodations for the wide diversity of students that is likely to be in your classroom.

Specific Learning Disabilities

The predominant instructional model for students with learning disabilities has historically viewed the learner as passive, with the mastery of skills taking precedence over understanding (Poplin, 1988a). Although popular, various skills-oriented models have produced very limited results.

A Perspective on Learning Disabilities

Students with learning disabilities have very specific problems with perceptual or cognitive processing. These problems may affect memory or the ability to speak or express ideas in writing, perceive auditory or written information, or integrate abstract ideas. It is insufficient simply to label a child "LD." The following insights offered by Borasi (1994) are an important point of departure for teachers who have children with learning disabilities in their classes:

- Students with learning disabilities are mentally capable; they are not slow or retarded.
- The classification of LD is not useful to the classroom teacher without a clear understanding of specific learning problems.
- Learning disabilities are not easily remediated and perhaps cannot be remediated.
- Learning disabilities should be compensated for by helping students use their strengths.
- Instructional modifications will be needed to accommodate children with specific learning disabilities.

Borasi suggests that teachers accept the fact that learning disabilities are real in the same sense that being blind or deaf is a real disability. You would not ask a blind person to "look more closely" or a deaf person to "listen more carefully." Hence, we should never ask a child with learning disabilities to do things that depend heavily on his or her area of deficit.

Adaptations for Specific Learning Difficulties

Note that cognitive deficits or processing disabilities may be present as auditory problems, visual processing problems, or sometimes both. If the child has already been evaluated by the school psychologist, test information will be available to help pinpoint specific weaknesses and also strengths. Working with the psychologist, you can find ways to adapt instructional strategies to avoid weaknesses and capitalize on strengths *without major modification of the curriculum.*

Adaptations for Perceptual Deficits

There are many variations of perceptual problems; some are visual and others auditory. All involve confusion of input in one way or another.

The entire area of perceptual problems is perhaps the clearest area in which the maxim "avoid weaknesses and

capitalize on strengths" is best observed. The following are simply a few specific suggestions:

- Seat the child near you and the chalkboard.
- Keep the child's desk or workspace free of distractions.
- Maintain a moderate voice. Repeat main ideas.
- When using the overhead projector or other technology with the whole class, show only one main idea, problem, or exercise at a time. (Avoid complex visual displays.)
- Maintain a classroom environment that values the importance of only one person talking at a time so that each child's voice is respected and the focus on one person is easier to attend to.
- Enunciate words clearly and attempt to face students when speaking to them.
- Design text or worksheet pages for the child. Provide templates to block out all but one problem or exercise at a time.
- Utilize methods for organizing written work. Have computations done on centimeter grid paper writing one number per square. Provide paper with columns or turn notebook paper sideways. Use drawn templates for traditional algorithms.
- Use a tape recorder (headphones) with instructions explaining what may be difficult to discern from the visual materials.
- Provide geometric models whenever possible instead of relying on pictures. Use geoboards and tiles such as pattern blocks for constructions to keep drawing to a minimum.
- Assign a buddy to help read, explain, or repeat directions.

Adaptations for Memory Deficits

Memory deficits can also be specifically visual or auditory. Children with *short-term memory* deficits can have trouble recalling things for even a few seconds, as when copying from the board or recalling information in a word problem or directions. Children with *long-term memory* deficits may show no difficulty with material when presented but appear to have not learned at all a day or a week later. Mastery of basic facts is a hallmark problem for children with this disability.

You can diminish the load on short-term memory by breaking tasks and directions into small steps and providing a buddy to help with recall. Long-term memory problems require overlearning, frequent practice, and as many associations with other ideas as possible. The following additional specific suggestions may be useful:

- Rather than a series of instructions, provide only one at a time.
- After giving instructions, ask one or more students to state the instructions in their own words as a way to check for broad understanding of the instructions and

to allow other students to hear the instructions from a peer's perspective.

- Write instructions on the board or make written copies to distribute.
- When working on oral exercises or problems, allow students the option of using written versions as well.
- For basic facts, use strategies and number relationships to promote memorization (see Chapter 11).
- Allow use of a calculator at all times.
- Use frequent brief reviews—distributed practice.

Memory deficits tend to be exhibited in procedural work. Remember that no routine procedural knowledge, including mastery of basic facts, should prevent a student from progress in mathematical ideas. Exploration of new concepts is never dependent on mastery of skills.

Adaptations for Integrative Deficits

Children with integrative problems seem to have difficulty with abstract ideas and conceptualization. These children often have difficulty making the cognitive connections that others may find easy. Children with an integrative disorder may do quite well at rote procedures such as computational algorithms, but these are no longer the focus of the mathematics curriculum. A general principle for helping these children integrate concepts and develop understanding is to use experiences and ideas most familiar to them: their own invented procedures for solving problems, familiar models or personal drawings that make sense to them, and their own words in either written or oral form to express their ideas. The following more specific approaches may be helpful for children with integrative difficulties:

- Use familiar physical models for longer than the usual period of time.
- Have students verbalize what they do as often as possible using words, pictures, and numbers. Use oral reports as well as written.
- Frequently require explanations and justifications to heighten the children's awareness of new ideas and to assist them in making connections.
- Allow for repetition or practice of new conceptual ideas.
- Encourage students to restate word problems in their own words.
- Provide students with opportunities to teach a concept to a peer or younger child, hence organizing and reconceptualizing their own thoughts about the concept.
- Use multiple representations of abstract concepts (e.g., words, symbols, drawings, concrete objects, acting it out).

Adaptations for Attention Deficits

Many (not all) students with learning disabilities also are identified as having attention deficit disorder or attention deficit–hyperactivity disorder. These children have chronic difficulties with attention span, impulse control, and sometimes hyperactivity. The following strategies have proved useful:

- Establish simple, predictable routines and discuss them with the child. Make expectations and consequences clear.
- Design learning activities that are active and involving rather than tedious or requiring lengthy periods of silent seatwork.
- Plan for the child to do independent work in an environment free of distractions or intense visual stimuli.
- Use highlighters to attract attention to important key ideas in textual material.
- Keep assignments and exercise lists short. Plan smaller subtasks within larger explorations or projects.
- Assign a buddy, and impress on both that the agenda is to stay on task.
- Instead of placing the child in a cooperative group of three or four, use a buddy to form a separate group of two.

Intellectual Disabilities

All of us possess different mental capacities that modify our individual strengths and weaknesses or learning styles. Children with moderate or severe intellectual disabilities (generally with IQ scores between 50 and 70) will be limited in the kind and degree of mathematical reasoning they can perform. The essential requirement is for significantly more time for learning than would be given under standard circumstances. Although severely disabled children are generally best served in a special classroom, a wide range of intellectual disabilities are likely to be present in the regular classroom.

Modifications in Instruction

Limited cognitive abilities do not in any way alter the way that children learn, but these limited abilities do alter the means by which children experience and acquire their learning. For example, a child with limited cognitive abilities can learn the part/whole concept of addition just as a child without limitations can. However, much more time, repetitiveness, and use of concrete learning tools will likely be required. In general, these special children learn *much* more slowly than do their peers (Bley, 1994; NRC, 2001).

Though a fast-paced, highly interactive classroom may be somewhat overwhelming for children who need more time to learn, they can benefit from many of the same experiences as the rest of the class. They can and should participate in projects and hands-on activities with their peer group. They can participate in cooperative groups by taking on less demanding roles, such as materials organizer or encourager. They can learn to perform calculations on a calculator and can serve as the person in a group who performs this activity. Many such children are good at drawing or making graphs. These helping roles are potentially consistent with the kinds of jobs they are likely to have in the adult world.

Partner the child with limited abilities with different students periodically, and have the partner help the child with the same task or idea. In this way, there is opportunity for needed repeated exposure or overlearning, and other students also will gain from serving as the explainer. It is important for all children in the room to involve children who need more time to learn in activities and projects. All children gain an appreciation for and acceptance of human differences.

Modifications in Curriculum

Since children with limited abilities need more time to learn than other children, it follows that less content can be learned during the years they are in school. It makes sense to focus the available instructional time on those areas that are going to be of the most value to these students as adults. Computational skill is the most obvious area where changes in curricular expectations should be made. There is no reason to be obsessive about fact mastery. Traditional computational algorithms should be eliminated from their curriculum altogether.

These students should have a calculator handy for all mathematics work. The child with limited abilities should be given careful instruction and lots of practice in using the calculator. A calculator with a printer is useful because it creates a printed record of work done.

Whereas calculations can be mastered via the calculator, the meanings of numbers in the real world cannot. Do not confuse number meaning with place-value concepts. What is important here is to realize that a bag of flour weighs 5 pounds, that $100 buys a pair of fancy shoes, or that it takes about 20 minutes to walk a mile. Numbers in the abstract will be of little use in their conceptual development.

Culturally and Linguistically Diverse Students

The United States has been called both a melting pot and a salad bowl. In reality, it is both. Many students in our classrooms have parents or grandparents of mixed heritage, yet they have been raised in the United States and their first language is English. The United States also has many students who have not been blended into mainstream American culture. They are first- or second-

generation children from another culture and may speak another language as their first language. You will serve the needs of your students better if you consider them more of the mosaic than the melting pot, valuing their culture and language, and not trying to force them into local culture and language. This section discusses ways to address students whose culture or language varies from what is commonplace in the United States. These students are referred to as culturally and linguistically diverse (CLD).

Culturally Relevant Mathematics Instruction

You have probably heard it said that "mathematics is a universal language." This is a common misconception that can lead to inequities in the classroom. Unfortunately, since this is a common belief, language needs for CLD students tend to be ignored in mathematics instruction (Lee & Jung, 2004). Here are three different perspectives on how best to meet the needs of CLD students in mathematics:

1. Limit the use of language and focus primarily on symbols.
2. Implement the NCTM *Principles and Standards*, using a lot of language-rich tasks.
3. Integrate a standards-based curriculum with CLD strategies (Bay-Williams & Herrera, forthcoming).

We will look briefly at each of these three approaches, including their advantages and disadvantages.

The rationale for the limited-language approach is that the student will understand the symbols, which are universal. There are many problems with this viewpoint. First, symbols are not universal. For example, in Mexico textbooks may refer to angle B as $\hat{B}$ or $\overset{\frown}{ABC}$ rather than $\angle B$ or $\angle ABC$ as in the United States. An English language learner may not recognize the angle symbol and might confuse it with the "less than" symbol. The numeral 9 as written in Latin American countries can easily be confused with a lowercase *g*. What is called "billions" in the United States is called "thousand millions" in Mexico (Perkins & Flores, 2002). Second, symbols are abstract. As discussed in Chapter 3, students should begin with concrete materials and problems that provide a situation familiar to the student. Third, the use of language, in written and oral forms, is essential to developing a deep understanding of mathematics (Khisty, 1997). Finally, a belief that symbols are easier for CLD students often causes a teacher too quickly to use symbolic representations and, therefore, limits a student's understanding (Garrison & Mora, 1999).

The second perspective on teaching CLD students is to embrace the recommendations outlined in *Principles and Standards*. A standards-based teacher may use inquiry, student–student interactions (pairs and small groups), discussions, and alternative assessments. All of these can support the learning of a student who is also learning English or who is not familiar with particular aspects of U.S. culture (Echevarria, Vogt, & Short, 2004).

Standards-based teaching supports the ELL more effectively than traditional teaching because many strategies are helpful not only for CLD students but for other students as well. For example, the *Standards* encourages a learning environment in which students solve a problem using a strategy of their own choosing and later explain how they solved the problem. A student from a different culture may have learned different strategies for that concept or for related skills. In addition, explaining their strategy allows students opportunities to develop their language skills.

However, even in classrooms where teachers incorporate many standards-based practices, an achievement gap may still exist. What is often lacking is an intentional effort to help students develop their language skills. This is what the third approach offers.

Creating effective learning for CLD students involves integrating principles of bilingual education with standards-based content instruction. That is, lessons must be based on problems and discussions while also attending to the culture and the language of the students. In order to operate from this perspective, it is important to explore how to embrace culture and to support language development. Both are discussed separately in the next two sections, even though they are interrelated and should not be separated in instruction.

Ethnomathematics

When culture, mathematics, and education activities are combined, this mixture is often referred to as *ethnomathematics*. Many societies have different mathematical traditions and have developed various strands of mathematical thought. Teaching mathematics with respect to culture is one way to respect diversity within the classroom. Students can be personally engaged in mathematics by examining their own culture's impact on the ways they use, practice, and think about mathematics. A study of mathematics within other cultures provides an opportunity for students to "put faces" on mathematics instead of erroneously thinking that mathematics is a result of some mystical phenomenon.

There are many ways to approach mathematics from a cultural perspective (e.g., biographies of mathematicians, historical development of concepts, games, children's literature, and thematic units). Mathematics is the by-product of human ideas, creativity, problem solving, recreation, beliefs, values, and survival. Contributions to the field of mathematics come from diverse people all over the world. Many women and people of color who made important contributions to mathematics have been overlooked. There are Web sites and resources available that provide links to contributions of CLD mathematicians and ideas for teaching ethnomathematics. Two are listed with the resources at the end of the chapter.

English Language Learners (ELLs)

How many students are in schools who are not fluent in English? In California, one in four students is an ELL; in Texas one in seven. Nationally, 4 million students (8 percent of the student population) were receiving ELL services in 2003. This is not just a statistic for coastal states; this is true for every state in the United States and every province in Canada. For example, in Kansas, the number of students identified as ELL (or LEP, limited English proficient) doubled between 1995 and 2005.

English language learners enter the mathematics classroom from homes in which English is not the primary language of communication. Although a person might develop conversational English language skills in a few years, it takes as much as seven years to learn "academic language," which is the language that is specific to a content area, such as mathematics (Cummins, 1994). Academic language is harder to learn because it is not used in a student's everyday world. When learning about mathematics, students might be learning content in English that they have no words for in their native language. For example, in studying the measures of central tendency (*mean, median,* and *mode*), they may not know words for these terms in their first language, increasing the challenge for learning academic language in their second language. In addition, story problems are difficult for ELLs not just due to the language but also to the fact that sentences in story problems are often structured differently than sentences in conversational English.

Teachers of English to Speakers of Other Languages (TESOL) developed standards for effective instruction of English as a second language (ESL) to pre-K–12 students in the United States (TESOL, 1997). TESOL's vision of effective education for students learning English includes developing proficiency in English and the maintenance and promotion of students' native languages. TESOL standards state that students will use English to

1. "interact in the classroom,"
2. "obtain, process, construct, and provide subject matter information in spoken and written form," and
3. "use appropriate learning strategies to construct and apply academic knowledge" (TESOL, 1997, p. 9).

Notice that students are to use English in their academic content courses. This does not mean "English only," but rather an approach that encourages the use of native language and the development of English. Also note that the emphasis for ELLs is providing these language opportunities: reading, writing, speaking, and listening. When these are incorporated effectively into instruction, both mathematical understanding and language can be learned.

Specific Strategies for Teaching Mathematics to English Language Learners

Among the many ways to support the ELL in the classroom, the six strategies discussed in this section are critical to mathematics instruction. They are among the ideas that teachers and researchers most commonly mention as increasing the academic achievement of ELLs in mathematics classrooms.

1. Write and State the Content and Language Objectives

Every lesson should begin with telling students what they will be learning. You do not give away what they will discover in their exploration, but you state the larger purpose of what they are doing; in other words, provide a road map. If students know the purpose of the lesson, they are better able to make sense of the details in light of the bigger picture. Look quickly at the lesson, "Building on Numbers You Know" (see p. 250), which is about using different strategies for multiplication and division. When teaching this lesson, you would write student-friendly objectives on the board such as:

Today you will:

1. Find different ways to multiply and divide numbers. (content)
2. Explain how you completed a multiplication and division problem when you were given the first step. (language and content)
3. Write the way you would pick to solve the division problem. (language)

2. Build Background

This is similar to building on prior knowledge, but it takes into consideration language and culture as well as content. If possible, use a context and any appropriate visuals to help students understand the task you want them to solve. Link the lesson to prior learning: yesterday's lesson, a real-world problem, or something you did earlier in the month. For the noncontextual lesson in "Building on Numbers You Know," you might have a discussion of what 22×37 could refer to (perhaps it refers to the measurements of a picture hanging on the wall or the amount of money it will cost to buy stamps for each member of a class of 22 students).

3. Encourage Use of Native Language

Research shows that students' cognitive development proceeds more readily in their native language. In a mathe-matics classroom, students should be encouraged to communicate in their native language and to continue with their English language development. For example, when students are working in small groups, a good strategy is having a group of students who speak Spanish first discuss the problem in Spanish as they try to solve. If a student knows enough English, then the presentation during the *after* phase of the lesson can be assigned as "English preferred." If the student knows little or no English, then he or she can explain in Spanish and have a translator.

4. Comprehensible Input

Comprehensible input is a term used in bilingual education that means that the message you are communicating is understandable to students. It means to simplify sentence structures and limit the use of nonessential vocabulary; it does not mean to lower the expectations for the lesson. It also means to use strategies to help students understand the language they encounter. Sometimes teachers put many unnecessary words and phrases into questions making them less clear to nonnative speakers. Compare the following two teacher questions:

Not Modified: You have a labsheet in front of you that I just gave out. For every situation, I want you to determine the total area for the shapes. You will be working with your partners, but each of you needs to write your answers on your own paper and explain how you got your answer. If you get stuck on a problem raise your hand.

Modified: Please look at your paper. (Holds paper and points to it. Pointing to the first picture.) You will find the area. What does area mean? (Allows wait time.) How can you calculate area? ("Calculate" is more like the Spanish word *calcular*, so it is more accessible to Spanish speakers.) Talk to your partners. (Points to mouth and then to a pair of students as she says this.) Write your answers. (Makes a writing motion over paper.)

Notice that three things have been done: sentences shortened, removal of unnecessary words, and use of gestures and motions that link to the vocabulary. Also notice the "wait time" the teacher gives. It is very important to provide extra time after posing a question or giving instructions to allow ELLs time to translate and make sense of the request and then participate.

Another way to provide comprehensible input is to use a variety of tools to help students visualize and understand what is verbalized. This is particularly critical for students who may not have strong verbal skills. Modeling is important. In the preceding example, the teacher is modeling the instructions. When introducing a lesson, include pictures, real objects, and diagrams. For example, if teaching integers, having a real thermometer, as well as an overhead of a thermometer, will help provide a visual (and a context) for exploring the number line. You might even add pictures of places covered in snow and position it near the low temperatures and so on. Students should also be expected to include multiple representations in their work. Expect students to draw, write, and explain what they have done. This is helpful to them and to their peers who will be seeing their solutions. Supplemental materials you should consider using include manipulatives, real objects, pictures, visuals, multimedia, demonstrations, children's books, and adapted text (Echevarria, Vogt, & Short, 2004).

5. Explicitly Teach Vocabulary

One popular technique to reinforce vocabulary development is a mathematics word wall. As you encounter vocabulary essential for learning mathematics, students participate in creating and adding to the word wall. When a word is selected, students can create cards that include the word in English, translations to languages represented in your room, pictures, and a student-made description (not a formal definition) in English or in several languages.

In addition to word walls, there are many ways to explicitly teach vocabulary. For example, students can create concept maps, linking concepts and terms as they study the relationship among fractions, decimals, and percents. Students can keep "personal math dictionaries" of terms they need to know, which include the word, illustrations, and examples. As you use a mathematical term that has been previously addressed, stop and make sure that students remember the term. As new terms are introduced, the word itself should be discussed, sharing the root and related words (Rubenstein, 2000). There are many terms that have different meanings in mathematics than in everyday activities. Here are some examples: *product, mean, sum, factor, acute, foot, division, difference, similar, angle.*

6. Use Cooperative Groups

English language learners need opportunities to use language in nonthreatening situations. They also need to speak, write, talk, and listen. The best way to accomplish both is through cooperative groups. In grouping, you must consider a student's language skills. Placing an ELL with two English-speaking students may result in the ELL being left out entirely. It is better to place a bilingual student in this group, or to place students that have the same first language together (Garrison, 1997; Khisty, 1997). Pairs may be more appropriate than groups of three or four. As with all group work, rules or structures should be in place to make sure that each student is able to participate and is accountable for the activity assigned.

The single most important thing you can do is create an environment that is supportive and nurturing and that values a culture where children are willing to risk making mistakes in front of others. ELLs will recognize that you have established such a haven when they find that you see their culture and language as a resource to be valued rather than a drawback to be managed.

From Gender Bias to Gender Equity

Based on the results of NAEP tests, gender gaps in mathematics achievement remained small but fairly consistent from 1990 to 2000, with males outperforming females in grades 4, 8, and 12. Over that time, both male and female performance has improved. Differences are generally greater at the higher percentile rankings and males do significantly better on test items rated as "most difficult" (Lubinski, McGraw, & Strutchins, 2004). There persists in our society a common belief that boys are better than girls at mathematics—what Damarin (1995) refers to as the "maleness of mathematics." After high school more males than females enter fields of study that include heavy emphases on mathematics and science. It remains important to be aware of and address gender equity issues in your classroom.

Possible Causes of Gender Inequity

As Becker and Jacobs (2001) point out, most of the research "is moving away from 'sex differences' to 'gender differences' in acknowledgment that gender is socially constructed and the differences are not biologically determined" (p. 2). We can find some of the causes of gender inequity in the classroom.

Teacher Interactions and Gender

Teachers may not consciously seek to stereotype students by gender; however, the gender-based biases of our society often affect teachers' interactions with students (Martin, Sexton, Wagner, & Gerlovich, 1997). For example, observations of teachers' gender-specific interactions in the classroom indicate that boys get more attention and different kinds of attention than girls do. Boys receive more criticism for wrong answers as well as more praise for correct answers. Boys also tend to be more involved in discipline-related attention and have their work monitored more carefully (Campbell, 1995; Leder, 1995). Attention is interpreted as value, with a predictable effect on both sexes. The increased attention, both positive and negative, that teachers unconsciously provide males contributes to the impression of mathematics as a male domain.

Research has found that teachers wait longer for responses from boys than from girls (Leder, 1995). In one study, females received more wait time on low-level questions concerning facts and procedures, whereas males received longer wait times on more difficult, more challenging, and higher-cognitive questions. Over time, these subtle but real differences suggest to girls that they are not perceived as capable of quality thinking, and they eventually adopt this belief themselves.

Belief Systems Related to Gender

The belief that mathematics is a male domain persists in our society and is held by both sexes. In adolescent years, when girls are significantly interested in and influenced by boys, many girls are afraid to act "too smart" for fear of alienating boys. Campbell (1995) points out that "unless boys as well as girls are convinced that 'real women do math,' efforts toward gender equity in mathematics will encounter obstacles based on stereotyped social roles" (p. 229).

Working Toward Gender Equity: What Can Be Done?

Campbell (1995) makes a compelling argument that we have tended to address gender inequity as a "girl problem." This places the focus of our solution efforts on girls—to make them somehow like mathematics more or take more courses in mathematics. This approach, she says, makes it seem that there really is something wrong with girls. "If you change a girl so that she 'loves math,' but then you put her back into the same environment and situations that caused her to hate mathematics in the first place, she will revert to hating mathematics" (p. 226). As already noted, the causes of girls' perceptions of themselves vis-à-vis mathematics are largely a function of the educational environment. That is where we should look for solutions.

Become Aware

As a teacher, you need to be aware whether you treat boys and girls differently. Work at ensuring equitable treatment. As you interact with students, try to be aware of the interactions with both gender groups in relationship to the

- Number and type of questions you ask
- Amount of attention given to disturbances
- Kinds and topics of projects and activities assigned
- Praise given in response to students' participation
- Makeup of small groups
- Contexts of problems

Being aware of your gender-specific actions is more difficult than it may sound. To receive feedback, try video-recording a class or two on a periodic basis. Tally the number of questions asked of boys and girls. Also note which students ask questions and what kind of questions are being asked. Where do you stand in class? At first, you will be surprised at how gender-biased your interaction is. Awareness takes effort.

Involve All Students

Find ways to involve all students in your class, not just those who seem eager. Girls tend to shy away from involvement and are not as quick to seek help. Perhaps the best sugges-

tion for involving students is to follow the tenets of this book—use a problem-based approach to instruction. Mau and Leitze (2001) make the case that when teachers are in a show-and-tell mode, there is significantly more opportunity for the teacher to reinforce the more overt behaviors of boys and allow girls to be passive. In a classroom influenced by constructivist theory, all students are expected to both talk and listen. More mathematics is constructed with less teacher intervention. Authority resides in the students and in their arguments. The result is that girls are on an equal footing with the boys.

 pause and reflect _____

Stop for a moment and envision the directive teaching that most likely was the model you experienced. Can you see situations in which males are favored, encouraged, or assisted by the teacher—even without consciously being aware of any differential treatment? How would these differences possibly disappear in a problem-based, student-oriented environment?

Providing for the Mathematically Promising

Children who are typically known as "gifted" no doubt deserve consideration in the educational decisions required to provide *all* children with the best possible education. Considerable research is available on the education of the gifted but offers little consensus. Alternative views have typically focused on two major questions: What does it mean to be gifted, and should the program for gifted children focus on acceleration or enrichment? In addition, there are practical considerations, not the least of which is how to deliver an appropriate program. Alternatives include pull-out designs, after-school models, and in-class programs. There are also questions of time, teachers, and materials.

Identification of Mathematically Promising Students

In 1995, NCTM convened the Task Force on the Mathematically Promising to prepare recommendations and draft a policy statement concerning the mathematically talented. The task force preferred to use the term *promising* rather than *gifted* or *talented* because under common definitions of the gifted and talented, many mathematically adept students have been overlooked or excluded. The task force explained that mathematical promise was a function of *ability*, *motivation*, *belief*, and *experience or opportunity*.

The literature on mathematically promising students suggests that they may not be especially talented in other areas. Nor can mathematical promise be equated with general school achievement or facility with computational algorithms. Promising students generally have good verbal skills, curiosity, imagination, analytic thinking skills, and the ability to concentrate and work independently (House, 1999).

What all of this means for the identification of promising students is that simple criteria built on test scores, IQ, or high grades may exclude those who have a high probability of developing into exceptional mathematical students.

Acceleration, Enrichment, and Depth

For years, one of the primary debates related to the talented mathematics student was over the relative merits of acceleration versus enrichment. *Acceleration* occurs when students are either placed in a grade ahead of their normal age group or when the pace at which they progress through the regular curriculum is speeded up. *Enrichment* refers to the expansion of the regular curriculum to include additional topics.

Acceleration and Enrichment

Both merits and cautions are associated with acceleration and enrichment. Capable and promising students should be challenged to move at an appropriate pace through the curriculum and should be exposed to as much quality mathematics as time permits. The NCTM task force chose not to endorse either approach. Acceleration can have the effect of developing a large array of meaningless skills as students are pushed to learn more without exploring the ideas in a full conceptual manner. Without adequate time, the guidance of a skilled teacher, and the benefit of directed discourse and exploration, students in acceleration programs tend to focus on mechanical skills. This will often be the case as well when students are left to study independently.

Too often enrichment programs result in little more than "fun math time" with topics such as geometric puzzles, computer games, or the "problem of the day." Although enrichment mathematics activities can be fun, they should accomplish much more. They should broaden students' mathematical horizons, require students to think deeply, make connections to earlier ideas and to real contexts, and challenge them to ask questions, make conjectures, and reason about important ideas.

The Addition of Depth

Recognizing the strengths and pitfalls of enrichment and acceleration, Sheffield (1999) argues for a three-dimensional approach: breadth (enrichment), rate (acceleration), and depth or complexity. That is, the benefits of both acceleration and enrichment should be coupled with the opportunity for studying the complexities of new mathematical ideas, both those in the regular curriculum and those that go beyond it. Sheffield writes that promising students should be introduced to the "joys and frustrations of thinking deeply about a wide range of original, open-ended, or complex problems that encourage them to respond creatively in ways that are original, fluent, flexible, and elegant" (p. 46).

In the regular classroom, teachers often "reward" highly capable students for finishing routine tasks quickly by having them do more exercises or more tedious exercises than those required of the rest of the class. For example, if the full class is working on the multiplication algorithm for multidigit numbers, there is no redeeming value in having promising students who complete their work quickly do more exercises or exercises with more digits. However, they may be asked what would produce the largest or smallest products given four distinct digits to make two factors. Is there a general rule? Why does the rule work? Would the rule work if there were five digits?

Even more interesting than the max/min task is that for some products, interchanging the digits in each two-digit factor produces the same result:

$$
\begin{array}{r} 24 \\ \times\ 63 \\ \hline 1512 \end{array}
\qquad
\begin{array}{r} 42 \\ \times\ 36 \\ \hline 1512 \end{array}
$$

However, this is obviously not always the case, as a little experimentation will quickly show. When will this interchanging of the digits produce equal products and why? Students working on tasks such as these are engaged in a deeper exploration of the multiplication algorithm than simply understanding how it works and being able to use it.

There is no simple formula for adding depth to mathematical explorations, but some valuable insights may be learned from the Japanese. According to Hashimoto and Becker (1999), the Japanese approach to mathematical problem solving involves making the problem open in one of three ways: the process is open (multiple paths to a solution are explored), the end product is open (there are multiple correct answers to be discovered), or the formulation of new problems is open (students explore new problems related to the one solved).

These three approaches to open-ended problem solving are explored in depth in *The Open-Ended Approach: A New Proposal for Teaching Mathematics* (Becker & Shimada, 1997). Application of the open-ended methods is an excellent way to add depth to both acceleration and enrichment for special students.

Reflections on Chapter 7

Writing to Learn

1. How is equity in the classroom different from teaching all students equally?
2. What are some of the negative effects of tracking or homogeneous grouping?
3. Distinguish between accommodation and modification. How can a modification be used as a scaffolding for the same high expectations held for the whole class?
4. Briefly describe each of the following specific learning disabilities, and give some indication of how the disability may affect mathematics learning or ability. For each disability, also list at least two accommodations that can be used by the classroom teacher to help the child.
   a. Perceptual deficits
   b. Memory deficits (short term and long term)
   c. Integrative deficits
   d. Attention deficits
5. For children with intellectual disabilities and special learning needs, how should content and instruction each be modified?
6. Three options were discussed for CLD classrooms. The second was to use a standards-based approach—like the one described in this book. How did the third and most preferable option differ from this?
7. Describe ethnomathematics in your own words. Why is it important to consider culture in mathematics instruction?
8. What are some of the specific difficulties English language learners may encounter in the mathematics class?
9. TESOL advocates that English language learners use English in their academic classes. How can students who do not know English do this?
10. Six specific strategies were described for teaching mathematics to English language learners. Select three that you think are most important and describe these in your own words.
11. What are some factors that contribute to gender inequity, and what are the long-term effects of that inequity?
12. How can teachers in the elementary or middle school work to erase gender inequity?
13. Describe what is meant by enrichment and by acceleration. What are the dangers of each for mathematically promising students?
14. In the context of providing for the mathematically promising, what is meant by depth? How can the Japanese open-ended approaches help provide depth?

For Discussion and Exploration

1. Two common threads in this chapter are the beliefs that all children will benefit from a developmental or constructivist approach to teaching and that there is real value in teaching children in diverse, heterogeneous classrooms. Some teachers may argue with this position, contending that it is best for the majority of children if "special needs" students are isolated. And besides, the argument continues, their special needs are best met by special teachers in classes with fewer students. Pick a position in this argument, and articulate it in writing or in a classroom discussion.
2. Develop your own philosophical statement for "all students" or "every child." Design a visual representation for your statement. Read the Equity Principle in *Principles and Standards* and see if your position is in accord with that principle.
3. Find and observe a mathematics class in a room that could be described as CLD, especially one that includes ELLs. Identify as many specific adaptations as you can that are made by the teacher in the course of the lesson. Compare these adaptations to those you have found in this chapter. If modifications were made, did these modifications maintain high expectations for students equal to those for all students?
4. Develop a mathematics lesson plan that reflects a cultural approach to mathematics. What mathematics concepts does your lesson address?
5. What would you do if you found yourself teaching a class with one exceptionally talented child who had no equal in the room? Assume that acceleration to the next grade has been ruled out due to social adjustment factors.

Recommendations for Further Reading

Berry, R. Q., III. (2004). The Equity Principle through the voices of African American males. *Mathematics Teaching in the Middle School, 10,* 100–103.

With both quotations and anecdotes, Berry provides the reader with a realistic view of adolescent African American males who can and do find their way in mathematics. It is clear that it is the teacher who makes a difference.

Lee, H., & Jung, W. S. (2004). Limited English-proficient (LEP) students and mathematical understanding. *Mathematics Teaching in the Middle School, 9,* 269–272.

The article is intended to help teachers design instruction to assist students who know little or no English. The article is reflective of the ideas discussed in this chapter. Specific examples will help the reader go beyond guiding principles.

National Council of Teachers of Mathematics. (2004). Teaching mathematics to special needs students [Focus Issue]. *Teaching Children Mathematics, 11.*

The first article in this focus issue by Karp and Howell is worth the rest of the journal by itself. They tackle the reality that children with special needs truly are different and need special help to meet high standards. The suggestions are specific and excellent. Other articles address assessment issues for special students, strategies for differentiation, and more.

Robert, M. (2002). Problem solving and the at-risk students: Making "mathematics for all" a classroom reality. *Teaching Children Mathematics, 8,* 290–295.

This tale of a year in a fifth-grade classroom of seriously disadvantaged children, by a teacher who had previously spent 2 years in an affluent suburban school, will support and sustain teachers who think their class is simply too difficult. Robert tells about how she initially struggled and yet worked throughout the year to use a problem-based approach. Children began to catch on. This is an important story from a teacher for teachers.

Secada, W. G. (Series Ed.). (1999–2002). *Changing the faces of mathematics* (6 volumes). Reston, VA: National Council of Teachers of Mathematics.

These six books present perspectives on four categories of cultures: Asian Americans and Pacific Islanders, Native Americans, Latinos, and African Americans. Two volumes address multiculturalism and gender equity. Each culture-specific volume explores curriculum, instruction, and assessment issues relevant to the culture for all grade levels. The authors stress pedagogical strategies, classroom environment, and positive practices that support the learning of students. These are unique, excellent resources.

Sheffield, L. J. (Ed.). (1999). *Developing mathematically promising students.* Reston, VA: National Council of Teachers of Mathematics.

This book is the result of the work of an NCTM Task Force on Mathematically Promising Students. The book has a wealth of ideas and perspectives for working with our most talented students and adds depth to any discussion of mathematics for the talented.

Online Resources

Suggested Applets and Web Links

The Society for Advancement of Chicanos and Native Americans in Science (SACNAS) Biography Project
www2.sacnas.org/biography/default.asp

An online resource for K–12 educators who are interested in teaching their students about the accomplishments of Chicano/Latino and Native American scientists.

LD Online
www.ldonline.org

This site offers a vast array of information on a variety of topics related to special students. Click on *LD-InDepth* for articles, research findings, and useful forums, including an area specifically devoted to dyscalculia. Also see *Learning Disorders in Math.*

Special Education Resources on the Internet
http://seriweb.com

SERI is a collection of Internet-accessible information and resources of interest to those involved in fields related to special education.

The International Study Group on Ethnomathematics
www.rpi.edu/~eglash/isgem.htm

The ISGEm is dedicated to the understanding of the cultural diversity of mathematical practices and to applying this knowledge to education and development. Its Web page provides links to other useful sites.

An additional list of books and articles related to the ideas in this chapter can be found on the Companion Web site at **www.ablongman.com/vandewalle6e.**

chapter 8

Technology and School Mathematics

Technology is an essential tool for teaching and learning mathematics effectively; it extends the mathematics that can be taught and enhances students' learning.

www.nctm.org/about/position_statements/
position_statement_13.htm

The term *technology* in the context of school mathematics refers primarily to calculators of all sorts and computers, including access to the Internet and the available resources for use with these devices. The simple position statement of the NCTM (just quoted) is quite clear with regard to technology: It is an *essential tool* for both learning and teaching mathematics. It is important not to think of technology as an extra burden added on to the list of things you are trying to accomplish in your classroom. Rather, technology should be another of the many real tools at your disposal for helping children learn mathematics. Seen as an integral part of your instructional arsenal of tools for learning, technology can enlarge the scope of the content students can learn and broaden the range of problems that students are able to tackle (Ball & Stacey, 2005; NCTM Position Statement, 2003).

That technology is one of the six principles in the *Principles and Standards* document further highlights the importance that NCTM gives to technology (see Chapter 1).

Calculators and computer software (including Internet-based applications, or "applets") are highlighted throughout this text, with references to specific activities and programs where they are appropriate. The purpose of this chapter is to examine technology and the teaching of mathematics in a more general way so that you will be able to make informed judgments about truly integrating technology into your array of instructional tools.

Calculators in the Mathematics Classroom

Mathematics educators have long understood the value of calculators in the study of mathematics. Since 1976, NCTM has published numerous articles, books, and position statements, all advocating the regular use of calculators in the teaching of mathematics at all grade levels. In its 2005 position statement on computation and calculators, NCTM clarified its long-standing view that there is an important place in the curriculum for both calculator use and the development of a variety of computational skills (www.nctm.org).

Unfortunately, the everyday use of calculators in society, coupled with professional support of calculators in schools, has had a muted impact on the mathematics classroom, especially at the elementary level. Resistance to the use of calculators has diminished but not disappeared. The vocal minority of detractors to the reform movement often assail the use of calculators as "dumbing down" the curriculum or as a "crutch." Their inflammatory rhetoric often resonates with parents, who want what is best for their children. Parents must be made aware of the fact that calculator use will in no way prevent children from learning mathematics; in fact, calculators used thoughtfully and appropriately can enhance the learning of mathematics. Furthermore, parents must learn that the use of both calculators and computers requires the student to be a "problem solver." Calculators always calculate according to the input information. Calculators cannot substitute for understanding.

Benefits of Calculator Use

Rather than fearing potential damage that calculators might do, it is important to understand how calculators can contribute to the learning of mathematics. In this section, the focus is on simple calculators. A discussion of graphing calculators is reserved for later.

Calculators Can Be Used to Develop Concepts

The calculator can be much more than a device for calculation. It can be used effectively to develop concepts. *Adding It Up: Helping Children Learn Mathematics* (NRC, 2001) cites several long-term studies that have shown that students in grades 4–6 who used calculators improved their conceptual understanding. Activities for developing concepts with the calculator are suggested throughout this book, especially in the areas of numeration and computation. Here are two simple examples. On the calculator, 796 ÷ 42 = 18.95348. Consider the task of using the calculator to determine the whole-number remainder. Another example is to use the calculator to find a number that when multiplied by itself will produce 43. In this situation, a student can press 6.1 ⊠ ▣ to get the square of 6.1. For students who are just beginning to understand decimals, the activity will demonstrate that numbers such as 6.3 and 6.4 are between 6 and 7. Furthermore, 6.55 is between 6.5 and 6.6. For students who already understand decimals, the same activity serves as a meaningful and conceptual introduction to square roots.

Calculators Can Be Used for Drill

The calculator is an excellent drill device that requires no computer or software. For example, students who want to practice the multiples of 7 can press 7 ⊠ 3 and delay pressing the ▣. The challenge is to answer the fact to themselves before pressing the ▣ key. Subsequent multiples of 7 can be checked by simply pressing the second factor and the ▣. The TI-10 and TI-15 calculators now have built-in problem-solving modes in which students can practice facts, develop lists of related facts, and test equations or inequalities with arithmetic expressions on both sides of the relationship symbol (http://education.ti.com/us/product/tech/10/features/1015getstart.html).

A class can be split in half with one half required to use a calculator and the other required to do the computations mentally. For 3000 + 1765, the mental group wins every time. It will also win for simple facts and numerous problems that lend themselves to mental computation. Of course, there are many computations, such as 537 × 32, where the calculator is preferred and that side will win. Not only does this simple exercise provide practice with mental math, but it also demonstrates to students that it is not always appropriate to reach for the calculator. Studies have found that for average-ability learners, calculator use enhanced basic skills acquisition (NRC, 2001).

Calculators Enhance Problem Solving

Several research studies have found that calculator use improved the problem-solving abilities of learners at all abil-ity levels for all grades (NRC, 2001). The mechanics of computation can often distract students' attention from the meaning of the problem they are working on. As students come to understand the meanings of the operations, they should be exposed to realistic problems with realistic numbers. The numbers may be beyond their abilities to compute, but the calculator makes these realistic problems accessible.

Calculators Save Time

By-hand computation is time consuming, especially for young students who have not developed a high degree of mastery. Why should time be wasted having students add numbers to find the perimeter of a polygon? Why compute averages, find percents, convert fractions to decimals, or solve problems of any sort with pencil-and-paper methods when computation skills are not the objective of the lesson?

Calculators Are Commonly Used in Society

Nowadays, almost everyone uses calculators in every facet of life that involves any sort of exact computation—everyone except schoolchildren. Students should be taught how to use this commonplace tool effectively and also learn to judge when it is appropriate to use it. Many adults have not learned how to use the automatic constant feature of a calculator and are not practiced in recognizing gross errors that are often made on calculators. Effective use of calculators is an important skill that is best learned by using them regularly and meaningfully.

Addressing Myths and Fears About Using Calculators

The lingering opposition to calculators is largely based on misinformation. Myths and fears about students not learning because of using calculators still persist, even in the face of evidence to the contrary.

Myth: If Kids Use Calculators, They Won't Learn the "Basics"

Every advocate of calculator use must make it clear to parents that basic fact mastery and flexible computational skills, including mental computation, remain important goals of the curriculum. By and large, research has demonstrated that the availability of calculators has no negative effect on traditional skills (NRC, 2001). Although the eighth NAEP assessment data suggest a decrease in achievement for fourth graders who use calculators either weekly or every day, it is important to note that the same data also show that only 5 percent of teachers report everyday calculator use and only 21 percent report weekly use (http://nces.ed.gov/nationsreportcard/mathematics/results). Moreover, evidence from a meta-analysis of calculator use shows a slight negative effect of calculators among fourth graders but not among students of any other grade (NRC,

2001). This may be an artifact of conditions specific to those studies of calculator use that included fourth graders. Most important, the performance of tedious by-hand computations does not involve thinking or reasoning or solving problems. Employers want employees who can think and solve novel problems.

Myth: Calculators Make Students Lazy

Almost no mathematical thinking is involved in doing routine computations by hand. People who use calculators when solving problems are, therefore, using their intellect in more important ways—reasoning, conjecturing, testing ideas, and solving problems. When used appropriately, calculators enhance learning; they do not get in the way of learning.

Myth: Students Should Learn the "Real Way" Before Using Calculators

Following rules for pencil-and-paper computation does little to help students understand the ideas behind them. A glaring example is the invert-and-multiply method for division of fractions. Few parents and elementary teachers can explain why this method makes sense. And yet they all had extensive practice with that technique. To one degree or another, the same is true of nearly all computational procedures.

It is essential to point out that by-hand techniques are not to be totally abandoned and that introductory explorations are often best done without a calculator. The teacher must play a role in setting the necessary explorations in the classroom.

Myth: Students Will Become Overly Dependent on Calculators

Calculators kept from students are like forbidden fruit. When finally allowed to use them, students often use them for the simplest of tasks. Teachers in the upper grades often complain that students are using their calculators all the time.

It is essential that mastery of basic facts, mental computation, and some attention to by-hand techniques continue to be requirements for all students. In lessons in which these skills are the objective, the calculator should simply be off limits. When students learn these essential noncalculator skills, they rarely use the calculator inappropriately. Furthermore, if the calculator is always available for appropriate uses, students learn when and how to use it wisely.

Calculators for Every Student, Every Day

> **Calculators should be in or on students' desks at all times from kindergarten through high school.**

In addition to the benefits already described, here are a few arguments in favor of calculator access at all times:

- First and foremost, it does no harm. Any teacher can conduct an activity or pose tasks in which calculators are set off limits. Availability of calculators does not detract from the development of basic skills.
- Many excellent explorations that happen spontaneously in a problem-solving environment will be enhanced by the use of calculators. Students should not have to leave their desks or ask permission to use a calculator when solving a problem.
- When calculators are kept from students, they tend to be used for special "calculator lessons," promoting the student belief that calculators are not common tools for solving problems.
- Students must learn to make wise choices about when to use calculators—for tedious computations—and when to use mental math—for simple computations and estimations. They learn this only by making such choices independently and on a regular basis.

Graphing Calculators

The graphing calculator, once thought useful only in high school, is so important to middle school mathematics that it deserves some special attention. Today, a graphing calculator makes sense for all middle school students. Cost is still a possible deterrent. Several models are available for under $75, less than the cost of a pair of sneakers or a few CDs. A calculator purchased in the sixth grade may be the only one the student will need through high school. A school can purchase a classroom set for less than the price of a single computer.

What the Graphing Calculator Offers

It is a mistake to think that graphing calculators are only for doing "high-powered" mathematics usually studied by honors students in high school. Here is a list of some features the graphing calculator offers, every one of which is useful within the standard middle school curriculum.

- The display window permits compound expressions such as $3 + 4(5 - 6/7)$ to be shown completely before being evaluated. Furthermore, once evaluated, previous expressions can be recalled and modified. This promotes an understanding of notation and order of operations. The device is also a significant tool for exploring patterns and solving problems. Expressions can include exponents, absolute values, and negation signs, with no restrictions on the values used. (Note that this same feature is now found on many simpler calculators such as the TI-15.)
- Even without using function definition capability, students can insert values into expressions or formulas

without having to enter the entire formula for each new value. The results can be entered into a list or table of values and stored directly on the calculator for further analysis.

- Variables can be used in expressions and then assigned different values to see the effect on expressions. This simple method helps with the idea of a variable as something that varies.

- The distinction between "negative" and "minus" is clear and very useful. A separate key is used to enter the negative of a quantity. The display shows the negative sign as a superscript. If $^-5$ is stored in the variable B, then the expression $^-2 - {}^-B$ will be evaluated correctly as $^-7$. This feature is a significant aid in the study of integers and variables.

- Points can be plotted on a coordinate screen either by entering coordinates and seeing the result or by moving the cursor to a particular coordinate on the screen.

- Very large and very small numbers are managed without error. The calculator will quickly compute factorials, even for large numbers, as well as permutations and combinations. Graphing calculators use scientific notation so that large and small numbers do not result in error statements. For example, $23! = 1.033314797 \times 10^{40}$.

- Built-in statistical functions allow students to examine the means, medians, and standard deviations of large sets of realistic data without a computer. Data are easily entered, ordered, added to, or changed almost as easily as on a spreadsheet.

- Graphs for data analysis are available, including box-and-whisker plots, histograms, and, on some calculators, pie charts, bar graphs, and pictographs.

- Random number generators allow for the simulation of a variety of probability experiments that would be difficult without such a device.

- Scatter plots for ordered pairs of real data can be entered, plotted, and examined for trends. The calculator will calculate the equations of best-fit linear, quadratic, cubic, or logarithmic functions.

- Functions can be explored in three modes: equation, table, and graph. Because the calculator easily switches from one to the other and because of the trace feature, the connections between these modes become quite clear. Even sixth-grade students can explore a variety of types of functions along with their graphs and function tables. There is no need to wait until high school to let students explore how the m and b in $y = mx + b$ affect the graph.

- The graphing calculator is programmable. Programs are very easily written and understood. For example, a program involving the Pythagorean theorem can be used to find the length of sides of right triangles.

- Data, programs, and functions can be shared from one graphing calculator to another and, thus, to the display calculator for the overhead or TV monitor. This permits students to share and discuss work with the rest of the class. Calculators also connect to computers to store data and programs and to print out anything that can be seen on the calculator screen.

- Students can share data from one calculator to another, connect their calculators to a classroom display screen, save information on a computer, and download software applications that give additional functionality for special uses.

Most of the ideas on this list are explored briefly in appropriate chapters in this book.

Arguments against graphing calculators are similar to those for other calculators—and are equally hollow and unsubstantiated. These amazing tools have the potential of significantly opening up real mathematics for students. It is time that graphing calculators became a regular tool in the middle grades.

Electronic Data Collection

In addition to the capabilities of the graphing calculator alone, electronic data collection devices make them even more remarkable. Texas Instruments calls its version the CBL (for *computer-based laboratory*), and such calculators are often referred to by that acronym. The current Texas Instruments version is the CBL-2. Casio's current version is called the EA-200 and is nearly identical in design. These devices accept a variety of data collection probes, such as temperature or light sensors and motion detectors, that can be used to gather real physical data. The data can be transferred to the graphing calculator, where they are stored in one or more lists. The calculator can then produce scatter plots or prepare other analyses. With appropriate software, the data can also be transferred to a computer.

A number of excellent resource books are available that describe experiments in detail. Most include disks with calculator programs that make the interface with the CBL quite easy. With a CBL, science and mathematics meet head-on.

The most popular probe for mathematics teachers is the motion detector. Texas Instruments has a special motion detector called a Ranger or CBR that connects directly to the calculator without requiring a CBL unit. Experiments with a motion detector include analysis of objects rolling down an incline, bouncing balls, or swinging pendulums. The motion actually determines the distance an object is from the sensor. When distance is plotted against time, the graph shows velocity. Students can plot their own motion walking toward or away from the detector. The concept of rate when interpreted as the slope of a distance-to-time curve can become quite dramatic.

Though not as widely used as calculators, personal digital assistants (PDAs) such as the PalmPilot or Handspring

Visor have similar capabilities to the CBL. As with the CBL, PDAs can use software and available probes to collect and analyze data. The ImagiProbe from ImagiWorks (www.imagiworks.com) connects to a PDA for distance and temperature data. The Technology Enhanced Elementary and Middle School Science site from the Concord Consortium (www.concord.org/teemss) offers strategies and ideas for using these devices.

The Computer as a Tool in Mathematics

Tool software is a generic term for software that performs a function that makes doing something easier. A very common software tool is the word processor. Other popular tools include spreadsheets, databases, and presentation software such as PowerPoint. A number of powerful tools have been created for use in the mathematics classroom. These exist in two formats: as stand-alone programs that can be purchased from software publishers and as Internet-based applications or *applets* (for "little applications") accessible through Web browsers such as Netscape Browser, Microsoft Internet Explorer, and Apple's Safari.

Applets are always much smaller, more targeted programs than commercial software. A significant advantage is that they are freely accessed on the Internet. Many can also be downloaded so that an Internet connection is not required for student use. Some of these applets are described briefly throughout this book and at the end of each chapter. At the end of this chapter, sites are listed that collectively offer well over 100 applets. You are strongly urged to browse and play. Many of these are lots of fun!

In addition to applets on the Web, another excellent source is the CD-ROMs that come with every volume of the NCTM *Navigations* series. This newest collection of resources from NCTM is designed to help teachers translate *Principles and Standards for School Mathematics* into the classroom. As of 2005, grade-band books are available on the topics of Algebra, Geometry, Number and Operations, Data Analysis, Probability, and Problem Solving and Reasoning. Most of the applets on the *Navigations* CDs can also be found on NCTM's *Illuminations* Web site.

A mathematical software tool is somewhat like a physical manipulative; by itself, it does not teach. However, the user of a well-designed tool software package has an electronic "thinker toy" with which to explore mathematical ideas.

Electronic Manipulatives for Numeration

In these programs, screen versions of popular manipulative models for counting, place value, and fractions are available for students to work with freely without the computer posing problems, evaluating results, or telling the students what to do.

At the earliest level, there are programs that provide "counters" such as colored tiles, pictures of assorted objects, or in one specific case, Unifix cubes.* Typically, students can drag counters to any place on the screen, change the colors, and put them in groupings. Some programs have options that turn on counters for the screen or subsets of the screen. Nonmathematical programs such as *Kid Pix Deluxe 4 for Schools* (Riverdeep, 2005) can also be used to "stamp" discrete objects on the screen, explore shapes, word process, and more.

Base-ten blocks (ones, tens, and hundreds models), assorted fraction pieces, and Cuisenaire rods (centimeter rods) are available in some software packages as well as in Web-based applets. These include both pure tool programs and instructional software programs that attempt to teach or tutor. Some fraction models are more flexible than physical models. For example, a circular region might be subdivided into many more fractional parts than is reasonable with physical models. When the models are connected with on-screen counters, it is possible with some programs to have fraction or decimal representations shown so that connections between fractions and decimals can be illustrated. *Mighty Math Number Heroes* (Riverdeep, 2005) does a nice job of connecting these types of representations for fractions with denominators as small as twelfths. Many of these commercial programs, however, are not completely open to student use without some constraints. For example, in *MathKeys: Unlocking Whole Numbers, Grades 3–5* (Riverdeep, 2005), pieces can be combined or taken apart only by adding or subtracting two quantities.

Web-based tools or applets exist that are designed so that students may manipulate them without constraint. For example, the Base Ten Block Applet (www.arcytech.org/java/b10blocks/b10blocks.html) allows children to collect as many flats, rods, and units as they wish, gluing together groups of ten, or breaking a flat into ten rods or a rod into ten units. Other than providing a description of the pieces, there is no attempt to teach or tutor.

The obvious question is, Why not simply use the actual physical models? Especially for electronic tools (as opposed to instructional software), electronic or virtual manipulatives have some advantages that merit integrating them into your instruction—not just adding them on as extras.

- *Qualitative Differences in Use.* Usually it is at least as easy to manipulate virtual manipulatives as it is to use their physical counterparts. However, control of

---

*Unifix® is the registered trademark for a set of plastic connecting cubes. The cubes are about 2 cm in width and snap easily into bars of any length. They are popular materials for grades K–2.

materials on the screen requires a different, perhaps more deliberative, mental action that is "more in line with the *mental actions* that we want children to carry out" (Clements & Sarama, 2005, p. 53). For example, the base-ten rod representing a ten can be broken into 10 single blocks by clicking on it with a hammer icon. With physical blocks, the ten must be traded for the equivalent blocks counted out by the student.

- *Connection to Symbolism.* Most virtual manipulatives for number include dynamic numerals or odometers that change as the representation on the screen changes. This direct and immediate connection to numeral representation is impossible with physical models.

- *Unlimited Materials with Easy Cleanup.* With virtual manipulatives, a student can easily erase the screen and begin a new problem with the click of a mouse. He or she will never run out of materials. For place value, even the large 1000 cubes are readily available in quantity. And there is no storage or cleanup to worry about.

- *Accommodations for Special Purposes.* For English language learners, some programs come with speech enhancements so that the students hear the names of the materials or the numbers. Some programs and applets are available in Spanish. For students with physical disabilities, the computer models are often easier to access and use than physical models.

Many software-based programs also offer a word-processing capability connected to the workspace. This allows students to write a sentence or two to explain what they have done or perhaps to create a story problem to go with their work. Printing a picture of the workspace, with or without a written attachment, creates a record of the work for the teacher or parent that is not possible with physical models. Web-based applets typically do not have print capabilities.

Geometry Tools

Computer tools for geometric exploration are much closer to pure tools than those just described for numeration. That is, students can use most of these tools without any constraints. They typically offer some significant advantages over physical models, although the computerized tools should never replace physical models in the classroom.

Blocks and Tiles

Programs that allow students to "stamp" geometric tiles or blocks on the screen are quite common. Typically, there is a palette of blocks, often the same as pattern blocks or tangrams, from which students can choose by clicking the

mouse. Often the blocks can be made "magnetic" so that when they are released close to another block, the two will snap together, matching like sides. Blocks can usually be rotated, either freely or in set increments. Different programs offer different variations and features. Figure 8.1 shows a simple yet powerful applet that permits a student to slice any of the three shapes in any place and then manipulate any of the pieces. This is a good example of something a student can do with a computer that would be difficult or impossible with physical models. You may find the following:

- The ability to enlarge or reduce the size of blocks, usually by set increments
- The ability to "glue" blocks together to make new blocks
- The ability to reflect one or more blocks across a mirror line or to rotate them about a point
- Puzzle tasks built into the program
- The ability to measure area or perimeters
- The ability to select polygons with a variable number of sides
- The possibility of creating three-dimensional shapes and rotating them in space

For students who have poor motor coordination or a physical disability that makes block manipulation difficult, the computer versions of blocks are a real plus. Colorful printouts can be displayed, discussed, and taken home if that option is available.

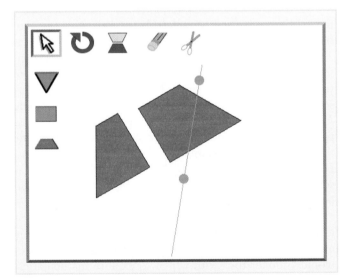

FIGURE 8.1 The "Cutting Shapes Tool."

Drawing Programs

For younger students, drawing shapes on a grid is much easier and more useful for geometric exploration than free-form drawing. Several programs offer electronic geoboards on which lines can be drawn between points on a grid. When a shape such as a triangle is formed, it can typically be altered just as you would a rubber band on a geoboard. For examples, check the NCTM e-*Standards* or NCTM's Illuminations Web site. Addresses are at the end of this chapter. The electronic geoboard programs offer a larger grid on which to draw, ease of use, and the ability to save and print. Some include measuring capabilities as well as reflection and rotation of shapes, things that are difficult or impossible to do on a physical geoboard. An example of a good Internet applet for drawing is the Isometric Drawing Tool found at NCTM's Web site (see Figure 8.2).

Dynamic Geometry Software

Dynamic geometry programs are much more than simple drawing packages. These exciting programs allow students to create shapes on the computer screen and then manipulate and measure them by dragging vertices. The most well-known programs of this type are *The Geometer's Sketchpad* (Key Curriculum Press) and *Cabri Geometry II* (Texas Instruments). Dynamic geometry programs allow the creation of geometric objects (lines, circles) so that their relationship to another screen object is established. For example, a new line can be drawn through a point and perpendicular to another line. A midpoint can be established on any line segment. Once created, these relationships are preserved no matter how the objects are altered. Once thought of as programs for high school students, they are now commonly used in middle school classrooms and are appropriate in classrooms even as early as grade 3. Dynamic geometry software can dramatically both change and improve the teaching of geometry. The ability of students to explore geometric relationships with this software is unmatched with any noncomputer mode. More detailed discussion of these programs can be found in Chapter 21.

Probability and Data Analysis Tools

These computer tools allow for the entry of data and a wide choice of graphs made from the data. In addition, most will produce typical statistics such as mean, median, and range. Some programs are designed for students in the primary grades. Others are more sophisticated and can be used through the middle grades. These programs make it possible to change the emphasis in data analysis from "how to construct graphs" to "which graph best tells the story."

It should be noted that the spreadsheet and the graphing calculator provide much the same capabilities as dedicated data graphing software. Generally, the data programs, described in Chapter 22, offer more graphing options and easier use than a spreadsheet since they are designed to assist in the development of data analysis concepts.

Probability Tools

These programs, also described in Chapter 23, make it easy to conduct controlled probability experiments and see graphical representations of the results. The young student using these programs must accept that when the computer "flips a coin" or "spins a spinner," the results are just as random and have the same probabilities as if done with real coins or spinners. The value of these programs is found in the ease with which experiments can be designed and large numbers of trials conducted.

Spreadsheets and Data Graphers

Spreadsheets are programs that can manipulate rows and columns of numeric data. Values taken from one position in the spreadsheet can be used in formulas to determine entries elsewhere in the spreadsheet. When an entry is changed, the spreadsheet updates all values immediately.

Because the spreadsheet is among the most popular pieces of standard tool software outside of schools, it is often available in integrated packages you may already have on your computer. The spreadsheet program *Excel* is available separately or included in the Microsoft *Office* suite. A spreadsheet similar to *Excel* is found in the *Apple Works* programs. Students as early as third grade can use these programs to organize data, display data graphically in

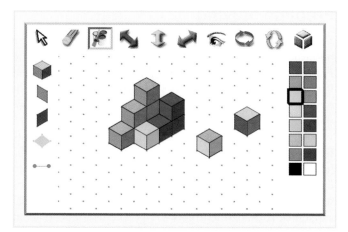

FIGURE 8.2 The "Isometric Drawing Tool" applet from NCTM's Illuminations Web site.

various ways, and do numeric calculations such as finding the total or the mean. Students only need to know how to use the capabilities of the spreadsheet that they will be using. These functions are well within the grasp of the elementary student.

As an alternative to these commercial packages, the *Illuminations* Web site from NCTM offers a couple of very nice spreadsheet Internet applets, *Spreadsheet* and *Spreadsheet and Graphing Tool*. They can be used while connected to the Internet, or they can be downloaded to your computer.

Programs that do the tedious work of creating graphs will permit students in the primary grades to focus on how different graphs convey the information they have gathered. Nice examples in this category are *The Graph Club* for students in grades K to 3 and *Graph Master* for grades 4 to 8 (both from Tom Snyder Productions). *TinkerPlots* (Key Curriculum Press) is a new program developed with NSF funding for students in grades 4 to 8. This program not only creates graphs but also encourages the manipulation of data so that students learn statistical concepts and big ideas about the shape of data.

A number of very nice applets that offer graphing capabilities are freely available on the Web.

Function Graphers

Function graphing software permits the user to create the graph of almost any function very quickly. Multiple functions can be plotted on the same axis. It is usually possible to trace along the path of a curve and view the coordinates at any point. The dimensions of the viewing area can be changed easily so that it is just as easy to look at a graph for x and y between -10 and $+10$ as it is to look at a portion of the graph thousands of units away from the origin. By "zooming in" on the intersection of two graphs, it is possible to find points of intersection without algebraic manipulation. Similarly, the point where a graph crosses the axis can be found to as many decimal places as is desired.

All of the features just described are available on all graphing calculators. Computer programs add speed, color, visual clarity, and a variety of other interesting features to help students analyze functions.

Instructional Software

Instructional software is designed for student interaction in a manner similar to the textbook or a tutor. It is designed to teach. The distinction between tool and instructional software is not always clear since some packages include a tool-only component. Nor is it always clear how to categorize particular instructional programs. In the following discussion, the intent is to provide some perspective on the different kinds of input to your mathematics program that instructional software might offer.

Concept Instruction

A growing number of programs make an effort to offer conceptual instruction. Some, like the *Fizz & Martina's Math Adventures* series of programs (Tom Snyder Productions) and the *Prime Time Math* series (Tom Snyder Productions), rely on real-world contexts to illustrate mathematical ideas. These are problem-solving situations in which specific concepts are developed in a guided manner to solve the problem.

More common in this category is the use of a visual model and much more directed instruction. *MathKeys* programs (Riverdeep), and the Tenth Planet series (Sunburst) use this approach. In *MathKeys*, the models are set up in a noncontextual manner. The Tenth Planet packages embed models into a contextual format, but these stop short of being real world.

What is most often missing is a way to make the mathematics problem based or to connect the conceptual activity with the symbolic techniques. Furthermore, when students work on a computer, there is little opportunity for discourse, conjecture, or original ideas. Some software even presents concepts in such a fashion as to remove learners from thinking and constructing their own understanding. In some instances, the programs might be best used with the teacher controlling the program on a large display screen with the class. In this way, the teacher can pose questions and entertain discussion that is simply not possible with one student on a computer.

Problem Solving

With the current focus on problem solving, more software publishers purport to teach students to solve problems. The *Fizz & Martina* and *Prime Time Math* series can be included in the problem-solving category. Here the problems are not typical story problems awaiting a computation but more thoughtful stories set in real contexts.

At the other end of the spectrum are programs that offer little more than a large library of typical story problems. Usually, the teacher can control for problem difficulty and the operations to be used. These programs would be more valuable if they offered some conceptual assistance if the student gets the problems incorrect, but that is rarely the case.

Logic problem solving is another variant of problem-solving software. This category includes attribute activities, as in *The Zoombinis Logical Adventure* (The Learning Company/Riverdeep) and *Math Arena* (Sunburst), spatial reasoning, as in *Factory Deluxe* (Sunburst), and number patterns and operation sense, as in *Splish Splash Math* (Sunburst).

Drill

Drill programs give students practice with skills that are assumed to have been taught prior to using the programs. In general, a drill program poses questions that are answered directly or by selecting from a multiple-choice list. Many of these programs are set in arcade formats that make them exciting for students who like that sort of video game, but the format has nothing to do with the practice involved.

Drill programs evaluate responses immediately. How they respond to the first or second incorrect answer is one important distinguishing feature. At one extreme, the answer is simply recorded as wrong. There may be a second or third chance to correct it. At the other extreme, the program may branch to an explanation of the correct response. Others may provide a useful hint or supply a visual model to help with the task. Some programs offer record-keeping features for the teacher to keep track of individual student's progress.

Although computer drill is convenient, there is little evidence to suggest that it is any more effective than non-computer drills. A major advantage is in the formats, which can add motivation to an otherwise boring drill.

Guidelines for Selecting and Using Software

There is so much software for mathematics today. Commercially published software is becoming increasingly expensive. Even though most Internet-based applets are free to use, schools must still provide for Internet access and the appropriate hardware. In either case, it is important to make informed decisions when investing limited resources.

How to Select Software

The most important thing to do before purchasing software is to be well informed about the product and to evaluate its merits in an objective manner.

Gathering Information

One of the best sources of information concerning new software is the review section of the NCTM journals or other journals that you respect. Typically, two or three pieces of software are reviewed each issue, or approximately 20 titles per year. Search through 2 or 3 years of back issues to find software that appeals. Many Web sites offer reviews on both commercially available software and Internet-based applets. The Illuminations Web site by NCTM (http://illuminations.nctm.org) is one such site. Another is The Math Forum at Drexel University at http://mathforum.org. When selecting any computer-based tool or instructional software, it is important to evaluate it appropriately.

Next, try to get a preview copy or at least a demonstration version. The latter may not let you actually interact with the software but rather view a form of commercial on your computer. Many distributors will send their software to you for 30-day approval. If this option is available, take advantage of it. Before purchasing, try the software with kids in the grade that will be using it.

Catalogs are useful for finding prices and titles. They are of limited value for understanding how the software works or even what the content is. A title that says it treats "addition and subtraction" does not tell you if this is basic facts, concepts, contextual problems, or multidigit computation. Drill-and-practice software is rarely distinguished from concept software. Remember, it is the content you are interested in, not the game the students will be playing.

Criteria

Here are some things to think about as you review software before purchasing it or using it in your classroom:

- What does this do better than can be done without the computer? Don't select or use software just to put your students on the computer. Be sure to get past the clever graphics and the games. Focus on what students will be learning.
- How are students likely to be engaged with the *content* (not the bells and whistles)? Remember that student reflective thought is the most significant factor in effective instruction. Is the mathematics presented so that it is problematic for the student?
- How easy is the program to use? Students need not be able to learn the program on their own; you can teach them to use it. But there should not be so much tedium in using the program that attention is diverted from the content or students become frustrated.
- What sort of conceptual information is provided? In drill programs, how are wrong answers handled? Are the models or explanations going to aid in student understanding?
- What controls are provided to the teacher? Are there options that can be turned on and off (e.g., sound, types of feedback or help, levels of difficulty)? Is there a provision for record keeping so that you will know what progress individual students have made?
- Is a manual or online instruction available? What is the quality of the manual or instructions? Minimally, the manual should make it clear how the program is to operate and provide assistance for troubleshooting.
- Is printable material available? What is the quality of this material? Many programs come with extensive off-computer activities, lesson plans, Blackline Masters, and suggestions for ways to use the program with your class.

- What is the nature of the licensing agreement? In the case of purchased software, is a site license or network license available? If you purchase a single-user package, it is not legal to install the software on multiple computers. Note also that many programs that come on a CD must have the CD in the computer to run the program. Internet applets require the computer to be connected to the Internet. Do these constraints fit with your school situation?

- Be sure that the program will run on the computers at your school. The software description should indicate the compatible platform(s) (Windows/Macintosh) and the version of the required operating systems.

Guidelines for Using Software

How software is used in mathematics instruction will vary considerably with the topic, the grade level, and the software itself. The following are offered as considerations that you should keep in mind.

- Software should contribute to the objectives of the lesson or unit. It should not be used as an add-on or substitute for more accessible approaches. Its use should take advantage of what technology can do efficiently and well.

- For individualized or small group use, plan to provide specific instructions for how the software is used, and plan to provide time for students to freely explore or practice using the software.

- Combine software activities with off-computer activities (e.g., collect measurement data in the classroom to enter into a spreadsheet).

- Create a management plan for using the software. This could include a schedule for when the software is used (e.g., during centers, during small group work) and a way to assess the effectiveness of the software use. Although some software programs include a way to keep track of student performance, you may need to rely on other assessment strategies to determine whether the software is being effective at meeting the objectives of the lesson or unit.

Mathematics Education Resources on the Internet

In addition to access to Internet-based software applications, or applets, the World Wide Web is a wellspring of information and resources for both teachers and students interested in mathematics and teaching mathematics.

Instead of using a standard search engine to find mathematics-related information, it is better to have some places to begin. Several good Web sites in different categories will usually provide you with more links to other sites than you will have time to search. One place to get good Web sites is from the NCTM's *News Bulletin*, a newsletter sent free to all members nine times each year. For several years, the *Bulletin* has featured information about useful Web sites. Make it a habit to check these out in each issue.

At the end of the chapter you will find a list of Web-based resources arranged by the type of information the site provides. A brief description accompanies each listing but you are encouraged to check these out yourself as Web sites are frequently modified. The types of resources you can expect to find are described here.

Professional Information

Most professional organizations have established Web sites that provide information about their organizations, conferences, current issues and events, publications, and other matters. Often these sites provide useful links to related resources or information. Periodic visits to these sites are a good way to stay current with what is going on.

Teacher Resources

The Internet is a wonderful source of creative and useful lesson ideas. It is also a good way to find out about materials and software. The sites listed in this category were selected because of the quantity of information that is available on them and because the site addresses are not likely to change or disappear quickly. However, these few suggestions only scratch the surface. A large number of other resources are accessible through these sites.

Applets

Collections of applets are usually found on a single Web site. The sites listed in this category are some that have been found to be the most useful collections across content and grade levels. Selected individual applets for particular content areas are listed at the end of each chapter in Section 2 of this book.

Remember that all applets are not equal, just as all software is not equal. Applets vary in how much freedom they offer the student. Some can be considered pure tool software and others are closer to instructional devices. Some applets come packaged with detailed lessons or investigations and questions for students to answer.

Some applets can be downloaded to your computer so that you do not need to be connected to the Web in order to use them. Even in an off-line mode, however, you will still need a current version of a Web browser such as Netscape Browser, Microsoft Internet Explorer, or Apple's Safari to run them.

Writing to Learn

1. Technology has affected the mathematics curriculum and how it is taught in three ways. Explain each, and give an example to support your explanation. Can you think of examples that are not included in this chapter?
2. Describe some of the benefits of using calculators regularly in the mathematics classroom. Which of these seem to you to be the most compelling? What are some of the arguments against using calculators? Answer each of the arguments against calculators as if you were giving a speech at your PTA meeting or arguing for regular use of calculators before your principal.
3. Aside from the special features of graphing calculators, what are some of the benefits that come simply from having a large display screen and the ability to recall prior statements?
4. What are at least three features of graphing calculators that truly improve the learning of mathematics in the middle grades?
5. Describe what is meant by tool software in mathematics. Describe several types.
6. Describe the three categories of computer instructional software. If you have seen or used examples from these categories, use those in your descriptions.
7. What are some criteria that seem most important to you when selecting software?
8. What kind of information can you expect to find on the Internet?

For Discussion and Exploration

1. Talk with some teachers about their use or nonuse of calculators in the classroom. How do the teachers who use them go about doing so? What are the main reasons for not using them? Read the Technology Principle in *Principles and Standards for School Mathematics*. How do the reasons the teachers you talked with compare to the NCTM position?
2. Among the software kept at your school, find one example of drill software and one of some other form of instructional software for mathematics. Try each and decide how it would be used in your classroom (if at all). Be sure to check the documentation for suggested grade levels.
3. Check out at least three of the Web sites suggested below for teacher resources. Be sure to follow some of the links to other sites. Share at least two good ideas with a friend. Get the friend to do the same.
4. Explore three or four applets from one or more of the sites listed under Applets (see below). Select one and try it with children. Teach a lesson that incorporates the applet as either a teacher tool or student activity.

Recommendations for Further Reading

Crown, W. D. (2003). Using technology to enhance a problem-based approach to teaching: What will and what won't work. In F. K. Lester & R. I. Charles (Eds.), *Teaching mathematics through problem solving: pre-K to 6*. Reston, VA: National Council of Teachers of Mathematics.

Crown offers an overview of both calculators and computers for problem-based mathematics. In his discussion of computers, he describes six categories of educational software. For each category, he explains why that particular type of software is or is not particularly useful in problem-based instruction. Crown's categories of software alone make it worth taking a look at this article.

Hillman, S. L., & Malotka, C. M. (2004). Changing views: Fearless families conquering technology together. *Mathematics Teaching in the Middle School, 10*, 169–173.

The authors offer descriptions of three workshops for parents (including two with students attending) designed to illustrate the power of calculator technology. They used both the TI-Math Explorer and the TI-73.

Masalski, W. J., & Elliott, P. C. (Eds.). (2005). *Technology-supported mathematics learning environments: Sixty-seventh yearbook*. Reston, VA: National Council of Teachers of Mathematics.

An excellent collection of perspectives on the use of technology across the grades by noted authorities and practicing teachers alike. Topics include strategies for effective use of technology, examination of virtual manipulatives for young students, dynamic geometry software, the spreadsheet, and much more. A CD is included to illustrate many of the ideas found in the book plus additional sources.

McGehee, J., & Griffith, L. K. (2004). Technology enhances student learning across the curriculum. *Mathematics Teaching in the Middle School, 9*, 344–349.

Five examples of using technology are explored. Understanding graphs (rate of change), decimals, geometry, measurement, and data analysis are the areas the examples cover. This is a good introduction to the use of technology in any of these domains.

National Council of Teachers of Mathematics. (2002). Learning and teaching mathematics with technology [Focus Issue]. *Teaching Children Mathematics, 8*(6).

In the practical manner of *TCM*, this special issue provides excellent articles on all aspects of technology in the classroom for young children.

Thompson, T., & Sproule, S. (2005). Calculators for students with special needs. *Teaching Children Mathematics, 11*, 391–395.

An excellent argument is made for the use of calculators for students who have learning problems that affect their mathematical skills. A framework or flowchart that is easily used to make decisions about when to allow calculator use is not only appropriate for special students but also for every child. This short article can blunt the objections raised by the calculator critics.

Online Resources

Suggested Applets and Web Links

Professional Information

National Council of Teachers of Mathematics (NCTM)
www.nctm.org

The NCTM Web site is a must for every elementary teacher and teacher of mathematics. It includes specific information for teachers, parents, leaders, and researchers. The home page changes almost monthly, providing up-to-date information about conferences, publications, news, and more. The site also provides a mechanism for joining the council, registering for conferences, purchasing publications and products, and linking to the Illuminations site (see separate entry). Members can access their journals online, subscribe to a special electronic journal, and renew memberships. You can choose to receive a monthly e-mail update informing you of recent additions to the Web site.

Eisenhower National Clearinghouse (ENC)
www.enc.org

This is a site of links to information about standards-based curriculum materials for K–12 mathematics and science, information and articles on standards-based issues, information about TIMSS, and ideas for classroom use. Look especially at ENC Features.

American Association for the Advancement of Science
www.aaas.org

This is the association for Project 2061, a national science standards document. Access to this and other information concerning science education is available.

Association for Supervision and Curriculum Development (ACSD)
www.ascd.org

ASCD is an international nonprofit educational association that is committed to successful teaching and learning for all.

EQUALS and Family Math
http://equals.lhs.berkeley.edu

The EQUALS program is dedicated to equal opportunity for females in mathematics and science. It publishes Family Math and other valuable resources. For those interested in issues surrounding gender equity and parental involvement, this is a good place to begin.

Mathematically Sane
www.mathematicallysane.com

This is an important and unique Web site that provides evidence for and discussion of the success of standards-based initiatives in mathematics education. Its mission statement identifies the site as created by a "grassroots organization of teachers, administrators, teacher educators, parents, and mathematicians concerned about the future of mathematics education."

Teacher Resources

NCTM Illuminations
http://illuminations.nctm.org

This is an incredible site developed by NCTM to provide Internet resources for teaching and learning intended to "illuminate" *Principles and Standards for School Mathematics*. You can find resources from lesson ideas to "math-lets" (applets designed to provide tools for developing understanding in mathematics). Also at this site are multimedia investigations for students and links to video vignettes designed to promote professional reflection.

The Math Forum
http://mathforum.org

Along with the NCTM sites, this may be your most important source of information and links to useful sites. The forum has resources for both teachers and students. There are suggestions for lessons, puzzles, and activities, plus links to other sites with similar information. There are forums where teachers can talk with other teachers. Two pages accept questions about mathematics from students or teachers (Ask Dr. Math) and about teaching mathematics from teachers (Teacher 2 Teacher). Problems are regularly posted, and solutions can be entered via the Internet. Information is available about software, and some can be downloaded free.

MegaMath!
www.c3.lanl.gov/mega-math

This is a great site! A project of the Computer Research and Applications Group at Los Alamos National Laboratory, it is intended to bring unusual and important mathematical ideas to elementary classrooms.

Math Archives: K–12 Internet Sites
http://archives.math.utk.edu/k12.html

This page contains a very large collection of links to lessons, software, information (both public domain and commercial), and curriculum materials. Each of the hundreds of sites has a brief description. If you are looking for an Internet address for a mathematics resource, this may be a good place to look.

EdWeb Home Page
www.edwebproject.org

This site explores issues of educational reform and contains links to online resources around the world.

Home Page for New Math Teachers
http://people.clarityconnect.com/webpages/terri/terri.html

A veteran teacher, Terri Husted, offers advice on a list of subjects challenging the new teacher. In addition, she provides clever problems to pose to students, links to a huge number of useful sites, and much more.

Annenberg/CPB Projects
www.learner.org

The site lists free online learning activities, including information about all sorts of interesting uses of mathematics and science in the real world, resources for free and inexpensive materials from Annenberg, and information about funding opportunities. It is a tremendous resource.

Center for Implementing Technology in Education (CITEd): Math Matrix
www.citeducation.org/mathmatrix/default.asp

CITEd's Math Matrix is a small but useful database of technology products that supports instruction in mathematics for students with special needs. Each product evaluation includes a link to the supplier's Web site.

U.S. Census Data
www.census.gov

Copious statistical information by state, county, or voting district.

The World Fact Book
www.odci.gov/cia/publications/factbook/index.html

This page provides demographic information for every nation in the world, including population, age distributions, death and birth rates, and information on the economy, government, transportation, and geography. Maps are included as well.

Applets

National Council of Teachers of Mathematics e-Examples
http://standards.nctm.org/document/eexamples/index.htm

Many of these applets are referenced in and directly support the text of *Principles and Standards for School Mathematics*. They are also available on the CD version of the Standards. Most are also available on the *Illuminations* site.

NCTM Illuminations
http://illuminations.nctm.org

Check both the i-Math Investigations (interactive math lessons, most built around applets) and Interactive Math-lets (a collection of applets). The Math-let applications cover the K–12 spectrum. They are ordered alphabetically, so be sure to check out the full list. This is a good collection of quality tools. The i-Math Investigations include all of the applets from the e-examples.

The National Library for Virtual Manipulatives (NLVM)
http://matti.usu.edu/nlvm/nav/vlibrary.html

This NSF-funded site is located at Utah State University. It contains a huge collection of applets organized by the five content strands of the *Standards* and also by the same four grade bands. You may not find all of these applets equally interesting or usable but there is a lot more to like than not. Give the site a thorough look.

Arcytech
http://arcytech.org/java

At the time this was written this site included tool applets for base-ten blocks, pattern blocks, Cuisenaire rods, fraction bars, and integer bars. There is also an extended interactive lesson developing the Pythagorean theorem.

Shodor Interactivate (Shodor Education Foundation)
http//www.shodor.org/interactive

The site contains a huge list of applets that continues to grow. In addition, there are lessons and activities, many that include the use of applets. Applets (referred to as "activities") are arranged by content rather than grade level, so be sure to look through the full list. This is a valuable site, especially for teachers in the upper grades and middle school.

Count On
www.mathsyear2000.org

This site is sponsored by the National Grid for Learning and contains all sorts of resources in addition to applets for mathematics. Click on the Explorer button to find a number of applets as well as other useful features such as a mathematics dictionary. Check out other areas of this site as well.

An additional list of books and articles related to the ideas in this chapter can be found on the Companion Web site at **www.ablongman.com/vandewalle6e.**

chapter 9

Developing Early Number Concepts and Number Sense

Number is a complex and multifaceted concept. A rich understanding of number, a relational understanding, involves many different ideas, relationships, and skills. Children come to school with many ideas about number. These ideas should be built upon as we work with children and help them develop new relationships. It is sad to see the large number of students in grades 4, 5, and above who essentially know little more about number than how to count. It takes time and lots of experiences for children to develop a full understanding of number that will grow and enhance all of the further number-related concepts of the school years.

This chapter looks at the development of number ideas for numbers up to about 20. These foundational ideas can all be extended to larger numbers, operations, basic facts, and computation.

Big Ideas

1. Counting tells how many things are in a set. When counting a set of objects, the last word in the counting sequence names the quantity for that set.

2. Numbers are related to each other through a variety of number relationships. The number 7, for example, is more than 4, two less than 9, composed of 3 and 4 as well as 2 and 5, is three away from 10, and can be quickly recognized in several patterned arrangements of dots. These ideas further extend to an understanding of 17, 57, and 370.

3. Number concepts are intimately tied to the world around us. Application of number relationships to the real world marks the beginning of making sense of the world in a mathematical manner.

Mathematics Content Connections

Early number development is related to other areas in the curriculum in two ways: content that interacts with and enhances the development of number and content that is directly affected by how well early number concepts have been developed. Measurement, data, and operation meanings fall in the first category. Basic facts, place value, and computation fall in the second.

- **Operations** (Chapter 10): As children solve story problems for any of the four operations, they count on, count back, make and count groups, and make comparisons. In the process, they form new relationships and methods of working with numbers.

- **Measurement** (Chapter 20): The determination of measures of length, height, size, or weight is an important use of number for the young child. Measurement involves meaningful counting and comparing (number relationships) and connects number to the world in which the child lives.

- **Data** (Chapter 22): Data, like measurement, involve counts and comparisons to both aid in developing number and connecting it to the real world.

- **Basic Facts** (Chapter 11): A rich and thorough development of number relationships is a critical foundation for mastering basic facts. Without number relationships, facts must be rotely memorized. With number understanding, facts for addition and subtraction are relatively simple extensions.

- **Place Value and Computation** (Chapters 12 and 13): Many of the ideas that contribute to computational fluency and flexibility with numbers are clear extensions of how numbers are related to ten and how numbers can be taken apart and recombined in different ways.

Number Development in Pre-K and Kindergarten

Parents help children count their fingers, toys, people at the table, and other small sets of objects. Questions concerning "who has more?" or "are there enough?" are part of the daily lives of children as young as 2 or 3 years of age. Considerable evidence indicates that these children have some understanding of the concepts of number and counting (Baroody & Wilkins, 1999; Fuson, 1988; Gelman & Gallistel, 1978; Gelman & Meck, 1986; NRC, 2001).

The Relationships of More, Less, and Same

The concepts of "more," "less," and "same" are basic relationships contributing to the overall concept of number. Children begin to develop these ideas before they begin school. An entering kindergarten child can almost always choose the set that is *more* if presented with two sets that are quite obviously different in number. In fact, Baroody (1987) states, "A child unable to use 'more' in this intuitive manner is at considerable educational risk" (p. 29). Classroom activities should help children build on this basic notion and refine it.

Though the concept of less is logically equivalent to the concept of more (selecting the set with more is the same as *not* selecting the set with less), the word *less* proves to be more difficult for children than *more*. A possible explanation is that children have many opportunities to use the word *more* but have limited exposure to the word *less*. To help children with the concept of less, frequently pair it with the word *more* and make a conscious effort to ask "which is less?" questions as well as "which is more?" questions. For example, suppose that your class has correctly selected the set that has more from two that are given. Immediately follow with the question "Which is less?" In this way, the less familiar term and concept can be connected with the better-known idea.

For all three concepts (more, less, and same), children should construct sets using counters as well as make comparisons or choices between two given sets. The activities described here include both types. These activities should be conducted in a spirit of inquiry followed whenever possible with requests for explanations. "Why do you think this set has less?"

activity 9.1

Make Sets of More/Less/Same
At a workstation or table, provide about eight cards with sets of 4 to 12 objects, a set of small counters or blocks, and some word cards labeled *More, Less,* and *Same.* Next to each card have students make three collections of counters: a set that is more, one that is less, and one that is the same. The appropriate labels are placed on the sets (see Figure 9.1).

In Activity 9.1, students create a set with counters, which gives them the opportunity to reflect on the sets and adjust them as they work. The next activity is done without counters. Although it addresses the same basic ideas, it provides a different problem situation.

activity 9.2

Find the Same Amount
Give children a collection of cards with sets on them. Dot cards are one possibility (see the Blackline Masters). Have the children pick up any card in the collection and then find another card with the same amount to form a pair. Continue to find other pairs.

Activity 9.2 can be altered to have children find dot cards that are "less" or "more."

Observe children as they do this task. Children whose number ideas are completely tied to counting and nothing more will select cards at random and count each dot. Others will begin by selecting a card that appears to have about the same number of dots. This is a significantly higher level of understanding. Also observe how the dots are counted. Are the counts made accurately? Is each counted only once? A significant milestone for children occurs when they begin recognizing small patterned sets without counting.

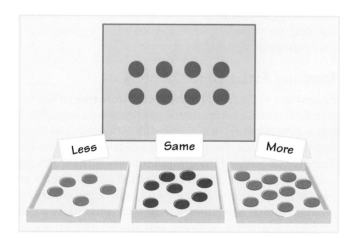

FIGURE 9.1 Making sets that are more, less, and the same.

pause and reflect ————————————

You have begun to see some of the early foundational ideas about number. Stop now and make a list of all of the important ideas that you think children should *know about* 8 by the time they finish first grade. (The number 8 is used as an example. The list could be about any number from, say, 6 to 12.) Put your thoughts aside and we will revisit these ideas later.

Early Counting

Meaningful counting activities can begin in preschool. Generally, children at midyear in kindergarten should have a fair understanding of counting, but children must construct this idea. It cannot be forced. Only the counting sequence is a rote procedure. The *meaning* attached to counting is the key conceptual idea on which all other number concepts are developed.

The Development of Counting Skills

Counting involves at least two separate skills. First, one must be able to produce the standard list of counting words in order: "One, two, three, four, ..." Second, one must be able to connect this sequence in a one-to-one manner with the items in the set being counted. Each item must get one and only one count.

Experience and guidance are the major factors in the development of these counting skills. Many children come to kindergarten able to count sets of ten or beyond. At the same time, children from impoverished backgrounds may require considerable practice to make up their experience deficit. The size of the set is also a factor related to success in counting. Obviously, longer number strings require more practice to learn. The first 12 counts involve no pattern or repetition, and many children do not recognize a pattern in the teens. Children still learning the skills of counting—that is, matching oral number words with objects—should be given sets of blocks or counters that they can move or pictures of sets that are arranged for easy counting.

Meaning Attached to Counting

Fosnot and Dolk (2001) make it very clear that an understanding of cardinality and the connection to counting is not a simple matter for 4-year-olds. Children will learn *how* to count (matching counting words with objects) before they understand that the last count word indicates the *amount* of the set or the *cardinality* of the set. Children who have made this connection are said to have the *cardinality principle*, which is a refinement of their early ideas about quantity. Most, but certainly not all, children by age $4\frac{1}{2}$ have made this connection (Fosnot & Dolk, 2001; Fuson & Hall, 1983).

 Young children who can count orally may not have attached meaning to their counts. Show a child a card with five to nine large dots in a row so that they can be easily counted. Ask the child to count the dots. If the count is accurate, ask "How many dots are on the card?" Many children will count again. One indication of understanding the first count will be a response that reflects the first count without recounting. Now have the child get that same number of counters from a collection of counters: "Please get the same number of counters as there are dots on the card." There are several indicators to watch for. Will the child recount to know how many to get? Does the child count the counters or place them one-to-one on the dots? Is the child confident that there is the same number of counters as dots? ∎

Fosnot and Dolk discuss a class of 4-year-olds in which children who knew there were 17 children in the class were unsure how many milk cartons they should get so that each could have one.

To develop their understanding of counting, engage children in almost any game or activity that involves counts and comparisons. The following is a simple suggestion.

activity **9.3**

Fill the Chutes

Create a simple game board with four "chutes." Each consists of a column of about twelve 1-inch squares with a star at the top. Children take turns rolling a die and collecting the indicated number of counters. They then place these counters in one of the chutes. The object is to fill all of the chutes with counters. As an option, require that the chutes be filled exactly. A roll of 5 cannot be used to fill a chute with four spaces.

This "game" provides opportunities for you to talk with children about number and assess their thinking. Watch how the children count the dots on the die. Ask, "How do you know you have the right number of counters?" and "How many counters did you put in the chute? How many more do you need to fill the chute?"

Activities 9.1 and 9.2 also provide opportunities for diagnosis. Regular classroom activities, such as counting how many napkins are needed at snack time, are additional opportunities for children to learn about number and for teachers to listen to their students' ideas.

Numeral Writing and Recognition

Helping children read and write single-digit numerals is similar to teaching them to read and write letters of the alphabet. Neither has anything to do with number concepts. Traditionally, instruction has involved various forms of repetitious practice. Children trace over pages of numerals, repeatedly write the numbers from 0 to 10, make the numerals from clay, trace them in sand, write them on the chalkboard or in the air, and so on.

The calculator is a good instructional tool for numeral recognition. In addition to helping children with numerals, early activities can help develop familiarity with the calculator so that more complex activities are possible.

---

activity **9.4**

Find and Press

Every child should have a calculator. Always begin by having the children press the clear key. Then you say a number, and the children press that number on the calculator. If you have an overhead calculator, you can then show the children the correct key so that they can confirm their responses, or you can write the number on the board for children to check. Begin with single-digit numbers. Later, progress to two or three numbers called in succession. For example, call, "Three, seven, one." Children press the complete string of numbers as called.

Perhaps the most common kindergarten exercises have children match sets with numerals. Children are given pictured sets and asked to write or match the number that tells how many. Alternatively, they may be given a number and told to make or draw a set with that many objects. Many teacher resource books describe cute learning center activities where children put a numeral with the correct-sized set—numbered frogs on lily pads (with dots), for example. It is important to note that these frequently overworked activities involve only the skills of counting sets and numeral recognition or writing. When children are successful with these activities, little is gained by continuing to do them.

Computer software that allows children to create sets on the screen with the click of a mouse is quite common. *Unifix Software* (Hickey, 1996) is an electronic version of the popular Unifix cubes, plastic cubes that snap together to make bars. The software allows the teacher to add features to counting activities that are not available with the cubes alone. In its most basic form, children can click to create as many single cubes as they wish. They can link cubes to make bars of cubes, break the bars, move them around, add sounds to each cube, and more. The teacher can choose to have a numeral appear on each bar showing the total. From one to

four loops can be created, with the loop total another option. Not only can students count to specified numbers and have the numerals appear for reinforcement, but also they can informally begin to explore the idea that two quantities can form a larger amount. ■

Counting On and Counting Back

Although the forward sequence of numbers is relatively familiar to most young children, counting on and counting back are difficult skills for many. Frequent short practice drills are recommended.

---

activity **9.5**

Up and Back Counting

Counting up to and back from a target number in a rhythmic fashion is an important counting exercise. For example, line up five children and five chairs in front of the class. As the whole class counts from 1 to 5, the children sit down one at a time. When the target number, 5, is reached, it is repeated; the child who sat on 5 now stands, and the count goes back to 1. As the count goes back, the children stand up one at a time, and so on, "1, 2, 3, 4, 5, 5, 4, 3, 2, 1, 1, 2, ..." Kindergarten and first-grade children find exercises such as this both fun and challenging. Any movement (clapping, turning around, doing jumping jacks) can be used as the count goes up and back in a rhythmic manner.

The last activity is designed only to help students become fluent with the number words in both forward and reverse order and to begin counts with numbers other than 1. Although not at all easy for young students, these activities do not address counting on or counting back in a meaningful manner. Fosnot and Dolk (2001) describe the ability to count on as a "landmark" on the path to number sense. The next two activities are designed for that purpose.

---

activity **9.6**

Counting On with Counters

Give each child a collection of 10 or 12 small counters that the children line up left to right on their desks. Tell them to count four counters and push them under their left hands or place them in a cup (see Figure 9.2). Then say, "Point to your hand. How many are there?" (Four.) "So let's count like this: f-o-u-r (pointing to their hand), five, six, ..." Repeat with other numbers under the hand.

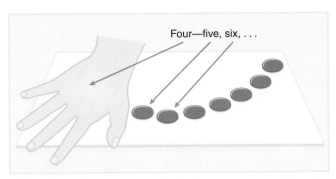

FIGURE 9.2 Counting on: "Hide four. Count, starting from the number of counters hidden."

The following activity addresses the same concept in a bit more problem-based manner.

activity **9.7**

Real Counting On

This "game" for two children requires a deck of cards with numbers 1 to 7, a die, a paper cup, and some counters. The first player turns over the top number card and places the indicated number of counters in the cup. The card is placed next to the cup as a reminder of how many are there. The second child rolls the die and places that many counters next to the cup. (See Figure 9.3.) Together they decide how many counters in all. A record sheet with columns for "In the Cup," "On the Side," and "In All" is an option. The largest number in the card deck can be adjusted if needed.

Watch how children determine the total amounts in this last activity. Children who are not yet counting on may want to dump the counters from the cup or will count up from one without dumping out the counters. Be sure to permit these strategies. As children continue to play, they will eventually count on as that strategy becomes meaningful and useful.

FIGURE 9.3 How many in all? How do children count to tell the total? Dump the counters? Count up from 1 without dumping the counters? Count on?

Early Number Sense

Number sense was a term that became popular in the late 1980s, even though terms such as this have somewhat vague definitions. Howden (1989) described number sense as a "good intuition about numbers and their relationships. It develops gradually as a result of exploring numbers, visualizing them in a variety of contexts, and relating them in ways that are not limited by traditional algorithms" (p. 11). This may still be the best definition.

NCTM Standards In *Principles and Standards*, the term *number sense* is used freely throughout the Number and Operations standard. This example is from the K–2 level: "As students work with numbers, they gradually develop flexibility in thinking about numbers, which is a hallmark of number sense. . . . Number sense develops as students understand the size of numbers, develop multiple ways of thinking about and representing numbers, use numbers as referents, and develop accurate perceptions about the effects of operations on numbers" (p. 80).

The discussion of number sense begins in this book with the remainder of this chapter as we look at the kinds of relationships and connections children should be making about smaller numbers up to about 20. But "good intuition about numbers" does not end with these smaller whole numbers. Children continue to develop number sense as they begin to use numbers in operations, build an understanding of place value, and devise flexible methods of computing and making estimates involving large numbers. Flexible, intuitive thinking with numbers—number sense—should continue to be developed throughout the school years as fractions, decimals, and percents are added to students' repertoire of number ideas.

The early number ideas that have been discussed to this point in the chapter are the rudimentary aspects of number. Unfortunately, too many traditional programs move directly from these beginning ideas to addition and subtraction, leaving students with a very limited collection of ideas about number to bring to these new topics. The result is often that children continue to count by ones to solve simple story problems and have difficulty mastering basic facts. Early number sense development should demand significantly more attention than it is given in most traditional K–2 programs.

Relationships Among Numbers 1 Through 10

Once children have acquired a concept of cardinality and can meaningfully use their counting skills, little more is to be gained from the kinds of counting activities described so far. More relationships must be created for children to develop number sense, a flexible concept of number not completely tied to counting.

A Collection of Number Relationships

Figure 9.4 illustrates the four different types of relationships that children can and should develop with numbers:

- *Spatial relationships:* Children can learn to recognize sets of objects in patterned arrangements and tell how many without counting. For most numbers, there are several common patterns. Patterns can also be made up of two or more easier patterns for smaller numbers.
- *One and two more, one and two less:* The two-more-than and two-less-than relationships involve more than just the ability to count on two or count back two. Chil-

dren should know that 7, for example, is 1 more than 6 and also 2 less than 9.

- *Anchors or "benchmarks" of 5 and 10:* Since 10 plays such a large role in our numeration system and because two fives make up 10, it is very useful to develop relationships for the numbers 1 to 10 to the important anchors of 5 and 10.
- *Part-part-whole relationships:* To conceptualize a number as being made up of two or more parts is the most important relationship that can be developed about numbers. For example, 7 can be thought of as a set of 3 and a set of 4 or a set of 2 and a set of 5.

The principal tool that children will use as they construct these relationships is the one number tool they possess: counting. Initially, then, you will notice a lot of counting, and you may wonder if you are making progress. Have patience! Counting will become less and less necessary as children construct these new relationships and begin to use the more powerful ideas.

Spatial Relationships: Patterned Set Recognition

Many children learn to recognize the dot arrangements on standard dice due to the many games they have played that use dice. Similar instant recognition (also known as *subitizing*) can be developed for other patterns as well. The activities suggested here encourage reflective thinking about the patterns so that the relationships will be constructed. Quantities up to 10 can be known and named without the routine of counting. This can then aid in counting on (from a known patterned set) or learning combinations of numbers (seeing a pattern of two known smaller patterns).

A good set of materials to use in pattern recognition activities is a set of dot plates. These can be made using small paper plates and the peel-off dots commonly available in office supply stores. A reasonable collection of patterns is shown in Figure 9.5. Note that some patterns are combinations of two smaller patterns or a pattern with one or two additional dots. These should be made in two colors. Keep the patterns compact. If the dots are spread out, the patterns are hard to see.

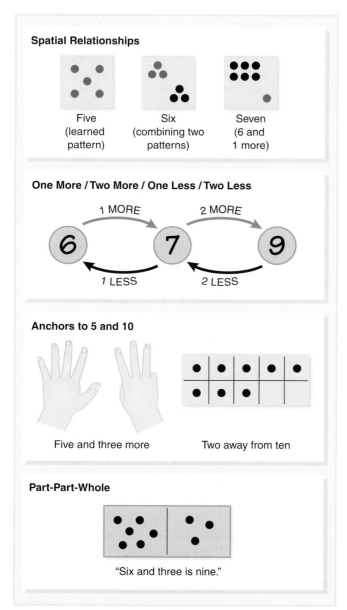

FIGURE 9.4 Four relationships to be developed involving small numbers.

Learning Patterns

To introduce the patterns, provide each student with about ten counters and a piece of construction paper as a mat. Hold up a dot plate for about 3 seconds. "Make the pattern you saw using the counters on the mat. How many dots did you see? How did you see them?" Spend some time discussing the configuration of the pattern and how many dots. Do this with a few new patterns each day.

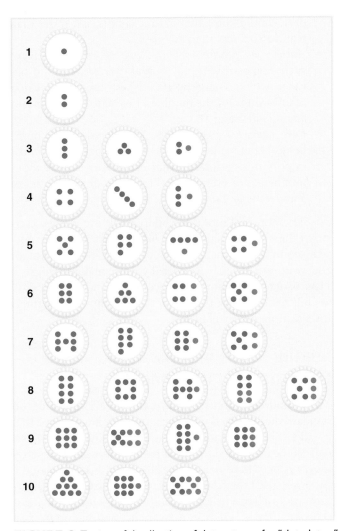

FIGURE 9.5 A useful collection of dot patterns for "dot plates."

---

dominoes in the regular way, matching up the ends. As a speed activity, spread out all of the dominoes and see how fast the children play all of the dominoes or play until no more can be played. Regular dominoes could also be used, but there are not as many patterns.

The instant recognition activities with the plates are exciting and can be done in 5 minutes at any time of day or between lessons. There is value in using them at any primary grade level and at any time of year.

One and Two More, One and Two Less

When children count, they have no reason to reflect on the way one number is related to another. The goal is only to match number words with objects until they reach the end of the count. To learn that 6 and 8 are related by the twin relationships of "two more than" and "two less than" requires reflection on these ideas within tasks that permit counting. Counting on (or back) one or two counts is a useful tool in constructing these ideas.

Note that the relationship of "two more than" is significantly different than "comes two counts after." This latter relationship is applied to the string of number words, not to the quantities they represent. A comes-two-after relationship can be applied to letters of the alphabet. The letter *J* comes two after the letter *H*. However, there is no numeric or quantitative difference between *H* and *J*. The quantity 8 would still be two more than 6 even if there were no number string to count these quantities. It is the numeric relationship you want to develop even though initially students will use counting in different ways to develop it.

The following activity is a good place to begin helping children with these relationships. As described, it focuses on the two-more-than relationship although it can be used just as well for any of the four relationships.

> **EXPANDED LESSON**
>
> An expanded lesson based on Activity 9.11 can be found at the end of Chapter 5.

---

activity **9.9**

Dot Plate Flash
Hold up a dot plate for only 1 to 3 seconds. "How many? How did you see it?" Children like to see how quickly they can recognize and say how many dots. Include lots of easy patterns and a few with more dots as you build their confidence. Students can also flash the dot plates to each other as a workstation activity.

---

activity **9.10**

Dominoes
Make a set of dominoes out of poster board and put a dot pattern on each end. The dominoes can be about 2 inches by 4 inches. The same patterns can appear on lots of dominoes with different pairs of patterns making up each one. Let the children play

---

activity **9.11**

Make a Two-More-Than Set
Provide students with about six dot cards. Their task is to construct a set of counters that is two more than the set shown on the card. Similarly, spread out eight to ten dot cards, and find another card for each that is two less than the card shown. (Omit the 1 and 2 cards for two less than, and so on.)

In activities in which children find a set or make a set, they can add a numeral card (a small card with a number written on it) to all of the sets involved. They can also be encouraged to take turns reading a number sentence to their partner. If, for example, a set has been made that is two more than a set of four, the child can read this by saying the number sentence, "Two more than four is six" or "Six is two more than four."

The next activity combines the relationships so children will need to be more attentive to which idea they need to be thinking about.

activity 9.12

More or Less

This is an activity for two players or a small group. Use the Blackline Masters to make a deck of More-or-Less cards as shown in Figure 9.6. Make four or five of each type of card. You will also need a set of cards with the numbers 3 to 10 (2 each). One child draws a number card and places it face up where all can see. That number of counters are put into a cup. Next, another child draws one of the More-or-Less cards and places it next to the number card. For the More cards, counters are added accordingly to the cup. For the Less cards, counters are removed from the cup. For Zero cards, no change is made. Once the cup has been adjusted, each child predicts how many counters are now in the cup. The counters are dumped out and counted, ending that round of the game and a new number card is drawn.

"More or Less" can be played with the class. You announce how many counters you are placing in the cup and write this number on the board. Have a student draw a card and have students predict the new amount. The words *more* and *less* can be paired or substituted with *plus* and *minus* to connect these ideas with the arithmetic operations, even if they have not yet been formally introduced.

The calculator can be an exciting device to practice the relationships of one more than, two more than, one less than, and two less than.

activity 9.13

A Calculator Two-More-Than Machine

Teach children how to make a two-more-than machine. Press 0 ⊞ 2 ⊟. This makes the calculator a two-more-than machine. Now press any number—for example, 5. Children hold their finger over the ⊟ key and predict the number that is two more than 5. Then they press ⊟ to confirm. If they do not press any of the operation keys (+, −, ×, ÷), the "machine" will continue to perform in this way.

FIGURE 9.6 To play "More or Less," children draw a number card to tell how many counters to put in the cup. Then they draw a More-or-Less card and adjust the number of counters accordingly. Then they predict how many counters are in the cup.

What is really happening in the two-more-than machine is that the calculator "remembers" or stores the last operation, in this case "+2," and adds that to whatever number is in the window when the ⊟ key is pressed. If the child continues to press ⊟, the calculator will count by twos. At any time, a new number can be pressed followed by the equal key. To make a two-less-than machine, press 2 ⊟ 2 ⊟. (The first press of 2 is to avoid a negative number.) In the beginning, students forget and press operation keys, which change what their calculator is doing. Soon, however, they get the hang of using the calculator as a machine.

The calculator two-more-than machine will, of course, give the number two more than any number pressed, including those with two or more digits. Although not found in traditional curricula, the two-more-than relationship should be extended to two-digit numbers as soon as students are exposed to them. One way to do this is to ask for the number that is two more than 7. After getting the correct answer, ask "What is two more than 37?" and similarly for other numbers that end in 7. When you try this for 8 or 9, expect difficulties and unusual responses such as two more than 28 is "twenty-ten." In the first grade, this struggle can prove quite valuable. The "More or Less" activity can also be extended to larger numbers if no actual counters are used.

Anchoring Numbers to 5 and 10

Here again, we want to help children relate a given number to other numbers, specifically 5 and 10. These

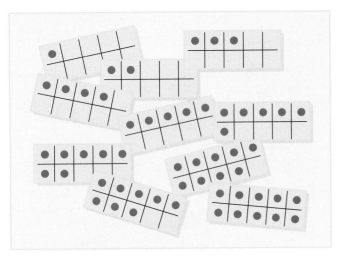

FIGURE 9.7 Ten-frames.

relationships are especially useful in thinking about various combinations of numbers. For example, in each of the following, consider how the knowledge of 8 as "5 and 3 more" and as "2 away from 10" can play a role: 5 + 3, 8 + 6, 8 − 2, 8 − 3, 8 − 4, 13 − 8. (It may be worth stopping here to consider the role of 5 and 10 in each of these examples.) Later similar relationships can be used in the development of mental computation skills on larger numbers such as 68 + 7.

The most common and perhaps most important model for this relationship is the ten-frame. The ten-frame is simply a 2 × 5 array in which counters or dots are placed to illustrate numbers (see Figure 9.7). Ten-frames can be simply drawn on a full sheet of construction paper (or use the Blackline Master). Nothing fancy is required, and each child can have one. The ten-frame has been incorporated into a variety of activities in this book and is now popular in standard textbooks for children.

For children in kindergarten or early first grade who have not yet explored a ten-frame, it is a good idea to begin with a five-frame. This row of five sections is also drawn on a sheet of construction paper (or use the Blackline Master). Provide children with about ten counters that will fit in the five-frame sections and conduct the following activity.

activity **9.14**

Five-Frame Tell-About
Explain that only one counter is permitted in each section of the five-frame. No other counters are allowed on the five-frame mat. Have the children show 3 on their five-frame. "What can you tell us about 3 from looking at your mat?" After hearing from several children, try other numbers from 0 to 5. Children may place their counters on the five-frame in any

manner. What they observe will differ a great deal from child to child. For example, with four counters, a child with two on each end may say, "It has a space in the middle" or "It's two and two." There are no wrong answers. Focus attention on how many more counters are needed to make 5 or how far away from 5 a number is. Next try numbers between 5 and 10. The rule of one counter per section still holds. As shown in Figure 9.8, numbers greater than 5 are shown with a full five-frame and additional counters on the mat but not in the frame. In discussion, focus attention on these larger numbers as 5 and some more: "Eight is five and three more."

Notice that the five-frame really focuses on the relationship to 5 as an anchor for numbers but does not anchor numbers to 10. When five-frames have been used for a week or so, introduce ten-frames. You may want to play a ten-frame version of a "Five-Frame Tell-About" but soon introduce the following rule for showing numbers on the ten-frame: *Always fill the top row first, starting on the left, the same way you read. When the top row is full, counters can be placed in the bottom row, also from the left.* This will produce the "standard" way to show numbers on the ten-frame as in Figure 9.7.

The horizontal orientation of the ten-frame is not essential, although it is the one generally shown in this book. However, some educators place the dots in a vertical ten-frame and fill the bottom sections first rather than fill a row of five first (e.g., Losq, 2003, 2005). In this format, 5 is shown as two dots in one row or column and three in the other. Although there is a strong case to be made for this arrangement, it does not accentuate the relationship to 5 and 10 as strongly as the row-at-a-time configuration shown in Figure 9.7.

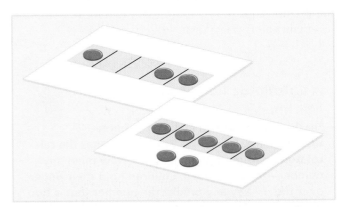

FIGURE 9.8 A five-frame focuses on the 5 anchor. Counters are placed one to a section, and students tell how they see their number in the frame.

For a while, many children will count every counter on their ten-frame. Some will take all counters off and begin each number from a blank frame. Others will soon learn to adjust numbers by adding on or taking off only what is required, often capitalizing on a row of five without counting. Do not pressure students. With continued practice, all students will grow. How they are using the ten-frame provides insight into students' current number concept development.

activity 9.15

Crazy Mixed-Up Numbers

This activity is adapted from *Mathematics Their Way* (Baratta-Lorton, 1976). All children make their ten-frame show the same number. The teacher then calls out random numbers between 0 and 10. After each number, the children change their ten-frames to show the new number. Children can play this game independently by preparing lists of about 15 "crazy mixed-up numbers." One child plays "teacher," and the rest use the ten-frames. Children like to make up their own number lists.

"Crazy Mixed-Up Numbers" is much more of a problem than it first appears. How do you decide how to change your ten-frame? Some children will wipe off the entire frame and start over with each number. Others will have learned what each number looks like. To add another dimension, have the children tell, *before changing their ten-frames*, how many more counters need to be added ("plus") or removed ("minus"). They then call out plus or minus whatever amount is appropriate. If, for example, the frames showed 6, and the teacher called out "four," the children would respond, "Minus two!" and then change their ten-frames accordingly. A discussion of how they know what to do is valuable.

Ten-frame flash cards are an important variation of ten-frames. Make cards from tagboard about the size of a small index card, with a ten-frame on each and dots drawn in the frames. A set of 20 cards consists of a 0 card, a 10 card, and two each of the numbers 1 to 9. The cards allow for simple drill activities to reinforce the 5 and 10 anchors as in the following activity.

activity 9.16

Ten-Frame Flash

Flash ten-frame cards to the class or group and see how fast the children can tell how many dots are shown. This activity is fast-paced, takes only a few minutes, can be done at any time, and is a lot of fun if you encourage speed.

Important variations of "Ten-Frame Flash" include

- Saying the number of spaces on the card instead of the number of dots
- Saying one more than the number of dots (or two more, and also less than)
- Saying the "ten fact"—for example, "Six and four make ten"

Ten-frame tasks are surprisingly problematic for students. Students must reflect on the two rows of five, the spaces remaining, and how a particular number is more or less than 5 and how far away from 10. The early discussions of how numbers are seen on the five-frames or ten-frames are examples of brief *after* activities in which students learn from one another.

How well students can respond to the cards in "Ten-Frame Flash" is one good indicator of their number concepts and should be included in any quick assessment of a child's current number concept level. Include as well the variations of the activity that were listed. Since the distance to 10 is so extremely important, another assessment is to point to a numeral less than ten and ask, "If this many dots were on a ten-frame, how many spaces would there be?" Or you can also simply ask, "If I have seven, how many more do I need to make ten?" ■

Part-Part-Whole Relationships

 *pause and reflect* _____

Before reading on, get some simple counters or coins. Count out a set of eight counters in front of you as if you were a first- or second-grade child counting them.

Any child who has learned how to count meaningfully can count out eight objects as you just did. What is significant about the experience is what it did *not* cause you to think about. Nothing in counting a set of eight objects will cause a child to focus on the fact that it could be made of two parts. For example, separate the counters you just set out into two piles and reflect on the combination. It might be 2 and 6 or 7 and 1 or 4 and 4. Make a change in your two piles of counters and say the new combination to yourself. Focusing on a quantity in terms of its parts has important implications for developing number sense. A noted researcher in children's number concepts, Lauren Resnick (1983) states:

> Probably the major conceptual achievement of the early school years is the interpretation of numbers in terms of part and whole relationships. With the application of a Part-Whole schema to quantity, it becomes possible for children to think about numbers as compositions of other numbers. This enrichment of number understanding

permits forms of mathematical problem solving and interpretation that are not available to younger children. (p. 114)

A study of kindergarten children examined the effects of part-part-whole activities on number concepts (Fischer, 1990). With only 20 days of instruction to develop the part-part-whole structure, children showed significantly higher achievement than the control group on number concepts, word problems, and place-value concepts.

Basic Ingredients of Part-Part-Whole Activities

Most part-part-whole activities focus on a single number for the entire activity. Thus, a child or group of children working together might work on the number 7 throughout the activity. Either children build the designated quantity in two or more parts, or else they start with the full amount and separate it into two or more parts. A group of two or three children may work on one number in one activity for 5 to 20 minutes. Kindergarten children will usually begin these activities working on the number 4 or 5. As concepts develop, the children can extend their work to numbers 6 to 12. A wide variety of materials and formats for these activities can help to maintain student interest. It is not unusual to find children in the second grade who have not developed firm part-part-whole constructs for numbers in the 7-to-12 range.

When children do these activities, have them say or "read" the parts aloud or write them down on some form of recording sheet (or do both). Reading or writing the combinations serves as a means of encouraging reflective thought focused on the part-whole relationship. Writing can be in the form of drawings, numbers written in blanks (_____ and _____), or addition equations if these have been introduced (3 + 5 = 8). There is a clear connection between part-part-whole concepts and addition and subtraction ideas.

Part-Part-Whole Activities

The following activity and its variations may be considered the "basic" part-part-whole activity.

activity **9.17**

Build It in Parts

Provide children with one type of material, such as connecting cubes or squares of colored paper. The task is to see how many different combinations for a particular number they can make using two parts. (If you wish, you can allow for more than two parts.) Each different combination can be displayed on a small mat, such as a quarter-sheet of construction paper. Here are just a few ideas, each of which is illustrated in Figure 9.9.

- Use two-color counters such as lima beans spray painted on one side (also available in plastic).
- Make bars of connecting cubes. Make each bar with two colors. Keep the colors together.
- Color rows of squares on 1-inch grid paper.
- Make combinations using two dot strips—strips of poster board about 1 inch wide with stick-on dots. (Make lots of strips with from one to four dots and fewer strips with from five to ten dots.)
- Make combinations of "two-column strips." These are cut from tagboard ruled in 1-inch squares. All pieces except the single squares are cut from two columns of the tagboard.

As you observe children working on the "Build It in Parts" activity, ask them to "read" a number sentence to go with each of their designs. Encourage children to read their designs to each other. Two or three children work-

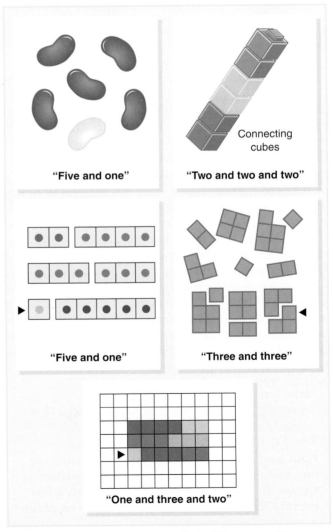

"Five and one"   "Two and two and two"
Connecting cubes

"Five and one"   "Three and three"

"One and three and two"

FIGURE 9.9 Assorted materials for building parts of 6.

ing together with the same materials may have quite a large number of combinations including lots of repeats.

A note about the "two-column cards" mentioned in the activity and shown in Figure 9.9: In her unpublished research, Kuske (2001) makes the case that this two-column model for numbers is more valuable than dot patterns and ten-frames. Her reasoning is that the pieces are "additive." That is, the combination of any two of the pieces is another piece in the set, as can be seen in Figure 9.9. Of course, this is not true of dot patterns or ten-frames. The squares in two-column cards are arranged the same as the dots in the alternative version of ten-frame cards (Losq, 2005). In both Kuske's and Losq's work, sets of ten are given special importance and used as precursors to place value. For example, a 6 and a 7 piece make a 10 and 3 piece. Their research is quite interesting and, if nothing else, reinforces the importance of helping children think about numbers in terms of two parts.

In the "Build It in Parts" activity, the children are focusing on the combinations. To add some interest, vary the activity by adding a design component. Rather than create a two-part illustration for a number, they create an interesting design with an assigned number of elements. For each design, they are then challenged to see and read the design in two parts. Here are some ideas.

- Make arrangements of wooden cubes.
- Make designs with pattern blocks. It is a good idea to use only one or two shapes at a time.
- Make designs with flat toothpicks. These can be dipped in white glue and placed on small squares of construction paper to create a permanent record.
- Make designs with touching squares or triangles. Cut a large supply of small squares or triangles out of construction paper. These can also be pasted down.

It is both fun and useful to challenge children to see their designs in different ways, producing different number combinations. In Figure 9.10, decide how children look at the designs to get the combinations listed under each.

The following activity is strictly symbolic. However, children should use counters if they feel they need to.

activity 9.18

Two out of Three

Make lists of three numbers, two of which total the whole that children are focusing on. Here is an example list for the number 5:

2—3—4
5—0—2
1—3—2
3—1—4
2—2—3
4—3—1

With the list on the board, overhead, or worksheet, children can take turns selecting the two numbers that make the whole. As with all problem-solving activities, children should be challenged to justify their answers.

Missing-Part Activities

A special and important variation of part-part-whole activities is referred to as *missing-part* activities. In a missing-part activity, children know the whole amount and use their already developed knowledge of the parts of that whole to try to tell what the covered or hidden part is. If they do not know or are unsure, they simply uncover the

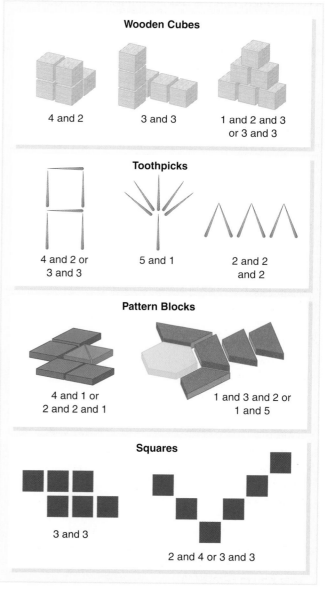

FIGURE 9.10 Designs for 6.

unknown part and say the full combination as they would normally. Missing-part activities provide maximum reflection on the combinations for a number. They also serve as the forerunner to subtraction concepts. With a whole of 8 but with only 3 showing, the child can later learn to write "8 – 3 = 5."

Missing-part activities require some way for a part to be hidden or unknown. Usually this is done with two children working together or else in a teacher-directed manner with the class. Again, the focus of the activity remains on a single designated quantity as the whole. The next four activities illustrate variations of this important idea.

activity 9.19

Covered Parts

A set of counters equal to the target amount is counted out, and the rest are put aside. One child places the counters under a margarine tub or piece of tagboard. The child then pulls some out into view. (This amount could be none, all, or any amount in between.) For example, if 6 is the whole and 4 are showing, the other child says, "Four and *two* is six." If there is hesitation or if the hidden part is unknown, the hidden part is immediately shown (see Figure 9.11).

activity 9.20

Missing-Part Cards

For each number 4 to 10, make missing-part cards on strips of 3-by-9-inch tagboard. Each card has a numeral for the whole and two dot sets with one set covered by a flap. For the number 8, you need nine cards with the visible part ranging from zero to eight dots. Students use the cards as in "Covered Parts," saying, "Four and two is six" for a card showing four dots and hiding two (see Figure 9.11).

activity 9.21

I Wish I Had

Hold out a bar of connecting cubes, a dot strip, a two-column strip, or a dot plate showing 6 or less. Say, "I wish I had six." The children respond with the part that is needed to make 6. Counting on can be used to check. The game can focus on a single whole, or the "I wish I had" number can change each time.

The following activity is completely symbolic but is an effective method of practicing part-whole combinations.

activity 9.22

Calculator Parts of 8 Machine

Make a parts of 8 machine by pressing 8 ☐ 8 ☐. Now if any number from 0 to 8 is pressed followed by ☐, the display shows the other part. The second part shows as a negative number. Tell students that is how they can tell it is the second part. Children should try to say the other part before they press ☐. Though this is basically a drill activity, a discussion with any child concerning his or her reasoning returns it to a problem orientation. Machines can be made for any number in the same way.

 There are lots of ways you can use computer software to create part-part-whole activities. All that is needed is a program that permits students to create sets of objects on the screen.

Scott Foresman's *eTools* (Pearson Education, 2004) includes a variety of background screens for counters. In the version shown in Figure 9.12, children can stamp three different

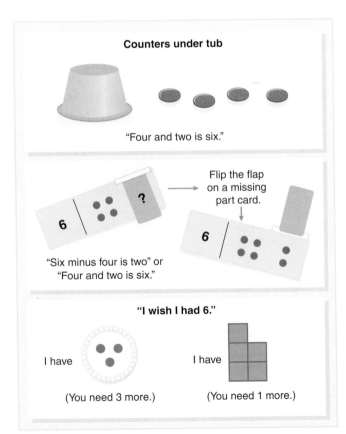

Counters under tub

"Four and two is six."

Flip the flap on a missing part card.

"Six minus four is two" or "Four and two is six."

"I wish I had 6."

I have (You need 3 more.)

I have (You need 1 more.)

FIGURE 9.11 Missing-part activities.

(a)

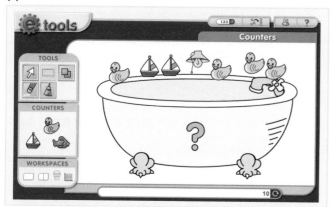

(b)

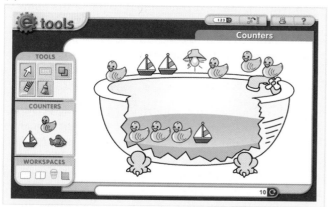

FIGURE 9.12 The counters tool in Scott Foresman's *eTools* software (Pearson Education, 2004) is a useful tool for exploring part-part-whole and missing-part ideas as well as earlier number concepts and early addition/subtraction ideas.

types of bathtub toys either in the tub (unseen) or outside the tub. The numeral on the tub shows how many are in the tub or it can be fixed to show a question mark (?) for missing-part thinking. The odometer at the bottom shows the total or whole. It also can be turned off. By clicking on the light, the contents of the tub can be seen (Figure 9.12b). In the hands of a teacher, this program offers a great deal of diversity and challenge for both part-part-whole and missing-part activities.

Combining and Breaking Apart Numbers (Tenth Planet, 1998a) is specifically designed for part-part-whole activities. Although the early activities in this package are fairly passive and slow, the "Through" or last section makes the mathematics reasonably problematic. In various animated settings, children attempt to make a number either in two parts or by adding two groups and then removing one or two groups. This is an example of software that requires some teacher guidance to create good problems or else students will not stay engaged. The printed support material includes suggestions for corresponding off-line activities that make this a worthwhile program. ■

 pause and reflect _____

Remember the list you made earlier in the chapter about what children should know about the number 8? Get it out now and see if you would add to it or revise it based on what you have read to this point. Do this before reading on.

Here is a possible list of the kinds of things that children should know about the number 8 (or any number up to about 12) by the end of the first grade. Children should be able to:

- Count to eight (know the number words).
- Count eight objects and know that the last number word tells how many.
- Write the numeral 8.
- Recognize the numeral 8.

The preceding list represents the minimal skills of number. In the following list are the relationships students should have that contribute to number sense:

- More and less by 1 and 2: 8 is one more than 7, one less than 9, two more than 6, and two less than 10.
- Spatial patterns for 8 such as

- Anchors to 5 and 10: 8 is 5 and 3 more and 2 away from 10.
- Part-whole relationships: 8 is 5 and 3, 2 and 6, 7 and 1, and so on. This includes knowing the missing part of 8.
- Other relationships such as

    Doubles: double 4 is 8.

    Relationships to the real world: 8 is one more than the days of the week, my brother is 8 years old, my reading book is 8 inches wide.

Dot Card Activities

Many good number development activities involve more than one of the relationships discussed so far. As children learn about ten-frames, patterned sets, and other relationships, the dot cards in the Blackline Masters provide a wealth of activities (see Figure 9.13). The cards contain dot patterns, patterns that require counting, combinations of two and three simple patterns, and ten-frames with "standard" as well as unusual placements of dots. When children use these cards for almost any activity that involves number concepts, the cards make them think about numbers in many different ways. The dot cards add another dimension to many of the activities already described and can be used effectively in the following activities.

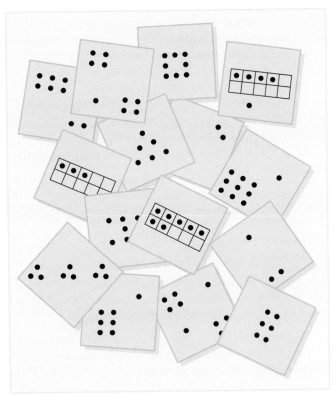

FIGURE 9.13 Dot cards can be made using the Blackline Masters.

activity 9.23

Double War

The game of "Double War" (Kamii, 1985) is played like war, but on each play, both players turn up two cards instead of one. The winner is the one with the larger total number. Children playing the game can use many different number relationships to determine the winner without actually finding the total number of dots.

activity 9.24

Dot-Card Trains

Make a long row of dot cards from 0 up to 9, then go back again to 1, then up, and so on. Alternatively, begin with 0 or 1 and make a two-more/two-less train.

activity 9.25

Difference War

Besides dealing out the cards to the two players as in regular "War," prepare a pile of 30 to 40 counters. On each play, the players turn over their cards as usual. The player with the greater number of dots wins as many counters from the pile as the difference between the two cards. The players keep their cards. The game is over when the counter pile runs out. The player with the most counters wins the game.

activity 9.26

Number Sandwiches

Select a number between 5 and 12, and find combinations of two cards that total that number. With the two cards students make a "sandwich" with the dot side out. When they have found at least ten sandwiches, the next challenge is to name the number on the other "slice" of the sandwich. The sandwich is turned over to confirm. The same pairs can then be used again to name the hidden part.

To assess the important part-whole relationships, use a missing-part assessment similar to Activity 9.19 ("Covered Parts") on p. 132. Begin with a number you believe the child has "mastered," say, 5. Have the child count out that many counters into your open hand. Close your hand around the counters and confirm that she knows how many are hidden there. Then remove some and show them in the palm of your other hand. (See Figure 9.14.) Ask the child, "How many are hidden?" Repeat with different amounts removed, although it is only necessary to check three or four missing parts for each number. If the child responds quickly and correctly and is clearly not counting in any way, call that a "mastered number." If a number is mastered, repeat the entire process with the next higher number. Continue un-

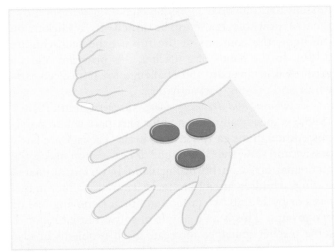

FIGURE 9.14 A missing-part number assessment. Eight in all. "How many are hidden?"

Investigations
in Number, Data, and Space

Grade K, How Many in All?
Investigation 2: Six Tiles

Context
The activities in this investigation take place over one to two weeks near the end of the year but could be done earlier. The entire investigation focuses on the number 6. The authors explain that 6 is an amount most kindergarten children can count, even early in the year. Children need more than one hand to show 6. It provides enough two-part combinations to be interesting, and it is an amount that can be visually recalled and manipulated. Furthermore, most kindergarten children will turn 6 years old during the year.

Task Descriptions
In "Cover Up," the teacher draws an arrangement of six squares on a grid so that all can see. For example:

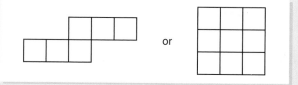

Students are told to look at the drawings and discuss different ways they could remember what they see. Then the picture is covered up and students try to describe the drawing. The discussion is focused on ideas that get at the parts of the picture, not just that there are six squares. "Cover Up" is repeated with several different drawings. "Six Tiles in All" is a follow-up activity in which students paste down six squares on grid paper in as many ways as they can find. Squares have to

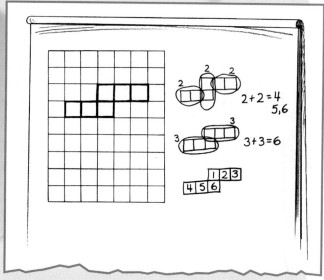

From *Investigations in Number, Data, and Space: Kindergarten* by Marlene Kliman et al. Copyright © 1998 by Dale Seymour Publications. Reprinted by permission of Pearson Education, Inc.

touch on a full side. The different arrangements are shared and the teacher helps students see number combinations for 6 as in the teacher notes shown here. This investigation provides just one opportunity to naturally introduce the symbolism for addition as children say the combinations they see.

The authors point out that it is tempting to think that the activities in this unit could profitably be repeated for other numbers as well. Their experience, however, is that students get bored doing the same thing over and over. These ideas are important for other numbers, but students need different contexts and materials to maintain interest.

---

til the child begins to stumble. In early first grade you will find a range of mastered numbers from 4 to 7 or 8. By spring of the first grade, most children should have mastered numbers to 10. ■

The *Investigations in Number, Data, and Space* curriculum for kindergarten integrates number development throughout most of the year. Four of seven units focus on the development of number, including the unit on data and measurement. The activity described in this excerpt provides some flavor of the *Investigations* program's early approach to number.

Relationships for Numbers 10 to 20

Even though kindergarten, first-, and second-grade children daily experience numbers up to 20 and beyond, it should not be assumed that they will automatically extend the set of relationships they have developed on smaller numbers to the numbers beyond 10. And yet these numbers play a big part in many simple counting activities, in basic facts, and in much of what we do with mental computation. Relationships with these numbers are just as important as relationships involving the numbers through 10.

A Pre-Place-Value Relationship with 10

A set of ten should play a major role in children's early understanding of numbers between 10 and 20. When children see a set of six with a set of ten, they should know without counting that the total is 16. However, the numbers between 10 and 20 are not an appropriate place to discuss place-value concepts. That is, prior to a much more complete development of place-value concepts (appropriate for second grade and beyond), children should not be asked to explain the 1 in 16 as representing "one ten."

 *pause and reflect* ——————————

Say to yourself, "One ten." Now think about that from the perspective of a child just learning to count to 20! What could one ten possibly mean when ten tells me how many fingers I have and is the number that comes after nine? How can it be one?

Initially, children do not see a numeric pattern in the numbers between 10 and 20. Rather, these number names are simply ten additional words in the number sequence. The concept of a single ten is just too strange for a kindergarten or early first-grade child to grasp. Some would say that it is not appropriate for grade 1 at all (Kamii, 1985). The inappropriateness of discussing "one ten and six ones" (what's a one?) does not mean that a set of ten should not figure prominently in the discussion of the teen numbers. The following activity illustrates this idea.

activity **9.27**

Ten and Some More
Use a simple two-part mat and have children count out ten counters onto one side. Next have them put five counters on the other side. Together count all of the counters by ones. Chorus the combination: "Ten and five is fifteen." Turn the mat around: "Five and ten is fifteen." Repeat with other numbers in a random order but without changing the 10 side of the mat.

Activity 9.27 is designed to teach new number names and, thus, requires a certain amount of directed teaching. Following this activity, explore numbers to 20 in a more open-ended manner. Provide each child with two ten-frames drawn one under the other on a construction paper mat or use the Blackline Master provided. In random order, have children show numbers to 20 on their mats. That is, play "Crazy Mixed-Up Numbers" (Activity 9.15) with two ten-frames and numbers to 20. There is no preferred way to do this as long as there are the correct number of counters. What is interesting is to discuss how the coun-

ters can be placed on the mat so that it is easy to see how many are there. Have children share their ideas. Not every child will use a full set of ten, but as this idea becomes more popular, the notion that ten and some more is a teen amount will soon be developed. Do not forget to include numbers less than 10 as well. As you listen to your children, you may want to begin challenging them to find ways to show 26 counters or even more.

Extending More and Less Relationships

The relationships of one more than, two more than, one less than, and two less than are important for all numbers. However, these ideas are built on or connected to the same concepts for numbers less than 10. The fact that 17 is one less than 18 is connected to the idea that 7 is one less than 8. Children may need help in making this connection.

activity **9.28**

More and Less Extended
On the overhead, show seven counters, and ask what is two more, or one less, and so on. Now add a filled ten-frame to the display (or 10 in any pattern) and repeat the questions. Pair up questions by covering and uncovering the ten-frame as illustrated in Figure 9.15.

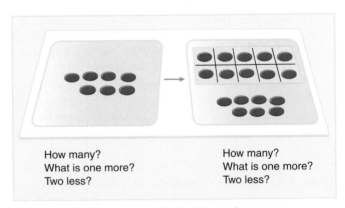

How many?
What is one more?
Two less?

How many?
What is one more?
Two less?

FIGURE 9.15 Extending relationships to the teens.

Double and Near-Double Relationships

The use of doubles (double 6 is 12) and near-doubles (13 is double 6 and 1 more) is generally considered a strategy for memorizing basic addition facts. There is no reason why children should not begin to develop these relationships long before they are concerned with memorizing basic facts. Doubles and near-doubles are simply special cases of the general part-part-whole construct.

Relate the doubles to special images. Thornton (1982) helped first graders connect doubles to these visual ideas:

Double 3 is the bug double: three legs on each side.

Double 4 is the spider double: four legs on each side.

Double 5 is the hand double: two hands.

Double 6 is the egg carton double: two rows of six eggs.

Double 7 is the two-week double: two weeks on the calendar.

Double 8 is the crayon double: two rows of eight crayons in a box.

Double 9 is the 18-wheeler double: two sides, nine wheels on each side.

Children can draw pictures or make posters that illustrate the doubles for each number. There is no reason that the images need be restricted to those listed here. Any images that are strong ideas for your children will be good for them.

Periodically conduct oral exercises in which students double the number you say. Ask children to explain how they knew a particular double. Many will not use the pictures.

activity 9.29

The Double Maker

Make the calculator into a "double maker" by pressing 2 ☒ ☐. Now a press of any digit followed by ☐ will produce the double of that number. Children can work in pairs or individually to try to beat the calculator.

As a related oral task, say a number, and ask students to tell what double it is. "What is fourteen?" (Double 7!) When students can do this well, use any number up to 20. "What is seventeen?" (Double 8 and 1 more.)

Number Sense and the Real World

Here we examine ways to broaden the early knowledge of numbers in a different way. Relationships of numbers to real-world quantities and measures and the use of numbers in simple estimations can help children develop the flexible, intuitive ideas about numbers that are most desired.

Estimation and Measurement

One of the best ways for children to think of real quantities is to associate numbers with measures of things. In the early grades, measures of length, weight, and time are good places to begin. Just measuring and recording results will not be very effective, however, since there is no reason for children to be interested in or think about the result. To help children think or reflect a bit on what number might tell how long the desk is or how heavy the book is, it would be good if they could first write down or tell you an estimate. To produce an estimate is, however, a very difficult task for young children. They do not understand the concept of "estimate" or "about." For example, suppose that you have cut out of poster board an ample supply of very large footprints, say, about 18 inches long. All are exactly the same size. You would like to ask the class, "About how many footprints will it take to measure across the rug in our reading corner?" The key word here is *about*, and it is one that you will need to spend a lot of time helping children understand. To this end, the request of an estimate can be made in ways that help with the concept of "about" yet not require students to give a specific number.

The following estimation questions can be used with most early estimation activities:

- *More or less than* _____? Will it be more or less than 10 footprints? Will the apple weigh more or less than 20 wooden blocks? Are there more or less than 15 connecting cubes in this long bar?
- *Closer to* _____ *or to* _____? Will it be closer to 5 footprints or closer to 20 footprints? Will the apple weigh closer to 10 blocks or closer to 30 blocks? Does this bar have closer to 10 cubes or closer to 50 cubes?
- *About* _____. Use one of these numbers: 5, 10, 15, 20, 25, 30, 35, 40, ... About how many footprints? About how many blocks will the apple weigh? About how many cubes are in this bar?

Asking for estimates using these formats helps children learn what you mean by "about." Every child can make an estimate without having to pull a number out of the air.

To help with numbers and measures, estimate several things in succession using the same unit. For example, suppose that you are estimating and measuring "around things" using a string. To measure, the string is wrapped around the object and then measured in some unit such as craft sticks. After measuring the distance around Demetria's head, estimate the distance around the wastebasket or around the globe or around George's wrist. Each successive measure helps children with the new estimates. See Chapter 20 for a complete discussion of measurement.

More Connections

Here are some additional activities that can help children connect numbers to real situations.

activity 9.30

Add a Unit to Your Number

Write a number on the board. Now suggest some units to go with it and ask the children what they can think of that fits. For example, suppose the number is 9. "What do you think of when I say 9 *dollars*? 9 *hours*? 9 *cars*? 9 *kids*? 9 *meters*? 9 *o'clock*? 9 *hand spans*? 9 *gallons*?" Spend some time in discussion of each. Let children suggest units as well. Be prepared to explore some of the ideas either immediately or as projects or tasks to share with parents at home.

activity 9.31

Is It Reasonable?

Select a number and a unit—for example, 15 feet. Could the teacher be 15 feet tall? Could your living room be 15 feet wide? Can a man jump 15 feet high? Could three children stretch their arms 15 feet? Pick any number, large or small, and a unit with which children are familiar. Then make up a series of these questions.

Once children are familiar with Activity 9.31, have them select the number and the unit or things (10 kids, 20 bananas, . . .), and see what kinds of questions children make up. When a difference of opinion develops, capitalize on the opportunity to explore and find out. Resist the temptation to supply your adult-level knowledge. Rather, say, "Well, how can we find out if it is or is not reasonable? Who has an idea about what we could do?"

These activities are problem-based in the truest sense. Not only are there no clear answers, but children can easily begin to pose their own questions and explore number in the part of the environment most interesting to them. Children will not have these real-world connections when you begin, and you may be disappointed in their limited ideas about number. Howden (1989) writes about a first-grade teacher of children from very impoverished backgrounds who told her, "They all have fingers, the school grounds are strewn with lots of pebbles and leaves, and pinto beans are cheap. So we count, sort, compare, and talk about such objects. We've measured and weighed almost everything in this room and almost everything the children can drag in" (p. 6). This teacher's children had produced a wonderfully rich and long list of responses to the question "What comes to your mind when I say twenty-four?" In another school in a professional community where test scores are high, the same question brought almost no response from a class of third graders. It can be a very re-

warding effort to help children connect their number ideas to the real world.

Graphs

Graphing activities are another good way to connect children's worlds with number. Chapter 22 discusses ways to make graphs with children in grades K–2. Graphs can be quickly made of almost any data that can be gathered from the students: favorite ice cream, color, sports team, pet; number of sisters and brothers; kids who ride different buses; types of shoes; number of pets; and so on. Graphs can be connected to content in other areas. A unit on sea life might lead to a graph of different categories of sea life.

Once a simple bar graph is made, it is very important to take a few minutes to ask as many number questions as is appropriate for the graph. In the early stages of number development (grades K–1), the use of graphs for number relationships and for connecting numbers to real quantities in the children's environment is a more important reason for building graphs than the graphs themselves. The graphs focus attention on counts of realistic things. Equally important, bar graphs clearly exhibit comparisons between and among numbers that are rarely made when only one number or quantity is considered at a time. See Figure 9.16 for an example of a graph and questions that can be asked. At first, children will have trouble with the questions involving differences, but repeated exposure to these ideas in a bar graph format will improve their understanding. These comparison concepts add considerably to children's understanding of number.

NCTM Standards The *Standards* clearly recognizes the value of integrating number development with other areas of the curriculum. "Students' work with numbers should be connected to their work with other mathematics topics. For example, computational fluency . . . can both enable and be enabled by students' investigations of data; a knowledge of patterns supports the development of skip counting and algebraic thinking; and experiences with shape, space, and number help students develop estimation skills related to quantity and size" (p. 79).

Literature Connections

Children's literature abounds with wonderful counting books. Involving children with books in a variety of ways can serve to connect number to reality, make it a personal experience, and provide ample opportunities for problem solving. Be sure to go beyond simply reading a counting book or a number-related book and looking at the pictures. Find a way to extend the book into the chil-

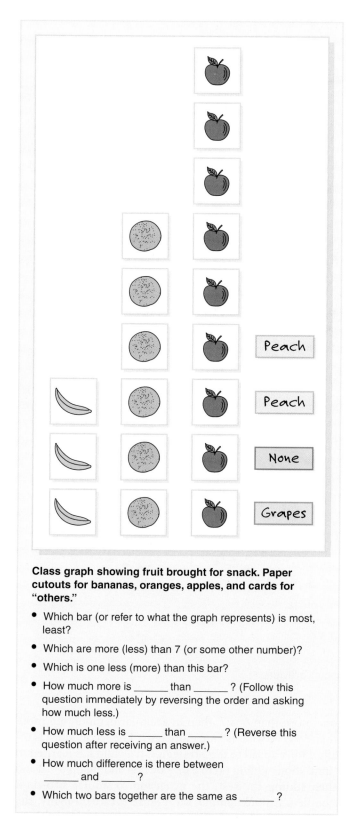

Class graph showing fruit brought for snack. Paper
cutouts for bananas, oranges, apples, and cards for
"others."

- Which bar (or refer to what the graph represents) is most,
least?

- Which are more (less) than 7 (or some other number)?

- Which is one less (more) than this bar?

- How much more is _____ than _____ ? (Follow this
question immediately by reversing the order and asking
how much less.)

- How much less is _____ than _____ ? (Reverse this
question after receiving an answer.)

- How much difference is there between
_____ and _____ ?

- Which two bars together are the same as _____ ?

FIGURE 9.16 Relationships and number sense in a bar graph.

dren's world. Create problems related to the story. Have children write a similar story. Extend the numbers and see what happens. Create a mural, graphs, or posters. The

ideas are as plentiful as the books. Here are a few ideas for making literature connections to number concepts and number sense.

Anno's Counting House
Anno, 1982

In the beautiful style of Anno, this book shows ten children in various parts of a house. As the pages are turned, the house front covers the children, and a few are visible through cutout windows. A second house is on the opposite page. As you move through the book, the children move one at a time to the second house, creating the potential for a 10–0, 9–1, 8–2, . . . , 0–10 pattern of pairs. But as each page shows part of the children through the window, there is an opportunity to discuss how many in the missing part. Have children use counters to model the story as you "read" it the second or third time.

What if the children moved in pairs instead of one at a time? What if there were three houses? What if there were more children? What else could be in the house to count? How many rooms, pictures, windows? What about your house? What about two classrooms or two buses instead of houses?

The Very Hungry Caterpillar
Carle, 1969

This is a predictable-progression counting book about a caterpillar who eats first one thing, then two, and so on. Children can create their own eating stories and illustrate them. What if more than one type of thing were eaten at each stop? What combinations for each number are there? Are seven little things more or less than three very large things? What does all of this stuff weigh? How many things are eaten altogether?

Two Ways to Count to Ten
Dee, 1988

This Liberian folktale is about King Leopard in search of the best animal to marry his daughter. The task devised involves throwing a spear and counting to 10 before the spear lands. Many animals try and fail. Counting by ones proves too lengthy. Finally, the antelope succeeds by counting "2, 4, 6, 8, 10."

The story is a perfect lead-in to skip counting. Can you count to 10 by threes? How else can you count to 10? How many ways can you count to 48? What numbers can you reach if you count by fives? The size of the numbers you investigate is limited only by the children. A hundreds board or counters are useful thinker toys to help with these problems. Be sure to have children write about what they discover in their investigations.

Another fun book to use is *The King's Commissioners* (Friedman, 1994), a hilarious tale that also opens up opportunities to count by different groupings or skip counting. ∎

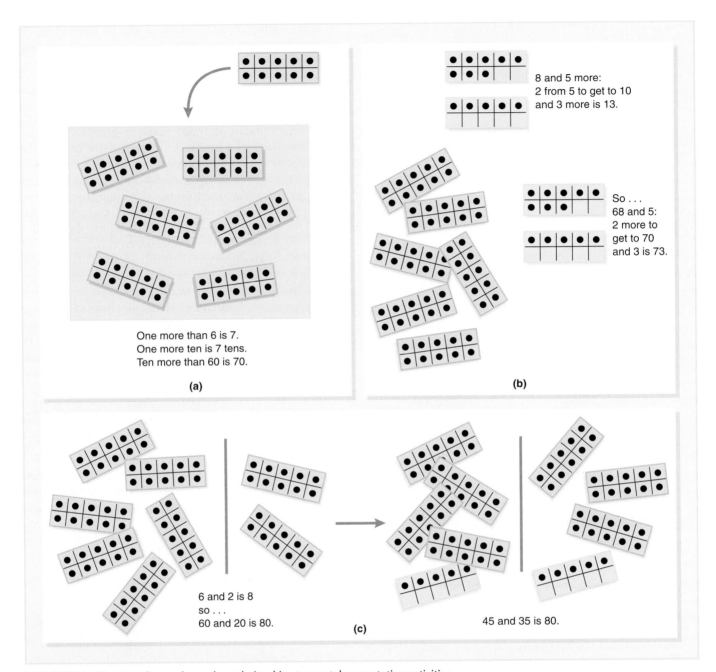

One more than 6 is 7.
One more ten is 7 tens.
Ten more than 60 is 70.

(a)

8 and 5 more:
2 from 5 to get to 10
and 3 more is 13.

So . . .
68 and 5:
2 more to
get to 70
and 3 is 73.

(b)

6 and 2 is 8
so . . .
60 and 20 is 80.

45 and 35 is 80.

(c)

FIGURE 9.17 Extending early number relationships to mental computation activities.

Extensions to Early Mental Mathematics

Teachers in the second and third grades can capitalize on some of the early number relationships and extend them to numbers up to 100. A useful set of materials to help with these relationships is the little ten-frames found in the Blackline Masters. Each child should have a set of 10 tens and a set of frames for each number 1 to 9 with an extra 5.

The following three ideas are illustrated with the little ten-frames in Figure 9.17. First are the relationships of one more than and one less than. If you understand that one more than 6 is 7, then in a similar manner, ten more than 60 is 70 (that is, one more ten). The second idea is really a look ahead to fact strategies. If a child has learned to think about adding on to 8 or 9 by first adding up to 10 and then adding the rest, the extension to similar two-digit numbers is quite simple; see Figure 9.17(b). Finally, the most powerful idea for small numbers is thinking of them in parts. It is a very useful idea (though not one found in textbooks) to take apart larger numbers to begin to develop some flexibility in the same way. Children can begin by thinking of ways to take apart a multiple of 10 such as 80. Once they do it with tens, the challenge can be to think of ways to take apart 80 when one part has a 5 in it, such as 25 or 35.

More will be said about early mental computation in Chapter 13. The point to be made here is that early num- ber relationships have a greater impact on what children know than may be apparent at first. Even teachers in the upper grades may profitably consider the use of ten-frames and part-part-whole activities.

Reflections on Chapter 9

Writing to Learn

1. Describe an activity that deals with a basic concept of number that does not require an understanding of counting. Explain the purpose of this activity.
2. What things must a child be able to do in order to count a set accurately?
3. When does a child have the *cardinality principle*? How can you tell if this principle has been acquired?
4. Describe an activity that is a "set-to-numeral match" activity. What ideas must a child have to do these activities meaningfully and correctly?
5. How can "Real Counting On" (Activity 9.7, p. 124) be used as an assessment to determine if children understand counting on or are still in a transitional stage?
6. What are the four types of relationships that have been described for small numbers? Explain briefly what each of these means and suggest at least one activity for each.
7. Describe a missing-part activity. What should happen if the child trying to give the missing part does not know it?
8. How can a teacher assess each of the four number relationships? Give special attention to part-whole ideas.
9. How can a calculator be used to develop early counting ideas connected with number? How can a calculator be used to help a child practice number relationships such as part-part-whole or one less than?
10. For numbers between 10 and 20, describe how to develop each of these ideas:
    a. The idea of the teens as a set of ten and some more
    b. Extension of the one-more/one-less concept to the teens
11. Describe briefly your own idea of what number sense is.
12. What are three ways that children can be helped to connect numbers to real-world ideas?
13. Give two examples of how early number relationships can be used to develop some early mental computation skills.

For Discussion and Exploration

1. Examine a textbook series for grades K–2. Compare the treatment of counting and number concept development with that presented in this chapter. What ideas are stressed? What ideas are missed altogether? If you were teaching in one of these grades, how would you plan your number concept development program? What part would the text play?
2. Many teachers in grades 3 and above find that their children do not possess the number relationships discussed in this chapter but rely heavily on counting. Given the pressures of other content at these grades, how much effort should be made to remediate these number concept deficiencies?

Recommendations for Further Reading

Burton, G. (1993). *Number sense and operations: Addenda series, grades K–6.* Reston, VA: National Council of Teachers of Mathematics.
   Either this book or the *Number Sense and Operations* addenda series book for your grade level should be a must for developing number concepts. The activities are developed in sufficient detail to give you clear guidance and yet allow considerable flexibility.
Fosnot, C. T., & Dolk, M. (2001). *Young mathematicians at work: Constructing number sense, addition, and subtraction.* Portsmouth, NH: Heinemann.
   One of three books in a series by these authors, they describe clearly the development of number concepts. Dolk represents the view of the Freudenthal Institute in the Netherlands and Fosnot is a respected mathematician and theoretician in the United States. This book demonstrates a sensitivity for children and a detailed perspective on children's number development.
Fuson, K. C., Grandau, L., & Sugiyama, P. A. (2001). Achievable numerical understandings for all young children. *Teaching Children Mathematics, 7,* 522–526.
   Researchers who have long worked with the number development of young children provide the reader with a concise overview of number development from ages 3 to 7. This practical reporting of their research is quite useful.
Griffin, S. (2003). Laying the foundation for computational fluency in early childhood. *Teaching Children Mathematics, 9,* 306–309.
   This short article lays out clearly five stages of number development based on a simple addition story problem task. This is followed by activities to develop number at each stage. A useful article, especially for diagnosis and remediation of early number development.
Richardson, K. (2002). *Assessing math concepts: The hiding assessment.* Rowley, MA: Didax.
   One of a series of nine assessment books covering number topics from counting through two-digit numbers. The assessments are designed for one-on-one interviews. Extensive

explanations and levels with examples are provided. The hiding assessment is a missing-part task. Richardson is a leading expert on early number development and assessment. The other books in the series are recommended although there is overlap in the front portions.

Online Resources

Suggested Applets and Web Links

Count Us In
www.abc.net.au/countusin/default.htm
  A site full of downloadable activities and games for early number development.

Let's Count to Twenty
http://illuminations.nctm.org/index_o.aspx?id=153
  A series of seven lessons designed to develop students' number understanding up to 20. Blackline Masters are included. One of several early number lessons on the *Investigations* Web site.

Math Tools: Math 1, Number Sense
http://mathforum.org/mathtools/cell/m1,3.2,ALL,ALL
  On this one page of the Math Tools Web site you will find activities and lessons appropriate for first-grade number sense. Explore other options on the site as well.

Ten Frame (NCTM illuminations Tools)
http://illuminations.nctm.org/tools/tool_detail.aspx?id=75
  A nice manipulative version of the ten-frame (applet). Probably best used by the teacher because the text is quite small. Students use counters and enter a number that answers a question. There is also a five-frame applet.

An additional list of books and articles related to the ideas in this chapter can be found on the Companion Web site at **www.ablongman.com/vandewalle6e.**

Companion Website

chapter 10

Developing Meanings for the Operations

This chapter is about helping children connect different meanings, interpretations, and relationships to the four operations of addition, subtraction, multiplication, and division so that they can effectively use these operations in real-world settings.

The main thrust of this chapter is helping children develop what might be termed *operation sense*, a highly integrated understanding of the four operations and the many different but related meanings these operations take on in real contexts.

As you read this chapter, pay special attention to the impact on number development, basic fact mastery, and computation. As children develop their understanding of operations, they can and should simultaneously be developing additional ideas about number and ways to think about basic fact combinations. Story problems for operations meaning are also a method of developing computational skills.

▼ Big Ideas

1. Addition and subtraction are connected. Addition names the whole in terms of the parts, and subtraction names a missing part.

2. Multiplication involves counting groups of like size and determining how many are in all (multiplicative thinking).

3. Multiplication and division are related. Division names a missing factor in terms of the known factor and the product.

4. Models can be used to solve contextual problems for all operations and to figure out what operation is involved in a problem regardless of the size of the numbers. Models also can be used to give meaning to number sentences.

Mathematics Content Connections

The ideas in this chapter are most directly linked to concepts of numeration and the development of invented computation strategies.

- **Number Development** (Chapter 9): As children learn to think about number in terms of parts and missing parts, they should be relating these ideas to addition and subtraction. Multiplication and division require students to think about numbers as units: In 3 × 6 each of the three sixes is counted as a unit. In some sense, operations can be seen as simply a way to record ideas about numbers using symbols.

- **Basic Facts** (Chapter 11): A good understanding of the operations can firmly connect addition and subtraction so that subtraction facts are a natural consequence of having learned addition. For example, 12 − 5 is 7 since 5 + 7 is 12. A firm connection between multiplication and division provides a similar benefit.

- **Whole-Number Place Value and Computation** (Chapters 12 and 13): Students can work with and develop ideas about the base-ten number system as they solve story problems involving larger numbers. Although computational strategies have been traditionally taught separately from the meanings of the operations, it is reasonable to have children invent strategies for computing with two-digit numbers as they build their understanding of the operations.

- **Algebraic Thinking** (Chapter 15): Representing contextual situations in equations is at the heart of algebraic thinking. This is exactly what students are doing as they learn to write equations to go with their solutions to story problems.

- **Fraction and Decimal Computation** (Chapters 17 and 18): These topics for the upper elementary and middle grades depend on a firm understanding of the operations.

Addition and Subtraction Problem Structures

A significant method of developing meaning for the operations is to have children solve contextual problems or story problems.

Researchers have separated addition and subtraction problems into categories based on the kinds of relationships involved. These include *join* problems, *separate* problems, *part-part-whole* problems, and *compare* problems (Carpenter, Carey, & Kouba, 1990; Carpenter, Fennema, Franke, Levi, & Empson, 1999; Gutstein & Romberg, 1995). The basic structure for each of these four types of problems is illustrated in Figure 10.1. Each structure involves a number "family" such as 3, 5, 8. A different problem results depending on which of the three quantities in the structure is unknown.

Examples of Problems for Each Structure

The number family 4, 8, 12 is used in each of the story problems that follow and can be connected to the structure in Figure 10.1. These drawings are not intended for children but to help you as a teacher consider the different structures. Also note that the problems are described in terms of their structure and not as addition or subtraction problems. Contrary to what you may have thought, a joining action does not always mean addition, nor does separate or remove always mean subtraction.

Join Problems

For the action of joining, there are three quantities involved: an initial or starting amount, a change amount (the part being added or joined), and the resulting amount (the total amount after the action is over). Any one of these three quantities can be unknown in a problem as shown here.

JOIN: RESULT UNKNOWN

Sandra had 8 pennies. George gave her 4 more. How many pennies does Sandra have altogether?

JOIN: CHANGE UNKNOWN

Sandra had 8 pennies. George gave her some more. Now Sandra has 12 pennies. How many did George give her?

JOIN: INITIAL UNKNOWN

Sandra had some pennies. George gave her 4 more. Now Sandra has 12 pennies. How many pennies did Sandra have to begin with?

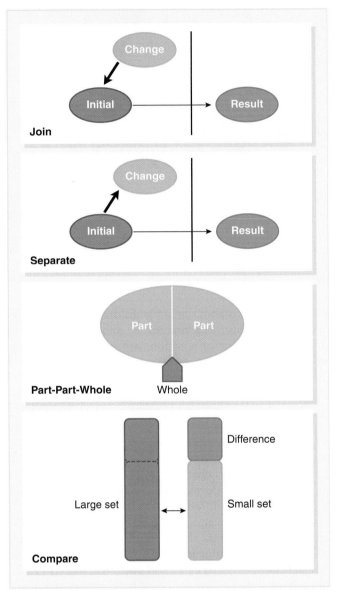

FIGURE 10.1 Four basic structures for addition and subtraction story problems. Each structure has three numbers. Any one of the three numbers can be the unknown in a story problem.

Separate Problems

Notice that in the separate problems, the initial amount is the whole or the largest amount, whereas in the join problems, the result was the whole. Again, refer to Figure 10.1 as you consider these problems. Be sure you can identify the two given quantities and the unknown amount with the initial, change, and result amounts.

SEPARATE: RESULT UNKNOWN

Sandra had 12 pennies. She gave 4 pennies to George. How many pennies does Sandra have now?

SEPARATE: CHANGE UNKNOWN

Sandra had 12 pennies. She gave some to George. Now she has 8 pennies. How many did she give to George?

SEPARATE: INITIAL UNKNOWN

Sandra had some pennies. She gave 4 to George. Now Sandra has 8 pennies left. How many pennies did Sandra have to begin with?

Part-Part-Whole Problems

Part-part-whole problems involve two parts that are combined into one whole. The combining may be a physical action, or it may be a mental combination where the parts are not physically combined.

There is no meaningful distinction between the two parts in a part-part-whole situation, so there is no need to have a different problem for each part as the unknown. For each possibility (whole unknown and part unknown), two problems are given here. The first is a mental combination where there is no action. The second problem involves a physical action.

PART-PART-WHOLE: WHOLE UNKNOWN

George has 4 pennies and 8 nickels. How many coins does he have?

George has 4 pennies and Sandra has 8 pennies. They put their pennies into a piggy bank. How many pennies did they put into the bank?

PART-PART-WHOLE: PART UNKNOWN

George has 12 coins. Eight of his coins are pennies, and the rest are nickels. How many nickels does George have?

George and Sandra put 12 pennies into the piggy bank. George put in 4 pennies. How many pennies did Sandra put in?

Compare Problems

Compare problems involve the comparison of two quantities. The third amount does not actually exist but is the difference between the two amounts. There are three types of compare problems, corresponding to which quantity is unknown (smaller, larger, or difference). For each of these, two examples are given: one problem where the difference is stated in terms of more and another in terms of less.

COMPARE: DIFFERENCE UNKNOWN

George has 12 pennies and Sandra has 8 pennies. How many more pennies does George have than Sandra?

George has 12 pennies. Sandra has 8 pennies. How many fewer pennies does Sandra have than George?

COMPARE: LARGER UNKNOWN

George has 4 more pennies than Sandra. Sandra has 8 pennies. How many pennies does George have?

Sandra has 4 fewer pennies than George. Sandra has 8 pennies. How many pennies does George have?

COMPARE: SMALLER UNKNOWN

George has 4 more pennies than Sandra. George has 12 pennies. How many pennies does Sandra have?

Sandra has 4 fewer pennies than George. George has 12 pennies. How many pennies does Sandra have?

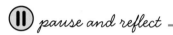 *pause and reflect*

Go back through all of these problems and match the numbers in the problems with the components of the structures in Figure 10.1. For each problem, do two additional things. First, use a set of counters to model (solve) the problem as you think children in the primary grades might do. Second, for each problem, write either an addition or subtraction equation that you think best represents the problem as you did it with counters.

Reflections on the Four Structures

In most curricula, the overwhelming emphasis is on the easier join and separate problems with the result unknown. These become the de facto definitions of addition and subtraction: Addition is "put together" and subtraction is "take away." The fact is, these are *not* the definitions of addition and subtraction.

When students develop these limited put-together and take-away definitions for addition and subtraction, they often have difficulty later when addition or subtraction is called for but the structure is other than put together or take away. It is important that children be exposed to all forms within these structures.

Computational and Semantic Forms of Equations

If you wrote an equation for each of the problems as just suggested, you may have some equations where the unknown quantity is not isolated on one side of the equal sign. For example, a likely equation for the join problem with initial part unknown is $\square + 4 = 12$. This is referred to as the *semantic* equation for the problem since the numbers are listed in the order that follows the meaning of the

Quantity Unknown	Join Problems	Separate Problems
Result	8 + 4 = [ ]	12 − 4 = [ ]
Change	8 + [ ] = 12	12 − [ ] = 8
Initial	[ ] + 4 = 12	[ ] − 4 = 8

FIGURE 10.2 The *semantic* equation for each of the six join and separate problems on pages 144–145. Notice that for results-unknown problems the semantic form is also the computational form. The computational form for the other four problems is an equivalent equation that isolates the unknown quantity.

problem. Figure 10.2 shows the semantic equation for the six join and separate problems. Note that the two result-unknown problems place the unknown alone on one side of the equal sign. An equation that isolates the unknown in this way is referred to as the *computational* form of the equation. When the semantic form is not also the computational form, an equivalent equation can be written. For example, the equation $\square + 4 = 12$ can be written equivalently as $12 - 4 = \square$. The computational form is the one you would need to use if you were to solve these equations with a calculator. As numbers increase in size and children are not solving equations with counters, they must eventually learn to see the equivalence between different forms of the equations.

Problem Difficulty

The various types of problems are not at all equal in difficulty for children. The change problems in which the initial part is unknown are among the most difficult, probably because children modeling the problems directly do not know how many counters to put down to begin with. Problems in which the change amounts are unknown are also difficult.

Many children will solve compare problems as part-part-whole problems without making separate sets of counters for the two amounts. The whole is used as the large amount, one part for the small amount and the second part for the difference. Which method did *you* use? There is absolutely no reason this should be discouraged as long as children are clear about what they are doing.

Teaching Addition and Subtraction

So far you have seen a variety of types of story problems for addition and subtraction and you probably have used some counters to help you understand how these problems can

be solved by children. These two methods, contextual problems and models (counters, drawings, number lines), are the main teaching tools that you have to help students construct a rich understanding of these two operations. Let's examine how each approach can be used in the classroom.

Using Contextual Problems

There is more to think about than simply giving students problems to solve.

Context or Story Problems

In contrast with the rather sterile story problems in the previous section, consider the following problem.

Yesterday we were measuring how tall we were. You remember that we used the connecting cubes to make a big train that was as long as we were when we were lying down. Dion and Rosa were wondering how many cubes long they would be if they lay down head to foot. Dion had measured Rosa and she was 84 cubes long. Rosa measured Dion and she was 102 cubes long. Let's see if we can figure out how long they will be end to end, and then we can check by actually measuring them.

Fosnot and Dolk (2001) point out that in story problems, children tend to focus on getting the answer, probably in the way that the teacher wants. "Context problems, on the other hand, are connected as closely as possible to children's lives, rather than to 'school mathematics.' They are designed to anticipate and to develop children's mathematical modeling of the real world" (p. 24). Contextual problems might derive from recent experiences in the classroom, a field trip, a discussion you have been having in art or social studies, or from children's literature.

Lessons Built on Context or Story Problems

The tendency in the United States is to have students solve a lot of problems in a single class period. The focus of these lessons seems to be on how to get answers. In Japan, however, a complete lesson will often revolve around one or two problems and the related discussion (Reys & Reys, 1995).

What might a good lesson look like for second grade that is built around word problems? The answer comes more naturally if you think about students not just solving the problems but also using words, pictures, and numbers to explain how they went about solving the problem and why they think they are correct. Children should be allowed to use whatever physical materials they feel they need to help them, or they can simply draw pictures. Whatever they put on their paper should explain what they did well enough to allow someone else to understand it (allow at least a half page of space for a problem).

Choosing Numbers for Problems

Even kindergarten children should be expected to solve story problems. Their methods of solution will typically involve using counters in a very direct modeling of the problems. This is what makes the join and separate problems with the initial parts unknown so difficult. For these problems, children initially use a trial-and-error approach (Carpenter, Fennema, Franke, Levi, & Empson, 1999).

Although the structure of the problems will cause the difficulty to vary, the numbers in the problems should be in accord with the number development of the children. Kindergarten children can use numbers as large as they can count meaningfully, which is usually to about 10 or 12.

Second-grade children are also learning about two-digit numbers and are beginning to understand how our base-ten system works. Rather than wait until students have learned about place value and have developed techniques for computing numbers, word problems are a problem-based opportunity to learn about number and computation at the same time. For example, a problem involving the combination of 30 and 42 has the potential to help students focus on the sets of ten. As they begin to think of 42 as 40 and 2, it is not at all unreasonable to think that they will add 30 and 40 and then add 2 more. As you learn more about invented strategies for computation in Chapter 13, you will develop a better understanding of how to select numbers to aid in computational development.

NCTM Standards The *Standards* authors make clear the value of connecting addition and subtraction. "Teachers should ensure that students repeatedly encounter situations in which the same numbers appear in different contexts. For example, the numbers 3, 4, and 7 may appear in problem-solving situations that could be represented by 4 + 3, 3 + 4, or 7 − 3, or 7 − 4. . . . Recognizing the inverse relationship between addition and subtraction can allow students to be flexible in using strategies to solve problems" (p. 83).

Introducing Symbolism

Very young children have no need for the symbols +, −, and =. However, these symbolic conventions are important. When you feel your students are ready to use these symbols, introduce them in the discussion portion of a lesson where students have solved story problems. Say, "You had the whole number of 12 in your problem and the number 8 was one of the parts of 12. You found out that the part you did not know was 4. Here is a way we can write that: 12 − 8 = 4." The minus sign should be read as

"minus" or "subtract" but not as "take away." The plus sign is easier since it is typically a substitute for "and."

Some care should be taken with the equal sign. The equal sign means "is the same as." However, most children come to think of it as a symbol that tells you that the "answer is coming up." It is interpreted in much the same way as the on a calculator. That is, it is the key you press to get the answer. An equation such as 4 + 8 = 3 + 9 has no "answer" and is still true because both sides stand for the same quantity. A good idea is to often use the phrase "is the same as" in place of or in conjunction with "equals" as you read equations with students.

Assessment Notes Watching how children solve story problems will give you a lot of information about children's understanding of number as well as the more obvious information about problem solving and their understanding of addition and subtraction. The CGI project (Carpenter et al., 1999) has found that children progress in their problem-solving strategies from kindergarten to grade 2. These strategies are a reflection of students' understanding of number and of their emerging mastery of basic fact strategies. For example, early on, students will use counters and count each addend and the entire set for a join-result-unknown problem. Later, they will count on from the first set. This strategy will be modified to count on from the larger set; that is, for 4 + 7 the child will begin with 7 and count on, even though 4 is the initial set in the problem. Eventually, students will begin to use facts retrieved from memory and rely on counters or other models only when necessary. Watching how students solve problems provides cues to help you decide what numbers to use in problems and how to challenge children to continue to build their number concepts and problem-solving skills. ■

Using Model-Based Problems

Many children will use counters or number lines (models) to solve story problems. The model is a thinking tool to help them both understand what is happening in the problem and a means of keeping track of the numbers and solving the problem. Problems can also be posed using models when there is no context involved. The part-part-whole concept as discussed in Chapter 9 is a good way to help students think about addition and subtraction when they are focused on models.

Addition

When the parts of a set are known, addition is used to name the whole in terms of the parts. This simple, albeit sterile, definition of addition serves both action situations (join and separate) and static or no-action situations.

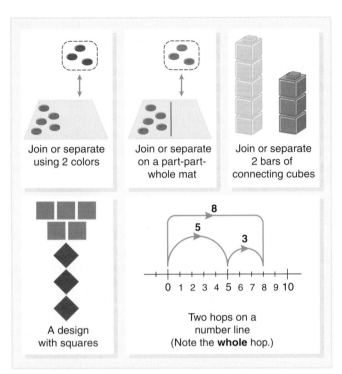

Join or separate using 2 colors

Join or separate on a part-part-whole mat

Join or separate 2 bars of connecting cubes

A design with squares

Two hops on a number line (Note the **whole** hop.)

FIGURE 10.3 Part-part-whole models for 5 + 3 = 8 and 8 – 3 = 5.

Each of the part-part-whole models shown in Figure 10.3 is a model for 5 + 3 = 8. Some of these are the result of a definite put-together or joining action, and some are not. Notice that in every example, both of the parts are distinct, even after the parts are joined. If counters are used, the two parts should be kept in separate piles or in separate sections of a mat or should be two distinct colors. For children to see a relationship between the two parts and the whole, the image of the 5 and 3 must be kept as two separate sets. This helps children reflect on the action after it has taken place. "These red chips are the ones I started with. Then I added these five blue ones, and now I have eight altogether."

A number line presents some real conceptual difficulties for first and second graders. Its use as a model at that level is generally not recommended. A number line measures distances from zero the same way a ruler does. In the early grades, children focus on the dots or numerals on a number line instead of the spaces. However, if arrows (hops) are drawn for each number in an exercise, the length concept is more clearly illustrated. To model the part-part-whole concept of 5 + 3, start by drawing an arrow from 0 to 5, indicating, "This much is five." Do not point to the dot for 5, saying "This is five."

activity **10.1**

Equations with Number Patterns
Recall Activity 9.17 (p. 130) called "Build It in Parts" and its variations, in which children made designs

or built sets for a specific number. When children seem ready to deal with written symbolism, simply show them how to write a plus or addition number sentence (equation) for each design. In those initial activities, children said a combination, such as "Four and five is nine." Now they have a new symbolic way to match what they say.

Two children can work together, do something with a model, say the combination, and together write the equation. The children can vary the total amounts they construct each time—within appropriate limits, of course. Remember that what makes "Equations with Number Patterns" problem based is the challenge to find different combinations for a number.

Subtraction

In a part-part-whole model, when the whole and one of the parts are known, subtraction names the other part. This definition is in agreement with the drastically overused language of "take away." If you start with a whole set of 8 and remove a set of 3, the two sets that you know are the sets of 8 and 3. The expression 8 – 3, read "eight minus three," names the five remaining. Therefore, eight minus three is five. Notice that the models in Figure 10.3 are models for subtraction as well as addition (except for the action). Helping children see that they are using the same models or pictures aids in connecting the two operations.

activity **10.2**

Missing-Part Subtraction
A fixed number of counters is placed on a mat. One child separates the counters into two parts while the other child hides his or her eyes. The first child covers one of the two parts with a sheet of tagboard, revealing only the other part (see Figure 10.4). The second child says the subtraction sentence. For example, "Nine minus four [the visible part] is five [the covered part]." The covered part can be revealed if necessary for the child to say how many are there. Both the subtraction equation and the addition equation can then be written.

Subtraction as Think-Addition

Note that in Activity 10.2, the situation ends with two parts clearly distinct, even when there is a remove action. The removed part remains in the activity or on the mat as a model for an addition equation to be written after writing the subtraction equation. A discussion of how these two equations can be written for the same model situation

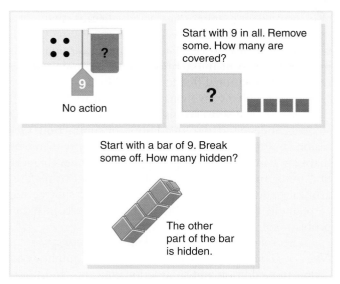

FIGURE 10.4 Models for 9 − 4 as a missing-part problem.

is an important opportunity to connect addition and subtraction. This is significantly better than the traditional worksheet activity of "fact families" in which children are given a family of numbers such as 3, 5, and 8 and are told to write two plus equations and two minus equations. Very quickly this becomes a matter of dropping the numbers in the various slots.

Subtraction as "think-addition" rather than "take-away" is extremely significant for mastering subtraction facts. Because the counters for the remaining or unknown part are left hidden under the cover, when children do these activities, they are encouraged to think about the hidden part: "What goes with the part I see to make the whole?" For example, if the total or whole number of counters is 9, and 6 are removed from under the cover, the child is likely to think in terms of "6 and what makes 9?" or "What goes with 6 to make 9?" The mental activity is "think-addition" instead of a "count what's left" approach. Later, when working on subtraction facts, a subtraction fact such as 9 − 6 = ☐ should trigger the same thought pattern: "6 and what makes 9?"

Comparison Models

Comparison situations involve two distinct sets or quantities and the difference between them. Several ways of modeling the difference relationship are shown in Figure 10.5. The same kind of model can be used whether the difference or one of the two quantities is unknown.

Note that it is not immediately clear how you would associate either the addition or subtraction operations with a comparison situation. From an adult vantage point, you can see that if you match part of the larger amount with the smaller amount, the large set is now a part-part-whole model that can solve the problem. In fact, many children

do model compare problems in just this manner. But that is a very difficult idea to show children if they do not construct the idea themselves.

Have children make two amounts, perhaps with two bars of connecting cubes. Discuss the difference between the two bars to generate the third number. For example, if the children make a bar of 10 and a bar of 6, the difference is 4. "What equations can we make with these three numbers?" Have children make up story problems that involve two amounts of 10 and 6. Discuss which equations go with the problems that are created.

The Order Property and the Zero Property

The *order* property (or *commutative* property) for addition says that it makes no difference in which order two numbers are added. Although the order property may seem obvious to us (simply reverse the two piles of counters on the part-part-whole mat), it may not be as obvious to children as you may think. Since it is quite useful in problem solving, mastering basic facts, and mental mathematics, there is value in spending some time helping children construct the relationship. The name of the property is not important, but the idea is. Schifter (2001) describes a class of early second-grade students who discovered the "turn-around" property while examining sums to ten. Later, the teacher wondered if they really understood this idea and asked the children if they thought it would always work. Many in the class were unsure if it worked all of the time and were especially unsure about it working with large

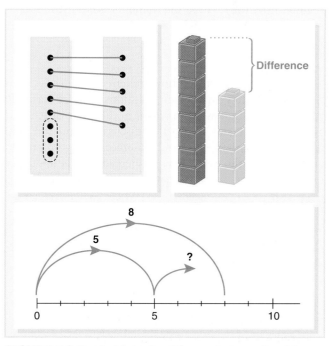

FIGURE 10.5 Models for the difference between 8 and 5.

numbers. The point is that children may see and accept the order property for sums they've experienced but not be able to explain or even believe that this simple yet important property works for all addition combinations.

To help children focus on the order property, pair problems that have the same addends but in different orders. The context for each problem should be different. For example:

Tania is on page 32 in her book. Tomorrow she hopes to read 15 more pages. What page will she be on if she reads that many pages?

The milk tray in the cafeteria was down to only 15 cartons. Before lunch, the delivery person brought in some more milk. She filled up the tray with 32 more cartons. How many cartons does the milk tray hold?

Ask if anyone notices how these problems are alike. If done as a pair, some (not all) students will see that having solved one they have essentially solved the other.

The following activity is also important and helps with the same idea.

activity **10.3**

More Than Two Addends

Give students six sums to find involving three or four addends. Prepare these on one page divided into six sections so that there is space to write beneath each sum. Within each, include at least one pair with a sum of ten or perhaps a double: 4 + 7 + 6, 5 + 9 + 9, or 3 + 4 + 3 + 7. Students should show how they added the numbers. Allow students to find the sums without any other directions.

Figure 10.6 illustrates how students might show what they did. As they share their solutions, almost certainly there will be students who added in different orders but got the same result. From this discussion you can help them conclude that you can add numbers in any order. You are also using the associative property but it is the order or commutative property that is more important. This is

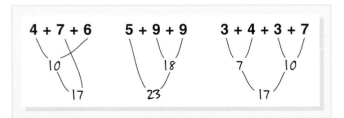

FIGURE 10.6 Students show how they added.

also an excellent number sense activity because many students will find combinations of ten in these sums or will use doubles (easy facts for many students). Learning to adjust strategies to fit the numbers is the beginning of the road to computational fluency.

Story problems involving zero and or using zeros in the three-addend sums are also a good method of helping students understand zero in addition or subtraction. Occasionally students feel that 6 + 0 must be more than 6 or that 12 − 0 must be 11 since "plus makes numbers bigger" or "minus makes numbers smaller." Instead of making arbitrary-sounding rules about adding and subtracting zero, build opportunities for discussing zero into the problem-solving routine.

The second-grade curriculum of *Investigations in Number, Data, and Space* places a significant emphasis on connecting addition and subtraction concepts. In the excerpt shown here, you can see an activity involving word problems for addition and subtraction and a discussion of this portion of the curriculum. Take special note of the envelope technique used. This allows for all students to solve as many problems as their pace and time permit without having to face blank, incomplete work. The technique mixes the problems so that it will be possible to discuss all of the problems as a class.

The *Fizz & Martina* series (Tom Snyder Productions, 1998) embed problems in "real-life" adventures of Fizz and Martina. The stories require students to pay attention and take notes. A story is stopped when the problem is posed, and students work in groups without the video or computer. Printed support material is included. This model fits nicely with the *before*, *during*, and *after* format of a problem-solving lesson.

At present, few programs offer addition and subtraction word problems with the variety of problem types we have just explored. However, there are two other ways that you can take advantage of your classroom computers using almost any basic tool software you happen to have. First, you can provide problems yourself using your word processor or any program that allows shapes to be easily drawn and words to be typed. An example of the latter type is *Kid Pix* (Riverdeep Interactive Learning, 2005). Open a new file and write a word problem in an appropriate space. Students open the file and use the drawing capabilities to record their solution. The students' work is either not saved or renamed so that your file remains as an activity.

A first-grade teacher notes that her children were much better at writing story problems on the computer than they were by hand, and she often had students write problems for pictures she created. Make a file with a drawing involving counters in two parts or with a whole specified and one part showing. Students write and solve a story problem on the computer to go with the drawing. ■

▲ Investigations
in Number, Data, and Space

Grade 2, Coins, Coupons, and Combinations
Investigation 3: Making Sense of Addition and Subtraction

Context

The *Coins, Coupons, and Combinations* unit occurs early in the second grade. It is one of two units in which the work on addition and subtraction is undertaken. In the first portion of the unit, the focus is on developing strategies for addition combinations (the ideas you will encounter in Chapter 11 of this book). Children are not only working with small addition "facts" but also are solving two-digit addition problems with invented strategies before they begin to work on story problems.

Task Description

As you can see from the problems shown here, *Investigations* has students explore addition and subtraction problems together. In the discussions surrounding these problems there is a definite effort to use the story problems to connect the concepts of addition and subtraction.

The problems on the page shown are duplicated and cut apart. Problems are put in six envelopes, one problem per envelope. Students may select any envelope, take a problem, and paste it on their paper. In this manner, page format in no way suggests what is to be done or how much space is required for showing work. When one problem is complete, they can select another problem, and paste it on the page. Most students will complete from two to three problems on a sheet. The envelope technique is a useful way to attend to individual differences and pacing issues.

Students are to use whatever methods and materials they wish to solve the problems but are required to "show their solution so that someone else can understand it" (p. 104). In fact, for this lesson, children must show their solution to another student to check that what they wrote can be understood by someone else.

In this unit, all of the problems are *result unknown* (join and separate) or *part-whole* problems. In a later unit, *change unknown* problems are included.

1. Kira and Jake were eating peanuts. There were 39 peanuts in the bag. Kira ate 18 of them and Jake ate the rest. How many peanuts did Jake eat?

2. Kira and Jake were making snowballs. They both made 19 snowballs. How many did they make in all?

3. There were 47 students in the gym. One class of 23 students went back to their room. How many students were left in the gym?

4. The second grade class went on a trip to the zoo. There were 32 students and 12 adults on the trip. How many people went on the zoo trip?

5. Marcel and Shawn were counting pennies. Marcel had 33 pennies and Shawn had 36 pennies. How many pennies did they have in all?

6. Lin has 50 pennies in a cup. She spent 29 pennies at the store on a pencil. How much money does Lin have left?

7. Make up a problem to go with 30 – 13. Write about how you solved the problem. Use words, numbers, or pictures to show your thinking.

Page 163 from *The Number System: Coins, Coupons, and Combinations* by K. Economopoulos & S. J. Russell. *Investigations in Number, Data, and Space.* Copyright © 1998 by Dale Seymour Publications. Reprinted by permission of Pearson Education, Inc.

In a full-class session following this activity, students are given two story problems involving children getting on and off a bus. The first is a separate problem for 29 – 13 and the second is a part-whole problem for 16 + 13. After sharing how they would do these problems, students are asked if they see anything about the problems that is alike or how solving one might help them solve the other. They are also asked what equations they would write for each problem. This is a good example of how to focus on connecting the concepts of addition and subtraction.

Problem Structures for Multiplication and Division

Like addition and subtraction, there are problem structures that will help you as the teacher in formulating and assigning multiplication and division tasks. As with the additive structures, these are for you, not for students.

Most researchers identify four different classes of multiplicative structures (Greer, 1992). Of these, the two described in Figure 10.7, *equal groups* (*repeated addition*, *rates*) and *multiplicative comparison*, are by far the most prevalent in the elementary school. Problems matching these structures can be modeled with sets of counters, number lines, or arrays. They represent a large percentage of the multiplicative problems in the real world. (The term *multiplicative* is used here to describe all problems that involve multiplication and division structure.)

Examples of Problems for Each Structure

In multiplicative problems one number or *factor* counts how many sets, groups, or parts of equal size are involved. The other factor tells the size of each set or part. These two factors have traditionally been referred to as the *multiplier* (number of parts) and the *multiplicand* (size of each

part). These terms are not particularly useful to children and will not be used here unless needed for clarity. The third number in each of these two structures is the *whole* or *product* and is the total of all of the parts. The parts and wholes terminology is useful in making the connection to addition.

Equal-Group Problems

When the number and size of groups are known, the problem is a multiplication situation. When either the number of sets or the size of sets is unknown, division results. But note that these latter two situations are not alike. Problems in which the size of the sets is unknown are called *fair-sharing* or *partition* problems. The whole is shared or distributed among a known number of sets to determine the size of each. If the number of sets is unknown but the size of the equal sets is known, the problems are called *measurement* or sometimes *repeated-subtraction* problems. The whole is "measured off" in sets of the given size. These terms are used with the examples to follow. Keep in mind the structure in Figure 10.7 to see which numbers are given and which is unknown.

There is also a subtle difference between problems that might be termed *repeated-addition* problems (If three children have four apples each, how many apples are there?) and those that might be termed *rate* problems (If there are four apples per child, how many apples would three children have?). For each category, two examples of rate problems are provided.

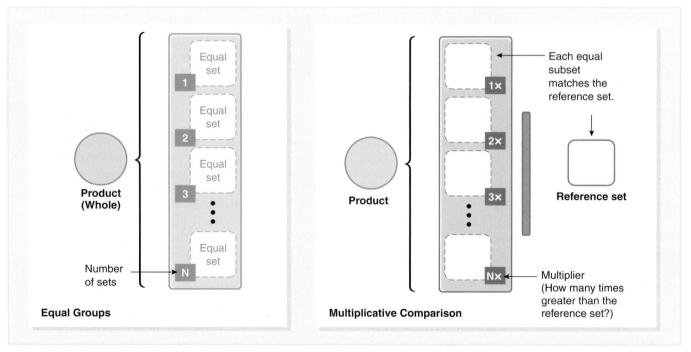

FIGURE 10.7 Two of the four basic structures for multiplication and division story problems. Each structure has three numbers. Any one of the three numbers can be the unknown in a story problem.

EQUAL GROUPS: WHOLE UNKNOWN (MULTIPLICATION)

Mark has 4 bags of apples. There are 6 apples in each bag. How many apples does Mark have altogether?

If apples cost 7 cents each, how much did Jill have to pay for 5 apples? (*rate*)

Peter walked for 3 hours at 4 miles per hour. How far did he walk? (*rate*)

EQUAL GROUPS: SIZE OF GROUPS UNKNOWN (PARTITION DIVISION)

Mark has 24 apples. He wants to share them equally among his 4 friends. How many apples will each friend receive?

Jill paid 35 cents for 5 apples. What was the cost of 1 apple? (*rate*)

Peter walked 12 miles in 3 hours. How many miles per hour (how fast) did he walk? (*rate*)

EQUAL GROUPS: NUMBER OF GROUPS UNKNOWN (MEASUREMENT DIVISION)

Mark has 24 apples. He put them into bags containing 6 apples each. How many bags did Mark use?

Jill bought apples at 7 cents apiece. The total cost of her apples was 35 cents. How many apples did Jill buy? (*rate*)

Peter walked 12 miles at a rate of 4 miles per hour. How many hours did it take Peter to walk the 12 miles? (*rate*)

Multiplicative Comparison Problems

In multiplicative comparison problems, there are really two different sets, as there were with comparison situations for addition and subtraction. One set consists of multiple copies of the other. Two examples of each possibility are provided here. In the former, the comparison is an amount or quantity difference. In multiplicative situations, the comparison is based on one set's being a particular multiple of the other.

COMPARISON: PRODUCT UNKNOWN (MULTIPLICATION)

Jill picked 6 apples. Mark picked 4 times as many apples as Jill. How many apples did Mark pick?

This month Mark saved 5 times as much money as last month. Last month he saved $7. How much money did Mark save this month?

COMPARISON: SET SIZE UNKNOWN (PARTITION DIVISION)

Mark picked 24 apples. He picked 4 times as many apples as Jill. How many apples did Jill pick?

This month Mark saved 5 times as much money as he did last month. If he saved $35 this month, how much did he save last month?

COMPARISON: MULTIPLIER UNKNOWN (MEASUREMENT DIVISION)

Mark picked 24 apples, and Jill picked only 6. How many times as many apples did Mark pick as Jill did?

This month Mark saved $35. Last month he saved $7. How many times as much money did he save this month as last?

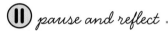 *pause and reflect*

What you just read is a lot to take in without reflection. Stop now and get a collection of counters—at least 35. Use the counters to solve each of the problems. Look first at the equal-group problems and do the "Mark problems" or the first problem in each set. Match the numbers with the structure model in Figure 10.7. How are these problems alike and how are they different, especially the two division problems? Repeat the exercise with the "Jill problems" and then the "Peter problems." Can you see how the problems in each group are alike and how the problems across groups are related?

When you are comfortable with the equal-group problems, repeat the same process with the multiplicative comparison problems. Again, start with the first problem in all three sets and then the second problem in all three sets. Reflect on the same questions posed earlier.

Reflections on the Multiplicative Structures

There is evidence that kindergarten and first-grade children are quite successful at solving multiplication and division problems, even division involving remainders (Carpenter, Ansell, Franke, Fennema, & Weisbeck, 1993; Carpenter, Carey, & Kouba, 1990; Carpenter et al., 1999). Mulligan and Mitchelmore (1997), based on their own research and that of others, make a strong argument that students should be exposed to all four operations from the first year of school and that multiplication and division should be much more closely linked in the curriculum.

Teaching Multiplication and Division

Multiplication and division are taught separately in most traditional programs, with multiplication preceding division. It is important, however, to combine multiplication and division soon after multiplication has been introduced in order to help students see how they are related. In most curricula, these topics are a main focus of the third grade with continued development in the fourth and fifth grades.

One of the major conceptual hurdles of working with multiplicative structures is that of understanding groups of things as single entities while also understanding that a group contains a given number of objects (Clark & Kamii, 1996; Kouba, 1989; Steffe, 1988). Children can solve the problem *How many apples in 4 baskets of 8 apples each?* by counting out four sets of eight counters and then counting all. To think multiplicatively about this problem as four *sets of eight* requires children to conceptualize each group of eight as a single item to be counted. Experiences with making and counting groups, especially in contextual situations, are extremely useful. (See the discussion of the book *Each Orange Had 8 Slices* at the end of this chapter.)

Using Contextual Problems

Many of the issues surrounding addition and subtraction also apply to multiplication and need not be discussed in depth again. It remains important to use contextual problems whenever reasonable instead of more sterile story problems. Just as with additive structures, it is a good idea to build lessons around only two or three problems. Students should solve problems using whatever techniques they wish. What is important is that they explain—preferably in writing—what they did and why it makes sense. Words, pictures, and numbers remain important.

Symbolism for Multiplication and Division

When students solve simple multiplication story problems before learning about multiplication symbolism, they will most likely write repeated-addition equations to represent what they did as an equation. This is your opportunity to introduce the multiplication sign and explain what the two factors mean.

The usual convention is that 4×8 refers to four sets of eight, not eight sets of four. There is absolutely no reason to be rigid about this convention. The important thing is that the students can tell you what each factor in *their* equations represents. In vertical form, it is usually the bottom factor that indicates the number of sets. Again, this distinction is not terribly important.

The quotient 24 divided by 6 is represented in three different ways: $24 \div 6$, $6\overline{)24}$, and $\frac{24}{6}$. The fraction notation becomes important at the middle school level. The computational form $6\overline{)24}$ would probably not exist if it were

not for the standard pencil-and-paper procedure that utilizes it. Children have a tendency to read this as "6 divided by 24" due to the left-right order of the numerals. Generally this error does not match what they are thinking.

Compounding the difficulty of division notation is the unfortunate phrase, "six goes into twenty-four." This phrase carries little meaning about division, especially in connection with a fair-sharing or partitioning context. The "goes into" (or "guzinta") terminology is simply engrained in adult parlance and has not been in textbooks for years. If you tend to use that phrase, it is probably a good time to consciously abandon it.

Choosing Numbers for Problems

When selecting numbers for multiplicative story problems or activities, there is a tendency to think that large numbers pose a burden to students or that 3×4 is somehow easier to understand than 4×17. An understanding of products or quotients is not affected by the size of numbers as long as the numbers are within the grasp of the students. Little is gained by restricting early explorations of multiplication to small numbers. Even in early third grade, students can work with larger numbers using whatever counting strategies they have at their disposal. A contextual problem involving 14×8 is not at all too large for third graders even before they have learned a computation technique. When given these challenges, children are likely to invent computational strategies.

Remainders

More often than not, division does not result in a simple whole number. For example, problems with 6 as a divisor will "come out even" only one time out of six. In the absence of a context, a remainder can be dealt with in only two ways: It can either remain a quantity left over or be partitioned into fractions. In Figure 10.8, the problem $11 \div 4$ is modeled to show fractions.

In real contexts, remainders sometimes have three additional effects on answers:

> The remainder is discarded, leaving a smaller whole-number answer.
> The remainder can "force" the answer to the next highest whole number.
> The answer is rounded to the nearest whole number for an approximate result.

The following problems illustrate all five possibilities.

You have 30 pieces of candy to share fairly with 7 children. How many pieces of candy will each child receive?
Answer: 4 pieces of candy and 2 left over. (left over)

Each jar holds 8 ounces of liquid. If there are 46 ounces in the pitcher, how many jars will that be?
Answer: 5 and $\frac{6}{8}$ jars. (partitioned as a fraction)

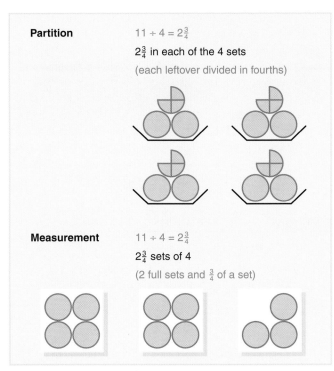

FIGURE 10.8 Remainders expressed as fractions.

The rope is 25 feet long. How many 7-foot jump ropes can be made?
  Answer: 3 jump ropes. (*discarded*)

The ferry can hold 8 cars. How many trips will it have to make to carry 25 cars across the river?
  Answer: 4 trips. (*forced to next whole number*)

Six children are planning to share a bag of 50 pieces of bubble gum. About how many pieces will each child get?
  Answer: About 8 pieces for each child. (*rounded, approximate result*)

Students should not just think of remainders as "R 3" or "left over." Remainders should be put in context and dealt with accordingly.

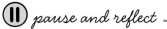 *pause and reflect* _____
It is useful for you to make up problems in different contexts. Include continuous quantities such as length, time, and volume. See if you can come up with problems in each division category for equal-group and comparison problems that would have remainders dealt with as fractions or as rounded-up or rounded-down results.

 It is important to provide story problems for both multiplication and division in the same lesson so that you can be certain children are interpreting the meaning of the problems and not simply taking the two numbers and using today's operation.

When modeling multiplicative problems or using their own strategies for solving them, children will not always use an approach that matches the problem. For example, if solving a problem involving 12 sets of 4, many children will add 4 twelves rather than 12 fours. Rather than be concerned about this, view it as an indication that students likely accept or understand that 12×4 and 4×12 give the same result. However, when students solve a problem such as this in different ways, it is a great opportunity for profitable discussion. ■

Using Models-Based Problems

In the beginning, children will be able to use the same models—sets and number lines—for all four operations. A model not generally used for addition but extremely important and widely used for multiplication and division is the array. An *array* is any arrangement of things in rows and columns, such as a rectangle of square tiles or blocks.

To make clear the connection to addition, early multiplication activities should also include writing an addition sentence for the same model. A variety of models are shown in Figure 10.9. Notice that the products are not included—only addition and multiplication "names" are written. This is another way to avoid the tedious counting of large sets. A similar approach is to write one sentence that expresses both concepts at once, for example, $9 + 9 + 9 + 9 = 4 \times 9$.

Multiplication and Division Activities

As with additive problems, children can benefit from a few activities with models and no context. The purpose of such activities is to focus on the meaning of the operation and the associated symbolism. Activity 10.4 has a good problem-solving spirit. The language you use depends on what you have used with your children in the past.

activity **10.4**

Finding Factors
Start by assigning a number that has several factors—for example, 12, 18, 24, 30, or 36. Have students find multiplication expressions for their assigned number. With counters, students attempt to find a way to separate the counters into equal subsets. With arrays (perhaps made from square tiles or cubes or drawn on grid paper), students try to build rectangles that have the given number of squares. For each such arrangement of sets or appropriate rectangles, both an addition and a multiplication equation should be written.

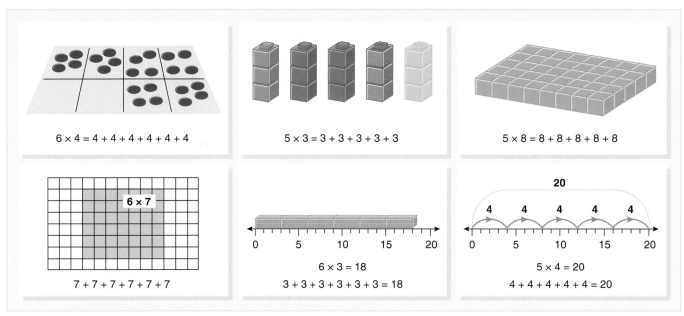

FIGURE 10.9 Models for equal-group multiplication.

Activity 10.4 can also include division concepts. When children have learned that 3 and 6 are factors of 18, they can write the equations $18 \div 3 = 6$ and $18 \div 6 = 3$ along with $3 \times 6 = 18$ and $6 + 6 + 6 = 18$ (assuming that three sets of six were modeled). The following variation of the same activity focuses on division. Having children create word problems is another excellent elaboration of this activity. Require children to explain how their story problems fit with what they did with the counters.

activity 10.5

Learning About Division

Provide children with an ample supply of counters and some way to place them into small groups. Small paper cups work well. Have children count out a number of counters to be the whole or total set. They record this number: "Start with 31." Next specify either the number of equal sets to be made or the size of the sets to be made: "Separate your counters into four equal-sized sets," or "Make as many sets of four as is possible." Next have the children write the corresponding multiplication equation for what their materials show; under that, have them write the division equation.

Be sure to include both types of exercises: number of equal sets and size of sets. Discuss with the class how these two are different, yet each is related to multiplication and each is written as a division equation. You can show both

ways to write division equations at this time. Do Activity 10.5 several times. Start with whole quantities that are multiples of the divisor (no remainders) but soon include situations with remainders. (Note that it is technically incorrect to write $31 \div 4 = 7$ R 3. However, in the beginning, that form may be the most appropriate to use.)

The activity can be varied by changing the model. Have children build arrays using square tiles or blocks or by having them draw arrays on centimeter grid paper. Present the exercises by specifying how many squares are to be in the array. You can then specify the number of rows that should be made (partition) or the length of each row (measurement). How could children model fractional answers using drawings of arrays on grid paper?

Tech Notes

The applet "Rectangle Division" on the NLVM Web site (http://nlvm.usu.edu/en/nav/vlibrary. html) is an excellent interactive illustration of division with remainders. A division problem is presented with an array showing the number of squares in the product. The dimensions of the array can be modified but the number of squares stays constant. If, for example, the task is to show the problem $52 \div 8$, the squares can be adjusted to show an 8 by 6 array with 4 extra squares in a different color $(8 \times 6 + 4)$ as well as any other variation of 52 squares in a rectangle plus a shorter column for the remainder. Division is very vividly related to multiplication with this applet. ∎

activity 10.6

The Broken Multiplication Key

The calculator is a good way to relate multiplication to addition. Students can be told to find various products on the calculator without using the $\boxed{\times}$ key. For example, 6 × 4 can be found by pressing $\boxed{+}$ 4 $\boxed{=}$ $\boxed{=}$ $\boxed{=}$ $\boxed{=}$ $\boxed{=}$ $\boxed{=}$. (Successive presses of $\boxed{=}$ add 4 to the display each time. You began with zero and added 4 six times.) Students can be challenged to demonstrate their result with sets of counters. But note that this same technique can be used to determine products such as 23 × 459 ($\boxed{+}$ 459 and then 23 presses of $\boxed{=}$). Students will want to compare to the same product using the $\boxed{\times}$ key.

"The Broken Multiplication Key" can profitably be followed by "The Broken Division Key."

activity 10.7

The Broken Division Key

Have children work in groups to find methods of using the calculator to solve division exercises without using the divide key. The problems can be posed without a story context. "Find at least two ways to figure out 61 ÷ 14 without pressing the divide key." If the problem is put in a story context, one method may actually match the problem better than another. Good discussions may follow different solutions with the same answers. Are they both correct? Why or why not?

ⅠⅠ *pause and reflect* ————————

There is no reason ever to show children how to do Activity 10.7. However, it would be a good idea for *you* to see if you can find *three* ways to solve 61 ÷ 14 on a calculator without using the divide key. For a hint, see the footnote.*

NCTM Standards "In grades 3–5, students should focus on the meanings of, and relationship between, multiplication and division. It is important that students understand what each number in a multiplication or division expression represents. . . . Modeling multiplication problems with pictures, diagrams, or concrete materials helps students learn what the factors and their product represent in various contexts" (p. 151).

---

*There are two measurement approaches or two ways to find out how many 14s are in 61. A third way is essentially related to partitioning or finding 14 times what number is close to 61.

Useful Multiplication and Division Properties

As with addition and subtraction, there are some multiplicative properties that are useful and, thus, worthy of attention. The emphasis should be on the ideas and not terminology or definitions.

The Order Property in Multiplication

It is not intuitively obvious that 3 × 8 is the same as 8 × 3 or that, in general, the order of the numbers makes no difference (the *order* or *commutative* property). A picture of 3 sets of 8 objects cannot immediately be seen as 8 piles of 3 objects. Eight hops of 3 land at 24, but it is not clear that 3 hops of 8 will land at the same point.

The array, by contrast, is quite powerful in illustrating the order property, as is shown in Figure 10.10. Children should draw or build arrays and use them to demonstrate why each array represents two different multiplications with the same product.

The Role of Zero and One in Multiplication

Zero and, to a lesser extent, 1 as factors often cause difficulty for children. In one recent third-grade text (Charles et al., 1998), a lesson on factors of 0 and 1 has children use a calculator to examine a wide range of products involving 0 or 1 (423 × 0, 0 × 28, 1536 × 1, etc.) and look for patterns. The pattern suggests the rules for factors of 0 and 1 but not a reason. In the same lesson, a word problem asks how many grams of fat there are in 7 servings of celery with 0 grams of fat in each serving. This approach is far

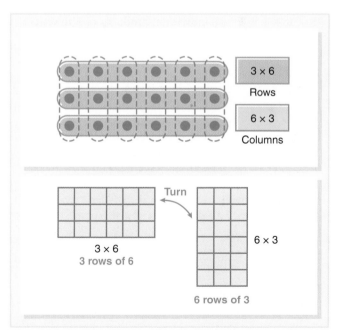

FIGURE 10.10 Two ways an array can be used to illustrate the order (commutative) property for multiplication.

preferable to an arbitrary rule, since it asks students to reason. Make up interesting word problems involving 0 or 1, and discuss the results. Problems with 0 as a first factor are really strange. Note that on a number line, 5 hops of 0 land at 0 (5 × 0). What would 0 hops of 5 be? Another fun activity is to try to model 6 × 0 or 0 × 8 with an array. (Try it!) Arrays for factors of 1 are also worth investigating.

The Distributive Property

The *distributive property* refers to the idea that one of two factors in a product can be split into two or more parts and each part multiplied separately and then added. The result is the same as when the original factors are multiplied. For example, 6 × 9 is the same as (6 × 5) + (6 × 4). The 9 has been split into 5 and 4. The concept involved is very useful in relating one basic fact to another, and it is also involved in the development of two-digit computation. Figure 10.11 illustrates how the array model can be used to illustrate that a product can be broken up into two parts.

The next activity is designed to help children discover how to partition factors or, in other words, learn about the distributive property.

activity 10.8

Slice It Up

Supply students with several sheets of centimeter grid paper. Assign each pair of students a product such as 6 × 8. (Products can vary across the class or all be the same.) The task is to find all of the different ways to make a single slice through the rectangle. For each slice students write an equation. For a slice of one row of 8, students would write 6 × 8 = 5 × 8 + 1 × 8. The individual products can be written in the arrays as was done in Figure 10.11.

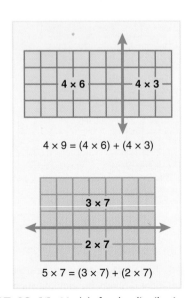

FIGURE 10.11 Models for the distributive property.

Why Not Division by Zero?

Some children are simply told "Division by zero is not allowed." To avoid an arbitrary rule, pose problems to be modeled that involve zero: "Take thirty counters. How many sets of zero can be made?" or "Put twelve blocks in zero equal groups. How many in each group?"

The *Fizz & Martina* series (Tom Snyder Productions, 1998) was mentioned earlier as a vehicle for embedding story problems into real contexts. For the upper grades, the problems are both one- and two-step and involve a wider range of mathematical concepts than has been discussed here. Many teachers like the idea of a video format for its ease of use.

Figure This! is a wonderful collection of explorations that is available for free on the NCTM Web site (www.NCTM.org). The 80 challenges are designed for middle grades students. Although not simple story problems, many involve an understanding of the operations. Each problem has interesting follow-up questions and all are designed to engage students in real-world applications of mathematics. A CD version is available. ■

Strategies for Solving Contextual Problems

So far our focus has been on either additive or multiplicative problems. The purpose has been to help students learn about these operations and in the process to begin to develop some informal computational strategies.

In the upper grades (although not exclusively so) students see context or story problems and are at a loss for what to do. In this section you will learn some techniques for helping them.

Analyzing Context Problems

Consider the following problem:

In building the road through the subdivision, a low section in the land was filled in with dirt that was hauled in by trucks. The complete fill required 638 truckloads of dirt. The average truck carried $6\frac{1}{4}$ cubic yards of dirt, which weighed 17.3 tons. How many tons of dirt were used in the fill?

Typically, in fifth- to eighth-grade books, problems of this type are found as part of a series of problems revolving around a single context or theme. Data may be found in a graph or chart or perhaps a short news item or story. Most likely the problems will include all four of the operations. Students have difficulty deciding on the correct operation and even finding the appropriate data for the problem. Many students will find two numbers in the problem and guess at the correct operation. These children simply do not have any tools for analyzing problems. At least two strategies can be taught that are very helpful: Think about the answer before solving the problem, or solve a simpler problem that is just like this one.

Think About the Answer Before Solving the Problem

Poor problem solvers fail to spend adequate time thinking about the problem and what it is about. They rush in and begin doing calculations, believing that "number crunching" is what solves problems. That is simply not the case. Rather, students should spend time talking about (later, thinking about) what the answer might look like. For our sample problem, it might go as follows:

> *What is happening in this problem?* Some trucks were bringing dirt in to fill up a hole.
>
> *What will the answer tell us?* How many tons of dirt were needed in the fill.
>
> *Will that be a small number of tons or a large number of tons?* Well, there were 17.3 tons on a truck, but there were a lot of trucks, not just one. It's probably going to be a whole lot of tons.
>
> *About how many do you think it will be?* It's going to be really big. If there were just 100 trucks, it would be 1730 tons. It might be close to 10,000 tons. That's a lot of tons!

In this type of discussion, three things are happening. First, the students are asked to focus on the problem and the meaning of the answer instead of on numbers. The numbers are not important in thinking about the structure of the problem. Second, with a focus on the structure of the problem, students can identify the numbers that are important or data that they must look up in a table or graph as well as numbers that are not important to the problem. Third, the thinking leads to a rough estimate of the answer. Sometimes, for everyday things, this can simply be based on common sense. In any event, thinking about what the answer tells and about how large it might be is a useful first step.

Work a Simpler Problem

The reason that models are rarely used with problems such as the dirt problem is that the numbers are impossible to model easily. Dollars and cents, distances in thousands of miles, and time in minutes and seconds are all examples of data likely to be found in the upper grades, and all are difficult to model. The general problem-solving strategy of "try a simpler problem" can almost always be applied to problems with unwieldy numbers.

A simple strategy has the following steps:

1. Substitute small whole numbers for all relevant numbers in the problem.

2. Model the problem using the new numbers (counters, drawing, number line, array).
3. Write an equation that solves the small-number version of the problem.
4. Write the corresponding equation with the original numbers used where the small-number substitutes were.
5. Use a calculator to do the computation.
6. Write the answer in a complete sentence, and decide if it makes sense.

Figure 10.12 shows what might be done for the dirt problem. It also shows an alternative in which only one of the numbers is made smaller and the other number is illustrated symbolically. Both methods are effective.

The idea is to provide a tool students can use to analyze a problem and not just guess at what computation to do. It is much more useful to have students do a few

FIGURE 10.12 Working a simpler problem: two possibilities.

problems where they must use a model of a drawing to justify their solution than to give them a lot of problems where they guess at a solution but don't know if their guess is correct.

Caution: Avoid the Key Word Strategy!

It is often suggested that students should be taught to find "key words" in story problems. Some teachers even post lists of key words with their corresponding meanings. For example, "altogether" and "in all" mean you should add and "left" and "fewer" indicate you should subtract. The word "each" suggests multiplication. To some extent, teachers have been reinforced by the overly simple and formulaic story problems often found in textbooks. When problems are written in this way, it may appear that the key word strategy is effective.

In contrast with this belief, researchers and mathematics educators have long cautioned against the strategy of key words (e.g., Burns, 2000; Carpenter, 1985; Goldin, 1985; Kliman & Russell, 1998). Here are three arguments against the key word approach.

1. Key words are misleading. Often the key word or phrase in a problem suggests an operation that is incorrect. For example:

Maxine took the 28 stickers she no longer wanted and gave them to Zandra. Now Maxine has 73 stickers *left*. How many stickers did Maxine have to begin with?

If you look through the story problems in this chapter, you will find other examples of misleading key words.

2. Many problems have no key words. Especially when you get away from the overly simple problems found in primary textbooks, you will find that a large percentage of problems have no key words. A child who has been taught to rely on key words is left with no strategy. In both the additive and the multiplicative problems in this chapter, you will find numerous examples of problems with no key words. And this is from a collection of overly simple problems designed to help you with structure.

3. The key word strategy sends a terribly wrong message about doing mathematics. The most important approach to solving any contextual problem is to analyze its structure—to make sense of it. The key word approach encourages students to ignore the meaning and structure of the problem and look for an easy way out. Mathematics is about reasoning and making sense of situations. A sense-making strategy will *always* work.

Two-Step Problems

Students often have difficulty with multistep problems. If your students are going to work with multistep problems, be sure they can analyze one-step problems in the way that we have discussed. The following ideas, adapted from suggestions by Huinker (1994), are designed to help children see how two problems can be chained together.

1. Give students a one-step problem and have them solve it. Before discussing the answer, have each student or group make up a second problem that uses the answer to the first problem. The rest of the class can then be asked to use the answer to the first problem to solve the second problem. Here is an example:

Given problem: It took $3\frac{1}{3}$ hours for the Joneses to drive the 195 miles to Washington. What was their average speed?

Second problem: The Jones children remember crossing the river at about 10:30, or 2 hours after they left home. About how far from home is the river?

---

2. Make a "hidden question." Repeat the first exercise by beginning with a one-step problem. You might give different problems to different groups. This time have students write out both problems as before. Then write a single related problem that leaves out the question from the first problem. That question from the first problem is the "hidden question." Here is a simple example:

Given problem: Tony bought three dozen eggs for 89 cents a dozen. How much was the bill?

Second problem: How much change did Tony get back from $5?

Hidden-question problem: Tony bought three dozen eggs for 89 cents a dozen. How much change did Tony get back from $5?

Have other students identify the hidden question. Since all students are working on a similar task but with different problems (be sure to mix the operations), they will be more likely to understand what is meant by a hidden question.

3. Pose standard two-step problems, and have the students identify and answer the hidden question. Consider the following problem:

> Willard Sales decides to add widgets to its line of sale items. To begin with, Willard bought 275 widgets wholesale for $3.69 each. In the first month, the company sold 205 widgets at $4.99 each. How much did Willard make or lose on the widgets? Do you think Willard Sales should continue to sell widgets?

Begin by considering the questions that were suggested earlier: "What's happening in this problem?" (Something is being bought and sold at two different prices.) "What will the answer tell us?" (How much profit or loss there was.) These questions will get you started. If students are stuck, you can ask, "Is there a hidden question in this problem?"

NCTM Standards The value of student discussions to help develop meaning throughout mathematics including understanding the operations is quite evident in the *Standards.* At the K–2 level: "When students struggle to communicate ideas clearly, they develop a better understanding of their own thinking" (p. 129). At the 3–5 level: "The use of models and pictures provides a further opportunity for understanding and conversation. Having a concrete referent helps students develop understandings that are clearer and more easily shared" (p. 197).

Two Additional Concepts of Multiplication

Two types of multiplicative concepts exist in addition to the equal-groups and multiplicative comparisons that we have discussed in this chapter: *combinations* or *Cartesian products* and *product-of-measures* problems (e.g., length times width equals area). These concepts are rarely mentioned within the multiplication and division sections of most curricula.

Combinations Problems

Combinations problems involve counting the number of possible pairings that can be made between two sets. The product consists of pairs of things, one member of each pair taken from each of the two given sets.

COMBINATIONS: PRODUCT UNKNOWN

Sam bought 4 pairs of pants and 3 jackets, and they all can be worn together. How many different outfits consisting of a pair of pants and a jacket does Sam have?

> An experiment involves tossing a coin and rolling a die. How many different possible results or outcomes can this experiment have?

In these two examples, the product is unknown and the size of the two sets is given. It is possible to have related division problems for the combinations concept. However, such problems are rarely encountered.

Figure 10.13 shows two common methods of modeling combination problems: an array and a tree diagram. Counting how many combinations of two or more things or events are possible is important in determining probabilities. For example, to determine the probability of a head and either a 1 or a 6, one needs to know that there are 12 possible outcomes for the head and die experiment. The combinations concept is most often found in the probability strand.

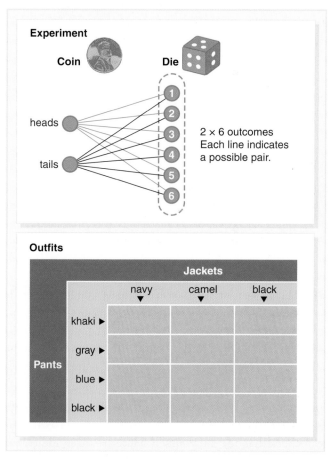

FIGURE 10.13 Models for combinations situations.

Product-of-Measures Problems

What distinguishes product-of-measures problems from the others is that the product is literally a different type of thing from the other two factors. In a rectangle, the product of two lengths (length × width) is an area, usually square units. Figure 10.14 illustrates how different the square units are from each of the two factors of length: 4 feet times 7 feet is not 28 feet but 28 *square* feet. The factors are each one-dimensional entities, but the product consists of *two*-dimensional things.

Two other fairly common examples in this category are number of workers × hours worked = worker-hours and kilowatts × hours = kilowatt-hours.

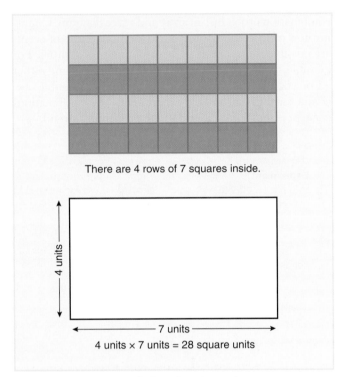

There are 4 rows of 7 squares inside.

4 units

7 units

4 units × 7 units = 28 square units

FIGURE 10.14 Length times length equals area.

Literature Connections

Finding an exciting and fun way to use literature to develop or expand understanding of the operations is extremely easy. There are lots of books with stories or pictures concerning sets of things, buying things, measures, and so on, that can be used to pose problems or, better, to stimulate children to invent their own problems. Perhaps the most widely mentioned book in this context is *The Doorbell Rang* by Pat Hutchins (1986). You can check that one out yourself. Here are three additional suggestions.

How Many Snails?
Giganti, 1988

Appropriate for the K–2 set, this book includes a variety of pictures where the objects belonging to one collection have various subcollections (parts and wholes). For example, a sky full of clouds has various types of clouds. The text asks,

"How many clouds are there? How many clouds are big and fluffy? How many clouds are big and fluffy and gray?" These pages lead directly to addition and subtraction situations matching the part-part-whole concepts. Of special note is the opportunity to have missing-part thinking for subtraction. Children can think of collections that they would like to draw so that subcollections have a variety of attributes. They can then pose their own questions about the drawing and add appropriate number sentences. In discussion, children could explain why they selected the particular equation and how it fits the picture.

More Than One
Hoban, 1981

The wonderful black-and-white photos of Tana Hoban are designed to introduce group words such as a *crowd* of people, a *herd* of elephants, or a *bundle* of wood. A discussion of group words (animal groups fit nicely with science—*flock, pride, covey,* etc.) beyond those that are in the book can be interesting in and of itself. Do different groups typically contain different numbers of things? Is it likely that there would be two elephants in a herd? Could there be 50? What is typical? These grouping words provide a real opportunity for children to develop *group* as a single entity but with separate things inside. Now suppose that there are many groups (herds, flocks, crowds). If we know the size of one, and we know how many herds, do we know how many elephants in all? Imagine a situation where that was always the case—all groups with group names have the same number of things. If there are 87 pieces of wood in 3 bundles, how many in a bundle? Clever one- and two-step multiplication and division stories can be generated.

Each Orange Had 8 Slices
Giganti, 1992

Each two-page spread shows objects grouped in three ways. For example, one spread has four trees, three bird's nests in each tree, and two eggs in each nest. The author asks three questions: "How many trees? How many nests? How many eggs?" The three questions with each picture extend multiplication to a three-factor product. In the case of the trees, nests, and eggs, the product is 4 × 3 × 2. After children get a handle on the predictable arrangement of the book's pictures, they can not only write multiplication stories that go with the pictures but also make up situations of their own. What similar situations can be found in the classroom? Perhaps desks, books, and pages or bookshelves, shelves, and books. There is no need to restrict the discussion to three nestings of objects. The same idea is present in measurements: yards, feet, inches or gallons, quarts, pints, cups, ounces. New problems can be posed that require division. What if there were some boxes with six cartons in each? Each carton has four widgets. If there are 72 widgets, how many boxes are there? ■

Reflections on Chapter 10

Writing to Learn

1. Make up a context for some story problems and make up six different join and separate problems: three with a join action and three with a separate action. For all six problems, use the same number family: 9, 4, 13.
2. Make up a comparison word problem. Next change the problem to provide an example of all six different possibilities for comparison problems.
3. Why might a contextual problem be more effective than a simple story problem?
4. What considerations would you take into account when selecting numbers for addition and subtraction problems? Grade level will make a difference.
5. How can you use models in a problem-based way for addition and for subtraction?
6. Explain how missing-part activities prepare students for mastering subtraction facts.
7. Make up multiplication word problems to illustrate the difference between equal groups and multiplicative comparison. Can you create problems involving rates or continuous quantities?
8. Make up two different word problems for $36 \div 9$. For one, the modeling should result in four sets of nine, and for the other, the modeling should result in nine sets of four. Which is which? Which of your problems is a measurement problem and which is a partition problem?
9. Explain the meaning of the first and second factors in $3 \times 8 = 24$. What is 24 called in this equation?
10. Describe multiplication and division activities that begin with models rather than with word problems.
11. How would you help students learn these properties of multiplication: order or commutative property, distributive property, and property of zero? How would you help students discover that division by zero is not well defined and so is not really possible?
12. Make up realistic measurement and partition division problems where the remainder is dealt with in each of these three ways: (a) it is discarded (but not left over); (b) it is made into a fraction; (c) it forces the answer to the next whole number.
13. Explain how to help students analyze problems when the numbers are not small whole numbers but rather are large or are fractions or decimals that do not lend themselves to using counters.
14. Why is the use of key words not a good strategy to teach children?
15. Describe the sequence of steps suggested for helping children deal with two-step problems.

For Discussion and Exploration

1. *Cognitively Guided Instruction* is not a curriculum program but a professional development program in which teachers learn to use students' thinking to guide instruction. The predominant thrust of CGI is the use of story problems, not only for learning the operations but also for number and fact development and even for computation development with larger numbers. Select either basic fact mastery or computation development and describe how you think these goals might be achieved primarily through story problems. If possible, view some of the video clips on the CD that comes with *Children's Mathematics: Cognitively Guided Instruction* (Carpenter et al., 1999) to compare your thoughts with theirs.
2. Examine a basal textbook at one or more grade levels. Identify how, and in what chapters, the meanings for the operations are developed. Discuss the relative focus on meanings of the operations with one-step story problems, use of models, mastery of basic facts, and where computation fits in.
3. See how many different types of story problems you can find in a basal textbook. In the primary grades, look for join, remove, part-part-whole, and compare problems. For grades 4 and up, look for the four multiplicative types. (Look in the multiplication and division chapters and also at special problem-solving lessons.) Are the various types of problems well represented?

Recommendations for Further Reading

Carpenter, T. P., Fennema, E., Franke, M. L., Levi, L., & Empson, S. (1999). *Children's mathematics: Cognitively guided instruction.* Portsmouth, NH: Heinemann. (Also published by NCTM)

For teachers, this is the best book available for understanding the CGI approach to operations and the use of story problems to develop number, basic facts, and computational procedures. The classifications of word problems for all operations, as discussed in this chapter, are explained in detail along with methods for using these problems with students. With the book come two CDs, one with classroom clips of CGI classrooms and the other showing children using the various strategies described in the book.

Fosnot, C. T., & Dolk, M. (2001). *Young mathematicians at work: Constructing number sense, addition, and subtraction.* Portsmouth, NH: Heinemann.

Fosnot, C. T., & Dolk, M. (2001). *Young mathematicians at work: Constructing multiplication and division.* Portsmouth, NH: Heinemann.

Either of these two small books will provide you with excellent ideas and insights for helping children construct number and operation sense. Catherine Fosnot, a leader in U.S. mathematics education and a proponent of constructivism, has teamed with Maarten Dolk from the Netherlands where student-centered methods have been used for many years.

Together they share ideas from their respective research. These books are written for teachers as practical guides by leading experts in the field. Each is filled with detailed examples and student work.

Kouba, V. L., & Franklin, K. (1993). Multiplication and division: Sense making and meaning. In R. J. Jensen (Ed.), *Research ideas for the classroom: Early childhood mathematics* (pp. 103–126). Old Tappan, NJ: Macmillan.

This chapter, which seeks to help teachers understand the intricacies of multiplicative concepts, is complete and readable, providing teachers at the 3–4 level with a good perspective without being too technical.

Schifter, D., Bastable, V., & Russell, S. J. (1999b). *Developing mathematical understanding: Numbers and operations, Part 2, Making meaning for operations (Casebook).* Parsippany, NJ: Dale Seymour Publications.

In this casebook, teachers in grades K–7 share their stories of working with children as they develop meanings for the four operations. The teachers discuss the kinds of actions and situations that students use as they come to understand the operations. This is a companion book to an extended in-service guide. There is also a video available to augment the series. However, the casebook is easily worthwhile by itself.

Online Resources

Suggested Applets and Web Links

The Factor Game

http://illuminations.nctm.org/tools/tool_detail.aspx?id=12

A challenging game in which players need to think of all of the factors of selected numbers.

Factorize

http://illuminations.nctm.org/tools/tool_detail.aspx?id=64

With this applet, the connection between factors and dimensions of a rectangle is made as students build rectangles to match a factorization of a number.

Rectangle Division

http://nlvm.usu.edu/en/nav/frames_asid_193_g_1_t_1.html

The challenge is to build a rectangle on a grid plus additional squares to match an equation of this form: $43 = 9 \times \underline{\quad} + \underline{\quad}$.

An additional list of books and articles related to the ideas in this chapter can be found on the Companion Web site at **www.ablongman.com/vandewalle6e.**

chapter 11

Helping Children Master the Basic Facts

Basic facts for addition and multiplication refer to combinations where both addends or both factors are less than 10. Subtraction and division facts correspond to addition and multiplication facts. Thus, 15 − 8 = 7 is a subtraction fact because both parts are less than 10.

Mastery of a basic fact means that a child can give a quick response (in about 3 seconds) without resorting to nonefficient means, such as counting. Work toward mastery of addition and subtraction facts typically begins in the first grade. Most books include all addition and subtraction facts for mastery in the second grade, although often additional work is required in grade 3 and even after. Multiplication and division facts are generally a target for mastery in the third grade. Typically, more work is required in grades 4 and 5. Unfortunately, many children in grade 8 and above do not have a complete command of the basic facts.

All children are able to master the basic facts—including children with learning disabilities. All children can construct efficient mental tools that will help them. This chapter is about helping children develop those tools.

▼| Big Ideas

1. Number relationships provide the foundation for strategies that help students remember basic facts. For example, knowing how numbers are related to 5 and 10 helps students master facts such as 3 + 5 (think of a ten-frame) and 8 + 6 (since 8 is 2 away from 10, take 2 from 6 to make 10 + 4 = 14).

2. "Think-addition" is the most powerful way to think of subtraction facts. Rather than 13 "take away 6," which requires counting backward while also keeping track of how many counts, students can think 6 and what makes 13. They might add up to 10 or they may think double 6 is 12 so it must be 13.

3. All of the facts are conceptually related. You can figure out new or unknown facts from those you already know. For example, 6 × 8 can be thought of as five 8s (40) and one more 8. It might also be three 8s doubled.

Mathematics Content Connections

As should be clear from the Big Ideas, basic fact mastery is not really new mathematics; rather, it is the development of fluency with ideas that have already been learned.

■ **Number and Operations** (Chapters 9 and 10): Fact mastery relies significantly on how well students have constructed relationships on numbers and how well they understand the operations.

Fluency with basic facts allows for ease of computation, especially mental computations, and, therefore, aids in the ability to reason numerically in every number-related area. Although calculators and tedious counting are available for students who do not have command of the facts, reliance on these methods for simple number combinations is a serious handicap to mathematical growth.

Approaches to Fact Mastery

In attempting to help children master their basic facts, three somewhat different approaches can be identified. The most overused method is an extensive program of drill. A second approach that can be traced at least as far back as the 1970s (Rathmell, 1978) suggests that we teach students a collection of strategies or thought patterns for various classes of basic facts. These strategies have been found to be efficient and teachable. The third approach is to spend most of our efforts on the concepts and number relationships on which these strategies depend. Armed with this background, students are then guided to develop strategies that are useful and meaningful to them although not all students will develop the same approaches.

Pros and Cons of Each Approach

Drill is easily the most popular approach used in schools. However, the very fact that many students in the fourth and fifth grades have not mastered addition and subtraction facts and students in middle school and beyond do not know their multiplication facts strongly suggests that this method simply does not work well. You may be tempted to respond that you learned your facts in this manner, as did many other students. Studies by Brownell and Chazal (1935) long ago concluded that children develop a variety of different thought processes for basic facts in spite of the amount of drill that they endure. They found that children invent and hold on to procedures that develop from their own number concepts and that drill does not help students develop any new or more efficient strategies. As we will see, drill can be used once a student has acquired an efficient strategy. Premature drill, however, will certainly be ineffective, waste valuable time, and for many students contribute to a strong distaste for and a faulty view of learning mathematics.

For approximately three decades, it has been popular to show students an efficient strategy that is applicable to a collection of facts. Students then practice the strategy as it was shown to them. There is strong evidence to indicate that such a method can be effective (e.g., Baroody, 1985; Bley & Thornton, 1995; Fuson, 1984, 1992; Rathmell, 1978; Thornton & Toohey, 1984). An all-too-quickly taught version of this approach is found in all traditional textbooks. Many of the ideas developed and tested by these researchers are found in this chapter. Although significantly more effective than drill, this approach is not without its limitations. When students attempt to apply a strategy that does not emanate from their own set of number relationships, they are essentially following rules rather than thinking about number relationships. For instance, a popular strategy for addition of facts that are almost doubles (e.g., 6 + 7) is to double the smaller number and add one. Many students will simply double the first number or the top number (vertical format) and add one so that their response for 7 + 6 might be 15 rather than 13. Furthermore, when students are not working on a specific strategy drill, they often forget to use a strategy and revert to inefficient counting methods. When strategies are imposed on students, they often develop these ideas in a rote manner rather than integrating a strategy with their own ideas.

The third option might be called "guided invention" (Gravemeijer & van Galen, 2003). In this preferred approach, fact mastery is intricately connected to students' collection of number relationships. Some students may think of 6 + 7 as "double 6 is 12 and one more is 13." In the same class, others may note that 7 is 3 away from 10 and so take 3 from the 6 to put with the 7 to make 10. They then add on the remaining 3. Still other students may take 5 from each addend to make 10 and then add the remaining 1 and 2. What is significant is that students are not necessarily aware of using a strategy but rather they are thinking about number combinations and relationships that they own and that make sense to them. This is quite different from following a rule, even if the rule is an efficient strategy. Because the strategies are not rules to apply but applications of their own ideas, they will be used whenever they are needed, not just in structured drills.

Gravemeijer and van Galen call this approach *guided invention* because many of the strategies that are efficient, especially those for multiplication, will not be developed by all students without some exposure to them. That is, we cannot simply place all of our efforts on number relationships and the meanings of the operations and assume that fact mastery will happen by magic. Class discussions based on student solutions to story problems and other number tasks and games will bring a variety of strategies into the classroom. Because they come from students and not the authority of the teacher, children can select and adapt the ideas that are meaningful to them. The teacher's task is to design tasks and problems that will promote the invention of effective strategies by students and to be sure that these strategies are clearly articulated and shared in the classroom. It is also important that teachers attend to the development of a rich collection of number relationships, as described in Chapter 9. The *Cognitively Guided Education* project (Carpenter et al., 1999) and the three elementary standards-based curricula are designed with this approach. All have shown the approach to be effective.

In order for you to guide your students to the invention of effective strategies, you yourself need to have a command of as many good strategies as possible, even if you have never used them. With this knowledge, you will be able to recognize effective strategies as your students develop them and help others capitalize on their ideas.

Guiding Strategy Development

You need to plan lessons in which specific strategies are likely to be developed. There are two basic types of lessons suggested for this purpose. The first and more important is to use simple story problems designed in such a manner that students are most likely to develop a strategy as they solve it. In the discussion of these solution methods, you can focus attention on the methods that are most useful.

Suppose that Aidan explains how she figured out 3×7 by starting with double 7 (14) and then adding 7 more. She knew that 6 more onto 14 is 20 and one more is 21. You can ask another student to explain what Aidan just shared. This requires students to attend to ideas that come from their classmates. Now explore with the class to see what other facts would work with Aidan's strategy. This discussion may go in a variety of directions. Some may notice that all of the facts with a 3 in them will work. Others may say that you can always add one more set on if you know the smaller fact. For example, for 6×8 you can start with 5×8 and add 8.

Don't expect to have a strategy introduced and understood with just one word problem or one exposure such as this. Try on several successive days problems in which the same type of strategy might be used. Children need lots of opportunities to make a strategy their own. Many children will simply not be ready to use an idea the first few days, and then all of a sudden something will click and a useful idea will be theirs.

It is a good idea to write new strategies on the board or make a poster of strategies students develop. Give the strategies names that make sense. (*Double and add one more set. Aidan's idea. Use with 3s.* Include an example.)

No student should be forced to adopt someone else's strategy, but every student should be required to understand strategies that are brought to the discussion.

The *Thinking with Numbers* program (Rathmell, Leutzinger, & Gabriele, 2000) uses just such an approach. It consists of a large collection of simple story problems developed in sets designed to promote particular strategies or ways of thinking about a particular collection of facts. Teachers pose one problem each day for students to solve mentally. This is followed by a brief discussion of the ideas that students use. Teachers are guided to focus on efficient methods but no student is forced to adopt any particular approach. The authors have strong evidence of the effectiveness of this approach. Other research has found that when a strong emphasis is placed on students' solving problems, they not only become better problem solvers but also they master more basic facts than students in a fact drill program (NRC, 2001).

A second possible approach is a bit more direct. A lesson may be designed to have students examine a special collection of facts for which a particular type of strategy is appropriate. You can discuss how these facts might all be alike in some way, or you might suggest an approach and see if students are able to use it on similar facts.

There is a huge temptation simply to tell students about a strategy and then have them practice it. Though this can be effective for some students, many others will not personally relate to your ideas or may not be ready for them. Continue to discuss strategies invented in your class and plan lessons that encourage strategies.

Drill of Efficient Methods

If you have read the section entitled "Drill or Practice?" in Chapter 5 (p. 67), you will recall a distinction between what drill means and what practice means. In the context of fact mastery, "practice" applies to those lessons just discussed, that is, problem-based experiences in which students are encouraged to develop flexible and useful strategies that are personally meaningful.

Drill—repetitive non-problem-based activity—is appropriate for children who have a strategy that they understand, like, and know how to use but have not yet become facile with it. Drill with an in-place strategy focuses students' attention on that strategy and helps to make it more automatic.

Drill Established Strategies

Drill plays a significant role in fact mastery, and the use of old-fashioned methods such as flash cards and fact games can be effective if used wisely.

When you are comfortable that children are able to use a strategy and are beginning to use it mentally, it may be appropriate to create drill activities for special groupings of facts. You might have as many as ten different activities for each strategy or group of facts. File folder or boxed activities can be used by children individually, in pairs, or even in small groups. With a large number of activities, children can work on strategies they understand and on the facts that they need the most.

Flash cards are among the most useful approaches to fact strategy practice. For each strategy or related group of facts, make several sets of flash cards using all of the facts that fit that strategy. On the cards, you can label the strategy or use drawings or cues to remind the children of the strategy. Examples appear throughout the chapter.

Other activities involve the use of special dice made from wooden cubes or foam rubber, teacher-made spinners, matching activities where a helping fact or a relationship is matched with the new fact being learned, and games of all sorts. A game or drill suggested for one strategy can usually be adapted to another.

Avoid Premature Drill

It is critical that you do not introduce drill too soon. Suppose that a child does not know the $9 + 5$ fact and has no way to deal with it other than to count fingers or use counters. These are inefficient methods. Premature drill introduces no new information and encourages no new connections. It is both a waste of time and a frustration to the child.

Many of the activities suggested in the chapter are simple drills—flash cards, matching games, dice, or spinner activities—in which the objective is quick response. Do not misinterpret these activities that are clearly drills as the way to introduce or develop strategies. Drill should only be used when an efficient strategy is in place.

Individualize

To some extent, you want to individualize drills in such a way that students are using their preferred strategy in the drills. This is not as difficult as it may seem at first.

Different students will likely invent or adopt different strategies for the same collection of facts. For example, there are several methods or strategies that use 10 when adding 8 or 9. Therefore, a drill that includes all of the addition facts with an 8 or a 9 can accommodate any child who has a strategy for that collection. Two children can be playing a spinner drill game, each using different strategies.

It is imperative that you listen to your students. Keep track of what strategies different students are using. This will help you occasionally create groups of students that can all benefit from the same drills. This will also help you know which students have yet to develop an efficient strategy for one or more collection of facts. If you are not sure who knows what facts, gather small groups of students to take a diagnostic test, a simple fact test with facts mixed randomly. Explain that you want them to first answer only those facts that they "know" without any counting. Then they should go back and attempt the unknown facts. Listen to find out how they approach these strategies.

NCTM Standards Critics of the reform movement in mathematics education often try to suggest that the *Standards* are "soft on the basics," especially mastery of facts. Nothing could be further from the truth. Among several similar statements that could be selected from the *Standards* document is this rather unambiguous quote: "Knowing the basic number combinations—single-digit addition and multiplication pairs and their counterparts for subtraction and division—is essential" (p. 32).

Strategies for Addition Facts

The strategies that students can and will invent for addition facts are directly related to one or more number relationships. In Chapter 9, numerous activities were suggested to develop these relationships. The teaching task is to help children connect these number relationships to the basic facts.

One-More-Than and Two-More-Than Facts

Each of the 36 facts highlighted in the chart has at least one addend of 1 or 2. These facts are a direct application of the one-more-than and two-more-than relationships.

Join or part-part-whole problems in which one of the addends is a 1 or a 2 are easy to make up. For example, *When Tommy was at the circus, he saw 8 clowns come out in a little car. Then 2 more clowns came out on bicycles. How many clowns did Tommy see in all?* Ask different students to explain how they got the answer of 10. Some will count on from 8. Some may still need to count 8 and 2 and then count all. Others will say they knew that 2 more than 8 is 10. The last response gives you an opportunity to talk about facts where you can use the two-more-than idea.

The different responses will provide you with a lot of information about students' number sense. As students are ready to use the two-more-than idea without counting all, they can begin to practice with activities such as the following.

activity **11.1**

One-/Two-More-Than Dice
Make a die labeled +1, +2, +1, +2, "one more," and "two more." Use with another die labeled 4, 5, 6, 7, 8, and 9. After each roll of the dice, children should say the complete fact: "Four and two is six."

activity **11.2**

One-/Two-More-Than Match
In a matching activity, children can begin with a number, match that with the one that is two more, and then connect that with the corresponding basic fact.

Figure 11.1 illustrates some of these activities and shows several possibilities for flash cards. Notice that activities such as the dice or spinner games can be modified for almost all of the strategies in the chapter. These are not repeated for each strategy.

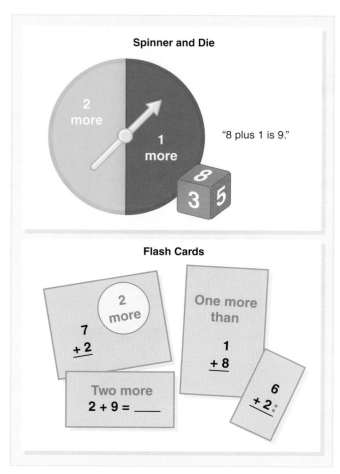

FIGURE 11.1 One-more and two-more facts.

activity **11.3**

What's Alike? Zero Facts
Write about ten zero facts on the board, some with the zero first and some with the zero second. Discuss how all of these facts are alike. Have children use counters and a part-part-whole mat to model the facts at their seats.

Doubles

There are only ten doubles facts from $0 + 0$ to $9 + 9$, as shown here. These ten facts are relatively easy to learn and become a powerful way to learn the near-doubles (addends one apart). Some children use them as anchors for other facts as well.

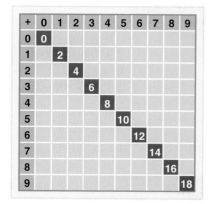

Facts with Zero

Nineteen facts have zero as one of the addends. Though such problems are generally easy, some children overgeneralize the idea that answers to addition are bigger. Word problems involving zero will be especially helpful. In the discussion, use drawings that show two parts with one part empty.

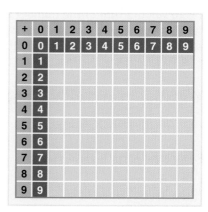

activity **11.4**

Double Images
Have students make picture cards for each of the doubles, and include the basic fact on the card as shown in Figure 11.2.

A simple "machine" can be drawn on the board or on a sheet of tagboard as shown in Figure 11.2. In this case the machine is labeled as the "Double" machine. Cards are made with an "input number" on one side and the double of the number on the reverse. A pair of students or a small group can use input/output machines, or you can lead the activity with a larger group.

Word problems can focus on pairs of like addends. *Alex and Zack each found 7 seashells at the beach. How many did they find together?*

FIGURE 11.2 Doubles facts.

the display. (Note that the calculator is also a good way to practice +1 and +2 facts.)

Near-Doubles

Near-doubles are also called the "doubles-plus-one" facts and include all combinations where one addend is one more than the other. The strategy is to double the smaller number and add 1. Be sure students know the doubles before you focus on this strategy.

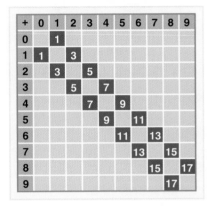

In addition to story problems involving near-doubles, you can introduce the strategy to the class by writing about ten near-doubles facts on the board. Use vertical and horizontal formats and vary which addend is the smaller.

Have students work independently to write the answers. Then discuss their ideas for "good" (that is, efficient) methods of answering these facts. Some may double the smaller number and add one and others may double the larger and subtract. If no one uses a near-double strategy, write the corresponding doubles for some of the facts and ask how these facts could help.

activity 11.6

Double Dice Plus One
Students roll a single die with numerals or dot sets. Their task is to say the sum of the number shown plus the number that is one greater. That is, for 7, students should say, "Seven plus eight is fifteen."

Figure 11.3 illustrates additional activities for near-doubles.

Make-Ten Facts

These facts all have at least one addend of 8 or 9. One strategy for these facts is to build onto the 8 or 9 up to 10

activity 11.5

Calculator Doubles
Use the calculator and enter the "double maker" (2 ⊗ =). Let one child say, for example, "Seven plus seven." The child with the calculator should press 7, try to give the double (14), and then press = to see the correct double on

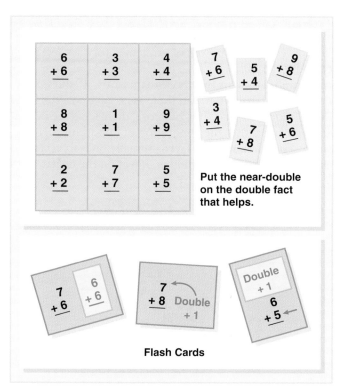

FIGURE 11.3 Near-doubles facts.

and then add on the rest. For 6 + 8, start with 8, then take 2 from the 6 to make 10, and that leaves 4 more for 14.

+	0	1	2	3	4	5	6	7	8	9
0										
1										10
2									10	11
3									11	12
4									12	13
5									13	14
6									14	15
7									15	16
8		10	11	12	13	14	15	16	17	
9		10	11	12	13	14	15	16	17	18

Before using this strategy, be sure that children have learned to think of the numbers 11 to 18 as 10 and some more. Many second- and third-grade children have not constructed this relationship. (Refer to "Relationships for Numbers 10 to 20" in Chapter 9.)

The next activity is a good way to introduce the make-ten strategy.

activity **11.7**

Make 10 on the Ten-Frame

Give students a mat with two ten-frames (see Figure 11.4). Flash cards are placed next to the ten-

frames, or a fact can be given orally. The students model each number in the two ten-frames and then decide on the easiest way to find the total without counting. The obvious (but not the only) choice is to move counters into the frame showing either 8 or 9. Get students to explain what they did. Focus especially on the idea that 1 (or 2) can be taken from the other number and put with the 9 (or 8) to make 10. Then you have 10 and whatever is left.

Provide a lot of time with the make-ten activity. Encourage discussion and exploration of "easy ways" to think about adding two numbers when one of them is 8 or 9. Perhaps discuss why this is not a useful idea for a fact such as 6 + 5 where neither number is near 10.

Note that children will have many other ways of using 10 to add with 8 or 9. For example, with the fact 9 + 5, some will add 10 + 5 and subtract 1. This is a perfectly good strategy, and it uses 10. You may want to give efficient strategies unique names determined by the children and discuss which ones seem especially useful.

When children seem to have the make-ten idea or a similar strategy, try the same activity without counters. Use the little ten-frame cards found in the Blackline Masters.

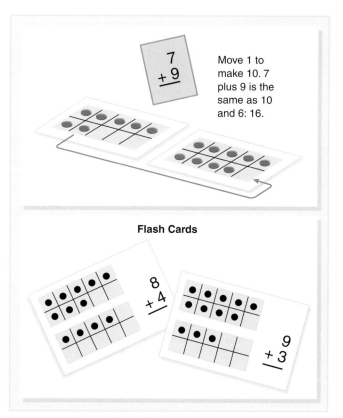

FIGURE 11.4 Make-ten facts.

Make a transparency set for the overhead. Show an 8 (or 9) card on the overhead. Place other cards beneath it one at a time as students respond with the total. Have students say orally what they are doing. For 8 + 4, they might say, "Take 2 from the 4 and put it with 8 to make 10. Then 10 and 2 left over is 12." The activity can be done independently with the little ten-frame cards.

 pause and reflect ————————————————

As has been noted, there is more than one way to efficiently use 10 in a strategy for facts involving 8 or 9. Imagine two or three children who have on the table a small ten-frame card for 9 so that all can see. One at a time, other cards are turned up and the students are to name the total of the two cards. How many different efficient methods involving 10 can you think of that can be accommodated by this simple activity?

A Generic Task

So far the suggested activities each focus on a particular strategy. In contrast, the next activity can be thought of as a generic task that can be posed for any fact. Use it as a possible introduction to strategies for a new collection, or use it after several strategies for a collection of facts have already been introduced. This activity gives every student the message that their ideas are OK. For those students who do not think of a good strategy, they will benefit from the discussion.

 **activity 11.8**

If You Didn't Know

Pose the following task to the class: If you did not know the answer to 8 + 5 (or any fact that you want students to think about), what are some really good ways you can use to get the answer? Explain that "really good" means that you don't have to count and you can do it in your head. Encourage students to come up with more than one way. Use a think-pair-share approach in which students discuss their ideas with a partner before they share them with the class.

In the event that no one comes up with a practical strategy you can offer one that a fictional friend shared with you—perhaps a student that you heard about in another school. You can also use this ploy to introduce a strategy that no one has thought about but which you think is possibly more efficient than those that have been suggested thus far. You are only offering ideas for consideration, not forcing them on students. You don't always have to rely on the students to come up with every strategy that they need.

Other Strategies and the Last Six Facts

To appreciate the power of strategies for fact learning, consider the following. We have discussed only five ideas or strategies (one or two more than, zeros, doubles, near-doubles, and make-ten), yet these ideas have covered 88 of the 100 addition facts! Furthermore, these ideas are not really new but rather the application of important relationships. The 12 remaining facts are really only six facts and their respective turnarounds as shown on the chart.

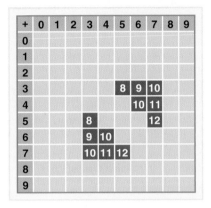

Before trying to develop any particular strategies for these facts, spend several days with word problems where these facts are the addends. Listen carefully to the ideas that students use in figuring out the answers.

Doubles Plus Two, or Two-Apart Facts

Of the six remaining facts, three have addends that differ by 2: 3 + 5, 4 + 6, and 5 + 7. There are two possible relationships that might be useful here, each depending on knowledge of doubles. Some children find it easy to extend the idea of the near-doubles to double plus 2. For example, 4 + 6 is double 4 and 2 more. A different idea is to take 1 from the larger addend and give it to the smaller. Using this idea, the 5 + 3 fact is transformed into the double 4 fact—*double the number in between.*

Make-Ten Extended

Three of the six facts have 7 as one of the addends. The make-ten strategy is frequently extended to these facts as well. For 7 + 4, the idea is *7 and 3 more makes 10 and 1 left is 11.* You may decide to suggest this idea at the same time that you initially introduce the make-ten strategy. It is interesting to note that Japan, mainland China, Korea, and Taiwan all teach an addition strategy of building through 10 and do so in the first grade. Many U.S. second graders do not know what 10 plus any number is (Fuson, 1992).

Counting On

Counting on is a common strategy found in textbooks. It is generally taught as a strategy for all facts that have 1, 2, or

3 as one of the addends and, thus, includes the one- and two-more-than facts. For the fact 3 + 8, the child starts with 8 and counts three counts: *9, 10, 11.* There are several reasons this approach is downplayed in this text. First, it is frequently applied to facts where it is not efficient, such as 8 + 5. It is difficult to explain to young children that they should count for some facts but not others. Second, it is much more procedural than conceptual. Finally, if other strategies are used, it is not necessary.

Ten-Frame Facts

If you have been keeping track, all of the remaining six facts have been covered by the discussion so far, with a few being touched by two different thought patterns. The ten-frame model is so valuable in seeing certain number relationships that these ideas cannot be passed by in thinking about facts. The ten-frame helps children learn the combinations that make 10. Ten-frames immediately model all of the facts from 5 + 1 to 5 + 5 and the respective turnarounds. Even 5 + 6, 5 + 7, and 5 + 8 are quickly seen as two fives and some more when depicted with these powerful models (see Figure 11.5).

A good idea might be to group the facts shown in the chart here and practice them using one or two ten-frames as a cue to the thought process.

The next two activities suggest the type of relationships that can be developed.

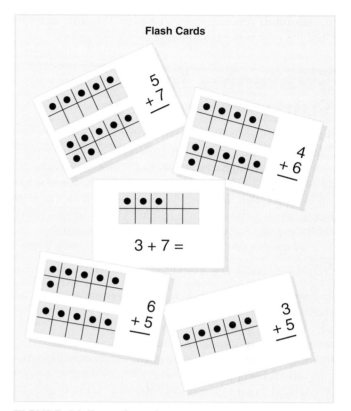

FIGURE 11.5 Ten-frame facts.

Obviously, the calculator can be made into a machine for adding any number and is a powerful drill device.

activity **11.10**

Say the Ten Fact

Hold up a ten-frame card, and have children say the "ten fact." For a card with seven dots, the response is "seven and three is ten." Later, with a blank ten-frame drawn on the board, say a number less than 10. Children start with that number and complete the "ten fact." If you say, "four," they say, "four plus six is ten." Use the same activities in independent or small group modes.

 Many students will have latched on to counting strategies for addition facts. Often these children become so adept at counting that you may not be aware that they are doing so. Speed in counting is not a substitute for fact mastery. It is useful to find out just how your students are thinking when they respond to facts. This may require a short interview. Prepare a page with no more than 25 facts selected to sample the fact groups that you think the student may not have mastered. Have the child complete the page as you watch. You should be able to tell if counting is being used. If you

activity **11.9**

A Plus-Five Machine

Use the calculator to practice adding five. Enter ⊞ 5 ⊜. Next enter any number and say the sum of that number plus 5 before pressing ⊜. Continue with other numbers. (The ⊞ 5 ⊜ need not be repeated.) If a ten-frame is present, the potential for strengthening the 5 and 10 relationships is heightened.

are doubtful, you can point to a particular fact and ask, "Tell me how you were thinking to get this answer." ■

Strategies for Subtraction Facts

Subtraction facts prove to be more difficult than addition. This is especially true when children have been taught subtraction through a "count-count-count" approach; for 13 − 5, *count* 13, *count* off 5, *count* what's left. There is little evidence that anyone who has mastered subtraction facts has found this approach helpful. Unfortunately, many sixth, seventh, and eighth graders are still counting.

Subtraction as Think-Addition

In Figure 11.6, subtraction is modeled in such a way that students are encouraged to think, "What goes with this part to make the total?" When done in this *think-addition* manner, the child uses known addition facts to produce the unknown quantity or part. (You might want to revisit the discussion of missing-part activities in Chapter 9 and part-part-whole subtraction concepts in Chapter 10.) If this important relationship between parts and wholes—between addition and subtraction—can be made, subtraction facts will be much easier. When children see 9 − 4, you want them to think spontaneously, "Four and *what* makes nine?" By contrast, observe a third-grade child who struggles with this fact. The idea of thinking addition never occurs. Instead, the child will begin to count either back from 9 or up from 4. The value of think-addition cannot be overstated.

Word problems that promote think-addition are those that sound like addition but have a missing addend: *join, initial part unknown; join, change unknown;* and *part-part-whole, part unknown* (see Chapter 10). Consider this prob-

lem: *Janice had 5 fish in her aquarium. Grandma gave her some more fish. Then she had 12 fish. How many fish did Grandma give Janice?* Notice that the action is join and, thus, suggests addition. There is a high probability that students will think *5 and how many more makes 12.* In the discussion in which you use problems such as this, your task is to connect this thought process with the subtraction fact, 12 − 5.

Subtraction Facts with Sums to 10

Think-addition is most immediately applicable to subtraction facts with sums of 10 or less. These are generally introduced with a goal of mastery in the first grade. Sixty-four of the 100 subtraction facts fall into this category.

If think-addition is to be used effectively, it is essential that addition facts be mastered first. Evidence suggests that children learn very few, if any, subtraction facts without first mastering the corresponding addition facts. In other words, mastery of 3 + 5 can be thought of as prerequisite knowledge for learning the facts 8 − 3 and 8 − 5.

Facts involving 0, 1, and 2 may be solved by different children in many different ways including think-addition. These facts are closely related to important basic number relationships. If children experience difficulties with facts such as 8 − 0 or 7 − 2, it would be a good idea to investigate their number concepts. A child who says that 7 − 0 is 6 may have overgeneralized that subtraction makes the number smaller.

The 36 "Hard" Subtraction Facts: Sums Greater Than 10

Ⅱ *pause and reflect* _____

Before reading further, look at the three subtraction facts shown here, and try to reflect on what thought process you use to get the answers. Even if you "just know them," think about what a likely process might be.

$$\begin{array}{ccc} 14 & 12 & 15 \\ -\ 9 & -\ 6 & -\ 6 \end{array}$$

Many people will use a different strategy for each of these facts. For 14 − 9, it is easy to start with 9 and work up through 10: *9 and 1 more is 10, and 4 more makes 5.* For the 12 − 6 fact, it is quite common to hear "double 6," a think-addition approach. For the last fact, 15 − 6, 10 is used again but perhaps by working backward from 15—a take-away process: *Take away 5 to get 10, and 1 more leaves 9.* We could call these three approaches, respectively, build up through 10, think-addition, and back down through 10. Each of the remaining 36 facts with sums of 11 or more can be learned using one or more of these strategies.

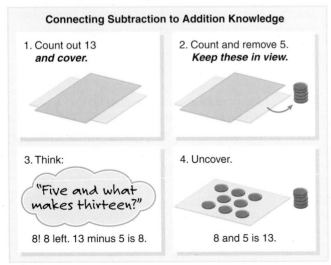

Connecting Subtraction to Addition Knowledge

1. Count out 13 *and cover.*

2. Count and remove 5. *Keep these in view.*

3. Think:

"Five and what makes thirteen?"

8! 8 left. 13 minus 5 is 8.

4. Uncover.

8 and 5 is 13.

FIGURE 11.6 Using a think-addition model for subtraction.

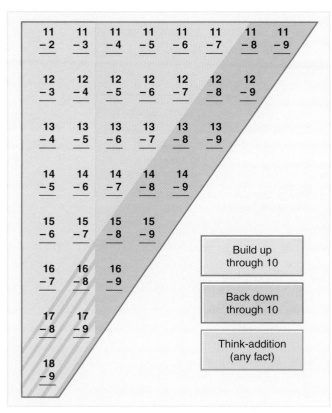

FIGURE 11.7 The 36 "hard" subtraction facts.

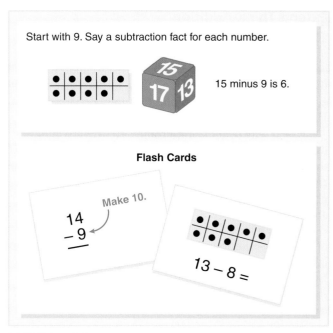

FIGURE 11.8 Build up through 10.

Figure 11.7 shows how these facts, in three overlapping groups, correspond to these three strategies. Keep in mind that these are not required strategies. Some children may use a think-addition method for all. Others may have a completely different strategy for some or all of these. The three approaches suggested here are based on ideas already developed: the relationship between addition and subtraction and the power of 10 as a reference point.

Build Up Through 10

This group includes all facts where the part or subtracted number is either 8 or 9. Examples are 13 − 9 and 15 − 8.

activity 11.11

Build Up Through the Ten-Frame

On the board or overhead, draw a ten-frame with nine dots. Explain that you are going to say a number greater than ten. The students' task is to say how many more dots are needed to make that number. After playing this "game" for a while, ask students to describe how they are getting their answers. On another day, repeat the activity with only eight dots on the ten-frame. Note that not all students will use ten in the way that we've been discussing. Do not force your method but rather listen to the ideas of all students and allow them to share their ideas.

Figure 11.8 shows a dice version of this activity and also some suggested flash cards. Do not forget to use story problems. Here is an example: *On the shelf there are 8 books. If the shelf will hold 13 books, how many more can be put on the shelf?*

Back Down Through 10

Here is one strategy that is really take-away and not think-addition. It is useful for facts where the ones digit of the whole is close to the number being subtracted. For example, with 15 − 6, you start with the total of 15 and take off 5. That gets you down to 10. Then take off 1 more to get 9. For 14 − 6, just take off 4 and then take off 2 more to get 8. Here we are working backward with 10 as a "bridge."

activity 11.12

Subtract to Ten

On the board write five or six pairs of facts where the difference for the first fact is 10 and the second fact is either 8 or 9: for example, 16 − 6 and 16 − 7, 14 − 4, and 14 − 6. Have students complete all of the facts and then discuss their strategies. The idea is to connect the two facts in each pair. The second fact is either one or two less than 10. If your discussion proves fruitful, on a subsequent day repeat the activity using only the facts with differences of 8 or 9.

A useful story problem for this strategy might be one like the following: *Becky had 16 cents. She spent 7 cents to buy a small toy. How much money does she have left?*

Extend Think-Addition

Think-addition remains one of the most powerful ways to think about subtraction facts. When the think-addition concept of subtraction is well developed, many children will use that approach for all subtraction facts. (Notice that virtually everyone uses a think-multiplication approach for division. Why?)

What may be most important is to listen to children's thinking as they attempt to answer subtraction facts that they have not yet mastered. If they are not using one of the three ideas suggested here, it is a good bet that they are counting—an inefficient method.

The activities that follow are all of the think-addition variety. There is of course no reason why these activities could not be used for all of the subtraction facts. They need not be limited to the "hard facts."

> **EXPANDED LESSON**
>
> An expanded lesson based on Activity 11.13 is on the Companion Web site at www.ablongman.com/vandewalle6e.

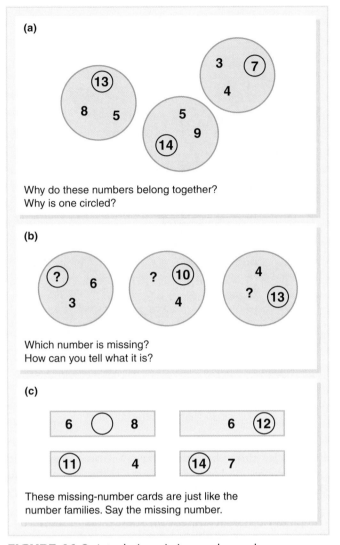

(a)

Why do these numbers belong together?
Why is one circled?

(b)

Which number is missing?
How can you tell what it is?

(c)

These missing-number cards are just like the number families. Say the missing number.

FIGURE 11.9 Introducing missing-number cards.

---

activity 11.13

Missing-Number Cards

Show children, without explanation, families of numbers with the sum circled as in Figure 11.9(a). Ask why they think the numbers go together and why one number is circled. When this number family idea is understood, show some families with one number replaced by a question mark, as in Figure 11.9(b), and ask what number is missing. When students understand this activity, explain that you have made some missing-number cards based on this idea. Each card has two of three numbers that go together in the same way. Sometimes the circled number is missing (the sum), and sometimes one of the other numbers is missing (a part). The object is to name the missing number.

---

activity 11.14

Missing-Number Worksheets

Make copies of the blank form found in the Blackline Masters to make a wide variety of drill exercises. In a row of 13 "cards," put all of the combinations from two families with different numbers missing, some parts and some wholes. Put blanks in different positions. An example is shown in Figure 11.10. After filling in numbers, make copies, and have students fill in the missing numbers. Another idea is to group facts from one strategy or number relation or perhaps mix facts from two strategies on one page. Have students write

an addition fact and a subtraction fact to go with each missing-number card. This is an important step because many children are able to give the missing part in a family but do not connect this knowledge with subtraction.

---

activity 11.15

Find a Plus Fact to Help

Select a group of subtraction facts that you wish to practice. Divide a sheet of paper into small cards, about 10 or 12 to a sheet. For each subtraction fact, write the corresponding addition fact on one of the cards. Two subtraction facts can be related to each addition fact. Duplicate the sheet and have students

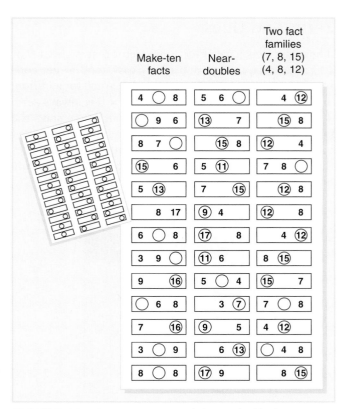

| | | Two fact families |
| Make-ten facts | Near-doubles | (7, 8, 15) (4, 8, 12) |

FIGURE 11.10 Missing-part worksheets. The blank version can be used to fill in any sets of facts you wish to emphasize (see Blackline Masters).

---

cut the cards apart. Now write one of the subtraction facts on the board. Rather than call out answers, students find the addition fact that helps with the subtraction fact. On your signal, each student holds up the appropriate fact. For 12 − 4 or 12 − 8, the students would select 4 + 8. The same activity can be made into a matching card game.

Assessment Notes For all students working on subtraction facts it is a good idea to assess their knowledge of addition facts. Be sure these are fairly well mastered first.

The connection between addition and subtraction is critical for mastery of subtraction facts. Activities 11.14 and 11.15 can both be used as assessment tools for individual or small groups of students. Students having difficulty with either of these activities but who do know their addition facts are likely thinking about subtraction strictly as take-away. For these students, explore the think-addition concept of subtraction as illustrated in Figure 11.6. ■

NCTM Standards Teachers often ask when students should have mastered the addition and subtraction facts. According to the *Standards*, "By the end of grade 2, students should know the basic addition and subtraction combinations" (p. 35).

Strategies for Multiplication Facts

Multiplication facts can also be mastered by relating new facts to existing knowledge.

It is imperative that students completely understand the commutative property (go back and review Figure 10.10). For example, 2×8 is related to the addition fact double 8. But the same relationship also applies to 8×2 that many children think about as $2 + 2 + 2 + 2 + 2 + 2 + 2 + 2$. Most of the fact strategies are more obvious with the factors in one order than in the other, but turn-around facts should always be learned together.

Of the five groups or strategies discussed next, the first four strategies are generally easier and cover 75 of the 100 multiplication facts. You are continually reminded that these strategies are suggestions, not rules, and that the most general approach with children is to have them discuss ways that *they* can use to think of facts easily.

Doubles

Facts that have 2 as a factor are equivalent to the addition doubles and should already be known by students who know their addition facts. The major problem is to realize that not only is 2×7 double 7, but so is 7×2. Try word problems where 2 is the number of sets. Later use problems where 2 is the size of the sets. *George was making sock puppets. Each puppet needed 2 buttons for eyes. If George makes 7 puppets, how many buttons will he need for the eyes?*

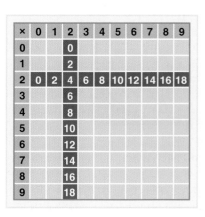

Fives Facts

This group consists of all facts with 5 as the first or second factor, as shown here.

×	0	1	2	3	4	5	6	7	8	9
0						0				
1						5				
2						10				
3						15				
4						20				
5	0	5	10	15	20	25	30	35	40	45
6						30				
7						35				
8						40				
9						45				

Practice counting by fives to at least 45. Connect counting by fives with rows of five dots. Point out that six rows is a model for 6 × 5, eight rows is 8 × 5, and so on.

activity 11.16

Clock Facts

Focus on the minute hand of the clock. When it points to a number, how many minutes after the hour is it? Draw a large clock face and point to numbers 1 to 9 in random order. Students respond with the minutes after. Now connect this idea to the multiplication facts with 5. Hold up a flash card and then point to the number on the clock corresponding to the other factor. In this way, the fives facts become the "clock facts."

Include the clock idea on flash cards or to make matching activities (see Figure 11.11).

Zeros and Ones

Thirty-six facts have at least one factor that is either 0 or 1. These facts, though apparently easy, tend to get confused with "rules" that some children learned for addition. The fact 6 + 0 stays the same, but 6 × 0 is always zero. The 1 + 4 fact is a one-more idea, but 1 × 4 stays the same. The concepts behind these facts can be developed best through story problems. Above all else, avoid rules that sound arbitrary and without reason such as "Any number multiplied by zero is zero."

×	0	1	2	3	4	5	6	7	8	9
0	0	0	0	0	0	0	0	0	0	0
1	0	1	2	3	4	5	6	7	8	9
2	0	2								
3	0	3								
4	0	4								
5	0	5								
6	0	6								
7	0	7								
8	0	8								
9	0	9								

Nifty Nines

Facts with a factor of 9 include the largest products but can be among the easiest to learn. The table of nines facts includes some nice patterns that are fun to discover. Two of these patterns are useful for mastering the nines: (1) The tens digit of the product is always one less than the "other" factor (the one other than 9), and (2) the sum of the two digits in the product is always 9. These two ideas can be used together to get any nine fact quickly. For 7 × 9, *1 less than 7 is 6, 6 and 3 make 9, so the answer is 63.*

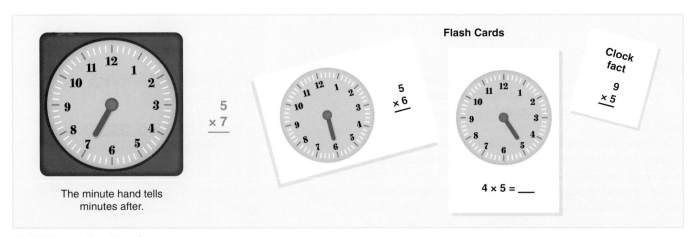

The minute hand tells minutes after.

Flash Cards

Clock fact

FIGURE 11.11 Fives facts.

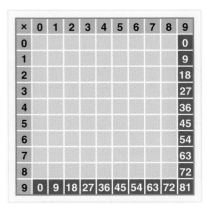

Children are not likely to invent this strategy simply by solving word problems involving a factor of 9. Therefore, consider building a lesson around the following task.

activity 11.17

Patterns in the Nines Facts

In column form, write the nines table on the board ($9 \times 1 = 9, 9 \times 2 = 18, \ldots, 9 \times 9 = 81$). The task is to find as many patterns as possible in the table. (Do not ask students to think of a strategy.) As you listen to the students work on this task, be sure that somewhere in the class the two patterns necessary for the strategy have been found. After discussing all the patterns, a follow-up task is to use the patterns to think of a clever way to figure out a nine fact if you didn't know it. (Note that even for students who know their nines facts, this remains a valid task.)

Once children have invented a strategy for the nines, practice activities such as those shown in Figure 11.12 are appropriate. Also consider word problems with a factor of 9 and check to see if the strategy is in use.

Warning: Although the nines strategy can be quite successful, it also can cause confusion. Because two separate rules are involved and a conceptual basis is not apparent, children may confuse the two rules or attempt to apply the idea to other facts. It is not, however, a "rule without reason." It is an idea based on a very interesting pattern that exists in the base-ten numeration system. One of the values of patterns in mathematics is that they help us do seemingly difficult things quite easily. The nifty-nine pattern illustrates clearly one of the values of pattern and regularity in mathematics.

An alternative strategy for the nines is almost as easy to use. Notice that 7×9 is the same as 7×10 less one set

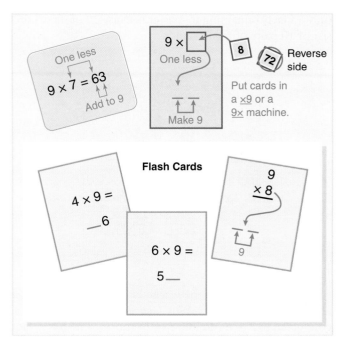

FIGURE 11.12 "Nifty nines" rule.

of 7, or $70 - 7$. This can easily be modeled by displaying rows of ten cubes, with the last one a different color, as in Figure 11.13. For students who can easily subtract 6 from 60, 7 from 70, and so on, this strategy may be preferable.

You might introduce this idea by showing a set of bars such as those in the figure with only the end cube a different color. After explaining that every bar has ten cubes, ask students if they can think of a good way to figure out how many are yellow.

Helping Facts

The chart shows the remaining 25 multiplication facts. It is worth pointing out to children that there are actually

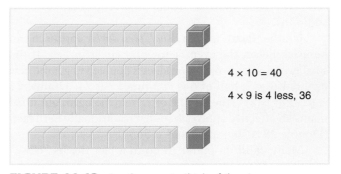

FIGURE 11.13 Another way to think of the nines.

only 15 facts remaining to master because 20 of them consist of 10 pairs of turnarounds.

×	0	1	2	3	4	5	6	7	8	9
0										
1										
2										
3				9	12		18	21	24	
4				12	16		24	28	32	
5										
6				18	24		36	42	48	
7				21	28		42	49	56	
8				24	32		48	56	64	
9										

These 25 facts can be learned by relating each to an already known fact or *helping* fact. For example, 3 × 8 is connected to 2 × 8 (double 8 and 8 more). The 6 × 7 fact can be related to either 5 × 7 (5 sevens and 7 more) or to 3 × 7 (double 3 × 7). The helping fact must be known, and the ability to do the mental addition must also be there. For example, to go from 5 × 7 is 35 and then add 7 for 6 × 7, a student must be able to add 35 and 7. If you see finger counting at that stage, the idea of make-ten can be extended: 35 and 5 more is 40 and 2 left makes 42.

How to find a helping fact that is useful varies with different facts and sometimes depends on which factor you focus on. Figure 11.14 illustrates models for four overlapping groups of facts and the thought process associated with each.

The *double and double again* approach is applicable to all facts with 4 as one of the factors. Remind children that the idea works when 4 is the second factor as well as when it is the first. For 4 × 8, double 16 is also a difficult fact. Help children with this by noting, for example, that 15 + 15 is 30, 16 + 16 is two more, or 32. Adding 16 + 16 on paper defeats the purpose.

Double and one more set is a way to think of facts with one factor of 3. With an array or a set picture, the double part can be circled, and it is clear that there is one more set. Two facts in this group involve difficult mental additions.

If either factor is even, a *half then double* approach can be used. Select the even factor, and cut it in half. If the smaller fact is known, that product is doubled to get the new fact. For 6 × 7, half of 6 is 3. 3 times 7 is 21. Double 21 is 42. For 8 × 7, the double of 28 may be hard, but it remains an effective approach to that traditionally hard fact. (Double 25 is 50 + 2 times 3 is 56.)

Many children prefer to go to a fact that is "close" and then *add one more set* to this known fact. For example, think of 6 × 7 as 6 sevens. Five sevens is close: That's 35. Six sevens is one more seven, or 42. When using 5 × 8 to

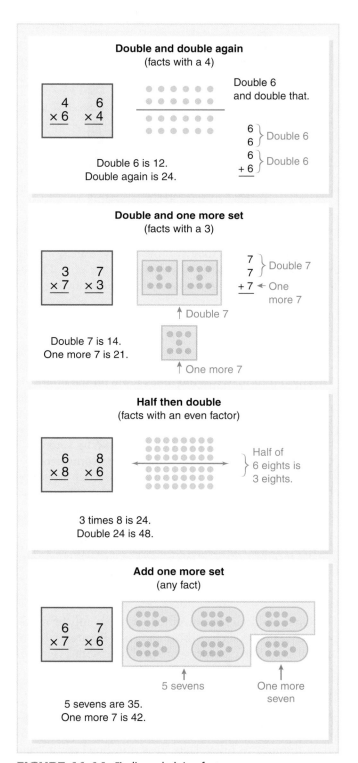

FIGURE 11.14 Finding a helping fact.

help with 6 × 8, the set language "6 eights" is very helpful in remembering to add 8 more and not 6 more. Admittedly difficult, this approach is used by many children, and it becomes the best way to think of one or two particularly difficult facts. "What is seven times eight? Oh, that's 49 and 7 more—56." The process can become almost automatic.

The relationships between easy and hard facts are fertile ground for good problem-based tasks. Rather than tell students what helping facts to use and how to use them, select a fact from one of the strategies. Use the same formulation as in Activity 11.8, "If You Didn't Know" (p. 172). For example, "If you didn't know what 6×8 is, how could you figure it out by using something that you do know?" Students should be challenged to find as many as possible interesting and useful ways to answer a hard multiplication fact.

 *pause and reflect* —————

Go through each of the 20 "hard facts" and see how many of the strategies in Figure 11.14 you can use for each one. Many children will not think in terms of the arrays shown but rather will use a symbolic representation. For example, for 6×8 they might think of a vertical sum of six 8s or eight 6s. Try to see how this type of representation works for the ideas in Figure 11.14.

Since arrays are a powerful thinking tool for these strategies, provide students with copies of the ten-by-ten dot array (Figure 11.15, also in Blackline Masters). A tagboard *L* is used to outline arrays for specific products. The lines in the array make counting the dots easier and often suggest the use of the easier fives facts as helpers. For example, 7×7 is 5×7 plus double 7 $\longrightarrow$ 35 + 14.

Don't forget to use word problems as a vehicle for developing these harder facts. Consider this problem: *Con-*

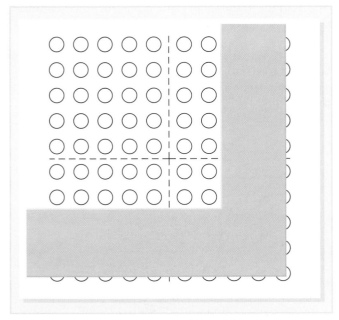

FIGURE 11.15 An array is a useful model for developing strategies for the hard multiplication facts. An array like this can be found in the Blackline Masters.

nie bundled up all of her old crayons into bags of 7 crayons each. She was able to make 8 bags with 3 crayons left over. How many crayons did she have? As students work to get an answer, many of the strategies just discussed are possible. Plus there is the added benefit of the assessment value gained by listening to the methods different children bring to a situation that does not look like a fact drill.

Word problems can also be structured to prompt a strategy. *Carlos and Jose kept their baseball cards in albums with 6 cards on each page. Carlos had 4 pages filled, and Jose had 8 pages filled. How many cards did each boy have?* (Do you see the half-then-double strategy?)

It should be clear that the array plays a large part in helping students establish multiplication facts and relationships. In both third and fourth grades, the *Investigations in Number, Data, and Space* curriculum places a significant emphasis on arrays. They are used to help with multiplication facts, the relationship between multiplication and division, and in the development of computational procedures for multiplication. On page 182, several array activities from *Investigations* are described.

Division Facts and "Near Facts"

 *pause and reflect* —————

What thought process do you use to recall facts such as 48 ÷ 6 or 36 ÷ 9?

If we are trying to think of 36 ÷ 9, we tend to think, "Nine times what is thirty-six?" For most, 42 ÷ 6 is not a separate fact but is closely tied to 6×7. (Would it not be wonderful if subtraction were so closely related to addition? It can be!)

An interesting question to ask is, "When children are working on a page of division facts, are they practicing division or multiplication?" There is undoubtedly some value in limited practice of division facts. However, mastery of multiplication facts and connections between multiplication and division are the key elements of division fact mastery. Word problems continue to be a key vehicle to create this connection.

Exercises such as 50 ÷ 6 might be called "near facts." Divisions that do not come out evenly are much more prevalent in computations and in real situations than division facts or division without remainders. To determine the answer to 50 ÷ 6, most people run through a short sequence of the multiplication facts, comparing each product to 50: "6 times 7 (low), 6 times 8 (close), 6 times 9 (high). Must be 8. That's 48 and 2 left over." This process can and should be drilled. That is, children should be able to do problems with one-digit divisors and one-digit answers plus remainders mentally and with reasonable speed.

Investigations
in Number, Data, and Space

Grade 3, Things That Come in Groups
Investigation 3: Arrays and Skip Counting

Context

This unit is scheduled for early in the third grade and is the main focus on multiplication and division for the grade. Prior to this investigation, students will have explored the idea of counting things in groups and will have considerable practice with skip counting using the hundreds chart. This investigation continues skip counting by counting rows and columns on an array. In this way skip counting is connected to groups of things, patterns on the hundreds chart, arrays, and later as a possible strategy for solving problems.

Page 49 from *Multiplication and Division: Things That Come in Groups* by C. Tierney, M. Berle-Carman, & J. Akers. *Investigations in Number, Data, and Space.* Copyright © 1998 by Dale Seymour Publications. Reprinted by permission of Pearson Education, Inc.

Task Description

The materials for this investigation consist of a collection of arrays made of half-inch grids, cut out by the students so that each child has a complete set. The set consists of 51 rectangles representing every product in the multiplication table from 1 × 2 to 12 × 12 with products between 2 and 50. For example, there is a 2 by 1, a 5 by 10, and a 12 by 4 rectangle but not a 7 by 8 or 9 by 6. On the grid side of the array or rectangle, students write the dimensions as a product (e.g., 3 × 7 and 7 × 3). On the blank side they write the product without the factors.

For the activity "Multiplication Pairs," two students spread out all of the array cards, some turned with the factors and grid side up and others showing the blank rectangle with the product. Students take turns selecting an array by placing their finger on it but not picking it up. Their task is to name either the factors or the product on the reverse side. When the grid side is down, the shape of the rectangle is a clue to the possible factors. When the grid side is up, the grid can aid students who are just learning the combinations. Students might skip-count or use a related array product that they do know. Students are encouraged to keep track of the facts they "know" and "don't know yet" and keep this information in their folders.

At grade 4, the same game is played, however, the collection of arrays includes all of the products through 12 × 12.

Other activities with the arrays include building larger arrays from smaller arrays, skip counting with the arrays, and using the arrays in a compare game similar to "war."

---

activity 11.18

How Close Can You Get?

To practice "near facts," try this exercise. As illustrated, the idea is to find the one-digit factor that makes the product as close as possible to the target without going over. Help children develop the process of going through the multiplication facts that was just described. This can be a drill with the full class by preparing a list for the overhead, or it can be a worksheet activity.

> Find the largest factor without going over the target number.
>
> 4 × ☐ ⟶ 23, ☐ left over
> 7 × ☐ ⟶ 52, ☐ left over
> 6 × ☐ ⟶ 27, ☐ left over
> 9 × ☐ ⟶ 60, ☐ left over

NCTM Standards What does the *Standards* document tell us about multiplication and division facts? "Through skip-counting, using area models, and relating unknown combinations to known ones, students will learn and become fluent with unfamiliar combinations [multiplication facts]. . . . If by the end of the fourth grade, students are not able to use multiplication and division strategies efficiently, then they must either develop strategies so that they are fluent with these combinations or memorize the 'harder' combinations" (p. 153).

Effective Drill

There is little doubt that strategy development and general number sense (number relationships and operation meanings) are the best contributors to fact mastery. Drill in the absence of these factors has repeatedly been demonstrated as ineffective. However, the positive value of drill should not be completely ignored. Drill of nearly any mental activity strengthens memory and retrieval capabilities (Ashcraft & Christy, 1995).

When and How to Drill

Teachers and parents hold tenaciously to their belief in drill. Undoubtedly, far too much time is devoted to inefficient drill of basic facts, often with a negative impact on students' attitudes toward mathematics and beliefs in their abilities.

Avoid Inefficient Drill

Adopt this simple rule and stick with it: *Do not subject any student to fact drills unless the student has developed an efficient strategy for the facts included in the drill.* Drill can strengthen strategies with which students feel comfortable—ones they "own"—and will help to make these strategies increasingly automatic. Therefore, drill of strategies such as those discussed in this chapter will allow students to use them with increased efficiency, even to the point of recalling the fact without being conscious of using a strategy. Counting on fingers and making marks on paper can never result in automatic fact recall regardless of the amount of drill. Short-term gains from inefficient drill are almost certain to be lost over time. Drill prior to development of efficient methods is simply a waste of precious instructional time.

It is worth mentioning that the preceding statement applies equally to students in the upper grades or middle school grades who have not yet mastered facts. Because the curriculum at these levels typically does not include strategy development, drill is often the only approach offered. Alternatives to this serious error are discussed later in the chapter.

Individualize Drill

It is unreasonable to expect every student in your class to develop and be comfortable with the same strategies. As you have seen, there are multiple paths to most facts. Different students will bring different number tools to the task and will develop strategies at different rates. This means that there are few drills that are likely to be efficient for a full class at any given time. That is why so many of the suggested activities are designed as flash cards, games, or simple repeatable worksheets. By creating a large number of drill activities promoting different strategies and addressing different collections of facts, it is not at all unreasonable to direct students to activities that are most useful for them.

 There are literally hundreds of software programs that offer drill of basic facts. Nearly all fact programs offer games or exercises at various difficulty levels. Unfortunately, there do not seem to be any programs that organize facts the way they are organized in this chapter. It should be clear that computerized fact practice should be used only after students have developed some strategies.

A few representative programs are described here.

In *Math Munchers Deluxe* (Riverdeep Interactive Learning, 2005), students move their muncher in a three dimensional grid format. By answering questions, they can avoid six Troggles that chase the muncher and try to eat it. Like many programs, *Math Munchers* encourages speed and is highly motivating. It is aimed at grades 3 to 6 and could profitably be used through grade 8.

Math Blaster (Knowledge Adventure) promotes speed through an arcade format. There are children who are attracted to this approach and many who are not. For some, the formats in fancy, high-paced programs are a distraction to the mathematical thinking you want to promote. Like most programs, *Math Blaster* includes drills for more than just facts. It is not uncommon to see drills with multidigit computation, decimals, fractions, percents, estimation, and other topics, all in the same format.

One aspect of a program you should be aware of is how a student inputs answers. For fact practice, numbers are usually typed left to right. But in the same program, multidigit computation may be entered beginning with the ones place or right to left. A multiple-choice format is not uncommon, especially for programs designed for younger children, but is less effective for basic facts.

Many commercial programs automatically keep performance records of individual students. There are numerous sites on the Internet that offer fact practice (for examples, see *Flashcards for Kids* at www.edu4kids.com/index.php?TB=2&page=12 or *Arithm Attack* at www.dep.anl.gov/aattack.htm). Almost all provide immediate feedback and many provide options for the number of problems, the size of the numbers, and whether or not to time the student. ■

What About Timed Tests?

Consider the following:

> Teachers who use timed tests believe that the tests help children learn basic facts. This makes no instructional sense. Children who perform well under time pressure display their skills. Children who have difficulty with skills, or who work more slowly, run the risk of reinforcing wrong learning under pressure. In addition, children can become fearful and negative toward their math learning. (Burns, 2000, p. 157)

Think about this quotation whenever you are tempted to give a timed test. Reasoning and pattern searching are never facilitated by restricting time. Some children simply cannot work well under pressure or in situations that provoke stress.

Although speed may encourage children to memorize facts, it is effective only for students who are goal oriented and who can perform in pressure situations. The pressure of speed can be debilitating and provides no positive benefits.

The value of speed drills or timed tests as a learning tool can be summed up as follows:

Timed tests

- Cannot promote reasoned approaches to fact mastery
- Will produce few long-lasting results
- Reward few
- Punish many
- Should generally be avoided

 If there is any defensible purpose for a timed test of basic facts it may be for diagnosis—to determine which combinations are mastered and which remain to be learned. Even for diagnostic purposes there is little reason for a timed test more than once every couple of months. ■

Fact Remediation with Upper-Grade Students

Students who have not mastered their basic facts by the fifth or sixth grade are in need of something other than more drill. They have certainly seen and practiced facts countless times in previous grades. There is no reason to believe that the drills *you* provide will somehow be more effective than last year's. These students need something better. The following key ideas can guide your efforts to help these older students.

1. *Recognize that more drill will not work.* Students' fact difficulties are due to a failure to develop or to connect concepts and relationships such as those that have been discussed in this chapter, not a lack of drill. At best, more drill will provide temporary results. At worst, it will cause negative attitudes about mathematics.

2. *Provide hope.* Students who have experienced difficulty with fact mastery often believe that they cannot learn facts or that they are doomed to finger counting forever. Let these children know that you will help them and that you will provide some new ideas that will help them as well. Take that burden on yourself, and spare them the prospect of more defeat.

3. *Inventory the known and unknown facts for each student in need.* Find out from each student what facts are known quickly and comfortably and which are not. Fifth-grade or older students can do this diagnosis for you. Provide sheets of all facts for one operation in random order, and have the students circle the facts they are hesitant about and answer all others. Suggest that finger counting or making marks in the margin is not permitted. To achieve an honest assessment, emphasize that you need this information so that you can help the student.

4. *Diagnose strengths and weaknesses.* Find out what students do when they encounter one of their unknown facts. Do they count on their fingers? Add up numbers in the margins? Guess? Try to use a related fact? Write down times tables? Are they able to use any of the relationships that might be helpful as suggested in this chapter? Some of this you may be able to accomplish by having students write about how they approach two or three specific facts. More efficiently, you should conduct a 10-minute diagnostic interview with each student in need. Simply pose unknown facts and ask the student how he or she approaches them. Don't try to teach; just find out. Again, students can provide some of this information by writing about what they do when they don't know a fact.

5. *Suggest strategies.* Because students will likely be working alone or with a small group in this remediation program, they will not have the benefit of class discussion nor the time required over weeks and months to develop their own strategies. Therefore, with these students, it is reasonable to share with them strategies that "you have seen other students use." That is, in the interest of time, show these older students a useful strategy for a collection of facts they have not mastered. Be certain that they have a conceptual understanding of the strategy and are able to use it.

6. *Build in success.* As you begin a well-designed fact program for a child who has experienced failure, be sure that successes come quickly and easily. Begin with easy strategies, and introduce only a few new ideas at a time. Success builds success! With strategies as an added assist, success comes even more quickly. Point out to students how one idea, one strategy, is all that is required to learn many facts. Use fact charts to show what set of facts you are working on. It is surprising how the chart quickly fills up with mastered facts. Keep reviewing newly learned facts and those that were already known. This is success. It feels good, and failures are not as apparent. Short practice exercises can be designed as homework. Have students write about which ideas are helpful and which are not. Use this information to design the next exercise.

Your extra effort beyond class time can be a motivation to a student to make some personal effort on his or her own time. During class, these students should continue to work with all students on the regular curriculum. You must believe and communicate to these students that the reason they have not mastered basic facts is not a reflection of their ability. With efficient strategies and individual effort, success will come. Believe!

Facts: No Barrier to Good Mathematics

Students who have total command of basic facts do not necessarily *reason better* than those who, for whatever reason, have not yet mastered facts. Today, mathematics is not about computation, especially pencil-and-paper computation. Mathematics is about reasoning and patterns and making sense of things. Mathematics is problem solving. There is no reason that a child who has not yet mastered all basic facts should be excluded from real mathematical experiences.

The most obvious alternative is the calculator. It should be on the desk every day for all students. There is absolutely no evidence that the presence of a calculator will impede basic fact mastery. On the contrary, the more students use the calculator, the more proficient they will be with it. This will make many of the calculator fact drills more effective and provide students with ready access to electronic flash cards. In a classroom climate where most students do know their facts and where students help one another and share thinking strategies as has been suggested, very few students will rely on the calculator for any prolonged period.

Students who are relegated to drill of facts when the rest of the class is engaged in meaningful experiences will soon feel stupid and incapable of doing "real" mathematics. By contrast, when students who have not mastered facts are engaged in exciting and meaningful experiences, they have real motivation to learn facts and real opportunities to develop relationships that can aid in that endeavor. Do not allow students who are behind in fact mastery to fall behind in mathematics.

Reflections on Chapter 11

Writing to Learn

1. Of the three different approaches to teaching basic facts that were discussed, drill and the direct teaching of strategies each have serious limitations. Describe what is wrong with these two methods.
2. Provide a general description of the third and recommended approach to helping students master basic facts.
3. How are story problems used in a good fact development program?
4. Besides story problems, what is the other approach that is suggested?
5. For each addition fact strategy:
   a. List at least three facts for which the strategy can be used.
   b. Explain the thinking process or concepts that are involved in using the strategy. Use a specific fact as an illustration.
6. What is meant by subtraction as "think-addition"? How can you help children develop a think-addition thought pattern for subtraction?
7. What kinds of story problems are useful for promoting a think-addition strategy for subtraction facts? Give an example.
8. For subtraction facts with sums greater than 10, it is reasonable that as many as three different thought patterns or strategies might be used. Describe each of those suggested in the text.

9. Why is the turnaround property (commutative property) more important in multiplication fact mastery than in addition?
10. For each multiplication strategy except "use a helping fact," answer the questions in item 5.
11. The "last 25" multiplication facts involve using a fact that has already been learned and working from that fact to the new or harder fact. Four different ways to make this connection with a helping fact were described. Some are applicable only to certain facts. Describe each of these approaches, and list the facts for which the approach is applicable.
12. Describe when it is appropriate to use drill and how it can help. What is "premature" drill?
13. Why not use speed drills to learn facts?
14. How do you help children who have been drilling their basic facts for years and still have not mastered them?

For Discussion and Exploration

1. Explore a computer software program that drills basic facts. What features does your program have that are good? Not so good? Explain. In general, do you think these programs are effective? How would you use such software in a classroom with only one or two available computers?

2. One view of thinking strategies is that they are little more than a collection of tricks for kids to memorize. Discuss the question, "Is teaching children thinking strategies for basic fact mastery in keeping with a constructivist view of teaching mathematics?" Carole Thornton (1990), a leading researcher in the area of basic-fact strategies, suggests a fairly direct approach to teaching strategies.

3. Examine a recently published second-, third-, or fourth-grade textbook to determine how thinking strategies for the basic facts have been developed. Compare what you find with the groupings of facts in this chapter. How would you use the text effectively in your program?

Recommendations for Further Reading

Baron, C. (2004). *Thinking strategies: Addition. Building mastery of addition facts.* Winnipeg, Manitoba: Portage and Main Press. (One of a series of four books addressing each of the four operations.)

There are numerous books available as resource materials for teachers aimed at basic fact teaching. Nearly all use a strategy approach. This is one of the most recent series of its type and certainly one of the best. Each book contains a sequence of detailed lessons complete with excellent explanations of strategies as well as pages and pages of useful and practical Blackline Masters. One might argue that the approach is somewhat directed in contrast to the student-centered approach described in this chapter. Having said that, there are too many good ideas and games in these books to pass them by. They will certainly prove to be a help.

Buchholz, L. (2004). Learning strategies for addition and subtraction facts: The road to fluency and the license to think. *Teaching Children Mathematics, 10,* 362–367.

Lisa Buchholz is a second-grade teacher who tells an amazing story complete with examples of children's written work. Over several months her students developed and named their strategies and even extended them to work with two-digit numbers. She found that some of her "lower ability" students were really some of her best thinkers. This inspiring story provides a look into the way that an effective fact program can work. This is also a story of a teacher who became convinced of the power of a constructivist approach while working on a task usually seen as mundane—teaching basic facts.

Fennema, E., & Carpenter, T. P. (with Levi, L., Franke, M. L., & Empson, S.) (1997). *Cognitively guided instruction: Professional development in primary mathematics.* Madison, WI: Wisconsin Center for Education Research.

The CGI program believes that students develop their own strategies for mastering the basic facts. They are helped in this process by solving well-selected story problems. Teachers listen carefully to students' emerging processes and encourage increasingly efficient methods. This book provides detailed explanations. (See the annotation of this same book in Chapter 7.)

Kamii, C., & Anderson, C. (2003). Multiplication games: How we made and used them. *Teaching Children Mathematics, 10,* 135–141.

Constance Kamii is a strict constructivist who often tells teachers to use games involving numbers that will encourage students to develop number concepts. In this article she teams up with an experienced third-grade teacher and describes a collection of games that were used to help children in a Title I school master their multiplication facts. Each game is described in detail. At the end of the school year their students performed nearly perfectly on 100 multiplication facts in 10 minutes. This is another success story of how students can master facts without drill and by invention of their own strategies.

Rathmell, E. C., Leutzinger, L. P., & Gabriele, A. J. (2000). *Thinking with numbers.* Cedar Falls, IA: Thinking with Numbers, Inc.

Rathmell was one of the first to write about the use of thinking strategies for basic facts. (See the 1978 NCTM Yearbook.) He and his colleagues have developed a large set of small cards, each with several simple story problems. The cards are organized by strategies for each of the operations. As children solve these problems (5 minutes per day), they invent their own strategies and share them with the class. The nature of the story problems encourages development of the strategies you have read about. This set of materials has been well tested in classrooms and supports the approach in this chapter.

Online Resources

Suggested Applets and Web Links

Arithmaattack
www.dep.anl.gov/aattack.htm

A very straightforward fact drill program that can be used online or downloaded free of charge (Department of Energy's Argonne National Laboratory).

Arithmetic Four
www.shodor.org/interactivate/activities/agame/index.html

The game is like "Connect Four." Players must answer an arithmetic fact to be able to enter a piece of their color on the board. Operations can be selected and timer set for answering each fact. Difficulty levels can be adjusted as can the operations used.

Cross the Swamp (BBC)
www.bbc.co.uk/schools/starship/maths/crosstheswamp. shtml

This British applet asks students to supply a missing operation (+/− or ×/÷) and a number to complete an equation (e.g., 4 __ __ = 12). There are five questions in a set, each with three levels of difficulty.

SpeedMath Deluxe (Jefferson Lab)
http://education.jlab.org/smdeluxe/index.html

Players are given four numbers between which they must enter one of the four operation signs so that the resulting expression equals a given number. Requires an understanding of order of operations and occasionally integers but a very nice applet.

An additional list of books and articles related to the ideas in this chapter can be found on the Companion Web site at **www.ablongman.com/vandewalle6e.**

Companion Website

chapter **12**

Whole-Number Place-Value Development

A complete understanding of place value, including the extension to decimal numeration, develops across the elementary and middle grades. For whole numbers, the most critical period in this development occurs in grades K to 3. In grades K and 1 children count and are exposed to patterns in the numbers to 100. Most importantly, they begin to think about groups of ten things as a unit. By second grade, these initial ideas of patterns and groups of ten are formally connected to our place-value system of numeration. In grades 3 and 4 children explore numbers with three or more digits. In fourth and fifth grades, the ideas of whole numbers are extended to decimals.

As a significant part of this development, students should begin to work at putting numbers together and taking them apart in a wide variety of ways as they solve addition and subtraction problems with two- and three-digit numbers. Computation and place-value development need not be entirely separated as they have been traditionally. Children's struggles with the invention of their own methods of computation will both enhance their understanding of place value and provide a firm foundation for flexible methods of computation.

Big Ideas

1. Sets of ten (and tens of tens) can be perceived as single entities. These sets can then be counted and used as a means of describing quantities. For example, three sets of ten and two singles is a base-ten method of describing 32 single objects. This is the major principle of *base-ten* numeration.

2. The positions of digits in numbers determine what they represent—which size group they count. This is the major principle of *place-value* numeration.

3. There are patterns to the way that numbers are formed. For example, each decade has a symbolic pattern reflective of the 1-to-9 sequence.

4. The groupings of ones, tens, and hundreds can be taken apart in different ways. For example, 256 can be 1 hundred, 14 tens, and 16 ones but also 250 and 6. Taking numbers apart and recombining them in flexible ways is a significant skill for computation.

5. "Really big" numbers are best understood in terms of familiar real-world referents. It is difficult to conceptualize quantities as large as 1000 or more. However, the number of people that will fill the local sports arena is, for example, a meaningful concept for those who have experienced that crowd.

Mathematics Content Connections

The base-ten place-value system is the way that we communicate and represent anything that we do with whole numbers and later with decimals.

■ **Whole-Number Computation and Number Sense** (Chapters 13 and 14): Flexible methods of computation including various mental methods, pencil-and-paper methods, estimation skills, and even effective use of calculators and computer computations depend completely on an understanding of place value. Computational strategies for addition and subtraction can and should be developed along with an understanding of place value.

■ **Decimal and Percents** (Chapter 18): Whole-number place-value ideas are extended to allow for representation of the full range of rational numbers and approximations of irrational numbers.

■ **Measurement** (Chapter 20): Problem-based tasks involving real measures can be used to help students structure ideas about grouping by tens. Through measures, people develop benchmarks and meaningful referents for numbers.

187

Pre-Base-Ten Concepts

It is tempting to think that children know a lot about numbers with two digits (10 to 99) even as early as kindergarten. After all, most kindergartners can and should learn to count to 100 and count out sets of things with as many as 20 or 30 objects. They do daily calendar activities, count children in the room, turn to specified page numbers in their books, and so on. However, their understanding is quite different from yours. It is based on a one-more-than or count-by-ones approach to quantity.

Children's Pre-Base-Ten View of Number

Ask first- or second-grade children to count out 53 tiles, and most will be able to do so or will make only careless errors. It is a tedious but not formidable task. If you watch closely, you will note that the children count out the tiles one at a time and put them into the pile with no use of any type of grouping. Have the children write the number that tells how many tiles they just counted. Most children will be able to write it. Some may write "35" instead of "53," a simple reversal.

So far, so good. Now ask the children to write the number that is 10 more than the number they just wrote. Most will begin to count, probably starting from 53. When counting on from 53, they find it necessary to keep track of the counts, probably on their fingers. Many, if not most, children in the first and early second grades will not be successful at this task, and almost none will know immediately that 10 more is 63. Asking for the number that is 10 less is even more problematic.

Finally, show a large collection of cards, each with a ten-frame drawn on it. Explain that the cards each have ten spaces and that each will hold ten tiles. Demonstrate putting tiles on the cards by filling up one of the ten-frames with tiles. Now ask, "How many cards like this do you think it will take if we want to put all of these tiles [the 53 counted out] on the cards?" A response of "53" is not unusual. Other children will say they do not know, and a few will try to put the tiles on the cards to figure it out.

Quantity Tied to Counts by Ones

The children just described know that there are 53 tiles "because I counted them." Writing the number and saying the number are usually done correctly, but their understanding of 53 derives from and is connected to the count by ones. Children do not easily or quickly develop a meaningful use of groups of ten to represent quantities.

With minimal instruction, children can tell you that in the numeral 53, the 5 is in the tens place or that there are "3 ones." However, it is likely that this is simply a naming of the positions with little understanding. If children have been exposed to base-ten materials, they may name a rod of ten as a "ten" and a small cube as a "one." These same children, however, may not be readily able to tell how many ones are required to make a ten. It is easy to attach words to both materials and groups without realizing what the materials or symbols represent.

Children do know that 53 is "a lot" and that it's more than 47 (because you count past 47 to get to 53). They think of the "53" that they write as a single numeral. They do not know that the 5 represents five groups of ten things and the 3 three single things (Fuson et al., 1997; Ross, 1989). Fuson and her colleagues refer to children's pre-base-ten understanding of number as "unitary." That is, there are no groupings of ten, even though a two-digit number is associated with the quantity. They rely on unitary counts to understand quantities.

Basic Ideas of Place Value

Place-value understanding requires an integration of new and difficult-to-construct concepts of grouping by tens (the base-ten concept) with procedural knowledge of how groups are recorded in our place-value scheme, how numbers are written, and how they are spoken.

Integration of Base-Ten Groupings with Counts by Ones

Recognizing that children can count out a set of 53, we want to help them see that making groupings of tens and leftovers is a way of counting that same quantity. Each of the groups in Figure 12.1 has 53 tiles. We want children to construct the idea that all of these are the same and that the sameness is clearly evident by virtue of the groupings of tens.

There is a subtle yet profound difference between two groups of children: those who know that group B is 53 because they understand the idea that 5 groups of 10 and 3 more is the same amount as 53 counted by ones and those who simply say, "It's 53," because they have been told that when things are grouped this way, it's called 53. The latter children may not be sure how many they will get if they count the tiles in set B by ones or if the groups were "ungrouped" how many there would then be. The children who understand will see no need to count set B by ones. They understand the "fifty-threeness" of sets A and B to be the same.

 *pause and reflect* ⎯⎯⎯⎯⎯⎯⎯⎯

The ideas in the preceding paragraph are important for you to understand so that the activities discussed later will make sense. Be sure you can talk about children who do and children who do not understand place value.

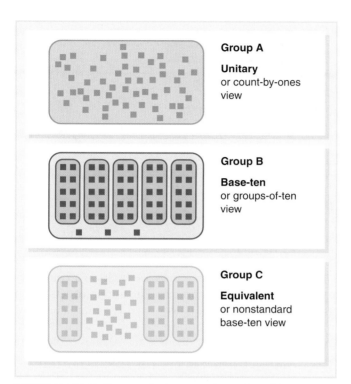

FIGURE 12.1 Three equivalent groupings of 53 objects. Group A is 53 because "I counted them (by ones)." Group B has 5 tens and 3 more. Group C is the same as B, but now some groups are broken into singles.

Recognition of the equivalence of groups B and C is another step in children's conceptual development. Groupings with fewer than the maximum number of tens can be referred to as *equivalent groupings* or *equivalent representations*. Understanding the equivalence of B and C indicates that grouping by tens is not just a rule that is followed but that any grouping by tens, including all or some of the singles, can help tell how many. Many computational techniques are based on equivalent representations of numbers.

The Role of Counting in Constructing Base-Ten Ideas

Counting plays a key role in constructing base-ten ideas about quantity and connecting these concepts to symbols and oral names for numbers.

Children can count sets such as those in Figure 12.1 in three different ways. Each way helps children think about the quantities in a different way (Thompson, 1990).

1. *Counting by ones.* This is the method children have to begin with. Initially, a count by ones is the only way they are able to name a quantity or "tell how many." All three of the sets in Figure 12.1 can be counted by ones. Before base-ten ideas develop, a count by ones is the only way children can be convinced that all three sets are the same.

2. *Counting by groups and singles.* In group B in Figure 12.1, counting by groups and singles would go like this: "One, two, three, four, five bunches of ten, and one, two, three singles." Consider how novel this method would be for a child who had never thought about counting a group of things as a single item. Also notice how this counting does not tell directly how many items there are. This counting must be coordinated with a count by ones before it can be a means of telling "how many."

3. *Counting by tens and ones.* This is the way adults would probably count group B and perhaps group C: "Ten, twenty, thirty, forty, fifty, fifty-one, fifty-two, fifty-three." While this count ends by saying the number that is there, it is not as explicit as the second method in counting the number of groups. Nor will it convey a personal understanding of "how many" unless it is coordinated with the more meaningful count by ones.

Regardless of the specific activity that you may be doing with children, helping them integrate the grouping-by-tens concept with what they know about number from counting by ones should be your foremost objective. Children should frequently have the opportunity to count sets of objects in several ways. If first counted by ones, the question might be, "What will happen if we count these by groups and singles (or by tens and ones)?" If a set has been grouped into tens and singles and counted accordingly, "How can we be really certain that there are 53 things here?" or "What do you think we will get if we count by ones?" It is inadequate to *tell* children that these counts will all be the same. That is a relationship they must construct themselves through reflective thought, not because the teacher says it works that way.

Integration of Groupings with Words

The way we say a number such as "fifty-three" must also be connected with the grouping-by-tens concept. The counting methods provide a connecting mechanism. The count by tens and ones results in saying the number of groups and singles separately: "five tens and three." This is an acceptable, albeit nonstandard, way of naming this quantity. Saying the number of tens and singles separately in this fashion can be called *base-ten language* for a number. Children can associate the base-ten language with the usual language: "five tens and three—fifty-three."

There are several variations of the base-ten language for 53—5 tens and 3; 5 tens and 3 ones; 5 groups of ten and 3 leftovers; 5 tens and 3 singles; and so on. Each may be used interchangeably with the standard name, "fifty-three."

It can easily be argued that base-ten language should be used throughout the second grade, even in preference to standard oral names.

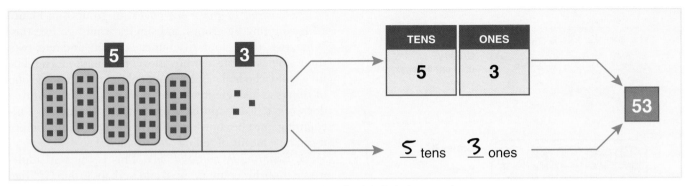

FIGURE 12.2 Groupings by 10 are matched with numerals, placed in labeled places, and eventually written in standard form.

Integration of Groupings with Place-Value Notation

In like manner, the symbolic scheme that we use for writing numbers (ones on the right, tens to the left of ones, and so on) must be coordinated with the grouping scheme. Activities can be designed so that children physically associate a tens and ones grouping with the correct recording of the individual digits, as Figure 12.2 indicates.

Language again plays a key role in making these connections. The explicit count by groups and singles matches the individual digits as the number is written in the usual left-to-right manner.

A similar coordination is necessary for hundreds.

NCTM Standards "Making a transition from viewing 'ten' as simply the accumulation of 10 ones to seeing it both as 10 ones *and* as 1 ten is an important first step for students toward understanding the structure of the base-ten number system" (p. 33).

Figure 12.3 summarizes the ideas that have been discussed so far.

- The conceptual knowledge of place value consists of the base-ten grouping ideas.

   When a collection of objects is grouped in sets of ten and some leftover singles, counting the groups of ten and adding the singles tells how many are in the collection.

   There can be equivalent representations with fewer than the maximum groupings.

- The base-ten grouping ideas must be integrated with oral and written names for numbers.

- In addition to counting by ones, children use two other ways of counting: by groups and singles separately and by tens and ones. All three methods of counting are coordinated as the principal method of integrating the concepts, the written names, and the oral names.

Remember that these ideas are built on a count-by-ones understanding of number. The notion of sets of ten as single entities must be constructed as a completely new way of thinking about number. Simply showing children groups of ten and telling them that "10 ones is the same as 1 ten" will not construct that idea for them.

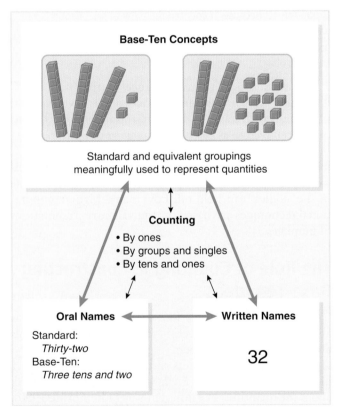

FIGURE 12.3 Relational understanding of place value integrates three components, shown as the corners of the triangle: base-ten concepts, oral names for numbers, and written names for numbers. Counting is a key activity by which children can construct and integrate these three ideas and connect them to the pre-place-value concepts of number that they have to begin with.

Think of Figure 12.3 as a triangle with the conceptual ideas of place value at the top. The procedural ideas of how we say and write numbers are the other two corners. Counting is the main tool children use to help connect these ideas. Before moving further, be sure that you have a good feel for how these ideas are related. Remember that the conceptual ideas must first be built on the count-by-ones concept of quantity that children bring to this array of ideas.

Models for Place Value

Physical models for base-ten concepts can play a key role in helping children develop the idea of "a ten" as both a single entity and as a set of ten units. Remember, though, that the models do not "show" the concept to the children. The children must construct the concept and impose it on the model.

Base-Ten Models and the Ten-Makes-One Relationship

A good base-ten model for ones, tens, and hundreds is *proportional*. That is, a ten model is physically ten times larger than the model for a one, and a hundred model is ten times larger than the ten model. Base-ten models can be categorized as *groupable* and *pregrouped*.

Groupable Models

Models that most clearly reflect the relationships of ones, tens, and hundreds are those for which the ten can actually be made or grouped from the singles. When children put ten beans in a portion cup, the cup of ten literally *is the same as* the ten single beans. Examples of these groupable models are shown in Figure 12.4(a). These could also be called "put-together-take-apart" models.

Of the groupable models, beans or counters in cups are the cheapest and easiest for children to use. (Plastic portion cups can be purchased from stores specializing in paper supplies.) Plastic connecting cubes are attractive and provide a good transition to pregrouped tens sticks. Plastic chain links in ten-link chains are another popular model. Bundles of Popsicle sticks or coffee stirrers are a well-known model, but small hands have trouble with rubber bands and actually making the bundles. With most groupable materials, hundreds are possible but are generally not practical for most activities in the classroom.

As children become more and more familiar with these models, collections of tens can be made up in advance by the children and kept as ready-made tens. Lids can be purchased for the plastic portion cups, and the con-

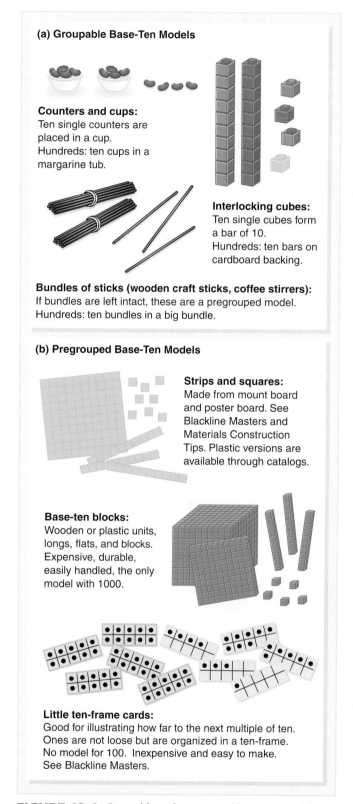

(a) Groupable Base-Ten Models

Counters and cups:
Ten single counters are placed in a cup.
Hundreds: ten cups in a margarine tub.

Interlocking cubes:
Ten single cubes form a bar of 10.
Hundreds: ten bars on cardboard backing.

Bundles of sticks (wooden craft sticks, coffee stirrers):
If bundles are left intact, these are a pregrouped model.
Hundreds: ten bundles in a big bundle.

(b) Pregrouped Base-Ten Models

Strips and squares:
Made from mount board and poster board. See Blackline Masters and Materials Construction Tips. Plastic versions are available through catalogs.

Base-ten blocks:
Wooden or plastic units, longs, flats, and blocks. Expensive, durable, easily handled, the only model with 1000.

Little ten-frame cards:
Good for illustrating how far to the next multiple of ten. Ones are not loose but are organized in a ten-frame. No model for 100. Inexpensive and easy to make. See Blackline Masters.

FIGURE 12.4 Groupable and pregrouped base-ten models.

necting cubes or the links can be left prebundled. This is a good transition into the pregrouped models described next.

Pregrouped or Trading Models

Models that are pregrouped are commonly shown in text-books and are commonly used. With pregrouped models such as those in Figure 12.4(b), children cannot actually take pieces apart or put them together. When ten single pieces are accumulated, they must be exchanged or *traded* for a ten, and likewise, tens must be traded for hundreds.

The chief advantage of these models is their ease of use and the efficient way they model large numbers. A significant disadvantage is the potential for children to use them without reflecting on the ten-to-one relationships or without really understanding what they are doing. For example, if children are told to trade 10 ones for a ten, it is quite possible for them to make this exchange without attending to the "tenness" of the piece they call a ten. Similarly, children can learn to "make the number 42" by simply selecting 4 tens and 2 ones pieces without understanding that if the pieces all came apart there would be 42 ones pieces that could be counted by ones.

In this category, the little ten-frame cards are somewhat unique. If children have been using ten-frames to think about numbers to 20 as discussed in Chapter 9, the value of the filled ten-frame may be more meaningful than it is with strips and squares of base-ten blocks. Although the ones are fixed on the cards, this model has the distinct advantage of always showing the distance to the next multiple of ten. When 47 is shown with 4 ten cards and a seven card, it is clear that three more will make 50. With all other models, the ones must continually be counted to tell how many and the distance to the next ten is obscure. The commercial materials called *DecaDots 10-Frame Tiles* (ETA/Cuisenaire) are a plastic version of these tiles. Note that the tiles with fewer than ten dots have the dots arranged differently than the ten-frame cards in this book.

No model, including a groupable model, will guarantee that children are reflecting on the ten-to-one relationships in the materials. With pregrouped models we need to make an extra effort to see that children understand that a ten piece really is the same as 10 ones.

(See the Blackline Masters and Materials Construction Tips for making base-ten strips and squares and the ten-frame cards.)

 Electronic versions of base-ten manipulatives are becoming more popular. Usually these are computer representations of the three-dimensional base-ten blocks, including the thousands piece. With simple mouse clicks children can place units, rods, flats, or cubes on the screen. In the Base Block applets at the National Library of Virtual Manipulatives (NLVM) at Utah State University (http://matti.usu.edu/nlvm/nav/vlibrary.html), the models are placed on a place-value chart. If ten of one type are dragged to the column to the left, they snap together. If a piece is dragged one column to the right,

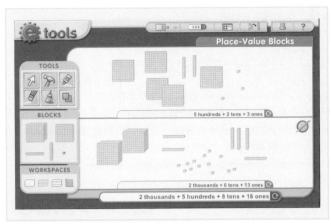

FIGURE 12.5 Pearson Scott Foresman's *eTools* includes a computer model of base-ten blocks. Students can model one, two, or three separate numbers. The odometers show the value of each number as well as the total. The hammer and glue bottle are used to break pieces apart and put pieces together.

Source: From *eTools*, Scott Foresman (2004). Reprinted by permission of Pearson Education, Inc.

the pieces break apart. The NLVM applets are free online. Pearson Education's *eTools* has a similar place-value tool with a bit more flexibility. (See Figure 12.5.) With the *eTools Number Blocks*, place-value columns can be turned off, and up to three different numbers can be modeled separately. The "odometer" option can show the number 523 as *5 hundreds + 2 tens + 3 ones*, as *500 + 20 + 3*, or as *five hundred twenty-three*. A hammer icon will break a piece into smaller pieces and a glue bottle icon is used to group ten pieces together.

Virtual versions of place-value blocks have become increasingly popular. Compared to real base-ten models, virtual blocks are cheap, are easily grouped and ungrouped, can be shown to the full class on a monitor, and are available in "endless" supply, even the thousands blocks. Computer models allow students to print their work and, thus, create a written record of what they've done. For this reason, electronic blocks should be considered a groupable model.

On the other hand, the computer model is no more conceptual than a physical model and, like the physical model, is only a representation for students who understand the relationships involved. ■

Developing Base-Ten Concepts

Now that you have a sense of the task of helping children develop place-value concepts, we can begin to focus on activities that can help with this task. This section focuses on the top of the triangle of ideas in Figure 12.3: base-ten concepts or grouping by tens. The central idea of counting groups of ten to describe quantities is clearly the most important component to be developed. The connections of these critical ideas with the place-value system of writing numbers and with the way we say numbers—the bottom two corners of the triangle—are discussed separately to help you focus on the conceptual objective. However, in the classroom, the oral and written names for numbers can and should be developed in concert and nearly always with connections to conceptual ideas using models.

Grouping Activities

Because children come to their development of base-ten concepts with a count-by-ones idea of number, you must begin there. You cannot arbitrarily impose grouping by ten on children. We want children to experiment with showing amounts in groups of like size and perhaps to come to an agreement that ten is a very useful size to use. The following activity could be done in late first grade or second grade and is designed as an example of a first effort at developing grouping concepts.

activity **12.1**

Counting in Groups

Find a collection of things that children might be interested in counting—perhaps the number of eyes in the classroom or the number of shoes, a mystery jar of buttons or cubes, a long chain of plastic links, or the number of crayons in the crayon box. The quantity should be countable, somewhere between 25 and 100. Pose the question, "How could we count our shoes in some way that would be easier than counting by ones?" Whatever suggestions you get, try to implement them. After trying several methods, you can have a discussion of what worked well and what did not. If no one suggests counting by tens, you might casually suggest that as possibly another idea.

One teacher had her second-grade students find a good way to count all the connecting cubes being held by the children after each had been given a cube for each of their pockets. The first suggestion was to count by sevens. That was tried but did not work very well because none of the second graders could count by sevens. In search of a faster way, the next suggestion was to count by twos. This did not seem to be much better than counting by ones. Finally, they settled on counting by tens and realized that this was a pretty good method, although counting by fives worked pretty well also.

This and similar activities provide you with the opportunity to suggest that materials actually be arranged into groups of tens before the "fast" way of counting is

begun. Remember that children may count "ten, twenty, thirty, thirty-one, thirty-two" but not fully realize the "thirty-two-ness" of the quantity. To connect the count-by-tens method with their understood method of counting by ones, the children need to count both ways and discuss why they get the same result.

The idea in the next activity is for children to make groupings of ten and record or say the amounts. Number words are used so that children will not mechanically match tens and ones with individual digits. It is important that children confront the actual quantity in a manner meaningful to them.

activity **12.2**

Groups of 10

Prepare bags of counters of different types. Bags may have toothpicks, buttons, beans, plastic chips, connecting cubes, craft sticks, or other items. Children have a record sheet similar to the top example in Figure 12.6. The bags can be placed at stations around the room, or each pair of children can be given one. Children dump out and count the contents. The amount is recorded as a number word. Then the counters are grouped in as many tens as possible. The groupings are recorded on the form. Bags are traded, or children move to another station after returning all counters to the bag.

If children have difficulty writing the number words, a chart can be displayed for students to copy from (see Figure 12.7).

Variations of the "Groups of 10" activity are suggested by the other recording sheets in Figure 12.6. In "Get This Many," the children count the dots and then count out the corresponding number of counters. Small cups in which to put the groups of ten should be provided. Notice that the activity requires students to first count the set in a way they understand, record the amount in words, and then make the groupings. The activity starts with meaningful student counts and develops the idea of groups.

"Fill the Tens" and "Loop This Many" begin with a verbal name (number word), and students must count the indicated amount and then make groups.

 As you watch children doing these activities, you will be able to learn a lot about their base-ten concept development. For example, how do children count out the objects? Do they make groupings of ten as they go? Do they count to 10 and then start again at 1? Children who do that are already using the base-ten structure. But what you will more likely see early on is children counting a full set without any stopping at tens and without any effort to group the materials in piles.

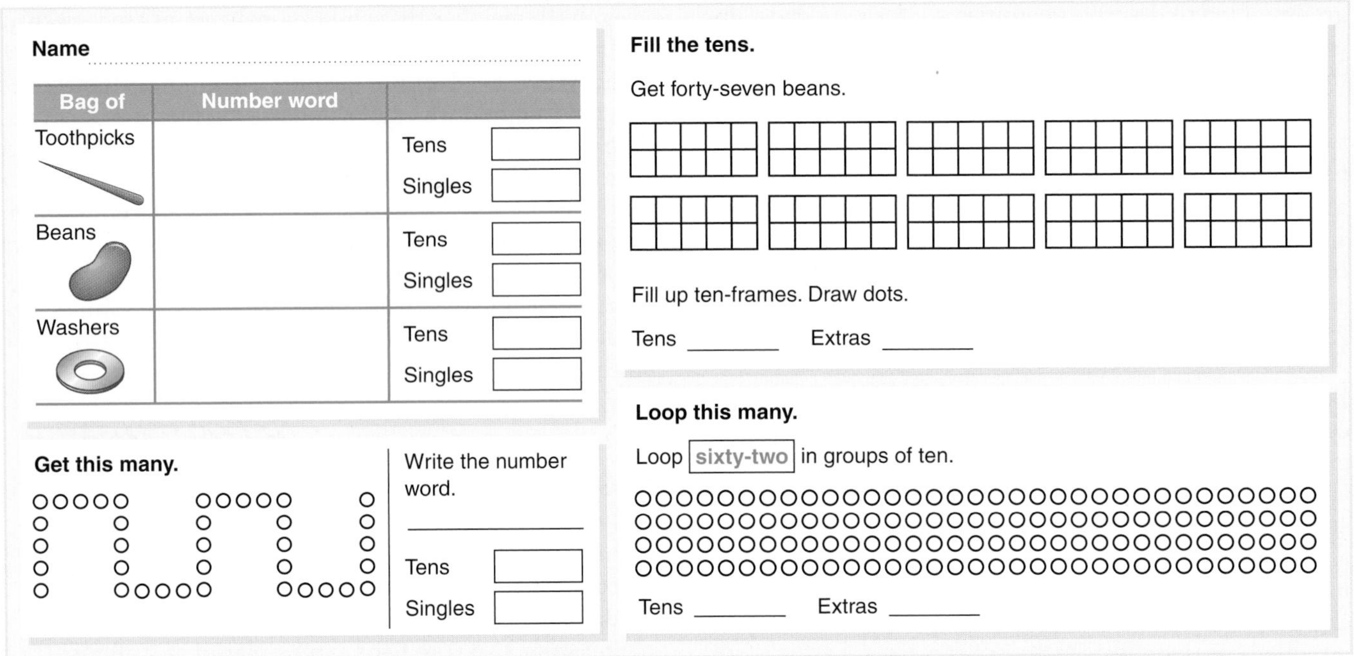

Name ....

Bag of	Number word		
Toothpicks		Tens	
		Singles	
Beans		Tens	
		Singles	
Washers		Tens	
		Singles	

Get this many.

○○○○○   ○○○○○   ○
○　○　○　○　○
○　○　○　○　○
○　○　○　○　○
○　○○○○○　○○○○○

Write the number word.

_____

Tens	
Singles	

Fill the tens.

Get forty-seven beans.

Fill up ten-frames. Draw dots.

Tens _____   Extras _____

Loop this many.

Loop [sixty-two] in groups of ten.

Tens _____   Extras _____

FIGURE 12.6 Activities involving number words and making groups of 10.

A second-grade teacher had her students count a jar of small beans. After they had recorded the number, they were to ask for plastic cups in which to make cups of ten. Several children, when asked how many cups they thought they might need, had no idea or made random guesses. ■

It is quite easy to integrate grouping concepts along with measurement activities. This will save time in your curriculum as well as add interest to both areas. As you will read in Chapter 20, adding an estimation component to early measurement activities is important to help students understand measurement concepts. In the following measurement activity, the estimation also serves to help students think about quantities as groupings of ten.

Number Words

eleven	ten	one
twelve	twenty	two
thirteen	thirty	three
fourteen	forty	four
fifteen	fifty	five
sixteen	sixty	six
seventeen	seventy	seven
eighteen	eighty	eight
nineteen	ninety	nine

FIGURE 12.7 A chart to help children write number words.

activity **12.3**

Estimating Groups of Tens and Ones
Show students a length that they are going to measure—for example, the length of a student lying down or the distance around a sheet of newspaper. At one end of the length, line up ten units (e.g., ten cubes in a bar, ten toothpicks, rods, or blocks). On a recording sheet (see Figure 12.8), students write down a guess of how many groups of ten and leftovers they think will fit into the length. Next they find the actual measure, placing units along the full length. These are counted by ones and also grouped in tens. Both results are recorded.

Notice that all place-value components are included in Activity 12.3. Children can work in pairs to measure several lengths around the room. A similar estimation approach could be added to "Groups of 10" (Activity 12.2), where students first estimate the quantity in the bags. Estimation requires reflective thought concerning quantities expressed in groups.

 Listening to students' estimates is also a useful assessment opportunity that tells you a lot about children's concepts of numbers in the range of your current activities. ■

In *Investigations in Number, Data, and Space*, first-grade students learn the oral sequence of numbers to 100, especially through the use of a hundreds chart. (See hundreds

NAME _Jessica_

OBJECT	ESTIMATE	ACTUAL

desk   __5__ TENS __6__ SINGLES   __3__ TENS __2__ SINGLES

                                                 __ThirTy-Two__
                                                 Number Word

_____   _____ TENS _____ SINGLES   _____ TENS _____ SINGLES

                                                 _____
                                                 Number Word

FIGURE 12.8 Recording sheet for estimating groups of tens and ones.

chart activities later in this chapter.) However, the authors are aware of the fact that most students rely on their counts by ones to understand quantity. The excerpt on page 196 illustrates how the *Investigations* curriculum nudges children gently to a more advanced understanding of counting.

The Strangeness of *Ones*, *Tens*, and *Hundreds*

Reflect for a moment on how strange it must sound to say "seven ones." Certainly children have never said they were "seven ones" years old. The use of the word *ten* as a singular group name is even more mysterious. Consider the phrase "Ten ones makes one ten." The first *ten* carries the usual meaning of 10 things, the amount that is 1 more than 9 things. But the other *ten* is a singular noun, a thing. How can something the child has known for years as the name for a lot of things suddenly become one thing? Bunches, bundles, cups, and groups of 10 make more sense in the beginning than "a ten."

As students begin to make groupings of 10, the language of these groupings must also be introduced. At the start, language such as "groups of 10 and leftovers" or "bunches of tens and singles" is most meaningful. For tens, use whatever terminology fits: bars of 10, cups of 10, bundles of 10. Eventually you can abbreviate this simply to "ten." There is no hurry to use the word "ones" for the leftovers. Language such as "four tens and seven" works very well.

The word *hundred* is equally strange and yet usually gets less attention. It must be understood in three ways: as 100 single objects, as 10 tens, and as a singular thing. These word names are not as simple as they seem!

Grouping Tens to Make 100

So far we have focused mainly on helping students move from counting by ones to understanding how groups of ten can be used more effectively. In late second grade and into

third grade, numbers from 100 to 999 become important. Here the issue is not one of connecting a count-by-ones concept to a group of 100, but rather, seeing how a group of 100 can be understood as a group of 10 tens as well as 100 single ones. In textbooks, this connection is usually illustrated on one page showing how 10 sticks of ten can be put together to make 1 hundred. This quick demonstration may be lost on many students.

As a means of introducing hundreds as groups of 10 tens and also 100 singles, consider the following estimation activity.

activity **12.4**

Too Many Tens

Show students any quantity with 150 to 1000 items. For example, you might use a jar of lima beans. Alternatives include a long chain of connecting links or paper clips or a box of Styrofoam packing peanuts. First, have students make and record estimates of how many beans are in the jar. Discuss with students how they came to select their estimates. Give portions of the beans to pairs or triads of students to put into cups of ten beans. Collect leftover beans and put these into groups of ten as well. Now ask, "How can we use these groups of ten to tell how many beans we have?" Although someone will likely suggest it for you, suggest that you could make groups of the groups. Point out that ten groups of ten is called 100. If using cups of beans, be prepared with some larger containers into which ten cups can be placed. When all groups are made, count the hundreds, the tens, and the ones separately. Record on the board as "4 hundreds + 7 tens + 8 ones."

In the last activity it is important to use a groupable model so that students can see the 100 items in the ten groups. This is often lost in the rather simple display of a 100 flat or square in the pregrouped base-ten models.

Investigations
in Number, Data, and Space

Grade 1, Number Games and Story Problems
Investigation 2: Twos, Fives, and Tens

Context

In the introductory pages of this unit, the authors say, "By the end of the year, many students will have learned the oral counting sequence to 100, will recognize some patterns in the sequence of written numbers from 1 to 100, and will have a solid grasp of quantities up to about 25" (p. I-18). Within the unit, students learn to recognize numbers in groups and begin to skip count with the aid of the hundreds chart. The Number Games and Story Problems unit occurs in the latter half of the year.

Task Description

In a series of tasks called "How Many Squares?" students count the number of paper 1-inch squares prepared for them. One set has 8 single squares and 6 pairs (a strip of 2 squares). A second set has 7 single squares and 4 strips of 5 squares, and the third set has 5 single squares, 5 pairs, and 2 strips of 5.

Using the overhead to lead a discussion, the teacher encourages students to make an arrangement of the squares in the first set in order to count them in different ways. Initially students count each square one at a time and many continue in this manner regardless of how they arrange the squares. Some children will place the squares in sets of two or sets of three and either skip count or add up the squares as they go.

After the activity is introduced, children take a set of squares, arrange them in some manner for counting, record on paper how they arranged them, and show using words and/or numbers how they counted. The children's work shown here is taken from the assessment notes.

The child labeled (a) organizes her squares into groups of four and then puts the remainder in a row. She recognizes the sets of four as 4 but has difficulty when she attempts to skip count and eventually counts by ones. Child (b) makes several different groupings including the 2 fives to make 10. She records each group and then writes addition combinations to determine the totals. She is using known facts and there is some evidence that she uses 10 for small numbers. Students (c) and (d) are beginning to use the structure of place value. Child (d) counts the 5 twos by two and then "five, ten" for the fives.

It is interesting to note that no base-ten models are used at all in the *Investigations* program. In both the first and second grades, a lot of emphasis is placed on the hundreds chart in ways somewhat reflected in activities found in this book.

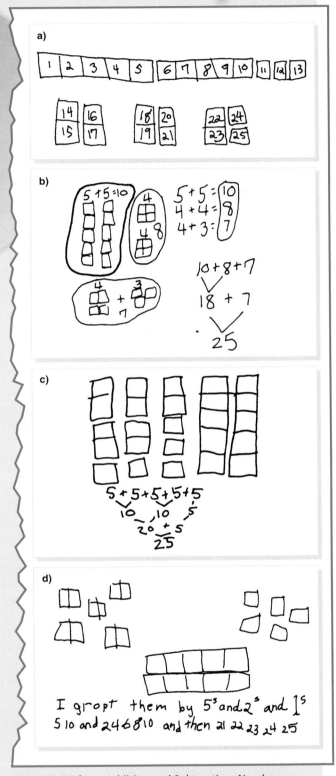

Pages 95–97 from *Addition and Subtraction: Number Games and Story Problems* by M. Kliman & S. J. Russell. *Investigations in Number, Data, and Space.* Copyright © 1998 by Dale Seymour Publications. Reprinted by permission of Pearson Education, Inc.

Equivalent Representations

An important variation of the grouping activities is aimed at the equivalent representations of numbers. For example, with children who have just completed the "Groups of 10" activity for a bag of counters, ask, "What is another way you can show your 42 besides 4 groups and 2 singles? Let's see how many ways you can find." Interestingly, most children will go next to 42 singles. The following activities are also directed to the idea of equivalent representations.

activity **12.5**

Odd Groupings

Show a collection of materials that are only partly grouped in sets of ten. For example, you may have 5 chains of 10 links and 17 additional links. Be sure the children understand that the groups each have ten items. Count the number of groups, and also count the singles. Ask, "How many in all?" Record all responses, and discuss before you count. Let the children use whatever way they wish to count. Next change the groupings (make a ten from the singles, or break apart one of the tens) and repeat the questions and discussion. Do not change the total number from one time to the next. Once students begin to understand that the total does not change, ask in what other ways the items could be grouped if you use tens and singles.

If you are teaching in grade 3 or 4, equivalent representations for hundreds as groups of tens can help with the concept of a hundred as 10 tens. The next activity is similar to "Odd Groupings" but is done using pregrouped materials and includes hundreds.

activity **12.6**

Three Other Ways

Students work in groups or pairs. First they show "four hundred sixty-three" on their desks with strips and squares in the standard representation. Next they find and record at least three other ways of showing this number.

A variation of "Three Other Ways" is to challenge students to find a way to show an amount with a specific number of pieces. "Can you show 463 with 31 pieces?" (There is more than one way to do this.) Students in grades 3 or 4 can get quite involved with finding all the ways to show a three-digit number.

After children have had sufficient experiences with pregrouped materials, a "dot, stick, and square" notation

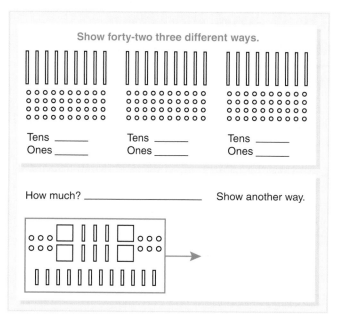

FIGURE 12.9 Equivalent representation exercises using square-stick-dot pictures.

can be used for recording ones, tens, and hundreds. By third grade, children can use small squares for hundreds, as shown in Figure 12.9. Use the drawings as a means of telling the children what materials to get out to solve the problems and also as a way for children to record results.

The next activity begins to incorporate oral language with equivalent representation ideas.

activity **12.7**

Base-Ten Riddles

Base-ten riddles can be presented orally or in written form. In either case, children should use base-ten materials to help solve them. The examples here illustrate a variety of possibilities with different levels of difficulty.

I have 23 ones and 4 tens. Who am I?

I have 4 hundreds, 12 tens, and 6 ones. Who am I?

I have 30 ones and 3 hundreds. Who am I?

I am 45. I have 25 ones. How many tens do I have?

I am 341. I have 22 tens. How many hundreds do I have?

I have 13 tens, 2 hundreds, and 21 ones. Who am I?

If you put 3 more tens with me, I would be 115. Who am I?

I have 17 ones. I am between 40 and 50. Who am I?

I have 17 ones. I am between 40 and 50. How many tens do I have?

Oral and Written Names for Numbers

In this section we focus on helping children connect the bottom two corners of the triangle in Figure 12.3—oral and written names for numbers—with their emerging base-ten concepts of using groups of ten as efficient methods of counting. Note that the ways we say and write numbers are conventions rather than concepts. Students must learn these by being told rather than through problem-based activities. It is also worth remembering that for ELL students, the structure or pattern in our English number words is probably not the same as it is in their native language. This is especially true of the numbers 11 to 19.

Two-Digit Number Names

In first and second grades, children need to connect the base-ten concepts with the oral number names they have used many times. They know the words but have not thought of them in terms of tens and ones.

Almost always use base-ten models while teaching oral names. Initially, rather than using standard number words, a more explicit *base-ten language* can be used. In base-ten language, rather than saying "forty-seven" you would say "four tens and seven ones." Base-ten language is rarely misunderstood as children are working with groupings of ten. As it seems appropriate, begin to pair base-ten language with standard language. Emphasize the teens as exceptions. Acknowledge that they are formed "backward" and do not fit the patterns. The next activity is useful for introducing oral names for numbers.

activity **12.8**

Counting Rows of 10

Use a 10 × 10 array of dots on the overhead projector. Cover up all but two rows, as shown in Figure 12.10(a). "How many tens? (2.) Two tens is called *twenty.*" Have the class repeat. "Sounds a little like *twin.*" Show another row. "Three tens is called *thirty.* Four tens is *forty.* Five tens should have been *fivety* rather than *fifty.*" The names *sixty, seventy, eighty,* and *ninety* all fit the pattern. Slide the cover up and down the array, asking how many tens and the name for that many.

Use the same 10 × 10 array to work on names for tens and ones. Show, for example, four full lines, "forty." Next expose one dot in the fifth row. "Four tens and one. Forty-one." Add more dots one at a time. "Four tens and two. Forty-two." "Four tens and three. Forty-three." This is shown in Figure 12.10(b). When that pattern is established, repeat with other decades from twenty through ninety.

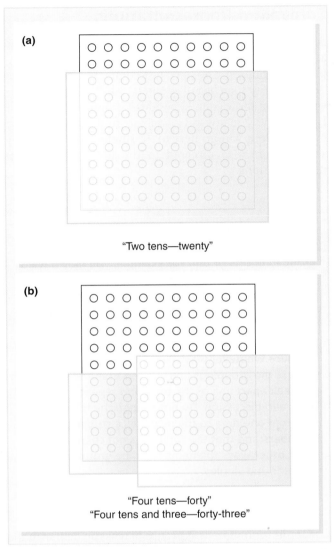

FIGURE 12.10 10 × 10 dot arrays are used to model sets of ten and singles.

Repeat this basic approach with other base-ten models. The next activity shows how this might be done.

activity **12.9**

Counting with Base-Ten Models

Show some tens pieces on the overhead in a mixed arrangement as shown in Figure 12.11. Ask how many tens. Add a ten or remove a ten and repeat the questions. Next add some ones. Always have children give the base-ten name and the standard name. Continue to make changes in the materials displayed by adding or removing 1 or 2 tens and by adding and removing ones. By avoiding the standard left-to-right order for tens and ones, the emphasis is on the names of the materials, not the order they are in.

Reverse the activity by having children use base-ten pieces at their desks. For example, you say, "Make 63." The children make the number with the models and then give the base-ten name.

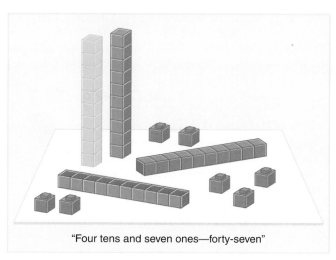

"Four tens and seven ones—forty-seven"

FIGURE 12.11 Mixed model of 47.

Note that Activities 12.8 and 12.9 will be much enhanced by discussion. Have children explain their thinking. If you don't require children to reflect on these responses, they soon learn how to give the response you want, matching number words to models, without actually thinking about the total quantities. The next activity has the same objective.

activity 12.10

Tens, Ones, and Fingers
Ask your class, "How can you show 37 fingers?" (It is fun to precede this question by asking for different ways to show 6 fingers, 8 fingers, and other amounts less than 10.) Soon children will figure out that four children are required. Line up four children, and have three hold up 10 fingers and the last child 7 fingers. Have the class count the fingers by tens and ones. Ask for other children to show different numbers. Emphasize the number of sets of 10 fingers and the single fingers (base-ten language) and pair this with the standard language.

In the last three activities, it is important occasionally to count an entire representation by ones. Remember that the count by ones is the young child's principal linkage with the concept of quantity. For example, suppose you have just had children use connecting cubes to make 42. Try asking, "Do you think there really are 42 blocks

there?" Many children are not convinced, and the count by ones is very significant.

Three-Digit Number Names

The approach to three-digit number names is essentially the same as for two-digit names. Show mixed arrangements of base-ten materials. Have children give the base-ten name and the standard name. Vary the arrangement from one example to the next by changing only one type of piece. That is, add or remove only ones or only tens or only hundreds.

Similarly, have children at their desks model numbers that you give to them orally using the standard names. By the time that children are ready for three-digit numbers, the two-digit number names, including the difficulties with the teens, have usually been mastered. The major difficulty is with numbers involving no tens, such as 702. As noted earlier, the use of base-ten language is quite helpful here. The zero-tens difficulty is more pronounced when writing numerals. Children frequently write 7002 for "seven hundred two." The emphasis on the meaning in the oral base-ten language form will be a significant help.

Written Symbols

Place-value mats are simple mats divided into two or three sections to hold ones and tens or ones, tens, and hundreds pieces as shown in Figure 12.12. You can suggest to your students that the mats are a good way to organize their materials when working with base-ten pieces. Explain that the

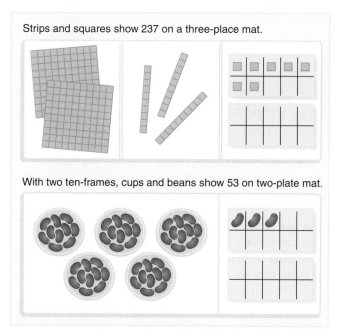

Strips and squares show 237 on a three-place mat.

With two ten-frames, cups and beans show 53 on two-plate mat.

FIGURE 12.12 Place-value mats with two ten-frames in the ones place to organize the counters and promote the concept of groups of ten.

standard way to use a place-value mat is with the space for the ones on the right and tens and hundreds places to the left.

Though there is no requirement to have anything printed on the mats, it is strongly recommended that two ten-frames be drawn in the ones place as shown. (See Blackline Masters.) That way, the amount of ones on the ten-frames is always clearly evident, eliminating the need for frequent and tedious counting. The ten-frame also makes it very clear how many additional counters would be needed to make the next set of ten. If children are modeling two numbers at the same time, one ten-frame can be used for each number. Most illustrations of place-value mats in this book will show two ten-frames, even though that feature is not commonly seen in standard texts.

As children use their place-value mats, they can be shown how the left-to-right order of the pieces is also the way that numbers are written. The place-value mat becomes a link between the base-ten models and the written form of the numbers. Once again, be aware of how easy it would be for a child to show a number on a mat using tens and ones pieces and learn to write the number without any understanding of what the number represents. First- and second-grade textbooks often show a model and have children record numbers in this manner:

_7_ tens and _3_ ones is _73_ in all.

It is all too easy to copy down the number of sticks and single blocks and rewrite these digits in a single number 73 and not confront what these symbols stand for.

The next three activities are designed to help children make connections among all three representations: models, oral language, and written forms. They can be done with two- or three-digit numbers in grades 1–4.

activity 12.11

Say It/Press It

Display some ones and tens (and hundreds) so that the class can see. (Use the overhead projector or simply draw on the board using the square-stick-dot method.) Arrange the materials in a mixed design, not in the standard left-to-right format. Students say the amount shown in base-ten language ("four hundreds, one ten, and five") and then in standard language ("four hundred fifteen"), and finally they enter it on their calculators. Have someone share his or her display and defend it. Make a change in the materials and repeat.

"Say It/Press It" is especially good for helping with teens (note the example in the activity description) and for

three-digit numbers with zero tens. If you show 7 hundreds and 4 ones, the class says "seven hundreds, zero tens, and four—seven hundred (*slight pause*) four." The pause and the base-ten language suggest the correct three-digit number to press or write. Many students have trouble with this example and write "7004," writing exactly what they hear in the standard name. Similarly, first- and second-grade children often write "504" for fifty-four. This activity will help. The next activity simply changes the first representation that is presented to the students.

activity 12.12

Show It/Press It

Say the standard name for a number (with either two or three digits). At their desks, students use their own base-ten models to show that number and press it on their calculators (or write it). Again, pay special attention to the teens and the case of zero tens.

The following activity has been popular for decades and remains a useful challenge for students in the early stages of place-value development.

activity 12.13

Digit Change

Have students enter a specific two- or three-digit number on the calculator. The task is to then change one of the digits in the number without simply entering the new number. For example, change 48 to 78. Change 315 to 305 or to 295. Changes can be made by adding or subtracting an appropriate amount. Students should write or discuss explanations for their solutions.

Assessment Notes

Children are often able to disguise their lack of understanding of place value by following directions, using the tens and ones pieces in prescribed ways, and using the language of place value.

The diagnostic tasks presented here are designed to help you look more closely at children's understanding of place value. They are not suggested as definitive tests but as means of obtaining information for the thoughtful teacher. These tasks have been used by several researchers and are adapted primarily from Labinowicz (1985), Kamii (1985), and Ross (1986). The tasks are designed for one-on-one settings. They should not be used as instructional activities.

Write the number 342. Have the child read the number. Then have the child write the number that is 1 more than the number. Next ask for the number that is 10 more than the number. You may wish to explore further with models. One less and 10 less can be checked the same way.

The next task is referred to as the *Digit Correspondence Task* and has been used widely in the study of place-value development. Dump out 36 blocks. Ask the child to count the blocks, and then have the child write the number that tells how many there are. Circle the 6 in 36 and ask, "Does this part of your 36 have anything to do with how many blocks there are?" Then circle the 3 and repeat the question exactly. Do not give clues. Based on responses to the task, Ross (1989) has identified five distinct levels of understanding of place value:

1. *Single numeral.* The child writes 36 but views it as a single numeral. The individual digits 3 and 6 have no meaning by themselves.
2. *Position names.* The child identifies correctly the tens and ones positions but still makes no connections between the individual digits and the blocks.
3. *Face value.* The child matches 6 blocks with the 6 and 3 blocks with the 3.
4. *Transition to place value.* The 6 is matched with 6 blocks and the 3 with the remaining 30 blocks but not as 3 groups of 10.
5. *Full understanding.* The 3 is correlated with 3 groups of 10 blocks and the 6 with 6 single blocks. ■

Patterns and Relationships with Multidigit Numbers

Up to this point in the chapter, the focus has been on helping students read and write multidigit numbers with understanding—the triangle of ideas described in Figure 12.3. Generally the focus has been on the meaning of only one number at a time and the meaning of each digit—*show me 346 with base-ten blocks.*

So, what is wrong with this approach? Although there is much to commend in the efforts to help students connect representations of base-ten concepts with written and oral forms for numbers, restricting our attention to this approach fails to help students develop a sense of how any number is connected to close, important numbers such as multiples of 10, 25, and 100.

Although not suggesting that the curriculum should abandon the connections described in Figure 12.3, in this section we want to move beyond this snapshot view of individual numbers toward an orientation that looks at the full number rather than the digits. Here the focus will be on the patterns in our number system and how numbers are related to one another. We are interested in the relationships of numbers to important special numbers—relationships that begin to overlap with or are a readiness for computation. In the standards-based curricula, ideas simi-

lar to those found in this section comprise nearly all of the place-value development with little or no attention given to the ideas that were discussed earlier.

The Hundreds Chart

The hundreds chart (Figure 12.13) is such an important tool in the development of place-value concepts that it deserves special attention. K–2 classrooms should have a hundreds chart displayed prominently.

An extremely useful version of the chart is made of transparent pockets into which each of the 100 numeral cards can be inserted. You can hide a number by inserting a blank card in front of a number in the pocket. You can insert colored pieces of paper in the slots to highlight various number patterns. And you can remove the number cards and have students replace them in their correct slots.

An overhead transparency of a hundreds chart is almost as flexible as the pocket chart version. Numbers can be hidden by placing opaque counters on them. Patterns can be marked with a pen or with transparent counters. A transparency of a blank 10 × 10 grid serves as an empty hundreds chart on which you can write numbers. These transparencies can be made from the Blackline Masters and are also available commercially. (A set of four smaller charts on one page is also available in the Blackline Masters and is useful for many student activities.)

At the kindergarten and first-grade levels, students can be helped to count and recognize two-digit numbers with the hundreds chart long before they develop a base-ten understanding of these numbers. There are many useful hundreds-chart activities for the K–2 level.

1	2	3	4	5	6	7	8	9	10
11	12	13	14	15	16	17	18	19	20
21	22	23	24	25	26	27	28	29	30
31	32	33	34	35	36	37	38	39	40
41	42	43	44	45	46	47	48	49	50
51	52	53	54	55	56	57	58	59	60
61	62	63	64	65	66	67	68	69	70
71	72	73	74	75	76	77	78	79	80
81	82	83	84	85	86	87	88	89	90
91	92	93	94	95	96	97	98	99	100

FIGURE 12.13 A hundreds chart.

activity **12.14**

Patterns on the Hundreds Chart

Have children work in pairs to find patterns on the hundreds chart. Solicit ideas orally from the class. Have children explain patterns found by others to be sure that all understand the ideas that are being suggested.

There are lots of patterns on the hundreds chart. In a discussion, different children will describe the same pattern in several ways. Accept all ideas. Here are some of the patterns they may point out:

- The numbers in a column all end with the same number, which is the same as the number at the top.
- In a row, one number "counts" (the ones digit goes 1, 2, 3, . . . , 9, 0); the "second" number goes up by ones, but the first number (tens digit) stays the same.
- In a column, the first number (tens digit) "counts" or goes up by ones.
- You can count by tens going down the right-hand column.
- The numbers under the 2 are all even numbers. (Every other number is even.)
- If you count by fives, you get two columns, the last column and the 5 column.

For children, these patterns are not at all obvious or trivial. For example, one child may notice the pattern in the column under the 4—every number ends in a 4. Two minutes later another child will "discover" the parallel pattern in the column headed by 7. That there is a pattern like this in every column may not be completely obvious.

Other patterns you might have students explore include numbers that have a 7 in them, numbers where the digits add up to four, and various skip-count patterns.

activity **12.15**

Skip-Count Patterns

As a full class activity, have students skip count by twos, threes, fours, and so on. After skip counting as a class, have students record a specific skip-count pattern on their own copy of the hundreds chart by coloring in each number they count. Every skip count produces an interesting pattern on the chart. You should also discuss the patterns in the numbers. For example, when you skip-count by fours, you only land on numbers that you get when you count by twos. Which counts make column patterns and which counts make diagonal patterns?

In the beginning, skip counting may be quite difficult for children. As they become more comfortable with skip counts, you can challenge students to skip-count without the aid of the hundreds chart. Skip-counting skills show a readiness for multiplication combinations and also help children begin to look for interesting and useful patterns in numbers.

activity **12.16**

Missing Numbers

Provide students with a hundreds chart on which some of the number cards have been removed. Use the classroom pocket chart or, for a full-class activity, you can use the overhead transparency. The students' task is to replace the missing numbers or tell what they are. Beginning versions of this activity have only a random selection of individual numbers removed. Later, remove sequences of several numbers from three or four different rows. Finally, remove all but one or two rows or columns. Eventually, challenge children to replace all of the numbers in a blank chart.

Replacing the number cards or tiles from a blank chart is a good station activity for two students to work on together. By listening to how students go about finding the correct places for numbers you can learn a lot about how well they have constructed an understanding of the 1-to-100 sequence.

activity **12.17**

More and Less on the Hundreds Chart

Begin with a blank or nearly blank chart. Circle a particular missing number. Students are to fill in the designated number and its "neighbors," the numbers to the left, right, above, and below. This can be done with the full class on the overhead projector, or worksheets can be prepared using a blank hundreds chart or 10 × 10 grid. After students become comfortable naming the neighbors of a number, ask what they notice about the neighbor numbers. The numbers to the left and right are one more and one less than the given number. Those above and below are ten less and ten more, respectively. By discussing these relationships on the chart, students begin to see how the sequence of numbers is related to the numeric relationships in the numbers.

Notice that children will first use the hundreds chart to learn about the patterns in the sequence of numbers. Many students, especially at the K or grade-1 level, will not understand the corresponding numeric relationships such as those discussed in the last activity. In the following activity, number relationships on the chart are made more explicit by including the use of base-ten models.

activity **12.18**

Models with the Hundreds Chart

This activity has several variations that can be conducted with the full class or can be made into an activity in which two students work together to explore an idea and write about what they have discovered. Use any physical model for two-digit numbers with which the students are familiar. The little ten-frame cards are recommended.

- **Give children one or more numbers to first make with the models and then find on the chart. Use groups of two or three numbers either in the same row or the same column.**
- **Indicate a number on the chart. What would you have to change to make each of its neighbors (the numbers to the left, right, above, and below)?**

To accentuate how the hundreds chart can extend even very young students' concepts of number, consider Figure 12.14, which shows the results of kindergarten discussion in which children were using a hundreds chart to find combinations for six. These students likely had very little understanding of base-ten concepts but used patterns on the chart to see how big numbers are related in a similar manner as little numbers.

It is becoming more and more popular to have a chart that extends to 200, even in the first grade. Perhaps a more powerful idea is to extend the hundreds chart to 1000.

activity **12.19**

The Thousands Chart

Provide students with several sheets of the blank hundreds charts from the Blackline Masters. Assign groups of three or four students the task of creating a 1-to-1000 chart. The chart is made by taping ten charts together in a long strip. Students should decide how they are going to divide up the task with different students taking different parts of the chart.

The thousands chart should be discussed as a class to examine how numbers change as you count from 1 hundred to the next, what the patterns are, and so on. In fact, the earlier hundreds chart activities can all be extended to a thousands chart. You may want to make a blank thousands chart (clearly indicating each 100-square). Use the students' charts for other discussions.

Several software packages include hundreds charts that allow students to explore patterns. Many of these offer little advantage over a physical chart. *Learning About Number Relationships* is an e-example from NCTM's *e-Standards* that has a calculator and hundreds chart and allows for a fairly open exploration. Patterns are colored on the chart as students

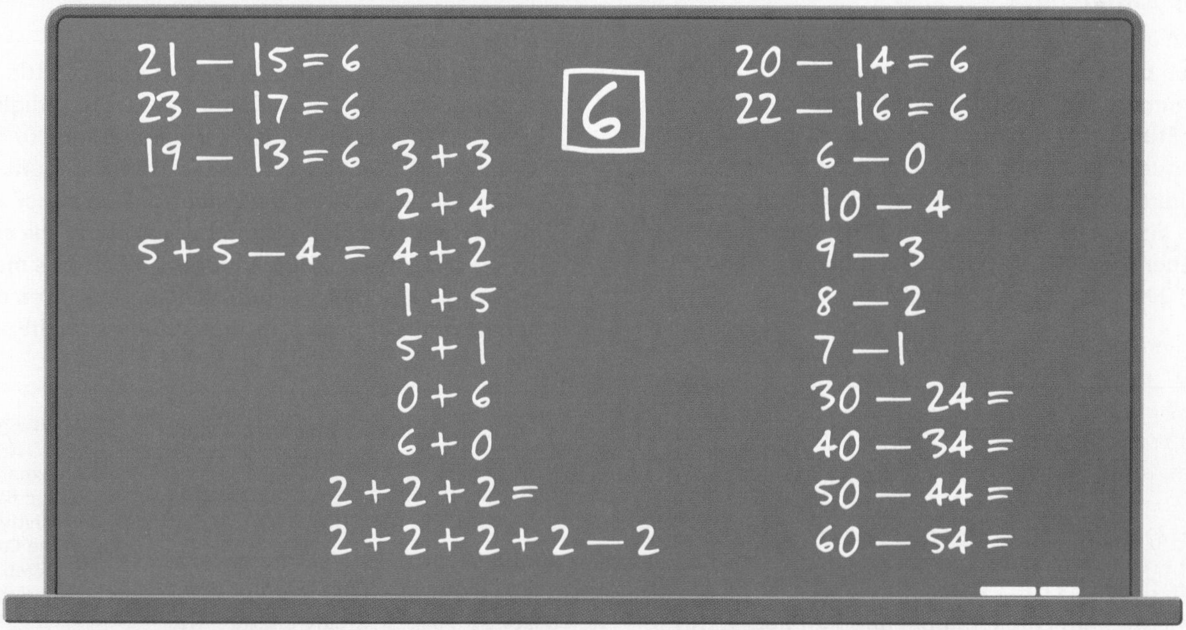

$$21 - 15 = 6$$
$$23 - 17 = 6$$
$$19 - 13 = 6 \quad 3 + 3$$
$$2 + 4$$
$$5 + 5 - 4 = 4 + 2$$
$$1 + 5$$
$$5 + 1$$
$$0 + 6$$
$$6 + 0$$
$$2 + 2 + 2 =$$
$$2 + 2 + 2 + 2 - 2$$

$$\boxed{6}$$

$$20 - 14 = 6$$
$$22 - 16 = 6$$
$$6 - 0$$
$$10 - 4$$
$$9 - 3$$
$$8 - 2$$
$$7 - 1$$
$$30 - 24 =$$
$$40 - 34 =$$
$$50 - 44 =$$
$$60 - 54 =$$

FIGURE 12.14 Kindergarten children used a hundreds chart to find these combinations for six (reproduction of an actual chalkboard from a kindergarten class).

skip-count with the calculator. Students can skip-count by any number and also begin their counts at any number. Any two patterns can be overlapped using two colors. Patterns are easily cleared to try another. The chart also extends to 1000. The *Number Patterns* applet from the NLVM (http://matti.usu.edu/nlvm/nav/vlibrary.html) presents students with number patterns to complete. ■

Relationships with Landmark Numbers

One of the most valuable features of both the hundreds chart and the little ten-frame cards is how clearly they illustrate the distance to the next multiple of ten—the end of the row on the chart or the blank spaces on the ten-frame card. Multiples of 10, 100, and occasionally other special numbers such as multiples of 25, are referred to in the *Investigations in Number, Data, and Space* program as *landmark numbers.* Students learn to use this term as they work with informal methods of computation. When finding the difference between 74 and 112, a child might say, "First I added 6 onto 74 to get to a landmark number. Then I added 2 more tens onto 80 to get to 100 because that's another landmark number. . . ." Whatever terminology is used, understanding how numbers are related to these special numbers is an important step in students' number sense development.

In addition to the hundreds chart, the number line is an excellent way to get at these relationships. The next two activities are suggestions for using number lines.

activity 12.20

Who Am I?
Sketch a line labeled 0 and 100 at opposite ends. Mark a point with a ? that corresponds to your secret number. (Estimate the position the best you can.) Students try to guess your secret number. For each guess, place and label a mark on the line. Continue marking each guess until your secret number is discovered. As a variation, the endpoints can be other than 0 and 100. For example, try 0 and 1000, 200 and 300, or 500 and 800.

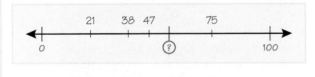

activity 12.21

Who Could They Be?
Label two points on a number line (not necessarily the ends) with landmark numbers.

Ask students what numbers they think different points labeled with letters might be and why they think that. In the example shown here, B and C are

less than 100 but probably more than 60. E could be about 180. You can also ask where 75 might be or where 400 is. About how far apart are A and D? Why do you think D is more than 100?

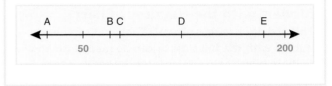

The next two activities are extensions of part-part-whole ideas that were explored in Chapter 9. In the first of these, one of the parts is a landmark number. In the second, the landmark number is the whole.

activity 12.22

50 and Some More
Say or write a number between 50 and 100. Students respond with "50 and ____." For 63, the response is "50 and 13." Any landmark number can be used instead of 50. For example, you could use any number that ends in 50. You can also do this with numbers such as 70 or 230.

Landmark numbers are often broken apart in computations. The next activity is aimed at what may be the most important landmark number, 100.

activity 12.23

The Other Part of 100
Two students work together with a set of little ten-frame cards. One student makes a two-digit number. Then both students work mentally to determine what goes with the ten-frame amount to make 100. They write their solutions on paper and then check by making the other part with the cards to see if the total is 100. Students take turns making the original number. Figure 12.15 shows three different thought processes that students might use.

Being able to give the other part of 100 should become a skill focus at grades 2 to 4 because it is so useful for flexible methods of computation.

If your students are adept at parts of 100, you can change the whole from 100 to another number. At first try other multiples of 10 such as 70 or 80. Then extend the whole to any number less than 100.

EXPANDED LESSON
An expanded lesson based on Activity 12.23 is on the Companion Web site at www. ablongman.com/ vandewalle6e.

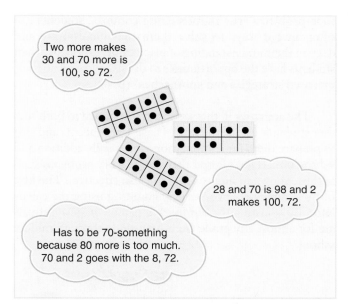

FIGURE 12.15 Using little ten-frames to help think about the "other part of 100."

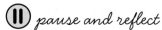

(II) *pause and reflect* _____

Suppose that the whole is 83. Sketch four little ten-frame cards showing 36. Looking at your "cards," what goes with 36 to make 83? How did you think about it?

_____

What you just did in finding the other part of 83 was subtract 36 from 83. You did not borrow or regroup. Most likely you did it in your head. With more practice you (and students as early as the third grade) can do this without the aid of the cards.

Compatible numbers for addition and subtraction are numbers that go together easily to make nice numbers. Numbers that make tens or hundreds are the most common examples. Compatible sums also include numbers that end in 5, 25, 50, or 75, since these numbers are easy to work with as well. The teaching task is to get students accustomed to looking for combinations that work together and then looking for these combinations in computational situations.

activity **12.24**

Compatible Pairs

Searching for compatible pairs can be done as a worksheet activity or with the full class using the overhead projector. Prepare a transparency or duplicate a page with a search task. Four possibilities of different difficulty levels are shown in Figure 12.16. Students call out or connect the compatible pairs as they see them.

The next activity has children apply some of the same ideas about landmark numbers that we have been exploring.

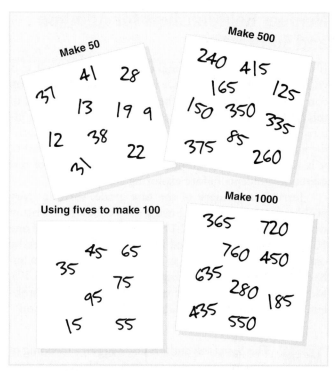

FIGURE 12.16 Compatible-pair searches.

activity **12.25**

Close, Far, and In Between

Put any three numbers on the board. If appropriate, use two-digit numbers.

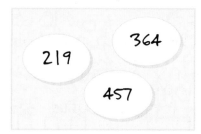

With these three numbers as referents, ask questions, such as the following, and encourage discussion of all responses:

Which two are closest? Why?

Which is closest to 300? To 250?

Name a number between 457 and 364.

Name a multiple of 25 between 219 and 364.

Name a number that is more than all of these.

About how far apart are 219 and 500? 219 and 5000?

If these are "big numbers," what are some small numbers? Numbers that are about the same? Numbers that make these seem small?

Number Relationships for Addition and Subtraction

If you examine any traditional textbook for grades 1 to 5 you will find chapters on place value and other chapters on computational strategies. The same, of course, is true of this book. However, evidence suggests that there is an interaction between learning about numeration and learning about computational techniques (NRC, 2001). That is, it is not necessary to complete the development of numeration concepts before exploring computation.

Jerrika, in January of the first grade, solves a story problem for 10 + 13 + 22 using snap cubes. Her written work is shown in Figure 12.17. She is beginning to use one 10 but most likely counted on the remaining cubes by ones. Her classmate, Monica, solved the same problem but has clearly utilized more base-ten ideas (Figure 12.17). Ideas such as these continue to grow with additional problem solving and sharing of ideas during class discussion.

NCTM Standards The *Standards* authors also suggest a blending of numeration and computation. "It is not necessary to wait for students to fully develop place-value understandings before giving them opportunities to solve problems with two- and three-digit numbers. When such problems arise in interesting contexts, students can often invent ways to solve them that incorporate and deepen their understanding of place value, especially when students have the opportunities to discuss and explain their invented strategies and approaches" (p. 82).

The activities in this section are designed to both further students' understanding of base-ten concepts and also to prepare them for computation—especially addition and subtraction. (Don't forget that simple story problems such as those shown in Figure 12.17 are also effective.) The first of these activities involves skip counting using the calculator. By adjusting the numbers, it can be made appropriate for almost any grade from first grade through middle school.

activity **12.26**

Calculator Challenge Counting

Students press any number on the calculator (e.g., 7) and then [+] 4. They say the sum before they press [=]. Then they continue to add 4 mentally, challenging themselves to say the number before they press [=]. A challenge is to see how far they can go without making a mistake.

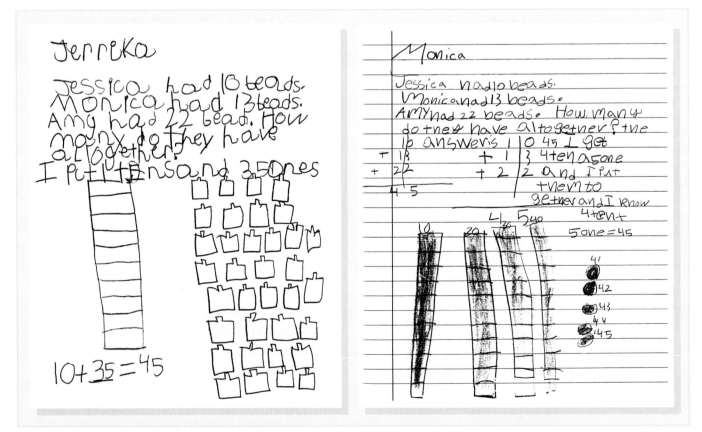

FIGURE 12.17 The work of two first-grade children in January. They both solved the problem 10 + 13 + 22. Jerrika's work shows she does not yet use tens in her computation whereas Monica is clearly adding groups of ten.

The constant addend (+ 4) in "Calculator Challenge Counting" can be any number, even a two- or three-digit number. Generally, the starting number is less than ten but there is no reason that students cannot begin, for example, with 327 or any other number. Young students will even find jumps of five fairly challenging if the starting number is not also a multiple of five. Skip-counting by 20 or 25 will be easier than counting by 7 or 12 and will help to develop important patterns and relationships.

"Calculator Challenge Counting" can also go in reverse. That is, enter a number such as 123 in the calculator and press – 6. As before, students say the result before pressing =. Each successive press will subtract six or whatever constant was entered.

The skip-counting in this activity can, of course, be done with a full class. However, the usual mode of leaders and followers may diminish the value. Two children can work together quite profitably. The flexibility of the activity allows for it to be used over and over at various skill levels, always challenging students and improving their mental skills with numbers.

The next activity combines symbolism with base-ten representations.

activity **12.27**

Numbers, Squares, Sticks, and Dots

As illustrated in Figure 12.18, prepare a worksheet or a transparency on which a numeral and some base-ten pieces are shown. Use small squares, sticks, and dots to keep the drawings simple. The task is to mentally compute the totals.

If this activity is done as a full class, discuss each exercise before going to the next. If you use a worksheet format, include only a few examples and have students write how they went about solving them. It is still important to have a discussion with the class.

The next activity extends the use of the hundreds board.

activity **12.28**

Hundreds Board Addition

For this activity it is best to have a classroom hundreds board (or a thousands board) that all students can see. An alternative is to provide individual hundreds boards on paper (see Blackline Masters). Students are to use the hundreds board to add two numbers. Because there are many ways that the hundreds board can be used for addition, the value is in class discussions. Therefore, it is a good idea to do only one sum at a time and then have a discussion of different methods.

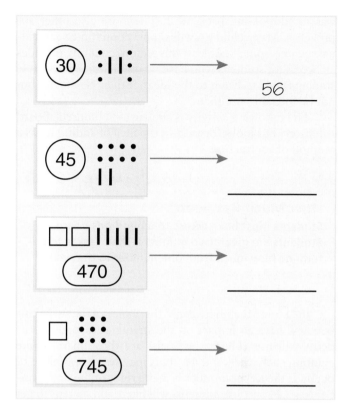

FIGURE 12.18 Flexible counting on or addition using both models and numerals.

The hundreds chart can be seen as a folded-up number line—one that accentuates the distance from any number to the next multiple of ten. A jump down a row is the same as adding ten and up a row is ten less. Consider how a child might use the hundreds chart to help think about the sum of 38 and 25. As illustrated in Figure 12.19(a), one approach is to begin at 38 and count over 2 to 40. From there a student might count down two rows to 60 for a total of 22 and then add 3 more in the next row. Figure 12.19(b) shows adding 38 beginning at 25. Here the idea

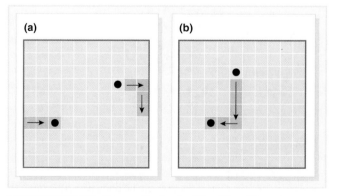

FIGURE 12.19 Two methods of adding 38 + 25 on the hundreds chart. It is important to stress the idea that moving down a row is the same as adding 10.

was to add 40 and back off 2. There are also other approaches. Many children will simply count on 25 individual squares from 38. At least this tedious counting provides an access for students who have no other strategies. These students need to listen to the ideas of their classmates but not be forced to use them.

The following activity is similar to "Hundreds Board Addition" but looks forward to the idea of adding up as a method of subtraction.

activity **12.29**

How Much Between?
Students must have access to a hundreds board. Students are given two numbers. Their task is to determine how much from one number to the next.

In "How Much Between?" the choice of the two numbers will have an impact on the strategies that some students will use. The easiest pairs are those in the same column, such as 24 and 64. This may be a good place to begin. If the larger number is to the right of the first number (e.g., 24 and 56), students will likely add on tens to get to the target number's row and then add ones. Of course, this is also a reasonable strategy for any two numbers. But consider 17 and 45 where 45 is left of 17 on the chart. With this pair, a reasonable strategy is to move down 3 rows (+30) to 47 and then count back 2 (−2) to 45. The total count is now 30 − 2 or 28. There are also other possible approaches.

The next two activities are mathematically parallel to the previous two but they use little ten-frame cards instead of the hundreds chart.

activity **12.30**

Little Ten-Frame Sums
Provide pairs of students with two sets of little ten-frame cards. Each child chooses a number. An example is shown in Figure 12.20(a). Students then work together to find the total number of dots. Each pair of numbers and the sum should be written on paper with the agreed-upon answer.

The activity can also be done by showing the two numbers on the overhead projector and having students work in pairs at their desks.

activity **12.31**

How Far to My Number?
Students work in pairs with a single set of little ten-frame cards. One student uses the cards to make a number less than 50. In the meantime, the other student writes a number larger than 50 on a piece of paper, as shown in Figure 12.20(b). You may choose to limit the size of this number but it is not necessary. The task is for the students to work together to find out how much more must be added to the ten-frame number to get to the written number. Students should try to do this without using any more cards. Once an answer is determined, they should make their answer with cards and see if the total is the same as the written numbers.

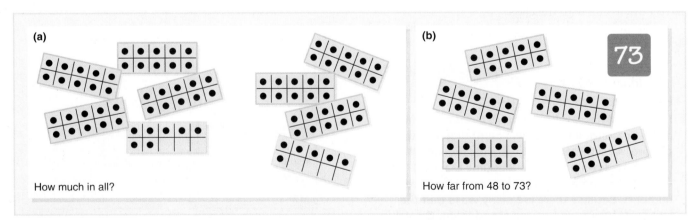

(a) How much in all?

(b) How far from 48 to 73?

FIGURE 12.20 Two tasks that can be done with little ten-frame cards. Students working on problems such as these are learning about place value and also are preparing for addition and subtraction.

(II) *pause and reflect* _____

Try your hand at the two examples in Figure 12.20. How many ways can you imagine that two students might do these? Share your ideas with a colleague.

_____

Chapter 13 will discuss a variety of solution strategies that students use to add and subtract numbers. Students should have ample opportunities to develop their ideas in activities like those in this section. Notice, however, that students may still be developing their ideas about numbers and the distances between them. These ideas are as much about place-value understanding as about addition and subtraction. The little ten-frames and the hundreds chart are good models to help with these relationships.

 Students who exhibit difficulty with any of these activities may also have difficulty with almost any type of invented computation. For example, how do students go about the exercises in Activity 12.27, "Numbers, Squares, Sticks, and Dots"? That activity requires that children have sufficient understanding of base-ten concepts to use them in meaningful counts. If students are counting by ones, perhaps on their fingers, then more practice with these activities may be misplaced. Rather, consider additional counting and grouping activities in which students have the opportunity to see the value of groups of ten. Using the little ten-frame cards may also help.

"How Far to My Number?" (Activity 12.31) is also a useful diagnostic task. As you listen to how children solve these problems, you will realize that there is a lot more information to be found out about their thinking beyond simply getting the correct answer. ■

Connections to Real-World Ideas

We should not permit children to study place-value concepts without encouraging them to see number in the world about them. You do not need a prescribed activity to bring real numbers into the classroom.

Children in the second grade should be thinking about numbers under 100 first and, soon after, numbers up to 1000. Quantities larger than that are difficult to think about. Where are numbers like this? Around your school: the number of children in each class, the numbers on the school buses, the number of minutes devoted to mathematics each day and then each week, the number of cartons of chocolate and plain milk served in the cafeteria each day, the numbers on the calendar (days in a week, month, year), the number of days since school has started. And then there are measurements, numbers at home, numbers on a field trip, and so on.

What do you do with these numbers? Turn them into interesting graphs, write stories using them, make up problems, devise contests.

As children get a bit older, the interest in numbers can expand beyond the school and classroom. All sorts of things can and should be measured to create graphs, draw inferences, and make comparisons. For example, what numbers are associated with the "average" fifth grader? Height, weight, arm span, age in months, number of siblings, number of grandparents, distance from home to school, length of standing broad jump, number of pets, hours spent watching TV in a week. How can you find the average for these or other numbers that may be of interest to the students in your room? Is anyone really average?

The particular way you bring number and the real world together in your class is up to you. But do not underestimate the value of connecting the real world to the classroom.

Helping Children Work with Money

Money skills are perennial problems for the primary teacher. Although no easy answers exist, it is useful to consider what skills and concepts are required for working with money. Here is a list of the money ideas and skills typically required in the primary grades:

- Coin recognition
- Values of coins
- Using the values of coins
- Counting sets of coins (including comparing two sets)
- Equivalent collections of coins (same amounts, different coins)
- Selecting coins for a given amount
- Making change

These ideas and skills will be discussed in the following sections.

Coin Recognition and Values

The names of our coins are conventions of our social system. Students learn these names the same way that they learn the names of any physical objects in their daily environment—through exposure and repetition.

The value of each coin is also a convention that students must simply be told. For these values to make sense, students must have an understanding of 5, 10, and 25. More than that, they need to be able to think of these quantities without seeing countable objects. Nowhere else do we say, "this is five," while pointing to a single item. A child whose number concepts remain tied to counts of objects is not going to be able to understand the values of coins. Coin value lessons should focus on purchase power—a dime can *buy the same thing* that 10 pennies can buy.

Using Coin Values

The remaining items in the list of skills are all a form of mental computation and/or compound skip-counting. To name the total value of a group of coins is the same as mentally adding their values except that there are no numerals visible. Ironically, most state standards require coin counting before they require students to do the symbolic sum mentally.

There is nothing wrong with asking second-grade students to do the mental math required in counting a collection of coins. Even though it is actually mental computation, the numbers are fortunately restricted to multiples of five and ten with some ones added at the end. The next activity is a preparation for counting money.

activity 12.32

Money Skip Counts

Explain to the students that they will start skip-counting by one number and at your signal they will shift to a count by a different number. Begin with only two different amounts, say, 25 and 10. Write these numbers on the board. Point to the larger number (25), and have students begin to skip-count. After three or more counts, raise your hand to indicate a pause in the counting. Then lower your hand and point to the smaller number (10). Children continue the skip count from where they left off but now count by 10s. Use any two of these numbers: 100, 50, 25, 10, 5, 1. Always start with the larger. Later, try three numbers, still in descending order.

Remember that working with coins requires not only adding up the values but also first mentally giving each coin a value and then ordering the coins. A good readiness activity is the following one in which students add a mixed collection of numbers, each of which is the value of a coin.

activity 12.33

Coin-Number Addition

On the board or overhead, write a small collection of numbers in haphazard form. All numbers are the same as coin values.

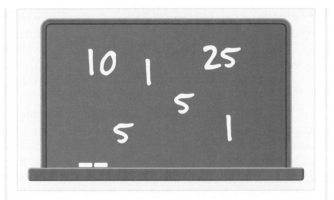

Begin with only 10s and 1s. Then add some 5s and eventually 25s (and 50s, if these are in your curriculum). The students' task is to add the numbers mentally. Do not suggest how they add the numbers or in what order. Depending on the particular collection, there is generally more than one good way to do this. Discuss with students how they added the collection.

When discussing solutions to this last activity, be sure to value any approach that works. However, pay special attention to those students who begin with the larger values and those who put nice combinations together utilizing thinking with tens. There is no reason to require students to add in any particular order, not with this activity or with coins.

After students have gathered experiences with coin-numbers, try the same activity with coins. Simply spill some plastic coins on the overhead or draw "coins" on the board. (Draw circles with P, N, D, or Q inside but no numbers.) Equivalent exercises are found in most standard textbooks.

Making Change

Last in the list of money skills is making change. In traditional curricula, making change is the only time that students are asked to add on to find a difference, so it is a very foreign type of task. Furthermore, children are generally asked to create the difference or change in a prescribed manner. Finally, they must do it with coins instead of numerals.

Because adding on to find a difference is such a valuable skill—much easier than using the usual subtraction algorithm—it makes sense to give students a lot of experience with adding on to find differences before asking them to make change. As students become more skillful at adding on, they can see the process of making change as an extension of a skill already acquired.

Good places to begin are with the activity "The Other Part of 100" (Activity 12.23) and "How Far to My Number?" (Activity 12.31). The use of the little ten-frame cards in these activities encourages students to first add up to the next ten, although that is not the only method.

This sequence of suggested activities is not a surefire solution to the difficulties students experience with money. It is designed to build on prerequisite number and place-value skills and concepts without or before using coins.

Numbers Beyond 1000

For children to have good concepts of numbers beyond 1000, the conceptual ideas that have been carefully developed must be extended. This is sometimes difficult to do because physical models for thousands are not commonly available. At the same time, number sense ideas must also be developed. In many ways, it is these informal ideas about very large numbers that are the most important.

Extending the Place-Value System

Two important ideas developed for three-digit numbers should be extended to larger numbers. First, the grouping idea should be generalized. That is, ten in any position makes a single thing (group) in the next position, and vice versa. Second, the oral and written patterns for numbers in three digits are duplicated in a clever way for every three digits to the left. These two related ideas are not as easy for children to understand as adults seem to believe. Because models for large numbers are so difficult to have or picture, textbooks must deal with these ideas in a predominantly symbolic manner. That is not sufficient!

activity **12.34**

What Comes Next?

Have a "What Comes Next?" discussion with the use of base-ten strips and squares. The unit or ones piece is a 1-centimeter (cm) square. The tens piece is a 10 × 1 strip. The hundreds piece is a square, 10 cm × 10 cm. What is next? Ten hundreds is called a thousand. What shape? It could be a strip made of 10 hundreds squares. Tape 10 hundreds together. What is next? (Reinforce the idea of "ten makes one" that has progressed to this point.) Ten one-thousand strips would make a square measuring 1 meter (m) on a side. Once the class has figured out the shape of the thousand piece, the problem-based task is "What comes next?" Let small groups work on the dimensions of a ten-thousand piece.

If your students become interested in seeing the big pieces from "What Comes Next?" engage them in measuring them out on paper. Ten ten-thousand squares (100,000) go together to make a huge strip. Draw this strip on a long sheet of butcher paper, and mark off the ten squares that make it up. You will have to go out in the hall.

How far you want to extend this square, strip, square, strip sequence depends on your class. The idea that 10 in one place makes 1 in the next can be brought home dramatically. It is quite possible with older children to make the next 10 m × 10 m square using chalk lines on the playground. The next strip is 100 m × 10 m. This can be measured out on a large playground with kids marking the corners. By this point, the payoff includes an appreciation of the increase in size of each successive amount as well as the ten-makes-one progression. The 100 m × 10 m strip is the model for 10 million, and the 10 m × 10 m square models 1 million. The difference between 1 million and 10 million is dramatic. Even the concept of 1 million tiny centimeter squares is dramatic.

The three-dimensional wooden or plastic base-ten materials are all available with a model for thousands, which is a 10-cm cube. These models are expensive, but having at least one large cube to show and talk about is a good idea.

Try the "What Comes Next?" discussion in the context of these three-dimensional models. The first three shapes are distinct: a *cube*, a *long*, and a *flat*. What comes next? Stack ten flats and they make a cube, same shape as the first one only 1000 times larger. What comes next? (See Figure 12.21.) Ten *cubes* make another *long*. What comes next? Ten big *longs* make a big *flat*. The first three shapes have now repeated! Ten big flats will make an even bigger cube, and the triplet of shapes begins again.

Each cube has a name. The first one is the *unit* cube, the next is a *thousand*, the next a *million*, then a *billion*, and so on. Each long is 10 cubes: 10 units, 10 thousands, 10 millions. Similarly, each flat shape is 100 cubes.

To read a number, first mark it off in triples from the right. The triples are then read, stopping at the end of each to name the unit (or cube shape) for that triple (see

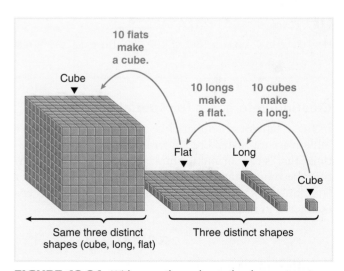

FIGURE 12.21 With every three places, the shapes repeat. Each cube represents a 1, each long represents a 10, and each flat represents a 100.

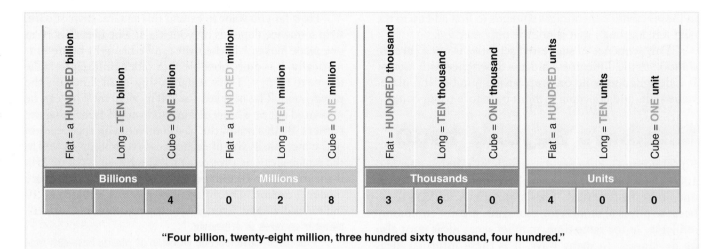

"Four billion, twenty-eight million, three hundred sixty thousand, four hundred."

FIGURE 12.22 The triples system for naming large numbers.

Figure 12.22). Leading zeros in each triple are ignored. If students can learn to read numbers like 059 (fifty-nine) or 009 (nine), they should be able to read any number. To write a number, use the same scheme. If first mastered orally, the system is quite easy.

It is important for children to realize that the system does have a logical structure, is not totally arbitrary, and can be understood.

Conceptualizing Large Numbers

The ideas just discussed are only partially helpful in thinking about the actual quantities involved in very large numbers. For example, in extending the square, strip, square, strip sequence, some appreciation for the quantities of 1000 or of 100,000 is included. But it is hard for anyone to translate quantities of small squares into quantities of other items, distances, or time.

Ⅱ *pause and reflect* —————————

How do you think about 1000 or 100,000? Do you have any real concept of a million?

————————————————————————

Creating References for Special Big Numbers

In these activities, numbers like 1000, 10,000, or even 1 million are translated literally or imaginatively into something that is easy or fun to think about. Interesting quantities become lasting reference points or benchmarks for large numbers and thereby add meaning to numbers encountered in real life.

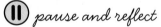 **12.35**

Collecting 10,000

Collections. As a class or grade-level project, collect some type of object with the objective of reaching some specific quantity—for example, 1000 or 10,000

buttons, walnuts, old pencils, jar lids, or pieces of junk mail. If you begin aiming for 100,000 or 1 million, be sure to think it through. One teacher spent nearly 10 years with her classes before amassing a million bottle caps. It takes a small dump truck to hold that many!

activity **12.36**

Showing 10,000

Illustrations. Sometimes it is easier to create large amounts. For example, start a project where students draw 100 or 200 or even 500 dots on a sheet of paper. Each week different students contribute a specified number. Another idea is to cut up newspaper into pieces the same size as dollar bills to see what a large quantity would look like. Paper chain links can be constructed over time and hung down the hallways with special numbers marked. Let the school be aware of the ultimate goal.

activity **12.37**

How Long?/How Far?

Real and imagined distances. How long is a million baby steps? Other ideas that address length: toothpicks, dollar bills, or candy bars end to end; children holding hands in a line; blocks or bricks stacked up; children lying down head to toe. Real measures can also be used: feet, centimeters, meters.

activity **12.38**

A Long Time

Time. How long is 1000 seconds? How long is a million seconds? A billion? How long would it take to count to 10,000 or 1 million? (To make the counts all the same, use your calculator to do the counting. Just press the [=].) How long would it take to do some task like buttoning a button 1000 times?

Estimating Large Quantities

Activities 12.35 through 12.38 focus on a specific number. The reverse idea is to select a large quantity and find some way to measure, count, or estimate how many.

activity 12.39

Really Large Quantities

Ask how many

- Candy bars would cover the floor of your room
- Steps an ant would take to walk around the school building
- Grains of rice would fill a cup or a gallon jug
- Quarters could be stacked in one stack floor to ceiling
- Pennies can be laid side by side down the entire hallway
- Pieces of notebook paper would cover the gym floor
- Seconds you have lived

Big-number projects need not take up large amounts of class time. They can be explored over several weeks as take-home projects or group projects or, perhaps best of all, be translated into great schoolwide estimation contests.

NCTM Standards The *Standards* document also recognizes the need for relating large numbers to the real world. "A third-grade class might explore the size of 1000 by skip-counting to 1000, building a model of 1000 using ten hundred charts, gathering 1000 items such as paper clips and developing efficient ways to count them, or using strips that are 10 or 100 centimeters long to show the length of 1000 centimeters" (p. 149).

Literature Connections

Books that emphasize groups of things, even simple counting books, are a good beginning to the notion of ten things in a single group. Many books have wonderful explorations of large quantities and how they can be combined and separated.

Moira's Birthday
Munsch, 1987

As Moira plans her birthday party, she invites more and more children until she has invited all the children in the kindergarten, first, second, third, fourth, fifth, and sixth grades. Then she needs to order food. She orders 200 cakes and 200 pizzas. Wonderful bedlam ensues as the food and the children all arrive at the party. A second-grade teacher, Diane Oppedal (1995), used this story as a background for the question "How can you show 200 things in different ways?" As children work on this or similar projects, they can be encouraged to use some form of groups to keep track of their collections.

The same book can also be used to motivate a variety of computation situations that could be used prior to structured computation instruction. "How many children are in three classrooms?" "What if everyone at the party got two pieces of pizza?" "If Moira gave 37 of her 94 presents back to the children who helped her clean up, how many presents did she have left?"

How to Count Like a Martian
St. John, 1975

This book explores number systems from different ancient cultures (Chinese, Roman, Egyptian, etc.) and so has a culture connection as well as a mathematics connection. The contrast of the different systems, most of which are not place-value systems, can be a good way for children in the fourth and fifth grades to appreciate and discuss the base-ten place-value system. Most other numeration systems do not have a zero, for example. Several numeration systems use the same symbol repeatedly to express multiples of a certain quantity. Children could write numbers in different systems, try to compute in another system, or discuss how they might make up a system of their own. Why is it that most of the world has adopted the system we use?

The King's Commissioners
Friedman, 1994

The king has so many commissioners, he can't keep track of how many there are. In a hilarious tale, the commissioners are marched into the throne room to be counted. One person tries to count them by twos and another by fives. The princess convinces the king that there are many other excellent ways to count. The story is a natural background for place-value concepts, including grouping and different counting methods, large numbers, and informal early computation challenges. Stephanie Sheffield (1995) offers specific suggestions for using this story with children at about the second-grade level.

A Million Fish . . . More or Less
McKissack, 1992

This story, which takes place in lower Louisiana, is a tall tale of a boy who catches three fish . . . and then a million more. The story is full of exaggerations such as a turkey that weighs 500 pounds and a jump-rope contest (using a snake) where the story's hero wins with 5553 jumps. "Could these things really be? How long would it take to jump 5553 times? Could Hugh put a million fish in his wagon? How do you write half of a million?" Rusty Bresser (1995) suggests a number of excellent ways this tale can be used to investigate large numbers and how they are written. The connections to real things and real ideas is just the ticket to add number sense to an upper-grade unit on place value.

Many other excellent books investigate very large numbers in interesting contexts. *How Much Is a Million?* (1985) and *If You Made a Million* (1989), both by David Schwartz, have become very popular. Wanda Gag's *Millions of Cats* (1928) is a classic that is still worth the time to investigate. Just one more of many possibilities is *Six Dogs, Twenty-Three Cats, Forty-Five Mice, and One Hundred Sixteen Spiders* (Chalmers, 1986). The imagination that these books inspire can lead children into fascinating investigations of large numbers, and with a bit of guidance, good place-value concepts can be visited along the way. ■

Reflections on Chapter 12

Writing to Learn

1. Explain how a child who has not yet developed base-ten concepts understands quantities as large as, say, 85. Contrast this with a child who understands these same quantities in terms of base-ten groupings.
2. What is meant by *equivalent representations?*
3. Explain the three ways one can count a set of objects and how these methods of counting can be used to coordinate concepts and oral and written names for numbers.
4. Describe the two types of physical models for base-ten concepts. What is the significance of the difference between these two types of models?
5. Describe an activity for developing base-ten grouping concepts, and reflect on how the activity encourages children to construct base-ten concepts.
6. How do children learn to write two- and three-digit numbers in a way that is connected to the base-ten meanings of ones and tens or ones, tens, and hundreds?
7. What ideas about numbers are overlooked if the curriculum restricts place-value development to the triad of ideas (concepts, oral names, and written names) found in Figure 12.3?
8. Describe some patterns that can be found on the hundreds chart. In addition to looking for patterns, describe another activity with the hundreds chart.
9. What are landmark numbers? Describe the relationships that you want children to develop with respect to landmark numbers. Describe an activity that addresses this relationship.
10. How can place-value concepts and computation skills be developed at the same time? Describe two activities that can be used to address these dual agendas.
11. Explain why determining the value of a collection of coins is essentially a mental addition skill. Why is this more difficult than doing the same addition with numbers? Describe at least one activity that can help children work with money.
12. What are two different ideas that you would want children to know about very large numbers (beyond 1000)? Describe one or two activities for each.

For Discussion and Exploration

1. Based on the suggestions in this chapter and on the content of a standard basal textbook, design a diagnostic interview for a child at a particular grade level and conduct the interview. It is a good idea to take a friend to act as an observer or to use a tape recorder or video recorder to keep track of how the interview went.
2. A popular collection of activities, sometimes referred to as "trading activities," are done with base-ten models. In all of these activities, children have a place-value mat on which they accumulate materials or from which they remove materials. The activities generally take a game format. Usually a die is rolled to tell the child how many ones are to be placed on the mat or how many may be removed. Whenever 10 pieces in one section are accumulated, a trade is made for a single piece in the next place: 10 ones for a ten, 10 tens for a hundred. Similarly, in the process of removing pieces, trades are made in the reverse manner: 1 ten for 10 ones.

   Do these trading activities contribute any new connections or ideas to place-value understanding? If so, what are they? Are trading activities problem based? Are there any activities in this chapter that get at the same ideas?
3. The *Investigations in Number, Data, and Space* second-grade module entitled *Coins, Coupons, and Combinations: The Number System* (Economopoulos & Russell, 1998) is the principal unit addressing numeration. Numeration concepts are also addressed in a later unit on addition and subtraction. Examine the *Number System* book and see if you can describe how the *Investigations* program develops base-ten and place-value concepts. Keep in mind that number is also addressed in the introductory module, in the addition and subtraction module, and to a lesser extent in other modules. Compare the *Investigations* approach with the ideas you've read about here as well as the way that place value is taught in a standard basal textbook.

Recommendations for Further Reading

Burns, M. (1994). *Math by all means: Place value, grade 2.* Sausalito, CA: Math Solutions Publications.
  Burns provides 25 days of very detailed lessons in place value for second-grade children. In her usual style, there are ample examples of children's written work and descriptions of interactions that took place in the classroom. It is possible to take issue with the claims the author makes for the complete

development resulting from these lessons, but that does not detract from the value of most of the activities. Perhaps most important is the way that Burns brings you into the classroom to get a feel for how these activities will work with children.

Ellett, K. (2005). Making a million meaningful. *Teaching Children Mathematics, 10,* 416–423.

This amazing collection of ideas for helping students think about large numbers, especially 1 million, is found in the *TCM* focus issue on Mathematics and Literature. Ellett shares lists of examples of student projects and ways for students to conceptualize a million, shows student work, and connects many of these ideas to literature. Easily one of the best resources for working with large-number concepts.

Jones, G. A., Thornton, C. A., Putt, I. J., Hill, K. M., Mogill, A. T., Rich, B. S., & Van Zoest, L. R. (1996). Multidigit number sense: A framework for instruction and assessment. *Journal for Research in Mathematics Education, 27,* 310–336.

Based on a two-year study of first- and second-grade children, this research refined an earlier framework for place-value development. It consists of four constructs: counting, partitioning, grouping, and number relationships. Within each, five levels of understanding were identified. Although in a research journal, there is ample practical information for the first- through third-grade teacher, for both instructional purposes and for assessment.

Kari, A. R., & Anderson, C. B. (2003). Opportunities to develop place value through student dialogue. *Teaching Children Mathematics, 10,* 78–82.

These two teachers describe a mixed first/second-grade classroom illustrating in vivid detail how children's understanding of two-digit numbers can at first be quite mistaken and then developed conceptually with the aid of discussion in the classroom. Much of the discussion revolves around one child's belief that any 1 in a number stands for ten. This student is convinced that 11 + 11 +11 is 60. Reading this article will highlight the need to listen carefully to children about their ideas surrounding multidigit numbers. It also emphasizes the wide range of student ideas and the value of classroom discourse.

Richardson, K. (1990). *A look at children's thinking: Video II and study guide.* Norman, OK: Educational Enrichment, Inc.

This tape showing diagnostic interviews is must viewing for anyone interested in how children develop number concepts and place value in particular. Richardson uses the same series of questions with several children at different stages of development. Her commentary clearly describes why the questions are asked, what she is looking for, and an analysis of the students' responses. You cannot watch this tape and not fully appreciate the complexity of place-value concepts and the difficulty children have developing them.

Schifter, D., Bastable, V., & Russell, S. J. (1999a). *Developing mathematical understanding: Numbers and operations, Part 1, Building a system of tens (Casebook).* Parsippany, NJ: Dale Seymour Publications.

Schifter and her colleagues at TERC have compiled in this book a wonderful collection of cases, each written by a classroom teacher, in which the complexities of place-value development truly come to light. Although this is a companion book to an in-service program, the cases by themselves are worth reading. They will provide useful insights into children's thinking and useful points of discussion. The book includes 29 different cases from grades 1 to 6 and covers situations involving invented computations and decimals as well as whole number meanings.

Online Resources

Suggested Applets and Web Links

Base-Ten Blocks
http://nlvm.usu.edu/en/nav/category_g_2_t_1.html

There are several variations of the basic base-ten blocks applet here. Blocks appear on a place-value chart and can be grouped or broken apart. The addition and subtraction versions pose problems and allow blocks in two colors to model two separate numbers.

Comparison Estimator and Estimator
www.shodor.org/interactivate/activities/estim2/index.html

www.shodor.org/interactivate/activities/estim/index.html

Two sets of small objects are shown and the task is to decide which set has more. The actual counts are then given. The same applet also allows for comparisons of length and areas. *Estimator* asks for a numeric estimate rather than a comparison. Try to get *close, really close,* or *almost perfect.*

Hundreds Board and Calculator
http://standards.nctm.org/document/eexamples/chap4/4.5/index.htm

A calculator is used to create skip-counting patterns on a hundreds chart. You can start the pattern on any number and skip by any number. The chart extends to 1000. A second pattern will show with red dots on top of the first pattern.

Lots of Dots and A Million Dots on One Page
www.vendian.org/envelope/

These explorations of big numbers are only a hint at the array of ideas found on this Web site. A lot is beyond the elementary school, but anyone interested in big numbers and measures will certainly be intrigued. See a dot for every second of the day!

The MegaPenny Project
www.kokogiak.com/megapenny/default.asp

A fascinating look at large numbers in terms of stacks of pennies. Stacks from 1 penny to a trillion pennies are shown with visual referents, value, weight, height if stacked, and more. Great for large-number concepts.

The Place Value Game (Jefferson Lab)
http://education.jlab.org/placevalue/index.html

The goal is to make the largest possible number from the digits the computer gives you. Digits are presented one at a time. The player must place the digit in the number without knowing what the next digits will be. It's fun and also good for understanding ordering of numbers.

An additional list of books and articles related to the ideas in this chapter can be found on the Companion Web site at **www.ablongman.com/vandewalle6e.**

chapter 13

Strategies for Whole-Number Computation

M uch of the public sees computational skill as the hallmark of what it means to know mathematics at the elementary school level. Although this is far from the truth, the issue of computational skills with whole numbers is, in fact, a very important part of the elementary curriculum, especially in grades 2 to 6.

Rather than a single method of subtracting (or any operation), the most appropriate method can and should change flexibly as the numbers and the context change. In the spirit of the *Standards*, the issue is no longer a matter of "knows how to subtract three-digit numbers"; rather it is the development over time of an assortment of flexible skills, including the ability to compute mentally, that will best serve students in the real world.

It is quite possible that you do not have these skills, but you can acquire them. Work at them as you learn about them. Equip yourself with a flexible array of computational strategies.

▼ Big Ideas

1. Flexible methods of computation involve taking apart and combining numbers in a wide variety of ways. Most of the partitions of numbers are based on place value or "compatible" numbers—number pairs that work easily together, such as 25 and 75.

2. "Invented" strategies are flexible methods of computing that vary with the numbers and the situation. Successful use of the strategies requires that they be understood by the one who is using them—hence, the term *invented*. Strategies may be invented by a peer or the class as a whole; they may even be suggested by the teacher. However, they must be constructed by the student.

3. Flexible methods for computation require a good understanding of the operations and properties of the operations, especially the turnaround property and the distributive property for multiplication. How the operations are related—addition to subtraction, addition to multiplication, and multiplication to division—is also an important ingredient.

4. The traditional algorithms are clever strategies for computing that have been developed over time. Each is based on performing the operation on one place value at a time with transitions to an adjacent position (trades, regrouping, "borrows," or "carries"). Traditional algorithms tend to make us think in terms of digits rather than the composite number that the digits make up. These algorithms work for all numbers but are often far from the most efficient or useful methods of computing.

▲▲ *Mathematics* Content Connections

Flexible computation is built on the ideas found in the preceding three chapters. Flexible methods for computing, especially mental methods, allow one to reason much more effectively in every area of mathematics involving numbers.

■ **Operation Meanings and Fact Mastery** (Chapters 10 and 11): The need for understanding the ideas in these chapters is evident. Children can and should explore contextual problems involving multidigit numbers as they develop their understanding of the operations. Without basic facts, students will be severely disadvantaged in any computational endeavor. Furthermore, many strategies and number concepts used to master basic facts can be extended to computation.

■ **Place Value** (Chapter 12): Place value is not only a basis for computation; students can also develop place-value understanding as a *result* of finding their own methods of computing. In the process of making sense of different computational methods, students explore and develop place-value concepts.

■ **Computational Estimation** (Chapter 14): Computational estimation involves substituting "nice" numbers in a computation so that the new computation can be done mentally or at least with minimal effort. Without good computational skills—especially methods other than the traditional algorithms—estimation is nearly impossible.

Toward Computational Fluency

With today's technology the need for doing tedious computations by hand has essentially disappeared. A study done in 1957, well before the commonplace use of calculators, found that adults used pencil-and-paper computation methods for only 25 percent of the calculations they did (Wandt & Brown in McIntosh, 1998). We now know that there are numerous methods of computing that can be handled either mentally or with pencil-and-paper support. In most everyday instances, these alternative strategies for computing are easier and faster, can often be done mentally, and contribute to our overall number sense. The traditional algorithms (procedures for computing) do not have these benefits.

Consider the following problem.

Mary had 114 spaces in her photo album. So far she has 89 photos in the album. How many more photos can she put in before the album is full?

 *pause and reflect*

Try solving the photo album problem using some method other than the one you were taught in school. If you want to begin with the 9 and the 4, try a different approach. Can you do it mentally? Can you do it in more than one way? Work on this before reading further.

Here are just four of many methods that have been used by students in the primary grades to solve the computation in the photo album problem:

89 + 11 is 100. 11 + 14 is 25.

90 + 10 is 100 and 14 more is 24 plus 1 (for 89, not 90) is 25.

Take away 14 and then take away 11 more or 25 in all.

89, 99, 109 (that's 20). 110, 111, 112, 113, 114 (keeping track on fingers) is 25.

Strategies such as these can be done mentally, are generally faster than the traditional algorithms, and make sense to the person using them. Every day, students and adults resort to error-prone, traditional strategies when other, more meaningful methods would be faster and less

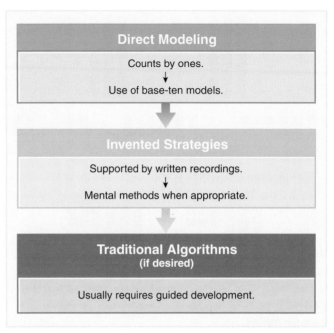

FIGURE 13.1 Three types of computational strategies.

susceptible to error. Flexibility with a variety of computational strategies is an important tool for successful daily living. It is time to broaden our perspective of what it means to compute.

Figure 13.1 lists three general types of computing. The initial, inefficient direct modeling methods can, with guidance, develop into an assortment of invented strategies that are flexible and useful. As noted in the diagram, many of these methods can be handled mentally, although no special methods are designed specifically for mental computation. The traditional pencil-and-paper algorithms remain in the mainstream curricula. However, the attention given to them should, at the very least, be debated.

NCTM Standards "Equally essential [with basic facts] is computational fluency—having and using efficient and accurate methods for computing. Fluency might be manifested in using a combination of mental strategies and jottings on paper or using an algorithm with paper and pencil, particularly when the numbers are large, to produce accurate results quickly. Regardless of the particular methods used, students should be able to explain their method, understand that many methods exist, and see the usefulness of methods that are efficient, accurate, and general" (p. 32).

Direct Modeling

The developmental step that usually precedes invented strategies is called *direct modeling*: the use of manipulatives or drawings along with counting to represent directly the

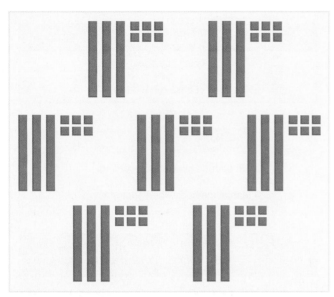

FIGURE 13.2 A possible direct modeling of 36 × 7 using base-ten models.

meaning of an operation or story problem. Figure 13.2 provides an example using base-ten materials, but often students use simple counters and count by ones.

Students who consistently count by ones most likely have not developed base-ten grouping concepts. That does not mean that they should not continue to solve problems involving two-digit numbers. As you work with these children, suggest (don't force) that they group counters by tens as they count. Perhaps instead of making large piles, they might make bars of ten from connecting cubes or organize counters in cups of ten. Some students will use the ten-stick as a counting device to keep track of counts of ten, even though they are counting each segment of the stick by ones.

Students using direct modeling will soon transfer their ideas to methods that do not rely on materials or counting. The direct-modeling phase provides a necessary background of ideas. These developmental strategies are also important because they provide students who are not ready for more efficient methods a way to explore the same problems as classmates who have progressed beyond this stage. It is important not to push students prematurely to abandon manipulative approaches.

Invented Strategies

Carpenter, Franke, Jacobs, Fennema, and Empson (1998) refer to any strategy other than the traditional algorithm and that does not involve the use of physical materials or counting by ones an *invented strategy*. We will use this term also, although *personal and flexible strategies* might be equally appropriate. At times, invented strategies become mental methods after the ideas have been explored, used, and understood. For example, 75 + 19 is not difficult to

do mentally (75 + 20 is 95, less 1 is 94). For 847 + 256, some students may write down intermediate steps to aid in memory as they work through the problem. (Try that one yourself.) In the classroom, some written support is often encouraged as strategies develop. Written records of thinking are more easily shared and help students focus on the ideas. The distinction between written, partially written, and mental is not important, especially in the development period.

Over the past two decades, a number of research projects have focused attention on how children handle computational situations when they have not been taught a specific algorithm or strategy.* The *Investigations* curriculum bases the development of computational methods entirely on student-invented strategies. "There is mounting evidence that children both in and out of school can construct methods for adding and subtracting multi-digit numbers without explicit instruction" (Carpenter et al., 1998, p. 4). Data supporting students' construction of useful methods for multiplication and division have also been gathered (Baek, 1998; Fosnot & Dolk, 2001; Kamii & Dominick, 1997; Schifter, Bastable, & Russell, 1999b).

Not all students invent their own strategies. Strategies invented by class members are shared, explored, and tried out by others. However, no student should be permitted to use any strategy without understanding it (Campbell, Rowan, & Suarez, 1998).

Contrasts with Traditional Algorithms

There are significant differences between invented strategies and the traditional algorithms.

1. *Invented strategies are number oriented rather than digit oriented.* For example, an invented strategy for 68 × 7 begins 7 × 60 is 420 and 56 more is 476. The first product is 7 times *sixty*, not the digit 6, as would be the case in the traditional algorithm. Using the traditional algorithm for 45 + 32, children never think of 40 and 30 but rather 4 + 3. Kamii, long a crusader against standard algorithms, claims that they "unteach" place value (Kamii & Dominick, 1998).

2. *Invented strategies are left-handed rather than right-handed.* Invented strategies begin with the largest parts of numbers, those represented by the leftmost digits. For 26 × 47, invented strategies will begin with 20 ×

---

*The Cognitively Guided Instruction (CGI) project, directed by Carpenter, Fennema, and Franke at the University of Wisconsin; the Conceptually Based Instruction (CBI) project, directed by Hiebert and Wearne at the University of Delaware; the Problem Centered Mathematics Project (PCMP), directed by Human, Murray, and Olivier at the University of Stellenbosch, South Africa; the Supporting Ten-Structured Thinking (STST) project, directed by Fuson at Northwestern University; and ongoing research by Kamii at the University of Alabama are all examples of efforts that have informed thinking about invented strategies for computation.

40 is 800, providing some sense of the size of the eventual answer in just one step. The traditional algorithm begins with 7 × 6 is 42. By beginning on the right with a digit orientation, traditional methods hide the result until the end. Long division is an exception.

3. *Invented strategies are flexible rather than rigid.* Invented strategies tend to change with the numbers involved in order to make the computation easier. Try each of these mentally: 465 + 230 and 526 + 98. Did you use the same method? The traditional algorithm suggests using the same tool on all problems. The traditional algorithm for 7000 − 25 typically leads to student errors, yet a mental strategy is relatively simple (Carroll & Porter, 1997).

Benefits of Invented Strategies

The development of invented strategies delivers more than computational facility. Both the development of these strategies and their regular use have positive benefits that are difficult to ignore.

- *Students make fewer errors.* Research indicates that students using methods they understand make many fewer errors than when strategies are learned without understanding (Gravemeijer & van Galen, 2003; Kamii & Dominick, 1997). After decades of good intentions with the standard algorithms, far too many students do not understand the concepts that support them. Not only do these students make errors, but also the errors are often systematic and difficult to remediate. Errors with invented strategies are less frequent and almost never systematic.
- *Less reteaching is required.* Teachers often complain that students' early efforts with alternative strategies are slow and time consuming. The time-consuming struggle in these early stages, however, results in ideas that are meaningful and well integrated in a web of ideas that are robust and long lasting. An increase in development time is more than made up for with a significant decrease in the need for reteaching and remediation.
- *Students develop number sense.* "More than just a means to produce answers, computation is increasingly seen as a window on the deep structure of the number system" (NRC, 2001, p. 182). Students' development and use of number-oriented, flexible algorithms offer them a rich understanding of the number system. In contrast, students frequently use traditional algorithms without being able to explain why they work (Carroll & Porter, 1997). Such rules without reasons have few benefits.
- *Invented strategies are the basis for mental computation and estimation.* The methods we are calling invented strategies are exactly those that are used for mental computation. When invented strategies are the norm

for computation, there is no need to teach other methods or even to talk about mental computation as if it were a separate skill. Often students who have been taught to record their thinking with invented strategies or to write down intermediate steps will ask if this writing is really required since they find they can do the procedures more efficiently mentally. Computational estimation does involve a separate set of skills; the development of flexible, number-oriented strategies plays a significant role in most of these skills (NRC, 2001).

- *Flexible methods are often faster than the traditional algorithms.* Consider the product 64 × 8. A simple invented strategy might involve 60 × 8 = 480 and 8 × 4 = 32. The sum of 480 and 32 is 500 + 12 more—512. This is easily done mentally, or even with some recording, in much less time than the multiple steps of the traditional algorithm. Those who become adept with nonstandard methods will consistently perform addition and subtraction computations more quickly than those using a traditional algorithm.
- *Algorithm invention is itself a significantly important process of "doing mathematics."* All students who invent a strategy for computing, or who adopt a strategy from a classmate, are involved intimately in the process of making sense of mathematics and they develop a confidence in their ability to do so. This development of procedures is a process that traditionally has been hidden from elementary school students. By engaging in this aspect of mathematics, a significantly different and valuable view of "doing mathematics" is opened to young children.

In addition to these benefits, there is a growing body of evidence that students' computational skills do not suffer in contrast to those taught the traditional strategies. Data have been collected from school systems using either *Everyday Mathematics* (before it began to include the traditional algorithms) or *Investigations in Number, Data, and Space* and compared with similar schools using traditional programs. Students in these standards-based programs consistently outperform their traditional program counterparts on measures of understanding and problem solving. In the area of multidigit computation, most studies find that the standards-based students are either on a par with students in traditional programs or outperform them (Fuson, 2003). Students in the Netherlands are not taught to use traditional algorithms and they perform at least as well as U.S. students (Gravemeijer & van Galen, 2003; Torrence, 2003).

Mental Computation

A mental computation strategy is simply any invented strategy that is done mentally. What may be a mental strategy for one student may require written support by another. Initially, students should not be asked to do computations mentally, as this may threaten students who have not yet developed a reasonable invented strategy or who are still at the direct-modeling stage. At the same time, you may be quite amazed at the ability of students (and at your own ability) to do computations mentally.

Try your own hand with this example:

$$342 + 153 + 481$$

 pause and reflect ————————————

For the addition task just shown, try this method: Begin by adding the hundreds, saying the totals as you go—*3 hundred, 4 hundred, 8 hundred.* Then add on to this the tens in successive manner and finally the ones. Do it now.

When the computations are a bit more complicated, the challenge is more interesting and generally there are more alternatives. For 7 × 28, the *Standards* lists three paths to a solution but there are at least two more (NCTM, 2000, p. 152). How many ways can you find?

As your students become more adept, they can and should be challenged from time to time to do appropriate computations mentally. Do not expect the same skills of all students.

Traditional Algorithms

With the exception of *Investigations*, every commercial curriculum teaches the traditional algorithms. More than a century of tradition plus pressures from parents are at least partly responsible for our unwillingness to abandon these approaches. Other arguments generally revolve around efficiency and the need for methods that will work with all numbers. For addition and subtraction, one can easily counter that well-understood and practiced invented strategies are more than adequate. However, it is certainly true that a computation such as 486 × 372 is difficult with invented strategies. But shouldn't computations like that be done with technology?

No matter the growing interest in invented strategies, and no matter how compelling the arguments against the traditional algorithms may be, few classroom teachers will be able to independently abandon the traditional approaches.

Delay! Delay! Delay!

Students are not going to invent the traditional algorithms. You will need to introduce and explain each algorithm to them and help them understand how and why they work using a direct-instruction approach. No matter how carefully you introduce these algorithms into your classroom as simply another alternative, students are likely to sense that "this is the real way" or the "right way" to compute. "This is the way the teacher taught us to do it and it is the way my mom

and dad compute." Once having begun with traditional methods, it is extremely difficult to suggest to students that they learn other methods. Notice how difficult it is for you to begin computations by working from the left rather than the right and to think in terms of whole numbers rather than digits. These habits, once established, are difficult to break.

Can the traditional algorithms be taught meaningfully? Absolutely! Meaningful approaches for teaching each algorithm are discussed later in this chapter. If you plan to teach the traditional algorithms, you are well advised to first spend a significant time with invented strategies—months, not weeks. Do not feel that you must rush to the traditional methods. Delay! Spend most of your effort on invented methods. The understanding children gain from working with invented strategies will make it much easier for you to teach the traditional methods.

Traditional Algorithms Will Happen

You probably cannot keep the traditional algorithms out of your classroom. Children pick up the traditional algorithms from older siblings, last year's teacher, well-meaning parents ("My dad showed me an easy way"). Traditional algorithms are in no way evil, and so to forbid their use is somewhat arbitrary. However, students who latch on to a traditional method often resist the invention of more flexible strategies. What do you do then?

First and foremost, apply the same rule to traditional algorithms as to all strategies: *If you use it, you must understand why it works and be able to explain it.* In an atmosphere that says, "Let's figure out why this works," students can profit from making sense of these algorithms just like any other. But the responsibility should be theirs, not yours.

Accept a traditional algorithm (once it is understood) as one more strategy to put in the class "tool box" of methods. But reinforce the idea that like the other strategies, it may be more useful in some instances than in others. Pose problems where a mental strategy is much more useful, such as 504 − 498 or 75 × 4. Discuss which method seemed best. Point out that for a problem such as 4568 + 12,813, the traditional algorithm has some advantages. But in the real world, most people do those computations on a calculator.

Development of Student-Invented Strategies

Students do not spontaneously invent wonderful computational methods while the teacher sits back and watches. Among different experimental programs, students tended to develop or gravitate toward different strategies suggesting that teachers and the programs do have an effect on what methods students develop (Fuson et al., 1997). This section discusses general pedagogical methods for helping children develop invented strategies that are appropriate at all grades and for all four operations.

Integrate Computation with Place Value and Fact Development

Invented strategies are developed out of a strong understanding of numbers. The standard development of place value often leaves students ill prepared for the challenges of inventing computational strategies. For example, many third- and fourth-grade students have difficulty naming a number that is ten more or ten less than a given two-digit number without resorting to counting. The difficulty is greater if the result crosses 100, as in 94 and 10 more or 10 less than 106. Activities that focus on the patterns in our number system and that explore addition and subtraction using the hundreds chart, the little ten-frame cards, or base-ten blocks can both prepare students for invented strategies and improve their number sense. A collection of appropriate activities focusing on number relationships and informal addition and subtraction strategies can be found in Chapter 12. (See pp. 201 to 209.)

Note also that many of the strategies for addition and subtraction are extensions of basic fact strategies, especially those that use 10 as a bridge. (See Chapter 11.) For example, as students are exploring methods for mastering facts with an 8 or 9, extend these ideas to 38 or 69. As another example, double 4 can be extended to double 40.

Use Story Problems Frequently

When computational tasks are embedded in simple contexts, students seem to be more engaged than they are with bare computations. Furthermore, the choice of story problems influences the strategies students use to solve them. Compare these two problems:

Max had already saved 68 cents when Mom gave him some money for running an errand. Now Max has 93 cents. How much did Max earn for his errand?

George took 93 cents to the store. He spent 68 cents. How much does he have left?

The computation 93 − 68 solves both problems, but the first is more likely than the second to be solved by an add-on method. In a similar manner, fair-share division problems are more likely to encourage a share strategy than a measurement or repeated subtraction problem.

Not every task need be a story problem. Especially when students are engaged in figuring out a new strategy, bare arithmetic problems are quite adequate.

Use the Three-Part Lesson Format

The three-part lesson format described in Chapter 4 is a good structure for an invented-strategy lesson. The task can be one or two story problems or even a bare computation but always with the expectation that the method of solution will be discussed. Sometimes you can provide variations with different numbers to different groups to adjust for difficulty.

Allow plenty of time to solve a problem. Listen to the different strategies students are using, but do not interject your own. Challenge able students to find a second method, solve a problem without models, or improve on a written explanation. Allow children who are not ready for thinking with tens to use simple counting methods.

The most important portion of the lesson comes when students explain their solution methods. Encourage students to ask questions of their classmates. Occasionally have the class try a particular method with different numbers to see how it works. When students find a particular idea worthwhile, record it on a "strategies chart," perhaps labeled with the student's name or a name that suggests the approach. Remember, not every student will invent strategies. However, students can and will try strategies that they have seen and that make sense to them.

Record Students' Processes

As students report how they completed a computation, record each step on the board. Avoid vertical formats as those tend to encourage traditional algorithms. Try using arrows or lines to indicate how two computations are joined together as shown in Figure 13.3(a). The notion of "splitting" a number into parts is a useful strategy for all operations. Both the word *split* and the use of a visual diagram, as shown, have been found to help students develop strategies (Sáenz-Ludlow, 2004).

The *empty number line* (see Figure 13.3(b)) is a technique developed in the Netherlands that is increasingly being suggested in the United States (Fosnot & Dolk, 2001; Gravemeijer & van Galen, 2003; McClain, Cobb, Gravemeijer, & Estes, 1999.) Initially, the empty number line is a good way to help you model a student's thinking for the class. Soon it will become a tool for students to use in creating their own thinking (Klein, Beishuizen, & Treffers, 1998). These researchers found that the empty number line is much more flexible than the usual number line because it can be used with any numbers and students are not confused with tic marks and the spaces between them.

The hops on the line can be recorded as the students share or explain each step of their solution.

(a) How much is 86 and 47?

S: I know that 80 and 20 more is 100.

T: Where do the 80 and the 20 come from?

S: I split the 47 into 20 and 20 and 7 and the 86 into 80 and 6.

T: (illustrates the splitting with lines)
So then you added one of the 20s to 80?

S: Yes, 80 and 20 is 100. Then I added the other 20 and got 120.

T: (writes the equations on the board)

S: Then I added the 6 and the 7 and got 13.

T: (writes this equation)

S: Then I added the 120 to the 13 and got 133.

T: Indicates with joining lines.

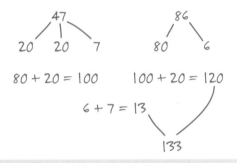

(b) How much is 4 times 68?

S: I used 70s because they were easier than 68s. First I did 70 and 70 is 140.

Then I doubled 140 to get 280.

T: Why did you double 140?

S: Because that would make four 70s, and I already had two 70s. Then I had to take off four sets of 2 because I used 70 instead of only 68. That got me to 272.

FIGURE 13.3 Two methods of recording students' thought processes on the board so that the class can see the strategy. The splitting process and the empty number line may both become strategies that the students use to help with their thinking in future problems.

Invented Strategies for Addition and Subtraction

Research has demonstrated that children will invent a lot of different strategies for addition and subtraction. Your goal might be that each of your children has at least one or two methods that are reasonably efficient, mathematically correct, and useful with lots of different numbers. Expect different children to settle on different strategies.

It is not at all unreasonable for students to be able to add and subtract two-digit numbers mentally by third grade. However, many children will continue to require written support for their thinking. Daily recording of strategies on the board not only helps communicate ideas but also helps children who need the short-term memory assistance of recording intermediate steps.

There is no clear-cut progression to follow that will dictate what problems you should pose to your students. You must learn to listen to the kind of reasoning they are using and the strategies that are being suggested. The numbers involved in a computation and also the type of story problems used will tend to influence how students approach a problem. Even so, you will discover many variations of thought processes in any classroom. The following sections suggest a variety of strategies that children often use. These are presented not as a curriculum but rather to give you some idea of the range of possibilities.

Adding and Subtracting Single Digits

When adding or subtracting a small amount, or finding the difference between two numbers that are reasonably close, many students will use counting to solve the problems. One goal should be to extend students' knowledge of basic facts and the ten-structure of the number system so that counting is not required. When the difference crosses a ten (e.g., 58 + 6), using the distance up to or down to the multiple of ten is extremely helpful.

Tommy was on page 47 of his book. Then he read 8 more pages. What page did he end up on?

How far is it from 68 to 75?

Ruth had 52 cents. She bought a small toy for 8 cents. How much does she have left?

Each of these problems crosses a multiple of ten and involves a change or a difference of less than ten. Listen for children who are counting on or counting back without paying attention to the ten. For these children, you might suggest using either the hundreds chart or the little ten-frames as shown in Figure 13.4. Also, find out how they solve fact combinations such as 8 + 6 or 13 − 5. The use of ten for these facts is essentially the same as for the higher-decade problems. Related activities are "Calculator Challenge Counting" (12.25), "How Much Between?" (12.28), or "Little Ten-Frame Sums" (12.29), all found in Chapter 12. ■

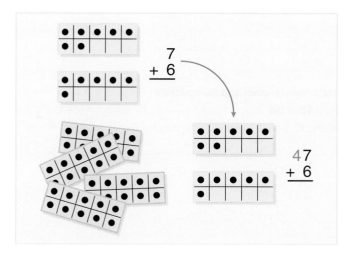

FIGURE 13.4 Little ten-frame cards can help children extend the make-ten idea to larger numbers.

Adding and Subtracting Tens and Hundreds

Sums and differences involving multiples of 10 or 100 are easily computed mentally. Write a problem such as the following on the board:

$$300 + 500 + 20$$

Challenge children to solve it mentally. Ask students to share how they did it. Look for use of place-value words: "3 *hundred* and 5 *hundred* is 8 *hundred*, and 20 is 820."

Use base-ten models to help children begin to think in terms of tens and hundreds. Early examples should not include any trades. The exercise 420 + 300 involves no trades, whereas 70 + 80 may be more difficult.

Adding Two-Digit Numbers

Problems involving the sum of 2 two-digit numbers will provoke a wide variety of strategies. Some of these will involve starting with one or the other number and working from that point, either by adding on to get to the next ten or by adding tens from one number to the other. That is, for 46 + 35 a student may add on 4 to the 46 to get to 50 and then add 31 more, or, first add 30 to 46 and then add 4 to get to 80 and 1 more. In either case there is a clear advantage to the utilization of ten. Many children will count past these multiples without stopping at ten.

Other approaches involve splitting the numbers into parts and adding the easier parts separately. Usually the split will involve tens and ones, or students may use other parts of numbers such as 50 or 25 as a "nice" part of a number to work with.

Students will often use a counting-by-tens-and-ones technique. That is, instead of "46 + 30 is 76," they may count "46 ⟶ 56, 66, 76." These counts can be written down as they are said to help students keep track.

Figure 13.5 illustrates four different strategies for addition of 2 two-digit numbers. The ways that the solutions are recorded are suggestions. Note the use of the empty number line. The following story problem is a suggestion.

The two Scout troops went on a field trip. There were 46 Girl Scouts and 38 Boy Scouts. How many Scouts went on the trip?

The *move to make ten* and *compensation* strategies are useful when one of the numbers ends in 8 or 9. To promote that strategy, present problems with addends like 39 or 58. Note that it is only necessary to adjust one of the two numbers.

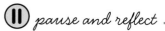 *pause and reflect* ─────────────
Try adding 367 + 155 in as many different ways as you can. How many of your ways are like those in Figure 13.5?

Subtracting by Counting Up

This is an amazingly powerful way to subtract. Students working on the *think-addition* strategy for their basic facts can also be solving problems with larger numbers. The concept is the same. For 38 − 19, the idea is to think, "How much do I add to 19 to get to 38?" Notice that this strategy is probably not efficient for 42 − 6. Using *join with change unknown* problems or *missing-part* problems will encourage the counting-up strategy. Here is an example of each.

Sam had 46 baseball cards. He went to a card show and got some more cards for his collection. Now he has 73 cards. How many cards did Sam buy at the card show?

Juanita counted all of her crayons. Some were broken and some not. She had 73 crayons in all. 46 crayons were not broken. How many were broken?

The numbers in these problems are used in the strategies illustrated in Figure 13.6. Simply asking for the difference between two numbers may also prompt this strategy.

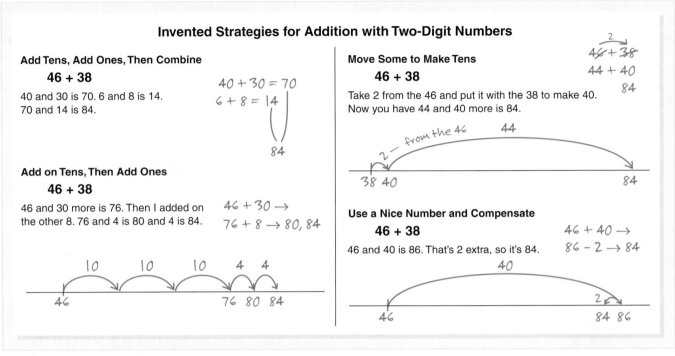

FIGURE 13.5   Four different invented strategies for adding 2 two-digit numbers.

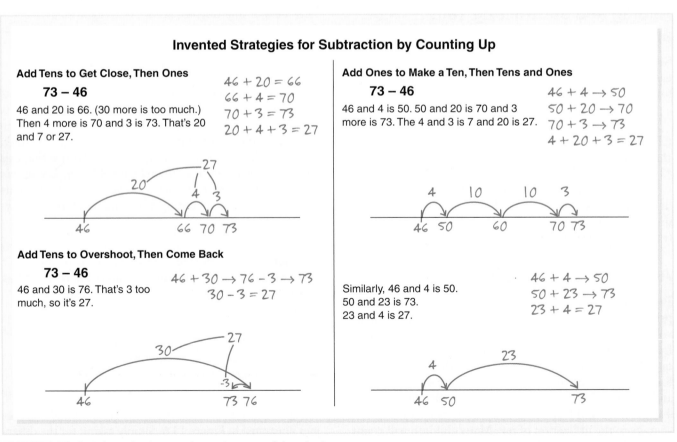

FIGURE 13.6   Subtraction by counting up is a powerful method.

Take-Away Subtraction

EXPANDED LESSON

An expanded lesson plan for having students explore subtraction strategies can be found on the Companion Web site at www.ablongman.com/vandewalle6e.

Using take-away is considerably more difficult to do mentally. However, take-away strategies are common, probably because traditional textbooks emphasize take-away as the meaning of subtraction. When the subtracted number is a multiple of ten or close to a multiple of ten, take-away can be an easy method to use. Four different strategies are shown in Figure 13.7.

> **There were 73 children on the playground. The 46 second-grade students came in first. How many children were still outside?**

The two methods that begin by taking tens from tens are reflective of what most students do with base-ten pieces (Madell, 1985). The other two methods leave one of the numbers intact and subtract from it. Try 83 − 29 in your head by first taking away 30 and adding 1 back. This is a good mental method when subtracting a number that is close to a multiple of ten.

Sometimes we need to be reminded of what comes naturally to children. Campbell (1997) tested over 2000 students in Baltimore who had not been taught the traditional algorithm for subtraction. Not one student began with the ones place!

 pause and reflect _____

Try computing 82 − 57. Use both take-away and counting up methods. Can you use all of the strategies in Figures 13.6 and 13.7 without looking?

Assessment Notes For many subtraction problems, especially those with three digits, adding on is significantly easier than a take-away approach. Try not to force the issue for students who do not use an add-on method. However, you may want to return to simple missing-part activities that are more likely to encourage that type of thinking. Try Activity 12.30, "How Far Is My Number?" or simply show a number such as 28 with little ten-frame cards and ask, "What goes with 28 to make 53?"

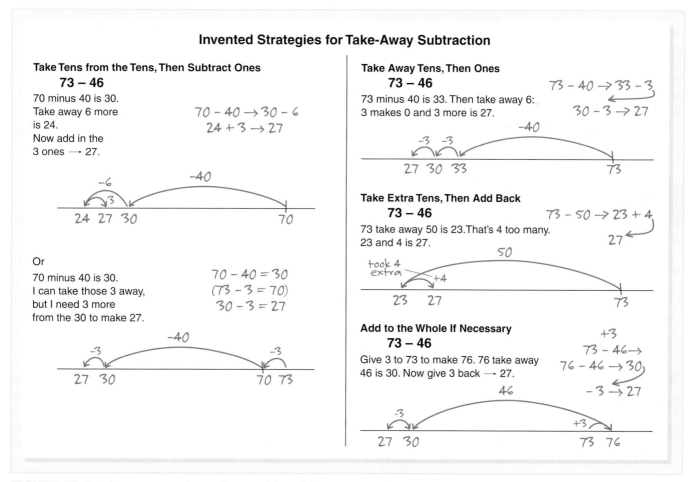

FIGURE 13.7 Take-away strategies work reasonably well for two-digit problems. They are a bit more difficult with three digits.

You can do the same with three-digit numbers without the use of models. ■

Extensions and Challenges

Each of the examples in the preceding sections involved sums less than 100 and all involved *bridging* or *crossing a ten*; that is, if done with a traditional algorithm, they require carrying or borrowing. Bridging, the size of the numbers, and the potential for doing problems mentally are all issues to consider.

Bridging

For most of the strategies, it is easier to add or subtract when bridging is not required. Try each strategy with 34 + 52 or 68 − 24 to see how it works. Easier problems instill confidence. They also permit you to challenge your students with a "harder one." There is also the issue of bridging 100 or 1000. Try 58 + 67 with different strategies. Bridging across 100 is also an issue for subtraction. Problems such as 128 − 50 or 128 − 45 are more difficult than ones that do not cross 100.

Larger Numbers

Most curricula will expect third graders to add and subtract three-digit numbers. Your state standards may even require work with four-digit numbers. Try seeing how *you* would do these without using the traditional algorithms: 487 + 235 and 623 − 247. For subtraction, a counting-up strategy is usually the easiest. Occasionally, other strategies appear with larger numbers. For example, "chunking off" multiples of 50 or 25 is often a useful method. For 462 + 257, pull out 450 and 250 to make 700. That leaves 12 and 7 more ⟶ 719.

 A reading of the Number and Operation standard in both the pre-K–2 and 3–5 chapters will clearly demonstrate that the *Standards* are supportive of the approaches described in this chapter. For example, "When students compute with strategies they invent or choose because they are meaningful, their learning tends to be robust—they are able to remember and apply their knowledge. Children with specific learning disabilities can actively invent and transfer strategies if given well-designed tasks that are developmentally appropriate" (p. 86).

Traditional Algorithms for Addition and Subtraction

If you must teach the traditional computation strategies for addition and subtraction, remember that a serious effort of several months with invented strategies is still well worth it. Because your students will not invent the traditional algorithms, your instruction will necessarily be more directed. Students will infer from this that this "new" way that you are explaining must be preferred and many will abandon their invented strategies. In the short run, it is also true that the traditional strategies appear easier to students. If they remember the rules, only basic facts are required. Try to avoid this complete switch to the traditional algorithms by presenting them as another alternative and then maintain practice with invented methods.

The traditional algorithms require an understanding of *regrouping*, exchanging 10 in one place-value position for 1 in the position to the left—or the reverse, exchanging 1 for 10 in the position to the right. The corresponding terms *carrying* and *borrowing* are obsolete and conceptually misleading. The word *regroup* also has little meaning for young children. A preferable term is *trade*. Ten ones are *traded* for a ten. A hundred is *traded* for 10 tens. Notice that none of the invented strategies involves regrouping.

It is a serious error to work for mastery of nonregrouping problems before tackling regrouping. To keep these problems separate has been the documented source of many error patterns. Teaching nonregrouping problems first causes bad habits that children must later unlearn.

The Addition Algorithm

Explain to the students that they are going to learn a method of adding that most "big people" learned when they were in school. It is not the only way or even the best way; it is just a method you want them to learn.

Begin with Models Only

In the beginning, avoid any written work except for the possible recording of an answer. Provide children with place-value mats and base-ten models. The mat with two ten-frames in the ones place (Blackline Masters) is suggested.

Have students make one number at the top of the mat and a second beneath it as shown in the top portion of Figure 13.8. If children are still developing base-ten concepts, a groupable model such as counters in cups is most helpful.

Explain this one rule: *You begin in the ones column.* "This is a way people came up with a long time ago, and it worked for them." Let students solve the problem on their own. Provide plenty of time, and then have students explain what they did and why. Let students use overhead models or magnetic pieces to help with their explanations.

One or two problems in a lesson with lots of discussion is much more productive than a lot of problems based on rules children don't understand.

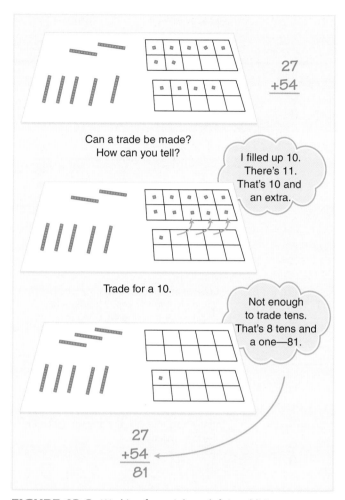

FIGURE 13.8 Working from right to left in addition.

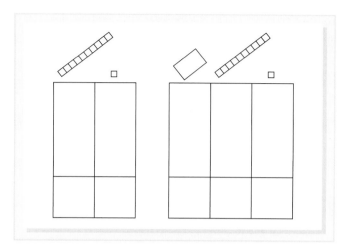

FIGURE 13.9 Blank recording charts are helpful (see Blackline Masters).

The Subtraction Algorithm

The general approach to developing the subtraction algorithm is the same as for addition. When the procedure is completely understood with models, a do-and-write approach connects it with a written form.

Begin with Models Only

Start by having children model the top number in a subtraction problem on the top half of their place-value mats. For the amount to be subtracted, have children write each digit on a small piece of paper and place these pieces near the bottom of their mats in the respective columns, as in Figure 13.12 (p. 229). To avoid inadvertent errors, suggest making all trades first. That way, the full amount on the paper slip can be taken off at once. Also explain to children that they are to begin working with the ones column first, as they did with addition.

Anticipate Difficulties with Zeros

Exercises in which zeros are involved anywhere in the problem tend to cause special difficulties. Give extra attention to these cases while still using models.

The very common error of "borrowing across zero" is best addressed at the modeling stage. For example, in 403 − 138, children must make a double trade, exchanging a hundreds piece for 10 tens and then one of the tens for 10 ones.

Develop the Written Record

The process of recording each step as it is done is the same as was suggested for addition. The same recording sheets (Figure 13.9) are also recommended.

When children can explain symbolism, that is a signal for moving children on to a completely symbolic level. Again, be attentive to problems with zeros.

Develop the Written Record

Reproduce pages with simple place-value charts similar to those shown in Figure 13.9. The charts will help young children record numerals in columns. The general idea is to have children record on these pages each step of the procedure they do with the base-ten models *as it is done*. The first few times you do this, guide each step carefully, as illustrated in Figure 13.10. A similar approach would be used for three-digit problems.

A suggestion is to have children work in pairs. One child is responsible for the models and the other for recording the steps. Children reverse roles with each problem.

Figure 13.11 shows a variation of the traditional recording scheme that is quite reasonable, at least for up to three digits. It avoids the little "carried ones" and focuses attention on the value of the digits. If students were permitted to start adding on the left as they are inclined to do, this is just a vertical recording scheme for the invented strategy "Add tens, add ones, then combine" (Figure 13.5, p. 224).

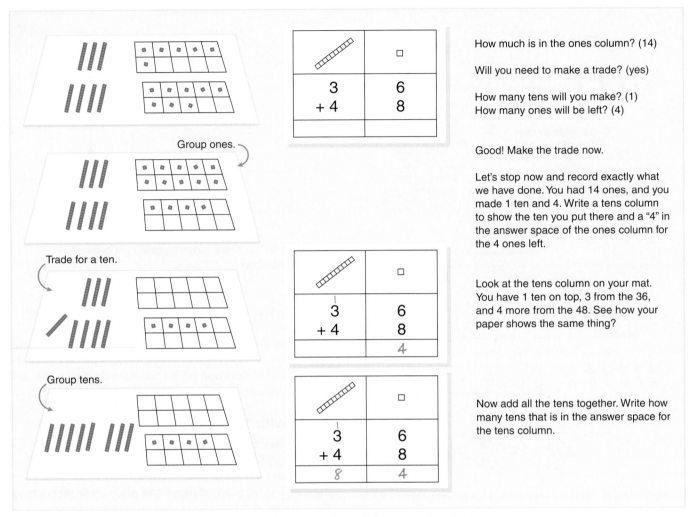

How much is in the ones column? (14)

Will you need to make a trade? (yes)

How many tens will you make? (1)
How many ones will be left? (4)

Good! Make the trade now.

Let's stop now and record exactly what we have done. You had 14 ones, and you made 1 ten and 4. Write a tens column to show the ten you put there and a "4" in the answer space of the ones column for the 4 ones left.

Look at the tens column on your mat. You have 1 ten on top, 3 from the 36, and 4 more from the 48. See how your paper shows the same thing?

Now add all the tens together. Write how many tens that is in the answer space for the tens column.

FIGURE 13.10 Help students record on paper each step they do on their mats as they do it.

If students are permitted to follow their natural instincts and begin with the big pieces (from the left instead of the right), recording schemes similar to that shown in Figure 13.13 are possible. The trades are made from the pieces remaining *after* the subtraction in the column to the left has been done. A "borrow across zero" difficulty will still occur, but in problems like this: 462 − 168. Try it.

⏸ pause and reflect _____

Contrast the difficulties of teaching children to borrow in subtraction, especially borrowing across zero, with the ease of adding on. For example, try solving this: 428 and how much makes 703? Now think about teaching students to borrow across zero to solve 703 − 428.

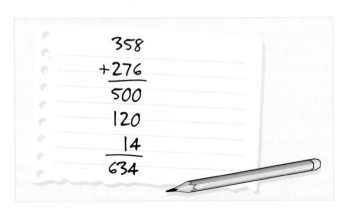

FIGURE 13.11 An alternative recording scheme for addition. Notice that this can be used from left to right as well as from right to left.

Invented Strategies for Multiplication

For multiplication, the ability to break numbers apart in flexible ways is even more important than in addition or subtraction. The distributive property is another concept that is important in multiplication computation. For example, to multiply 43 × 5, one might think about

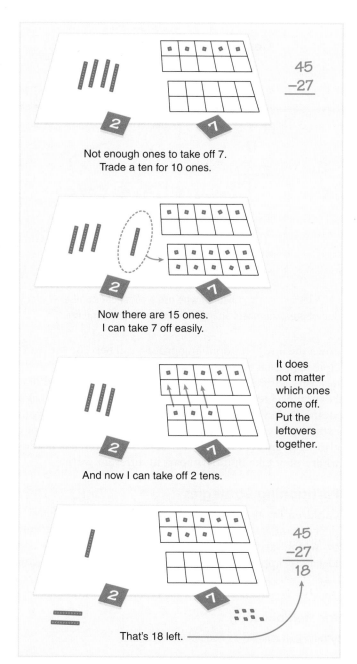

Not enough ones to take off 7.
Trade a ten for 10 ones.

Now there are 15 ones.
I can take 7 off easily.

It does not matter which ones come off. Put the leftovers together.

And now I can take off 2 tens.

That's 18 left.

FIGURE 13.12 Two-place subtraction with models.

breaking 43 into 40 and 3, multiplying each by 5, and then adding the results. Children require ample opportunities to develop these concepts by making sense of their own ideas and those of their classmates.

Useful Representations

The problem 34 × 6 may be represented in a number of ways, as illustrated in Figure 13.14. Often the choice of a model is influenced by a story problem. To determine how many Easter eggs 34 children need if each colors 6 eggs, children may model 6 sets of 34 (or possibly 34 sets of 6). If the problem is about the area of a rectangle that is 34 cm

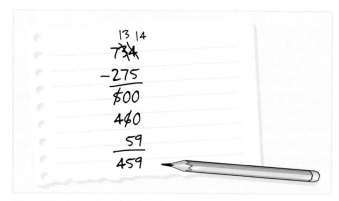

FIGURE 13.13 A left-hand recording scheme for subtraction. Other methods can also be devised.

by 6 cm, then some form of an array is likely. But each representation is appropriate for thinking about 34 × 6 regardless of the context, and students should get to a point where they select ways to think about multiplication that are meaningful to them.

How children represent a product interacts with their methods for determining answers. The groups of 34 might suggest repeated additions—perhaps taking the sets two at a time. Double 34 is 68 and there are three of those, so 68 + 68 + 68. From there a variety of methods is possible.

The six sets of base-ten pieces might suggest breaking the numbers into tens and ones: 6 times 3 tens or

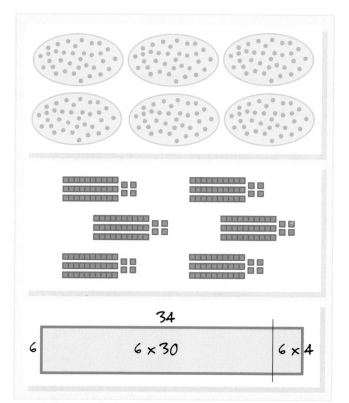

FIGURE 13.14 Different ways to model 34 × 6 may support different computational strategies.

6 × 30 and 6 × 4. Some children use the tens individually: 6 tens make 60. So that's 60 and 60 and 60 (180). Then add on the 24 to make 204.

All of these ideas should be part of students' repertoire of models for multidigit multiplication. Introduce different representations (one at a time) as ways to explore multiplication until you are comfortable that the class has a collection of useful ideas. At the same time, do not force students who reason very well without drawings to use models when they are not needed.

Multiplication by a Single-Digit Multiplier

As with addition and subtraction, it is helpful to place multiplication tasks in contextual story problems. Let students model the problems in ways that make sense to them. Do not be concerned about mixing of factors (6 sets of 34 or 34 sets of 6). Nor should you be timid about the numbers you use. The problem 3 × 24 may be easier than 7 × 65, but the latter provides challenge. The types of strategies that students use for multiplication are much more varied than for addition and subtraction. However, the following three categories can be identified from the research to date.

Complete-Number Strategies

Children who are not yet comfortable breaking numbers into parts will approach the numbers in the sets as single groups. Most likely these early strategies will be based on repeated addition. Often students will list long columns of numbers and add them up. In an attempt to shorten this tedious process, students soon realize that if they add two numbers, the next two will have the same sum and so on

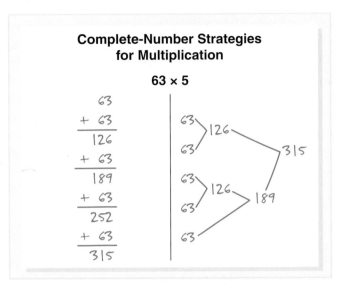

FIGURE 13.15 Children who use a complete-number strategy do not break numbers apart into decades or tens and ones.

down the line. This doubling process can become the principle approach for many students, although it is certainly not very efficient (Ambrose, Baek, & Carpenter, 2003; Fosnot & Dolk, 2001b). Figure 13.15 illustrates two methods they may use. These children will benefit from listening to children who use base-ten models. They may also need more work with base-ten grouping activities where they take numbers apart in different ways.

Partitioning Strategies

Children break numbers up in a variety of ways that reflect an understanding of base-ten concepts, at least four of which are illustrated in Figure 13.16. The "By Decades" approach is the same as the standard algorithm

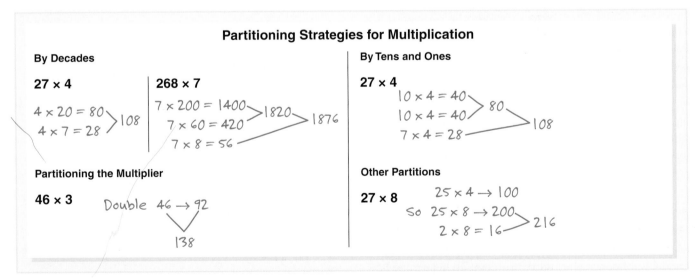

FIGURE 13.16 Numbers can be broken apart in different ways to make easier partial products, which are then combined. Partitioning by decades is useful for mental computation and is very close to the standard algorithm.

except that students always begin with the large values. It extends easily to three digits and is very powerful as a mental math strategy. Another valuable strategy for mental methods is found in the "Other Partitions" example. It is easy to compute mentally with multiples of 25 and 50 and then add or subtract a small adjustment. All partition strategies rely on the distributive property.

Compensation Strategies

Children look for ways to manipulate numbers so that the calculations are easy. In Figure 13.17, the problem 27×4 is changed to an easier one, and then an adjustment or compensation is made. In the second example, one factor is cut in half and the other doubled. This is often used when a 5 or a 50 is involved. Because these strategies are so dependent on the numbers involved, they can't be used for all computations. However, they are powerful strategies, especially for mental math and estimation.

Compensation Strategies for Multiplication

27 × 4

$$27 + 3 \rightarrow 30 \times 4 \rightarrow 120$$
$$3 \times 4 = 12 \rightarrow \underline{-12}$$
$$108$$

250 × 5

I can split 250 in half and multiply by 10.
$$125 \times 10 = 1250$$

17 × 70

$$3 \times 70 \searrow$$
$$20 \times 70 \rightarrow 1400 - 210 \rightarrow 1190$$

FIGURE 13.17 Compensation methods use a product related to the original. A compensation is made in the answer, or one factor is changed to compensate for a change in the other factor.

Using Multiples of 10 and 100

There is a value in exposing students early to products involving multiples of 10 and 100.

The Scout troop wanted to package up 400 fire starter kits as a fund-raising project. If each pack will have 12 fire starters, how many fire starters are the Scouts going to need?

Children will use $4 \times 12 = 48$ to figure out that 400×12 is 4800. There will be discussion around how to say and

write "forty-eight hundred." Be aware of students who simply tack on zeros without understanding why. Try problems such as 30×60 or 210×40 where tens are multiplied by tens.

Two-Digit Multipliers

A problem such as this one can be solved in many different ways:

The parade had 23 clowns. Each clown carried 18 balloons. How many balloons were there altogether?

Some children look for smaller products such as 6×23 and then add that result three times. Another method is to do 20×23 and then subtract 2×23. Others will calculate four separate partial products: $10 \times 20 = 200$, $8 \times 20 = 160$, $10 \times 3 = 30$, and $8 \times 3 = 24$. And still others may add up a string of 23s. Two-digit multiplication is both complex and challenging. But students can solve these problems in a variety of interesting ways, many of which will contribute to the development of the traditional algorithm or one that is just as efficient. Figure 13.18 shows the work of three fourth-grade students who had not been taught the traditional method for multiplication. Kenneth's "parting" refers to *partitioning*, a strategy label provided earlier by the teacher. Briannon is content with adding. She needs to see other strategies developed by her classmates. Nick's method is conceptually very similar to the traditional algorithm. As students begin partitioning numbers along place-value lines, the strategies are often like the traditional algorithm but without the traditional recording schemes.

Cluster Problems

In the fourth and fifth grades of *Investigations in Number, Data, and Space*, one approach to multidigit multiplication is called "cluster problems." (See the *Investigations* excerpt on p. 233 explaining this approach and showing a sample of student work.)

It is useful to have students make an estimate of the final product before doing any of the problems in the cluster. In the first example cluster on p. 233, 3×50 and 10×50 may be helpful in thinking about 30×50. The results of 30×50 and 4×50 combine to give you 34×50. It may seem that 34×25 is harder than 34×50. However, if you know 34×25, it need only be doubled to get the desired product. Students should be encouraged to add problems to the cluster if they need them. Think how you could use 10×34 (and some other related problems) to find 34×25.

The cluster-problem approach begins with students being provided with the cluster problems. After they have become familiar with the approach, students should make

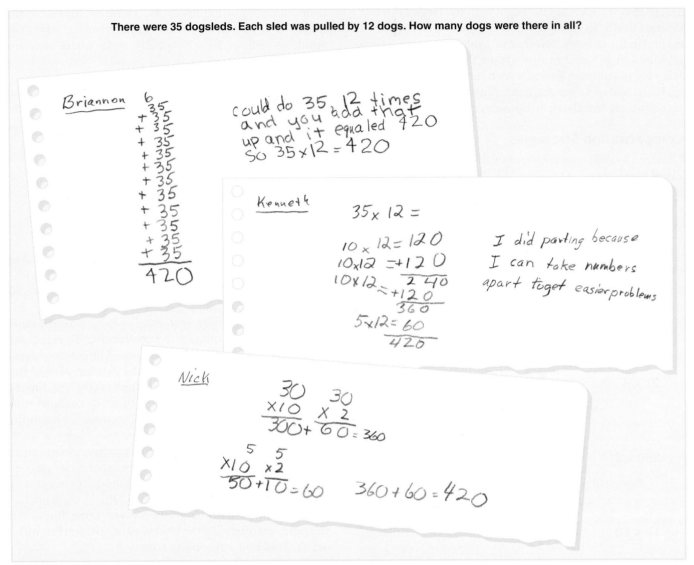

FIGURE 13.18 Three fourth-grade students solve a multiplication problem using their own invented strategies. Each is at a different place in developing a reasonably efficient method for multiplication. None has been taught a traditional multiplication algorithm.

up their own cluster of problems for a given product. At first, have students brainstorm clusters together as a class.

(II) *pause and reflect* _____

Try your hand at making up a cluster of problems for 86 × 42. Include all possible problems that you think might be helpful, even if they are not all related to one approach to finding the product. Then use your cluster to find the product. Is there more than one way?

_____

Here are some problems that might be in your cluster.

$$2 \times 80 \quad 4 \times 80 \quad 2 \times 86 \quad 40 \times 80$$
$$6 \times 40 \quad 10 \times 86 \quad 40 \times 86$$

Of course, your cluster may have included products not shown here. All that is required to begin the cluster-problem approach is that your cluster eventually leads to a solution. Besides your own cluster, see if you can use the problems in this cluster to find 86 × 42.

Cluster problems help students think about ways that they can break numbers apart—or split numbers—into easier parts. The strategy of splitting numbers and multiplying the parts—the distributive property—is an extremely valuable technique for flexible computation. It is also fun to find different clever paths to the solution. For many problems, finding a workable cluster is actually faster than using an algorithm. You do not need to be teaching the *Investigations* curriculum to use cluster problems with your students.

Investigations
in Number, Data, and Space

Grade 4, Packages and Groups
Investigation 2: Double-Digit Multiplication

Context

This unit occurs in the latter half of the fourth grade. Earlier in the same grade, children are introduced to the general approach of cluster problems, which is the topic of the task described here. In the earlier unit, students explored ways to multiply two-digit numbers by one-digit numbers. Here they are working on more difficult tasks. The same approach is used later for division.

Task Description

Cluster problems are a major feature of this unit and are found in quite a few of the investigations. This rather unique approach to the topic encourages students to use facts and combinations they know in order to figure out complex computations. For example, the following cluster is used in an introductory lesson in the unit: 3×7, 5×7, 10×7, 50×7, and **53×7**. The goal is to figure out the last product. Students solve all of the problems and explain what problems were helpful in solving the last problem. Not every problem in the cluster needs to be used to solve the final problem.

The figure here is taken from the teacher notes showing how a student completed one of the cluster problem worksheets. Notice how students draw lines to show connections and add new problems.

Here are two cluster problems taken from a worksheet found later in the unit:

3×50, 10×50, 34×25, 30×50, **34×50**

60×20, 62×10, 62×3, **62×23**

Students are asked to make an estimate of the last problem before they solve the cluster problems includ-

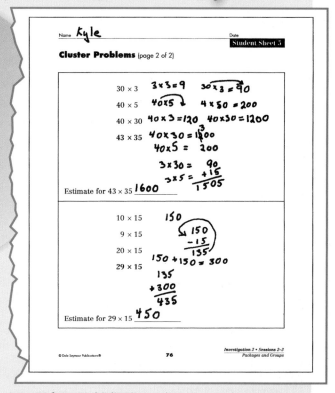

Page 76 from *Multiplication and Division: Packages and Groups* by K. Economopoulos, S. J. Russell, & C. Tierney. *Investigations in Number, Data, and Space.* Copyright © 1998 by Dale Seymour Publications. Reprinted by permission of Pearson Education, Inc.

ing the last problem. Students are encouraged to add their own helping problems to the clusters if they wish. Later, students make up their own cluster problems for a given problem. That is essentially solving the problems without any assistance—using easier related problems is a general strategy for invented approaches to multiplication.

Area Models

A valuable exploration is to prepare large rectangles for each group of two or three students. The rectangles should be measured carefully, with dimensions between 25 cm and 60 cm, and drawn accurately with square corners. (Use the corner of a piece of poster board for a guide.) The students' task is to determine how many small ones pieces (base-ten materials) will fit inside. Wooden or plastic base-

ten pieces are best, but cardboard strips and squares are adequate. Alternatively, rectangles can be drawn on base-ten grid paper (see Blackline Masters), or students can simply be given the task verbally: *What is the area of a rectangle that is 47 cm by 36 cm?*

Most children will fill the rectangle first with as many hundreds pieces as possible. One obvious approach is to put the 12 hundreds in one corner. This will leave narrow

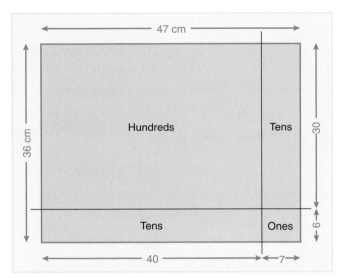

FIGURE 13.19 Ones, tens, and hundreds pieces fit exactly into the four sections of this 47 × 36 rectangle. Figure the size of each section to determine the size of the whole rectangle.

regions on two sides that can be filled with tens pieces and a final small rectangle that will hold ones. Especially if students have had earlier experiences with finding products in arrays, figuring out the size of each subrectangle is not terribly difficult. The sketch in Figure 13.19 shows the four regions.

 *pause and reflect* ————————

If you did not already know the algorithm, how would you determine the size of the rectangle? Use your method (not the standard algorithm) on a rectangle that measures 68 cm × 24 cm. Make a sketch to show and explain your work.

———————————————————————

As you will see in the discussion of the traditional algorithm, the area model leads to a fairly reasonable approach to multiplying numbers.

The Traditional Algorithm for Multiplication

The traditional multiplication algorithm is probably the most difficult of the four algorithms if students have not had plenty of opportunities to explore their own strategies. The multiplication algorithm can be meaningfully developed using either a repeated addition model or an area model. For single-digit multipliers, the difference is minimal. When you move to two-digit multipliers, the area model has some advantages. For that reason, the discussion here will use the area model. Again, you are reminded of the need for a more directed approach than when developing invented strategies.

One-Digit Multipliers

As with the other algorithms, as much time as necessary should be devoted to the conceptual development of the algorithm with the recording or written part coming later. In contrast, most textbooks spend less time on development and more time on drill.

Begin with Models

Give students a drawing of a rectangle 47 cm by 6 cm. *How many small square centimeter pieces will fit in the rectangle?* (What is the area of the rectangle in square centimeters?) Let students solve the problem in groups before discussing it as a class. This simple task can be made into a good problem for students. Challenge them to find a way to determine the number of unit squares on the inside of the rectangle by slicing it into two or more parts in such a way that they can tell the size of each part. For example, it could be sliced into two sections of 20 × 6 and one of 7 × 6.

As shown in Figure 13.20, the rectangle can be sliced or separated into two parts so that one part will be 6 ones by 7 ones, or 42 ones, and the other will be 6 ones by 4 tens, or 24 tens. Notice that the base-ten language "6 ones times 4 tens is 24 tens" tells how many *pieces* (sticks of ten) are in the big section. To say "6 times 40 is 240" is also correct and tells how many units or square centimeters are in the section. Each section is referred to as a *partial product*. By adding the two partial products, you get the total product or area of the rectangle.

To avoid the tedium of drawing large rectangles and arranging base-ten pieces, use the base-ten grid paper found in the Blackline Masters. On the grid paper, students can easily draw accurate rectangles showing all of the pieces. Do not force any recording technique on students until they understand how to use the two dimensions of a rectangle to get a product.

Develop the Written Record

To help with a recording scheme, provide sheets with base-ten columns on which students can record problems.

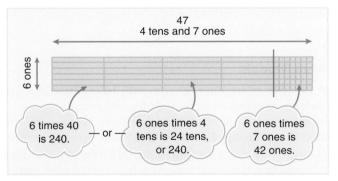

FIGURE 13.20 A rectangle filled with base-ten pieces is a useful model for two-digit-by-one-digit multiplication.

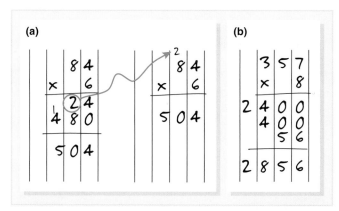

FIGURE 13.21 (a) In the standard form, the product of ones is recorded first. The tens digit of this first product can be written as a "carried" digit above the tens column. (b) It is quite reasonable to abandon the carried digit and permit the partial products to be recorded in any order.

When the two partial products are written separately as in Figure 13.21(a), there is little new to learn. Students simply record the products and add them together. As illustrated, it is possible to teach students how to write the first product with a carried digit so that the combined product is written on one line. This traditional recording scheme is known to be a source of errors. The little carried digit is often the difficulty—it gets added in before the second multiplication or is forgotten.

There is absolutely no practical reason why students can't be allowed to record both partial products and avoid the errors related to the carried digit. When you accept that, it makes no difference in which order the products are written. Why not simply permit students to do written multiplication as shown in Figure 13.21? When the factors are in a word problem, chart, or other format, all that is really necessary is to write down all the partial products and add. Furthermore, that is precisely how this is done mentally.

Most standard curricula progress from two digits to three digits with a single-digit multiplier. Students can make this progression easily. They still should be permitted to write all three partial products separately and not have to bother with carrying.

Two-Digit Multipliers

With the area model, the progression to a two-digit multiplier is relatively straightforward. Rectangles can be drawn on base-ten grid paper, or full-sized rectangles can be filled in with base-ten pieces. There will be four partial products, corresponding to four different sections of the rectangle.

Several variations in language might be used. Consider the product 47 × 36 as illustrated in Figure 13.22. In the partial product 40 × 30, if base-ten language is used—*4 tens times 3 tens is 12 hundreds*—the result tells how many

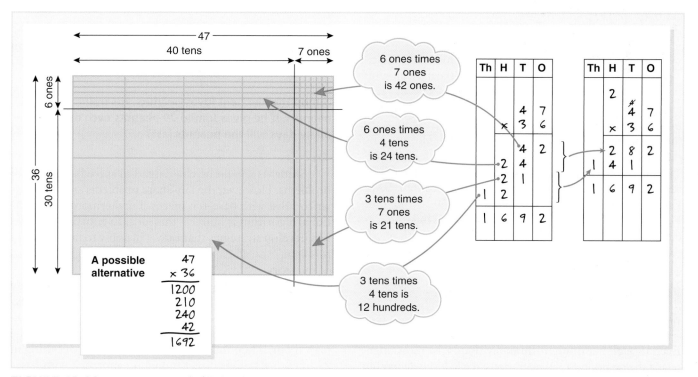

FIGURE 13.22 47 × 36 rectangle filled with base-ten pieces. Base-ten language connects the four partial products to the traditional written format. Note the possibility of recording the products in some other order.

hundreds pieces are in that section. Verbally, the product "forty times thirty" is formidable. Try to avoid "four times three," which promotes thinking about digits rather than numbers. It is well worth stressing the idea that in all cases, a product of *tens times tens is hundreds.*

Figure 13.22 also shows the recording of four partial products in the traditional order and how these can be collapsed to two lines if carried digits are used. Here the second "carry" technically belongs in the hundreds column but it rarely is written there. Often it gets confused with the first and is thus an additional source of errors. The lower left of the figure shows the same computation with all four products written in a different order. This is quite an acceptable algorithm. In the rare instance when someone multiplies numbers such as 538×29 with pencil and paper, there would be six partial products. But far fewer errors would occur, requiring less instructional time and much less remediation.

NCTM Standards "As students move from third to fifth grade, they should consolidate and practice a small number of computational algorithms for addition, subtraction, multiplication and division that they understand well and can use routinely. . . . Having access to more than one method for each operation allows students to choose an approach that best fits the numbers in a particular problem. For example, 298×42 can be thought of as $(300 \times 42) - (2 \times 42)$, whereas 41×16 can be computed by multiplying 41×8 to get 328 and then doubling 328 to get 656" (p. 155).

 Computer versions of the area model for multiplication can alleviate some of the difficulties of physically filling in place-value blocks into rectangles. On the NLVM Web site, the Rectangle Multiplication applet will model any rectangle up to 30×30 (http://nlvm.usu.edu/en/nav/category_g_2_t_l.html). The rectangle is split into two parts rather than four, corresponding to the tens and ones digits in the multiplier. The result is nicely correlated to the standard algorithm. Scott Foresman's *eTools* permits rectangles up to 50×100. (See Figure 13.23.) Students must stamp the blocks into the rectangle just as if they were placing them by hand with physical blocks. The total can be shown or hidden. ■

Invented Strategies for Division

Even though many adults think division is the most onerous of the computational operations, it can be considerably easier than multiplication. Typically, division computation strategies are developed in the third and fourth grades.

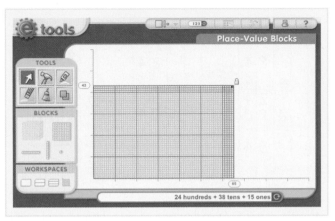

FIGURE 13.23 The *eTools* software (Scott Foresman, 2004) will allow the creation of a rectangle up to 50 by 100 that can be filled in with base-ten blocks the same as would be done with physical blocks.

Source: From *eTools*, Scott Foresman (2004). Reprinted by permission of Pearson Education, Inc.

Recall that there are two concepts of division. First there is the partition or fair-sharing idea, illustrated by this story problem:

The bag has 783 jelly beans, and Aidan and her four friends want to share them equally. How many jelly beans will Aidan and each of her friends get?

Then there is the measurement or repeated subtraction concept:

Jumbo the elephant loves peanuts. His trainer has 625 peanuts. If he gives Jumbo 20 peanuts each day, how many days will the peanuts last?

Students should be challenged to solve both types of problems. However, the fair-share problems are often easier to solve with base-ten pieces. Furthermore, the traditional algorithm is built on this idea. Eventually, students will develop strategies that they will apply to both types of problem, even when the process does not match the action of the story.

Figure 13.24 shows some strategies that fourth-grade children have used to solve division problems. The first example illustrates $92 \div 4$ using base-ten pieces and a sharing process. A ten is traded when no more tens can be passed out. Then the 12 ones are distributed, resulting in 23 in each set. This direct modeling approach with base-ten pieces is quite easy even for third-grade students to understand and use.

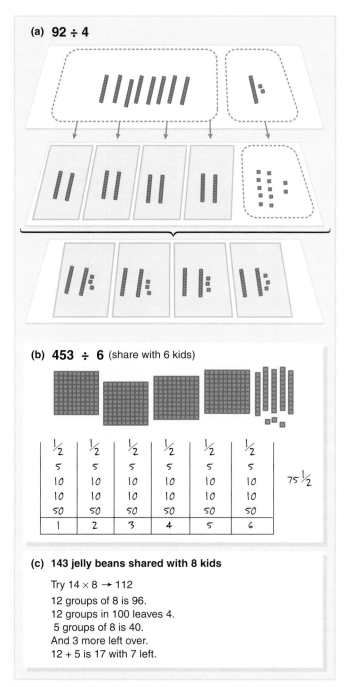

(a) 92 ÷ 4

(b) 453 ÷ 6 (share with 6 kids)

½	½	½	½	½	½	
5	5	5	5	5	5	
10	10	10	10	10	10	75 ½
10	10	10	10	10	10	
50	50	50	50	50	50	
1	2	3	4	5	6	

(c) 143 jelly beans shared with 8 kids

Try 14 × 8 → 112

12 groups of 8 is 96.
12 groups in 100 leaves 4.
5 groups of 8 is 40.
And 3 more left over.
12 + 5 is 17 with 7 left.

FIGURE 13.24 Students use both models and symbols to solve division tasks.

Source: Adapted from *Developing Mathematical Ideas: Numbers and Operations, Part I: Building a System of Tens—Casebook* by Deborah Schifter, Virginia Bastable, and Susan Jo Russell. © 2002 by Educational Development Center, Inc. Published by Dale Seymour Publications, an imprint of Pearson Learning Group, a division of Pearson Education, Inc. Used by permission.

In the second example, the student sets out the base-ten pieces and draws a "bar graph" with six columns. After noting that there are not enough hundreds for each kid, he splits the 3 hundreds in half, putting 50 in each column.

That leaves him with 1 hundred, 5 tens, and 3 ones. After trading the hundred for tens (now 15 tens), he gives 20 to each, recording 2 tens in each bar. Now he is left with 3 tens and 3 ones, or 33. He knows that 5×6 is 30, so he gives each kid 5, leaving him with 3. These he splits in half and writes $\frac{1}{2}$ in each column.

The child in the third example is solving a sharing problem but tries to do it as a measurement process. She wants to find out how many eights are in 143. Initially she guesses. By multiplying 8 first by 10, then by 20, and then by 14, she knows the answer is more than 14 and less than 20. After some more work (not shown), she rethinks the problem as how many eights in 100 and how many in 40.

Missing-Factor Strategies

Notice in Figure 13.24(a) how the use of base-ten blocks tends to develop a digit-oriented approach—first share the hundreds, then the tens, and finally the ones. Although this is good background for the traditional algorithm, it does not help develop complete-number strategies that are also quite useful. In Figure 13.24(c), the student is using a multiplicative approach. She is trying to find out, "What number times 8 will be close to 143 with less than 8 remaining?"

 *pause and reflect*

Try to determine the quotient of 318 ÷ 7 by figuring out *what number times 7* (or *7 times what number*) is close to 318 without going over. Do not use the standard algorithm.

There are several places to begin solving this problem. For instance, since 10×7 is only 70 and 100×7 is 700, the answer has to be between 10 and 100. You might start with multiples of 10. Thirty 7s are 210. Forty 7s are 280. Fifty 7s are 350. So 40 is not enough and 50 is too much. It has to be forty-something. At this point you could guess at numbers between 40 and 50. Or you might add on 7s. Or you could notice that forty 7s (280) leaves you with 20 plus 18 or 38. Five 7s will be 35 of the 38 with 3 left over. In all, that's $40 + 5$ or 45 with a remainder of 3.

This missing-factor approach is likely to be invented by some students if they are solving measurement problems such as the following:

Grace can put 6 pictures on one page of her photo album. If she has 82 pictures, how many pages will she need?

Alternatively, you can simply pose a task such as 82 ÷ 6 and ask students, "What number times 6 would be close to 82?" and continue from there.

Cluster Problems

Another approach to developing missing-factor strategies is to use cluster problems as discussed for multiplication. Here are two examples:

100 × 4	10 × 72
500 ÷ 4	5 × 70
4 × 25	2 × 72
6 × 4	4 × 72
527 ÷ 4	5 × 72
	381 ÷ 72

Notice that the missing-factor strategy works equally well for one-digit divisors as for two-digit divisors. Also notice that it is okay to include division problems in the cluster. In the preceding example, 125 × 4 could easily have replaced 500 ÷ 4, and 400 ÷ 4 could replace 100 × 4. The idea is to keep multiplication and division as closely connected as possible.

Cluster problems accentuate a flexible approach to computation, helping students realize that there are many different good ways to compute. Another way to develop flexibility is to pose a division problem (or a multiplication problem) and have students solve the problem using two different approaches. Of course, neither of the methods should be the traditional algorithm or a calculator.

Cluster problems provide students with a sense that problems can be solved in different ways and with different starting points. Therefore, rather than cluster problems, you can provide students with a variety of first steps for solving a problem. Their task is to select one of the starting points and solve the problem from there. For example, here are four possible starting points for 514 ÷ 8:

     10 × 8   400 ÷ 8   60 × 8   80 ÷ 8

 When students are first asked to solve problems using two methods, they often use a primitive or completely inefficient method for their second approach (or revert to a standard algorithm). For example, to solve 514 ÷ 8, a student might perform a very long string of subtractions (514 − 8 = 506, 506 − 8 = 498, 498 − 8 = 490, and so on) and count how many times he or she subtracted 8. Others will actually draw 514 tally marks and loop groups of 8. These students have not developed sufficient flexibility to think of other efficient methods. The idea just suggested of posing a variety of starting points can nudge students into other more profitable alternatives. Class discussions will also help students begin to see more flexible approaches. ■

The Traditional Algorithm for Division

Long division is the one traditional algorithm that starts with the left-hand or big pieces. The conceptual basis for

FIGURE 13.25 In the division algorithm shown, the numbers on the side indicate the quantity of the divisor being subtracted from the dividend. As the two examples indicate, the divisor can be subtracted from the dividend in any amount desired.

the algorithm most often taught in textbooks is the partition or fair-share method, the method we will explore in detail. Another well-known algorithm is based on repeated subtraction and may be viewed as a good way to record the missing-factor approach with partial products recorded in a column to the right of the division computation. As shown by the two examples in Figure 13.25, one advantage is that there is total flexibility in the factors selected at each step of the way.

One-Digit Divisors

Typically, the division algorithm with one-digit divisors is introduced in the third grade. If done well, it should not have to be retaught, and it should provide the basis for two-digit divisors. Students in the upper grades who are having difficulty with the division algorithm can also benefit from a conceptual development.

Begin with Models

Traditionally, if we were to do a problem such as 4)583, we might say "4 goes into 5 one time." This is quite mysterious to children. How can you just ignore the "83" and keep changing the problem? Preferably, you want students to think of the 583 as 5 hundreds, 8 tens, and 3 ones, not as the independent digits 5, 8, and 3. One idea is to use a context such as candy bundled in boxes of ten with 10 boxes to a carton. Then the problem becomes *We have 5 boxes, 8 cartons, and 3 pieces of candy to share between 4 schools evenly.* In this context, it is reasonable to share the cartons first until no more can be shared. Those remaining are "unpacked," and the boxes shared, and so on. Money ($100, $10, and $1) can be used in a similar manner.

⏸ *pause and reflect* —————————————————
Try this yourself using base-ten pieces and the problem 524 ÷ 3. Try to talk through the process without using "goes into." Think sharing.

————————————————————————————————

Language plays an enormous role in thinking about the algorithm conceptually. Most adults are so accustomed to the "goes into" language that it is hard to let it go. For the problem 583 ÷ 4, here is some suggested language:

* I want to share 5 hundreds, 8 tens, and 3 ones among these four sets. There are enough hundreds for each set to get 1 hundred. That leaves 1 hundred that I can't share.
* I'll trade the hundred for 10 tens. That gives me a total of 18 tens. I can give each set 4 tens and have 2 tens left over. Two tens is not enough to go around the four sets.
* I can trade the 2 tens for 20 ones and put those with the 3 ones I already had. That makes a total of 23 ones. I can give 5 ones in each of the four sets. That leaves me with 3 ones as a remainder. In all I gave out 1 hundred, 4 tens, and 5 ones with 3 left over.

Develop the Written Record

The recording scheme for the long-division algorithm is not completely intuitive. You will need to be quite directive in helping children learn to record the fair sharing with models. There are essentially four steps:

1. *Share* and record the number of pieces put in each group.
2. *Record* the number of pieces shared in all. Multiply to find this number.
3. *Record* the number of pieces remaining. Subtract to find this number.
4. *Trade* (if necessary) for smaller pieces, and combine with any that are there already. Record the new total number in the next column.

When students model problems with a one-digit divisor, steps 2 and 3 seem unnecessary. Explain that these steps really help when you don't have the pieces there to count.

Record Explicit Trades

Figure 13.26 details each step of the recording process just described. On the left, you see the traditional algorithm. To the right is a suggestion that matches the actual action with the models by explicitly recording the trades. Instead of the somewhat mysterious "bring-down" procedure, the traded pieces are crossed out, as is the number of existing pieces in the next column. The combined number of pieces is

written in this column using a two-digit number. In the example, 2 hundreds are traded for 20 tens, combined with the 6 that were there for a total of 26 tens. The 26 is, therefore, written in the tens column.

Students who are required to make sense of the long-division procedure find the explicit-trade method easier to follow. Blank division charts with wide place-value columns are highly recommended. These can be found in the Blackline Masters. Without the charts, it is important to spread out the digits in the dividend when writing down the problem. (*Author note:* The explicit-trade method is an invention of mine. It has been used successfully in grades 3 to 8. You will not find it in textbooks.)

Both the explicit-trade method and the use of place-value columns will help with the problem of leaving out a middle zero in a problem (see Figure 13.27).

Two-Digit Divisors

There is almost no justification for having children master division with two-digit divisors. A large chunk of the fourth, fifth, and sometimes sixth grade is frequently spent on this outdated skill. The cost in terms of time and students' attitudes toward mathematics is enormous. Only a few times in any adult's life will an exact result to such a computation be required and a calculator not be available. If you can possibly influence the removal of this outdated skill from your school's curriculum, you are encouraged to speak up.

With a two-digit divisor, it is hard to come up with the right amount to share at each step. A guess too high or too low means you have to erase and start all over.

An Intuitive Idea

Suppose that you were sharing a large pile of candies with 36 friends. Instead of passing them out one at a time, you conservatively estimate that each person could get at least 6 pieces. So you give 6 to each of your friends. Now you find there are more than 36 pieces left. Do you have everyone give back the 6 pieces so you can then give them 7 or 8? That would be silly! You simply pass out more.

The candy example gives us two good ideas for sharing in long division. First, always underestimate how much can be shared. You can always pass out some more. Second, if there is enough left to share some more, just do it! To avoid ever overestimating, always pretend there are more sets among which to share than there really are. For example, if you are dividing 312 by 43 (sharing among 43 sets or "friends"), pretend you have 50 sets instead. Round *up* to the next multiple of 10. You can easily determine that 6 pieces can be shared among 50 sets because 6 × 50 is an easy product. Therefore, since there are really only 43 sets, clearly you can give *at least* 6 to each. Always consider a larger divisor; *always round up*. If your underestimate leaves you with more to share, simply pass out some more.

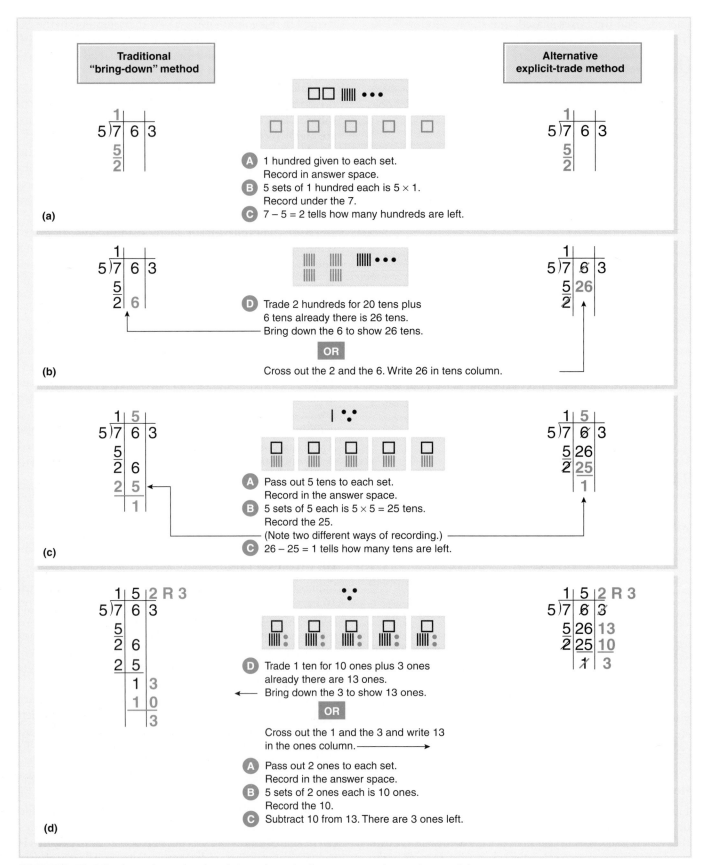

FIGURE 13.26 The traditional and explicit-trade methods are connected to each step of the division process. Every step can and should make sense.

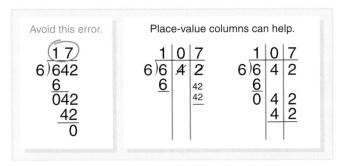

FIGURE 13.27 Using lines to mark place-value columns can help avoid forgetting to record zeros.

Using the Idea Symbolically

These ideas are used in Figure 13.28. Both the traditional method and the explicit-trade method of recording are illustrated. The rounded-up divisor, 70, is written in a little "think bubble" above the real divisor. Rounding up has another advantage: It is easy to run through the multiples of 70 and compare them to 374. Think about sharing base-ten pieces (thousands, hundreds, tens, and ones). Work through the problem one step at a time, saying exactly what each recorded step stands for.

This approach has proved successful with children in the fourth grade learning division for the first time and

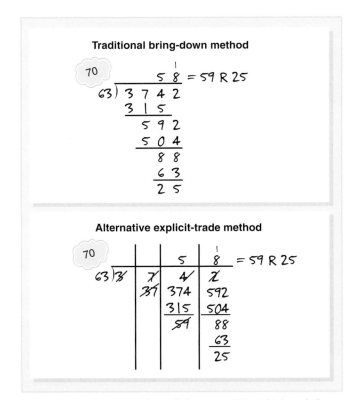

FIGURE 13.28 Round the divisor up to 70 to think with, but multiply what you share by 63. In the ones column, share 8 with each set. Oops! 88 left over. Just give 1 more to each set.

with children in the sixth to eighth grades in need of remediation. It reduces the mental strain of making choices and essentially eliminates the need to erase. If an estimate is too low, that's okay. And if you always round up, the estimate will never be too high. Nor is there any reason ever to change to the more familiar approach. It is just as good for adults as for children. The same is true of the explicit-trade notation. It is certainly an idea to consider.

NCTM Standards The following comes from the 3–5 chapter of the *Standards:* "Although the expectation is that students develop fluency in computing with whole numbers, frequently they should use calculators to solve complex computations involving large numbers or as part of an extended problem" (p. 155).

Assessment Notes When teaching a traditional algorithm for any operation, you will undoubtedly give periodic quizzes or use chapter-end tests found in your textbook. When students do well on these tests, both teachers and parents are pleased. Whether they do well or not so well, it is important to ask yourself if you really can tell what students understand or do not understand from a strictly computational test. You can always check for fact errors or carelessness. When students make a systematic error in an algorithm, it will likely show up in the same way in repeated problems. What you do not know is what conceptual knowledge children are using—or not using. Don't mistake correct use of a standard algorithm for understanding.

To assess this very important background understanding for algorithms, it is important to do more than test skills. During class discussions, call on different students to explain individual steps. Keep track of students' responses in a simple chart or other recording technique, indicating how well they seem to understand the algorithm you are working on. For students experiencing trouble, you may want to conduct a short 5- to 10-minute interview to explore in a bit more detail their level of understanding.

An interview might begin by having the student complete a computation. When finished, ask for explanations for specific steps in the process. If there is difficulty explaining the symbolic process, have the student use base-ten blocks to perform the same computation. Assuming that the student can do this, ask for connections between what was done with the models and what was done symbolically. ∎

Literature Connections

Children's literature can play a very useful role in helping you develop problems for your invented strategies and mental computation lessons. Your simple story problems every day may be great, but children deserve a change. Turn to children's books. There are a great many fascinating books that involve large numbers and opportunities to compute. Some are about real data, and others are fictional.

Cookies
Jaspersohn, 1993

This is the true story of Wally Amos and his Famous Amos Chocolate Chip Cookies. (Are you interested already?) The text includes a large number of color and black-and-white photos that show the production and distribution of Famous Amos cookies. Because it is filled with facts about the cookies—numbers sold, number the average person eats in a year, and so on—you can easily pose questions that require computation and that children will find interesting. Although actual computations can be done on a calculator, this context clearly suggests that estimates and round numbers make more sense. As you discuss ideas generated by the book, some computations can be done mentally to determine exact answers. Other computations will be estimates. Students can extend the story to a project to research cookie consumption in their home, data from grocery stores about other cookies, or the number of trucks or miles required to get cookies to market. The possibilities are endless. During these projects, suggest that students pay attention to where an estimate makes more sense than an exact computation. Find out if there are places as they are working on their project where they made a quick mental estimate or did a mental computation.

Is a Blue Whale the Biggest Thing There Is?
Wells, 1993

This is one of the most intriguing books you will find about large things and large distances. Blue whales look small next to Mount Everest, which in turn looks small next to the earth. The data in the book allow children to make other comparisons, such as the number of fourth graders that would have the same weight or volume as a blue whale or would fill the gymnasium. As with the Famous Amos data, these comparisons are the perfect place for estimations and discussions about how much accuracy is necessary to make a meaningful comparison. Bresser (1995) provides excellent insights into the use of this story with fourth-, fifth-, and sixth-grade students. ■

Reflections on Chapter 13

Writing to Learn

1. What is the difference between solving a problem with direct modeling and solving a problem with an invented strategy? What is a traditional algorithm?

2. How are traditional algorithms different from invented strategies? Explain the benefits of invented strategies over traditional algorithms.

3. When a problem has been solved, how do you manage all of the different methods that students may propose, and what should you do about students who propose no ideas of their own?

4. What do you do when someone brings a traditional algorithm into the classroom before you have introduced it? What if you never plan to teach the traditional algorithm but students want to use it anyway?

5. Explain how strategies for problems such as 58 + 6 or 72 − 5 are similar to the make-ten strategies for basic facts. How can you help children extend their basic fact strategies to these larger numbers?

6. Illustrate three different strategies for adding 46 + 39. Which ones are easy to do mentally? Is there a strategy that is easier because 39 is close to 40? What strategies work well for sums such as 538 + 243? For each strategy you work with, think about how you could record it on the board so that other students will be able to follow what is being done.

7. Use two different adding-up strategies for 93 − 27 and for 545 − 267. Make up a story problem that would encourage an adding-up strategy.

8. Describe how you would go about developing the traditional algorithms for addition and subtraction. How would you deal with the issue of beginning on the right with the ones place when students' natural tendency is to begin on the left? Use 385 + 128 to illustrate a reasonable written algorithm that begins on the left instead of the right. Do the same for 453 − 278.

9. Draw pictures showing how 57 × 4 could be modeled: with counters, with base-ten pieces, with rectangles or arrays on base-ten grids.

10. What would you do if your students seemed to persist in using complete-number strategies for multiplication (variations of repeated addition without really doing any multiplication)?

11. What is a cluster problem? Make up cluster problems for 46 × 5 and 73 × 18.

12. Try to develop some skill using an invented strategy for multiplying by single-digit numbers. Can you do 327 × 6 mentally? How would you record the steps on the chalkboard if a student gave them to you the way you did it?

13. Use a compensation strategy for these: 68 × 20, 5 × 46, 25 × 480.

14. Draw a rectangle for 28 × 57, and explain how it could be used to compute the product.

15. Which division concept, measurement or partition, is easier for direct modeling and is also the one used to develop the usual long-division algorithm? Make up an appropriate word story with that concept to go with 735 ÷ 6.

16. Explain a missing-factor strategy for division. Use that approach to solve 264 ÷ 12. Repeat the problem using a different starting point.

17. Use the traditional algorithm for 735 ÷ 6, and then repeat the process using the text's suggestion of recording trades explicitly. With the two algorithms side by side, explain every recorded number in terms of what it stands for when sharing base-ten pieces.

18. To avoid erasures in long division, a rounded-up divisor can be used to make estimates of the quotient in each place value. Show how this method works and avoids erasures using the problem 4589 ÷ 62.

19. Why is some form of assessment that gets at student understanding so important when teaching traditional algorithms?

For Discussion and Exploration

1. Conduct a four-person panel discussion debating whether or not the traditional computational algorithms for whole numbers should continue to be taught. Have two persons represent each view. Arguments should show the benefits of each approach, efficiency of various methods, students' understanding of "doing mathematics," the issue of available technology in the real world, the need for computation of various types outside of the classroom, high-stakes testing, and the desires of parents (valid or not). Two intermediate views are also possible: including traditional algorithms only for multiplication and division, and withholding teaching of the traditional algorithms until seventh or eighth grade after flexible strategies and better number sense have been developed. Have separate panel members for these views.

2. Select any grade between 2 and 6, and discuss what you feel is an appropriate skill level for whole-number computation at that grade. Should these skills be taught at that grade or earlier? How do your views compare with the treatment given whole-number computation in a traditional textbook for that grade level? How does the textbook treatment compare with the general position offered in this chapter?

3. Examine one of the three standards-based curricula (see Chapter 1, p. 10) for the elementary grades. How is whole-number computation developed? Note that only *Investigations* relies completely on invented strategies.

Recommendations for Further Reading

Campbell, P. F., & Johnson, M. L. (1995). How primary students think and learn. In I. M. Carl (Ed.), *Prospects for school mathematics* (pp. 21–42). Reston, VA: National Council of Teachers of Mathematics.

Campbell and Johnson describe a project in an urban school system that is completely based in a constructivist paradigm. The purpose of the chapter is to describe how children are able to construct their own ideas. Interestingly, most of the examples provided surround computation and student-invented methods. Absolutely worth reading.

Fosnot, C. T., & Dolk, M. (2001). *Young mathematicians at work: Constructing multiplication and division.* Portsmouth, NH: Heinemann.

Fosnot, C. T., & Dolk, M. (2001). *Young mathematicians at work: Constructing number sense, addition, and subtraction.* Portsmouth, NH: Heinemann.

These are two in a series of three books that are the product of Fosnot (a U.S. mathematics educator and expert in constructivism) and Dolk (a mathematics educator at the Freudenthal Institute in the Netherlands). The books are products of a collaborative effort begun in 1988, of working with teachers, examining how children learn, and how to support that learning. They show children constructing ideas about number, operations, and computation in ways not found elsewhere. The authors talk about the "landscape of learning" and ideas "on the horizon"—the places where children are working and the ideas they are working toward. Refreshing, thoughtful, and informative. (Their third book is on fractions and decimals.)

Morrow, L. (Ed.). (1998). *The teaching and learning of algorithms in school mathematics.* Reston, VA: National Council of Teachers of Mathematics.

Mastery of algorithms is and always has been a topic that antireformers choose to attack, usually because they believe that reform means stop teaching computation. In this NCTM yearbook we find well-articulated perspectives on the issue. More important, there are numerous articles with practical teaching suggestions at the elementary, middle, and secondary levels.

National Council of Teachers of Mathematics. (2003). Computational fluency [Focus Issue]. *Teaching Children Mathematics, 9.*

How to help children achieve skills and understanding in the area of computation is the focus of this entire journal, which can be purchased separately from the NCTM. Each of the nine articles is well worth reading. These include a discussion of teaching computation to English language learners, an article on computational fluency written by an internationally prominent mathematician, a reprint of a classic article on meaning and skill by William Brownell, plus other worthwhile papers by both classroom teachers and researchers in the area of computation.

Russell, S. J. (2000). Developing computational fluency with whole numbers. *Teaching Children Mathematics, 7,* 155–158.

In just four pages, Russell provides an articulate view of what *Principles and Standards* means by computational fluency. Russell accompanies each of her points with examples from children. She talks about connecting understanding with procedures and how to assess computational fluency. She ends this little article by explaining that teaching for fluency is a complex task requiring the teacher's understanding of the mathematics, selecting appropriate tasks, and recognizing when to capitalize on students' ideas.

Online Resources

Suggested Applets and Web Links

Base Blocks Addition
http://nlvm.usu.edu/en/nav/frames_asid_154_g_1_t_1.html

Base Blocks Subtraction
http://nlvm.usu.edu/en/nav/frames_asid_155_g_1_t_1.html

These two similar applets use base-ten blocks on a place-value chart. You can form any problem you wish through four digits. The subtraction model shows the bottom number in red instead of blue. When the top blocks are dragged onto the red blocks, they disappear. Although you can begin in any column, the model forces a regrouping strategy as well as a take-away model for subtraction. Good for the traditional algorithms.

Rectangle Multiplication
http://nlvm.usu.edu/en/nav/frames_asid_192_g_1_t_1.html

This applet nicely models two-digit by two-digit products up to 30×30.

An additional list of books and articles related to the ideas in this chapter can be found on the Companion Web site at **www.ablongman.com/vandewalle6e.**

chapter 14

Computational Estimation with Whole Numbers

Recall that *Principles and Standards* defined computational fluency as "having and using efficient and accurate methods for computing" (NCTM, 2000, p. 32). Computational estimation skills round out a full development of flexible and fluent thinking with whole numbers. Estimation skills with whole numbers also form the foundation for most estimation skills with fractions, decimals, and percents.

Mental computation and computational estimation are highly related yet quite different skills. Estimates are made using mental computations with numbers that are easier to work with than the actual numbers involved. Thus, estimation depends on students' mental computational skills. However, because of the importance of estimation—both in the real world and in much of mathematics—and because the strategies for computational estimation are quite different from those discussed in the preceding chapter, it makes sense to address this topic separately.

▼ Big Ideas

1. Multidigit numbers can be built up or taken apart in a wide variety of ways. When the parts of numbers are easier to work with, these parts can be used to create estimates in calculations rather than using the exact numbers involved. For example, 36 is 30 and 6 or 25 and 10 and 1. 483 can be thought of as 500 − 20 + 3.

2. Nearly all computational estimations involve using easier-to-handle parts of numbers or substituting difficult-to-handle numbers with close "nice" numbers so that the resulting computations can be done mentally.

Mathematics Content Connections

Estimation skills once developed are a tool for everyday living as well as a tool for sense making in other areas of mathematics.

- **Operations, Place Value, and Whole-Number Computation** (Chapters 10, 12, and 13): Many of the skills of estimation grow directly out of invented strategies for computation. For example, to estimate 708 ÷ 27 you might compute 20 × 27 (540) and then 5 × 27 (135, for a total of 675). Thus, the quotient is a little more than 25. To compute these two products requires an understanding of place value. To understand how multiplication can help with the division estimate requires an understanding of how multiplication and division are related.

- **Estimation with Fractions, Decimals, and Percents** (Chapters 17 and 18): Once students have an understanding of what an estimate is and have developed strategies for whole-number estimation, few new strategies are required for estimation with other types of numbers. To estimate 3.45 + 24.06 − 0.0057 requires no new estimation skills, only a good conceptual understanding of the decimals involved. Similar statements are true of fractions and percents.

Introducing Computational Estimation

The long-term goal of computational estimation is to be able quickly to produce an approximate result for a computation that will be adequate for the situation. In everyday life, estimation skills are valuable time savers. Many situations do not require an exact answer, so reaching for a calculator or a pencil is not necessary if one has good estimation skills.

Good estimators tend to employ a variety of computational strategies they have developed over time. Teaching these strategies to children has become a regular part of the curriculum. Beginning about grade 3, we can help children develop an understanding of what it means to estimate a computation and start to develop some early strategies that may be useful. From then on through middle school, children should continue to develop and add to their estimation strategies and skills.

Understanding Computational Estimation

By itself, the term *estimate* refers to a number that is a suitable approximation for an exact number given the particular context. This concept of an estimate is applied not only to computation but also to measures and quantities.

Three Types of Estimation

In the K–8 mathematics curriculum, *estimation* refers to three quite different ideas:

- *Measurement estimation*—determining an approximate measure without making an exact measurement. For example, we can estimate the length of a room or the weight of a watermelon in the grocery store.
- *Quantity estimation*—approximating the number of items in a collection. For example, we might estimate the number of students in the auditorium or jelly beans in the "guessing jar."
- *Computational estimation*—determining a number that is an approximation of a computation that we cannot or do not wish to determine exactly. For example, we might want to know the approximate gas mileage in our car if we travel 326 miles on 16 gallons of gas (326 ÷ 16). In some instances, it is sufficient to know that a computation is either more or less than a given number. Do I have enough money to buy six boxes at $3.29 each? We have 28 dozen donuts. Are there enough for the 117 students to have two each?

This chapter addresses only computational estimation.

Estimate or Guess

Many children confuse the idea of estimation with guessing. None of the three types of estimation involves outright guessing. Each involves some form of reasoning. Computational estimation involves some computation; it is not a guess at all. Since it is based on computation, how can there be different answers to estimates? The answer, of course, is that any particular estimate depends on the strategy used and the kinds of adjustments in the numbers that might be made. Estimates also tend to vary with the need for the estimate. Estimating your gas mileage is quite different from trying to decide if your last $5 will cover the three items you need at the Fast Mart. These are new and difficult ideas for young students.

Choosing a Form of Computation

Whenever we are faced with a computation in real life or even in school, we have a variety of choices to make concerning how we will handle the computation. As pointed out in the 1989 *Standards* document, the first decision is: "Do we need an exact answer or will an approximate answer be okay?" If an exact answer is called for, we can use an invented or mental strategy, a pencil-and-paper algorithm, a calculator, or even a computer. A computer is called for when there are many repetitive computations that lend themselves to spreadsheet formats. Often, however, we do not need an exact answer and so we can use an estimate. How good an estimate—how close it must be to the actual computation—is a matter of context, as was the original decision to be satisfied with an estimate.

NCTM Standards "Teachers should help students learn how to decide when an exact answer or an estimate would be more appropriate, how to choose the computational methods that would be best to use, and how to evaluate the reasonableness of answers to computations. Most calculations should arise as students solve problems in context" (p. 220).

Suggestions for Estimation Instruction

Here are some general principles that are worth keeping in mind as you help your students develop estimation skills.

Find Real Examples of Estimation

Discuss situations in which computational estimations are used in real life. Some simple examples include dealing with grocery store situations (doing comparative shopping, determining if there is enough to pay the bill), adding up distances in planning a trip, determining approximate yearly or monthly totals of all sorts of things (school supplies, haircuts, lawn-mowing income, time watching TV), and figuring the cost of going to a sporting event or show including transportation, tickets, and snacks. Discuss why exact answers are not necessary in some instances and why they are necessary in others. Look in a newspaper or magazine to find where numbers are the result of estimation and where they are the result of exact computations.

Use the Language of Estimation

Words and phrases such as *about, close, just about, a little more* (or *less*) *than*, and *between* are part of the language of estimation. Students should understand that they are trying to get as close as possible using quick and easy methods, but there is no correct estimate. Language can help convey that idea.

Use Context to Help with Estimates

A real-world number sense also plays a role in estimation. For thirty 69-cent soft drinks, is $2.10, $21, or $210 most reasonable? It is much easier to focus on 7 × 3 and use a result that makes sense than to compute 0.69 × 30 and try to place the decimal correctly. Similar assists come from knowing if the cost of a car would likely be $950 or $9500. Could attendance at the school play be 30 or 300 or 3000? A simple computation can provide the important digits, with number sense providing the rest.

Accept a Range of Estimates

What estimate would you give for 27 × 325? If you use 20 × 300, you might say 6000. Or you might use 25 for the 27, noting that four 25s make 100. Since 325 ÷ 4 is about 81, that would make 8100. If you use 30 × 300, your estimate is 9000, and 30 × 320 gives an estimate of 9600. Is one of these "right"?

By listing the estimates of many students and letting students discuss how and why different estimates resulted, they can begin to see that estimates generally fall in a range around the exact answer. Different approaches provide different results. And don't forget the context. Some situations call for more careful estimates than others.

Focus on Flexible Methods, Not Answers

Remember that your primary concern is to help students develop strategies for making estimates. It is, therefore, reflection on the strategies that will lead to strategy development. Class discussion of strategies for estimation is just as important as it was for the development of invented methods of computation. For any given estimation, there are often several very good but different methods of estimation. Students will learn strategies from each other.

The discussion of different strategies will also help students understand that there is no "right" estimate. Different strategies produce different estimates.

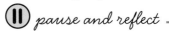 **pause and reflect** ⎯⎯⎯⎯⎯⎯⎯⎯⎯

Estimate this product: 438 × 62. Use the first idea that comes to your head and write down the result. Then return to the task and try a different approach, perhaps using different numbers in your approach to the estimate.

Sometimes different strategies produce the same estimates. For 438 × 62, you might have thought about using 450 × 60 as a first step. Then suppose you think 10 × 450 is 4500. Double 4500 is 9000 and 3 × 9000 is 27,000. You might also have thought 6 × 45 is 240 + 30 or 270. But this is not 6 × 45 but 60 times 450 so you add two more zeros— 27,000. Here two good strategies produce the same result.

Alternatively, you could have used 400 × 60 and gotten 24,000 and then recognized that you rounded both

numbers down. You lost at least 38 sets of 62 or about 40 × 60. So add 2400 to the 24,000 to get 26,400.

If just a "ballpark" estimate were OK, you might have thought 500 × 60 is 30,000 and realized that it was a bit high. But the exact answer is also at least 400 × 60 or 24,000. So it's between 24 and 30 thousand.

You've just seen four of many possible estimation strategies for one computation. The more strategies you experience, the more you will learn. The more strategies you have, the better you can select one to use for the situation at hand. Students will learn like this as well. In contrast, if you tell students to use a given strategy (e.g., round each number to one significant digit and multiply), everyone will get the same answer or they will be "wrong." Different strategies are useful to learn. Different strategies often give different estimates.

Estimation Without Estimates

Consider the threat a third-grade student perceives when you ask for an estimate of the sum $349.29 + $85.99 + $175.25. The requirement is to come up with *a number*. Even textbooks, in an attempt to teach a particular estimation strategy, will lead students through a series of rounding and adding and come up with a singular answer. This is contrary to the idea of what an estimate really is: producing answers that are "good enough" for the purposes. The purposes often determine what we need to know. For the three prices, the question "About how much?" is quite different from "Is it more than $600?" How would you answer each of those questions?

Each activity that follows suggests a format for estimation in which a specific numeric response is not required.

activity **14.1**

Over or Under?

Prepare several estimation exercises on a transparency. With each, provide an "over or under number." In Figure 14.1, each is either over or under $1.50, but the number need not be the same for each task.

The last activity need not be very elaborate. Here are some more "over/under" examples:

37 + 75	over/under 100
712 − 458	over/under 300
17 × 38	over/under 400
349 ÷ 45	over/under 10

FIGURE 14.1 "Over or Under?" is a good beginning estimation activity.

Simple, noncontextual tasks such as these can be prepared quickly. After presenting each, have students select their choice and then discuss their reasoning. The next activity is similar. It is adapted from an activity in the *Investigations in Number, Data, and Space* fifth-grade materials.

> **EXPANDED LESSON**
> An expanded lesson plan based on Activity 14.2 can be found on the Companion Web site www. ablongman.com/ vandewalle6e.

activity **14.2**

High or Low?

Display a computation and three or more possible computations that might be used to create an estimate. The students' task is to decide if the estimation will be higher or lower than the actual computation. For example, present the computation 736 × 18. For each of the following, decide if the result will be higher or lower than the exact result and explain why you think so.

750 × 10	730 × 15
700 × 20	750 × 20

activity **14.3**

Best Choice

For any single estimation task, offer three or four possible estimates.

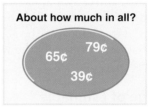

About how much in all?

65¢　79¢　39¢

How close the choices are will determine the difficulty of the task. Sometimes it is a good idea to use multiples of ten, such as $21, $210, and $2100.

With all of these tasks, the three-part lesson format remains useful. Present the exercise, have students quickly write their choice on paper (this commits them to an answer), and then discuss why the choice was made. All three parts may take only 10 minutes. In the discussion, a wide variety of estimates and estimation methods will be shared. This will help students see that estimates fall in a range and that there is no single correct estimate or method.

Estimations from Invented Strategies

Suppose that you were asked to compute the sum of 64 and 28. You might begin by adding 60 and 20 or 64 and 30. For each of these beginnings, you would need to make one or two additional computations before arriving at the answer. However, each of these beginnings is actually a reasonable estimate.

Stop Before the Details

Often it is the first step or two in an invented computation that is good enough for the estimate. In the 64 + 28 example, even a third grader would probably continue to the exact answer. But estimations are generally called for because an exact answer is too tedious or not necessary. When students have a good repertoire of invented strategies, one approach to an estimate is to simply begin to compute until you've gotten close enough to the result.

activity **14.4**

That's Good Enough

Present students with a computation that is reasonably difficult for their skills. For example: *T-shirts* *with the school logo cost $6 wholesale. The Pep Club has saved $257. How many shirts can they buy for their fund-raiser?* **The task is to describe the steps they would take to get an exact answer but not do them.**

Share students' ideas. Next, have students actually do as many of the steps as they can in their heads. When it begins to get too tough, stop and see if that is a good estimate or if it can be used for an estimate. Complete the steps using paper and pencil to help. Compare the various estimates with the exact amount.

4 + 5 + 6
400 + 500 + 600
400 + 600
60 + 30 + 100
60 + 20 + 90
467 + 528 + 693

600 − 300
600 − 400
85 + 15
15 + 13
85 − 13
613 − 385

10 ÷ 7
70 ÷ 7
7 × 11
7 × 12
87 ÷ 7

6 × 7
6 × 8
70 × 7
60 × 7
68 × 7

40 × 20
50 × 4
48 × 2
48 × 4
50 × 20
48 × 24

5 × 20
5 × 22
5 × 10
22 × 10
2 × 22
147 ÷ 22

The example in "That's Good Enough" may have seemed difficult to you. Try the same idea with a sum of four to six numbers: 47 + 29 + 74 + 55. Try it with a nasty difference: 7021 − 4583. Try it with a product: 86 × 29. The methods that students will come up with will be based on the ideas that they have learned for computing. In most instances, the beginnings of these computations are good estimates. By completing the steps, students are also improving their understanding of invented strategies and computations. For older students, use computations in this task that typically they would use a calculator to do. For younger students (grades 3 or 4), the tasks need not be terribly difficult. It is fun to see if you can do tough calculations without a standard algorithm or a calculator.

Cluster Problems

In Chapter 13, the use of cluster problems was explained as a technique to help students develop invented strategies for multiplication and division. (See p. 231.) The cluster-problem approach, adapted from the *Investigations* curriculum, has students solve a collection of problems related to but easier than the target problem. These problems are then used to solve the harder problem. An important aspect of the cluster-problem approach is that students first make (and write down) an estimate of the target computation.

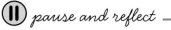

pause and reflect ——————

What follows are some cluster problems for each of the operations. The last problem is the target problem. Give these a try. Don't forget to first make an estimate of the target. Then solve all of the problems in the cluster. Use any of the cluster problems and any additional problems to solve the target. Indicate how you solved the target problem. No traditional methods allowed!

There are many possible paths to the results. Notice how in your own work, however, the cluster problems (not the target) are actually good problems to use in making estimates.

Once students have gotten comfortable with cluster problems, try the following task.

activity **14.5**

Make a Little Cluster
Give students a target problem for a cluster. It can be any operation that you are working on. The task is to create a cluster of no more than two problems that will help produce a reasonable estimate. Once students have made the little cluster, they should use their problems to estimate the target.

The excerpt from *Investigations in Number, Data, and Space* on the next page shows another activity in the same spirit as those just discussed. In the activity, students continue to solve the problems to get exact answers. However, the activity is designed to help students choose places to begin when making an estimate.

Investigations
in Number, Data, and Space

Grade 5, Building on Numbers You Know
Investigation 3: Ways to Multiply and Divide

Context

In this investigation, cluster problems are used for both multiplication and division targets. The students are always encouraged to make an estimate of the target computation before beginning the cluster problems. The task described here follows the work with cluster problems. The unit is designed for about midway in the year.

Task Description

To introduce an activity called "Solving a Problem with the First Step Given," the teacher puts the problem 133 ÷ 6 on the board. Instead of students solving the problem using their own methods, the teacher explains that she wants them to start in a certain way. "Suppose someone said that when she solved this problem, the first thing she did was solve 6 × 10. Think about it: How could solving 6 × 10 have helped her? What's one thing she could have done next?" (p. 92). Students discuss ways to approach the problem with this beginning and solve it accordingly. In a similar manner, they consider starting the same problem with 12 ÷ 6. Students are also asked to suggest other possible first steps.

There are several first-step worksheets to follow this introduction. The one shown here is the second of five that are available for both in-class work and for homework. The pages show three to five possible first steps toward a solution. The students are to select two of the first steps and show how they could solve the problem with those first steps.

Note that this activity remains quite flexible. If students do not know how to begin with one of the given steps, they may solve the problem in a way that makes sense for them. Solutions are discussed in class. There

---

Name _____ Date _____
Student Sheet 27

How Did I Solve It? (page 2 of 3)

For each problem, choose **two** first steps to complete.

3. 22 × 37 =

  a. Start by solving 22 × 10 =

  b. Start by solving 37 × 10 =

  c. Start by solving 20 × 30 =

4. 754 ÷ 30 =

  a. Start by solving 30 × 10 =

  b. Start by solving 30 × 2 =

  c. Start by solving 300 ÷ 30 =

  d. Start by solving 25 × 30 =

  e. Start by solving 75 ÷ 3 =

© Dale Seymour Publications®   **187**   *Investigation 3 • Sessions 7–9 Building on Numbers You Know*

Page 187 from *Computation and Estimation Strategies: Building on Numbers You Know* by M. Kliman, S. J. Russell, C. Tierney, & M. Murray. *Investigations in Number, Data, and Space.* Copyright © 1998 by Dale Seymour Publications. Reprinted by permission of Pearson Education, Inc.

is often more than one path to a solution from a given first step.

In a later activity, students are given a problem and are asked to suggest two first steps on their own and to solve the problem using each first step.

Computational Estimation Strategies

Estimation strategies are specific algorithms that produce approximate results rather than exact results. The strategies discussed in this section are the ones good estimators use.

As you work through the strategies in this section, you should recognize many of the same approaches that students are likely to have developed from their invented

methods. However, it is also likely that many of the strategies in this section will not have been developed. You should feel free to suggest these to your students as additional alternatives to estimation. Be very clear whenever you suggest a strategy that the intention is to create a good full "basket" of strategies. Those that you introduce are no more correct or important than ideas that they have devised. After introducing a strategy, you can have students practice it so that it is clearly understood.

When students have seen a variety of strategies, stop specifying which strategy to use. Rather, provide a task, and let students come up with an estimate using whatever strategy makes sense to them. Even in groups of three or four, students can each make an estimate and then compare both estimates and strategies. This helps in the selection of a strategy as well as in allowing for a range of answers.

Front-End Methods

Front-end methods focus on the leading or leftmost digits in numbers, ignoring the rest. After an estimate is made on the basis of only these front-end digits, an adjustment can be made by noticing how much has been ignored.

For students who have had a lot of experience with invented strategies, the front-end strategy will make a lot of sense since all invented strategies begin with the large part of the numbers involved. The front-end approach is an especially good place to begin the topic of estimation for students who use only the traditional algorithms. They will have to work hard at the idea of looking first at the left portion of numbers in a computation.

Front-End Addition and Subtraction

A front-end approach is reasonable for addition or subtraction when all or most of the numbers have the same number of digits. Figure 14.2 illustrates the idea. Notice

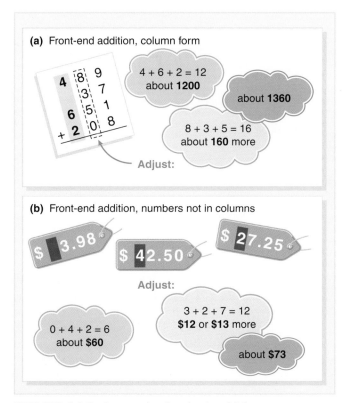

(a) Front-end addition, column form

$$4 + 6 + 2 = 12$$
about **1200**

about **1360**

$$8 + 3 + 5 = 16$$
about **160** more

Adjust:

(b) Front-end addition, numbers not in columns

$ 3.98 $ 42.50 $ 27.25

Adjust:

$$0 + 4 + 2 = 6$$
about **$60**

$$3 + 2 + 7 = 12$$
$12 or **$13** more

about **$73**

FIGURE 14.2 Front-end estimation in addition.

that when a number has fewer digits than the rest, that number is ignored completely.

After adding or subtracting the front digits, an adjustment is made to correct for the digits or numbers that were ignored. Making an adjustment is actually a separate skill. For young children, practice first just using the front digits. Pay special attention to numbers of uneven length when not in a column format.

The leading-digit strategy is easy to use and easy to teach because it does not require rounding or changing numbers. The numbers used are there and visible, so children can see what they are working with. It is a good first strategy for children as early as the third grade.

Front-End Multiplication and Division

For multiplication and division, the front-end method uses the first digit in each factor. The computation is then done using zeros in the other positions. For example, a front-end estimation of 48×7 is 40 times 7, or 280. When both numbers have more than one digit, the front ends of both are used. For 452×23, consider 400×20, or 8000.

For division, the best approach to estimation is to think multiplication. Avoid presenting problems using the computational form $(7 \overline{)3482})$ because this tends to suggest a computation rather than an estimate and encourages a "goes into" approach. Present problems in context or using the algebraic form: $3482 \div 7$. For this problem the front-end digit is determined by first getting the correct position. (100×7 is too low. 1000×7 is too high. It's in the hundreds.) There are 34 hundreds in the dividend, so since $34 \div 7$ is between 4 and 5, the front-end estimate is 400. In this example, since $34 \div 7$ is almost 5, a closer estimate is 500.

Rounding Methods

Rounding is the most familiar form of estimation. Estimation based on rounding is a way of changing the problem to one that is easier to work with mentally. Good estimators follow their mental computation with an adjustment to compensate for the rounding. To be useful in estimation, rounding should be flexible and well understood conceptually.

Rounding Concept

To round a number simply means to substitute a "nice" number that is close so that some computation can be done more easily. The close number can be any nice number and need not be a multiple of 10 or 100, as has been traditional. It should be whatever makes the computation or estimation easier or simplifies numbers sufficiently in a story, chart, or conversation. You might say, "Last night it took me 57 minutes to do my homework" or "Last night it took me about one hour to do my homework." The first expression is more precise; the second substitutes a rounded number for better communication.

FIGURE 14.3 A blank number line can be labeled in different ways to help students with near and nice numbers.

A number line with nice numbers highlighted can be useful in helping children select near nice numbers. An unlabeled number line like the one shown in Figure 14.3 can be made using three strips of poster board taped end to end. Labels are written above the line on the chalkboard. The ends can be labeled 0 and 100, 100 and 200, . . . , 900 and 1000. The other markings then show multiples of 25, 10, and 5. Indicate a number above the line that you want to round. Discuss the marks (nice numbers) that are close. (*Author note:* The term *nice number* is not found in standard textbooks. It is my invention. There is no established definition.)

Rounding in Addition and Subtraction

When a lot of numbers are to be added, it is usually a good idea to round them to the same place value. Keep a running sum as you round each number. In Figure 14.4, the same total is estimated two ways using rounding. A combination of the two is also possible.

In subtraction situations, there are only two numbers to deal with. For subtraction and for additions involving only two addends, it is generally necessary to round only one of the two numbers. For subtraction, round only the subtracted number. In 6724 − 1863, round 1863 to 2000. Then it is easy: 6724 − 2000 is 4724. Now adjust. You took away a bigger number, so the result must be too small. Adjust to about 4800. For 627 + 385, you might round 627 to 625 because multiples of 25 are almost as easy to work with as multiples of 10 or 100. After substituting 625 for 627, you may or may not want to round 385 to 375 or 400. The point is that there are no rigid rules. Choices depend on the relationships held by the estimator, on how quickly the estimate is needed, and on how accurate an estimate is required.

Rounding in Multiplication and Division

The rounding strategy for multiplication is no different from that for other operations. However, the error involved can be significant, especially when both factors are rounded. In Figure 14.5, several multiplication situations are illustrated, and rounding is used to estimate each.

If one number can be rounded to 10, 100, or 1000, the resulting product is easy to determine without adjusting the other factor.

When one factor is a single digit, examine the other factor. Consider the product 7 × 836. If 836 is rounded to 800, the estimate is relatively easy and is low by 7 × 36. If a more accurate result is required, round 836 to 840, and add two partial products. Then the estimate is 5600 plus 280, or 5880 (7 × 800 and 7 × 40).

If possible, round only one factor—select the larger one if it is significantly larger. (Why?) For example, in 47 × 7821, 47 × 8000 is 376,000, but 50 × 8000 is 400,000.

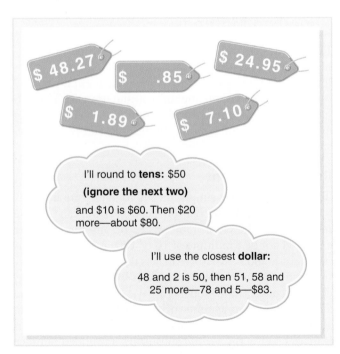

FIGURE 14.4 Rounding in addition.

FIGURE 14.5 Rounding in multiplication.

Another good rule of thumb with multiplication is to round one factor up and the other down (even if that is not the closest round number). When estimating 86 × 28, 86 is between 80 and 90, but 28 is very close to 30. Try rounding 86 down to 80 and 28 up to 30. The actual product is 2408, only 8 off from the 80 × 30 estimate. If both numbers were rounded to the nearest 10, the estimate would be based on 90 × 30, with an error of nearly 300.

With one-digit divisors, it is almost always best to search for a compatible dividend rather than to round off. For example, 4325 ÷ 7 can be estimated by using the close compatible number, 4200, to yield an estimate of 600. Rounding would suggest a dividend of 4000 or 4300, neither of which is very helpful.

Using Compatible Numbers

When adding a long list of numbers, it is sometimes useful to look for two or three numbers that can be grouped to make 10 or 100. If numbers in the list can be adjusted slightly to produce these groups, that will make finding an estimate easier. This approach is illustrated in Figure 14.6.

FIGURE 14.7 Compatibles can mean an adjustment that produces an easy difference.

In subtraction, it is often possible to adjust only one number to produce an easily observed difference, as illustrated in Figure 14.7.

Frequently in the real world, an estimate is needed for a large list of addends that are relatively close. This might happen with a series of prices of similar items, attendance at a series of events in the same arena, cars passing a point on successive days, or other similar data. In these cases, as illustrated in Figure 14.8, a nice number can be selected as representative of each, and multiplication can be used to determine the total. This is more of an *averaging technique* than a compatible-numbers strategy.

One of the best uses of the compatible-numbers strategy is in division. The two exercises shown in Figure 14.9 illustrate adjusting the divisor or dividend (or both) to create a division that comes out even and is, therefore, easy to do mentally. Many percent, fraction, and rate situations involve division, and the compatible-numbers strategy is quite useful, as shown in Figure 14.10.

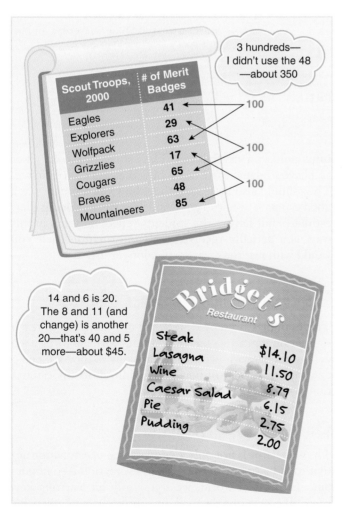

FIGURE 14.6 Compatibles used in addition.

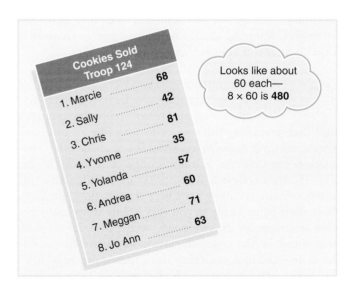

FIGURE 14.8 Estimating sums using averaging.

FIGURE 14.9 Adjusting to simplify division.

Source: From *GUESS (Guide to Using Estimation Skills and Strategies)* (box II, cards 2 and 3), by B. J. Reys and R. E. Reys, 1983, White Plains, NY: Dale Seymour Publications. Copyright 1983 by Dale Seymour Publications. Reprinted by permission of Dale Seymour Publications.

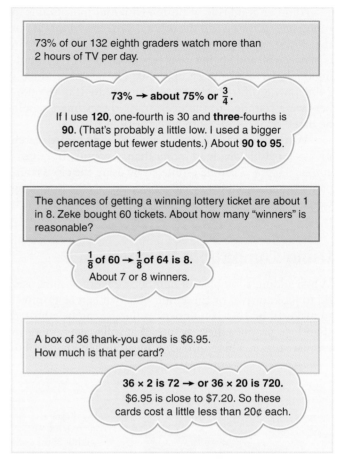

FIGURE 14.10 Using compatible numbers in division.

NCTM Standards "Instructional attention and frequent modeling by the teacher can help students develop a range of computational estimation strategies including flexible rounding, the use of benchmarks, and front-end strategies. Students should be encouraged to frequently explain their thinking as they estimate" (p. 156).

 Since estimation involves a certain element of speed, teachers often wonder how they can test it so that students are not computing on paper and then rounding the answer to look like an estimate. One method is to prepare a short list of about three estimation exercises on a transparency. The cards in the GUESS boxes (Reys & Reys, 1983) are a ready source for these, or you can simply write bare computations. Students have their paper ready as you very briefly show one exercise at a time on the overhead, perhaps for 20 seconds, depending on the task. Students write their estimate immediately and indicate if they think their estimate is "low" or "high"—that is, lower or higher than the exact computation. They are not to do any written computation. Con-

tinue until you are finished. Then show all the exercises and have students write down how they did each estimate. They should also indicate if they think the estimate was a good estimate or not so good and why. By only doing a few estimates but having the students reflect on them in this way, you actually receive more information than you would with just the answers to a longer list. ■

Estimation Exercises

The examples presented here are not designed to teach estimation strategies but offer useful formats to provide your students with practice using skills as they are being developed. These will be a good addition to any estimation program.

Calculator Activities

The calculator is not only a good source of estimation activities but also one of the reasons estimation is so important. In the real world, we frequently hit a wrong key, leave off a zero or a decimal, or simply enter numbers incorrectly. An estimate of the expected result alerts us to these errors. The calculator as an estimation-teaching tool lets students work independently or in pairs in a challenging, fun way without fear of embarrassment. With a calculator for the overhead projector, some of the activities described here work very well with a full class.

---

activity 14.6

The Range Game

This is an estimation game for any of the four operations. First pick a start number and an operation. The start number and operation are stored in the calculator. Students then take turns entering a number and pressing $=$ to try to make the result land in the target range. The following example for multiplication illustrates the activity: Suppose that a start number of 17 and a range of 800 to 830 are chosen. Press 17 $\times$ $=$ to store 17 as a factor. Press a number and then $=$. Perhaps you try 25. (Press 25 $=$.) The result is 425. That is about half the target. Try 50. The result is 850—maybe 2 or 3 too high. Try 48. The result is 816—in the target range! Figure 14.11 gives examples for all four operations. Prepare a list of start numbers and target ranges. Let students play in pairs to see who can hit the most targets on the list (Wheatley & Hersberger, 1986).

"The Range Game" can be played with an overhead calculator with the whole class, by an individual, or by two or three children with calculators who can race one another. The speed element is important. The width of the range and the type of numbers used can all be adjusted to suit the level of the class.

---

activity 14.7

The Range Game: Sequential Versions

Select a target range as before. Next enter the starting number in the calculator, and hand it to the first player. For addition and subtraction, the first player then presses either $+$ or $-$, followed by a number, and then $=$. The next player begins his or her turn by entering $+$ or $-$ and an appropriate number, operating on the previous result. If the target is 423 to 425, a sequence of turns might go like this:

Start with 119.

$+$ 350 $=$ ⟶ 469 (too high)

$-$ 42 $=$ ⟶ 427 (a little over)

$-$ 3 $=$ ⟶ 424 (success)

For multiplication or division, only one operation is used through the whole game. After the first or second turn, decimal factors are usually required. This variation provides excellent understanding of multiplication or division by decimals. A sequence for a target of 262 to 265 might be like this:

Start with 63.

$\times$ 5 $=$ ⟶ 315 (too high)

$\times$ 0.7 $=$ ⟶ 220.5 (too low)

$\times$ 1.3 $=$ ⟶ 286.65 (too high)

$\times$ 0.9 $=$ ⟶ 257.985 (too low)

$\times$ 1.03 $=$ ⟶ 265.72455 (very close!)

(What would you press next?)

Try a target of 76 to 80, begin with 495, and use only division.

After entering the setup with the start # as shown, players take turns pressing a number, then $=$ to try to get a result in the target range.

Addition:

Press: 0 $+$ (start #) $=$

START		TARGET
153	⟶	790 → 800
216	⟶	400 → 410
53	⟶	215 → 220

Subtraction:

Press: 0 $-$ (start #) $=$

START		TARGET
18	⟶	25 → 30
41	⟶	630 → 635
129	⟶	475 → 485

Multiplication:

Press: (start #) $\times$ 0 $=$

START		TARGET
67	⟶	1100 → 1200
143	⟶	3500 → 3600
39	⟶	1600 → 1700

Division:

Press: 0 $\div$ (start #) $=$

START		TARGET
20	⟶	25 → 30
39	⟶	50 → 60
123	⟶	15 → 20

FIGURE 14.11 "The Range Game"—a calculator game.

More Estimation Activities

Most of the discussion in this chapter has had students focus on their strategies for estimating. The following game adapted from the *Investigations in Number, Data, and Space* curriculum challenges students to make estimates that are as close as possible to the actual computation.

activity 14.8

How Close?

Decide which type of problem (the operation and the number of digits) you want students to practice and create a "structure page." For example, if you want students to practice estimations of two-digit by two-digit products, the structure would be ___ ___ × ___ ___. Draw this on a sheet of paper. The game is played in groups of three to six students. One student leads a round by drawing numbers one at a time from a set of 1 to 9 numeral cards or tiles. These numbers are placed into the structure from left to right. The students then have 30 seconds (use an egg timer or other timer controlled by the leader) to come up with an estimate. Players are required to work mentally without paper but must write down their estimate before the 30 seconds is up. Next, the exact answer is computed with a calculator. Students record both their estimate and the exact answer and subtract the smaller from the larger to determine their score for that round. After three rounds, scores are totaled. The goal is to have the smallest score.

The following activity works well on the overhead projector as do many full-class estimation activities. This activity is also good for engaging students in discussions of estimation strategies.

activity 14.9

What Was Your Method?

Select a problem with an estimation given. For example, 139 × 43 might be estimated as 6000. Ask questions concerning this estimate: "How do you think that estimate was arrived at? Was that a good approach? How should it be adjusted? Why might someone select 150 instead of 140 as a substitute for 139?" Almost every estimate can involve different choices and methods. Alternatives make good discussions, helping students see different methods and learn that there is no single correct estimate.

 Estimation skills are often embedded in software drill-and-practice packages, although very few are designed for estimation skills alone. *Math Blaster* (Knowledge Adventure) and *CornerStone ATS 3.2: Mathematics* (Riverdeep Interactive Learning) are a couple of examples. The estimation activities in *Math Blaster* are in an arcade format. This adds the useful element of speed but may be a turn-off for students who do not care for the format. *CornerStone ATS 3.2: Mathematics* has test-generating materials that are useful for evaluation and practice in test taking.

The *Blue Falls Elementary* title in *Fizz & Martina's Math Adventures* (Tom Snyder Productions, 1998) includes three estimation problems in each of the four episodes. (The *Fizz & Martina* programs are each built around adventure stories with group problem solving in a realistic context.) Students are encouraged to estimate and then explain the strategy they have used. At least one strategy is provided. ■

Estimating with Fractions, Decimals, and Percents

It might be argued that much of the estimation in the real world involves fractions, decimals, and percents. A few examples are suggested here:

SALE! $51.99. Marked one-fourth off. What was the original price?

About 62 percent of the 834 students bought their lunch last Wednesday. How many bought lunch?

Tickets sold for $1.25. If attendance was 3124, about how much was the total gate?

I drove 337 miles on 12.35 gallons of gas. How many miles per gallon did my car get?

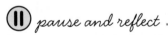 *pause and reflect*

Suppose you were to make estimates in each of the previous situations. Without actually getting an estimate, decide what numbers you would use in each case. For instance, in the first example you would not use 51.99 but perhaps 50 or 52. What about the fractions, decimals, and percents in the other problems? Think about that now before reading on.

The first example asks for an estimate of $\frac{3}{4}$ of $51.99. To get $\frac{3}{4}$ of a quantity requires dividing by 4 and multiplying by 3. Those are whole-number computations, but they require an understanding of fraction multiplication.

In the next example, the problem is finding a way to deal with 62 percent. Well, that's close to 60 percent, which is $\frac{3}{5}$ or equivalently, 6 times 10 percent. In either case, the required computations involve whole numbers. The translation of 62 percent requires an understanding of percents.

In the third example, an understanding of decimals and fractions converts the problem to $1\frac{1}{4}$ of 3125. The computations involve dividing 3125 (perhaps 3200) by 4 and adding that to 3125—all whole-number computations. Similarly, the final example requires an understanding of decimals followed by whole-number computations.

The point is that when fractions, decimals, and percents are involved, an understanding of numeration is often the first thing required to make an estimate. That understanding often translates the situation into one involving only whole-number computations.

Of course, this is not always the case for fractions and decimals. Consider what is required to make estimates for the following:

$$2\frac{3}{8} + 4\frac{1}{9} - \frac{1}{12}$$

$$4.0178 + 73.4$$

A reasonable estimate in each case relies almost entirely on an understanding of the numbers involved. There are very few new estimation skills required.

In any good curriculum, computational estimation will be coupled with computational skill development. Therefore, when computation involving fractions, decimals, and percents is discussed, estimation should certainly be a part of that development (as it will be in this book). Most if not all of the computational skills required involve whole-number strategies as discussed in this chapter.

Literature Connections

Interesting literature often provides a diversionary context in which the mathematics may be a bit more fun and possibly more realistic. Even if realism in these two books is a bit stretched, the context makes a welcome change of pace.

The Twelve Circus Rings
Chwast, 1993

Based on the same pattern as "The Twelve Days of Christmas," the 12 circus rings each contain more animals or more acts: "six acrobats, five dogs a-barking, four aerialists zooming, three monkeys playing, two elephants, and a daredevil on high wire." The colorful illustrations add to the excitement of the circus and the growing number of performers. After 12 days, how many aerialists are zooming? Remember that there are four aerialists not only in ring 4 but also in rings 5 through 12. The story lends itself to some early estimation but can easily be extended to create some fun questions. "About how much do the bows cost for all the dogs a-barking if each bow costs \$1.29?" Both you and your students can make up estimation questions that challenge the skills you've been developing. In addition to the potential for both estimation and mental computation, the author also considers patterns as another extension.

The 329th Friend
Sharmat, 1979

This book not only offers the opportunity to examine mental math strategies and practice in the context of the story but is also about friendship and the need to be liked. The story is about Emery Raccoon, who has no friends. Because he is lonely, Emery invites 328 strangers to lunch to make new friends. There are considerations about the number of dishes, knives, forks, and spoons that suggest multiplying 329 by small numbers and different ways of doing this. The story is easily expanded into other similar number questions. At the end, Emery discovers that although his guests ignored him, there was one friend that was there all along—himself. ■

Reflections *on* Chapter 14

Writing to Learn

1. How is computational estimation different from other types of estimation?
2. Why might the idea of an estimate for a computation be strange to students?
3. Describe each of the general strategies that were offered for conducting estimation activities.
4. Young children often find it difficult to come up with an estimate. What are the suggested techniques where students are required to estimate but not to actually produce an estimate?
5. Describe in general terms how estimation can grow out of the development of invented strategies.
6. What is a cluster problem and how is it used for developing both invented strategies and estimation skills? Make up cluster problems for 72×16 and for $342 \div 13$.
7. Describe each of these estimation strategies. Be able to make up a good example and use it in your explanation.
   a. Front-end addition and subtraction.
   b. Front-end multiplication.
   c. Rounding in addition.
   d. Rounding in subtraction.

   e. Rounding in multiplication.

   f. Compatible numbers in addition and subtraction.

   g. Compatible numbers in division.

8. How can the calculator be used to practice estimation strategies?

9. Describe an estimation practice activity that you think is especially useful. Why do you think it is good?

For Discussion and Exploration

1. In the past, the computation curriculum focused only on the traditional algorithms. There was only one way to compute. In the K–8 curriculum today, how much emphasis should be given to each of the forms of computation that have been discussed (invented strategies both with pencil and paper and mental, traditional algorithms and variations, and finally estimation)? Try to support your argument on the basis of real-world use.

2. Do the curriculum standards for your state require computational estimation? Mental computation? For "straightforward computation," is there any requirement that a particular algorithm or method of computation be used? How do your state's computational guidelines influence what computation methods are taught in school? Do you agree with what is required?

3. *Adding It Up* (NRC, 2001) devotes less than five pages to the topics of mental arithmetic and estimation (pp. 214–218). Read these few pages with special attention to the discussion of estimation and the related skills that are needed for estimation. You can access the full text of *Adding It Up* on the Web at www.nap.edu/books/0309069955/html/index.html and read the excerpt there. How does this view of mental computation and estimation both agree and disagree with the ideas in this chapter and Chapter 13?

Recommendations for Further Reading

Bresser, R., & Holtzman, C. (1999). *Developing number sense: Grades 3–6.* Sausalito, CA: Math Solutions Publications. Bresser and Holtzman are classroom teachers who have compiled 13 worthwhile number-sense activities covering a range of topics including mental computation, number meanings, and estimation. With each activity the authors provide pages of extensions, practical suggestions, and answers to questions concerning using the activity in the classroom. Most activities include examples of students' work.

Reys, R. E., & Nohda, N. (Eds.). (1994). *Computational alternatives for the twenty-first century: Cross-cultural perspectives from*
Japan and the United States. Reston, VA: National Council of Teachers of Mathematics.

This book addresses similarities and differences between computation in the United States and Japan. Divided into three sections, the articles discuss mental computation, estimation, and the use of calculators in the two countries. Respected researchers from both countries have contributed to this work. Although not designed as a resource book, the thoughtful teacher will certainly find practical ideas as well as interesting perspectives.

Reys, R. E., & Reys, B. J. (1983). *Guide to using estimation skills and strategies (GUESS) Boxes I & II.* Palo Alto, CA: Dale Seymour. Still among the best materials for teaching computational estimation strategies, these two hefty boxes of cards provide the fourth- through eighth-grade teacher with a complete program. Two of the cards are shown in Figure 14.9. Use them as transparencies, in small groups, or as independent work.

Online Resources

Suggested Applets and Web Links

Beat Calc
http://mathforum.org/k12/mathtips/beatcalc.html
   This site contains an enormous list of "tricks" for getting an exact computation for very specific types of problems. For example, adding two consecutive numbers, multiplying a two-digit number by 51, dividing a two-digit number by 15, squaring various types of numbers, finding percentages, and more. The patterns include an example and an explanation.

Estimation—Hundreds
www.quia.com/mc/65924.html
   Players select squares on a board that round to the same hundred. A concentration version is also available.

Estimator Four
http://mathforum.org/k12/mathtips/beatcalc.html
   Two players must enter an acceptable estimate to a computation within a time limit to be able to place a game piece on the board.

An additional list of books and articles related to the ideas in this chapter can be found on the Companion Web site at **www.ablongman.com/ vandewalle6e.**

Companion Website

chapter 15

Algebraic Thinking: Generalizations, Patterns, and Functions

Algebra is an established content strand in most, if not all, state standards for grades K to 12 and it is one of the five content standards in NCTM's *Principles and Standards*. Although there is much variability in what is required in algebra at the elementary and middle school levels, one thing is clear: The algebra envisioned for these grades—and for high school as well—is not the algebra that you most likely experienced in high school. That typical algebra course of the eighth or ninth grade consisted primarily of symbol manipulation procedures and artificial applications with little connection to the real world. The focus now is on the type of thinking and reasoning that prepares students to think mathematically across all areas of mathematics.

Algebraic thinking or *algebraic reasoning* involves forming generalizations from experiences with number and computation, formalizing these ideas with the use of a meaningful symbol system, and exploring the concepts of pattern and functions. Far from a topic with little real-world use, algebraic thinking pervades all of mathematics and is essential for making mathematics useful in daily life.

Big Ideas

1. Structure in our number system and the methods we use to compute can be generalized. These generalizations become powerful ideas for doing mathematics.

2. Symbolism, especially that involving equations and variables, is used to express the generalizations from arithmetic and the structure of the number system. For example, the generalization that $a + b = b + a$ tells us that $83 + 27 = 27 + 83$ without computing the sums on each side.

3. Variables are symbols that take the place of numbers or ranges of numbers. They are used to represent quantities that vary or change, as specific unknown values, and as placeholders in generalized expressions or formulas.

4. Patterns, a regular occurrence in all of mathematics, can be recognized, extended, and generalized.

5. Functions are relationships or rules that uniquely associate members of one set with members of another set.

6. Functional relationships can be represented in real-world contexts, graphs, symbolic equations, tables, and words. Each representation provides a different view of the same relationship. Different representations serve different purposes in making the function useful.

Mathematics Content Connections

As Kaput (1998) notes, it is difficult to find an area of mathematics that does not involve generalizing and formalizing in some central way. In fact, this type of reasoning is at the heart of mathematics as a science of pattern and order.

■ **Number, Place Value, Basic Facts, and Computation** (Chapters 9, 11, 12, and 13): The most important generalizations at the core of algebraic thinking are those made about number and computation—arithmetic. Not only does algebraic thinking generalize from number and computation, but also the generalizations themselves add to the understanding and facility with computation. We can use our understanding of 10 to add $5 + 8$ ($5 + 8 = 3 + 2 + 8 = 3 + 10$), and $5 + 38$ ($5 + 38 = 3 + 2 + 38 = 3 + 40$). These ideas can be generalized so that adding a number less than 10 to any number ending in 8 involves the same reasoning.

■ **Operation Concepts** (Chapter 10): As children learn about the operations, they also learn that there are regularities in the way that the operations work. Examples include the commutative properties $a + b = b + a$ and $a \times b = b \times a$ as well as the way that operations are related to one another.

- **Proportional Reasoning** (Chapter 19): Every proportional situation gives rise to a linear (straight-line function) with a graph that goes through the origin. The constant ratio in the proportion is the slope of the graph.

- **Measurement** (Chapter 20): Measures are a principal means of describing relationships in the physical world. These relationships can be mathematized so that the generalities of algebra can be used to better understand them. Measurement formulas are functions, a special form of algebraic generalization.

- **Geometry** (Chapter 21): Geometric patterns are some of the first that children experience. Growing patterns give rise to functional relationships. Coordinates are used to generalize distance concepts and to control transformations. And, of course, functions are graphed on the coordinate plane to visually show algebraic relationships.

- **Data Analysis** (Chapter 22): When data are gathered, the algebraic thinker is able to examine them for regularities and patterns. Functions are used to approximate trends or describe the relationships in mathematically useful ways.

Algebraic Thinking

Kaput (1999), a leader in crafting appropriate algebra curriculum across the grades, talks about algebra that "involves generalizing and expressing that generality using increasingly formal languages, where the generalizing begins in arithmetic, in modeling situations, in geometry, and in virtually all the mathematics that can or should appear in the elementary grades" (pp. 134–135). Although many authors and researchers have written about algebraic thinking, Kaput's description is the most complete and encompasses the ideas of others. He describes five different forms of algebraic reasoning:

1. Generalization from arithmetic and from patterns in all of mathematics.
2. Meaningful use of symbolism.
3. Study of structure in the number system.
4. Study of patterns and functions.
5. Process of mathematical modeling, which integrates the first four.

So algebraic thinking is not a singular idea but is composed of different forms of thought and an understanding of symbolism. It is a separate strand of the curriculum but should also be imbedded in all areas of mathematics. There is general agreement that we must begin the development of these forms of thinking from the very beginning of school so that students will learn to think productively with the powerful ideas of mathematics—so that they can think mathematically.

Generalization in Number and Operations

The process of creating generalizations from number and arithmetic begins as early as kindergarten and continues as students learn about all aspects of number and computation, including basic facts and meanings of the operations. Therefore, algebraic thinking is very much connected to the ideas in Chapters 9 through 14.

In order to make generalizations, it is helpful to use symbolism. Thus, both generalizations and an understanding of variables and symbolism are developed at the same time.

The Meaning of the Equal Sign

The equal sign is one of the most important symbols in elementary arithmetic, in algebra, and in all mathematics using numbers and operations. At the same time, research dating from 1975 to the present indicates clearly that "=" is a very poorly understood symbol.

Ⅱ *pause and reflect* ─────────────

In the following expression, what number do you think belongs in the box?

$$8 + 4 = \square + 5$$

How do you think students in the early grades or in middle school typically answer this question?

─────────────────────────

In a recent study, no more than 10 percent of students at any grade from 1 to 6 put the correct number (7) in the box. The common responses were 12 and 17. In grade 6, not one student out of 145 put a 7 in the box (Falkner, Levi, & Carpenter, 1999). Earlier studies found similar results (Behr, Erlwanger, & Nichols, 1975; Erlwanger & Berlanger, 1983).

Certainly, students are told in first grade that the equal sign means "is the same as" and students are told that the expressions on each side must be the same. However, students' experiences lead them to believe that one side of the equal sign—usually the left side—is the problem and the other side is the answer. Their understanding of = is more like the button on the calculator—it is what you press to get the answer. In written form it separates the problem from the answer.

Why is it so important that students correctly understand the equal sign? First, it is important for students to see and understand the relationships in our number system. The equal sign is a principal method of representing these relationships. For example, $6 \times 7 = 5 \times 7 + 7$. We don't expect students to think about this fact strategy in these symbolic terms. However, this is not only a fact strategy but also represents several basic ideas in arithmetic. A number can be expressed as a sum: $6 = 1 + 5$. The distributive property allows us to multiply each of the parts separately: $(1 + 5) \times 7 = (1 \times 7) + (5 \times 7)$. Even further number properties convert this last expression to $5 \times 7 + 7$. When these ideas, initially and informally developed through arithmetic, are generalized and expressed symbolically, powerful relationships are available for working with other numbers in a generalized manner.

A second reason is that when students fail to understand the equal sign, they typically have difficulty when it is encountered in algebraic expressions. Even solving a simple equation such as $5x - 24 = 81$ requires students to see both sides of the equal sign as equivalent expressions. It is not possible to "do" the left-hand side. However, if both sides are the same, then they will remain the same when 24 is added to each side.

True/False and Open Sentences

Carpenter, Franke, and Levi (2003) suggest that a good starting point for helping students with the equal sign is to explore equations as either true or false. The meaning of the equal sign is just one of the outcomes of this type of exploration as seen in the following activity.

activity 15.1

True or False

Introduce true/false sentences or equations with simple examples to explain what is meant by a true equation and a false equation. Then put several simple equations on the board, some true and some false. The following are appropriate for primary grades:

$5 + 2 = 7$ $4 + 1 = 6$
$4 + 4 = 8$ $8 = 10 - 1$

Your collection might include other operations but keep the computations simple. The students' task is to decide which of the equations are true equations and which are not. For each response they are to explain their reasoning.

After this initial exploration of true/false sentences, have students explore equations that are less traditional in form:

$4 + 5 = 8 + 1$ $3 + 7 = 7 + 3$ $6 - 3 = 7 - 4$ $8 = 8$
$4 + 5 = 4 + 5$ $9 + 5 = 14$ $9 + 5 = 14 + 0$

Do not try to explore all variations in a single lesson. Listen to the types of reasons that students are using to justify their answers and plan additional equations accordingly for subsequent days.

Students will generally agree on equations where there is an expression on one side and a single number on the other, although initially, the less familiar form of $7 = 2 + 5$ may cause some discussion. For an equation with no operation ($8 = 8$), the discussion may be heated. Students often believe that there must be an operation on one side. Equations with an operation on both sides of the equal sign can be the most interesting. It is all right to remind students that the equal sign means *is the same as*. Their internalization of this idea will come from the discussions. It is also reasonable to explore inequalities in the same manner.

After students have experienced true/false sentences, introduce an open sentence—one with a box to be filled in or letter to be replaced.

activity 15.2

Open Sentences

Write several open sentences on the board. To begin with, these can be similar to the true/false sentences that you have been exploring.

$5 + 2 = \square$ $4 + \square = 6$ $4 + 5 = \square - 1$ $3 + 7 = 7 + \square$

$\square + 4 = 8$ $\square = 10 - 1$ $6 - \square = 7 - 4$ $\square + 5 = 5 + 8$

The task is to decide what number can be put into the box to make the sentence true. Of course, an explanation is also required.

For grades 3 and above, include multiplication as well as addition and subtraction.

Initially, some students will revert to doing computations and putting the answer in the box. This is a result of too many exercises where an answer is to be written as a single number following an equal sign. In fact, the box is a forerunner of a variable, not an answer holder.

Relational Thinking

Consider two distinctly different explanations for why a 5 goes in the box for the open sentence $7 - \square = 6 - 4$.

a. Since $6 - 4$ is 2, you need to take away from 7 to get 2. $7 - 5$ is 2, so 5 goes in the box.

b. Seven is one more than the 6 on the other side. That means that you need to take one more away on the left side to get the same number. One more than 4 is 5 so 5 goes in the box.

 *pause and reflect* ─────────

How are these two correct responses actually quite different? How would each of these students solve this open sentence? $534 + 175 = 174 + \square$

The first student computes the result on one side and adjusts the result on the other to make the sentence true. The second student is using a relationship between the expressions on either side of the equal sign. This student does not need to compute the values on each side. When the numbers are large, the relationship approach is much more useful. Since 174 is one less than 175, the number in the box must be one more than 134 to make up the difference. The first student will need to do the computation and will perhaps have difficulty finding the correct addend.

When a student observes and uses numeric relationships between the two sides of the equal sign rather than actually computing the amounts, the thinking involved is referred to as *relational thinking*. Relational thinking goes beyond simple computation and instead focuses on how one operation or series of operations is related to another. Relational thinking is at the heart of many fact strategies. For example, think about the near-doubles strategy for 6 + 7 or the half-and-double strategy for 6 × 8. Each of these strategies involves utilizing a relationship between the required fact and one that is known: 6 + 7 is one more than 6 + 6, and 3 × 8 is half of 6 × 8. Fact strategies are just a simple example of the value of relational thinking. Similar relationships are *used in* invented strategies and *abstracted from* invented strategies. In a broader context, relational thinking of this sort is a first step toward generalizing relationships found in arithmetic so that these same relationships can be used when variables are involved and not just numbers.

Do not try to impose relational thinking on students. Rather, continue to explore an ever increasingly complex series of true/false and open sentences with your class. Select equations designed to elicit good thinking and challenges rather than computation. Use large numbers that make computation difficult (not impossible) to push them toward relational thinking.

$$674 - 389 = 664 - 379 \qquad 5 \times 84 = 10 \times 42$$
$$37 \times 54 = 38 \times 53 \qquad 64 \div 14 = 32 \div 28$$
$$73 + 56 = 71 + \square \qquad 126 - 37 = \square - 40$$
$$20 \times 48 = \square \times 24 \qquad 68 + 58 = 57 + 69 + \square$$

Ⅱ *pause and reflect* ──────────────

In the preceding true/false equations, one is false. Try to use relational thinking to confirm that the others are true and also to find the numbers that will make the open sentences true.

───────────────────────────

The following activity is another good way to promote relational thinking.

activity **15.3**

Writing True/False Sentences
After students have had ample time to discuss true/false and open sentences, challenge them to

make up their own true/false sentences that they can use to challenge their classmates. Each student should write a collection of three or four sentences with at least one true and at least one false sentence. Encourage them to include one "tricky" one. Their equations can either be traded with a partner or can be used in full-class discussions.

When students write their own true/false sentences, they often are intrigued with the idea of using large numbers and lots of numbers in their sentences. This encourages them to create sentences involving relational thinking. Early approaches generally involve the use of zeros and adding and subtracting the same number. The order property will also be commonly used.

A similar activity has students create expressions for the day of the month.

activity **15.4**

Incredible Expressions
This is a good calendar-time activity. If, for example, the date is November 21, the students' task is to write expressions using any or all of the operations that equal 21.

In "Incredible Expressions" students will initially use simple expressions such as 20 + 1 or 25 − 4. With a little encouragement to write "really incredible" expressions, students will begin to construct expressions such as 100 − 80 + 1 or 1 + 1 + 1 + 1 + 1 + 1 + 1 + 1 + 1 + 1 + 10. Eventually you may decide to outlaw certain common tricks such as a series of + 1s, − 1s, or adding and subtracting the same number. Students will often build ideas upon those of their classmates. For example, if one student suggests 40 − 20 + 1, another may say 140 − 120 + 1 and another suggest 340 − 320 + 1.

 As students explore true/false and open-sentence activities, look for two things. First, are students developing an appropriate understanding of the equal sign? Look to see if they are comfortable using operations on both sides of the equal sign and can use the meaning of *equal* as "is the same as" to solve open sentences.

Second, look for an emergence of relational thinking. Students who rely on relationships found in the operations on each side of the equal sign rather than on direct computation have moved up a step in their algebraic thinking. ■

Variables in Equations

Variables are an extremely powerful representation device that allow for the expression of generalizations. A goal is for students to work with expressions involving variables without even thinking about the specific number or numbers that the letters may stand for. This is what Kaput (1999) refers to as manipulation of *opaque formalisms*—we can look at and work with the symbols themselves rather than looking through or into the symbols at what they might represent. Variables can be used as unique unknown values or as quantities that vary.

Variables Used as an Unknown Value

Students first experience variables used as symbols that stand for an unknown value. In the open sentence explorations, the □ is a precursor of a variable used in this way. Early on, you can begin using various letters instead of a box in your open sentences. Rather than ask students what number goes in the box, ask what number the letter could stand for to make the sentence true. Initial work with finding the value of the variable that makes the sentence true—solving the equation—should initially rely on relational thinking. Later, students will develop specific techniques for solving equations when these relationships are insufficient.

Consider the following open sentence: □ + □ + 7 = □ + 17 (or, equivalently, $n + n + 7 = n + 17$). Without a convention for the use of multiple variables, there would be no unique solution. However, there is a convention. Carpenter et al. (2003) refer to it as *the mathematician's rule*, which simply states that if the same symbol or letter appears more than once in an equation, then it must stand for the same number every place it occurs. In our example, relational thinking might suggest that □ + 7 on the left must be the same as the 17 on the right. That means that the □ must stand for 10.

Variables Used as Quantities That Vary

When there are different symbols or variables in a single equation, the different variables may have different values. For example, in the equation $a + 6 = 10 - b$, one solution is $a = 3$ and $b = 1$. Another solution is for both a and b to = 2. In this equation, the two variables can vary. As one variable changes, so must the other. Many students believe that because the two variables are different, their values must be different. This is not so.

In the primary grades, the use of two or even three variables is a forerunner of variables that are used to describe functions as in $y = 3x - 5$. It is also a good opportunity to continue to explore and generalize ideas about numbers and operations.

For situations in which variables vary, context is often useful, as illustrated in Figure 15.1. With a problem such as this or even with a simple open sentence such as $n - w = 8$, suggest that students make some form of a table like the one begun in the figure. For the two-tree task, students will begin by finding ways to partition 7 into two parts. At the first-grade level, this will be somewhat random. Stu-

FIGURE 15.1 Seven monkeys want to play in two trees, one big and one small. Show all the different ways that the seven monkeys could play in the two trees.

(Adapted from a task by Yackel, 1997. Carpenter, Franke, and Levi, 2003, explored a similar task.)

dents may not think to use 0, and many will only come up with three or four solutions. As the discussion continues, students will discover that 2 and 7 is a different solution from 7 and 2 (a reason for making the trees different sizes).

The significant question is how to decide when all of the solutions have been found. At one level, students will just not be able to think of any more and many will forget about using 0. Other children may try to use each number from 0 to 7 for one tree. The student who explains that for each number 0 to 7 there are two solutions is no longer partitioning 7 into parts but is making a generalization that yields the number of solutions without even listing them (Yackel, 1997). That reasoning can be generalized to the number of ways 376 monkeys occupy the two trees. At the second grade, Carpenter et al. (2003) found students who articulated that there is always one more solution than the number of monkeys. Notice how this is a generalization that no longer depends on the numbers involved.

The context of the monkeys in the trees restricted the number of solutions to whole numbers with a maximum value of 7. These restrictions help young children see generalizations. Had the problem been presented as $B + S = 7$ with no context, the solutions would include numbers such as $2\frac{1}{2}$ and $4\frac{1}{2}$, as well as negative numbers. Generalizations are still possible (as one variable increases, the other decreases by the same amount) but are more difficult for young learners.

Solving Equations or Inequalities

Through about the fourth grade, it is reasonable to allow students to find solutions to open sentences with one or more variables by simply using trial and error, and relational thinking. By about the fifth or sixth grade, students

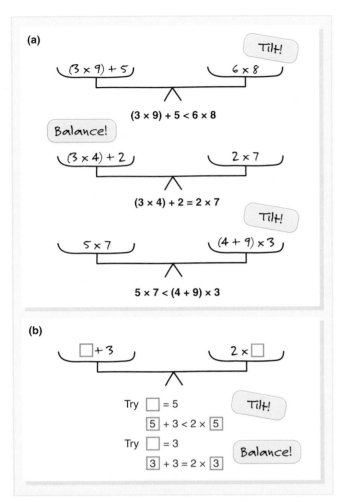

FIGURE 15.2 Using expressions and variables in equations and inequalities. The two-pan balance helps develop the meaning of =, <, and >.

and ask which pan will go down or whether the two will balance (see Figure 15.2). Challenge students to write expressions for each side of the scale to make it balance. For each, write a corresponding equation to illustrate the meaning of =. Note that when the scale "tilts," either a "greater than" or "less than" symbol (> or <) is used.

After a short time, add variables to the expressions and allow students to solve them using whatever methods they wish. Do not make the task so easy that the solutions can be found by simple inspection.

The balance makes it reasonably clear to students that if you add or subtract a value from one side, you must add or subtract a like value from the other side to keep the scales balanced.

activity **15.6**

Adjust the Balance

Show a balance with variable expressions on each side. Use only one variable. Make the tasks such that a solution by trial and error is not reasonable. For example, the solution to $3x + 2 = 11 - x$ is not a whole number. Suggest that adjustments can be made to the quantities in each pan as long as the balance is maintained. If you begin with simple equations such as $x - 17 = 31 - x$, students should be able to develop skills and explain their rationale. Students should also be challenged to devise a method of proving that their solutions are correct.

need to develop some procedures that will allow them to solve equations when these informal methods are no longer adequate.

The need for understanding equality in equations cannot be overstated. Students in the upper grades will still benefit from explorations of true/false and open sentences, perhaps with slightly more difficult numbers than those used in the examples to this point. A useful model for equality is a sketch of a simple two-pan balance with numeric expressions shown in each pan, as in Figure 15.2. This two-pan-balance model also illustrates that the expressions on each side are names for numbers rather than problems to work. The next activity can be used to introduce the model.

activity **15.5**

Tilt or Balance

On the board or overhead, draw a simple two-pan balance. In each pan, write a numeric expression

Figure 15.3 shows solutions for two equations, one in a balance and the other without. Even after you have stopped using the balance, it is a good idea to refer to the scale or balance-pan concept of equality and the idea of keeping the scales balanced.

As students begin to develop equations they wish to graph, the equations will often be in a form in which neither variable is isolated. For example, in the equation $3A - B = 2A$, they may want A in terms of B or B in terms of A. The same technique of solving for one variable can be used to solve for one variable in terms of the other by adjusting the expressions on both sides while keeping the equation in balance.

Another format for equations and equation solving has become popular. These problems also involve scales but with only variables on the pans in the form of geometric shapes. In Figure 15.4, a series of examples shows scale problems in which each shape on the scales repre-

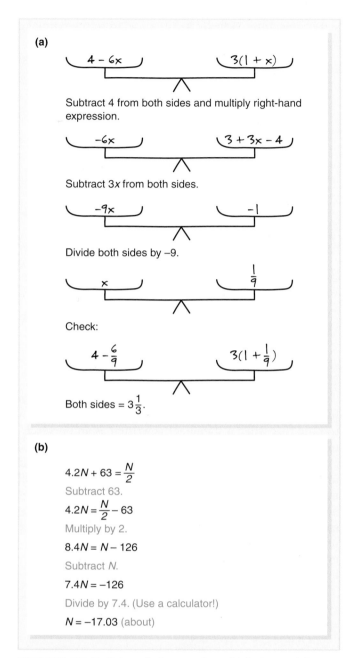

(a)

Subtract 4 from both sides and multiply right-hand expression.

Subtract 3x from both sides.

Divide both sides by −9.

Check:

Both sides = $3\frac{1}{3}$.

(b)

$4.2N + 63 = \frac{N}{2}$

Subtract 63.

$4.2N = \frac{N}{2} - 63$

Multiply by 2.

$8.4N = N - 126$

Subtract N.

$7.4N = -126$

Divide by 7.4. (Use a calculator!)

$N = -17.03$ (about)

FIGURE 15.3 Using a balance scale to think about solving equations.

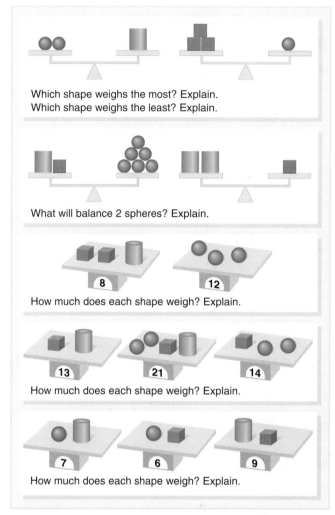

Which shape weighs the most? Explain.
Which shape weighs the least? Explain.

What will balance 2 spheres? Explain.

How much does each shape weigh? Explain.

How much does each shape weigh? Explain.

How much does each shape weigh? Explain.

FIGURE 15.4 Examples of problems with multiple scales (equations).

sents a different value. Two or more scales for a single problem provide different information about the shapes or variables. Problems of this type can be adjusted in difficulty for children throughout first to eighth grades. Greenes and Findell (1999a, b) have developed a whole collection of these and similar activities in books for grades 1 to 7.

When no numbers are involved, as in the top two examples of Figure 15.4, students can find combinations of numbers for the shapes that make all of the balances balance. If an arbitrary value is given to one of the shapes, then values for the other shapes can be found accordingly.

In the second example, if the sphere = 2, then the cylinder must be 4 and the cube = 8. If a different value is given to the sphere, the other shapes will change accordingly.

The scale problems (with a number for each scale) are to be solved for a unique value for each shape. There are usually several paths to finding a solution.

⏸ pause and reflect

How would you solve the last problem in Figure 15.4? Can you solve it in two ways?

You (and students) can tell if you are correct by checking your solutions with the original scale positions. Believe it or not, you have just solved a series of simultaneous equations, a skill generally left to a formal algebra class.

Making Structure in the Number System Explicit

In Chapter 10 a few properties are discussed for each operation (p. 149 and p. 157) that are important for students as they learn basic facts and strategies for computation. For example, the commutative or order property for both addition and multiplication reduces substantially the number of facts necessary to learn. These and other properties are likely to be used informally as students develop relational thinking while working with true/false and open sentences as described in the previous sections.

A next step is to have students examine these structures or properties explicitly and express them in general terms without reference to specific numbers. For example, a student solving $394 + 176 = N + 394$ may say that N must be 176 because $394 + 176$ is the same as $176 + 394$. This is a specific instance of the commutative property. To articulate this (and other structural properties of our number system) in a form such as $a + b = b + a$, and to note that it is true for all numbers, is the goal of looking at structure. When made explicit and understood, these structures not only add to students' tools for computation, but also they enrich the understanding of the number system and provide a base for even higher levels of abstraction (Carpenter et al., 2003).

Making Conjectures

Properties of the number system can be built into students' explorations with true/false and open-number sentences. For example, third-grade students will generally agree that the true/false sentence $41 \times 3 = 3 \times 41$ is true. The pivotal question, however, is, "Is this true for any numbers?" Some students will argue that while it seems to be true all of the time, there may be two numbers that haven't been tried yet for which it does not work.

With general or even partial agreement, ask a student to try to state the idea in words without using a specific number. *When you multiply any two numbers, you will get the same answer if you multiply them in the reverse order.* If a formulation is ambiguous or not entirely correct, have students discuss the wording until all agree that they understand what it means. Write this verbal statement of the property on the board as a *conjecture*—not an absolute fact. Call it a conjecture and explain that it is not necessarily a true statement just because we think that it is true. Until someone either proves it or finds a counterexample—an instance for which the conjecture is not true—it remains a conjecture.

Students can make conjectures as early as the second grade. By third or fourth grade, students should be challenged to translate verbal conjectures into open sentences. The preceding conjecture can be written using any two letters as follows: $A \times B = B \times A$. It is best to have students

state conjectures verbally before moving to the symbolic statement of the same idea.

activity **15.7**

Conjecture Creation

Once students have seen a couple of conjectures developed out of your explorations of true/false sentences, challenge students to make up conjectures on their own—to create statements about numbers and computation that they believe are always true. It is best to have them state the conjectures in words. Alternatively, challenge students to write an open sentence that they believe will be true for all numbers. The full class should discuss the various conjectures. They should edit each conjecture for clarity or challenge the conjecture with a counterexample. Conjectures agreed upon by all should be added to a class list of conjectures and, if not done already, written as open sentences as well as stated verbally.

Table 15.1 lists basic properties of the number system for which students may make conjectures. It is important to note that when a statement is written as an open sentence it is assumed to be true for all numbers.

Students are almost certainly not going to know or understand why division by zero is not possible. You will need to point this exception out to them. Table 15.1 does not include the associative properties for addition and subtraction, nor is the distributive property included. These properties are somewhat difficult to state verbally. However, they are just as important as the others. They are listed here as open sentences:

$$(a + b) + c = a + (b + c)$$
$$(a \times b) \times c = a \times (b \times c)$$
$$a \times (b + c) = a \times b + a \times c$$

The associative properties may arise when students are adding or multiplying three or more numbers. Some students may add in one order and others in the reverse order. *Will you always get the same answer if you add (multiply) the first two and then the last as when you do the last ones first?* The distributive property is fundamental to almost all methods of multiplying two-digit numbers. For example, 37×5 is the same as $5 \times 30 + 5 \times 7$. To fit this to the foregoing form, write 37 as $30 + 7$.

"Proving" Conjectures

Attempting to establish that a conjecture is true is a significant form of algebraic reasoning and is at the heart of what it means to do mathematics. How young students attempt to prove that something is always true is a relatively

TABLE 15.1
Properties of the Number System

Number Sentence	Student Statement of Conjecture
Addition and Subtraction	
$a + 0 = a$	When you add zero to a number, you get the same number you started with.
$a - 0 = a$	When you subtract zero from a number, you get the number you started with.
$a - a = 0$	When you subtract a number from itself, you get zero.
$a + b = b + a$	You can add numbers in one order and then change the order and you will get the same number.
Multiplication and Division	
$a \times 1 = a$	When you multiply a number by 1, you get the number you started with.
$a \div 1 = a$	When you divide a number by 1, you get the number you started with.
$a \div a = 1, a \neq 0$	When you divide a number that is not zero by itself, you get 1.
$a \times 0 = 0$	When you multiply a number times zero, you get zero.
$0 \div a = 0, a \neq 0$	When you divide zero by any number except zero, you get zero.
$a \times b = b \times a$	When you multiply two numbers, you can do it in any order and you will get the same number.
Conjectures Derived from Basic Properties	
$a + b - b = a$	When you add a number to another number and then subtract the number that you added, you will get the number that you started with.
$a \times b \div b = a, b \neq 0$	When you multiply a number by another number that is not zero and then divide by the same number, you get the number you started with.

Adapted from Carpenter, Franke, and Levi (2003) and used with permission.

new and interesting area of research (Ball & Bass, 2003; Carpenter, Franke, & Levi, 2003; Schifter, 1999; Schifter, Bastable, Monk, & Russell, in press). These researchers all believe that there is a real value in challenging students even as early as second grade to establish that the conjectures they make are always true. Therefore, as conjectures are made in class, regardless of the grade level, the next step is to ask, "Is that always true? How can we tell?"

Students' attempts tend to fall into three categories. At the lowest level, students appeal to authority: "I learned this last year from Mrs. Wilson." Of course, this is not true justification. Students need to reason through ideas based on their own thinking. Challenge them to come up with their own reasons and not to rely simply on the word of others.

In the elementary school, the most common form of "proof" is the use of examples. Students will try lots of specific numbers in a conjecture. "See, it works for any number you try." They may try very large numbers as substitutes for "any" number. Often there will be students in the class who will not accept this approach as proof. "How do we know there aren't some numbers that it doesn't work for?"

Finally, students will attempt to use some form of logic. Often these efforts include the use of physical materials to show the reasoning behind the conjecture. For example, a student attempting to prove that $a + b = b + a$ might show two bars of snap cubes, one with 8 cubes and the other with 6. The bars are used to show that the number of blocks does not change when the order of the two bars is reversed. What moves this beyond just an example is the student's statement or explanation that the number of cubes in the bars is not part of the argument: "It would work this way no matter how many blocks are in each bar."

Students will not be able to fully prove a property as basic as the commutative property without use of a model or the use of language indicating that their reasons are not tied to specific numbers. There are, however, properties that can be proven. The conjectures $a + b - b = a$ and $a \times 0 = 0$ can be proven by appealing to other more basic properties and definitions.

At the elementary level, not all students will be able to create arguments and some may not even follow those constructed by others (Carpenter et al., 2003). However, at all levels it is important to push students to reason using logic and not be content with appeals to authority or the use of examples. Remember that your goal is the students' thinking involved in these justifications. There is little value in making a good argument for your students.

Odd and Even Relationships

An interesting category of conjectures surrounds the concepts of odd and even numbers. Students will often observe that the sum of two even numbers is even, that the sum of two odd numbers is even, or that the sum of an even and an odd number is always odd. Similar statements can be made about multiplication. Odd and even numbers are not really basic properties of the number system but the result of definitions imposed on the numbers. A number is *even* if it can be divided by 2 with no remainder. Alternatively, a quantity is *even* if it can be made up entirely of pairs of two. An *odd* number is one that is not even.

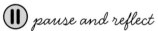 *pause and reflect*

Before reading on, think for a moment about how you might prove that the sum of two odd numbers is always even.

Students will provide a variety of interesting proofs of odd/even conjectures. As with other conjectures, they typically begin by trying lots of numbers. But here it is a bit easier to imagine that there just might be two numbers "out there" that don't work. Then students turn to the definition or a model that illustrates the definition. For example, if a number is odd and you split it in two, there will be a leftover. If you do this with the second odd number, it will have a leftover also. So if you put these two numbers together, the two leftovers will go together so there won't be a leftover in the sum. Students frequently use models such as bars of snap cubes to strengthen their arguments.

Because students have access to more avenues for reasoning with odd and even numbers, explorations of conjectures involving them is a good place to have students explore proofs. Students from second grade through middle school will benefit from these challenges.

 It is not important that all students initiate conjectures. It is important that all students actively consider the validity of all conjectures made by classmates. When deciding if a conjecture is always true, have students write their ideas before sharing with the class. If you begin with a class discussion, only a few students are likely to participate, with others content to listen whether or not they are following the arguments. You can then use both what the students write as well as their input in discussions to assess what level of reasoning they are at: authority, lots of examples, or an appeal to logic. ∎

Repeating Patterns

Patterns are found in all areas of mathematics. Learning to search for patterns and how to describe, translate, and extend them is part of doing mathematics and thinking algebraically. At the pre-K to 3 level, a good place to begin is with the exploration of repeating patterns.

The concept of a repeating pattern and how a pattern is extended or continued can be introduced to the full class in several ways. One possibility is to draw simple shape patterns on the board and extend them in a class discussion. Oral patterns can be joined in by all children. For example, "do, mi, mi, do, mi, mi, . . ." is a simple singing pattern. Up, down, and sideways arm positions provide three elements with which to make patterns: up, side, side, down, up, side, side, down, . . . Boy-girl patterns or stand-sit patterns are also fun. From these ideas, the youngest children learn quickly the concept of patterns. Students can begin to work more profitably in small groups or even independently once a general notion of patterns is developed.

activity **15.8**

Pattern Strips

Students can work independently or in groups of two or three to extend patterns made from simple materials: buttons, colored blocks, connecting cubes, toothpicks, geometric shapes—items you can gather easily. For each set of materials, draw two or three complete repetitions of a pattern on strips of tagboard about 5 cm by 30 cm. The students' task is to use actual materials, copy the pattern shown, and extend it as far as they wish. Figure 15.5 illustrates possible patterns for a variety of materials. Make 10 to 15 different pattern strips for each set of materials. With six to eight sets, your entire class can work at the same time, in small groups working with different patterns and different materials.

The *core* of a repeating pattern is the shortest string of elements that repeats. Notice in Figure 15.5 that the core is always fully repeated and never only partially shown. If the core of a pattern is –oo, a card might have –oo–oo (two repetitions of the core), but it would be ambiguous if the card showed –oo–oo– or –oo–.

A significant step forward mathematically is to see that two patterns constructed with different materials are actually the same pattern. For example, the first pattern in Figure 15.5 and the first pattern in Figure 15.6 can both be "read" A-B-B-A-B-B-, and the pattern below those in both figures is A-B-C-C-A-B-C-C-.

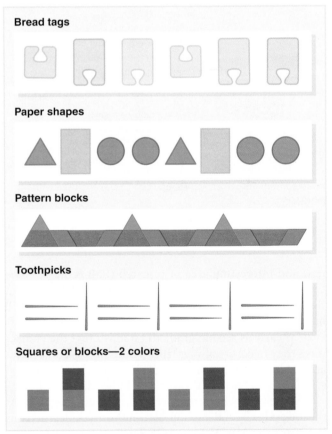

Bread tags

Paper shapes

Pattern blocks

Toothpicks

Squares or blocks—2 colors

FIGURE 15.5 Examples of pattern cards drawn on tagboard. Each pattern repeats completely and does not split in the middle of a core.

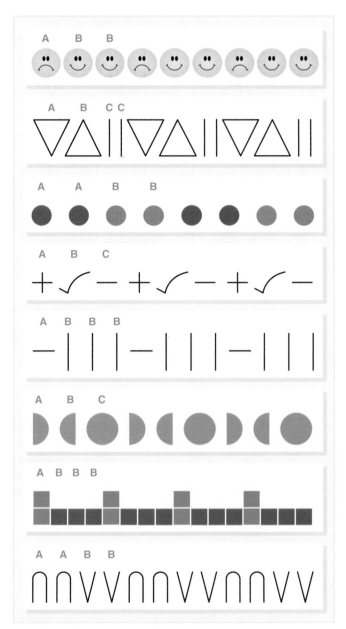

FIGURE 15.6 More examples of repeating patterns.

"... students should recognize that the color pattern 'blue, blue, red, blue, blue, red' is the same in form as 'clap, clap, step, clap, clap, step.' This recognition lays the foundation for the idea that two very different situations can have the same mathematical features and thus are the same in some important ways. Knowing that each pattern above could be described as having the form AABAAB is for students an early introduction to the power of algebra" (pp. 91–92).

The following activities reflect the powerful algebraic concept of repeating patterns just described in the quotation from *Principles and Standards*.

---

activity **15.9**

Pattern Match
Using the chalkboard or overhead projector, show six or seven patterns with different materials or pictures. Teach students to use an A, B, C method of reading a pattern. Half of the class can close their eyes while the other half uses the A, B, C scheme to read a pattern that you point to. After hearing the pattern, the students who had their eyes closed examine the patterns and try to decide which pattern was read. If two of the patterns in the list have the same structure, the discussion can be very interesting.

The following independent activity involves translation of a pattern from one medium to another, which is another way of helping students separate the relationship in a pattern from the materials used to build it.

---

activity **15.10**

Same Pattern, Different Stuff
Have students make a pattern with one set of materials given a pattern strip showing a different set. This activity can easily be set up by simply switching the pattern strips from one set of materials to another. A similar idea is to mix up the pattern strips for four or five different sets of materials and have students find strips that have the same pattern. To test if two patterns are the same, children can translate each of the strips into a third set of materials or can write down the A, B, C pattern for each.

The challenge in the next activity is a forerunner to looking at the function aspect of patterns.

---

activity **15.11**

Predict Down the Line
For most repeating patterns, the elements of the pattern can be numbered 1, 2, 3, and so on. Provide students with a pattern to extend. Before students begin to extend the pattern, have them predict exactly what element will be in, say, the fifteenth position. Students should be required to provide a reason for their prediction, preferably in writing. A slightly different challenge reverses the task: What position is the thirteenth red block in? Students can extend their patterns if necessary to check their reasoning.

The prediction activity may be quite challenging before the second grade. Eventually, students will figure out that the length of the core of the pattern plays a significant role in predicting "down the line." If you ask for a prediction of the hundredth element students will not be able to check the prediction by extending the pattern. Verification focuses on the rationale for the prediction. Students may need to use a calculator to skip-count or multiply. But it is always the reasoning that is most important.

Charts and Other Number Patterns

Patterns with numbers offer wonderful opportunities for students to extend their understanding of mathematical patterns. Number patterns found in charts or number sequences based on a particular rule provide appropriate algebraic thinking challenges for all grade levels, K to 8.

Patterns on the Hundreds Chart

The hundreds chart is a rich field for exploring number relationships and should not be thought of solely as a device for teaching numeration.

In Chapter 12, children colored skip counts on the hundreds chart and looked for patterns (see Activities 12.14–12.19 and Activity 12.28). Here are some additional tasks you might explore in a similar manner.

- Which numbers make diagonal patterns? Which make column patterns?
- What skip-count patterns will land on 24? On 35? How many counts will it take to land on 60 if you count by 5s?
- Can you find two skip-count patterns with one "on top of" the other? That is, all of the squares for one pattern are part of the pattern for the other. How are these two skip-count numbers related? Are there other patterns that are on top of each other?
- What two patterns only have some squares in common but not all? On what numbers do the patterns cross? Can you tell without looking at the charts?

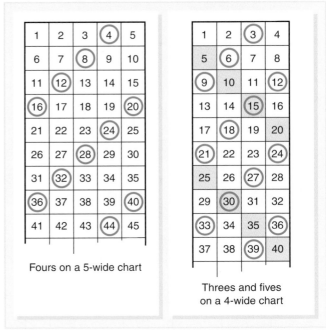

Fours on a 5-wide chart

Threes and fives on a 4-wide chart

FIGURE 15.7 Patterns on hundreds charts of different widths.

Students will find that the same patterns are on top of each other as with the regular chart. However, patterns go in columns only when skip counting by a factor or a multiple of the chart width. For example, on a chart of width 9, the threes make columns but the twos make diagonals. What will sixes do on a 9-wide chart? What if the width of the chart is a prime number? You can also explore charts that are wider than 10.

Number Patterns

Many worthwhile patterns can be observed with numbers alone. These can be simple repeating patterns such as 1, 2, 1, 2, ... Even very young children can use numbers in patterns like these. Generally, however, numeric patterns involve some form of progression. The pattern 1, 2, 1, 3, 1, 4, 1, 5, . . . is a simple example that even young students can discover. Here are some more numeric patterns:

2, 4, 6, 8, 10, . . .	(even numbers; add 2 each time)
1, 4, 7, 10, 13, . . .	(start with 1; add 3 each time)
1, 4, 9, 16, . . .	(squares: 1^2, 2^2, 3^2, etc.)
0, 1, 5, 14, 30, . . .	(add the next square number)
2, 5, 11, 23, . . .	(double the number and add 1)
2, 6, 12, 20, 30, . . .	(multiply pairs of counting numbers)
3, 3, 6, 9, 15, 24, . . .	(add the two preceding numbers—an example of a Fibonacci sequence)

The challenge in these patterns or sequences of numbers is not only to find and extend the pattern but also to make generalizations. As in "Predict Down the Line," have students predict the thirteenth number or one hundredth number. Then work toward a general rule to produce the *n*th number in the sequence.

The calculator provides a powerful approach to patterns. For a good example, see the discussion of "Start and Jump Numbers" in Chapter 2 (p. 14).

Growing Patterns—A First Look at Functions

Beginning at about the fourth grade and extending through the middle school years, students can explore patterns that involve a progression from step to step. In technical terms, these are called *sequences;* we will simply call them *growing patterns.* With these patterns, students not only extend patterns but also look for a generalization or an algebraic relationship that will tell them what the pattern will be at any point along the way. Growing patterns also demonstrate the concept of function and can be used as an entry point to this very important mathematical idea.

Figure 15.8 illustrates some growing patterns that are built with various materials or drawings. The patterns consist of a series of separate steps, each new step related to the previous one according to a rule.

The first thing to do with patterns in the upper and middle grades is to get students comfortable with building patterns and talking about how they can be extended in a logical manner. Building the patterns with physical materials such as tiles, counters, or flat toothpicks allows students to make changes if necessary and to build on to one step to make a new step. It is also more fun! The following activity will introduce growing patterns.

activity **15.13**

Extend and Explain
Show students the first three or four steps of a pattern such as those in Figure 15.8. Provide them with appropriate materials or grid paper, have them extend the patterns, and explain why their extension indeed follows the pattern.

Growing patterns have a numeric component, the number of objects in each step. As shown in Figure 15.9, a table can be made for any growing pattern. One row of the table or chart is always the number of steps, and the other is for recording how many objects are in that step. Frequently, a pattern grows so quickly and requires so many blocks or spaces to draw it that it is only reasonable to build or draw the first five or six steps. This leads to the following activity.

activity **15.14**

Predict How Many
Have students begin to extend a growing pattern you provide. They should also make a table showing how many items are needed to make each step of the pattern. The task is to predict the number of items in the twentieth step of the pattern. The challenge is to see if there is a way to do this without filling in the first 19 entries of the table. Predictions should also be accompanied by an explanation.

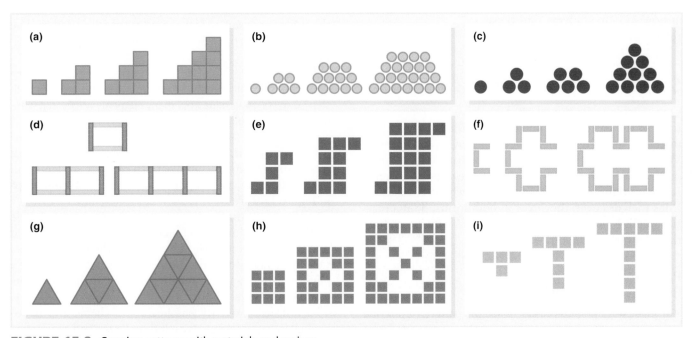

FIGURE 15.8 Growing patterns with materials or drawings.

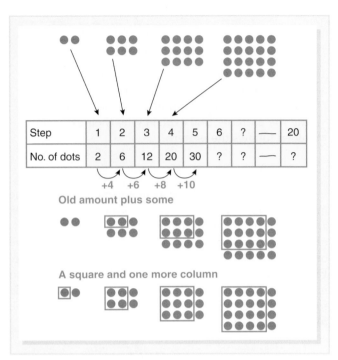

FIGURE 15.9 Two different relationships in a visual pattern.

For some patterns it is much easier to find a general rule than it is for others. In Figure 15.8, patterns (c) and (i) are easier than (a) or (e). Finding a way to determine the twentieth or even the hundredth entry in the table gets at the heart of finding a relationship that later students will understand is an example of a function. We next look at how to help students find these relationships.

Searching for Relationships

Once a table is developed, students have two representations of the pattern: the one created with the drawing or materials and the numeric version that is in the table. When looking for relationships, some students will focus on the table and others will focus on the physical pattern. It is important for students to see that whatever relationships they discover, they exist in both forms. So if a relationship is found in a table, challenge students to see how that plays out in the physical version.

Patterns from Step to Step: Recursive Relationships

For most students, it is easier to see the patterns from one step to the next. When you have a table constructed, the differences from one step to the next can be written next to

or below it, as in Figure 15.9. In that example, the number in each step can be determined from the previous step by adding successive even numbers. The description that tells how a pattern changes from step to step is known as a *recursive relationship*.

Whenever students notice a pattern in the table, see if they can find that same pattern in the physical version. In Figure 15.9, notice that in each step, the previous step has been outlined. That lets you examine the amount added and see how it creates the pattern of adding on even numbers. The picture or physical pattern and the table should be as closely connected as possible.

Patterns from Step Number to Step: Functional Relationships

The recursive step-to-step pattern is almost certainly the first that your students will observe. However, to find the table entry for the hundredth step, the only way a recursive pattern can help is to find all of the prior 99 entries in the table. If a rule or relationship can be discovered that connects the number of objects in a step to the number of the step, any table entry can be determined without building or calculating all of the intermediate entries. A rule that determines the number of elements in a step from the step number is an example of a *functional relationship*.

There is no single best method for finding this relationship between step number and step. Some students may get insight by simply "playing around" with the numbers and asking, "How can I operate on the number of the step to get the corresponding number in the table?" Most will benefit from examining the physical pattern for regularities. At the bottom of Figure 15.9, a square array is outlined for each step. Each successive square is one larger on a side. What relationship might exist between this subset of the pattern and the step numbers? In this example, the side of each square is the same as the step number. The row to the right of each square is also the step number.

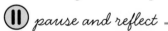 *pause and reflect* —————

With that information, how would you describe the twentieth step? Can you determine how many elements will be in it without drawing the picture?

At this point, writing a numeric expression for each step number using the same pattern can help students find the functional relationship. For example, the first four steps in Figure 15.9 are $1^2 + 1$, $2^2 + 2$, $3^2 + 3$, and $4^2 + 4$.

The most interesting and perhaps most valuable method of searching for a functional relationship is to find it in the physical pattern rather than in the numeric table. One method of doing this is to examine only one step of a physical pattern and ask students to find a method of counting the elements without simply counting each by one. The following activity has become a classic and is described in many resources including Burns and McLaughlin (1990) and Boaler and Humphreys (2005).

activity **15.15**

The Border Problem

On centimeter grid paper, have students draw an 8 × 8 square representing a swimming pool. Next, have them shade in the surrounding squares, the tiles around the pool. (See Figure 15.10.) The task is to find a way to count the border tiles without counting them one by one. Students should use their drawings, words, and number sentences to show how they counted the squares.

For each method of counting that they find, they should write the number sentences that would be used for a 6 × 6 pool and a 75 × 75 pool if the same method is used.

There are at least five different methods of counting the border tiles around a square other than counting them one at a time.

⏸ *pause and reflect* ──────────

Before reading further, see if you can find four or five different counting schemes for the border tiles problem. Apply your method to a square border of other dimensions.

A very common solution is to notice that there are ten squares across the top and also across the bottom, leaving eight squares on either side. This might be written as:

$$10 + 10 + 8 + 8 = 36 \text{ or } 2 \times 10 + 2 \times 8 = 36$$

Each of the following expressions can likewise be traced to looking at the squares in various groupings:

$$4 \times 9$$
$$4 \times 8 + 4$$
$$4 \times 10 - 4$$
$$10^2 - 8^2$$

FIGURE 15.10 How many different ways can you find to count the border tiles of an 8 × 8 pool without counting them one at a time?

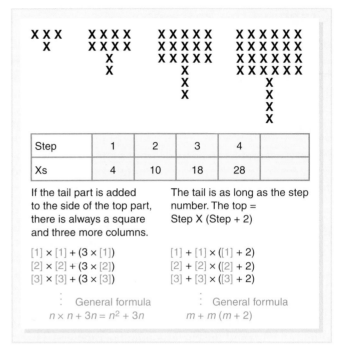

Step	1	2	3	4	
Xs	4	10	18	28	

If the tail part is added to the side of the top part, there is always a square and three more columns.

The tail is as long as the step number. The top = Step X (Step + 2)

[1] × [1] + (3 × [1])   [1] + [1] × ([1] + 2)
[2] × [2] + (3 × [2])   [2] + [2] × ([2] + 2)
[3] × [3] + (3 × [3])   [3] + [3] × ([3] + 2)

⋮ General formula   ⋮ General formula
$n \times n + 3n = n^2 + 3n$ $m + m(m + 2)$

FIGURE 15.11 Finding functional relationships in a pattern.

Addition may be used instead of multiplication for equivalent expressions. Be sure that you can decide how each is derived from the grid of squares. The last expression is based on areas. If the pool was 75 × 75, the 4 × 8 + 4 expression becomes 4 × 75 + 4. The 75 is the number of squares on each side, not counting the corners.

In "The Border Problem" there is no table, forcing students to look only at the picture or physical situation and not at numbers. Another approach is to have students build each step of the pattern, create a table of elements in each step, and then find a way to count the elements of each step using the step numbers in the same manner at each step. Figure 15.11 shows how this might be done.

General Function Statements from Patterns

Notice in Figure 15.11 that a general expression for the *n*th step was written for each of the two ways that the pattern was developed. If students can relate their counting method to the step numbers, they should then be able to write a general formula that will give them the number for any step. In "The Border Problem," the 2 × 10 + 2 × 8 approach becomes $t = 2(n + 2) + 2n$. The formula is actually a *function*, a rule that uniquely associates elements of one set with elements of another set. In this case, the first set is the set of lengths of one edge of the pool and these are represented by the *independent variable n*. The second set is the numbers of tiles required to surround the pools. Values from this set are represented by the *dependent variable t*.

Graphing the Patterns

So far, growing patterns have been represented by the physical materials or drawings, by a chart, and by a symbolic rule. A graph adds a fourth representation. Figure 15.12 shows the graph for "The Border Problem" and the pattern in Figure 15.11. Notice that the first is a straight-line (linear) relationship and the other is a curved line that would make half of a parabola if the points were joined. Note that a graph can be made from a table without finding a general formula. The horizontal axis is always used for the step numbers, the independent variable.

Do not forget how easy it is both to plot points and to draw curves on the graphing calculator. The second graph in Figure 15.12 is also shown on a graphing calculator with the function $y = x^2 + 3x$ (same as $n^2 + 3n$) drawn through it. ∎

Consider strings of a single color of pattern blocks (Figure 15.13) and the corresponding perimeters. This is a good pattern to explore in the same manner as "The Bor-

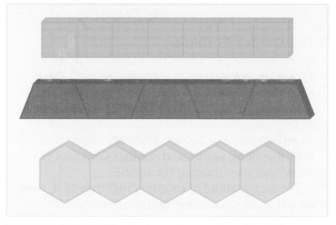

FIGURE 15.13 What is the perimeter of a string of *N* pattern blocks?

der Problem," beginning with a string of seven or eight blocks and finding schemes for determining the perimeter without counting. Any block can be used and the schemes will be the same with a few exceptions for the trapezoids. (Note that the long edge of the red trapezoid is two units and the other edges are one unit.) For the other shapes there are again five different ways to find the perimeter, each resulting in a general formula that appears on the surface to be different from the others.

⏸ *pause and reflect* ───────

For the string of hexagons in Figure 15.13, find at least two different ways to find the perimeter and write a general formula for each method.

───────────────────────────

Two of the five possible perimeter methods for hexagons result in these formulas or functions:

$$P = 6 + (N - 1)4 \text{ and } P = (N - 2)4 + (2 \times 5)$$

For the first expression, note that one hexagon has six sides and each additional block adds four units to the total perimeter. The second expression is based on the lengths of the tops and bottoms plus the two end blocks. Can you find other ways to get the perimeters? The perimeter graphs for the three shapes in Figure 15.13 are shown in Figure 15.14.

A challenge for the perimeter task is to add a second variable *S* to the formulas, where *S* represents the perimeter of a single block. The resulting formula will then give the perimeter for all pattern blocks as well as for strings of regular polygons of any size.

If you make a table for the hexagon perimeter task, you will notice that the recursive pattern (the pattern from step to step) is a constant 4. For the squares, the recursive pattern is a constant 2. The rate of change from one step to the next is constant. As a result, the graphs of these patterns fall in a straight line. However, examine the recur-

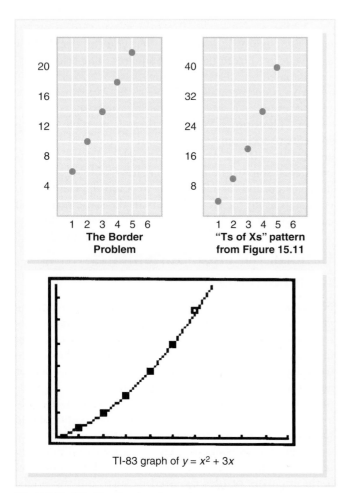

FIGURE 15.12 Graphs of growing patterns.

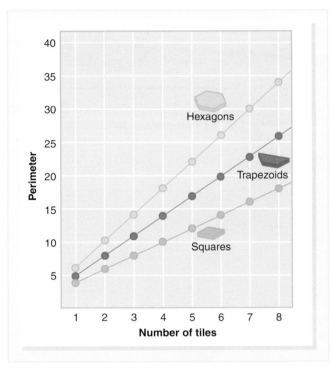

FIGURE 15.14 Graphs of the perimeters of three different pattern-block strings. The lines are drawn only to show that the points align. They are not part of the graph.

sive pattern for the Ts in Figure 15.12. The change from step to step increases with each step: + 6, + 8, + 10, ... Since the rate of change (the recursive pattern) increases, the graph gets steeper and steeper from step to step, resulting in a curved graph rather than a straight line. You can always look at the recursive relationship and determine if the graph will be a straight line or a curve. Straight lines have a constant recursive pattern. Using the information about recursive patterns, can you tell which of the patterns in Figure 15.8 will have straight graphs and which curved graphs? Can you find the general functional relationships for those patterns?

In the fifth grade of *Investigations in Number, Data, and Space*, an entire unit focuses specifically on this rate-of-change aspect in functional relationships. As you can see in the excerpt on page 276, the recursive relationship is recorded on a third column of the table and is also graphed.

 As you work with students exploring patterns, you want to first see that they understand the concept of a pattern. They should be able to describe the pattern and extend it. Next you want to see if they can abstract the mathematical ideas from the pattern. For repeating patterns, can students identify the core, translate the pattern to another set of materials, and make predictions about elements further down the pattern? For growing patterns, look for students' ability to find a gen-

eral rule or functional relationship as well as the recursive relationship in the pattern. This is almost always easier with a linear relationship. With growing patterns, it is also important for students to begin to see the connections between the pattern, the table of values, and the graphs. ■

NCTM Standards "In grades 3–5, students should investigate numerical and geometric patterns and express them mathematically in words or symbols. They should analyze the structure of the pattern and how it grows or changes, organize this information systematically, and use their analysis to develop generalizations about the mathematical relationships in the pattern" (p. 159).

Function Concepts and Representations

Earlier, we defined a *function* as a rule that uniquely associates elements of one set with elements of another set. This may be a bit formal for elementary and middle grade students. For these students the function concept best evolves from contextual situations in which a change in one thing (independent variable) causes a corresponding change in another thing (dependent variable). The height of a bean plant changes as the number of days elapse since it sprouted. The height of the plant is a function of the days it has grown. There are endless examples of functional relationships in our daily lives. The size of the paycheck is a function of the number of hours worked. The level in the gas tank is a function of the miles driven since filling up. Profit is a function of sales. These are all examples of a change in one variable causing a corresponding change in a second variable. Functions are used to better understand change in all sorts of contexts.

Five Representations of Functions

Look back at the different ways growing patterns are represented. First, there is the physical or pictorial pattern itself. Both the recursive and functional relationships are "in" the pattern. Next, we created a chart or table for the pattern. Again the relationships can be found in the table, although often it seems easier to find the functional relationships in the pattern. Using either the table or the pattern, the functional relationship is generalized into a formula or symbolic statement of the function. Clearly, the functional relationship is in the formula. Next we created a graph of the pattern, probably using the table to get the numbers or by plugging numbers into the formula. The graph shows us the relationship in a picture form. We can see how quickly the step values increase depending on how steep the graph rises from left to right. We even know that straight-line graphs have a constant recursive

Investigations
in Number, Data, and Space

Grade 5, Patterns of Change
Investigation 1: Number Patterns in Changing Shapes

Context

This unit occurs in the second half of the fifth grade. In this first investigation, students explore growing block patterns and graph them. For most of the remainder of the unit, instead of geometric patterns, students look at graphs of distance traveled away from a starting point with the steps being intervals of time. Nowhere in the unit are students asked to find general formulas. However, they do learn about rates of change.

Task Description

During the first two days of this investigation, students make tables and plot the graphs of growing patterns made with square tiles. The patterns grow from one step to the next by adding on to the previous step. When students add on to their patterns, they change the color of tile they are using.

By using the change-of-color approach, students need only draw one picture to show all of the steps of the tile pattern. This is recorded in the upper left portion of the worksheet shown here where the first three steps of the pattern are given. Based on the pattern, students fill in the table for the first eight steps. These tables have three columns, not just two. The middle column, labeled "New tiles (step size)," is actually the recursive relationship or the slope of the graph for that step. Next, students make two graphs: one of the steps and the step size, and the second of the step and the number of tiles. For a pattern such as this one in which two new tiles are added at each step, the first graph is a horizontal line two units up. The graph of the total tiles is a straight line increasing upward, always with a slope of 2. For the student page shown here, the first graph is a straight line going up with a slope of 1. The graph of the total is a curve.

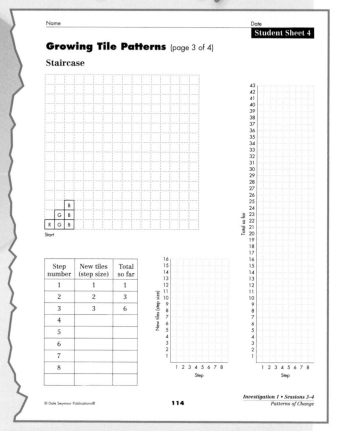

When students begin graphing distances from a starting point, they explore a full variety of curves, including those that decrease and are horizontal. For example, in one activity, students look at walking rates and positions from the start point. Not only can walking speed (step size) be fast, slow, or even zero, but it can also be negative (walking backward or toward the start). Therefore, graphs of step sizes are both above and below the horizontal axis, and the corresponding position graphs go up or down with differing rates of change.

relationship. That constant recursive relationship could be determined from the graph. We can also add language as a fifth representation. For example, we can say, "The perimeter of the row of hexagons is a function of the number of blocks. The perimeter is four times the number of blocks plus 2 more."

Thus, we have five representations for growing patterns: (1) the pattern itself, which we can refer to as the context; (2) the chart or table; (3) the symbolic equation; (4) the graph; and (5) language. Each of these five representations embodies the same functional and recursive relationships. The same five representations are used for all functions, not just patterns. It is important to see that each representation is a way of looking at the function, yet each provides a different way of looking at or thinking about the function. The value of each representation is in the way that it helps us see and understand the function in a different manner than the others do.

To explore these five representations further, we will use the context of a hot-dog vendor.

Brian is trying to make money to help pay for college by selling hot dogs from a hot-dog cart at the coliseum during major performances and ball games. He pays the cart owner $35 per night for the use of the cart. He sells hot dogs for $1.25 each. His costs for the hot dogs, condiments, napkins, and other paper products are about 60 cents per hot dog on average. The profit from a single hot dog is, therefore, 65 cents.

Contextual Representations of Functions

This function begins with a context: selling hot dogs and the resulting profit. We are interested in Brian's profit in terms of the number of hot dogs sold: The more hot dogs Brian sells, the more profit he will make. Brian does not begin to make a profit immediately because he must pay the $35 rent on the vending cart. Nonetheless, Brian's profit is dependent on—*is a function of*—the number of hot dogs he sells.

Not every function has a real-world context, but at the middle school level, it is useful to place functions in contexts that make sense to students. Here are some other contexts in which functional relationships are to be found:

- Suppose that the value of a new car depreciates at the rate of 20 percent each year. There is a definite relationship between the age of the car and its current value.
- If you measure the height and arm span of a lot of different people, from very short to very tall, you will likely find that there is a predictable relationship between these two measures. Arm span is related to height.
- A ride on a roller coaster has several possible relationships. As time passes from the beginning of the ride to the end of the ride, the height of the cars above the ground changes. It increases slowly at first, then most likely has a fast decrease followed by a series of lesser increases and decreases. The speed of the cars on the roller coaster is also a function of time. The speed of the cars has an effect on how loud the passengers scream, and so it is reasonable to say that speed and screams are related, although perhaps not as precisely as the height is related to the time.
- If you build rectangles so that all have the same fixed perimeter, the length of the rectangles will decrease as

the widths increase. If you begin with a very small width and a longer length, the area of the rectangles first increases as the width increases from zero and then decreases.

These are all contexts in which there is a functional relationship. For the height versus arm span and the loudness of roller coaster passengers, a relationship is not easy to determine precisely. Riders will not always scream at exactly the same decibel level, nor will everyone's height-to-arm span ratio be the same. However, all of these situations illustrate functions in meaningful contexts. Each has at least two values that vary, with one being dependent on or related to the other.

Table Representations of Functions

Brian the hot-dog vendor might well sit down and calculate some possible income figures based on hypothetical sales. This will give him some idea of how many franks he must sell to break even and what his profit might be for an evening. For example, if he sells no hot dogs, he will be $35 in the hole, or his profit will be negative $35. Selling 70 hot dogs would yield a profit of $70 \times 0.65 - 35 = 45.50 - 35$, or $10.50. A table of similar values might look like this:

Hot Dogs	Profit
0	−35.00
70	10.50
100	30.00
150	62.50

The number of hot dogs shown in the table is purely a matter of choice. One could calculate the profit for 10,000 hot dogs ($10,000 \times 0.65 - 35$), even though it is not reasonable to expect Brian to sell that many. One of the values of contexts in thinking about functions is to see how mathematical representations can ignore reality. The person who interprets the table must take the context into consideration.

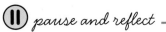 *pause and reflect* ———————————

When a set of data such as the height and arm span is organized in a table, it does not yet create a function. Why not?

A function must *uniquely* define the value of one variable in terms of the other. Heights can predict arm span but not precisely. There may be many different persons in the data set with the same height who have different arm spans. As you will see in Chapter 22, a function can approximate data that are not perfectly organized.

Language Expressions for Functions

Functional relationships are dependent relationships or rules of correspondence. In the hot-dog vendor situation,

Brian's profit depends on the number of hot dogs that are sold. In functional language, we can say, "Profit *is a function of* the number of hot dogs sold." The phrase "is a function of" expresses the dependent relationship. The profit *depends on*—is a function of—the hot-dog sales.

Looking at the other examples, we would say that the current value of a car is a function of its age or its value depends on its age. If someone were to ask what speed the roller coaster is going, you might respond, "It depends on the time since the ride began," or, in functional terms, "That depends. The speed is a function of the time since the ride began."

Graphical Representations of Functions

They say that a picture is worth a thousand words. This is certainly true of functions. In the case of a function the picture is a graph. In Figure 15.15, six different values of hot-dog sales are plotted on a graph. The horizontal axis represents the number of hot dogs sold, and the vertical axis, the profit. As we have already established, the profit goes up as the sales go up. There is, in this situation, a very clear pattern to the six values.

The graph shows that the relationship between sales and profits is *linear*—a straight line—and is increasing. It also allows us easily to answer questions about Brian's profits. How many hot dogs must be sold to break even? The graph shows zero profit (the break-even point) where the line crosses the horizontal axis. (Why?) It looks to be near 53 or 54. What is Brian's profit for 130 hot dogs?

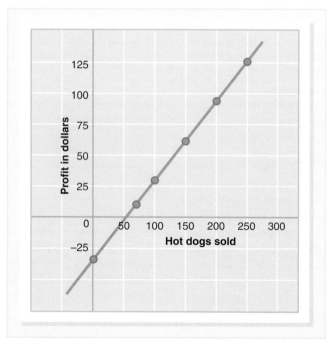

FIGURE 15.15 A graph showing profit as a function of hot-dog sales.

How many hot dogs must be sold to make a profit of $100? The context gives meaning to the graph, and the graph adds understanding to the context.

The graph is another mathematical model that, in terms of the context, does not make sense for all portions of the picture. If the line is extended indefinitely, there would be values where Brian's sales were negative (to the left of the vertical axis). This clearly does not make sense. Nor is it reasonable to talk about sales of millions of hot dogs even though the graph can extend as far as is wished.

Not all functions have straight-line graphs. If you start with a rectangle that has a fixed perimeter of 24 inches and increase the length beginning at 1 inch, both the width and the area will vary accordingly (see Figure 15.16). The width graph is linear. It decreases at a constant rate. By contrast, the area graph rises in a curve, reaches a maximum value, and then goes back down.

Figure 15.17 shows a simple roller coaster. Suppose that it takes just 120 seconds to ride.

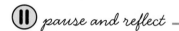 *pause and reflect* _____

Try to sketch a graph that shows the *height* of the roller coaster throughout the ride. Why will your graph not be exactly the same as the path of the roller coaster? Now make another graph that shows the *speed* of the car over the 120 seconds of the ride. Share your sketches with a friend. How are these two graphs related to each other?

Equations to Represent Functions

Suppose that we pick a letter, say, H, to represent the number of hot dogs Brian sells. For each hot dog sold, his income is $1.25 \times H$ dollars. But to determine his profit, we have to subtract from his income the rental cost of the cart and 60 cents cost per hot dog. Therefore, Brian's profit is represented by $(1.25 \times H) - (0.60 \times H) - 35$, or $(0.65 \times H) - 35$. To make an equation, we can assign another letter to stand for profit: $P = (0.65 \times H) - 35$. This equation defines a mathematical relationship between two values or two variables, profit and hot dogs. Taken out of context, it is simply a relationship between P and H. It is the same as the relationship between x and y in the equation $y = 0.65x - 35$.

By expressing a function as an equation, it can be examined in its most abstract form. Different types of equations have different properties. When the properties are understood, they can be applied to the context as well. In our hot-dog example, the equation has the general form of a linear equation, $Y = mX + b$. In this form, the value of m tells us how quickly or steeply the line goes up or down moving from left to right. The value of b tells where the graph will cross the vertical axis.

In the rectangle context, the following two equations represent the width and area, respectively, as functions of

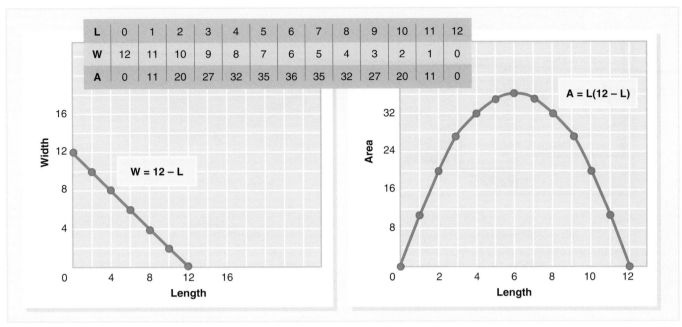

L	0	1	2	3	4	5	6	7	8	9	10	11	12
W	12	11	10	9	8	7	6	5	4	3	2	1	0
A	0	11	20	27	32	35	36	35	32	27	20	11	0

FIGURE 15.16 The width and area graphs as functions of the length of a rectangle with a fixed perimeter of 24 units.

the length (assuming that the perimeter is fixed at 24 units):

$$W(L) = \frac{24 - 2L}{2} = 12 - L$$

$$A(L) = L(12 - L) = 12L - L^2$$

In this example, the function notations $W(L)$ and $A(L)$ were used instead of a single letter for each. $W(L)$ stands for the width. Within this efficient notation is an indication that the width is a function of the length L. "The

width when the length is 3" can now be represented symbolically as $W(3)$. The symbolic name for the function itself—the relationship between the length and width—is represented by the letter W. Similarly for the area function A: $A(L)$ is the area for any given value of L; $A(4)$ is the area when the length is 4. The area is a function of the length.

Equations also make it easier to calculate values of the function. The equation can be entered into a graphing calculator, and the calculator can do the calculations to produce a table or draw a graph. Without the equation

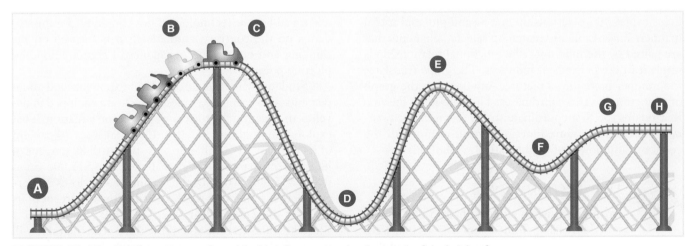

FIGURE 15.17 If it takes 120 seconds to ride this roller coaster, sketch a graph of the height of the car as a function of time. How should the points A through H be spaced along the time line? Sketch a second graph of the speed as a function of time. The time axis with points A to H should be the same. What would a graph of "scream decibels" look like?

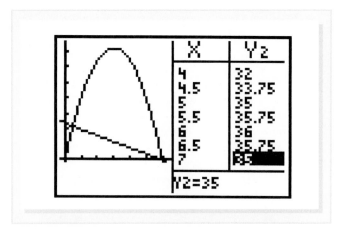

FIGURE 15.18 This graphing calculator shows graphs of both the width and the area of a rectangle of fixed perimeter as functions of the length. The table can show all possible length and area values.

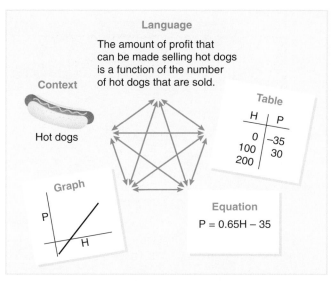

FIGURE 15.19 Five different representations of a function. For any given function, students should see that all these representations are connected and illustrate the same relationship. Each representation provides a different perspective on the function.

representation of the function, the graphing calculator is much less useful. Figure 15.18 shows the screen of a TI-83 calculator with both the width and the area graphs drawn. The table to the right computes the area for every length in steps of one-half. It requires very little expertise to do this on the calculator and allows the middle school child the chance to see and explore graphs without the tedium of having to plot points.

Connect Different Representations

Figure 15.19 illustrates the five representations of functions. The most important idea is to see that, for a given function, each of these representations illustrates the same relationship. The *context* provides an embodiment of the relationship outside the world of mathematics. *Language* helps express the relationship in a meaningful and useful manner. *Tables* explicitly match up selected elements that are paired by the function. The functional relationship is implicit in the pairings of numbers. The *graph* translates the number pairs into a picture. Any point on the graph of a function has two coordinates. The function is the rule that relates the first coordinate to the second. The *equation* expresses the same functional relationship with the economy and power of mathematical symbolism.

Use Technology

In the past, when students had to plot points and do by hand all the computations that were involved, functions were limited to very simple examples. Eighth-grade students would probably never see a function with an equation much more complicated than $y = 3x + 2$. The tedium of computing and plotting function values meant that examples had to use numbers that were small

and relatively easy to work with, making the link to real contexts almost impossible. Thanks to technology, we can now explore realistic contexts involving not-so-nice numbers. Students can investigate all sorts of functions as long as a relationship can be identified.

Consider the examples mentioned earlier. The profit example is the easiest to work with and could probably be examined without technology. The car depreciation is an exponential function. The area for a fixed perimeter is a quadratic function. If students can come up with an equation to go with a function rule, technology can be used to make a graph and do the necessary number crunching to make a table. The technology is not "thinking" for the students; on the contrary, student effort is focused on the thinking and not on the mechanics of computation and plotting points.

Students who have talked about exponents and about percents—both middle grades topics—are equipped to develop an equation for the car depreciation situation. That exploration might go like this: If the car loses 20 percent of its value in 1 year, then it must be worth 80 percent of its value after a year. So after 1 year, the $15,000 car is worth $15,000 × 0.8. In the second year, it loses 20 percent of that value, so it will be worth only 80 percent of its value at the end of year one: ($15,000 × 0.8) × 0.8 = $15,000 × 0.8^2. At the end of the third year, the value will be $15,000 × 0.8^3, and so on. In general, at the end of n years, the value of the car can be expressed in this equation: $V = \$15{,}000 \times 0.8^n$. Figure 15.20 shows the graph and the table of values on a graphing calculator. This equation is no more difficult to enter into a graphing calcula-

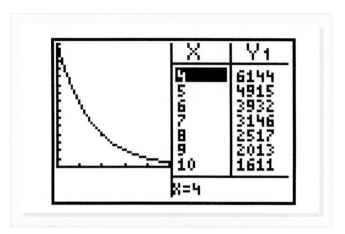

FIGURE 15.20 The graph and table for $V = 15,000 \times 0.8^n$. The graph shows n for values 0 to 15. The vertical axis runs from 0 to 15,000.

tor or a computer graphing utility than $y = 3x + 2$. The idea is to see that there are functional relationships and that these can be expressed in different ways. ■

NCTM Standards "By the middle grades, students should be able to understand the relationships among tables, graphs, and symbols and to judge the advantages and disadvantages of each way of representing relationships for practical purposes. As they work with multiple representations of functions—including numeric, graphic, and symbolic—they will develop a more comprehensive understanding of functions" (p. 38).

Explorations with Functional Relationships

Growing patterns are good first examples of functions for students in the upper grades because they extend the general idea of looking for and extending patterns. The tables, graphs, and formulas are generally accessible to younger students. By fifth or sixth grade, students can and should begin to explore the concept of function in a variety of real-world situations as well as from other areas of the curriculum.

Relationships Found in the Real World

Students can explore real-world situations, such as the example of Brian selling hot dogs, using several representations of functions. After computing several entries in a table, students will begin to see a pattern develop. Consider the following activity.

activity **15.16**

How Many Gallons Left?
Present this situation to students: A car gets 23 miles per gallon of gas. It has a gas tank that holds 20 gallons. Suppose that you were on a trip and had filled the tank at the outset. Make a table showing the number of gallons remaining in the tank for at least three different points in a trip of 350 miles. Plot the data on a graph. Show how you calculated each entry in your table, and be prepared to discuss with the class what you did.

Notice that very little direction is given in this activity. However, the situation presented to the students is fairly clear. Some teachers may prefer to use numbers that would be easier to compute, but that takes much of the realism out of the situation. If a student decides to make a table entry for 50 miles, he or she will first have to figure out what to do. On a calculator, $50 \div 23 = 2.173913$. This amount should be subtracted from 20 to find out how many gallons remain in the tank. Should you subtract 2 or 2.17 or 2.173913? This is a good example to use to discuss numbers in real contexts. Avoid being prescriptive so that students will do their own thinking and not rely on your directions. Students are bound to make errors in reasoning as well as in computation. Class discussion will sort things out.

As part of the discussion, help students develop functional language to represent the situation. Here the number of gallons in the tank is dependent on how far the car has been driven. Thus, the number of gallons remaining *is a function of* the miles driven. In addition to the language, work toward student development of an equation that represents the relationship in the situation. In this case, one possible equation is $g = 20 - \frac{m}{23}$. Or, using functional notation, you might say $G(m) = 20 - \frac{m}{23}$.

Students can draw a line through their plotted points, or with a computer or graphing calculator they can enter the equation and have technology do the graphing. In either case, use the graph to answer questions about the situation: "How can you tell from the graph how much gas will be left after driving 300 miles?" "How many miles can you drive before the gas tank has only 3 gallons left?" "What will happen to the graph if the driver stops to fill the tank after driving 350 miles?" The *trace* feature on a graphing calculator is a great help for getting values from a graph.

Here are a few suggestions for similar explorations.

Mr. Calloway wants to build a fenced pen against one side of his shed. The shed is 15 feet long, and he wants to use the full side of the shed. The pen is to be in the shape of a rectangle with two sides 15 feet long. How much fence will he have to buy if he knows how long

the other two sides of the pen will be (side versus fence length)? Add in a gate that is 3 feet long and costs $32. If fencing is $4.25 per foot, rethink the problem in terms of side versus cost. You can also discuss area and side length.

Mark is an avid cyclist. He can average 17 miles per hour for about 4 hours. He leaves home and travels for $2\frac{1}{2}$ hours at this rate, stops for lunch for $\frac{1}{2}$ hour, and then starts home. What is his distance from home at any given time? Suppose he goes faster for 1 hour and slower for 2 more hours and then returns home. Suppose he has a flat tire and has to stop for 15 minutes to repair it. How fast will he have to go in order to return home at the same time as scheduled, including the same lunch break? Does it make any difference where the breakdown occurs?

Pleasant's Hardware buys widgets for $4.17 each, marks them up 35 percent over wholesale, and sells them at that price. Relate widgets sold to total income. Consider profit instead of income. Incorporate a sale using a reduced price.

 The NCTM *E-Examples* has two applets that demonstrate the connection between a real-world context and graphs, tables, and equations. In Applet 5.2 students can adjust the speed, direction, and starting position of two runners. As the runners are set in motion, a time–distance graph is generated dynamically for each runner (see Figure 15.21). In Applet 6.2, when the cost per minute of a phone call is adjusted,

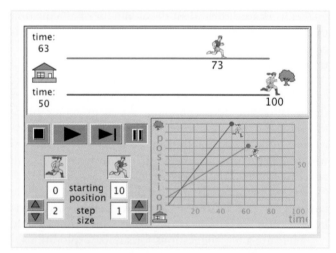

FIGURE 15.21 Applet 6.2, "Understanding Distance, Speed, and Time Relationships Using Simulation Software."

a graph and equation of the total cost are adjusted accordingly. Two rates on the same graph help illustrate rate (slope) visually. ■

The two applets just described each involve two functions that are graphed on the same axes and are compared. Many real-world situations are like this. For example, suppose that our hot-dog vendor, Brian, has a competitor, Sasha, who rents a small storefront shop rather than a cart. Sasha has a much larger investment in her shop; she might charge more per hot dog to try to make up the difference. Who will make the most profit for a given number of hot dogs sold? Is there a number of hot dogs sold at which they both have the same profit? This problem is similar to the phone call rate task found in the NCTM applet.

The following problem was posed to and solved by a group of fourth-grade students (Carraher, Schliemann, Martinez, & Earnst, 2005).

Mike has $8 in his hand and the rest of his money in his wallet. Robin has three times as much money as Mike has in his wallet. Who has the most money?

This problem lends itself to the general process of setting up a table, entering some data, and eventually finding a formula or equation—two equations in this case. If the two equations are graphed, it becomes clear that there is a value for which both Mike and Robin have the same amount of money—the intersection of the graphs. This will also be seen in the table. On one side of this intersection, Mike has more money, and on the other, Robin. The solutions are intervals rather than single values.

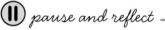 *pause and reflect* ──────────

Find the two equations for the Mike and Robin wallet problem.

The seventh-grade *Connected Mathematics* curriculum has an entire unit in which students explore and use both graphs and tables to represent functions found in real contexts. As you can see from the excerpt on the next page, the initial focus is on these two representations with almost no concern for equations.

Proportional Situations

Many relationships involving rates or proportions offer a valuable opportunity for examining functions. The following is a typical proportion problem.

Two out of every three students who eat in the cafeteria drink a pint of white milk. If 450 students eat in the cafeteria, how many gallons of milk are consumed?

Connected Mathematics

Grade 7, Variables and Patterns
Investigation 3: Analyzing Graphs and Tables

Context

Much of this unit is built on the context of a group of students who take a multiday bike trip from Philadelphia to Williamsburg, Virginia, and who then decide to set up a bike tour business of their own. Students explore a variety of functional relationships between time, distance, speed, expenses, profits, and so on. When data are plotted as discrete points, students consider what the graph might look like between points. For example, what interpretations could be given to each of these five graphs showing speed change from 0 to 15 mph in the first 10 minutes of a trip?

Task Description

In this investigation, the fictional students in the unit are gathering data in preparation for setting up their tour business. For the first task, data are given from two different bike rental companies as shown here—from one company in the form of a table and from the other in the form of a graph. The task is interesting because of the firsthand way in which students experience the value of one representation over another, depending on the need of the situation. In this unit students are frequently asked whether a graph or a table is the better source of information.

In the tasks that follow, students are given a table of data showing results of a phone poll that asked at which price former tour riders would take a bike tour. Students must find the best way to graph this data. After a price for a bike tour is established, graphs for estimated profits are created with corresponding questions about profits depending on different numbers of customers.

3.1 Renting Bicycles

The tour operators decided to rent bicycles for their customers rather than having customers bring their own bikes. They called two bike shops and asked for estimates of rental fees.

Rocky's Cycle Center sent a table of weekly rental fees for various numbers of bikes.

Number of bikes	5	10	15	20	25	30	35	40	45	50
Rental fee	$400	535	655	770	875	975	1070	1140	1180	1200

Adrian's Bike Shop sent a graph of their weekly rental fees. Since the rental fee depends on the number of bikes, they put the number of bikes on the *x*-axis.

Adrian's Bike Shop Fees

Problem 3.1

A. Which bike shop should Ocean and History Bike Tours use? Explain your choice.

B. Explain how you used the information in the table and the graph to make your decision.

From *Connected Mathematics: Variables and Patterns: Introducing Algebra.* © 2002 by Michigan State University, Glenda Lappan, James T. Fey, William M. Fitzgerald, Susan N. Friel, & Elizabeth Difanis Phillips. Published by Pearson Education, Inc., publishing as Pearson Prentice Hall. Used by permission.

The investigations use no formulas to this point. The subsequent investigation is called "Patterns and Rules" and begins the exploration of connecting equations or rules to the representations of graphs and tables. In the final investigation, students use graphing calculators to explore how graphs change in appearance when the rules that produce the graphs change.

As the problem is stated, there are a fixed number of students (450) and a single answer to the problem. Students would be expected to set up a proportion and solve for the unknown. But if only the first sentence of the problem is provided, students can be asked to create a table

showing the number of pints (or gallons) of milk consumed for four or five different numbers of students, plot the data on a graph, and create an equation that shows the relationship between students in the cafeteria and milk consumed. Functional language can be discussed: The number of pints of milk consumed in the cafeteria *is a function of* the number of students who eat there. The graph can be used to answer the question about milk for 450 students. Students can be challenged to find an equation that gives the amount of milk in terms of the number of students.

The following problem has been converted to a function investigation by asking for an answer in terms of an unknown instead of a specific number.

If each lemonade recipe will serve 20 people, how many recipes are needed to serve *n* people? If it takes three cans of concentrate to make one recipe, how many cans should be purchased to serve *n* people?

This example has two questions. One equation can be written to relate the number of recipes as a function of the number of people [$R = f(p)$], and a second equation to give the number of cans of concentrate as a function of the number of recipes [$C = g(R)$]. Using these equations you can find an equation that gives cans of concentrate as a function of the number of people.

Notice that the graphs of all proportional situations are straight lines that pass through the origin. Students will find that the slope of these lines is also the rate between the two variables.

Functions and Measurement

Geometric formulas relate various dimensions, areas, and volumes of shapes. Each of these formulas involves at least one functional relationship.

Consider any familiar formula for measuring a geometric shape. For example, $V = \frac{1}{3}\pi r^2 h$ is the formula for the volume of a circular cone. Here the volume is related to both the height of the cone and the radius. If the radius is held constant, the volume is a function of the height. Similarly, for a fixed height, the volume is a function of the radius. Figure 15.22 shows how both of these ideas might be illustrated and the graph that would be associated with each.

Maximum/Minimum Problems

Many real situations revolve around the issue of determining the best price, the greatest profit, the least expense, the shortest time, and so on. A general method of answering these questions is to establish a functional relationship and look for the maximum or minimum values in the graph and/or in a table of values. Earlier, in Figure 15.16 (p. 279), we saw that rectangles with a perimeter of 24 units have a maximum area at the top of the length versus area curve, where the length is 6 or the rectangle is a 6×6 square. The following activity is similarly related to measurement.

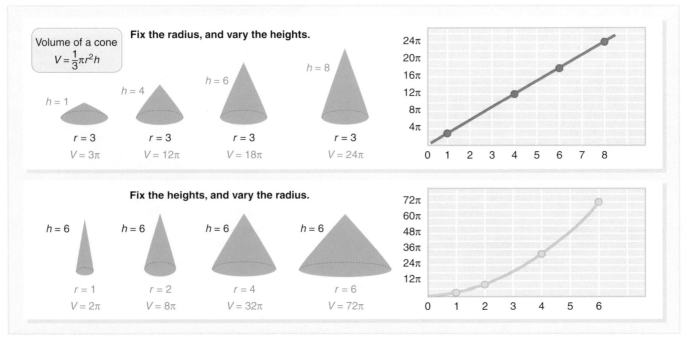

FIGURE 15.22 Volume as a function of height or radius. If the radius is fixed, changes in height produce a straight-line graph, but if the height is fixed, changes in the radius produce a curved line.

Designing the Largest Box

Begin with a rectangular sheet of cardboard, and from each corner, cut a square. Fold up the four resulting flaps, and tape them together to form an open box. The volume of the box will vary, depending on the size of the squares. (The sheet in Figure 15.23 measures 9 by 12 inches.) Write a formula that gives the volume of the box as a function of the size of the cutout squares. Use the function to determine what size the squares should be to create the box with the largest volume.

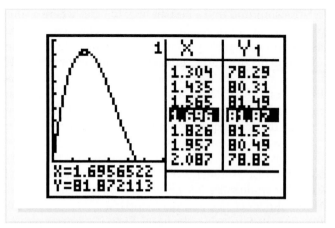

FIGURE 15.24 A graphing calculator plot of the volume function for the problem in Figure 15.23.

In "Designing the Largest Box," the resulting equation is a cubic or third-power polynomial. However, any seventh-grade student who knows that the volume of a box is the product of the three dimensions could develop this formula. A table of values and a graph are easily produced on a graphing calculator.

As with some other contexts we have looked at, this function is defined for values that do not make sense in the context. The largest square that could be cut out is 4.5 inches on a side, in which case the squares from adjacent corners would touch and there would be no flap to turn up. But the function will produce "negative volumes" for values between 4.5 and 6 and positive volumes for values of the variable greater than 6. The equation representation of the function makes sense in this context *only* for values between 0 and 4.5. This is a useful discussion for students to help them realize that a mathematical model cannot be completely divorced from the context. Figure 15.24 shows

the graph on a calculator. The tracer is near the point at which a maximum volume will occur.

Functions from Scatter Plot Data

Often in the real world, phenomena are observed that seem to suggest a functional relationship but not necessarily as clean or as well defined as the situations we have observed so far. In these cases, the data are generally plotted on a graph to produce a scatter plot of points. A visual inspection of the graphed data may suggest what kind of relationship, if any, exists. When a functional relationship seems to be suggested, an equation can be sought that defines a function approximating the data.

In Chapter 22, data representing the heights and weights of people are plotted, one point for each person in the sample. As we might expect, weights tend to increase as people get taller. On page 470 an algorithm is described that will produce a straight line that "best" approximates a collection of accurately plotted points without doing any calculations. Depending on the skills of the students, the equation of the line can be determined. Alternatively, a graphing calculator will compute the equation of the same line.

Not all scatter plots will show a straight-line relationship. Suppose students were to rank lemonade formulas on a scale of 1 to 10. If the only change in the formula was the amount of sugar used, the ratings might go up for a while until the lemonade became too sweet and then the ratings would decline. A parabola, rather than a straight line, might be a better approximating curve. Graphing calculators can also find best-fitting curves, although the actual computations are too difficult, even at the high school level.

Students in the middle grades might easily gather data found in an interesting context and perform this same type of analysis—that is, plot the data, look for a possible

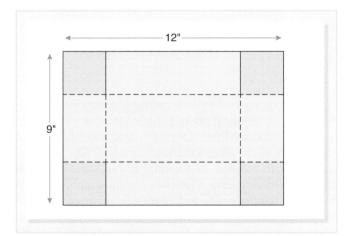

FIGURE 15.23 If squares are cut from a 9-by-12-inch piece of cardboard so that the four flaps can be folded up, what size squares should be cut so that the volume of the box is the largest possible?

relationship, and find a best-fit line. In cases where a simple equation is not readily accessible technology can be used to produce the equation. There seems little reason to stop students from using graphing calculators or curve-fitting software to see that methods do exist for finding best-fit curves. The calculator permits students to see what these best-fit curves and equations may look like, even though the techniques of finding the equations without technology will have to wait.

Consider gathering information that may be of personal interest to students. For example, do grades earned in social studies predict grades earned in mathematics? What about science and mathematics? What would the functional relationships be here? Even if a scatter plot of some information that was gathered showed no particular trend, functional language could still be employed—for example, "The grades on last week's mathematics test do *not* appear to be a function of the number of hours' sleep students got the night before the test."

Data can also be obtained from sports records, census reports, the business section of the newspaper, and many other sources. As noted toward the end of Chapter 8, the Internet has lots of sites where data can be found.

NCTM Standards "When doing experiments or dealing with real data, students may encounter 'messy data,' for which a line or a curve may not be an exact fit. They will need experience with such situations and assistance from the teacher to develop their ability to find a function that fits the data well enough to be useful as a prediction tool" (p. 228).

Fun Experiments

There are all sorts of experiments that students can invent to see what functional relationships, if any, exist between two variables.

activity 15.18

Fun Function Experiments

The task is to try to develop a functional relationship between two variables by conducting an experiment. Data should be entered in a table and plotted on a graph. The goal is to determine an equation (function) that can be used to make predictions. A graphing calculator or computer will be a useful tool for curve fitting, although for some experiments that may not be necessary. Students should explain which is the independent variable and which the dependent. Here are some ideas for experiments:*

- How long would it take for 100 students standing in a row to complete a wave like the ones done at football games? Experiment with different numbers of students from 5 to 25. Can the relationship predict how many students it would take for a given wave time?
- How far will a Matchbox car roll off of a ramp, based on the height the ramp is raised?
- How is the flight time of a paper airplane affected by the number of paper clips attached to the nose of the plane?
- What is the relationship between the number of dominoes in a row and the time required for them to fall over? (Use multiples of 100 dominoes.)
- Make wadded newspaper balls using different numbers of sheets of newspaper. Rubber bands help hold the paper in a ball. What is the relationship between the number of sheets and the distance the ball can be thrown?
- If colored water is dropped on a paper towel, what is the relationship between the number of drops and the diameter of the spot? Is the relationship different for different brands of towels?
- How much weight can a toothpick bridge hold? Lay toothpicks in a bunch to span a 2-inch gap between two boards. From the toothpicks, hang a bag or other container into which weights can be added until the toothpicks break. Begin with only one toothpick.

Experiments like these are fun. They also provide an opportunity for students to engage in experimental design. Students need practice in identifying independent and dependent variables, controlling experiments for other variables, measuring and recording results, and analyzing data. This is a perfect blend of mathematics and science.

Assessment Notes Students' understanding of functions is an extension of their knowledge of growing patterns. Most importantly, you want them to see that all five of the representations for a function are nothing more than ways of looking at the same function through different eyes. Can they use the graph, table, or formula interchangeably to find specific values of the function? Can they use these various representations to discuss what is happening within the context of the function? Be sure to distinguish between the less important skill of drawing an accurate graph and understanding what the graph represents. Try to use graphing technology to avoid penalizing students who do not have good motor skills for making graphs. ■

---

*Most of these experiments were inspired by the article "Algebra: Real-Life Investigations in a Lab Setting" (McCoy, 1997), which contains additional ideas and useful suggestions.

Generalizations About Functions

It is useful to return to the notion that algebraic thinking involves observing and making generalizations from mathematical experiences. As students explore functions in a variety of contexts, they can begin to take note of specific attributes that groups of functions have in common. For example, we have already noted that certain functions are linear—they have graphs that are straight lines. Linear functions can also be described in terms of their formulas. Although the analysis of functions will continue in high school, students in the middle grades should begin to look at some general ideas about functions.

Analysis of Rate of Change

An analysis of change is the fourth goal in the NCTM Algebra standard. (See Appendix A.) Change can be found in all functional relationships. Is the profit increasing quickly or slowly? How is it increasing? Does it stay the same for any period? Generalizations about change can help us better understand the situations that the functions represent.

Graphs and Contexts

It is both fun and profitable to interpret and construct graphs related to real situations but without using any specific data, equations, or numbers. The advantage of activities such as these is the focus on how a graph can express the relationships involved.

activity **15.19**

Sketch a Graph

Sketch a graph for each of these situations. No numbers or formulas are to be used.

a. The temperature of a frozen dinner from 30 minutes before it is removed from the freezer until it is removed from the microwave and placed on the table. (Consider time 0 to be the moment the dinner is removed from the freezer.)
b. The value of a 1970 Volkswagen Beetle from the time it was purchased to the present. (It was kept by a loving owner and is in top condition.)
c. The level of water in the bathtub from the time you begin to fill it to the time it is completely empty after your bath.
d. Profit in terms of number of items sold.
e. The height of a baseball in terms of time from when it is thrown straight up to the time it hits the ground.
f. The speed of the baseball in the situation in (e).

 *pause and reflect*

Stop for a moment and sketch graphs for each of the situations in the last activity.

In a classroom, it is fun to have students sketch their graphs on transparencies without identifying which situation is being graphed (no labels on the graphs). Let students examine the graphs to see if they can determine which situation goes with each graph that is presented. Examine the graphs for one situation drawn by several students to decide which graph represents a situation best and why. Figure 15.25 contains six graphs that match the six situations described in the "Sketch a Graph" activity. Can you match these graphs with the six situations?

Graphs and Rate of Change

Notice that the analysis of the graphs focuses on how the graphs increase or decrease and how steeply or gradually. A graph is a picture of the rate of change of one variable in terms of the other. Essentially, graphs can only have one

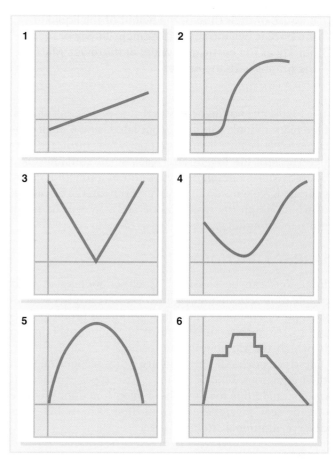

FIGURE 15.25 Match each graph with the situations described in Activity 15.19. Talk about what is happening in each case.

FIGURE 15.26 Seven ways that graphs can change. A given graph may have combinations of these characteristics.

of the seven characteristics shown in Figure 15.26 or some combination of these. In the first three segments, the graphs are increasing, either steadily (linearly), with an increasing rate, or with a decreasing rate. The three decreasing options can be characterized the same way. The final option is no change, indicated by a horizontal graph.

The types of change shown in Figure 15.26 will be seen in the following activity that focuses on rates of change as seen in graphs, again, without any numbers being involved.

activity 15.20

Bottles and Volume Graphs

Figure 15.27 shows six bottles and six graphs. Assume that the bottles are filled at a constant rate. Because of their shapes, the height of the liquid in the bottles will increase either more slowly or more quickly as the bottle gets wider or narrower. Match the graphs with the bottles.

Find some bottles or glasses that have different shapes. One place to look is in the science lab. Using a small container such as a medicine cup, pour water into each bottle. Measure the height after each small containerful is poured. Make a graph of the heights as a function of the volume. If students do an actual experiment, the discussion of which graph fits which bottle and why will be much more meaningful.

Linear Functions

Functions can be classified by either looking at their graphs and/or at their equations. We have already seen an example of a parabola in the fixed perimeter problem (Figure 15.16) and also an example of an exponential function in which the variable in the formula was an exponent. These categories of functions are easily recognized from their equations. One of the most basic types of functions has a straight line for a graph—a *linear* function. We have already seen several examples of these. Linear functions deserve additional attention here.

Slope

In Figure 15.26, the first three graphs are increasing, meaning they increase from left to right. Graphs tell us how the variable represented by the vertical axis changes

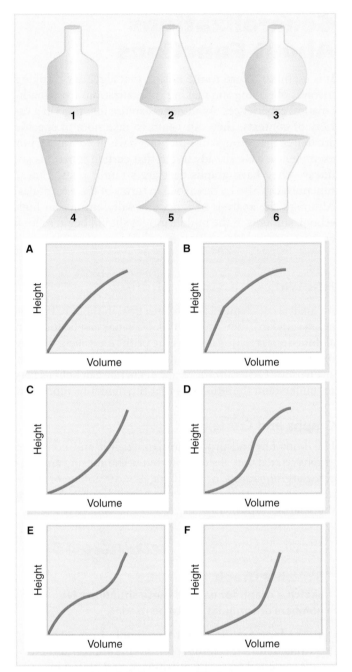

FIGURE 15.27 If the bottles are filled at a constant rate, match the graphs with the bottles.

as the variable on the horizontal axis increases. For straight lines the rate of change is constant. The rate at which the function values increase or decrease is evident in the steepness of the line, either up or down. The "steepness" of the line is called the *slope* of the line.

It is very useful to be able to assign a number to the attribute of slope. The convention for doing so is based on the ideas of *rise* and *run* between any two points on the line. As illustrated in Figure 15.28, the rise is the vertical change from one point to a point to the right on the line—positive for upward changes and negative for downward changes. The run is the horizontal distance from the left

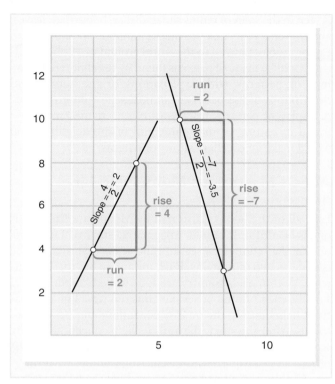

FIGURE 15.28 The slope of a line = rise ÷ run.

point to the right point. Slope is then defined as *rise ÷ run*, the ratio of the vertical change to the horizontal change. The convention is that vertical lines have no slope.

To find the rate of change, or the slope, you must determine how much y changes when x increases by 1. If a line contains the points (2, 4) and (3, −5), then you can see that as x increases by 1, y decreases by 9. So the rate of change is −9. For the points (4, 3) and (7, 9), you can see that when x increases by 3, y increases by 6. Therefore, an increase of 1 in x results in a change of 2 in y. Upon further exploration, you (and your students) will begin to notice that you can find the rate of change or slope by finding the difference in the y values and dividing by the difference in the x values.

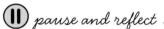 *pause and reflect* ———————

Can you see from the definition of slope that a horizontal line has a slope of 0?

Linear Equations

The equations of all linear functions can be put into the form: $y = mx + b$. The fixed value m in this formula is the slope of the line or the rate of change. Thus, if the equation is $P = .65H − 35$ (Brian's hot-dog profit function), the slope of the line is .65. If the slope and any one point on the line are known, then the equation of the line can also be found.

The value of a function where the graph crosses the vertical axis is important because it often represents the initial value of the function. For Brian's hot dogs, this value is the profit when no hot dogs have been sold. We can find out where the graph of any equation will cross the y-axis (or whatever the dependent variable is) by substituting 0 for x in the equation. (Do you see why?) In the case of the equation $y = mx + b$, substituting $x = 0$ tells us that $y = b$. That is, in the equation of a straight line b tells where the line will cross the y-axis. Brian's profit function began at negative 35 on the P-axis. That is, when he had sold 0 hot dogs, he was $35 in the hole.

Sometimes an equation may not look like the familiar form $y = mx + b$. For example, in the fixed perimeter example, if the L and W represent the length and width, and the perimeter is 24, then $2L + 2W = 24$ is an equation that relates the length to the width. If we solve this equation for W, we end up with $W = (24 − 2L)/2$ or $W = 12 − L$. This can also be written as $W = −1L + 12$, a linear equation with a slope of negative 1 that crosses the W-axis or vertical axis at +12. The graph of this equation is found in Figure 15.16 (p. 279).

In general we can say that any equation in two variables will have a straight-line graph if both variables appear only to the first power (after all multiplications have been done.)

Parallel and Perpendicular Lines

Consider the situation of Larry and Mary, each earning $3 a week for the summer months. Mary starts the summer $5 dollars in the hole and Larry already has $2. When will Mary and Larry have the same amount of money? In week 3, how much more money does Larry have? How much more does he have in week 7? In any week, what is the difference in their wealth? The rate of increase in wealth is the same for Larry and Mary and the graphs of their wealth would go up at the same rate; that is, the slopes would be the same.

In general, if two lines have the same slope, it means that the lines are either increasing or decreasing at exactly the same rate and the two lines are parallel. We can tell that the graphs of $y = 3x + 2$ (Larry's money) and $y = 3x − 5$ (Mary's money) are parallel without even making the graphs.

Slopes can also tell us when two lines are perpendicular, but it is less obvious. A little bit of analysis using similar triangles will show that for perpendicular lines, the slope of one is the negative reciprocal of the other.

The point here is not to get you deeply into symbolic manipulations and formulas that may dredge up negative memories of an old algebra class. What is important to see is that an analysis of change, especially as seen in graphs, is well within reach of middle school students. Furthermore, this analysis can easily provide the necessary foundation for a study of linear functions in general. An understanding of rate of change—the slope of a graph—is also a significant factor in any mathematical analysis that involves functions and change. We should help students early on to develop an understanding of this fundamental concept.

Mathematical Modeling

Kaput (1999) defines *modeling* as the process of beginning with real phenomena and an attempt to mathematize them. That means that, in some way, mathematics is used to both record the phenomena and search for patterns or regularities that can then be expressed using mathematical models such as equations, tables, and graphs. The models not only allow for a good description of the phenomena but also permit predictions without the necessity of actually engaging in further experiments. In Kaput's description of algebraic thinking, modeling reflects algebra as a "web of languages" that permeates all the other aspects of mathematics.

This does not mean that modeling should be kept until last in the development of algebraic thinking. In fact, we have already seen many examples and opportunities for modeling. For example, the relationships derived from the various real-world situations (gas remaining in the car, dimensions of a pen against a barn, the sale of widgets, finding the box with maximum volume, and exploring the relationships between two children's amounts of money) are all phenomena that can be modeled using the various representations of functions.

How is modeling used to predict? Take the example of selling widgets marked up at some percentage over whole-sale. Once a formula is derived for a given price and markup, it can be used to identify what the profit would be at different sales levels. Furthermore, it is relatively easy to make adjustments in the price and the markup percentage, allowing for further predictions. That is, the model allows us to see points in the function (in the table or on the graph) that we may not have observed in the real phenomenon and also permits changes mathematically that were not part of the original experiment. The case of the two runners in the NCTM applet (see Figure 15.21) allows us to control the speed and starting points for each runner and see the results for each trial. Using the mathematical model is certainly more efficient than running every possible race.

Creating the functional relationships and using them to observe, find out, or predict is all part of the integrating aspect of algebraic thinking known as mathematical modeling.

Literature Connections

Many teachers find pattern explorations sufficiently interesting that they may not think of using literature to provide a springboard for student explorations. However, here are three examples of books that are excellent beginnings for patterns and chart building.

Pattern
Pluckrose, 1988

This book brings pattern from the real world to the classroom in the form of brilliantly colored photographs. Pattern is seen in the soles of tennis shoes, dishes, butterflies, leaves, and flowers. The book provides a jumping-off point for an exploration of pattern in the world around us. A photo collage could be made of patterns found by the children. Drawings of patterns with explanations of the source and descriptions of the patterns can be assembled into a book. A display of patterns from your class activities and those found in nature, in the home, and in the neighborhood would make an excellent show for parents.

Anno's Mysterious Multiplying Jar
Anno & Anno, 1983

Like all of the books illustrated by Mitsumasa Anno, this one is beautiful. It tells an imaginative story of a mysterious jar that contains a sea. On the sea is one island. The island has two mountains. Each mountain has three countries. Within each country are four walled kingdoms. . . . Finally, each of nine boxes contains ten jars. The illustrations help develop the quickly expanding numbers of factorials. After the story, the authors help conceptualize the size of each factorial with arrays of tiny stars and suggest other ways to explore this fascinating number pattern.

Children of almost any age are likely to be interested in exploring the factorial concept due to the large numbers. A simple idea is to create a multiplying story and illustrate it or collect objects to show how many items are involved. Another idea is to examine nested situations in the real world even if they are not factorials. For example, talk to a grocery store about how small items such as chewing gum are shipped to the store. There will likely be cartons in which there are smaller boxes. In each box there may possibly be packages. Each package might contain several packs of gum and then finally single sticks. How many in all is determined by the same multiplication process.

Anno's Magic Seeds
Anno, 1994

Another wonderful book by Mitsumasa Anno, *Magic Seeds* develops a pattern that changes throughout, becoming a bit more elaborate with each change. A wise man gives Jack two magic seeds. He is told to eat one and plant the other. The seed he eats will keep him from hunger for a whole year, and the planted seed will produce two new seeds by the following year. Several years later, Jack decides to plant both seeds rather than eating one. This new pattern continues until he marries, has a child, and starts to sell seeds.

At each stage of the story, there is an opportunity to develop a chart and extend the current pattern into the future. Austin and Thompson (1997) outline in considerable detail how they used the story to develop patterns and charts with sixth- and seventh-grade students. Their article is worth looking up. However, you will have no problem developing good pattern lessons from this book without any assistance. ■

Writing to Learn

1. Kaput lists five types of algebraic thinking. Rather than list each of these, describe algebraic thinking in no more than three sentences in a manner that encompasses Kaput's main ideas and the spirit of this chapter.
2. Describe true/false sentences and open sentences. How are each used in the early grades?
3. What is the correct meaning of the equal sign? How does the use of true/false and open sentences help students understand this symbol?
4. Explain what is meant by *relational thinking* in the context of how students might solve an open sentence. Give an example.
5. Distinguish between the two uses of a variable. Give examples.
6. Explain how to solve the equation $4x + 3 = x + 12$ using the pan-balance approach.
7. Give examples of conjectures that students might make about operations in the number system. As students try to justify these conjectures, what are three levels of thinking that you will likely observe?
8. Make up three pattern strips showing repeating patterns for some common objects that might be found in the classroom. Label each using an A, B, C scheme. No two schemes should be alike, but all should use the same materials. What is the core of each pattern? What will be the twenty-fifth element of each?
9. What is a *recursive relationship?* Where in a table for a growing pattern would you look for the recursive relationship? What would it mean in terms of the pattern itself? In terms of growing patterns, what is meant by a *functional relationship?*
10. How can you tell from the recursive relationship whether the graph of the growing pattern will be straight or curved?
11. For pattern (d) in Figure 15.8, find two different ways to count the number of rods used to make six windows. Use one of your methods to determine a functional relationship for this pattern. For this example, why does the recursive relationship indicate that the function is linear?
12. Describe in your own words the five different representations of a function and how they actually all represent the same functional relationship.
13. Make up a real-world situation that defines a functional relationship. Use your example to do the following:
    a. Sketch a possible graph of the relationship.
    b. State the relationship using the language of functions.
    c. Build a table with numbers that might go with your relationship. Your table should reflect the same relationship as in your graph.
    d. Explain how your graph meets the formal definition of a function.
14. A scatter plot graph of data is not a function. Why not? How are functions developed from these sorts of data? Why would you want to have a function built from data?
15. Sketch some graphs showing different rates of change. Explain the idea of increasing or decreasing rates of change using your graphs. In Figure 15.26, how do the three increasing graphs differ in terms of rate of change?
16. Describe the slope of a straight line. How is a number assigned to the attribute of slope?
17. What is mathematical modeling?

For Discussion and Exploration

1. The idea of having students make generalizations about the number system is a relatively new idea for the elementary curriculum. Do you think that there is a practical value in beginning this generalization process in the primary grades? Are the generalizations themselves (conjectures) as important as the reasoning that goes into trying to justify these conjectures? Is the whole area of algebraic generalizations reflected in any way in your state's standards? If not, should it be?
2. The Disney film *Donald Duck in Mathmagic Land* is a classic animation originally released for TV in 1959 and now available in VHS (see Amazon.com or ebay.com). The film explores pattern and other interesting ideas in mathematics in a timeless manner. Your mathematics education is not quite complete if you have not seen it. Find ways to use this 27-minute animated film with students from third grade to high school. Or just watch it with some classmates and discuss its potential for use in school.
3. Develop a lesson or lessons for middle school students using a graphing calculator to explore the function concept. If the students do not have access to graphing calculators, you can (a) use only one calculator and a display screen or monitor so that students can at least see the graphs, tables, and functions and interact with the lesson, or (b) ask your college instructor to arrange with Texas Instruments to loan a classroom set of graphing calculators.

Recommendations for Further Reading

Carpenter, T. P., Franke, M. L., & Levi, L. (2003). *Thinking mathematically: Integrating arithmetic & algebra in elementary school.* Portsmouth, NH: Heinemann.

This book is a detailed look at helping children in the primary grades develop the thinking and create the generalizations of algebra. The included CD shows classroom-based examples of the ideas discussed. Many of the ideas about equality, true/false sentences, and generalizations discussed in this chapter were influenced by this book.

Coburn, T. G. (1993). *Patterns: Addenda series, grades K–6.* Reston, VA: National Council of Teachers of Mathematics.

This is one of the best resource books on patterns for the K–6 grades. Examples of virtually every type of pattern activity are included. What you get in this book are not only good activities but also a longitudinal view of how pattern can easily progress from kindergarten to grade 6. (The same activities are found in each of the grade-level books.)

Driscol, M. (1999). *Fostering algebraic thinking: A guide for teachers, grades 6–10.* Portsmouth, NH: Heinemann.

For the indicated grade levels, Driscol's book has become a standard. It is easy to read and includes many excellent problems and explorations. You will find it to be a good expansion of the ideas in this chapter.

Fulton, B. S., & Lombard, B. (2001). *The pattern and function connection.* Emeryville, CA: Key Curriculum Press.

This resource provides the teacher with clear lesson plans and Blackline Masters for a complete development of functions. Each new idea is developed from a pattern. After learning how to graph functions, students learn about slopes, intercepts, and nonlinear functions. Most of the book is accessible to middle school students. This is an extremely practical and innovative approach to the topic.

NCTM's *Navigations Series*

Greenes, C., Cavanagh, M., Dacey, L., Findell, C., & Small, M. (2001). *Navigating through algebra in prekindergarten–grade 2.* Reston, VA: National Council of Teachers of Mathematics.

Cuevas, G. J., & Yeatts, K. (2001). *Navigating through algebra in grades 3–5.* Reston, VA: National Council of Teachers of Mathematics.

Friel, S., Rachlin, S., & Doyle, D. (2001). *Navigating through algebra in grades 6–8.* Reston, VA: National Council of Teachers of Mathematics.

If you want some high quality algebra activities that are directly reflective of *Principles and Standards*, it would be hard to go wrong with any of these three books from NCTM's *Navigations* Series. The authors discuss the standards in the introductory portion of the book and then follow with representative activities presented with just the right level of detail. Each book includes a CD-ROM with Blackline Masters for the activities, several very nice applets, and the full text of selected articles related to the topic.

Joram, E., Hartman, C., & Trafton, P. R. (2004). "As people get older, they get taller": An integrated unit on measurement, linear relationships, and data analysis. *Teaching Children Mathematics, 10,* 344–351.

The article delivers what the title says! This is a wonderful unit for second grade showing how students used real data to answer the question of how much taller were students in their grade compared to students in the fourth grade. They even use the idea of a best-fit line to create a function from the scatter plot data. Great!

Mann, R. L. (2004). Balancing act: The truth behind the equals sign. *Teaching Children Mathematics, 11,* 65–69.

Mann shows us how she guided students' development of equations through a series of activities involving real balance beams, visual balance problems, and open sentences. The activities are conducted with third graders.

Schifter, D. (1999). Reasoning about operations: Early algebraic thinking, grades K through 6. In L. Stiff & F. Curcio (Eds.), *Developing mathematical reasoning in grades K–12* (pp. 62–81). Reston, VA: National Council of Teachers of Mathematics.

Found in the NCTM Yearbook devoted to reasoning, Schifter's chapter focuses on the reasoning that prepares students for algebra. Classroom examples from solving story problems in grades 1 and 2 to reasoning about properties of the number system provide an insight into the type of reasoning called algebraic thinking. Schifter also provides a compelling rationale for engaging students in this way.

Van Dyke, F., & Tomback, J. (2005). Collaborating to introduce algebra. *Mathematics Teaching in the Middle School, 10,* 236–242.

The authors share details of a sixth-grade unit that includes a heavy emphasis on graphing and an understanding of rate of change. An explicit effort is made to help students connect the representations of equation, table, graph, and language.

Online Resources

Suggested Applets and Web Links

Algebra Balance Scales and Algebra Balance Scales—Negative
http://nlvm.usu.edu/en/nav/frames_asid_201_g_4_t_2.html

Linear equations are presented on a two-pan balance with variables on each side. The user can solve equations in the same way as described in the text. The Negative version uses balloons for negative values and negative variables.

Function Machine
www.fi.uu.nl.toepassingen/02022/toepassing_wisweb.en.html

A function machine is shown with a secret rule. Numbers are put into the machine and the output is recorded in a table. The goal is to determine the function rule. A very good example of many function machine applets you might find.

Graph Sketcher
www.shodor.org/interactiv/activities/sketcher/index.html

Works very much like a graphing calculator for graphing functions of any type. A good demonstration tool for making graphs of equations.

Learning About Rate of Change
http://standards.nctm.org/document/eexamples/chap6/6.2/index.htm

A nice interactive lesson in which the cost per minute to make a phone call (the slope) can be adjusted and then the graph of the cost can be displayed. A slider helps connect points on the two graphs.

Pan Balance—Shapes
http://illuminations.nctm.org/tools/tool_detail.aspx?id=33#

With each problem, four shapes are assigned unknown values. By stacking shapes on the two balance pans, the user attempts to balance the scale and then create additional balances. A numbers version and an expressions version are extensions of this applet.

Slope Slider
www.shodor.org/interactivate/activities/slopeslider/index.html

A good interactive tool for illustrating the meaning of slope and the y-intercept for a linear equation of the form $y = mx + b$. The user can use a slider to change the value of m or b and see the graph change dynamically.

Understanding Distance, Speed, and Time
http://standards.nctm.org/document/eexamples/chap5/5.2/index.htm

The speed and starting position of two runners can be set. Runners can even go in opposite directions. Graphs of each runner are created dynamically as the runners are set in motion.

An additional list of books and articles related to the ideas in this chapter can be found on the Companion Web site at **www.ablongman.com/vandewalle6e.**

chapter 16

Developing Fraction Concepts

Fractions have always represented a considerable challenge for students, even into the middle grades. Results of NAEP testing have consistently shown that students have a very weak understanding of fraction concepts (Wearne & Kouba, 2000). This lack of understanding is then translated into untold difficulties with fraction computation, decimal and percent concepts, the use of fractions in measurement, and ratio and proportion concepts.

Traditional programs for primary grades typically offer students limited exposure to fractions with most of the work on fraction development occurring in the third and/or fourth grades. Few, if any, programs provide students with adequate time or experiences to help them with this complex area of the curriculum. State objectives are quite varied with respect to fractions. This chapter explores a conceptual development of fraction concepts that can help students at any level construct a firm foundation, preparing them for the skills that are later built on these ideas.

▼ Big Ideas

1. Fractional parts are equal shares or equal-sized portions of a whole or unit. A unit can be an object or a collection of things. More abstractly, the unit is counted as 1. On the number line, the distance from 0 to 1 is the unit.

2. Fractional parts have special names that tell how many parts of that size are needed to make the whole. For example, *thirds* require three parts to make a whole.

3. The more fractional parts used to make a whole, the smaller the parts. For example, eighths are smaller than fifths.

4. The denominator of a fraction indicates by what number the whole has been divided in order to produce the type of part under consideration. Thus, the denominator is a divisor. In practical terms, the denominator names the kind of fractional part that is under consideration. The numerator of a fraction counts or tells how many of the fractional parts

(of the type indicated by the denominator) are under consideration. Therefore, the numerator is a multiplier—it indicates a multiple of the given fractional part.

5. Two equivalent fractions are two ways of describing the same amount by using different-sized fractional parts. For example, in the fraction $\frac{6}{8}$, if the eighths are taken in twos, then each pair of eighths is a fourth. The six-eighths then can be seen to be three-fourths.

Mathematics Content Connections

What students bring to the topic of fractions is an understanding of fair sharing. So there is a minimal connection to division of whole numbers. Other whole-number ideas actually interfere in early fraction development. However, fraction concepts are intimately connected to other areas of the curriculum.

- **Fraction Computation** (Chapter 17): Without a firm conceptual understanding of fractions, computation with fractions is relegated to rules without reasons.

- **Decimals and Percents** (Chapter 18): A key idea for students is that decimal notation and percent notation are simply two other methods of representing fractions. By making the connections between these three representations, the load of new ideas to be learned is significantly reduced.

- **Ratio and Proportion** (Chapter 19): A part-to-whole concept of a fraction is just one form of ratio. However, because the same fraction notation is often used for other ratios (e.g., the ratio of boys to girls in the room is 3 to 5 or $\frac{3}{5}$), it is important to understand what a fraction is so that concepts are not confused. Equivalent ratio concepts are very similar to equivalent fraction ideas.

In addition to the clear content connections just listed, fractions are used frequently in measurement (Chapter 20) and in probability (Chapter 23).

Sharing and the Concept of Fractional Parts

The first goal in the development of fractions should be to help children construct the idea of *fractional parts of the whole*—the parts that result when the whole or unit has been partitioned into *equal-sized portions* or *fair shares.*

Children seem to understand the idea of separating a quantity into two or more parts to be shared fairly among friends. They eventually make connections between the idea of fair shares and fractional parts. Sharing tasks are, therefore, good places to begin the development of fractions.

Sharing Tasks

Considerable research has been done with children from first through eighth grades to determine how they go about the process of forming fair shares and how the tasks posed to students influence their responses (e.g., Empson, 2002; Lamon, 1996; Mack, 2001; Pothier & Sawada, 1983).

Sharing tasks are generally posed in the form of a simple story problem. *Suppose there are four square brownies to be shared among three children so that each child gets the same amount. How much (or show how much) will each child get?* Task difficulty changes with the numbers involved, the types of things to be shared (regions such as brownies, discrete objects such as pieces of chewing gum), and the presence or use of a model.

Students initially perform sharing tasks (division) by distributing items one at a time. When this process leaves leftover pieces, it is much easier to think of sharing them fairly if the items can be subdivided. Typical "regions" to share are brownies (rectangles), sandwiches, pizzas, crackers, cake, candy bars, and so on. The problems and variations that follow are adapted from Empson (2002).

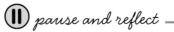

Four children are sharing ten brownies so that each one will get the same amount. How much can each child have?

Problem difficulty is determined by the relationship between the number of things to be shared and the number of sharers. Because children's initial strategies for sharing involve halving, a good place to begin is with two, four, or even eight sharers. For ten brownies and four sharers, many children will deal out two to each child and then halve each of the remaining brownies. (See Figure 16.1.)

Consider these variations in numbers:

5 brownies shared with 2 children

2 brownies shared with 4 children

5 brownies shared with 4 children

4 brownies shared with 8 children

3 brownies shared with 4 children

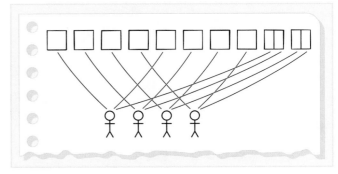

FIGURE 16.1 Ten brownies shared with four children.

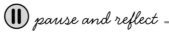

Try drawing pictures for each of the preceding sharing tasks. Which do you think is most difficult? Which of these represent essentially the same degree of difficulty? What other tasks involving two, four, or eight sharers would you consider as similar, easier, or more difficult than these?

When the numbers allow for some items to be distributed whole (five shared with two), some students will first share whole items and then cut up the leftovers. Others will slice every piece in half and then distribute the halves. When there are more sharers than items, some partitioning must happen at the beginning of the solution process.

When students who are still using a halving strategy try to share five things among four children, they will eventually get down to two halves to give to four children. For some, the solution is to cut each half in half; that is, "each child gets a whole (or two halves) and a half of a half."

It is a progression to move to three or six sharers because this will force children to confront their halving strategies.

pause and reflect ——————————————

Try solving the following variations using drawings. Can you do them in different ways?

4 pizzas shared with 6 children

7 pizzas shared with 6 children

5 pizzas shared with 3 children

To subdivide a region into a number of parts other than a power of two (four, eight, etc.) requires an odd subdivision at some point. This is difficult for young children.

Several types of sharing solutions might be observed. Figure 16.2 shows some different approaches.

Use a variety of representations for these problems. The items to be shared can be drawn on worksheets as

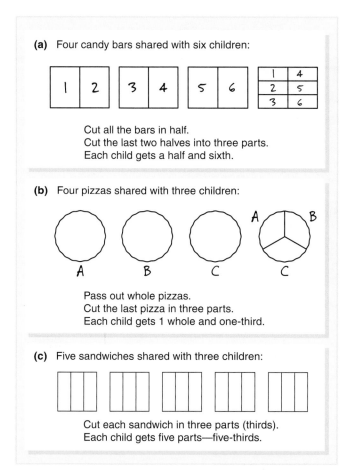

(a) Four candy bars shared with six children:

Cut all the bars in half.
Cut the last two halves into three parts.
Each child gets a half and sixth.

(b) Four pizzas shared with three children:

Pass out whole pizzas.
Cut the last pizza in three parts.
Each child gets 1 whole and one-third.

(c) Five sandwiches shared with three children:

Cut each sandwich in three parts (thirds).
Each child gets five parts—five-thirds.

FIGURE 16.2 Three different sharing processes.

rectangles or circles along with a statement of the problem. Another possibility is to cut out construction paper circles or squares. Some students may need to cut and physically distribute the pieces. Students can use connecting cubes to make bars that they can separate into pieces. Or they can use more traditional fraction models such as circular "pie" pieces.

Sharing Tasks and Fraction Language

During the discussions of students' solutions (and discussions are essential!) is a good time to introduce the vocabulary of fractional parts. This can be quite casual and, at least for younger children, should not involve any fraction symbolism. When a brownie or other region has been broken into equal shares, simply say, "We call these *fourths*. The whole is cut into four parts. All of the parts are the same size—fourths."

Children need to be aware of two aspects or components of fractional parts: (1) the number of parts and

(2) the equality of the parts (in size, not necessarily in shape). Emphasize that the number of parts that make up a whole determines the name of the fractional parts or shares. They will be familiar with halves but should quickly learn to describe thirds, fourths, fifths, and so on.

Models for Fractions

There is substantial evidence to suggest that the use of models in fraction tasks is important (Cramer & Henry, 2002). Unfortunately, many teachers in the upper grades, where manipulative materials are not as common, fail to use models for fraction development. Models can help students clarify ideas that are often confused in a purely symbolic mode. Sometimes it is useful to do the same activity with two quite different models; from the viewpoint of the students, the activity will be quite different. In this chapter we will distinguish among three types of models: area or region models, length models, and set models.

Region or Area Models

In the discussion of sharing, all of the tasks involved sharing something that could be cut into smaller parts. The fractions are based on parts of an area or region. This is a good place to begin and is almost essential when doing sharing tasks. There are many good region models, as shown in Figure 16.3.

Circular "pie" piece models are by far the most commonly used area model. (See the Blackline Masters for masters of pie models.) The main advantage of the circular region is that it emphasizes the amount that is remaining to make up a whole. The other models in Figure 16.3 are more flexible and allow for different-sized units or wholes. Paper grids, several of which can be found in the Blackline Masters, are especially flexible and do not require management of materials.

Commercial versions of area models are available in a wide variety, including circular and rectangular regions. Many of these have fraction labels stamped on them. Printing fraction labels on the pieces may seem useful at first but there are two significant disadvantages. First, the label denies students the opportunity to reflect on the size of the piece relative to the whole and to decide for themselves what the fraction is. Second, labeling the pieces presumes which shape is the whole and removes flexibility from the materials.

Length or Measurement Models

With measurement models, lengths are compared instead of areas. Either lines are drawn and subdivided, or physical materials are compared on the basis of length, as shown

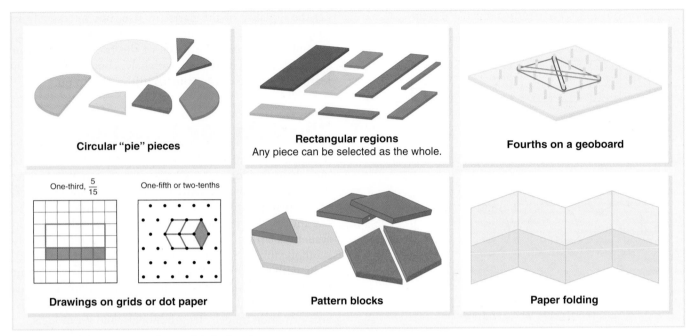

FIGURE 16.3 Area or region models for fractions.

in Figure 16.4. Manipulative versions provide more opportunity for trial and error and for exploration.

Fraction strips are a teacher-made version of Cuisenaire rods. Both the strips and the rods have pieces that are in lengths of 1 to 10 measured in terms of the smallest strip or rod. Each length is a different color for ease of identification. Strips of construction paper or adding-machine tape can be folded to produce equal-sized subparts.

The rod or strip model provides the most flexibility while still having separate pieces for comparisons. To make fraction strips, cut 11 different colors of poster board into strips 2 cm wide. Cut the smallest strips into 2-cm squares. Other strips are then 4, 6, 8, . . . , 20 cm, producing lengths 1 to 10 in terms of the smallest strip. Cut the last color into strips 24 cm long to produce a 12 strip. If you are using Cuisenaire rods, tape a red 2 rod to an orange 10 rod to make a 12 rod. In this chapter's illustrations, the colors of the strips will be the same as the corresponding lengths of the Cuisenaire rods:

1 White	7 Black
2 Red	8 Brown
3 Light green	9 Blue
4 Purple	10 Orange
5 Yellow	12 Pink or red-orange
6 Dark green	

The number line is a significantly more sophisticated measurement model (Bright, Behr, Post, & Wachsmuth, 1988). From a child's vantage point, there is a real difference between putting a number on a number line and

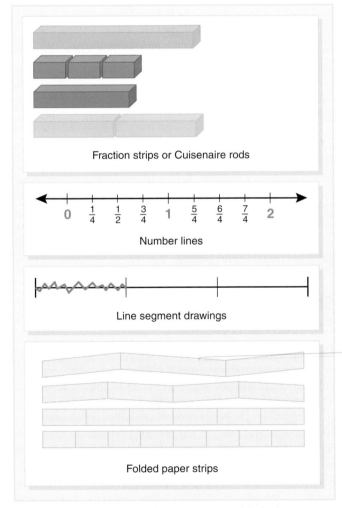

FIGURE 16.4 Length or measurement models for fractions.

comparing one length to another. Each number on a line denotes the distance of the labeled point from zero.

Set Models

In set models, the whole is understood to be a set of objects, and subsets of the whole make up fractional parts. For example, three objects are one-fourth of a set of 12 objects. The set of 12, in this example, represents the whole or 1. It is the idea of referring to a collection of counters as a single entity that makes set models difficult for some children. Students will frequently focus on the size of the set rather than the number of equal sets in the whole. For example, if 12 counters make a whole, then a set of 4 counters is one-*third*, not one-fourth, since 3 equal sets make the whole. However, the set model helps establish important connections with many real-world uses of fractions and with ratio concepts. Figure 16.5 illustrates several set models for fractions.

Counters in two colors on opposite sides are frequently used. They can easily be flipped to change their color to model various fractional parts of a whole set.

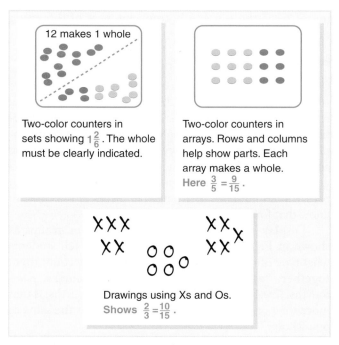

FIGURE 16.5 Set models for fractions.

From Fractional Parts to Fraction Symbols

As already discussed, one of the best ways to introduce the concept of fractional parts is through sharing tasks. However, the idea of fractional parts is so fundamental to a strong development of fraction concepts that it should be explored further with additional tasks.

Fractional Parts and Words

In addition to helping children use the words *halves*, *thirds*, *fourths*, *fifths*, and so on, be sure to make regular comparison of fractional parts to the whole. Make it a point to use the terms *whole*, or *one whole*, or simply *one* so that students have a language that they can use regardless of the model involved.

The following activity is a simple extension of the sharing tasks. It is important that students can tell when a region has been separated into a particular type of fractional part.

activity **16.1**

Correct Shares

As in Figure 16.6, show examples and nonexamples of specified fractional parts. Have students identify the wholes that are correctly divided into requested fractional parts and those that are not. For each response, have students explain their reasoning. The activity should be done with a variety of models, including length and set models.

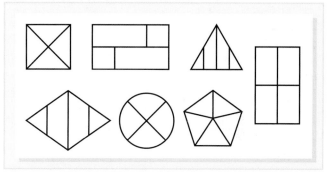

FIGURE 16.6 Students learning about fractional parts should be able to tell which of these figures are correctly partitioned in fourths. They should also be able to explain why the other figures are not showing fourths.

In the "Correct Shares" activity, the most important part is the discussion of the nonexamples. The wholes are already partitioned either correctly or incorrectly, and the children were not involved in the partitioning. It is also useful for children to create designated equal shares given a whole, as they are asked to do in the next activity.

activity **16.2**

Finding Fair Shares

Give students models and have them find fifths or eighths or other fractional parts using the models. (The models should never have fractions written on them.) The activity is especially interesting when

different wholes can be designated in the same model. That way, a given fractional part does not get identified with a special shape or color but with the relationship of the part to the designated whole. Some ideas are suggested in Figure 16.7.

Notice when partitioning sets that children frequently confuse the number of counters in a share with the name of the share. In the example in Figure 16.7, the 12 counters are partitioned into 4 sets—*fourths*. Each share or part has three counters, but it is the number of shares that makes the partition show *fourths*.

 Be aware that some manipulative models for fractions can mask students' true understanding. For example, if using pattern blocks with the outline of two hexagons as the whole (as shown in Figure 16.7), a student may correctly show sixths using the blue rhombuses. This student apparently understands that sixths are made of six parts. However, this same student may draw a partition of a circle or even a rectangle into

"sixths" in which the parts are not at all equal. Does the student understand that the parts must be the same size, or is the incorrect drawing due to weak motor skills?

The physical model also may indicate to students that the fractional parts must be the same *shape* as well as the same size. Challenge students' thinking with a drawing such as this that shows thirds but in different shapes:

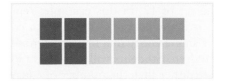

Class discussions that challenge students' thinking and expose their ideas are the best ways to both help students develop accurate concepts and to find out what they understand. ■

Understanding Fraction Symbols

Fraction symbolism represents a fairly complex convention that is often misleading to children. It is well worth your time to help students develop a strong understanding of what the top and bottom numbers of a fraction tell us.

Fractional-Parts Counting

Counting fractional parts to see how multiple parts compare to the whole creates a foundation for the two parts of a fraction. Students should come to think of counting fractional parts in much the same way as they might count apples or any other objects. If you know the kind of part you are counting, you can tell when you get to one, when you get to two, and so on. Students who understand fractional parts should not need to arrange pie pieces into a circle to know that four fourths make a whole.

Display some pie-piece fraction parts in groups as shown in Figure 16.8. For each collection, tell students what type of piece is being shown and simply count them together: "*one*-fourth, *two*-fourths, *three*-fourths, *four*-fourths, *five*-fourths." Ask, "If we have five-fourths, is that more than one whole, less than one whole, or the same as one whole?"

As students count each collection of parts, discuss the relationship to one whole. Make informal comparisons between different collections. "Why did we get almost two wholes with seven-fourths, and yet we don't even have one whole with ten-twelfths?"

Also take this opportunity to lay verbal groundwork for mixed fractions. "What is another way that we could say seven-thirds?" (Two wholes and one more third or one whole and four-thirds.)

With this introduction, students are ready for the following task.

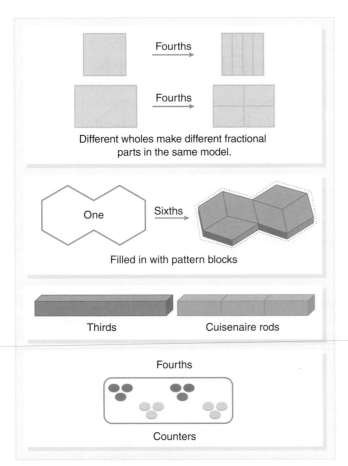

FIGURE 16.7 Given a whole, find fractional parts.

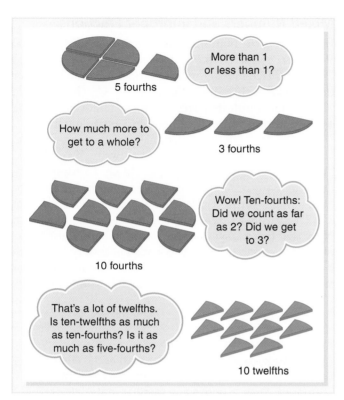

FIGURE 16.8 Counting fractional parts.

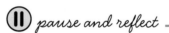

activity **16.3**

More, Less, or Equal to One Whole

Give students a collection of fractional parts (all the same type) and indicate the kind of fractional part they have. Parts can be drawn on a worksheet or physical models can be placed in plastic baggies with an identifying card. For example, if done with Cuisenaire rods or fraction strips, the collection might have seven light green rods/strips with a caption or note indicating "these are eighths." The task is to decide if the collection is less than one whole, equal to one whole, or more than one whole. Students must draw pictures and/or use numbers to explain their answer. They can also tell how close the set is to a complete whole. Several collections constitute a reasonable task.

Try Activity 16.3 with several different fraction models (although pie pieces are too much of a giveaway). Pattern blocks make a good manipulative format and are also easily drawn with a template. The same is true of Cuisenaire rods. A set model may cause students some initial difficulty but it is especially important, even if they have been successful with region or length models. For example, show a collection of 15 counters (dots or actual coun-

ters) and indicate that a set of 5 counters is one-fourth. How much is the set of 15 counters?

Top and Bottom Numbers

The way that we write fractions with a top and a bottom number and a bar between is a convention—an arbitrary agreement for how to represent fractions. (By the way, always write fractions with a horizontal bar, not a slanted one. Write $\frac{3}{4}$, not 3/4.) As a convention, it falls in the category of things that you simply tell students. However, a good idea is to make the convention so clear by way of demonstration that students will tell *you* what the top and bottom numbers stand for. The following procedure is recommended even if your students have been "using" symbolic fractions for several years.

Display several collections of fractional parts in a manner similar to those in Figure 16.8. Have students count the parts together. After each count, write the correct fraction, indicating that this is how it is written as a symbol. Include sets that are more than one, but write them as simple or "improper" fractions and not as mixed numbers. Include at least two pairs of sets with the same top numbers such as $\frac{4}{8}$ and $\frac{4}{3}$. Likewise, include sets with the same bottom numbers. After the class has counted and you have written the fraction for at least six sets of fractional parts, pose the following questions:

What does the bottom number in a fraction tell us?

What does the top number in a fraction tell us?

Ⅱ *pause and reflect* ————————————

Before reading further, answer these two questions in your own words. Don't rely on formulations you've heard before. Think in terms of what we have been talking about—namely, fractional parts and counting fractional parts. Imagine counting a set of 5 eighths and a set of 5 fourths and writing the fractions for these sets. Use children's language in your formulations and try to come up with a way to explain these meanings that has nothing to do with the type of model involved.

Here are some reasonable explanations for the top and bottom numbers.

• *Top number:* This is the counting number. It tells how many shares or parts we have. It tells how many have been counted. It tells how many parts we are talking about. It counts the parts or shares.

• *Bottom number:* This tells what is being counted. It tells what fractional part is being counted. If it is a 4, it means we are counting *fourths*; if it is a 6, we are counting *sixths*; and so on.

This formulation of the meanings of the top and bottom numbers may seem unusual to you. It is often said that the top number tells "how many." (This phrase seems unfinished. How many *what*?) The bottom number is said to tell "how many parts it takes to make a whole." This may be correct but can be misleading. For example, a $\frac{1}{6}$ piece is often cut from a cake without making any slices in the remaining $\frac{5}{6}$ of the cake. That the cake is only in two pieces does not change the fact that the piece taken is $\frac{1}{6}$. Or if a pizza is cut in 12 pieces, two pieces still make $\frac{1}{6}$ of the pizza. In neither of these instances does the bottom number tell how many pieces make a whole.

There is evidence that an iterative notion of fractions, one that views a fraction such as $\frac{3}{4}$ as a count of three things called *fourths*, is an important idea for children to develop (Post, Wachsmuth, Lesh, & Behr, 1985; Tzur, 1999). The iterative concept is most clear when focusing on these two ideas about fraction symbols:

- The top number *counts*.
- The bottom number tells *what is being counted*.

The *what* of fractions are the fractional parts. They can be counted. Fraction symbols are just a shorthand for saying *how many* and *what*.

Smith (2002) points out a slightly more "mathematical" definition of the top and bottom numbers that is completely in accord with the one we've just discussed. For Smith, it is important to see the bottom number as the divisor and the top as the multiplier. That is, $\frac{3}{4}$ is three *times* what you get when you *divide* a whole into four parts. This multiplier and divisor idea is especially useful when students are asked later to think of fractions as an indicated division; that is, $\frac{3}{4}$ also means $3 \div 4$.

 The *Standards* supports a strong conceptual development of fractions in grades 3 to 5 but suggests that computation be primarily a middle school topic. "During grades 3–5, students should build their understanding of fractions as parts of a whole and as division. They will need to see and explore a variety of models of fractions, focusing primarily on fractions such as halves, thirds, fourths, fifths, sixths, eighths, and tenths" (p. 150).

Numerator and *Denominator*

To count a set is to *enumerate* it. *Enumeration* is the process of counting. The common name for the top number in a fraction is the *numerator*.

A $1 bill, a $5 bill, and a $10 bill are said to be different *denominations* as are branches of religions (such as Baptists, Presbyterians, Episcopalians, and Catholics). A denomination is the name of a class or type of thing. The common name for the bottom number in a fraction is the *denominator*.

The words *numerator* and *denominator* have no common referent for children. Whether these words are used or not, the words themselves will not help young children understand the meanings.

Mixed Numbers and Improper Fractions

In the fourth National Assessment of Educational Progress, about 80 percent of seventh graders could change a mixed number to an improper fraction, but fewer than half knew that $5\frac{1}{4}$ was the same as $5 + \frac{1}{4}$ (Kouba et al., 1988a). The result indicates that many children are using a symbolism convention without understanding it.

If you have counted fractional parts beyond a whole, your students already know how to write $\frac{13}{6}$ or $\frac{11}{3}$. Ask, "What is another way that you could say 13 *sixths*?" Students may suggest "two wholes and one-sixth more," or "two plus one-sixth." Explain that these are correct and that $2 + \frac{1}{6}$ is usually written as $2\frac{1}{6}$ and is called a *mixed number*. Note that this is a symbolism convention and must be explained to children. What is not at all necessary is to teach a rule for converting mixed numbers to common fractions and the reverse. Rather, consider the following task.

activity **16.4**

Mixed-Number Names

Give students a mixed number such as $3\frac{2}{5}$. Their task is to find a single fraction that names the same amount. They may use any familiar materials or make drawings, but they must be able to give an explanation for their result. Similarly, have students start with a fraction greater than 1, such as $\frac{17}{4}$, and have them determine the mixed number and provide a justification for their result.

Repeat the "Mixed-Number Names" task several times with different fractions. After a while, challenge students to figure out the new fraction name without the use of models. A good explanation for $3\frac{1}{4}$ might be that there are 4 fourths in one whole, so there are 8 fourths in two wholes and 12 fourths in three wholes. The extra fourth makes 13 fourths in all, or $\frac{13}{4}$. (Note the iteration concept playing a role.)

There is absolutely no reason ever to provide a rule about multiplying the whole number by the bottom number and adding the top number. Nor should students need a rule about dividing the bottom number into the top to convert fractions to mixed numbers. These rules can readily be developed by the students but in their own words and with complete understanding.

activity **16.5**

Calculator Fraction Counting

Calculators that permit fraction entries and displays are now quite common in schools. Many, like the TI-15, now display fractions in correct fraction format and offer a choice of showing results as mixed numbers or simple fractions. Counting by fourths with the TI-15 is done by first storing $\frac{1}{4}$ in one of the two operation keys: [OP₁] [+] **1** [n] **4** [d] [OP₁]. To count, press 0 [OP₁] [OP₁] [OP₁] . . . . The display will show the counts by fourths and also the number of times that the [OP₁] key has been pressed. Students should coordinate their counts with fraction models, adding a new fourths piece to the pile with each count. At any time the display can be shifted from mixed form to simple fractions with a press of a key. The TI-15 can be set so that it will not simplify fractions automatically, the appropriate setting prior to the introduction of equivalent fractions.

Fraction calculators provide a powerful way to help children develop fractional symbolism. A variation on Activity 16.5 is to show children a mixed number such as $3\frac{1}{8}$ and ask how many counts of $\frac{1}{8}$ on the calculator it will take to count that high. The students should try to stop at the correct number $\left(\frac{25}{8}\right)$ before pressing the mixed-number key.

Parts-and-Whole Tasks

The exercises presented here can help children develop their understanding of fractional parts as well as the meanings of the top and bottom numbers in a fraction. Models are used to represent wholes and parts of wholes. Written or oral fraction names represent the relationship between the parts and wholes. Given any two of these—whole,

part, and fraction—the students can use their models to determine the third.

Any type of model can be used as long as different sizes can represent the whole. Traditional pie pieces do not work because the whole is always the circle, and all the pieces are *unit fractions*. (A *unit fraction* is a single fractional part. The fractions $\frac{1}{3}$ and $\frac{1}{8}$ are unit fractions.)

Examples of each type of exercise are provided in Figure 16.9, Figure 16.10, and Figure 16.11. Each figure includes examples with a region model (freely drawn rectangles), a length model (Cuisenaire rods or fraction strips), and set models.

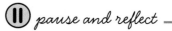 *pause and reflect* ——————

It would be a good idea to work through these exercises before reading on. For the rectangle models, simply sketch a similar rectangle on paper. For the rod or strip models, use Cuisenaire rods or make fraction strips. The colors used correspond to the actual rod colors. Lengths are not given in the figures so that you will not be tempted to use an adult-type numeric approach. If you do not have access to rods or strips, just draw lines on paper. The process you use with lines will correspond to what is done with rods.

————————————————————

The questions that ask for the fraction when given the whole and part require a lot of trial and error and can

If this rectangle is one whole,
—find one-fourth.
—find two-thirds.
—find five-thirds.

If brown is the whole,
find one-fourth.

If dark green is one whole,
what rod is two-thirds?

If dark green is one whole,
what rod is three-halves?

If 8 counters are a whole set,
how many are in
one-fourth of a set?

If 15 counters are a whole,
how many counters make
three-fifths?

If 9 counters are a whole,
how many are in five-thirds
of a set?

FIGURE 16.9 Given the whole and the fraction, find the part.

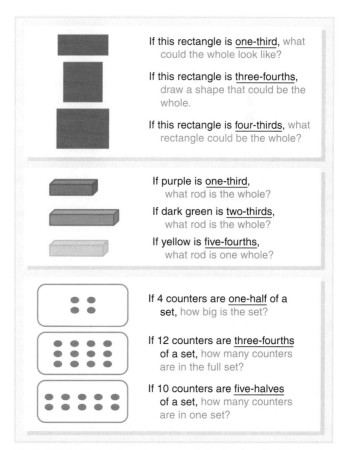

If this rectangle is one-third, what could the whole look like?

If this rectangle is three-fourths, draw a shape that could be the whole.

If this rectangle is four-thirds, what rectangle could be the whole?

If purple is one-third, what rod is the whole?

If dark green is two-thirds, what rod is the whole?

If yellow is five-fourths, what rod is one whole?

If 4 counters are one-half of a set, how big is the set?

If 12 counters are three-fourths of a set, how many counters are in the full set?

If 10 counters are five-halves of a set, how many counters are in one set?

FIGURE 16.10 Given the part and the fraction, find the whole.

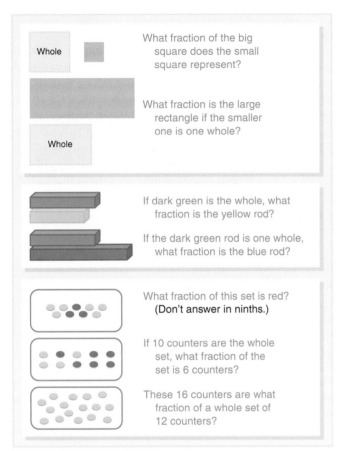

FIGURE 16.11 Given the whole and the part, find the fraction.

frustrate young students. Be sure that appropriate fractional parts are available for the region and length versions of these questions.

Two or three challenging parts-and-whole questions can make an excellent lesson. The tasks should be presented to the class in just the same form as in the figures. Physical models are often the best way to present the tasks so that students can use a trial-and-error approach to determine their results. As with all tasks, it should be clear that an explanation is required to justify each answer. For each task, let several students supply answers and explanations.

Sometimes it is a good idea to create simple story problems that ask the same questions.

Mr. Samuels has finished $\frac{3}{4}$ of his patio. It looks like this:

Draw a picture that might be the shape of the finished patio.

The problems can also involve numbers instead of models:

If the swim team sold 400 raffle tickets, it would have enough money to pay for new team shirts. So far the swimmers have $\frac{5}{8}$ of the necessary raffle tickets sold. How many more tickets do they need to sell?

With some models, it is necessary to be certain that the answer exists within the model. For example, if you were using fraction strips, you could ask, "If the blue strip (9) is the whole, what strip is two-thirds?" The answer is the 6 strip, or dark green. You could not ask students to find "three-fourths of the blue strip" because each fourth of 9 would be $2\frac{1}{4}$ units, and no strip has that length. Similar caution must be taken with rectangular pieces.

Questions involving unit fractions are generally the easiest. The hardest questions usually involve fractions greater than 1. For example, *If 15 chips are five-thirds of one whole set, how many chips are in a whole?* However, in every question, the unit fraction plays a significant role. If you have $\frac{5}{3}$ and want the whole, you first need to find $\frac{1}{3}$.

 The parts-and-whole questions are challenging yet very effective at helping students reflect on the meanings of the numerator and denominator. They also are a good way to see if students really understand the meanings of the numerator and denominator since the tasks force students to *use* those meanings, not simply recite a definition. The second type of task (Figure 16.10) may be the most useful as a diagnostic tool. This task is rarely found in textbooks. Give students two or at most three parts-and-whole tasks and have them supply both answers and their rationale. Avoid being the answer book for these tasks since the validity of the answers is built into the task when it is understood. ■

 Representing Fractions (Sunburst) is software that offers a range of challenges for fraction development. In two of the four activities, students build given fractions using models of unit fractions. Though not open-ended, these activities may reinforce the iterative concept of fractions. The computer orally counts to the fraction target when a solution is offered: "One-fourth, two-fourths, three-fourths." Another task area requires students to build a whole based on a given fractional part. This activity is similar to building a whole with fraction strips, given the fraction and the part as described earlier in this chapter.

"Open-Ended Build and Play" is a component of *Representing Fractions* in which the user can slice up squares, circles, or triangles by connecting equally spaced dots on the edges. Parts can then be cut into even smaller pieces. The individual pieces can be painted different colors and dragged to any part of the screen. This open-ended model provides teachers or students with a tool that is more flexible than any physical model. Note that this is a pure model or tool. No fraction symbols are provided, nor are any problems posed. The computer does no evaluation. The teacher can pose tasks and let students use the program to work on solutions. Alternatively, students can devise their own challenges for each other using the drawing tool. As with all Sunburst activities, a journal permits students to copy a picture of their work, write about it, and even record a short message. ■

Fraction Number Sense

The focus on fractional parts is an important beginning. But number sense with fractions demands more—it requires that students have some intuitive feel for fractions. They should know "about" how big a particular fraction is and be able to tell easily which of two fractions is larger.

Benchmarks of Zero, One-Half, and One

The most important reference points or benchmarks for fractions are 0, $\frac{1}{2}$, and 1. For fractions less than 1, simply comparing them to these three numbers gives quite a lot of information. For example, $\frac{3}{20}$ is small, close to 0, whereas $\frac{3}{4}$ is between $\frac{1}{2}$ and 1. The fraction $\frac{9}{10}$ is quite close to 1. Since any fraction greater than 1 is a whole number plus an amount less than 1, the same reference points are just as helpful: $3\frac{3}{7}$ is almost $3\frac{1}{2}$.

activity 16.6

Zero, One-Half, or One

On the board or overhead, write a collection of 10 to 15 fractions. A few should be greater than 1 ($\frac{9}{8}$ or $\frac{11}{10}$), with the others ranging from 0 to 1. Let students sort the fractions into three groups: those close to 0, close to $\frac{1}{2}$, and close to 1. For those close to $\frac{1}{2}$, have them decide if the fraction is more or less than $\frac{1}{2}$. The difficulty of this task largely depends on the fractions. The first time you try this, use fractions such as $\frac{1}{20}$, $\frac{53}{100}$, or $\frac{9}{10}$ that are very close to the three benchmarks. On subsequent days, use fractions with most of the denominators less than 20. You might include one or two fractions such as $\frac{2}{8}$ or $\frac{3}{4}$ that are exactly in between the benchmarks. As usual, require explanations for each fraction.

The next activity is also aimed at developing the same three reference points for fractions. In "Close Fractions," however, the students must come up with the fractions rather than sort them.

activity 16.7

Close Fractions

Have your students name a fraction that is close to 1 but not more than 1. Next have them name another fraction that is even closer to 1 than that. For the second response, they have to explain why they believe the fraction is closer to 1 than the previous fraction. Continue for several fractions in the same manner, each one being closer to 1 than the previous fraction. Similarly, try close to 0 or close to $\frac{1}{2}$ (either under or over). The first several times you try this activity, let the students use models to help with their thinking. Later, see how well their explanations work when they cannot use models or drawings. Focus discussions on the relative size of fractional parts.

Understanding why a fraction is close to 0, $\frac{1}{2}$, or 1 is a good beginning for fraction number sense. It begins to focus on the size of fractions in an important yet simple manner. The next activity also helps students reflect on fraction size.

activity 16.8

About How Much?

Draw a picture like one of those in Figure 16.12 (or prepare some ahead of time for the overhead). Have each student write down a fraction that he or she thinks is a good estimate of the amount shown

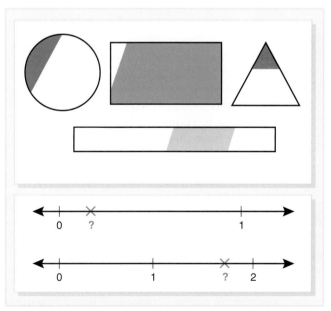

FIGURE 16.12 About how much? Name a fraction for each drawing, and explain why you chose that fraction.

(or the indicated mark on the number line). Listen without judgment to the ideas of several students, and discuss with them why any particular estimate might be a good one. There is no single correct answer, but estimates should be "in the ballpark." If children have difficulty coming up with an estimate, ask if they think the amount is closer to 0, $\frac{1}{2}$, or 1.

Thinking About Which Is More

The ability to tell which of two fractions is greater is another aspect of number sense with fractions. That ability is built around concepts of fractions, not on an algorithmic skill or symbolic tricks. In the 2000 NAEP test, only 21 percent of fourth-grade students could explain why one unit fraction was larger or smaller than another (Kloosterman et al., 2004). At the eighth grade, only 41 percent of students were able to correctly order three fractions given in reduced form (Sowder, Wearne, Martin, & Strutchens, 2004). As these researchers note, "How students can work meaningfully with fractions if they do not have a sense of the relative size of the fractions is difficult to imagine" (p. 116).

Concepts, Not Rules

Children have a tremendously strong mind-set about numbers that causes them difficulties with the relative size of fractions. In their experience, larger numbers mean "more." The tendency is to transfer this whole-number concept to fractions: Seven is more than four, so sevenths should be bigger than fourths (Mack, 1995). The inverse relationship between number of parts and size of parts cannot be told but must be a creation of each student's own thought process.

activity 16.9

Ordering Unit Fractions

List a set of unit fractions such as $\frac{1}{3}$, $\frac{1}{8}$, $\frac{1}{5}$, and $\frac{1}{10}$. Ask children to put the fractions in order from least to most. Challenge children to defend the way they ordered the fractions. The first few times you do this activity, have them explain their ideas by using models.

This idea is so basic to the understanding of fractions that arbitrary rules ("Larger bottom numbers mean smaller fractions") are not only inappropriate but dangerous. Come back to this basic idea periodically. Children will seem to understand one day and revert to their more comfortable ideas about big numbers a day or two later. It is also important to repeat Activity 16.9 with all numerators equal to some number other than 1. You may be surprised to see a change in students' thinking.

You have probably learned rules or algorithms for comparing two fractions. The usual approaches are finding common denominators and using cross-multiplication. These rules can be effective in getting correct answers but require no thought about the size of the fractions. This is especially true of the cross-multiplication procedure. If children are taught these rules before they have had the opportunity to think about the relative size of various fractions, there is little chance that they will develop any familiarity with or number sense about fraction size. Comparison activities (which fraction is more?) can play a significant role in helping children develop concepts of relative fraction sizes. But keep in mind that reflective thought is the goal, not an algorithmic method of choosing the correct answer.

Ⅱ *pause and reflect* ————————

Before reading further, try the following exercise. Assume for a moment that you know nothing about equivalent fractions or common denominators or cross-multiplication. Assume that you are a fourth- or fifth-grade student who was never taught these procedures. Now examine the pairs of fractions in Figure 16.13 and select the larger of each pair. Write down or explain one or more reasons for your choice in each case.

Which fraction in each pair is greater?
Give one or more reasons. Try not to use drawings or models.
Do <u>not</u> <u>use</u> common denominators or cross-multiplication.
Rely on concepts.

A.	$\frac{4}{5}$ or $\frac{4}{9}$		G.	$\frac{7}{12}$ or $\frac{5}{12}$
B.	$\frac{4}{7}$ or $\frac{5}{7}$		H.	$\frac{3}{5}$ or $\frac{3}{7}$
C.	$\frac{3}{8}$ or $\frac{4}{10}$		I.	$\frac{5}{8}$ or $\frac{6}{10}$
D.	$\frac{5}{3}$ or $\frac{5}{8}$		J.	$\frac{9}{8}$ or $\frac{4}{3}$
E.	$\frac{3}{4}$ or $\frac{9}{10}$		K.	$\frac{4}{6}$ or $\frac{7}{12}$
F.	$\frac{3}{8}$ or $\frac{4}{7}$		L.	$\frac{8}{9}$ or $\frac{7}{8}$

FIGURE 16.13 Comparing fractions using concepts.

Conceptual Thought Patterns for Comparison

The first two comparison schemes listed here rely on the meanings of the top and bottom numbers in fractions and on the relative sizes of unit fractional parts. The third and fourth ideas use the additional ideas of 0, $\frac{1}{2}$, and 1 as convenient anchors or benchmarks for thinking about the size of fractions.

1. *More of the same-size parts.* To compare $\frac{3}{8}$ and $\frac{5}{8}$, it is easy to think about having 3 of something and also 5 of the same thing. It is common for children to choose $\frac{5}{8}$ as larger simply because 5 is more than 3 and the other numbers are the same. Right choice, wrong reason. Comparing $\frac{3}{8}$ and $\frac{5}{8}$ should be like comparing 3 apples and 5 apples.

2. *Same number of parts but parts of different sizes.* Consider the case of $\frac{3}{4}$ and $\frac{3}{7}$. If a whole is divided into 7 parts, the parts will certainly be smaller than if divided into only 4 parts. Many children will select $\frac{3}{7}$ as larger because 7 is more than 4 and the top numbers are the same. That approach yields correct choices when the parts are the same size, but it causes problems in this case. This is like comparing 3 apples with 3 melons. You have the same number of things, but melons are larger.

3. *More and less than one-half or one whole.* The fraction pairs $\frac{3}{7}$ versus $\frac{5}{8}$ and $\frac{5}{4}$ versus $\frac{7}{8}$ do not lend themselves to either of the previous thought processes. In the first pair, $\frac{3}{7}$ is less than half of the number of sevenths needed to make a whole, and so $\frac{3}{7}$ is less than a half. Similarly, $\frac{5}{8}$ is more than a half. Therefore, $\frac{5}{8}$ is the larger fraction. The second pair is determined by noting that one fraction is less than 1 and the other is greater than 1.

4. *Distance from one-half or one whole.* Why is $\frac{9}{10}$ greater than $\frac{3}{4}$? Not because the 9 and 10 are big numbers, although you will find that to be a common student response. Each is one fractional part away from one whole, and tenths are smaller than fourths. Similarly, notice that $\frac{5}{8}$ is smaller than $\frac{4}{6}$ because it is only one-eighth more than a half, while $\frac{4}{6}$ is a sixth more than a half. Can you use this basic idea to compare $\frac{3}{5}$ and $\frac{5}{9}$? (*Hint:* Each is half of a fractional part more than $\frac{1}{2}$.) Also try $\frac{5}{7}$ and $\frac{7}{9}$.

How did your reasons for choosing fractions in Figure 16.13 compare to these ideas? It is important that you are comfortable with these informal comparison strategies as a major component of your own number sense as well as for helping children develop theirs.

Tasks you design for your students should assist them in developing these and possibly other methods of comparing two fractions. It is important that the ideas come from your students and their discussions. To teach "the four ways to compare fractions" would be adding four more mysterious rules and would be defeating for many students.

activity **16.10**

Choose, Explain, Test
Present two or three pairs of fractions to students. The students' task is to decide which fraction is greater (choose), to explain why they think this is so (explain), and then to test their choice using any model that they wish to use. They should write a description of how they made their test and whether or not it agreed with their choice. If their choice was incorrect, they should try to say what they would change in their thinking. In the student explanations, rule out drawing as an option. Explain that it is difficult to draw fraction pictures accurately and for this activity pictures may cause them to make mistakes.

Rather than directly teach the different possible methods for comparing fractions, select pairs that will likely elicit desired comparison strategies. On one day, for example, you might have two pairs with the same denominators and one with the same numerators. On another day, you might pick fraction pairs in which each fraction is exactly one part away from a whole. Try to build strategies over several days by the appropriate choice of fraction pairs.

The use of a model in Activity 16.10 is an important part of students' development of strategies as long as the model is helping students create the strategy. However, after several experiences, change the activity so that the testing portion with a model is omitted. Place greater emphasis on students' reasoning. If class discussions yield different choices, allow students to use their own arguments for their choices in order to make a decision about which fraction is greater.

The next activity extends the comparison task a bit more.

activity **16.11**

Line 'Em Up
Select four or five fractions for students to put in order from least to most. Have them indicate approximately where each fraction belongs on a number line labeled only with the points 0, $\frac{1}{2}$, and 1. Students should include a description of how they decided on the order for the fractions. To place the fractions on the number line, students must also make estimates of fraction size in addition to simply ordering the fractions.

Including Equivalent Fractions

The discussion to this point has somewhat artificially ignored the idea that students might use equivalent fraction concepts in making comparisons. Equivalent fraction concepts are such an important idea that a separate section is devoted to the development of that idea. However, equivalent fraction concepts need not be put off until last and certainly should be allowed in the discussions of which fraction is more.

Smith (2002) thinks that it is essential that the comparison question is asked as follows: "Which of the following two (or more) fractions is greater, *or are they equal?*" (p. 9, emphasis added). He points out that this question leaves open the possibility that two fractions that may look different can, in fact, be equal.

In addition to this point, with equivalent fraction concepts, students can adjust how a fraction looks so that they can use ideas that make sense to them. Burns (1999) told of fifth graders who were comparing $\frac{6}{8}$ to $\frac{4}{5}$. (You might want to stop for a moment and think how you would compare these two.) One child changed the $\frac{4}{5}$ to $\frac{8}{10}$ so that both fractions would be two parts away from the whole and he reasoned from there. Another changed both fractions to a common *numerator* of 12.

Be absolutely certain to revisit the comparison activities and include pairs such as $\frac{8}{12}$ and $\frac{2}{3}$ in which the fractions are equal but do not appear to be. Also include fractions that are not in lowest terms.

Only One Size for the Whole

A key idea about fractions that students must come to understand is that a fraction does not say anything about the size of the whole or the size of the parts. A fraction tells us only about the *relationship between* the part and the whole. Consider the following situation.

Mark is offered the choice of a third of a pizza or a half of a pizza. Since he is hungry and likes pizza, he chooses the half. His friend Jane gets a third of a pizza but ends up with more than Mark. How can that be? Figure 16.14 illustrates how Mark got misdirected in his choice. The point of the "pizza fallacy" is that whenever two or more fractions are discussed in the same context, the correct assumption (the one Mark made in choosing a half of a pizza) is that the fractions are all parts of the same size whole.

Comparisons with any model can be made only if both fractions are parts of the same whole. For example, $\frac{2}{3}$ of a light green strip cannot be compared to $\frac{2}{5}$ of an orange strip.

In the fourth grade of the *Investigations in Number, Data, and Space* program, many of the same ideas just discussed are developed very carefully. The excerpt on the next page is an example.

Estimation

A frequently quoted result from the Second National Assessment (Post, 1981) concerns the following item:

Estimate the answer to $\frac{12}{13} + \frac{7}{8}$. You will not have time to solve the problem using paper and pencil.

Here is how 13-year-olds answered:

Response	Percent of 13-Year-Olds
1	7
2	24
19	28
21	27
Don't know	14

A more recent study of sixth- and eighth-grade Taiwanese students included this same item. The results were nearly identical to those in the NAEP study (Reys, 1998). In the Taiwanese study, a significantly higher percentage of students (61 percent and 63 percent) was able to correctly compute the sum, a process that requires finding the common denominator of thirteenths and eighths! Notice that to estimate this sum requires no skill whatsoever with computation—only a feeling for the size of the two fractions.

The development of fraction number sense should most certainly include estimation of fraction sums and differences—even before computational strategies are introduced. The following activity can be done regularly as a short full-class warm-up for any fraction lesson.

activity **16.12**

First Estimates

Tell students that they are going to estimate a sum or difference of two fractions. They are to decide only if the exact answer is more or less than one. On the overhead projector show, for no more than about 10 seconds, a fraction addition or subtraction problem involving two proper fractions. Students write down on paper their choice of more or less than one. Do several problems in a row. Then return to each problem and discuss how students decided on their estimate.

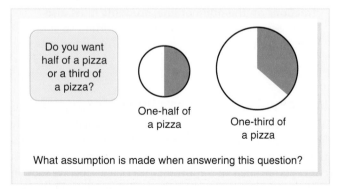

Do you want half of a pizza or a third of a pizza?

One-half of a pizza

One-third of a pizza

What assumption is made when answering this question?

FIGURE 16.14 The "pizza fallacy."

Investigations *in Number, Data, and Space*

Grade 4, Different Shapes, Equal Pieces
Investigation 2: Parts of Rectangles: Thirds, Sixths, and Twelfths

Context

In the first three sessions of this investigation, students work with 5×7 dot grids (4 squares by 6 squares) to show different ways to make thirds, sixths, and twelfths. In the previous investigation, they explored halves, fourths, eighths, and sixteenths—building on students' propensity for halving. Ordering or comparing fractions and an informal development of equivalent fractions are the focus of the investigation that follows this one.

Task Description

This session or class period is entitled "Working with $\frac{2}{3}$, $\frac{3}{4}$, $\frac{5}{6}$, and $\frac{7}{8}$." Notice that each of these fractions is one part away from a whole. The session begins with a class discussion of these two squares. Students are asked, "How much is colored and how much is not colored?"

After this introductory discussion, students are told to color four squares of their own, one showing $\frac{3}{4}$ colored, one showing $\frac{2}{3}$, one showing $\frac{5}{6}$, and one showing $\frac{7}{8}$. For their drawings students use squares with either six or eight equal spaces marked on the edges. They are told that the colored parts need not be all connected. Given prior experiences, students will likely color their fractions in many different ways. They do not label the squares.

Next, they exchange their drawings with other students. With their exchanged designs, they work in pairs to determine what fraction is shown on each square. To this point no comparisons have been involved. The

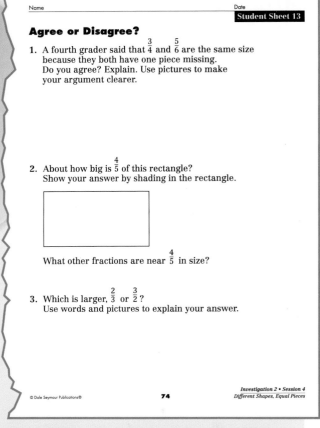

squares are collected and posted under the names of the four fractions.

The coloring of squares is followed with the worksheet shown here. After completing this, there is a class discussion of students' reasoning. Notice how this entire lesson focuses on the idea of one part missing, yet never directly tells this to students. The last question on the sheet is a review.

Restricting Activity 16.12 to proper fractions keeps the difficulty to a minimum. When students are ready for a tougher challenge, choose from the following variations:

- Use fractions that are less than one. Estimate to the nearest half $(0, \frac{1}{2}, 1, 1\frac{1}{2}, 2)$.

- Use both proper and mixed fractions. Estimate to the nearest half.

- Use proper and mixed fractions. Estimate the best answer you can.

In the discussions following these estimation exercises, ask students if they think that the exact answer is more or less than the estimate that they gave. What is their reasoning?

Figure 16.15 shows six sample sums and differences that might be used in a "First Estimates" activity.

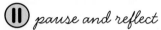 *pause and reflect*

Test your own estimation skills with the sample problems in Figure 16.15. Look at each computation for only about 10 seconds and write down an estimate. After writing down all six of your estimates, look at the problems and decide if your estimate is higher or lower than the actual computation. Don't guess! Have a good reason.

In most cases students' estimates should not be much more than $\frac{1}{2}$ away from the exact sum or difference.

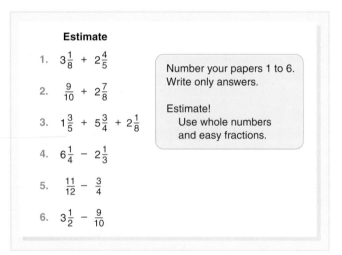

Estimate

1. $3\frac{1}{8} + 2\frac{4}{5}$

2. $\frac{9}{10} + 2\frac{7}{8}$

3. $1\frac{3}{5} + 5\frac{3}{4} + 2\frac{1}{8}$

4. $6\frac{1}{4} - 2\frac{1}{3}$

5. $\frac{11}{12} - \frac{3}{4}$

6. $3\frac{1}{2} - \frac{9}{10}$

Number your papers 1 to 6. Write only answers.

Estimate!
Use whole numbers and easy fractions.

FIGURE 16.15 Fraction estimation drill.

 NCTM Standards "The development of rational-number concepts is a major goal for grades 3–5, which should lead to informal methods for calculating with fractions. For example, a problem such as $\frac{1}{4} + \frac{1}{2}$ should be solved mentally with ease because students can picture $\frac{1}{2}$ and $\frac{1}{4}$ or can use decomposition strategies, such as $\frac{1}{4} + \frac{1}{2} = \frac{1}{4} + (\frac{1}{4} + \frac{1}{4})$" (p. 35).

 A sense of fraction size and the ability to make comparisons between two fractions are extremely important. Any of the activities in this section on fraction sense, especially "Choose, Explain, Test" (Activity 16.10) and the estimation of sums and differences, are excellent assessments of student understanding. Even after full-class discussions of these activities, they can be repeated as an assessment with students writing their explanations. To continue in your fraction unit without students having a good understanding of fraction size is a mistake. ■

Equivalent-Fraction Concepts

 *pause and reflect*

How do you know that $\frac{4}{6} = \frac{2}{3}$? Before reading further, think of at least two different explanations.

Concepts Versus Rules

Here are some possible answers to the question just posed:

1. They are the same because you can reduce $\frac{4}{6}$ and get $\frac{2}{3}$.

2. If you have a set of 6 things and you take 4 of them, that would be $\frac{4}{6}$. But you can make the 6 into groups of 2. So then there would be 3 groups, and the 4 would be 2 groups out of the 3 groups. That means it's $\frac{2}{3}$.

3. If you start with $\frac{2}{3}$, you can multiply the top and the bottom numbers by 2, and that will give you $\frac{4}{6}$, so they are equal.

4. If you had a square cut into 3 parts and you shaded 2, that would be $\frac{2}{3}$ shaded. If you cut all 3 of these parts in half, that would be 4 parts shaded and 6 parts in all. That's $\frac{4}{6}$, and it would be the same amount.

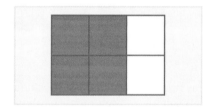

All of these answers are correct. But let's think about what they tell us. Responses 2 and 4 are very conceptual, although not very efficient. The procedural responses, 1 and 3, are quite efficient but indicate no conceptual knowledge. All students should eventually be able to write an equivalent fraction for a given fraction. At the same time, the rules should never be taught or used until the students understand what the result means. Consider how different the algorithm and the concept appear to be.

Concept: Two fractions are equivalent if they are representations for the same amount or quantity—if they are the same number.

Algorithm: To get an equivalent fraction, multiply (or divide) the top and bottom numbers by the same nonzero number.

In a problem-based classroom, students can develop an understanding of equivalent fractions and also develop from that understanding a conceptually based algorithm.

As with most algorithms, a serious instructional error is to rush too quickly to the rule. Be patient! Intuitive methods are always best at first.

Equivalent-Fraction Concepts

The general approach to helping students create an understanding of equivalent fractions is to have them use models to find different names for a fraction. Consider that this is the first time in their experience that a fixed quantity can have multiple names (actually an infinite number). The following activities are possible starting places.

activity 16.13

Different Fillers

Using an area model for fractions that is familiar to your students, prepare a worksheet with two or at most three outlines of different fractions. Do not limit yourself to unit fractions. For example, if the model is circular pie pieces, you might draw an outline for $\frac{2}{3}$, $\frac{1}{2}$, and $\frac{3}{4}$. The students' task is to use their own fraction pieces to find as many single-fraction names for the region as possible. After completing the three examples, have students write about the ideas or patterns they may have noticed in finding the names. Follow the activity with a class discussion.

In the class discussion following the "Different Fillers" activity, a good question to ask involves what names could be found if students had any size pieces that they wanted. For example, ask students "What names could you find if we had sixteenths in our fraction kit? What names could you find if you could have any piece at all?" The idea is to push beyond filling in the region in a pure trial-and-error approach.

The following activity is just a variation of "Different Fillers." Instead of a manipulative model, the task is constructed on dot paper.

activity 16.14

Dot Paper Equivalencies

Create a worksheet using a portion of either isometric or rectangular dot grid paper. (These can be found in the Blackline Masters.) On the grid, draw the outline of a region and designate it as one whole. Draw a part of the region within the whole. The task is to use different parts of the whole determined by the grid to find names for the part. Figure 16.16

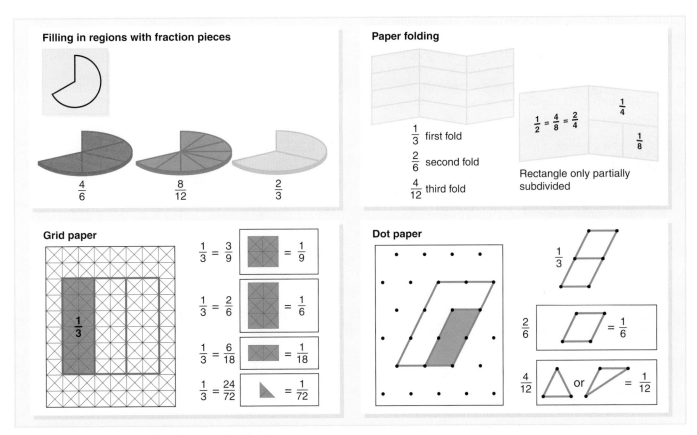

FIGURE 16.16 Area models for equivalent fractions.

includes an example drawn on an isometric grid. Students should draw a picture of the unit fractional part that they use for each fraction name. The larger the size of the whole, the more names the activity will generate.

The "Dot Paper Equivalencies" activity is a form of what Lamon (2002) calls "unitizing," that is, given a quantity, finding different ways to chunk the quantity into parts in order to name it. She points out that this is a key ability related not only to equivalent fractions but also to proportional reasoning, especially in the comparison of ratios. (See also Lamon, 1999a, b.)

EXPANDED LESSON

An expanded lesson plan based on Activity 16.14, "Dot Paper Equivalencies," can be found on the Companion Web site at www.ablongman.com/vandewalle6e.

Length models can be used to create activities similar to the "Different Fillers" task. For example, as shown in Figure 16.17, rods or strips can be used to designate both a whole and a part. Students use smaller rods to find fraction names for the given part. To have larger wholes and, thus, more possible parts, use a train of two or three rods for the whole and the part. Folding paper strips is another method of creating fraction names. In the example shown in Figure 16.17, one half is subdivided by successive folding in half. Other folds would produce other names and these possibilities should be discussed if no one tries to fold the strip in an odd number of parts.

The following activity is also a unitizing activity in which students look for different units or chunks of the whole in order to name a part of the whole in different ways. This activity is significant because it utilizes a set model.

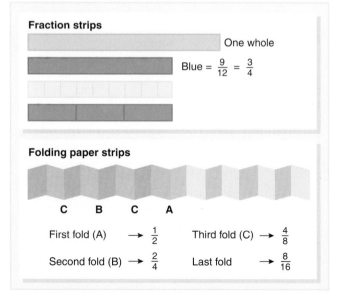

FIGURE 16.17 Length models for equivalent fractions.

activity **16.15**

Group the Counters, Find the Names

Have students set out a specific number of counters in two colors—for example, 24 counters, 16 of them red and 8 yellow. The 24 make up the whole. The task is to group the counters into different fractional parts of the whole and use the parts to create fraction names for the red and the yellow counters. In Figure 16.18, 24 counters are arranged in different array patterns. You might want to suggest arrays or allow students to arrange them in any way they wish. Students should record their different groupings and explain how they found the fraction names. They can simply use Xs and Os for the counters.

In Lamon's version of the last activity, she prompts students with questions such as, "If we make groups of four, what part of the set is red?" With these prompts you can suggest fraction names that students are unlikely to think of. For our example in Figure 16.18, if we make groups of one-half counters, what would the yellow set be

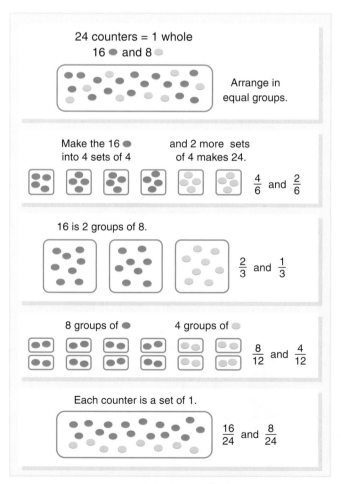

FIGURE 16.18 Set models for equivalent fractions.

called? Suppose we made groups of six? (Groups of six result in a fractional numerator. Why?)

In the activities so far, there has only been a hint of a rule for finding equivalent fractions. The following activity moves a bit closer but should still be done before development of a rule.

activity 16.16

Missing-Number Equivalencies

Give students an equation expressing an equivalence between two fractions but with one of the numbers missing. Here are four different examples:

$$\frac{5}{3} = \frac{\square}{6} \qquad \frac{2}{3} = \frac{6}{\square} \qquad \frac{8}{12} = \frac{\square}{3} \qquad \frac{9}{12} = \frac{3}{\square}$$

The missing number can be either a numerator or a denominator. Furthermore, the missing number can either be larger or smaller than the corresponding part of the equivalent fraction. (All four of these possibilities are represented in the examples.) The task is to find the missing number and to explain your solution. The examples shown involve simple whole-number multiples between equivalent fractions. As a challenge, consider pairs such as $\frac{6}{8} = \frac{\square}{12}$ or $\frac{9}{12} = \frac{6}{\square}$. In these pairs, neither fraction is in lowest terms, making the task more difficult and, therefore, more interesting.

When doing "Missing-Number Equivalencies" you may want to specify a particular model, such as sets or pie pieces. Alternatively, you can allow students to select whatever methods they wish to solve these problems. One or two equivalencies followed by a discussion is sufficient for a good lesson. This activity is surprisingly challenging, especially if students are required to use a set model.

Before continuing with development of an algorithm for equivalent fractions with your class, you should revisit the comparison tasks as children begin to realize that they can change the names of fractions in order to help reason about which fraction is greater or if they are equal.

Developing an Equivalent-Fraction Algorithm

Kamii and Clark (1995) argue that undue reliance on physical models does not help children construct equivalence schemes. When children understand that fractions can have different names, they should be challenged to develop a method for finding equivalent names. It might also be argued that students who are experienced at looking for patterns and developing schemes for doing things can invent an algorithm for equivalent fractions without further assistance. However, the following approach will certainly improve the chances of that happening.

An Area Model Approach

Your goal is to help students see that if they multiply both the top and bottom numbers by the same number, they will always get an equivalent fraction. The approach suggested here is to look for a pattern in the way that the fractional parts in both the part as well as the whole are counted. Activity 16.17 is a good beginning, but a good class discussion following the activity will also be required.

activity 16.17

Slicing Squares

Give students a worksheet with four squares in a row, each approximately 3 cm on a side. Have them shade in the same fraction in each square using vertical dividing lines. For example, slice each square in fourths and shade three-fourths as in Figure 16.19. Next, tell students to slice each square into an equal number of horizontal slices. Each square is sliced with a different number of slices, using anywhere from one to eight slices. For each sliced square, they should write an equation showing the equivalent fraction. Have them examine their four equations and the drawings and challenge them to discover any patterns in what they have done. You may want them to repeat this with four more squares and a different fraction.

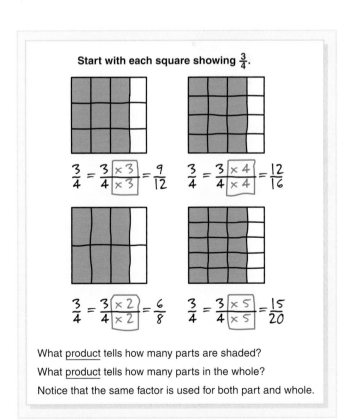

Start with each square showing $\frac{3}{4}$.

$$\frac{3}{4} = \frac{3 \boxed{\times 3}}{4 \boxed{\times 3}} = \frac{9}{12} \qquad \frac{3}{4} = \frac{3 \boxed{\times 4}}{4 \boxed{\times 4}} = \frac{12}{16}$$

$$\frac{3}{4} = \frac{3 \boxed{\times 2}}{4 \boxed{\times 2}} = \frac{6}{8} \qquad \frac{3}{4} = \frac{3 \boxed{\times 5}}{4 \boxed{\times 5}} = \frac{15}{20}$$

What <u>product</u> tells how many parts are shaded?

What <u>product</u> tells how many parts in the whole?

Notice that the same factor is used for both part and whole.

FIGURE 16.19 A model for the equivalent-fraction algorithm.

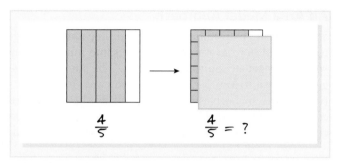

FIGURE 16.20 How can you count the fractional parts if you cannot see them all?

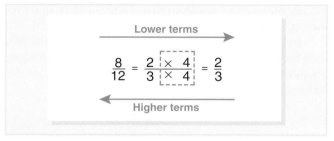

FIGURE 16.21 Using the equivalent-fraction algorithm to write fractions in simplest terms.

Following this activity, write on the board the equations for four or five different fraction names found by the students. Discuss any patterns they found. To focus the discussion, show on the overhead a square illustrating $\frac{4}{5}$ made with vertical slices as in Figure 16.20. Turn off the overhead and slice the square into six parts in the opposite direction. Cover all but two edges of the square as shown in the figure. Ask, "What is the new name for my $\frac{4}{5}$?"

The reason for this exercise is that many students simply count the small regions and never think to use multiplication. With the covered square, students can see that there are four columns and six rows to the shaded part, so there must be 4×6 parts shaded. Similarly, there must be 5×6 parts in the whole. Therefore, the new name for $\frac{4}{5}$ is $\frac{4 \times 6}{5 \times 6}$.

Using this idea, have students return to the fractions on their worksheet to see if the pattern works for other fractions.

Examine examples of equivalent fractions that have been generated with other models, and see if the rule of multiplying top and bottom numbers by the same number holds there also. If the rule is correct, how can $\frac{6}{8}$ and $\frac{9}{12}$ be equivalent? What about fractions like $2\frac{1}{4}$? How could it be demonstrated that $\frac{9}{4}$ is the same as $\frac{27}{12}$?

Writing Fractions in Simplest Terms

The multiplication scheme for equivalent fractions produces fractions with larger denominators. To write a fraction in *simplest terms* means to write it so that numerator and denominator have no common whole number factors. (Some texts use the name *lowest terms* instead of *simplest terms.*) One meaningful approach to this task of finding simplest terms is to reverse the earlier process, as illustrated in Figure 16.21. Try to devise a problem-based task that will help students develop this reverse idea.

Of course, finding and eliminating a common factor is the same as dividing both top and bottom by the same number. The search for a common factor keeps the process of writing an equivalent fraction to one rule: Top and bottom numbers of a fraction can be multiplied by the

same nonzero number. There is no need for a different rule for rewriting fractions in lowest terms.

Two additional notes:

1. Notice that the phrase *reducing fractions* was not used. This unfortunate terminology implies making a fraction smaller and is rarely used anymore in textbooks.

2. Many teachers seem to believe that fraction answers are incorrect if not in simplest or lowest terms. This is also unfortunate. When students add $\frac{1}{6} + \frac{1}{2}$ and get $\frac{4}{6}$, they have added correctly and have found the answer. Rewriting $\frac{4}{6}$ as $\frac{2}{3}$ is a separate issue.

Multiplying by One

Many middle school textbooks use a strictly symbolic approach to equivalent fractions. It is based on the multiplicative property that says that any number multiplied by 1 remains unchanged. Any fraction of the form $\frac{n}{n}$ can be used as the identity element. Therefore, $\frac{3}{4} = \frac{3}{4} \times 1 = \frac{3}{4} \times \frac{2}{2} = \frac{6}{8}$. Furthermore, the numerator and denominator of the identity element can also be fractions. In this way, $\frac{6}{12} = \frac{6}{12} \times \left(\frac{1/6}{1/6}\right) = \frac{1}{2}$.

This explanation relies on an understanding of the multiplicative identity property, which most students in grades 4 to 6 do not fully appreciate. It also relies on the procedure for multiplying two fractions. Finally, the argument uses solely deductive reasoning based on an axiom of the rational number system. It does not lend itself to intuitive modeling. A reasonable conclusion is to delay this important explanation until at least seventh or eighth grade in an appropriate prealgebra context and not as a method or a rationale for producing equivalent fractions.

 In the NCTM e-examples (http://standards. nctm.org/document/eexamples/index.htm), there is a very nice fraction game for two players (*Applet 5.1, Fraction Tracks*). The game uses a number-line model, and knowledge of equivalent fractions plays a significant role.

The NLVM Web site (http://nlvm.usu.edu/en/nav/ vlibrary.html) has a limited applet tool for exploring equivalent fractions, *Fractions—Equivalent.* Proper fractions are presented randomly in either square or circular formats.

Students can slice the model in as many parts as they wish to see which slicings create equivalent fractions. For squares, the new slices go in the same direction as the original slices. For circles, it is a bit hard to distinguish new slices from old. Students enter an equivalent fraction and then click a button to check their response. ■

Literature Connections

Fractions in textbooks and even in the activities in this chapter lack context. Context takes children away from rules and encourages them to explore ideas in a more open and informal manner. The way that children approach fraction concepts in these contexts may surprise you.

The Doorbell Rang
Hutchins, 1986

Often used to investigate whole-number operations of multiplication and division, this book is also an excellent early introduction to fractions. The story is a simple tale of two children preparing to share a plate of 12 cookies. Just as they have figured out how to share the cookies, the doorbell rings and more children arrive. This continues to happen until there are more children than cookies. Grandma saves the day. By changing the number of children to create an uneven division, children have to figure out how to divide the remaining cookies fairly. If given drawings of circles for cookies, investigations of situations such as four cookies for six children provide a variety of ways to solve fraction problems and discuss the need for fractional parts consisting of equal shares.

Gator Pie
Mathews, 1979

Appropriate even for grades 5 and 6, this delightful book has Alvin, Alice, and other alligators sharing a pie they find in the woods. As more and more gators arrive, the need for cutting the pie into more and more pieces is evident, finally ending in hundredths, making a nice connection between decimals and fractions. An interesting exploration involves cutting a pie (or a rectangle) into halves or thirds and then deciding how to share it among a larger number once already cut. To go from halves to sixths is reasonably easy but may surprise you. What if the pie is cut in thirds and then we want to share it in tenths?

The Man Who Counted: A Collection of Mathematical Adventures
Tahan, 1993

This book contains a story, "Beasts of Burden," about a wise mathematician, Beremiz, and the narrator, who are traveling together on one camel. They are asked by three brothers to solve an argument. Their father has left them 35 camels to divide among them: half to one brother, one-third to another, and one-ninth to the third. The story provides an excellent context for discussing fractional parts of sets and how fractional parts change as the whole changes. However, if the whole is changed from 35 to, say, 36 or 34, the problem of the indicated shares remains unresolved. The sum of $\frac{1}{2}$, $\frac{1}{3}$, and $\frac{1}{9}$ will never be one whole, no matter how many camels are involved. Bresser (1995) describes three full days of wonderful discussions with his fifth graders, who proposed a wide range of solutions. Bresser's suggestions are worth considering. ■

Reflections on Chapter 16

Writing to Learn

1. Describe what is meant by sharing activities. What is the goal of these activities? When would you use them? Distinguish between early and later sharing activities. What makes them different?
2. Give examples of three categories of fraction models. Why are set models more difficult for younger children?
3. Describe fractional parts. What are the two distinct requirements of fractional parts? Explain how children's concepts of partitioning need to be refined to produce a concept of fractional parts.
4. What are children learning in activities in which you count fractional parts? How can this type of activity help children learn to write fractions meaningfully?
5. Give a fourth-grade explanation of the meaning of the top number and the bottom number in a fraction.
6. Using a length model, make up part-and-whole questions for each of the following cases:
   a. Given a part and a nonunit fraction less than 1, find the whole.
   b. Given a part and a nonunit fraction greater than 1, find the whole.
   c. Given a whole and a nonunit fraction less than 1, find the part.
   d. Given a whole and a nonunit fraction greater than 1, find the part.

Try your questions with a friend. Then change each question so that it is in terms of sets. With sets, be sure that a unit fraction is never a single counter. That is, if the question is about fourths, use whole sets of size 8 or 12 or more. What is the main purpose of these activities?

7. Describe several types of ideas for number sense with fractions and an activity for each.

8. Make up pairs of fractions that can be compared ("select the larger") without using an algorithm. See if you can make up examples that use the four different ideas that were suggested for comparing fractions. How do these activities change as students begin to use equivalent fractions?

9. Explain the difference between understanding the concept of equivalent fractions and knowing the algorithm for writing an equivalent fraction.

10. Describe some activities that will help children develop the equivalent-fraction concept.

11. How can you help children develop the algorithm for equivalent fractions?

For Discussion and Exploration

1. A common error that children make is to write $\frac{3}{5}$ for the fraction represented here:

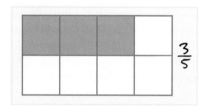

Why do you think that they do this? In this chapter, the notation of fractional parts and counting by unit fractions were introduced before any symbols. How could this help avoid the type of thinking that is involved in this common error?

2. Do you know what the requirements for fraction concepts are according to your state standards? There is considerable variation in state objectives relative to fractions, and many state objectives are not very helpful when it comes to what students should understand about fractions (as opposed to what they should be able to do). Compare your state objectives for two consecutive grades—third and fourth are suggested—with the ideas in this chapter. Then look at the textbooks used in your locality. How do all of these match up? What should you do as a teacher?

3. In an editorial in *Mathematics Teaching in the Middle School*, Patrick Groff (1996) questions the importance of teaching fractions in the upper-elementary and middle grades. His arguments are based in part on the difficulty of learning fraction ideas at this level, the decreased use of fractions in everyday life, and the press for space in the curriculum from other topics that have recently been introduced. His opinion is rebutted in the "Readers Write" section of the September–October 1996 issue by a former physicist and by a current teacher.

A few years later, a similar discussion appeared in *Teaching Children Mathematics* concerning teaching fractions in the primary grades. Watanabe (2001) argued against frac-

tions in the primary grades and then Powell and Hunting (2003) responded. The existence of these arguments alone is interesting. Read at least one pair of these short articles and take a stance that you can defend.

Recommendations for Further Reading

Burns, M. (2001). *Teaching arithmetic: Lessons for introducing fractions, grades 4–5*. Sausalito, CA: Math Solutions Publications.

Typical of Marilyn Burns, this book offers well-designed lessons with lots of details, sample student dialogue, and Blackline Masters. These are introductory ideas for fraction concepts. Five lessons cover one-half as a benchmark. Assessments are also included.

Flores, A., & Klein, E. (2005). From students' problem-solving strategies to connections in fractions. *Teaching Children Mathematics, 11*, 452–457.

This article offers a very realistic view (complete with photos of student work) of how children develop initial fraction concepts and an understanding of notation as they engage in sharing tasks like those described in this chapter. The information here is significant for anyone wishing to help students make this important connection.

Reys, B. J., Kim, O., & Bay, J. M. (1999). Establishing fraction benchmarks. *Mathematics Teaching in the Middle School, 4*, 530–532.

This short article describes a simple three-question interview administered to 20 fifth-grade students. The results are both sad and surprising. A significant conclusion is that the teaching of benchmarks for fractions, specifically 0, $\frac{1}{2}$, and 1, is generally neglected in the standard curriculum. The questions used in the interview can profitably be used with children in grades 4 to 7.

Stump, S. (2003). Designing fraction counting books. *Teaching Children Mathematics, 9*, 546–549.

This little article describes the work of several preservice teachers whose students created counting books in which they count by unit fractions as described in this chapter. Some nice examples are shared and the author describes difficulties and insights gained from this simple activity.

Tzur, R. (1999). An integrated study of children's construction of improper fractions and the teacher's role in promoting learning. *Journal for Research in Mathematics Education, 30*, 390–416.

Don't shy away from this research article. Tzur's teaching experiment is described in detail, providing the reader with a real understanding of the construction of fraction concepts at the fourth-grade level.

Watanabe, T. (1996). Ben's understanding of one-half. *Teaching Children Mathematics, 2*, 460–464.

This provocative article examines three very interesting tasks that were presented to a second-grade child. Even if you are interested in the upper grades, this is a worthwhile article. Not only are the tasks or variations of them quite interesting for all children, but the implications are also worth considering. Listening carefully to children informs us best.

Online Resources

Suggested Applets and Web Links

Fraction Bars

http://nlvm.usu.edu/en/nav/frames_asid_203_g_1_t_1.html

A very versatile model that is similar to the use of Cuisenaire rods except that bars are segmented. Students can create bars of any size from 1 to 10 in any color and place them anywhere on the screen. Multiple bars are easily made. There are no numbers or evaluation of what is being done.

Fraction Pieces

http://nlvm.usu.edu/en/nav/frames_asid_274_g_2_t_1. html?open=activities

A virtual version of both a circular model and a rectangular model for fraction pieces. Completely open-ended manipulation. If the square or circle is accepted as the whole, appropriate labels can be turned on.

Fraction Track

http://standards.nctm.org/document/eexamples/chap5/ 5.1/index.htm

Players position fractions on number lines with different denominators. Fractions can be split into parts. A challenging game involving equivalent-fraction concepts.

Fraction Pointer

www.shodor.org/interactive/activities/fracfinder1/ index.html

A good applet for connecting an area model with the number line. After creating area models for two fractions, the user must then create a new fraction between the first two. Similar to the *Illuminations* applet, Equivalent Fractions.

Fractions—Comparing

http://nlvm.usu.edu/en/nav/frames_asid_159_g_2_t_1.html

Students use models to find common denominators in order to compare two fractions and then locate both fractions on the number line and a new fraction between the first two.

Fractions—Visualizing

http://nlvm.usu.edu/en/nav/frames_asid_103_g_1_t_1.html

Users are given a fraction and a model that can be subdivided into as many sections as desired. By clicking on sections the fraction model is shaded to match the given fraction. Two even simpler versions are also available.

Who Wants Pizza? A Fun Way to Learn Fractions

http://math.rice.edu/%7Elanius/fractions/index.html

Not an applet but a series of interactive, albeit straightforward, lessons on fractions from the meaning of fractions through multiplication.

Companion Website

An additional list of books and articles related to the ideas in this chapter can be found on the Companion Web site at **www.ablongman.com/vandewalle6e.**

chapter 17

Computation with Fractions

 fifth-grade student asks, "Why is it when we times 29 times two-ninths that the answer goes down?" (Taber, 2002, p. 67). Although generalizations from whole numbers can confuse students, you should realize that their ideas about the operations were developed with whole numbers. Students need to build on their ideas of whole-number operations. This is where students are. We can use their understanding of what the operations mean to give meaning to fraction computation.

However, as you will discover in this chapter, a firm understanding of fractions is the most critical foundation for fraction computation. Without this foundation, your students will almost certainly be learning rules without reasons, an unacceptable goal.

▼ Big Ideas

1. The meanings of each operation on fractions are the same as the meanings for the operations on whole numbers. Operations with fractions should begin by applying these same meanings to fractional parts.
   - For addition and subtraction, it is critical to understand that the numerator tells the number of parts and the denominator the type of part.
   - For multiplication by a fraction, it is useful to recall that the denominator is a divisor. This idea allows us to find parts of the other factor. (See Chapter 16, p. 300.)
   - For division by a fraction, the two ways of thinking about the operation—partition and measurement—are extremely important. The partition or fair-sharing concept of division will lead to a very different division procedure than will the measurement or repeated subtraction concept.

2. Estimation of fraction computations is tied almost entirely to concepts of the operations and of fractions. A compu-

tation algorithm is not required for making estimates. Estimation should be an integral part of computation development to keep students' attention on the meanings of the operations and the expected size of the results.

▲ Mathematics
Content Connections

Computation with fractions is built on an understanding of the operations and on fraction sense. The ability to compute and estimate with fractions will serve the user well whenever these skills are required. However, understanding fraction computation has a special connection in two areas.

- **Decimals and Percents** (Chapter 18): Because decimals and percents are alternative representations for fractions, they can often help with computational fluency, especially in the area of estimation. For example, 2.452×0.513 is about $2\frac{1}{2} \times \frac{1}{2}$ or $1\frac{1}{4} = 1.25$. Twenty-five percent off of the $132 list price is easily computed as $\frac{1}{4}$ of 132.

- **Proportional Reasoning** (Chapter 19): Fraction multiplication helps us to think about fractions as operators. This in turn is connected to the concepts of ratio and proportion, especially the ideas of scaling and scale factors.

Number Sense and Fraction Algorithms

Today it is important to be able to compute with fractions, primarily for the purpose of making estimates, for understanding computations done with technology, and for relatively simple calculations. Even standardized testing reflects an emphasis on less-tedious computations with fractions.

The Dangerous Rush to Rules

It is important to give students ample opportunity to develop fraction number sense as described in the previous chapter and not immediately to start talking about common denominators and other rules of computation. Even in grade 7 or 8 it makes sense to delay computation and work on concepts if students are not conceptually ready.

Premature attention to rules for fraction computation has a number of serious drawbacks. None of the rules helps students think about the operations and what they mean. Armed only with rules, students have no means of assessing their results to see if they make sense. Surface mastery of rules in the short term is quickly lost. When mixed together, the myriad rules of fraction computation soon become a meaningless jumble. Students ask, "Do I need a common denominator, or do you just add the bottom numbers like in multiplication?" "Which one do you invert, the first or the second number?" The algorithm rules do not immediately apply to mixed numbers. More rules! And perhaps most important is that this approach to mathematics is immensely defeating to the child.

NCTM Standards *Principles and Standards* suggests that the main focus on fractions and decimals in grades 3–5 should be on the development of number sense and informal approaches to addition and subtraction. In grades 6–8, students should expand their skills to include all operations with fractions, decimals, and percents.

A Problem-Based, Number Sense Approach

Even if your curriculum guidelines call for teaching all four of the operations with fractions in the fifth grade, you are still advised to delay a rush to algorithmic procedures until it becomes clear that students are ready. (Very few states call for multiplication and division of fractions before the fifth grade.) Students can become adequately proficient using informal, student-invented methods that they understand.

The following guidelines should be kept in mind when developing computational strategies for fractions:

1. *Begin with simple contextual tasks.* Huinker (1998) makes an excellent case for the use of contextual problems and for letting students develop their own methods of computation with fractions. Problems or contexts need not be elaborate. What you want is a context for both the meaning of the operation and the fractions involved.

2. *Connect the meaning of fraction computation with whole-number computation.* To consider what $2\frac{1}{2} \times \frac{3}{4}$ might mean, we should ask, "What does 2×3 mean?" The concepts of each operation are the same, and benefits can be had by connecting these ideas.

3. *Let estimation and informal methods play a big role in the development of strategies.* "Should $2\frac{1}{2} \times \frac{3}{4}$ be more or less than 1? More or less than 3?" Estimation keeps the focus on the meanings of the numbers and the operations, encourages reflective thinking, and helps build informal number sense with fractions.

4. *Explore each of the operations using models.* Use a variety of models. Have students defend their solutions using the models including simple student drawings. You will find that sometimes it is possible to get answers with models that do not seem to help with pencil-and-paper approaches. That's fine! The ideas will help children learn to think about the fractions and the operations, contribute to mental methods, and provide a useful background when you eventually do get to the standard algorithms.

In the discussions that follow, informal exploration is encouraged for each operation. There is also a guided development of each traditional algorithm.

Addition and Subtraction

As with whole-number computation, provide computational tasks without giving rules or procedures for completing them. Expect that students will use a variety of methods and that the methods will vary widely with the fractions encountered in the problems.

No attempt is made in this chapter to describe all of the solution strategies that students might develop. Students will continue to find ways to solve problems with fractions, and their informal approaches will contribute to the development of more standard methods (Huinker, 1998; Lappan & Mouck, 1998; Schifter, Bastable, & Russell, 1999c).

Informal Exploration

Consider the following problem.

Mark bought $4\frac{1}{4}$ pounds of candy for his mom. The candy looked so good that he ate $\frac{7}{8}$ of a pound of it. How much did he give to his mom?

A fifth-grade class was asked to solve this problem in two ways. Many students attempted or correctly used a standard subtraction algorithm for mixed numbers as one method. However, not a single drawing or other explanation could be found in the class for the algorithm. As shown in Figure 17.1, Christian makes an error with the algorithm but draws a correct picture showing $4\frac{1}{4} = \frac{34}{8}$ and gets a correct answer of $\frac{27}{8}$. However, he is not confident in his drawing and crosses it out. Although many students do not understand their procedural methods, those who are not used to justifying their methods will believe in the algorithm more than their own reasoning.

A drawing method used by many in the class involved taking the $\frac{1}{8}$ left from the $\frac{7}{8}$ and adding it onto the $\frac{1}{4}$ as shown in Brandon's drawing. Only DaQuawn does this first in a symbolic manner. His "second method" is a drawing supporting his work. When DaQuawn shares with the class he says, "I took this from eighths so I could minus it from $\frac{7}{8}$. That leaves $\frac{1}{8}$. Then change [points to quarter circle] to $\frac{2}{8}$. Minus $\frac{1}{8}$ from . . . no, add it to $\frac{1}{8}$ equals $\frac{2}{8}$ plus $\frac{1}{8}$ equals $\frac{3}{8}$." DaQuawn's teacher notes that he "struggles with reading and writing although he has good number sense." This teacher correctly values students' thinking and distinguishes it from their abilities to express ideas.

These examples not only illustrate how written work can force students to explain their thinking, but they also illustrate that students have great difficulty with any explanation for algorithms that they have not developed themselves.

Students seem to have a preference for drawing circles to represent fractions. Perhaps that says something about an overuse of that model. The drawings in Figure 17.1 are not accurate. However, the students are not making conclusions based on the size of the pieces, but rather they are drawing to explain their reasoning. When students are using drawings in this manner, do not be concerned with poorly drawn fractions.

How you ask students to solve a problem can make a difference in what will happen in the classroom. For example, consider this problem:

Jack and Jill ordered two medium pizzas, one cheese and one pepperoni. Jack ate $\frac{5}{6}$ of a pizza and Jill ate $\frac{1}{2}$ of a pizza. How much pizza did they eat together?

⏸ *pause and reflect* ——————————

Try to think of two ways that students might solve this problem without using a common denominator symbolic approach.

———————————————————————

If students draw circles as in the earlier example, some will try to fill in the $\frac{1}{6}$ gap in the pizza. Then they will need to figure out how to get $\frac{1}{6}$ from $\frac{1}{2}$. If they can think of $\frac{1}{2}$ as $\frac{3}{6}$, they can use one of the sixths to fill in the gap. Another approach, after drawing the two circular pizzas, is to notice that there is a half plus 2 more sixths in the $\frac{5}{6}$ pizza. Put the two halves together to make one whole and there are $\frac{2}{6}$ more—$1\frac{2}{6}$. These are certainly good solutions that represent the type of informal thinking that you want to encourage.

Now suppose that you had asked the students to solve the same pizza problem using Cuisenaire rods or fraction strips. The first decision that must be made is what strip to use as the whole. That decision is not required with a circular model. The whole must be the same for both fractions although there is a tendency to use the easiest whole for each fraction. Again, this issue does not arise with circles. In this case, the smallest strip that will work is the 6 strip or the dark green strip. Figure 17.2(a) illustrates a solution. The thinking required in this task helps pave the way for a common-denominator approach. Figure 17.2(b) illustrates how a similar addition might be done with a set model.

As we saw in the very first example (Figure 17.1), students can and do use informal methods for subtraction as well as addition. This informal reasoning is extremely important. Students should become comfortable with different methods of taking simple fractions apart and recombining them in ways that make sense. Keep the fractions in your problems "friendly" with denominators no greater than 12. There is no need to add fifths and sevenths or even fifths and twelfths. With numbers like that,

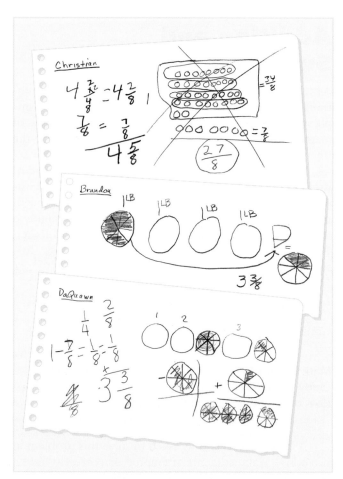

FIGURE 17.1 Fifth-grade students show how they solved the problem $4\frac{1}{4} - \frac{7}{8}$ For most students, their methods based on drawings have little to do with their symbolic algorithms. The work of DaQuawn, a student who struggles, is an exception.

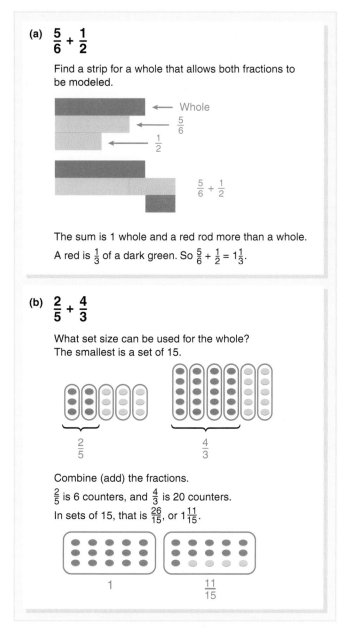

FIGURE 17.2 Using models to add fractions can force students to think about common denominators.

drawings are next to impossible and very large common denominators are almost required. Although forcing the use of a model such as fraction strips or sets can cause students to prepare for common denominators, it is best to delay that emphasis in the beginning.

The Myth of Common Denominators

Teachers commonly tell students, "In order to add or subtract fractions, you must first get common denominators." The explanation usually goes something like, "After all, you can't add apples and oranges." This well-intentioned statement is essentially false. A correct state-

ment might be, "In order *to use the standard algorithm* to add or subtract fractions, you must first get common denominators." And the explanation is then, "The algorithm is designed to work only with common denominators."

Using their own invented strategies, students will see that many correct solutions are found without ever getting a common denominator. Consider these sums and differences:

$$\frac{3}{4} + \frac{1}{8} \qquad \frac{1}{2} - \frac{1}{8} \qquad \frac{2}{3} + \frac{1}{2} \qquad 1\frac{1}{2} - \frac{3}{4} \qquad 1\frac{2}{3} + \frac{3}{4}$$

Working with the ways different fractional parts are related one to another often provides solutions without common denominators. For example, halves, fourths, and eighths are easily related. Also, picture three-thirds making up a whole in a circle as in Figure 17.3. Have you ever noticed that one-half of the whole is a third plus a half of a third or a sixth? Similarly, the difference between a third and a fourth is a twelfth. Another helpful model is a clock face where each five-minute interval is one-twelfth of the whole. With relationships such as these, many fraction computations can be solved without first getting common denominators.

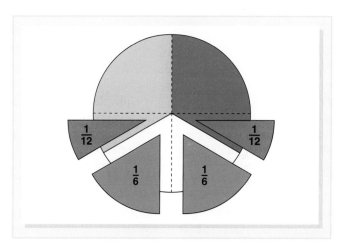

FIGURE 17.3 There are lots of fractional relationships that can be observed simply by looking at how halves, thirds, fourths, sixths, and twelfths fit into a partitioned circle.

Developing the Algorithm

The foregoing notwithstanding, it is reasonable to develop an algorithm for addition and subtraction, and children will likely need some guidance in doing so. At the same time, they can easily build on their informal explorations and see that the common-denominator approach is meaningful.

Like Denominators

Most lists of objectives first specify addition and subtraction with like denominators. This is both unfortunate and unnecessary! If students have a good foundation with fraction concepts, they should be able to add or subtract like fractions immediately. Students who are not confident solving problems such as $\frac{3}{4} + \frac{2}{4}$ or $3\frac{7}{8} - 1\frac{3}{8}$ almost certainly do not have good fraction concepts and will be lost in any further development. The idea that the top number counts and the bottom number tells what is counted makes addition and subtraction of like fractions the same as adding and subtracting whole numbers.

 The ease with which students can or cannot add like-denominator fractions should be viewed as an important concept assessment before pushing students forward to an algorithm. As just noted, students who do not see these sums or differences as trivial likely do not understand the meanings of the numerator and denominator. Any further symbolic development will almost certainly be without understanding.

An understanding of the algorithms for addition and subtraction also is heavily dependent on a conceptual understanding of fraction equivalence. Have students complete a sum such as $\frac{3}{8} + \frac{4}{8}$ and write the finished equation on the board. Then, beneath this equation, write a second sum made of easily seen equivalents for each fraction as shown here:

$$\frac{3}{8} + \frac{4}{8} = \frac{7}{8}$$
$$\frac{6}{16} + \frac{1}{2} = ?$$

Discuss briefly the fact that $\frac{3}{8}$ is equivalent to $\frac{6}{16}$ as is $\frac{4}{8}$ to $\frac{1}{2}$. Now have students write the answer to the second equation and give a reason for their answer. Students should see that the answer is $\frac{7}{8}$. The second sum is the same as the first because although the fractions *look* different, they are actually the same numbers. Students who do not readily pick up on this may not understand the concept of equivalence and additional work with equivalence may be warranted. ■

Unlike Denominators

To get students to move to common denominators, consider a task such as $\frac{5}{8} + \frac{2}{4}$ where only one fraction needs to be changed. Let students use any method to get the result of $1\frac{1}{8}$. Many will note that the models for the two fractions make one whole and there is $\frac{1}{8}$ extra. The key question to ask at this point is, "How can we change this problem into one that is just like the easy ones where the parts are the same?" For this example, it is relatively easy to see that fourths could be changed into eighths. Have students use models or drawings to explain why the original problem and also the converted problem should have the same answer.

Next try some examples where both fractions need to be changed—for example, $\frac{2}{3} + \frac{1}{4}$. Encourage students to solve these problems without use of models or drawings if possible. Suggest (don't require) that the use of equivalent

fractions might be an easier tool than a drawing. In the discussion of student solutions, focus attention on the idea of *rewriting the problem* to make it easier. Be certain that students understand that the rewritten problem is the same as the original and, therefore, must have the same answer. Of course, this can and should be confirmed by modeling both forms of the sum. However, if your students express any doubt about the equivalence of the two problems ("Is $\frac{11}{12}$ really the answer to $\frac{2}{3} + \frac{1}{4}$?"), that should be a clue that the concept of equivalent fractions is not well understood.

As students continue to explore solutions to sums and differences of fractions, models should remain available for use. The three examples in Figure 17.4 show how models might be used. Note that fraction strips and set models require students to think about the size of a whole that can be used with both fractions.

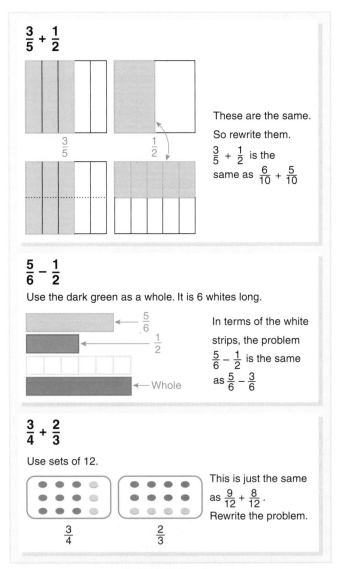

FIGURE 17.4 Rewriting addition and subtraction problems involving fractions.

The most common error in adding fractions is to add both numerators and denominators. Rather than jump in and attempt to correct this error directly, capitalize on the opportunity for a wonderful class discussion. One idea is to show students the following solution for adding $\frac{1}{2} + \frac{1}{3}$ that you "saw" offered by a fictional student in another class:

Therefore, $\frac{1}{2} + \frac{1}{3} = \frac{2}{5}$.

Add tops and bottoms.

Ask students to decide if the student could be right. If not, what is wrong with the solution?

Ⅱ *pause and reflect* ────────────

Why can't the answer be $\frac{2}{5}$ and what is wrong with the student's reasoning?

─────────────────────

Focus first on the answer. The sum of $\frac{2}{5}$ is smaller than $\frac{1}{2}$ when, in fact, $\frac{1}{2} + \frac{1}{3}$ must be more than $\frac{1}{2}$. When students are convinced that the sum cannot be $\frac{2}{5}$, there is real value in letting them decide what is wrong with the reasoning. The flaw is an easy error for students to make when using a fraction model where the whole is not a fixed size as it is with circular pie pieces. In the example here, each of the fractions in the equation is modeled with a different whole. Refer back to the pizza fallacy discussed in Chapter 16 (p. 306).

Common Multiples

Many students have trouble with finding common denominators because they are not able to come up with common multiples of the denominators quickly. That is a skill that you may wish to drill. It also depends on having a good command of the basic facts for multiplication. Here is an activity aimed at the skill of finding least common multiples or common denominators.

activity **17.1**

LCM Flash Cards

Make flash cards with pairs of numbers that are potential denominators. Most should be less than 16. For each card, students try to give the least common multiple, or LCM (see Figure 17.5). Be sure to include pairs that are prime, such as 9 and 5; pairs in which one is a multiple of the other, such as 2 and 8; and pairs that have a common divisor, such as 8 and 12.

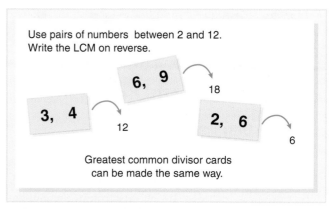

FIGURE 17.5 Least common multiple (LCM) flash cards.

Mixed Numbers

A separate algorithm for mixed numbers in addition and subtraction is not necessary even though mixed numbers are often treated as separate topics in traditional textbooks and in some lists of objectives. Avoid layering fractions with yet another rule. Include mixed numbers in all of your activities with addition and subtraction, and let students solve these problems in ways that make sense to them. Furthermore, it is almost certain that students will add the whole numbers first and then deal with the fractions using the algorithm or whatever method makes sense.

For subtraction, dealing with the whole numbers first still makes sense. Consider this problem: $5\frac{1}{8} - 3\frac{5}{8}$. After subtracting 3 from 5, students will need to deal with the $\frac{5}{8}$. Some will take $\frac{5}{8}$ from the whole part, 2, leaving $1\frac{3}{8}$, and then $\frac{1}{8}$ more is $1\frac{4}{8}$. Others may take away the $\frac{1}{8}$ that is there and then $\frac{4}{8}$ from the remaining 2. A third but unlikely method is to trade one of the wholes for $\frac{8}{8}$, add it to the $\frac{1}{8}$, and then take $\frac{5}{8}$ from the resulting $\frac{9}{8}$. This last method is the same as the traditional algorithm.

Estimation and Simple Methods

With denominators of 16 or less, estimation using "nice" fractions like halves and fourths is usually possible and should be encouraged. Estimation also leads to informal methods that are often easier than traditional algorithms for getting exact answers.

Consider $7\frac{1}{8} - 2\frac{3}{4}$. A first estimate might be 5, ignoring the fractions. Will it be more or less than 5? Others may begin by thinking $7\frac{1}{8}$ is close to 7 and $2\frac{3}{4}$ is close to 3 ──→ about 4, maybe a little more. Once students begin to think in these terms, a meaningful method for an exact answer is often possible without using an algorithm.

Examine the fraction exercises for addition and subtraction in a middle grades textbook. See how many of them you can do without pencil and paper. Challenge students to do the same.

At the sixth grade, the *Connected Mathematics* program does not spend a great deal of time with addition and

Connected *Mathematics*

Grade 6, Bits and Pieces II
Investigation 4: Adding and Subtracting Fractions

Context

Bits and Pieces II is the second full unit of the sixth grade that explores fractions. In the earlier unit, the emphasis is placed on fraction meanings and connections to decimals and percents. In this unit, strategies for all four of the operations are explored as well as computations with decimals and percents.

Task Description

This problem builds on students' understanding of fractions as part of a region. Two sections of land are shown on the map, each section being 640 acres (1 square mile). The problem is in two parts. First, students are to determine what fraction of a section (one square) each person owns. As a follow-up they also find the number of acres each person owns, an early application of a fraction times a whole number.

The second part of the problem includes a small logic task, as well as addition of fractions, involving owners of some parcels sold to other landowners. Students are given clues about the transactions. Their task is to redraw the map, find out how much land each of the remaining four owners has, and to explain their reasoning. Here are the transaction clues:

Clue 1: When all the sales are completed, four people—Theule, Fuentes, Wong, and Gardella—own all of the land in the two sections.

Clue 2: Theule bought from one person and now owns land equivalent to $\frac{1}{2}$ of one section.

Clue 3: Fuentes bought from three people and now owns the equivalent of $\frac{13}{32}$ of one section.

Clue 4: Gardella now owns the equivalent of $\frac{1}{2}$ of a section.

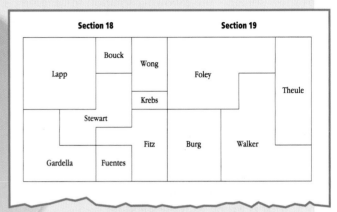

From *Connected Mathematics: Bits and Pieces II: Using Rational Numbers.* © 2002 by Michigan State University, Glenda Lappan, James T. Fey, William M. Fitzgerald, Susan N. Friel, & Elizabeth Difanis Phillips. Published by Pearson Education, Inc., publishing as Pearson Prentice Hall. Used by permission.

Clue 5: Wong now owns all of the rest of the land in the two sections.

Clue 6: Each of the four owners can walk around all of their land without having to cross onto another person's land.

According to the manual, most students end up subdividing each section with an 8 × 8 grid and use this to determine the fractional part of each parcel. In the discussion, students are encouraged not only to use their drawings but also to use addition of fractions to justify their conclusions from the clues.

The logical reasoning component and the contextual setting for this problem make it engaging for sixth graders. In the next lesson, students are challenged to design at least one algorithm for adding fractions and one for subtracting fractions. Notice how the land problem can help students see a value in a common denominator and prepare them for designing their own procedures.

subtraction of fractions. However, it pays considerable attention to connecting fractions, decimals, and percents. The activity described here involves an open-ended approach to fraction addition appropriate at that grade level.

Multiplication

When working with whole numbers, we would say that 3 × 5 means "3 sets of 5." The first factor tells how much of

the second factor you have or want. This is a good place to begin. Simple story problems are a significant help in this development.

Informal Exploration

The story problems that you use to pose multiplication tasks to children need not be elaborate, but it is important to think about the numbers that you use in the problems.

A possible progression of problem difficulty is developed in the sections that follow.

Beginning Concepts

Consider these two problems as good starting tasks:

There are 15 cars in Michael's toy car collection. Two-thirds of the cars are red. How many red cars does Michael have?

Suzanne has 11 cookies. She wants to share them with her three friends. How many cookies will Suzanne and each of her friends get?

Finding the fractional part of a whole number, which is the task in both problems, is not unlike the task of finding a fractional part of a whole. In Michael's car problem, think of the 15 cars as the whole and you want $\frac{2}{3}$ of the whole. First, find thirds by dividing 15 by 3. Multiplying by thirds, regardless of how many thirds, involves dividing by 3. The denominator is a divisor.

Suzanne's cookie problem is the same as the sharing problems discussed in the last chapter. Dividing by 4 is the same as multiplication by $\frac{1}{4}$. Or think of the 11 cookies as the whole. How many in one-fourth? Cookies are used so that the items can be subdivided. The many ways that students solve these sharing problems were discussed in Chapter 16.

Problems in which the first factor or multiplier is a whole number are also important.

Wayne filled 5 glasses with $\frac{2}{3}$ liter of soda in each glass. How much soda did Wayne use?

This problem may be solved in different ways. Some children will put the thirds together, making wholes as they go. Others will count all of the thirds and then find out how many whole liters are in 10 thirds.

Unit Parts Without Subdivisions

To expand on the ideas just presented, consider these three problems:

You have $\frac{3}{4}$ of a pizza left. If you give $\frac{1}{3}$ of the leftover pizza to your brother, how much of a whole pizza will your brother get?

Someone ate $\frac{1}{10}$ of the cake, leaving only $\frac{9}{10}$. If you eat $\frac{2}{3}$ of the cake that is left, how much of a whole cake will you have eaten?

Gloria used $2\frac{1}{2}$ tubes of blue paint to paint the sky in her picture. Each tube holds $\frac{4}{5}$ ounce of paint. How many ounces of blue paint did Gloria use?

Notice that the units or fractional parts in these problems do not need to be subdivided further. The first problem is $\frac{1}{3}$ of three things, the second is $\frac{2}{3}$ of nine things, and the last is $2\frac{1}{2}$ of four things. The focus remains on the number of unit parts in all, and then the size of the parts determines the number of wholes. Figure 17.6 shows how problems of this type might be modeled. However, it is very important to let students model and solve these problems in their own way, using whatever models or drawings they choose. Require only that they be able to explain their reasoning.

Subdividing the Unit Parts

When the pieces must be subdivided into smaller unit parts, the problems become more challenging.

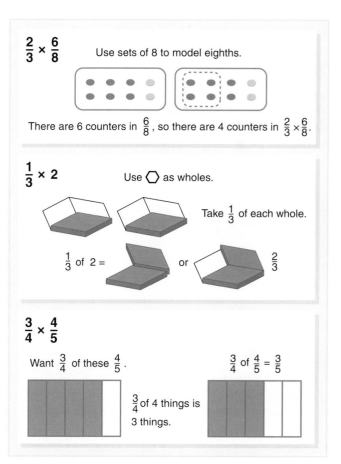

FIGURE 17.6 Modeling multiplication problems in which the unit pieces do not require further subdivision.

Zack had $\frac{2}{3}$ of the lawn left to cut. After lunch, he cut $\frac{3}{4}$ of the grass he had left. How much of the whole lawn did Zack cut after lunch?

The zookeeper had a huge bottle of the animals' favorite liquid treat, Zoo Cola. The monkey drank $\frac{1}{5}$ of the bottle. The zebra drank $\frac{2}{3}$ of what was left. How much of the bottle of Zoo Cola did the zebra drink?

Ⅱ *pause and reflect* _____

Pause for a moment and figure out how you would solve each of these problems. Draw pictures to help you, but do not use a computational algorithm.

In Zack's lawn problem, it is necessary to find fourths of two things, the 2 *thirds* of the grass left to cut. In the Zoo Cola problem, you need thirds of four things, the 4 *fifths* of the cola that remain. Again, the concepts of the top number counting and the bottom number naming what is counted play an important role. Figure 17.7 shows two possible solutions for Zack's lawn problem. Similar approaches can be used for the Zoo Cola problem. You may have used different drawings, but the ideas should be the same.

If students use counters to model problems where the units require subdivision, an added difficulty arises. Figure 17.8 illustrates what might happen solving the problem $\frac{3}{5} \times \frac{2}{3}$. (*Three-fifths of $\frac{2}{3}$ of a whole is how much of a whole?*) Here the representation of a whole must be changed so that the thirds can be subdivided. Sets of 6, 9, and 12 can all be used to show thirds. For each of these,

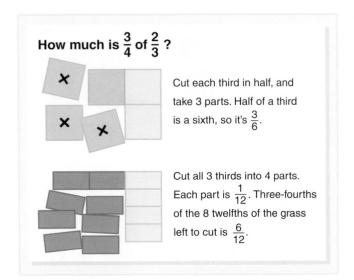

How much is $\frac{3}{4}$ of $\frac{2}{3}$?

Cut each third in half, and take 3 parts. Half of a third is a sixth, so it's $\frac{3}{6}$.

Cut all 3 thirds into 4 parts. Each part is $\frac{1}{12}$. Three-fourths of the 8 twelfths of the grass left to cut is $\frac{6}{12}$.

FIGURE 17.7 Solutions to fraction products when the unit parts must be subdivided.

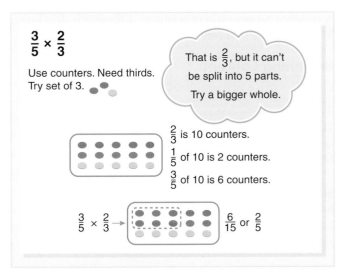

FIGURE 17.8 Modeling multiplication of fractions with counters.

however, $\frac{2}{3}$ of a whole cannot be broken into 5 parts to get $\frac{3}{5}$. When a set of 15 is used as the whole, $\frac{2}{3}$ is shown with 10 counters and the problem can be solved. Do not discourage students from using counters, but be prepared to help them find ways to show thirds using larger sets.

The problem in Figure 17.8 offers another possible twist worth mentioning. Since there is no context to the problem, why not use the commutative property—turn the factors around and consider $\frac{2}{3}$ of $\frac{3}{5}$. Wow! Do you see that the answer is $\frac{2}{5}$ almost immediately?

EXPANDED LESSON

An expanded lesson plan for having students explore multiplication of fractions can be found on the Companion Web site at www.ablongman.com/vandewalle6e.

Developing the Algorithm

If you have spent adequate time with your students exploring multiplication of fractions as just described, the traditional multiplication algorithm will be relatively simple to develop. Shift from contextual problems to a straight computation. Have students use a square or a rectangle as the model.

A Beginning Task

To make a problem-based task for students, provide them with a drawing of $\frac{3}{4}$ of a square as shown in Figure 17.9. The task is to use the drawing to determine the product $\frac{3}{5} \times \frac{3}{4}$ (three-fifths of three-fourths of a whole) and explain the result. Remember, you want to find a fractional part of the shaded part. The *unit*, however, the way the parts are measured, must remain the whole square.

Drawn as shown, the easiest way to get $\frac{3}{4}$ of the shaded region is to divide it into fourths using lines in the

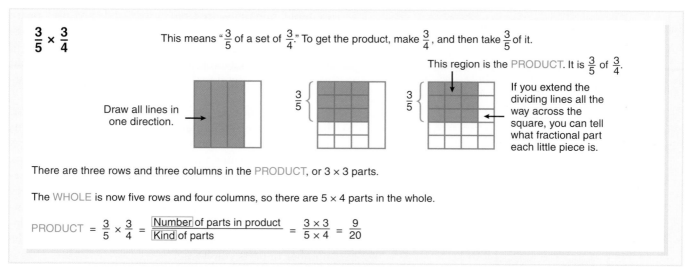

FIGURE 17.9 Development of the algorithm for multiplication of fractions.

opposite direction. Then the problem is to determine what types of unit pieces these are. Although students may not think of it, an easy method of doing this is to extend the lines, subdividing the entire whole into fourths. Then the product of the denominators tells how many pieces are in the whole (the kind of unit), and the product of the numerators tells the number of pieces in the product.

Avoid pushing students to formalize the rule or algorithm of multiplying tops and bottoms. Many students will simply count each small part in the drawings and not notice that the numbers of rows and columns are actually the two numerators and the two denominators, respectively. You might steer students in this direction by posing a problem with the initial sketch but asking them to determine the product without additional drawing. Try this with $\frac{7}{8} \times \frac{4}{5}$, where the numbers make it almost mandatory that you multiply.

A cautionary note: Many texts make this sliced-square approach so mechanical that it actually becomes a meaningless algorithm in itself. Students are told to shade a square one way for the first factor and the opposite way for the second factor. Without rationale, they are told that the product is the region that is double-shaded. You might as well give students the rule and forget about explanations.

Factors Greater Than One

Many textbooks have students change mixed numbers to improper fractions in order to multiply them. In that way, the same algorithm can be applied. Although there is nothing mathematically wrong with this method, it is not necessary. As students are exploring multiplication, begin to include tasks where one of the factors is a mixed number. For example, $\frac{3}{4} \times 2\frac{1}{2}$. Students who understand that $2\frac{1}{2}$ means $2 + \frac{1}{2}$ will almost certainly multiply $\frac{3}{4} \times 2$ and $\frac{3}{4} \times \frac{1}{2}$ and add the results—the distributive property.

When both factors are mixed numbers, there are four partial products, just as there are when multiplying 2 two-digit numbers.

⏸ *pause and reflect* _____

Find the four partial products in this multiplication: $3\frac{2}{3} \times 2\frac{1}{4}$.

_____

Figure 17.10 shows how this product might be worked out by multiplying the individual parts. In most cases, the resulting fractions are not likely to be difficult to work with. More importantly, the process is more conceptual and also lends itself to estimation—either before the partial products are determined or after.

Figure 17.11 shows how the same product is modeled using the area approach that was used for fractions less than 1. Notice that by changing this relatively simple problem to improper fractions and applying the algorithm, the result is $\frac{99}{12}$, a rather formidable-looking fraction. The partial product method of Figure 17.10 seems to make

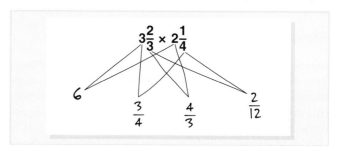

FIGURE 17.10 When multiplying two mixed numbers, there will be four partial products. These can then be added up to get the total product or an estimate may be enough. Here the answer is about 8.

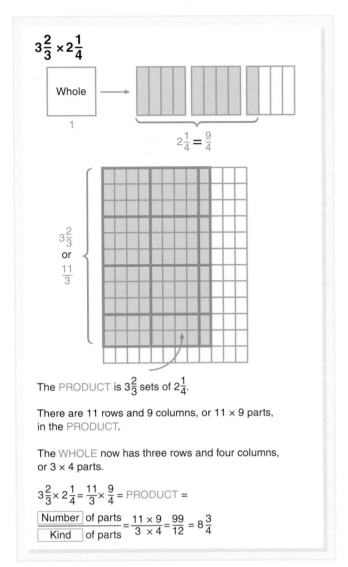

$3\frac{2}{3} \times 2\frac{1}{4}$

The PRODUCT is $3\frac{2}{3}$ sets of $2\frac{1}{4}$.

There are 11 rows and 9 columns, or 11 × 9 parts, in the PRODUCT.

The WHOLE now has three rows and four columns, or 3 × 4 parts.

$3\frac{2}{3} \times 2\frac{1}{4} = \frac{11}{3} \times \frac{9}{4} = $ PRODUCT =

$\dfrac{\boxed{\text{Number}} \text{ of parts}}{\boxed{\text{Kind}} \text{ of parts}} = \dfrac{11 \times 9}{3 \times 4} = \dfrac{99}{12} = 8\frac{3}{4}$

FIGURE 17.11 The same approach used to develop the algorithm for fractions less than 1 can be expanded to mixed numbers.

much more sense. Notice that the same four partial products of Figure 17.10 can be found in the rectangle in Figure 17.11.

Mental Techniques and Estimation

Staying with the same product of $3\frac{2}{3} \times 2\frac{1}{4}$ for a moment, how would you estimate the answer? Using the estimation technique of rounding one factor up and the other down, this product might be estimated as 4 × 2. That simple estimation may be all that is required in a real setting. It is also good enough to help students know if their calculated answer is in the right ballpark.

In the real world, there are many instances when the product of a whole number times a fraction occurs, and a mental estimate or even an exact answer is quite useful. For

example, sale items are frequently listed as "$\frac{1}{4}$ off," or we read of a "$\frac{1}{3}$ increase" in the number of registered voters. Fractions are excellent substitutes for percents, as you will see in the next chapter. To get an estimate of 60 percent of \$36.69, it is useful to think of 60 percent as $\frac{3}{5}$ or as a little less than $\frac{2}{3}$.

These products of fractions with large whole numbers can be calculated mentally by thinking of the meanings of the top and bottom numbers. For example, $\frac{3}{5}$ is 3 *one*-fifths. So if you want $\frac{3}{5}$ of 350, for example, first think about *one*-fifth of 350, or 70. If *one*-fifth is 70, then *three*-fifths is 3 × 70, or 210. Although this example has very accommodating numbers, it illustrates a process for mentally multiplying a large number by a fraction: First determine the unit fractional part, and then multiply by the number of parts you want.

When numbers are not so nice, encourage students to use compatible numbers. To estimate $\frac{3}{5}$ of \$36.69, a useful compatible is \$35. One-fifth of 35 is 7, so three-fifths is 3 × 7, or 21. Now adjust a bit—perhaps add an additional 50 cents, for an estimate of \$21.50.

Students should practice estimating fractions times whole numbers in lots of real contexts: $3\frac{1}{4}$ gallons of paint at \$14.95 per gallon or $\frac{7}{8}$ of the 476 students who attended Friday's football game. When working with decimals and percents, these skills will be revisited, and once again mathematics will seem more connected than disconnected.

Division

Invert the divisor and multiply is probably one of the most mysterious rules in elementary mathematics. We want to avoid this mystery at all costs. However, first it makes sense to examine division with fractions from a more familiar perspective.

As with the other operations, go back to the meaning of division with whole numbers. Recall that there are two meanings of division: partition and measurement. We will review each briefly and look at some story problems that involve fractions. (Can you make up a word problem right now that would go with the computation $2\frac{1}{2} \div \frac{1}{4}$?)

You should have students explore both measurement and partition problems. Here we will discuss each type of problem separately for the purpose of clarity. In the classroom, the types of problems should probably be mixed. As with multiplication, how the numbers relate to each other in the problems tends to affect the difficulty.

Informal Exploration: Partition Concept

Too often we think of the partition problems strictly as sharing problems: 24 apples to be shared with 4 friends. How many will each friend get? Recall from Chapter 10, however, that this same sharing structure applies to rate problems: If you walk 12 miles in 3 hours, how many miles do you walk per hour? Both of these problems, in fact, all partition problems, ask the questions, "How much is one?" "How much is the amount for *one* friend?" "How many miles are walked in *one* hour?" The 24 is the amount for the 4 friends. The 12 miles is the amount for the 3 hours.

Whole-Number Divisors

Having the total amount be a fraction with the divisor a whole number is not really a big leap. These problems still are easy to think of as sharing situations. However, as you work through these questions, notice that you are answering the question, "How much is the whole?" or "How much for one?"

Cassie has $5\frac{1}{4}$ yards of ribbon to make three bows for birthday packages. How much ribbon should she use for each bow if she wants to use the same length of ribbon for each?

When the $5\frac{1}{4}$ is thought of as fractional parts, there are 21 fourths to share, or 7 fourths for each ribbon. Alternatively, one might think of first allotting 1 yard per bow, leaving $2\frac{1}{4}$ yards, or 9 fourths. These 9 fourths are then shared, 3 fourths per bow, for a total of $1\frac{3}{4}$ yards for each bow. Regardless of the particular process, the unit parts required no further subdivision in order to do the division. In the following problem, the parts must be split into smaller parts.

Mark has $1\frac{1}{4}$ hours to finish his three household chores. If he divides his time evenly, how many hours can he give to each?

Note that the question is, "How much for one chore?" The 5 fourths of an hour that Mark has do not split neatly into three parts. So some or all of the parts must be subdivided. Figure 17.12 shows three different models for figuring this out. In each case, all of the fourths are subdivided into three equal parts, producing twelfths. There are a total of 15 twelfths, or $\frac{5}{12}$ hour for each chore. (Test this answer against the solution in minutes: $1\frac{1}{4}$ hours is 75 minutes, which divided among 3 chores is 25 minutes per chore.)

Fractional Divisors

The sharing concept appears to break down when the divisor is a fraction. However, it is enormously helpful to keep in mind that for partition and rate problems the fundamental question is, "How much is one?" Interestingly,

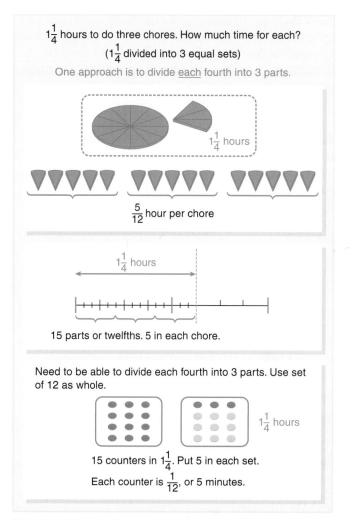

FIGURE 17.12 Three models of partition division with a whole-number divisor.

this is exactly the second type of question in the parts-and-whole tasks from Chapter 16: Given the part, find the whole—how much is one? For example, if a set of 18 counters is $2\frac{1}{4}$, how much is a whole set? In solving these problems, the first task is to find the number in one-fourth and then multiply by 4 to get four-fourths or *one*. Let's see if we can see the same process in the following problem:

Elizabeth bought $3\frac{1}{3}$ pounds of tomatoes for $2.50. How much did she pay per pound?

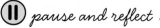 *pause and reflect*

The given amount of $2.50 is distributed across $3\frac{1}{3}$ pounds. How much is distributed to 1 pound? Solve the problem the same way as you would a parts-and-whole problem. Try it now before reading on.

In $3\frac{1}{3}$ there are 10 thirds. Since the $2.50 covers (or is distributed across) ten-thirds, 1 third is covered by one-tenth of the $2.50 or 25 cents. There are 3 thirds in one. Therefore, 75 cents must cover 1 pound, or 75 cents per pound.

Try the following problems using a similar strategy.

Dan paid $2.40 for a $\frac{3}{4}$-pound box of candy. How much is that per pound?

Aidan found out that if she walks really fast during her morning exercise, she can cover $2\frac{1}{2}$ miles in $\frac{3}{4}$ of an hour. She wonders how fast she is walking in miles per hour.

With both problems, first find the amount of one-fourth and then the value of one whole. Aidan's walking problem is a bit harder because the $2\frac{1}{2}$ miles, or 5 half-miles, do not neatly divide into three parts. If this was difficult for you, try dividing each half into three parts. Draw pictures or use models if that will help.

Informal Exploration: Measurement Concept

Almost all division explorations with fractions found in the elementary and middle school curriculum involve the measurement concept. To review, 13 ÷ 3 with this concept means "How many sets of 3 are in 13?" Here is a contextual setting: *If you have 13 quarts of lemonade, how many canteens holding 3 quarts each can you fill?* A key idea to get from this example involves how to deal with that last quart after filling the first four canteens. If you continue to fill a fifth canteen, it will get only one quart. It will be only one-third full. So one answer is $4\frac{1}{3}$ *canteens*.

Since this is the concept of division that is almost always seen in textbooks and will be used to develop an algorithm for dividing fractions, it is important for students to explore this idea in contextual situations.

Whole-Number Results

Students readily understand problems such as the following:

You are going to a birthday party. From Ben and Jerry's ice cream factory, you order 6 pints of ice cream. If you serve $\frac{3}{4}$ of a pint of ice cream to each guest, how many guests can be served? (Schifter, Bastable, & Russell, 1999b, p. 120)

Students typically draw pictures of six things divided into fourths and count out how many sets of $\frac{3}{4}$ can be found. The difficulty is in seeing this as $6 \div \frac{3}{4}$, and that part will require some direct guidance on your part. One idea is to compare the problem to one involving whole numbers (6 pints, 2 per guest) and make a comparison.

Here is a slightly more complex problem:

Farmer Brown found that he had $2\frac{1}{4}$ gallons of liquid fertilizer concentrate. It takes $\frac{3}{4}$ gallon to make a tank of mixed fertilizer. How many tankfuls can he mix?

Try solving this problem yourself. Use any model or drawing you wish to help explain what you are doing. Notice that you are trying to find out *How many sets of 3 fourths are in a set of 9 fourths?* Your answer should be 3 tankfuls (not 3 fourths). Here is another problem to try:

Linda has $4\frac{2}{3}$ yards of material. She is making baby clothes for the bazaar. Each dress pattern requires $1\frac{1}{6}$ yards of material. How many dresses will she be able to make from the material she has?

What makes this problem a bit different is that the given quantity is in thirds and the divisor is in sixths. Since you want to measure off "sets" of $1\frac{1}{6}$, someplace in the solution, sixths will need to be used. Two ideas are shown in Figure 17.13.

Answers That Are Not Whole Numbers

If Linda had 5 yards of material, she could still make only four dresses because a part of a dress does not make sense. But suppose that Farmer Brown began with 4 gallons of concentrate. After making five tanks of mix, he would have used $\frac{15}{4}$, or $3\frac{3}{4}$ gallons, of the concentrate. With the $\frac{1}{4}$ gallon remaining he could make a *partial* tank of mix. He could make $\frac{1}{3}$ of a tank of mix, since it takes 3 fourths to make a whole, and he has 1 fourth of a gallon.

Here is another problem to try:

John is building a patio. Each section requires $\frac{2}{3}$ of a cubic yard of concrete. The concrete truck holds $2\frac{1}{4}$ cubic yards of concrete. If there is not enough for a full section at the end, John can put in a divider and make a partial section. How many sections can John make with the concrete in the truck?

 *pause and reflect*

You should first try to solve this problem in some way that makes sense to *you*. Stop and do this now.

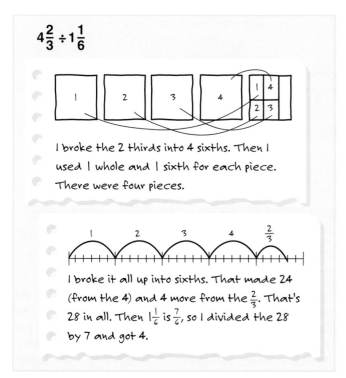

FIGURE 17.13 Two solutions to the problem: *How many lengths of $1\frac{1}{6}$ yards can be cut from $4\frac{2}{3}$ yards of cloth?*

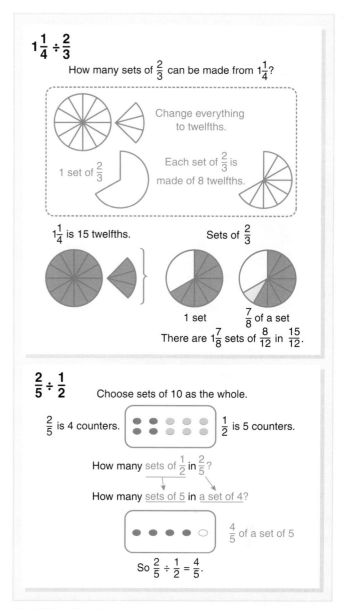

FIGURE 17.14 Models for the measurement concept of fraction division.

After you have solved it your way, try this method. Change all of the numbers to the same unit (twelfths). Then the problem becomes: *How many sets of 8 twelfths are in a set of 27 twelfths?* Figure 17.14 shows two noncontextual problems solved in this same way, each with a different model. That is, both the dividend or given quantity and the divisor are expressed in the same type of fractional parts. This results in a whole-number division problem. (In the concrete problem, the answer is the same as 27 ÷ 8.) In the classroom, after students have solved problems such as this using their own methods, suggest this common-unit approach.

Developing the Algorithms

There are two different algorithms for division of fractions. Methods of teaching both algorithms are discussed here.

The Common-Denominator Algorithm

The common-denominator algorithm relies on the measurement or repeated subtraction concept of division. Consider the problem $\frac{3}{5} \div \frac{1}{2}$. As shown in Figure 17.15, once each number is expressed in terms of the same fractional part, the answer is exactly the same as the whole-number problem 10 ÷ 3. The name of the fractional part (the denominator) is no longer important, and the problem is one of dividing the numerators. The resulting rule or algorithm, therefore, is as follows: *To divide fractions, first get common denominators, and then divide numerators.* For example, $\frac{5}{3} \div \frac{1}{4} = \frac{20}{12} \div \frac{3}{12} = 20 \div 3 = \frac{20}{3} = 6\frac{2}{3}$.

Try using pie pieces, fraction strips, and then sets of counters to model $1\frac{2}{3} \div \frac{3}{4}$ and $\frac{5}{8} \div \frac{1}{2}$ to help yourself develop this algorithm.

The Invert-and-Multiply Algorithm

To invert the divisor and multiply may be one of the most poorly understood procedures in the K–8 curriculum. (Do you know why invert-and-multiply works?) Interestingly,

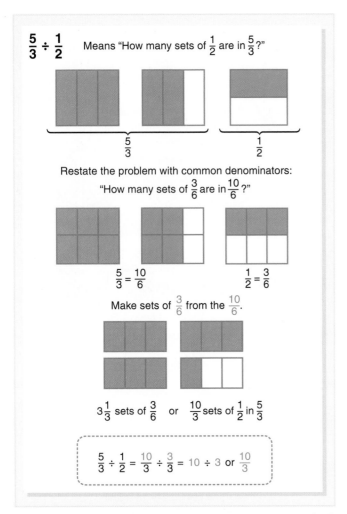

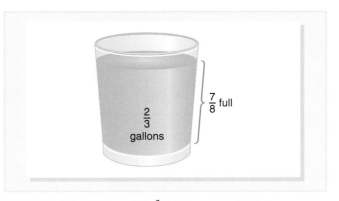

FIGURE 17.16 The pail is $\frac{7}{8}$ full. One-seventh of the water times 8 will be how much it takes to fill the entire pail.

FIGURE 17.15 Models for the common-denominator method for fraction division.

in a much discussed study of Chinese and U.S. teachers, Liping Ma (1999) found that most Chinese teachers not only use and teach this algorithm, but they also understand why it works. U.S. teachers were found to be sadly lacking in their understanding of fraction division.

If you return to the few partition problems that were discussed, you will find that solving these problems almost immediately gives rise to the invert-and-multiply algorithm. Let's look at one more example in which both the dividend and the divisor are proper fractions.

A small pail can be filled to $\frac{7}{8}$ full using $\frac{2}{3}$ of a gallon of water. How much will the pail hold if filled completely?

Ignore temporarily that the amount is $\frac{2}{3}$ of a gallon of water. Draw a simple picture like the one in Figure 17.16.

Again, recall the parts-and-whole problems in which the task was to find the whole. That is what is done here—find the *whole* pail if the given water is $\frac{7}{8}$ of the whole. A full pail is $\frac{8}{8}$. Because the water in the pail is seven of the eight parts needed to fill the pail, dividing the water by 7 and multiplying that amount by 8 solves the problem. Therefore, take the $\frac{2}{3}$, divide by 7, and multiply by 8.

Now recall the meanings of the denominator and numerator. The denominator in a fraction divides the whole into parts, thus indicating the type of part. The denominator is a divisor. The numerator tells us the number of those parts. The numerator is a multiplier. In the problem we divided the $\frac{2}{3}$ by 7 and multiplied by 8. Therefore, we multiplied the $\frac{2}{3}$ by $\frac{8}{7}$.

In many middle school textbooks, a more symbolic justification for the invert-and-multiply procedure is offered. That explanation goes something like the one shown in Figure 17.17.

 *pause and reflect* ————

Read through the explanation in Figure 17.17. Is that rationale more or less meaningful to you than the one based on the problem with the pail of water? Given your choice, which algorithm—common denominator or invert-and-multiply—would you select to teach to your students?

Curricular Decisions

Your answers to the questions just posed may have an influence on how you teach division of fractions. It matters very little *how* students do operations, only that they can do them meaningfully and accurately in a reasonably efficient manner. Each of the algorithms has value. Regardless of which algorithm is your goal, you are strongly advised to build on informal work with story problems. Most textbook story problems for fraction division seem to be mea-

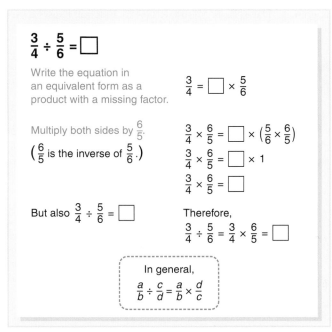

$$\frac{3}{4} \div \frac{5}{6} = \square$$

Write the equation in an equivalent form as a product with a missing factor.

$$\frac{3}{4} = \square \times \frac{5}{6}$$

Multiply both sides by $\frac{6}{5}$.

($\frac{6}{5}$ is the inverse of $\frac{5}{6}$.)

$$\frac{3}{4} \times \frac{6}{5} = \square \times \left(\frac{5}{6} \times \frac{6}{5}\right)$$

$$\frac{3}{4} \times \frac{6}{5} = \square \times 1$$

$$\frac{3}{4} \times \frac{6}{5} = \square$$

But also $\frac{3}{4} \div \frac{5}{6} = \square$

Therefore,

$$\frac{3}{4} \div \frac{5}{6} = \frac{3}{4} \times \frac{6}{5} = \square$$

In general,

$$\frac{a}{b} \div \frac{c}{d} = \frac{a}{b} \times \frac{d}{c}$$

FIGURE 17.17 To divide, invert the divisor and multiply.

surement problems. This is not the case in China. In the United States, very little research has been done to explore the partition approach to invert-and-multiply.

 The NLVM Web site (http://nlvm.usu.edu/en/nav/vlibrary.html) has a nice collection of fraction applets. Number Line Bars allows the user to place bars of any fractional length along a number line. The number line can be adjusted to have increments from $\frac{1}{2}$ to $\frac{1}{15}$, but the user must decide. For example, if bars of $\frac{1}{4}$ and $\frac{1}{3}$ are placed end to end, the result cannot be read from the applet until the increments are in twelfths. A division task is nicely illustrated with the bars when the applet opens initially.

Rectangle Multiplication (also at NLVM) shows the area model for multiplication of any two fractions up to 2×2. Although the applet does an excellent job of connecting the model to the equation, much of the thinking work is taken from the user. This is still recommended.

Tenth Planet's *Fraction Operations* (Sunburst) is one of the few software programs that does a reasonably good job of developing the concepts of the operations with fractions via clever graphics and audio. Multiplication and division are especially well done. The downside is that there is very little reflective thinking required of the user. One suggestion for this and similar programs is to use them with the entire class, stopping at appropriate places so that the students can work on the problem in the spirit of a problem-based approach. ∎

Reflections on Chapter 17

Writing to Learn

1. Make up an example, and use pie pieces (or draw pictures) to show how two fractions with unlike denominators can be added without first getting a common denominator. In your example, did you get your answer by either looking at the part that was more than a whole or at the missing part that was just less than a whole? Explain both of these ideas.

2. Suppose that you got pie pieces out to show $\frac{2}{3} + \frac{1}{2}$ and by some informal means your students are now convinced that the sum is $1\frac{1}{6}$. Now suppose that you substitute $\frac{16}{24}$ for the $\frac{2}{3}$ and $\frac{7}{14}$ for the $\frac{1}{2}$. "What is this sum ($\frac{16}{24} + \frac{7}{14}$)?" Explain why you would want students to say *immediately* that the sum was $1\frac{1}{6}$. Why is this idea important to the use of common denominators in addition and subtraction?

3. Explain why it is obvious that $\frac{3}{4} \times \frac{8}{5} = \frac{6}{5}$ without using the algorithm and without first getting $\frac{24}{20}$.

4. Draw pictures of squares for the whole to illustrate these products and explain each:

$$3 \times \frac{2}{5} \qquad \frac{3}{4} \times \frac{2}{3} \qquad 2\frac{1}{2} \times \frac{2}{3}$$

5. Explain at least one mental method (estimation or mental computation) for each of these:

$$\frac{3}{4} \times 5\frac{1}{2} \qquad 1\frac{1}{8} \text{ of } 679$$

6. Make up a word problem with a fraction as a divisor. Is your problem a measurement problem or a partition problem? Make up a second word problem with fractions of the other type (measurement or partition).

7. Draw pictures to explain each of these divisions using a measurement approach:

$$\frac{2}{4} \div \frac{1}{4} \qquad 2\frac{1}{3} \div \frac{2}{3} \qquad \frac{3}{4} \div \frac{1}{8} \qquad 2\frac{3}{4} \div \frac{2}{3}$$

In the second and fourth examples, the answer is not a whole number. To help you explain the fractional part of the answer, use a set of counters to explain why $13 \div 5 = 2\frac{3}{5}$ also using a measurement approach. (That is, how many sets of 5 are in a set of 13?)

8. Use the same problems you modeled in item 7 to explain a common-denominator algorithm for division. Use the same rationale to explain why $\frac{13}{79} \div \frac{5}{79} = 13 \div 5 = \frac{13}{5}$.

9. What is one strong reason for not teaching "invert and multiply"?

For Discussion and Exploration

1. Imagine teaching fraction computation in the seventh or eighth grade, a subject required by your curriculum. You quickly find that your students have a very weak understanding of fractions. Your textbook primarily targets computation. Where would you begin? Some teachers argue that there is no time to reteach the concepts of fractions. Others would argue that it is necessary to teach the meanings of numerators and denominators and equivalent fractions or else all the computation will be meaningless rules.

2. Examine a textbook series, and see where each fraction algorithm is first introduced. Does the preparation for the algorithm seem appropriate? How guided is the development? Will students develop an understanding of the rule or simply apply it to the exercises?

3. Several calculators are now available that do computations in fractional form as well as in decimal form. Some of these automatically give results in simplest terms. If you have access to such a calculator, discuss how it might be used in teaching fractions and especially fraction computation. If such calculators become commonplace, should we continue to teach fraction computation?

Recommendations for Further Reading

Huinker, D. (1998). Letting fraction algorithms emerge through problem solving. In L. J. Morrow (Ed.), *The teaching and learning of algorithms in school mathematics* (pp. 170–182). Reston, VA: National Council of Teachers of Mathematics.
Huinker takes the idea of students inventing algorithms as described for whole numbers in Chapter 10 and applies it to problems involving fractions. With examples of children's work, this article makes a good case for avoiding rules and letting students work with ideas that make sense. As always, Huinker is worth reading.

Kamii, C., & Warrington, M. A. (1999). Teaching fractions: Fostering children's own reasoning. In L. V. Stiff (Ed.), *Developing mathematical reasoning in grades K–12* (pp. 82–92). Reston, VA: National Council of Teachers of Mathematics.
Kamii begins with a quick review of Piagetian constructivism but quickly moves to apply this theory to the development of fraction operations. As always, Kamii avoids the use of models and relies on carefully selected word problems. All four operations are discussed.

Kieren, T., Davis, B., & Mason, R. (1996). Fraction flags: Learning from children to help children learn. *Mathematics Teaching in the Middle School, 2,* 14–19.
The authors began with a simple area model involving rectangular pieces cut from a standard sheet of paper. When smaller pieces were placed on larger pieces with spaces in between, the results looked like flags and presented interesting problem-based tasks for the students. These researchers have a long history of work with fractions and this article offers useful insights as well as a suggestion for an easily made model.

Perlwitz, M. D. (2005). Dividing fractions: Reconciling self-generated solutions with algorithmic answers. *Mathematics Teaching in the Middle School, 10,* 278–282.
On the surface, this article is about dealing with the remainder in fraction division. When dividing 10 yards by $\frac{3}{4}$ yard, there is $\frac{1}{4}$ yard left over. Why is the answer $13\frac{1}{3}$ and not $13\frac{1}{4}$? The discussions in this class of preservice teachers and the reflections of the author get at the deeper question of understanding algorithms, wrestling with the minimal knowledge that many teachers bring to this subject, and the value of classroom discourse.

Online Resources

Suggested Applets and Web Links

Fraction Bars
http://nlvm.usu.edu/en/nav/frames_asid)265_g_1_t_1.html?open=activities
Much like Cuisenaire rods, this applet encourages students to think in a good way. Bars are placed over a number line on which the step size can be adjusted. A flexible model that can be used for all four operations.

Fractions—Adding
http://nlvm.usu.edu/en/nav/frames_asid_106_g_2_t_1.html
Two fractions and an area model for each are given. The user must find a common denominator to rename and add the fractions. Very conceptual although rigidly adhering to the algorithm. You cannot set your own problem.

Fractions—Rectangle Multiplication
http://nlvm.usu.edu/en/nav/frames_asid_194_g_2_t_1.html
An easily adjusted area model for multiplication of two fractions up to 2 × 2. You cannot set your own problems but the presentation is quite good.

Companion Website

An additional list of books and articles related to the ideas in this chapter can be found on the Companion Web site at **www.ablongman.com/vandewalle6e.**

chapter 18

Decimal and Percent Concepts and Decimal Computation

In the U.S. curriculum, decimals are typically introduced in the fourth grade and most of the computation work with decimals occurs in the fifth grade and is repeated later in grades 6 and 7. This fractions-first, decimals-later sequence is arguably the best approach. However, the unfortunate fact is that the topics of fractions and decimals are too often developed separately. Linking the ideas of fractions to decimals can be extremely useful, both from a pedagogical view as well as a practical, social view. Most of this chapter focuses on that connection.

▼ Big Ideas

1. Decimal numbers are simply another way of writing fractions. Both notations have value. Maximum flexibility is gained by understanding how the two symbol systems are related.

2. The base-ten place-value system extends infinitely in two directions: to tiny values as well as to large values. Between any two place values, the ten-to-one ratio remains the same.

3. The decimal point is a convention that has been developed to indicate the units position. The position to the left of the decimal point is the unit that is being counted as singles or ones.

4. Percents are simply hundredths and as such are a third way of writing both fractions and decimals.

5. Addition and subtraction with decimals are based on the fundamental concept of adding and subtracting the numbers in like position values—a simple extension from whole numbers.

6. Multiplication and division of two numbers will produce the same digits, regardless of the positions of the decimal point. As a result, for most practical purposes, there is no reason to develop new rules for decimal multiplication and division. Rather, the computations can be performed as whole numbers with the decimal placed by way of estimation.

▲▼▲ Mathematics Content Connections

The most important connections for decimals are built within this chapter—between decimal numbers and the concepts of fractions.

- **Fraction Concepts** (Chapter 16): Both decimal and fraction symbolism represents the same ideas—the rational numbers.

- **Measurement** (Chapter 20): The metric system is modeled after the base-ten system, and all metric measures are expressed in decimals rather than fractions. Conversion from one metric measure to another is quite simple, given an understanding of the decimal system.

- **Real Number System** (Chapter 24): Decimal numeration is helpful in characterizing and understanding the density of the rational numbers and also for approximating irrational numbers.

Connecting Two Different Representational Systems

The symbols 3.75 and $3\frac{3}{4}$ represent the same quantity, yet on the surface the two appear quite different. For children especially, the world of fractions and the world of decimals are very distinct. Even adults tend to think of fractions as sets or regions (three-fourths *of* something), whereas we think of decimals as being more like numbers. When we tell children that 0.75 is the same as $\frac{3}{4}$, this can be especially confusing. Even though different ways of writing the numbers have been invented, the numbers themselves are not different. A significant goal of instruction in decimal and fraction numeration should be to help students see that both systems represent the same concepts.

To help students see the connection between fractions and decimals, we can do three things. First, we can use familiar fraction concepts and models to explore rational numbers that are easily represented by decimals: tenths, hundredths, and thousandths. Second, we can help them see how the base-ten system can be extended to include numbers less than 1 as well as large numbers. Third, we can help children use models to make meaningful translations between fractions and decimals. These three components are discussed in turn.

Base-Ten Fractions

Fractions that have denominators of 10, 100, 1000, and so on will be referred to in this chapter as *base-ten fractions*. This is simply a convenient label and is not one commonly found in the literature. Fractions such as $\frac{7}{10}$ or $\frac{63}{100}$ are examples of base-ten fractions.

Base-Ten Fraction Models

Most of the common models for fractions are somewhat limited for the purpose of depicting base-ten fractions. Generally, the familiar fraction models cannot show hundredths or thousandths. It is important to provide models for these fractions using the same conceptual approaches that were used for fractions such as thirds and fourths.

Two very important region models can be used to model base-ten fractions. First, to model tenths and hundredths, circular disks such as the one shown in Figure 18.1 can be printed on cardstock (see Blackline Masters). Each disk is marked with 100 equal intervals around the edge and is cut along one radius. Two disks of different colors, slipped together as shown, can be used to model any fraction less than 1. Fractions modeled on this hundredths disk can be read as base-ten fractions by noting the spaces around the edge but are still reminiscent of the traditional pie model.

The most common model for base-ten fractions is a 10 × 10 square. These squares can be run off on paper for students to shade in various fractions (see Figure 18.2 and Blackline Masters). Another important variation is to use base-ten place-value strips and squares. As a fraction model, the 10-cm square that was used as the hundreds model for whole numbers is taken as the whole or 1. Each strip is then 1 tenth, and each small square is 1 hundredth. In the Blackline Masters you will find a large square that is subdivided into 10,000 tiny squares. When shown on an overhead projector, individual squares or ten-thousandths can easily be identified and shaded in with a pen on the transparency.

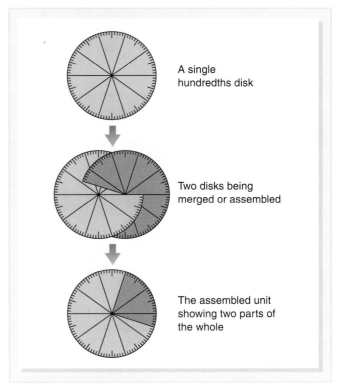

FIGURE 18.1 A hundredths disk for modeling base-ten fractions.

A single hundredths disk

Two disks being merged or assembled

The assembled unit showing two parts of the whole

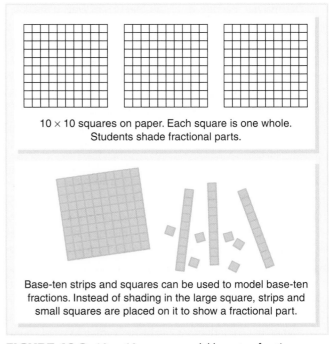

10 × 10 squares on paper. Each square is one whole. Students shade fractional parts.

Base-ten strips and squares can be used to model base-ten fractions. Instead of shading in the large square, strips and small squares are placed on it to show a fractional part.

FIGURE 18.2 10 × 10 squares model base-ten fractions.

One of the best length models is a meter stick. Each decimeter is one-tenth of the whole stick, each centimeter is one-hundredth, and each millimeter is one-thousandth. Any number-line model broken into 100 subparts is likewise a useful model for hundredths.

Many teachers use money as a model for decimals, and to some extent this is helpful. However, for children, money is almost exclusively a two-place system: Numbers like 3.2 or 12.1389 do not relate to money. Children's initial contact with decimals should be more flexible, and so money is not recommended as a decimal model, at least not at the introductory level. Money is certainly an important *application* of decimal numeration.

Multiple Names and Formats

Early work with base-ten fractions is designed primarily to acquaint students with the models, to help them begin to think of quantities in terms of tenths and hundredths, and to learn to read and write base-ten fractions in different ways.

Have students show a base-ten fraction using any base-ten fraction model. Once a fraction, say, $\frac{65}{100}$, is modeled, the following things can be explored:

- Is this fraction more or less than $\frac{1}{2}$? Than $\frac{2}{3}$? Than $\frac{3}{4}$? Some familiarity with these fractions can be developed by comparison with fractions that are easy to think about.
- What are some different ways to say this fraction using tenths and hundredths? ("6 tenths and 5 hundredths," "65 hundredths") Include thousandths when appropriate.
- Show two ways to write this fraction ($\frac{65}{100}$ or $\frac{6}{10} + \frac{5}{100}$).

The last two questions are very important. When base-ten fractions are later written as decimals, they are usually read as a single fraction. That is, 0.65 is read "sixty-five hundredths." But to understand them in terms of place value, the same number must be thought of as 6 tenths and 5 hundredths. A mixed number such as $5\frac{13}{100}$ is usually read the same way as a decimal: 5.13 is "five and thirteen-hundredths." For purposes of place value, it should also be understood as $5 + \frac{1}{10} + \frac{3}{100}$.

The expanded forms will be helpful in translating these fractions to decimals. Exercises at this introductory level should include all possible connections between models, various oral forms, and various written forms. Given a model or a written or oral fraction, students should be able to give the other two forms of the fraction, including equivalent forms where appropriate.

Extending the Place-Value System

Before considering decimal numerals with students, it is advisable to review some ideas of whole-number place value.

One of the most basic of these ideas is the 10-to-1 relationship between the value of any two adjacent positions. In terms of a base-ten model such as strips and squares, 10 of any one piece will make 1 of the next larger, and vice versa.

A Two-Way Relationship

The 10-makes-1 rule continues indefinitely to larger and larger pieces or positional values. This concept is fun to explore in terms of how large the strips and squares will actually be if you move six or eight places out.

If you are using the strip-and-square model, for example, the strip and square shapes alternate in an infinite progression as they get larger and larger. Having established the progression to larger pieces, focus on the idea that each piece to the right in this string gets smaller by one-tenth. The critical question becomes "Is there ever a smallest piece?" In the students' experience, the smallest piece is the centimeter square or unit piece. But couldn't even that piece be divided into 10 small strips? And couldn't these small strips be divided into 10 very small squares, and so on? In the mind's eye, there is no smallest strip or smallest square.

The goal of this discussion is to help students see that a 10-to-1 relationship can extend *infinitely in two directions*. There is no smallest piece and no largest piece. The relationship between adjacent pieces is the same regardless of which two adjacent pieces are being considered. Figure 18.3 illustrates this idea.

The Role of the Decimal Point

An important idea to be realized in this discussion is that there is no built-in reason why any one position should naturally be chosen to be the unit or ones position. In terms of strips and squares, for example, which piece is the ones piece? The small centimeter square? Why? Why not a larger or a smaller square? Why not a strip? *Any piece could effectively be chosen as the ones piece.*

As shown in Figure 18.4, a given quantity can be written in different ways, depending on the choice of the unit or what piece is used to count the entire collection. The decimal point is placed between two positions with the convention that the position to the left of the decimal is the units or ones position. Thus, the role of the decimal point is *to designate the units position*, and it does so by sitting just to the right of that position.

A fitting caricature for the decimal is shown in Figure 18.5. The "eyes" of the decimal always focus up toward the name of the units or ones. A cardstock disk of this decimal-point face can be used between adjacent base-ten models or on a place-value chart (found with the hundredths disk in the Blackline Masters). If such a decimal point were placed between the squares and strips in Figure 18.4, the squares would then be designated as the units, and 16.24 would be the correct written form for the model.

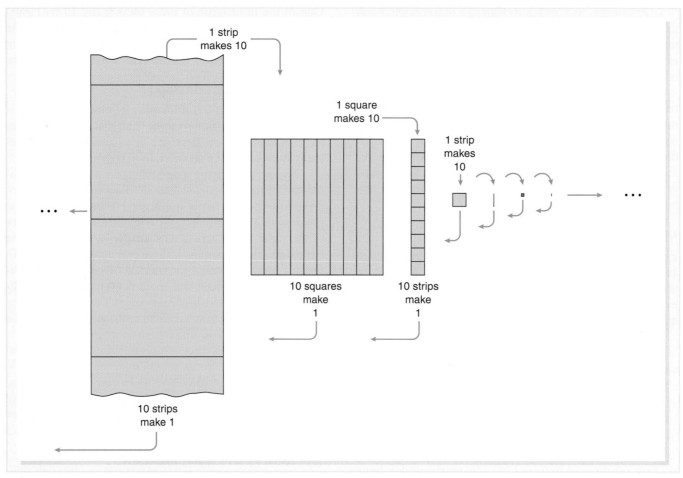

FIGURE 18.3 Theoretically, the strips and squares extend infinitely in both directions.

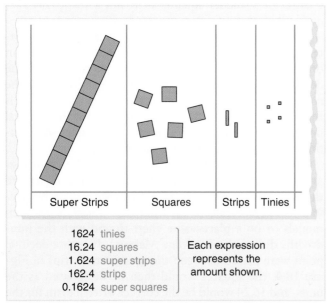

Super Strips	Squares	Strips	Tinies

1624 tinies
16.24 squares   Each expression
1.624 super strips   represents the
162.4 strips   amount shown.
0.1624 super squares

FIGURE 18.4 The decimal point indicates which position is the units.

activity **18.1**

The Decimal Names the Unit

Have students display a certain number of base-ten pieces on their desks. For example, put out three squares, seven strips, and four tinies. Refer to the pieces as "squares," "strips," and "tinies," and reach an agreement on names for the theoretical pieces both smaller and larger. To the right of tinies can be "tiny strips" and "tiny squares." To the left of squares can be "super strips" and "super squares." Each student should also have a smiley decimal point. Now ask students to write and say how many squares they have, how many super strips, and so on, as in Figure 18.4. The students position their decimal point accordingly and both write and say the amounts.

Activity 18.1 illustrates vividly the convention that the decimal indicates the named unit and that the unit can change without changing the quantity.

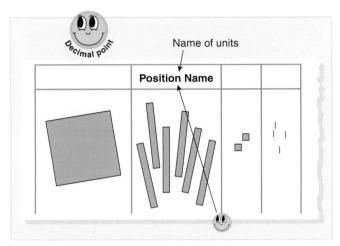

FIGURE 18.5 The decimal point always "looks up at" the name of the units position.

The Decimal with Measurement and Monetary Units

The notion that the decimal "looks at the units place" is useful in a variety of contexts. For example, in the metric system, seven place values have names. As shown in Figure 18.6, the decimal can be used to designate any of these places as the unit without changing the actual measure. Our monetary system is also a decimal system. In the amount $172.95, the decimal point designates the dollars position as the unit. There are 1 hundred (of dollars), 7 tens, 2 singles, 9 dimes, and 5 pennies or cents in this amount of money regardless of how it is written. If pennies were the designated unit, the same amount would be written as 17,295 cents or 17,295.0 cents. It could just as correctly be 0.17295 thousands of dollars or 1729.5 dimes.

In the case of measures such as metric lengths or weights or the U.S. monetary system, the name of the unit is written after the number rather than above the digit as on a place-value chart. You may be 1.62 meters tall, but it does not make sense to say you are "1.62 tall." In the paper, we may read about Congress spending $7.3 billion. Here the units are billions of dollars, not dollars. A city may have a population of 2.4 million people. That is the same as 2,400,000 individuals.

 The number blocks component of *eTools* (Scott Foresman) allows the user to put any number of base-ten blocks on the screen with the total shown either in words, expanded form, or simply as a number. Of interest in the current discussion is that any of the four sizes of blocks can be designated as the unit. When a change of unit is made, the total is changed accordingly.

The applet Base Blocks—Decimals from NLVM (http://nlvm.usu.edu/en/nav/vlibrary.html) allows this same change of unit but in a different manner. In Base Blocks you can choose the number of decimal places you want to show, but only a discussion would indicate how the unit changes with a change of decimal places. ■

Making the Fraction–Decimal Connection

To connect the two numeration systems, fractions and decimals, students should make concept-oriented translations; that is, translations based on understanding rather than a rule or algorithm. The purpose of such activities has less to do with the skill of converting a fraction to a decimal than with construction of the concept that both systems are used to express the same ideas. The place to begin is with base-ten fractions.

activity **18.2**

Base-Ten Fractions to Decimals
For this activity, have students use their place-value strips and squares. Agree that the large square

kilometer	hectometer	dekameter	meter	decimeter	centimeter	millimeter
		4	3	8	5	

4 dekameters, 3 meters, 8 decimeters, and 5 centimeters =

43.85	meters
43850	millimeters
0.04385	kilometers
4385	centimeters

Unit names

FIGURE 18.6 In the metric system, each place-value position has a name. The decimal point can be placed to designate which length is the unit length.

represents one. Have students cover a base-ten fractional amount of the square using their strips and tinies. For example, have them cover $2\frac{35}{100}$ of the square. Whole numbers require additional squares. The task is to decide how to write this fraction as a decimal and demonstrate the connection using their physical models.

For the last activity, a typical (and correct) reason why $2\frac{35}{100}$ is the same as 2.35 is that there are 2 wholes, 3 tenths, and 5 hundredths. It is important to see this physically. The exact same materials that are used to represent $2\frac{35}{100}$ of the square can be rearranged or placed on an imaginary place-value chart with a paper decimal point used to designate the units position as shown in Figure 18.7.

The reverse of this activity is also worthwhile. Give students a decimal number such as 1.68 and have them show it with base-ten pieces. Their task is to write it as a fraction and show it as a fractional part of a square.

Although these translations between decimals and base-ten fractions are rather simple, the main agenda is for students to learn from the beginning that decimals are simply fractions.

The calculator can also play a significant role in decimal concept development.

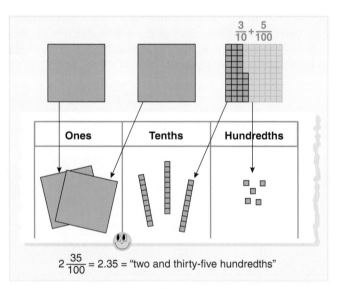

$2\frac{35}{100}$ = 2.35 = "two and thirty-five hundredths"

FIGURE 18.7 Translation of a base-ten fraction to a decimal.

activity 18.3

Calculator Decimal Counting
Recall how to make the calculator "count" by pressing ⊞ 1 ⊟ ⊟ . . . . Now have students press ⊞ 0.1 ⊟ ⊟ . . . . When the display shows 0.9, stop and discuss what this means and what the display will look like with the next press.

Many students will predict 0.10 (thinking that 10 comes after 9). This prediction is even more interesting if, with each press, the students have been accumulating base-ten strips as models for tenths. One more press would mean one more strip, or 10 strips. Why should the calculator not show 0.10? When the tenth press produces a display of 1 (calculators never display trailing zeros to the right of the decimal), the discussion should revolve around trading 10 strips for a square. Continue to count to 4 or 5 by tenths. How many presses to get from one whole number to the next? Try counting by 0.01 or by 0.001. These counts illustrate dramatically how small one-hundredth and one-thousandth really are. It requires 10 counts by 0.001 to get to 0.01 and 1000 counts to reach 1.

The fact that the calculator counts 0.8, 0.9, 1, 1.1 instead of 0.8, 0.9, 0.10, 0.11 should give rise to the question "Does this make sense? If so, why?"

Calculators that permit entry of fractions also have a fraction–decimal conversion key. On some calculators a decimal such as 0.25 will convert to the base-ten fraction $\frac{25}{100}$ and allow for either manual or automatic simplification. Graphing calculators can be set so that the conversion is either with or without simplification. The ability of fraction calculators to go back and forth between fractions and decimals makes them a valuable tool as students begin to connect fraction and decimal symbolism.

Developing Decimal Number Sense

So far, the discussion has revolved around the connection of decimals with base-ten fractions. Number sense implies more. It means having intuition about or a friendly understanding of numbers. To this end, it is useful to connect decimals to the fractions with which children are familiar, to be able to compare and order decimals readily, and to approximate decimals with useful familiar numbers.

Familiar Fractions Connected to Decimals

Chapter 16 showed how to help students develop a conceptual familiarity with simple fractions, especially halves, thirds, fourths, fifths, and eighths. We should extend this familiarity to the same concepts expressed as decimals. One way to do this is to have students translate familiar fractions to decimals by means of a base-ten model.

The following two activities have the same purpose— to help students think of decimals in terms of familiar fraction equivalents and to make this connection in a conceptual manner.

activity 18.4

Friendly Fractions to Decimals

Students are given a "friendly" fraction to convert to a decimal. They first model the fraction using either a 10 × 10 grid or the base-ten strips and squares. With the model as a guide, they then write and draw an explanation for the decimal equivalent. If strips and squares are used, be sure that students draw pictures as part of their explanations.

A good sequence is to start with halves and fifths, then fourths, and possibly eighths. Thirds are best done as a special activity.

Figure 18.8 shows how translations in the last activity might go with a 10 × 10 grid. For fourths, students will often shade a 5 × 5 section (half of a half). The question then becomes how to translate this to decimals. Ask these students how they would cover $\frac{1}{4}$ with strips and squares if they were only permitted to use nine or fewer tinies. The fraction $\frac{3}{8}$ represents a wonderful challenge. A hint might be to find $\frac{1}{4}$ first and then notice that $\frac{1}{8}$ is half of a fourth. Remember that the next

EXPANDED LESSON

An expanded lesson plan based on Activity 18.4, "Friendly Fractions to Decimals," can be found on the Companion Web site at www.ablongman.com/vandewalle6e.

smaller pieces are tenths of the little squares. Therefore, a half of a square is $\frac{5}{1000}$.

Because the circular model carries such a strong mental link to fractions, it is well worth the time to do some fraction-to-decimal conversions with the hundredths disk.

activity 18.5

Estimate, Then Verify

With the blank side of the disk facing them, have students adjust the disk to show a particular friendly fraction, for example, $\frac{3}{4}$. Next they turn the disk over and record how many hundredths were in the section they estimated (note that the color reverses when the disk is turned over). Finally, they should make an argument for the correct number of hundredths and the corresponding decimal equivalent.

The estimation component of the last activity adds interest, and the visual "feeling" for fractions is greater than with strips and squares. In one fifth-grade class that was having difficulty finding a decimal equivalent for their hundredths disk fraction, the teacher cut up some extra disks into tenths and hundredths so that these parts of the fraction could be placed on a chart. (See Figure 18.9.)

The exploration of modeling $\frac{1}{3}$ as a decimal is a good introduction to the concept of an infinitely repeating decimal. Try to partition the whole square into 3 parts using strips and squares. Each part receives 3 strips with 1 left over. To divide the leftover strip, each part gets 3 small

FIGURE 18.8 Familiar fractions converted to decimals using a 10 × 10 square.

$$\frac{1}{4} = \frac{25}{100} = .25$$

$$\frac{3}{8} = \frac{37}{100} + \frac{5}{1000} = .375$$

Same amount

$\frac{1}{4}$ is $\frac{2}{8}$

$\frac{3}{8}$ is $\frac{1}{4}$ and $\frac{1}{8}$ together.

$$\frac{3}{5} = \frac{6}{10} = .6$$

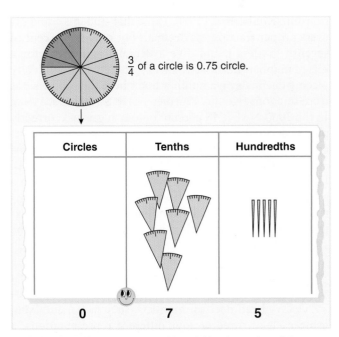

$\frac{3}{4}$ of a circle is 0.75 circle.

Circles	Tenths	Hundredths
0	7	5

FIGURE 18.9 Fraction models could be decimal models.

squares with 1 left over. To divide the small square, each part gets 3 tiny strips with 1 left over. (Recall that with base-ten pieces, each smaller piece must be $\frac{1}{10}$ of the preceding size piece.) Each of the 3 parts will get 3 tiny strips with 1 left over. It becomes obvious that this process is never-ending. As a result, $\frac{1}{3}$ is the same as 0.333333 . . . or $0.\overline{3}$. For practical purposes, $\frac{1}{3}$ is about 0.333. Similarly, $\frac{2}{3}$ is a repeating string of sixes, or about 0.667. Later, students will discover that many fractions cannot be represented by a finite decimal.

The number line is another good connecting model. Students are more apt to think of decimals as numbers that appear on the number line than they are to think of fractions in that way. The following activity continues the development of fraction–decimal equivalences.

activity 18.6

Decimals on a Friendly Fraction Line

Give students five decimal numbers that have friendly fraction equivalents. Keep the numbers between two consecutive whole numbers. For example, use 3.5, 3.125, 3.4, 3.75, and 3.66. On a worksheet, show a number line encompassing the same whole numbers. The subdivisions on the number line should be only fourths, only thirds, or only fifths but without labels. The students' task is to locate each of the decimal numbers on the number line and to provide the fraction equivalent for each.

Results of National Assessment of Educational Progress (NAEP) examinations consistently reveal that students have difficulties with the fraction–decimal relationship. Kouba et al. (1988a) note that students could express proper fractions as decimals but only 40 percent of seventh graders could give a decimal equivalent for a mixed number. In the sixth NAEP, students had difficulty placing decimals on a number line where the subdivisions were fractions (Kouba, Zawojewski, & Strutchens, 1997). In the 2000 NAEP, 48 percent of fourth graders correctly placed decimal numbers on a number line when the increments were multiples of 0.1—not even in fraction increments (Sowder, Wearne, Martin, & Strutchens, 2004). Division of the numerator by the denominator may be a means of converting fractions to decimals, but it contributes nothing to understanding the resulting equivalence. Note that this method has not been and will not be suggested in this chapter.

Assessment Notes A simple yet powerful assessment of decimal understanding has students represent two related decimal numbers, such as 0.6 and 0.06, using each of three or four different representations: a number line (not provided but student drawn), a 10 × 10 grid, money, and base-ten materials (Martinie & Bay-

Williams, 2003). For additional information, have students give reasons for their representations. If students have significantly more difficulty with one model than others, this may mean that they have learned how to use certain models but have not necessarily developed true understanding of decimals. Placement of decimals on a blank number line is perhaps the most interesting—and the most telling. (See Figure 18.10.) ■

Approximation with a Nice Fraction

In the real world, decimal numbers are rarely those with exact equivalents to nice fractions. What fraction would you say approximates the decimal 0.52? In the sixth NAEP exam, only 51 percent of eighth graders selected $\frac{1}{2}$. The other choices were $\frac{1}{50}$ (29 percent), $\frac{1}{5}$ (11 percent), $\frac{1}{4}$ (6 percent), and $\frac{1}{3}$ (4 percent) (Kouba et al., 1997). Again, the most plausible explanation for this performance is a reliance on rules. Students need to wrestle with the size of decimal numbers and begin to develop a sense of familiarity with them.

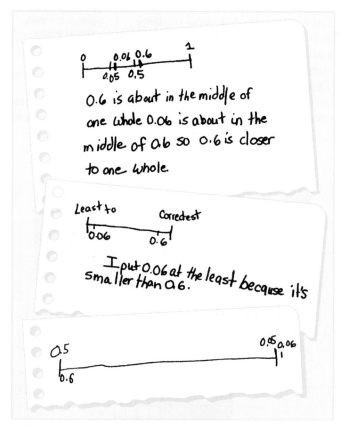

FIGURE 18.10 Three different sixth-grade students attempt to draw a number line and show the numbers 0.6 and 0.06.

Source: Reprinted with permission from Martinie, S. L., & Bay-Williams, J. (2003). Investigating students' conceptual understanding of decimal fractions using multiple representations. *Mathematics Teaching in the Middle School, 8,* 244–247 at p. 246. Copyright © 2003 by the National Council of Teachers of Mathematics. All rights reserved.

As with fractions, the first benchmarks that should be developed are 0, $\frac{1}{2}$, and 1. For example, is 7.3962 closer to 7 or 8? Why? (Would you accept this response: "Closer to 7 because 3 is less than 5"?) Is it closer to 7 or $7\frac{1}{2}$? Often the 0, $\frac{1}{2}$, or 1 benchmarks are good enough to make sense of a situation. If a closer approximation is required, students should be encouraged to consider the other friendly fractions (thirds, fourths, fifths, and eighths). In this example, 7.3962 is close to 7.4, which is $7\frac{2}{5}$. A good number sense with decimals would imply the ability to think quickly of a meaningful fraction that is a close substitute for almost any number.

To develop this type of familiarity with decimals, children do not need new concepts or skills. They do need the opportunity to apply and discuss the related concepts of fractions, place value, and decimals in activities such as the following.

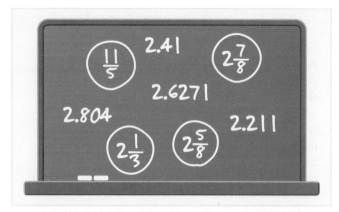

FIGURE 18.11 Match the decimal numbers with the closest fraction expression.

activity 18.7

Close to a Friendly Fraction

Make a list of about five decimals that are close to but not exactly equal to a nice or friendly fraction equivalent. For example, use 24.8025, 6.59, 0.9003, 124.356, and 7.7.

The students' task is to decide on a decimal number that is close to each of these decimals and that also has a friendly fraction equivalent that they know. For example, 6.59 is close to 6.6, which is $6\frac{3}{5}$. They should write an explanation for their choices. Different students may select different equivalent fractions providing for a discussion of which is closer.

activity 18.8

Best Match

On the board, list a scattered arrangement of five familiar fractions and at least five decimals that are close to the fractions but not exact. Students are to pair each fraction with the decimal that best matches it. Figure 18.11 is an example. The difficulty is determined by how close the various fractions are to one another.

In Activities 18.7 and 18.8, students will have a variety of reasons for their answers. Sharing their thinking with the class provides a valuable opportunity for all to learn. Do not focus on the answers but on the rationales.

 The connections between models and the two symbol systems for rational numbers—fractions and decimals—provide a good schema for assessment. Provide students with a number represented in any one of these three ways and have them provide the

other two along with an explanation. Here are a few examples:

- Write the fraction $\frac{5}{8}$ as a decimal. Use a drawing or a physical model (meter stick or 10×10 grid) and explain why your decimal equivalent is correct.
- What fraction is also represented by the decimal 2.6? Use words, pictures, and numbers to explain your answer.
- Use both a fraction and a decimal to tell what point might be indicated on this number line. Explain your reasoning.

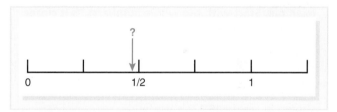

In the last example, it is especially interesting to see which representation students select first—fraction or decimal. Furthermore, do they then translate this number to the other representation or make a second independent estimate? ■

Ordering Decimal Numbers

Putting a list of decimal numbers in order from least to most is a skill closely related to the one just discussed. Consider the following list: 0.36, 0.058, 0.375, and 0.4. The most common error is to select the number with more digits as largest, an incorrect application of whole-number ideas. Some students later pick up the idea that digits far to the right represent very small numbers. They then incorrectly identify numbers with more digits as smaller. Both errors reflect a lack of conceptual understanding of how decimal numbers are constructed. The following activities can help promote discussion about the relative size of decimal numbers.

activity **18.9**

Line 'Em Up

Prepare a list of four or five decimal numbers that students might have difficulty putting in order. They should all be between the same two consecutive whole numbers. Have students first predict the order of the numbers, from least to most. Require students to use a model of their choice to defend their ordering. As students wrestle with representing the numbers with a model (perhaps a number line with 100 subdivisions or the 10,000 grid), they will necessarily confront the idea of which digits contribute the most to the size of a decimal.

In the world outside of classrooms, we almost never have to even think about the order of "ragged" decimals—decimals with different numbers of digits after the decimal point. The real purpose of exercises such as "Line 'Em Up" is not to develop a skill—but rather to create a better understanding of decimal numeration. Tasks such as this will, however, continue to be on standardized tests because they are good assessments of decimal understanding.

activity **18.10**

Close "Nice" Numbers

Write a four-digit decimal on the board—3.0917, for example. Start with the whole numbers: "Is it closer to 3 or 4?" Then go to the tenths: "Is it closer to 3.0 or 3.1?" Repeat with hundredths and thousandths. At each answer, challenge students to defend their choices with the use of a model or other conceptual explanation. A large number line without numerals, shown in Figure 18.12, is useful.

The drill program *Math Munchers Deluxe* (Riverdeep) provides useful drill of decimal–fraction equivalence in a format students seem to like. An array of 25 fractions, decimals, fraction region models, percents, and ratios is presented. The student is to find all instances that are equivalent to a given decimal number. The game can also be played with less than or greater than rather than equivalent. The 17 levels of difficulty provide ample challenge. This is a good example of worthwhile drill. However, it must come after conceptual ideas are well developed. The program offers no feedback or conceptual assistance. ■

Other Fraction–Decimal Equivalents

Recall that the denominator is a divisor and the numerator is a multiplier. For example, $\frac{3}{4}$, therefore, means the same as $3 \times (1 \div 4)$ or $3 \div 4$. So how would you express $\frac{3}{4}$ on a simple four-function calculator? Simply enter $3 \div 4$. The display will read 0.75.

Too often students think that dividing the denominator into the numerator is simply an algorithm for converting fractions to decimals, and they have no understanding of why this might work. Use the opportunity to help students develop the idea that in general $a/b = a \div b$. (See Chapter 16, p. 300, and Chapter 24, p. 504.)

Finding the decimal equivalents with a calculator can produce some interesting patterns and observations. For example, here are some questions to explore:

- Which fractions have decimal equivalents that terminate? Is the answer based on the numerator, the denominator, or both?
- For a given fraction, how can you tell the maximum length of the repeating part of the decimal? Try dividing by 7 and 11 and 13 to reach an answer.
- Explore all of the ninths—$\frac{1}{9}, \frac{2}{9}, \frac{3}{9}, \ldots \frac{8}{9}$. Remember that $\frac{1}{3}$ is $\frac{3}{9}$ and $\frac{2}{3}$ is $\frac{6}{9}$. Use only the pattern you discover to predict what $\frac{9}{9}$ should be. But doesn't $\frac{9}{9} = 1$?
- How can you find what fraction produced this repeating decimal: 3.454545. . . ?

The final task in this list can be generalized for any repeating decimal, illustrating that every repeating decimal is a rational number. It is not at all useful for students to become skillful at this.

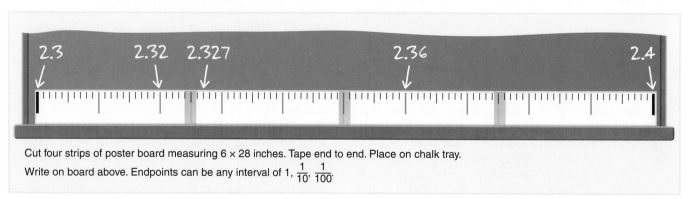

Cut four strips of poster board measuring 6 × 28 inches. Tape end to end. Place on chalk tray.

Write on board above. Endpoints can be any interval of 1, $\frac{1}{10}$, $\frac{1}{100}$.

FIGURE 18.12 A decimal number line.

Much of what was discussed in this section is recommended by the *Standards*. "Students in [grades 3 to 5] should use models and other strategies to represent and study decimal numbers. For example, they should count by tenths (one-tenth, two-tenths, three-tenths, . . .) verbally or use a calculator to link and relate whole numbers with decimal numbers. . . . They should also investigate the relationship between fractions and decimals, focusing on equivalence" (p. 150).

Introducing Percents

Textbooks have traditionally treated percents as a separate topic from fractions and decimals or stuck them in a chapter on ratios. The connection of percents to fraction and decimal concepts is so strong that it also makes sense to discuss percents as students begin to have a good grasp of the fraction–decimal relationships.

A Third Operator System

The results of the NAEP tests and numerous other studies have consistently shown that students have difficulty with problems involving percents (Wearne & Kouba, 2000). For example, on the seventh NAEP, only 35 percent of eighth graders could determine an amount following a given percent of increase. Almost half selected the answer obtained by adding the percent itself to the original amount. That is, for a 7 percent increase, they selected the answer that was 7 more than the original amount. A good reason for this continual dismal performance is a failure to develop percent concepts meaningfully. In this book we explore percentages twice. Here we will connect them to fractions and decimals. In the next chapter we will revisit percent as a ratio as part of the study of proportional reasoning. It can be argued that the connection to fractions is more important for daily understanding.

Another Name for Hundredths

The term *percent* is simply another name for *hundredths*. If students can express common fractions and simple decimals as hundredths, the term *percent* can be substituted for the term *hundredth*. Consider the fraction $\frac{3}{4}$. As a fraction expressed in hundredths, it is $\frac{75}{100}$. When $\frac{3}{4}$ is written in decimal form, it is 0.75. Both 0.75 and $\frac{75}{100}$ are read in exactly the same way, "seventy-five hundredths." When used as operators, $\frac{3}{4}$ of something is the same as 0.75 or 75 percent of that same thing. Thus, percent is merely a new notation and terminology, not a new concept.

Models provide the main link among fractions, decimals, and percents, as shown in Figure 18.13. Base-ten fraction models are suitable for fractions, decimals, and percents, since they all represent the same idea.

Another helpful approach to the terminology of percent is through the role of the decimal point. Recall that

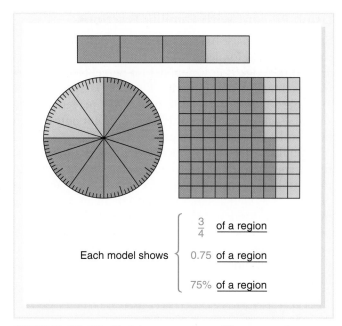

Each model shows
$\frac{3}{4}$ of a region
0.75 of a region
75% of a region

FIGURE 18.13 Models connect three different notations.

the decimal identifies the units. When the unit is ones, a number such as 0.659 means a little more than 6 tenths of 1. The word *ones* is understood (6 tenths of 1 *one* or one *whole*). But 0.659 is also 6.59 tenths and 65.9 hundredths and 659 thousandths. The name of the unit must be explicitly identified, or else the unit would change with each position of the decimal. Since *percent* is another name for *hundredths*, when the decimal identifies the hundredths position as the units, the word *percent* can be specified as a synonym for *hundredths*. Thus, 0.659 (of some whole or 1) is 65.9 hundredths or 65.9 percent of that same whole. As illustrated in Figure 18.14, the notion of placing the decimal point to *identify the percent position* is conceptually more meaningful than the apparently arbitrary rule: "To change a decimal to a percent, move the decimal two places to the right." A better idea is to equate hundredths with percent both orally and in notation.

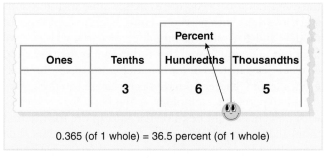

Ones	Tenths	Percent Hundredths	Thousandths
		3	6	5

0.365 (of 1 whole) = 36.5 percent (of 1 whole)

FIGURE 18.14 Hundredths are also known as percents.

Using Percent with Familiar Fractions

Students should use base-ten models for percents in much the same way as for decimals. The disk with 100 markings around the edge is now a model for percents as well as a fraction model for hundredths. The same is true of a 10 × 10 square. Each tiny square inside is 1 percent of the square. Each row or strip of 10 squares is not only a tenth but also 10 percent of the square.

Similarly, the familiar fractions (halves, thirds, fourths, fifths, and eighths) should become familiar in terms of percents as well as decimals. Three-fifths, for example, is 60 percent as well as 0.6. One-third of an amount is frequently expressed as $33\frac{1}{3}$ percent instead of 33.3333 . . . percent. Likewise, $\frac{1}{8}$ of a quantity is $12\frac{1}{2}$ percent or 12.5 percent of the quantity. These ideas should be explored with base-ten models and not as rules about moving decimal points.

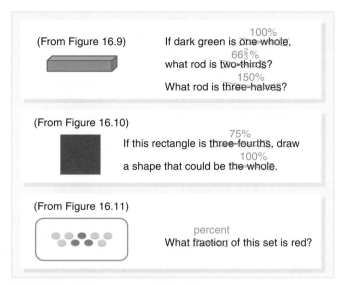

FIGURE 18.15 Part-whole-fraction exercises can be translated into percent exercises.

Realistic Percent Problems

The Three Percent Problems

Middle school teachers talk about "the three percent problems." The sentence "_____ is _____ percent of _____" has three spaces for numbers; for example, "20 is 25 percent of 80." The classic three percent problems come from this sterile expression; two of the numbers are given, and the students are asked to produce the third. Students learn very quickly that you either multiply or divide the two given numbers, and sometimes you have to move a decimal point. But they have no way of determining when to do what, which numbers to divide, or which way to shift the decimal. As a result, performance on percentage problems is very poor. Furthermore, commonly encountered expressions using percent terminology, such as sales figures, taxes, census data, political information, and trends in economics, are almost never in the "_____ is _____ percent of _____" format. So when asked to solve a realistic percent problem, students are frequently at a loss.

Chapter 16 explored three types of exercises with fractions, in which one element—part, whole, or fraction—was unknown. Students used models and simple fraction relationships in those exercises. Those three types of exercises are precisely the same as the three percent problems. Developmentally, then, it makes sense to help students make the connection between the exercises done with fractions and those done with percents. How? Use the same types of models and the same terminology of parts, wholes, and fractions. The only thing that is different is that the word *percent* is used instead of *fraction*. In Figure 18.15, three exercises from Chapter 16 have been changed to the corresponding percent terminology. A good idea for early work with percents would be to review (or explore for the first time) all three types of exercises in terms of percents. The same three types of models can be used (refer to Figures 16.9, 16.10, and 16.11 on pp. 301–302).

Realistic Percent Problems and Nice Numbers

Though students must have some experience with the noncontextual situations in Figure 18.15, it is important to have them explore these relationships in real contexts. Find or make up percent problems, and present them in the same way that they appear in newspapers, on television, and in other real contexts. In addition to realistic problems and formats, follow these maxims for your unit on percents:

- Limit the percents to familiar fractions (halves, thirds, fourths, fifths, and eighths) or easy percents ($\frac{1}{10}$, $\frac{1}{100}$), and use numbers compatible with these fractions. The focus of these exercises is the relationships involved, not complex computational skills.
- Do not suggest any rules or procedures for different types of problems. Do not categorize or label problem types.
- Use the terms *part*, *whole*, and *percent* (or *fraction*). *Fraction* and *percent* are interchangeable. Help students see these percent exercises as the same types of exercises they did with simple fractions.
- Require students to use models or drawings to explain their solutions. It is better to assign three problems requiring a drawing and an explanation than to give 15 problems requiring only computation and answers. Remember that the purpose is the exploration of relationships, not computational skill.
- Encourage mental computation.

The following sample problems meet these criteria for easy fractions and numbers. Try working each problem, identifying each number as a part, a whole, or a fraction. Draw length or area models to explain or work through your thought process. Examples of this informal reasoning are illustrated with additional problems in Figure 18.16.

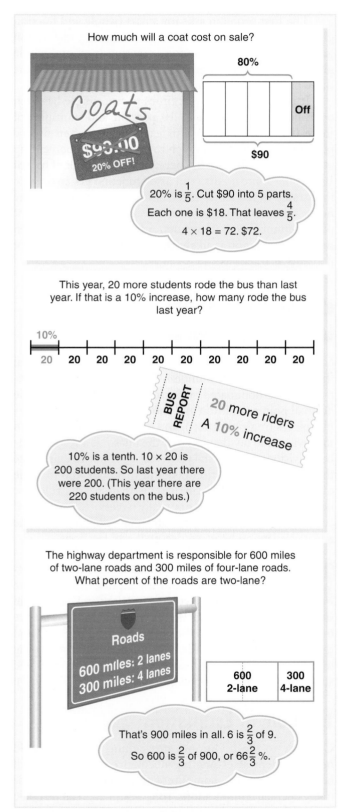

FIGURE 18.16 Real percent problems with nice numbers. Simple drawings help with reasoning.

1. **The PTA reported that 75 percent of the total number of families were represented at the meeting last night. If children from 320 families go to the school, how many were represented at the meeting?**
2. **The baseball team won 80 percent of the 25 games it played this year. How many games were lost?**
3. **In Mrs. Carter's class, 20 students, or $66\frac{2}{3}$ percent, were on the honor roll. How many students are in her class?**
4. **George bought his new computer at a $12\frac{1}{2}$ percent discount. He paid $700. How many dollars did he save by buying it at a discount?**
5. **If Joyce has read 60 of the 180 pages in her library book, what percent of the book has she read so far?**
6. **The hardware store bought widgets at 80 cents each and sold them for $1 each. What percent did the store mark up the price of each widget?**

(**II**) *pause and reflect* ───────────

Examine the examples in Figure 18.16. Notice how each problem is solved with simple fractions and mental math. Then try each of the six problems just listed. Each can be done easily and mentally using friendly fraction equivalents.

Assessment Notes Realistic percent problems are still the best way to assess a student's understanding of percent. Assign one or two, and have students explain why they think their answer makes sense. You might take a realistic percent problem and substitute fractions for percents (e.g., use $\frac{1}{8}$ instead of 12.5 percent) to see how students handle these problems with fractions compared to decimal numbers.

If your focus is on reasons and justifications rather than number of problems correct, you will be able to collect all the information you need. ■

Estimation in Percent Problems

Of course, not all real percent problems have nice numbers. Frequently in real life an approximation or estimate in percent situations is all that is required or is enough to help one think through the situation. Even if a calculator will be used to get an exact answer, an estimate based on an understanding of the relationship can confirm that a correct operation was performed or that the decimal was positioned correctly.

To help students with estimation in percent situations, two ideas that have already been discussed can be applied. First, when the percent is not a "nice" one, substitute a close percent that is easy to work with. Second, select numbers that are compatible with the percent involved, to make the calculation easy to do mentally. In essence, convert the not-nice percent problem into one that is nice. Here are some examples.

1. The 83,000-seat stadium was 73 percent full. How many people were at the game?
2. The treasurer reported that 68.3 percent of the dues had been collected, for a total of $385. How much more money could the club expect to collect if all dues are paid?
3. Max McStrike had 217 hits in 842 at-bats. What was his batting average?

 **pause and reflect** _____

Use friendly fractions and compatible numbers to solve each of these last three problems. Do this before reading on.

_____

Possible Estimates

1. (Use $\frac{3}{4}$ and 80,000) ⟶ about 60,000
2. (Use $\frac{2}{3}$ and $380; will collect $\frac{1}{3}$ more) ⟶ about $190
3. (4 × 217 > 842; $\frac{1}{4}$ is 25 percent, or 0.250) ⟶ a bit more than 0.250

The following activity is also useful in helping students with estimation in percent situations.

activity 18.11

Estimate with Nice Fractions

Provide students with realistically stated percent problems. For percentages in the problems, use values that are close to but not the same as the nice percents or friendly fractions. Choose the other numbers in the problems so that they are compatible with the close friendly fraction. The students' task is to make estimates of the answers using easy computations or mental mathematics. As always, they should write down their procedures and rationale. Do not expect that every student will estimate in the same manner.

Here are three percent problems with two sets of numbers. The first set involves nice numbers that allow the problem to be worked mentally using fraction equivalents. The second set of numbers requires that the numbers be substituted with approximations allowing for an estimate as in the last activity.

1. The school enrolls {480, 547} students. Yesterday {$12\frac{1}{2}$ percent, 13 percent} of the students were absent. How many came to school?
2. Mr. Carver sold his lawn mower for {$45, $89}. This was {60 percent, 62 percent} of the price he paid for it new. What did the mower cost when it was new?

3. When the box fell off the shelf {90, 63} of the {720, 500} widgets broke. What percentage was lost in the breakage?

The first problem asks for a part (whole and fraction given), the second asks for a whole (part and fraction given), and the third asks for a fraction (part and whole given). Notice again that these are exactly the same as the three parts-and-whole questions found in Chapter 16.

It is also convenient at times to use simple base-ten equivalents: 1 percent and 10 percent and multiples of these (including halves). For example, we often use 10 percent plus half of that much to compute a 15 percent tip at a restaurant. To find 0.5 percent we can think of half of 1 percent. Some adults (and also students) get so used to the strategies related to these base-ten fractions that they never think to use other fraction equivalents that might produce more accurate results. A focus on these base-ten percentages is not as likely to help students conceive of percents as fractions.

Computation with Decimals

Certainly, students should develop some computational fluency with decimal numbers. In the past, decimal computation was dominated by the following rules: Line up the decimal points (addition and subtraction), count the decimal places (multiplication), and shift the decimal point in the divisor and dividend so that the divisor is a whole number (division). Traditional textbooks continue to emphasize these rules. The position taken in this book and in some of the standards-based curricula is that specific rules for decimal computation are not really necessary, especially if computation is built on a firm understanding of place value and a connection between decimals and fractions.

NCTM Standards At the 3–5 level, the *Standards* says that students should "develop and use strategies to estimate computations involving fractions and decimals in situations relevant to students' experience" (p. 148). At the 6–8 level, students are to "select appropriate methods and tools for computing with fractions and decimals from among mental computation, estimation, calculators or computers, and paper and pencil, depending on the situation" (p. 214).

The Role of Estimation

Contrary to the traditional curriculum, students should become adept at estimating decimal computations well before they learn to compute with pencil and paper. For many decimal computations, rough estimates can be made easily by rounding the numbers to nice whole numbers or simple base-ten fractions. A minimum goal for your students should be to have the estimate contain the correct number of digits to the left of the decimal—the whole-number part. Select problems for which estimates are not terribly difficult.

 **pause and reflect** _____

Before going on, try making easy whole-number estimates of the following computations. Do not spend time with fine adjustments in your estimates.

1. 4.907 + 123.01 + 56.1234
2. 459.8 − 12.345
3. 24.67 × 1.84
4. 514.67 ÷ 3.59

Your estimates might be similar to the following:

1. Between 175 and 200
2. More than 400, or about 425 to 450
3. More than 25, closer to 50 (1.84 is more than 1 and close to 2)
4. More than 125, less than 200 (500 ÷ 4 = 125 and 600 ÷ 3 = 200)

In these examples, an understanding of decimal numeration and some simple whole-number estimation skills can produce rough estimates. When estimating, thinking focuses on the meaning of the numbers and the operations and not on counting decimal places. However, students who are taught to focus on the pencil-and-paper rules for decimal computation do not even consider the actual values of the number much less estimate.

Therefore, a good *place* to begin decimal computation is with estimation. Not only is it a highly practical skill, but it also helps children look at answers in ballpark terms and can form a check on calculator computation.

A good *time* to begin computation with decimals is as soon as a conceptual background in decimal numeration has been developed. Learning the rules for decimal computation will do little or nothing to help students understand decimal numeration and will interfere with a more robust development of number sense. An emphasis on estimation is very important, even for students in the seventh and eighth grades who have been exposed to and have used rules for decimal computation, especially for multiplication and division. Many students who are totally reliant on rules for decimals make mistakes without being aware.

Addition and Subtraction

Consider this problem:

Max and Moe each timed his own quarter-mile run with a stopwatch. Max says that he ran the quarter in 74.5

seconds. Moe was more accurate. He reported his run as 81.34 seconds. How many seconds faster did Max run than Moe?

Students who understand decimal numeration should first of all be able to tell approximately what the difference is—close to 7 seconds. With an estimate as a beginning, students should then be challenged to figure out the exact difference. The estimate will help them avoid the typical error of lining up the 5 under the 4. A variety of student strategies are possible. For example, students might note that 74.5 and 7 is 81.5 and then figure out how much extra that is. Others may count on from 74.5 by adding 0.5 and then 6 more seconds to get to 81 seconds and then add on the remaining 0.34 second. These and other strategies will eventually confront the difference between the one-place decimal (.5) and the two-place decimal (.34). Students can resolve this issue by returning to their understanding of place value. Similar story problems for addition and subtraction, some involving different numbers of decimal places, will help develop students' understanding of these two operations. Always request an estimate prior to computation.

After students have had several opportunities to solve addition and subtraction story problems, the following activity is reasonable.

activity **18.12**

Exact Sums and Differences

Give students a sum involving different numbers of decimal places. For example: 73.46 + 6.2 + 0.582. The first task is to make an estimate and explain the way the estimate was made. The second task is to compute the exact answer and explain how that was done (no calculators). In the third and final task students devise a method for adding and subtracting decimal numbers that they can use with any two numbers.

When students have completed these three tasks, have students share their strategies for computation and test them on a new computation that you provide.

The same task can be repeated for subtraction.

The earlier estimation practice will focus students' attention on the meanings of the numbers. It is reasonable to expect that students will develop an algorithm that is essentially the same as aligning the decimal points.

 If students have difficulty with Activity 18.12, it is an indication that they have a weak understanding of decimal concepts and the role of the decimal point. This is true even for students who get a correct sum by using a rule they learned in an earlier grade but who have difficulty with their explanations. Rather than focus on how to add or subtract decimals, return or shift your focus to decimal concepts as discussed earlier in the chapter. ∎

Multiplication

Estimation should play a significant role in developing an algorithm for multiplication. As a beginning point, consider this problem:

The farmer fills each jug with 3.7 liters of cider. If you buy 4 jugs, how many liters of cider is that?

Begin with an estimate. It is more than 12 liters. What is the most it could be? Could it be 16 liters? Once an estimate of the result is decided on, let students use their own methods for determining an exact answer. Many will use repeated addition: 3.7 + 3.7 + 3.7 + 3.7. Others may begin by multiplying 3 × 4 and then adding up 0.7 four times. Eventually, students will agree on the exact result of 14.8 liters. Explore other problems involving whole-number multipliers. Multipliers such as 3.5 or 8.25 that involve nice fractional parts—here, one-half and one-fourth—are also reasonable.

As a next step, have students compare a decimal product with one involving the same digits but no decimal. For example, how are 23.4 × 6.5 and 234 × 65 alike? Interestingly, both products have exactly the same digits: 15210. (The zero may be missing from the decimal product.) Using a calculator, have students explore other products that are alike except for the decimals involved. The digits in the answer are always alike. After seeing how the digits remain the same for these related products, do the following activity.

activity 18.13

Where Does the Decimal Go?: Multiplication

Have students compute the following product: 24 × 63. Using only the result of this computation and estimation, have them give the exact answer to each of the following:

   0.24 × 6.3   24 × 0.63   2.4 × 63   0.24 × 0.63

For each computation they should write a rationale for their answers. They can check their results with a calculator. Any errors must be acknowledged, and the rationale that produced the error adjusted.

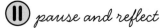

pause and reflect

The product of 24 × 63 is 1512. Use this information to give the answer to each of the products in the previous activity. Do *not* count decimal places. Remember your fractional equivalents.

The method of placing the decimal point in a product by way of estimation is more difficult as the product gets smaller. For example, knowing that 54 × 83 is 4482 does not make it easy to place the decimal in the product 0.0054 × 0.00083. Even the product 0.054 × 0.83 is hard. The practical question is this: Can you think of any situation outside of school in which someone might require an exact answer to a product such as one of these but would not have access to a calculator? When precision is important, technology makes sense and is always available. Yes, there is a conceptual rationale for counting the decimal places. Even if learned, it focuses attention on the smallest part of the product and provides absolutely no practice with estimation. It is a non-number-sense method that need not be used or taught today.

Assessment Notes Questions such as the following keep the focus on number sense and provide useful information about your students' understanding.

1. Consider these two computations: $3\frac{1}{2} \times 2\frac{1}{4}$ and 2.276 × 3.18. Without doing the calculations, which do you think is larger? Provide a reason for your answer that can be understood by someone else in this class.
2. How much larger is 0.76 × 5 than 0.75 × 5? How can you tell without doing the computation (Kulm, 1994)?

Student discussions and explanations as they work on these or similar questions can provide insights into their decimal and fraction number sense and the connections between the two representations. ∎

Division

Division can be approached in a manner exactly parallel to multiplication. In fact, the best approach to a division estimate generally comes from thinking about multiplication rather than division. Consider the following problem:

The trip to Washington was 282.5 miles. It took exactly $4\frac{1}{2}$ hours or 4.5 hours to drive. What was the average miles per hour?

To make an estimate of this quotient, think about what times 4 or 5 is close to 280. You might think 60 × 4.5 = 240 + 30 = 270. So maybe about 61 or 62 miles per hour.

Here is a second example without context. Make an estimate of 45.7 ÷ 1.83. Think only of what times $1\frac{8}{10}$ is close to 45.

❙❙ *pause and reflect* ─────────

Will the answer be more or less than 45? Why? Will it be more or less than 20? Now think about 1.8 being close to 2. What times 2 is close to 46? Use this to produce an estimate.

─────────

Since 1.83 is close to 2, the estimate is near 22. And since 1.83 is less than 2 the answer must be greater than 22—say 25 or 26. (The actual answer is 24.972677.)

Okay, so estimation can produce a reasonable result, but you may still require a pencil-and-paper algorithm to produce the digits the way it was done for multiplication. Figure 18.17 shows division by a whole number and how that can be carried out to as many places as you wish. (The explicit-trade method described in Chapter 13 is shown on the right.) It is not necessary to move the decimal point up into the quotient. Leave that to estimation.

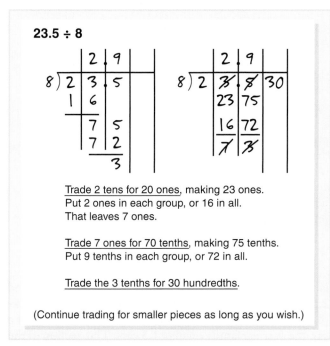

23.5 ÷ 8

Trade 2 tens for 20 ones, making 23 ones.
Put 2 ones in each group, or 16 in all.
That leaves 7 ones.

Trade 7 ones for 70 tenths, making 75 tenths.
Put 9 tenths in each group, or 72 in all.

Trade the 3 tenths for 30 hundredths.

(Continue trading for smaller pieces as long as you wish.)

FIGURE 18.17 Extension of the division algorithm.

activity **18.14**

Where Does the Decimal Go?: Division

Provide a quotient such as 146 ÷ 7 = 20857 correct to five digits but without the decimal point. The task is to use only this information and estimation to give a fairly precise answer to each of the following:

146 ÷ 0.7   1.46 ÷ 7   14.6 ÷ 0.7   1460 ÷ 70

For each computation students should write a rationale for their answers and then check their results with a calculator. Any errors should be acknowledged, and the rationale that produced the error adjusted.

❙❙ *pause and reflect* ─────────

Give the answer to each of the products in the previous activity.

─────────

A reasonable algorithm for division is parallel to that for multiplication: *Ignore the decimal points, and do the computation as if all numbers were whole numbers. When finished, place the decimal by estimation.* This is reasonable for divisors with no more than two significant digits. If students have a method for dividing by 45, they can divide by 0.45 and 4.5 and even 0.045.

It is interesting to notice how different programs deal with computation beyond whole numbers. *Investigations in Number, Data, and Space*, a K–5 program, does not mention computation with decimals but works hard to connect decimal numeration to fractions and percents. Traditional programs develop addition and subtraction skills in the fifth grade, all four operations in the sixth grade, and review them again in the seventh. The *Connected Mathematics* program provides five or six days of development work on the addition, subtraction, and multiplication with decimals in the sixth grade but no division. No further work with these skills is found in the seventh and eighth grades. The next page shows an interesting multiplication activity from *Connected Mathematics*.

📖 Literature Connections

Few interesting stories inspire exploration of decimals and percents for children in the fifth grade and higher. One notable exception is *The Phantom Tollbooth*, a story that should not be missed regardless of its mathematical significance.

In the daily paper and weekly magazines, you will find decimal and percent situations with endless real-world connections. One issue with percents in news stories is the frequent omission of the base amount or the whole on which the percent is determined. "March sales of widgets were reported to be up 3.6 percent." Does that mean an increase over February or over March of the previous year? Increase and decrease by percents are interesting to project over

MIDDLE GRADES

Grade 6, Bits and Pieces II
Investigation 6: Computing with Decimals

Context

"Computing with Decimals" is the only place in the whole *Connected Mathematics* program in which decimal computation is explicitly addressed. The investigation is scheduled for approximately five days. Prior to this, students have worked at computation with fractions. The first two lessons in the investigation develop the addition and subtraction algorithm. The lesson just prior to the activity described here explores patterns in products with factors of 0.1, 0.01, 0.001, and 0.0001.

Task Description

Rather than begin with the factors, this activity begins with the product and has students explore the factors. In a full-class discussion, students find pairs of numbers with a product of 1560. This is based on earlier work with prime factorization. Given a list of four pairs with a product of 1560, the students are asked to find a pair with a product of 156.0 and a pair with a product of 1.560. Students use calculators to work on these tasks and find that the factors involve the exact same digits as for the whole-number product. For example, 2.4×0.65, 0.024×65, 0.39×4, and so on, all have a product of 1.560. With this introduction, students are given the task shown here.

The teaching notes suggest that part B of the task is more difficult because students have no specific number to begin with. Each student in a group is encouraged to come up with different factors so that as a group there will be a variety of examples. Once there are num-

bers that satisfy part B1, the task is about how to adjust these numbers to get products in different ranges. Notice that there is no direct discussion in this task of how to multiply decimal numbers.

The last lesson of the unit is built on a contextual problem about fencing a rectangular pen for a dog. Students must determine the amount of fence, the number of posts, and the number of staples needed. Unit prices are given, and a 7 percent sales tax must also be computed. The problem involves addition and multiplication of decimal numbers in context. Calculators are permitted.

> **Problem 6.4**
>
> **A.** 1. Find two numbers with a product of 1344.
>   2. Find two numbers with a product of 134.4.
>   3. Find two numbers with a product of 1.344.
>   4. Find two numbers with a product of 0.1344.
>   5. Explain how you got your answers and why you think they are correct.
>
> **B.** 1. Find two numbers with a product between 2000 and 3000.
>   2. By moving decimal points, change the value of each of the numbers you found in part 1 so that their product is between 200 and 300.
>   3. By moving decimal points, change the value of each of the numbers you found in part 1 so that their product is between 20 and 30.
>   4. By moving decimal points, change the value of each of the numbers you found in part 1 so that their product is between 2 and 3.
>   5. Explain what you did to get your answers and why you think they are correct.

From *Connected Mathematics: Bits and Pieces II: Using Rational Numbers.* © 2002 by Michigan State University, Glenda Lappan, James T. Fey, William M. Fitzgerald, Susan N. Friel, & Elizabeth Difanis Phillips. Published by Pearson Education, Inc., publishing as Pearson Prentice Hall. Used by permission.

---

several years. If the consumer price index rises 3 percent a year, how much will a $50 basket of groceries cost by the time your students are 21 years old?

The Phantom Tollbooth
Juster, 1961

References to mathematical ideas abound throughout this book. Milo enters a world of crazy places and imaginative creatures after driving his toy car through a model of a turnpike tollbooth. Several chapters involve adventures in Digitopolis, where everything is number-oriented. In Digitopolis, Milo meets a boy who is only half of a boy, appearing in the drawing to be the left half of a boy cut top to bottom. As it turns out, the boy is actually 0.58 since he

is a member of the average family: a mother, father, and 2.58 children. The boy is the 0.58. One advantage, he explains, is that he is the only one who can drive the $\frac{3}{10}$ of a car, the average family owning 1.3 cars. This section of the tale involves a great discussion of averages that come out in decimal numbers.

An obvious extension of the story is to explore averages of things that are interesting to the students (average number of siblings, average arm span, etc.) and see where these odd decimal parts come from. In the case of measures of length, for example, an average length can be a real length even if no one has it. But an average number of something like cars or sisters can be very humorous as discussed in the story. Where else are fractions and decimals used in this way? ■

Writing to Learn

1. Describe three different base-ten models for fractions and decimals, and use each to illustrate how base-ten fractions can easily be represented.
2. Explain why the place-value system extends infinitely in two directions. How can this idea be developed with students in the fifth or sixth grade?
3. Use an example involving base-ten pieces to explain the role of the decimal point in identifying the units position. Relate this idea to changing units of measurement as in money or metric measures.
4. What are the suggested "familiar fractions"? How can these fractions be connected to their decimal equivalents in a conceptual manner?
5. What should be emphasized if you want children to have good number sense with decimals?
6. Describe one or two ways in which a calculator can be used to develop number ideas with decimals.
7. What does rounding mean? What type of rounding can we do that is different from rounding to the nearest tenth or hundredth? Explain how a number line can be used in rounding.
8. Make up three realistic percent problems in which the percents are actually nice fractions and the numbers involved are compatible with the fractions. One problem should ask for the part, given the whole and the percent. One should ask for the percent, given the whole and the part. The third should ask for the whole, given the part and the percent. Model each, and show how each can be solved using fraction ideas.
9. For addition and subtraction, the line-up-the-decimals rule can be reasonably taught without much trouble. Explain.
10. Why does the multiplication procedure of counting decimal places to determine decimal-point placement not help with number sense? What are the contrasting values of using the estimation approach described in the chapter?
11. Give an example explaining how, in most problems, multiplication and division with decimals can be replaced with estimation and whole-number methods.

For Discussion and Exploration

1. For each of the four operations, discuss what computational skill with decimals is necessary for children to have. For example, if you believe that division with decimal numbers is important, what is the most tedious problem you would consider having students master? What alternatives to traditional pencil-and-paper computation do you think should be included in the curriculum?
2. One way to order a series of decimal numbers is to annex zeros to each number so that all numbers have the same number of decimal places. For example, rewrite

0.34		0.3400
0.3004	as	0.3004
0.059		0.0590

Now ignore the decimal points and any leading zeros, and order the resulting whole numbers. Discuss the merits of teaching this approach to children. If taught this procedure, what would students learn about decimal numeration?
3. Talk individually with some seventh- or eighth-grade students. First find out if they can do simple fraction exercises that ask for the part, the whole, or the fraction given the other two (as in Chapter 16). Encourage them to make drawings and give explanations. Next ask them to solve simple percent word problems that require the same type of reasoning using simple fractions and compatible numbers. Compare students' abilities with these mathematically identical problems.

Recommendations for Further Reading

Bennett, A. B., & Nelson, L. T. (1994). A conceptual model for solving percent problems. *Mathematics Teaching in the Middle School, 1,* 20–25.
　This article introduces a useful twist on using the 10×10 grid to understand percents. The authors provide a series of increasingly difficult tasks that can easily be used in a constructivist environment to challenge a range of students. Realistic percent problems are used throughout.

Irwin, K. C. (2001). Using everyday knowledge of decimals to enhance understanding. *Journal for Research in Mathematics Education, 4,* 399–420.
　Irwin's article describes her work with 16 children, ages 11 and 12. The students worked in eight pairs, half of which solved problems given in contexts. The other four pairs solved the same problems but without contexts. The article is enlightening on a number of fronts, not the least of which are the transcriptions that clearly indicate the students' misconceptions of decimal numeration. Don't be afraid of this because it is a research article. It is readable, interesting, and valuable for anyone considering teaching decimal numeration.

Martinie, S. L., & Bay-Williams, J. (2003). Investigating students' conceptual understanding of decimal fractions using multiple representations. *Mathematics Teaching in the Middle School, 8,* 244–247.
　This little article describes the results of 43 sixth-grade students who were asked to represent 0.6 and 0.06 with four different representations: a number line, a 10×10 grid, money, and base-ten materials. The results indicate that students may appear to understand decimals with one model but not with another. The authors make an argument for using multiple models in teaching decimals.

McIntosh, A., Reys, B., Reys, R., & Hope, J. (1997). *Number SENSE: Simple effective number sense experiences [Grades 3–4, Grades 4–6, Grades 6–8].* White Plains, NY: Cuisenaire–Dale Seymour.
　These three activity resource books provide Blackline Masters that are designed to help students develop a wide range

of useful number relationships. Of special note are activities that use benchmarks of 0, $\frac{1}{2}$, and 1 for fractions and for decimals. There are also good activities for connecting fractions and decimals. The pages can be used with a full class as overhead transparencies or for individual use.

Owens, D. T., & Super, D. B. (1993). Teaching and learning decimal fractions. In D. T. Owens (Ed.), *Research ideas for the classroom: Middle grades mathematics* (pp. 137–158). Old Tappan, NJ: Macmillan.

Owens and Super offer useful insights from research on how children develop decimal concepts and the difficulties involved. The chapter also provides a variety of useful activities for decimal concept development. The authors have also included results of NAEP testing that give some perspective on what is typical student development.

Online Resources

Suggested Applets and Web Links

Base Blocks—Decimals
http://nlvm.usu.edu/en/nav/frames_asid_264_g_2_t_1.html
Base-ten blocks can be placed on a place-value chart the same as for whole numbers. The number of decimal places can be selected, thus designating any of the four blocks as the unit. Addition and subtraction problems can be created or can be generated randomly by the applet.

Fractions Bar Applet
www.arcytech.org/java/fractions/fractions.html
A very nice applet for developing the relationships among fractions, decimals, and percents. Bars for one whole are displayed and can be partitioned according to selected fraction, decimal, or percent values and then labeled in any of these representations. This makes equivalencies easy to explore without being too leading.

Fraction Model—Version 3
http://illuminations.nctm.org/tools/tool_detail.aspx?id=45
The equivalence of fraction, decimal, and percent representations in a circle, set, or rectangle model is demonstrated. Versions 1 and 2 are the same but the numerators and denominators are restricted to 20.

Percentages
http://nlvm.usu.edu/en/nav/frames_asid_160_g_2_t_1.
html?open=activities
The user enters any two of the values—whole, part, and percent—and clicks on Compute. Although the computer does the work, the applet nicely models percent problems.

An additional list of books and articles related to the ideas in this chapter can be found on the Companion Web site at **www.ablongman.com/vandewalle6e.**

chapter 19
Proportional Reasoning

Proportional reasoning has been referred to as the capstone of the elementary curriculum and the cornerstone of algebra and beyond (Lesh, Post, & Behr, 1987). It represents the ability to begin to understand multiplicative relationships where most arithmetic concepts are additive in nature. The development of proportional reasoning is one of the most important goals of the 5–8 curriculum.

Big Ideas

1. A ratio is a multiplicative comparison of two quantities or measures. A key developmental milestone is the ability of a student to begin to think of a ratio as a distinct entity, different from the two measures that made it up.

2. Ratios and proportions involve multiplicative rather than additive comparisons. Equal ratios result from multiplication or division, not from addition or subtraction.

3. Proportional thinking is developed through activities involving comparing and determining the equivalence of ratios and solving proportions in a wide variety of problem-based contexts and situations without recourse to rules or formulas.

Mathematics Content Connections

Proportional reasoning is indeed the cornerstone of a wide variety of topics in the middle and high school curriculum.

■ **Fractions** (Chapter 16): Equivalent fractions are found through a multiplicative process; numerators and denominators are multiplied or divided by the same number. Equivalent ratios can be found in the same manner. In fact, part-whole relationships (fractions) are an example of ratio.

Fractions are also one of the principal methods of representing ratios.

■ **Algebra** (Chapter 15): Much of algebra concerns a study of change and, hence, rates of change (ratios) are particularly important. In this chapter you will see that the graphs of equivalent ratios are straight lines passing through the origin. The slope of the line is the unit ratio. Slope itself is a rate of change and is an important component in understanding algebraic representations of related quantities.

■ **Similarity** (Chapter 21): When two figures are the same shape but different sizes (i.e., similar), they constitute a visual example of a proportion. The ratios of linear measures in one figure will be equal to the corresponding ratios in the other.

■ **Data Graphs** (Chapter 22): A relative frequency histogram shows the frequencies of different related events compared to all outcomes (visual part-to-whole ratios). A box-and-whisker plot shows the relative distribution of data along a number line and can be used to compare distributions of populations of very different sizes.

■ **Probability** (Chapter 23): A probability is a ratio that compares the number of outcomes in an event to the total possible outcomes. Proportional reasoning helps students understand these ratios, especially in comparing large and small sample sizes.

Ratios, Proportions, and Proportional Reasoning

Regardless of how the objectives are stated in your curriculum concerning the ability to solve proportions or percent problems, the ultimate goal for your students should be focused on the development of proportional reasoning, not a collection of skills. To this end it is useful to have a good idea of what constitutes a ratio and a proportion and in what contexts these mathematical ideas appear. With this information we can then examine what it means to reason proportionally and begin to work toward helping students achieve that goal.

Examples of Ratios in Different Contexts

A *ratio* is a number that relates two quantities or measures within a given situation in a multiplicative relationship (in contrast to a difference or additive relationship). A ratio can be applied to another situation where the relative amounts of the quantities or measures are the same as in the first situation (Smith, 2002). Ratios appear in a variety of different contexts. Part of proportional reasoning is the ability to recognize ratios in these various settings. To the student just beginning to develop an understanding of ratio, different settings or contexts may well seem like different ideas even though they are essentially the same from a mathematical viewpoint.

Part-to-Whole Ratios

Ratios can express comparisons of a part to a whole, for example, the ratio of the number of girls in a class to the number of students in the class. Because fractions are also part-whole ratios, it follows that every fraction is also a ratio. In the same way, percentages are ratios, and in fact, percentages are sometimes used to express ratios. Probabilities are ratios of a part of the sample space to the whole sample space.

Part-to-Part Ratios

A ratio can also express one part of a whole to another part of the same whole. For example, the number of girls in the class can be compared to the number of boys. For other examples, consider Democrats to Republicans or peanuts to cashews. Although the probability of an event is a part-to-whole ratio, the *odds* of an event happening is a ratio of the number of ways an event can happen to the number of ways it cannot happen—a part-to-part ratio.

Rates as Ratios

Both part-to-whole and part-to-part ratios compare two measures of the same type of thing. A ratio can also be a *rate*. A rate is a comparison of the measures of two different things or quantities; the measuring unit is different for each value.

For example, if 4 similar boats carry 36 passengers, then the comparison of 4 boats to 36 passengers is a ratio.

Boats and passengers are different types of things. Similarly, all rates of speed are comparisons of time and distance: for example, driving at 55 miles per hour or jogging at 9 minutes per mile.

Miles per gallon, square yards of coverage per gallon of paint, passengers per busload, and roses per bouquet are all rates. Relationships between two units of measure are also rates or ratios, for example, inches per foot, milliliters per liter, and centimeters per inch.

Other Examples of Ratio

In geometry, the ratios of corresponding parts of similar geometric figures are always the same. The diagonal of a square is always $\sqrt{2}$ times a side; that is, the ratio of the diagonal of a square to its side is $\sqrt{2}$. π (pi) is the ratio of the circumference of a circle to the diameter. The trigonometric functions can be developed from ratios of sides of right triangles.

The slope of a line or of a roof is a ratio of rise for each unit of horizontal distance or run. Slope is an extremely important ratio in algebra. Not only does it describe the steepness of a line, but also it tells us the rate of change of one variable in terms of another.

In nature, the ratio known as the *golden ratio* is found in many spirals, from nautilus shells to the swirls of a pinecone or a pineapple. Artists and architects have used the same ratio in creating shapes that are naturally pleasing to the eye.

Proportions

Recall that a ratio is a number that expresses a multiplicative relationship that can be applied to a second situation where the relative quantities or measures are the same as in the first situation. A *proportion* is a statement of equality between two ratios. If 4 boats carry 36 passengers, then 2 boats of the same size will carry 18 passengers, 3 boats will carry 27 passengers, and 20 boats will carry 180 passengers. Here the ratio of 4 to 36 can be applied to each of these situations even though the measures are different in each case.

For students to begin to understand ratio as a single value that can be applied to different yet proportional situations, they must learn to recognize these relationships in the different settings or to learn that in each setting the two quantities are *in the same ratio*. Similarly, they must be able to compare situations where the measures are not in the same ratio and decide how these ratios are different. In fact, many of the most valuable activities to develop proportional reasoning do not involve solving proportions at all but rather comparing ratios in similar but nonproportional settings.

Solving a proportion involves applying a known ratio to a situation that is proportional (relevant measures are in the same ratio) and finding one of these measures when the other is given. For example, given that 4 boats carry 36 passengers (known ratio is 4 to 36), how many passengers can 7 boats carry (equal ratio is 7 to x)?

Different notations for proportions can be used, for example:

$$3 : 9 = 4 : 12 \quad \text{or} \quad \tfrac{3}{9} = \tfrac{4}{12}$$

These might be read "3 is to 9 as 4 is to 12" or "3 and 9 are in the same ratio as 4 and 12."

A ratio that is a rate usually includes the units of measure when written, for example:

$$\frac{\$12.50}{1 \text{ gallon}} = \frac{\$37.50}{3 \text{ gallons}}$$

Proportional Reasoning

Proportional reasoning is difficult to define in a simple sentence or two. It is not something that you either can or cannot do. It is both a qualitative and quantitative process. According to Lamon (1999), the following are a few of the characteristics of proportional thinkers:

- Proportional thinkers have a sense of covariation. That is, they understand relationships in which two quantities vary together and are able to see how the variation in one coincides with the variation in another.
- Proportional thinkers recognize proportional relationships as distinct from nonproportional relationships in real-world contexts.
- Proportional thinkers develop a wide variety of strategies for solving proportions or comparing ratios, most of which are based on informal strategies rather than prescribed algorithms.
- Proportional thinkers understand ratios as distinct entities representing a relationship different from the quantities they compare.

It is estimated that more than half of the adult population cannot be viewed as proportional thinkers (Lamon, 1999). That means that we do not acquire the habits and skills of proportional reasoning simply by getting older. On the other hand, Lamon's research and that of others indicate that instruction can have an effect, especially if rules and algorithms for fraction computation, for comparing ratios, and for solving proportions are delayed. Students may need as much as three years' worth of opportunities to reason in multiplicative situations in order to adequately develop proportional reasoning skills. Chinese students begin their formal exploration of ratio and proportion in the elementary grades (Cai & Sun, 2002). In the United States, these concepts are typically taught in grades 6 to 9. Premature use of rules encourages students to apply rules

without thinking and, thus, the ability to reason proportionally often does not develop.

Additive Versus Multiplicative Situations

Consider the following problem adapted from the book *Adding It Up* (National Research Council, 2001).

Two weeks ago, two flowers were measured at 8 inches and 12 inches, respectively. Today they are 11 inches and 15 inches tall. Did the 8-inch or 12-inch flower grow more?

 *pause and reflect* _____

Before reading further, find and defend two different answers to this problem.

One answer is that they both grew the same amount— 3 inches. This correct response is based on additive reasoning. That is, a single quantity was added to each measure to result in the two new measures. A second way to look at the problem is to compare the amount of growth to the original height of the flower. The first flower grew $\tfrac{3}{8}$ of its height while the second grew $\tfrac{3}{12}$. Based on this multiplicative view ($\tfrac{3}{8}$ *times as much* more), the first flower grew more. This is a proportional view of this change situation. Here, both the additive reasoning and multiplicative reasoning produce valid, albeit different, answers. The value in comparisons of this type is that discussion will focus on the nature of the comparison and, thus, highlight the distinction between additive and multiplicative comparisons. An ability to understand the difference between these situations is an indication of proportional reasoning.

Considerable research has been conducted to determine how children reason in various proportionality tasks and to determine if developmental or instructional factors are related to proportional reasoning (for example, see Bright, Joyner, & Wallis, 2003; Karplus, Pulos, & Stage, 1983; Lamon, 1993, 2002; Lo & Watanabe, 1997; Noelting, 1980; and Post, Behr, & Lesh, 1988).

The research provides direction for how to help children develop proportional thought processes. Some of these ideas are outlined here.

1. Provide ratio and proportion tasks in a wide range of contexts. These might include situations involving measurements, prices, geometric and other visual contexts, and rates of all sorts.
2. Encourage discussion and experimentation in predicting and comparing ratios. Help children distinguish

between proportional and nonproportional comparisons by providing examples of each and discussing the differences.

3. Help children relate proportional reasoning to existing processes. The concept of unit fractions is very similar to unit rates. Research indicates that the use of a unit rate for comparing ratios and solving proportions is the most common approach among junior high students even when cross-product methods have been taught. (This approach is explained later.)

4. Recognize that symbolic or mechanical methods, such as the cross-product algorithm, for solving proportions do not develop proportional reasoning and should not be introduced until students have had many experiences with intuitive and conceptual methods.

NCTM Standards   In 1989, the *Curriculum Standards* noted that proportional reasoning "was of such great importance that it merits whatever time and effort must be expended to assure its careful development" (NCTM, 1989, p. 82). The emphasis on proportional reasoning is similarly reflected in the 2000 *Standards*. The *Principles and Standards* authors have focused on the need for an integrative approach, one that involves "percent, similarity, scaling, linear equations, slope, relative frequency histograms, and probability" (NCTM, 2000, p. 212).

As a further aid in helping you understand the complexities of proportional reasoning, consider the five-item assessment shown in Figure 19.1, devised to examine students' appropriate use of additive or multiplicative reasoning (Bright, Joyner, & Wallis, 2003). Notice the way that each item deals with the possibility of using additive versus multiplicative reasoning. This instrument could easily be used in the classroom as a preassessment, as a series of good classroom tasks to then be discussed, or as a summative assessment to see how well students have acquired an understanding of multiplicative comparisons. In item 1, you might want to explain that the 200 percent setting doubles each dimension of the photo. ■

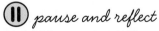 *pause and reflect* ⎯⎯⎯⎯⎯⎯⎯⎯⎯⎯⎯

Answer the questions in Figure 19.1. Discuss your answers with your colleagues. Can you find the item that is not a proportional situation? What is the difference between items 2 and 4?

Notice that the items involving rectangles (1, 2, and 5) cannot be answered correctly using additive reasoning, as could the flower-growth problem on p. 355. For a group of 132 eighth- and ninth-grade students, item 2 was the

---

For each problem, circle the correct answer.

1. Mrs. Allen took a 3-inch by 5-inch photo of the Cape Hatteras Lighthouse and made an enlargement on a photocopier using the 200% option. Which is "more square," the original photo or the enlargement?

   a. The original photo is "more square."
   b. The enlargement is "more square."
   c. The photo and the enlargement are equally square.
   d. There is not enough information to determine which is "more square."

2. The Science Club has four separate rectangular plots for experiments with plants:

1 foot by 4 feet	7 feet by 10 feet
17 feet by 20 feet	27 feet by 30 feet

   Which rectangular plot is most square?

   a. 1 foot by 4 feet
   b. 7 feet by 10 feet
   c. 17 feet by 20 feet
   d. 27 feet by 30 feet

3. Sue and Julie were running equally fast around a track. Sue started first. When Sue had run 9 laps, Julie had run 3 laps. When Julie completed 15 laps, how many laps had Sue run?

   a. 45 laps
   b. 24 laps
   c. 21 laps
   d. 6 laps

4. At the midway point of the basketball season, you must recommend the best free-throw shooter for the all-star game. Here are the statistics for four players:

Novak: 8 of 11 shots	Peterson: 22 of 29 shots
Williams: 15 of 19 shots	Reynolds: 33 of 41 shots

   Which player is the best free-throw shooter?

   a. Novak   b. Peterson   c. Williams   d. Reynolds

5. Write your answer to this problem.

   A farmer has three fields. One is 185 feet by 245 feet, one is 75 feet by 114 feet, and one is 455 feet by 508 feet. If you were flying over these fields, which one would seem most square? Which one would seem least square? Explain your answers.

FIGURE 19.1 Five items to assess proportional reasoning.

Source: Reprinted with permission from G. W. Bright, J. J. Joyner, and C. Wallis, "Assessing Proportional Thinking," *Mathematics Teaching in Middle School 9*(3), p. 167, copyright © 2003 by the National Council of Teachers of Mathematics. All rights reserved.

easiest (67 percent). The percentage correct on the other three multiple-choice items ranged only from 45 percent to 59 percent. The open-response item, number 5, proved quite difficult (37 percent most square, 28 percent least square). Over 52 percent of the students selected the 75×114 rectangle as the most square, and 45 percent selected the 185×245 rectangle as the least square. The authors speculate that there is a qualitative difference between open-response and multiple-choice items. Among other recommendations, they suggest that students engage in rich classroom discussions of proportional reasoning situations to improve their understanding.

Informal Activities to Develop Proportional Reasoning

Five categories of informal activities are suggested here: identification of multiplicative relationships, selection of equivalent ratios, comparison of ratios, scaling with ratio tables, and construction and measurement activities. Each provides a different opportunity for the development of proportional reasoning. The first category includes activities designed to help, students distinguish between proportional situations and additive or nonproportional ones. The remaining categories are not in any definitive sequence, nor are they designed to teach specific methods for solving proportions. Note that these are informal, exploratory activities. They are not intended to directly produce algorithmic skills or procedures. However, it is critical that students spend ample time with these or similar activities to properly develop proportional reasoning.

Identifying Multiplicative Relationships

Consider the following situation suggested by Cai and Sun in their discussion of how Chinese teachers introduce the concept of ratio (2002, p. 196):

> Miller Middle School has 16 sixth-grade students, and 12 of them say that they are basketball fans. The remaining students are not basketball fans.

Students are asked to describe whatever relationships they can between students who are basketball fans and those who are not. Once it is determined that there are four nonfans, there are now several different possibilities including these:

- There are eight more fans than nonfans.
- There are three times as many fans as nonfans.
- For every three students who like basketball, there is one who does not.

Of these, the first is an additive relationship—focusing on the difference between the two numbers. The other two are variations of the multiplicative relationship, each expressing the 3-to-1 ratio of fans to nonfans in a slightly

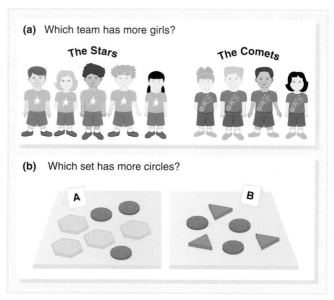

FIGURE 19.2 Two pictorial situations that can be interpreted with either additive or multiplicative comparisons.

different way. A discussion helps to contrast the multiplicative relationship with the additive one.

In the following activities, two ratios are considered rather than one, and a comparison is required. As with the earlier flower-growing problem, the choices can be made using either additive or multiplicative reasoning, providing your class with a helpful distinction between the two types of relationships without your attempt to define ratio for them.

activity **19.1**

Which Has More?

Provide students with two or three situations similar to those in Figure 19.2. Whether students work individually or in groups, a follow-up class discussion is imperative. This discussion can provide you with insights into how students are thinking and can also provide opportunities for students to help others see the situations from different perspectives.

Do not prompt students by telling them to look for a multiplicative relationship, but wait to see what sort of answers the students provide.

The situations in Figure 19.2 can be interpreted either additively or multiplicatively. The ambiguity is the key: If students recognize and understand the difference between the additive and multiplicative approaches, this is an indication of proportional reasoning. As with the flower problem, both interpretations are correct. You are looking for an awareness that there is a different way of looking at the situation. If at first they do not voluntarily suggest another way, ask a different question: for example, "Which class team has a larger proportion of girls?"

Return for a moment to item 3 in Figure 19.1. This item has been used in other studies that have shown that students try to solve this as a proportion problem when it is strictly an additive situation. The two runners will end up six laps apart, which is how they began. Not only is this a useful question to ask students, but also it points to the influence that being in a unit on proportional reasoning can have on students. Watson and Shaughnessy (2004) note that often the way that we word problems is a dead giveaway that a proportion is involved.

The following task is similar in nature to the flower problem.

activity **19.2**

Weight Loss

Show students the data in the following chart:

Week	Max	Moe	Minnie
0	210	158	113
2	202	154	108
4	196	150	105

Max, Moe, and Minnie are each on a diet and have recorded their weight at the start of their diet and at two-week intervals. After four weeks, which person is the most successful dieter?

The task is to make three different arguments—one that would favor each of the three dieters.

The way that the task in "Weight Loss" is presented, the students are forewarned that there are differing arguments and the results will assure a good discussion. (The argument for Moe is that he is the most steady in his loss.)

Equivalent-Ratio Selections

In selection activities, a ratio is presented, and students select an equivalent ratio from others presented. The focus should be on an intuitive rationale for why the pairs selected are in the same ratio. Sometimes numeric values will play a part to help students develop numeric methods to explain their reasoning. In later activities, students will be asked to construct an equivalent ratio without choices being provided.

It is extremely useful in these activities to include pairs of ratios that are not proportional but have a com-

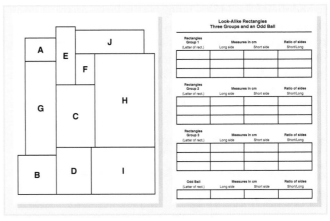

FIGURE 19.3 These two Blackline Masters for Activity 19.3 are available on the Companion Web site at www.ablongman.com/vandewalle6e.

mon difference. For example, $\frac{5}{8}$ and $\frac{9}{12}$ are not equivalent ratios, but the corresponding differences are the same: $8 - 5 = 12 - 9$. Students who focus on this additive relationship are not seeing the multiplicative relationship of proportionality.

activity **19.3**

Look-Alike Rectangles

Provide groups of students with a copy of the Blackline Master shown in Figure 19.3 and have them cut out the ten rectangles. Three of the rectangles (A, I, and D) have sides in the ratio of 3 to 4. Rectangles C, F, and H have sides in the ratio of 5 to 8. J, E, and G have sides in the ratio of 1 to 3. Rectangle B is a square, so its sides are in the ratio of 1 to 1.

The task is to group the rectangles into three sets of three that "look alike" with one "oddball." If your students know the word *similar* from geometry, you can use that instead of "look alike." To explain what "look alike" means, draw three rectangles on the board with two that are similar and one that is clearly dissimilar to the other two, as in the following example. Have students use their language to explain why rectangles 1 and 3 are alike.

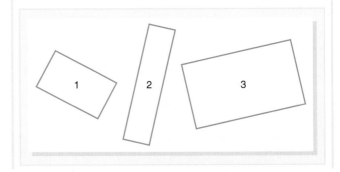

When students have decided on their groupings, stop and discuss the reasons they classified the rectangles as they did. Be prepared for some students to try to match sides or look for rectangles that have the same amount of difference between them. Do not evaluate any rationale offered. Next have them measure and record the sides of each rectangle to the nearest half-centimeter and calculate the ratios of the short to long sides for each. The Blackline Master can be used to record the data. Discuss these results and ask students to offer explanations. If the groups are formed of proportional (similar) rectangles, the ratios within each group will all be the same.

From a geometric standpoint, "Look-Alike Rectangles" is an activity about similarity. The two concepts—proportionality and similarity—are closely connected. However, if the activity were done with figures other than rectangles, the congruent angles of similar figures would defeat the purpose.

Another characteristic of proportional rectangles can be observed by stacking like rectangles aligned at one corner, as in Figure 19.4. Place a straightedge across the diagonals, and you will see that opposite corners also line up. If the rectangles are placed on a coordinate axis with the common corner at the origin, the slope of the line joining the corners is the ratio of the sides. Here is a connection between proportional reasoning and algebra.

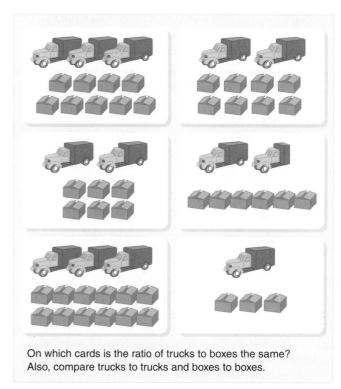

On which cards is the ratio of trucks to boxes the same? Also, compare trucks to trucks and boxes to boxes.

FIGURE 19.5 Rate cards: Match cards with the same rate of boxes per truck.

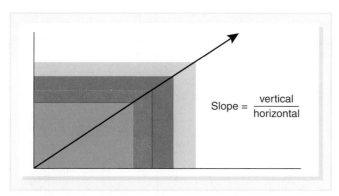

Slope = $\dfrac{\text{vertical}}{\text{horizontal}}$

FIGURE 19.4 The slope of a line through a stack of proportional rectangles is equal to the ratio of the two sides.

troduces the notion of ratios as rates. A unit rate is depicted on a card that shows exactly one of either of the two types of objects. For example, the card with three boxes and one truck provides one unit rate. A unit rate for the other ratio is not shown. What would it be?

Comparing Ratios

An understanding of proportional situations includes being able to compare two ratios as well as to identify equivalent ratios. The following activity has been used in various studies of proportional reasoning.

EXPANDED LESSON

An expanded lesson plan based on Activity 19.5, "Lemonade," can be found on the Companion Web site at www. ablongman.com/ vandewalle6e.

activity **19.4**

Different Objects, Same Ratios

Prepare cards with distinctly different objects, as shown in Figure 19.5. Given one card, students are to select a card on which the ratio of the two types of objects is the same. This task moves students to a numeric approach rather than a visual one and in-

activity **19.5**

Lemonade

Show students a picture of two lemonade pitchers as in Figure 19.6. The pitchers each have the same amount of lemonade. The little squares indicate the recipes used in each pitcher. A yellow square is a cup of lemonade concentrate and the blue square is

a cup of water. The task is to decide which pitcher will have the stronger lemonade flavor or if they will both taste the same. Explanations are required.

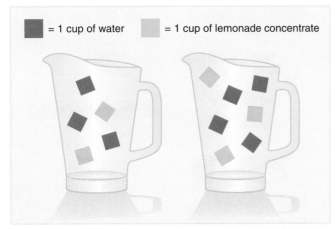

FIGURE 19.6 Assume that each pitcher is filled with the same amount of lemonade. The little squares indicate the recipe used in each pitcher. Which pitcher will have the stronger lemon flavor, or will they be the same?

 *pause and reflect* _____

Solve the problem in "Lemonade" and jot down your reasoning. Can you think of more than one argument to support your conclusion?

The task in "Lemonade" is challenging for many students. The interesting thing about the task, however, is how many different ways there are to make the comparison. A common method is to figure out how much water goes with each cup of lemonade mix. As we will see later, this is using a unit rate: cups of water per cup of lemonade mix ($1\frac{1}{2}$ vs. $1\frac{1}{3}$). Other approaches use fractions instead of unit rates and attempt to compare the fractions: lemonade mix compared to water ($\frac{2}{3}$ vs. $\frac{3}{4}$) or the reverse, and also lemonade mix as a fraction of the total ($\frac{2}{5}$ vs. $\frac{3}{7}$). This can also be done with water as a fraction of the total. Some students may also use percentages instead of fractions creating the same arguments. Another argument involves considering duplicates of one or both of the pitchers until either the water or the lemonade mix is equal in both. (Make sure that you can both create and justify each of these various solutions.)

One of the most interesting arguments is that the pitchers will taste the same: If the lemonade mix and water are matched up in each pitcher, then there will be one cup of water left in each recipe. Although incorrect (can you tell why?), your class will likely have a spirited discussion of these ideas.

The lemonade task can be adjusted for difficulty. As given, the two mixtures are reasonably close and there are

no simple relationships between the two pitchers. If the solutions are 3 to 6 and 4 to 8 (equal flavors), the task is much simpler. For a 2-to-5 recipe versus a 4-to-9 recipe, it is easy to double the first and compare it to the second. When a 3-to-6 recipe is compared to a 2-to-5 recipe, the unit rates are perhaps more likely (1 to 2 vs. 1 to $2\frac{1}{2}$).

The following problem also is adapted from the research literature.

Two camps of Scouts are having pizza parties. The Bear Camp ordered enough so that every 3 campers will have 2 pizzas. The leader of the Raccoons ordered enough so that there would be 3 pizzas for every 5 campers. Did the Bear campers or the Raccoon campers have more pizza to eat?

Figure 19.7 shows two different possibilities for informal methods.

When the pizzas are sliced up into fractional parts (Figure 19.7(a)), the approach is to look for a unit rate—pizzas per camper. A sharing approach has been used for each ratio just as described for fractions in Chapter 16. But notice that this problem does not say that the camps have only 3 and 5 campers, respectively. Any multiples of 2 to 3 and 3 to 5 can be used to make the appropriate comparison, the same as making multiple pitchers of lemonade. This is the approach used in Figure 19.7(b). Three "clones" of the 2-to-3 ratio and two clones of the 3-to-5 ratio are made so that the number of campers getting a like number of pizzas can be compared. From a vantage of fractions, this is like getting common numerators. Because there are more campers in the Raccoon ratio (larger denominator), there is less pizza for each camper.

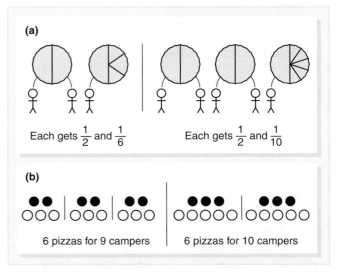

FIGURE 19.7 Two informal methods for comparing two ratios.

Here is a list of similar problems in which students can compare two ratios. As with the lemonade task and the pizza problem, there are usually numerous ways to solve these. Let students use any method they wish and always require an explanation. You will find that context as well as the numbers involved will influence the solution strategies. In fact, students with good proportional reasoning tend to alter their thinking strategies from one situation to another. The value of using a variety of problems is to generate this flexibility.

1. Terry can run 4 laps in 12 minutes. Susan can run 2 laps in 5 minutes. Who is the faster runner, or do they run the same?

2. Jack and Jill were picking strawberries at the Pick Your Own Berry Patch. Jack "sampled" 5 berries every 25 minutes. Jill ate 3 berries every 10 minutes. If they both continue to pick at about the same speed, who will bring home more berries, or will they each pick the same?

3. Some of the hens in Farmer Brown's chicken farm lay brown eggs and the others lay white eggs. Farmer Brown noticed that in the large hen house he collected about four brown eggs for every ten white ones. In the smaller hen house the ratio of brown to white was 1 to 3. In which hen house do the hens lay more brown eggs, or are the two the same?

4. Mike drove his car 120 miles in 2 hours and Carl drove 180 miles in 3 hours. Who drove faster, or did they drive the same speed?

5. Two parking garages, A and B, have 30 and 40 total spaces respectively. If lot A has 18 cars parked and lot B has 28 cars, which lot is more filled?

6. Talks-A-Lot phone company charges 70¢ for every 15 minutes. Reaching Out phone company charges $1.00 for 20 minutes. Which company is offering the cheaper rate, or are the two rates alike?

7. Which rectangle is more like a square?: a 3×5 rectangle or an 8×14 rectangle?

Notice that all questions except 5 and 7 allow for the possibility that the two ratios are alike. Tasks 5 and 7 essentially are asking which ratio is closer to 1. In the parking garage task, the difference for each lot (additive relationship) is the same (12), a feature not found in the other problems. The numbers in tasks such as these can always be adjusted to make them easier or harder. Problems like these are easy to make up, and other examples can most likely be found in your textbook.

 How your students solve problems such as those in the preceding list is a good clue to your students' emerging proportional reasoning. Be careful to watch for students who always use the same approach—perhaps always finding a unit rate—since

they may have latched onto a procedure that works without really understanding it. Challenge these students to explain a different procedure used by another classmate or to find a second method of solving the problem. ■

Scaling with Ratio Tables

Ratio tables or charts that show how two variable quantities are related are often good ways to organize information. Consider the following table:

Acres	5	10	15	20	25	
Pine trees	75	150	225			

If the task is to find the number of trees for 65 acres of land or the number of acres needed for 750 trees, students can easily proceed by using addition. That is, they can add 5s along the top row and 75s along the bottom row until the problems are solved. Although this is efficient and orderly, it is an additive procedure and does little as a task to promote proportional reasoning. As illustrated in the next activity, the instructional "trick" is to select numbers that require some form of multiplicative thinking.

activity **19.6**

Using Ratio Tables

Given a situation like one of the following, the task is to build a ratio table and use it to answer the question. Tasks are adapted from Lamon (1999, p. 183).

a. **A person who weighs 160 pounds on Earth will weigh 416 pounds on the planet Jupiter. How much will a person weigh on Jupiter who weighs 120 pounds on earth?**

b. **At the local college, five out of every eight seniors live in apartments. How many of the 30 senior math majors are likely to live in an apartment?**

c. **The tax on a purchase of $20 is $1.12. How much tax will there be on a purchase of $45.50?**

d. **When in Australia you can exchange $4.50 in U.S. dollars for $6 Australian. How much is $17.50 Australian in U.S. dollars?**

The tasks in this activity are typical "solve the proportion" tasks. One ratio and part of a second are given with the task being to find the fourth number. However, tasks such as these should come long before any formal approach is suggested. Further note that in no case is it easy to simply add or subtract to get to the desired entry. Rather, the student should use a ratio table to solve the

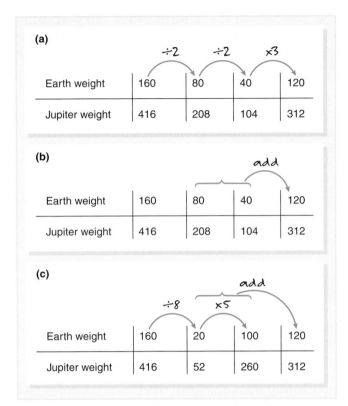

FIGURE 19.8 160 pounds on Earth is 416 pounds on Jupiter. If something weighs 120 pounds on Earth, how many pounds would it weigh on Jupiter? Three solutions using ratio tables.

problem. Figure 19.8 shows three different ways to solve the Jupiter weight task using ratio tables.

The format of these ratio tables is not at all important. Some students may not use a table format at all and simply draw arrows and explain in words how they got from one ratio to another. You may find value in a more structured format. The following problem and the table in Figure 19.9 are taken from Lamon (1999, p. 233). Notice that the numbers are not "nice" at all.

Cheese is $4.25 per pound. How much will 12.13 pounds cost?

The format in Figure 19.9 allows for easier tracing of what was done at each step. The format is just that—a format. It is not the same as an algorithm. For any problem there are likely to be several different reasonable ratio tables. In applying this technique, students are using multiplicative relationships to transform a given ratio into an equivalent ratio. As Lamon points out, the process is not at all random. Students should mentally devise a plan for getting from one number to another. Consider the following problem:

How many pounds of grass seed can be purchased for $18 if you can buy 28 pounds for $35?

	Pounds	Cost	Notes
A	1	4.25	Given
B	10	42.50	A × 10
C	2	8.50	A × 2
D	0.1	0.425	A ÷ 10
E	12.1	51.425	B + C + D
F	0.01	0.0425	D ÷ 10
G	0.03	0.1275	F × 3
H	12.13	51.5525	E + G

FIGURE 19.9 A more structured ratio table. The Notes column shows what was done in each step. The task is to find the cost of 12.13 pounds.

 pause and reflect _____

Before reading further, write down a plan for moving from 35 to 18. Then create a ratio table using your plan to solve the problem. Compare your strategy with someone else's, or try to find another one yourself.

One possible plan for getting from 35 to 18 is as follows: $35 \div 5$ is 7; 7×2 is 14. (Now you need 4 more.) Go back to 7: $7 \div 7$ is 1; 1×4 is 4. Now add 4 and 14 to make 18. When these same steps are applied to 28, the foregoing problem is solved.

The tasks suggested in Activity 19.6 have quite reasonable numbers. However, as you can see from the cheese example, it is quite possible to use this technique with almost any numbers. By using easy multiples and divisors, often the arithmetic can be done mentally.

Assessment Notes It should be clear to students why the same factor must be used on both entries in a ratio table. For example, in row A of Figure 19.9, both the 1 and 4.25 are multiplied by 10. In row G, both parts are multiplied by 3. Each pair of entries comprises a ratio. An equivalent ratio is found by multiplying both parts by the same number. ■

Any ratio table provides data that can be graphed. Make each axis correspond to one of the quantities in the table. This idea is developed in the next activity.

activity **19.7**

Graphs Showing Ratios
Have students make a graph of the data from a collection of equal ratios that they have scaled or discussed. The graph in Figure 19.10 is of the ratios of

two sides of similar rectangles. If only a few ratios have actually been computed, the graph can be drawn carefully and then used to determine other equivalent ratios. This is especially interesting when there is a physical model to coincide with the ratio. In the rectangle example, students can draw rectangles with sides determined by the graphs and compare them to the original rectangles. A unit ratio can be found by locating the point on the line that is directly above or to the right of the number 1 on the graph. (There are actually two unit ratios for every ratio. Why?) Students can then use the unit ratio to scale up to other values and check to see that they are on the graph as well. Note that the slope of any line through the origin is a ratio.

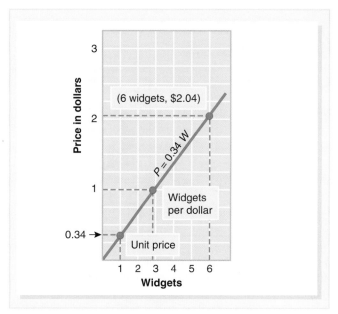

FIGURE 19.11 Graph of price-to-item ratios.

Construction and Measurement Activities

In these activities, students make measurements or construct physical or visual models of equivalent ratios in order to provide a tangible example of a proportion as well as look at numeric relationships.

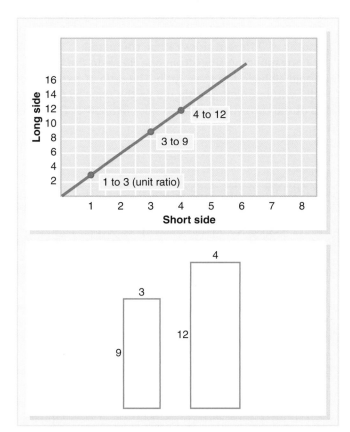

FIGURE 19.10 Graphs show ratios of sides in similar rectangles.

Graphs provide another way of thinking about proportions, and they connect proportional thought to algebraic interpretations. All graphs of equivalent ratios fall along straight lines that pass through the origin. If the equation of one of these lines is written in the form $y = mx$, the slope m is always one of the equivalent ratios. Note that the slope of any line through the origin is the ratio of the y-coordinate at any point with the x-coordinate of the same point. Figure 19.11 shows the graph of the prices of widgets.

activity **19.8**

Different Units, Equal Ratios
Cut strips of adding machine tape all the same length, and give one strip to each group in your class. Each group is to measure the strip using a different unit. Possible units include different Cuisenaire rods, a piece of chalk, a pencil, the edge of a book or index card, or standard units such as inches or centimeters. When every group has measured the strip, ask for the measure of one of the groups, and display the unit of measure. Next, hold up the unit of measure used by another group, and have the class compare it with the first unit. See if the class can estimate the measurement that the second group found. The ratio of the measuring units should be the inverse of the measurements made with those units. For example, if two units are in a ratio of 2 to 3, the respective measures will be in a ratio of 3 to 2. Examine measurements made with other units. Finally, present a unit that no group has used, and see if the class can predict the measurement when made with that unit.

Activity 19.8 can be profitably extended by providing each group with an identical set of four strips of quite different

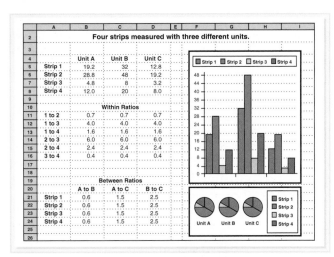

FIGURE 19.12 A spreadsheet can be used to record data, create tables of interesting ratios, and produce bar and circle graphs.

Source: Screen reprinted with permission from Apple Computer, Inc.

lengths. Good lengths might be 20, 50, 80, and 120 cm. As before, each group measures the strips using a different unit.

This time, have each group enter data into a common spreadsheet. (Alternatively, share group data so that all groups can enter data on their own spreadsheets.) Figure 19.12 shows what a spreadsheet might look like for three groups. A template can be prepared ahead of time, or students can create their own spreadsheets. Almost all spreadsheets will offer a variety of graphing options. In this activity, bar graphs show the actual measurements for each group and circle graphs show each measure in ratio to the sum of the measures (i.e., a percentage of total measures.)

Once the graphs are completed, there are numerous opportunities to observe and explore proportions. The bar graphs, though different in size, all look "alike." Since the circle graphs illustrate the ratios rather than the actual measurements, they will be identical or nearly so. Within ratios (for a set of strips) and between ratios (one unit to another) are easily calculated with the spreadsheet. (Within and between ratios are discussed later in the chapter.)

Continue the exploration by introducing a new strip. If you know its measure with any one of the units, what will its measure be with the other units? Similarly, if a new unit of measure is introduced, how can the measures of the strips be determined? Can this be done by comparing the new unit with an old one? If a known strip is measured with the new unit, can all other measures and ratios be determined?

Bar graphs and circle plots are also easily made with a TI-73 graphing calculator. If technology is not available, this same activity can be done by hand. To make circle graphs, use the hundredths disk in the Blackline Masters.

The connection between proportional reasoning and the geometric concept of similarity is very important. Similar figures provide a visual representation of proportions, and proportional thinking enhances the understanding of similarity. Whenever similarity is discussed, ratios in the figures should almost certainly be explored. The next two activities are aimed at this connection.

activity **19.9**

Scale Drawings

On grid or dot paper (see the Blackline Masters), have students draw a simple shape using straight lines with vertices on the dots. After one shape is complete, have them draw a larger or smaller shape that is the same as or similar to the first. This can be done on a grid of the same size or a different size, as shown in Figure 19.13. After completing two or three pictures of different sizes, the ratios of the lengths of different sides can be compared.

Corresponding sides from one figure to the next should all be in the same ratio. The ratio of two sides within one figure should be the same as the ratio of the corresponding two sides in another figure.

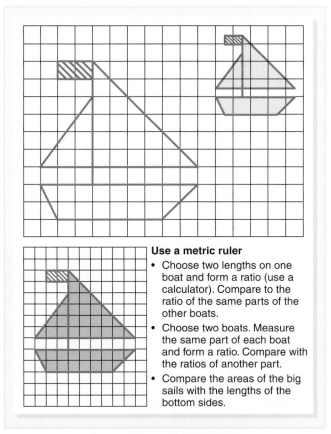

Use a metric ruler
- Choose two lengths on one boat and form a ratio (use a calculator). Compare to the ratio of the same parts of the other boats.
- Choose two boats. Measure the same part of each boat and form a ratio. Compare with the ratios of another part.
- Compare the areas of the big sails with the lengths of the bottom sides.

FIGURE 19.13 Comparing similar figures drawn on grids.

activity 19.10

Length, Surface, and Volume Ratios

A three-dimensional version of Activity 19.9 can be done with blocks, as shown in Figure 19.14. Using 1-inch or 2-cm wooden cubes, make a simple "building." Then make a similar but larger building and compare measures. A different size can also be made using different-sized blocks. To measure buildings made with different blocks, use a common unit such as centimeters.

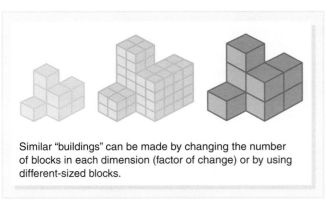

Similar "buildings" can be made by changing the number of blocks in each dimension (factor of change) or by using different-sized blocks.

FIGURE 19.14 Similar constructions.

Activities 19.9 and 19.10 involve area and volume as well as length. Comparisons of corresponding lengths, areas, and volumes in proportional figures lead to some interesting ratios. If two figures are proportional (similar), any two linear dimensions you measure will be in the same ratio on each, say, 1 to k. Corresponding areas and surface areas, however, will be in the ratio of 1 to k^2, and corresponding volumes in the ratio of 1 to k^3. If the edge of a block building is tripled ($k = 3$), the surface area will increase by a factor of 9 ($k^2 = 9$) and the volume by a factor of 27 ($k^3 = 27$). The new building will require 27 times as many blocks to construct.

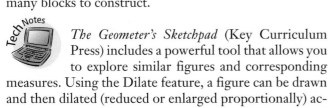 *The Geometer's Sketchpad* (Key Curriculum Press) includes a powerful tool that allows you to explore similar figures and corresponding measures. Using the Dilate feature, a figure can be drawn and then dilated (reduced or enlarged proportionally) according to any scale factor of your choosing. The ratios of beginning and ending measures (lengths and areas) can then be compared to the scale factor. All of the computations can be done within the software program. ■

As a means of contrasting proportional situations with additive ones, try starting with a figure on a grid or a building made with blocks and adding two units to every dimension in the figure. The result will be larger but will not look at all the same. Try this with a simple rectangle that is 1 cm by 15 cm. The new rectangle is twice as "thick" (2 cm) but only a bit longer. It will not appear to be the same shape as the original.

Dynamic geometry software such as *The Geometer's Sketchpad* (Key Curriculum Press) offers a very effective method of exploring the idea of ratio. In Figure 19.15, two lengths are drawn on a grid using the "snap-to-grid" option. The lengths are measured, and two ratios are computed. As the length of either line is changed, the measures and ratios are updated instantly. A screen similar to this could be used to discuss ratios of lengths as well as inverse ratios with your full class. In this example, notice that the second pair of lines has the same difference but that the ratios are not the same. A similar drawing could be prepared for the overhead on a transparency of a centimeter dot grid if software was not available. ■

The *Connected Mathematics* program places the main emphasis on proportional reasoning in the seventh grade. In the eighth grade, the proportional concepts are applied

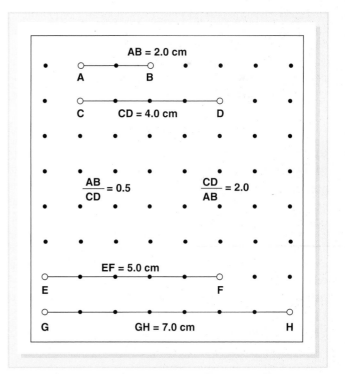

FIGURE 19.15 Dynamic geometry software or just a centimeter grid can be used to discuss ratios of two lengths.

Source: From *The Geometer's Sketchpad.* Key Curriculum Press. Used by permission.

Connected *Mathematics*

MIDDLE GRADES

Grade 7, Comparing and Scaling
Investigation 3: Comparing and Using Ratios

Context

This investigation occurs in the second week of the unit on ratio and proportions. In earlier activities, students explored ratios and percents to compare survey data from large populations with similar data gathered from their own class. Students used fractions, decimals, and percents to express ratios, and they compared ratios using their own strategies.

Task Description

The problem shown here is introduced in the context of students deciding on the best mix of juice for a camping trip.

Within the same investigation are two similar problems that are paraphrased here:

1a. A can of tomatoes will make sauce for 5 to 6 campers. How many cans should be purchased to make spaghetti for 240 campers? Five cans cost $4. How much will the cans of tomatoes cost?

2a. If pizzas are shared evenly, will a camper get more pizza sharing 4 pizzas with 10 campers or 3 pizzas with 8 campers?

2b. The ratio of 10-seat tables to 8-seat tables is 8 to 5. If there are just enough tables for all 240 campers, how many of each type are there?

Problem 3.1

Arvind and Mariah tested four juice mixes.

Mix A
2 cups concentrate
3 cups cold water

Mix B
1 cup concentrate
4 cups cold water

Mix C
4 cups concentrate
8 cups cold water

Mix D
3 cups concentrate
5 cups cold water

A. Which recipe will make juice that is the most "orangey"? Explain your answer.

B. Which recipe will make juice that is the least "orangey"? Explain your answer.

C. Assume that each camper will get $\frac{1}{2}$ cup of juice. For each recipe, how much concentrate and how much water are needed to make juice for 240 campers? Explain your anwer.

From *Connected Mathematics: Comparing and Scaling: Ratio, Proportion, and Percent.* © 2002 by Michigan State University, Glenda Lappan, James T. Fey, William M. Fitzgerald, Susan N. Friel, & Elizabeth Difanis Phillips. Published by Pearson Education, Inc., publishing as Pearson Prentice Hall. Used by permission.

The full unit contains six investigations, each with numerous real contexts. Scaling, the use of unit rates, and percentages are suggested techniques. However, no particular method is forced on the students.

---

throughout the curriculum. The sample activity is similar to the comparing ratio ideas you have read about earlier.

NCTM Standards "Attention to developing flexibility in working with rational numbers contributes to students' understanding of, and facility with, proportionality. Facility with proportionality involves much more than setting two ratios equal and solving for a missing term. It involves recognizing quantities that are related proportionally and using numbers, tables, graphs, and equations to think about the quantities and their relationship" (p. 217).

Solving Proportions

The activities to this point have been designed to lead students to an intuitive concept of ratio and proportion to help in the development of proportional reasoning.

One practical value of proportional reasoning is to use observed proportions to find unknown values. Knowledge of one ratio can often be used to find a value in the other. Comparison pricing, using scales on maps, and solving percentage problems are just a few everyday instances where solving proportions is required. Students need to learn to set up proportions symbolically and to solve them.

Within and Between Ratios

When examining two ratios, it is sometimes useful to think of them as being either *within* ratios or *between* ratios. A ratio of two measures in the same setting is a *within* ratio. For example, in the case of similar rectangles, the ratio of length to width for any one rectangle is a within ratio, that is, it is "within" the context of that rectangle. For all similar rectangles, corresponding within ratios will be equal.

A *between* ratio is a ratio of two corresponding measures in different situations. In the case of similar rectangles, the ratio of the length of one rectangle to the length of another is a between ratio; that is, it is "between" the two rectangles. For two similar rectangles, all of the between ratios will be equal. However, the between ratios for each pair of similar rectangles will be different.

⏸ *pause and reflect* _____

Consider three rectangles *A*, *B*, and *C*. *A* measures 2 × 6, *B* measures 3 × 9, and *C* measures 8 × 24. Find the within ratio for each rectangle. This should convince you that the rectangles are similar. Now examine the between ratios for *A* and *B* and for *A* and *C*. Why are these ratios different?

Figure 19.5 (p. 359) shows six pictures of trucks and boxes. The within ratios are trucks to boxes (within one picture). The between ratios are from trucks to trucks and boxes to boxes. Be sure that you can distinguish within and between ratios in that figure.

The simple drawing in Figure 19.16 is a nice generic way of looking at two ratios and determining if a ratio is between or within. A drawing similar to this will be very helpful to students in setting up proportions. Pick any two equivalent truck and box pictures and place the numbers in this figure.

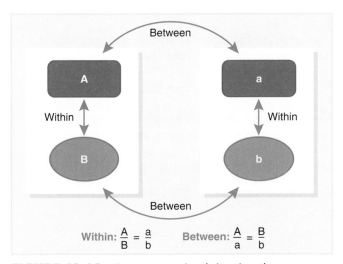

FIGURE 19.16 Given a proportional situation, the two between ratios and the two within ratios will be the same.

An Informal Approach

Traditional textbooks show students how to set up an equation of two ratios involving an unknown, "cross-multiply," and solve for the unknown. This can be a very mechanical approach and will almost certainly lead to confusion and error. Although you may wish eventually to cover the cross-product algorithm, it is well worth the time for students to find ways to solve proportions using their own ideas first. If you have been exploring pro-

portions informally, students will have a good foundation on which to build their own approaches.

To illustrate some intuitive approaches for solving proportions, consider the following tasks:

Tammy bought 3 widgets for $2.40. At the same price, how much would 10 widgets cost?

Tammy bought 4 widgets for $3.75. How much would a dozen widgets cost?

⏸ *pause and reflect* _____

Before reading further, solve these two problems using an approach for each that seems most reasonable to you.

In the first situation, it is perhaps easiest to determine the cost of one widget—the unit rate or unit price. This can be found by dividing the price of three widgets by 3. Multiplying this unit rate of $0.80 per widget by 10 will produce the answer. This approach is referred to as a *unit-rate* method of solving proportions. Notice that the unit rate is a within ratio.

In the second problem, a unit-rate approach could be used, but the division does not appear to be easy. Since 12 is a multiple of 4, it is easier to notice that the cost of a dozen is 3 times the cost of 4. This is called a *factor-of-change* method. It could have been used on the first problem but would have been awkward. The factor of change between 3 and 10 is $3\frac{1}{3}$. Multiplying $2.40 by $3\frac{1}{3}$ will produce the correct answer. (When you multiply entries in a ratio table, you are using a factor of change.) Although the factor-of-change method is a useful way to think about proportions, it is most frequently used when the numbers are compatible. Students should be given problems in which the numbers lend themselves to both approaches so that they will explore both methods. The factor of change is a between ratio.

For each of the following two problems, place the numbers in a little drawing of two ratios in Figure 19.16. Solve each problem. Think about within or between ratios matching up. Do not use cross-multiplication.

At the Office Super Store, you can buy plain #2 pencils, 4 for 59 cents. The store also sells the same pencils in a large box of 5 dozen pencils for $7.79. How much do you save by buying the large box?

The price of a box of 2 dozen candy bars is $4.80. Bridget wants to buy 5 candy bars. What will she have to pay?

To solve the pencil problem, you might notice that the between ratio of pencils to pencils is 4 to 60, or 1 to 15. If you multiply the 59 cents by 15, the factor of change, you will get the price of the box of 60 if the pencils were sold at the same price. In the candy problem, the within ratio of 24 to $4.80 is easy to use to get the unit rate of 20 cents per candy bar. But what do you do if the numbers don't "come out nicely" like they do in these problems?

Try solving the same problems with new numbers that do not work out so easily. If you are having difficulty with the new problems, discuss them with a friend.

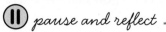 *pause and reflect* —————————

Try the following problem. Make a little sketch as before, and use a technique you have figured out yourself. (Do this now before reading on.)

Brian can run 5 km in 18.4 minutes. If he keeps on running at the same speed, how far can he run in 23 minutes?

The first situation for your sketch is Brian's 5-km run (5 km and 18.4 minutes). The second situation is the unknown distance and 23 minutes. There are at least two things you might consider, and one is no easier than the other. You could look at the between ratios of minutes to minutes in order to find a factor of change. That is, what do you multiply 18.4 by to get 23? On the calculator, compute 23 ÷ 18.4 to get 1.25, the factor of change. Now 5 km × 1.25 is 6.25 km.

The second possibility is to get a unit rate for the 5 km and multiply by 23. That would mean divide both the 5 and the 18.4 by 18.4 (like simplifying a fraction to a denominator of 1). The calculator yields 0.2717391, or about 0.27 km per minute. Multiply this unit rate by 23 minutes and you get 6.2499993 km. In both cases, the longer distance is 6.25 km.

Before asking students to solve problems such as Brian's run, it is extremely important that they have worked with the slightly easier problems first, where either the factor of change or the unit rate are easily computed. Notice that both of the explanations you have just read rely on these ideas. Students should be permitted to wrestle with the more difficult problems and come up with their own methods of solution. If students struggle, refer them to one of the easier problems and suggest that they use an idea that they have tried before. The sketch of the two ratios helps keep things straight and avoids ambiguous cross-multiplying.

The Cross-Product Algorithm

"The central challenge of developing students' capacity to think with ratios (to reason proportionally) is to teach ideas and restrain the quick path to computation" (Smith, 2002, p. 15).

The methods just described come close to being well-defined algorithms, though they are a bit more flexible than cross-product methods. The reality is that the computations involved are exactly the same as in cross-multiplication. Sixth- and seventh-grade students rarely use cross-multiplication to solve proportion problems, even when that method has been taught (Smith, 2002). A possible reason is that, although the method is relatively efficient, it does not appear on the surface to look like the earlier conceptual approaches. Yet some teachers may still want to teach cross-multiplication.

Draw a Simple Model

Given a ratio word problem, the greatest difficulty students have is setting up a correct proportion or equation of two ratios, one of which includes the missing value. "Which fractions do I make? Where does the *x* go?"

Rather than drill and drill in the hope that they will somehow eventually get it, show students how to sketch a simple picture that will help them determine what parts are related. In Figure 19.17, a simple model is drawn for a typical rate or price problem. The two equations in the figure come from setting up within and between ratios.

Solve the Proportion

Examine the left (within) ratios in the same way as for Brian's 5-km race: Find out what to multiply the left fraction by to get the right. To do this, we would divide 5 by 3 and then multiply that result by 89:

$$\frac{5}{3} \times 89$$

Looking at the same left equation in Figure 19.17, we could also determine the unit price or the price for 1 pound by dividing the 89 cents by 3 and then multiplying this result by 5 to determine the price of 5 pounds:

$$\frac{89}{3} \times 5$$

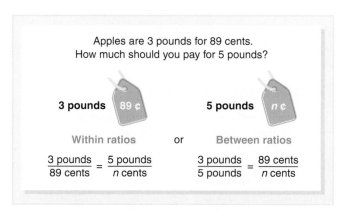

Apples are 3 pounds for 89 cents. How much should you pay for 5 pounds?

3 pounds [89 ¢]   5 pounds [n ¢]

Within ratios   or   Between ratios

$$\frac{3 \text{ pounds}}{89 \text{ cents}} = \frac{5 \text{ pounds}}{n \text{ cents}} \qquad \frac{3 \text{ pounds}}{5 \text{ pounds}} = \frac{89 \text{ cents}}{n \text{ cents}}$$

FIGURE 19.17 A simple drawing helps to establish correct proportion equations.

Now look what happens if we cross-multiply in the original equation:

$$3n = 5 \times 89$$

$$n = \frac{5 \times 89}{3}$$

This equation can be solved by dividing the 5 by 3 and multiplying by 89 or dividing 89 by 3 and multiplying by 5. These are exactly the two devices we employed in our more intuitive approach. If you cross-multiply the between ratios, you get exactly the same result. Furthermore, you get the same result if you had written the two ratios inverted, that is, with the reciprocals of each fraction. Try it!

So if you want to develop a cross-product algorithm, it is not unreasonable to do problems like these while encouraging students to use their own methods. If you write out the computations involved, a very small amount of direct teaching can develop the cross-product approach. But why hurry?

In Figure 19.18, a problem involving rates of speed is modeled with simple lines representing the two distances. The distance and the time for each run are modeled with the same line. You cannot see time, but it fits into the distance covered. All equal-rates-of-speed problems can be modeled this way. There really is no significant difference from the drawing used for the apples. Again, it is just as acceptable to write between ratios as within ratios, and students need not worry about which one goes on top as long as the ratios are written in the same order. The model helps with this difficulty.

Activities That Require Proportions

In the preceding discussion, simple rate problems were used to help students develop a technique for solving proportions. The next two activities illustrate other common uses of proportional reasoning.

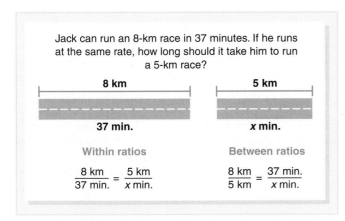

FIGURE 19.18 Line segments can be used to model both time and distance.

Scale Drawings

Provide students with a drawing of a simple geometric figure, including its dimensions. The task is to create a new drawing that is either larger or smaller than the given one. One dimension of the new drawing is specified (see Figure 19.19 for an example). Students can set up between or within ratios and determine the other dimensions by solving the proportion.

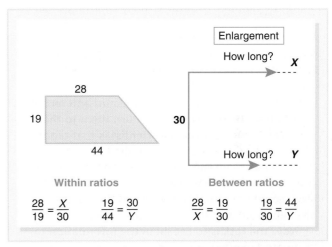

FIGURE 19.19 Pictures help in establishing equal ratios.

This scale drawing activity is somewhat simplistic, but it provides students with the essential ideas for setting up proportions. Here are some more interesting situations to consider:

- If you wanted to make a scale model of the solar system and use a Ping-Pong ball for the earth, how far away should the sun be? How large a ball would you need?
- What scale should be used to draw a scale map of your city (or some interesting region) so that it will nicely fit onto a standard piece of poster board?
- Use the scale on a map to estimate the distance and travel time between two points of interest.
- Roll a toy car down a ramp, timing the trip with a stopwatch. How fast was the car traveling in miles per hour? If the speed is proportional to the size of the car, how fast would this have been for a real car?
- Your little sister wants a table and chair for her doll. Her doll is 14 inches tall. How big should you make the table?
- Determine the various distances that a ten-speed bike travels in one turn of the pedals. You will need to count the sprocket teeth on the front and back gears.

Have you ever wondered how scientists estimate wildlife counts such as the number of bass in a lake or the number of monarch butterflies that migrate each year to Mexico? One method often used is a capture-recapture technique modeled in the next activity.

activity 19.12

Capture-Recapture

Prepare a shoebox full of some uniform small object such as centicubes or plastic chips. You could also use a larger box filled with Styrofoam packing "peanuts." If the box is your lake and the objects are the fish you want to count, how can you estimate the number without actually counting them? Remember, if they were fish, you couldn't even see them! Have a student reach into the box and "capture" a representative sample of the "fish." For a large box, you may want to capture more than a handful. "Tag" each fish by marking it in some way—marking pen or sticky dot. Count and record the number tagged and then return them to the box. The assumption of the scientist is that tagged animals will mix uniformly with the larger population, so mix them thoroughly. Next, have five to ten students make a recapture of fish from the box. Each counts the total captured and the number in the capture that are tagged. Accumulate these data.

    Now the task is to use all of the information to estimate the number of fish in the lake. The recapture data provide an estimated ratio of tagged to untagged fish. The number tagged to the total population should be in the same ratio. After solving the proportion, have students count the actual items in the box to see how close their estimate is.

For a more detailed description of the "Capture-Recapture" activity, see the NCTM Addenda Series book *Understanding Rational Numbers and Proportions* (Curcio & Bezuk, 1994).

Percent Problems as Proportions

Percent has traditionally been included as a topic with ratio and proportion because percent is one form of ratio, a part-to-whole ratio. In Chapter 18, it was shown that percent problems can be connected to fraction concepts. Here the same part-to-whole fraction concept of percent will be extended to ratio and proportion concepts. Ideally, all of these ideas (fractions, decimals, ratio, proportion, and percent) should be conceptually integrated. The better that students connect these ideas, the more flexible and useful their reasoning and problem-solving skills will be.

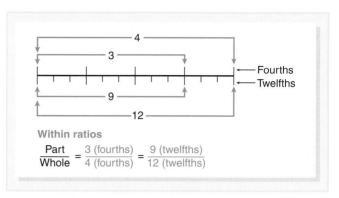

FIGURE 19.20 Equivalent fractions as proportions.

Equivalent Fractions as Proportions

First consider how equivalent fractions can be interpreted as a proportion using the same simple models already used. In Figure 19.20, a line segment is partitioned in two different ways: in fourths on one side and in twelfths on the other. In the previous examples, proportions were established based on two amounts of apples, two different distances or runs, and two different sizes of drawings. Here only one thing is measured—the part of a whole—but it is measured or partitioned two ways: in fourths and in twelfths.

    The within ratios are ratios of part to whole within each measurement. Within ratios result in the usual equivalent fraction equation, $\frac{3}{4} = \frac{9}{12}$ (3 fourths are to 4 fourths as 9 twelfths are to 12 twelfths). The between proportion equates a part-to-part ratio with a whole-to-whole ratio, or $\frac{3}{9} = \frac{4}{12}$ (3 fourths are to 9 twelfths as 4 fourths are to 12 twelfths).

    A simple line segment drawing similar to the one in Figure 19.20 could be drawn to set up a proportion to solve any equivalent-fraction problem, even ones that do not result in whole-number numerators or denominators. An example is shown in Figure 19.21.

Percent Problems

All percent problems are exactly the same as the equivalent-fraction examples. They involve a part and a whole measured in some unit and the same part and whole measured in hundredths—that is, in percents. A simple line segment drawing can be used for each of the three types of percent problems. Let the measures on one side of the line correspond to the numbers or measures in the problem. On the opposite side of the line, indicate the corresponding values in terms of percents. It is useful to label the segments of the line rather than endpoints as in a number line. Using this model as a guide, a proportion can be written and solved by the cross-product algorithm. Examples of each type of problem are shown in Figure 19.22.

    Notice how flexible this simple line model is for every type of percent problem. It allows modeling of not only part-whole scenarios but also increase-decrease situations

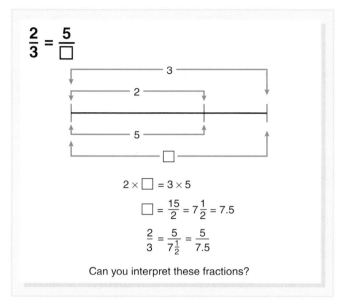

$$\frac{2}{3} = \frac{5}{\square}$$

$2 \times \square = 3 \times 5$

$\square = \frac{15}{2} = 7\frac{1}{2} = 7.5$

$\frac{2}{3} = \frac{5}{7\frac{1}{2}} = \frac{5}{7.5}$

Can you interpret these fractions?

FIGURE 19.21 Solving equivalent-fraction problems as equivalent ratios using cross-products.

and those in which there is a comparison between two distinct quantities. One of each of these is included in Figure 19.22. Another advantage of the line model is that it does not restrict students from thinking about percents greater than 100 as does a circle graph or a 10 × 10 grid (Parker, 2004).

It is tempting to teach all percent problems in this one way. Developmentally, such an approach is not recommended. Even though the approach is conceptual, it does not translate easily to intuitive ideas, mental arithmetic, or estimation as discussed in Chapter 18. The modeling and proportion approach of Figure 19.22 is suggested only as a way to help students analyze problems that may verbally present some difficulty. The approach of Chapter 18, which relates percent to part-whole fraction concepts, should probably receive more emphasis.

Literature Connections

Literature brings an exciting dimension to the exploration of proportional reasoning. Many books and stories discuss comparative sizes; concepts of scale as in maps; giants and miniature people who are proportional to regular people; comparative rates, especially rates of speed; and so on. A book may not appear to explore proportions, and the author may not have had that in mind at all, but comparisons are the stuff of many excellent stories and are at the heart of proportional ideas. For example, Beckman, Thompson, and Austin (2004) explore the popular *Harry Potter* stories, *The Lord of the Rings*, and *The Perfect Storm* for exciting contexts for proportional reasoning activities. In addition to their suggestions, those that follow are intended to give you a hint of how you might explore proportional reasoning with literature.

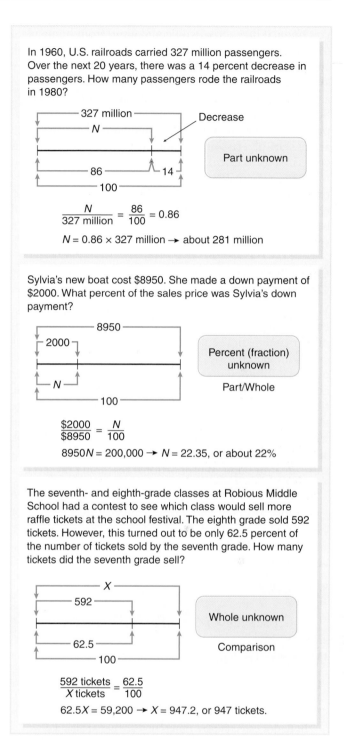

In 1960, U.S. railroads carried 327 million passengers. Over the next 20 years, there was a 14 percent decrease in passengers. How many passengers rode the railroads in 1980?

$$\frac{N}{327\text{ million}} = \frac{86}{100} = 0.86$$

$N = 0.86 \times 327$ million → about 281 million

Sylvia's new boat cost $8950. She made a down payment of $2000. What percent of the sales price was Sylvia's down payment?

$$\frac{\$2000}{\$8950} = \frac{N}{100}$$

$8950N = 200,000$ → $N = 22.35$, or about 22%

The seventh- and eighth-grade classes at Robious Middle School had a contest to see which class would sell more raffle tickets at the school festival. The eighth grade sold 592 tickets. However, this turned out to be only 62.5 percent of the number of tickets sold by the seventh grade. How many tickets did the seventh grade sell?

$$\frac{592\text{ tickets}}{X\text{ tickets}} = \frac{62.5}{100}$$

$62.5X = 59,200$ → $X = 947.2$, or 947 tickets.

FIGURE 19.22 The three percentage problems solved by setting up a proportion using a simple line segment model.

If You Hopped Like a Frog
Schwartz, 1999

David Schwartz, the author of *How Much Is a Million?* and *If You Made a Million*, has found some wonderful mathematics in nature with this new book. Here Schwartz uses proportional reasoning to determine what it would be like if we had the powers or dimensions of familiar animals. "If you hopped like a frog, you could jump from home plate to first base in one mighty leap." This short picture book contains 12 of these fascinating proportions: if you were as strong as an ant . . . , if you flicked your tongue like a chameleon . . . , and so on. At the end of the book, Schwartz provides some factual data on which the proportions are based. The book could be read at least twice at the start of a lesson, and students could find their own comparisons to calculate. This is a wonderful connection to science. There is no reason the comparisons need be between animals and humans as in this book. The toy-car to real-car ratio is an example of comparisons students could be encouraged to explore using this delightful book as a springboard.

Counting on Frank
Clement, 1991

We will refer to this wonderful book again when we discuss measurement in Chapter 20. It is hard to imagine that more mathematics could spring from 24 pages mostly covered with pictures. But the ideas appeal to all ages, and the potential for good investigations is clearly there for older children. The narrator and his pet dog, Frank, estimate, figure, and ponder interesting facts, usually about large numbers in odd settings (enough green peas to be level with the kitchen tabletop). But three spreads of the book are wonderful fantasies of proportions that could easily inspire an entire unit of proportional reasoning projects.

* "If I had grown at the same speed as the tree—6 feet per year—I'd now be almost 50 feet tall!" How

fast do we grow? What if we kept growing at the same rate? How old is the narrator? How old would he be when he is 75 feet tall? Is this a multiplicative situation?

* If the mosquito that bothers him were 4 million times bigger. . . . What would any common object be like if it were a million times bigger?

* If the toaster that shoots toast 3 feet in the air were as big as the house. . . .

The Borrowers
Norton, 1953

This is the classic tale of little folk living in the walls of a house. The furnishings and implements are created from odds and ends from the full-size human world. The potential to make scale comparisons is endless.

A similar tale unfolds in Shel Silverstein's poem "One Inch Tall" (1974), in which you are invited to imagine being 1 inch tall.

At the other extreme are stories about giants and dinosaurs, but the concepts of scale are similar. Suppose that a giant were 18 feet tall, or 3 times the height of a tall man. All linear dimensions (arm span, foot length, etc.) would also be three times that of the man. But the surface area would be 3^2 or 9 times as large, and the giant's volume and hence his weight would be 3^3 or 27 times as much as the man's. That would make the giant weigh about 5400 pounds. With a cross-sectional area of the bones only 9 times more, the bones would not be able to hold the weight. This is one reason there are no real giants. ■

Reflections *on* Chapter 19

Writing to Learn

1. Describe the idea of a ratio in your own words. Explain how your idea fits with each of the following statements:
   a. A fraction is a ratio.
   b. Ratios can compare things that are not at all alike.
   c. Ratios can compare two parts of the same whole.
   d. Rates such as prices or speeds are ratios.
2. What is a proportion? For each of the statements in item 1, give an example of a proportion. Also give an example of a comparison that is additive rather than proportional.
3. Describe a situation in which the comparison involved could be interpreted both in an additive sense as well as multiplicatively. Why might you want to explore a situation such as this early on in your discussion of ratio and proportion?
4. Much of this chapter is about activities that help students observe ratios and develop proportional reasoning abilities. These activities were grouped into five categories:

   a. Identification of multiplicative relationships
   b. Selection of equivalent ratios
   c. Comparisons of ratios
   d. Scaling activities using ratio tables
   e. Construction and measurement
      For each of these categories, pick one activity presented in the book that you did not do as part of your class experiences. Do the activity and briefly describe how you think the activity would contribute to students' proportional reasoning.
5. What can you say about the graph of a collection of equivalent ratios?
6. Make up a realistic proportional situation that can be solved by a factor-of-change approach and another that can be solved by a unit-rate approach. Explain each.
7. Consider this problem: If 50 gallons of fuel oil cost $56.95, how much can be purchased for $100? Draw a sketch to illustrate the proportion, and set up the equation in two dif-

ferent ways. One equation should equate within ratios and the other between ratios.

8. Make up a realistic percentage problem and set up a proportion. Draw a line-segment model to help explain why the proportion makes sense. Illustrate how this method could be used for any of the three types of percentage problems.

For Discussion and Exploration

1. Examine a teacher's edition of a basal textbook for the sixth, seventh, or eighth grade. How is the topic of ratio developed? What is the emphasis? Select one lesson, and write a lesson plan that extends the ideas found on the student pages and actively involves the students.

2. In Chapter 18, the three percent problems were developed around the theme of which element was missing—the part, the whole, or the fraction that related the two. In this chapter, percent is related to proportions, an equality of two ratios with one of these ratios a comparison to 100. How are these two approaches alike? How are they different? Explain how 100 percent could, in some problems, be a part rather than a whole.

Recommendations for Further Reading

Lamon, S. J. (1999). *Teaching fractions and ratios for understanding: Essential content knowledge and instructional strategies for teachers*. Mahwah, NJ: Lawrence Erlbaum.

Lamon is one of the most prolific researchers and writers on the subject of fractions, ratios, and proportional reasoning. Her work is full of specific practical examples of activities and is freely illustrated with children's work. At the same time this is a serious, research-based, and thought-provoking book. Many of the ideas found in this chapter are adapted from this book and other works by Lamon. Anyone seriously interested in the development of proportional reasoning needs to have this book. There is a companion volume with additional examples to elaborate the ideas found here. (See the other suggested readings that follow.)

Langrall, C. W., & Swafford, J. (2000). Three balloons for two dollars. *Mathematics Teaching in the Middle School, 6*, 254–261.

If you cannot find the Lamon book just mentioned and would like to see an overview of her ideas in a short article, then try this one. The authors describe and give examples of four levels of proportional reasoning using examples from the classroom. A good article on a difficult topic.

Litwiller B. (Ed.). (2002). *Making sense of fractions, ratios, and proportions: 2002 yearbook*. Reston, VA: National Council of Teachers of Mathematics.

Eleven of the 26 short chapters in this NCTM yearbook discuss explicitly the issue of multiplicative relationships and/or proportional reasoning. The remaining chapters are on various aspects of fraction concepts and fraction computation, many illustrating the connection with proportional thinking. Several articles were referenced in this chapter. This is an important reference book to have either in your own collection or in your school library. Accompanying the yearbook is a book of *Classroom Activities* complete with Blackline Masters.

Lo, J., Watanabe, T., & Cai, J. (2004). Developing ratio concepts: An Asian perspective. *Mathematics Teaching in the Middle School, 9*, 362–367.

These well-known researchers discuss the way that the concepts of ratio and proportion are developed in Asian countries. They share a sequence of activities adapted from textbooks used in China, Taiwan, and Japan. They also look at the notes that are found in the teacher's guides. You will likely be amazed at the level of mathematical discussion in these notes. The series of examples will certainly be useful in your classroom. This combination of activities and discussion is a very useful companion to the present chapter.

Online Resources

Suggested Applets and Web Links

Fibonacci Sequence

http://nlvm.usu.edu/en/nav/frames_asid_315_g_3_t_1.html

The applet simply computes successive terms of the Fibonacci sequence and shows in both fraction and decimal forms the ratio of successive terms of the sequence. This ratio converges to the *golden ratio*. For what may be the most information assembled anywhere on the Fibonacci sequence, go to www.mcs.surrey.ac.uk/Personal/R.Knott/Fibonacci.

Fish Simulation Applet I

http://mathforum.org/escotpow/puzzles/fish/applet.html

A collection of two colors of fish is to be placed into three ponds to create specified ratios within each pond. Students should find out if there is more than one solution and then make up similar problems for their classmates.

Learning about Length, Area, Volume, Surface Area of Similar Objects

http://standards.ncrm.org/document/eexamples/chap6/6.3/part2.htm

A two-part exploration complete with extensive teacher notes. The applets compare two rectangles or two prisms showing ratios of measures in both numeric and graphical form.

Understanding Ratios of Inscribed Figures

http://standards.nctm.org/document/eexamples/chap7/7.3/index.htm

A nice geometry/measurement link to ratio. The user explores the ratio of figures inscribed in polygons formed by joining midpoints of sides. These points can also be adjusted. The supporting lesson and activity suggestions are quite good.

 An additional list of books and articles related to the ideas in this chapter can be found on the Companion Web site at **www.ablongman.com/vandewalle6e.**

chapter 20

Developing Measurement Concepts

That measurement was given its own standard in *Principles and Standards* points not only to the importance of this topic across the grades but also to its complexity. Measurement is not an easy topic for students to understand. Data from both international studies (TIMSS) and from NAEP consistently indicate that students are weaker in the area of measurement than any other topic in the curriculum (Thompson & Preston, 2004). Various hypotheses exist for this poor performance. Although learning both the metric and the customary measurement systems may be a contributing factor, the poor performance is more likely a function of how the subject is taught—too much reliance on pictures and worksheets rather than hands-on experiences and a focus on skills with less attention to the concepts of measurement.

In this chapter you will learn how to help students develop a conceptual understanding of the measurement process and the tools of measurement. You will also learn about informal and standard units of measurement, estimation in measurement including the use of benchmarks, and the development of measurement formulas for area and volume.

Big Ideas

1. Measurement involves a comparison of an attribute of an item or situation with a unit that has the same attribute. Lengths are compared to units of length, areas to units of area, time to units of time, and so on. Before anything can be measured meaningfully, it is necessary to understand the attribute to be measured.

2. Meaningful measurement and estimation of measurements depend on a personal familiarity with the unit of measure being used.

3. Estimation of measures and the development of personal benchmarks for frequently used units of measure help

students increase their familiarity with units, prevent errors in measurements, and aid in the meaningful use of measurement.

4. Measurement instruments are devices that replace the need for actual measurement units. It is important to understand how measurement instruments work so that they can be used correctly and meaningfully.

5. Area and volume formulas provide a method of measuring these attributes by using only measures of length.

6. Area, perimeter, and volume are related to each other, although not precisely or by formula. For example, as the shapes of regions or three-dimensional objects change but maintain the same areas or volumes, there is a predictable effect on the perimeters and surface areas.

Mathematics Content Connections

Measurement has traditionally been paired in the curriculum with geometry. However, measurement is actually more closely connected to other mathematical topics. In order to provide more time for students to engage in meaningful measurement activities, measurement should be integrated across the mathematics curriculum as well as the science curriculum.

- **Number** (Chapter 9): Early measurement activities are a very meaningful context for counting. Measurement of important objects in the familiar environment connects ideas of number to the real world, enhancing number sense.

- **Place Value** (Chapter 10): Multiples of ten are profitably used by young children in counting informal measures such as the height of the door in terms of connecting cubes. The metric system of measurement is built on the base-ten system of numeration. An understanding of each topic enhances the use of and understanding of the other.

374

■ **Algebra** (Chapter 15): Functions are used to study and describe the relationships between various phenomena, especially things that are measured. Measurement formulas are themselves functions. Measurement provides data from which generalizations and functional relationships can be derived.

■ **Proportional Reasoning** (Chapter 19): The use of benchmarks in estimating measures (e.g., a door is about 3 feet wide so the room is about seven "doors" or 21 feet) promotes multiplicative thinking, a fundamental aspect of proportional reasoning. Measures are used in scale drawings. Proportions are used to find unknown measures of similar figures.

■ **Fractions** (Chapter 16): The need for increased precision leads to fractional parts of units.

■ **Geometry** (Chapter 21): The development and understanding of perimeter, area, and volume formulas require an understanding of the shapes and relationships involved. Measures help to describe shapes, and angular measures play a significant role in the properties of shapes.

■ **Data** (Chapter 22): Statistics and graphs are used to describe our world and help us answer questions about it. Often this description is in terms of measures. Graphing and measurement are easily blended into the same units or activities.

The Meaning and Process of Measuring

Suppose that you asked your students to measure an empty bucket. The first thing they would need to know is *what* about the bucket is to be measured. They might measure the height or depth, diameter (distance across), or circumference (distance around). All of these are length measures. The surface area of the side could be determined. A bucket also has volume (or capacity) and weight. Each of these aspects that can be measured is an *attribute* of the bucket.

Once they determine the attribute to be measured, they need to choose a unit of measure. The unit must have the attribute that is being measured. Length is measured with units that have length, volume with units that have volume, and so on.

Technically, a *measurement* is a number that indicates a comparison between the attribute of the object (or situation, or event) being measured and the same attribute of a given unit of measure. We commonly use small units of measure to determine in some way a numeric relationship (the measurement) between what is measured and the unit. For example, to measure a length, the comparison can be done by lining up copies of the unit directly against the length being measured. To measure weight, which is a pull of gravity or a force, the weight of the object might first be

applied to a spring. Then the comparison is made by finding out how many units of weight produce the same effect on the spring. In either case, the number of units is the measure of the object.

For most of the attributes that are measured in schools, we can say that *to measure* means that the attribute being measured is "filled" or "covered" or "matched" with a unit of measure with the same attribute (as illustrated in Figure 20.1). This concept of filling or covering is a good way to talk with students about measurement. It is appropriate with this understanding, then, to say that the measure of an attribute is a count of how many units are needed to fill, cover, or match the attribute of the object being measured.

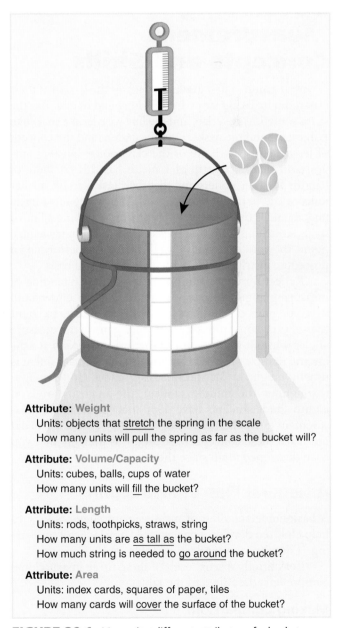

Attribute: Weight
   Units: objects that <u>stretch</u> the spring in the scale
   How many units will pull the spring as far as the bucket will?

Attribute: Volume/Capacity
   Units: cubes, balls, cups of water
   How many units will <u>fill</u> the bucket?

Attribute: Length
   Units: rods, toothpicks, straws, string
   How many units are <u>as tall as</u> the bucket?
   How much string is needed to <u>go around</u> the bucket?

Attribute: Area
   Units: index cards, squares of paper, tiles
   How many cards will <u>cover</u> the surface of the bucket?

FIGURE 20.1 Measuring different attributes of a bucket.

In summary, to measure something, one must perform three steps:

1. Decide on the attribute to be measured.
2. Select a unit that has that attribute.
3. Compare the units, by filling, covering, matching, or some other method, with the attribute of the object being measured.

Measuring instruments such as rulers, scales, protractors, and clocks are devices that make the filling, covering, or matching process easier. A ruler lines up the units of length and numbers them. A protractor lines up the unit angles and numbers them. A clock lines up units of time and marks them off.

Developing Measurement Concepts and Skills

A typical group of first graders measures the length of their classroom by laying strips 1 meter long end to end. But the strips sometimes overlap, and the line weaves in a snakelike fashion around the desks. Do they understand the concept of length as an attribute of the classroom? Do they understand that each strip of 1 meter has this attribute of length? Do they understand that their task is to fill smaller units of length into the longer one? What they most likely understand is that they are supposed to be making a line of strips stretching from wall to wall (and from their vantage point, they are doing quite well). They are performing a procedure instrumentally, without a conceptual basis.

Reflect for a moment on your own understanding of measuring angles with a protractor. Do you understand what the units are and how the protractor helps to count them? Can you think of a way that you might measure angles without a protractor? How are your skills at estimating the size of angles? Although angle measurement is usually taught in the intermediate grades (and retaught throughout the middle grades), the majority of U.S. eighth-grade students have poor concepts of angle measurement (Strutchens, Martin, & Kenney, 2003). If you did not learn these concepts in school, it is unlikely that you have developed them since then.

A General Plan of Instruction

A basic understanding of measurement suggests how to help children develop a conceptual knowledge of measuring. These are summarized in Table 20.1.

Let's briefly discuss each of these three instructional components described in the table.

Making Comparisons

The first and most critical goal is for students to understand the attribute they are going to measure. When stu-

TABLE 20.1
Plan for Measurement Instruction

Step One
Goal: Students will understand the attribute to be measured.
Type of Activity: Make comparisons based on the attribute. For example, longer/shorter, heavier/lighter. Use direct comparisons whenever possible.
Notes: When it is clear that the attribute is understood, there is no further need for comparison activities.

Step Two
Goal: Students will understand how filling, covering, matching, or making other comparisons of an attribute with measuring units produces a number called a measure.
Type of Activity: Use physical models of measuring units to fill, cover, match, or make the desired comparison of the attribute with the unit.
Notes: In most instances it is appropriate to begin with informal units. Progress to the direct use of standard units when appropriate and certainly before using formulas or measuring tools.

Step Three
Goal: Students will use common measuring tools with understanding and flexibility.
Type of Activity: Make measuring instruments and use them in comparison with the actual unit models to see how the measurement tool is performing the same function as the individual units. Be certain to make direct comparisons between the student-made tools and the standard tools.
Notes: Student-made tools are usually best made with informal units. Without a careful comparison with the standard tools, much of the value in making the tools can be lost.

dents compare objects on the basis of some measurable attribute, that attribute becomes the focus of the activity. For example, is the capacity of one box more than, less than, or about the same as the capacity of another? No measurement is required, but some manner of comparing one volume to the other must be devised. The attribute of "capacity" (how much a container can hold) is inescapable.

Many attributes can be compared directly, such as placing one length directly in line with another. In the case of volume or capacity, some indirect method is probably required, such as filling one box with beans and then pouring the beans into the other box. Using a string to compare the height of a wastebasket to the distance around is another example of an indirect comparison. The string is the intermediary. It is impossible to compare these two lengths directly.

Constructing or making something that is the same in terms of a measurable attribute is another type of comparison activity—for example, "Cut the straw to be just as long as this piece of chalk" or "Draw a rectangle that is about the same size (has the same area) as this triangle."

Using Models of Units

The second goal is for students to understand what units of measure might be for the particular attribute in question and how these units are used to produce a measurement.

Regardless of the grade level, you should make no assumptions that students have an understanding of measuring units for the attribute being considered. For most attributes that are measured in elementary schools, it is possible to have physical models of the units of measure. Time and temperature are exceptions. (Many other attributes not commonly measured in school also do not have physical units of measure. Light intensity, speed, loudness, viscosity, and radioactivity are just a few examples.) Unit models can be found for both informal units and standard units. For length, for example, drinking straws (informal) or tagboard strips 1 foot long (standard) might be used as units.

The most easily understood use of unit models is actually to use as many copies of the unit as are needed to fill or match the attribute measured. To measure the area of the desktop with an index card unit, you can literally cover the entire desk with index cards. Somewhat more difficult, especially for younger children, is to use a single copy of the unit with an iteration process. The same desktop area can be measured with a single index card by moving it from position to position and keeping track of which areas the card has covered although this iteration process may not adequately portray the measurement concept.

It is useful to measure the same object with different-sized units. Results should be predicted in advance and discussed afterward. This will help students understand that the unit used is as important as the attribute being measured. The fact that smaller units produce larger numeric measures, and vice versa, is hard for young children to understand. This inverse relationship can only be constructed by reflecting on measurements with varying-sized units. Predictions and discussions of results add to the reflective nature of the activities.

Making and Using Measuring Instruments

An understanding of the devices we use to measure is the third goal. In the sixth National Assessment of Educational Progress (Kenney & Kouba, 1997), only 24 percent of fourth-grade students and 62 percent of eighth-grade students could give the correct measure of an object not aligned with the end of a ruler, as in Figure 20.2. These results point to the difference between using a measuring device and understanding how it works. Students also experienced difficulty when the increments on a measuring device were other than one unit.

If students actually make simple measuring instruments using unit models with which they are familiar, it is more likely that they will understand how an instrument

measures. A ruler is a good example. If students line up physical units along a strip of tagboard and mark them off, they can see that it is the *spaces* on rulers and not the marks or numbers that are important. It is essential that the measurement with actual unit models be compared with the measurement using an instrument. Without this comparison, students may not understand that these two methods are really two means to the same end. Always have students explain how the ruler, scale, or other device compares to using actual units.

A discussion of student-made measuring instruments for each attribute is provided in the text that follows. Of course, children should also use standard, ready-made instruments such as rulers and scales and should compare the use of these devices with the use of the corresponding unit models.

Informal Units and Standard Units: Reasons for Using Each

It is common in primary grades to use nonstandard or informal units to measure length and sometimes area. Unfortunately, measurement activities in the upper grades, where other attributes are measured, often do not begin with informal units. The use of informal units for beginning measurement activities is beneficial at all grade levels.

- Informal units make it easier to focus directly on the attribute being measured. For example, in a discussion of how to measure the area of an irregular shape, units such as lima beans, square tiles, or circular counters may be suggested. Each unit covers area and each will give a different result. The discussion focuses on what it means to measure area.
- The use of informal units can avoid conflicting objectives in the same beginning lesson. Is your lesson about what it means to measure area or about understanding square centimeters?
- Informal units provide a good rationale for standard units. A discussion of the need for a standard unit can have more meaning after groups in your class have measured the same objects with their own units and arrived at different answers.
- Using informal units can be fun.

The use of standard units is also important in your measurement program at any grade level.

- Knowledge of standard units is a valid objective of a measurement program and must be addressed. Students must not only develop a familiarity with standard units but must also learn appropriate relationships between them.
- Once a measuring concept is fairly well developed, it is frequently just as easy to use standard units. If there is no good instructional reason for using informal units, why not use standard units and provide the exposure?

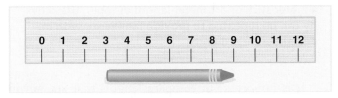

FIGURE 20.2 "How long is this crayon?"

There is no simple rule for when to use standard or informal units. Children's initial measurement of any attribute should probably begin with informal units and progress over time to the use of standard units and standard measuring tools. The amount of time that should be spent using informal unit models varies with the age of the children and the attributes being measured. First-grade children need a lot of experience with a variety of informal units of length, weight, and capacity. Informal units might be used at this level all year. Conversely, the benefits of nonstandard measuring units may last only a day or two for measurements of angles at the middle school level. When informal units have served their purpose, move on.

The Role of Estimation in Learning Measurement

It is very important to have students estimate a measurement before they make it. This is true with both informal and standard units. There are at least four good reasons for including estimation in measurement activities:

- Estimation helps students focus on the attribute being measured and the measuring process. Think how you would estimate the area of the front of this book with standard playing cards as the unit. To do so, you have to think about what area is and how the units might be fitted into the book cover.
- Estimation provides intrinsic motivation to measurement activities. It is fun to see how close you can come in your estimate or if your team can make a better estimate than the other teams in the room.
- When standard units are used, estimation helps develop familiarity with the unit. If you estimate the height of the door in meters before measuring, you have to devise some way to think about the size of a meter.
- The use of a benchmark to make an estimate promotes multiplicative reasoning. The width of the building is about one-fourth of the length of a football field—perhaps 25 yards.

The Approximate Nature of Measurement

In all measuring activities, emphasize the use of approximate language. The desk is *about* 15 orange rods long. The chair is *a little less than* 4 straws high. The use of approximate language is very useful for younger children because many measurements do not come out even. Older children will begin to search for smaller units or will use fractional units to try to measure exactly. Here is an opportunity to develop the idea that all measurements include some error. Each smaller unit or subdivision does produce a greater degree of *precision*. For example, a length measure

can never be more than one-half unit in error. And yet, since there is mathematically no "smallest unit," there is always some error involved.

NCTM Standards The Measurement Standard in *Principles and Standards* has two main parts. The first emphasizes the need for students to understand the attributes of things they will be measuring and the process of using units to create measures. The second part focuses on the use of measurement tools and the use of formulas. The *Standards* authors stress that students should have ample opportunities to use informal units and similar meaningful experiences with measurement—regardless of grade level—before focusing on tools and formulas.

Measuring Length

Length is usually the first attribute students learn to measure. Be aware, however, that length measurement is not immediately understood by young children.

Comparison Activities

At the kindergarten level, children should begin with direct comparisons of two or more lengths.

activity 20.1

Longer, Shorter, Same

Make a sorting-by-length station at which students sort objects as longer, shorter, or about the same as a specified object. It is easy to have several such stations in your room. The reference object can be changed occasionally to produce different sorts. A similar task is to put objects in order from shortest to longest.

activity 20.2

Length (or Unit) Hunt

Give pairs of students a strip of tagboard, a stick, a length of rope, or some other object with an obvious length dimension. The task on one day might be to find five things in the room that are shorter than, longer than, or about the same length as their object. They can draw pictures or write the names of the things they find.

By making the target length a standard unit (e.g., a meter stick or a 1-meter length of rope), the activity can be repeated to provide familiarity with important standard units.

It is important to compare lengths that are not in straight lines. One way to do this is with string or rope.

Students can wrap string around objects in a search for things that are, for example, as long around as the distance from the floor to their belly button or as long as the distance around one's head or waist. Body measures are always fun.

Indirect comparisons are used in the next activity.

EXPANDED LESSON

An expanded lesson plan based on Activity 20.3, "Crooked Paths," can be found on the Companion Web site at www.ablongman.com/vandewalle6e.

activity 20.3

Crooked Paths

Make some crooked or curvy paths on the floor with masking tape. The task is to determine which path is longest, next longest, and so on. The students should find a way to make straight paths that are just as long as the crooked paths so that they can be compared easily. (You may or may not wish to offer this suggestion.) Provide pairs of students with a long piece of rope. The task is easier if the rope is longer than the crooked paths. The students can draw their straight paths on the board, mark them with tape on the floor, or use some other method that you devise. Have students explain how they solved the problem. (This is a good outdoor activity also.)

Using Units of Length

Students can use a variety of informal units to begin measuring length, for example:

- *Giant footprints:* Make about 20 copies of a large footprint about $1\frac{1}{2}$ to 2 feet long cut out of poster board.
- *Measuring ropes:* Cut cotton clothesline into lengths of 1 m. These are useful for measuring curved lines and the circumference of large objects such as the teacher's desk.
- *Plastic straws:* Drinking straws are inexpensive and provide large quantities of a useful unit. Straws are easily cut into smaller units. You can link straw units together with a long string. The string of straws is an excellent bridge to a ruler or measuring tape.
- *Short units:* Toothpicks, connecting cubes, wooden cubes, and paper clips are all useful units for measuring shorter lengths. Cuisenaire rods are one of the nicest sets of units because they come in ten different lengths, are easily placed end to end, and can be related to each other. Paper clips can readily be made into chains as can plastic chain links, available from suppliers of manipulatives.

The temptation is to carefully explain to students how to use these units to measure and then send them off to practice measuring. This approach will shift students' attention to the procedure (following your instruction) and away from developing an understanding of measurement using units. In the following activity students are provided with a measuring task but are required to develop their own approach. Correct ideas about measurement can be developed out of a discussion of the results.

activity 20.4

How Long Is the Teacher?

Explain that you have just received an important request from the principal. She needs to know exactly how tall each teacher is. The students are to decide how to measure the teachers and write a note to the principal explaining how tall their teacher is and how they decided. Next, explain that it may be easier if you lay down and students measure how long you are instead of how tall. Do this at several stations around the room. Have students make marks at your feet and head and draw a straight line between these marks.

Explain that the principal says you can use any ONE of these units to measure with. (Provide several choices. For each choice of unit, supply enough units to more than cover your length.) Put students in pairs and allow them to select one unit with which to measure.

The value of the last activity will come from the discussion. Good questions include "How did you get your measurement?" "Did students who measured with the same unit get the same answers? Why not?" "How could the principal make a line that was just as long as the teacher?" In your discussion, focus on the value of lining units up carefully, end to end. Discuss what happens if you overlap units or don't stay in a straight line.

Repeat the basic task of "How Long Is the Teacher?" with other measuring tasks, each time providing a choice of units and the requirement that students explain their measures. It is always helpful if the same lengths (heights, distances around) are measured by several pairs of students so that possible errors can be discussed and the measuring process refined. The following similar activity adds an estimation component.

activity 20.5

Guess and Measure

Make lists of things in the room to measure (see Figure 20.3). For younger children, run a piece of masking tape along the dimension of each object to be measured. On the list, designate the units to be used. Do not forget to include curves or other

distances that are not straight lines. Include estimates before the measures. Young children will not be very good at estimating distances at first.

Name _____

Around your outline

Unit: ▭▭▭▭
straw

Guess _____ straws

Measured _____ straws

The teacher's desk

Unit: ▭▭
orange rod

Guess _____ rods

Measured _____ rods

Around math book

Math Book

Unit: ▭
paper clip

Guess _____ clips

Measured _____ clips

FIGURE 20.3 Recording sheet for measuring with informal length units.

For students beginning to learn about two-digit numbers, add the following component to the "Guess and Measure" activity: Have students make a row or chain of exactly ten units to use in helping them with their estimates. They first lay ten units against the object and then make their guess.

It is fruitless to attempt explaining to students that larger units will produce a smaller measure and vice versa. Instead, engage students in an activity like the following where this issue is a focus.

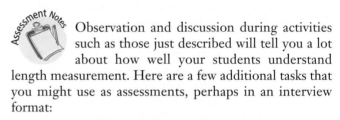

activity **20.6**

Changing Units

Have students measure a length with a specified unit. Then provide them with a different unit that is either twice as long or half as long as the original unit. Their task is to predict the measure of the same length using the new unit. Students should write down their predictions and explanations of

how they were made. Stop and have a discussion about their predictions and then have them make the actual measurement. Cuisenaire rods are excellent for this activity. Older students can be challenged with units that are more difficult multiples of the original unit.

In "Changing Units," you are looking first for the basic idea that when the unit is longer the measure is smaller and vice versa. The actual computation of the second measure is an additional challenge and depends somewhat on the age of the students.

"Changing Units" is a good activity to do just before you discuss unit conversion with standard units. For example, if the doorway is 80 inches high, how many feet is that? Changing measurement units is an excellent proportional reasoning task for middle school students.

Assessment Notes Observation and discussion during activities such as those just described will tell you a lot about how well your students understand length measurement. Here are a few additional tasks that you might use as assessments, perhaps in an interview format:

- Provide a box with assorted units of different sizes. Cuisenaire rods would be suitable. Have the students use the materials in the box to measure a given length. Observe if the students understand that all units must be of like size. If different lengths of units are used, ask how the students would describe their measurement.
- Ask students to draw a line or mark off a distance of a prescribed number of units. Observe whether the students know to align the units in a straight line without overlaps or gaps.
- Have students measure two different objects. Then ask how much longer is the longer object. Observe if the students can use the measurements to answer or if a third measurement must be made of the difference.
- Provide a length of string. Tell students that the string is 6 units long. How could they use the string to make a length of 3 units? How could they make a length of 9 units? In this task, you are looking to see if students can mentally subdivide the given length (string) based on an understanding of its measure. That is, can students visualize that 6 units are matched to the string length and half of these is 3 units? ■

Two Units and Fractional Parts of Units

Children are sometimes perplexed when their measurements do not come out evenly. One suggestion you might

Width = 5 orange and 4 red

FIGURE 20.4 Using two units to measure length.

make to younger students is to use a smaller unit to fill in the remaining gap as in Figure 20.4. Another idea is to suggest that fractions be used. Both ideas are used in standard measurements. In the metric system, units are rarely mixed, and fractional units are expressed in decimal form (e.g., 3.2 m). In the customary system, both approaches are used. A measurement of 4 feet 3 inches is sometimes reported as 51 inches or as $4\frac{1}{4}$ feet. The use of fractional units is a good readiness for subdivision marks on a ruler. The children's book *Inchworm and a Half* provides a nice way to introduce the idea of fractional units (see p. 405).

Making and Using Rulers

The jump from using units to measure to using rulers is challenging. One of the best methods of helping students understand rulers is to have them make their own rulers out of actual units.

activity 20.7

Make Your Own Ruler

Precut narrow strips of construction paper 5 cm long and about 2 cm wide. Use two different colors of paper. Discuss how the strips could be used to measure by laying them end to end. Provide long strips of tagboard about 3 cm wide. Without explicit guided direction, have students make their own ruler by pasting the units onto the tagboard. Have a list of a few things to measure. Students use their new rulers to measure the things on the list. Discuss the results. It is very likely that there will be discrepancies due to rulers that were not made properly or to a failure to understand how a ruler works.

The same activity can be done using larger units such as tracings of students' footprints pasted onto strips of adding machine tape. Older children can use a standard unit (inch, foot, centimeter) to make marks on the strips and color in the spaces with alternating colors.

This activity makes the construction of a ruler a problem-based experience. By not overguiding students in how to make their rulers, you will get information concerning students' understanding of the measurement process. More importantly, the ideas about how a ruler can be made to get correct measures will come from the students' own ideas, avoiding blindly following rules. At the conclusion of this process, all students should have personally made a ruler correctly. The unit copies on the student-made rulers (rather than markings and numbers) maximize the connection between the spaces on the ruler and the actual units. Students should use their rulers to measure lengths that are longer than their rulers and discuss how that can be done. Another important challenge is to find more than one way to measure a length with a ruler. Do you have to begin at the end? What if you begin in the center?

Students should eventually put numbers on their homemade rulers, as shown in Figure 20.5. For young children, numbers can be written in the center of each unit to make it clear that the numbers are a way of precounting the units. When numbers are written in the standard way, at the ends of the units, the ruler becomes a number line. This format is more sophisticated and should be carefully discussed with children.

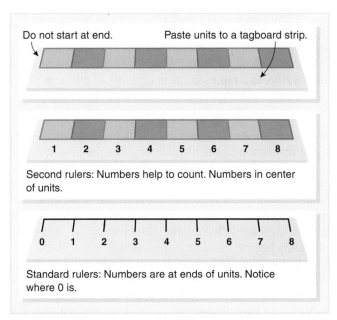

FIGURE 20.5 Give meaning to numbers on rulers.

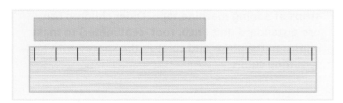

FIGURE 20.6 Use an unmarked ruler and ask students to measure an object. Does the student count spaces or hash marks? In the example shown, the correct length is 8 units. A student counting hash marks would respond with 9 units.

Assessment Notes Research indicates that when students see standard rulers with the numbers on the hash marks, they often believe that the numbers are counting the marks rather than indicating the units or spaces between the marks. This is an incorrect understanding of rulers that can lead to wrong answers when using them. As an assessment, provide students with a ruler, as shown in Figure 20.6, with hash marks but no numbers. Have students use the ruler to measure an item that is shorter than the ruler. A correct understanding of rulers is indicated if students count spaces between the hash marks.

Another good assessment of ruler understanding is to have students measure with a "broken" ruler, one with the first two units broken off. Some students will say that it is impossible to measure with such a ruler because there is no starting point. Those who understand rulers will be able to match and count the units meaningfully in their measures. (See Barrett, Jones, Thornton, & Dickson, 2003, for a complete discussion of student development of length measurement including the use of rulers.)

Observing how children use a ruler to measure an object that is longer than the ruler is also informative. Children who are simply reading the last mark on the ruler may not be able to do this task because they do not understand how a ruler is a representation of a row of units. ■

Much of the value of student-made rulers can be lost if you do not transfer this knowledge to standard rulers. Give children a standard ruler, and discuss how it is like and how it differs from the ones they have made. What are the units? Could you make a ruler with paper units the same as this? Could you make some cardboard units and measure the same way as with the ruler? What do the numbers mean? What are the other marks for? Where do the units begin?

In contrast with many traditional texts, the *Investigations in Number, Data, and Space* curriculum has first-grade children exploring a variety of attributes (length, weight, capacity, and area), but in the second and third grades the entire measurement units are devoted to length. See the excerpt from the third grade on the next page.

 In the Pre-K–2 section of the *Standards*, it is suggested that students become familiar with the attributes of length, volume, area, and time. However, the authors stress that "linear measurements are the main emphasis" of the primary years (p. 103). "Teachers cannot assume that students understand measurement fully even when they are able to tell how long an object is when it is aligned with a ruler" (p. 106).

Measuring Area

Area is the two-dimensional space inside a region. As with other attributes, students must first understand the attribute of area before measuring. Data from the seventh NAEP suggest that fourth- and eighth-grade students have an incomplete understanding of area (Martin & Strutchens, 2000).

Comparison Activities

One of the purposes of comparison activities with areas is to help students distinguish between size (or area) and shape, length, and other dimensions. A long, skinny rectangle may have less area than a triangle with shorter sides. This is an especially difficult concept for young children to understand. Piagetian experiments indicate that many 8- or 9-year-olds do not understand that rearranging areas into different shapes does not affect the amount of area.

Direct comparison of two areas is nearly always impossible except when the shapes involved have some common dimension or property. For example, two rectangles with the same width can be compared directly, as can any two circles. Comparison of these special shapes, however, fails to deal with the attribute of area. Instead, activities in which one area is rearranged are suggested. Cutting a shape into two parts and reassembling it in a different shape can show that the before and after shapes have the same area, even though they are different shapes. This idea is not at all obvious to children in the K–2 grade range.

activity **20.8**

Two-Piece Shapes

Cut a large number of rectangles of the same size, about 3 inches by 5 inches. Each pair of students will need six rectangles. Have students fold and cut the rectangles on the diagonal, making two identical triangles. Next, have them rearrange the triangles into different shapes, including the original rectangle. The rule is that only sides of the same length can be matched up and must be matched exactly. Have each group find all the shapes that

Investigations
in Number, Data, and Space

Grade 3, From Paces to Feet
Investigation 2: Measuring Centers

Context

The activities described here occur roughly halfway through a unit of at least three weeks that focuses on linear measurement including estimation, the use of standard and nonstandard units (customary and metric), and rulers. In addition, students graph their measurement data as they develop graphing techniques and examine the "shape" of data.

Task Description

In this investigation, students spend roughly one day working through four centers and another session developing a graph of the data from one of the centers. The centers are described briefly here.

> *Measure and Compare.* Students complete the sheet shown here and a second that is similar to it.
> *Body Benchmarks.* With another worksheet for guidance, students find personal references on their bodies for lengths of 1, 6, and 12 inches.
> *How Far Can a Third Grader Jump?* Students each complete a standing jump, measure the distance, and record measurements on a line plot posted on the wall. Students make decisions about how to measure their jumps and other details such as number of trial jumps.
> *How Far Can You Blow a Pattern Block?* Students blow a pattern block on a flat table surface, again determining their own rules and gathering class data.

Students select their own methods of measurement and make their own decisions concerning precision (e.g., half units or "about"). The entire measurement unit is nicely integrated with learning about data representation. Real measurements collected by students offer numeric data that are graphed on a line plot. The concept of median is also explored. A final investigation in the unit offers two activities involving early concepts of scale and proportion in a measurement context.

Name _____   Date _____

Student Sheet 8

Measure and Compare (page 1 of 2)

1. Measure each of these things. Write down your measurements.
2. Write a sentence saying how much bigger one thing is than the other. Show or tell how you figured it out.

scissors	marker

ruler	pencil

length of table	length of bookshelf

© Dale Seymour Publications®   90   *Investigation 2 • Sessions 3–4*
From Paces to Feet

Page 90 from *Measuring Data: From Paces to Feet* by K. Economopoulos, J. Mokros, & S. J. Russell. *Investigations in Number, Data, and Space.* Copyright © 1998 by Dale Seymour Publications. Reprinted by permission of Pearson Education, Inc.

---

can be made this way, pasting the triangles on paper as a record of each shape (see Figure 20.7). Discuss the size and shape of the different results. Is one shape bigger than the rest? How is it bigger? Did one take more paper to make, or do they all have the same amount of paper? Help children conclude that although each figure is a different shape, all the figures have the same *area*. (*Size* in this context is a useful substitute for *area* with very young children, although it does not mean exactly the same thing.)

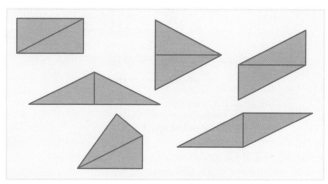

FIGURE 20.7 Different shapes, same size.

activity 20.9

Rectangle Compare—No Units

Provide students with pairs of rectangles as follows.

Pair A: A1 is 2 × 9 and A2 is 3 × 6.
Pair B: B1 is 1 × 10 and B2 is 3 × 5.
Pair C: C1 is 3 × 8 and C2 is 4 × 5.

The rectangles should be blank except for the labels. The students' task is to decide in each pair which rectangle has the greater area or if the two are the same size. They are allowed to cut or fold the rectangles in any way they wish, but they must include an explanation for their decision in each pair. Pair C will cause the most difficulty and you may wish to reserve it as a challenge.

In the first two pairs, the skinny rectangle can be folded and cut to either match (pair A) or be easily compared (pair B) to the second rectangle. For pair C, one rectangle can be placed on the other and then the extended pieces compared.

Tangrams, a very old and popular set of puzzle shapes, can be used for the same purpose. The standard set of seven tangram pieces is cut from a square, as shown in Figure 20.8. The two small triangles can be used to make the parallelogram, the square, and the medium triangle. Four small triangles will make the large triangle. This permits a similar discussion about the pieces having the same size (area) but different shapes (Seymour, 1971). (Tangram pieces can be found in the Blackline Masters.)

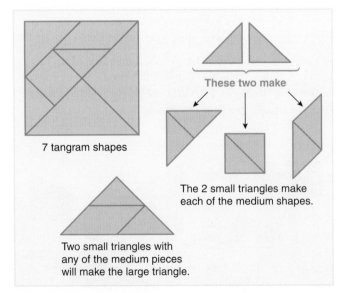

FIGURE 20.8 Tangrams provide a nice opportunity to investigate size and shape concepts.

The following activity uses tangrams to compare areas.

activity 20.10

Tangram Areas

Draw the outline of several shapes made with tangram pieces, as in Figure 20.9. Let students use tangrams to decide which shapes are the same size, which are larger, and which are smaller. Shapes can be duplicated on paper, and children can work in groups. Let students explain how they came to their conclusions. There are several different approaches to this task, and it is best if students determine their own solutions rather than blindly follow your directions.

 *pause and reflect* _____

You might pause here, get a set of tangrams, and make the area comparisons suggested in Figure 20.9.

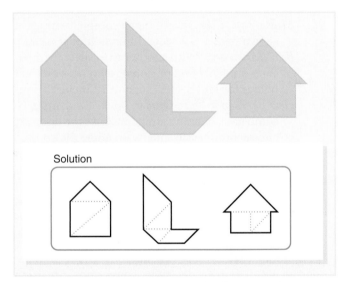

FIGURE 20.9 Compare shapes made of tangram pieces.

Using Units of Area

Although squares are very nice units of area (and the most commonly used), any tile that conveniently fills up a plane region can be used. Even filling a region with uniform circles or lima beans provides a useful idea of what it means to measure areas. Here are some suggestions for area units that are easy to gather or make in the large quantities you will need.

- Round plastic chips, pennies, or lima beans can be used. It is not necessary at a beginning stage that the area units fit with no gaps.

- Color Tiles (1-inch plastic squares).
- Squares cut from cardboard. Large squares (about 20 cm on a side) work well for large areas. Smaller units should be about 5 to 10 cm on a side.
- Sheets of newspaper make excellent units for very large areas.

Children can use units to measure surfaces in the room such as desktops, bulletin boards, or books. Large regions can be outlined with masking tape on the floor. Small regions can be duplicated on paper so that students can work at their desks. Odd shapes and curved surfaces provide more challenge and interest. The surfaces of a watermelon or of the side of the wastebasket provide useful challenges.

In area measurements, there may be lots of units that only partially fit. You may wish to begin with shapes in which the units fit by building a shape with units, and drawing the outline. By third or fourth grade, students should begin to wrestle with partial units and mentally put together two or more partial units to count as one (see Figure 20.10).

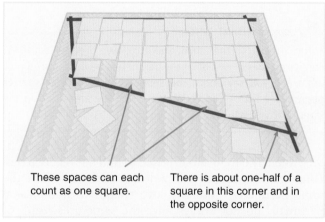

These spaces can each count as one square.

There is about one-half of a square in this corner and in the opposite corner.

FIGURE 20.10 Measuring the area of a large shape drawn with tape on the floor. Units are pieces of tagboard all cut to the same shape.

The following activity is a good starting point to see what ideas your students bring to their understanding of area measurement.

activity **20.11**

Fill and Compare
Draw two rectangles and a blob shape on a sheet of paper. Make it so that the three areas are not the same but with no area that is clearly largest or smallest. The students' task is to first make a guess about which is the smallest and the largest of the three shapes. After recording their guess, they should use a filler of their choice to decide. Provide small units such as circular disks, Color Tiles, or lima beans. Students should explain in writing what they found out.

Your objective in the beginning is to develop the idea that area is measured by covering. Do not introduce formulas. Groups are very likely to come up with different measures for the same region. Discuss these differences with the children, and point to the difficulties involved in making estimates around the edges. Avoid the idea that there is a "right" answer.

It is important to stress that filling areas with units to determine a measure has almost no impact on students' understanding of formulas such as $L \times W$ for determining area. The filling process does not help them focus on the dimensions or on multiplying as a means of counting units. The only goal of these activities is to understand the meaning of area measurement.

By no later than fourth grade, students should begin to relate the concept of multiplication using arrays to the area of rectangles. The following activity is a good first step in that direction.

activity **20.12**

Rectangle Comparison—Square Units
Students are given a pair of rectangles that are either the same or very close in area. They are also given a model or drawing of a single square unit and an appropriate ruler. (The ruler should clearly measure the appropriate unit. Students must be familiar with rulers.) The students are not permitted to cut out the rectangles. They may draw on them if they wish. The task is to use their rulers to determine, in any way that they can, which rectangle is larger or whether they are the same. They should use words, drawings, and numbers to explain their conclusions. Some suggested pairs are as follows:

4×10 and 5×8
5×10 and 7×7
4×6 and 5×5

The goal of the preceding activity is not necessarily to develop an area formula but to apply students' developing concepts of multiplication to the area of rectangles. Not all students will use a multiplicative approach. In order to count a single row of squares along one edge, and then multiply by the length of the other edge, the first row must be thought of as a unit that is then replicated to fill in the rectangle (Outhred, Mitchelmore, McPhail, & Gould, 2003). Many students will attempt to draw in all

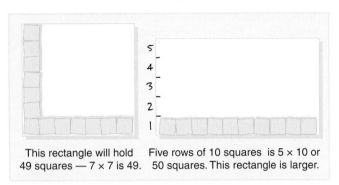

This rectangle will hold 49 squares — 7 × 7 is 49.

Five rows of 10 squares is 5 × 10 or 50 squares. This rectangle is larger.

FIGURE 20.11 Some students will be able to figure out how many squares fit along each side and know that multiplication will tell the total number.

the squares. However, some may use their rulers to determine the number of squares that will fit along each side and, from that, use multiplication to determine the total area. (See Figure 20.11.) By having students share their strategies, more students can be exposed to the use of multiplication in this context.

Using Grids

With the exception of computer drafting equipment, there really are no instruments designed for measuring area. However, grids of various types can be thought of as a kind of "area ruler." A grid of squares for area does exactly what a ruler does for length. It lays out the units for you. Square grids are available in the Blackline Masters. Note that triangular grids can also be used. Make transparencies of any grid paper. Have students place the grid over a region to be measured and count the units inside. An alternative method is to trace around a region on a paper grid.

Area and Perimeter

Area and perimeter (the distance around a region) are continually a source of confusion for students. Perhaps it is because both involve regions to be measured or because students are taught formulas for both concepts and tend to get formulas confused. Whatever the reason, expect that students even in the fifth and sixth grades will confuse these two ideas. Several good books are available that address this confusion. (See Rectanus, 1997; Shroyer & Fitzgerald, 1986.)

An interesting approach to alleviating this confusion is to contrast the two ideas as in the next activities.

activity 20.13

Fixed Perimeters

Give students a loop of string that is exactly 24 units long. (Use a nonstretchy string. Double the string and make a mark 1 foot from the loop. Tie a knot just beyond the marks so that the resulting

loop is 24 inches.) The task is to decide what different-sized rectangles can be made with a perimeter of 24 inches. Students may want to use a 1-inch grid to place their strings on. Each different rectangle can be recorded on grid paper with the area noted.

An alternative to the string loop is to simply use centimeter grid paper and ask students to find rectangles with a perimeter of 24.

activity 20.14

Fixed Areas

Provide students with 36 square tiles such as Color Tiles. The task is to see how many rectangles can be made with an area of 36—that is, using all 36 tiles to make filled-in rectangles, not just borders. Each new rectangle should be recorded by sketching the outline and the dimensions on grid paper. Centimeter or half-centimeter grids are good for recording. For each rectangle, students should determine and record the perimeter.

❚❚ *pause and reflect* ——————————

Before reading further, think about the two previous activities. For "Fixed Areas," will all of the perimeters be the same? If not, what can you say about the shapes with longer or shorter perimeters? For "Fixed Perimeters," will the areas remain the same? Why or why not?

——————————————————————————

You may have been surprised to find out that two rectangles having the same area do not necessarily have the same perimeter. Similarly, two shapes with the same perimeter do not always have the same area. And, of course, this fact is not restricted to rectangles.

As students do Activities 20.13 and 20.14, have them keep track of the new areas and perimeters they find in a table. Using the table, they can make graphs that illustrate the relationships between the side of the rectangle and both the area and perimeter. For the data found in the "Fixed Perimeters" activity, suggest that students plot the length against the width of the various rectangles. They should also plot the length against the area of the rectangles. The relationships in the graphs and tables are good early examples of functions. For the "Fixed Areas" activity, students will be able to find nine different rectangles, assuming that the 2 × 18 rectangle and the 18 × 2 rectangle are considered to be different. The graph of the length against the perimeter (Figure 20.12) shows that as the rectangle approaches a square shape, the perimeter gets smaller.

Even though the equation of the graph in Figure 20.12 may be too difficult for students to determine, they can plot the points and draw the curve. To get the formula,

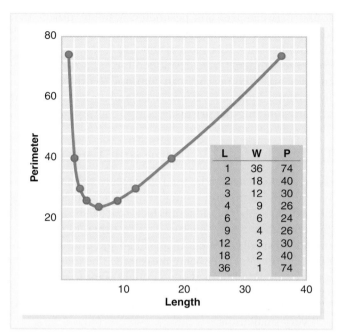

L	W	P
1	36	74
2	18	40
3	12	30
4	9	26
6	6	24
9	4	26
12	3	30
18	2	40
36	1	74

FIGURE 20.12 Rectangles are made using 36 square tiles. The graph shows how the length of each rectangle affects the perimeter. The smallest perimeter will always occur when the rectangle is the "fattest" or, in this case, a square. The graph can be drawn with no skills other than the ability to plot points.

note that $A = 36 = LW$. Therefore, $W = 36/L$. Substitute this in the formula $P = 2L + 2W$ and get $P = 2L + 2(36/L)$.

There is a relationship of sorts that is fairly interesting. If you have explored the last two activities, you may have noticed that, when the area is fixed, the shape with the smallest perimeter is a square. For a fixed perimeter, the rectangle with the largest area is also a square. If you allow for any shapes whatsoever, the shape with the smallest perimeter and a fixed area is a circle. That is, the "fatter" a shape, the smaller its perimeter and the skinnier a shape, the larger its perimeter, assuming the areas are the same. (A corresponding result is true in three dimensions. Replace perimeter with surface area and area with volume.)

Measuring Volume and Capacity

Volume and *capacity* are both terms for measures of the "size" of three-dimensional regions. The term *capacity* is generally used to refer to the amount that a container will hold. Standard units of capacity include quarts and gallons, liters and milliliters—units used for liquids as well as the containers that hold them. The term *volume* can be used to refer to the capacity of a container but is also used for the size of solid objects. Standard units of volume are expressed in terms of length units, such as cubic inches or cubic centimeters.

Comparison Activities

Comparing the volumes of solid objects is very difficult. For children at the primary level, it is appropriate to focus on capacity. A simple method of comparing capacity is to fill one container with something and then pour this amount into the comparison container. By third grade most students will understand the concept of "holds more" with reference to containers. The concept of volume for solid objects may not be as readily understood. Even if these ideas are understood, one or two comparison activities can be fun.

Young children should have lots of experiences directly comparing the capacities of different containers. Collect a large assortment of cans, small boxes, and plastic containers. Gather as many different shapes as possible. Also gather some plastic scoops. Cut a plastic 2-liter bottle in half, and use the top portion as a funnel. Rice or dried beans are good fillers to use. Sand and water are both considerably messier.

activity 20.15

Capacity Sort

Provide a collection of labeled containers, with one marked as the "target." The students' task is to sort the collection into those that hold more than, less than, or about the same amount as the target container. Provide a recording sheet on which each container is listed and a place to circle "holds more," "holds less," and "holds about the same." List the choices twice for each container. The first choice is to record a guess made by observation. The second is to record "what was found." Provide a filler (such as beans or rice), scoops, and funnels. Avoid explicit directions, but later discuss students' ideas for solving the task.

activity 20.16

Capacity Lineup

Given a series of five or six labeled containers of different sizes and shapes, the task is to order them from least volume to most. This can be quite challenging. Do not provide answers. Let students work in groups to come up with a solution and also explain how they arrived at it.

Do not expect students to be able to accurately predict which of two containers holds more. Even adults have difficulty making this judgment. Try the following task yourself as well as with students. Take two sheets of construction paper. Make a tube shape (cylinder) of one by taping the two long edges together. Make a shorter, fatter tube from the other sheet by taping the short edges together. When placed upright, which cylinder holds more, or do they have the same capacity?

This task is a good exploration for older students, and the results may be surprising. Before doing this with your class, survey them to see how many select which option. Most groups split roughly in thirds: short and fat, tall and skinny, same. Without using formulas, try using a filler such as Styrofoam packing peanuts or lima beans. Place the skinny cylinder inside the fat one. Fill the inside tube and then lift it up, allowing the filler to empty into the fat cylinder.

The apparent volumes of solid objects are sometimes misleading, and a method of comparison is also difficult. To compare volumes of solids such as a ball and an apple, some method of displacement must be used. Provide students with two or three containers that will each hold the objects to be compared and a filler such as rice or beans. With this equipment some students may be able to devise their own comparison method. One approach is to first fill a container completely and then pour it into an empty holding container. Next, place an object in the first container and fill it again to the top, using filler from the holding container. The volume of filler remaining is equal to the volume of the object. Mark the level of the leftover filler in the holding container before repeating the experiment with other objects. By comparing the level of the leftover filler for two or more objects, the volumes of the objects can be compared.

The following activity is a three-dimensional version of the "Fixed Areas" activity. Here the volume is fixed and students look for changes in surface area.

activity 20.17

Fixed Volume: Comparing Prisms
Give each pair of students a supply of multilink cubes or wooden cubes. Their task is, for a fixed number of cubes, to build different rectangular prisms and record the surface area for each prism formed. A good number of cubes to suggest is 64, since a minimal surface area will occur with a 4 × 4 × 4 cube. With 64 cubes a lot of prisms can be made. However, if you are short of cubes, other good choices are 24 or 36 cubes. Using the tables students construct, they should observe any patterns that occur. In particular, what happens to the surface area as the prism becomes less like a tall, skinny box and more like a cube?

The goal here is for students to realize that volume does not dictate surface area and to recognize the pattern between surface area and volume that is similar to the one

found between area and perimeter. Namely, prisms that are more cubelike have less surface area than prisms with the same volume that are less cubelike.

Once students have developed formulas for computing area and volume, they can continue to explore the relationships between surface area and volume without actually building the prisms.

Using Units of Volume and Capacity

Two types of units can be used to measure volume and capacity: solid units and containers. Solid units are things like wooden cubes or old tennis balls that can be used to fill the container being measured. The other type of unit model is a small container that is filled and poured repeatedly into the container being measured. The following are a few examples of units that you might want to collect.

- Plastic caps and liquid medicine cups are all good for very small units.
- Plastic jars and containers of almost any size can serve as a unit.
- Wooden cubic blocks or blocks of any shape can be units as long as you have a lot of the same size.
- Styrofoam packing peanuts can be used. Even though they do not pack perfectly, they still produce conceptual measures of volume.

Measuring activities for capacity are similar to those for length and area. Estimation of capacity is a lot more fun because it is much more difficult. Finding ways to measure containers such as a large cardboard carton in terms of a relatively small container-type unit can be an excellent challenge for groups of fourth or fifth graders. This can be done long before volume formulas are developed.

Volumes of rectangular boxes such as a shoebox can be determined by filling with any of the units mentioned earlier. However, here is an opportunity to prepare students for volume formulas in a manner similar to what was discussed for the area of rectangles. If students are given a box and sufficient cubes to fill it, they will most likely count the cubes rather than use any multiplicative structure. The following activity is similar to "Rectangle Comparison— Square Units" (Activity 20.12).

activity 20.18

Box Comparison—Cubic Units
Provide students with a pair of small boxes that you have folded up from poster board. (See Figure 20.13.) Use unit dimensions that match the blocks that you have. Students are given two boxes, exactly one block, and an appropriate ruler. (If you use 2-cm cubes, make a ruler with the unit equal to 2 centimeters.) The students' task is to decide which

box has the greater volume or if they have the same volume.

Here are some suggested box dimensions ($L \times W \times H$):

6 × 3 × 4   5 × 4 × 4   3 × 9 × 3   6 × 6 × 2   5 × 5 × 3

Students should use words, drawings, and numbers to explain their conclusions.

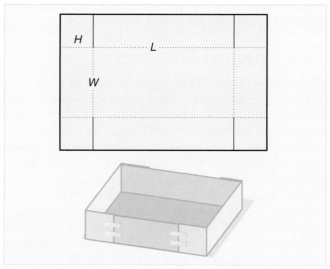

FIGURE 20.13 Make small boxes by starting with a rectangle and drawing a square on each corner as shown. Cut on the solid lines and fold the box up, wrapping the corner squares to the outside and tape or glue them to the sides as shown.

A useful hint in the last activity is to first figure out how many cubes will fit on the bottom of the box. Some students, although certainly not all, will discover a multiplicative rule for the volume. The boxes can be filled with cubes to confirm conclusions. No formulas should be used unless students can explain them. The development of a formula is not necessarily the goal of this activity.

Making and Using Measuring Cups

Instruments for measuring capacity are generally used for small amounts of liquids or pourable materials such as rice or water. These tools are commonly found in kitchens and laboratories. As with other instruments, if children make their own, they are likely to develop a better understanding of the units and the approach to the measuring process.

A measuring cup can be made by using a small container as a unit. Select a large, transparent container for the cup and a small container for a unit. Fill the unit with beans or rice, empty it into the large container, and make a mark indicating the level. Repeat until the cup is nearly full. If the unit is small, marks may only be necessary after every 5 units. Numbers need not be written on the container for every marking. Students frequently have difficulty reading scales in which not every mark is labeled or where each

mark represents more than one unit. This is an opportunity to help them understand how to interpret lines on a real measuring cup.

Students should use their measuring cups and compare the measures with those made by directly filling the container from the unit. The cup is likely to produce errors due to inaccurate markings. This is an opportunity to point out that measuring instruments themselves can be a source of error in measurement. The more accurately made the instrument, and the finer the calibration, the less the error from that source.

Measuring Weight and Mass

Weight is a measure of the pull or force of gravity on an object. *Mass* is the amount of matter in an object and a measure of the force needed to accelerate it. On the moon, where gravity is much less than on earth, an object has a smaller weight but the identical mass as on earth. For practical purposes, on the earth, the measures of mass and weight will be about the same. In this discussion, the terms *weight* and *mass* will be used interchangeably.

Making Comparisons

The most conceptual way to compare the weights of two objects is to hold one in each hand, extend your arms, and experience the relative downward pull on each—effectively communicating to a young child what "heavier" or "weighs more" means. This personal experience can then be transferred to one of two basic types of scales—balances and spring scales. Figure 20.14 shows a homemade version

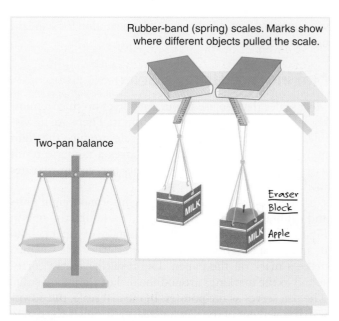

FIGURE 20.14 Two simple scales.

of each. Simple scales of each type are available through school-supply catalogs.

Children should first use their hands to estimate which of two objects is heavier. When they then place the objects in the two pans of a balance, the pan that goes down can be understood to hold the heavier object. Even a relatively simple balance will detect small differences. If two objects are placed one at a time in a spring scale, the heavier object pulls the pan down farther. Both balances and spring scales have real value in the classroom. (Technically, spring scales measure weight and balance scales measure mass. Why?)

With either scale, sorting and ordering tasks are possible with very young children. For older children, comparison activities for weight are not necessary. (Why?)

Using Units of Weight or Mass

Any collection of uniform objects with the same mass can serve as weight units. For very light objects, wooden or plastic cubes work well. Large metal washers found in hardware stores are effective for weighing slightly heavier objects. You will need to rely on standard weights to weigh things as heavy as a kilogram or more.

Weight cannot be measured directly. Either a two-pan balance or a spring scale must be used. In a balance scale, place an object in one pan and weights in the other until the two pans balance. In a spring scale, first place the object in and mark the position of the pan on a piece of paper taped behind the pan. Remove the object and place just enough weights in the pan to pull it down to the same level. Discuss how equal weights will pull the spring or rubber band with the same force.

While the concept of heavier and lighter is learned rather early, the notion of units of weight or mass is a bit more mysterious. At any grade level, even a brief experience with informal unit weights is good preparation for standard units and scales.

Making and Using a Scale

Most scales that we use in our daily lives produce a number when an object is placed on or in it. There are no visible unit weights. How does the scale produce the right number? By making a scale that gives a numeric result without recourse to units, students can see how scales work in principle.

By third grade students can use informal weight units and calibrate a simple rubber-band scale like the one in Figure 20.14. Mount the scale with a piece of paper behind it, and place weights in the pan. After every five weights, make a mark on the paper. The resulting marks correspond to the markings around the dial of a standard scale. The pan serves as the pointer. In the dial scale, the downward movement of the pan mechanically causes the dial to turn. The value of this activity is seeing how scales are made. Even digital readout scales are based on the same principle.

Measuring Time

Time is a bit different from the other attributes that are commonly measured in school because it cannot be seen or felt and because it is more difficult for students to comprehend units of time or how they are matched against a given time period or duration.

Comparison of Durations

Time can be thought of as the duration of an event from its beginning to its end. As with other attributes, for students to adequately understand the attribute of time, they should make comparisons of events that have different durations. If two events begin at the same time, the shorter duration will end first and the other last longer. For example, which top spins longer? However, this form of comparison focuses on the ending of the duration rather than the duration itself. In order to think of time as something that can be measured, it is helpful to compare two events that do not start at the same time. This requires that some form of measurement of time be used from the beginning.

An informal unit of time might be the duration of a pendulum swing made with a tennis ball suspended on a long string from the ceiling. The long string produces a slow swing and, thus, keeps the counting manageable. The steady drip of a water faucet into an empty container is another option. The level of the water is marked at the end of the period. When the marked container is emptied and used to time a second duration, the two markings can be compared. One advantage of the water drip method is that there are no units to count. Simple tasks that might be compared include the following:

- Stacking ten blocks one at a time and then removing them one at a time
- Printing the alphabet
- Walking slowly around a designated path
- Making a bar of 15 Unifix cubes

Only one student does each task, so that there is no competition or racing.

Clock Reading

The common instrument for measuring time is the clock. However, learning to tell time has little to do with time measurement and more to do with the skills of learning to read a dial-type instrument. Clock reading is a difficult skill to teach.

Some Difficulties

Young children's problems with clock reading may be due to the curriculum. Children are usually taught first to read clocks to the hour, then the half and quarter hours, and finally to 5- and 1-minute intervals. In the early stages of this sequence, children are shown clocks set exactly to the hour or half hour. Many children who can read a clock at 7:00 or 2:30 have no idea what time it is at 6:58 or 2:33.

Digital clocks permit students to read times easily but do not relate times very well. To know that a digital reading of 7:58 is nearly 8 o'clock, the child must know that there are 60 minutes in an hour, that 58 is close to 60, and that 2 minutes is not a very long time. These concepts have not been developed by most first-grade and many second-grade children. The analog clock (with hands) shows "close to" times without the need for understanding big numbers or even how many minutes in an hour.

Furthermore, the standard approach to clock reading ignores the distinctly different actions and functions of the two hands. The little hand indicates broad, approximate time (nearest hour), and the big hand indicates time (minutes) before or beyond an hour. When we look at the hour hand, we focus on where it is pointing. With the minute hand, the focus is on the distance that it has gone around the clock or the distance yet to go for the hand to get back to the top.

Suggested Approach

The following suggestions can help students understand and read analog clocks.

1. Begin with a one-handed clock. A clock with only an hour hand can be read with reasonable accuracy. Use lots of approximate language: "It's about 7 o'clock." "It's a little past 9 o'clock." "It's halfway between 2 o'clock and 3 o'clock" (see Figure 20.15).

2. Discuss what happens to the big hand as the little hand goes from one hour to the next. When the big hand is at 12, the hour hand is pointing exactly to a number. If the hour hand is about halfway between numbers, about where would the minute hand be? If the hour hand is a little past or before an hour (10 to 15 minutes), about where would the minute hand be?

3. Use two real clocks, one with only an hour hand and one with two hands. (Break off the minute hand from an old clock.) Cover the two-handed clock. Periodically during the day, direct attention to the one-handed clock. Discuss the time in approximate language. Have students predict where the minute hand should be. Uncover the other clock and check.

4. Teach time after the hour in 5-minute intervals. After step 3 has begun, count by fives going around the clock. Instead of predicting that the minute hand is pointing at the 4, encourage students to say it is about 20 minutes after the hour. As skills develop, suggest that students always look first at the little or hour hand to learn approximately what time it is and then focus on the minute hand for precision.

5. Predict the reading on a digital clock when shown an analog clock, and vice versa; set an analog clock when shown a digital clock. This can be done with both one-handed and two-handed clocks.

Related Concepts

Students also need to learn about seconds, minutes, and hours and to develop some concept of how long these units are. You can help by making a conscious effort to note the duration of short and long events during the day. Timing small events of $\frac{1}{2}$ minute to 2 minutes is fun and useful. TV shows and commercials are a good standard. Have students time familiar events in their daily lives: brushing teeth, eating dinner, riding to school, spending time in the reading group.

As students learn more about two-digit numbers, the time after the hours can also be related to the time left before the hour. This is helpful not only for telling time but for number sense as well. Note that in the sequence suggested, time after the hour is stressed almost exclusively. Time before or till the hour can come later.

The following activity can be used to help students in the second grade and beyond, even if the earlier sequence of one-handed clocks has not been followed.

activity 20.19

One-Handed Clocks
Prepare a page of clock faces (see the Blackline Masters). On each clock draw an hour hand. Include placements that are approximately a quarter past the hour, a quarter until the hour, half past the hour, and some that are close to but not on the hour. For each clock face, the students' task is to write the digital time and draw a minute hand on the clock where they think it would be.

"One-Handed Clocks" is a good assessment of students' clock reading. If students in the third grade or above are having difficulty reading clocks, working with a one-handed clock as suggested earlier will offer a different approach. ∎

"About 7 o'clock" "Halfway between 2 o'clock and 3 o'clock" "A little bit past 9 o'clock"

FIGURE 20.15 Approximate time with one-handed clocks.

Elapsed Time

Determining elapsed time is a skill required by most state curricula. It is also a skill that can be difficult for students, especially when the period of time includes noon. Students must know how many minutes are in an hour. In one national assessment, only 58 percent of eighth-grade students could tell how many hours are equal to 150 minutes (Jones & Arbaugh, 2004). If given the digital time or the time after the hour, students must be able to tell how many minutes to the next hour. This should certainly be a mental process for multiples of five minutes. Avoid having students use pencil and paper to subtract 25 from 60.

Figuring the time from, say, 8:15 A.M. to 11:45 A.M. is a multistep task regardless of how it is done. Keeping track of the intermediate steps is difficult, as is deciding what to do first. In this case you could count hours from 8:15 to 11:15 and add on 30 minutes. But then what do you do if the endpoints are 8:45 and 11:15? To propose a singular method or algorithm is not helpful.

Next is the issue of A.M. and P.M. The problem is due less to the fact that students don't understand what happens on the clock at noon and midnight, as it is that they now have trouble counting the intervals.

In the discussion so far, we have only addressed one form of the problem. There is also the task of finding the end time given the start time and elapsed time, or finding the start time given the end time and the elapsed time. In keeping with the spirit of problem solving and the use of models, consider the following.

As a general model for all of these elapsed time problems, suggest that students sketch a an empty time line (similar to the empty number line discussed in Chapter 13 for computation). Examples are shown in Figure 20.16. It is important not to be overly prescriptive in telling students how to use the time line since there are various alternatives. For example, in Figure 20.16(a), a student might count by full hours from 10:45 (11:45, 12:45, 1:45, 2:45, 3:45) and then subtract 15 minutes.

Measuring Angles

Angle measurement causes difficulty for two reasons: The attribute of angle size is often misunderstood, and protractors are introduced and used without understanding how they work.

Comparing Angles

The attribute of angle size might be called the "spread of the angle's rays." Angles are composed of two rays that are infinite in length with a common vertex. The only difference in their size is how widely or narrowly the two rays are spread apart.

(a) School began late today at 10:45 A.M. If you get out at 3:30, how much time will you be in school today?

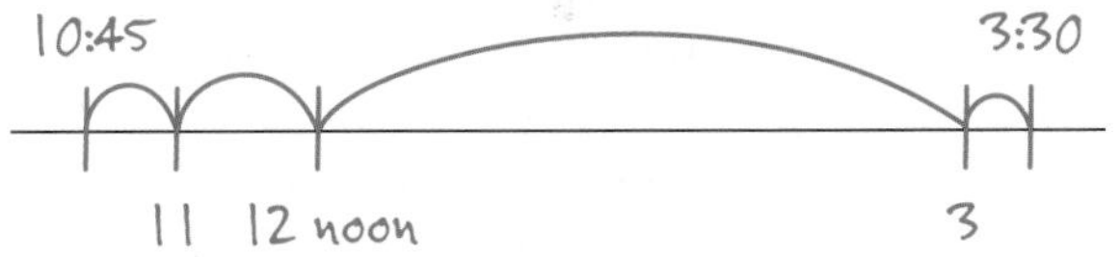

Four hours from 11 to 3 (1 and 3). Then 15 minutes in front and 30 minutes at the end—45 minutes. Three hours 45 minutes in all.

(b) The game begins at 11:30 A.M. If it lasts 2 hours and 15 minutes, when will it be over?

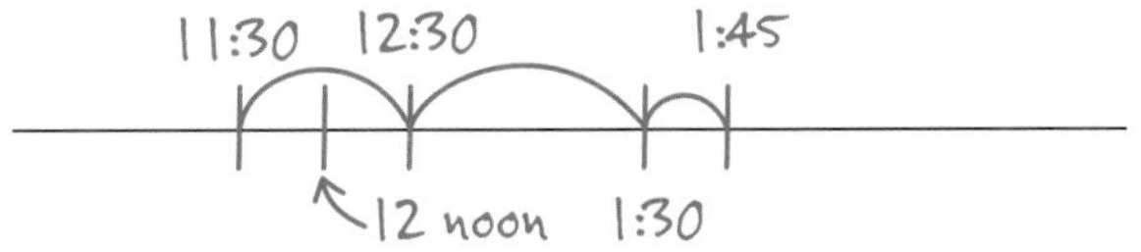

One hour after 11:30 is 12:30 and a second hour gets you to 1:30 and then 15 minutes more is 1:45. It's P.M. because it is after noon.

FIGURE 20.16 A simple sketch of a line can be useful in solving elapsed time problems. Students should not be told how to use the time line. For each of the examples here, the problem can be solved in a different manner. The value of the time line is in seeing where noon is and keeping track of the different parts of the interval.

Some authors have students think of how much one ray has rotated away from the other. Two rulers held together near the ends can be used to demonstrate this idea. As one ruler is rotated, the size of the angle is seen to get larger. However, when we see angles, the rays have already been spread—there is no rotation. Do you think of the angles in a triangle as one side being rotated away from the other?

To help children conceptualize the attribute of the spread of the rays, two angles can be directly compared by tracing one and placing it over the other. Be sure to have students compare angles with sides of different lengths. A wide angle with short sides may seem smaller than a narrow angle with long sides. This is a common misconception among students. As soon as students can tell the difference between a large angle and a small one, regardless of the length of the sides, you can move on to measuring angles.

Using Units of Angular Measure

A unit for measuring an angle must be an angle. Nothing else has the same attribute of spread that we want to measure. (Contrary to popular opinion, you do not need to use degrees to measure angles.)

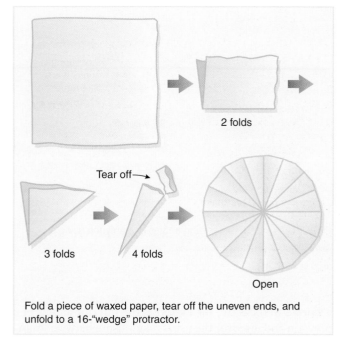

Fold a piece of waxed paper, tear off the uneven ends, and unfold to a 16-"wedge" protractor.

FIGURE 20.18 Making a waxed-paper protractor.

activity **20.20**

A Unit Angle

Give each student an index card or a small piece of tagboard. Have students draw a narrow angle on the tagboard using a straightedge and then cut it out. The resulting wedge can then be used as a unit of angular measure by counting the number that will fit in a given angle as shown in Figure 20.17. Pass out a worksheet with assorted angles on it, and have students use their unit to measure them. Because students made their own unit angles, the results will differ and can be discussed in terms of unit size.

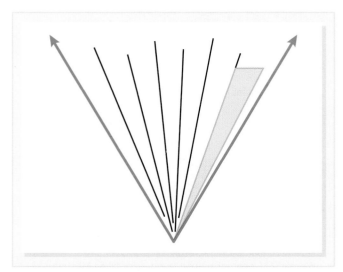

FIGURE 20.17 Using a small wedge cut from an index card as a unit angle, this angle measures about $7\frac{1}{2}$ wedges. Accuracy of measurement with these nonstandard angles is less important than the idea of how an angle is used to measure the size of another angle.

Activity 20.20 illustrates that measuring an angle is the same as measuring length or area; unit angles are used to fill or cover the spread of an angle just as unit lengths fill or cover a length. Once this concept is well understood, you can move on to the use of measuring instruments.

Making a Protractor

The protractor is one of the most poorly understood measuring instruments found in schools. Part of the difficulty arises because the units (degrees) are so very small. It would be physically impossible to cut out a single degree and use it in, say, Activity 20.20. Another problem is that there are no visible angles showing; there are only little marks around the outside edge of the protractor. Finally, the numbering that appears on most protractors runs both clockwise and counterclockwise along the marked edges. "Which num-

bers do I use?" By making a protractor with a large unit angle, all of these mysterious features can be understood. A careful comparison with a standard protractor will then permit that instrument to be used with understanding.

Tear off about a foot of ordinary waxed paper for each student. Have the students fold the paper in half and crease the fold tightly. Fold in half again so that the folded edges match. Repeat this two more times, each time bringing the folded edges together and creasing tightly. Cut or tear off the resulting wedge shape about 4 or 5 inches from the vertex and unfold. If done correctly, there will be 16 angles surrounding the center, as in Figure 20.18. This serves as an excellent protractor with a unit angle that is one-eighth of a straight angle. It is sufficiently transparent that it can be placed over an angle on paper, on the blackboard, or on the overhead projector to measure angles, as shown in Figure 20.19. Reasonable estimates of angle measures can be made with a waxed-paper protractor as small as the one in Figure 20.19. In that figure, one angle of a free-form polygon is measured for you. Use a waxed-paper protractor to measure the other four angles in this polygon as carefully as possible. Use fractional estimates. Your sum for all five interior angles should be very close to 24 wedges. There are two possible ways to get the measure of the angle indicated with the arrow. How would you measure that angle if your protractor was only a half circle instead of a full circle?

The waxed-paper protractor makes it quite clear how a protractor fits unit angles into an angle for measurement. When measuring angles, students can easily estimate halves, thirds, or fourths of a "wedge," a possible name for this informal unit angle. This is sufficiently

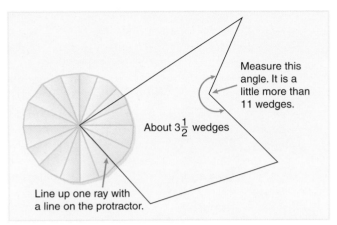

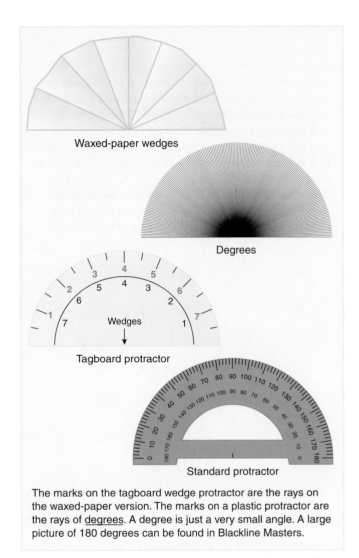

FIGURE 20.19 Measuring angles in a polygon using a waxed-paper protractor.

accurate to measure, for example, the interior angles of a polygon and discover the usual relationship between number of sides and sum of the interior angles. For a triangle, the sum is 8 wedges, recorded as 8^w. For a quadrilateral, the sum is 16^w. And in general, the sum for an n-sided polygon is $(n - 2) \times 8^w$. The superscript w is a forerunner of the degree symbol (°).

Figure 20.20 illustrates how a tagboard semicircle can be made into a protractor to measure angles in wedges. This tagboard version is a bit closer to a standard protractor, since the rays do not extend down to the vertex and the markings are numbered in two directions. The only difference between this protractor and a standard one is the size of the unit angle. The standard unit angle is the *degree*, which is simply a very small angle. A standard protractor is not very helpful in teaching the meaning of a degree. But an analogy between wedges and degrees and between these two protractors is a very effective approach (see the Blackline Masters).

Introducing Standard Units

As pointed out earlier, there are a number of reasons for teaching measurement using nonstandard units. However, measurement sense demands that children be familiar with the common measurement units and that they be able to make estimates in terms of these units and meaningfully interpret measures depicted with standard units.

Perhaps the biggest error in measurement instruction is the failure to recognize and separate two types of objectives: first, understanding the meaning and technique of measuring a particular attribute and, second, learning about the standard units commonly used to measure that attribute. These two objectives can be developed separately; when both objectives are attempted together, confusion is likely.

The marks on the tagboard wedge protractor are the rays on the waxed-paper version. The marks on a plastic protractor are the rays of <u>degrees</u>. A degree is just a very small angle. A large picture of 180 degrees can be found in Blackline Masters.

FIGURE 20.20 Comparisons of protractors and unit angles.

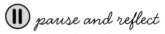 *pause and reflect* ——————

How many of the four reasons why you might use informal units can you recall? Which of these seem most important to you and why?

Reread the list of reasons for using informal units on p. 377. Not all reasons apply to every situation you may face. To avoid wasting time in your measurement program it is important to know why you are or are not using informal or nonstandard units. It is only when students are comfortable with measurement of an attribute that they can focus on things like cups and quarts or the number of inches in a foot or feet in a yard or have a feel for grams and kilograms.

Instructional Goals

Three broad goals relative to standard units of measure can be identified:

1. *Familiarity with the unit.* Familiarity means that students should have a basic idea of the size of commonly used units and what they measure. Without this familiarity, measurement sense is impossible. It is more important to know about how much 1 liter of water is or to be able to estimate a shelf as 5 feet long than to have the ability to measure either of these accurately.

2. *Ability to select an appropriate unit.* Related to unit familiarity is knowing what is a reasonable unit of measure in a given situation. The choice of an appropriate unit is also a matter of required precision. (Would you measure your lawn to purchase grass seed with the same precision as you would use in measuring a window to buy a pane of glass?) Students need practice in using common sense in the selection of appropriate standard units.

3. *Knowledge of a few important relationships between units.* The emphasis should be kept to those relationships that are commonly used, such as inches, feet, and yards or milliliters and liters. Tedious conversion exercises do little to enhance measurement sense. The goal of unit relationships is the least important of all measurement objectives.

Developing Unit Familiarity

Two types of activities can help develop familiarity with standard units: (1) comparisons that focus on a single unit and (2) activities that develop personal referents or benchmarks for single units or easy multiples of units.

activity **20.21**

About One Unit

Give students a model of a standard unit, and have them search for things that measure about the same as that one unit. For example, to develop familiarity with the meter, give students a piece of rope 1 meter long. Have them make lists of things that are about 1 meter. Keep separate lists for things that are a little less (or more) or twice as long (or half as long). Encourage students to find familiar items in their daily lives. In the case of lengths, be sure to include circular lengths. Later, students can try to predict if a given object is more than, less than, or close to 1 meter.

The same activity can be done with other unit lengths. Parents can be enlisted to help students find familiar distances that are about 1 mile or about 1 kilometer. Suggest in a letter that they check the distances around the neighborhood, to the school or shopping center, or along other frequently traveled paths.

For capacity units such as cup, quart, and liter, students need a container that holds or has a marking for a single unit. They should then find other containers at home and at school that hold about as much, more, and

less. Remember that the shapes of containers can be very deceptive when estimating their capacity.

For the standard weights of gram, kilogram, ounce, and pound, students can compare objects on a two-pan balance with single copies of these units. It may be more effective to work with 10 grams or 5 ounces. Students can be encouraged to bring in familiar objects from home to compare on the classroom scale.

Standard area units are in terms of lengths such as square inches or square feet, so familiarity with lengths is important. Familiarity with a single degree is not as important as some idea of 30, 45, 60, and 90 degrees.

The second approach to unit familiarity is to begin with very familiar items and use their measures as references or benchmarks. A doorway is a bit more than 2 meters high. A bag of flour is a good reference for 5 pounds. Your bedroom may be about 10 feet long. A paper clip weighs about a gram and is about 1 centimeter wide. A gallon of milk weighs a little less than 4 kilograms.

activity **20.22**

Familiar References

For each unit of measure you wish to focus on, have students make a list of at least five familiar things and measure those things using that unit. For lengths, encourage them to include long and short things; for weight, to find both light and heavy things; and so on. The measures should be rounded off to nice whole numbers. Discuss lists in class so that different ideas are shared.

Of special interest for length are benchmarks found on our bodies. These become quite familiar over time and can be used as approximate rulers in many situations. Even though young children grow quite rapidly, it is useful for them to know the approximate lengths that they carry around with them.

activity **20.23**

Personal Benchmarks

Measure your body. About how long is your foot, your stride, your hand span (stretched and with fingers together), the width of your finger, your arm span (finger to finger and finger to nose), the distance around your wrist and around your waist, and your height to waist, to shoulder, and to head? Perhaps you cannot remember all of these, but some may prove to be useful benchmarks, and some may be excellent models for single units. (The average child's fingernail width is about 1 cm, and most people can find a 10-cm length somewhere on their hands.)

To help remember these references, they must be used in activities in which lengths, volumes, and so on are compared to the benchmarks to estimate measurements.

Choosing Appropriate Units

Should the room be measured in feet or inches? Should the concrete blocks be weighed in grams or kilograms? The answers to questions such as these involve more than simply knowing how big the units are, although that is certainly required. Another consideration involves the need for precision. If you were measuring your wall in order to cut a piece of molding or woodwork to fit, you would need to measure it very precisely. The smallest unit would be an inch or a centimeter, and you would also use small fractional parts. But if you were determining how many 8-foot molding strips to buy, the nearest foot would probably be sufficient.

activity 20.24

Guess the Unit

Find examples of measurements of all types in newspapers, on signs, or in other everyday situations. Present the context and measures but without units. The task is to predict what units of measure were used. Have students discuss their choices.

Important Standard Units and Relationships

Both the customary and metric systems include many units that are rarely if ever used in everyday life. Table 20.2 lists the units that are most common in each system. Your state or local curriculum is the best guide to help you decide which units your students should learn. Remember that textbooks are written to satisfy the needs of many states, and so they may touch on units not in your curriculum. This excess information can be boring. Familiarity with the most popularly used units should be the principal focus of almost all instruction with standard units. (See Activities 20.21, 20.22, and 20.23.)

The relationships between units within either the metric or customary systems are conventions. As such, students must simply be told what the relationships are, and exercises must be devised to reinforce them. It can be argued that knowing about how much liquid makes a cup or a quart, or being able to pace off 3 yards—unit familiarity—is more important than knowing how many cups in a quart or inches in a yard. However, in the intermediate grades, knowing basic relationships becomes more important for testing purposes. Your curriculum should be your guide.

TABLE 20.2

Commonly Encountered Units of Measure

	Metric System	Customary System
Length	millimeter	inch
	centimeter	foot
	meter	yard
	kilometer	mile
Area	square centimeter	square inch
	square meter	square foot
		square yard
Volume	cubic centimeter	cubic inch
	cubic meter	cubic foot
		cubic yard
Capacity	milliliter	ounce*
	liter	cup
		quart
		gallon
Weight	gram	ounce*
	kilogram	pound
	metric ton	ton

*In the U.S. customary system, the term *ounce* refers to a weight or *avoirdupois* unit, 16 of which make a pound, and also a volume or capacity unit, 8 of which make a cup. Though the two units have the same name, they are not related.

The customary system has very few patterns or rules to guide students in converting units. Liquid or capacity units involve mostly multiples of 2, 4, and 8, but there is no consistent pattern. The relationships between inches, feet, and yards are quite common and can be the source of good word problems involving multiplication and division.

On the other hand, the metric system was designed systematically around powers of ten. An understanding of the role of the decimal point as indicating the units position is a powerful concept for making metric conversions. (See Chapter 18, Figure 18.6.) As students begin to appreciate the structure of decimal notation, the metric system can and should be developed with all seven places: three prefixes for smaller units (*deci-*, *centi-*, *milli-*) and three for larger units (*deka-*, *hecto-*, *kilo-*). Avoid mechanical rules such as "To change centimeters to meters, move the decimal point two places to the left." When the students themselves do not create conceptual, meaningful methods for conversions, arbitrary-sounding rules are bound to be misused and forgotten.

Exact conversions between the metric and the customary system should never be done. As long as we live in a country that uses two systems of measurement, "soft" or "friendly" conversions are useful. For example, a liter is a "gulp more" than a quart, and a meter is a bit longer than a yard. The same is true of familiar references. One hundred meters is about one football field plus one end zone, or about 110 yards.

In assessing students' understanding and familiarity with standard units, there is a danger of focusing on the traditional conversion tasks. Consider these two tasks:

1. 4 feet = _____ inches.
2. Estimate the length of this rope in feet and then in inches. How did you decide on your estimate?

Both tasks relate feet and inches. However, the second task requires students to have a familiarity with the units as well. With the estimation task we can observe whether the student uses the first estimate to make the second (understanding and *using* the feet–inches relationship) or rather makes two separate estimates. This task also allows us to see how an estimate is made; information that is unavailable in the narrower, more traditional task. ■

Estimating Measures

Measurement estimation is the process of using mental and visual information to measure or make comparisons without the use of measuring instruments. It is a practical skill. Almost every day, we make estimates of measures. Do I have enough sugar to make the cookies? Can you throw the ball 50 feet? Is this suitcase over the weight limit? About how long is the fence?

Besides its value outside the classroom, estimation in measurement activities helps students focus on the attribute being measured, adds intrinsic motivation, and helps develop familiarity with standard units. Therefore, measurement estimation both improves measurement instruction and develops a valuable life skill.

Techniques of Measurement Estimation

Just as for computational estimation, specific strategies exist for estimating measures. Four strategies can be taught specifically:

1. *Develop and use benchmarks or referents for important units.* This strategy was also mentioned as a way to develop familiarity with units. Research has shown that students who have both acquired mental benchmarks or reference points for measurements *and* have practiced using them in class activities are much better estimators than students who have not learned to use benchmarks (Joram, 2003). Referents should be things that are easily envisioned by the student. One example is a bed, as shown in Figure 20.21. Students should have a good referent for single units and also useful multiples of standard units.

2. *Use "chunking" when appropriate.* Figure 20.21 shows an example. It may be easier to estimate the shorter chunks along the wall than to estimate the whole length as one. The weight of a stack of books is easier if some estimate is given to an "average" book.

3. *Use subdivisions.* This is a similar strategy to chunking, with the chunks imposed on the object by the estimator. For example, if the wall length to be estimated has no useful chunks, it can be mentally divided in half and then in fourths or even eighths by repeated halving until a more manageable length is arrived at. Length, volume, and area measurements all lend themselves to this technique.

4. *Iterate a unit mentally or physically.* For length, area, and volume, it is sometimes easy to mark off single units visually. You might use your hands or make marks or folds

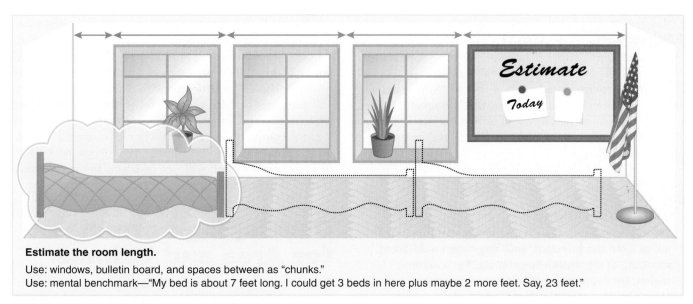

Estimate the room length.

Use: windows, bulletin board, and spaces between as "chunks."
Use: mental benchmark—"My bed is about 7 feet long. I could get 3 beds in here plus maybe 2 more feet. Say, 23 feet."

FIGURE 20.21 Estimating measures by chunking.

to keep track as you go. For length, it is especially useful to use a body measure as a unit and iterate with that. If you know, for example, that your stride is about $\frac{3}{4}$ meter, you can walk off a length and then multiply to get an estimate. Hand and finger widths are useful for shorter measures.

Tips for Teaching Estimation

Each of the four strategies just listed should be taught directly and discussed with students. Suggested benchmarks for useful measures can be developed and recorded on a class chart. Include items found at home. But the best approach to improving estimation skills is to have students do a lot of estimating. Keep the following tips in mind:

1. Help students learn strategies by having them use a specified approach. Later activities should permit students to choose whatever techniques they wish.

2. Periodically discuss how different students made their estimates. This will help students understand that there is no single right way to estimate and also remind them of different approaches that are useful.

3. Accept a range of estimates. Think in relative terms about what is a good estimate. Within 10 percent for length is quite good. Even 30 percent off may be reasonable for weights or volumes.

4. Sometimes have students give a range of measures that they believe includes the actual measure. This not only is a practical approach in real life but also helps focus on the approximate nature of estimation.

5. Make measurement estimation an ongoing activity. A daily measurement to estimate can be posted on the bulletin board. Students can turn in their estimates on paper and discuss them in a 5-minute period. Older students can even be given the task of making up the things to estimate, with a team assigned this task each week.

Measurement Estimation Activities

Estimation activities need not be elaborate. Any measurement activity can have an "estimate first" component. For more emphasis on the process of estimation itself, simply think of things that can be estimated, and have students estimate. Here are two suggestions.

activity **20.25**

Estimation Quickie
Select a single object such as a box, a watermelon, a jar, or even the principal. Each day, select a different attribute or dimension to estimate. For a watermelon, for example, students can estimate its length, girth, weight, volume, and surface area.

activity **20.26**

Estimation Scavenger Hunt
Conduct measurement scavenger hunts. Give teams a list of measurements, and have them find things that are close to having those measurements. Permit no measuring instruments. A list might include the following items:

> **A length of 3.5 m**
> **Something that weighs more than 1 kg but less than 2 kg**
> **A container that holds about 200 ml**

Let students suggest how to judge results in terms of accuracy.

Estimation of angle size is sometimes overlooked with too much attention given to measurement with protractors. Students should have a good understanding of 90 degrees, the angle formed by perpendicular lines. Since 45 degrees is a just half of a right angle, that is also an important reference, and students should be able to estimate an angle to be more, less, or about the same as 90 degrees and also 45 degrees. Angles greater than 90 degrees should then be compared to 135 degrees (90 + 45) and 180 degrees. Multiples of 30 degrees, or thirds of a right angle, are also useful for even better estimates.

 In the 3–5 grade band, the *Principles and Standards* document suggests several estimation strategies that are similar to those you have just read about. It points out that the techniques of estimation will vary with the situation at hand. The authors encourage teachers to have students share both their estimates and their strategies for estimation as well.

 Estimation tasks are a good way to assess students' understanding of both measurement and standard units. Use real objects and distances within the room as well as outside. Time and long distances should be estimated with comparisons to events and distances that are meaningful to the students. Have students explain how they arrived at their estimates to get a more complete picture of their measurement knowledge. Asking only for a numeric estimate can mask a lack of understanding and will not give you the information you need to provide appropriate remediation. ■

Developing Formulas for Area and Volume

Do not make the mistake of bypassing formula development with your students even if your state and local testing programs allow students access to formulas during the test. A conceptual development of formulas does much more than provide formulas for students. When students develop formulas, they gain conceptual understanding of the ideas and relationships involved and they are engaging in one of the real processes of doing mathematics. There is less likelihood that students will confuse area and perimeter or that they will select the incorrect formula on the test. General relationships are developed. For example, students can see how all area formulas are related to one idea: length of the base times the height. And students who understand where formulas come from do not see them as mysterious, tend to remember them, and are reinforced in the idea that mathematics makes sense. Rote use of formulas from a book offers none of these advantages.

Common Difficulties

The results of National Assessment of Educational Progress (NAEP) testing indicate clearly that students do not have a very good understanding of formulas. For example, in the sixth NAEP, only 19 percent of fourth-grade students and 65 percent of eighth-grade students were able to give the area of a carpet 9 feet long and 6 feet wide (Kenney & Kouba, 1997). A common error is to confuse formulas for area and perimeter. Performances such as this are largely due to an overemphasis on formulas with little or no conceptual background. Simply telling students how a formula was derived does not work.

The tasks in Figure 20.22 cannot be solved with simple formulas; they require an understanding of concepts and how formulas work. "Length times width" is not a definition of area.

Another common error when students use formulas comes from failure to conceptualize the meaning of height and base in both two- and three-dimensional geometric figures. The shapes in Figure 20.23 each have a slanted side and a height given. Students tend to confuse these two. Any side or flat surface of a figure can be called a *base* of the figure. For each base that a figure has, there is a cor-

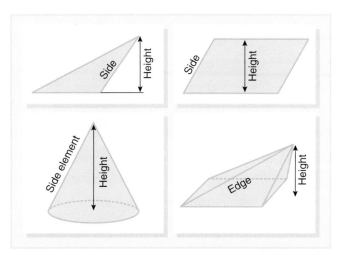

FIGURE 20.23 Heights of figures are not always measured along an edge or a surface.

responding height. If the figure were to slide into a room on a selected base, the *height* would be the height of the shortest door it could pass through without bending over—that is, the perpendicular distance to the base. Students have a lot of early experiences with the length-times-width formula for rectangles, in which the height is exactly the same as the length of a side. Perhaps this is the source of the confusion. Before formulas involving heights are discussed, students should be able to identify where a height could be measured for any base that a figure has.

The Area of Rectangles, Parallelograms, Triangles, and Trapezoids

The formula for the area of a rectangle is one of the first that is developed and is usually given as $A = L \times W$, "area equals length times width." Looking forward to other area formulas, an equivalent but more unifying idea might be $A = b \times h$, "area equals *base* times *height*." The base-times-height formulation can be generalized to all parallelograms (not just rectangles) and is useful in developing the area formulas for triangles and trapezoids. Furthermore, the same approach can be extended to three dimensions, where volumes of cylinders are given in terms of the *area of the base* times the height. Base times height, then, helps connect a large family of formulas that otherwise must be mastered independently.

Rectangles

Before thinking about formulas for rectangles, it is important that students have a clear understanding of area. Research suggests, however, that it is a significant leap for students to move from counting squares inside of a rectangle to a conceptual development of a formula. Battista (2003) found that students often try to fill in empty

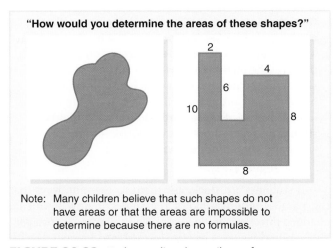

"How would you determine the areas of these shapes?"

2
4
6
10
8
8

Note: Many children believe that such shapes do not have areas or that the areas are impossible to determine because there are no formulas.

FIGURE 20.22 Understanding the attribute of area.

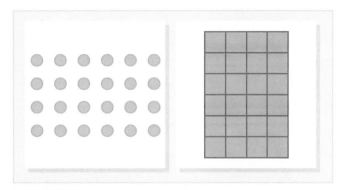

FIGURE 20.24 In preparation for the area formula, review the concept of multiplication as applied to arrays. One factor tells us how many in a row or column. The other factor tells how many rows or columns.

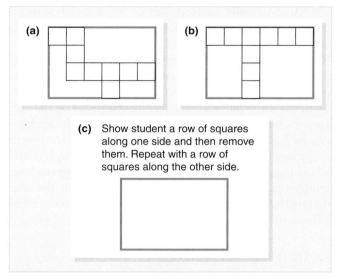

(c) Show student a row of squares along one side and then remove them. Repeat with a row of squares along the other side.

FIGURE 20.25 Three different activities in sequential order for determining area. Students in each case are to tell how many squares will fill the rectangles. (Based on suggestions by Battista, 2003.)

rectangles with drawings of squares and then count the result one square at a time.

An important concept to review is the meaning of multiplication as seen in arrays. Show students rows and columns of objects or of squares, as in Figure 20.24, and discuss why multiplication tells the total amount. You are not multiplying squares by squares or dots by dots. Rather, we count either a single row or column and then find out how many columns or rows there are in all. This is the same concept that they will need to apply to the area of a rectangle. When we multiply a length times a width, we are not multiplying "squares times squares." Rather, the *length* of one side indicates how many squares will fit on that side. If this set of squares is taken as a unit, then the *length* of the other side (not a number of squares) will tell how many of these *rows of squares* can fit in the rectangle.

A good activity to begin your exploration of area formulas is Activity 20.12, "Rectangle Comparison—Square Units" (p. 385). Students who are drawing in all of the squares and counting them have not thought about a row of squares as a single row that can be replicated. Related tasks, based on the work of Battista (2003), are shown in Figure 20.25.

As your students discuss their methods for determining the area of rectangles in these activities, listen for and highlight the thinking of students who talk about a row or column of squares as a group. Challenge students to find the area of a rectangle given only the rectangle and a ruler. However, require that they use words and pictures to explain their results.

When your students have formulated an approach to area based on the idea of a row of squares (determined by the length of a side) multiplied by the number of these rows that will fit the rectangle (determined by the length of the other side), it is time to consolidate these ideas. Explain to students that you like the idea of measuring one side to tell how many squares will fit in a row along that side. You would like them to call or think of this side as the

base of the rectangle even though some people call it the length or the width. Then the other side you can call the *height*. But which side is the base? Be sure that students conclude that either side could be the base. If you use the formula $A = b \times h$, then the same area will result using either side as the base.

From Rectangles to Other Parallelograms

Once students understand the base-times-height formula for rectangles, the next challenge is to determine the areas of parallelograms. Do not provide a formula or other explanation. Rather, try the following activity, which again asks students to devise their own formula.

activity **20.27**

Area of a Parallelogram

Give students two or three parallelograms either drawn on grid paper or, for a slightly harder challenge, drawn on plain paper. If drawn on plain paper, provide all dimensions—the lengths of all four sides and the height. Their task is to use what they have learned about the area of rectangles to determine the area of these parallelograms. Students should find a method that will work for any parallelogram, even if not drawn on a grid.

If students are stuck, ask them to examine ways that the parallelogram is like a rectangle or how it can be changed into a rectangle. As shown in Figure 20.26, a parallelogram can always be transformed into a rectangle with the same base, the same height, and the same area. Thus,

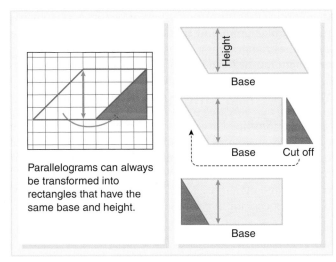

FIGURE 20.26 Area of a parallelogram.

the formula for the area of a parallelogram is exactly the same as for a rectangle: base times height.

From Parallelograms to Triangles

It is very important for students to understand the parallelogram formula before exploring triangle area. With that background, the area of a triangle is relatively simple. Again, use a problem-based approach as in the next activity.

activity 20.28

Area of a Triangle

Provide students with at least two triangles drawn on grid paper. Avoid right triangles because they are an easier special case. The challenge for students is to use what they have learned about the area of parallelograms to find the area of each of the triangles and to develop a method that will work for any triangle. They should be sure that their method works for all the triangles given to them as well as at least one more that they draw.

There are several hints that you might offer if students are stuck. *Can you find a parallelogram that is somehow related to your triangle?* If this is not sufficient, suggest that they fold a piece of paper in half, draw a triangle on the folded paper, and cut it out, making two identical copies. They should use the copies to find out how a triangle is related to a parallelogram.

As shown in Figure 20.27, two congruent triangles can always be arranged to form a parallelogram with the same base and the same height as the triangle. The area of the triangle will, therefore, be one-half as much as the parallelogram. Have students further explore all three possible parallelograms, one for each triangle side serving as base. Will the computed areas always be the same?

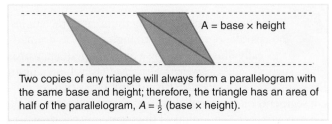

Two copies of any triangle will always form a parallelogram with the same base and height; therefore, the triangle has an area of half of the parallelogram, $A = \frac{1}{2}$ (base × height).

FIGURE 20.27 Two triangles always make a parallelogram.

From Parallelograms to Trapezoids

After developing formulas for parallelograms and triangles, your students may be interested in tackling trapezoids without any further assistance. (See Figure 4.1, p. 41, for an example of a completely open challenge.) There are at least ten different methods of arriving at a formula for trapezoids, each related to the area of parallelograms or triangles. One of the nicest methods uses the same general approach that was used for triangles. Suggest that students try working with two trapezoids that are identical, just as they did with triangles. Figure 20.28 shows how this method results in the formula. Now, not only are all of these formulas connected, but similar methods were used to develop them as well.

Here are a few hints, each leading to a different approach to finding the area of a trapezoid.

- Make a parallelogram inside the given trapezoid using three of the sides.
- Make a parallelogram using three sides that surround the trapezoid.
- Draw a diagonal forming two triangles.
- Draw a line through the midpoints of the nonparallel sides. The length of that line is the average of the lengths of the two parallel sides.
- Draw a rectangle inside the trapezoid leaving two triangles and then put those two triangles together.

❙❙ *pause and reflect*

Do you think that students should learn special formulas for the area of a square? Why or why not? Do you think students need formulas for the perimeters of squares and rectangles?

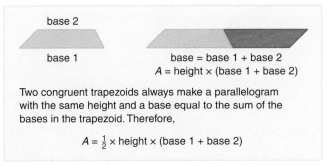

base = base 1 + base 2
$A = \text{height} \times (\text{base 1} + \text{base 2})$

Two congruent trapezoids always make a parallelogram with the same height and a base equal to the sum of the bases in the trapezoid. Therefore,

$$A = \frac{1}{2} \times \text{height} \times (\text{base 1} + \text{base 2})$$

FIGURE 20.28 Two trapezoids always form a parallelogram.

The relationship among the areas of rectangles, parallelograms, and triangles can be dramatically illustrated using a dynamic geometry program such as *The Geometer's Sketchpad* (Key Curriculum Press) or *Geometry Inventor* (Riverdeep). Draw two congruent segments on two parallel lines, as shown in Figure 20.29. Then connect the endpoints of the segments to form a parallelogram and two triangles. A segment between the parallel lines and perpendicular to each indicates the height. Either of the two line segments can be dragged left or right to "sheer" the parallelogram and triangle but without changing the base or height. All area measures remain fixed! ■

Circle Formulas

The relationship between the *circumference* of a circle (the distance around or the perimeter) and the length of the *diameter* (a line through the center joining two points on the circle) is one of the most interesting that children can discover. The circumference of every circle is about 3.14 times as long as the diameter. The exact ratio is an irrational number close to 3.14 and is represented by the Greek letter π. So $\pi = C/D$, the circumference divided by the diameter. In a slightly different form, $C = \pi D$. Half the diameter is the radius (r), so the same equation can be written $C = 2\pi r$. (Chapter 21 will discuss in detail the concept of π and how students can discover this important ratio.)

Figure 20.30 presents an argument for the area formula $A = \pi r^2$. This development is one commonly found in textbooks.

Regardless of the approach you use to develop the area formula, students should be challenged to figure it out on their own. For example, show students how to arrange 8 or 12 sectors of a circle into an approximate parallelogram. Their task should be to use this as a hint toward development of an area formula for the circle. You may need to help

them notice that the arrangement of sectors is an approximate parallelogram and that the smaller the sectors, the closer the arrangement gets to a rectangle. But the complete argument for the formula should come from your students.

Volumes of Common Solid Shapes

The relationships between the formulas for volume are completely analogous to those for area. As you read, notice the similarities between rectangles and prisms, between parallelograms and "sheered" (oblique) prisms, and between triangles and pyramids. Not only are the formulas related, but the process for development of the formulas is similar.

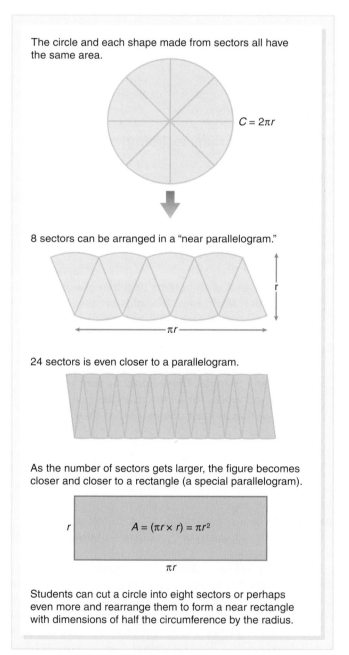

The circle and each shape made from sectors all have the same area.

$C = 2\pi r$

8 sectors can be arranged in a "near parallelogram."

r

πr

24 sectors is even closer to a parallelogram.

As the number of sectors gets larger, the figure becomes closer and closer to a rectangle (a special parallelogram).

r

$A = (\pi r \times r) = \pi r^2$

πr

Students can cut a circle into eight sectors or perhaps even more and rearrange them to form a near rectangle with dimensions of half the circumference by the radius.

FIGURE 20.30 Development of the circle area formula.

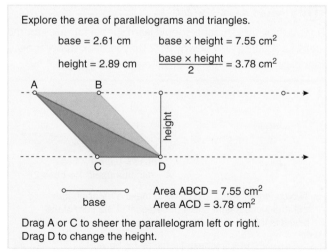

Explore the area of parallelograms and triangles.

base = 2.61 cm base × height = 7.55 cm²

height = 2.89 cm $\dfrac{\text{base} \times \text{height}}{2}$ = 3.78 cm²

A B

height

C D

base

Area ABCD = 7.55 cm²
Area ACD = 3.78 cm²

Drag A or C to sheer the parallelogram left or right.
Drag D to change the height.

FIGURE 20.29 Dynamic geometry software shows that figures with the same base and height maintain the same area.

Volumes of Cylinders

A *cylinder* is a solid with two congruent parallel bases and sides with parallel elements that join corresponding points on the bases. There are several special classes of cylinders, including *prisms* (with polygons for bases), *right prisms*, *rectangular prisms*, and *cubes* (see Chapter 21). Interestingly, all of these solids have the same volume formula, and that one formula is analogous to the area formula for parallelograms.

activity 20.29

Volume of Boxes

Provide students with some cardboard shoe boxes or similar cardboard boxes, a few cubes, and a ruler. As was done with rectangles, the task is to determine how many cubes will fit inside the box. Most likely your boxes will not have whole-number dimensions, so tell students to ignore any fractional parts of cubes. Although they may have seen or used a volume formula before, for this task they may not rely on a formula. Rather, they must come up with a method or formula that they can explain or justify. If a hint is required, suggest that they begin by finding out how many cubes will fit on the bottom of the box.

The development of the volume formula from this box exploration is exactly parallel to the development of the formula for the area of a rectangle. Figure 20.31 illustrates how this development is like that for area. The *area* of the base (instead of *length* of the base for rectangles) determines how many *cubes* can be placed on the base forming a single unit—a layer of cubes (instead of *squares*). The *height* of the box then determines how many of these *layers* will fit in the box just as the height of the rectangle determined how many *rows* of squares would fill the rectangle.

Recall that a parallelogram can be thought of as a "sheered" rectangle, as was illustrated with the dynamic geometry software (Figure 20.29). Show students a stack of three or four decks of playing cards (or a stack of books

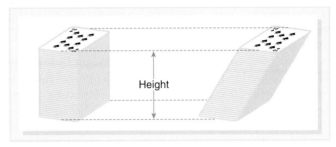

FIGURE 20.32 Two cylinders with the same base and height have the same volume.

or paper). When stacked straight, they form a rectangular solid. The volume, as just discussed, is $V = A \times h$, with A equal to the area of one card. Now if the stack is sheered or slanted to one side as shown in Figure 20.32, what will the volume of this new figure be? Students should be able to argue that this figure has the same volume (and same volume formula) as the original stack.

What if the cards in this activity were some other shape? If they were circular, the volume would still be the area of the base times the height; if they were triangular, still the same. The conclusion is that the volume of *any* cylinder is equal to the *area of the base* times the *height*.

Volumes of Cones and Pyramids

Recall that when parallelograms and triangles have the same base and height, the areas are in a 2-to-1 relationship. Interestingly, the relationship between the volumes of cylinders and cones with the same base and height is 3 to 1. That is, *area* is to *two*-dimensional figures what *volume* is to *three*-dimensional figures. Furthermore, triangles are to parallelograms as cones are to cylinders.

To investigate this relationship use plastic models of these related shapes such as Power Solids. Have students estimate the number of times the pyramid will fit into the prism. Then have them test their prediction by filling the pyramid with water or rice and emptying it into the prism. They will discover that exactly three pyramids will fill a prism with the same base and height. (See Figure 20.33.)

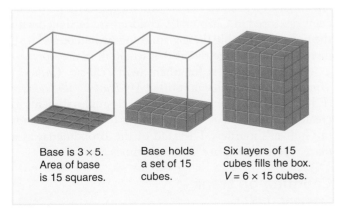

Base is 3 × 5.
Area of base
is 15 squares.

Base holds
a set of 15
cubes.

Six layers of 15
cubes fills the box.
$V = 6 \times 15$ cubes.

FIGURE 20.31 Volume of a right prism: *Area* of the base × height.

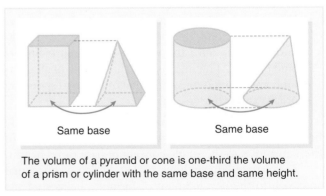

Same base   Same base

The volume of a pyramid or cone is one-third the volume of a prism or cylinder with the same base and same height.

FIGURE 20.33 Comparing volumes of prisms to pyramids and cones to cylinders.

The volume of a cone or pyramid is exactly one-third the volume of the corresponding cylinder with the same base and height.

Using the same idea of base times height, it is possible to explore the surface area of a sphere (4 times the area of a circle with the same radius) and the volume of a sphere ($\frac{1}{3}$ times the surface area times the radius). That is, the surface area of a sphere is $4\pi r^2$ and the volume is $\frac{1}{3}(4\pi r^2)r$ or $\frac{4}{3}\pi r^3$. A description of this exploration is found in Van de Walle & Lovin (2006).

Reviewing the Formulas

Notice how all of the formulas that we have discussed tie together:

- Parallelograms are really just rectangles that have been shifted to make the sides slanted. The area for both is $B \times h$ or *length of the base × height*.
- Triangles turn out to simply be half of a parallelogram with the same base and height. The area of a triangle is $\frac{1}{2}(B \times h)$.
- Trapezoids are also related to parallelograms and triangles. For example, all trapezoids can be made into two triangles. The heights of each are the same. Use B for the longer parallel side and b for the shorter, and the area of the trapezoid is $\frac{1}{2}(B \times h) + \frac{1}{2}(b \times h)$. (Although this can be simplified, this version of the formula is one easy way to remember it.)
- The area of a circle is found by using smaller and smaller sectors so that it can be rearranged into a parallelogram. The base of the near-parallelogram is half of the circumference (πr) and the height is the radius. So, $B \times h$ becomes ($\pi r) \times r$ or πr^2.

And then we moved to three dimensions and found very similar results.

- All cylinders (i.e., right prisms or boxes, slanted prisms, circular cylinders, and, in fact, cylinders with any shaped base) have the same volume formula. It is nearly identical to the formula for parallelograms: $B \times h$ where B represents the *area* of the base instead of the *length* of the base.
- Whereas triangles are *one-half* the area of related parallelograms, cones (including the special case of pyramids) are *one-third* the volume of related cylinders (and prisms). That means that the volume of all pyramids and cones is one-third that of the corresponding prisms and cylinders: $\frac{1}{3}(B \times h)$.

The connectedness of mathematical ideas can hardly be better illustrated than with the connections of all of these formulas to the single concept of base times height.

As illustrated throughout this last section, a conceptual approach to the development of formulas helps students understand these tools as meaningful yet efficient ways to measure different attributes of objects around us. After having developed formulas in meaningful ways, students are no longer required to memorize them as isolated pieces of mathematical facts, but they can derive formulas from what they already know. Mathematics does make sense!

 The *Standards* points out that the development of area and volume formulas is a "particularly accessible and rich domain" for investigation at the sixth- to eighth-grade level (p. 244) and that middle school students should connect their study of length, area, and volume measures to the study of similarity and proportions. This includes examining the ratios of measures of similar figures and looking for relationships.

Literature Connections

Various fantasy books about giants, or strange lands, and unusual occurrences prompt comparisons of measures with our everyday world. There are also a large number of "concept books" for measurement, books that are designed to help children explore interesting aspects of measurement. The selections here are offered as examples.

How Big Is a Foot?
Myller, 1990

The story in this concept book is very attractive to younger children. The king measures his queen (crown included) using his feet and orders a bed made that is 6 feet long and 3 feet wide. The chief carpenter's apprentice, who is very small, makes the bed according to his own feet. The problems give rise to the need for standard units. But children are also motivated to use their own measuring methods for different purposes. Lubinski and Thiessen (1996) show how students create a "ruler" with footprints linked together and share activities conducted in a first-grade class.

Jim and the Beanstalk
Briggs, 1970

A variation on the classic tale of *Jack and the Beanstalk*, Jim helps the giant, who is growing quite old. Jim makes him a giant-sized pair of glasses and eventually measures the giant for false teeth and a wig. As with the books for ratio concepts discussed in Chapter 19, children are intrigued with the notion of how big these giant things would be and with discussing other large things that would fit in the story.

A similar story is Jonathan Swift's classic, *Gulliver's Travels*. A fourth-grade unit titled *My Travels with Gulliver* (Education Development Center, 1991) guides students to create drawings and use measurements to explore the lands in Gulliver's journey. The land of the Brobdingnag is a place where objects are about ten times normal size.

Counting on Frank
Clement, 1991

The dog, Frank, and his young master, the narrator of the story, engage in a series of estimations of everyday things:

the length of a line that can be drawn by the average ball-point pen, the number of Franks that would fit in the bedroom, or the time it would take to fill the entire bathroom with water if the tap were left on. These fanciful ideas and hilarious drawings easily motivate students to make their own estimates. Younger children may not be able to go further than a guess of one of their own ideas. By third grade, students can investigate how well their estimate agrees with reality. This book can lead children to investigate length, weight, volume, area, and time and connect each to their personal world. "If I filled my room with stuffed duffel bags, I estimate it would take 3000 bags. Altogether these bags would weigh over 15,000 pounds. If the duffel bags were each as big as my dad's car, they would take a space as big as the football stadium." Ideas such as this are fun to imagine but can also be tested against reality through measurement and calculations. One idea is to have class members contribute to their very own Frank book and provide an appendix that explains their estimates.

Inchworm and a Half
Pinczes, 2001

In this wonderfully illustrated book, an inchworm happily goes about measuring various garden vegetables. One day

the measurement does not come out even, and the worm is very upset. Fortunately, a smaller worm drops onto the vegetable and measures a one-half unit. Eventually, other fraction-measuring worms appear. The story provides a great connection between fractions and measurement concepts, especially for the introduction of fractional units in measurement. Moyer and Mailley (2004) describe a nice series of activities inspired by the book.

8,000 Stones
Wolkstein, 1972

This is an interesting folktale concerning the Supreme Governor of China, who wishes to find a method of weighing an elephant that has been received as a gift. The emperor's son solves the problem by putting the elephant in a boat and noticing the water level on the side. The amount of weight to produce the same effect is that of the elephant. This is a wonderful introduction to indirect methods of measurement for middle grade students. Not only can the same weighing method be explored, but students can research other measurements and find out how they are made. For example, how do we measure temperature with a mercury thermometer, and how is it done with a bimetal thermometer, the kind that causes a dial to rotate? ■

Reflections on Chapter 20

Writing to Learn

1. Explain what it means to measure something. Does your explanation work equally well for length, area, weight, volume, and time?
2. A general instructional plan for measurement has three steps. Explain how the type of activity to use at each step accomplishes the instructional goal.
3. Four reasons were offered for using informal units instead of standard units in instructional activities. Which of these seem most important to you, and why?
4. For each of the following attributes, describe a comparison activity, one or two possible informal units, and a group activity that includes an estimation component:
   a. Length   **d.** Weight
   b. Area   **e.** Capacity
   c. Volume   **f.** Time
5. With a straightedge, draw a triangle, a quadrilateral, and a five-sided figure. Make each about as large as a sheet of notebook paper. Make a waxed-paper protractor, and measure each interior angle. Did the sum of the angles for each figure come close to what is predicted?
6. What is a degree? How would you help children learn what a degree is?

7. What do students need to know about standard units? Of these, which is the most and least important?
8. Develop in a connected way the area formulas for rectangles, parallelograms, triangles, and trapezoids. Draw pictures and provide explanations.
9. Explain how the volume formula for a right rectangular prism can be developed in an analogous manner to the area formula for a rectangle.
10. Explain how the area of a circle can be determined using the basic formula for the area of a parallelogram. (If you have a set of fraction "pie pieces," these can be used as sectors of a circle.)
11. Describe the differences between the typical approach for teaching clock reading and the one-handed approach discussed in this chapter.

For Discussion and Exploration

1. Make your own measuring instrument for an informal unit of measure. Use your instrument to measure, and then make the same measurement directly with a unit model. What are the values and limitations of each method? Can you see the importance of having children do this both ways?

2. Frequently, a textbook chapter on measurement will cover length, area, volume, and capacity with both metric and customary units. This means a very light treatment of each. An alternative for the publisher is to focus on one area of measurement in each grade and risk not matching the curriculum guides for many states and districts. Get a teacher's edition of a basal textbook for any grade level, and look at the chapters on measurement. How well does the book cover measurement ideas? How would you modify or expand on the lessons found there?

Recommendations for Further Reading

Clements, D. H. (Ed.). (2003). *Learning and teaching measurement: 2003 Yearbook*. Reston, VA: National Council of Teachers of Mathematics.

A valuable source of information, this book brings a practical and a research perspective on measurement that expands and provides additional details concerning the ideas in this chapter. Grant and Kline discuss beginning measurement in the K–2 classroom. Clark and his colleagues from Australia offer assessment strategies along with a framework for teaching measurement. Joram details the importance of benchmarks in estimation. The two chapters that discuss research related to teaching area and volume helped to shape the ideas in this chapter. It is important to read these chapters in full. Schifter and Szymszek offer teachers' perspective as well as valuable tasks. And there is more.

Nitabach, E., & Lehrer, R. (1996). Developing spatial sense through area measurement. *Teaching Children Mathematics, 2,* 473–476.

This is a superb article. The authors describe six principles of measurement, giving special attention to area measurement. They then proceed to describe some nice activities with first and second graders and the children's responses. Too often we take simple measurement ideas for granted. This article provides a research-based view of reality.

National Council of Teachers of Mathematics. (2004). Measurement [Focus Issue]. *Mathematics Teaching in the Middle School, 9.*

Often the subject of measurement is skipped over in the upper grades. This focus issue of NCTM's middle school journal is full of great information for teachers at that level. Of particular note are several articles that involve scale drawings or other aspects of proportional reasoning, which is a great way to integrate measurement into the curriculum. In addition, there is a full article addressing curricular integration. This journal would be a good addition to your reference materials.

Pumala, V. A., & Klabunde, D. A. (2005). Learning measurement through practice. *Mathematics Teaching in the Middle School, 10,* 452–460.

A mathematics teacher and a science teacher, each lamenting that their students knew too little about measurement, collaborated on a series of six activities to help their students both learn about measurement and learn by doing. Included in the article are descriptions of the activities and detailed rubrics along with samples of student work. These teachers gave a lot of thought to this instructional sequence and you can benefit from their work. A superb article!

Online Resources

Suggested Applets and Web Links

Clockwise
www.shodor.org/interactive/activities/clock2/index.htm
A clock face is shown and the user enters the digital time. Three difficulty levels.

Cubes
http://illuminations.nctm.org/tools/tool_detail.aspx?id=6
An excellent interactive applet that illustrates the volume of a rectangular prism (box). Units of single cubes, rows of cubes, or layers of cubes can be used to fill a prism.

Geoboard
http://nlvm.usu.edu/en/nav/frames_asid_279_g_4_t_3.html
This electronic geoboard measures the area and perimeter of any shape made. What is nice is that the measures are not shown until the user clicks the Measure button. Students can be challenged to make shapes with specified areas and/or perimeters.

How High
http://nlvm.usu.edu/en/nav/frames_asid_275_g_3_t_4.html
Two cylinders are shown along with the area of the base shown as a grid of squares. One cylinder is filled to a specified height. The task is to determine the height of this same liquid when it is poured into the second container.

Image Tool
www.shodor.org/interactive/activities/imagetool/index.html
The user can measure angles, distances, and areas in several different images (choices include maps, aerial photos, and others). A scale feature allows the user to set the scale used for measuring distances and areas. Unique!

Match Clocks
http://nlvm.usu.edu/en/nav/frames_asid_317_g_2_t_4.html
The user matches either a digital time to an analog or the reverse. Problems are posed randomly and there are no controls for difficulty.

Perimeter Explorer
www.shodor.org/interactive/activities/permarea/index.html
The user sets a fixed number of square units and the applet randomly creates shapes on a grid with this area. The object is to determine the perimeter. There is also an *Area Explorer* (fixes the perimeter) and a *Shape Explorer,* which asks the user for both the area and perimeter of the randomly produced shapes.

Turtle Pond
http://illuminations.nctm.org/tools/tool_detail.aspx?id=83
In this activity the user enters distance and angle commands in a sequence (like Logo) to maneuver a turtle to a pond. Helps with distance and angle estimation.

What Time Will It Be?
http://nlvm.usu.edu/en/nav/frames_asid_318_g_2_t_4.html
Elapsed-time problems are presented in word format. Two clocks are shown, one with the start time and the other to be set. Some problems are digital, others analog.

An additional list of books and articles related to the ideas in this chapter can be found on the Companion Web site at **www.ablongman.com/vandewalle6e.**

chapter 21

Geometric Thinking and Geometric Concepts

Geometry in K–8 is finally being taken seriously. Geometry used to be the chapter that was skipped or put off until late in the year. Many teachers were not comfortable with geometry, associating it with high school and proofs. Nor was geometry seen as important because it was only minimally tested on standardized tests. Now geometry is a strand of the curriculum in nearly every state and district.

This change is due in large part to the influence of the NCTM standards movement beginning in 1989. A second significant influence is an attention to a theoretical perspective that has helped us understand how students reason about spatial concepts.

Big Ideas

1. What makes shapes alike and different can be determined by an array of geometric properties. For example, shapes have sides that are parallel, perpendicular, or neither; they have line symmetry, rotational symmetry, or neither; they are similar, congruent, or neither.

2. Shapes can be moved in a plane or in space. These changes can be described in terms of translations (slides), reflections (flips), and rotations (turns).

3. Shapes can be described in terms of their location in a plane or in space. Coordinate systems can be used to describe these locations precisely. In turn, the coordinate view of shape offers another way to understand certain properties of shapes, changes in position (transformations), and how they appear or change size (visualization).

4. Shapes can be seen from different perspectives. The ability to perceive shapes from different viewpoints helps us understand relationships between two- and three-dimensional figures and mentally change the position and size of shapes.

Mathematics Content Connections

A rich understanding of geometry has clear and important implications for other areas of the curriculum. Take advantage of these connections whenever possible.

- **Measurement** (Chapter 20): Measurement and geometry are clearly aligned in the development of area and volume formulas and in an understanding of area/perimeter and surface/volume relationships. Coordinate geometry provides new ways to determine lengths, areas, and volumes. The Pythagorean relationship is at once an algebraic, geometric, and metric relationship.

- **Proportional Reasoning** (Chapter 19): Similar geometric objects have proportional dimensions and provide visual representation of proportionality.

- **Algebra** (Chapter 15): Coordinate graphing provides an analytic view of the concept of slope, and in turn, of perpendicular and parallel relationships. The Pythagorean relationship gives us an algebraic approach to the distance between points in a plane. Transformations of shapes (slides, flips, and turns) can be described in terms of coordinates, allowing for the digital manipulation of shapes. The entire world of computer animation is based on a marriage of geometry and algebra.

- **Integers** (Chapter 24): The coordinate plane provides a connection because both positive and negative numbers are used in the description of position in the plane and in space.

Since children study fractional parts of shapes, fractions have a relationship to geometry. This connection is probably more pedagogical than mathematical.

Geometry Goals for Students

It is useful to think about your geometry objectives in terms of two quite different yet related frameworks: spatial reasoning, or spatial sense, and the specific content such as that most likely found in your state or district objectives. The first of these frameworks has to do with the way students think and reason about shape and space. There is a well-researched theoretical basis for organizing the development of geometric thought that guides this framework. The second framework is content in the more traditional sense—knowing about symmetry, triangles, parallel lines, and so forth. The NCTM *Principles and Standards for School Mathematics* authors have helped describe content goals across the grades. We need to understand both of these aspects of geometry—reasoning and content—so that we can best help students grow.

Spatial Sense and Geometric Reasoning

Spatial sense can be defined as an intuition about shapes and the relationships among shapes. Individuals with spatial sense have a feel for the geometric aspects of their surroundings and the shapes formed by objects in the environment.

Spatial sense includes the ability to visualize mentally objects and spatial relationships—to turn things around in your mind. It includes a comfort with geometric descriptions of objects and position. People with spatial sense appreciate geometric form in art, nature, and architecture. They are able to use geometric ideas to describe and analyze their world.

Many people say they aren't very good with shape or that they have poor spatial sense. The typical belief is that you are either born with spatial sense or not. This simply is not true! We now know that rich experiences with shape and spatial relationships, when provided consistently over time, can and do develop spatial sense. Without geometric experiences, most people do not grow in their spatial sense or spatial reasoning. Between 1990 and 1996, NAEP data indicated a steady, continuing improvement in students' geometric reasoning at all three grades tested, 4, 8, and 12 (Martin & Strutchens, 2000). Students did not just get smarter. More likely there has been an increasing emphasis on geometry at all grades. Still, much more needs to be done if U.S. children are to rise to the same level as their European and Asian counterparts.

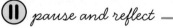 *pause and reflect* —————

Reflect for a moment about your own beliefs concerning an individual's abilities in the area of spatial sense. What do you think causes some people to have better spatial sense than others?

 The *Standards* supports the notion that all students can grow in their geometric skills and understandings. "The notion of building understanding in geometry across the grades, from informal to more formal thinking, is consistent with the thinking of theorists and researchers" (p. 41).

Geometric Content

For too long, the geometry curriculum in the United States has been somewhat of an eclectic mix of activities and lists of "bold print words"—too much emphasis has been placed on learning terminology. At the same time, the growing emphasis placed on geometry has spawned a huge assortment of wonderful tasks for students. The geometry standard in *Principles and Standards* is a useful guide for the pre-K–12 curriculum. As with each of the content standards, the geometry standard has a number of goals that apply to all grade levels. The four goals for geometry can be loosely summarized with these headings: *Shapes and Properties, Transformation, Location,* and *Visualization.*

- *Shapes and Properties* includes a study of the properties of shapes in both two and three dimensions, as well as a study of the relationships built on properties.
- *Transformation* includes a study of translations, reflections, rotations (slides, flips, and turns), the study of symmetries, and the concept of similarity.
- *Location* refers primarily to coordinate geometry or other ways of specifying how objects are located in the plane or in space.
- *Visualization* includes the recognition of shapes in the environment, developing relationships between two- and three-dimensional objects, and the ability to draw and recognize objects from different perspectives.

The value of these content goals is that a content framework finally exists that cuts across grades so that both teachers and curriculum planners can examine growth from year to year. To get a more detailed look at these areas of the curriculum, turn to Appendix A in this book and examine the NCTM goals and expectations for each of these areas across the grades. The activities in this chapter are grouped according to these four categories to further assist you.

The Development of Geometric Thinking

Not all people think about geometric ideas in the same manner. Certainly, we are not all alike, but we are all capable of growing and developing in our ability to think and reason in geometric contexts. The research of two Dutch educators, Pierre van Hiele and Dina van Hiele-Geldof, has provided insight into the differences in geometric thinking and how the differences come to be.

The van Hieles' work began in 1959 and immediately attracted a lot of attention in the Soviet Union but for nearly two decades got little notice in this country (Hoffer, 1983; Hoffer & Hoffer, 1992). But today, the van Hiele theory has become the most influential factor in the American geometry curriculum.

The van Hiele Levels of Geometric Thought

The most prominent feature of the model is a five-level hierarchy of ways of understanding spatial ideas. Each of the five levels describes the thinking processes used in geometric contexts. The levels describe how we think and what types of geometric ideas we think about, rather than how much knowledge we have. A significant difference from one level to the next is the objects of thought—what we are able to think about geometrically.

Level 0: Visualization

The objects of thought at level 0 are shapes and what they "look like."

Students at this first level recognize and name figures based on the global, visual characteristics of the figure—a gestaltlike approach to shape. These students are able to make measurements and even talk about properties of shapes, but these properties are not abstracted from the shapes at hand. It is the appearance of the shape that defines it for the student. A square is a square "because it looks like a square." Because appearance is dominant at this level, appearances can overpower properties of a shape. For example, a square that has been rotated so that all sides are at a 45-degree angle to the vertical may now be a diamond and no longer a square. Students at this level will sort and classify shapes based on their appearances—"I put these together because they are all pointy" (or "fat," or "look like a house," or are "dented in sort of," and so on). With a focus on the appearances of shapes, students are able to see how shapes are alike and different. As a result, students at this level can create and begin to understand classifications of shapes.

The products of thought at level 0 are classes or groupings of shapes that seem to be "alike."

The emphasis at level 0 is on the shapes that students can observe, feel, build, take apart, or work with in some manner. The general goal is to explore how shapes are alike and different and to use these ideas to create classes of shapes (both physically and mentally). Some of these classes of shapes have names—rectangles, triangles, prisms, cylinders, and so on. Properties of shapes, such as parallel sides, symmetry, right angles, and so on, are included at this level but only in an informal, observational manner.

Although the van Hiele theory applies to all students learning any geometric content, it may be easier to apply

FIGURE 21.1   An assortment of shapes for sorting. See the Blackline Masters for a larger collection of shapes.

the theory to the shapes-and-property category. The following activity is a good representation of one appropriate for level 0.

activity **21.1**

Shape Sorts

Have students work in groups of four with a set of 2-D shapes similar to those in Figure 21.1. Here are several related activities that might be done in order:

- **Each child randomly selects a shape. In turn, the students tell one or two things they find interesting about their shape. There are no right or wrong responses.**

- **Children each randomly select two shapes. The task is to find something that is alike about their two shapes and something that is different. (Have them select their shapes before they know the task.)**

- **The group selects one shape at random and places it in the center of the workspace. Their task is to find all other shapes that are like the target shape, but all according to the same rule. For example, if they say "This one is like our shape because it has a curved side and a straight side," then all other shapes that they put in the collection must have these properties. Challenge them to do a second sort with the same target shape but using a different property.**

- Have students share their sorting rules with the class and show examples. All students then draw a new shape that will also fit in the group according to the same rule. They should write about their new shape and why it fits the rule.
- Do a "secret sort." You or one of the students creates a small collection of about five shapes that fit a secret rule. Leave others that belong in your group in the pile. The other students try to find additional pieces that belong to the set and/or guess the secret rule.

Depending on the grade level, this activity will elicit a wide variety of ideas as students examine the shapes. For the most part these will be ideas such as "curvy" or "looks like a rocket" rather than typical geometric concepts. But students may begin to notice more sophisticated properties and the teacher can take the opportunity to attach appropriate names to them as the students describe them. For example, students may notice that some shapes have corners "like a square" (right angles) or that "these shapes are the same on both sides" (line symmetry).

What clearly makes this a level-0 activity, however, is not the presence or the absence of traditional geometric properties or terms. Rather, students are operating on the shapes that they see in front of them. Furthermore, for level-0 students, the shapes may even "change" or have different properties as they are rearranged or rotated. The objective of the activity is for students to begin to see that there are likenesses and differences in shapes. By forming groups of shapes, they may begin to imagine shapes belonging to these classes that are not there.

Level 1: Analysis

The objects of thought at level 1 are classes of shapes rather than individual shapes.

Students at the analysis level are able to consider all shapes within a class rather than a single shape. Instead of talking about *this* rectangle, it is possible to talk about *all* rectangles. By focusing on a class of shapes, students are able to think about what makes a rectangle a rectangle (four sides, opposite sides parallel, opposite sides same length, four right angles, congruent diagonals, etc.). The irrelevant features (e.g., size or orientation) fade into the background. At this level, students begin to appreciate that a collection of shapes goes together because of properties. Ideas about an individual shape can now be generalized to all shapes that fit that class. If a shape belongs to a particular class such as cubes, it has the corresponding properties of that class. "All cubes have six congruent faces, and each of those faces is a square." These properties were only implicit at level 0. Students operating at level 1 may be able to list all the properties of squares, rectangles, and parallelograms but not see that these are subclasses of one an-

other, that all squares are rectangles and all rectangles are parallelograms. In defining a shape, level-1 thinkers are likely to list as many properties of a shape as they know.

The products of thought at level 1 are the properties of shapes.

A significant difference between level 1 and level 0 is the object of students' thought. While level-1 students will continue to use models and drawings of shapes, they begin to see these as representatives of classes of shapes. Their understanding of the properties of shapes—such as symmetry, perpendicular and parallel lines, and so on—continues to be refined.

In the following activity, students call into play as many properties of shapes as they can. They will have learned these properties in earlier activities, possibly while operating at level 0. These would include ideas such as symmetry, angle classification (right, obtuse, acute), parallel and perpendicular, and the concept of congruent line segments and angles.

activity **21.2**

Property Lists for Quadrilaterals

Prepare worksheets for parallelograms, rhombi, rectangles, and squares. (See the Blackline Masters.) On each sheet are three or four examples of that category of shape. Examples are illustrated in Figure 21.2. Assign students working in groups of three or four to one type of quadrilateral. Their task is to list as many properties as they can. Each property listed must be applicable to all of the shapes on their sheet. They will need a simple index card to check right angles, to compare side lengths, and to draw straight lines. Mirrors (to check line symmetry) and tracing paper (for angle congruence and rotational symmetry) are also useful tools. Encourage students to use the words "at least" when describing how many of something: for example, "rectangles have at least two lines of symmetry," since squares—included in the rectangles—have four.

Have students prepare their property lists under these headings: Sides, Angles, Diagonals, and Symmetries. Groups then share their lists with the class and eventually a class list for each shape will be developed.

Both this activity and the earlier classification activity involve an examination of shapes. Although this activity will focus more on traditional geometric properties, we saw that those same properties might have developed during the earlier activity as well. What distinguishes this activity from the level-0 classification activity is the object of students' thinking. While there are a few shapes available, students must imagine that the properties apply to all shapes in the category. If they are working on the squares,

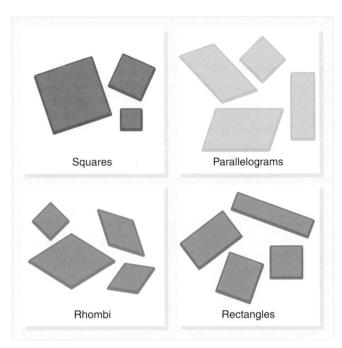

Squares   Parallelograms

Rhombi   Rectangles

FIGURE 21.2 Shapes for "Property Lists for Quadrilaterals" worksheets can be found in the Blackline Masters.

for example, their observations must apply to a square mile as well as a square inch.

Level 2: Informal Deduction

The objects of thought at level 2 are the properties of shapes.

As students begin to be able to think about properties of geometric objects without the constraints of a particular object, they are able to develop relationships between and among these properties. "If all four angles are right angles, the shape must be a rectangle. If it is a square, all angles are right angles. If it is a square, it must be a rectangle." With greater ability to engage in "if-then" reasoning, shapes can be classified using only minimum characteristics. For example, four congruent sides and at least one right angle can be sufficient to define a square. Rectangles are parallelograms with a right angle. Observations go beyond properties themselves and begin to focus on logical arguments *about* the properties. Students at level 2 will be able to follow and appreciate an informal deductive argument about shapes and their properties. "Proofs" may be more intuitive than rigorously deductive. However, there is an appreciation that a logical argument is compelling. An appreciation of the axiomatic structure of a formal deductive system, however, remains under the surface.

The products of thought at level 2 are relationships among properties of geometric objects.

The hallmark of level-2 activities is the inclusion of informal logical reasoning. Students have developed an understanding of various properties of shapes. Now it is time

to encourage conjecture and to ask "Why?" or "What if?" Contrast the required thinking in the following activity with that of the "Property Lists" activity that is designed as a follow-up to that one. (The two activities form a pair that can be done over several days.)

activity **21.3**

Minimal Defining Lists

(This activity must be done as a follow-up to the "Property Lists" activity described earlier.) Once property lists for the parallelogram, rhombus, rectangle, and square (and possibly the kite and trapezoid) have been agreed upon by the class, have these lists posted or type them up and duplicate them. In groups, the task is to find "minimal defining lists," or MDLs, for each shape. An MDL is a subset of the properties for a shape that is "defining" and "minimal." "Defining" here means that any shape that has all the properties on the MDL must be that shape. Thus, an MDL for a square will guarantee that you have a square. "Minimal" means that if any single property is removed from the list it is no longer defining. For example, one MDL for a square is a quadrilateral with four congruent sides and four right angles. Students should attempt to find at least two or three MDLs for their shape. A proposed list can be challenged as either not minimal or not defining. A list is not minimal if a property can be removed yet the list still defines the shape. A list is not defining if a counterexample—a shape other than one being described—can be produced using only the properties on the list.

Of particular note in the "Minimal Defining Lists" activity is the logic component. "*If* a quadrilateral has these properties, *then* it must be a square." Logic is also involved in proving that a list is faulty—either not minimal or not defining. Here students begin to learn the nature of a definition and the value of counterexamples. In fact, any minimal defining list (MDL) is a potential definition. This logical thinking was not required in the "Property Lists" activity. The other aspect of this activity that clearly sets it into the level-2 category is that students are focusing here on the lists of properties of the shapes – the very things that were products of the earlier level-1 activity. As a result of the MDL activity, students are creating a collection of new relationships that exist between and among properties.

Level 3: Deduction

The objects of thought at level 3 are relationships among properties of geometric objects.

At level 3, students are able to examine more than just the properties of shapes. Their earlier thinking has produced conjectures concerning relationships among properties. Are these conjectures correct? Are they "true"? As this analysis of the informal arguments takes place, the structure of a system complete with axioms, definitions, theorems, corollaries, and postulates begins to develop and can be appreciated as the necessary means of establishing geometric truth. At this level, students begin to appreciate the need for a system of logic that rests on a minimum set of assumptions and from which other truths can be derived. The student at this level is able to work with abstract statements about geometric properties and make conclusions based more on logic than intuition. A student operating at level 3 can clearly observe that the diagonals of a rectangle bisect each other, just as a student at a lower level of thought can. However, at level 3, there is an appreciation of the need to prove this from a series of deductive arguments. The level-2 thinker, by contrast, follows the argument but fails to appreciate the need.

The products of thought at level 3 are deductive axiomatic systems for geometry.

The type of reasoning that characterizes a level-3 thinker is the same that is required in a typical high school geometry course. There students build on a list of axioms and definitions to create theorems. They also prove theorems using clearly articulated logical reasoning, whereas the reasoning at level 2 may be quite informal. In the best geometry courses, students would engage in activities in which they would discover the relationships they later prove. This is similar to the discoveries students make in creating minimal defining lists.

In a very global sense, high school geometry students are working on the creation of a complete geometric deductive system. Usually this is the Euclidean system that describes best the world in which we live. They may also explore other geometric systems, such as the geometry where all lines are drawn on the surface of a sphere or "taxicab geometry" where lines may only follow a rectan-gular grid of "streets." These systems are the product of their thinking.

Level 4: Rigor

The objects of thought at level 4 are deductive axiomatic systems for geometry.

At the highest level of the van Hiele hierarchy, the objects of attention are axiomatic systems themselves, not just the deductions within a system. There is an appreciation of the distinctions and relationships between different axiomatic systems. For example, spherical geometry is based on lines drawn on a sphere rather than in a plane or ordinary space. This geometry has its own set of axioms and theorems. This is generally the level of a college mathematics major who is studying geometry as a branch of mathematical science.

The products of thought at level 4 are comparisons and contrasts among different axiomatic systems of geometry.

Characteristics of the van Hiele Levels

You no doubt noticed that the products of thought at each level are the same as the objects of thought at the next. This object–product relationship between levels of the van Hiele theory is illustrated in Figure 21.3. The objects (ideas) must be created at one level so that relationships among these objects can become the focus of the next level. In addition to this key concept of the theory, four related characteristics of the levels of thought merit special attention.

1. **The levels are sequential.** To arrive at any level above level 0, students must move through all prior levels. To move through a level means that one has experienced geometric thinking appropriate for that level and has created in one's own mind the types of objects

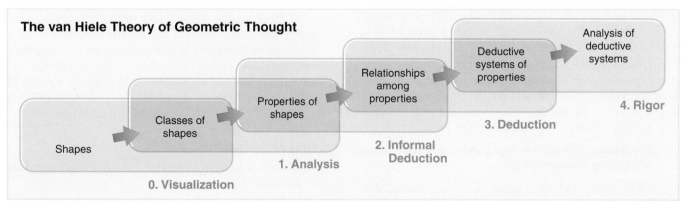

FIGURE 21.3 At each level of geometric thought, the ideas created become the focus or object of thought at the next level.

or relationships that are the focus of thought at the next level.

2. The levels are not age-dependent in the sense of the developmental stages of Piaget. A third grader or a high school student could be at level 0. Indeed, some students and adults remain forever at level 0, and a significant number of adults never reach level 2. But age is certainly related to the amount and types of geometric experiences that we have. Therefore, it is reasonable for all children in the K–2 range to be at level 0, as well as the majority of children in grades 3 and 4.

3. Geometric experience is the greatest single factor influencing advancement through the levels. Activities that permit children to explore, talk about, and interact with content at the next level, while increasing their experiences at their current level, have the best chance of advancing the level of thought for those children.

4. When instruction or language is at a level higher than that of the student, there will be a lack of communication. Students required to wrestle with objects of thought that have not been constructed at the earlier level may be forced into rote learning and achieve only temporary and superficial success. A student can, for example, memorize that all squares are rectangles without having constructed that relationship. A student may memorize a geometric proof but fail to create the steps or understand the rationale involved (Fuys, Geddes, & Tischler, 1988; Geddes & Fortunato, 1993).

Implications for Instruction

If the van Hiele theory is correct—and there is much evidence to support it—then a major goal of the K–8 curriculum must be to advance students' level of geometric thought. If students are to be adequately prepared for the deductive geometry curriculum of high school, then it is important for their thinking to have grown to level 2 by the end of the eighth grade.

Not every teacher will be able to move children to the next level. However, all teachers should be aware that the experiences they provide are the single most important factor in moving children up this developmental ladder. Every teacher should be able to see some growth in geometric thinking over the course of the year.

The van Hiele theory and the developmental perspective of this book highlight the necessity of teaching at the child's level of thought. However, almost any activity can be modified to span two levels of thinking, even within the same classroom. For many activities, how we interact with individual children will adapt the activity to their levels and encourage them or challenge them to operate at the next higher level.

The following sections contain descriptions of the types of activity and questioning that are appropriate for each of the first three levels. Apply these descriptors to the tasks that you pose to students, and use them to guide your interaction with students. The use of physical materials, drawings, and computer models is a must at every level.

Instruction at Level 0

Instructional activities in geometry appropriate for level 0 should:

* Involve lots of sorting and classifying. Seeing how shapes are alike and different is the primary focus of level 0. As students learn more content, the types of things that they notice will become more sophisticated. At an early stage they may talk about very non-geometric-sounding attributes of shape such as "fat" or even the color of the pieces. When properties such as symmetry and numbers of sides and corners are introduced, students should be challenged to use these features to classify shapes.

* Include a sufficient variety of examples of shapes so that irrelevant features do not become important. Students need ample opportunities to draw, build, make, put together, and take apart shapes in both two and three dimensions. These activities should be built around specific characteristics or properties so that students develop an understanding of geometric properties and begin to use them naturally.

To help students move from level 0 to level 1, students should be challenged to test ideas about shapes for a variety of examples from a particular category. Say to them, "Let's see if that is true for other rectangles," or "Can you draw a triangle that does *not* have a right angle?" In general, students should be challenged to see if observations made about a particular shape apply to other shapes of a similar kind.

Instruction at Level 1

Instructional activities in geometry appropriate for level 1 should:

* Focus more on the properties of figures rather than on simple identification. As new geometric concepts are learned, the number of properties that figures have can be expanded.

* Apply ideas to entire classes of figures (e.g., *all* rectangles, *all* prisms) rather than on individual models. Analyze classes of figures to determine new properties. For example, find ways to sort all possible triangles into groups. From these groups, define types of triangles. Dynamic geometry software such as *The Geometer's Sketchpad* (Key Curriculum Press) is especially useful for exploring many examples of a class of shapes.

To assist students in moving from level 1 to level 2, challenge them with questions such as "Why?" and those that involve some reasoning. For example, "If the sides of a four-sided shape are all congruent, will you always have a square?" and "Can you find a counterexample?"

Instruction at Level 2

Instructional activities in geometry appropriate for level 2 should:

- Encourage the making and testing of hypotheses or conjectures. "Do you think that will work all the time?" "Is that true for all triangles or just equilateral ones?"
- Examine properties of shapes to determine necessary and sufficient conditions for different shapes or concepts. "What properties of diagonals do you think will guarantee that you will have a square?"
- Use the language of informal deduction: *all, some, none, if . . . then, what if,* and so on.
- Encourage students to attempt informal proofs. As an alternative, require them to make sense of informal proofs that other students or you have suggested.

Task Selection and Levels of Thought

If you teach at the K–3 level, nearly all of your students will be at level 0. However, by at least grade 3 you certainly want to begin to challenge students who seem able. In the upper grades you may have children at two or even all three levels within the same classroom. How do you discover the level of each student? Once you know, how will you select the right activities to match your students' levels?

No simple test exists to pigeonhole students at a certain level. However, examine the descriptors for the first two levels. As you conduct an activity, listen to the types of observations that students make. Can they talk about shapes as classes? Do they refer, for example, to "rectangles" rather than basing discussion around a particular rectangle? Do they generalize that certain properties are attributable to a type of shape or simply the shape at hand? Do they understand that shapes do not change when the orientation changes? With simple observations such as these, you will soon be able to distinguish between levels 0 and 1.

At the upper grades, attempt to push students from level 1 to level 2. If students are not able to follow or appreciate logical arguments and are not comfortable with conjectures and if-then reasoning, these students are likely still at level 1 or below.

The remainder of this chapter offers a sampling of activities organized broadly around the four content goals of the NCTM standards: Shapes and Properties, Location, Transformations, and Visualization. Within each of these content groupings, activities are further sorted according to the first three van Hiele levels. Understand that all of these subdivisions are quite fluid. An activity found at one level can easily be adapted to an adjacent level simply by the way it is presented to the students. As you will see, even the content subdivisions overlap.

The activities that most clearly reflect the van Hiele levels are found in the Shapes and Properties section. As you explore some of the activities in each section, you should begin to get a feeling for why an activity is appropriate for one level or the other. Do not become so concerned about matching levels and activities that you agonize over task selection. As a rough guide, if you teach K–2, begin with level 0; for 3–5, look at levels 0 and 1; at the 6–8 level, look at level-1 and level-2 activities.

Learning About Shapes and Properties

This is the content area that most people think about when they think about geometry in the K–8 classroom; children are working with both two- and three-dimensional shapes. They are finding out what makes these shapes alike and different and in the process they begin to discover properties of the shapes. As properties are discovered and described, the conventional names for them can be given. Students will, with sufficient experiences, develop classifications of special shapes—triangles, parallelograms, cylinders, pyramids, and so on—and learn that some properties apply to full classes. Eventually, they will investigate how properties of shapes impose logical consequences on geometric relationships and the ability to reason about shapes and properties will be developed.

Shapes and Properties for Level-0 Thinkers

Young children need experience with a rich variety of both two- and three-dimensional shapes. Triangles should be more than just equilateral. Shapes should have curved sides, straight sides, and combinations of these. Along the way, the names of shapes and their properties can be introduced casually.

Sorting and Classifying

As young students work at classification of shapes, be prepared for them to notice features that you do not consider to be "real" geometric attributes, such as "curvy" or "looks like a rocket." Children at this level will also attribute to shapes ideas that are not part of the shape, such as "points up" or "has a side that is the same as the edge of the board."

For variety in two-dimensional shapes, create your own materials. A good set found in the Blackline Masters is called 2-D Shapes. Make multiple copies so that groups of children can all work with the same shapes. Once you have your sets constructed, a good beginning activity is the one described earlier—"Shape Sorts"—on p. 409.

In any sorting activity, the students should decide how to sort, not the teacher. This allows the students to do the activity using ideas *they* own and understand. By listening

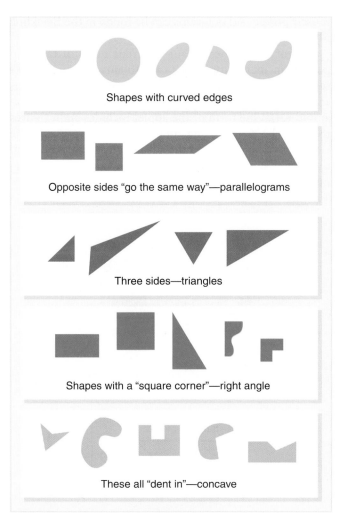

FIGURE 21.4 By sorting shapes, students begin to recognize properties.

to the kinds of attributes that they use in their sorting, you will be able to tell what properties they know and use and how they think about shapes. Figure 21.4 illustrates a few of the many possible ways a set might be sorted.

The secret sorting portion of Activity 21.1 is one option for introducing a new property. For example, sort the shapes so that all have at least one right angle or "square corner." When students discover your rule, you have an opportunity to talk more about that property.

The following activity is also done with the 2-D Shapes.

activity 21.4

What's My Shape?
From the Blackline Masters, make a set of 2-D Shapes on paper. Cut out about a third of the shapes and paste each inside a folded half-sheet of construction paper to make "secret shape" folders.

In a group, one student is designated the leader and given a secret-shape folder. The other students

are to find the shape that matches the shape in the folder. To this end, they ask questions to which the leader can answer only "yes" or "no." The group can sort the shapes as they ask questions to help narrow down the possibilities. They are not allowed to point to a piece and ask, "Is it this one?" Rather, they must continue to ask questions that reduce the choices to one shape. The final piece is tested against the one in the leader's folder.

The difficulty of Activity 21.4 is largely dependent on the shape in the folder. The more shapes in the collection that resemble the secret shape, the more difficult the task.

Most of the activities in "Shape Sorts" can and should be done with three-dimensional shapes as well. The difficulty is finding or making a collection that has sufficient variability. Geoblocks are a large set of wooden blocks available through various distributors. The variety is good, but no blocks have curved surfaces. Check catalogs for other collections. Consider combining several different sets to get variation. Another option is to collect real objects such as cans, boxes, balls, and Styrofoam shapes. Figure 21.5 illustrates some classifications of solids.

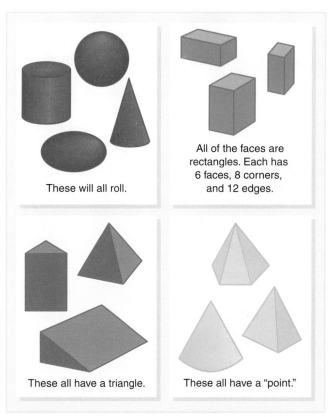

FIGURE 21.5 Early classifications of three-dimensional shapes.

The ways in which children describe shapes in "Shape Sorts" and similar activities with three-dimensional shapes are a good clue to their level of thinking. The classifications made by level-0 thinkers will generally be restricted to the shapes that they can actually put into a group. As they begin to think in terms of the properties of shapes, they will create categories based on properties and their language will indicate that there are many more shapes in the group than those that are physically present. Students may say things like, "These shapes have square corners sort of like rectangles," or "These look like boxes. All the boxes have square [rectangular] sides." ■

Constructing and Dissecting Shapes

Children need to freely explore how shapes fit together to form larger shapes and how larger shapes can be made of smaller shapes. Among two-dimensional shapes for these activities, pattern blocks and tangrams are the best known. In a 1999 article, Pierre van Hiele describes an interesting set of tiles he calls the mosaic puzzle (see Figure 21.6). Another excellent tile set for building is a set of triangles cut from squares (isosceles right triangles). Patterns for the

mosaic puzzle and tangrams can be found in the Blackline Masters.

Figure 21.7 shows four different types of tangram puzzles in increasing order of difficulty. Numerous resource books are available devoted entirely to tangrams and NCTM's *e-Standards* includes a tangram applet (Example 4.4). One form of the applet includes eight figures that can be made using all seven of the pieces. The e-version of tangrams has the advantage of motivation and the fact that you must be much more deliberate in arranging the shapes. *Investigations in Number, Data, and*

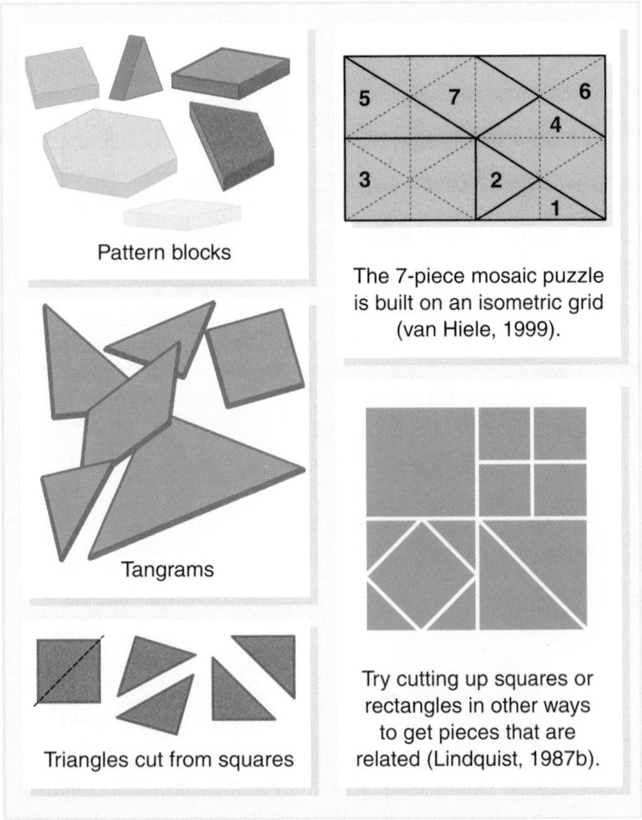

Pattern blocks

The 7-piece mosaic puzzle is built on an isometric grid (van Hiele, 1999).

Tangrams

Triangles cut from squares

Try cutting up squares or rectangles in other ways to get pieces that are related (Lindquist, 1987b).

FIGURE 21.6 Activities with tiles can involve an assortment of shapes or can be designed with just one shape.

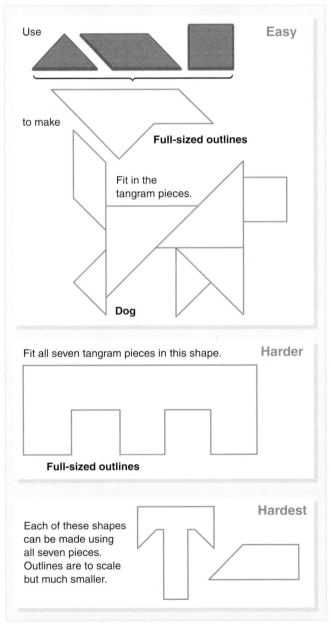

Use ... to make ... Full-sized outlines. Fit in the tangram pieces. Dog

Fit all seven tangram pieces in this shape. Harder

Full-sized outlines

Each of these shapes can be made using all seven pieces. Outlines are to scale but much smaller. Hardest

FIGURE 21.7 Four types of tangram puzzles illustrate a range of difficulty levels.

Investigations
in Number, Data, and Space

Grade 1, Quilt Squares and Block Towns
Investigation 1: 2-D Shapes and Patterns

Context

The activity is designed for the seventh class period of this investigation. The earlier sessions and some that follow are involved, as is this one, in finding different ways to fill an outline with pattern blocks. The *Investigations* program also has a computer component that uses the *Shapes* program (Clements & Sarama, 1995) described on p. 446. Most of the work prior to this lesson is done individually at stations. At this point, the computer program is also used in a free-play mode, in which students create their own designs on the screen. Other materials used in this unit include geoblocks and a set of shape cards for sorting.

Task Description

By this time, students are accustomed to filling in shapes with pattern blocks. They also have been recording their work in one of several possible ways: pasting in construction paper or sticker versions of pattern blocks or coloring in their designs freehand. In previous activities they recorded the number of times each type of block is used. In this activity they fill in the same shape at least three times, each time trying to use a different number of blocks. Students work in pairs, with one of the worksheets (shown here) for each pair of children. As the teacher interacts with the students, she or he focuses on what approach students take. Some children use the obvious shapes (the hexagon and trapezoid) and have difficulty finding other methods. Others use only triangles or only trapezoids.

Number is an added focus of the activity. Students are encouraged to try to find another way to fill in the design with *more* or *fewer* blocks or a number of blocks that is between two different totals. This focus on number has the potential to encourage students to substitute smaller blocks for an equivalent larger block (decom-

pose shapes) or larger blocks for smaller ones (combine shapes).

In the full class discussion, students list all of the different totals that they found. (There are eight different solutions.) Questions revolve around the possibility of a solution with even more blocks, or fewer blocks, or some additional solutions in between. The teacher is looking for students' comfort with reasoning and with manipulation of the shapes in making substitutions.

Name	Date
	Student Sheet 11

Different Ways to Fill, Shape A

Number of blocks
_____

Number of blocks
_____

Number of blocks
_____

© Dale Seymour Publications®   **187**   *Investigation 1 • Session 7*
Quilt Squares and Block Towns

Page 187 from *2-D and 3-D Geometry: Quilt Squares and Block Towns* by S. J. Russell, D. H. Clements, & J. Sarama. *Investigations in Number, Data, and Space.* Copyright © 1998 by Dale Seymour Publications. Reprinted by permission of Pearson Education, Inc.

Space uses pattern blocks in first grade in an activity similar to tangrams. As you can see in the excerpt on this page, pattern blocks, like the mosaic puzzle, offer considerable flexibility for young children in this type of activity.

The value of van Hiele's mosaic puzzle is partly due to the fact that the set contains five different angles (see

Figure 21.8). If appropriate, you can use the pieces to talk about square corners (*right* angles) and angles that are more and less than a right angle (*obtuse* and *acute* angles).

The geoboard is one of the best devices for "drawing" two-dimensional shapes. Here are just three of many possible activities appropriate for level 0.

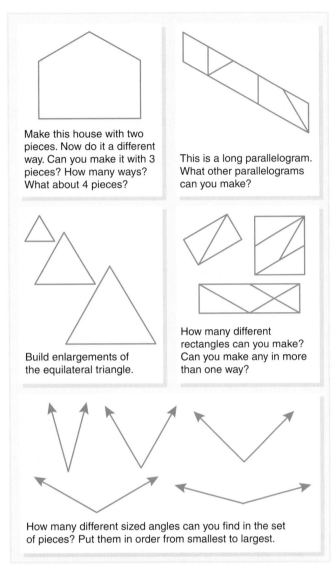

Make this house with two pieces. Now do it a different way. Can you make it with 3 pieces? How many ways? What about 4 pieces?

This is a long parallelogram. What other parallelograms can you make?

Build enlargements of the equilateral triangle.

How many different rectangles can you make? Can you make any in more than one way?

How many different sized angles can you find in the set of pieces? Put them in order from smallest to largest.

FIGURE 21.8 A sample of activities with the mosaic puzzle.

Based on van Hiele, P. M. (1999). Developing geometric thinking through activities that begin with play. *Teaching Children Mathematics*, 5, 310–316.

activity 21.5

Geoboard Copy

Copy shapes, designs, and patterns from prepared cards as in Figure 21.9. Begin with designs shown with dots as on a geoboard, and later have students copy designs drawn without dots.

activity 21.6

Congruent Parts

Copy a shape from a card, and have students subdivide or cut it into smaller shapes on their geoboards. Specify the number of smaller shapes. Also

specify whether they are all to be congruent or simply of the same type as shown in Figure 21.10. Depending on the shapes involved, this activity can be made quite easy or relatively challenging.

Have lots of geoboards available in the classroom. It is better for two or three children to have 10 or 12 boards at a station than for each to have only one. That way, a variety of shapes can be made and compared before they are changed.

Teach students from the very beginning to copy their geoboard designs. Paper copies permit students to create complete sets of drawings that fulfill a particular task. Drawings can be placed on the bulletin board for classification and discussion, made into booklets illustrating a new idea that is being discussed, and sent home to show parents what is happening in geometry.

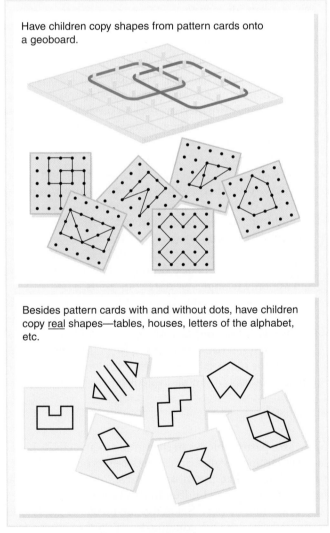

Have children copy shapes from pattern cards onto a geoboard.

Besides pattern cards with and without dots, have children copy <u>real</u> shapes—tables, houses, letters of the alphabet, etc.

FIGURE 21.9 Shapes on geoboards.

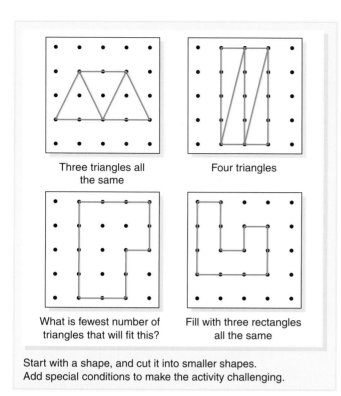

Three triangles all the same

Four triangles

What is fewest number of triangles that will fit this?

Fill with three rectangles all the same

Start with a shape, and cut it into smaller shapes.
Add special conditions to make the activity challenging.

FIGURE 21.10 Subdividing shapes.

Younger students can use paper with a single large geoboard on each sheet. Later, a paper board about 10 cm square is adequate. Older children can use centimeter dot grids. All are found in the Blackline Masters.

To help children in the very early grades copy geoboard designs, suggest that they first mark the dots for the corners of their shape ("second row, end peg"). With the corners identified, it is much easier for them to draw lines to make the shape.

The *e-Standards* provides a very good electronic geoboard (e-example 4.2). Although found in the K–2 section and entitled "Investigating the Concept of a Triangle," this is actually a great geoboard applet for any grade. It allows you to select and delete bands, and select and delete vertices. The *Geoboard* applet from the National Library of Virtual Manipulatives (http://nlvm.usu.edu/en/nav/vlibrary.html) is essentially the same but with instant calculation of perimeter and area with the click of a button and without vertex removal (other than to move a vertex to coincide with another). *Mighty Math: Number Heroes* (Riverdeep) also has a powerful electronic geoboard in the *GeoComputer* component. Students can move an entire shape to any part of the geoboard without changes. The shapes can be colored and flipped over or rotated 90 degrees—moves that are not simple to accomplish on a physical board. ■

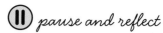
pause and reflect _____

If you have never used a geoboard, play around with one of these electronic geoboards. If you know about geoboards but have never used an e-geoboard, now would be a good time to try one.

Assorted dot and grid papers provide an alternative to geoboards. Virtually all of the activities suggested for tiles and geoboards can also be done on dot or grid paper. Changing the type of paper changes the activity and provides new opportunity for insight and discovery. The Blackline Masters have a variety of dot and grid paper.

Building three-dimensional shapes is a little more difficult compared with two-dimensional shapes. A variety of commercial materials permit fairly creative construction of geometric solids (for example, 3D Geoshapes, Polydron, and the Zome System). The 3D Geoshapes and Polydron are examples of materials consisting of plastic polygons that snap together to make three-dimensional models. The Zome System is a stick and connector set; skeletal models can be created with a great deal of variation. Zome is probably too difficult to use below the third grade. The following are three highly recommended homemade approaches to skeletal models.

- *Plastic coffee stirrers with modeling clay or pipe cleaners.* Plastic stirrers can be easily cut to different lengths. Use small chunks of clay (about 1 to 2 cm in diameter) to connect the corners. This is a good model as long as the structures are not too elaborate. For an alternative connection method, insert 2-inch lengths of pipe cleaners into the ends of the stirrers.
- *Plastic drinking straws with flexible joints.* Cut the straws lengthwise with scissors from the top down to the flexible joint. These slit ends can then be inserted into the uncut bottom ends of other straws, making a strong but flexible joint. Three or more straws are joined in this fashion to form two-dimensional polygons. To make skeletal solids, use tape or wire twist ties to join polygons side to side.
- *Rolled newspaper rods.* Fantastic superlarge skeletons can be built using newspaper and masking tape. Roll three large sheets of newspaper on the diagonal to form a rod. The more tightly the paper is rolled, the less likely the rod is to bend. Secure the roll at the center with a bit of masking tape. The ends of the rods are thin and flexible for about 6 inches where there is less paper. Connect rods by bunching this thin part together and fastening with tape. Use masking tape freely, wrapping it several times around each joint. Additional rods can be joined after two or three are already taped (see Figure 21.11).

With these homemade models, students should compare the rigidity of a triangle with the lack of rigidity of polygons with more than three sides. Point out that triangles are used in many bridges, in the long booms of

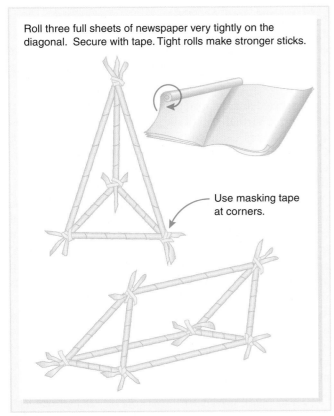

Roll three full sheets of newspaper very tightly on the diagonal. Secure with tape. Tight rolls make stronger sticks.

Use masking tape at corners.

FIGURE 21.11 Large skeletal structures and special shapes can be built with tightly rolled newspaper. Young children can build free-form sculptures. Older children can be challenged to build shapes with specific properties. Overlap the ends about 6 inches to ensure strength.

construction cranes, in gates, and in the structural parts of buildings. Discuss why this may be so. As children build large skeleton structures, they will find that they need to add diagonal members to form triangles. The more triangles, the less likely their structure will collapse.

The newspaper rod method is exciting because the structures quickly become large. Let students work in groups of four or five. They will soon discover what makes a structure rigid and ideas of balance and form. Primary-grade students can benefit from creating free-form structures. Older students can be challenged to make more well-defined shapes.

Tessellations

A *tessellation* is a tiling of the plane using one or more shapes in a repeated pattern with no holes or gaps. Making tessellations is an artistic way for level-0 students from first grade to eighth grade to explore patterns in shapes and to see how shapes combine to form other shapes. One-shape or two-shape tessellation activities can vary considerably in difficulty.

Even single-shape tessellations are more easily made with some shapes than others. For example, squares or equilateral triangles tessellate quite easily, although these pro-

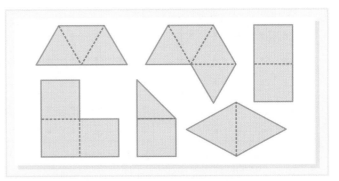

FIGURE 21.12 These simple shapes are good tiles to use for tessellations in the early grades. The dotted lines show how the shapes are made from squares or equilateral triangles. They are not included on the students' tiles.

vide only a minimal geometric challenge. Several shapes that make good early tessellation tiles are shown in Figure 21.12.

Some shapes are easier to tessellate than others (see Figure 21.13). When the shapes can be put together in more than one pattern, both the problem-solving level and the creativity increase. Literally hundreds of shapes can be used as tiles for tessellations.

For their first experiences with tessellations, most children will benefit from using actual tiles to create patterns. Simple construction paper tiles can be cut quickly on a paper cutter. Other tiles can be traced onto construction paper and several thicknesses cut at once with scissors. Older children may be able to use dot or line grids and plan their tessellations with pencil and paper. To plan a tessellation, use only one color so that the focus is on the spatial relationships. To complete an artistic-looking tessellation, add a color design. Use only two colors with younger children and never more than four. Color designs are also repeated regularly all over the tessellation.

Tessellations can be made by gluing paper tiles to large sheets of paper, by drawing them on dot or line grids, or by tracing around a poster board tile. Work from the center out, leaving ragged edges to indicate that the pattern goes on and on.

 *pause and reflect* ───────────

Look at the lower-left tessellation in Figure 21.13. What single tile (a combination of squares and half squares) made this pattern?

Shapes and Properties for Level-1 Thinkers

As students move to level-1 thinking, the attention turns more to properties possessed by the traditional classifications of shapes. During this period it makes sense for students to learn the proper names for shapes and their properties.

Tessellations can be drawn on grids or made of construction paper tiles. They are challenging and provide an opportunity for both artistic creativity and spatial reasoning.

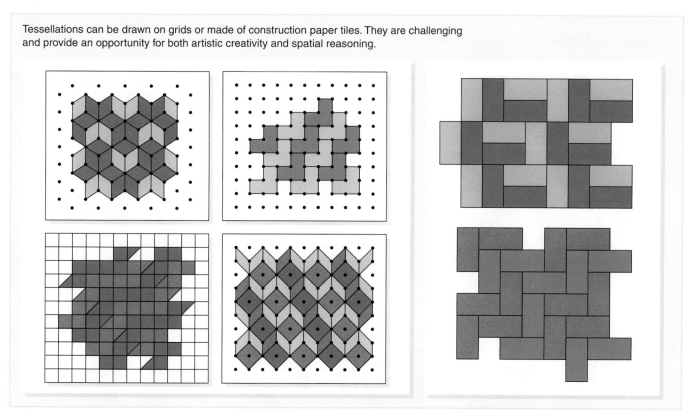

FIGURE 21.13 Tessellations.

For the sake of clarity, the important definitions of two- and three-dimensional shapes are provided here. You will notice that shape definitions include relationships between and among shapes.

Special Categories of Two-Dimensional Shapes

Table 21.1 lists some important categories of two-dimensional shapes. Examples of these shapes can be found in Figure 21.14.

TABLE 21.1

Categories of Two-Dimensional Shapes			
Shape	**Description**	**Shape**	**Description**
Simple Closed Curves		**Triangles**	
Concave, convex	An intuitive definition of *concave* might be "having a dent in it." If a simple closed curve is not concave, it is *convex*. A more precise definition of *concave* may be interesting to explore with older students.	Triangles	Polygons with exactly three sides.
		Classified by sides	
		Equilateral	All sides are congruent.
		Isosceles	At least two sides are congruent.
		Scalene	No two sides are congruent.
Symmetrical, nonsymmetrical	Shapes may have one or more lines of symmetry and may or may not have rotational symmetry. These concepts will require more detailed investigation.	*Classified by angles*	
		Right	Has a right angle.
		Acute	All angles are smaller than a right angle.
		Obtuse	One angle is larger than a right angle.
Polygons	Simple closed curves with all straight sides.	**Convex Quadrilaterals**	
Concave, convex		Convex quadrilaterals	Convex polygons with exactly four sides.
Symmetrical, nonsymmetrical		Kite	Two opposing pairs of congruent adjacent sides.
Regular	All sides and all angles are congruent.	Trapezoid	At least one pair of parallel sides.
		Isosceles trapezoid	A pair of opposite sides is congruent.
		Parallelogram	Two pairs of parallel sides.
		Rectangle	Parallelogram with a right angle.
		Rhombus	Parallelogram with all sides congruent.
		Square	Parallelogram with a right angle and all sides congruent.

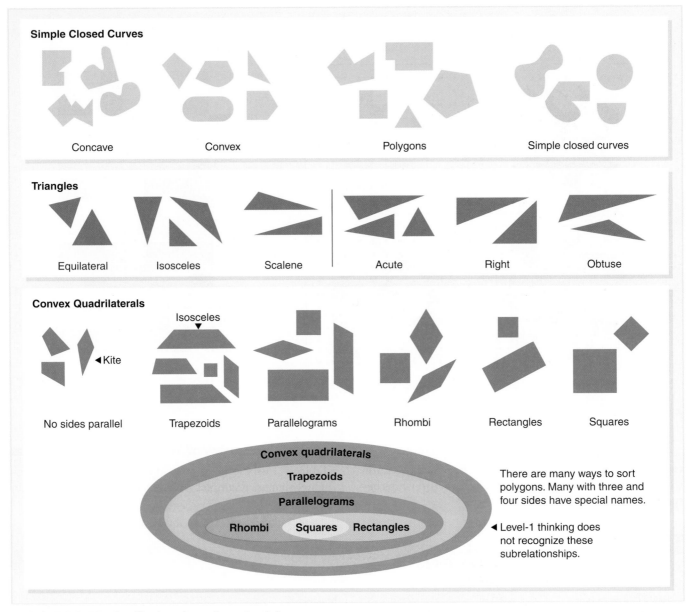

FIGURE 21.14 Classification of two-dimensional shapes.

In the classification of quadrilaterals and parallelograms, the subsets are not all disjoint. For example, a square is a rectangle and a rhombus. All parallelograms are trapezoids, but not all trapezoids are parallelograms.* Children at level 1 continue to have difficulty seeing this type of subrelationship. They may quite correctly list all the properties of a square, a rhombus, and a rectangle and still identify a square as a "nonrhombus" or a "nonrectangle." Is it

wrong for students to refer to subgroups as disjoint sets? By fourth or fifth grade, it is only wrong to encourage such thinking. Burger (1985) points out that upper elementary students correctly use such classification schemes in other contexts. For example, individual students in a class can belong to more than one club. A square is an example of a quadrilateral that belongs to two other clubs.

Special Categories of Three-Dimensional Shapes

Important and interesting shapes and relationships also exist in three dimensions. Table 21.2 describes classifications of solids. Figure 21.15 shows examples of cylinders

*Some definitions of trapezoid specify *only one* pair of parallel sides, in which case parallelograms would not be trapezoids. The University of Chicago School Mathematics Project (UCSMP) uses the "at least one pair" definition, meaning that parallelograms and rectangles are trapezoids.

TABLE 21.2

Categories of Three-Dimensional Shapes			
Shape	**Description**	**Shape**	**Description**
Sorted by Edges and Vertices		**Cylinders**	
Spheres and "egglike" shapes	Shapes with no *edges* and no *vertices* (corners). Shapes with *edges* but no *vertices* (e.g., a flying saucer). Shapes with *vertices* but no *edges* (e.g., a football).	Cylinder	Two congruent, parallel faces called *bases*. Lines joining corresponding points on the two bases are always parallel. These parallel lines are called *elements* of the cylinder.
		Right cylinder	A cylinder with elements perpendicular to the bases. A cylinder that is not a right cylinder is an *oblique cylinder*.
Sorted by Faces and Surfaces		Prism	A cylinder with polygons for bases. All prisms are special cases of cylinders.
Polyhedron	Shapes made of all faces (a *face* is a flat surface of a solid). If all surfaces are faces, all the edges will be straight lines.	Rectangular prism	A cylinder with rectangles for bases.
		Cube	A square prism with square sides.
	Some combination of faces and rounded surfaces (circular cylinders are examples, but this is not a definition of a cylinder).	**Cones**	
		Cone	A solid with exactly one face and a vertex that is not on the face. Straight lines (elements) can be drawn from any point on the edge of the base to the vertex. The base may be any shape at all. The vertex need not be directly over the base.
	Shapes with all curved surfaces. Shapes with and without edges and with and without vertices.		
		Circular cone	Cone with a circular base.
	Faces can be parallel. Parallel faces lie in planes that never intersect.	Pyramid	Cone with a polygon for a base. All faces joining the vertex are triangles. Pyramids are named by the shape of the base: *triangular* pyramid, *square* pyramid, *octagonal* pyramid, and so on. All pyramids are special cases of cones.

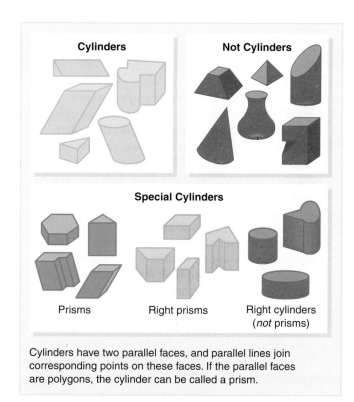

Cylinders have two parallel faces, and parallel lines join corresponding points on these faces. If the parallel faces are polygons, the cylinder can be called a prism.

FIGURE 21.15 Cylinders and prisms.

and prisms. Note that prisms are defined here as a special category of cylinder—a cylinder with a polygon for a base. Figure 21.16 shows a similar grouping of cones and pyramids.

 *pause and reflect* _____

Explain the following: Prisms are to cylinders as pyramids are to cones. How is this relationship helpful in learning volume formulas?

_____

Many textbooks define cylinders strictly as circular cylinders. These books do not have special names for other cylinders. Under that definition, the prism is not a special case of a cylinder. This points to the fact that definitions are conventions, and not all conventions are universally agreed upon. If you return to the volume formulas in Chapter 20, you will see that the more inclusive definition of cylinders and cones given here allows one formula for any type of cylinder—hence, prisms—with a similar statement that is true for cones and pyramids.

Sorting and Classifying Activities

The next activity provides a good method when you want to introduce a category of shapes.

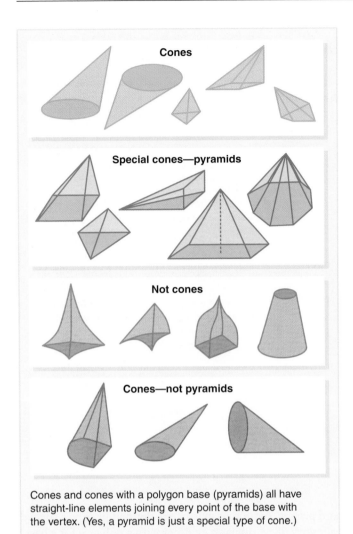

FIGURE 21.16 Cones and pyramids.

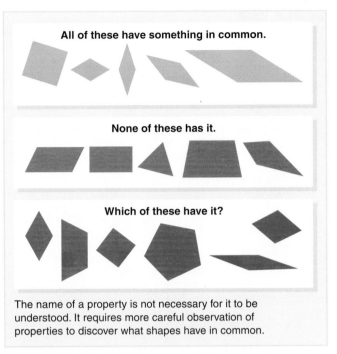

FIGURE 21.17 All of these, none of these: a mystery definition.

own concept development. After their definitions have been discussed and compared, you can offer the usual "book" definition for the sake of clarity.

For defining types or categories of triangles, the next activity is especially good and uses a different approach.

activity **21.7**

Mystery Definition

Use the overhead or chalkboard to conduct activities such as the example in Figure 21.17. For your first collection be certain that you have allowed for all possible variables. In Figure 21.17, for example, a square is included in the set of rhombi. Similarly, choose nonexamples to be as close to the positive examples as is necessary to help with an accurate definition. The third or mixed set should also include those nonexamples with which students are most likely to be confused.

Rather than confirm the choice of shapes in the third set, students should write an explanation for their choice.

The value of the "Mystery Definition" approach is that students develop ideas and definitions based on their

activity **21.8**

Triangle Sort

Make copies of the Assorted Triangles sheet found in the Blackline Masters. Note the examples of right, acute, and obtuse triangles; examples of equilateral, isosceles, and scalene triangles; and triangles that represent every possible combination of these categories. Have students cut them out. The task is to sort the entire collection into three groups so that no triangle belongs to two groups. When this is done and descriptions of the groupings have been written, students should then find a second criterion for creating three different groupings. Students may need a hint to look only at angle sizes or only at the issue of congruent sides, but hold these hints if you can.

"Triangle Sort" results in definitions of the six different types of triangles without having to list these definitions on the board and have students memorize them. As a follow-up activity, make a chart such as the one shown here. Challenge students to sketch a triangle in each of the nine cells.

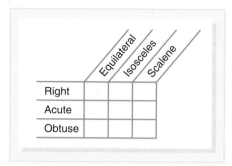

pause and reflect ——————

Of the nine cells in the chart, two of them are impossible to fill. Can you tell which ones and why?

Quadrilaterals (polygons with four sides) are an especially rich source of investigations. Once students are familiar with the concepts of right, obtuse, and acute angles, congruence of line segments and angles, and symmetry (both line and rotational), Activity 21.2, "Property Lists for Quadrilaterals" is a good way to bring these ideas together and to begin to see how different collections of properties apply to special classes of shapes. (Activity 21.2 on p. 410 was discussed briefly at the outset of the chapter. The development of symmetry concepts will be explored in the section on transformations later in the chapter.)

Recall that in "Property Lists for Quadrilaterals," students work to create lists of all the properties that they can find for a particular class of shapes. This may require two or three periods. Students should share lists beginning with parallelograms, then rhombi, then rectangles, and finally squares. Let one group present its list. Then others who worked on the same shape should add to or subtract from it. The class must agree with everything that is put on the list. As new relationships come up in this presentation-and-discussion period, you can introduce proper terminology. For example, if two diagonals intersect in a square corner, then they are *perpendicular*. Other terms such as *parallel, congruent, bisect, midpoint,* and so on can be clarified as you help students write their descriptions. This is also a good time to introduce symbols such as ≅ for "congruent" or ‖ for "parallel."

As an extension, repeat Activity 21.2 using kites and trapezoids. "Property Lists for Quadrilaterals" has some important follow-ups that are described in the section on level-2 activities (see p. 428). Furthermore, similar activities can be used to introduce three-dimensional shape definitions.

Construction Activities

Students' building or drawing shapes continues to be important at level 1. Dynamic geometry software (*The Geometer's Sketchpad* and *Cabri*) dramatically enhances the exploration of shapes at this level.

In the "Property Lists" activity, students examine the diagonals of various classes of quadrilaterals. If that activity has not been done already, the following exploration is very interesting. Rather than beginning with the shapes, it begins with the diagonals.

activity **21.9**

Diagonal Strips

For this activity, students need three strips of tagboard about 2 cm wide. Two should be the same length (about 30 cm) and the third somewhat shorter (about 20 cm). Punch nine holes equally spaced along the strip. (Punch a hole near each end. Divide the distance between the holes by 8. This will be the distance between the remaining holes.) Use a brass fastener to join two strips. A quadrilateral is formed by joining the four end holes as shown in Figure 21.18. Provide students with the list of possible relationships for angles, lengths, and ratios of parts. Their task is to use the strips to determine the properties of diagonals that will produce different quadrilaterals. The strips are there to help in the exploration. Students may want to make drawings on dot grids to test the various hypotheses.

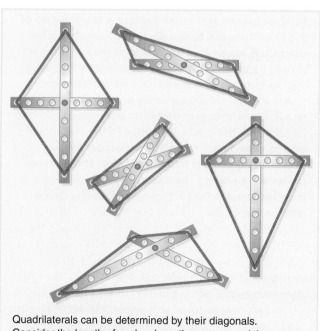

Quadrilaterals can be determined by their diagonals. Consider the length of each, where they cross, and the angles between them. What conditions will produce parallelograms? Rectangles? Rhombi? Challenge: What properties will produce a nonisosceles trapezoid?

FIGURE 21.18 Diagonals of quadrilaterals.

Every type of quadrilateral can be uniquely described in terms of its diagonals using only the conditions of length, ratio of parts, and whether or not they are perpendicular. Some students will work with the diagonal relationships to see what shapes can be made. Others will begin with examples of the shapes and observe the diagonal relationships. A dynamic geometry program such as *The Geometer's Sketchpad* is an excellent vehicle for this investigation.

Circles

Many interesting relationships can be observed between measures of different parts of the circle. Among the most astounding and important is the ratio between measures of the circumference and the diameter.

activity 21.10

Discovering Pi

Have groups of students carefully measure the circumference and diameter of many different circles. Each group measures different circles.

  Measure both the circumference and diameter of circular items such as jar lids, tubes, cans, and wastebaskets. To measure circumference, wrap string once around the object and then measure that length of string.

  Also measure large circles marked on gym floors and playgrounds. Use a trundle wheel or rope to measure the circumference.

  Collect measures of circumference and diameter from all groups and enter them in a table. Ratios of the circumference to the diameter should also be computed for each circle. A scatter plot of the data should be made with the horizontal axis representing diameters and the vertical axis circumferences.

  Most ratios should be in the neighborhood of 3.1 or 3.2. The scatter plot should approximate a straight line through the origin. The slope of the line should also be close to 3.1. (Recall from Chapter 19 that graphs of equivalent ratios are always straight lines through the origin.) The exact ratio is an irrational number, about 3.14159, represented by the Greek letter π (pi).

What is most important in Activity 21.10 is that students develop a clear understanding of π as the ratio of circumference to diameter in any circle. The quantity π is not some strange number that appears in math formulas; it is a naturally occurring and universal ratio.

As students begin to do more than build with geometric "blocks" (tangrams, pattern blocks, grid drawing, etc.), the computer begins to offer powerful tools for explorations. ∎

Dynamic Geometry Software

In a dynamic geometry program, points, lines, and geometric figures are easily constructed on the computer using only the mouse. Once drawn, the geometric objects can be moved about and manipulated in endless variety. Distances, lengths, areas, angles, slopes, and perimeters can be measured. As the figures are changed, the measurements update instantly.

Lines can be drawn perpendicular or parallel to other lines or segments. Angles and segments can be drawn congruent to other angles and segments. A point can be placed at the midpoint of a segment. A figure can be produced that is a reflection, rotation, or dilation of another figure. The most significant thing is that when a geometric object is created with a particular relationship to another, that relationship is maintained no matter how either object is moved or changed.

The best known dynamic geometry programs are *The Geometer's Sketchpad* (Key Curriculum Press), *Geometry Inventor* (Riverdeep), and *Cabri Geometry II* (Texas Instruments). Although each operates somewhat differently, they are sufficiently alike that separate descriptions are not required here. Originally designed for high school students, all can be used profitably and should be used starting about grade 4.

Dynamic Geometry Examples

To appreciate the potential (and the fun) of dynamic geometry software, you really need to experience it on a computer. In the meantime, an example is offered here in an attempt to illustrate how these programs work.

In Figure 21.19, the midpoints of a freely drawn quadrilateral ABCD have been joined. The diagonals of

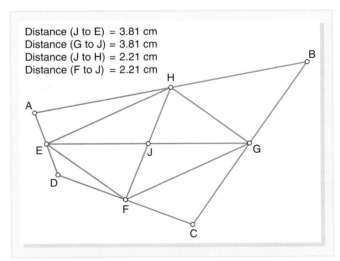

FIGURE 21.19 A *Sketchpad* construction illustrating an interesting property of quadrilaterals.

the resulting quadrilateral (EFGH) are also drawn and measured. No matter how the points A, B, C, and D are dragged around the screen, even inverting the quadrilateral, the other lines will maintain the same relationships (joining midpoints and diagonals), and the measurements will be instantly updated on the screen.

Remember that at level 1, the objects of thought are *classes* of shapes. In a dynamic geometry program, if a quadrilateral is drawn, only one shape is observed, as would be the case on paper or on a geoboard. But now that quadrilateral can be stretched and altered in endless ways. Students actually explore not one shape but an enormous number of examples from that class of shapes. If a property does not change when the figure changes, the property is attributable to the *class* of shapes rather than any particular shape.

Another example in Figure 21.20 shows how *Sketchpad* can be used to investigate quadrilaterals starting with the diagonals. The directions for creating the sketch are included and can be done quite simply with minimal experience with the software. By creating the drawing in this manner, the diagonals of ACBD will always bisect each other no matter how the drawing is altered. By dragging point C around, ACBD can be made into a parallelogram, rectangle, rhombus, and square. For each of these figures, additional information about the diagonals can be determined by looking at the drawing.

Dynamic geometry programs are also powerful for investigating concepts of symmetry and transformations (slides, flips, and turns). The publishers of these programs provide excellent activities that are appropriate for level-1 investigations. Many activities are included with the software, and others are found in supplemental publications.

Shapes and Properties for Level-2 Thinkers

At level 2, the focus shifts from simply examining properties of shapes to explorations that include logical reasoning. As students develop an understanding of various geometric properties and attach these properties to important categories of shapes, it is essential to begin to encourage conjecture and to explore informal deductive arguments. Students should begin to attempt—or at least follow—simple proofs and explore ideas that connect directly to algebra.

Definitions and Proofs

The partner activities of "Property Lists for Quadrilaterals" (Activity 21.2), which is a level-1 activity, and "Minimal Defining Lists" (Activity 21.3), a level-2 activity, really clarify the distinction between these two levels. (You may want to review these activities again before reading on. Refer to pp. 410–411.)

Finding MDLs (minimal defining lists) is the main challenge of Activity 21.3. The parallelogram, rhombus, rectangle, and square each have at least four MDLs. One of the most interesting MDLs for each shape consists only of the properties of its diagonals. For example, a quadrilateral with diagonals that bisect each other and are perpendicular (intersect at right angles) is a rhombus. Several MDLs consist of only one property. For example, a quadrilateral with rotational symmetry of at least order 2 is a parallelogram.

Notice that the MDL activity is actually more involved in logic than in examining shapes. Students are engaged in the general process of deciding, "*If we specify only this list of properties, will that guarantee this particular shape?*" A second feature is the opportunity to discuss what constitutes a definition. In fact, any MDL could be the definition of the shape. The definitions we usually use are MDLs that have been chosen probably due to the ease with which we can understand them. A quadrilateral with diagonals that bisect each other does not immediately call to mind a parallelogram although that is a defining list of

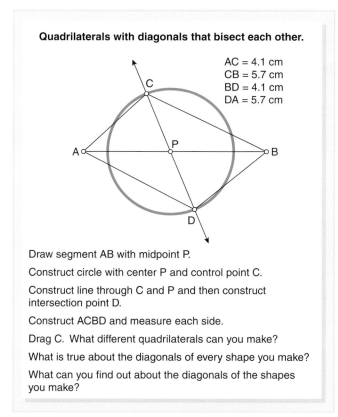

Quadrilaterals with diagonals that bisect each other.

AC = 4.1 cm
CB = 5.7 cm
BD = 4.1 cm
DA = 5.7 cm

Draw segment AB with midpoint P.

Construct circle with center P and control point C.

Construct line through C and P and then construct intersection point D.

Construct ACBD and measure each side.

Drag C. What different quadrilaterals can you make?

What is true about the diagonals of every shape you make?

What can you find out about the diagonals of the shapes you make?

FIGURE 21.20 With *The Geometer's Sketchpad* students can construct two line segments that will always bisect each other. When the endpoints are joined, the resulting quadrilateral will always be of the same class, regardless of how points A, B, C, and D are moved around.

properties. Recall that when students created their property lists, no definition was given, only a collection of shapes and a label. Theoretically, the lists could have been created without ever having heard of these shapes.

The next activity is also a good follow-up to the "Property Lists" activity, although it is not restricted to quadrilaterals and can include three-dimensional shapes as well. Notice again the logic involved.

activity **21.11**

True or False?

Prepare statements of the following forms: "If it is a _____, then it is also a _____." "All _____ are _____." "Some _____ are _____."

A few examples are suggested here but numerous possibilities exist.

- If it is a square, then it is a rhombus.
- All squares are rectangles.
- Some parallelograms are rectangles.
- All parallelograms have congruent diagonals.
- If it has exactly two lines of symmetry, it must be a quadrilateral.
- If it is a cylinder, then it is a prism.
- All prisms have a plane of symmetry.
- All pyramids have square bases.
- If a prism has a plane of symmetry, then it is a right prism.

The task is to decide if the statements are true or false and to present an argument to support the decision. Four or five true-or-false statements will make a good lesson. Once this format is understood, let students challenge their classmates by making their own lists of five statements. Each list should have at least one true statement and one false statement. Use the students' lists in subsequent lessons.

Ⅱ *pause and reflect* ————————

Use the property list for squares and rectangles to prove "All squares are rectangles." Notice that you must use logical reasoning to understand this statement. It does little good to simply force it on students who are not ready to develop the relationship.

———————————

Although logic has been involved in these activities, you may have difficulty understanding how middle school students can actually do proofs. The following activity was designed by Sconyers (1995) to demonstrate that students can create proofs in geometry well before high school.

activity **21.12**

Two Polygons from One
Pose the following problem:

Begin with a convex polygon with a given number of sides. Connect two points on the polygon with a line segment forming two new polygons. How many sides do the two resulting polygons have together?

Demonstrate with a few examples (see Figure 21.21). Have students explore by drawing polygons and slicing them. Encourage students to make a table showing sides in original and resulting sides. Students should first make conjectures about a general rule. When groups are comfortable with their conjecture, they should try to reason why their statement is correct—that is, prove their conjecture.

Obviously, the number of resulting sides depends on where the slice is made. With the exception of triangles, there are three possibilities. For each case, a clear argument can be made. The appropriate conjecture and proof are left to you, but trust that students working together can do this task.

Notice that in this task, as in others we have explored, the statements to be proved come from students. If you

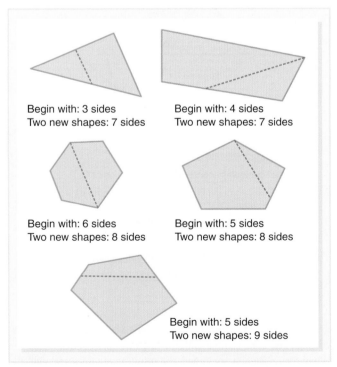

Begin with: 3 sides
Two new shapes: 7 sides

Begin with: 4 sides
Two new shapes: 7 sides

Begin with: 6 sides
Two new shapes: 8 sides

Begin with: 5 sides
Two new shapes: 8 sides

Begin with: 5 sides
Two new shapes: 9 sides

FIGURE 21.21 Start with a polygon, and draw a segment to divide it into two polygons. How many sides will the two new polygons have?

write a theorem on the board and ask students to prove it, you have already told them that it is true. If, by contrast, a student makes a statement about a geometric situation the class is exploring, it can be written on the board with a question mark as a *conjecture*, a statement whose truth has not yet been determined. You can ask, "Is it true? Always? Can we prove it? Can we find a counterexample?" Reasonable deductive arguments can be forged out of discussions.

The Pythagorean Relationship

The *Pythagorean relationship* is so important that it deserves some special attention. In geometric terms, this relationship states that if a square is constructed on each side of a right triangle, the areas of the two smaller squares will together equal the area of the square on the longest side, the hypotenuse. To discover this relationship, consider the following activity.

---

activity **21.13**

The Pythagorean Relationship

Have students draw a right triangle on half-centimeter grid paper. Assign each student a different triangle by specifying the lengths of the two legs. Students are to draw a square on each leg and the hypotenuse and find the area of all three squares. (For the square on the hypotenuse, the exact area can be found by making each of the sides the diagonal of a rectangle. See Figure 21.22.) Make a table of the area data (Sq. on leg 1, Sq. on leg 2, Sq. on hyp.), and ask students to look for a relationship between the squares.

As an extension to the last activity, students can explore drawing other figures on the legs of right triangles and computing areas. For example, draw semicircles or equilat-

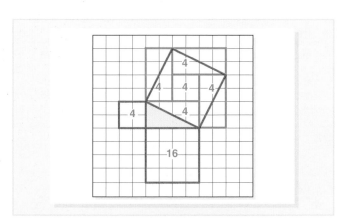

FIGURE 21.22 The Pythagorean relationship. Note that if drawn on a grid, the area of all squares is easily determined. Here 4 + 16 = area of the square on the hypotenuse.

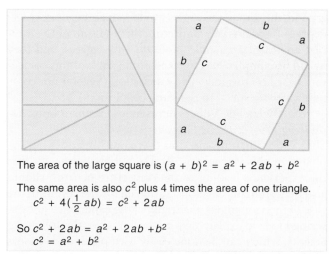

The area of the large square is $(a + b)^2 = a^2 + 2ab + b^2$

The same area is also c^2 plus 4 times the area of one triangle.
$$c^2 + 4(\tfrac{1}{2}ab) = c^2 + 2ab$$

So $c^2 + 2ab = a^2 + 2ab + b^2$
$$c^2 = a^2 + b^2$$

FIGURE 21.23 Two proofs of the Pythagorean relationship. The two squares together are a "proof without words." Can you supply the words? The second proof is the algebraic proof based on the right-hand figure.

eral triangles instead of squares. The areas of any regular polygons drawn on the three sides of right triangles will have the same relationship.

Activity 21.13 establishes the Pythagorean relationship. What about a proof? Figure 21.23 shows two proofs that students can follow. The first consists of only the two drawings. It is taken from the book *Proofs without Words* (Nelson, 1993). An algebraic proof is shown below the drawings, based on the second square.

 pause and reflect ⎯⎯⎯⎯⎯

Use the two drawings in Figure 21.23 to create a proof of the Pythagorean relationship.

 The *e-Standards* includes a dynamic proof without words that is worth sharing with your students (Applet 6.5). Because it requires knowing that parallelograms and rectangles with the same base and height have the same area (see Chapter 20), it is also a good review. ∎

Finding Versus Explaining Relationships

Dynamic geometry software such as *The Geometer's Sketchpad* allows students to explore an entire class of figures and observe properties or relationships that are attributable to that class. At level 2, however, the focus is on reasoning or deductive thinking. Can these computer programs help students develop deductive arguments to support the relationships they come to believe through inductive reasoning? Consider the following situation.

Suppose that you have students use a dynamic geometry program to draw a triangle, measure all of the angles, and add them up. As the triangle vertices are dragged around, the sum of the angles would remain steadfast at 180 degrees. Students can conjecture that the sum of the interior angles of a triangle is always 180 degrees, and they would be completely convinced of the truth of this conjecture based on this inductive experience. (Several noncomputer activities lead to the same conclusion.)

As Michael de Villiers notes in his excellent book *Rethinking Proof with the Geometer's Sketchpad* (1999), "The observation that the sun rises every morning does not explain why this is true" (p. 24). De Villiers points out that the experience leading to the conjecture or truth should also help students develop a rationale for the result. In the case of interior angles of a triangle, the experience just described fails to explain *why it is so.* Consider the following activity, which can be done easily with paper and scissors or quite dramatically with a dynamic geometry program.

activity 21.14

Angle Sum in a Triangle
Have all students cut out three congruent triangles. (Stack three sheets of paper, and cut three shapes at one time.) Place one triangle on a line and the second directly next to it in the same orientation. Place the third triangle in the space between the triangles as shown in Figure 21.24(a). Based on this experience, what conjecture can you make about the sum of the angles in a triangle?

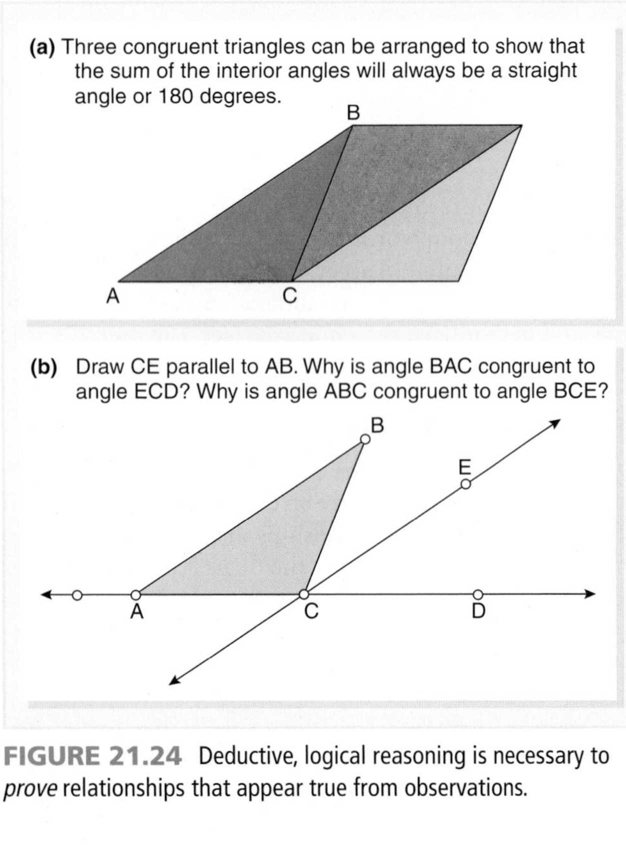

(a) Three congruent triangles can be arranged to show that the sum of the interior angles will always be a straight angle or 180 degrees.

(b) Draw CE parallel to AB. Why is angle BAC congruent to angle ECD? Why is angle ABC congruent to angle BCE?

FIGURE 21.24 Deductive, logical reasoning is necessary to *prove* relationships that appear true from observations.

In a dynamic geometry program, the three triangles in Figure 21.24(a) can be drawn by starting with one triangle, translating it to the right the length of AC, and then rotating the same triangle about the midpoint of side BC. When vertices of the original triangle are dragged, the other triangles will change accordingly and remain congruent. We still do not know why the angle sum is always a straight angle, but this exploration allows students to see why it might be so. In the figure, there are lines parallel to each side of the original triangle. By using properties of angles formed by cutting parallel lines with a transverse line, it is easy to argue that the sum of the angles will always be a straight line (see Figure 21.24(b); the proof is left to you).

Dynamic geometry software can be enormously powerful for helping students observe geometric relationships and make conjectures. The truth of the conjectures will often be obvious. At level 2, however, we must begin to ask why. The following activity further illustrates the point.

activity 21.15

Triangle Midsegments
Using a dynamic geometry program, draw a triangle, and label the vertices A, B, and C. Draw the segment joining the midpoints of AB and AC, and label this segment DE, as in Figure 21.25. Measure the length of DE and BC. Also measure angles ADE and ABC. Drag points A, B, and C. What conjectures can you make about the relationships between segment DE, the *midsegment* of ABC, and BC, the base of ABC?

It is very clear that the midsegment is half the length of the base and parallel to it, but why is this so? Students will need a bit more guidance, but you should not necessarily have to provide the argument for them. Suggest that

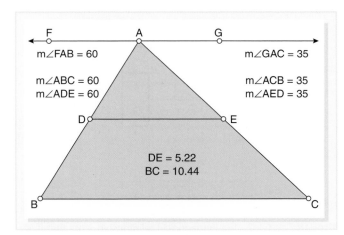

$m\angle FAB = 60$ $m\angle GAC = 35$

$m\angle ABC = 60$ $m\angle ACB = 35$
$m\angle ADE = 60$ $m\angle AED = 35$

DE = 5.22
BC = 10.44

FIGURE 21.25 The midsegment of a triangle is always parallel to the base and half as long.

they draw a line through A parallel to BC. List all pairs of angles that they know are congruent. Why are they congruent? Note that triangle ABC is similar to triangle ADE. Why is it similar? With hints such as these, many middle grade students can begin to make logical arguments for why the things they observe to be true are in fact true.

EXPANDED LESSON
An expanded lesson plan based on Activity 21.15, "Triangle Midsegments," can be found on the Companion Web site at www. ablongman.com/ vandewalle6e.

shape as the point of rotation and restrict reflections to vertical and horizontal lines through the center. These restrictions are not necessary and may even be misleading.

The Motion Man described in the next activity can also be used to introduce students to the terms *slide*, *flip*, and *turn*. In the activity, rotations are restricted to $\frac{1}{4}$, $\frac{1}{2}$, and $\frac{3}{4}$ turns in a clockwise direction. The center of the turn will be the center of the figure. Reflections will be flips over vertical or horizontal lines. These restrictions are for simplicity. In the general case, the center of rotation can be anywhere on or off the figure. Lines of reflection can also be anywhere.

Learning About Transformations

Transformations are changes in position or size of a shape. Movements that do not change the size or shape of the object moved are called "rigid motions." Usually, three rigid-motion transformations are discussed: *translations* or slides, *reflections* or flips, and *rotations* or turns. Interestingly, the study of symmetry is also included under the study of transformations. Do you know why?

Transformations for Level-0 Thinkers

Transformations at this level involve an introduction to the basic concepts of slides, flips, and turns and the initial development of line symmetry and rotational symmetry.

Slides, Flips, and Turns

At the primary level, the terms *slide*, *flip*, and *turn* are adequate. The early goal is to help students recognize these transformations and to begin to explore their effect on simple shapes. You can use a nonsymmetric shape on the overhead to introduce these terms (see Figure 21.26). Most likely your textbook will use only the center of a

activity **21.16**

Motion Man

Using the Motion Man Blackline Masters, make copies of the first Motion Man and then copy the mirror image on the backs of these copies. (See Figure 21.27.) Experiment first. You want the back image to match the front image when held to the light. Cut off the excess paper to leave a square. Give all students a two-sided Motion Man.

Demonstrate each of the possible motions. A slide is simply that. The figure does not rotate or turn over. Demonstrate $\frac{1}{4}$, $\frac{1}{2}$, and $\frac{3}{4}$ turns. Emphasize that only clockwise turns will be used for this activity. Similarly, demonstrate a horizontal flip (top goes to bottom) and a vertical flip (left goes to right). Practice by having everyone start with his or her Motion Man in the same orientation. As you announce one of the moves, students slide, flip, or turn Motion Man accordingly.

Then display two Motion Men side by side in any orientation. The task is to decide what motion or combination of motions will get the man on the left to match the man on the right. Students use their own man to work out a solution. Test the solutions that students offer. If both men are in the same position, call that a slide.

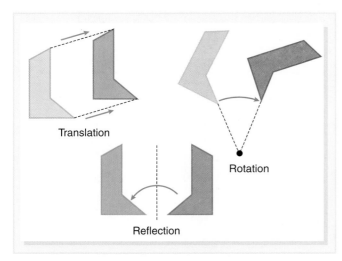

FIGURE 21.26 Translation (slide), reflection (flip), rotation (turn).

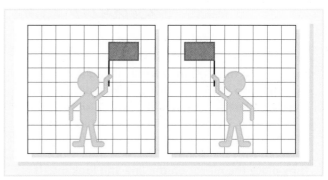

FIGURE 21.27 The Motion Man is printed back to back. Use to show slides, flips, and turns. (See Blackline Masters.)

pause and reflect ——————————

Begin with the Motion Man in the left position shown in Figure 21.27. Now place a second Motion Man next to the first. Will it take one move or more than one move (transformation) to get from the first to the second Motion Man? Can you describe all of the positions that require more than one move? Are there any positions that require more than two moves?

At first, students will be confused when they can't get their Motion Man into the new position with one move. This causes an excellent problem. Don't be too quick to suggest that it may take two moves. If flips across each of the two diagonals are added to the motions along with vertical and horizontal flips, Motion Man can assume any new position in exactly one move. This provides a challenge for students. Two students begin with their Motion Man figures in the same position. One student then changes his or her Motion Man and challenges the other student to say what motion is required to make the two Motion Men match. The solution is then tested and the roles reversed.

Line and Rotational Symmetry

If a shape can be folded on a line so that the two halves match, then it is said to have *line symmetry* (or *mirror symmetry*). Notice that the fold line is actually a line of reflection—the portion of the shape on one side of the line is reflected onto the other side. That is the connection between line symmetry and transformations.

One way to introduce line symmetry to children is to show examples and nonexamples using an all-of-these/none-of-these approach as in Figure 21.17, p. 424. Another possibility is to have students fold a sheet of paper in half and cut out a shape of their choosing. When they open the paper, the fold line will be a line of symmetry. A third way is to use mirrors. When you place a mirror on a picture or design so that the mirror is perpendicular to the table, you see a shape with symmetry when you look in the mirror.

Here is an activity with line symmetry.

activity 21.17

Pattern Block Mirror Symmetry

Students need a plain sheet of paper with a straight line through the middle. Using about six to eight pattern blocks, students make a design completely on one side of the line that touches the line in some way. The task is to make the mirror image of their design on the other side of the line. When finished, they use a mirror to check their work. They place the mirror on the line and look into it from the side of the original design. With the mirror in place they should see exactly the same image as they see when they lift the mirror. You can also challenge them to make designs with more than one line of symmetry.

Building symmetrical designs with pattern blocks tends to be easier if the line is "pointing" at the student, that is, with a left and a right side. With the line oriented horizontally or diagonally, the task is harder.

The same task can be done with a geoboard. First, stretch a band down the center or from corner to corner. Make a design on one side of the line and its mirror image on the other. Check with a mirror. This can also be done on either isometric or rectangular dot grids as shown in Figure 21.28.

A plane of symmetry in three dimensions is analogous to a line of symmetry in two dimensions. Figure 21.29 illustrates a shape built with cubes that has a plane of symmetry.

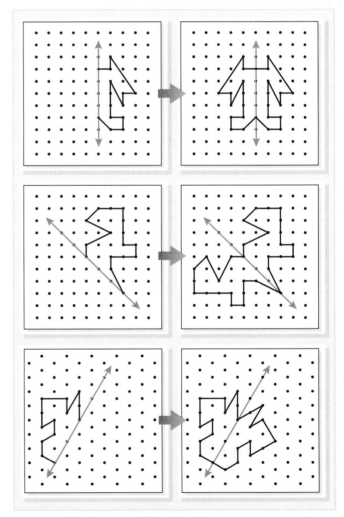

FIGURE 21.28 Exploring symmetry on dot grids.

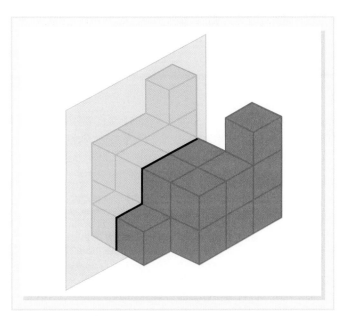

FIGURE 21.29 A block building with one plane of symmetry.

activity 21.18

Plane Symmetry Buildings
With cubes, build a building that has a plane of symmetry. If the plane of symmetry goes between cubes, slice the shape by separating the building into two symmetrical parts. Try making buildings with two or three planes of symmetry. Build various prisms. Do not forget that a plane can slice diagonally through the blocks.

A shape has *rotational symmetry* if it can be rotated about a point and land in a position exactly matching the one in which it began. A square has rotational symmetry as does an equilateral triangle.

A good way to understand rotational symmetry is to take a shape with rotational symmetry, such as a square, and trace around it on a piece of paper. Call this tracing the shape's "box." The order of rotational symmetry will be the number of ways that the shape can fit into its box without flipping it over. A square has rotational symmetry of *order* 4, whereas an equilateral triangle has rotational symmetry of *order* 3. The parallelogram in Figure 21.30 has rotational symmetry of order 2. Some books would call

order 2 symmetry "180-degree symmetry." The degrees refer to the smallest angle of rotation required before the shape matches itself or fits into its box. A square has 90-degree rotational symmetry.

activity 21.19

Pattern Block Rotational Symmetry
Have students construct designs with pattern blocks with different rotational symmetries. They should be able to make designs with order 2, 3, 4, 6, or 12 rotational symmetry. Which of the designs have mirror symmetry as well?

Rotational symmetry in the plane (also referred to as *point symmetry*) has an analogous counterpart in three dimensions. Whereas a figure in a plane is rotated about a point, a three-dimensional figure is rotated about a line. This line is called an *axis of symmetry*. As a solid with rotational symmetry revolves around an axis of symmetry, it will occupy the same position in space (its "box"), but in different orientations. A solid can have more than one axis of rotation. For each axis of symmetry, there is a corresponding order of rotational symmetry. A regular square pyramid has only one axis of symmetry that runs through the tip of the pyramid and the center of the square. A cube, by contrast, has a total of 13 axes of symmetry: three (through opposite faces) of order 4, four (through diagonally opposite vertices) of order 3, and six (through midpoints of diagonally opposite edges) of order 2.

activity 21.20

Find the Spin Lines
Give students a solid shape that has one or more axes of rotational symmetry. Color or label each face of the solid to help keep track. The task is to find all axes of rotational symmetry (spin lines) and determine the order of rotational symmetry for each. Suggest that students use one finger of each hand to hold the solid at the two points where the axis of symmetry emerges. A partner can then slowly turn the solid, and both can decide when the solid is again "in its box"—that is, in the same space it was in originally (see Figure 21.31).

Transformations for Level-1 Thinkers

Within the context of transformations, students moving into level-1 thinking can begin to analyze transformations a bit more analytically and to apply them to things that they see. Two types of activities seem appropriate at this level: compositions of transformations and using transformations to create tessellations.

FIGURE 21.30 This parallelogram fits in its box two ways without flipping it over. Therefore, it has rotational symmetry of order 2.

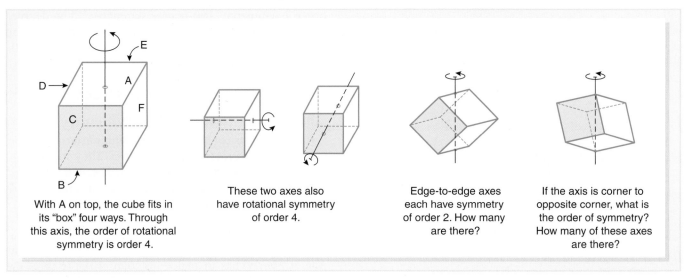

FIGURE 21.31 Rotations of a cube.

Composition of Transformations

One transformation can be followed by another. For example, a figure can be reflected over a line, and then that figure can be rotated about a point. A combination of two or more transformations is called a *composition*.

Have students experiment with compositions of two or even three transformations using a simple shape on a rectangular dot grid. For example, have students draw an L-shape on a dot grid and label it L_1. (Refer to Figure 21.32.) Reflect it through a line, and then rotate the image $\frac{1}{4}$ turn clockwise about a point not on the shape. Call this image L_2,

the image of a composition of a reflection followed by a rotation. Notice that if L_1 is rotated $\frac{1}{4}$ turn clockwise about the same point used before to L_3 there is a relationship between L_2 and L_3. Continue to explore different combinations of transformations. Don't forget to include translations (slides) in the compositions. Compositions do not have to involve different types of transformations. For example, a reflection can be followed by another reflection. When your students understand compositions of transformations on a grid, challenge them with the next task.

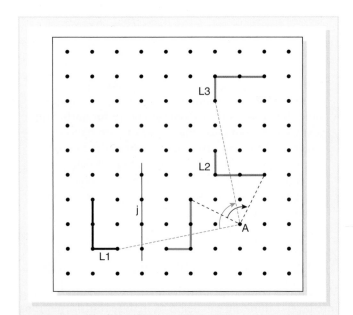

FIGURE 21.32 Shape L_1 was reflected across line j and rotated $\frac{1}{4}$ turn about point A resulting in L_2. L_1 was also rotated $\frac{1}{4}$ turn about point A. How are L_2 and L_3 related? Will this always work?

activity **21.21**

Mystery Transformations

Draw a small L-shaped figure near one corner of a rectangular dot grid. On this page, students draw a congruent L-shape somewhere near the center of the page. The second L can be flipped or turned in any orientation they wish. Then students trade papers with a partner. The task is to find some combination of slides, flips, and $\frac{1}{4}$ or $\frac{1}{2}$ turns that will take the shape in the corner onto the shape drawn by the students.

This is a challenging activity. To help students, ask if the L has been flipped over or not. If it is flipped over, then there will have to be one or three reflections. Regardless of how the two shapes are oriented, it can always be done in three or fewer transformations.

In NCTM's *e-Standards*, "Understanding Congruence, Similarity, and Symmetry" (Applet 6.4) is one of the best examples of a simple yet valuable interactive applet. In the first part of the applet, students develop an understanding of all three rigid motions. In the second part, a transformation is complete and the student uses a guess-and-check procedure to determine what exact transformation was done. In the last two parts, students can explore compositions of reflections and then other compositions of up to three transformations. This applet is strongly recommended.

Another vivid illustration of transformations is found in the dynamic geometry programs. These programs also allow you to create compositions of transformations. Students will likely require considerable guidance to create compositions. ■

Similar Figures and Proportional Reasoning

In Chapter 19 on proportional reasoning, we saw a good first definition of similar figures as shapes that "look alike but are different sizes" (see Activity 19.3, p. 358). More precisely, two figures are *similar* if all of their corresponding angles are congruent and the corresponding sides are proportional. Other proportional reasoning activities are also good connections to geometry. Activities 19.9, 19.10, and 19.11 involve scale drawings and proportional relationships in three-dimensional figures that are similar.

A *dilation* is a nonrigid transformation that produces similar figures. Figure 21.33 shows how a given figure can be *dilated* to make larger or smaller figures. If different groups of students dilate the same figure using the same scale factor, they will find that the resulting figures are all congruent, even with each group using different dilation points. Dynamic geometry software makes the results of this exercise quite dramatic. The software allows for the scale factors to be set at any value. Once a dilation is made, the dilation point can be dragged around the screen and the size and shape of the image clearly stay unchanged. Scale factors less than 1 produce smaller figures.

Tessellations Revisited

Either by using transformations or by combining compatible polygons, students at level 1 can create tessellations that are artistic and quite complex.

The Dutch artist M. C. Escher is well known for his tessellations, where the tiles are very intricate and often take the shape of things like birds, horses, angels, or lizards. Escher took a simple shape such as a triangle, parallelogram, or hexagon and performed transformations on the sides. For example, a curve drawn along one side might be translated (slid) to the opposite side. Another idea was to draw a curve from the midpoint of a side to the adjoining vertex. This curve was then rotated about the midpoint to form a totally new side of the tile. These two ideas are illustrated in part (a) of Figure 21.34. Dot paper is used to help draw the lines. *Escher-type tessellations*, as these have come to be called, are quite popular projects for students in grades 5 and up. Once a tile has been designed, it can be cut from two different colors of construction paper instead of drawing the tessellation on a dot grid.

A *regular tessellation* is made of a single tile that is a regular polygon (all sides and angles congruent). Each vertex

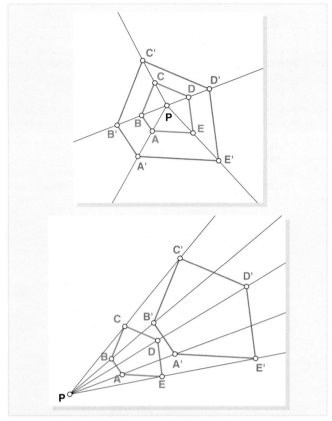

FIGURE 21.33 Begin with figure ABCDE and place point P anywhere at all. Draw lines from P through each vertex. Place point A' twice as far from P as A is from P (scale factor of 2). Do similarly for the other points. In this drawing, ABCDE is the same in both figures and the images are congruent.

of a regular tessellation has the same number of tiles meeting at that point. A checkerboard is a simple example of a regular tessellation. A *semiregular tessellation* is made of two or more tiles, each of which is a regular polygon. At each vertex of a semiregular tessellation, the same collection of regular polygons come together in the same order. A vertex (and, therefore, the complete semiregular tessellation) can be described by the series of shapes meeting at a vertex. Under each example of these tessellations in part (b) of Figure 21.34, the vertex numbers are given. Students can figure out what polygons are possible at a vertex and design their own semiregular tessellations.

Tessellations like these are very popular with teachers in grades 3 and above. A number of excellent resource books can be found in catalogs such as ETA Cuisenaire.

Transformations for Level-2 Thinkers

The following activity is a challenge for students to use their understanding of symmetries and transformations to establish an interesting relationship between these two ideas. The shapes used for this activity are called *pentominoes*—shapes made from 5 squares, each square

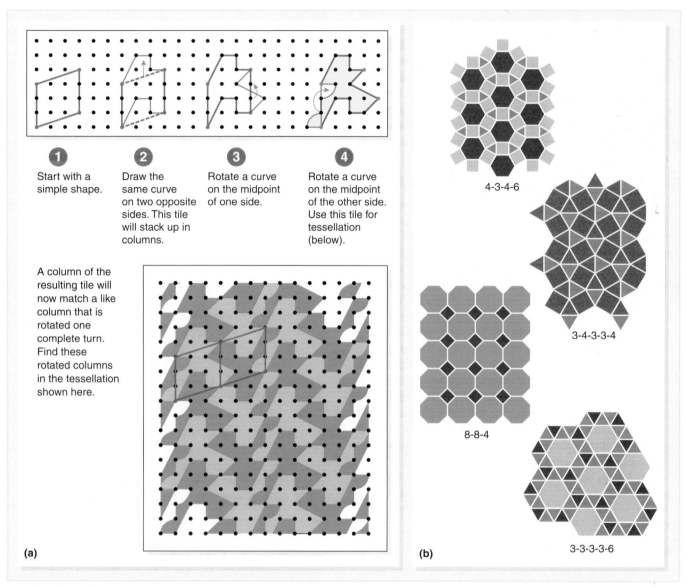

1. Start with a simple shape.

2. Draw the same curve on two opposite sides. This tile will stack up in columns.

3. Rotate a curve on the midpoint of one side.

4. Rotate a curve on the midpoint of the other side. Use this tile for tessellation (below).

A column of the resulting tile will now match a like column that is rotated one complete turn. Find these rotated columns in the tessellation shown here.

(a)

4-3-4-6

3-4-3-3-4

8-8-4

3-3-3-3-6

(b)

FIGURE 21.34 (a) One of many ways to create an Escher-type tessellation. (b) Examples of semiregular tessellations.

touching at least one other square with squares sharing a full side. Students may remember pentominoes from an earlier grade. The search to see how many different pentominoes there are is a well-known geometry activity. (See p. 444 for an introductory activity.) For our purposes in discussing transformations and symmetries, the collection of 12 pentominoes simply serves as a convenient collection of shapes. These are shown in Figure 21.35.

activity 21.22

Pentomino Positions

Have students cut out a set of 12 pentominoes from 2-cm grid paper. (See Figure 21.35.) Mark one side of each piece to help remember if it has been flipped over. The first part of the task is to determine how many different positions on the grid each piece has. Call positions "different" if a reflection or a turn is required to make them match. Therefore, the cross-shaped piece has only one position. The strip of five squares has two positions. Some pieces have as many as eight positions. The second part of the task is to find a relationship between the line symmetries and rotational symmetries for each piece and the number of positions it can have on the grid.

The first part of this activity was adapted from the classic book *Boxes, Squares, and Other Things* (Walter, 1970), which has many more excellent explorations. The second part of the problem is not hard if students make a table of what they know. The solutions to the task are left

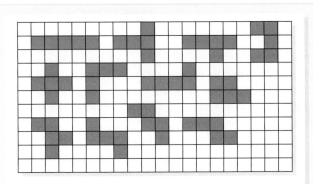

There are 12 pentominoes.

Finding all possible shapes made with five squares— or six squares (called "hexominoes") or six equilateral triangles and so on—is a good exercise in spatial problem solving.

FIGURE 21.35 There are 12 different pentomino shapes. An exploration to find these shapes is a visualization activity found on p. 436.

to you and your students. As a follow-up to Activity 21.22, examine the excerpt from the eighth-grade *Connected Mathematics* curriculum on page 439. Incidentally, a very similar exploration can be found in *Boxes, Squares, and Other Things.*

The next task challenges students to develop generalizations about certain compositions of transformations.

activity **21.23**

Double Reflections
There are two similar tasks in this activity:

1. **Verify that the composition of two reflections across parallel lines (first across one and then the other) is the same as a translation. Make a drawing on a dot grid to illustrate. Challenge: If you know the distance between the two parallel lines, what can you say about the translation— both its direction and its distance? Does it matter where the shape begins (between the lines or outside) or which line is used as the first reflection? Explain your conclusions.**

2. **Verify that the composition of two reflections across intersecting lines is the same as a rotation about the point of intersection of the lines. Make a drawing on a dot grid to illustrate. Challenge: How is the angle of rotation related to the angle between the lines? Explain your conclusions.**

In the first problem, the translation distance is always double the distance between the lines and is perpendicular to them. The direction is determined by which line is used for the first reflection in relation to the preimage. In the second problem, the angle of rotation is double the an-

gle between the lines. It is possible to construct reasonable arguments for these conclusions by examining drawings.

Learning About Location

The location standard in *Principles and Standards* says that students should "specify locations and describe spatial relationships using coordinate geometry and other representational systems" (NCTM, 2000, p. 42). After some everyday terms for how objects are located with respect to other objects (e.g., the ball is *under* the table), location activities involve analysis of paths from point to point as on a map and the use of coordinate systems. Coordinate systems are an extremely important form of representation. They allow us to analyze geometric ideas such as the transformations. Coordinates also play a significant role in algebra.

Location for Level-0 Thinkers

In kindergarten, children learn about everyday positional descriptions—*over, under, near, far, between, left,* and *right.* These are the beginnings of the *Standards'* goal of specifying locations. These informal indicators of location are useful for everyday interactions. However, helping students refine the way they answer questions of direction, distance, and location enhances spatial understandings. Geometry, measurement, and algebra are all supported by the use of a grid system with numbers or coordinates attached that can specify the location on a grid. As students become more sophisticated, their use of coordinates progresses along with them. However, there is no reason that students at the primary level cannot begin to think in terms of a grid system to identify location. This preparation for more sophisticated coordinate geometry is easily made in the early years of school.

The next activity can serve as a readiness task for coordinates and help students see the value of having a way to specify location without pointing.

activity **21.24**

Hidden Positions
For the game boards, draw an 8-inch square on tagboard. Subdivide the squares into a 3 × 3 grid. Two students sit with a "screen" separating their desktop space so that neither student can see the other's grid (see Figure 21.36.) Each student has four different pattern blocks. The first player places a block on four different sections of the grid. He then tells the other player where to put blocks on her grid to match his own. When all four pieces are positioned, the two grids are checked to see if they are alike. Then the players switch roles. Model the game once by taking the part of the first student. Use words such as *top row, middle, left,* and *right.* Students can play in pairs as a station activity.

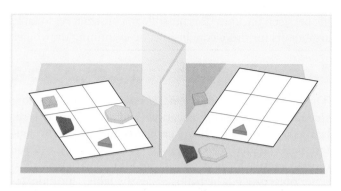

FIGURE 21.36 The "Hidden Positions" game. Players must communicate verbally the positions of their blocks on the grid.

The "Hidden Positions" game can easily be extended to grids up to 6 × 6. As the grid size increases, the need for a system of labeling positions increases. Students can begin to use a simple coordinate system as early as the first grade. Draw a coordinate grid on the board or on the overhead projector like the one shown in Figure 21.37. Explain how to use two numbers to designate an intersection point on the grid. The first number tells how far to move to the right. The second number tells how far to move up. For younger children use the words along with the numbers: 3 right and 0 up. Be sure to include 0 in your introduction. Select a point on the grid and have students decide what two numbers name that point. If your point is at (2, 4) and students incorrectly say "four, two," then simply indicate where the point is that they named. Emphasize that when they say or write the two numbers, the first number is the number of steps to the right and the second is the number of steps up.

The next activity explores the notion of different paths on a grid.

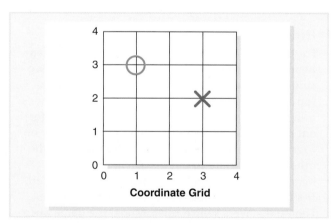

FIGURE 21.37 A simple coordinate grid. The X is at (3, 2) and the O is at (1, 3). Use the grid to play Three in a Row (like Tic-Tac-Toe). Put marks on intersections, not spaces.

activity **21.25**

Paths

On a sheet of 2-cm grid paper, mark two different points A and B as shown in Figure 21.38. Using the overhead or the chalkboard, demonstrate how to describe a path from A to B. For the points in the figure, one path is "up 5 and right 6." Another path might be "right 2, up 2, right 2, up 3, right 2." Count the length of each path. As long as you always move toward the target point (in this case either right or up), the path lengths will always be the same. Here they are 11 units long. Students draw three paths on their papers from A to B using different colored crayons. For each path they write directions that describe their paths. They should check the lengths of each path. Ask, "What is the greatest number of turns that you can make in your path?" "What is the smallest number?" "Where would A and B have to be in order to get there with no turns?"

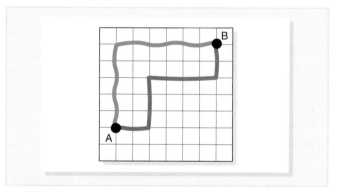

FIGURE 21.38 Coloring in different paths on a grid. What is the fewest number of turns needed to get from A to B? The most?

If you add a coordinate system on the grid in "Paths," students can describe their paths with coordinates: For example: (1, 2) ⟶ (3, 2) ⟶ (3, 5) ⟶ (7, 5) ⟶ (7, 7).

The NCTM *e-Standards* contains a nice applet (Applet 4.3) that is similar to the previous activity but offers some additional challenges. Students move a ladybug by issuing directions. The task is to make a list of directions to hide the ladybug beneath a leaf. When the directions are complete, the ladybug is set in motion to follow them. The ladybug is also used to draw shapes such as a rectangle in a tilted position or to travel through mazes. This applet is a very minimal version of the powerful computer programming language Logo.

Connected Mathematics

MIDDLE GRADES

Grade 8, Kaleidoscopes, Hubcaps, and Mirrors
Investigation 4: Symmetry and Algebra

Context

The interesting title of this unit comes from the first investigation, in which students examine symmetry in hubcap designs, designs made by kaleidoscopes (hexagonal), and those made by mirrors. Symmetry is actually *defined* in terms of transformations. "A geometric figure is *symmetric* if a reflection or rotation of the figure produces an image that matches the original figure exactly." A lot of the work in this unit is done with the coordinate grid.

Task Description

This lesson explores combinations of two symmetry transformations of an equilateral triangle and a square. Students make a table that resembles a multiplication table but represents the result of one transformation followed by another. The notation for reflections is related to which line of symmetry is used.

For example, L_1 is a reflection about line 1. Rotations are counterclockwise. R_{240} refers to a counterclockwise rotation of 240 degrees. By labeling the corners, students can keep track of each position of the triangle. The explanation above the table indicates how it is to be filled in.

After filling in the table, students are asked to look for patterns or other interesting results that may appear. They then complete an ordinary multiplication table for the numbers 1 to 6 and make comparisons of patterns found there and the patterns in the symmetry transformations table. Notice, for example, that R_{360} is placed in the same position as the number 1 in the multiplication table and behaves as an identity element. The commutative property works for some combinations but not others. None of the whole numbers in the multiplication table have a multiplicative inverse. How-

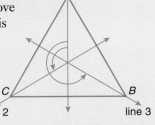

line 1

A

C   B

line 2   line 3

4.1 Transforming Triangles

The operations of arithmetic—addition, subtraction, multiplication, and division—define ways of putting two numbers together to get a single number. In a similar way, you can think of combining symmetry transformations as an operation that puts two transformations together to produce a single, equivalent transformation.

In this problem, you will explore combinations of symmetry transformations for an equilateral triangle. The notation L_n means a reflection over line n, and the notation R_n means a counterclockwise rotation of n degrees. The symbol $*$ represents the combining operation. You can read this symbol as "and then." For example, $L_1 * L_2 = R_{240}$ means that reflecting the triangle over line 1 "and then" reflecting it over line 2 is equivalent to rotating the triangle 240°.

Problem 4.1

The operation table below is reproduced on Labsheet 4.1B. Complete the table to show the results of combining symmetry transformations of an equilateral triangle. Each entry should be the result of performing the transformation in the left column followed by the transformation in the top row. The two entries already in the table represent the combinations you explored in the introduction:

$L_1 * L_2 = R_{240}$ $L_3 * R_{120} = L_2$

$*$	R_{360}	R_{120}	R_{240}	L_1	L_2	L_3
R_{360}						
R_{120}						
R_{240}						
L_1					R_{240}	
L_2						
L_3		L_2				

Note that transformation R_{360}, a 360° rotation, carries every point back to where it started. As you combine transformations, you will discover that many combinations are equivalent to R_{360}.

Problem 4.1 Follow-Up

1. Look carefully at the entries in your table. Describe any interesting patterns in the rows, columns, or blocks of entries. What do these patterns tell you about the results of combining rotations and line reflections?

60   Kaleidoscopes, Hubcaps, and Mirrors

From *Connected Mathematics: Kaleidoscopes, Hubcaps, and Mirrors: Symmetry and Transformations.* © 2002 by Michigan State University, Glenda Lappan, James T. Fey, William M. Fitzgerald, Susan N. Friel, & Elizabeth Difanis Phillips. Published by Pearson Education, Inc., publishing as Pearson Prentice Hall. Used by permission.

ever, recall that every rational number does. For example, 3 and $\frac{1}{3}$ are inverses of each other because their product is 1. For the symmetries of the triangle, every transformation has an inverse.

In addition to continuing their study of symmetry, this lesson really is a connection to algebra. It reviews the properties of operations and makes it clear that they really depend on the system being used.

Logo is technically a computer programming language. The *Turtle Math* version (Clements & Meredith, 1994) makes programming easy enough for third graders. Briefly, in Logo's graphics mode, a "turtle" (a small trian-

gle or a picture of a turtle) can be made to go forward or backward any distance and to turn left or right any number of degrees. The turtle draws a line in its path. The string of commands **fd 50 rt 90 fd 30 rt 90** will cause the turtle to draw a long and a short segment at right angles to each other. The command **rt 30 repeat 2[fd 60 rt 90 fd 30 rt 90]** will create a 60 × 30 rectangle tilted 30 degrees.

Logo brings a completely different perspective on geometric shapes and, thus, on geometric explorations and spatial development. Because students are required to draw shapes by issuing precise commands, Logo requires that a drawing be conceptualized in terms of its component parts—dimensions of sides, angle sizes, turn directions, and orientation in the plane. *Turtle Math* is used in the *Investigations in Number, Data, and Space* curriculum. (For a detailed discussion of Logo, see Clements & Battista, 2001.) ■

Location for Level-1 Thinkers

At level 1, one use of the coordinate grid is to examine transformations in a more analytic manner. There is not a lot of new knowledge about coordinates to learn except for the extension to four quadrants with the use of negative numbers. Even fourth- and fifth-grade students can use negative integers so that the full plane can be represented. The activities here suggest how coordinates can be used to examine transformations.

activity **21.26**

Coordinate Slides

Students will need a sheet of centimeter grid paper on which to draw two coordinate axes near the left and bottom edges. Have them plot and connect about five or six points on the grid to form a small shape. (See Figure 21.39.) If you direct them to use only coordinates between 5 and 12, the figure will be reasonably small and near the center of the paper. Next, students make a new shape by adding 6 to each of the first coordinates (typically called the *x*-coordinates) of their shape, leaving the second coordinates the same. That is, for the point (5, 10) a new point, (11, 10) is plotted. When new points for each point in the figure have been plotted, these are connected as before. This new figure should be congruent to the original and translated to the right. Students then create a third figure by adding 9 to each second coordinate of the original.

With these two slides as initial guidance, stop and discuss what should be done to the coordinates to move the figure along a slanted line up and to the right. Have students make and test their conjectures. Figure 21.39 shows a slide that was created by adding 6 to all of the first coordinates and adding 9 to all of the second coordinates. As long as all first coordinates are changed by the same amount and all second coordinates by the same amount, the figure will be translated without dis-

tortion. Challenge students to figure out how to change the coordinates to make the figure slide down and to the left instead of up and to the right. (Subtract from the coordinates instead of add.) Students' papers should show their original shape and four copies, each in a different location on the grid.

Help students summarize what they've learned: What does adding (or subtracting) a number from the first coordinates cause? What if the number is added or subtracted from the second coordinates? From both coordinates? Have students draw lines connecting corresponding points in the original figure with one of those where both coordinates were changed. What do they notice? (The lines are parallel and the same length.) Pick any two of the five shapes in the final drawing. How can you begin with one of the shapes and change the coordinates to get to the other?

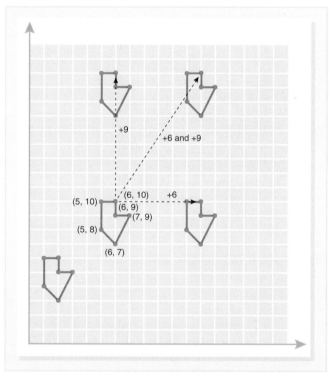

FIGURE 21.39 Begin with a simple shape and record the coordinates. By adding or subtracting from the coordinates, new shapes are found that are translations (slides) of the original.

In "Coordinate Slides" the figure did not twist, turn, flip over, or change size or shape. The shape "slid" along a path that matched the lines between the corresponding points. Reflections can be explored on a coordinate grid just as easily as translations. At this beginning level, it is advisable to restrict the lines of reflection to the *x*- or *y*-axis as in the following activity.

activity 21.27

Coordinate Reflections

Have students draw a five-sided shape in the first quadrant on coordinate grid paper using grid points for vertices. Label the Figure ABCDE and call it Figure 1. Use the *y*-axis as a line of symmetry and draw the reflection of the shape in the second quadrant. Call it Figure 2 (for second quadrant) and label the reflected points A'B'C'D'E'. Now use the *x*-axis as the line of symmetry. Reflect both Figure 2 and Figure 1 into the third and fourth quadrants, respectively, and call these Figures 3 and 4. Label the points of these figures with double and triple primes (A'' and A''', and so on). Write in the coordinates for each vertex of all four figures.

- How is Figure 3 related to Figure 4? How else could you have gotten Figure 3? How else could you have found Figure 4?
- How are the coordinates of Figure 1 related to its image in the *y*-axis, Figure 2? What can you say about the coordinates of Figure 4?
- Make a conjecture about the coordinates of a shape reflected in the *y*-axis and a different conjecture about the coordinates of a shape reflected in the *x*-axis.
- Draw lines from the vertices of Figure 1 to the corresponding vertices of Figure 2. What can you say about these lines? How is the *y*-axis related to each of these lines?

Refer to Figure 21.40 to answer these questions.

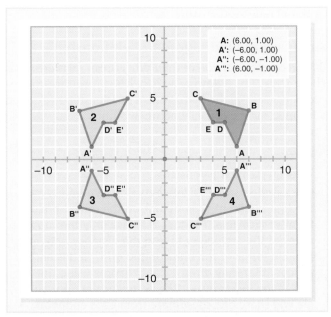

FIGURE 21.40 Figure 1 (ABCDE) is reflected across the *y*-axis. Then both Figures 1 and 2 are reflected across the *x*-axis.

Rotations can also be explored with the use of coordinates.

activity 21.28

Coordinate Rotations

Have students draw a small figure in the first quadrant. An L-shape drawing will help make the rotations easy to visualize. Use the origin as the center of rotation. Challenge students to rotate their figure a quarter turn counterclockwise into the second quadrant. Suggest rotating one point at a time by drawing a line from the origin to the point and then rotating this line a quarter turn to locate the rotated point. Repeat for other points until they are able to draw the rotated figure. (The rotation can be verified with tracing paper.) Next have students rotate the original figure a quarter turn clockwise to the fourth quadrant and a half turn to the third quadrant.

Students should explore their drawings for relationships between the coordinates of the original and rotated figures. They can test their ideas on a new figure by first making changes to the coordinates and then plotting the new points to see if they caused the desired rotation.

If your students have explored both rotations and reflections as in the last two activities, they can look for a relationship between a 180-degree turn and reflections through two perpendicular lines. (Can you tell what this relationship is?)

Students who have done the preceding activities should have a general way to describe translations, reflections across an axis, and 90-degree rotations about the origin all in terms of coordinates. In the following activity, multiplying a constant times the coordinates is a transformation that is not a rigid motion.

activity 21.29

Coordinate Dilations

Students begin with a four-sided shape in the first quadrant. They then make a list of the coordinates, and make a new set of coordinates by multiplying each of the original coordinates by 2. They plot the resulting shape. What is the result? Now have students multiply each of the original coordinates by $\frac{1}{2}$ and plot that shape. What is the result? Next, students draw a line from the origin to a vertex of the largest shape on their paper. Repeat for one or two additional vertices and ask for observations. (An example is shown in Figure 21.41.)

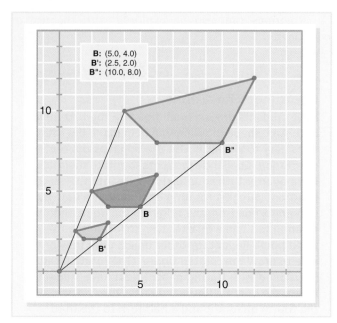

B: (5.0, 4.0)
B': (2.5, 2.0)
B": (10.0, 8.0)

FIGURE 21.41 Dilations with coordinates. Coordinates of the center figure were multiplied by 2 and also by 0.5 to create the other two figures.

Ⅱ *pause and reflect* —————

How do the lengths of sides and the areas of the shapes compare when the coordinates are multiplied by 2? What if they are multiplied by 3 or by $\frac{1}{2}$?

When the coordinates of a shape are multiplied as in the last activity, each by the same factor, the shape either gets larger or smaller. The size is changed but not the shape. The new shape is similar to the old shape. This is called a *dilation*, a transformation that is *not* rigid because the shape changes.

Your students may enjoy exploring this phenomenon a bit further. If they start with a line drawing of a simple face, boat, or some other shape drawn with straight lines connecting vertices, they will create an interesting effect by multiplying just the first coordinates, just the second coordinates, or using a different factor for each. When only the second coordinate is multiplied, the vertical dimensions alone are dilated, so the figure is proportionately stretched (or shrunk) in a vertical manner. Students can explore this process to distort shapes in various ways.

It is impressive to see how an arithmetic operation can control a figure. Imagine being able to control slides, flips, turns, and dilations, not just in the plane but also for three-dimensional figures. The process is identical to computer animation techniques.

Location for Level-2 Thinkers

On the surface, there may not be a clear distinction between coordinate activities for level 1 and those for level 2. However, as has been mentioned several times, the move to level-2 thinking is highlighted by the infusion of logical reasoning into the activities.

Coordinate Transformations Revisited

It is quite reasonable that a class has both level-1 and level-2 thinkers or at least students who are ready to move on to logical reasoning. While exploring the transformation activities in the last section, students who are ready might be challenged with questions such as the following that are a bit more than simple explorations:

- How should the coordinates be changed to cause a reflection if the line of reflection is not the *y*-axis but is parallel to it?
- Can you discover a single rule for coordinates that would cause a reflection across one of the axes followed by a rotation of a quarter turn? Is that rule the same for the reverse order—a quarter turn followed by a reflection?
- If two successive slides are made with coordinates and you know what numbers were added or subtracted, what number should be added or subtracted to get the figure there in only one move?
- What do you think will happen if, in a dilation, different factors are used for different coordinates?

 Once students begin to explore questions of this type, they may well come up with their own questions and explorations. The tedium of plotting points on a grid, however, can be a significant drawback. *The Geometer's Sketchpad* includes an optional coordinate grid. If drawings are made with the points "snapped" to the grid, coordinate transformations can be explored much more easily. ■

Applying the Pythagorean Relationship

The geometric version of the Pythagorean relationship is about areas. The following activity has students use the coordinate grid and the Pythagorean relationship to develop a formula for the distance between points.

activity **21.30**

The Distance Formula

Have students draw a line between two points in the first quadrant that are not on the same horizontal or vertical line. The task is to use only the coordinates of the endpoints to find the distance between them in terms of the units on the grid. To this end, suggest that they draw a right triangle using the line as the hypotenuse. The vertex at the right angle will share one coordinate from each endpoint. Students compute the areas of the squares on the legs and add to find the area of the square on the hypotenuse. Now the length of the original line

segment (the distance between the points) is the number whose square is the area of the square on the hypotenuse. (This last sentence is a geometric interpretation of square root.) Have students follow these directions to compute the length of the line.

Next, have them look through all of their calculations and see how the coordinates of the two endpoints were used. Challenge students to use the same type of calculations to get the distance between two new points without drawing any pictures.

Level-2 students do not necessarily construct proofs but should be able to follow the rationale if shown proofs. By leading students through the procedure of finding the length of one line (or the distance between the endpoints), you give them sufficient information to compute the lengths of other lines. Students will see that all they need are the coordinates of the two endpoints to compute the areas of all three squares and, hence, the length of the hypotenuse. If you then help them substitute letters for specific coordinates, a general distance formula results.

Slope

The topic of slope is another important connection between geometry and algebra and need not wait for the study of linear equations. To begin a discussion of slope, draw several different slanted lines on the board. Discuss how they are different. Some are steeper than others. Some go up, others go down. If you agree that "up" means sloping upward from left to right, then you can agree which ones go up and which go down. This "steepness" of a line is an attribute that can be measured like other measurable attributes. To give slope a number requires a reference line. The coordinate grid provides a reference (the *x*-axis) and the numbers to use in the measurement. Spend some time having students invent their own methods for attaching a number to the concept of steepness.

The convention for measuring the steepness of a line or the *slope* is based on the ideas of the *rise* and *run* between any two points on the line. The *rise* is the vertical change from the left point to the right point—positive if up, negative if down. The *run* is the horizontal distance from the left point to the right point. Slope is then defined as *rise ÷ run* or the ratio of the vertical change to the horizontal change (see Figure 21.42). By agreement, vertical lines have no slope or the slope is said to be "undefined." Horizontal lines have a slope of 0 as a result of the definition.

Once students are given the definition, they should be able to compute the slopes of any nonvertical line drawn on a coordinate grid without further assistance and *without formulas*.

A good problem-based task is to figure out what can be said about the slopes of parallel lines and perpendicular lines. (Is this geometry or algebra? Does it matter?)

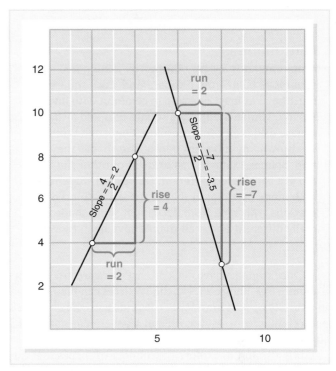

FIGURE 21.42 The slope of a line is equal to rise ÷ run.

Learning About Visualization

Visualization might be called "geometry done with the mind's eye." It involves being able to create mental images of shapes and then turn them around mentally, thinking about how they look from different perspectives—predicting the results of various transformations. It includes the mental coordination of two and three dimensions—predicting the unfolding of a box or understanding a two-dimensional drawing of a three-dimensional shape. Any activity that requires students to think about a shape mentally, to manipulate or transform a shape mentally, or to represent a shape as it is seen visually will contribute to the development of students' visualization skills.

Visualization for Level-0 Thinkers

At level 0, students are quite bound to thinking about shapes in terms of the way they look. Visualization activities at this level will have students using a variety of physical shapes and drawings and will challenge them to think about these shapes in different orientations.

Finding out how many different shapes can be made with a given number of simple tiles demands that students mentally flip and turn shapes in their minds and find ways to decide if they have found them all. That is the focus of the next activity.

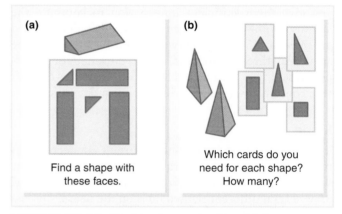

activity **21.31**

Pentominoes

A pentomino is a shape formed by joining five squares as if cut from a square grid. Each square must have at least one side in common with another. Provide students with five square tiles and a sheet of square grid paper for recording. Challenge them to see how many different pentomino shapes they can find. Shapes that are flips or turns of other shapes are not considered different. Do not tell students how many pentomino shapes there are. Good discussions will come from deciding if some shapes are really different and if all shapes have been found.

Once students have decided that there are just 12 pentominoes (see Figure 21.43), the 12 pieces can then be used in a variety of activities. Paste the grids with the children's pentominoes onto tagboard, and let them cut out the 12 shapes.

It is also fun to explore the number of shapes that can be made from six equilateral triangles or from four 45-degree right triangles (halves of squares). With the right tri-

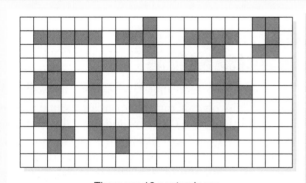

There are 12 pentominoes.

Finding all possible shapes made with five squares— or six squares (called "hexominoes") or six equilateral triangles and so on—is a good exercise in spatial problem solving.

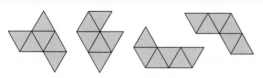

Four of the different shapes that six equilateral triangles will make.

Four of the different shapes that four "half-square" triangles will make.

FIGURE 21.43 Pentominoes and related shape challenges.

angles, sides that touch must be the same length. How many of each of these "ominoes" do you think there are?

Lots of activities can be done with pentominoes. For example, try to fit all 12 pieces into a 6×10 or 5×12 rectangle. Also, each of the 12 shapes can be used as a tessellation tile. Another task is to examine each of the 12 pentominoes and decide which will fold up to make an open box. For those that are "box makers," which square is the bottom?

Another aspect of visualization for young children is to be able to think about solid shapes in terms of their faces or sides. For these activities you will need to make "face cards" by tracing around the different faces of a shape, making either all faces on one card or a set of separate cards with one face per card (see Figure 21.44).

(a) Find a shape with these faces.

(b) Which cards do you need for each shape? How many?

FIGURE 21.44 Matching face cards with solid shapes.

activity **21.32**

Face Matching

There are two versions of the task: Given a face card, find the corresponding solid, or given a solid, find the face card. With a collection of single-face cards, students can select the cards that go with a particular block. For another variation, stack all of the single-face cards for one block face down. Turn them up one at a time as clues to finding the block.

The following activity has been adapted from NCTM's *Principles and Standards* book and is found in the pre-K–2 section on geometry (NCTM, 2000, p. 101). A similar activity is also found in the *Investigations* curriculum.

activity **21.33**

Quick Images

Draw some simple sketches on transparencies so that they can be shown to students one sketch at a time. They should be drawings that students can easily reproduce. Some examples are shown in Figure 21.45. On the overhead projector display one of

the sketches for about 5 seconds. Then have students attempt to reproduce the sketch on their own paper. Show the same sketch again for a few seconds and allow students to modify their drawings. Repeat with additional sketches.

In your discussions with students, ask them to tell how they thought about the sketch or to describe it in words that helped them remember what they saw. As students learn to verbally describe what they see, their visual memory will improve.

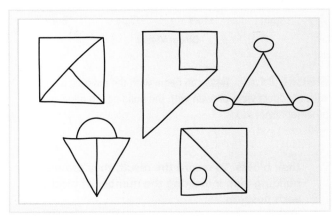

FIGURE 21.45 Examples of designs to use in the "Quick Images" activity. Draw each on acetate so that the design is about 4 to 5 inches across. Briefly show students the design and have them draw it on their paper from memory.

In the last activity, visual memory as well as the ability to create a sketch played a big role. Thinking about position of lines and features of the sketch is also important. In the next activity students must mentally move shapes and predict the results. The activity combines ideas about line symmetry (reflections) as well as visualization and spatial reasoning.

activity **21.34**

Notches and Holes

Use a half sheet of paper that will easily fit on the overhead. Fold it in half and then half again, making the second fold in the opposite direction from the first. Students make a sketch of the paper when it is opened, showing a line for each fold. With the paper folded, cut notches in one or two sides and/or cut off one or two corners. You can also use a paper punch to make a hole or two. While still folded, place the paper on the overhead showing the notches and holes (see Figure 21.46). The task is for students to draw the notches and holes that they think will appear when you open the paper.

To introduce this activity, begin with only one fold and only two cuts. Stay with one fold until students are ready for a more difficult challenge.

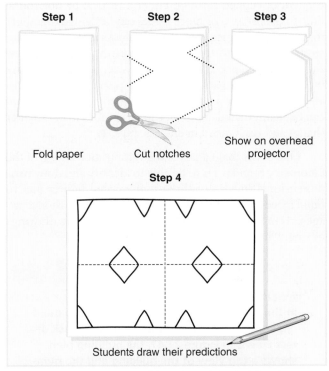

FIGURE 21.46 An example showing how the "Notches and Holes" activity is done. Make two folds and cut notches and/or punch holes in the folded paper. Before unfolding, students draw a sketch predicting the result when the paper is unfolded.

In "Notches and Holes" students will eventually learn which cuts create holes and how many and which cuts make notches in the edges or on the corners. Notice how line symmetry or reflection plays a major role in the activity. Symmetry determines the position, the shape, and the number of holes created by each cut.

Visualization for Level-1 Thinkers

In identifying a visualization task as either level 0 or level 1, one consideration is the degree of attention that must be given to the particular properties of shapes. The activities in this section are almost certainly too difficult for students at level 0.

 Geometry is one area of the curriculum for which a variety of fascinating computer programs exist. Many programs allow students to "stamp" geometric shapes such as tangrams or pattern blocks onto the screen and then manipulate them. We have already discussed e-geoboards, e-tangrams, and the computer program Logo. Here are some more examples.

Shape Up (Sunburst, 1995) and *Shapes* (Clements & Sarama, 1995) are two good examples of computer versions of physical tiles. Both programs include a pattern block and tangram format in which students can stamp pieces onto a blank screen. Pieces are easily moved around, rotated, or flipped through either a vertical or horizontal line. In *Shapes*, two or more pieces can be "glued together" to create new shapes. The pattern blocks include a quarter circle that adds to the variability. Both programs allow shapes to be enlarged or reduced in size. Some puzzles are included with the packages, and new puzzles are easily created. *Shape Up* has a third mode in which six regular shapes can be manipulated and each can be cut into many smaller shapes and rearranged in endless ways. ■

One of the main goals of the visualization strand of the Geometry Standard is to be able to identify and draw two-dimensional images of three-dimensional figures and to build three-dimensional figures from two-dimensional images. Activities aimed at this goal often involve drawings of small "buildings" made of one-inch cubes.

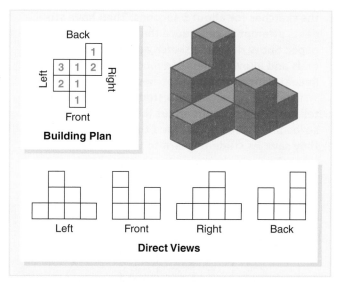

FIGURE 21.47 Tasks can begin with the building plan, or with the direct view, or even with the building. Students give the other representations.

activity 21.35

Viewpoints

a. In the first version, students begin with a building and draw the left, right, front, and back direct views. In Figure 21.47, the building plan shows a top view of the building and the number of blocks in each position. After students build a building from a plan like this, their task is to draw the front, right, left, and back direct views as shown in the figure.

b. In the reverse version of the task, students are given a right and front view. The task is to build the building that has those views. To record their solution, they draw a building plan (top view with numbers).

their blocks. To record the result, they draw a building plan indicating the number of blocks in each position.

b. In the second version, students are given either a block plan or the five direct views. They build the building accordingly and draw two or more of the perspective views. There are four possible perspectives from above the table: the front left and right, and the back left and right. It is useful to build the building on a sheet of paper with the words "front," "back," "left," and "right" written on the edges to keep from getting different viewpoints confused.

Notice that front and back direct views are symmetric, as are the left and right views. That is why only one of each is given in part b of the activity.

In "Viewpoints," students made "buildings" out of 1-inch cubes and coordinated these with direct views of the sides and top. A significantly more challenging activity is to draw perspective views of these block buildings or to match perspective drawings with a building. Isometric dot grids are used for the drawings. The next activity provides a glimpse at this form of visualization activity.

Figure 21.48 shows an example of this last activity. Some excellent resource books exist for this type of activity. It is not necessary to prepare these tasks yourself. Perhaps the best-known book is *Middle Grades Mathematics Project: Spatial Visualization* (Winter, Lappan, Phillips, & Fitzgerald, 1986). NCTM's *Navigating Though Geometry* books have similar activities in both the 3–5 and 6–8 grade books. (See Recommendations for Further Reading.)

 An amazing computer tool for drawing perspective views of block buildings such as in Activity 21.36 is available on the *Illuminations* Web site (http://illuminations.nctm.org/tools/isometric/isometric.asp). This applet requires only mouse clicks to draw either whole cubes, any single face of a cube, or just lines. The drawings, however, are actually "buildings" and can be viewed as three-dimensional objects. They can be rotated in space so that they can be seen from any vantage. Prepared investigations are informative and also lead stu-

activity 21.36

Perspective Drawings

a. In the first version, students begin with a perspective drawing of a building. The assumption is that there are no hidden blocks. From the drawing the students build the actual building with

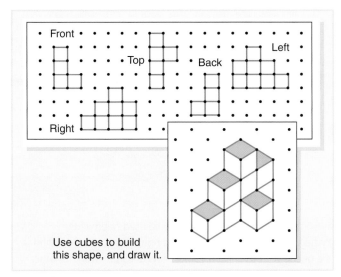

FIGURE 21.48 Develop perspective and visual perception with cubes and plain views. Draw block "buildings" on isometric grids.

Use cubes to build this shape, and draw it.

dents through the features of the tool. The NLVM applet, *Space Blocks*, is easier to use but only allows cubes to be arranged (http://nlvm.usu.edu/en/nav/vlibrary.html). ■

Another interesting connection between two and three dimensions is found in slicing solids in different ways. When a solid is sliced into two parts, a two-dimensional figure is formed on the slice faces. Figure 21.49 shows a cube being sliced off at the corner, leaving a triangular face. Slices can be explored with clay sliced with a potter's wire as shown in the figure. A niftier method is to partially fill a plastic solid with water. The surface of the water is the same as the face of a slice coinciding with the surface of the water. By tilting the shape in different ways, every possible "slice" can be observed. Small plastic solids such as *Power Solids* are excellent for this.

activity **21.37**

Water Slices

Students are given a solid and challenged to find out how to slice it to make a designated slice face. The list of challenges should include some that are impossible. Before water is poured into the solids, students must commit themselves on paper as to whether or not the slice is possible. If they think it is possible, they write and/or draw a description of where the slice must be made. Then water is put into the shape to test their predictions. If there are no plastic shapes available, clay models are the next best option. Here is a list of potential slice faces for a cube:

Square, nonsquare rectangle, nonrectangular parallelogram, isosceles trapezoid, nonisosceles trapezoid, equilateral triangle, isosceles right triangle, other isosceles triangle, scalene right triangle, other scalene triangle.

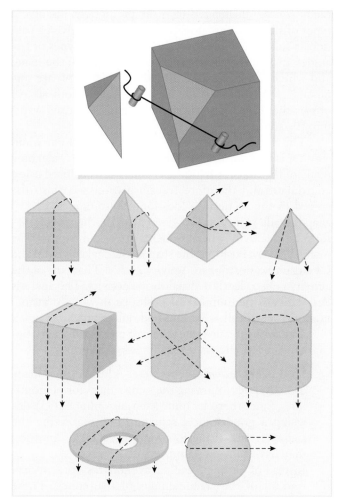

FIGURE 21.49 Predict the slice face before you cut a clay model with a piano wire.

A tetrahedron, a square pyramid, and prisms offer similar challenges. For other solids, it may be more interesting to find out how many different types of slice faces can be found and to describe each.

Visualization for Level-2 Thinkers

Once again, we see that logical reasoning is what distinguishes activities for level-2 thinkers from those for level 1. It is important to note, however, that this is an area of geometry where the distinction is not particularly sharp. In the upper grades, students within a classroom will almost certainly be at various levels. The activities described for level 1 can easily be modified to challenge level-2 thinkers. Likewise, the activities in this section will help to push level-1 students forward in their thinking.

Connecting Earlier Activities to Level-2 Visualization

A good example of the overlap in levels is found in the "Water Slices" activity (Activity 21.37). Students who are ready can be challenged to make predictions about the types of slices that are possible. For example, given a particular solid, they might go through a list of types of triangles and quadrilaterals and decide which can be made and which are impossible. For those they think are impossible, they should offer a reason for that hypothesis. All of this should be done without the help of putting water into the solids.

The distinction between one strand of geometry and another is also not always clear. We have already seen how many of the transformation activities were explored using coordinates and, therefore, transformations were also discussed in the section on location. Pentominoes, the 12 shapes made from 5 squares, were used earlier in a transformation activity where students are asked to find how many different positions the shapes could take in the plane ("Pentomino Positions," Activity 21.22). That part of the activity is also clearly a visualization activity. The analysis that explains the number of positions involves transformations, specifically rotations and reflections.

The following are extensions of pentomino activities that are appropriate visualization tasks for level 2:

- How many *hexominoes* are there? A hexomino is made of six squares following the same rule as for pentominoes. Since there are quite a few hexominoes (35), devising a good logical scheme for categorizing the shapes is one of the few ways there are of knowing they have all been found.

- Instead of putting together five squares, students can find all of the arrangements of five cubes. These shapes are called *pentominoids*. In general, shapes made of cubes in which adjoining cubes share a complete face are called *polyominoids*.

Proofs of the Pythagorean relationship are as much visualization tasks as they are about shapes and properties. Recall that the Pythagorean relationship says that a square built on the hypotenuse of a right triangle has an area equal to the sum of the areas of the squares built on the two legs. Figure 21.50 can be used to devise a proof of this relationship. As a visualization task, students may or may not be given any hints to help discover this proof. Once found, they can also explain how the proof will work for any right triangle, not just the one on which this figure is based.

The Platonic Solids

A *polyhedron* is a three-dimensional shape with polygons for all faces. Among the various polyhedra, the Platonic solids are especially interesting. *Platonic solids* is the name given to the set of completely regular polyhedrons. "Completely regular" means that each face is a regular polygon and every vertex has exactly the same number of faces joining at that point. An interesting visualization task appropriate for this level is to find and describe all of the Platonic solids.

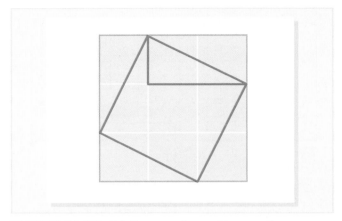

FIGURE 21.50 This figure can be used to prove the Pythagorean relationship. *Hint:* The right triangle to work with is the one in the upper right corner. How does this work for other right triangles?

activity 21.38

Search for the Platonic Solids
Provide students with a supply of equilateral triangles, squares, regular pentagons, and regular hexagons from one of the plastic sets for building solids (e.g., *Polydron* or *Geofix*). Explain what a completely regular solid is. The task is to find as many different completely regular solids as possible.

One approach to conducting this activity is to leave it as stated and allow students to work with no additional guidance. Success will depend on their problem-solving skills. Alternatively, you might suggest a systematic approach as follows. Since the smallest number of sides a face can have is three, begin with triangles, then squares, then pentagons, and so on. Furthermore, since every vertex must have the same number of faces, try three faces at a point, then four, and so on. (It is clearly impossible to have only two faces at a point.)

With this plan, students will find that for triangles they can have three, four, or five triangles coming to a point. For each of these, they can begin with a "tent" of triangles and then add more triangles so that each vertex has the same number. With three at a point you get a four-sided solid called a *tetrahedron* (*tetra* = four). With four at each point you get an eight-sided solid called an *octahedron* (*octa* = eight). It is really exciting to build the shape with five triangles at each point. It will have 20 sides and is called an *icosahedron* (*icosa* = twenty).

In a similar manner, students will find that there is only one solid made of squares—three at each point and six in all—a *hexahedron* (*hex* = six), also called a cube. And there is only one solid with pentagons, three at each point, 12 in all. This is called a *dodecahedron* (*dodeca* = twelve).

pause and reflect _____

Why are there no regular polyhedra with six or more triangles or four or more squares? Why are there no regular polyhedra made with hexagons or with polygons with more than six sides? The best way to answer these questions is to experiment with the polygons and explain the answers in your own words. Students should do the same.

A fantastic skeletal icosahedron can be built out of the newspaper rods described earlier. (See Figure 21.11, p. 420.) Since five triangles converge at each point, there are also five edges at each point. Simply work at bringing five rods to each vertex and remember that each face is a triangle. This icosahedron will be about 4 feet across and will be amazingly sturdy.

Assessment of Geometric Goals

At the beginning of this chapter we talked about two kinds of goals for your students: goals of spatial sense and geometric thinking, and goals of geometric content. This chapter has been organized to help you gain some perspective of these two agendas. By planning your assessment of geometric thinking as well as and separately from content, you can avoid the trap of teaching to content objectives in a superficial way. Activities that do not appear to directly match a content objective should at least have a growth objective.

Clarifying Your Geometry Objectives

Spatial Sense and van Hiele Objectives

In the early grades, when you can expect your students to be level-0 thinkers, you want to be sure that their thinking is increasing in its sophistication and is moving toward level 1. Here are suggestions for things to look for:

- Child attends to a variety of characteristics of shapes in sorting and building activities.
- Child uses language that is descriptive of geometric shapes.
- Child shows evidence of geometric reasoning in solving puzzles, exploring shapes, creating designs, and analyzing shapes.
- Child recognizes shapes in the environment.
- Child solves spatial problems.

Each of these statements can be assessed as indicative of either a level-0 thinker or a level-1 thinker. For example, at level 0, the types of characteristics that students are likely to pay attention to are not properties of general classes of shapes ("pointy," "fat," "has five sides," "goes up," etc.). Properties such as "parallel" or "symmetrical" may be used by level-0 thinkers as well as those at level 1. The distinction is found in what the properties are attributed to. At level 0, students are restricted in thought to the shapes they are currently working with, while at level 1, students attribute properties to classes of shapes (*all* rectangles or *all* cylinders). Language, reasoning, shape recognition, and spatial problem solving can all be assessed as being appropriate for level 0 or level 1. By thinking in this manner, teachers can begin to get a sense of the geometric growth of their students beyond the specific content knowledge that may have been developed.

At the upper elementary and middle grades, teachers can begin to think in terms of students being at level 1 or level 2 in their geometric thought. Before grade 6 or 7, very few students will have achieved level-2 thinking, but teachers need to be aware of progress in that direction. The following general indicators are more indicative of level-2 thinkers rather than level 1:

- Child shows improvement in spatial visualization skills.
- Child has an inclination to make and test conjectures in geometric situations.
- Child makes use of logical explanations in geometric problem solving.
- Child justifies conclusions in geometric contexts.
- Child assesses the validity of logical arguments in geometric situations.

Most of these indicators or objectives include elements of reasoning and logical sophistication that are not generally present in a level-1 thinker. As noted in the discussions of dynamic geometry software, a level-1 thinker is using inductive reasoning to discover relationships in shapes, whereas a level-2 thinker is, with guidance, beginning to develop arguments that explain why a particular relationship exists.

Geometric Concept Objectives

Principles and Standards is extremely helpful for articulating growth in geometric content across the grades. For each of the four goals articulated by the standards (shape and properties, location, transformations, and visualization) examine the grade-level expectations not only at your grade band but above and below as well. This chapter has been organized to help you obtain some sense of that growth across the K–8 span of grades.

Of course, you must attend to the content prescribed by your school system. That content may or may not align well with that outlined by the NCTM *Standards*. However, nearly all geometry taught in the K–8 span can be found within that standard. Try to include a sense of growth over time in your assessment of content. If you limit your assessment to a mastery of skills or definitions, the spirit of exploration that you want in your geometry program will be lost. We most often teach in a manner that reflects our assessment plans. Although mastery of some ideas is perhaps important, conceptual development is rarely reflected in memorizing definitions.

In deciding what to assess and how, it is best to take a long-term view of geometry rather than a more traditional mastery-oriented approach. Two major perspectives have been suggested:

- Growth in spatial sense and geometric thought
- Understanding of geometric concepts

Reflections on Chapter 21

Writing to Learn

1. Describe in your own words the first three van Hiele levels of geometric thought (levels 0, 1, and 2). Note in your description the object of thought and the product of thought. How do these ideas create a progression from one level to the next?
2. Describe the four characteristics of the van Hiele levels of thought. For each, reflect on why each characteristic might be important for teachers.
3. How would activities aimed at levels 0, 1, and 2 differ?
4. Briefly describe the nature of the content in each of the four geometric strands featured in this chapter and in the *Standards*: Shapes and Properties, Location, Transformations, and Visualization. In your description, note a progression across van Hiele levels.
5. Activities 21.1, 21.2, and 21.3 at the beginning of the chapter were used to highlight the differences in the three van Hiele levels of geometric thought. Select three different examples from the Shapes and Properties section, one for each level. What makes each activity appropriate for that level? Repeat this exercise three more times by selecting three activities representing the Transformation, Location, and Visualization strands of geometric content.
6. What can you do when the students in your classroom are at different van Hiele levels of thought?
7. Find one of the suggested applets for geometry or an example of geometry software and explain how it can be used. What are the advantages of using the computer in geometry instead of the corresponding hands-on materials or drawings?
8. How can a teacher assess students in terms of general geometric growth or spatial sense? Assuming that the van Hiele theory is correct, why is it important to understand where your students are in terms of that theory?

For Discussion and Exploration

1. How important should geometry be in the primary grades, the intermediate grades, and the middle school grades? Consider the competing demands of other areas of the mathematics curriculum, and suggest how many of the roughly 36 weeks of the year should be spent on geometry. What justification can you give for your position? Based on a review of a traditional textbook, how many weeks are typically spent on geometry?
2. Examine the teacher's edition of a basal textbook at any grade level. Select any lesson on geometry. Remember that the authors of the pupil's book are restricted to the printed page by the very nature of books. Teachers are not so restricted. How would you teach this lesson so that it was a *good* geometry lesson? Your lesson should include a hands-on activity and have a problem-solving spirit.
3. At the elementary and middle school levels, computer software should be an important component of your instructional tools. If you are not familiar with the types of software discussed in this chapter, find out what you have access to, and play around to learn what each program can do. (Learning about a dynamic geometry program is highly recommended.)

Recommendations for Further Reading

NCTM's *Navigations Series*

Findell, C. R., Small, M., Cavanagh, M., Dacey, L., Greenes, C. E., & Sheffield, L. J. (2001). *Navigating through geometry in prekindergarten–grade 2*. Reston, VA: National Council of Teachers of Mathematics.

Gavin, M. K., Sinelli, A. M., & St. Marie, J. (2001). *Navigating through geometry in grades 3–5*. Reston, VA: National Council of Teachers of Mathematics.

Pugalee, D. K., Frykholm, J., Johnson, A., Slovin, H., Malloy, C., & Preston, R. (2002). *Navigating through geometry in grades 6–8*. Reston, VA: National Council of Teachers of Mathematics.

Each of these three excellent books from the *Navigations Series* provides both a perspective on the geometry standard and also a collection of excellent activities appropriate for the grade band of the book. Activities are organized under the four strands of the Geometry Standard (as is this chapter). Each book includes a CD-ROM with the Blackline Masters, a small collection of excellent applets, plus the full text of selected articles. A great resource.

Glass, B. (2004). Transformations and technology: What path to follow? *Mathematics Teaching in the Middle School, 9*, 393–397.

Glass explored compositions of transformations with his middle school students. Part of their discourse revolved around this question: Is a composition of two or more transformations the same as the single transformation that will accomplish the same thing? For those exploring transformations at the upper grades, this is a useful article.

Koester, B. A. (2003). Prisms and pyramids: Constructing three-dimensional models to build understanding. *Teaching Children Mathematics, 9*, 436–442.

You may think that there is too much tedium to have children build models using straws and pipe cleaners. Koester's activities and explorations with third to fifth graders proves otherwise. The activities described involve classification and definitions of shapes and also Euler's formula relating faces, vertices, and edges.

National Council of Teachers of Mathematics. (1999). Geometry and geometric thinking [Focus Issue]. *Teaching Children Mathematics, 5*(6).

This focus issue of *TCM* is full of practical ideas and useful perspectives on geometry for the early grades. Of special note is a wonderful article by Pierre van Hiele, in which he describes a series of activities with a unique collection of shapes (the Mosaic Puzzle). For the small price, this focus issue is a very valuable resource for any teacher.

Renne, C. G. (2004). Is a rectangle a square? Developing mathematical vocabulary and conceptual understanding. *Teaching Children Mathematics, 10*, 258–263.

The voices of children in this article are clear examples of the difficulty that students at level-1 reasoning have in attempting to make logical conclusions about geometric properties and relationships. Renne's activities with fourth graders are very close to the property list activities (21.2 and 21.3) in this book.

Wyat, K. W., Lawrence, A., & Foletta, G. M. (1998). *Geometry activities for middle school students with* The Geometer's Sketchpad. Berkeley, CA: Key Curriculum Press.

As noted in this chapter, dynamic geometry software belongs in the upper elementary and middle grades. This book of explorations for *The Geometer's Sketchpad* can be used to introduce students (and *you*) to the software even if you have never used *Sketchpad* before. The activities explore triangles, quadrilaterals, symmetry, transformations, and constructions. With this book you will be convinced of the value of dynamic geometry in grades 4 to 8.

Online Resources

Suggested Applets and Web Links

Cube Nets
http://illuminations.nctm.org/tools/tool_detail.aspx?id=84
Great visualization challenge! Shows arrangements of squares. The challenge is to find the 11 arrangements that will fold into a cube.

Cut Out Nets
www.fi.uu.nl/toepassingen/00297/toepassing_ wisweb.en.html
Nets of the Platonic solids can be folded one side at a time and the shape rotated freely at any point in three dimensions. Fascinating!

Cutting Corners
http://illuminations.nctm.org/tools/CutTool/CutTool.asp
A cutting tool allows any one of three simple shapes to be sliced into parts along any straight line. Shapes can be re-arranged, rotated, and flipped.

Geoboards
http://nvlm.usu.edu/en/nav/vlibrary.html
The NLVM library has four geoboards. The first measures areas and perimeters. The circular board has pins in a circular arrangement. The isometric board has pins in a triangular arrangement (like isometric dot paper). The coordinate board shows coordinates for each peg when the cursor is on it. It measures the slope and distance between two points joined by a band and then the perimeter and area of banded shapes.

Isometric Drawing Tool
http://illuminations.nctm.org/tools/isometric/isometric.asp
Cubes and any face of a cube can be drawn on an isometric grid. The drawings created can be rotated on the grid. The drawing can also be viewed in a second window that shows the drawing as a three-dimensional object that can be slowly rotated around three separate axes. It takes a little practice but this is an amazing tool.

Maze Game
www.shodor.org/interactivate/activities/coords/index.html
Provides practice with coordinates. The user plots points to guide a robot through a mine field.

Mirror Tool
http://illuminations.nctm.org/tools/mirror/mirror.asp
A nice tool for early investigations of mirror or line symmetry.

Pythagorean Relationship
http://standards.nctm.org/document/eexamples/chap6/ 6.5/index.htm
This compelling, dynamic proof of the Pythagorean relationship uses the idea that rectangles and parallelograms with the same height and base have the same area.

Shape Sorter Tool
http://illuminations.nctm.org/tools/shapesorter/ shapesorter.asp
After selecting a Venn diagram and labels for each loop, shapes are produced and the user must correctly place them in the diagram. Labels are properties of angles and sides.

Slicing Platonic Solids
http://nlvm.usu.edu/en/nav/frames_asid_126_g_3_t_3.html
Any one of the five Platonic solids can be shown in a window that is a plane of intersection with the solid. As the solid is rotated freely, the portion above and below the plane changes. The plane intersection shape is always shown in a second window. This is a virtual version of "Water Slices," Activity 21.37.

Space Blocks
http://nlvm.usu.edu/en/nav/frames_asid_195_g_3_t_3. html?open=activities
This applet allows the user to create "buildings" made of cubic blocks rather easily. Each new block snaps to a block in the ongoing construction.

Tangrams
http://nlvm.usu.edu/en/nav/frames_asid_292_g_3_t_1.html
These virtual tangrams can be manipulated freely. Plus, there are 14 puzzle shapes to fill in with all 7 tangrams.

Visualizing Transformations
http://standards.nctm.org/document/eexamples/chap6/ 6.4/index.htm
This four-part applet provides an excellent exploration of the three rigid-motion transformations including composition of two transformations.

An additional list of books and articles related to the ideas in this chapter can be found on the Companion Web site at **www.ablongman.com/ vandewalle6e.**

chapter 22

Concepts of Data Analysis

Graphs and statistics bombard the public in areas such as advertising, opinion polls, reliability estimates, population trends, health risks, and progress of students in schools. We hear that the average amount of rainfall this summer is more than it was last summer; that the average American household consists of 2.53 people; that the national median value of a house is $185,200; that about 17 percent of the U.S. population has a college degree; and that 9 out of 10 dentists recommend a particular brand of toothpaste. Magazines and newspapers use various types of graphs to provide the reader with a snapshot of such information.

To deal with this information, students should have informal yet meaningful experiences with basic concepts of data analysis throughout their school years. At the K–3 level, students can begin this understanding by learning how data can be categorized and displayed in various graphical forms. By the time students are fifth graders, they should have had many experiences collecting and organizing sets of data as well as representing data in various graphical forms to best show what the data indicate. They should begin to learn about statistical concepts, such as mean, median, and mode. In the middle grades, students should continue to build on this basic knowledge, developing a better understanding of these representations and statistics as they learn about new representations such as box plots, stem-and-leaf plots, and scatter plots.

Big Ideas

1. A collection of objects with various attributes can be classified or sorted in different ways. A single object can belong to more than one class. Classification is the first step in the organization of data.

2. Data are gathered and organized in order to answer questions about the populations from which the data come.

With data from only a sample of the population, inferences are made about the population.

3. Different types of graphs and other data organizations provide different information about the data and, hence, the population from which the data were taken. The choice of graphical representation can impact how well the data are understood.

4. Measures that describe data with numbers are called *statistics*. Data can be organized in various graphical forms to visually convey information. The use of a particular graph or statistic can mediate what the data tell about the population.

5. Both graphs and statistics can provide a sense of the shape of the data, including how spread out or how centered they are. Having a sense of the shape of data is having a big picture of the data rather than a collection of numbers.

Mathematics Content Connections

The analysis of data involves both numbers and graphs to describe our world. Certainly, there are connections to the numeric areas of the curriculum. However, the connection to algebra is perhaps one of the most important mathematical connections.

- **Number Sense** (Chapter 9): Young children analyze graphs and use the graphs to talk about quantity. Graphs indicate numeric relationships of more, less, difference, and relative magnitude. Each bar of a graph is a part of the whole (part-part-whole relationships).

- **Fractions, Ratios, and Percents** (Chapters 16, 18, and 19): Fractions, decimals, and percents are used to describe data.

- **Measurement** (Chapter 20): Much of the real-world data that are gathered consist of measurements. Pedagogically, measurement can be interwoven with data analysis as students make measurements to answer questions and create data to be analyzed.

■ **Algebra** (Chapter 15): Algebra is used to analyze and describe relationships. Whenever data are gathered on two related variables (e.g., height and arm span, age and growth), algebra can be used to describe the relationship between the variables. The resulting relationship can then be used to predict outcomes for which no data have yet been gathered. The better that the data are approximated by the algebraic relationship or function, the more predictive value the function has.

Gathering Data to Answer Questions

Data analysis is about more than making graphs and calculating statistics. It includes both asking and answering questions about our world. To answer the questions, data must be gathered and organized and then analyzed. The first goal in the Data Analysis and Probability standard of *Principles and Standards* says that students should "formulate questions that can be addressed with data and collect, organize, and display relevant data to answer them" (NCTM, 2000, p. 48). Notice that data collection should be for a purpose, to answer a question, just as in the real world. The analysis of data should have the agenda of adding information about some aspect of our world. This is what political pollsters, advertising agencies, market researchers, census takers, wildlife managers, medical researchers, and hosts of others do: gather data to answer questions. Textbooks often provide students with questions to answer and also the data with which to answer them. Although these may be interesting contexts for data analysis, the questions are not necessarily of interest to your students. Students should be given opportunities to generate their own questions, decide on appropriate data to help answer these questions, and determine methods of collecting the data. Avoid gathering data simply to make a graph.

When students formulate the questions they want to ask, the data they gather become more meaningful. How they organize the data and the techniques for analyzing them have a purpose. For example, one class gathered data concerning which cafeteria foods were most often thrown in the garbage. As a result of these efforts, certain items were removed from the regular menu. The activity illustrated to students the power of organized data, and it helped them get food that they liked better.

Ideas for Questions and Data

Often the need to gather data will come from the class naturally in the course of discussion or from questions arising in other content areas. Science, of course, is full of

measurements and, thus, abounds in data requiring analysis. Social studies is also full of opportunities to pose questions requiring data analysis. The next few sections suggest some additional ideas.

Classroom Questions

Students often want to learn about themselves, their families and pets, measures such as arm span or time to get to school, their likes and dislikes, and so on. The easiest questions to deal with are those that can be answered by each class member contributing one piece of data. Here are a few ideas:

* *Favorites:* TV shows, games, movies, ice cream, video game platforms, sports teams, music CDs. (When there are lots of possibilities, suggest that students restrict the number of choices.)
* *Numbers:* Number of pets, sisters, or brothers; hours watching TV or hours of sleep; birthdays (month or day of month); bedtime; time spent on the computer.
* *Measures:* Height, arm span, area of foot, long-jump distance, shadow length, seconds to run around the track, minutes spent on the bus.

Beyond the Classroom

The questions in the previous section are designed for students to contribute data about themselves. This is appropriate for younger students who are interested in learning who they are as a class and how each fits into the class as an individual. Eventually, students should gather data for which they need to go outside the class or at least ask questions about things beyond the classroom. Discussions about communities provide a good way to integrate social studies and mathematics.

The newspaper suggests all sorts of data-related questions. For example, how many full-page ads occur on different days of the week? What types of stories are on the front page? Which comics are really for kids and which are not?

Science is another area where questions can be asked and data gathered. Students might collect leaves, rocks, or even insects from their own backyards. These objects can then be classified in various ways, creating categories for graphing. Experiments provide another type of question. How many times do different types of balls bounce when each is dropped from the same height? How many days does it take for different types of bean, squash, and pea seeds to germinate when kept in moist paper towels?

As children get older, they can begin to think about various populations and differences between them. For example, how are fifth

> **EXPANDED LESSON**
>
> A two-day expanded lesson plan dealing with using data to answer a question can be found on the Companion Web site at www.ablongman.com/vandewalle6e.

graders similar or different from middle school students? Students might examine questions concerning boys versus girls, adults or teachers versus students, or categories of workers or college graduates. These situations involve issues of sampling and making generalizations and comparisons.

The news media frequently report what the latest survey reveals about the "typical" family, business, teenager, drug addict, or member of some other population or group. How did they survey everyone, and what does "typical" mean? Do the students in your classroom believe they are typical? Are they like those in the next classroom or the next grade level? To describe a group usually involves asking a variety of questions, and deciding on which questions to ask is not nearly as easy as it may sound. How many questions should be asked? Should they be multiple choice? If not, how will the answers be handled? To describe a large group (say, the school), how many people should be surveyed? How should they be selected? Students should be involved in making these decisions as they formulate their questions and design surveys.

Much of the fifth-grade statistics unit in *Investigations in Number, Data, and Space* explores the issue of sampling. In the excerpt described on the next page, students first compare small samples from the class to the full class data. They also compare classroom data to national data.

Other Sources of Information

Gathering data can mean using data that have been collected by others. For example, newspapers, almanacs, sports record books, maps, and various government publications are sources of data that may be used to answer student questions. Students may be interested in facts about another country as a result of a social studies unit. Olympic records in various events over the years or data related to space flight are other examples of topics around which student questions may be formulated. For these and hundreds of other questions, data can be found on the World Wide Web. Here are three Web sites with a lot of interesting data.

- U.S. Census Bureau (www.census.gov): This Web site contains copious statistical information by state, county, or voting district.
- Economic Research Service, USDA (www.ers.usda.gov/data/foodconsumption): Here you can find wonderful data sets on the availability and consumption of hundreds of foods. Per capita estimates on a yearly basis often go back as far as 1909.
- The World Fact Book (www.odci.gov/cia/publications/factbook/index.html): This Web site provides demographic information for every nation in the world, including population, age distributions, death and birth rates, and information on the economy, government, transportation, and geography. Maps are included as well.

- Internet Movie Database (www.imdb.com): This Web site offers information about movies of all genres.

Classification and Data Analysis

Classification involves making decisions about how to categorize things. This basic activity is fundamental to data analysis. In order to formulate questions and decide how to represent data that have been gathered, decisions must be made about how things might be categorized. Farm animals, for example, might be grouped by number of legs; by type of product they provide; by those that work, provide food, or are pets; by size or color; by the type of food they eat; and so on. Each of these groupings is based on a different attribute of the animals.

Young children need experiences with categorizing things in different ways in order to learn to make sense of real-world data. Attribute activities are explicitly designed to develop this flexible reasoning about the characteristics of data.

Attribute Materials

Attribute materials are sets of objects that lend themselves to being sorted and classified in different ways. *Unstructured* attribute materials include such things as seashells, leaves, the children themselves, or the set of the children's shoes. The *attributes* are the ways that the materials can be sorted. For example, hair color, height, and gender are attributes of children. Each attribute has a number of different *values:* for example, blond, brown, or red (for the attribute of hair color); tall or short (for height); male or female (for gender).

A *structured* set of attribute pieces has exactly one piece for every possible combination of values for each attribute. For example, several commercial sets of plastic attribute materials have four attributes: color (red, yellow, blue), shape (circle, triangle, rectangle, square, hexagon), size (big, little), and thickness (thick, thin). The specific values, number of values, or number of attributes that a set may have is not important. Two teacher-made sets of structured attribute pieces are illustrated in Figure 22.1 on page 456.

The value of using structured attribute materials is that the attributes and values are clearly identified and easily described by students. There is no confusion about what values a particular piece possesses, so you can focus your attention on the reasoning skills that the activities are meant to serve.

NCTM Standards "Organizing data into categories should begin with informal sorting experiences, such as helping to put away groceries. . . . Young children should continue activities that focus on attributes of objects and data so that by the second grade, they can sort

Investigations
in Number, Data, and Space

Grade 5, Data: Kids, Cats, and Ads
Investigation 3: Sampling Ourselves

Context

In the first two investigations of this last unit of the fifth grade, students learn about a variety of different graphing techniques with an emphasis on line plots. No attention is given to measures of center (median or mean). Instead, students use both fractions and percents to compare data sets. Throughout the unit a clear effort is made to connect "nice" fractions (halves, thirds, fourths, etc.) to percents. This third investigation takes about four days. It is followed by two more units on sampling—one involving the percent of ad space in newspapers and one concerning play injuries on playgrounds. The data are very true to life.

Task Description

After a review of fractions, decimals, and percents (a one-hour activity), the next two days are devoted to exploring the implications of small samples to tell about a larger population. Using a list of six fun questions (e.g., Do you squeeze the toothpaste tube from the bottom or the middle? Do you put your ketchup to the side of the fries or on top of them?), students compare the results of samples of four students to the results for the full class. In addition to sampling issues, students must compare simple fractions such as $\frac{3}{4}$ to fractions such as $\frac{19}{26}$. Strips of paper are used to graphically show the part-whole relationships. The proportion issue of different-sized wholes (the sample of four versus the full class) is also revisited.

Next, class data are gathered for the seven questions shown here. The percentages given are from a national survey done in 1994. To make comparisons, students must convert their fractions to percents. Discussion concerns why the data from the class may be different from the national sample. Students are given information about the sample. It included children from ages 8 to 12 with equal numbers of each age. They came from all

Name			Date	
				Student Sheet 15

Survey Results

	Responses	National sample	Our class
1. When your family eats dinner, do you all eat together at the same time?	yes	82%	
	sometimes	8%	
	no	9%	
2. Do you watch television while you are eating dinner?	yes	29%	
	sometimes	19%	
	no	53%	
3. What's your favorite meal of the day—breakfast, lunch, or dinner?	breakfast	24%	
	lunch	33%	
	dinner	43%	
4. Do you get to choose what you eat for dinner?	yes	27%	
	sometimes	34%	
	no	40%	
5. Do you help set the table?	yes	57%	
	sometimes	19%	
	no	24%	
6. Do you help cook?	yes	26%	
	sometimes	37%	
	no	37%	
7. If you had a choice of cooking dinner, setting the table, or cleaning the dishes, which would you choose?	cook dinner	37%	
	set table	44%	
	clean dishes	18%	

Data (rounded to nearest percent) from "America's Children Talk About Family Time, Values, and Chores," 1994, Massachusetts Mutual Life Insurance Co.

© Dale Seymour Publications®   **139**   *Investigation 3 • Session 4*
Data: Kids, Cats, and Ads

Page 139 from *Statistics: Data: Kids, Cats, and Ads* by A. Rubin & J. Mokros. *Investigations in Number, Data, and Space.* Copyright © 1998 by Dale Seymour Publications. Reprinted by permission of Pearson Education, Inc.

parts of the nation. About 80 percent lived with their parents, and so on. Students can both see how they are alike and different and can also make judgments about their class as a suitable sample for the nation.

The combination of this activity with the earlier samples of four students to represent the whole classroom provides students with a good look at sampling, an approach that can be found every day in the newspaper and on the nightly news.

and classify simultaneously, using more than one attribute" (pp. 109–110).

Activities with Attribute Materials

Most attribute activities are best done with young children sitting on the floor in a large circle where all can see and

have access to the materials. All activities should be conducted in an easygoing manner that encourages risk taking, clear thinking, attentiveness, and discussion of ideas.

Most of the activities here will be described using the geometric shapes in Figure 22.1. However, each could be done with any structured set, and some could be done with nonstructured materials.

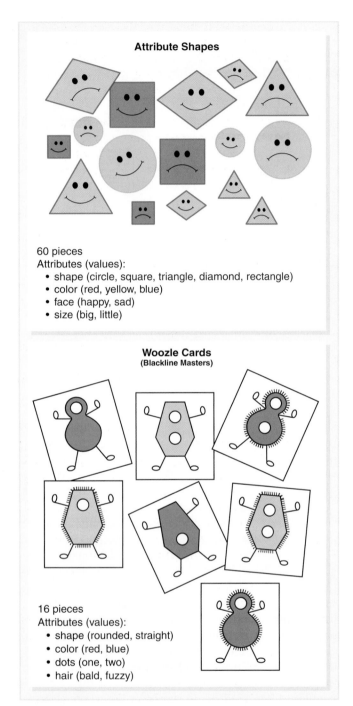

FIGURE 22.1 Three teacher-made attribute sets. Attribute shapes are made in large sizes from poster board and laminated. Woozle Cards can be duplicated on card stock, quickly colored in two colors, laminated, and cut into cards (see Blackline Masters).

Learning Classification Schemes

Several attribute activities involve using overlapping loops, each containing a designated class of materials such as pieces that are "red" or "not square." Loops can be made of yarn or drawn on large sheets of paper. When two loops overlap, the area that is inside both loops is for the pieces that have both properties. Children as young

as kindergarten can have fun with simple loop activities. With the use of words such as *and*, *or*, and *not*, the loop activities become quite challenging.

Before children can use loops in a problem-solving activity, the scheme itself must be understood. A good way to accomplish this is to do a few activities that involve the loops. Children find these interesting and fun. After several days of working with these initial activities, you can move on to problem-solving activities involving the same formats.

activity **22.1**

The First Loops
Give children two large loops of yarn or string. Direct them to put all the red pieces inside one string and all triangles inside the other. Let the children try to resolve the difficulty of what to do with the red triangles. When the notion of overlapping the strings to create an area common to both loops is clear, more challenging activities can be explored.

Later, "strings" or loops can be drawn on poster board or on large sheets of paper. If you happen to have a magnetic blackboard, try using small magnets on the backs of the pieces, and conduct full-class activities with the pieces on the board. Students can come to the board to place or arrange pieces inside loops drawn on the board with colored chalk.

Each loop can be given a label indicating a particular attribute. As shown in Figure 22.2, the labels need not be restricted to single attributes. Affix or draw labels on each loop and have students take turns placing pieces in the appropriate regions. If a piece does not fit in any region, it is placed outside of all of the loops.

It is important to introduce labels for negative attributes such as "not red" or "not small." Also important is the use of *and* and *or* connectives, as in "red and square" or "big or happy." This use of *and*, *or*, and *not* significantly widens children's classification schemes. It also will cause young children considerable difficulty as they attempt to place pieces in the correct regions of the loop diagrams.

Classification Problems

The activities described so far have students attempting to classify materials according to *our* schemes—the teacher creates a classification, and the children fit pieces into it. All that is required in these activities is an understanding of the loop method of classification and the ability to discriminate the attributes. Very limited logical reasoning is involved. A more significant activity is to infer how things have been classified when the scheme is not clearly articulated. The following activities require students to make and test conjectures about how things are being classified.

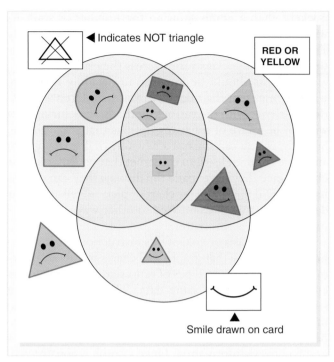

◀ Indicates NOT triangle

RED OR YELLOW

Smile drawn on card ▲

FIGURE 22.2 A three-loop activity with attribute pieces.

These activities more directly prepare students to analyze their world, formulate questions, and do data analysis.

activity **22.2**

Guess My Rule

For this activity, try using students instead of shapes as attribute "pieces." Decide on an attribute of your students such as "blue jeans" or "stripes on clothing," but do not tell your rule to the class. Silently look at one child at a time and move the child to the left or right according to this attribute rule. After a number of students have been sorted, have the next child come up and ask students to predict which group he or she belongs in. Before the rule is articulated, continue the activity for a while so that others in the class will have an opportunity to determine the rule. This same activity can be done with virtually any materials that can be sorted. When unstructured materials such as students, students' shoes, shells, or buttons are used, the classifications may be quite obscure, providing an interesting challenge.

activity **22.3**

Hidden Labels

Select label cards for the loops of string, and place the cards face down. Begin to sort pieces according to the turned-down labels. As you sort, have stu-

dents try to determine what the labels are for each of the loops. Let students who think they have guessed the labels try to place a piece in the proper loop, but avoid having them guess the labels aloud. Students who think they know the labels can be asked to "play teacher" and respond to the guesses of the others. Point out that one way to test an idea about the labels is to select pieces that you think might go in a particular section. Do not turn the cards up until most students have figured out the rule. With simple, one-value labels and only two loops, this activity can easily be played in kindergarten.

Connections to Data Analysis

"Guess My Rule" can and should be repeated with real-world materials connected to students' current explorations. For example, if you were doing a unit on animals in the backyard, you can use pictures of animals. The loops used with the attribute materials provide a first form of data presentation. The class can "graph" data about themselves by placing information in loops with labels. A graph of "Our Pets" might consist of a picture of each student's pet or favorite stuffed animal (in lieu of a pet) and be affixed to a wall display showing how the pets were classified. Different classifications would produce different graphs. For example, the graphs could show pets by the number of legs; by fur, feathers, or scales; by how long they have been with the family; and so on.

Numerous resource books contain exciting and challenging activities involving attribute materials. These are aimed primarily at logical reasoning and less at the skills of classification. These logic activities were first made popular in the 1960s and 1970s. The idea was that young children would learn reasoning skills by playing these games. But reasoning should not be a strand of the curriculum. Rather, it should pervade all of the mathematics that occurs in the classroom. Furthermore, research has not supported the hoped-for claims of logic activities. They have persisted in the early childhood curriculum primarily because they are fun and involve thinking. No harm is done by these activities, but they do not really fit into any of the content strands of the curriculum.

A popular program that encourages creation of classification schemes and using loop diagrams is *Tabletop, Jr.* (Sunburst). This program can be used by individuals or the full class. The program provides a wide variety of objects that can each be constructed with varying attributes. Various sorting choices are available, including the loop diagrams seen here. Objects can also be sorted according to a hidden rule specified by a user, a computer version of "Guess My Rule" with a lot of variation. Picture graphs can be constructed with the objects providing a direct link to data graphing. ∎

The Shape of Data

A big conceptual idea in data analysis can be referred to as the *shape of data:* a sense of how data are spread out or grouped, what characteristics about the data set as a whole can be described, and what the data tell us in a global way about the population from which they are taken.

There is no single technique that can tell us what the shape of the data is. Across the K–8 curriculum, students begin looking at the shape of data by looking at various graphs. Different graphing techniques or types of graphs can provide a different snapshot of the data as a whole. For example, bar graphs and circle graphs (percentage graphs) each show how the data cluster in different categories. The circle graph focuses more on the relative values of this clustering whereas the bar graph adds a dimension of quantity. The choice of which and how many categories to use in these graphs will cause different pictures of the shape of the data.

Part of understanding the shape of data is being aware of how spread out or clustered the data are. In the early grades this can be discussed informally by looking at almost any graph.

For numeric data, there are statistics that tell us how data are spread. The simplest of these is the *range*. Averages (the *mean* and the *median*) tell us where the "center" of the data is. In high school students will learn about the standard deviation statistic, which is a measure of spread. At the middle school level, a simple graphical technique called the *box-and-whisker plot* is designed to give us visual information about the spread of data.

Graphical Representations

How data are organized should be directly related to the question that caused you to collect the data in the first place. For example, suppose that students want to know how many pockets they have on their clothing, an idea suggested by Marilyn Burns (1996). Each student in the room counts his or her pockets and the data are collected.

 *pause and reflect* _____

If your second-grade class had collected these data, what are some ways that you might suggest they organize and graph them? Is one of your ideas better than others for answering the question about how many pockets? Think about this before reading on.

If a large bar graph is made with a bar for every student, that will certainly tell how many pockets each student has. However, is it the best way to answer the question? If the data were categorized by number of

pockets, then a graph showing the number of students with two pockets, three pockets, and so on will easily show which number of pockets is most common and how the number of pockets varies across the class.

Students should be involved in deciding how they want to represent their data. However, children with little experience with the various methods of picturing data will not be aware of the many options that are available. Sometimes you can suggest a new way of displaying data and have children learn to construct that type of graph or chart. Once they have made the display, they can discuss its value. Did this graph (or chart or picture) tell about our data in a clear way? Compared to other ways of displaying data, how is this better?

The emphasis or goal of this instruction should be to help children see that graphs and charts tell about information, that different types of representations tell different things about the same data. The value of having students actually construct their own graphs is not so much that they learn the techniques but that they are personally invested in the data and that they learn how a graph conveys information. Once a graph is constructed, the most important activity is discussing what it tells the people who see it, especially those who were not involved in making the graph. Discussions about graphs of real data that the children have themselves been involved in gathering will help them interpret other graphs and charts that they see in newspapers and on TV.

What we should *not* do is get overly anxious about the tedious details of graph construction. The issues of analysis and communication are your agendas and are much more important than the technique! In the real world, technology will take care of details.

There are two equally good possibilities you may consider when planning to have your students construct graphs or charts. First, you can simply encourage students to do their best and make charts and graphs that make sense to them and that they feel communicate the information they wish to convey. This is not to say that children do not need guidance. They should have seen and been involved in group constructions of various types of graphs and charts. This provides them with some ideas from which to choose for their own graphs. This informal approach may be best with younger students because they will be more personally invested in their work and not distracted by the techniques of technology. Care should be taken not to worry about fancy labeling or nice, neat pictures. The intent is to get the students involved in communicating a message about their data.

 The second option is to use technology. The computer and graphing calculators have provided us with many tools for constructing simple yet powerful representations. With the help of technology, it is possible to construct several different pic-

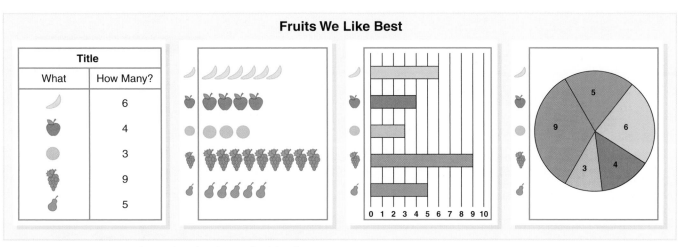

FIGURE 22.3 Four graphs produced with *Graph Club* software.

tures of the same data with very little effort. The discussion can then focus on the message or information that each format provides. Students can make their own selections of various graphs and can justify their choice based on their own intended purposes. As just one example, Figure 22.3 shows four graphs produced by *The Graph Club* (Tom Snyder, 1993). When two or more graphs are being created from the same data, it is possible to see all graphs change accordingly. How does a pie graph show information differently than a picture graph? ■

Cluster Graphs

As mentioned earlier in the discussion of attribute materials, a simple form of graph is a natural result of a classification activity. A *cluster graph* is nothing more than two or more labeled loops in which students write or place items that they have classified. For example, suppose students want to find out about different types of bugs and insects that are found in their backyards. After listing and describing the different bugs, students can draw pictures of the bugs on large index cards. They can then be challenged to think of different ways to sort the bugs. The question they are answering is "What kinds of bugs do we have in our backyards?" Figure 22.4 shows one possibility for a cluster graph that would help to answer this question. Other students may want to sort the bugs in different ways (e.g., where they are found, color, number of legs). The resulting collection of cluster graphs would tell the students a lot about the bugs in their backyards.

Bar Graphs and Tally Charts

Bar graphs and tally charts are among the first ways to group and present data and are especially useful in grades K–3. At this early level, bar graphs should be made so that each bar consists of countable parts such as squares, objects,

tallies, or pictures of objects. No numeric scale is necessary. Graphs should be simple and quickly constructed. Figure 22.5 illustrates a few techniques that can be used to make a graph quickly with the whole class.

A "real graph" uses the actual objects being graphed. Examples include types of shoes, seashells, and books. Each item can be placed in a square so that comparisons and counts are easily made.

Picture graphs use a drawing of some sort that represents what is being graphed. Students can make their own drawings, or you can duplicate drawings to be colored or cut out to suit particular needs.

Symbolic graphs use something like squares, blocks, tallies, or Xs to represent the things being counted in the graph. An easy idea is to use sticky notes as elements of a

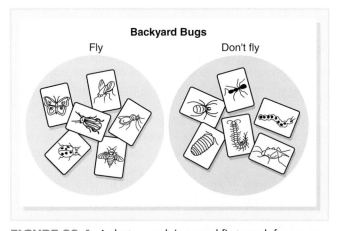

FIGURE 22.4 A cluster graph is a good first graph for young students. It is especially useful for situations in which classification of data is part of the activity. For one set of data (in this case, bugs found in the backyard) two or more different cluster graphs provide even more information. Some cluster graphs may have overlapping loops.

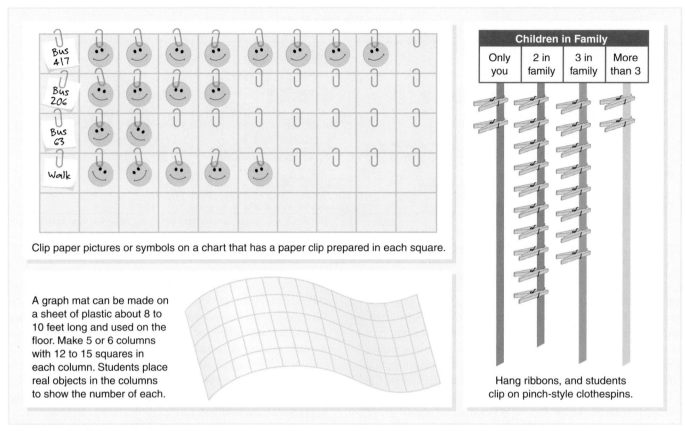

Clip paper pictures or symbols on a chart that has a paper clip prepared in each square.

A graph mat can be made on a sheet of plastic about 8 to 10 feet long and used on the floor. Make 5 or 6 columns with 12 to 15 squares in each column. Students place real objects in the columns to show the number of each.

Hang ribbons, and students clip on pinch-style clothespins.

FIGURE 22.5 Some ideas for quick graphs that can be used again and again.

graph. These can be stuck directly to the chalkboard or other chart and rearranged if needed.

To make a quick graph of class data, follow these steps:

1. Decide on what groups of data will make up the different bars. It is good to have two to six different bars in a graph.
2. Have each participant prepare a contribution to the graph before you begin. For real or picture graphs, the object or picture should be ready to be placed on the graph. For symbolic graphs, students should write down or mark their choice.
3. Have students, in small groups, quickly place or mark their entry on the graph. A graph mat can be placed on the floor, or a chart can be prepared on the wall or chalkboard. If tape or pins are to be used, have these items ready.

A class of 25 to 30 students can make a graph in less than 10 minutes, leaving ample time to use it for questions and observations.

Once a graph has been constructed, engage the class in a discussion of what information the graph tells or conveys. "What can you tell about our class by looking at this shoe graph?" Graphs convey factual information (more people wear sneakers than any other kind of shoe) and also provide opportunities to make inferences that are not directly observable in the graph (kids in this class do not like to wear leather shoes). The difference between actual facts and inferences is an important idea in graph construction and is also an important idea in science. Older students can examine graphs found in newspapers or magazines and discuss the *facts* in the graphs and the *message* that may have been intended by the person who made the graph.

As children begin to see different types of graphs, they can begin to make their own graphs of information gathered independently or by a group. A simple way to move graphing from the entire class to a small group is to assign different data collection tasks to different groups of children. The task is to gather the data and decide on and make a graph that displays as clearly as possible the information found.

Stem-and-Leaf Plots

Stem-and-leaf plots are a popular form of bar graph in which numeric data are plotted by using the actual numerals in the data to form the graph. By way of example, suppose that the American League baseball teams had posted the following record of wins over the past season:

Baltimore	45	Tampa Bay	91
Boston	94	Minnesota	98
Los Angeles	85	New York	100
Chicago	72	Oakland	101
Cleveland	91	Seattle	48
Detroit	102	Toronto	64
Kansas City	96	Texas	65

If the data are to be grouped by tens, list the tens digits in order and draw a line to the right, as in Figure 22.6(a). These form the "stem" of the graph. Next, go through the list of scores, and write the ones digits next to the appropriate tens digit, as in Figure 22.6(b). These are the "leaves." The process of making the graph groups the data for you. Furthermore, every piece of data can be retrieved from the graph. (Notice that stem-and-leaf plots are best made on graph paper so that each digit takes up the same amount of space.)

To provide more information, the graph can be quickly rewritten, ordering each leaf from least to most, as in Figure 22.6(c). In this form, it may be useful to identify the number that belongs to a particular team, indicating its relative place within the grouped listing.

Stem-and-leaf graphs are not limited to two-digit data. For example, if the data ranged from 600 to 1300, the stem could be the numerals from 6 to 13 and the leaves made of two-digit numbers separated by commas.

Figure 22.7 illustrates two additional variations. When two sets of data are to be compared, the leaves can extend in opposite directions from the same stem. In the same example, notice that the data are grouped by fives instead of tens. When plotting 62, the 2 is written next to the 6; for 67, the 7 is written next to the dot below the 6.

Stem-and-leaf plots are significantly easier for students to make than bar graphs, all of the data are maintained, they provide an efficient method of ordering data, and individual elements of data can be identified.

Continuous Data Graphs

Bar graphs or picture graphs are useful for illustrating categories of data that have no numeric ordering—for example, colors or TV shows. When data are grouped along a continuous scale, they should be ordered along a number line. Examples of such information include temperatures that occur over time, height or weight over age, and percentages of test takers scoring in different intervals along the scale of possible scores.

Line Plots

Line plots are useful *counts* of things along a numeric scale. To make a line plot, a number line is drawn and an X is made above the corresponding value on the line for every corresponding data element. One advantage of a line plot is that every piece of data is shown on the graph. It is also a very easy type of graph for students to make. It is

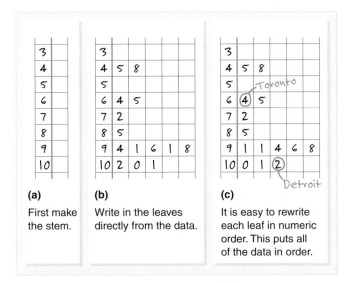

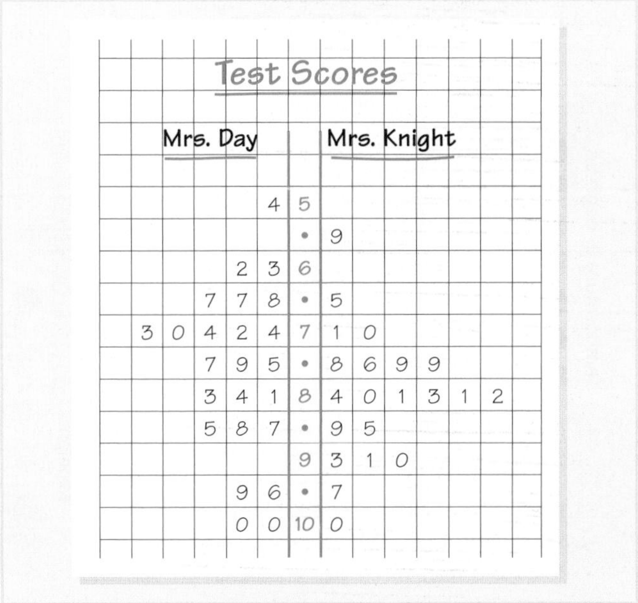

(a) First make the stem.

(b) Write in the leaves directly from the data.

(c) It is easy to rewrite each leaf in numeric order. This puts all of the data in order.

FIGURE 22.6 Making a stem-and-leaf plot.

FIGURE 22.7 Stem-and-leaf plots can be used to compare two sets of data.

essentially a bar graph with a potential bar for every possible value. A simple example is shown in Figure 22.8.

Histograms

A *histogram* is a form of bar graph in which the categories are consecutive equal intervals along a numeric scale. The height or length of each bar is determined by the number of data elements falling into that particular interval. Histograms are not difficult in concept but can cause problems for the students constructing them. What is the appropri-

ate interval to use for the bar width? What is a good scale to use for the length of the bars? That all of the data must be grouped and counted within each interval causes further difficulty. Technology helps us with all of these decisions, allowing children to focus on the graph and its message. Graphing calculators, for example, produce histograms without much difficulty. They allow for the size of the interval to be specified and easily changed. By connecting the calculator to a computer, the graphs can be printed out or pasted into a word processor for inclusion in a student report. Figure 22.8 shows an example of a histogram produced on a TI-83.

The little figure that looks like a bug on top of one of the bars is the trace indicator. It can be moved from bar to bar. For each bar, the trace indicates the number of data points in that interval. On this bar, there are six data points indicated by "$n = 6$" in the lower part of the screen.

Line Graphs

A *line graph* is used when there is a numeric value associated with equally spaced points along a continuous number scale. Points are plotted to represent two related pieces of data, and a line is drawn to connect the points. For example, a line graph might be used to show how the length of a flagpole shadow changed from one hour to the next during the day. The horizontal scale would be time, and the vertical scale would be the length of the shadow. Discrete points can be plotted and straight lines drawn connecting them. In the example of the shadow, a shadow did exist at all times, but its length did not jump or drop from one plotted value to the other. It changed continuously as suggested by the graph. See the example in Figure 22.8.

Students have a tendency to graph discrete data using continuous data graphs like the line graph. For example, consider Figure 22.9, in which a student has graphed the

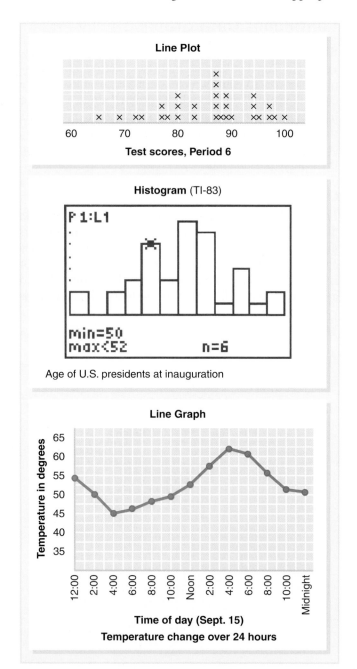

FIGURE 22.8 Three approaches to graphing data over continuous intervals. Notice that the horizontal scale must show some progression and is not just a grouping, as in a bar graph.

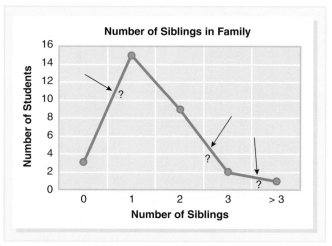

FIGURE 22.9 A line graph is used inappropriately to graph discrete data. What would the values be for the points indicated by the arrows?

number of siblings of each of his classmates using a line graph. The arrows have been added to the graph, highlighting the problem with displaying these types of data using a line graph. Every point on the line should have a value. What are the values where the arrows are pointing? A more appropriate choice would be a bar graph or a circle graph.

Similarly, a line graph would not be appropriate for a graph of students' favorite colors because there is no natural ordering, nor are there values between the colors. For these graphs, a bar graph would be more appropriate.

Circle Graphs

Typically, we think of circle graphs as showing percentages and, as such, these would probably not be appropriate for primary students. However, notice in Figure 22.3 that the circle graph only indicates the number of data points (in that case, students) in each of five categories. Many simple graphing programs will create a similar graph. An understanding of percentages is not required when the computer creates the graph.

Notice also that the circle graph shows information that is not easily available from the other graphs. For example, the peach and pear categories account for a bit more than half of the class, whereas the apple and orange groups are about one-fourth of the class. These fractional part ideas are quite appropriate at the primary level, even before students are able to make fractional estimates. As fraction concepts are developed in the third grade, making circle graphs is a good way to integrate different aspects of your curriculum.

When comparisons are made between two populations of very different size, the circle graph offers visual ratios that allow for these comparisons. In Figure 22.10, each of two graphs shows the percentages of students with different numbers of siblings. One graph is based on classroom data and the other on schoolwide data. Because pie graphs display ratios rather than quantities, the small set of class data can be compared to the large set of school data. That could not be done with bar graphs.

Easily Made Circle Graphs

Even without technology, there are a variety of ways that circle graphs can be made easily. Circle graphs of the students in your room can be made quickly and quite dramatically. Suppose, for example, that each student picked his or her favorite basketball team in the NCAA tournament's "Final Four." Line up all of the students in the room so that students favoring the same team are together. Now form the entire group into a circle of students. Tape the ends of four long strings to the floor in the center of the circle, and extend them to the circle at each point where the teams change. Voilà! A very nice pie graph with no measuring and no percentages. If you copy and cut out a hundredths disk (one is in the Blackline Masters) and place it on the center of the circle, the strings will show approximate percentages for each part of your graph (see Figure 22.11).

Another easy approach to circle graphs is similar to the human pie graph. Begin by having students make a bar graph of the data. Once complete, cut out the bars themselves, and tape them together end to end. Next, tape the

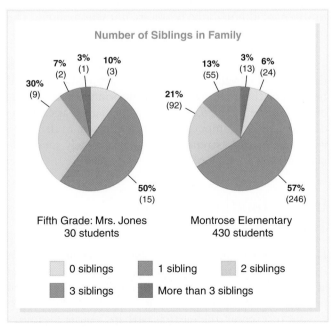

FIGURE 22.10 Circle graphs show ratios of part to whole and can be used to compare ratios.

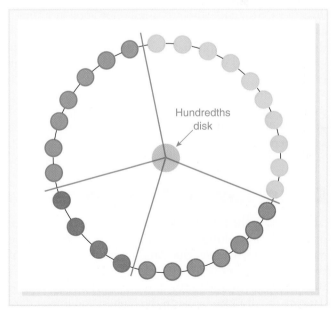

FIGURE 22.11 A human pie graph: Students are arranged in a circle, with string stretched between them to show the divisions.

two ends together to form a circle. Estimate where the center of the circle is, draw lines to the points where different bars meet, and trace around the full loop. You can estimate percentages using the hundredths disk as before.

From Percentages to Pie Graphs

If students have experienced either of the two methods just described, using their own calculations to make pie graphs will make more sense. The numbers in each category are added to form the total or whole. (That's the same as taping all of the strips together or lining up the students.) By dividing each of the parts by the whole with a calculator, numbers between 0 and 1 result—fractional parts of the whole. If rounded to hundredths, these numbers are now percentages of the whole. Rounding may cause some error. With a copy of the hundredths disk, students can easily make a pie chart and never have to mess with degrees and protractors. Trace around the disk to make the outline of the pie. Mark the center through a small hole in the disk, and draw a line to the circle. Start from that point, and use the disk to measure hundredths around the outside.

 As you evaluate students in the area of graphing, it is important not to focus undue attention on the skills of constructing a graph. It is more important to think about the choice of graphs that the students make to help answer their questions or complete their projects. Your goal is for students to understand that a graph helps answer a question and provides a picture of the data. Different graphs tell us different things about the data. If you make all of the decisions about what type of graphs to make and how they should be labeled and constructed, all that students are doing is following your directions. Students who are simply not good at graphic arts are likely to do poorly drawing graphs even though they may have exceptional understanding of what their graph shows and why they chose to make that particular type.

Students should write about their graphs, explaining what the graph tells and why they selected that type of graph to illustrate the data. Use this information for your assessment. ■

Descriptive Statistics

Although graphs provide visual images of data, measures of the data are a different and important way to describe data. Numbers that describe data are *statistics*, measures of the data that quantify some attribute of them. The things that are most often described numerically about a set of data are the distance between the highest and lowest data values (the *range*), some measure of where the center of the data is (an *average*), and how dispersed the data are within the range (the *variance* or *dispersion*). Students can get an idea of the importance of these statistics by exploring the ideas informally.

Averages

The term *average* is heard quite frequently in everyday usage. Sometimes it refers to an exact arithmetic average, as in "the average daily rainfall." Sometimes it is used quite loosely, as in "She is about average height." In either situation, an average is a single number or measure that is descriptive of a larger collection of numbers. If your test average is 92, it is assumed that somehow all of your test scores are reflected by this number.

The *mean, median,* and *mode* are specific types of averages or *measures of central tendency*. The *mode* is the value that occurs most frequently in the data set. Of these three statistics, the mode is the least useful and could perhaps be ignored completely. Consider the following set of numbers:

$$1, 1, 3, 5, 6, 7, 8, 9$$

The mode of this set is 1 and not a very good description of this set. If the 8 in this string of numbers were a 9, there would be two modes. If one of the ones were changed to a 2, there would be no mode at all. In short, the mode is a statistic that does not always exist, does not necessarily reflect the center of the data, and can be highly unstable, changeable with very small changes in the data.

The *mean* is computed by adding all of the numbers in the set and dividing the sum by the number of elements added. This is the statistic that is sometimes referred to as the *average*, although the terms are not synonymous. The mean of our sample set is 5 (40 ÷ 8). The mean is discussed in more detail in the next section.

The *median* is the middle value in an ordered set of data. Half of all values lie at or above the median and half below. For the eight numbers in our sample set, the median is between 5 and 6, or 5.5. The median is easier to understand and to compute and is not affected, as the mean is, by one or two extremely large or extremely small values outside the range of the rest of the data.

Understanding the Mean: Two Concepts

Due to ease of computation and stability, the median when compared to the mean has some advantages as a practical average. However, the mean will continue to be used in popular media and in books. For smaller sets of data such as your test scores, the mean is perhaps a more meaningful statistic. Finally, the mean is used in the computation of other statistics such as the standard deviation. Therefore, it remains important that students have a good concept of what the mean tells them about a set of numbers.

There are actually two different ways to think about the mean. First, it is a number that represents what all of the data items would be if they were leveled out. In this sense, the mean represents all of the data items. Statisticians prefer to think of the mean as a central balance point. This concept of the mean is more in keeping with the notion of a measure of the "center" of the data or a measure of central tendency. Both concepts are discussed in the following sections.

A Leveling Concept of the Mean

Suppose that the average number of family members for the students in your class is 5. One way to interpret this is to think about distributing the entire collection of moms, dads, sisters, and brothers to each of the students so that each would have a "family" of the same size. To say that you have an average of 93 for the four tests in your class is like spreading the total of all of your points evenly across the four tests. It is as if each student had the same family size and each test score were the same, but the totals matched the actual distributions. This concept of the mean is easy to understand and explain and has the added benefit that it leads directly to the algorithm for computing the mean.

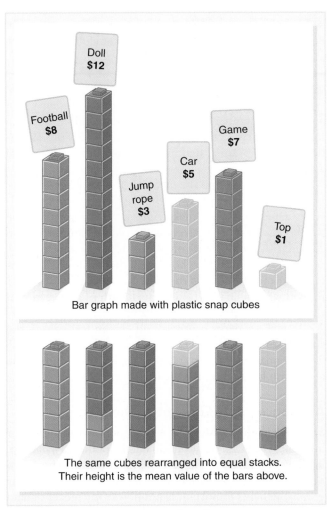

Bar graph made with plastic snap cubes

The same cubes rearranged into equal stacks. Their height is the mean value of the bars above.

FIGURE 22.12 Understanding the mean as a leveling of the data.

activity 22.4

Leveling the Bars

Have students make a bar graph of some data using plastic connecting cubes such as Unifix. Choose a situation with 5 or 6 bars with no more than 10 or 12 cubes in each. For example, the graph in Figure 22.12 shows prices for six toys. The task for students is to use the graph itself to determine what the price would be if all of the toys were the same price, assuming that the total for all the toys remained the same. Students will use various techniques to rearrange the cubes in the graph but will eventually create six equal bars, possibly with some leftovers that could mentally be distributed in fractional amounts. (In the example, the total number of cubes is a multiple of 6.) Do not tell students they are finding the average or mean, only that they are to find equal-length bars.

Explain to students that the size of the leveled bars is the *mean* of the data—the amount that each item would cost if all items cost the same amount but the total of the prices remained fixed.

Follow "Leveling the Bars" with the next activity to help students develop an algorithm for finding the mean.

activity 22.5

The Mean Foot

Pose the following question: What is the mean length of our feet in inches? Have each student cut a strip of adding machine tape that matches the length of his or her foot. Students record their names and the length of their feet in inches on the strips. Suggest that before finding a mean for the class, you will first get means for smaller groups. Put students into groups of four, six, or eight students. (Groups of five or seven will prove to be problematic.) In each group, have the students tape their foot strips end to end. The task for each group is to come up with a method of finding the mean without using any of the lengths written on the strips. They can only use the combined strip. Each group will share their method with the class. From this work, they will devise a method for determining the mean for the whole class.

Ⅱ *pause and reflect* _____

Before reading on, what is a method that the students could use in "The Mean Foot"?

_____

To evenly distribute the inches for each student's foot among the members of the group, they can fold the strip into equal parts so that there are as many sections as students in the group. Then they can measure the length of any one part.

How can you find the mean for the whole class? Suppose there are 23 students in the class. Using the strips already taped together, make one very long strip for the whole class. It is not reasonable to fold this long strip into 23 equal sections. But if you wanted to know how long the resulting strip would be, how could that be done? The total length of the strip is the sum of the lengths of the 23 individual foot strips. To find the length of one section if the strip were actually folded in 23 parts, simply divide by 23. In fact, students can mark off "mean feet" along the strip. There should be very close to 23 equal-length "feet." This dramatically illustrates the usual add-up-and-divide algorithm for finding the mean.

A Balance Point Concept of the Mean

Statisticians think about the mean as a point on a number line where the data on either side of the point are balanced. To help think about the mean in this way, it is useful to think about the data placed on a line plot rather than as bar graphs. What is important is not how many pieces of data are on either side of the mean or balance point but the distances of data from the mean that must balance.

To illustrate, draw a number line on the board, and arrange eight sticky notes above the number 3 as shown in Figure 22.13(a). Each sticky note represents one family. The notes are positioned on the line to indicate how many pets are owned by the family. Stacked up like this would indicate that all families have the same number of pets. The mean is three pets. But different families are likely to have different numbers of pets. So we could think of eight families with a range of numbers of pets. Some may have zero pets, and some may have as many as ten or even more. How could you change the number of pets for these eight families so that the mean remains at 3? Students will suggest moving the sticky notes in opposite directions, probably in pairs. This will result in a symmetrical arrangement. But what if one of the families has eight pets, a move of five spaces from the 3? This might be balanced by moving two families to the left, one three spaces to the 0 and one two spaces to the 1. Figure 22.13(b) shows one way the families could be rearranged to maintain a mean of 3. You should stop here and find at least two other distributions of the families, each having a mean of 3.

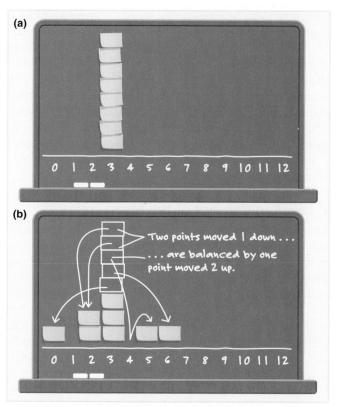

(a)

(b)

Two points moved 1 down . . .

. . . are balanced by one point moved 2 up.

FIGURE 22.13 (a) If all data points are the same, the mean is that value. (b) By moving data points away from the mean in a balanced manner, different distributions can be found that have the same mean.

Use the next activity to find the mean or balance point given the data.

activity **22.6**

Finding the Balance Point

Have students draw a number line from 0 to 12 with about an inch between the numbers. Use six small sticky notes to represent the prices of six toys as shown in Figure 22.14. Have them place a light pencil mark on the line where they think the mean might be. For the moment, avoid the add-up-and-divide computation. The task is to determine the actual mean by moving the sticky notes in toward the "center." That is, the students are finding out what price or point on the number line balances out the six prices on the line. For each move of a sticky one space to the left (a toy with a lower price), a different sticky must be moved one space to the right (a toy with a higher price). Eventually, all stickies should be stacked above the same number, the balance point or mean.

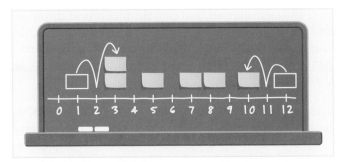

FIGURE 22.14 Move data points in toward the center or balance point without changing the balance around that point. When you have all points at the same value, that is the balance or the mean.

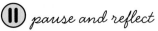 **pause and reflect** _____

Stop now and try this exercise yourself. Notice that after any pair of moves that keep the distribution balanced, you actually have a new distribution of prices with the same mean. The same was true when you moved the stickies out from the mean when they were all stacked on the same point.

The balance concept does not lead to the add-up-and-divide algorithm for computing the mean. However, it is useful to do the following side-by-side approach. Make bars of cubes for the original data in Figure 22.14. Level the bars by moving only one cube at a time from a longer bar to a shorter bar. Each time you move a cube off of a bar, the sticky note for that bar must be moved one space to the left. At the same time, the sticky note for the bar to which the cube was added must be moved one space to the right. As you continue to move cubes one at a time, adjust the sticky notes accordingly.

Changes in the Mean

Notice that the mean only defines a "center" of a set of data and so by itself is not a very useful description of the shape of the data. The balance approach to the mean clearly illustrates that many different distributions can have the same mean.*

Especially for small sets of data, the mean is significantly affected by extreme values. For example, suppose that another toy with a price of $20 is added to the six we have been using in the examples. How will the mean change? If the $1 toy were removed, how would the mean be affected? Suppose that one new toy is added that in-

creases the mean from $6 to $7. How much does the new toy cost? Students should be challenged with questions such as these using small sets of data and either the balance or the leveling concept.

NCTM Standards In NCTM's *e-Standards*, the applet "Comparing Properties of the Mean and the Median" shows seven data points that can be dragged back and forth along a number line with the mean and median updated instantly. The applet allows students to see how stable the median is and how changing one point can affect the mean.

Distribution of Data: Box-and-Whisker Plots

Box-and-whisker plots (or just *box plots*) are an easy method for visually displaying not only the median statistic but also information about the range and distribution or variance of data. In Figure 22.15, the ages in months for 27 sixth-grade

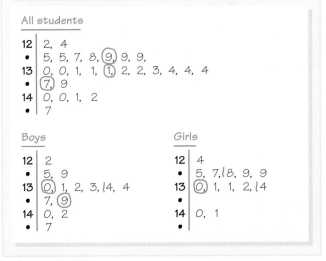

FIGURE 22.15 Ordered stem-and-leaf plots grouped by fives. Medians and upper and lower quartiles are found on the stem-and-leaf plots. Medians and quartiles are circled or are represented by a bar (I) if they fall between two elements.

_____

*The balance concept of the mean is the one developed in the Connected Math Project, one of the three standards-based programs for the middle grades. It is also developed in the *Used Numbers* book *Statistics: Middles, Means, and In-Betweens* (Friel, Mokros, & Russell, 1992).

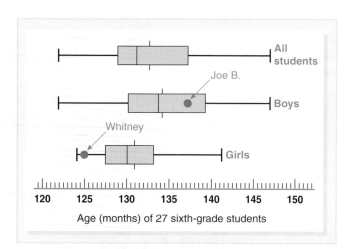

FIGURE 22.16 Box-and-whisker plots show a lot of information. In addition to showing how data are distributed, data points of particular interest can be shown.

students are given, along with stem-and-leaf plots for the full class and the boys and girls separately. Box-and-whisker plots are shown in Figure 22.16.

Each box-and-whisker plot has these three features:

1. A box that contains the "middle half" of the data, one-fourth to the left and right of the median. The ends of the box are at the *lower quartile*, the median of the lower half of the data, and the *upper quartile*, the median of the upper half of the data.
2. A line inside the box at the median of the data.
3. A line extending from the end of each box to the *lower extreme* and *upper extreme* of the data. Each line, therefore, covers the upper and lower fourths of the data.

Look at the information these box plots provide at a glance! The box and the lengths of the lines provide a quick indication of how the data are spread out or bunched together. Since the median is shown, this spreading or bunching can be determined for each quarter of the data. The entire class in this example is much more spread out in the upper half than the lower half. The girls are much more closely grouped in age than either the boys or the class as a whole. It is immediately obvious that at least three-fourths of the girls are younger than the median age of the boys. The *range* of the data (difference between upper and lower extremes) is represented by the length of the plot, and the extreme values can be read directly. A box plot provides useful visual information to help understand the shape of a data set.

Making box-and-whisker plots is quite simple. First, put the data in order. An easy and valuable method is to make a stem-and-leaf plot and order the leaves, providing another visual image as well. Next, find the median. Simply count the number of values and determine the middle one. This can be done directly on the stem-and-leaf plots as was done in Figure 22.15. To find the two quartiles, ig-

nore the median itself, and find the medians of the upper and lower halves of the data. Mark the two extremes, the two quartiles, and the median above an appropriate number line. Draw the box and the lines. Box plots can also be drawn vertically.

Note that the means for the data in our example are each just slightly higher than the medians (class = 132.4; boys = 133.9; girls = 130.8). For this example, the means themselves do not provide nearly as much information as the box plots. In Figure 22.16, the means are shown with small marks extending above and below each box.

Graphing calculators and several computer programs draw box-and-whisker plots, making this relatively simple process even more accessible. The TI-73 and TI-83 calculators can draw box plots for up to three sets of data on the same axis. In Figure 22.17, the data for the top box plot are based on 23 items. The second plot has 122 items. The third plot has 48 items of data. When you compare both large and small sets of data in this manner, the spread or lack of spread of the data becomes much more obvious.

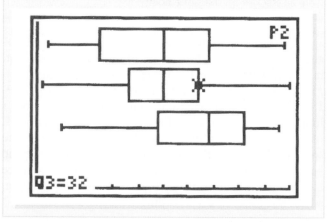

FIGURE 22.17 Three box plots of data falling between the values of 0 and 50. Twenty-three items are represented by the top plot, 122 by the middle plot, and 48 by the bottom plot. The cursor on the middle plot shows that the third quartile is 32. What other information can be determined from this plot?

 pause and reflect —————

Notice that in Figure 22.16 the box for the boys is actually a bit longer than the box for the whole class. How can that be when there are clearly more students in the full class than there are boys? How would you explain this apparent discrepancy to a class of seventh graders?

Assessment Notes When assessing students in the area of graphing and statistics, care should be taken to distinguish between the skills of making graphs or computing statistics and the quite different kind of knowledge that involves judgment and interpretation. Of course, you want your students to know how to make a stem-and-leaf plot and a box plot and how to find the mean and the median. But many students can learn to do these things without interpreting them. Choice and interpretation of graphs and statistics are more important than the ability to construct and compute.

Computers and calculators will make graphs even when they are inappropriate to your needs. Students must be able to select appropriate graphs and statistics to suit their purposes. It is important to pose situations that include a real context and have students decide what statistics and what graphs would best serve the purposes. Is a bar graph or a line graph more appropriate? Why? Which statistic is better in this situation, the mean or the median?

Nor does making a graph or computing a statistic, regardless of how it is done, indicate the ability to interpret graphs or statistics. Recall that data analysis is really about answering questions about the population from which the data are drawn. To assess students' interpretation skills, use good, contextual problems for which students create graphs and compute statistics. Within these contexts, a significant portion of the task should be an analysis of what the data tell about the population. If a particular statistic or graphing technique is omitted, have students return to the data and create the missing graph or compute the required statistic. Now you can ask for interpretations of these items as well. ∎

Scatter Plots and Relationships

Data are often analyzed to search for or demonstrate relationships between two sets of data or phenomena. For example, what are the relationships, if any, between time spent watching television and overall grades? Does the size of a college have anything to do with the cost of attending?

All sorts of real situations exist where we are interested in relationships between two variables or two numeric phenomena. The world of science abounds with experimental data. How far does a toy car roll down an inclined plane as compared to the angle of the plane? How tall do beans grow over a 21-day period from the day they sprout? Such data are generally gathered from some sort of experiment that is set up and observed, with measurements taken. The experiment defines the various variables to look at.

Data that may be related are gathered in pairs. For example, if you were going to examine the possible relationship between hours of TV watched and grades, each person in the survey or sample would produce a pair of numbers, one for TV time and one for grade point average.

Scatter Plots

Regardless of the source of the data, a good first attempt at examining them for possible relationships is to create a *scatter plot* of the two variables involved, a graph of points on a coordinate grid with each axis representing one of the two variables. Each pair of numbers from the two sets of data, when plotted, produces a visual image of the data as well as a hint concerning any possible relationships. Suppose that the following information was gathered from 25 eighth-grade boys: height in inches, weight in pounds, and number of letters in their last name. The two graphs in Figure 22.18 show two possibilities. Graph (a) is a scatter plot of height to weight, and graph (b) is a plot of name length to weight. Both were made with a graphing calculator.

As you would expect, the boys' weights seem to increase as their heights increase. However, the relationship is far from perfect. There is no reason to expect any relationship between name length and weight, and indeed the dots appear to be almost randomly distributed.

 "Teachers should encourage students to plot many data sets and look for relationships in the [scatter]plots; computer graphing software and

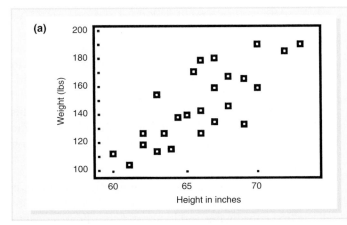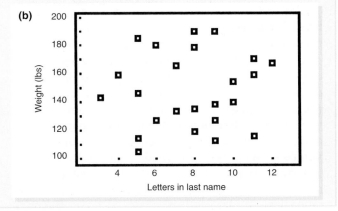

FIGURE 22.18 Scatter plots show potential relationships or lack of relationships.

graphing calculators can be very helpful in this work. Students should see a range of examples in which plotting data sets suggests linear relationships, and no apparent relationships at all" (p. 253).

Best-Fit Lines

If your scatter plot indicates a relationship, it can be simply described in words. "As boys get taller, they tend to get heavier." This is correct but not particularly useful. What exactly is the relationship? If I knew the height of a boy, could I predict what his weight might be based on this information? Like much of statistical analysis, the value of a statistic is to predict what has not yet been observed. We poll a small sample of voters before an election to predict how the full population will vote. Here, can a sample of 30 students predict the weights of other students?

The relationship in these cases is not a number like a mean or a standard deviation but rather a line or curve. Is there a line that can be drawn through the scatter plot that represents the "best" approximation of all of the dots and reflects the observed trend? If the scatter plot seems to indicate a steadily increasing or steadily decreasing relationship (as in the height–weight graph), you would probably try to find a straight line that approximates the dots. Sometimes the plot will indicate a curved relationship, in which case you might try to draw a smooth curve like a parabola to approximate the dots.

What Determines Best Fit?

From a strictly visual standpoint, the line you select defines the observed relationship and could be used to predict other values not in the data set. The more closely the dots in the scatter plot hug the line you select, the greater the confidence you would have in the predictive value of the line. Certainly you could draw a straight line somewhere in the name length–weight graph, but you would not have much faith in its predictive capability because the dots would be quite dispersed from any line you might draw.

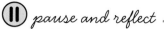

activity **22.7**

Best-Fit Line

Once students have collected related data and prepared a scatter plot, duplicate an accurate version of the plot for each group of students. Provide the groups with a piece of spaghetti to use as a line. The task is to tape the line on the plot so that it is the "best" line to represent the relationship in the dots. Furthermore, the students are to develop a rationale for why they positioned the line as they did.

Using an overhead transparency of the plot, compare the lines chosen by various groups and their rationales.

(II) *pause and reflect* _____

Before reading further, return to the height–weight plot in Figure 22.18(a) and draw a straight line that you think would make a good line of best fit. (You may want to make a photo enlargement of that figure to use with your class.) What reason would you offer for why you drew the line where you did?

Many of the reasons students will give for their best-fit line will be rather subjective: "It just looks right" or "There are just as many points above as below." Others will see how many points they can make the line touch. Most intuitive ideas fail to consider all of the points. Two different people using the same criteria might well come up with very different lines. There is a need for a better definition of a best-fit line.

Encourage students to use a more "mathematical" reason for why a line might be best. Since a good line is one around which most dots cluster, a good-fitting line is one where the distances from all of the dots to the line are minimal. This general notion of least distance to the line for all points can lead to an algorithm that will always produce a unique line for a given set of points. Two such algorithms are well known and used in statistics. The more complicated approach is called the *least squares regression* line. It is an algebraic procedure that is not accessible to middle grade students and is also rather tedious to compute. The second algorithm produces what is called the *median–median* line and is quite easy to determine.

Median-Median Line

The median-median line can be determined either directly from the graph or from the data. It is based on the simple median statistic. The method for determining the median-median line essentially consists of these steps:

1. Separate the data into three "equal" sets of points along the horizontal axis. (In the example of Figure 22.19, since there are 25 points, put the extra point into the middle third.)
2. Find the *median point* in each third of the points. (This is described in the text that follows.)
3. Connect the median points in the first and third sets of data. This line takes into consideration all points in these two sections but ignores the points in the middle third.
4. Draw a parallel line one-third of the distance from this first line to the center median point. This gives the center collection of points a proportional influence on the position of the line.

A *median point* in a scattered collection of points is the point with its first coordinate equal to the median of all the first coordinates and its second coordinate equal to the median of all the second coordinates. Another way of

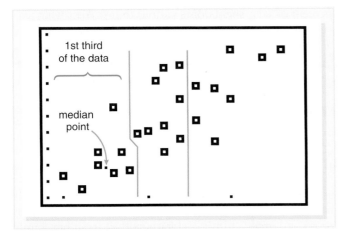

FIGURE 22.19 A height-versus-weight scatter plot. Use the graph to find the median-median line. The single pixel in the lower left is the median point for the left third of the points.

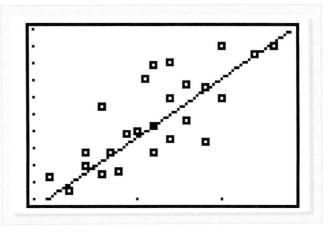

FIGURE 22.20 The median-median line for the points plotted in Figure 22.19.

saying this is that the median point is one that is midway vertically and midway horizontally. Using this second formulation, the median point can be found by counting points from the bottom up until you have half the points below and half above. With an odd number of points, draw a horizontal line through the middle point. With an even number of points, draw the line halfway between the two middle points. The median point will fall on this horizontal line. Repeat the process, moving from left to right. The vertical line you find this way will intersect the horizontal line at the median point. Note that it is not necessary for the median point to be a data point.

In Figure 22.19, the median point in the left-hand third of the data (the first eight points counting left to right) is shown as a single pixel.

 _pause and reflect_ _____

Find the other two median points on your own, and complete steps 3 and 4. Use Figure 22.19.

Median-Median Lines with a Calculator

The TI-73 and TI-83 calculators will compute the median-median line for you. Figure 22.20 shows the calculator plot of the median-median line for the same height-versus-weight data.

Thinking About Functional Relationships

It is worth noting that the median-median line is a graphical representation of a function relating the variable on the horizontal axis to the variable on the vertical axis. The best-fit line is a functional relationship that "best" describes an observed trend in the data. The functional relationship of the best-fit line is used to approximate this

trend. It can also be used to make best-guess predictions that extend beyond the data collected. Different methods of finding the best-fit line will likely develop slightly different lines.

Note that if the function (line) that we found accurately predicted the weight of a boy based on his height, all of the data points would fall along a perfectly straight line. That they do not is a vivid picture of the difference between data found in the world (the points on the graph) and a mathematical model of the real world (the line).

Scatter plots and best-fit lines are also discussed in the section on functions in Chapter 15. The connection among the real world, statistics, and algebraic ideas is a valuable one to make.

Technology or By-Hand Methods

Data analysis is an area of the curriculum in which technology really changes the way we teach. In the past, the emphasis was on _how_ to create the graph and _how_ to compute the statistic. Students had to labor over graph paper, drawing scales, labeling axes, coloring the graphs, and so on. Today, every graphical technique and every statistic mentioned in this chapter is readily available in a variety of technologies. An exception may be stem-and-leaf plots. With the help of technology, the focus of instruction in data analysis can and should shift to the big ideas of using graphs and statistics: to describe data, to get a sense of the shape of data, to answer questions with data, and to communicate this information to others.

At the primary level, it is useful to have a software program into which children can enter data and select from a variety of graphical representations. _The Graph Club_ (Sunburst), recently updated, is an excellent example of software in this category (see Figure 22.3). _The Cruncher 2.0_

(Sunburst) is a slightly simplified spreadsheet designed for grades 3 and up. Every popular spreadsheet will compute any statistic for columns or rows of data. If the data are changed, the statistics change instantly. Spreadsheets also make very nice bar graphs, line graphs, and circle graphs. Teachers should also check to see if the publisher of their textbook offers graphing software.

The graphing calculator puts data analysis technology in the hands of every student. The TI-73 calculator is designed for middle grade students. It will produce eight different kinds of plots or graphs, including pie charts, bar graphs, and picture graphs that are not available on the TI-83. All graphing calculators will compute and graph best-fit lines using either the median-median method or the regression method.

An argument can be made for having students do some graphing and computing of statistics without technology. Appropriate methods have been suggested in this chapter. However, the intent of by-hand methods should always be to help understand the graphs or the statistics. Given today's readily available technology, there is no reason for repetitive exercises with tedious by-hand methods.

Literature Connections

Literature is full of situations in which things must be sorted, compared, or measured. Each of these can be the springboard for a data collection and representation activity. Books of lists and interesting data also are fruitful beginnings for data explorations. Students can use the data in the books and/or compare similar data collected themselves. By making suggestions concerning the types of comparisons and graphs that may be useful, you can guide students to explore the graphing or statistical techniques that are on your agenda.

The Phantom Tollbooth
Juster, 1961/1989

This classic book is full of opportunities for mathematical discussions. (It was also mentioned in Chapter 18.) In Chapter 2, we are introduced to the Lethargians who inhabit the Doldrums. The Lethargians have a wonderful list of the things that they do all day, which can be "Anything as long as it's nothing, and everything as long as it isn't anything." Their day is separated into hour and half-hour intervals in which they spend their time daydreaming, dawdling and delaying, napping, lingering and loitering, and so on. This humorous accounting of how days are spent in the Doldrums easily leads to the question of how your students spend their days.

This is a good example of gathering data to answer a question. How to go about gathering the data is a good experience as that is not immediately obvious. One possibility for presenting the data is with circle graphs showing the percent of a day spent doing various things. Also, what percent of the class does given things at any time of the day? The amount of time spent doing things, such as playing outside, watching TV, playing video games, doing homework, and so on, will also vary. These data lend themselves to the use of box plots to show in what way the class varies in this regard.

The Best Vacation Ever
Murphy, 1997

This is just one book in the MathStart series, designed as a collection of single-concept books to generate simple activities in mathematics. In this book, appropriate for first or second grade, a little girl gathers data from her family to try to decide what is important to them. Her purpose is to use the data to decide where the family should go in order to have the best vacation and please everyone. It turns out that the place that serves best all of the family is their own backyard.

This book nicely introduces the concept of gathering data to answer a question. Your lesson might involve vacations, but perhaps you have another decision that needs to be made by the class. Use the book as an introduction to using data to answer a question. When data are gathered, how the information should be interpreted is another issue that will generate a useful discussion.

Frog and Toad Are Friends
Lobel, 1970

When Frog and Toad go walking, Frog loses a button. As they search to find the button, they find many buttons. Whenever one of Frog's friends asks, "Is this your button?" Frog responds (with a touch of anger), "No, that is not my button! That button is ____, but my button was ____." The phrase is repeated with each newly found button. It turns out that Frog did not lose the button on the walk but in his own home before they left. This provides another value to the story as Frog must find a way to make up for being so angry with his friends.

The approach to finding the button is very much like the game "One of These Things Is Not Like the Others." It is also a perfect lead-in to secret sorting activities as described in this chapter. Young students can model the story directly with sets of buttons, shells, attribute blocks, Woozle Cards, or other objects with a variety of attributes. With a highly varied set of geometric shapes, the children could play the game and explore their geometric language and perceptions of geometric attributes.

Incredible Comparisons
Ash, 1996

Not a story but an amazing collection of facts and comparisons, Ash's book includes 23 topics for comparison, each graphically displayed. For example, different-sized squares are used to compare the size of the continents.

Maps of major countries are layered on top of each other to indicate relative areas. Data about area and distances are also provided in different units of measure. The amount of time needed to travel the widths of countries is demonstrated as well. Data and drawings such as these can prompt students to find clever but acceptable ways to display the information or to research similar information in other resources. Other topics include big buildings, animal speeds, growth and age, and population. ■

Reflections on Chapter 22

Writing to Learn

1. Explain why attribute activities are important in the development of data analysis skills. Why would you use structured attribute materials for these activities instead of informal or unstructured materials such as buttons?
2. In initial loop activities, the teacher tells the students how to sort the attribute pieces. What is the purpose of these not so problem-based activities? What are students learning in activities where the loop labels are not shown or the sorting rule is a secret?
3. What is meant by the "shape of data"?
4. Data should be collected to answer questions. What are some examples of questions that students might explore with data at the K–2 level and in the upper grades?
5. What kinds of graphs can be used for data that can be put into categories? Which of these are most appropriate for K–2 students?
6. What is the difference between a bar graph and a histogram? What kinds of data are required for a histogram?
7. Describe a line plot and a line graph. Give an example of data that might be appropriate for these graphs. What is the distinct value of each?
8. Put at least 30 numbers in a stem-and-leaf plot, and use it to determine the median, the upper and lower quartiles, and the range and to draw a box-and-whisker plot.
9. What are three ways to make a circle graph? What does a circle graph tell you that a bar graph does not? What does it not tell?
10. What are three different forms of averages? Which is the most stable? Explain.
11. Describe two different concepts of the mean. How can each be developed? Which idea leads to the method of computing the mean?
12. Describe what is meant by a *best-fit line*. When would you want to find such a line? Does a scatter plot define a functional relationship? What about a best-fit line?
13. On a grid, make a scatter plot of about 30 points that appear to have a negative linear relationship or correlation. Use these points to draw the median-median line. Suppose that your points represented number of yearly visits to the mall as related to miles between home and mall. How could your best-fit line be used to predict the number of visits to the mall for a person who was not included in your data set? How much potential error would you assign to your prediction based solely on the scatter plot that you drew?

14. Technology makes it very easy to compute statistics and create graphs of all types. What is the value of using technology for these purposes?

For Discussion and Exploration

1. The three NCTM *Navigations Series* books (listed next) begin with an excellent overview of the development of data and probability concepts in the K–12 curriculum. (This introduction is the same in each book.) Read this introductory section and then compare what you found with the objectives in your state curriculum. How do these goals match up? How do they fit with the treatment of data analysis in the textbooks being used in your local district?

   Sheffield, L. J., Cavanagh, M., Dacey, L., Findell, C. R., Greenes, C. E., & Small, M. (2002). *Navigating through data analysis and probability in prekindergarten–grade 2.*

   Chapin, S., Koziol, A., MacPherson, J., & Rezba, C. (2002). *Navigating through data analysis and probability in grades 3–5.*

   Bright, G. W., Brewer, W., McClain, K., & Mooney, E. S. (2003). *Navigating through data analysis in grades 6–8.*

   Each of these books is strongly suggested as a reference for excellent activities and explorations with students.

2. Two types of graphs discussed in this chapter—stem-and-leaf plots and box-and-whisker plots—were originally created for student use in the K–12 curriculum. After two decades, these techniques are rarely or never seen outside of school classrooms. Why should schools continue to teach these graph forms?

3. Select a popular news weekly such as *Time* or *Newsweek*. Look through at least one issue carefully to see what graphs and statistical information a typical reader would be expected to understand. Note that you will not be able to do this by simply looking for graphs. Statistics are frequently used without any corresponding graphs.

Recommendations for Further Reading

Bolster, C. H., Scheaffer, R., Bereska, L., & Bolster, L. C. (1998). *Exploring statistics in the elementary grades: Book one (K–6), Book two (4–8).* White Plains, NY: Dale Seymour Publications. These two books consist of detailed lessons designed and field-tested to help students across the grades develop conceptual understanding of basic concepts and techniques of data analysis. Each lesson follows the format suggested by the American Statistical Association and is completely in accord with the spirit of this book. Blackline Masters are well designed to make the teaching of these lessons as easy as possible.

Curcio, F. R. (2001). *Developing data-graph comprehension in grades K–8* (2nd ed.). Reston, VA: National Council of Teachers of Mathematics.

Curcio has updated this valuable book, originally published in 1989. Here you will find useful discussion of graphs and how to help students understand and construct them. Every form of graph found in this chapter is discussed in Curcio's book. Most of the book consists of activities, each carefully coded by grade level and objective.

Harper, S. R. (2004). Students' interpretations of misleading graphs. *Mathematics Teaching in the Middle Grades, 9,* 340–343.

In this short article, Harper explores some of the types of misleading graphing techniques that are often seen in the popular press and discusses how she explored these graphs with students. This is a very short version of a few of the ideas found in the classic book *How to Lie with Statistics* (Huff, 1954/1993). The ideas discussed are not only important but also will clearly convey to the middle school student the value of graphs to convey information.

Manchester, P. (2002). The lunchroom project: A long-term investigative study. *Teaching Children Mathematics, 9,* 43–47.

A third-grade teacher describes how her class decided to do something about their dislike of the cafeteria food. She explains the difficulty of designing appropriate questions and gathering the data. Student work shows how the students dealt with the data collected. The project had the effect of making some desired changes in cafeteria offerings. Although the project could be replicated, Manchester's article highlights the importance of working with a question that is meaningful to students.

McClain, K., Cobb, P., & Gravemeijer, K. (2000). Supporting students' ways of reasoning about data. In M. J. Burke (Ed.), *Learning mathematics for a new century: 2000 Yearbook* (pp. 174–187). Reston, VA: National Council of Teachers of Mathematics.

This article provides an in-depth description of a seventh-grade instructional sequence involving data analysis. Students used two simple computer tools to represent data and make conclusions. Tasks included comparing two brands of batteries and also the speed of cars before and after passing through a speed trap. The value of the article is in seeing how students are using their own ideas to give meaning to graphs and statistics rather than simply following rules.

University of North Carolina Mathematics and Science Education Network. (1997). *Teach-stat activities: Statistics investigations for grades 1–3.* Palo Alto, CA: Dale Seymour Publications.

University of North Carolina Mathematics and Science Education Network. (1997). *Teach-stat activities: Statistics investigations for grades 3–6.* Palo Alto, CA: Dale Seymour Publications.

These two books contain a wealth of superb data activities developed through a National Science Foundation Grant under the direction of some of North Carolina's top mathematics educators. The activities are each designed to follow a four-stage model: pose the question, collect the data, analyze the data, interpret the results. That is, data are collected with the purpose of answering a question. The activities are each described in detail with all necessary blacklines included. A companion professional development manual is also available.

Online Resources

Suggested Applets and Web Links

Bar Graph (Shodor)
www.shodor.org/interactive/activities/bargraph/index.html
The user of this applet can enter data as well as manipulate the *y*-axis values to create a bar graph. The ability to manipulate the *y*-axis values allows the creation of potentially misleading graphs, a good source of discussion.

Box Plot (Shodor)
www.shodor.org/interactive/activities/boxplot/index.html
The user can enter data and create box plots.

Collecting, Representing, and Interpreting Data Using Spreadsheets and Graphing Software: Representing and Interpreting Data (NCTM's e-Examples)
http://standards.nctm.org/document/eexamples/chap5/5.5/part2.htm#applet
Data are provided in a spreadsheet. The data can be changed and/or ordered in different ways with simple buttons. Scatter plots and bar graphs are also easily made with various combinations of data. Lesson suggestions are provided.

Histograms and Box Plots
http://nlvm.usu.edu/en/nav/frames_asid_174_g_2_t_5.html
http://illuminations.nctm.org/tools/tool_detail.aspx?id=68#
www.shodor.org/interactivate/activities/histogram/index.html
Each of these sites offers an interactive applet allowing the user to create and manipulate histograms. User data can be entered or data are supplied on the NCTM applet. The NLVM applet also has a tool for box plots.

Plop It! (Shodor)
www.shodor.org/interactivate/activities/plot/what.html
The user can experiment with the concepts of mean, median, and mode by using a bar graph. The applet allows you to visually see the difference between these measures.

Stem-and-Leaf Plot (Shodor)
www.shodor.org/interactivate/activities/plop/what.html

An additional list of books and articles related to the ideas in this chapter can be found on the Companion Web site at **www.ablongman.com/vandewalle6e.**

chapter 23
Exploring Concepts of Probability

References to probability are all around us: The weather forecaster predicts a 60 percent chance of snow; medical researchers predict people with certain diets have a high chance of heart disease; airlines, in an effort to ensure the public's confidence in air travel, calculate the chance of a person dying in an airplane crash is 1 in 10,000,000. Simulations of complex situations are frequently based on probabilities and are then used in the design process of such things as spacecraft, highways and storm sewers, or plans for reactions to disasters. Because the ideas and methods of probability are so prevalent in today's world, this strand of mathematics has risen in visibility in the school curriculum.

Realistic concepts of chance require considerable development before children are ready to construct formal ideas about the probability of a future event. This development best occurs as children consider and discuss with their peers the outcomes of a wide variety of probabilistic situations. The emphasis should be on exploration rather than rules and formal definitions. If done well, these informal experiences will provide a useful background from which more formal ideas can be developed. Without these explorations, students will find it difficult to move from the relatively simple (and at times faulty) reasoning prevalent in elementary school to the more formal reasoning that will be developed after middle school.

▼ Big Ideas

1. Chance has no memory. For repeated trials of a simple experiment, the outcomes of prior trials have no impact on the next. The chance occurrence of six heads in a row has no effect on getting a head on the next toss of the coin. That chance remains 50–50.

2. The probability that a future event will occur can be characterized along a continuum from impossible to certain.

3. The *probability* of an event is a number between 0 and 1 that is a measure of the chance that a given event will occur. A probability of 0 indicates impossibility and that of 1 indicates certainty. A probability of $\frac{1}{2}$ indicates an even chance of the event occurring.

4. The relative frequency of outcomes of an event (*experimental probability*) can be used as an estimate of the exact probability of an event. The larger the number of trials, the better the estimate will be. The results for a small number of trials may be quite different than those experienced in the long run.

5. For some events, the exact probability can be determined by an analysis of the event itself. A probability determined in this manner is called a *theoretical probability*.

6. Simulation is a technique used for answering real-world questions or making decisions in complex situations in which an element of chance is involved. To see what is likely to happen in the real event, a model must be designed that has the same probabilities as the real situation.

▲▼ Mathematics Content Connections

Probability and data analysis have long been joined when talking about the mathematics curriculum and there is a real mathematical connection as students reach the upper grades. For most of the elementary grades, the connections are to other areas.

■ **Fractions and Percents** (Chapters 16 and 18): Since probabilities are measured with numbers between 0 and 1, there is a natural connection to these ideas. Students can see fractional parts of spinners or sets of counters in a bag and use these fractions to determine probabilities. Percents are useful because they are the most convenient common denominator for comparing ratios that do not have the same whole (e.g., rolling a 7 three times in the first 20 rolls, or 15%, and 16 times in 80 rolls, or 20%).

- **Ratio and Proportion** (Chapter 19): Comparing probabilities often involves comparing ratios that are parts of different wholes as in the example just illustrated. To understand these comparisons requires proportional reasoning.

- **Data Analysis** (Chapter 22): When performing a probability experiment, the results are data—a sample of the theoretically infinite experiments that could be done. The more experiments conducted, the better the observed frequencies will coincide with the actual probability. In the reverse situation, gathering of data and finding a best-fit line is a data-analysis activity. The greater the sample size, the greater the probability is that the observed relationship reflects the actual population.

Probability on a Continuum

Young children's concept of the likelihood of a future event is often bewildering to adults. Children can be absolutely convinced that the next roll of the die will be a 3 "because I just know it's going to happen" or "because 3 is my lucky number." Consider how engrossing the pre-K or kindergarten child finds a game of chance such as Old Maid or Candyland. These games of pure chance have become timeless because children do not comprehend that random chance makes each player equally likely to win. Rather, winning makes them proud of the accomplishment.

To change these early misconceptions, a good place to begin is with the extremes of the continuum. The following activity is designed for that purpose. In preparation for this activity, have a discussion of the words *impossible* and *certain*. Certain is the harder of these words for children. It means "absolutely for sure." It is the exact opposite of impossible.

activity **23.1**

Is It Likely?

Ask students to judge various events as *certain*, *impossible*, or *possible* ("might happen"). Consider these examples:

- **It will rain tomorrow.**
- **Drop a rock in water and it will sink.**
- **Trees will talk to us in the afternoon.**
- **The sun will rise tomorrow morning.**
- **Three students will be absent tomorrow.**
- **George will go to bed before 8:30 tonight.**
- **You will have two birthdays this year.**

Have children describe or make up events that are certain, impossible, or possible. For each event, they should justify their estimate of likelihood.

The key idea to developing chance or probability on a continuum is to help children see that some of these possible events are more likely or less likely than others. For instance, if a group of students has a running race, the chance that Gregg, a really fast runner, will be first is not certain but is very likely. It is more likely that Gregg will be near the front of the group than near the back of the pack.

The use of random devices that can be analyzed (e.g., spinners, number cubes, coins to toss, colored cubes drawn from a bag) can help students make predictions about the likelihood of an event. The following activity or variations of it should be repeated often using the same random devices and also with a variety of devices.

activity **23.2**

Race to the Top

Two players take turns spinning a spinner with two outcomes. Each game requires a simple recording sheet with ten rows or spaces. Figure 23.1 shows a sheet for a two-color spinner. In the simplest version of the game, use only one spinner: one-fourth red and three-fourths blue. Before playing, each student predicts which color will win, red or blue. (Note that it is *color* that wins, not a player!) After each spin, an X is drawn in the appropriate column. Play continues until one color reaches the top of the chart.

Students should play "Race to the Top" several times. After all students have played, ask "Which color won the most times? Why do you think so? If you play again, what color do you think will win?"

In activities such as "Race to the Top," use a variety of spinners. Notice that both equal spinners—each color hav-

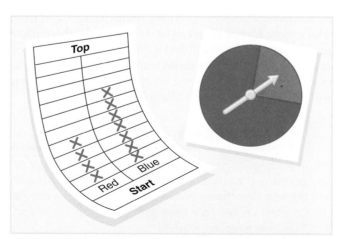

FIGURE 23.1 Students take turns spinning a spinner and recording the result. The first color to reach the top is the winner. The same game can be played with other random devices.

ing the same total area—and not equal spinners can be made using either two regions or more than two regions, as shown here.

As a random device, spinners have the advantage that students can see the relative portion of the whole given to each color or outcome. The other advantage is that spinner faces can easily be made to adjust the chances of different outcomes. Transparent plastic spinners can be purchased that have no partitions. Paper spinner faces that suit your current needs are taped to the bottom of these spinners and can be changed later. Transparent spinners can also be used on the overhead projector. Use an overhead pen to mark the sections. There are also several methods that can be used to make a spinner. One is shown in Figure 23.2.

Devices other than spinners should also be used for "Race to the Top" and similar activities. Colored dots can be stuck on the sides of a wooden cube to create different color probabilities. Similarly, opaque bags with eight red and two blue tiles or some other ratio of red to blue can

be used. Students draw a tile from the bag. Be sure that students return the tiles to the bag after each draw.

The following activity is a game of chance with unequal outcomes. However, students will not readily be able to predict which result is most likely, so it provides a good opportunity for discussion.

activity **23.3**

Add, Then Tally

Make number cubes with sides as follows: 1, 1, 2, 3, 3, 3. Each game requires two cubes. Students take turns rolling the two cubes and recording the sum of the two numbers. To record the results, run off tally sheets with five rows of ten squares, one for each sum 2 through 6. (See Figure 23.3.) Students continue to roll the cubes until one of the rows is full. They can repeat the game on a new tally sheet as long as time permits.

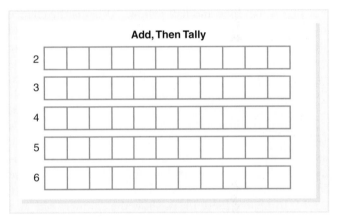

FIGURE 23.3 A recording sheet for "Add, Then Tally."

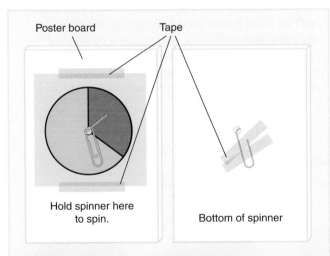

Draw spinner faces and duplicate them so that you can easily make lots of spinners. Cut these out and tape to poster board. Students can color the sections of the spinner. Make a small hole in the spinner center. Unbend one end of a sturdy paper clip and poke this upward from the bottom of the spinner. Tape the paper clip to the back leaving a paper clip post sticking up in the center of the spinner. To use the spinner, students put another paper clip on the post to act as the pointer. Hold the spinner flat to spin fairly. Spinner faces can be changed easily.

FIGURE 23.2 An easy way to make a spinner.

It is important to talk with students after they have played "Add, Then Tally." Which numbers "won" the most and the least often? If they were to play again, which number would they pick to win and why? Furthermore, all of the outcomes, 2 through 6, are possible. A sum of 4 is the most likely. Sums of 2 or 3 are the least likely. However, since few if any students will analyze the possible outcomes, their predictions for future games will tell you a lot about their probabilistic reasoning. Students who observe that 4 comes up a lot and, therefore, is the best choice to win have abandoned earlier subjective ideas about luck or of chance having a memory.

 Remember that students' ideas about chance must develop from experience. An explanation from a teacher will likely provide only superficial understanding. During discussions, your task is to elicit their ideas, not to explain or offer judgment. The main idea that you are looking for is a growth from a belief in pure chance or luck to one in which students begin to understand that some results are clearly more or less likely to happen than others regardless of luck. When you sense that this sort of growth has taken place, a significant milestone has been reached and you will know that your students are ready to move on and begin to refine their ideas of chance a bit more. ■

The Probability Continuum

To begin refining the concept that some events are more or less likely to occur than others, introduce the idea of a continuum of likelihood between impossible and certain. Draw a long line on the board. Label the left end "Impossible" and the right end "Certain." Write "Chances of Spinning Blue" above the line. Call this a "probability line" or a "chance line." Next, show students a spinner that is all yellow. "What is the chance of spinning blue with this spinner?" Indicate the left end of the probability line as showing this chance. Repeat with an all-blue spinner, indicating the right end, labeled Certain. Next, show a spinner that is half blue and half yellow. "What is the chance of spinning blue with this spinner?" The discussion should develop a consensus that it is about *equally likely* that blue will come up as not blue. Place a mark exactly in the center of the line to indicate this chance. You may want to note that this represents a chance of $\frac{1}{2}$ or 50 percent, although the position of the mark alone is actually sufficient.

Repeat the preceding discussion with a spinner that is less than $\frac{1}{4}$ blue and with one that is nearly all blue. Ask students where they would put a mark on the line to indicate the chance of spinning blue for each of these. These marks should be close to the ends of the line. (See Figure 23.4.) To review these ideas, show the spinners one at a time and ask which marks represent the chance of getting blue for that spinner.

In the next activity students design random devices that they think will create chances for various designated positions on the probability line. The activity suggests that students use a bag of colored tiles or cubes, which is a bit different than spinners. Even if the idea of drawing tiles from a bag seems new to your students, do not provide additional hints to help them with their reasoning.

activity **23.4**

Design a Bag

(Note that students must be introduced to the idea of a probability line as just described.)

Sketch a worksheet similar to that shown in Figure 23.5 and provide students with a copy. Be sure there are 12 squares drawn on the bag. On the board mark a place on a probability line at roughly the 20 percent position. At this time do not use percent or fraction language with the children. Students are to mark this position on their worksheet probability lines. Alternatively, you could mark the worksheets before making copies. Students should color the square indicated by "Color" at the top of the page. Explain that they are going to decide what color tiles should be put in bags of 12 total tiles so that the chance of drawing this designated color is about the same as the chance indicated on the probability line. Before students begin to design their bags, ask for ideas about what colors of tiles might be put in the bag if the mark were very close to the middle of the line. Show how the real bags will be filled based on the design on the page. Demonstrate with tiles, a bag, and a completed worksheet. Emphasize that the tiles will be shaken up so that which particular squares on the bag design are colored makes no difference.

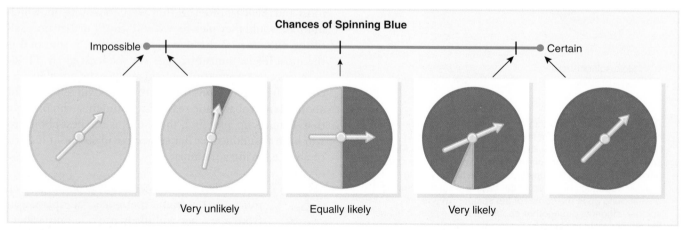

FIGURE 23.4 The probability line, or "chance line." Use these spinner faces to help students see how chance can be at different places on a continuum between impossible and certain.

At the bottom of each sheet (and on the reverse if needed), students explain why they chose their tiles. Give them an example: *We put in 8 red and 4 of other colors because _____.*

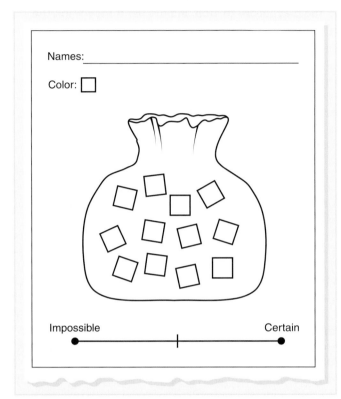

Names: _____

Color: ☐

Impossible ●————————|————————● Certain

FIGURE 23.5 A possible recording sheet for the "Design a Bag" activity. Students mark a point on the line between impossible and certain. Then they color the tiles in the bag to create a mix that will produce the estimated chance of the designated color being drawn.

Collect and display the designs made by the students in "Design a Bag." Discuss the ideas that students had for the number of designated colors to put in the bag. (Expect some variation.) Some students may think that the colors used for the other tiles make a difference, and this point should be discussed. Do not provide your opinion or comment on these ideas.

The "Design a Bag" activity provides useful information about how your students conceive of chance as appearing on a continuum. More importantly, however, you should follow up "Design a Bag" with the following related activity.

activity **23.5**

Testing Bag Designs

Select a bag design (from Activity 23.4) that most students seem to agree on for the 20 percent mark.

Distribute lunch bags and colored tiles or cubes to pairs of students to fill according to the selected design. Once filled, students shake the bag and draw out one tile. Tally marks are used to record a Yes (for the designated color) or No for any other color. This is repeated at least ten times. Be sure that students replace each tile after it is drawn.

Discuss with the class how their respective experiments turned out. Did it turn out the way they expected? With the small number of trials, there will be groups that get rather unexpected results.

Next, make a large bar graph or tally graph of the data from all of the groups together. This should show many more No's than Yes's. Here the discussion can help students see that if the experiment is repeated a lot of times, it is clearer that the chances are about as predicted.

The dual activities of "Design a Bag" and "Testing Bag Designs" can and should be repeated for two or three other marks on the probability line. Try marks at about $\frac{1}{3}$, $\frac{1}{2}$, and $\frac{3}{4}$.

"Design a Bag" and "Testing Bag Designs" are important activities. Because no numbers are used for the probabilities, there are no "right" answers. The small-group testing of a design shows students that chance is not an absolute predictor in the short run. The group graphs may help students with the difficult concept that the chance tends to approach what is expected in the long run. However, this latter idea involves comparing ratios in the small trials with ratios in large numbers using the accumulated data. For students below grade 5, this proportional reasoning may be elusive.

As another variation of "Design a Bag" have students design a spinner instead of a bag of tiles. This will allow you to revisit the concept at a later time without being repetitious.

EXPANDED LESSON

An expanded lesson plan based on Activity 23.5, "Testing Bag Designs," can be found on the Companion Web site at www.ablongman.com/vandewalle6e.

Theoretical Versus Experimental Probability

The *probability* of an event is a measure of the likelihood of an event occurring. Students to this point have only been asked to place events on a continuum from impossible to certain or to compare the likelihood of one event with another. So how do you measure a chance? In many situations, there are actually two ways to determine this measure. One way is through logical analysis of the situation (*theoretical probability*) and the other is generated through data collection (*experimental probability*). Let's consider a simple experiment as an illustration: What is the probability or likelihood of obtaining a head when tossing one coin?

Logically, we could argue that if it is a fair coin, obtaining a head is just as likely as obtaining a tail. Since there are two possible outcomes that are equally likely, each has a probability of $\frac{1}{2}$. Hence, the theoretical probability of obtaining a head is $\frac{1}{2}$. When all possible outcomes of a simple experiment are equally likely, the *theoretical probability* of an event is

$$\frac{\text{Number of outcomes in the event}}{\text{Number of possible outcomes}}$$

Now let's determine the probability of obtaining a head through data collection. Take a fair coin and toss it 10 times, recording the result of the toss in a frequency table (number of heads and number of tails). In 10 tosses, you might have had 3 tails and 7 heads ($\frac{7}{10}$ for heads), or 8 tails and 2 heads ($\frac{2}{10}$ for heads). These ratios are called *relative frequencies*. The *relative frequency* of an event is

$$\frac{\text{Number of observed occurrences of the event}}{\text{Total number of trials}}$$

These numbers ($\frac{7}{10}$ and $\frac{2}{10}$) are not close to the theoretical probability of $\frac{1}{2}$. Continue to collect data until you have completed 100 tosses. (A quick way to do this experiment is to work in groups. If 10 people each do 10 trials and pool their data, the time needed for 100 trials is not long.) The more tosses made, the closer the relative frequency gets to the theoretical probability, and you can become more confident in the results. Since it is impossible to conduct an infinite number of trials, we can only consider the relative frequency or *experimental probability* for a very large number of trials as an approximation of the theoretical probability. This emphasizes the notion that probability is more about predictions over the long term than predictions of individual events.

Theoretical Probability

In the following activity, students play a game and keep track of the outcomes for each turn—gathering data. The results of the game—the experimental probability—will very likely be contrary to students' intuitive ideas. This in turn will provide a real reason to analyze the game in a logical manner and find out why things happened as they did—theoretical probability.

activity **23.6**

Fair or Unfair?

Three students toss 2 like coins (e.g., 2 pennies or 2 nickels) and are assigned points according to the following rules: Player A gets 1 point if the coin toss results in "two heads"; player B gets 1 point if the toss results in "two tails"; and player C gets 1 point if the toss results are "mixed" (one head, one tail). The game is over after 20 tosses. The player who has the most points wins. Have students play the game at least two or three times. After each game, the players are to stop and discuss if they think the game is fair and make predictions about who will win the next game.

When the full class has played the game several times, conduct a discussion on the fairness of the game. Challenge students to make an argument *not* based on the data as to whether the game is fair or not and why.

A common analysis of the game in Activity 23.6 goes something like this: There are three outcomes: two tails, one head and one tail, or two heads. Each has an equal chance. The game should be fair. However, after playing "Fair or Unfair?" students will find that player C (gets points for a mixed result) appears to have an unfair advantage (especially if they have played several games or the class has pooled its data). This observation seems to contradict the notion that the outcomes are equally likely. If students cannot reconcile this discrepancy between their initial idea that the game is fair and the actual results, have them play the game once again. However, this time they should play the game using two different coins, say, a penny and a nickel. Have them record results separately for each coin. For example, a toss may result in "heads on both," "tails on both," "heads on the penny, tail on nickel," or "tail on penny, head on nickel." The distinction between these last two outcomes can help students understand why player C has an unfair advantage.

Some students may be able to analyze the situation and generate all the possible outcomes. An explanation may be as follows:

There is only one way for two heads to occur and one way for two tails to occur, but are two ways for a head and a tail to occur: Either the first coin is heads and the second tails, or vice versa. That makes a total of four possible outcomes, not three. (See Figure 23.6.) Getting a head and a tail happens in two out of the four possible outcomes. Since each outcome is equally likely, getting a head and a tail has a probability of $\frac{2}{4}$ or $\frac{1}{2}$.

This theoretical probability is based on a logical analysis of the experiment, not on experimental results.

Experimental Probability

In the preceding discussion, it should be clear that our intuition about the chance of an event is often misleading. It might seem, therefore, that we should always make an attempt to find the theoretical probability. But some situations cannot be analyzed mathematically to determine a

First Coin	Second Coin
Head	Head
Head	Tail
Tail	Head
Tail	Tail

FIGURE 23.6 Four possible outcomes of flipping two coins.

theoretical probability. In other words, the probability of some events can be determined only through data collection (experimental probability), conducting a sufficiently large number of trials to become confident that the resulting relative frequency is an approximation of the theoretical probability. The following activity provides students with such a situation.

activity **23.7**

Cup Toss

Provide a small plastic "portion" cup or other small cup to pairs of students. Ask them to list the possible ways that the cup could land if they tossed it in the air and let it land on the floor. Which of the possibilities (upside down, right side up, or on its side) do they think is most and least likely? Why? Inform them that they will toss the cup 20 times, each time recording how it lands on the floor. Students should agree on a uniform method of tossing the cups to ensure unbiased data (e.g., standing up, flipping the cups at the same height, and letting them land on the floor). Have students share their results for 20 trials. Discuss the differences and generate reasons for them. Have students predict what will happen if they pool their data. Pool the data and compute the three ratios (upside down, right side up, and on the side) to the total number of tosses at various points, say, after 100, 200, 300, 400, 500, and so on up to 1000 tosses. List the ratios in a chart with column headings: number of tosses, side, up, and down. As the pooled sample grows, continue to ask students to make and revise their predictions. The relative frequency should begin to converge toward and approximate the actual probability.

In the cup-tossing experiment (Activity 23.7), there is no practical way to determine the results before you start. However, once you have results for 200 flips, you would

undoubtedly feel more confident in predicting the results of the next 100 flips. After gathering data on that same cup for 1000 trials, you would feel even more confident. Say that your cup lands on its side 78 times out of the first 100 tosses. You might choose a round figure of 75 or 80 sideways landings for any 100 tosses as a possible probability. If, after 200 flips, there were 163 sideways landings, you would feel even more confident about a 4-out-of-5 ratio and predict about 800 sideways landings for 1000 tosses. The more flips that are made, the more confident you become. You have determined an *experimental probability* of $\frac{4}{5}$ or 80 percent for the cup to land on its side. It is experimental because it is based on the results of an experiment rather than a theoretical analysis of the cup.

The Law of Large Numbers

The phenomenon that the relative frequency becomes a closer approximation of the actual probability or the theoretical probability as the size of the data set (sample) increases is referred to as *the law of large numbers*. The larger the size of the data set, the more representative the sample is of the population. Thinking about statistics, a survey of 1000 people provides more reliable and convincing data about the larger population than a survey of 5 people. The larger the number of trials (people surveyed), the more confident you can be that the data reflect the larger population. The same is true when you are attempting to determine the probability of an event through data collection.

Using the actual fractions generated in a probability experiment and making comparisons assumes that students understand the proportional reasoning involved: How does 3 out of 7 compare to 250 out of 1000? Regardless of the age of students, a visual comparison may help students understand how the relative frequency of an event gets closer to a fixed probability as the number of trials gets very large. The next activity is designed to help students with this difficult idea without resorting to comparing ratios expressed as fractions.

activity **23.8**

Checking the Theory

Make a transparency of the Blackline Master shown in Figure 23.7. Provide pairs of students with a spinner face that is half red and half blue. Discuss the chances of spinning blue. After this discussion, students should agree that the chance of blue is one-half. Mark the $\frac{1}{2}$ point on the Impossible–Certain continuum and draw a vertical line down through all of the lines below this point. Then have each pair of students spin their spinner one time. Make a tally chart for Red and Blue results and tally these first spins. Collect the results of additional spins until you have a total of 20 spins. Mark the result of the

20 spins on the second line. For example, if there are 13 Blue and 7 Red, place a mark at about 13 on the 0-to-20 number line. If the result of these 20 spins was not exactly 10 and 10, discuss possible reasons why this may be so.

Now have student pairs each spin their spinners ten more times. Collect these results and add them to the tallies for the first 20 spins. Your total should be a multiple of ten. Mark the total in the right-hand box of the third line and indicate the number of Blue spins on the line as before. Repeat this at least two more times, continuing to add the results of new spins to the previous results. Each time, enter the total in the right-hand box to create a new number line but with the same length as before. If possible, try to get the total number of spins to be at least 1000.

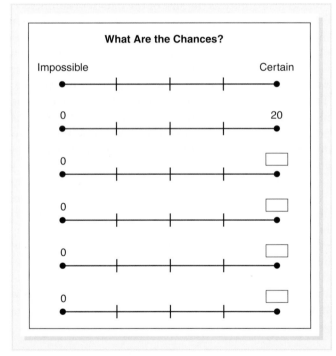

FIGURE 23.7 This worksheet is used to record accumulated data of an experiment collected in stages. Each number line represents the total number of trials at that stage. The number of desired outcomes is plotted at each stage. As the number of trials increases, the plotted point should become closer and closer to the theoretical probability (see Blackline Masters).

The successive number lines used in "Checking the Theory" each have the same length and each represent the total number of trials. When the results are plotted on any one number line, the position shows the fraction of the total spins as a visual portion of the whole line. If you try to be fairly accurate with your marks (perhaps measuring

with a centimeter ruler), successive marks will almost certainly get closer and closer to the $\frac{1}{2}$ line you drew earlier down the page. Note that 240 Blue spins out of 500 is 48 percent, or very close to one-half. This is so even though there are 20 more Red spins (260) than Blue. To be that close with only 100 spins, the results would need to be 48 and 52. For even larger numbers, the marks should be extremely close to the line you have drawn. If you draw much longer lines—say, 2 meters each—on the board, the results of "Checking the Theory" will be more dramatic. It will be clearer that the ratios are closing in on one-half.

Spinners sometimes are less than accurate due to spinning techniques, bent spinners, and so on. The same experiment can and should be conducted with other devices. For example, bags with two each of four colors could be used with the probability of each color marked on each line. Rolling a number cube with the event being an odd number is also a good idea.

The same Blackline Master and the same method of accumulating data in stages can and should be used for other experiments as well. For example, try using this approach with the "Cup Toss" experiment where the theoretical probability cannot be determined. Rather than draw a vertical line before collecting data, decide on the best guess at the actual probability after the numbers have gotten large. Then draw the vertical line at that time to observe how more and more trials brought the results closer to the line.

For students who have an understanding of percentages, the probabilities at each stage can be expressed in those terms. After plotting the point on the number line, divide the number of successful trials by the total trials. Record the resulting percentage on each number line. Note that the percentages are simply fractions with a common denominator of 100.

 Pose the following situation to students to assess their ideas about long-run results versus short-run results. Have students write about their ideas.

Margaret spun the spinner ten times. Blue turned up on three spins. Red turned up on seven spins. Margaret says that there is a 3-in-10 chance of spinning blue. Carla then spun the same spinner 100 times. Carla recorded 53 spins of blue and 47 spins of red. Carla says that the chance of spinning blue on this spinner is about even.

Who do you think is more likely to be correct: Margaret or Carla? Explain. Draw a spinner that you think they may have been using.

Look for evidence that students understand that even 10 spins is not very good evidence of the probability and that 100 spins tells us more about the chances.

Recall the first big idea in the chapter: Chance has no memory. You may want to see if students have developed this idea to any extent even though the activities explored have not explicitly addressed this idea. Have students either write about or discuss the following:

> Duane has a lucky coin that he has tossed many, many times. He is sure that it is a fair coin—that there is an even chance of heads or tails. Duane tosses his coin six times and heads come up six times in a row. Duane is sure that the next toss will be tails because he has never been able to toss heads seven times in a row. What do you think the chances are of Duane tossing heads on the next toss? Explain your answer.

In this case you are looking for the idea that each toss of the coin is independent of prior tosses. ■

Implications for Instruction

There are many reasons why an experimental approach to probability, actually conducting experiments and examining outcomes, is important in the middle grades classroom.

- It is significantly more intuitive. Results begin to make sense and do not come from some abstract rule.
- It eliminates guessing at probabilities and wondering, "Did I get it right?" Counting or trying to determine the number of elements in a sample space can be very difficult without some intuitive background information.
- It provides an experiential background for examining the theoretical model. When you begin to sense that the probability of two heads is $\frac{1}{4}$ instead of $\frac{1}{3}$, the analysis in Figure 23.6 seems more reasonable.
- It helps students see how the ratio of a particular outcome to the total number of trials begins to converge to a fixed number. For an infinite number of trials, the relative frequency and theoretical probability would be the same.
- It develops an appreciation for a simulation approach to solving problems. Many real-world problems are actually solved by conducting experiments or simulations.
- It is a lot more fun and interesting! Even searching for a correct explanation in the theoretical model is more interesting.

Try to use an experimental approach in the classroom whenever possible. If a theoretical analysis (such as with the two-coin experiment in "Fair or Unfair?") is possible, it should also be examined, and the results should be compared. Rather than correcting a student error in an initial analysis, we can let experimental results guide and correct student thinking.

Truly random events often occur in unexpected groups; a fair coin may turn up heads five times in a row. A 100-year flood may hit a town twice in ten years. Hands-on random devices such as spinners, dice, or cubes drawn from a bag give students an intuitive feel for the imperfect distribution of randomness. Students believe in the unbiased outcomes of these devices. The downside is that hands-on devices require a lot of time to produce a large number of trials. This is where technology can help enormously.

 Electronic devices, including some relatively simple calculators and graphing calculators, are designed to produce random outcomes at the press of a button. Computer software is available that flips coins, spins spinners, or draws numbers from a hat. Calculators produce random numbers that can then be interpreted in terms of the desired device. As long as students accept the results generated by the technology as truly random or equivalent to the hands-on device, they offer significant advantages for performing experiments. A possible downfall of using technology is that it may mask what is happening, such as how sample spaces are generated, which can hinder students' understanding of probability. Having students actually spin spinners, roll dice, draw chips out of bags, and so on is a useful first approach.

Software for exploring probability concepts can generally be described as computer-animated random devices. Graphics show students the coins being flipped or the spinner being spun. Most allow different speeds. In a slow version, students may watch each spin of a spinner or coin flip. Faster speeds show the recording of each trial but omit the graphics. An even quicker mode simply shows the cumulative results. The number of trials can be set by the user. *Tangible Math: The Probability Constructor* (Riverdeep, 2002), designed for students at the middle grades, is sophisticated and offers many options. Within each of six devices, the probability of the outcomes is adjustable and outcomes can be displayed in a variety of ways. Even with only one computer in the room, a good probability program is a worthwhile investment. ■

Sample Spaces and Computing Theoretical Probabilities

Understanding the concepts of outcome and sample space is central to understanding probability. The *sample space* for an experiment or chance situation is the set of all possible outcomes for that experiment. For example, if a bag contains two red, three yellow, and five blue tiles, the sample space consists of all ten tiles. An *event* is a subset of the sample space. The event of drawing a yellow tile has three elements or outcomes in the sample space and the event of drawing a blue tile has five elements in the sample space. For rolling a single number cube, the sample space always consists of the numbers 1 to 6. However, we might define several different events that split up the sample space in different ways. For example, rolling either an odd or an even number splits the sample space into two equal parts. Rolling either 5 or more or less than 5 splits the sample space into two unequal parts. When rolling a number cube, each number from 1 to 6 has an equal chance of occurring. Therefore, the chances of rolling an odd or an even number are equal. However, the chance of rolling a 5 or 6 is less than the chance of rolling a number less than 5.

Rolling a single die, drawing one colored chip from a bag, or the occurrence of rain tomorrow are all examples of what are called *single-stage* experiments. A *single-stage* or *one-stage* experiment is an experiment that requires only one activity to determine an outcome: one roll, one draw from the bag, one new day. A *two-stage* or *multistage* experiment is an experiment that requires two (or more) activities to determine an outcome. Examples include rolling two dice, drawing two cubes from a bag, and the occurrence of rain and forgetting your umbrella.

Determining the sample space for single-stage experiments should generally present no problem for students. However, some children are so influenced by their belief in luck that certain outcomes of an experiment may not seem possible even when they clearly are (Jones, Thornton, Langrall, & Tarr, 1999). Determining the sample spaces for experiments with two or more stages can often present a challenge, even for students in middle school.

When exploring two-stage experiments, there is another factor to consider: Does the occurrence of the event in one stage have an effect on the occurrence of the event in the other? In the following sections we will consider two-stage experiments of both types—those with independent events and those with dependent events.

Independent Events

Recall that in Activity 23.6, "Fair or Unfair?," students explored the results of tossing two coins. The toss of one coin had no effect on the other. These were examples of *independent events*; the occurrence or nonoccurrence of one event has no effect on the other. The same is true of rolling two dice—the result on one die does not affect the other. The common error for both tossing two coins or rolling two dice is a failure to distinguish between the two events, especially when the outcomes are combined, as in "a head and a tail" or adding the numbers on two dice.

We've already solved the problem of tossing two coins. Let's explore rolling two dice and adding the results. Suppose that your students tally the sums that they get for two dice. The results might look like Figure 23.8. Clearly, these events are not equally likely and in fact the sum of 7 appears to have the best chance of occurring. To explain this, students might look for the combinations that make 7: 1 and 6, 2 and 5, and 3 and 4. But there are also three combinations for 6 and for 8. It seems as though 6 and 8 should be just as likely as 7, and yet they are not.

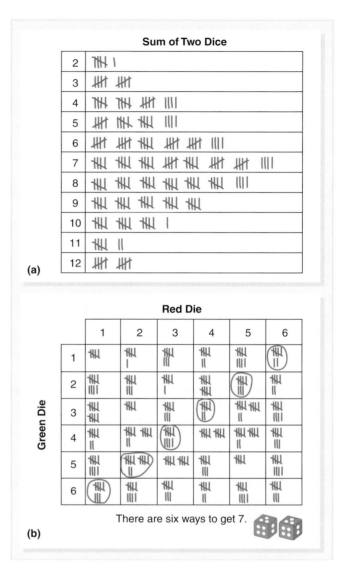

FIGURE 23.8 Tallies can account only for the total (a) or keep track of the individual dice (b).

Now suppose that the experiment is repeated. This time, for the sake of clarity, suggest that students roll two different-colored dice and that they keep the tallies in a chart like the one in part (b) of Figure 23.8.

The results of a large number of dice rolls indicate what one would expect, namely, that all 36 cells of this chart are equally likely. But there are more cells with a sum of 7 than any other number. Therefore, students were really looking for the event consisting of any of the six ways, not three ways, that two dice can add to 7. There are six outcomes in the desired event out of a total of 36, for a probability of $\frac{6}{36}$, or $\frac{1}{6}$.

To create the sample space for two independent events, it is helpful to use a chart or diagram that keeps the two events separate and illustrates the combinations. The matrix in Figure 23.8(b) is one good suggestion when there are only two events. A tree diagram (Figure 23.9) is another method of creating sample spaces that can be used with any number of events.

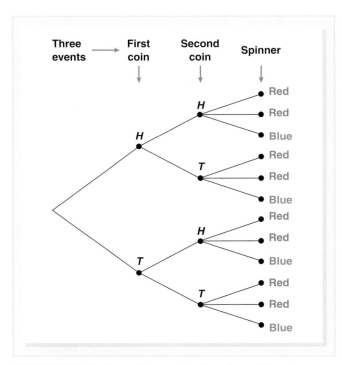

FIGURE 23.9 A tree diagram showing all possible outcomes for two coins and a spinner that is $\frac{2}{3}$ red.

⏸ *pause and reflect* _____

Use a chart and/or tree diagram to analyze the sum of two number cubes each with sides 1, 1, 2, 3, 3, and 3. (These were the cubes used in "Add, Then Tally," Activity 23.3.) What is the probability of each sum, 2 through 6?

---

activity **23.9**

Multistage Events

The following are examples of multistage events composed of independent events.

- Rolling an even sum with two dice
- Spinning blue and flipping a cup on end
- Getting two blues out of three spins (depends on spinner)
- Having a tack or a cup land up if each is tossed once
- Getting at *least* two heads from a toss of four coins

Have students first make and defend a prediction of the probability of the event. Then they should conduct an experiment with a large number of trials, comparing their results to their predicted probabilities. Finally, they should reconcile differences. Where appropriate, students can try to determine the theoretical probability as part of their final analysis of the experiment.

Words and phrases such as *and, or, at least*, and *no more than* can also cause children some trouble. Of special note is the word *or*, since its everyday usage is generally not the same as its strict logical use in mathematics. In mathematics, *or* includes the case of *both*. So in the tack-and-cup example, the event includes tack up, cup up, and *both* tack *and* cup up.

Theoretical Probabilities with an Area Model

One way to determine the theoretical probability of a multistage event is to list all possible outcomes and count those that are favorable, that is, those that make up the event. This is useful and intuitive as a first approach. However, it has some limitations. First, what if the events are not all equally likely? For example, the spinner may be only $\frac{1}{4}$ blue. Second, it is difficult to move from that approach to even slightly more sophisticated methods. An area model approach has been used successfully with fifth-grade students and is quite helpful for some reasonably difficult problems.

Suppose that after many experiences, you have decided that your cup lands on its side 82 percent of the time. The experiment is to toss the cup and then draw a card from a deck. What is the probability that the cup will land on its side *and* you will draw a spade? Draw a square to represent one whole. First partition the square to represent the cup toss, 82 percent and 18 percent, as in Figure 23.10(a). Now

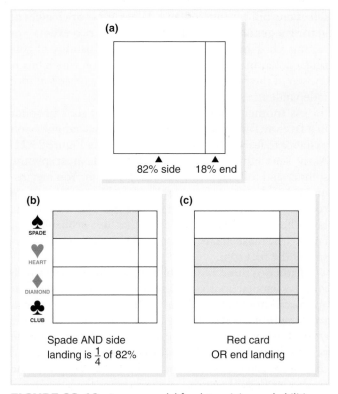

FIGURE 23.10 An area model for determining probabilities.

partition the square in the other direction to represent the four equal card suits. As shown in Figure 23.10(b), one region is the proportion of time that both events, sideways and spades, happen. The area of this region is $\frac{1}{4}$ of 82 percent, or 20.5 percent.

You can use the same drawing to determine the probability of other events in the same experiment. For example, what is the probability of the cup landing on either end *or* drawing a red card? As shown in Figure 23.10(c), half of the area of the square corresponds to drawing a red card. This section includes the case of drawing a red card *and* an end landing. The other half of the 18 percent end landings happen when a red card is not drawn. Half of 18 percent is 9 percent of the area. The total area for a red card *or* an end landing is 59 percent.

The area approach is easy for students to use and understand for experiments involving two independent events when the probability of each is known. For more than two independent events, further subdivision of each region is required but is still quite reasonable. The use of *and* and *or* connectives is easily dealt with. It is quite clear to students, without memorization of formulas, how probabilities should be combined.

Dependent Events

The next level of difficulty occurs when the probability of one event depends on the result of the first. For example, suppose that there are two identical boxes. In one box is a dollar bill and two counterfeit bills. In the other box is one of each. You may choose one box and from that box select one bill without looking. What are your chances of getting a genuine dollar? Here there are two events: selecting a box and selecting a bill. The probability of getting a dollar in the second event depends on which box is chosen in the first event. These events are *dependent*, not independent.

As another example, suppose that you are a prisoner in a faraway land. The king has pity on you and gives you a chance to leave. He shows you the maze in Figure 23.11. At the start and at each fork in the path, you must spin the spinner and follow the path that it points to. You may request that the key to freedom be placed in one of the two rooms. In which room should you place the key to have the best chance of freedom? Notice that the probability of ending the maze in any one room is dependent on the result of the first spin.

Either of these two problems could be explored with an experimental approach, a simulation. Remember, that approach should always be used first. A second approach to both problems is to use the area model to determine the theoretical probabilities. An area model solution to the prisoner problem is shown in Figure 23.12. How would the area model for the prisoner problem be different if the spinner at Fork II were a $\frac{1}{3}$ versus $\frac{2}{3}$ spinner?

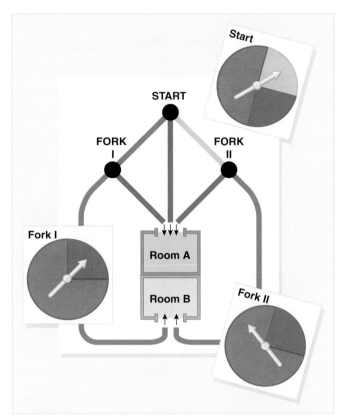

FIGURE 23.11 Should you place your key to freedom in Room A or Room B? At each fork, the spinner determines your path.

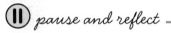 *pause and reflect*

It would be good to stop at this point and try the area approach for the problem of the counterfeit bills. The chance of getting a dollar is $\frac{5}{12}$. Can you get this result?

The area model will not solve all probability problems. However, it fits very well into a developmental approach to the subject because it is conceptual, it is based on existing knowledge of fractions, and more symbolic approaches can be derived from it. Figure 23.13 shows a tree diagram for the same problem, with the probability of each path of the tree written in. After some experience with probability situations, the tree diagram model is probably easier to use and adapts to a wider range of situations. You should be able to match up each branch of the tree diagram in Figure 23.13 with a section of the square in Figure 23.12. Use the area model to explain why the probability for each complete branch of the tree is determined by multiplying the probabilities along the branch.

Simulations

Simulation is a technique used for answering real-world questions or making decisions in complex situations where an element of chance is involved. Many times simulations

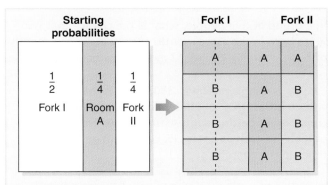

At Fork I, $\frac{3}{4}$ of the time you will go to Room B.

(Note: Not $\frac{3}{4}$ of the square but $\frac{3}{4}$ of the times you go to Fork I.)

At Fork II, $\frac{3}{4}$ of these times (or $\frac{3}{16}$ of total time) you will go to Room B.

Therefore, you will end up in Room A $\frac{7}{16}$ of the time and Room B $\frac{9}{16}$ of the time.

FIGURE 23.12 Using the area model to solve the maze problem.

are conducted because it is too dangerous, complex, or expensive to manipulate the real situation. To see what is likely to happen in the real event, a model must be designed that has the same probabilities as the real situation. For example, in designing a rocket, a large number of related systems all have some chance of failure. Various combinations of failures might cause serious problems with the rocket. Knowing the probability of serious failures will help determine if redesign or backup systems are required.

It is not reasonable to make repeated tests of the actual rocket. Instead, a model that simulates all of the chance situations is designed and run repeatedly with the help of a computer. The computer model can simulate thousands of flights, and an estimate of the chance of failure can be made.

Many real-world situations lend themselves to simulation analysis. In a business venture, the probability of selling a product might depend on a variety of chance factors, some of which can be controlled or changed and others not. Will advertising help? Should high-cost materials be used? What location provides the best chance of sales? If a reasonable model can be set up that simulates these factors, an experiment can be run before actually entering into the venture to determine the best choices.

The following problem and model are adapted from the excellent materials developed by the Quantitative Literacy Project (Gnanadesikan, Schaeffer, & Swift, 1987). In Figure 23.14, a diagram shows water pipes for a pumping system connecting A to B. The five pumps are aging, and it is estimated that at any given time, the probability of pump failure is $\frac{1}{2}$. If a pump fails, water cannot pass that station. For example, if pumps 1, 2, and 5 fail, water can flow only through 4 and 3. Consider the following questions that might well be asked about such a system:

- What is the probability that water will flow at any time?
- On the average, about how many stations need repair at any time?
- What is the probability that the 1–2 path is working at any time?

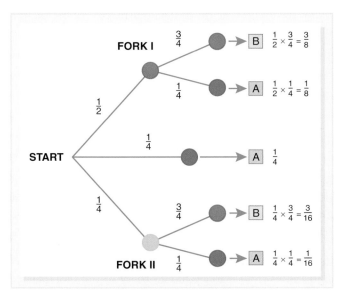

FIGURE 23.13 A tree diagram is another way to model the outcomes of two or more dependent events.

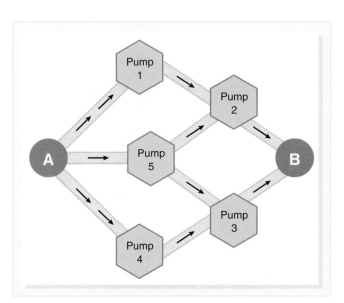

FIGURE 23.14 Each of these five pumps has a 50 percent chance of failure. What is the probability that some path from A to B is working?

For any simulation, a series of steps or a model can serve as a useful guide.

1. *Identify key components and assumptions of the problem.* The key component in the water problem is the condition of a pump. Each pump is either working or not. The assumption is that the probability that a pump is working is $\frac{1}{2}$.

2. *Select a random device for the key components.* Any random device can be selected that has outcomes with the same probability as the key component—in this case, the pumps. Here a simple choice might be tossing a coin, with heads representing a working pump.

3. *Define a trial.* A *trial* consists of simulating a series of key components until the situation has been completely modeled one time. In this problem, a trial could consist of tossing a coin five times, each toss representing a different pump.

4. *Conduct a large number of trials and record the information.* For this problem, it would be good to keep the record of heads and tails in groups of five because each set of five is one trial and represents all of the pumps.

5. *Use the data to draw conclusions.* There are four possible paths for the water, each flowing through two of the five pumps. As they are numbered in the drawing, if any one of the pairs 1–2, 5–2, 5–3, and 4–3 is open, it makes no difference whether the other pumps are working. By counting the trials in which at least one of these four pairs of coins both came up heads, we can estimate the probability of water flowing. To answer the second question, the number of tails per trial can be averaged.

 *pause and reflect* ─────────

How would you answer the third question concerning the 1–2 path's being open?

─────────────────────────────

Steps 4 and 5 are the same as solving a probability problem by experimental means. The interesting problem-solving aspects of simulation activities are in the first three steps, where the real-world situation is translated into a model. Translation of real-world information into models is the essence of applied mathematics.

Here are a few more examples of problems that can be solved by simulation and are easy enough to be tackled by middle school students.

In a true-or-false test, what is the probability of getting 7 out of 10 questions correct by guessing alone? (*Key component:* answering a question. *Assumption:* Chance of getting it correct is $\frac{1}{2}$.) What if the test were multiple choice with 4 choices?

In a group of five people, what is the chance that two were born in the same month? (*Key component:* month of birth. *Assumption:* All 12 months are equally likely.)

Casey's batting average is .350. What is the chance he will go hitless in a complete nine-inning game? (*Key component:* getting a hit. *Assumptions:* Probability of a hit for each at-bat is .35. Casey will get to bat four times in the average game.)

Krunch-a-Munch cereal packs one of five games in each box. About how many boxes should you expect to buy before you get a complete set? (*Key component:* getting one game. *Assumption:* Each game has a $\frac{1}{5}$ chance. *Trial:* Use a $\frac{1}{5}$ random device repeatedly until all five outcomes appear; the average length of a trial answers the question.) What is the chance of getting a set in eight or fewer boxes?

Students often have trouble selecting an appropriate random device for their simulations. Spinners are an obvious choice since faces can be adjusted to match probabilities. Coins or two-colored chips are useful for probabilities of $\frac{1}{2}$. A standard die can be used for probabilities that are multiples of $\frac{1}{6}$. There are also dice available from educational distributors with 4, 8, 12, and 20 sides.

 Many relatively simple calculators include a key that will produce a random number. Usually, the random numbers generated are between 0 and 1. Students who are going to use these random number generators will need some direction in using them to their advantage. Each number generated will likely have eight or more decimal places. A list of five numbers might look like this:

    0.8904433368
    0.0232028877
    0.1669322714
    0.1841957303
    0.5523714952

How could a list of decimals like this replace flipping a coin or spinning a spinner? Suppose each was multiplied by 2. The results would be between 0 and 2. If you ignore the decimal part, you would have a series of zeros and ones that could stand for heads and tails, boys and girls, true and false, or any other pair of equally likely outcomes. For three outcomes, the same as a $\frac{1}{4}$-$\frac{1}{4}$-$\frac{1}{2}$ spinner, you might decide to look at the first two digits of the number and assign values from 0 to 24 and 25 to 49 to the two quarter portions and values 50 to 99 for the one-half portion. Alternatively, each number could be multiplied by 4, the

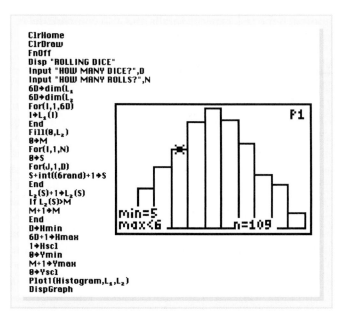

```
ClrHome
ClrDraw
FnOff
Disp "ROLLING DICE"
Input "HOW MANY DICE?",D
Input "HOW MANY ROLLS?",N
6D→dim(L₁
6D→dim(L₂
For(I,1,6D)
I→L₁(I)
End
Fill(0,L₂)
0→M
For(I,1,N)
0→S
For(J,1,D)
S+int((6rand)+1→S
End
L₂(S)+1→L₂(S)
If L₂(S)>M
M+1→M
End
0→Xmin
6D+1→Xmax
1→Xscl
0→Ymin
M+1→Ymax
0→Yscl
Plot1(Histogram,L₁,L₂)
DispGraph
```

```
F1
min=5
max<6                    n=109
```

FIGURE 23.15 This TI-83 program can be used to simulate thousands of dice rolls and accumulate the results.

decimal part ignored, resulting in random numbers 0, 1, 2, and 3. These could then be assigned to the desired outcomes. In effect, random numbers can simulate any simple random device.

With graphing calculators, the random number generator can be used inside of a simple program that produces the numbers and stores them in a list. The list can then be displayed graphically. The program in Figure 23.15 is for a TI-83 calculator. It will "roll" as many dice as you request. At the end of the program, a histogram displays the totals for each sum. With the TRACE feature, the value for each bar in the graph is displayed. The figure shows the result of rolling two dice 1000 times. It took about $2\frac{1}{2}$ minutes to run the program and produce the graph. (Computer programs produce the result almost instantly.) The TI-73 calculator designed for middle school has a built-in coin and dice function.

Although computer programs are much faster, allow for more variation, and include attractive graphics, the advantage of calculator approaches is availability. Every student can design and run an experiment individually. When computers are at a premium, this is a significant advantage. ■

Assessment Notes It is useful to have a list of the conceptual ideas that are involved in learning about probability so that, as you assess your students, you will not simply focus on the procedural skills. Nearly every idea we have discussed in this chapter is explored via a problem-based task that involves an analysis of an experiment. These tasks, or ones very similar to them, can be used as assessment activities. Instead of discussions with the class, have students write explanations to questions you include with the activity. Here is a list of the main ideas we have discussed in this chapter:

- *The distinction between theoretical and experimental probability.* Students can write about the results that occur in an experiment with, say, 50 or 100 trials and discuss the relationship of the relative frequency of an event to the true probability. What do you do if the theoretical probability cannot be determined? Ask for examples.
- *The law of large numbers.* Have students write about the results of an experiment in the short run and in the long run. Why are the relative frequencies usually different? Which results are most reliable?
- *Sample spaces and probabilities for independent and dependent events.* Have students determine the probabilities for two-stage experiments. Do they utilize the dependency of events if applicable? Do they use effectively a matrix, tree diagram, or area model? Do they use the models with understanding?
- *Simulations.* The most effective assessment is simply to have a student construct an assessment plan for a given simulation. It is not necessary for the student to actually conduct the simulation; rather, ask for written explanations for each decision made in designing the simulation. Within this task there are numerous ideas about probability that very likely will illustrate understanding of many of the concepts listed here. ■

Literature Connections

As with all mathematics topics, some books can be adapted to create an interesting mathematical problem in a manner that might never have occurred to either you or the author. Others offer us specific information that directly lends itself to the topic at hand. Both are represented in the selections here.

Do You Wanna Bet? Your Chance to Find Out About Probability
Cushman, 1991

The two characters in this book, Danny and Brian, become involved in everyday situations both in and out of school. Each situation has an element of probability involved. For example, two invitations to birthday parties are for the same day. What is the chance that two friends would have the same birthday? In another situation, Brian wonders if he should do his homework because the weather forecaster predicts a 60 percent chance that there will be enough snow to close schools. When it doesn't snow at all, the question is, was the forecaster wrong? Secret notes passed in class lead to the discussion of letter frequencies in our language. These and other situations woven into an interesting story can each lead to a probability experiment or discussion. Students might create simulations to examine some of the same ideas, or the story may provoke similar questions for exploration.

My Little Sister Ate One Hare
Grossman, 1996

This counting book will appeal to the middle school set as well as to young children due to the somewhat gross thought of a little girl eating one rabbit, two snakes, three ants, and so on, including bats, mice, worms, and lizards. Upon eating ten peas, she throws up everything she ate.

Bay-Williams and Martinie (2004) used this tale with primary-grade students to create a wonderful introductory lesson in probability. If one of the things the little sister "spilled" on the floor is picked up at random in the process of cleaning up, what is the probability of getting a polliwog (or other animal or category of animal)? Students can use cards for the correct number of each thing eaten and

approach the task experimentally and also compare the results to the theoretical probability.

Lotteries: Who Wins, Who Loses
Weiss, 1991

Lotteries are so popular in this country that they are by far our most favored form of gambling. This book for young adults provides all sorts of interesting information about money spent on legal and illegal gambling and also the odds of winning. The data in this book may be a bit out of date but that shouldn't matter much. If your state has a lottery or other form of gaming, students can explore the probabilities involved with current information. Comparisons to amounts of money spent in the late 1980s can be made to current data that can now easily be found on the Web. The social issues surrounding gambling can also be addressed. Lotteries have sometimes been described as a tax on those who don't know mathematics. The book notes that the chance of winning the lottery jackpot in one state was less than the chance of living to the age of 115. ■

Reflections on Chapter 23

Writing to Learn

1. What are the first ideas about the occurrence of future events that students should develop? How can you help students with these ideas?
2. Explain the idea that probability exists on a continuum. What are the numbers at either end of the continuum and what do they represent?
3. Activities 23.2 and 23.3 ("Race to the Top" and "Add, Then Tally") are each designed to help students see that some outcomes are more likely than others. What is the difference between these two activities? Why might this difference be useful in helping students?
4. Explain what is meant by the statement "Chance has no memory."
5. Describe the difference between experimental probability and theoretical probability. Will these ever be the same? Which is the "correct" probability?
6. Explain the law of large numbers. Describe an activity that might help students to appreciate this idea.
7. Describe the difference between a single-stage and a multistage experiment. Among multistage experiments, what are independent events and dependent events? Give an example of each.
8. What are the advantages of having students conduct experiments even before they attempt to figure out a theoretical probability?
9. What is the purpose of a simulation? Set up a simulation for at least one of the examples on p. 488. Conduct a few trials

to convince yourself that your simulation reflects the situation accurately.

10. Use an area model and a tree diagram to determine the theoretical probability for the following experiment:

    Dad puts a $5 bill and three $1 bills in the first box. In a second box, he puts another $5 bill with just one $1 bill. For washing the car, Junior gets to take one bill from the first box without looking and put it in the second box. After these are well mixed, he then gets to take one bill from the second box. What is the probability that he will get $5?

    Design a simulation for the problem and try it out. Does your simulation agree with your theoretical probability?

11. The three outcomes of an experiment have probabilities of $\frac{1}{3}$, $\frac{1}{6}$, and $\frac{1}{2}$. Describe how you could use a random number generator on a calculator or computer to simulate these probabilities.

For Discussion and Exploration

1. Read Michael Shaughnessy's chapter, "Research on Students' Understanding of Probability" (2003). This easily read paper in the *Research Companion to Principles and Standards for School Mathematics* highlights some interesting findings about students' understanding of probability and concludes with a number of recommendations for teaching probability. Select one or two ideas that you think are especially important and share them briefly with the class.

2. How important do you think it is to teach students the basic concepts of probability in grades K to 3? What about in grades 4 to 8? How much understanding of probability does the educated citizen require? Some experts have argued that the ability to understand probability (and statistical) ideas is so much more important than the related skills of being able to compute probabilities (and statistics) that the skills could be skipped in favor of increased reasoning in these areas. What position do you take on this issue? How do your state standards reflect your view?

3. The "Monty Hall Problem" has become a classic. In the game show, the contestant chooses from one of three doors. Behind one of the three doors is a big prize. Monty shows the contestant a goat behind one of the doors not selected and then offers the contestant the opportunity to switch doors. Does the contestant have a better chance of winning the big prize by switching, staying with the original choice, or is there no difference? There are numerous methods of answering this question. Make a convincing argument for your own answer based on the ideas and techniques in this chapter.

4. Examine one of the three NCTM books in the *Navigations Series* (*Data Analysis and Probability in Prekindergarten–Grade 2, Grades 3–5*, and *Probability in Grades 6–8*). These excellent books offer a wealth of useful activities along with Blackline Masters and detailed lessons.

Recommendations for Further Reading

Coffey, D. C., & Richardson, M. G. (2005). Rethinking fair games. *Mathematics Teaching in the Middle School, 10,* 298–303.

Students explore the fairness of a matching game both experimentally and using a theoretical model. They then set out to create a variation of the game that would be fair by assigning points to a match and to a mismatch. A TI-73 program is included that simulates the revised game.

Edwards, T. G., & Hensien, S. M. (2000). Using probability experiments to foster discourse. *Teaching Children Mathematics, 8,* 524–529.

Fifth-grade students experiment with outcomes of flipping a coin, spinning a spinner, and rolling a die. The discourse is directed to the disparity between the observed outcomes and the theoretical probabilities. For example, is it reasonable that there are 77 heads out of 150 tosses? The article well exhibits both students' understandings of these ideas and the art of engaging students in profitable discourse.

Jones, G. A., Thornton, C. A., Langrall, C. W., & Tarr, J. E. (1999). Understanding students' probabilistic reasoning. In L. V. Stiff (Ed.), *Developing mathematical thinking in grades K–12* (pp. 146–155). Reston, VA: National Council of Teachers of Mathematics.

These researchers identified four levels of student thinking that they observed in children in both elementary and middle school. They have applied their framework to key concepts such as experimental and theoretical probability and the independence/dependence of events. Examples and suggestions for instruction make this an important article.

Lawrence, A. (1999). From *The Giver* to *The Twenty-one Balloons:* Explorations with probability. *Mathematics Teaching in the Middle School, 8,* 504–509.

Lawrence uses two award-winning books to motivate some nontrivial explorations for her middle school students. One task was to decide how often in a series of 50 births there will be 25 boys and 25 girls. In a related task, students tried to find out if it was more likely to have the same number of girls and boys in a small family or a large family. The ideas here are quite challenging and the results are interesting.

Shaughnessy, J. M. (2003). Research on students' understanding of probability. In J. Kilpatrick, W. G. Martin, & D. Schifter (Eds.), *A research companion to Principles and Standards for School Mathematics* (pp. 216–226). Reston, VA: National Council of Teachers of Mathematics.

As noted in the first discussion question, Shaughnessy's chapter offers interesting insights from research and makes useful recommendations. Teachers serious about the teaching of probability will benefit from checking this out.

Online Resources

Suggested Applets and Web Links

Adjustable Spinner (Shodor)
www.shodor.org/interactivate/activities/spinner
A virtual spinner can be adjusted to have any number of sections of any size. It can then be spun any number of times in increments of 100,000.

Box Model (NLVM)
http://nlvm.usu.edu/en/nav/frames_asid_146_g_3_t_5.html
The applet permits creating a box of up to 16 colored cubes including the possibility of duplicates. Cubes can then be drawn at random (with replacement). A bar graph shows the results that can be compared to the theoretical results.

Coin Tossing (NLVM)
http://nlvm.usu.edu/en/nav/frames_asid_305_g_3_t_5.html
A single coin can be "tossed" any number of times. The results are shown in order, which can help with the concept of randomness. A bar graph shows results.

Probability (Shodor)
www.shodor.org/interactivate/activities/prob/index.html
A spinner can be created with up to four regions or two like dice can be made with each side adjustable from 1 to 6. The devices can then be used in experiments.

Probability Resources (Math Forum)
http://mathforum.org/library/topics/probability
Links to hundreds of articles, lessons, and applets related to probability.

 An additional list of books and articles related to the ideas in this chapter can be found on the Companion Web site at **www.ablongman.com/vandewalle6e.**

chapter 24

Developing Concepts of Exponents, Integers, and Real Numbers

Much of the middle grades curriculum has been discussed in other chapters, including decimals, ratio and proportion, percent, measurement, geometry, probability, statistics, and algebraic reasoning. Each of those topics has its initial development in earlier grades but continues in the middle school. Specifically, students in the middle grades need to develop a more complete understanding of the number system, extend whole numbers to integers, start to think of fractions as rational numbers (both positive and negative), and begin to appreciate the completeness of the real number system.

▼ Big Ideas

1. Exponential notation is a powerful way to express repeated products of the same number. Specifically, powers of 10 express very large and very small numbers in an economical manner.

2. Integers add to number the idea of opposite, so that every number has both size and a positive or negative relationship to other numbers. A negative number is the opposite of the positive number of the same size.

3. Every fraction, both positive and negative, is a rational number. Furthermore, every rational number can be expressed as a fraction.

4. Many numbers are not rational and can be expressed only symbolically or approximately using a close rational number. Examples include $\sqrt{2} \approx 1.41421\ldots$ and $\pi \approx 3.14159\ldots$.

▲ *Mathematics* Content Connections

The ideas in this chapter represent an expansion of the ways in which we represent numbers. These representations expand or enhance earlier ideas of whole numbers, fractions, and decimals.

■ **Whole-Number Place Value, Fractions, and Decimals** (Chapters 12, 16, and 18): When exponential notation is combined with decimal notation, very small and very large numbers can be written efficiently. Decimals and fractions help to describe the difference between rational and irrational numbers. Negative numbers extend the number line in both directions.

■ **Algebra** (Chapter 15): The symbolic manipulation of numbers, including the rules for order of operations, is exactly the same as is used with variables. An ease with manipulation and representations of numbers will translate to algebraic manipulations. The study of integers helps with the notion of "opposite," represented by a negative sign: $^-6$ is the opposite of $^+6$ and ^-x is the opposite of ^+x, regardless of whether x is negative or positive. Exponents can also be variables, giving rise to exponential functions.

Large Numbers, Small Numbers, and Exponents

As numbers in our technological world get very small or very large, expressing them in standard form is cumbersome. Exponential notation is much more efficient for conveying numeric or quantitative information.

Exponents

In algebra classes, students get confused trying to remember the rules of exponents. For example, when you raise numbers to powers, do you add or multiply the exponents? Here is an example of procedural knowledge that is often learned without supporting conceptual knowledge. Before algebra, students should have ample opportunity to explore working with exponents on whole numbers rather than with letters or variables. By doing so, they are able to deal directly with the concept and actually generate the rules themselves.

A *whole-number exponent* is simply shorthand for repeated multiplication of a number times itself; for example, $3^4 = 3 \times 3 \times 3 \times 3$. That is the only conceptual knowledge required.

Conventions of symbolism must also be learned. These are arbitrary rules with no conceptual basis. The first is that *an exponent applies to its immediate base*. For example, in the expression $2 + 5^3$, the exponent 3 applies only to the 5, so the expression is equal to $2 + (5 \times 5 \times 5)$. However, in the expression $(2 + 5)^3$, the 3 is an exponent of the quantity $2 + 5$ and is evaluated as $(2 + 5) \times (2 + 5) \times (2 + 5)$, or $7 \times 7 \times 7$.

The other convention involves the *order of operations:* Multiplication and division are always done before addition and subtraction. Since exponentiation is repeated multiplication, it also is done before addition and subtraction. In the expression $5 + 4 \times 2 - 6 \div 3$, 4×2 and $6 \div 3$ are done first. Therefore, the expression is evaluated as $5 + 8 - 2 = 13 - 2 = 11$.

Ⅱ *pause and reflect* _____

Try evaluating the same expression in left-to-right order. Do you get 4?

_____

Parentheses are used to group operations that are to be done first. Therefore, in $(5 + 4) \times 2 - 6 \div 3$, the addition can be done inside the parentheses first, or the distributive property can be used, and the final result is 16. The phrase "*P*lease *e*xcuse *m*y *d*ear *A*unt *S*ally" is sometimes used to help students recall that operations inside *p*arentheses are done first, then *e*xponentiation, and then *m*ultiplication and *d*ivision before *a*ddition and *s*ubtraction.

Calculators and Notation

Most scientific calculators employ "algebraic logic" that will evaluate expressions correctly and also allow grouping with parentheses. However, with the exception of the TI-MathMate and other newer calculators designed specifically for school use, simple four-function calculators generally do not use algebraic logic. Operations are processed as they are entered. On calculators without algebraic logic, the following two keying sequences produce the same results:

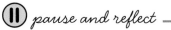

Whenever an operation sign is pressed, the effect is the same as pressing = and then the operation. Of course, neither result is correct for the expressions $3 + 2 \times 7$, which should be evaluated as $3 + 14$, or 17. Calculators designed for middle grades as well as the TI-Math Mate, the TI-10, and TI-15 do use algebraic logic and include parenthesis keys so that both $3 + 2 \times 7$ and $(3 + 2) \times 7$ can be keyed in the order that the symbols appear. Now all of the major manufacturers offer calculators that show an entire expression in the window, including parentheses, as do graphing calculators. Results are shown only after pressing the [Enter] key. With most scientific calculators, the display shows only one number at a time, as illustrated here.

| Key: → | 3 [+] 2 [×] 7 [=] |
| Display → 3 | 2   7   17 |

Notice that the display does not change when [×] is pressed and a right parenthesis is never displayed. Instead, the expression that the right parenthesis encloses is calculated and that result displayed.

| Key: → | [(] 3 [+] 2 [)] [×] 7 [=] |
| Display → [3 | 2 [5]   7   35 |

The newer "school" calculators and graphing calculators offer the best solution to these problems. When the expression $3 + 2 \times (6^2 - 4)$ is keyed in, the display shows the full expression. Nothing is evaluated until you press [Enter] or [EXE]. Then the result appears on the next line to the right of the screen:

| $3 + 2 * (6^2 - 4)$ | |
| | 67 |

Moreover, the last expression entered can be recalled and edited so that students can see how different expressions are evaluated. Only minimum key presses are required.

$3 + 2 * (6^2 - 4)$	
	67
$(3 + 2) * (6^2 - 4)$	
	160
$(3 + 2) * 6^2 - 4$	
	176
$3 + 2 * 6^2 - 4$	
	71

Nevertheless, the simple four-function calculator remains a powerful tool regardless of its limitations. For example, to evaluate 3^8, press 3 [×] [=] [=] [=] [=] [=] [=]. (The first press of [=] will result in 9, or 3×3.) Students will be fascinated by how quickly numbers grow. Enter any number, press ⊠, and then repeatedly press ⊜. Try two-digit numbers. Try 0.2.

Give students ample opportunity to explore expressions involving mixed operations and exponents with only the conventions and the meaning of exponents to guide them. No rules for exponents should be promoted. When experience has provided a firm background, the rules of exponents will make sense and should not require rote memorization.

activity 24.1

What's in an Expression?

Provide students with numeric expressions to evaluate with simple four-function calculators. Here are some examples of the types of expressions that can be valuable:

$3 + 4 \times 8$ $4 \times 8 + 3$	$3^6 + 2^6$ $(3 + 2)^6$	$3^4 \times 7 - 5^2$ $(3 \times 7)^4 - 5 \times 2$	$3^4 \times 5^2$ $(3 \times 5)^6$

$\dfrac{5^3 \times 5^2}{5^6}$	$4 \times 3 - 2^3 \times 5 + 23 \times 9$	$\dfrac{4 \times 3^5}{2}$ $4 + \dfrac{3^5}{2}$

When experiencing difficulty, students should write equivalent expressions without exponents or include parentheses to indicate explicit groupings. For example:

$$
\begin{aligned}
(7 \times 2^3 - 5)^3 &= (7 \times (2 \times 2 \times 2) - 5) \times \\
&\quad (7 \times (2 \times 2 \times 2) - 5) \times \\
&\quad (7 \times (2 \times 2 \times 2) - 5) \\
&= ((7 \times 8) - 5) \times \\
&\quad ((7 \times 8) - 5) \times \\
&\quad ((7 \times 8) - 5) \\
&= (56 - 5) \times (56 - 5) \times (56 - 5) \\
&= 51 \times 51 \times 51
\end{aligned}
$$

When discussing results, place all of the emphasis on the procedures rather than the answer. The fact that two groups got the same result does not help a group that got a different result. For many expressions, there is more than one way to proceed, and one may be easier to do or to understand than another.

Of course, calculators with algebraic logic will automatically produce correct results. Yet it remains important for students to know the correct order of operations. The calculator should not replace an understanding of the rules. The order-of-operation rules apply to symbolic manipulation in algebra and must also be understood if a calculator without algebraic logic is used.

Very Large Numbers

The real world is full of very large quantities and measures. We see references to huge numbers in the media all the time. Unfortunately, most of us have not developed an appreciation for extremely large numbers. Here are a few examples:

* A state lottery with 44 numbers from which to pick 6 has over 7 million possible combinations of 6 numbers. There are $44 \times 43 \times 42 \times 41 \times 40 \times 39$ possible ways that the balls could come out of the hopper (5,082,517,440). But generally the order in which they are picked is not important. Since there are $6 \times 5 \times 4 \times 3 \times 2 \times 1 = 720$ different arrangements of 6 numbers, each collection appears 720 times. Therefore, there are *only* 5,082,517,440 ÷ 720 possible lottery numbers, or in other words, 1 out of 7,059,052 chances to win.
* An estimate of the size of the universe is 40 billion light-years. One light-year is the number of miles light travels in *one year*. The speed of light is 186,281.7 miles per *second*, or 16,094,738,880 miles in a single day.
* The human body has about 100 billion cells.
* The distance to the sun is about 150 million kilometers.
* The population of the world in 2005 was about 6.5 billion.

Connecting these large numbers to meaningful points of reference can help students get a handle on their true magnitude. For example, suppose students determine the population in their city or town is about 500,000 people. They can then figure that it would take about 12,500 cities of the same population size to generate the population of the world. Or suppose students determine that it is about 4600 km between San Francisco, California, and Washington, DC. This would mean that it would take over 32,000 trips back and forth between these two cities to equal the distance between the earth and the sun. Building from such familiar or meaningful reference points can help students develop benchmarks to work with and make sense of large numbers.

Representation of Large Numbers: Scientific Notation

The more common it becomes to find very large numbers in our daily lives, the more important it is to have convenient ways to represent them. One option is to say and write numbers in their common form. However, this practice can at times be cumbersome. Another option is to use exponential notation and our base-ten place-value system.

Students in elementary school learn how to multiply by 10, by 100, and by 1000 by simply adding the appropriate number of zeros. Help students expand this idea by examining powers of 10 on a calculator that handles exponents. A graphing calculator is best but not the only option.

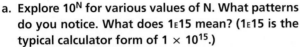

Exploring Powers of 10

Have students use any calculator that permits entering exponents to explore some of the following:

a. Explore 10^N for various values of N. What patterns do you notice. What does 1ᴇ15 mean? (1ᴇ15 is the typical calculator form of 1×10^{15}.)

b. Find different expressions for one thousand, one million, one billion, one trillion. What patterns are there in expressions you found?

c. Enter 45 followed by a string of zeros. How many will your calculator permit? What happens when you press ⎡Enter⎤? What does 4.5ᴇ10 mean?

d. What does 5.689ᴇ6 mean? Can you enter this another way?

e. Try sums like $(4.5 \times 10^N) + (27 \times 10^K)$ for different values of N and K. What can you find out?

f. What happens with products of numbers like those in item (e)?

It is useful to become comfortable with the power-of-10 expressions in Activity 24.2. Students should eventually discover that when scientific or graphing calculators display numbers with more digits than the display will hold, they use *scientific notation*—a decimal number between 1 and 10 times a power of 10. For example, on a TI-73, the product of $45,000,000 \times 8,000,000$ is displayed as 3.6ᴇ14, meaning 3.6×10^{14}, or $360,000,000,000,000$ (360 trillion).

Ask students why there are only 13 zeros. What happens when the numbers in the computation do not involve a lot of zeros?

pause and reflect ——————————

With each factor in the product expressed in scientific notation: $(4.5 \times 10^7) \times (8 \times 10^6)$, or 4.5ᴇ7 × 8.0ᴇ6, can you compute the result mentally?

Notice the advantages of scientific notation, especially for multiplication and division. Here the significant digits can be multiplied mentally ($4.5 \times 8 = 36$) and the exponents added to produce almost instantly 36×10^{13} or 3.6×10^{14}.

Different notations have different purposes and values. Consider this fact: In 1990, the population of the world was more than 5,050,700,000 persons, about 1 billion fewer than in the year 2000. This can be expressed in various ways:

5 billion 50 million 700 thousand

5,050,700,000

5.0507×10^9

Less than 5.1 billion

A little more than 5 billion

Each way of stating the number has value and purpose in different contexts. Rather than spend time with exercises converting numbers from standard form to scientific notation, consider large numbers found in newspapers, magazines, and atlases. How are they written? How are they said aloud? When are they rounded? When not and why? What forms of the numbers seem best for the purposes?

NCTM Standards The *Standards* reminds us that large numbers and scientific notation are used in various contexts. "A newspaper headline may proclaim, 'Clean-Up Costs from Oil Spill Exceed $2 Billion!' or a science textbook may indicate that the number of red blood cells in the human body is about 1.9×10^{13}" (p. 217).

In the eighth grade, the *Connected Mathematics* program looks at exponents as a particular type of function—exponential functions. The program uses real contexts throughout the development. An example is explored on the next page.

Negative Exponents

When students begin to explore exponents and have also experienced negative integers, it is interesting to consider what it might mean to raise a number to a negative power. For example, what does 2^{-4} mean? Two related options for exploring the possibilities of negative exponents seem reasonable. First, in the spirit of patterns in mathematics, examine a pattern of numbers, and see how it might best be expanded. As with large numbers, the powers of 10 seem the most profitable to explore because they are directly related to place value. Have students consider 10^N as follows:

$$10^4 = 10,000$$
$$10^3 = 1000$$
$$10^2 = 100$$
$$10^1 = 10$$
$$10^0 = ?$$
$$10^{-1} = ?$$

In this sequence, the most obvious entry for 10^0 is 1, and that is the *definition* of 10^0. That is, it is a convention that 10 or any other nonzero number raised to the power 0 is 1.

Grade 8, Growing, Growing, Growing: Exponential Relationships
Investigation 3: Growth Factors

Context

This entire unit, comprising approximately 20 days, is devoted to the concept of exponential growth as seen in real contexts. The unit begins with some fun examples to review the meaning of exponents. In the second investigation, the examples include the growth of single-celled organisms and the area covered by the growth of mold. The base of the exponent is called the *growth factor*. Through the first two units, growth factors are always small whole numbers. This and the next investigation explore growth factors that are not whole numbers.

Task Description

As a lead-in to this first task, students learn of the problem rabbit population in Australia. (Rabbits were introduced to Australia in 1859. In one year, a female rabbit can have as many as seven litters with five rabbits each.) The table provides hypothetical data that might have been collected during the first four years after the rabbits were introduced.

Time (years)	Rabbit population
0	100
1	180
2	325
3	580
4	1050

In the problem box shown here, notice how a recursive relationship is used to define the growth factor.

Problem 3.1

A. The table above shows that the rabbit population grows exponentially. What is the growth factor for this rabbit population? The growth factor from one year to the next is the fraction:

$$\frac{\text{population for year } n}{\text{population for year } n-1}$$

To find an approximate overall growth factor, compute the growth factors between several pairs of consecutive years and average your results.

B. If this growth pattern had continued, how many rabbits would there have been after 10 years? After 25 years? After 50 years?

C. How many years would it have taken the rabbit population to exceed 1 million?

D. Assume this growth pattern continued. Write an equation you could use to predict the rabbit population, P, for any year, n, after the rabbits were first counted.

From *Connected Mathematics: Growing, Growing, Growing: Exponential Mathematics.* © 2002 by Michigan State University, Glenda Lappan, James T. Fey, William M. Fitzgerald, Susan N. Friel, & Elizabeth Difanis Phillips. Published by Pearson Education, Inc., publishing as Pearson Prentice Hall. Used by permission.

This method of determining the growth factor was introduced earlier in the unit. The growth factor is a bit different for each year, as would be expected. Thus, the formula will be an approximation of the actual population of rabbits. This is a good example of the way that mathematical models often approximate real data.

As follow-up, students are asked related questions that involve changes in the basic formula developed in the initial problem, providing practice with the main idea.

In the fourth and final investigation of this unit, the growth factors are less than 1. These relationships are examples of "exponential decay" rather than of growth. One example from the text involves the rate at which water cools over time.

So what is 10^{-1}? If the pattern is to continue, the 1 should move to the right of the decimal:

$10^0 = 1$

$10^{-1} = 0.1$

$10^{-2} = 0.01$

$10^{-3} = 0.001$

and so on. Notice how each of these numbers is written as a fraction:

$$10^{-3} = 0.001 = \frac{1}{1000} = \frac{1}{10^3}$$

Students should be encouraged to explore these numbers on a calculator. That leads to the second way to explore negative exponents: Use a calculator to see if you can figure out what things like 4^{-3} or 2^{-5} mean. The calculator should, of course, never be seen as the *reason* for anything in mathematics, but here you are searching for a notation convention. Assuming that one exists, it is reasonable to believe that the calculator will have the correct convention incorporated. If the calculator has decimal-to-fraction conversion, suggest that students use that feature to help develop the meaning of negative exponents. Figure 24.1 gives an example of how this might look on a graphing calculator.

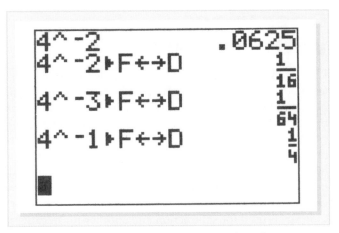

FIGURE 24.1 Graphing calculators routinely evaluate expressions as decimals. However, they also provide a way to convert decimals to fractions. This figure shows the screen of a TI-73 calculator. The F–D key converts fractions to decimals and also decimals to fractions as shown here.

Very Small Numbers

As with large numbers, it is extremely important to use real examples of very small numbers. Without real contexts, you may be tempted to resort to drill exercises that have little meaning for students. As with large numbers, connecting these small numbers to points of reference can help students conceptualize how very tiny these numbers really are. Here are a few examples of real-world values to explore:

- The length of a DNA strand in a cell is about 10^{-7} m. This is also measured as 1000 *angstroms*. (Based on this information, how long is an angstrom?) For perspective, the diameter of a human hair is about 2.54×10^{-5} m.
- Human hair grows at the rate of 10^{-8} miles per hour. Garden snails have been clocked at about 3×10^{-2} mph.
- The chances of winning the Virginia lottery, based on selecting six numbers from 1 to 44, is 1 in 7.059 million. That is a probability of less than 1.4×10^{-10}.
- The mass of one atom of hydrogen is 0.000 000 000 000 000 000 000 001 675 g while the mass of one paper clip is about 1 g.
- It takes sound 0.28 second (2.8×10^{-1}) to travel the length of a football field. In contrast, a TV signal travels a full mile in about 0.000005368 second, or 5.3×10^{-6} second. A TV viewer at home hears the football being kicked before the receiver on the field does.

Integer Concepts

Students almost daily have some interaction with negative numbers or experience phenomena that negative numbers can model. Some examples:

A loss of money is a negative cash flow.

Slowing down the car is negative acceleration, and driving in reverse is negative velocity.

Below-zero temperature and below-ground level are negatives relative to a scale.

In fact, almost any concept that is quantified and has direction probably has both a positive and a negative value.

Generally, negative values are introduced with *integers*—the whole numbers and their negatives or opposites—instead of with fractions or decimals.

Intuitive Models of Signed Quantities

As with any new types of numbers that students encounter, real models or examples are useful. Negative numbers or situations that model them do exist. It is a good idea to discuss some of these with your class before jumping directly into computation with signed numbers.

Debits and Credits

Suppose that you are the bookkeeper for a small business. At any time, your records show how many dollars the company has in its account. There are always so many dollars in cash (credits or receipts) and so many dollars in accounts payable (debits). The difference between the debit and credit totals tells the value of the account. If there are more credits than debits, the account is positive, or "in the black." If there are more debits than credits, the account is in debt, shows a negative cash value, or is "in the red." Suppose further that all transactions are handled by mail. The mail carrier can bring mail, a positive action, or take mail away, a negative action.

With this scenario, it is easy to discuss addition and subtraction of signed quantities. An example is illustrated in Figure 24.2.

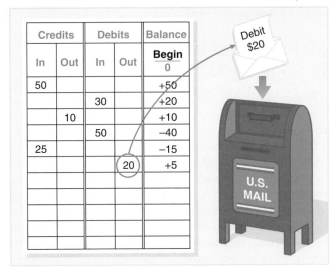

FIGURE 24.2 A ledger sheet model for integers.

Integer Football

An integer football field might have the center as the 0-yard line with one goal the +50 goal and the other the −50 goal. Any position on the field is determined by a signed number between +50 and −50. Gains or losses are like positive and negative quantities. A positive team moves toward the positive goal, and a negative team toward the negative goal. If the negative team starts on the −15-yard line and has a loss of 20 yards, it will be on the +5-yard line.

 *pause and reflect* ─────────────

You should sketch a picture of this example and convince yourself that it is numerically the same as the one in Figure 24.2 using the debit-credit model.

─────────────

Contrived situations such as mailing debits and credits and the football field are suggested as introductory discussion models. They can help students think intuitively about what happens to quantities when an action causes them to be less than 0. They also provide examples of a joining or positive action and a removal or negative action of both positive and negative quantities.

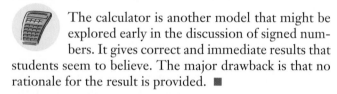 The calculator is another model that might be explored early in the discussion of signed numbers. It gives correct and immediate results that students seem to believe. The major drawback is that no rationale for the result is provided. ■

Have students explore subtraction problems such as 5 − 8 = ?, and discuss the results. (Be aware that the negative sign appears in different places on different calculators.)

Students can benefit by using the calculator along with the intuitive models and questions mentioned earlier. For example, how can you get from −5 to −17 by addition? 13 minus *what* is 15?

Mathematical Definition of Negative Numbers

The mathematician defines a negative number in terms of whole numbers. Therefore, the definition of negative 3 is the solution to the equation 3 + ? = 0. In general, the *opposite of n* is the solution to *n* + ? = 0. If *n* is a positive number, the *opposite of n* is a negative number. The set of integers, therefore, consists of the positive whole numbers, the opposites of the whole numbers, or negative numbers, and 0, which is neither positive nor negative. This is the definition found in student textbooks. Like many things in mathematics, abstract or symbolic definitions are best when there is some intuitive or conceptual framework with which to link the idea.

Operations with Integers

Until students encounter integers, the plus and minus signs are used only for the operations of addition and subtraction. Notation for signed numbers represents a real problem for many students. For example, the sum of 3 and negative 7 can be written as 3 + (−7) or as 3 + ⁻7. The latter form might be clear in a printed book but may be obscure in handwritten form. The use of parentheses is awkward, especially in expressions already involving parentheses. On graphing calculators, the distinction is forced on the user: One key is used for subtraction and another for negatives. They do not work interchangeably.

Two Models for Integer Operations

Two models are popular for helping students understand how the four operations (+, −, ×, and ÷) work with the integers. One model consists of counters in two different colors, one for positive counts and one for negative counts. Two counters, one of each type, cancel each other out. Thus, if yellows are positive and reds are negative, 5 yellows and 7 reds is the same as 2 reds and is an equivalent representation of ⁻2 (see Figure 24.3). It is important with this model that students understand that it is always possible to add to or remove from a pile any number of pairs consisting of one positive and one negative counter without changing the value of the pile. (Intuitively, this is like adding equal quantities of debits and credits.) The actions of addition and subtraction are the same as for whole numbers; addition is joining or adding counters, and subtraction is removing or taking away counters.

The other commonly used model is the number line. It is a bit more traditional and mathematical, yet many students find it confusing. The football field model provides an intuitive background. Positive and negative numbers are measured distances to the right and left of 0. It is important to remember that signed values are *directed distances* and not points on a line. The points on the number line are not models of integers; the directed distances are. To emphasize this for students, represent all integers with arrows, and avoid referring to the number line coordinates as "numbers." Poster board arrows of different

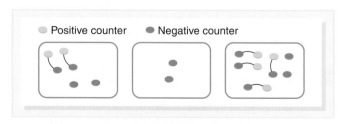

FIGURE 24.3 Each collection is a model of negative 2.

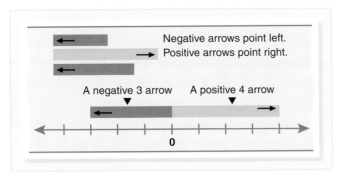

FIGURE 24.4 Number-line model for integers.

whole-number lengths can be made in two colors, yellow pointing to the right for positive quantities and red to the left for negative quantities (see Figure 24.4). The arrows help students think of integer quantities as directed distances. A positive arrow never points left, and a negative arrow never points right. Furthermore, each arrow is a quantity with both length (magnitude or absolute value) and direction (sign). These properties remain for each arrow regardless of its position on the number line. Small versions of the arrows can easily be cut from poster board for individual students to work with.

It is no doubt easier simply to give students the rules for integers than to develop them with arrows and counters. The conceptual explanations do not make the rules easier to use, and it is never intended that students continue to think in terms of these models as they practice integer arithmetic. Rather, it is important that students not view the procedural rules for manipulating integers as arbitrary and mysterious. Here is a case where we must make students responsible for the conceptual knowledge. If we emphasize only the procedural rules, there is little reason for students to attend to the conceptual justifications. Do not be content with right answers; always demand explanations.

Which Model to Use

Although the two models appear quite different, they are alike mathematically. Integers involve two concepts—*quantity* and *opposite*. Quantity is modeled by the number of counters or the length of the arrows. Opposite is represented as different colors or different directions.

Many teachers who have tried both models with their students report that students find one model easy and the other hard. (The counter model seems to be the favorite.) As a result, they decide to use only the model that students like or understand better. This is a mistake! Remember that the dual concepts of integers are not in the models but rather must be constructed by the students and imposed on the models. It may be that students find the operations easier when they use counters. This is not the same thing as understanding integer operations. Students should experience both models and, perhaps even more important, discuss how the two are alike. A parallel development using both models at the same time may be the most conceptual approach.

A Problem-Solving Approach for Integers

The following discussion is more a quick explanation of how counters and arrows can be used to model operations with integers than a suggested pedagogical approach. Once your students understand how integers are represented by each of the models, you can present the operations for the integers in the form of problems. In other words, rather than explaining how addition of integers works and showing students how to solve exercises with the models, you pose an integer computation and let students use their models to find a solution. It may be useful to assign half of the class the arrow model and the other half the counters. When solutions have been reached, the groups can compare and justify their results. Many incorrect ideas will surface, but the learning that will come from the discussion and clarification will be far superior to an expository approach.

Addition and Subtraction

Since middle school students may not have used counters or number lines for some time, it would be good to begin work with either of these models using positive whole numbers. After a few examples to help students become familiar with the model for addition or subtraction with whole numbers, have them work through an example with integers using exactly the same reasoning. Remember, the emphasis should be on the rationale and not on how quickly students can get correct answers.

Several examples of addition are modeled in Figure 24.5, each in two ways: with positive and negative counters and with the number-line-and-arrow model. First examine the counter model. After the two quantities are joined, any pairs of positive and negative counters cancel each other out, and students can remove these, making it easier to see the result.

To add using the arrow model, note that each added arrow begins at the point end of the previous arrow. Help students with the analogy between these arrows and the football situation: Players always face their own goal. They may go forward or backward, but they never face the opponents' goal. Addition is the advance of a team from the previous position. In the $^+3 + {}^-5$ example, the positive arrow (+ team) starts at 0 and ends at positive 3. From that point, the negative arrow begins (the negative team takes

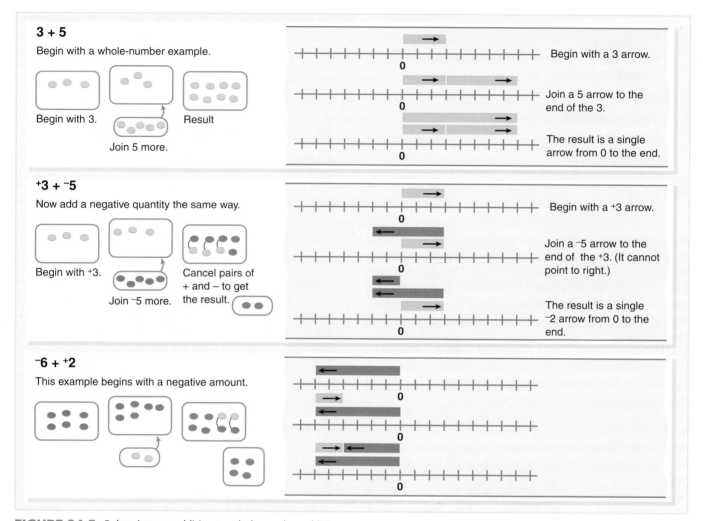

FIGURE 24.5 Relate integer addition to whole-number addition.

over and *advances* in the negative direction). The result, then, is an arrow beginning at 0 and ending where the second arrow ended.

Subtraction is represented as "remove" in terms of the counter model and "back up" in terms of the arrow model. In Figure 24.6, for ⁻5 – ⁺2, both models begin with a representation of ⁻5. To remove two positive counters from a set that has none, a different representation of ⁻5 must first be made. Since any number of neutral pairs (one positive, one negative) can be added without changing the value of the set, two pairs are added so that two positive counters can be removed. The net effect is to have more negative counters.

With the number-line-and-arrow model, subtraction means to back up or to move in the opposite direction. Using the football field analogy, teams move backward when penalized or they lose yardage. In the example of ⁻5 – ⁺2, the first arrow ends at ⁻5. Since a positive quantity is subtracted, use a positive arrow. To subtract it, move it in its

opposite direction (left). The forward movement ends at ⁻7. The result of the operation is an arrow from 0 to the back end of the ⁺2 arrow.

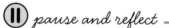 *pause and reflect* _____

Before reading further, go through each example in Figures 24.5 and 24.6. Solve the problems without examining the figure and then compare your results with those in the figures. You should become comfortable with both models.

_____

Have your students draw pictures to accompany integer computations. Set pictures are easy enough; they may consist of Xs and Os, for example. For the arrow model, there is no need for anything elaborate either. Figure 24.7 illustrates how a student might draw arrows for simple addition and subtraction exercises without even sketching the number line. Directions are shown by the arrows, and magnitudes are written on the arrows. For your initial

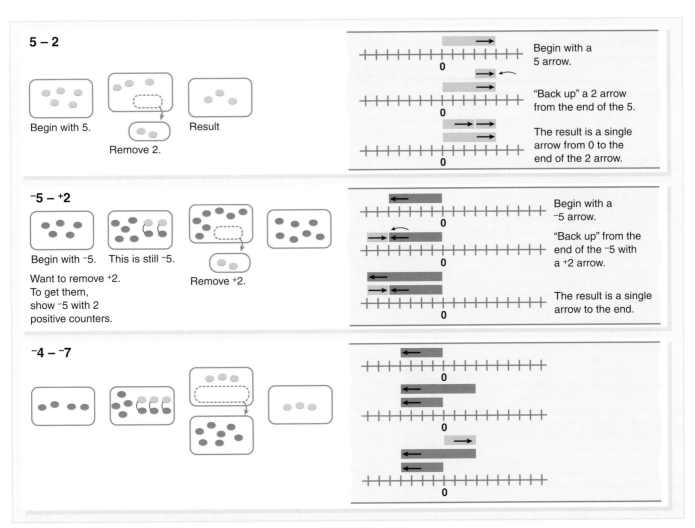

FIGURE 24.6 Integer subtraction is also related to whole numbers.

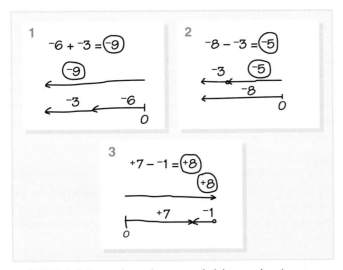

FIGURE 24.7 Students do not need elaborate drawings to think through the number-line model.

modeling, however, the poster board arrows in two colors will help students see that negative arrows always point left and that addition is a forward movement and subtraction is a backward movement for either type of arrow.

It is important for students to see that $^+3 + {}^-5$ is the same as $^+3 - {}^+5$ and that $^+2 - {}^-6$ is the same as $^+2 + {}^+6$. With the method of modeling addition and subtraction described here, these expressions are quite discernible and yet have the same result as they should have.

On graphing calculators, these expressions are entered using the "negative" key and the "subtraction" key. The difference is also evident in the display. The redundant superscript plus signs are not shown. Students can see that $3 + {}^-5$

EXPANDED LESSON

An expanded lesson plan for addition and subtraction of integers using the counter model can be found on the Companion Web site at www. ablongman.com/ vandewalle6e.

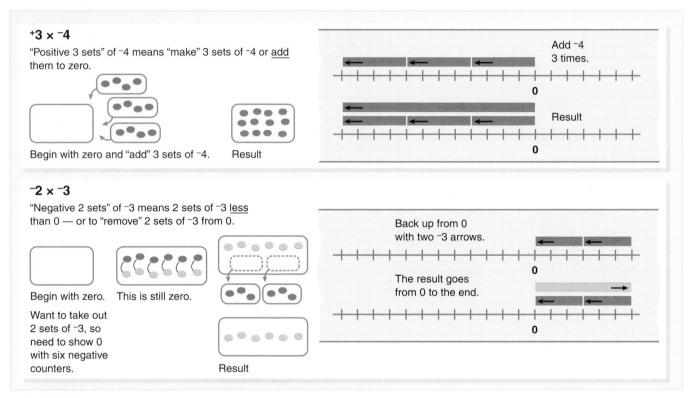

FIGURE 24.8 Multiplication by a positive first factor is repeated addition. Multiplication by a negative first factor is repeated subtraction.

and 3 − 5 each results in ⁻2 and that 3 − ⁻5 and 3 + 5 are also alike.

Multiplication and Division

Multiplication of integers should be a direct extension of multiplication for whole numbers, just as addition and subtraction were connected to whole-number concepts. We frequently refer to whole-number multiplication as repeated addition. The first factor tells how many sets there are or how many are added in all, beginning with 0. This translates to integer multiplication quite readily when the first factor is positive, regardless of the sign of the second factor. The first example in Figure 24.8 illustrates a positive first factor and a negative second factor.

What could the meaning be when the first factor is negative, as in ⁻2 × ⁻3? If a positive first factor means repeated addition (how many times added to 0), a negative first factor should mean repeated subtraction (how many times subtracted from 0). The second example in Figure 24.8 illustrates how multiplication with the first factor negative can be modeled.

The deceptively simple rules of "like signs yield positive products" and "unlike signs yield negative products" are quickly established. However, once more, it is just as important that your students be able to produce answers

correctly and skillfully as that they be able to supply a rationale.

With division of integers, again explore the whole-number case first. Recall that 8 ÷ 4 with whole numbers has two possible meanings corresponding to two missing-factor expressions: 4 × ? = 8 asks, "Four sets of *what* make eight?" whereas ? × 4 = 8 asks, "How many fours make eight?" Generally, the measurement approach (? × 4) is the one used with integers, although both concepts can be exhibited with either model. It is helpful to think of building the dividend with the divisor from 0, or repeated addition—to find the missing factor.

The first example in Figure 24.9 illustrates how the two models work for whole numbers. Following that is an example where the divisor is positive but the dividend is negative.

 *pause and reflect* —————

Try using both models to compute ⁻8 ÷ ⁺2. Draw pictures using Xs and Os and also arrows. Check your understanding with the examples in Figure 24.9. Once you understand that example, try ⁺9 ÷ ⁻3 and also ⁻12 ÷ ⁻4.

—————

The entire understanding of integer division rests on a good concept of a negative first factor for multipli-

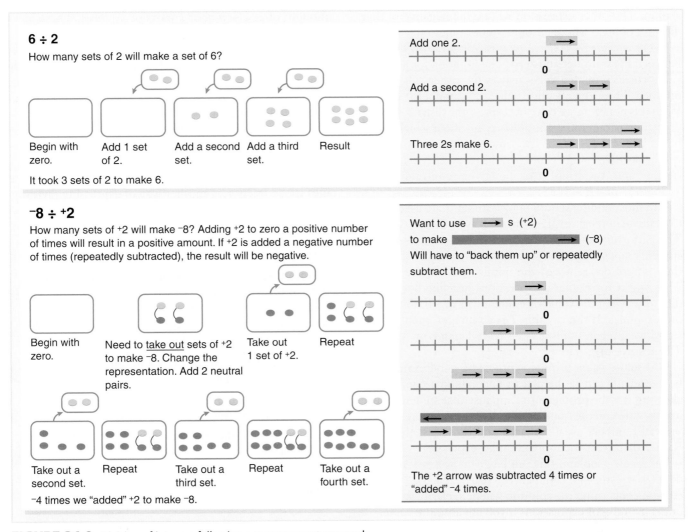

FIGURE 24.9 Division of integers following a measurement approach.

cation and a knowledge of the relationship between multiplication and division.

There is no need to rush your students on to some mastery of use of the models. It is much better that they first think about how to model the whole-number situation and then figure out, with some guidance from you, how to deal with integers.

NCTM Standards "Positive and negative integers should be seen as useful for noting relative changes or values. Students can also appreciate the utility of negative integers when they work with equations whose solution requires them, such as $2x + 7 = 1$" (p. 218).

Absolute Value

The distance between two points, either on the number line or in the plane, is often an important concern, especially in applications of mathematics. We need to be able,

for example, to tell a computer how far a train is from a station regardless of whether it is to the north or the south on the track. "Distance" can also refer to a mathematical distance as in the amount of possible error between a measurement and the true value. Here the measures could be weight, time, voltage, and so on.

When the two endpoint numbers that determine the distance are known, there is no problem—simply subtract the smaller from the larger. But how do you express this distance when the endpoints are variable? For example, if the true weight of an object is denoted by T and the measured weight is given as M, then what expression represents the amount of error between the true and measured values? Is it $T - M$ or $M - T$? You might say, "It depends on which is the greater value." But the values of T and M will change with different measurements. In the case of the train's distance from the station, denote the train's track position at any time t, as P_t. If the station is at mile marker 375, then either $375 - P_t$ or $P_t - 375$ will give the distance from the station. The other expression will be the negative of that distance. This is where absolute value comes in.

The *absolute value of a number* is defined as the distance between that number and zero. The notation for absolute value consists of two vertical bars on either side of the number. Thus, the absolute value of a number n is $|n|$. With this notation, we can now express the distances in the preceding paragraph without worrying about which number is larger. $|T - M|$ is the same as $|M - T|$ and both will be positive values. Similarly, the distance between the station and the train can be given equivalently as $|375 - P_t|$ or $|P_t - 375|$.

In most middle school books, students are asked only to evaluate numeric expressions such as $|-8|$ or $|6 - 10|$. The unfortunate consequence of these exercises is that students quickly learn to simply do the computation and then ignore or "remove" the minus sign if there is one. That works for numeric expressions just fine but causes difficulty when the values are unknowns or variables as in our examples. If the variable T is an integer, then $|T|$ is a positive integer. But is it T or ^-T? It depends on whether T is positive or negative.

Absolute value problems provide a good example of how students can be helped to understand a concept by allowing it to be problematic. Suppose that students have just sketched on the number line all of the solutions to $|x| > 3$ (all numbers greater than 3 and those less than $^-3$). Rather than treat the more complex expression $|2x + 3| > 3$ as a new problem, this can be given as a task for students to wrestle with (Hiebert & Wearne, 2003). The discussion concerning the solution will help clarify students' understanding of expressions involving absolute value.

Rational Numbers

Several number ideas that students have been exposed to in earlier grades, coupled with the ideas of the integers, need to come together in the middle grades. A complete understanding of the rational numbers as positive and negative decimals and equivalently as positive and negative fractions is an important development.

Fractions as Indicated Division

If four people were to share three pizzas, the amount that each would get can be expressed as $3 \div 4$; that is, three things divided four ways. Each person would receive three-fourths of a pizza. So $\frac{3}{4}$ and $3 \div 4$ are both expressions for the same idea: 3 things divided by 4.

In Chapter 15, we saw that this sharing idea is in fact compatible with the part-whole meaning of fractions. With $\frac{3}{4}$ of a pizza, each pizza can be divided into four parts (the denominator) and then each person gets 3 of these $\frac{1}{4}$ pieces (the numerator). And so any fraction $\frac{k}{n}$ can be

thought of as $k \div n$ or as k parts of $\frac{1}{n}$ pieces. These ideas appear quite different but in fact are not.

Students will likely find this division interpretation meaning of fractions unusual. Fractions are commonly thought of as parts of wholes, not as operations. Similarly, expressions such as $7 \div 3$ are thought of as operations (things to be done), not numbers. However, 4, 2 + 2, 12 ÷ 3, and $\frac{8}{2}$ are all symbolic expressions for the same number: $12 \div 3$ is not the question and 4 the answer; both are expressions for 4.

Here is one possible way to help students develop the idea that a fraction is another way of expressing division.

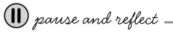
activity **24.3**

How Do You Write It?
Present students with a simple word problem similar to the following: *Zach has 18 meters of rope. He cuts off one-fifth of the rope to make a leash for his dog, Sam. How much rope did he use for the leash?* Three students have solved this problem.

> **Student A:** Zach cut off 3.6 meters because $18 \div 5 = 3.6$.
>
> **Student B:** I did $\frac{1}{5} \times 18$ like this: $\frac{1}{5} \times \frac{18}{1} = \frac{18}{5} = 3\frac{3}{5}$. So the answer is 3 and $\frac{3}{5}$ meters.
>
> **Student C:** I did the same thing, but I just said the answer was $\frac{18}{5}$ meters.

Which student is correct? Which one has the "best" answer?

❙❙ *pause and reflect* ─────────
How would you respond to the questions in Activity 24.3?

─────────────────

In the discussion of a problem situation like the one in Activity 24.3, you can lead students to see that $18 \div 5$ and $\frac{18}{5}$ mean exactly the same thing. All three students are correct.

Similarly, discuss the difference between these three expressions:

$$\frac{1}{4} \text{ of } 24 \qquad \frac{24}{4} \qquad 24 \div 4$$

This discussion can lead to a general development of the idea that a fraction can be thought of as division of the numerator by the denominator or that $\frac{a}{b}$ is the same as $a \div b$.

Fractions as Rational Numbers

Because children tend to think of fractions as parts of sets or objects, they remain, in the minds of children, more physical object than number. This is one reason that students can have such a difficult time placing fractions on a number line. A significant leap toward thinking about fractions as numbers is made when students begin to understand that a decimal is a representation of a fraction. In Chapter 18, we explored the idea of the "friendly" fractions (halves, thirds, fourths, fifths, eighths) in terms of their decimal equivalents.

In the middle grades, it is time to combine all of these ideas:

- $4\frac{3}{5}$ is 4.6 because $\frac{3}{5}$ is six-tenths of a whole, so 4 wholes and six-tenths is 4.6.
- $4\frac{3}{5}$ is $\frac{23}{5}$, and that is the same as $23 \div 5$, or 4.6 if I use decimals.
- 4.6 is read "four and six-tenths," so I can write that as $4\frac{6}{10} = 4\frac{3}{5}$.

What becomes clear in a discussion building on students' existing ideas is that any number, positive or negative, that can be written as a fraction can also be written as a decimal number. You can also reverse this idea and convert decimal numbers to fractions. Keep in mind that the purpose is to see that there are different symbolic notations for the same quantities—not to become skilled at conversions.

When a fraction is converted to a decimal, it is interesting to note that the decimal either terminates (e.g., 3.415) or repeats (e.g., 2.5141414...).

The result of this discussion is a reasonable definition of rational numbers: A *rational number* is any number that can be expressed as a fraction. Equivalently, a *rational number* is any number that can be written as either a terminating or repeating decimal number.

Is there a way to tell if a given fraction is a terminating decimal or a repeating decimal? The answer lies in the denominator. The following activity can be used to discover the rule.

activity 24.4

Repeater or Terminator

Have students generate a table listing in one column the first 20 unit fractions ($\frac{1}{2}, \frac{1}{3}, \frac{1}{4}, \ldots \frac{1}{21}$). In the second column they list the prime factorization of the denominators and in the third column the decimal equivalent for the fraction. Have students use calculators to get the decimal form.

After completing the table, the task is to see if they can discover a rule that will tell in advance if the decimal will repeat or terminate. They can test the rule with fractions with denominators beyond 21. They may also wish to confirm that it makes no difference what the numerator is.

If you try the last activity yourself, you will quickly discover that the only fractions with terminating decimals have denominators that factor with all 2s and/or 5s. The explanation for why this is so is also within the reach of students. For now, that is left to you and your students.

Armed with a reasonable characterization of rational numbers, the following activity can help students develop a better understanding of the structure of the rational number system.

activity 24.5

How Close Is Close?

Have students select any two fractions or any two decimals that they think are "really close." It makes no difference what numbers students pick or even how close together they really are. Now challenge them to find at least ten more numbers (fractions or decimals) that are between these two numbers. Do not be tempted to show students any clever methods for finding the numbers.

"How Close Is Close?" is an opportunity to find out how your students understand fractions and decimals. (The activity should be done in both forms eventually.) If students haven't been told a method, they must rely on their own ideas to come up with a solution. The activity offers a great opportunity for discussion, assessment of individual students' fraction and decimal concepts, and the introduction of perhaps the most interesting feature of the rational number system: density. The rational numbers are said to be *dense* because between any two rational numbers there exists an *infinite* number of other rational numbers.

The density of the rationals makes the irrationals even more amazing.

Real Numbers

As just noted, there are *irrational* numbers, numbers that are not rational. The irrationals together with the rational numbers make up the *real* numbers. The real numbers fill in all the holes on the number line even though the holes are infinitesimally small. Students' first experience with irrational numbers typically occurs when exploring roots of whole numbers.

Introducing the Concept of Roots

The following activity provides a good introduction to square roots and cube roots. From this beginning, the notion of roots of any degree is easily developed.

activity **24.6**

Edges of Squares and Cubes

Show students pictures of three squares (or three cubes) as in Figure 24.10. The edges of the first and last figure are consecutive whole numbers. The areas (volumes) of all three figures are provided. The students' task is to use a calculator to find the edge of the figure in the center. Use of the square root key is not permitted. Solutions will satisfy these equations:

$$\square \times \square = 45, \quad \text{or} \quad \square^2 = 45$$

and

$$\square \times \square \times \square = 30, \quad \text{or} \quad \square^3 = 30$$

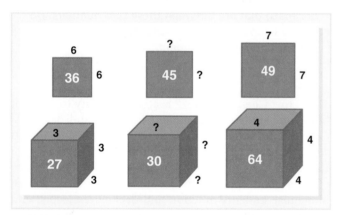

FIGURE 24.10 A geometric interpretation of square roots and cube roots.

In "Edges of Squares and Cubes," the calculator permits students to test a possible edge length to see if it is too long or too short. For example, to solve the cube problem, students might start with 3.5 and find that 3.5^3 is 42.875, much too large. Quickly, they will find that the solution is between 3.1 and 3.2. But where?

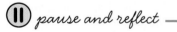 *pause and reflect* ————————————

Use a calculator to continue getting a better approximation of the cube root of 30 to two decimal places.

————————————

From this simple introduction, students can be challenged to find solutions to equations such as $\square^6 = 8$. These students are now prepared to understand the general definition of the *nth root* of a number N as the number that when raised to the *n*th power equals N. The *square* and *cube roots* are simply other names for the second and third roots. The notational convention of the radical sign comes last. It should then be clear that $\sqrt{6}$ is a number

and not an exercise to be done. The cube root of eight is the same as $\sqrt[3]{8}$ which is just another way of writing 2.

NCTM Standards "In grades 6–8, students frequently encounter squares and square roots when they use the Pythagorean relationship. They can use the inverse relationship to determine the approximate location of square roots between whole numbers on a number line" (p. 220). As examples, the authors note that $\sqrt{27}$ is a little more than 5 because $5^2 = 25$ and $\sqrt{99}$ is a little less than 10 since $10^2 = 100$.

Discussing Real Numbers

Eighth-grade students probably do not need a very sophisticated knowledge of the real number system. A few powerful ideas, however, deserve to be explored informally.

Irrational Numbers

One characterization of a rational number is that it can be written as a decimal where the decimal part is either finite or repeats infinitely. Thus, both 3.45 and 87.19363636 . . . are rational numbers and can each be converted to fractional form. But what about a decimal number that just goes on and on, with no repetition? Or what about the number 3.101001000100001000001 . . . ? These never repeat and are not finite and, therefore, are not rational. A real number that is not rational is called *irrational*.

The numbers π and $\sqrt{2}$ are both irrational numbers. The number π is a ratio of two measures in a circle, the circumference and the diameter. Although it is not possible to prove the irrationality of π at this level, the fact that it is irrational implies that it is impossible to have a circle with the lengths of both the circumference and the diameter rational. (Why?) A proof that $\sqrt{2}$ is irrational typically begins by assuming that $\sqrt{2}$ *is* rational, which then leads to a contradiction. This type of proof may be too difficult for middle school students.

Density of the Real Numbers

If the density of the rationals is impressive, even more astounding is that the irrationals are also dense. And the irrationals and the rationals are all mixed up together. The density of the irrationals is not as easy to demonstrate and is not within the scope of the middle school.

Rational Roots

One reason it is difficult to comprehend irrational numbers is that we have very little firsthand experience with them. The ones we are most familiar with are roots of numbers. For example, we just noted that students are frequently shown a proof for the irrationality of $\sqrt{2}$. An intuitive notion of that fact is difficult to come by. Most calculators will show only eight to ten digits, requiring a leap of faith to accept that the decimal representation is infinitely long and nonrepeating.

Unfortunately, what can happen is that whenever students see the radical sign, they think the number is irrational. A possible approach is to consider roots from the opposite direction. Rather than ask what is the square root of 64 or the cube root of 27, we might suggest that *every* number is the square root, the cube root, the fourth root, and so on, of some number (3 is the second root of 9, the third root of 27, etc.). From this vantage point, students can see that "square root" is just a way of indicating a relationship between two numbers. That the cube root of 27 is 3 indicates a special relationship between 3 and 27.

 Many books emphasize rules and exercises at the expense of opportunities for explorations. Activities like "What's in an Expression?" provide good opportunities to see how students reason, communicate ideas, go beyond the answer to generate their own ideas, and generally do mathematics. Once students have learned the relatively simple definition of what an exponent is, the search for easy tricks for multiplying and dividing should be left to students' discovery and their own reasoning. The discussions that ensue will be better than drilling rules about adding exponents when you multiply numbers with like bases. These are good opportunities to assess mathematical power.

With respect to integers, if the rules for operating on the integers are developed by the students themselves, not only will students have a deeper understanding, but you will have an opportunity to observe and assess their mathematical power.

Similar comments can be made about fractions and decimal relationships and rational numbers. The development of reasoning ability and students' belief that they can do mathematics is far more important than drilling rules. ■

Literature Connections

Some topics in this chapter present opportunities for "playing around" with ideas and numbers. Although most teachers in the middle grades do not think of using literature as a springboard for mathematics, here are a few ideas that offer a change of pace in the upper grades.

The Number Devil
Enzensberger, 1997

Full of humor and wit, of imagination like that found in *Alice in Wonderland*, and the author's clear passion for numbers and their relationships, *The Number Devil* lays out a collection of interesting ideas about numbers in 12 easily read chapters. Robert, a boy who hates mathematics, meets up with a crafty number devil in each of 12 dreams. The dreams cover intricacies of the Fibonacci sequence

and issues related to prime numbers, number tricks, Roman numerals, and more. On the fourth night, Robert learns about infinitely repeating decimals and the "Rutabaga of two" (the square root of two).

Reading any one chapter aloud to students in the middle grades would be 15 minutes well invested even without exploring the concepts further. The simple pictures add to the fun.

The Phantom Tollbooth
Juster, 1961

Milo's remarkable journey through the lands beyond the magic tollbooth are so full of wonderful words and ideas that the story is a must to read and discuss with adolescents regardless of the potential mathematical content. But the first page of Chapter 14, with its road sign indicating three directions to Digitopolis, is worthy of time in your mathematics class. The sign reads:

DIGITOPOLIS

5	Miles
1600	Rods
8800	Yards
26,400	Feet
316,800	Inches
633,600	Half inches

AND THEN SOME

The discussion about which road is shorter or quicker is just great. Three pages later, Milo is told, "Why, did you know that if a beaver two feet long with a tail a foot and a half long can build a dam twelve feet high and six feet wide in two days, all you would need to build Boulder Dam is a beaver sixty-eight feet long with a fifty-one foot tail?" (p. 175). In the next chapter is an equally humorous discussion of infinity. That is followed by the chapter in which Milo meets the 0.58 boy.

Not only are these fanciful ideas in a story filled with excellent language, but there are also opportunities to wonder what if or to create similar fantasies based on numbers. For example, students could write a new chapter for the book in which Milo journeys to a world in outer space where the distances are enormous and everyone uses scientific notation.

In the Next Three Seconds
Morgan, 1997

A fascinating book of numbers and amazing statistics is built around things that happen around the world in three seconds, three minutes, three days, . . . , three centuries. "In the next three minutes Americans will eat four and half head of cattle as take-out hamburgers." Thiessen, Mathias, and Smith (1998) write, "Written in a style that is entertaining and humorous, this book also astonishes readers as it raises their level of concern about the preservation of our earth and its resources" (p. 139). Here is a book that will illuminate real-life data and have students exploring their own ideas about things that are happening in our world.

Math Curse
Scieszka and Smith, 1995

This book was an instant hit probably because there are so many people out there who have math phobias. The first page sets the tone: "On Monday in math class Mrs. Fibonacci says, 'You know, you can think of almost everything as a math problem.' On Tuesday I start to have problems." Some may argue that this book is so anti-mathematics that it has no place in the middle grades. But it does provide an opportunity to show your human side as you discuss a wide range of mathematical ideas. ■

Reflections on Chapter 24

Writing to Learn

1. Explain the value of the graphing calculator's ability to display a complete arithmetic expression (with or without a variable) on a single line and to evaluate it on another line.
2. How can a calculator be used to explore the order-of-operations convention? Why is this rule something you must simply tell students?
3. Explain how powers of 10 are used to write very small and very large numbers. What is the particular form of the power-of-10 symbolism used in scientific notation and on calculators? What is the value of this notation?
4. Why is it probably better to use two different models for the integers even if one of the two seems to cause students some confusion?
5. Use both the arrow model and the counter model to demonstrate the following:

$$^-10 + {}^+13 = {}^+3 \qquad ^-4 - {}^-9 = {}^+5 \qquad ^+6 - {}^-7 = {}^+13$$

$$^-4 \times {}^-3 = {}^+12 \qquad ^+15 \div {}^-5 = {}^-3 \qquad ^-12 \div {}^-3 = {}^+4$$

6. How can you help students understand that a fraction such as $\frac{7}{8}$ means the same thing as $7 \div 8$?
7. How would you explain the difference between a rational and an irrational number to a middle school student?
8. What does $\sqrt{6}$ mean? How is $\sqrt{6}$ different from $\sqrt{4}$? How are they the same?
9. What does it mean to say that the rational numbers are dense?

For Discussion and Exploration

1. A traditional self-contained Algebra I course groups the content of this chapter with an additional focus on factoring polynomials and other symbolic manipulations. Does your local school system have an Algebra I course in grade 8? Do you think it should? What are some of the pros and cons of a special course?
2. Examine the table of contents in sixth-, seventh-, and eighth-grade books from two or three different publishers or books specifically intended for middle school mathematics. Using these books as a guide, how would you define "prealgebra"? How much of the curriculum of these three grade levels seems repetitious? Is this the same for all publishers?
3. Use a calculator for the following exercises:
   a. What do you think will happen if you enter 1000 in your calculator and then press ⊞ 2 ⊜ ⊜ ...? Try it.
   b. What do you think will happen if you enter 1000 in your calculator and then repeatedly press the √ key? Before you try it, try to explain why you think it will happen.

Recommendations for Further Reading

Fitzgerald, W., Winter, M. J., Lappan, G., & Phillips, E. (1986). *Middle grades mathematics project: Factors and multiples.* Menlo Park, CA: AWL Supplemental.
   This book is one in a series of five that has stood the test of time. The related topics of prime, factor, composite, prime factorization, divisor, multiple, common multiple, common factor, and relatively prime number are all developed in a series of interesting games and activities for the middle grades. The focus is on pattern development and logical connections. This is a good way to involve students in good mathematics without overwhelming them with tedious algebraic ideas.

Graeber, A. O., & Baker, K. M. (1992). Little into big is the way it always is. *Arithmetic Teacher, 39*(8), 18–21.
   This is one of the few articles that discusses the issue of a fraction as an indicated division. The authors look at practices in the elementary school that suggest why the difficulty exists and make practical suggestions for working with middle school students.

Phillips, E., Gardella, T., Kelly, C., & Stewart, J. (1991). *Patterns and functions: Addenda series, grades 5–8.* Reston, VA: National Council of Teachers of Mathematics.
   The *Addenda Series* is still a good place to go for excellent activities. In this volume, you will find sections on exponents

and growth patterns, number theory and counting patterns, and rational number patterns. Other topics in the book are related more to the concepts of function and variable.

Reeves, C. A., & Webb, D. (2004). Balloons on the rise: A problem-solving approach to integers. *Mathematics Teaching in the Middle School, 9*, 476–482.

Expanding on a discussion of the possibility of helium party balloons making you weigh less if held while on a scale, the fifth-grade students in this article generalize the concepts of integers and use their ideas for addition and subtraction. The authors point clearly to the value of a context to help students develop a new concept.

Online Resources

Suggested Applets and Web Links

Color Chips (NLVM)
http://nlvm.usu.edu/en/nav/frames_asid_161_g_2_t_1.html
This applet is an e-version of the chip model for integer arithmetic. Positive and negative chips or pairs of chips can be dragged to and from a workspace to model addition or subtraction.

The Evolution of the Real Numbers
www.themathpage.com/aReal/real-numbers.htm
This is an interesting description of many topics that lead up to the definition and exploration of the real number system. Although mostly text, the pages are filled with interactive questions. Useful information that is not too technical.

Tic-Tac-Go (Freudenthal Institute)
www.fi.uu.nl/toepassingen/03088/toepassing_wisweb.en.html
This applet provides simple drill of integer arithmetic.

An additional list of books and articles related to the ideas in this chapter can be found on the Companion Web site at **www.ablongman.com/vandewalle6e.**

appendix **A**

Principles and Standards for School Mathematics

Content Standards and Grade Level Expectations

Source: Reprinted with permission from *Principles and Standards for School Mathematics*. Copyright ©2000 by the National Council of Teachers of Mathematics. All rights reserved.

Number and Operations

STANDARD

Instructional programs from prekindergarten through grade 12 should enable all students to—

STANDARD	Pre-K–2 Expectations	Grades 3–5 Expectations
	In prekindergarten through grade 2 all students should—	In grades 3–5 all students should—
Understand numbers, ways of representing numbers, relationships among numbers, and number systems	• count with understanding and recognize "how many" in sets of objects; • use multiple models to develop initial understandings of place value and the base-ten number system; • develop understanding of the relative position and magnitude of whole numbers and of ordinal and cardinal numbers and their connections; • develop a sense of whole numbers and represent and use them in flexible ways, including relating, composing, and decomposing numbers; • connect number words and numerals to the quantities they represent, using various physical models and representations; • understand and represent commonly used fractions, such as 1/4, 1/3, and 1/2.	• understand the place-value structure of the base-ten number system and be able to represent and compare whole numbers and decimals; • recognize equivalent representations for the same number and generate them by decomposing and composing numbers; • develop understanding of fractions as parts of unit wholes, as parts of a collection, as locations on number lines, and as divisions of whole numbers; • use models, benchmarks, and equivalent forms to judge the size of fractions; • recognize and generate equivalent forms of commonly used fractions, decimals, and percents; • explore numbers less than 0 by extending the number line and through familiar applications; • describe classes of numbers according to characteristics such as the nature of their factors.
Understand meanings of operations and how they relate to one another	• understand various meanings of addition and subtraction of whole numbers and the relationship between the two operations; • understand the effects of adding and subtracting whole numbers; • understand situations that entail multiplication and division, such as equal groupings of objects and sharing equally.	• understand various meanings of multiplication and division; • understand the effects of multiplying and dividing whole numbers; • identify and use relationships between operations, such as division as the inverse of multiplication, to solve problems; • understand and use properties of operations, such as the distributivity of multiplication over addition.
Compute fluently and make reasonable estimates	• develop and use strategies for whole-number computations, with a focus on addition and subtraction; • develop fluency with basic number combinations for addition and subtraction; • use a variety of methods and tools to compute, including objects, mental computation, estimation, paper and pencil, and calculators.	• develop fluency with basic number combinations for multiplication and division and use these combinations to mentally compute related problems, such as 30×50; • develop fluency in adding, subtracting, multiplying, and dividing whole numbers; • develop and use strategies to estimate the results of whole-number computations and to judge the reasonableness of such results; • develop and use strategies to estimate computations involving fractions and decimals in situations relevant to students' experience; • use visual models, benchmarks, and equivalent forms to add and subtract commonly used fractions and decimals; • select appropriate methods and tools for computing with whole numbers from among mental computation, estimation, calculators, and paper and pencil according to the context and nature of the computation and use the selected method or tool.

Number and Operations

STANDARD

Instructional programs from prekindergarten through grade 12 should enable all students to—

STANDARD	Grades 6–8	Grades 9–12
	Expectations In grades 6–8 all students should—	**Expectations** In grades 9–12 all students should—
Understand numbers, ways of representing numbers, relationships among numbers, and number systems	• work flexibly with fractions, decimals, and percents to solve problems; • compare and order fractions, decimals, and percents efficiently and find their approximate locations on a number line; • develop meaning for percents greater than 100 and less than 1; • understand and use ratios and proportions to represent quantitative relationships; • develop an understanding of large numbers and recognize and appropriately use exponential, scientific, and calculator notation; • use factors, multiples, prime factorization, and relatively prime numbers to solve problems; • develop meaning for integers and represent and compare quantities with them.	• develop a deeper understanding of very large and very small numbers and of various representations of them; • compare and contrast the properties of numbers and number systems, including the rational and real numbers, and understand complex numbers as solutions to quadratic equations that do not have real solutions; • understand vectors and matrices as systems that have some of the properties of the real-number system; • use number-theory arguments to justify relationships involving whole numbers.
Understand meanings of operations and how they relate to one another	• understand the meaning and effects of arithmetic operations with fractions, decimals, and integers; • use the associative and commutative properties of addition and multiplication and the distributive property of multiplication over addition to simplify computations with integers, fractions, and decimals; • understand and use the inverse relationships of addition and subtraction, multiplication and division, and squaring and finding square roots to simplify computations and solve problems.	• judge the effects of such operations as multiplication, division, and computing powers and roots on the magnitudes of quantities; • develop an understanding of properties of, and representations for, the addition and multiplication of vectors and matrices; • develop an understanding of permutations and combinations as counting techniques.
Compute fluently and make reasonable estimates	• select appropriate methods and tools for computing with fractions and decimals from among mental computation, estimation, calculators or computers, and paper and pencil, depending on the situation, and apply the selected methods; • develop and analyze algorithms for computing with fractions, decimals, and integers and develop fluency in their use; • develop and use strategies to estimate the results of rational-number computations and judge the reasonableness of the results; • develop, analyze, and explain methods for solving problems involving proportions, such as scaling and finding equivalent ratios.	• develop fluency in operations with real numbers, vectors, and matrices, using mental computation or paper-and-pencil calculations for simple cases and technology for more-complicated cases; • judge the reasonableness of numerical computations and their results.

Algebra
STANDARD

Instructional programs from prekindergarten through grade 12 should enable all students to—

	Pre-K–2	Grades 3–5
	Expectations	**Expectations**
	In prekindergarten through grade 2 all students should—	In grades 3–5 all students should—
Understand patterns, relations, and functions	• sort, classify, and order objects by size, number, and other properties; • recognize, describe, and extend patterns such as sequences of sounds and shapes or simple numeric patterns and translate from one representation to another; • analyze how both repeating and growing patterns are generated.	• describe, extend, and make generalizations about geometric and numeric patterns; • represent and analyze patterns and functions, using words, tables, and graphs.
Represent and analyze mathematical situations and structures using algebraic symbols	• illustrate general principles and properties of operations, such as commutativity, using specific numbers; • use concrete, pictorial, and verbal representations to develop an understanding of invented and conventional symbolic notations.	• identify such properties as commutativity, associativity, and distributivity and use them to compute with whole numbers; • represent the idea of a variable as an unknown quantity using a letter or a symbol; • express mathematical relationships using equations.
Use mathematical models to represent and understand quantitative relationships	• model situations that involve the addition and subtraction of whole numbers, using objects, pictures, and symbols.	• model problem situations with objects and use representations such as graphs, tables, and equations to draw conclusions.
Analyze change in various contexts	• describe qualitative change, such as a student's growing taller; • describe quantitative change, such as a student's growing two inches in one year.	• investigate how a change in one variable relates to a change in a second variable; • identify and describe situations with constant or varying rates of change and compare them.

Algebra
STANDARD

Instructional programs from prekindergarten through grade 12 should enable all students to—

	Grades 6–8 **Expectations** In grades 6–8 all students should—	Grades 9–12 **Expectations** In grades 9–12 all students should—
Understand patterns, relations, and functions	• represent, analyze, and generalize a variety of patterns with tables, graphs, words, and, when possible, symbolic rules; • relate and compare different forms of representation for a relationship; • identify functions as linear or nonlinear and contrast their properties from tables, graphs, or equations.	• generalize patterns using explicitly defined and recursively defined functions; • understand relations and functions and select, convert flexibly among, and use various representations for them; • analyze functions of one variable by investigating rates of change, intercepts, zeros, asymptotes, and local and global behavior; • understand and perform transformations such as arithmetically combining, composing, and inverting commonly used functions, using technology to perform such operations on more-complicated symbolic expressions; • understand and compare the properties of classes of functions, including exponential, polynomial, rational, logarithmic, and periodic functions; • interpret representations of functions of two variables.
Represent and analyze mathematical situations and structures using algebraic symbols	• develop an initial conceptual understanding of different uses of variables; • explore relationships between symbolic expressions and graphs of lines, paying particular attention to the meaning of intercept and slope; • use symbolic algebra to represent situations and to solve problems, especially those that involve linear relationships; • recognize and generate equivalent forms for simple algebraic expressions and solve linear equations.	• understand the meaning of equivalent forms of expressions, equations, inequalities, and relations; • write equivalent forms of equations, inequalities, and systems of equations and solve them with fluency—mentally or with paper and pencil in simple cases and using technology in all cases; • use symbolic algebra to represent and explain mathematical relationships; • use a variety of symbolic representations, including recursive and parametric equations, for functions and relations; • judge the meaning, utility, and reasonableness of the results of symbol manipulations, including those carried out by technology.
Use mathematical models to represent and understand quantitative relationships	• model and solve contextualized problems using various representations, such as graphs, tables, and equations.	• identify essential quantitative relationships in a situation and determine the class or classes of functions that might model the relationships; • use symbolic expressions, including iterative and recursive forms, to represent relationships arising from various contexts; • draw reasonable conclusions about a situation being modeled.
Analyze change in various contexts	• use graphs to analyze the nature of changes in quantities in linear relationships.	• approximate and interpret rates of change from graphical and numerical data.

Geometry

STANDARD

Instructional programs from prekindergarten through grade 12 should enable all students to—

	Pre-K–2 Expectations	Grades 3–5 Expectations
	In prekindergarten through grade 2 all students should—	In grades 3–5 all students should—
Analyze characteristics and properties of two- and three-dimensional geometric shapes and develop mathematical arguments about geometric relationships	• recognize, name, build, draw, compare, and sort two- and three-dimensional shapes; • describe attributes and parts of two- and three-dimensional shapes; • investigate and predict the results of putting together and taking apart two- and three-dimensional shapes.	• identify, compare, and analyze attributes of two- and three-dimensional shapes and develop vocabulary to describe the attributes; • classify two- and three-dimensional shapes according to their properties and develop definitions of classes of shapes such as triangles and pyramids; • investigate, describe, and reason about the results of subdividing, combining, and transforming shapes; • explore congruence and similarity; • make and test conjectures about geometric properties and relationships and develop logical arguments to justify conclusions.
Specify locations and describe spatial relationships using coordinate geometry and other representational systems	• describe, name, and interpret relative positions in space and apply ideas about relative position; • describe, name, and interpret direction and distance in navigating space and apply ideas about direction and distance; • find and name locations with simple relationships such as "near to" and in coordinate systems such as maps.	• describe location and movement using common language and geometric vocabulary; • make and use coordinate systems to specify locations and to describe paths; • find the distance between points along horizontal and vertical lines of a coordinate system.
Apply transformations and use symmetry to analyze mathematical situations	• recognize and apply slides, flips, and turns; • recognize and create shapes that have symmetry.	• predict and describe the results of sliding, flipping, and turning two-dimensional shapes; • describe a motion or a series of motions that will show that two shapes are congruent; • identify and describe line and rotational symmetry in two- and three-dimensional shapes and designs.
Use visualization, spatial reasoning, and geometric modeling to solve problems	• create mental images of geometric shapes using spatial memory and spatial visualization; • recognize and represent shapes from different perspectives; • relate ideas in geometry to ideas in number and measurement; • recognize geometric shapes and structures in the environment and specify their location.	• build and draw geometric objects; • create and describe mental images of objects, patterns, and paths; • identify and build a three-dimensional object from two-dimensional representations of that object; • identify and build a two-dimensional representation of a three-dimensional object; • use geometric models to solve problems in other areas of mathematics, such as number and measurement; • recognize geometric ideas and relationships and apply them to other disciplines and to problems that arise in the classroom or in everyday life.

Geometry
STANDARD

Instructional programs from prekindergarten through grade 12 should enable all students to—

	Grades 6–8	Grades 9–12
	Expectations	**Expectations**
	In grades 6–8 all students should—	In grades 9–12 all students should—
Analyze characteristics and properties of two- and three-dimensional geometric shapes and develop mathematical arguments about geometric relationships	• precisely describe, classify, and understand relationships among types of two- and three-dimensional objects using their defining properties; • understand relationships among the angles, side lengths, perimeters, areas, and volumes of similar objects; • create and critique inductive and deductive arguments concerning geometric ideas and relationships, such as congruence, similarity, and the Pythagorean relationship.	• analyze properties and determine attributes of two- and three-dimensional objects; • explore relationships (including congruence and similarity) among classes of two- and three-dimensional geometric objects, make and test conjectures about them, and solve problems involving them; • establish the validity of geometric conjectures using deduction, prove theorems, and critique arguments made by others; • use trigonometric relationships to determine lengths and angle measures.
Specify locations and describe spatial relationships using coordinate geometry and other representational systems	• use coordinate geometry to represent and examine the properties of geometric shapes; • use coordinate geometry to examine special geometric shapes, such as regular polygons or those with pairs of parallel or perpendicular sides.	• use Cartesian coordinates and other coordinate systems, such as navigational, polar, or spherical systems, to analyze geometric situations; • investigate conjectures and solve problems involving two- and three-dimensional objects represented with Cartesian coordinates.
Apply transformations and use symmetry to analyze mathematical situations	• describe sizes, positions, and orientations of shapes under informal transformations such as flips, turns, slides, and scaling; • examine the congruence, similarity, and line or rotational symmetry of objects using transformations.	• understand and represent translations, reflections, rotations, and dilations of objects in the plane by using sketches, coordinates, vectors, function notation, and matrices; • use various representations to help understand the effects of simple transformations and their compositions.
Use visualization, spatial reasoning, and geometric modeling to solve problems	• draw geometric objects with specified properties, such as side lengths or angle measures; • use two-dimensional representations of three-dimensional objects to visualize and solve problems such as those involving surface area and volume; • use visual tools such as networks to represent and solve problems; • use geometric models to represent and explain numerical and algebraic relationships; • recognize and apply geometric ideas and relationships in areas outside the mathematics classroom, such as art, science, and everyday life.	• draw and construct representations of two- and three-dimensional geometric objects using a variety of tools; • visualize three-dimensional objects from different perspectives and analyze their cross sections; • use vertex-edge graphs to model and solve problems; • use geometric models to gain insights into, and answer questions in, other areas of mathematics; • use geometric ideas to solve problems in, and gain insights into, other disciplines and other areas of interest such as art and architecture.

Measurement

STANDARD

Instructional programs from prekindergarten through grade 12 should enable all students to—

	Pre-K–2	Grades 3–5
	Expectations	**Expectations**
	In prekindergarten through grade 2 all students should—	In grades 3–5 all students should—
Understand measurable attributes of objects and the units, systems, and processes of measurement	• recognize the attributes of length, volume, weight, area, and time; • compare and order objects according to these attributes; • understand how to measure using nonstandard and standard units; • select an appropriate unit and tool for the attribute being measured.	• understand such attributes as length, area, weight, volume, and size of angle and select the appropriate type of unit for measuring each attribute; • understand the need for measuring with standard units and become familiar with standard units in the customary and metric systems; • carry out simple unit conversions, such as from centimeters to meters, within a system of measurement; • understand that measurements are approximations and understand how differences in units affect precision; • explore what happens to measurements of a two-dimensional shape such as its perimeter and area when the shape is changed in some way.
Apply appropriate techniques, tools, and formulas to determine measurements	• measure with multiple copies of units of the same size, such as paper clips laid end to end; • use repetition of a single unit to measure something larger than the unit, for instance, measuring the length of a room with a single meterstick; • use tools to measure; • develop common referents for measures to make comparisons and estimates.	• develop strategies for estimating the perimeters, areas, and volumes of irregular shapes; • select and apply appropriate standard units and tools to measure length, area, volume, weight, time, temperature, and the size of angles; • select and use benchmarks to estimate measurements; • develop, understand, and use formulas to find the area of rectangles and related triangles and parallelograms; • develop strategies to determine the surface areas and volumes of rectangular solids.

Measurement

STANDARD

Instructional programs from prekindergarten through grade 12 should enable all students to—

	Grades 6–8	Grades 9–12
	Expectations	**Expectations**
	In grades 6–8 all students should—	In grades 9–12 all students should—
Understand measurable attributes of objects and the units, systems, and processes of measurement	• understand both metric and customary systems of measurement; • understand relationships among units and convert from one unit to another within the same system; • understand, select, and use units of appropriate size and type to measure angles, perimeter, area, surface area, and volume.	• make decisions about units and scales that are appropriate for problem situations involving measurement.
Apply appropriate techniques, tools, and formulas to determine measurements	• use common benchmarks to select appropriate methods for estimating measurements; • select and apply techniques and tools to accurately find length, area, volume, and angle measures to appropriate levels of precision; • develop and use formulas to determine the circumference of circles and the area of triangles, parallelograms, trapezoids, and circles and develop strategies to find the area of more-complex shapes; • develop strategies to determine the surface area and volume of selected prisms, pyramids, and cylinders; • solve problems involving scale factors, using ratio and proportion; • solve simple problems involving rates and derived measurements for such attributes as velocity and density.	• analyze precision, accuracy, and approximate error in measurement situations; • understand and use formulas for the area, surface area, and volume of geometric figures, including cones, spheres, and cylinders; • apply informal concepts of successive approximation, upper and lower bounds, and limit in measurement situations; • use unit analysis to check measurement computations.

Data Analysis and Probability

STANDARD

Instructional programs from prekindergarten through grade 12 should enable all students to—

	Pre-K–2 Expectations	Grades 3–5 Expectations
	In prekindergarten through grade 2 all students should—	In grades 3–5 all students should—
Formulate questions that can be addressed with data and collect, organize, and display relevant data to answer them	• pose questions and gather data about themselves and their surroundings; • sort and classify objects according to their attributes and organize data about the objects; • represent data using concrete objects, pictures, and graphs.	• design investigations to address a question and consider how data-collection methods affect the nature of the data set; • collect data using observations, surveys, and experiments; • represent data using tables and graphs such as line plots, bar graphs, and line graphs; • recognize the differences in representing categorical and numerical data.
Select and use appropriate statistical methods to analyze data	• describe parts of the data and the set of data as a whole to determine what the data show.	• describe the shape and important features of a set of data and compare related data sets, with an emphasis on how the data are distributed; • use measures of center, focusing on the median, and understand what each does and does not indicate about the data set; • compare different representations of the same data and evaluate how well each representation shows important aspects of the data.
Develop and evaluate inferences and predictions that are based on data	• discuss events related to students' experiences as likely or unlikely.	• propose and justify conclusions and predictions that are based on data and design studies to further investigate the conclusions or predictions.
Understand and apply basic concepts of probability		• describe events as likely or unlikely and discuss the degree of likelihood using such words as certain, equally likely, and impossible; • predict the probability of outcomes of simple experiments and test the predictions; • understand that the measure of the likelihood of an event can be represented by a number from 0 to 1.

Data Analysis and Probability

STANDARD

Instructional programs from prekindergarten through grade 12 should enable all students to—

STANDARD	Grades 6–8 Expectations	Grades 9–12 Expectations
	In grades 6–8 all students should—	In grades 9–12 all students should—
Formulate questions that can be addressed with data and collect, organize, and display relevant data to answer them	• formulate questions, design studies, and collect data about a characteristic shared by two populations or different characteristics within one population; • select, create, and use appropriate graphical representations of data, including histograms, box plots, and scatterplots.	• understand the differences among various kinds of studies and which types of inferences can legitimately be drawn from each; • know the characteristics of well-designed studies, including the role of randomization in surveys and experiments; • understand the meaning of measurement data and categorical data, of univariate and bivariate data, and of the term variable; • understand histograms, parallel box plots, and scatterplots and use them to display data; • compute basic statistics and understand the distinction between a statistic and a parameter.
Select and use appropriate statistical methods to analyze data	• find, use, and interpret measures of center and spread, including mean and interquartile range; • discuss and understand the correspondence between data sets and their graphical representations, especially histograms, stem-and-leaf plots, box plots, and scatterplots.	• for univariate measurement data, be able to display the distribution, describe its shape, and select and calculate summary statistics; • for bivariate measurement data, be able to display a scatterplot, describe its shape, and determine regression coefficients, regression equations, and correlation coefficients using technological tools; • display and discuss bivariate data where at least one variable is categorical; • recognize how linear transformations of univariate data affect shape, center, and spread; • identify trends in bivariate data and find functions that model the data or transform the data so that they can be modeled.
Develop and evaluate inferences and predictions that are based on data	• use observations about differences between two or more samples to make conjectures about the populations from which the samples were taken; • make conjectures about possible relationships between two characteristics of a sample on the basis of scatterplots of the data and approximate lines of fit; • use conjectures to formulate new questions and plan new studies to answer them.	• use simulations to explore the variability of sample statistics from a known population and to construct sampling distributions; • understand how sample statistics reflect the values of population parameters and use sampling distributions as the basis for informal inference; • evaluate published reports that are based on data by examining the design of the study, the appropriateness of the data analysis, and the validity of conclusions; • understand how basic statistical techniques are used to monitor process characteristics in the workplace.
Understand and apply basic concepts of probability	• understand and use appropriate terminology to describe complementary and mutually exclusive events; • use proportionality and a basic understanding of probability to make and test conjectures about the results of experiments and simulations; • compute probabilities for simple compound events, using such methods as organized lists, tree diagrams, and area models.	• understand the concepts of sample space and probability distribution and construct sample spaces and distributions in simple cases; • use simulations to construct empirical probability distributions; • compute and interpret the expected value of random variables in simple cases; • understand the concepts of conditional probability and independent events; • understand how to compute the probability of a compound event.

appendix B

Professional Standards for Teaching Mathematics

Teaching Standards

1. Worthwhile Mathematical Tasks

The teacher of mathematics should pose tasks that are based on

- Sound and significant mathematics
- Knowledge of students' understandings, interests, and experiences
- Knowledge of the range of ways that diverse students learn mathematics

and that

- Engage students' intellect
- Develop students' mathematical understandings and skills
- Stimulate students to make connections and develop a coherent framework for mathematical ideas
- Call for problem formulation, problem solving, and mathematical reasoning
- Promote communication about mathematics
- Represent mathematics as an ongoing human activity
- Display sensitivity to, and draw on, students' diverse background experiences and dispositions
- Promote the development of all students' dispositions to do mathematics

2. Teacher's Role in Discourse

The teacher of mathematics should orchestrate discourse by

- Posing questions and tasks that elicit, engage, and challenge each student's thinking
- Listening carefully to students' ideas
- Asking students to clarify and justify their ideas orally and in writing
- Deciding what to pursue in depth from among the ideas that students bring up during a discussion
- Deciding when and how to attach mathematical notation and language to students' ideas
- Deciding when to provide information, when to clarify an issue, when to model, when to lead, and when to let a student struggle with a difficulty
- Monitoring students' participation in discussions and deciding when and how to encourage each student to participate

3. Students' Role in Discourse

The teacher of mathematics should promote classroom discourse in which students

- Listen to, respond to, and question the teacher and one another
- Use a variety of tools to reason, make connections, solve problems, and communicate
- Initiate problems and questions
- Make conjectures and present solutions
- Explore examples and counterexamples to investigate a conjecture
- Try to convince themselves and one another of the validity of particular representations, solutions, conjectures, and answers
- Rely on mathematical evidence and argument to determine validity

4. Tools for Enhancing Discourse

The teacher of mathematics, in order to enhance discourse, should encourage and accept the use of

- Computers, calculators, and other technology
- Concrete materials used as models
- Pictures, diagrams, tables, and graphs
- Invented and conventional terms and symbols
- Metaphors, analogies, and stories
- Written hypotheses, explanations, and arguments
- Oral presentations and dramatizations

5. Learning Environment

The teacher of mathematics should create a learning environment that fosters the development of each student's mathematical power by

- Providing and structuring the time necessary to explore sound mathematics and grapple with significant ideas and problems
- Using the physical space and materials in ways that facilitate students' learning of mathematics
- Providing a context that encourages the development of mathematical skill and proficiency
- Respecting and valuing students' ideas, ways of thinking, and mathematical dispositions

and by consistently expecting and encouraging students to

- Work independently or collaboratively to make sense of mathematics
- Take intellectual risks by raising questions and formulating conjectures
- Display a sense of mathematical competence by validating and supporting ideas with mathematical argument

6. Analysis of Teaching and Learning

The teacher of mathematics should engage in ongoing analysis of teaching and learning by

- Observing, listening to, and gathering other information about students to assess what they are learning
- Examining effects of the tasks, discourse, and learning environment on students' mathematical knowledge, skills, and dispositions

in order to

- Ensure that every student is learning sound and significant mathematics and is developing a positive disposition toward mathematics
- Challenge and extend students' ideas
- Adapt or change activities while teaching
- Make plans, both short- and long-range
- Describe and comment on each student's learning to parents and administrators, as well as to the students themselves

appendix C

Guide to Blackline Masters

This Appendix contains images of all of the Blackline Masters that are listed below. The actual masters can be found in either of two places:

- In hard copy at the end of the Field Experience Guide
- On the Companion Web site (www.ablongman.com/vandewalle6e)

More-or-less cards   1
Number cards   2
Dot cards   3–8
Five-frame   9
Ten-frame   10
Double ten-frame   11
10 × 10 multiplication array   12
Missing-part blanks   13
Base-ten materials grid   14
Little ten-frames   15–16
Place-value mat (with ten-frames)   17
Base-ten grid paper   18
Addition and subtraction record blanks   19
Multiplication and division record blanks   20
Blank hundreds chart (10 × 10 square)   21
Hundreds chart   22
Four small hundreds charts   23
Circular fraction pieces   24–26
10 × 10 grids   27
Hundredths disk   28
10,000 grid   29
Look-alike rectangles   30
Look-alike rectangles recording sheet   31
Degrees and wedges   32
Clock faces   33
2-cm square grid   34
1-cm square grid   35
0.5-cm square grid   36
1-cm square dot grid   37
2-cm isometric grid   38
1-cm isometric dot grid   39
1-cm square/diagonal grid   40
Assorted shapes   41–47
Coordinate grid   48
Geoboard pattern   49
Geoboard recording sheets   50
Tangrams and Mosaic Puzzle   51
Motion Man   52–53
Property lists for quadrilaterals   54–57
Assorted triangles   58
Woozle Cards   59

Suggestions for Use and Construction of Materials

Card Stock Materials

A good way to have many materials made quickly and easily for students is to have them duplicated on card stock at a photocopy store. Card stock is a heavy paper that comes in a variety of colors. It is also called *cover stock* or *index stock*. The price is about twice that of paper.

Card stock can be laminated and then cut into smaller pieces, if desired. The laminate adheres very well. Laminate first, and then cut into pieces afterward. Otherwise you will need to cut each piece twice.

Materials are best kept in plastic bags with zip-type closures. Freezer bags are recommended for durability. Punch a hole near the top of the bag so that you do not store air. Lots of small bags can be stuffed into the largest bags. You can always see what you have stored in the bags.

The following list is a suggestion for materials that can be made from card stock using the masters in this section. Quantity suggestions are also given.

Dot Cards

One complete set of cards will serve four to six children. Duplicate each set in a different color so that mixed sets can be separated easily. Laminate and then cut with a paper cutter.

Five-Frames and Ten-Frames

Five-frames and ten-frames are best duplicated on light-colored card stock. Do not laminate; if you do, the mats will curl and counters will slide around.

10 × 10 Multiplication Array

Make one per student in any color. Lamination is suggested. Provide each student with an L-shaped piece of tagboard.

Base-Ten Pieces (Centimeter Grid)

Use the grid (number 11) to make a master as directed. Run copies on white card stock. One sheet will make 4 hundreds and 10 tens or 4 hundreds and a lot of ones. Mount the printed card stock on white poster board using either a dry-mount press or permanent spray adhesive. (Spray adhesive can be purchased in art supply stores. It is very effective but messy to handle.) Cut into pieces with a paper cutter. For the tens and ones pieces, it is recommended that you mount the index stock onto *mount board* or *illustration board*, also available in art supply stores. This material is thicker and will make the pieces easier to handle. It is recommended that you *not* laminate the base-ten pieces. A kit consisting of 10 hundreds, 30 tens, and 30 ones is adequate for each student or pair of students.

Little Ten-Frames

There are two masters for these materials. One has full ten-frames and the other has 1 to 9 dots, including two with 5 dots. Copy the 1-to-9 master on one color of card stock and the full ten-frames on another. Cut off most of the excess stock (do not trim) and then laminate. Cut into little ten-frames. Each set consists of 20 pieces: 10 full ten-frames and 10 of the 1-to-9 pieces, including 2 fives. Make a set for each child.

Place-Value Mat (with Ten-Frames)

Mats can be duplicated on any pastel card stock. It is recommended that you not laminate these because they tend to curl and counters slide around too much. Make one for every child.

Circular Fraction Pieces

First make three copies of each page of the master. Cut the disks apart and tape onto blank pages with three of the same type on a page. You will then have a separate master for each size with three full circles per master. Duplicate each master on a different color card stock. Laminate and then cut the circles out. A kit for one or two students should have two circles of each size piece.

Hundredths Disk

These disks can be made on paper but are much more satisfying on card stock. Duplicate the master on two contrasting colors. Laminate and cut the circles and also the slot on the dotted line. Make a set for each student. It's easy and worthwhile.

Tangrams and Mosaic Puzzle

Both tangrams and the Mosaic Puzzle should be copied on card stock. For younger children, the card stock should first be mounted on poster board to make the pieces a bit thicker and easier to put together in puzzles. You will want one set of each per student.

Woozle Cards

Copy the Woozle Card master on white or off-white card stock. You need two copies per set. Before laminating, color one set one color and the other a different color. An easy way to color the cards is to make one pass around the inside of each Woozle, leaving the rest of the creature white. If you color the entire Woozle, the dots may not show up. Make one set for every four students.

Transparencies and Overhead Models

A copy of any page can be made into a transparency with a photocopier. Alternatively, the PDF files can be printed directly onto transparency masters (use the appropriate transparency film for your printer). This method will avoid the minor distortions and blurring that sometimes occur with photocopying.

Some masters make fine transparency mats to use for demonstration purposes on the overhead. The 10 × 10 array, the blank hundreds board, and the large geoboard are examples. The five-frame and ten-frame work well with counters. The place-value mat can be used with strips and squares or with counters and cups directly on the overhead. The missing-part blank and the record blanks for the four algorithms are pages that you may wish to use as write-on transparencies.

A transparency of the 10,000 grid is the easiest way there is to show 10,000 or to model four-place decimal numbers.

A transparency of the degrees and wedges page is the very best way to illustrate what a degree is and also to help explain protractors.

All of the line and dot grids are useful to have available as transparencies. You may find it a good idea to make several copies of each and keep them in a folder where you can get to them easily.

For the Woozle Cards, dot cards, little ten-frames, and assorted shapes, make a reduction of the master on a photocopy machine. Then make transparencies of the small cards, cut them apart, and use them on the overhead.

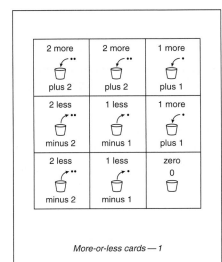

More-or-less cards — 1

Number cards — 2

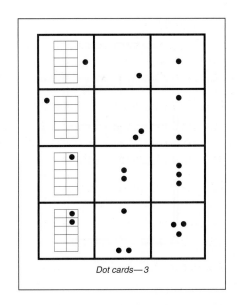

Dot cards — 3

Dot cards — 4

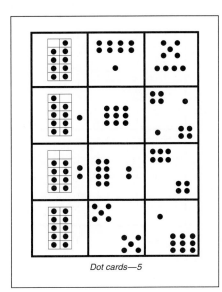

Dot cards — 5

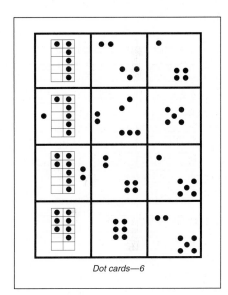

Dot cards — 6

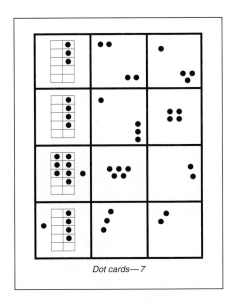

Dot cards — 7

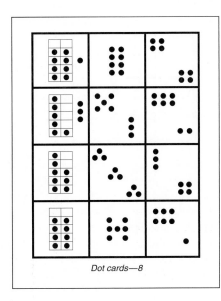

Dot cards — 8

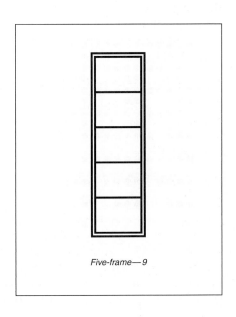

Five-frame — 9

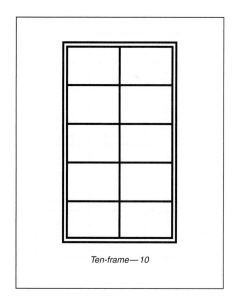

Ten-frame—10

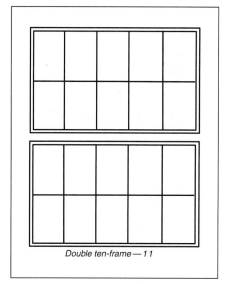

Double ten-frame—11

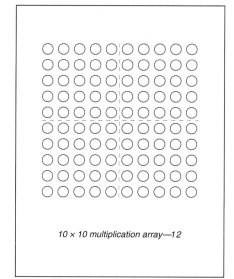

10 × 10 multiplication array—12

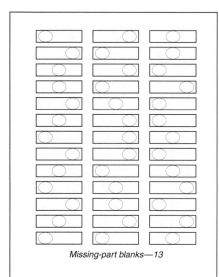

Missing-part blanks—13

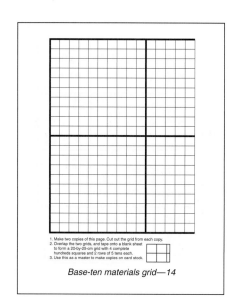

1. Make two copies of this page. Cut out the grid from each copy.
2. Overlap the two grids, and tape onto a blank sheet to form a 20-by-25-cm grid with 4 complete hundreds squares and 2 rows of 5 tens each.
3. Use this as a master to make copies on card stock.

Base-ten materials grid—14

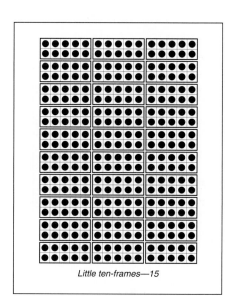

Little ten-frames—15

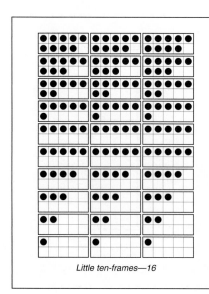

Little ten-frames—16

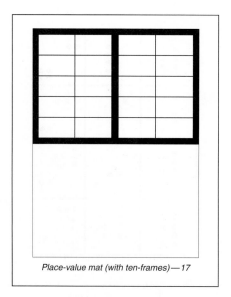

Place-value mat (with ten-frames)—17

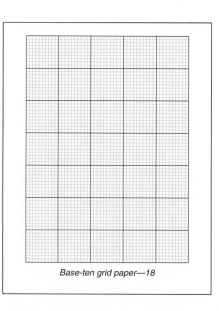

Base-ten grid paper—18

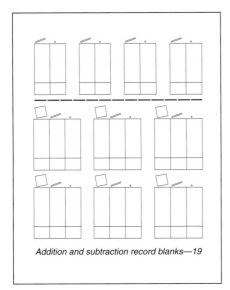

Addition and subtraction record blanks—19

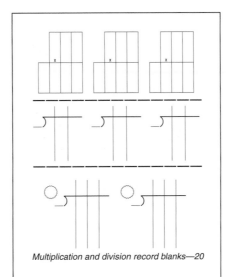

Multiplication and division record blanks—20

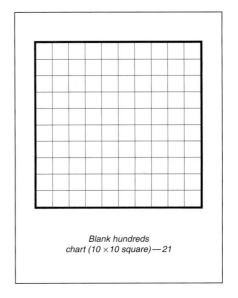

Blank hundreds
chart (10 × 10 square)—21

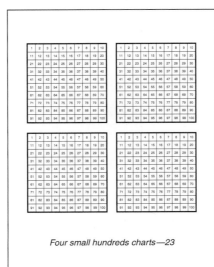

Hundreds chart—22

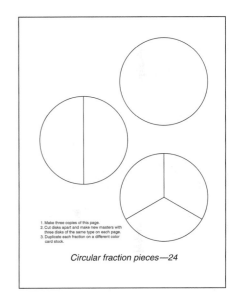

Four small hundreds charts—23

Circular fraction pieces—24

1. Make three copies of this page.
2. Cut disks apart and make new masters with three disks of the same type on each page.
3. Duplicate each fraction on a different color card stock.

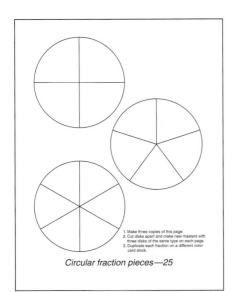

1. Make three copies of this page.
2. Cut disks apart and make new masters with three disks of the same type on each page.
3. Duplicate each fraction on a different color card stock.

Circular fraction pieces—25

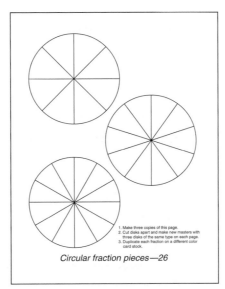

1. Make three copies of this page.
2. Cut disks apart and make new masters with three disks of the same type on each page.
3. Duplicate each fraction on a different color card stock.

Circular fraction pieces—26

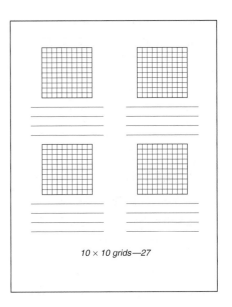

10 × 10 grids—27

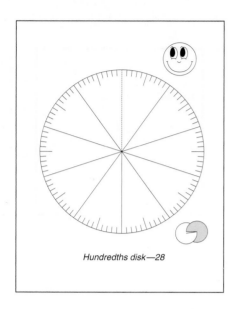

Hundredths disk—28

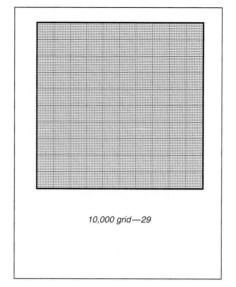

10,000 grid—29

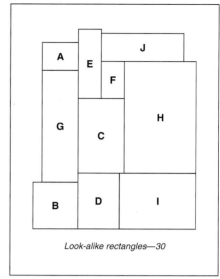

Look-alike rectangles—30

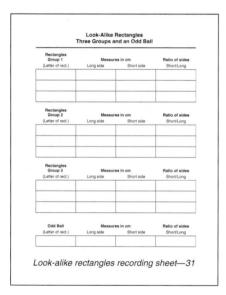

Look-alike rectangles recording sheet—31

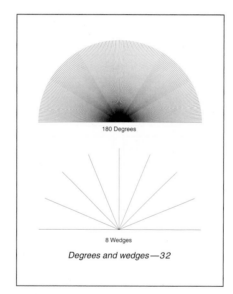

Degrees and wedges—32

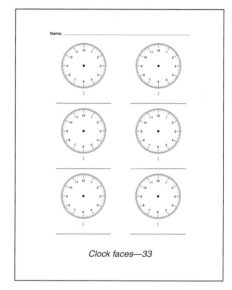

Clock faces—33

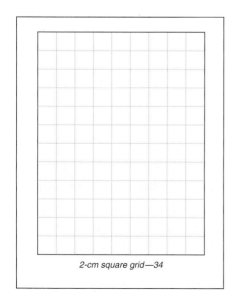

2-cm square grid—34

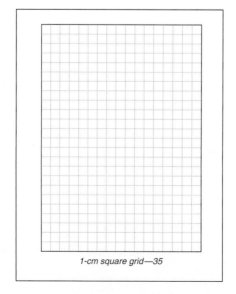

1-cm square grid—35

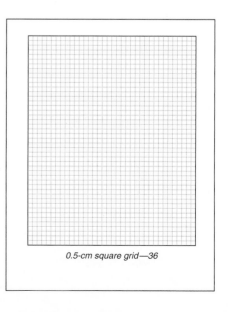

0.5-cm square grid—36

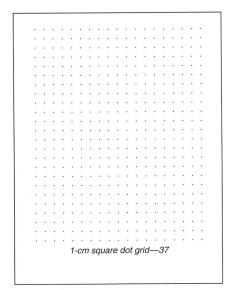

1-cm square dot grid—37

2-cm isometric grid—38

1-cm isometric dot grid—39

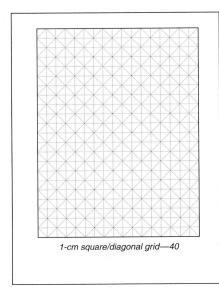

1-cm square/diagonal grid—40

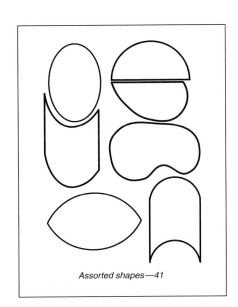

Assorted shapes—41

Assorted shapes—42

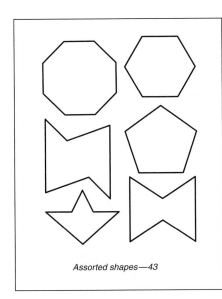

Assorted shapes—43

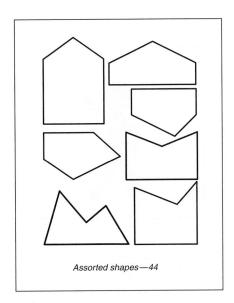

Assorted shapes—44

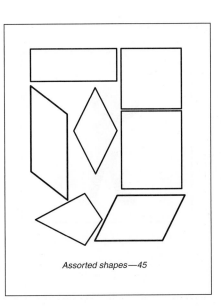

Assorted shapes—45

Assorted shapes—46

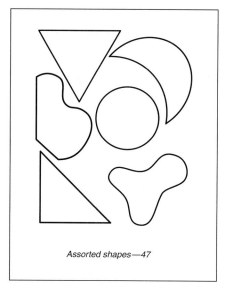

Assorted shapes—47

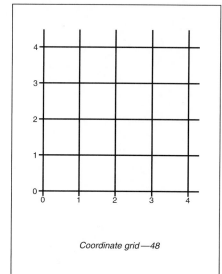

Coordinate grid—48

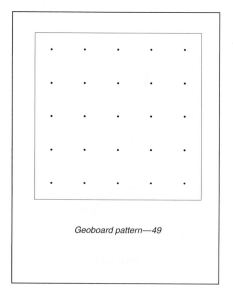

Geoboard pattern—49

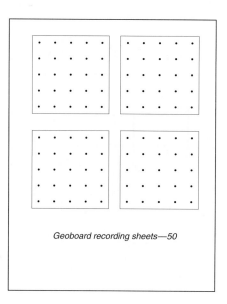

Geoboard recording sheets—50

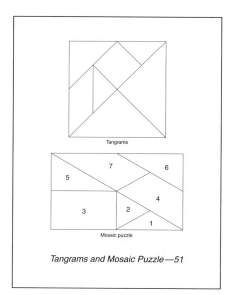

Tangrams and Mosaic Puzzle—51

Motion man—Side 1
Directions:
Make copies of Side 1. Then copy Side 2 on the reverse of Side 1. Check the orientation with one copy. When done correctly the two sides will match up when held to the light.

Motion Man—52

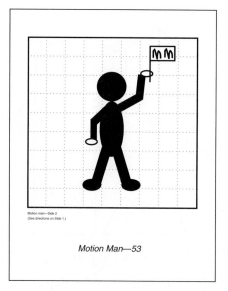

Motion man—Side 2
(See directions on Side 1.)

Motion Man—53

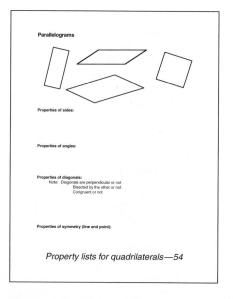

Parallelograms

Properties of sides:

Properties of angles:

Properties of diagonals:
Note: Diagonals are perpendicular or not
Bisected by the other or not
Congruent or not

Properties of symmetry (line and point):

Property lists for quadrilaterals—54

Rhombuses

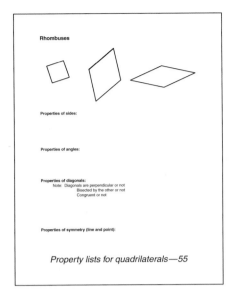

Properties of sides:

Properties of angles:

Properties of diagonals:
Note: Diagonals are perpendicular or not
Bisected by the other or not
Congruent or not

Properties of symmetry (line and point):

Property lists for quadrilaterals—55

Rectangles

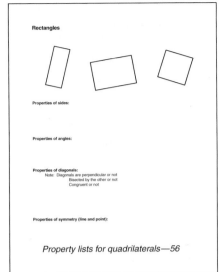

Properties of sides:

Properties of angles:

Properties of diagonals:
Note: Diagonals are perpendicular or not
Bisected by the other or not
Congruent or not

Properties of symmetry (line and point):

Property lists for quadrilaterals—56

Squares

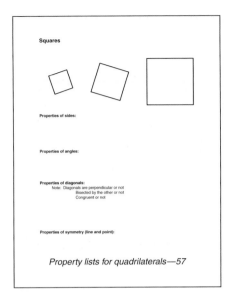

Properties of sides:

Properties of angles:

Properties of diagonals:
Note: Diagonals are perpendicular or not
Bisected by the other or not
Congruent or not

Properties of symmetry (line and point):

Property lists for quadrilaterals—57

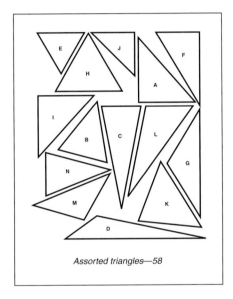

Assorted triangles—58

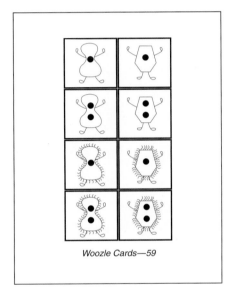

Woozle Cards—59

References

Ann Arbor Public Schools. (1993). *Alternative assessment: Evaluating student performance in elementary mathematics.* Palo Alto, CA: Dale Seymour.

ARC Center (2002). *The ARC tri-state student achievement study* [online]. Available: www.comap/elementary/projects/arc.

Ashcraft, M. H., & Christy, K. S. (1995). The frequency of arithmetic facts in elementary texts: Addition and multiplication in grades 1–6. *Journal for Research in Mathematics Education, 26,* 396–421.

Austin, R., & Thompson, D. (1997). Exploring algebraic patterns through literature. *Mathematics Teaching in the Middle School, 2,* 274–281.

Babcock, J. E. (1998). *U.S. TIMSS Report No. 8.* East Lansing, MI: TIMSS U.S. National Research Center, Michigan State University.

Backhouse, J., Haggarty, L., Pirie, S., & Stratton, J. (1992). *Improving the learning of mathematics.* Portsmouth, NH: Heinemann.

Baek, J. (1998). Children's invented algorithms for multidigit multiplication problems. In L. J. Morrow (Ed.), *The teaching and learning of algorithms in school mathematics* (pp. 151–160). Reston, VA: National Council of Teachers of Mathematics.

Baker, A., & Baker, J. (1991). *Math's in the mind: A process approach to mental strategies.* Portsmouth, NH: Heinemann.

Baker, J., & Baker, A. (1990). *Mathematics in process.* Portsmouth, NH: Heinemann.

Ball, D. L. (1992). Magical hopes: Manipulatives and the reform of math education. *American Educator, 16*(2), 14–18, 46–47.

Ball, L., & Bass, H. (2003). Making mathematics reasonable in school. In J. Kilpatrick, W. G. Martin, & D. Schifter (Eds.), *A research companion to Principles and Standards for School Mathematics* (pp. 27–44). Reston, VA: National Council of Teachers of Mathematics.

Ball, L., & Stacey, K. (2005). Teaching strategies for developing judicious technology use. In W. J. Masalski & P. C. Elliott (Eds.), *Technology-supported mathematics learning environments* (pp. 3–15). Reston, VA: National Council of Teachers of Mathematics.

Baratta-Lorton, M. (1976). *Mathematics their way.* Menlo Park, CA: AWL Supplemental.

Baroody, A. J. (1985). Mastery of the basic number combinations: Internalization of relationships or facts? *Journal for Research in Mathematics Education, 16,* 83–98.

Baroody, A. J. (1987). *Children's mathematical thinking: A developmental framework for preschool, primary, and special education teachers.* New York: Teachers College Press.

Baroody, A. J., & Wilkins, J. L. M. (1999). The development of informal counting, number, and arithmetic skills and concepts. In J. V. Copley (Ed.), *Mathematics in the early years* (pp. 48–65). Reston, VA: National Council of Teachers of Mathematics.

Barrett, J. E., Jones, G., Thornton, C., & Dickson, S. (2003). Understanding children's developing strategies and concepts of length. In D. H. Clements (Ed.), *Learning and teaching measurement* (pp. 17–30). Reston, VA: National Council of Teachers of Mathematics.

Battista, M. C. (1999). The mathematical miseducation of America's youth: Ignoring research and scientific study in education. *Phi Delta Kappan, 80,* 424–433.

Battista, M. T. (2003). Understanding students' thinking about area and volume measurement. In D. H. Clements (Ed.), *Learning and teaching measurement* (pp. 122–142). Reston, VA: National Council of Teachers of Mathematics.

Bay-Williams, J. M., & Martinie, S. L. (2004). *Math and literature: Grades 6–8.* Sausalito, CA: Math Solutions Publications.

Becker, J. P., & Shimada, S. (Eds.). (1997). *The open-ended approach: A new proposal for teaching mathematics.* Reston, VA: National Council of Teachers of Mathematics.

Becker, J. R., & Jacobs, J. E. (2001). Introduction. In J. E. Jacobs, J. R. Becker, & G. F. Gilmer (Eds.), *Changing the faces of mathe-* matics: *Perspectives on gender* (pp. 1–8). Reston, VA: National Council of Teachers of Mathematics.

Beckman, C. E., Thompson, D., & Austin R. A. (2004). Exploring proportional reasoning through movies and literature. *Mathematics Teaching in the Middle School, 9,* 256–262.

Bell, M. (1998–1999, Winter). Problems with implementing new curricula: The example of the K–6 *Everyday Mathematics* Curriculum. *UCSMP Newsletter, 24,* 1–2.

Bley, N. S. (1994). Accommodating special needs. In C. A. Thornton & N. S. Bley (Eds.), *Windows of opportunity: Mathematics for students with special needs* (pp. 137–163). Reston, VA: National Council of Teachers of Mathematics.

Bley, N. S., & Thornton, C. A. (1995). *Teaching mathematics to students with learning disabilities* (3rd ed.). Austin, TX: Pro-Ed.

Boaler, J. (1998). Open and closed mathematics: Student experiences and understandings. *Journal for Research in Mathematics Education, 29,* 41–62.

Boaler, J. (2002). *Experiencing school mathematics: Traditional and reform approaches to teaching and their impact on student learning.* Mahwah, NJ: Erlbaum.

Boaler, J., & Humphreys, C. (2005). *Connecting mathematical ideas: Middle school video cases to support teaching and learning.* Portsmouth, NH: Heinemann.

Borasi, R. (1994, April). Implementing the NCTM *Standards* in "inclusive" mainstream classrooms. Presented at the annual meeting of the National Council of Teachers of Mathematics, Indianapolis, IN.

Bresser, R. (1995). *Math and literature (grades 4–6).* White Plains, NY: Cuisenaire (distributor).

Bright, G. W., Behr, M. J., Post, T. R., & Wachsmuth, I. (1988). Identifying fractions on number lines. *Journal for Research in Mathematics Education, 19,* 215–232.

Bright, G. W., Joyner, J. M., & Wallis, C. (2003). Assessing proportional thinking. *Mathematics Teaching in the Middle School, 9,* 166–172.

Brooks, J. G., & Brooks, M. G. (1993). *In search of understanding: The case for the constructivist classroom.* Alexandria, VA: Association for Supervision and Curriculum Development.

Brownell, W., & Chazal, C. (1935). The effects of premature drill in third grade arithmetic. *Journal of Educational Research, 29,* 17–28.

Burger, W. F. (1985). Geometry. *Arithmetic Teacher, 32*(6), 52–56.

Burns, M. (1982). *Math for smarty pants.* New York: Little, Brown.

Burns, M. (1992). *Math and literature (K–3).* Sausalito, CA: Math Solutions Publications.

Burns, M. (1995a). Timed tests. *Teaching Children Mathematics, 1,* 408–409.

Burns, M. (1995b). *Writing in math class.* White Plains, NY: Cuisenaire (distributor).

Burns, M. (1996). *50 problem-solving lessons: Grades 1–6.* White Plains, NY: Cuisenaire (distributor).

Burns, M. (1999). *Making sense of mathematics: A look toward the twenty-first century.* Presentation at the annual meeting of the National Council of Teachers of Mathematics, San Francisco.

Burns, M. (2000). *About teaching mathematics: A K–8 resource* (2nd ed.). Sausalito, CA: Math Solutions Publications.

Burns, M., & McLaughlin, C. (1990). *A collection of math lessons from grades 6 through 8.* Sausalito, CA: Math Solutions Publications.

Buschman, L. (2003). *Share and compare: A teacher's story about helping children become problem solvers in mathematics.* Reston, VA: National Council of Teachers of Mathematics.

Cai, J., & Sun, W. (2002). Developing students' proportional reasoning: A Chinese perspective. In B. Litwiller (Ed.), *Making sense of fractions, ratios, and proportions* (pp. 195–205). Reston, VA: National Council of Teachers of Mathematics.

Campbell, P. B. (1995). Redefining the "girl problem in mathematics." In W. G. Secada, E. Fennema, & L. B. Adajian (Eds.), *New directions for equity in mathematics education* (pp. 225–241). New York: Cambridge University Press.

Campbell, P. F. (1996). Empowering children and teachers in the elementary mathematics classrooms of urban schools. *Urban Education, 30,* 449–475.

Campbell, P. F. (1997, April). Children's invented algorithms: Their meaning and place in instruction. Presented at the annual meeting of the National Council of Teachers of Mathematics, Minneapolis, MN.

Campbell, P. F., & Johnson, M. L. (1995). How primary students think and learn. In I. M. Carl (Ed.), *Prospects for school mathematics* (pp. 21–42). Reston, VA: National Council of Teachers of Mathematics.

Campbell, P. F., Rowan, T. E., & Suarez, A. R. (1998). What criteria for student-invented algorithms? In L. J. Morrow (Ed.), *The teaching and learning of algorithms in school mathematics* (pp. 49–55). Reston, VA: National Council of Teachers of Mathematics.

Campione, J. C., Brown, A. L., & Connell, M. L. (1989). Metacognition: On the importance of understanding what you are doing. In R. I. Charles & E. A. Silver (Eds.), *The teaching and assessing of mathematical problem solving* (pp. 93–114). Reston, VA: National Council of Teachers of Mathematics.

Carpenter, T. P. (1985). Learning to add and subtract: An exercise in problem solving. In E. A. Silver (Ed.), *Teaching and learning mathematical problem solving: Multiple research perspectives* (pp. 17–40). Hillsdale, NJ: Lawrence Erlbaum.

Carpenter, T. P., Ansell, E., Franke, M. L., Fennema, E., & Weisbeck, L. (1993). A study of kindergarten children's problem-solving processes. *Journal for Research in Mathematics Education, 24,* 428–441.

Carpenter, T. P., Carey, D. A., & Kouba, V. L. (1990). A problem-solving approach to the operations. In J. N. Payne (Ed.), *Mathematics for the young child* (pp. 111–131). Reston, VA: National Council of Teachers of Mathematics.

Carpenter, T. P., Fennema, E., Franke, M. L., Levi, L., & Empson, S. B. (1999). *Children's mathematics: Cognitively guided instruction.* Portsmouth, NH: Heinemann.

Carpenter, T. P., Franke, M. L., Jacobs, V. R., Fennema, E., & Empson, S. B. (1998). A longitudinal study of invention and understanding in children's multidigit addition and subtraction. *Journal for Research in Mathematics Education, 29,* 3–20.

Carpenter, T. P., Franke, M. L., & Levi, L. (2003). *Thinking mathematically: Integrating arithmetic & algebra in elementary school.* Portsmouth, NH: Heinemann.

Carraher, D., Schliemann, A., Martinez, M., & Earnst, D. (2005). Unexpected findings about how young students learn algebra. Presentation at the National Council of Teachers of Mathematics Research Pre-session, Anaheim, CA.

Carroll, W. M., & Porter, D. (1997). Invented strategies can develop meaningful mathematical procedures. *Teaching Children Mathematics, 3,* 370–374.

Charles, R. I., Chancellor, D., Harcourt, L., Moore, D., Schielack, J. F., Van de Walle, J., & Wortzman, R. (1998). *Scott Foresman—Addison Wesley MATH (Grades K to 5).* Glenview, IL: Addison Wesley Longman, Inc.

Clark, F. B., & Kamii, C. (1996). Identification of multiplicative thinking in children in grades 1–5. *Journal for Research in Mathematics Education, 27,* 41–51.

Clements, D. H., & Battista, M. T. (1990). Constructivist learning and teaching. *Arithmetic Teacher, 38*(1), 34–35.

Clements, D. H., & Battista, M. T. (2001). *Logo and geometry.* Reston, VA: National Council of Teachers of Mathematics.

Cobb, P. (1988). The tension between theories of learning and instruction in mathematics education. *Educational Psychologist, 23,* 87–103.

Cramer, K., & Henry, A. (2002). Using manipulative models to build number sense for addition of fractions. In B. Litwiller (Ed.), *Making sense of fractions, ratios, and proportions* (pp. 41–48). Reston, VA: National Council of Teachers of Mathematics.

Cummins, J. (1994). Primary language instruction and the education of language minority students. In C. F. Leyba (Ed.), *Schooling and language minority students: A theoretical framework* (pp. 3–46). Los Angeles, CA: California State University, National Evaluation, Dissemination and Assessment Center.

Curcio, F. R., & Bezuk, N. S. (1994). *Understanding rational numbers and proportions: Addenda Series, grades 5–8.* Reston, VA: National Council of Teachers of Mathematics.

Damarin, S. K. (1995). Gender and mathematics from a feminist standpoint. In W. G. Secada, E. Fennema, & L. B. Adajian (Eds.), *New directions for equity in mathematics education* (pp. 242–257). New York: Cambridge University Press.

Davis, R. B. (1986). *Learning mathematics: The cognitive science approach to mathematics education.* Norwood, NJ: Ablex.

De Villiers, M. D. (1999). *Rethinking proof with the Geometer's Sketchpad.* Emeryville, CA: Key Curriculum Press.

Echevarria, J., Vogt, M., and Short, D. J. (2004). *Making content comprehensible for English learners: The SIOP model* (2nd ed.). Boston: Pearson.

Elliott, P., & Garnett, C. (1994). Mathematics power for all. In C. A. Thornton & N. S. Bley (Eds.), *Windows of opportunity: Mathematics for students with special needs* (pp. 3–17). Reston, VA: National Council of Teachers of Mathematics.

Empson, S. B. (2002). Organizing diversity in early fraction thinking. In B. Litwiller (Ed.), *Making sense of fractions, ratios, and proportions* (pp. 29–40). Reston, VA: National Council of Teachers of Mathematics.

Falkner, K. P., Levi, L., & Carpenter, T. P. (1999). Children's understanding of equality: A foundation for algebra. *Teaching Children Mathematics, 6,* 232–236.

Fennema, E., Carpenter, T. P., Franke, M. L., & Carey, D. A. (1993). Learning to use children's mathematics thinking: A case study. In R. B. Davis & C. A. Maher (Eds.), *School, mathematics, and the world of reality* (pp. 93–117). Boston: Allyn & Bacon.

Fennema, E., Carpenter, T., Levi, L., Franke, M. L., & Empson, S. (1997). *Cognitively guided instruction: Professional development in primary mathematics.* Madison, WI: Wisconsin Center for Education Research.

Fischer, F. E. (1990). A part-part-whole curriculum for teaching number in the kindergarten. *Journal for Research in Mathematics Education, 21,* 207–215.

Fosnot, C. T. (1996). Constructivism: A psychological theory of learning. In C. T. Fosnot (Ed.), *Constructivism: Theory, perspectives, and practice* (pp. 8–33). New York: Teachers College Press.

Fosnot, C. T., & Dolk, M. (2001). *Young mathematicians at work: Constructing number sense, addition, and subtraction.* Portsmouth, NH: Heinemann.

Friel, S. N., Mokros, J. R., & Russell, S. J. (1992). *Statistics: Middles, means, and in-betweens.* A unit of study for grades 5–6 from *Used numbers: Real data in the classroom.* White Plains, NY: Cuisenaire—Dale Seymour.

Fuson, K. C. (1984). More complexities in subtraction. *Journal for Research in Mathematics Education, 15,* 214–225.

Fuson, K. C. (1988). *Children's counting and concepts of number.* New York: Springer-Verlag.

Fuson, K. C. (1992). Research on whole number addition and subtraction. In D. A. Grouws (Ed.), *Handbook of research on teaching and learning* (pp. 243–275). Old Tappan, NJ: Macmillan.

Fuson, K. C., Carroll, W. M., & Drueck, J. V. (2000). Achievement results for second and third graders using the *Standards*-based curriculum *Everyday Mathematics. Journal for Research in Mathematics Education, 31,* 277–295.

Fuson, K. C., & Hall, J. W. (1983). The acquisition of early number word meanings: A conceptual analysis and review. In H. P. Ginsburg (Ed.), *The development of mathematical thinking* (pp. 49–107). Orlando, FL: Academic Press.

Fuson, K. C., Wearne, D. Hiebert, J. C., Murray, H. G., Human, P. G., Olivier, A. I., Carpenter, T. P., & Fennema, E. (1997). Children's conceptual structures for multidigit numbers and methods of multidigit addition and subtraction. *Journal for Research in Mathematics Education, 28,* 130–162.

Fuys, D., Geddes, D., & Tischler, R. (1988). The van Hiele model of thinking in geometry among adolescents. *Journal for Research in Mathematics Education Monograph, 3.*

Garofalo, J. (1987). Metacognition and school mathematics. *Arithmetic Teacher, 34*(9), 22–23.

Garrison, L. (1997). Making the NCTM's Standards work for emergent English speakers. *Teaching Children Mathematics, 4,* 132–138.

Garrison, L., & Mora, J. K. (1999). Adapting mathematics instruction for English-language learners: The language-concept connection. In L. Ortiz-Franco, N. G. Hernandez, & Y. De La Cruz (Eds.), *Changing the faces of mathematics perspectives on Latinos* (pp. 45–47). Reston, VA: National Council of Teachers of Mathematics.

Geddes, D., & Fortunato, I. (1993). Geometry: Research and classroom activities. In D. T. Owens (Ed.), *Research ideas for the classroom: Middle grades mathematics* (pp. 199–222). New York: Macmillan.

Gelman, R., & Gallistel, C. R. (1978). *The child's understanding of number.* Cambridge, MA: Harvard University Press.

Gelman, R., & Meck, E. (1986). The notion of principle: The case of counting. In J. Hiebert (Ed.), *Conceptual and procedural knowledge: The case of mathematics* (pp. 29–57). Hillsdale, NJ: Erlbaum.

Ginsburg, H. P. (1977). *Children's arithmetic: The learning process.* New York: Van Nostrand.

Gnanadesikan, M., Schaeffer, R. L., & Swift, J. (1987). *The art and techniques of simulation: Quantitative literacy series.* Palo Alto, CA: Dale Seymour.

Goldin, G. A. (1985). Thinking scientifically and thinking mathematically: A discussion of the paper by Heller and Hungate. In E. A. Silver (Ed.), *Teaching and learning mathematical problem solving: Multiple research perspectives* (pp. 113–122). Hillsdale, NJ: Lawrence Erlbaum.

Gravemeijer, K., & van Galen, F., (2003). Facts and algorithms as products of students' own mathematical activity. In J. Kilpatrick, W. G. Martin, & D. Schifter (Eds.), *A research companion to Principles and Standards for School Mathematics* (pp. 114–122). Reston, VA: National Council of Teachers of Mathematics.

Greenes, C., & Findell, C. (1999a). *Groundworks: Algebra puzzles and problems* (separate books for grades 4 to 7). Chicago: Creative Publications.

Greenes, C., & Findell, C. (1999b). *Groundworks: Algebraic thinking* (separate books for grades 1, 2, and 3). Chicago: Creative Publications.

Greer, B. (1992). Multiplication and division as models of situations. In D. A. Grouws (Ed.), *Handbook of research on mathematics teaching and learning* (pp. 276–295). Old Tappan, NJ: Macmillan.

Groff, P. (1996). It is time to question fraction teaching. *Mathematics Teaching in the Middle School, 1,* 604–607.

Gutstein, E., & Romberg, T. A. (1995). Teaching children to add and subtract. *Journal of Mathematical Behavior, 14,* 283–324.

Hashimoto, Y., & Becker, J. (1999). The open approach to teaching mathematics—Creating a culture of mathematics in the classroom: Japan. In L. J. Sheffield (Ed.), *Developing mathematically promising students* (pp. 101–119). Reston, VA: National Council of Teachers of Mathematics.

Hiebert, J. (1990). The role of routine procedures in the development of mathematical competence. In T. J. Cooney (Ed.), *Teaching and learning mathematics in the 1990s* (pp. 31–40). Reston, VA: National Council of Teachers of Mathematics.

Hiebert, J. (2003). What research says about the NCTM standards. In J. Kilpatrick, W. G. Martin, & D. Schifter (Eds.), *A research companion to Principles and Standards for School Mathematics* (pp. 5–23). Reston, VA: National Council of Teachers of Mathematics.

Hiebert, J., & Carpenter, T. P. (1992). Learning and teaching with understanding. In D. A. Grouws (Ed.), *Handbook of research on mathematics teaching and learning* (pp. 65–97). Old Tappan, NJ: Macmillan.

Hiebert, J., Carpenter, T. P., Fennema, E., Fuson, K., Human, P., Murray, H., Olivier, A., & Wearne, D. (1996). Problem solving as a basis for reform in curriculum and instruction: The case of mathematics. *Educational Researcher, 25* (May), 12–21.

Hiebert, J., Carpenter, T. P., Fennema, E., Fuson, K., Wearne, D., Murray, H., Olivier, A., & Human, P. (1997). *Making sense: Teaching and learning mathematics with understanding.* Portsmouth, NH: Heinemann.

Hiebert, J., Gallimore, R., Garnier, H., Givvin, K. B., Hollingsworth, H., Jacobs, J., Chui, A. M–Y., Wearne, D., Smith, M., Kersting, N., Manaster, A., Tseng, E., Etterbeek, W., Manaster, C., Gonzales, P., & Stigler, J. (2003). *Teaching mathematics in seven countries: Results from the TIMSS 1999 video study.* Washington, D.C.: National Center for Education Statistics, U.S. Department of Education.

Hiebert, J., & Lindquist, M. M. (1990). Developing mathematical knowledge in the young child. In J. N. Payne (Ed.), *Mathematics for the young child* (pp. 17–36). Reston, VA: National Council of Teachers of Mathematics.

Hiebert, J., & Wearne, D. (1996). Instruction, understanding, and skill in multidigit addition and subtraction. *Cognition and Instruction, 14,* 251–283.

Hiebert, J., & Wearne, D. (2003). Developing understanding through problem solving. In H. L. Schoen & R. I. Charles (Eds.), *Teaching mathematics through problem solving* (pp. 3–14). Reston, VA: National Council of Teachers of Mathematics.

Hoffer, A. R. (1983). Van Hiele–based research. In R. A. Lesh & M. Landau (Eds.), *Acquisition of mathematics concepts and processes* (pp. 205–227). Orlando, FL: Academic Press.

Hoffer, A. R., & Hoffer, S. A. K. (1992). Ratios and proportional thinking. In T. R. Post (Ed.), *Teaching mathematics in grades K–8: Research-based methods* (2nd ed.) (pp. 303–330). Boston: Allyn & Bacon.

House, P. A. (1999). Promises, promises, promises. In L. J. Sheffield (Ed.), *Developing mathematically promising students* (pp. 1–7). Reston, VA: National Council of Teachers of Mathematics.

Howden, H. (1989). Teaching number sense. *Arithmetic Teacher, 36*(6), 6–11.

Huinker, D. (1994, April). Multi-step word problems: A strategy for empowering students. Presented at the annual meeting of the National Council of Teachers of Mathematics, Indianapolis, IN.

Huinker, D. (1998). Letting fraction algorithms emerge through problem solving. In L. J. Morrow (Ed.), *The teaching and learning of algorithms in school mathematics* (pp. 170–182). Reston, VA: National Council of Teachers of Mathematics.

Janvier, C. (Ed.). (1987). *Problems of representation in the teaching and learning of mathematics.* Hillsdale, NJ: Erlbaum.

Jones, D. L., & Arbaugh, F. (2004). What do students know about time? *Mathematics Teaching in the Middle School, 10,* 82–84.

Jones, G. A., Thornton, C. A., Langrall, C. W., & Tarr, J. E. (1999). Understanding students' probabilistic reasoning. In L. V. Stiff (Ed.), *Developing mathematical thinking in grades K–12* (pp. 146–155). Reston, VA: National Council of Teachers of Mathematics.

Joram, E. (2003). Benchmarks as tools for developing measurement sense. In D. H. Clements (Ed.), *Learning and teaching measurement* (pp. 57–67). Reston, VA: National Council of Teachers of Mathematics.

Kamii, C. K. (1985). *Young children reinvent arithmetic.* New York: Teachers College Press.

Kamii, C. K. (1989). *Young children continue to reinvent arithmetic: 2nd grade.* New York: Teachers College Press.

Kamii, C. K., & Clark, F. B. (1995). Equivalent fractions: Their difficulty and educational implications. *The Journal of Mathematical Behavior, 14,* 365–378.

Kamii, C. K., & Dominick, A. (1997). To teach or not to teach the algorithms. *Journal of Mathematical Behavior, 16*, 51–62.

Kamii, C. K., & Dominick, A. (1998). The harmful effects of algorithms in grades 1–4. In L. J. Morrow (Ed.), *The teaching and learning of algorithms in school mathematics* (pp. 130–140). Reston, VA: National Council of Teachers of Mathematics.

Kaput, J. J. (1998). Transforming algebra from an engine of inequity to an engine of mathematical power by "algebrafying" the K–12 curriculum. In *The nature and role of algebra in the K–12 curriculum: Proceedings of national symposium* (pp. 25–26). Washington, DC: National Academy Press.

Kaput, J. J. (1999). Teaching and learning a new algebra. In E. Fennema & T. A. Romberg (Eds.), *Mathematics classrooms that promote understanding* (pp. 133–155). Mahwah, NJ: Erlbaum.

Karplus, R., Pulos, S., & Stage, E. K. (1983). Proportional reasoning of early adolescents. In R. A. Lesh & M. Landau (Eds.), *Acquisition of mathematics concepts and processes* (pp. 45–90). Orlando, FL: Academic Press.

Kenney, P. A., & Kouba, V. L. (1997). What do students know about measurement? In P. A. Kenney & E. Silver (Eds.), *Results from the sixth mathematics assessment of the National Assessment of Educational Progress* (pp. 141–163). Reston, VA: National Council of Teachers of Mathematics.

Khisty, L. L. (1997). Making mathematics accessible to Latino students: Rethinking instructional practice. In M. Kenney & J. Trentacosta (Eds.), *Multicultural and gender equity in the mathematics classroom: The gift of diversity* (pp. 92–101). Reston, VA: National Council of Teachers of Mathematics.

Klein, A. S., Beishuizen, M., & Treffers, A. (1998). The empty number line in Dutch second grade: *Realistic* versus *gradual* program design. *Journal for Research in Mathematics Education, 29*, 443–464.

Kliman, M., & Russell, S. J. (1998). *The number system: Building number sense (Grade 1).* Glenview, IL: Scott Foresman.

Kloosterman P., & Lester, F. K., Jr. (2004). *Results and interpretations of the 1990–2000 mathematics assessments of the National Assessment of Educational Progress.* Reston, VA: National Council of Teachers of Mathematics.

Kloosterman, P., Warfield, J., Wearne, D., Koc, Y., Martin, W. G., & Strutchens, M. (2004). Fourth-grade students' knowledge of mathematics and perceptions of learning mathematics. In P. Kloosterman & F. K. Lester, Jr., *Results and interpretations of the 1990–2000 mathematics assessments of the National Assessment of Educational Progress* (pp. 71–103). Reston, VA: National Council of Teachers of Mathematics.

Kohn, A. (1993). *Punished by rewards: The trouble with gold stars, incentive plans, A's, praise, and other bribes.* Boston: Houghton Mifflin.

Kouba, V. L. (1989). Children's solution strategies for equivalent set multiplication and division word problems. *Journal for Research in Mathematics Education, 20*, 147–158.

Kouba, V. L., Brown, C. A., Carpenter, T. P., Lindquist, M. M., Silver, E. A., & Swafford, J. O. (1988a). Results of the fourth NAEP assessment of mathematics: Number, operations, and word problems. *Arithmetic Teacher, 35*(8), 14–19.

Kouba, V. L., Zawojewski, J. S., & Strutchens, M. E. (1997). What do students know about numbers and operations? In P. A. Kenney & E. Silver (Eds.), *Results from the sixth mathematics assessment of the National Assessment of Educational Progress* (pp. 87–140). Reston, VA: National Council of Teachers of Mathematics.

Kulm, G. (1994). *Mathematics and assessment: What works in the classroom.* San Francisco: Jossey-Bass.

Kuske, C. T. (2001). It all fits together: Number patterns that foster number sense in K–2 students—A brain-based model. Unpublished Masters Thesis, Antioch University Seattle.

Labinowicz, E. (1985). *Learning from children: New beginnings for teaching numerical thinking.* Menlo Park, CA: AWL Supplemental.

Lamon, S. J. (1993). Ratio and proportion: Connecting content and children's thinking. *Journal for Research in Mathematics Education, 24*, 41–61.

Lamon, S. J. (1996). The development of unitizing: Its role in children's partitioning strategies. *Journal for Research in Mathematics Education, 27*, 170–193.

Lamon, S. J. (1999a). *More: In-depth discussion of the reasoning activities in "Teaching fractions and ratios for understanding."* Mahwah, NJ: Lawrence Erlbaum.

Lamon, S. J. (1999b). *Teaching fractions and ratios for understanding: Essential content knowledge and instructional strategies for teachers.* Mahwah, NJ: Lawrence Erlbaum.

Lamon, S. J. (2002). Part-whole comparisons with unitizing. In B. Litwiller (Ed.), *Making sense of fractions, ratios, and proportions* (pp. 79–86). Reston, VA: National Council of Teachers of Mathematics.

Lappan, G., & Briars, D. (1995). How should mathematics be taught? In I. M. Carl (Ed.), *Prospects for school mathematics* (pp. 115–156). Reston, VA: National Council of Teachers of Mathematics.

Lappan, G., & Even, R. (1989). *Learning to teach: Constructing meaningful understanding of mathematical content* (Craft Paper 89–3). East Lansing: Michigan State University.

Lappan, G., & Mouck, M. K. (1998). Developing algorithms for adding and subtracting fractions. In L. J. Morrow (Ed.), *The teaching and learning of algorithms in school mathematics* (pp. 183–197). Reston, VA: National Council of Teachers of Mathematics.

Leder, G. C. (1995). Equity inside the mathematics classroom: Fact or artifact? In W. G. Secada, E. Fennema, & L. B. Adajian (Eds.), *New directions for equity in mathematics education* (pp. 209–224). New York: Cambridge University Press.

Lee, H., & Jung, W. S. (2004). Limited-English-Proficient (LEP) students' mathematical understanding. *Mathematics Teaching in the Middle School, 9*, 269–272.

Lesh, R. A., Post, T. R., & Behr, M. J. (1987). Representations and translations among representations in mathematics learning and problem solving. In C. Janvier (Ed.), *Problems of representation in the teaching and learning of mathematics* (pp. 33–40). Hillsdale, NJ: Erlbaum.

Lester, F. K., Jr. (1989). Reflections about mathematical problem-solving research. In R. I. Charles & E. A. Silver (Eds.), *The teaching and assessing of mathematical problem solving* (pp. 115–124). Reston, VA: National Council of Teachers of Mathematics.

Lo, J., & Watanabe, T. (1997). Developing ratio and proportion schemes: A story of a fifth grader. *Journal for Research in Mathematics Education, 28*, 216–236.

Lubienski, S. T., McGraw, R., & Strutchins, M. E. (2004). NAEP findings regarding gender: Mathematics achievement, student affect, and learning practices. In P. Kloosterman & F. K. Lester, Jr. (Eds.), *Results and interpretations of the 1990 through 2000 mathematics assessments of the National Assessment of Educational Progress* (pp. 305–336). Reston, VA: National Council of Teachers of Mathematics.

Lubinski, C. A., & Thiessen, D. (1996). Exploring measurement through literature. *Teaching Children Mathematics, 2*, 260–263.

Ma, L. (1999). *Knowing and teaching elementary mathematics: Teachers' understanding of fundamental mathematics in China and the United States.* Mahwah, NJ: Lawrence Erlbaum.

Mack, N. K. (1995). Confounding whole-number and fraction concepts when building on informal knowledge. *Journal for Research in Mathematics Education, 26*, 422–441.

Mack, N. K. (2001). Building on informal knowledge through instruction in a complex content domain: Partitioning, units, and understanding multiplication of fractions. *Journal for Research in Mathematics Education, 32*, 267–295.

Madell, R. (1985). Children's natural processes. *Arithmetic Teacher, 32*(7), 20–22.

Martin, G., & Strutchens, M. E. (2000). Geometry and measurement. In E. A. Silver & P. A. Kenney (Eds.), *Results from the seventh mathematics assessment of the National Assessment of Educational Progress* (pp. 193–234). Reston, VA: National Council of Teachers of Mathematics.

Martin, R., Sexton, C., Wagner, K., & Gerlovich, J. (1997). *Teaching science for all children.* Boston: Allyn & Bacon.

Mathematical Sciences Education Board, National Research Council. (1989). *Everybody counts: A report to the nation on the future of mathematics education.* Washington, DC: National Academy of Sciences Press.

Mau, T. S., & Leitze, A. R. (2001). Powerless gender or genderless power? The promise of constructivism for females in the mathematics classroom. In J. E. Jacobs, J. R. Becker, & G. F. Gilmer (Eds.), *Changing the faces of mathematics: Perspectives on gender* (pp. 37–41). Reston, VA: National Council of Teachers of Mathematics.

McClain, K., Cobb, P., Gravemeijer, K., & Estes, B. (1999). Developing mathematical reasoning in the context of measurement. In L. V. Stiff (Ed.), *Developing mathematical reasoning in grades K–12* (pp. 93–106). Reston, VA: National Council of Teachers of Mathematics.

McCoy, L. (1997). Algebra: Real-life investigations in a lab setting. *Mathematics Teaching in the Middle School, 2,* 220–224.

Mokros, J., Russell, S. J., & Economopoulos, K. (1995). *Beyond arithmetic: Changing mathematics in the elementary classroom.* Palo Alto, CA: Dale Seymour Publications.

Moyer, P. S., & Mailley, E. (2004). *Inchworm and a Half:* Developing fraction and measurement concepts using mathematical representations. *Teaching Children Mathematics, 10,* 244–252.

Mulligan, J. T., & Mitchelmore, M. C. (1997). Young children's intuitive models of multiplication and division. *Journal for Research in Mathematics Education, 28,* 309–330.

National Council of Teachers of Mathematics. (1989). *Curriculum and evaluation standards for school mathematics.* Reston, VA: Author.

National Council of Teachers of Mathematics. (1991). *Professional standards for teaching mathematics.* Reston, VA: Author.

National Council of Teachers of Mathematics. (1995). *Assessment standards for school mathematics.* Reston, VA: Author.

National Council of Teachers of Mathematics. (2000). *Principles and standards for school mathematics.* Reston, VA: Author.

National Council of Teachers of Mathematics. (2004). *News Bulletin 40*(6). Reston, VA: The Council.

National Research Council. (2001). *Adding it up: Helping children learn mathematics.* J. Kilpatrick, J. Swafford, & B. Findell (Eds.). Mathematics Learning Study Committee, Center for Education Division of Behavioral and Social Sciences and Education. Washington, DC: National Academy Press.

Nelson, R. B. (1993). *Proofs without words: Exercises in visual thinking.* Washington, DC: MAA.

Noddings, N. (1993). Constuctivism and caring. In R. B. Davis & C. A. Maher (Eds.), *Schools, mathematics, and the world of reality* (pp. 35–50). Boston: Allyn & Bacon.

Noelting, G. (1980). The development of proportional reasoning and the ratio concept: 1. Differentiation of stages. *Educational Studies in Mathematics, 11,* 217–253.

Oakes, Jeannie (1985). *Keeping track: How schools structure inequality.* New Haven: Yale University Press.

O'Brien, T. C. (1999). Parrot math. *Phi Delta Kappan, 80,* 434–438.

Oppedal, D.C. (1995). Mathematics is something good. *Teaching Children Mathematics, 2,* 36–40.

Papert, S. (1980). *Mindstorms: Children, computers, and powerful ideas.* New York: Basic Books.

Parker, M. (2004). Reasoning and working proportionally with percent. *Mathematics Teaching in the Middle School, 9,* 326–330.

Perkins, I., & Flores, A. (2002). Mathematical notations and procedures of recent immigrant students. *Mathematics Teaching in the Middle School, 7,* 346–351.

Poplin, M. S. (1988a). Holistic/constructivist principles of the teaching/learning process: Implications for the field of learning disabilities. *Journal of Learning Disabilities, 21,* 401–416.

Poplin, M. S. (1988b). The reductionistic fallacy in learning disabilities: Replicating the past by reducing the present. *Journal of Learning Disabilities, 21,* 389–398.

Post, T. R. (1981). Fractions: Results and implications from the national assessment. *Arithmetic Teacher, 28*(9), 26–31.

Post, T. R., Behr, M. J., & Lesh, R. A. (1988). Proportionality and the development of prealgebra understandings. In A. F. Coxford (Ed.), *The ideas of algebra, K–12* (pp. 78–90). Reston, VA: National Council of Teachers of Mathematics.

Post, T. R., Wachsmuth, I., Lesh, R. A., & Behr, M. J. (1985). Order and equivalence of rational numbers: A cognitive analysis. *Journal for Research in Mathematics Education, 16,* 18–36.

Pothier, Y., & Sawada, D. (1983). Partitioning: The emergence of rational number ideas in young children. *Journal for Research in Mathematics Education, 14,* 307–317.

Powell, C. A., & Hunting, R. P. (2003). Fractions in the early-years curriculum: More needed, not less. *Teaching Children Mathematics, 10,* 6–7.

Rasmussen, C., Yackel, E., & King, K. (2003). Social and sociomathematical norms in the mathematics classroom. In H. L. Schoen & R. I. Charles (Eds.), *Teaching mathematics through problem solving: Grades 6–12* (pp. 143–154). Reston, VA: National Council of Teachers of Mathematics.

Rathmell, E. C. (1978). Using thinking strategies to teach the basic skills. In M. N. Suydam (Ed.), *Developing computational skills* (pp. 13–38). Reston, VA: National Council of Teachers of Mathematics.

Rathmell, E. C., & Leutzinger, L. P. (2000). *Thinking with numbers.* (Separate packets for each operation.) Cedar Falls, IA: Thinking With Numbers.

Rectanus, C. (1997). *Math by all means: Area and perimeter, grades 5–6.* Sausalito, CA: Math Solutions Publications.

Resnick, L. B. (1983). A developmental theory of number understanding. In H. P. Ginsburg (Ed.), *The development of mathematical thinking* (pp. 109–151). New York: Academic Press.

Reys, B. J., & Reys, R. E. (1995). Japanese mathematics education: What makes it work. *Teaching Children Mathematics, 1,* 474–475.

Reys, B. J., Robinson, E., Sconiers, S., & Mark, J. (1999). Mathematics curricula based on rigorous national standards: What, why, and how? *Phi Delta Kappan, 80,* 454–456.

Reys, R. E. (1998). Computation versus number sense. *Mathematics Teaching in the Middle School, 4,* 110–113.

Reys, R. E., & Reys, B. J. (1983). *Guide to using estimation skills and strategies (GUESS)* (Boxes I and II). Palo Alto, CA: Dale Seymour.

Riordin, J. E. & Noyce, P. E. (2001). The impact of two *Standards*-based mathematics curricula on student achievement in Massachusetts. *Journal for Research in Mathematics Education, 32,* 368–398.

Ross, S. H. (1986). *The development of children's place-value numeration concepts in grades two through five.* Presented at the annual meeting of the American Educational Research Association, San Francisco. (ERIC Document Reproduction Service No. ED 2773 482.)

Ross, S. H. (1989). Parts, wholes, and place value: A developmental perspective. *Arithmetic Teacher, 36*(6), 47–51.

Rowan, T. E. (1995, March). Helping children construct mathematical understanding with IMPACT. Presented at the regional meeting of the National Council of Teachers of Mathematics, Chicago, IL.

Rowan, T. E., & Bourne, B. (1994). *Thinking like mathematicians: Putting the K–4 standards into practice.* Portsmouth, NH: Heinemann.

Rubenstein, R. N. (2000). Word origins: Building communication connections. *Mathematics Teaching in the Middle School, 5,* 493–498.

Russell, S. J. (1997, April). *Using video to study students' strategies for whole-number operations.* Paper presented at the annual meeting of the National Council of Teachers of Mathematics, Minneapolis, MN.

Sáenz-Ludlow, A. (2004). Metaphor and numerical diagrams in the arithmetical activity of a fourth-grade class. *Journal for Research in Mathematics Education, 35,* 34–56.

Schifter, D. (1999). Reasoning about operations: Early algebraic thinking, grades K through 6. In L. Stiff & F. Curcio (Eds.), *Developing mathematical reasoning in grades K–12* (pp. 62–81). Reston, VA: National Council of Teachers of Mathematics.

Schifter, D., Bastable, V., & Russell, S. J. (1999a). *Developing mathematical understanding: Numbers and operations, Part 1, Building a system of tens (Casebook).* Parsippany, NJ: Dale Seymour Publications.

Schifter, D., Bastable, V., & Russell, S. J. (1999b). *Developing mathematical understanding: Numbers and operations, Part 2, Making meaning for operations (Casebook).* Parsippany, NJ: Dale Seymour Publications.

Schifter, D., Bastable, V., & Russell, S. J. (1999c). *Developing mathematical understanding: Numbers and operations, Part 2, Making meaning for operations (Facilitator's Guide).* Parsippany, NJ: Dale Seymour Publications.

Schifter, D., Bastable, V., Monk, S., & Russell, S. J. (in press). *Developing mathematical ideas: Number and operations, Part 3, Reasoning algebraically about operations (Facilitator's Guide).* Parsippany, NJ: Dale Seymour Publications.

Schifter, D., & Fosnot, C. T. (1993). *Reconstructing mathematics education: Stories of teachers meeting the challenge of reform.* New York: Teachers College Press.

Schmidt, W. H., McKnight, C. C., & Raizen, S. A. (1996). *Executive summary of a splintered vision: An investigation of U.S. science and mathematics education.* Boston: Kluwer.

Schoenfeld, A. H. (1992). Learning to think mathematically: Problem solving, metacognition, and sense making in mathematics. In D. A. Grouws (Ed.), *Handbook of research on teaching and learning* (pp. 334–370). Old Tappan, NJ: Macmillan.

Schroeder, T. L., & Lester, F. K., Jr. (1989). Developing understanding in mathematics via problem solving. In P. R. Trafton (Ed.), *New directions for elementary school mathematics* (pp. 31–42). Reston, VA: National Council of Teachers of Mathematics.

Schwartz, S. L. (1996). Hidden messages in teacher talk: Praise and empowerment. *Teaching Children Mathematics, 2,* 396–401.

Sconyers, J. M. (1995). Proof and the middle school mathematics student. *Mathematics Teaching in the Middle School, 1,* 516–518.

Seymour, D. (1971). *Tangramath.* Palo Alto, CA: Creative Publications.

Shaughnessy, J. M. (2003). Research on students' understanding of probability. In J. Kilpatrick, W. G. Martin, & D. Schifter (Eds.), *A research companion to Principles and Standards for School Mathematics* (pp. 216–226). Reston, VA: National Council of Teachers of Mathematics.

Sheffield, L. J. (1999). Serving the needs of the mathematically promising. In L. J. Sheffield (Ed.), *Developing mathematically promising students* (pp. 43–55). Reston, VA: National Council of Teachers of Mathematics.

Sheffield, S. (1995). *Math and literature (K–3)* (Vol. 2). Sausalito, CA: Math Solutions Publications.

Shroyer, J., & Fitzgerald, W. (1986). *Mouse and elephant: Measuring growth.* Menlo Park, CA: AWL Supplemental.

Silver, E. A., & Kenney, P. A. (Eds.) (2000). *Results from the seventh mathematics assessment of the National Assessment of Educational Progress.* Reston, VA: National Council of Teachers of Mathematics.

Silver, E. A., Smith, M. S., & Nelson, B. S. (1995). The QUASAR project: Equity concerns meet mathematics education reform in the middle school. In W. G. Secada, E. Fennema, & L. B. Adajian (Eds.), *New directions for equity in mathematics education* (pp. 9–56). New York: Cambridge University Press.

Silver, E. A., & Stein, M. K. (1996). The QUASAR project: The "revolution of the possible" in mathematics instructional reform in urban middle schools. *Urban Education, 30,* 476–521.

Simon, M. A. (1995). Reconstructing mathematics pedagogy from a constructivist perspective. *Journal for Research in Mathematics Education, 26,* 114–145.

Skemp, R. (1978). Relational understanding and instrumental understanding. *Arithmetic Teacher, 26*(3), 9–15.

Smith, J. P., III. (2002). The development of students' knowledge of fractions and ratios. In B. Litwiller (Ed.), *Making sense of fractions, ratios, and proportions* (pp. 3–17). Reston, VA: National Council of Teachers of Mathematics.

Sowder, J. T., Wearne, D., Martin, W. G., & Strutchens, M. (2004). What do 8th-grade students know about mathematics? Changes over a decade. In P. Kloosterman & F. K. Lester, Jr., *Results and interpretations of the 1990–2000 mathematics assessments of the National Assessment of Educational Progress* (pp. 105–143). Reston, VA: National Council of Teachers of Mathematics.

Steffe, L. (1988). Children's construction of number sequences and multiplying schemes. In J. Hiebert & M. J. Behr (Eds.), *Number concepts and operations in the middle grades* (pp. 119–140). Hillsdale, NJ: Erlbaum.

Stein, M. K., Grover, B. W., & Henningsen, M. (1996). Building student capacity for mathematical thinking and reasoning: An analysis of mathematical tasks used in reform classrooms. *American Educational Research Journal, 33,* 455–488.

Stein, M. K., & Lane, S. (1996). Instructional tasks and the development of student capacity to think and reason: An analysis of the relationship between teaching and learning in a reform mathematics project. *Educational Research and Evaluation, 2*(1), 50–58.

Stenmark, J. K. (1989). *Assessment alternatives in mathematics: An overview of assessment techniques that promote learning.* Berkeley: EQUALS, University of California.

Stenmark, J. K. (Ed.). (1991). *Mathematics assessment: Myths, models, good questions, and practical suggestions.* Reston, VA: National Council of Teachers of Mathematics.

Stenmark, J. K., & Bush, W. S. (Eds.) (2001). *Mathematics assessment: A practical handbook for grades 3–5.* Reston, VA: National Council of Teachers of Mathematics.

Stephan, M., & Whitenack, J. (2003). Establishing classroom social and sociomathematical norms for problem solving. In F. K. Lester, Jr. & R. I. Charles (Eds.), *Teaching mathematics through problem solving: grades pre-K–6* (pp. 149–162). Reston, VA: National Council of Teachers of Mathematics.

Stoessiger, R., & Edmunds, J. (1992). *Natural learning and mathematics.* Portsmouth, NH: Heinemann.

Strutchens, M. E., Martin, W. G., & Kenney, P. A. (2003). What students know about measurement: Perspectives from the National Assessment of Educational Progress. In D. H. Clements (Ed.), *Learning and teaching measurement* (pp. 195–207). Reston, VA: National Council of Teachers of Mathematics.

Taber, S. B. (2002). Go ask Alice about multiplication of fractions. In B. Litwiller (Ed.), *Making sense of fractions, ratios, and proportions* (pp. 61–71). Reston, VA: National Council of Teachers of Mathematics.

Teachers of English to Speakers of Other Languages (TESOL). (1997). *TESOL ESL standards for pre-K–12 students.* Alexandria, VA: Author.

Theissen, D., Matthias, M., & Smith, J. (1998). *The wonderful world of mathematics: A critically annotated list of children's books in mathematics* (2nd ed.). Reston, VA: National Council of Teachers of Mathematics.

Thompson, C. S. (1990). Place value and larger numbers. In J. N. Payne (Ed.), *Mathematics for the young child* (pp. 89–108). Reston, VA: National Council of Teachers of Mathematics.

Thompson, P. W. (1994). Concrete materials and teaching for mathematical understanding. *Arithmetic Teacher, 41,* 556–558.

Thompson, T. D., & Preston, R. V. (2004). Measurement in the middle grades: Insights from NAEP and TIMSS. *Mathematics Teaching in the Middle School, 9,* 514–519.

Thornton, C. A. (1982). Doubles up—easy! *Arithmetic Teacher, 29*(8), 20.

Thornton, C. A. (1990). Strategies for the basic facts. In J. N. Payne (Ed.), *Mathematics for the young child* (pp. 133–151). Reston, VA: National Council of Teachers of Mathematics.

Thornton, C. A., & Toohey, M. A. (1984). *A matter of facts: (Addition, subtraction, multiplication, division)*. Palo Alto, CA: Creative Publications.

Tomlinson, C. A. (1999). *The differentiated classroom: Responding to the needs of all learners*. Alexandria, VA: Association for Supervision and Curriculum Development.

Torrence, E. (2003). Learning to think: An American third grader discovers mathematics in Holland. *Teaching Children Mathematics, 10*, 90–93.

Trafton, P. R., & Claus, A. S. (1994). A changing curriculum for a changing age. In C. A. Thornton & N. S. Bley (Eds.), *Windows of opportunity: Mathematics for students with special needs* (pp. 19–39). Reston, VA: National Council of Teachers of Mathematics.

Tsuruda, G. (1994). *Putting it together: Middle school math in transition*. Portsmouth, NH: Heinemann.

Tzur, R. (1999). An integrated study of children's construction of improper fractions and the teacher's role in promoting learning. *Journal for Research in Mathematics Education, 30*, 390–416.

U.S. Dept. of Education, Office of Educational Research and Improvement. (1996). *Pursuing excellence: A study of U.S. eighth-grade mathematics and science teaching, learning, curriculum, and achievement in international context*. NCES 97–198, by L. Peak. Washington, DC: U.S. Government Printing Office.

U.S. Dept. of Education, Office of Educational Research and Improvement. (1997a). *Introduction to TIMSS*. Washington, DC: U.S. Government Printing Office.

U.S. Dept. of Education, Office of Educational Research and Improvement. (1997b). *Moderator's guide to eighth-grade mathematics lessons: United States, Japan, and Germany*. Washington, DC: U.S. Government Printing Office.

U.S. Dept. of Education, Office of Educational Research and Improvement. (1997c). *Pursuing excellence: A study of U.S. fourth-grade mathematics and science achievement in international context*. NCES 97–255. Washington, DC: U.S. Government Printing Office.

Van de Walle, J. A., & Lovin, L. H. (2006). *Teaching student-centered mathematics: Grades 5–8*. Boston: Allyn and Bacon.

van Hiele, P. M. (1999). Developing geometric thinking through activities that begin with play. *Teaching Children Mathematics, 5*, 310–316.

von Glasersfeld, E., (1990). An exposition of constructivism: Why some like it radical. In R. B. Davis, C. A. Maher, & N. Noddings (Eds.), *Constructivist views on the teaching and learning of mathematics* (pp. 19–29). Reston, VA: National Council of Teachers of Mathematics.

von Glasersfeld, E. (1996). Introduction: Aspects of constructivism. In C. T. Fosnot (Ed.), *Constructivism: Theory, perspectives, and practice* (pp. 3–7). New York: Teachers College Press.

Wakefield, D. V. (2000). Math as a second language. *The Educational Forum, 64*, 272–279.

Walter, M. I. (1970). *Boxes, squares and other things: A teacher's guide for a unit in informal geometry*. Reston, VA: National Council of Teachers of Mathematics.

Watanabe, T. (2001). Let's eliminate fractions from the primary curricula! *Teaching Children Mathematics, 8*, 70–72.

Watson, J. M., & Shaughnessy, J. M. (2004). Proportional reasoning: Lessons learned from research in data and chance. *Mathematics Teaching in the Middle School, 10*, 104–109.

Wearne, D., & Kouba, V. L. (2000). Rational numbers. In E. A. Silver & P. A Kenney (Eds.), *Results from the seventh mathematics assessment of the National Assessment of Educational Progress* (pp. 163–191). Reston, VA: National Council of Teachers of Mathematics.

Welchman-Tischler, R. (1992). *How to use children's literature to teach mathematics*. Reston, VA: National Council of Teachers of Mathematics.

Wheatley, G. H., & Hersberger, J. (1986). A calculator estimation activity. In H. Schoen (Ed.), *Estimation and mental computation* (pp. 182–185). Reston, VA: National Council of Teachers of Mathematics.

Whitin, D. J., & Wilde, S. (1992). *Read any good math lately? Children's books for mathematical learning, K–6*. Portsmouth, NH: Heinemann.

Whitin, D. J., & Wilde, S. (1995). *It's the story that counts: More children's books for mathematical learning, K–6*. Portsmouth, NH: Heinemann.

Winter, M. J., Lappan, G., Phillips, E., & Fitzgerald, W. (1986). *Middle grades mathematics project: Spatial visualization*. Menlo Park, CA: AWL Supplemental.

Wood, T., Cobb, P., Yackel, E., & Dillon, D. (Eds.). (1993). *Rethinking elementary school mathematics: Insights and issues (Journal for Research in Mathematics Education* Monograph No. 6). Reston, VA: National Council of Teachers of Mathematics.

Wood, T., & Sellers, P. (1996). Assessment of a problem-centered mathematics program: Third grade. *Journal for Research in Mathematics Education, 27*, 337–353.

Wood, T., & Sellers, P. (1997). Deepening the analysis: Longitudinal assessment of a problem-centered mathematics program. *Journal for Research in Mathematics Education, 28*, 163–168.

Wood, T., & Turner-Vorbeck, T. (2001). Extending the conception of mathematics teaching. In T. Wood, B. S. Nelson, & Warfield, J. (Eds.), *Beyond classical pedagogy: Teaching elementary school mathematics* (pp. 185–208). Mahwah, NJ: Erlbaum.

Yackel, E. (1999). A foundation for algebraic reasoning in the early grades. *Teaching Children Mathematics, 3*, 276–280.

Yackel, E., & Cobb, P. (1996). Sociomathematical norms, argumentation, and autonomy in mathematics. *Journal for Research in Mathematics Education, 27*, 458–477.

Yackel, E., Cobb, P., Wood, T., Wheatley, G. H., & Merkel, G. (1990). The importance of social interaction in children's construction of mathematical knowledge. In T. J. Cooney (Ed.), *Teaching and learning mathematics in the 1990s* (pp. 12–21). Reston, VA: National Council of Teachers of Mathematics.

Children's Literature References

Anno, M. (1982). *Anno's counting house*. New York: Philomel Books.

Anno, M. (1994). *Anno's magic seeds*. New York: Philomel Books.

Anno, M., & Anno, M. (1983). *Anno's mysterious multiplying jar*. New York: Philomel Books.

Ash, R. (1996). *Incredible comparisons*. New York: Dorling Kindersley.

Briggs, R. (1970). *Jim and the beanstalk*. New York: Coward-McCann.

Carle, E. (1969). *The very hungry caterpillar*. New York: Putnam.

Chalmers, M. (1986). *Six dogs, twenty-three cats, forty-five mice, and one hundred sixteen spiders*. New York: HarperCollins.

Chwast, S. (1993). *The twelve circus rings*. San Diego, CA: Gulliver Books, Harcourt Brace Jovanovich.

Clement, R. (1991). *Counting on Frank*. Milwaukee: Gareth Stevens Children's Books.

Cushman, R. (1991). *Do you wanna bet? Your chance to find out about probability*. New York: Clarion Books.

Dee, R. (1988). *Two ways to count to ten*. New York: Holt.

Enzensberger, H. M. (1997). *The number devil*. New York: Metropolitan Books.

Friedman, A. (1994). *The king's commissioners*. New York: Scholastic.

Gag, W. (1928). *Millions of cats*. New York: Coward-McCann.

Giganti, P. (1988). *How many snails? A counting book*. New York: Greenwillow.

Giganti, P. (1992). *Each orange had 8 slices*. New York: Greenwillow.

Grossman, B. (1996). *My little sister ate one hare*. New York: Crown.

Hoban, T. (1981). *More than one*. New York: Greenwillow.

Hutchins, P. (1986). *The doorbell rang*. New York: Greenwillow.

Jaspersohn, W. (1993). *Cookies*. Old Tappan, NJ: Macmillan.

Juster, N. (1961). *The phantom tollbooth*. New York: Random House.

Lobal, A. (1970). *Frog and Toad are friends*. New York: HarperCollins.

Mathews, L. (1979). *Gator pie*. New York: Dodd, Mead.

McKissack, P. C. (1992). *A million fish . . . more or less*. New York: Knopf.

Munsch, R. (1987). *Moira's birthday*. Toronto: Annick Press.

Myller, R. (1990). *How big is a foot?* New York: Dell.

Norton, M. (1953). *The borrowers*. New York: Harcourt Brace.

Parker, T. (1984). *In one day*. Boston: Houghton Mifflin.

Pluckrose, H. (1988). *Pattern*. New York: Franklin Watts.

St. John, G. (1975). *How to count like a Martian*. New York: Walck.

Schwartz, D. (1985). *How much is a million?* New York: Lothrop, Lee & Shepard.

Schwartz, D. (1989). *If you made a million*. New York: Lothrop, Lee & Shepard.

Schwartz, D. M. (1999). *If you hopped like a frog*. New York: Scholastic Press.

Scieszka, J., & Smith, L. (1995). *Math curse*. New York: Viking Penguin.

Sharmat, M. W. (1979). *The 329th friend*. New York: Four Winds Press.

Silverstein, S. (1974). One inch tall. In *Where the sidewalk ends* (p. 55). New York: Harper & Row.

Tahan, M. (1993). *The man who counted: A collection of mathematical adventures* (Trans. L. Clark & A. Reid). New York: Norton.

Weiss, A. E. (1991). *Lotteries: Who wins, who loses*. Hillsdale, NJ: Enslow.

Wells, R. E. (1993). *Is a blue whale the biggest thing there is?* Morton Grove, IL: Whitman.

Wolkstein, D. (1972). *8,000 stones*. New York: Doubleday.

Computer Software

Broderbund. (1995a). *James discovers math*. Novato, CA: Author.

Broderbund. (1995b). *Tabletop, Jr*. Novato, CA: Author.

Broderbund. (1996a). *Kid pix*. Novato, CA: Author.

Broderbund. (1996b). *The zoombinis' logical adventure*. Novato, CA: Author.

Clements, D. H., & Meredith, J. S. (1994). *Turtle math*. Highgate Springs, VT: Logo Computer Systems.

Clements, D. H., & Sarama, J. (1995). *Shapes—Mathematical Thinking*. Highgate Springs, VT: Logo Computer Systems Inc. (LCSI).

Davidson & Associates. (n.d.). *Math for the real world*. Torrence, CA: Author.

Davidson & Associates. (n.d.). *Mega Math Blaster*. Torrence, CA: Author.

Edmark Corp. (1993). *Millie's math house*. Redmond, WA: Author.

Edmark Corp.(1996a). *GeoComputer*. Redmond, WA: Author.

Edmark Corp. (1996b). *Mighty math: Number heroes*. Redmond, WA: Author.

Education Development Center. (1991). *My travels with Gulliver*. Scotts Valley, CA: Wings for Learning.

EduQuest. (1994). *Math and more 3: Patterns on lattices*. Atlanta: IBM Corp.

EdVenture Software. (1997). *Gold medal mathematics*. Norwalk, CT: EdVenture Software.

Gamco Education Software. (1994). *Word problem square off*. Clayton, MO: Siboney Learning Group.

Hickey, A. (1996). *Unifix software*. Rowley, MA: Didax Educational Resources.

Jazz Interactive. *Performance math*. Glenview, IL: Scott Foresman–Addison Wesley.

Key Curriculum Press. (2001). *The geometer's sketchpad* (Version 4.0). Berkeley, CA: Key Curriculum Press.

Knowledge Adventure. (n.d.). *Math for the real world*. Pleasantville, NY: Author.

MECC. (1994). *TesselMania!* [Computer software]. Minneapolis, MN: Author.

MECC. (1995a). *MathKeys: Geometry, Vol. 1* [Computer Software]. Minneapolis, MN: Author.

MECC. (1995b). *MathKeys: Unlocking probability, Vols. 2 & 3* [Computer Software]. Minneapolis, MN: Author.

MECC. (1995c). *MathKeys: Unlocking whole numbers grades 3–5* [Computer Software]. Minneapolis, MN: Author.

MECC. (1996a). *MathKeys: Unlocking whole numbers grades K–2* [Computer Software]. Minneapolis, MN: Author.

MECC. (1996b). *MathKeys: Unlocking fractions and decimals grades 3–5* [Computer Software]. Minneapolis, MN: Author.

O'Brien, T. C. *Teasers by Tobbs: Numbers and operations* [Computer Software]. Pleasantville, NY: Sunburst Communications.

Pierian Spring Software. (1996). *CampOS Math* [Computer Software]. Portland, OR: Author.

Riverdeep. (1994a). *Tangible math: The geometry inventor*. Cambridge, MA: Author.

Riverdeep. (1994b). *Tangible math: The probability constructor*. Cambridge, MA: Author.

Riverdeep. (1994c). *TesselMania!* Mahwah, NJ: Author.

Riverdeep. (1995). *Math munchers deluxe*. Mahway, NJ: Author.

Riverdeep. (1996). *The new adventures of Jasper Woodbury*. Mahwah, NJ: Author.

Riverdeep. (1999). *Kid pix*. Mahwah, NJ: Author.

Riverdeep. (n.d.). *CornerStone ATS 3.2*. Mahwah, NJ: Author.

Sunburst Technology. (1995). *Shape up*. Pleasantville, NY: Author.

Sunburst Technology. (1997). *Grouping and place value*. Pleasantville, NY: Author.

Sunburst Technology. (1998a). *Combining and breaking apart numbers*. Pleasantville, NY: Author.

Sunburst Technology. (1998b). *Fraction operations*. Pleasantville, NY: Author.

Sunburst Technology. (1998c). *Number meanings and counting* [Computer Software]. Pleasantville, NY: Author.

Sunburst Technology. (1998d). *Representing fractions* [Computer Software]. Pleasantville, NY: Author.

Sunburst Technology. (n.d.). *Factory deluxe*. Pleasantville, NY: Author.

Sunburst Technology. (n.d.). *Math arena*. Pleasantville, NY: Author.

Sunburst Technology. (n.d.). *Splish splash math*. Pleasantville, NY: Author.

Sunburst Technology. (n.d.). *The cruncher 2.0*. Pleasantville, NY: Author.

Sunburst Technology. (n.d.) *The king's rule*. Pleasantville, NY: Author.

Texas Instruments. (1994). *Cabri geometry II* [Computer Software]. Dallas: Author.

Tom Snyder. (1993). *The graph club* [Computer Software]. Watertown, MA: Author.

Tom Snyder Productions. (1998). *Fizz & Martina's math adventures: Lights, camera, fractions* [Computer Software]. Watertown, MA: Author.

Tom Snyder Productions. (1999). *Prime time math*. Watertown, MA: Author.

Absolute value, 503–504
Acceleration, for mathematically promising students, 104
Accommodation, 23, 65–66, 112
Accountability, 8
Adding It Up (NRC), 96, 108
Addition, 144–151
  comparison models, 149
  computational estimation in, 251, 252
  contextual problems, 146–147
  of decimals, 347–348
  of fractions, 317–322
  invented strategies for, 222–223, 224
  model-based problems, 147–148, 226
  number relationships for, 206–209
  order property, 149–150
  in problem-solving approach with integers, 499–502
  problem structures, 144–146
  proportional reasoning and, 355–357
  strategies for mastery of basic facts, 168–174
  symbolism in, 147
  technology and, 150
  traditional algorithms for, 226–228, 319–321
  two-digit, 223
  zero property, 150, 169
African Americans. *See* Cultural and linguistic diversity
Algebraic reasoning, 259–290
  algebraic thinking and, 260
  charts and other number patterns, 270–271
  children's literature and, 289
  conjectures in, 266–267
  equal sign, meaning of, 260–262
  explicit structure in number system, 266–268
  functions in, 271–289
  generalization in number and operation, 260–265
  mathematical modeling in, 290
  odd-even relationships and, 267–268
  repeating patterns, 268–270
  sequences, 271–275
  variables in equations, 262–265
Algebra standard, 4
Alignment, grading and, 93
Alternative methods
  of assessment, 80–81
  in problem solving, 55
American Association for the Advancement of Science, 118
Analysis, in geometry, 410–411, 413–414, 420–427, 433–435, 440–442, 445–447
Analytic scale, 82–83
Anchoring numbers to 5 and 10, 125, 127–129
Anderson, C. B., 186, 215
Anecdotal notes, 85

Angles
  measurement of, 392–394
  units of, 392–393
Annenberg/CPB Projects, 118
Anno's Counting House (Anno), 139
Anno's Magic Seeds (Anno), 289
Anno's Mysterious Multiplying Jar (Anno & Anno), 289
Applets, 111, 116, 119, 204, 236, 282, 419, 439–440
Appropriate assessment, 80–82
  nature of, 80–81
  tasks in, 80–82
Approximation
  in fraction computation, 340–341
  in measurement, 378
Arcytech, 119
Area
  measuring, 382–387, 399–402
  perimeter and, 386–387
  units of, 384–386
Area models, 233–234, 236, 295, 311–313, 485–486
Arrays, 155, 181
Asian Americans. *See* Cultural and linguistic diversity
Assessment, 78–93
  appropriate, 80–82
  computational estimation and, 254
  of conceptual mathematics, 80
  of data analysis, 489
  disposition in, 80
  of functions, 286
  in geometry, 449–450
  grading in, 82, 92–93
  homogeneous grouping and, 96
  of mathematical processes, 80
  of measurement concepts, 380, 391
  nature of, 78
  observation in, 84–86, 241
  in place-value development, 193–194, 209
  of probability, 489
  problem solving approach and, 39
  of procedural mathematics, 80, 93
  purposes of, 79–80
  rubrics in, 82–84
  tests in, 90–92
  tracking and, 96
  of whole-number computation, 222–223, 241
  writing and journals in, 86–90
Assessment Principle (NCTM), 3
Assessment Standards for School Mathematics (NCTM), 2, 6, 78–80
Assimilation, 23
Association for Supervision and Curriculum Development, 118
Attention deficits, adaptations for, 98
Attitude inventories, 89–90

Attitudes, 58–59
  calculators and student, 108–109
  in problem solving, 58–59
  relational understanding and, 27
Attribute materials, 454–457
Authentic assessment, 80–81, 82
Automaticity, 69
Averages, 464–467
Awareness, gender equity and, 103
Axis of symmetry, 433

Background, in teaching English language learners (ELL), 101
Baker, K. M., 508
Ball, D. L., 35
Bar graphs, 459–460
Baron, C., 186
Base-ten blocks, electronic, 111
Base-ten concepts. *See* Place-value development
Base-ten language, 198–199
Basic facts. *See* Mastery of basic facts; Strategies for mastery of basic facts
  defined, 165
Basic skills, 2, 7, 14, 56, 108–109, 168
Bastable, V., 164, 215
Bay, J. M., 314
Bay-Williams, J., 351
Beliefs, 58
  gender and, 103
  relational understanding and, 27
Bennett, A. B., 351
Bereska, L., 473–474
Berry, R. Q. III, 105
Best-fit lines, 470
Best Vacation Ever, The (Murphy), 472
Big ideas, 27, 48, 91
Blacks. *See* Cultural and linguistic diversity
Blocks and tiles software, 112
Boaler, J., 59
Bolster, C. H., 473–474
Bolster, L. C., 473–474
Borrowers, The (Norton), 372
Bourne, B., 60
Box-and-whisker plots, 467–469
Brainstorming, 44, 88–89
Brandy, T., 35
Bresser, R., 258
Bridging, 226
Buchholz, L., 186
Burns, M., 76, 214–215, 314
Burton, G., 141
Buschmann, L., 35, 60
Bush, W. S., 94

Cabri Geometry II (Texas Instruments), 426
Cai, J., 373
Calculators, 107–113
  benefits of using, 107–108
  computational estimation activities, 254–255

counting and, 123
decimals and, 342
developmental approach and, 32
for every student, every day, 109
fractions and, 301
graphing, 109–111, 114, 472
myths and fears concerning, 108–109
notation and, 493–494
numeral recognition and, 123
place value and, 207
probability with, 488–489
for students with intellectual difficulties, 99
tests and, 90
Campbell, P. F., 243
Capacity
  measurement of, 387–389, 402–404
  units of, 388–389
Cardinality principle, 122
Carpenter, T. P., 60, 163, 186, 291
Cavanagh, M., 292, 450
CBI (Conceptually Based Instruction), 218n
CBL (computer-based laboratory), 110
Center for Implementing Technology in Education (CITEd), 119
Central tendency, measures of, 464–467
CGI (Cognitively Guided Instruction), 147, 163, 166, 186, 218n
Chance. *See* Probability
Charles, R. I., 60
Charts
  in algebraic reasoning, 270–271
  hundreds chart, 201–204, 207–208, 270
  in problem solving, 57
  thousands chart, 203
Checklists
  for full classes, 86
  for individuals, 85–86
Cherrington, A., 94
Children's literature
  algebraic reasoning and, 289
  computational estimation and, 257
  data analysis and, 472–473, 489–490
  decimals and, 349–350
  early number sense and, 138–139
  for exponents, integers, and real numbers, 507–508
  fractions in, 313
  mathematical operations and, 162
  measurement and, 404–405
  percents and, 349–350
  place-value development and, 213–214
  probability and, 472–473, 489–490

Children's literature (continued)
   in problem solving, 51–52
   proportional reasoning and,
      371–372
   whole-number computation
      and, 241–242
Children with learning problems,
   96–99
   intellectual disabilities, 98–99
   specific learning disabilities,
      96–98
Chunking, 397
Circle graphs, 463–464
Circles
   formulas for, 402
   nature of, 404
   relationships within, 426
Circumference of circle, 402
Clarification, in problem solving,
   55–56
Clements, D., 406
Clock reading, 390–391
Cluster graphs, 459
Cluster problems
   computational estimation, 249
   in division, 238
   in multiplication, 231–233
Cobb, P., 474
Coburn, T. G., 291
Coffey, D. C., 491
Cognitively Guided Instruction
   (CGI) (Fennema et al.), 147,
   163, 166, 186, 218n
Cognitive schemas, 23
Coherence Standard (NCTM), 79
Combination (Cartesian product)
   problems, 161
Combining and Breaking Apart
   Numbers (Tenth Planet), 133
Common denominators, 299–300,
   319–321, 329
Communication standard, 4, 5, 80
Communities of learners
   developmental approach and,
      30, 34
   in problem solving, 46–47, 56
Commutative property
   in addition, 149–150
   in multiplication, 157
Comparisons, 145
   in addition, 149
   fractions and, 304–306
   measurements and, 376,
      378–379, 382–384, 387–388,
      389–390, 392
   multiplicative, 152, 153
   ratios and, 359–361, 366
   in subtraction, 149
Compatible numbers, 253–254
Compensation strategies, 231
Complete-number strategies,
   230
Composition of transformations,
   434
Comprehensible input, for
   English language learners
   (ELL), 101–102
Computation, 25–26
   with decimals, 346–349
   fluency in, 217–220
   with fractions. See Fraction
      computation
   mental, 44, 140–141
   whole-number. See Whole-
      number computation

Computational estimation,
   245–257
   addition in, 251, 252
   assessment and, 254
   children's literature and, 257
   choosing form of, 246
   cluster problems and, 249
   with decimals, 256–257, 346–349
   defined, 246
   division in, 251, 252–253
   without estimates, 247–248
   exercises for, 254–256
   with fractions, 256–257,
      306–308, 321–322, 326
   from invented strategies,
      248–249
   multiplication in, 251, 252–253
   with percents, 256–257,
      345–346
   real-world applications of, 246
   strategies for, 250–254
   subtraction in, 251, 252
   suggestions for teaching,
      246–247
   technology in, 254, 256
   understanding, 246
Computational forms of
   equations, 145–156
Computer-based laboratory
   (CBL), 110
Computers in mathematics,
   111–114. See also Internet
   resources; Software;
   Technology in mathematics
Conceptually Based Instruction
   (CBI), 218n
Conceptual mathematics, 27. See
   also Early number concepts
   assessment of, 80
   calculators in, 108
   defined, 28
   examples of problem-based
      tasks in, 39–40
   instructional software for, 114
   interaction with procedural
      mathematics, 28
Cones, volume of, 403–404
Conjectures, in algebraic
   reasoning, 266–267
   making, 266
   "proving," 266–267, 268
Connected Mathematics, 8
   Grade 6: Bits and Pieces II,
      321–322, 349, 350
   Grade 7: Comparing and
      Scaling, 365–366
   Grade 7: Variables and
      Patterns, 283
   Grade 8: Growing, Growing,
      Growing, 496
   Grade 8: Kaleidoscopes,
      Hubcaps, and Mirrors, 439
Connections standard, 4, 5
Constructivism, 22–34
   classroom influences on
      learning and, 28–34
   developmental approach and,
      29–30, 34
   examples of constructed
      learning, 23–24
   models and, 32–33
   nature of, 22–24
   rote learning and, 24
   teaching approach for, 54–56
   understanding and, 24–28

Content standards (NCTM), 4
Contextual problems. See also
   Children's literature
   in addition, 146–147
   analyzing, 158–160
   in division, 154, 158–160
   to encourage invented strategy
      use, 221
   key word strategy in, 160
   in multiplication, 154, 158–160
   representations of functions,
      277, 280
   in subtraction, 146–147
   two-step, 160–161
Continuous data graphs, 461–463
Cookies (Jaspersohn), 242
Cooperative learning groups, for
   English language learners
   (ELL), 102
CornerStone ATS 3.2: Mathematics
   (Riverdeep Interactive
   Learning), 256
Counters, electronic, 111
Counting
   calculators and, 123
   in early number concepts,
      122–124, 172–173
   with subtraction, 223, 224
Counting on Frank (Clement), 372,
   404–405
Counting skills, 122, 123–124,
   172–173
   counts by groups and singles,
      189
   counts by ones, 188
   counts by tens and ones, 189
   fractional-parts counting,
      298–299
   place-value development and,
      188–189
Count On, 119
Credits, 497
Crown, W. D., 117
Cruncher, 2.0, The (Sunburst),
   471–472
Cubes, 403
Cuevas, G. J., 292
Cuisenaire Rods, electronic, 111
Cultural and linguistic diversity,
   99–102
   culturally relevant mathematics
      instruction, 99–100
   English language learners
      (ELL), 67, 100–102, 112
   ethnomathematics, 100
Curcio, F. R., 474
Curriculum
   modifications for intellectual
      disabilities, 95
   standards-based, 8, 10
   traditional, 8
Curriculum and Evaluation
   Standards for School
   Mathematics (NCTM), 2, 78
Curriculum Principle (NCTM), 3
Customary system, 396
Cylinders
   nature of, 404
   volume of, 403

Dacey, L., 292, 450
Data analysis and probability
   standard, 4, 452–473
   assessment and, 489
   attribute materials, 454–457

children's literature and,
      472–473, 489–490
   descriptive statistics, 464–467
   functional relationships,
      272–273, 471
   gathering data, 453–454
   graphical representations,
      458–464
   probability, 475–490
   scatter plots, 469–471
   shape of data, 458
   simulations, 486–489
   technology and, 457, 458–459,
      471–472
Davis, B., 332
Debits, 497
DecaDots 10-Frame Tiles, 192
Decimals, 333–350. See also
   Percents
   approximation, 340–341
   children's literature and,
      349–350
   computation with, 346–349
   connections with fractions,
      333–343
   estimation with, 256–257,
      346–349
   number sense, 338–343
   ordering decimal numbers,
      341–342
   technology and, 342
Deduction, in geometry, 411–414,
   427–431, 435–437, 442–443,
   447–448
Denominators, 299–300,
   319–321, 329
Dependent events, 486, 489
Depth, for mathematically
   promising students, 104
Descriptive statistics, 464–467
   averages, 464–467
   box-and-whisker plots, 467–469
   mean, 464–467
Developmental approach, 29–30,
   34
   calculators and, 32
   foundations of, 29–30
   strategies for effective teaching,
      34
Diagnostic interviews, in
   assessment of whole-number
   computation, 241
Diameter of circle, 402
Differentiated tasks, 65
Difficulty of problems, 146
Digit Correspondence Task, 201
Dilation, 435
Direct modeling, in whole-
   number computation,
   217–218
Discipline problems, 39
Discourse, in problem solving, 47,
   53–56
Disposition
   in assessment, 80
   nature of, 58
Distributive property, in
   multiplication, 158
Diversity, 64–67, 95–104
   accommodation for, 23, 65–66,
      112
   children with intellectual
      disabilities, 98–99
   children with learning
      problems, 96–99

cultural and linguistic, 99–102
differentiated tasks and, 65
drill and practice, 69
gender, 102–103
goal of equitable instruction, 96
heterogeneous groupings and, 65
homogeneous grouping, effects of, 96
instructional principles for, 96
listening to students, 66–67
mathematically promising students, 46, 103–104
meeting needs of all children and, 95–96
modification for, 65–66
multiple entry points and, 39, 40–41, 51, 64
tracking, effects of, 96
Division, 152–162
computational estimation in, 251, 252–253
contextual problems, 154, 158–160
of decimals, 348–349
of fractions, 326–331
fractions as indicated, 502–503
invented strategies for, 236–238
model-based problems, 155, 238–239
by one-digit divisors, 238–239
in problem-solving approach with integers, 502–503
problem structures, 152–153
strategies for mastery of facts, 181–183
symbolism in, 154, 241
traditional algorithms for, 238–241, 329–331
by two-digit divisors, 239–241
zero in, 158
Divisors
fractional, 327–328
one-digit, 238–239
two-digit, 239–241
whole-number, 327
Dodecahedron, 448–449
Doing mathematics, 12–20
basics in, 2, 7, 14, 56, 108–109, 168
environment for, 14, 20
helping students with, 20
mathematics as science of pattern and order, 13
sample problems for, 14–20
traditional views in, 12–13
verbs of, 13–14
Dolk, M., 141, 163–164, 243
Doorbell Rang, The (Hutchins), 51–52, 313
Dot card activities, 133–135
Double relationships, 136–137, 169–170, 172, 177, 180
Doyle, D., 292
Do You Wanna Bet? Your Chance to Find Out About Probability (Cushman), 489–490
Drawings
in journals, 88
tests and, 90
Drawing software, 114
Drill and practice, 24, 56–57, 67–69
appropriateness of, 69
avoiding premature drill, 167–168

calculators in, 108
deciding to use, 183
as homework, 70
individualization of drills, 168, 183
instructional software and, 115, 254, 256
new definitions of, 67
outcomes of, 67–69
in remediation with upper-grade students, 184
as strategy for mastery of basic facts, 165, 166, 167–168, 183–184
Driscol, M., 291–292
Dynamic geometry software, 113, 365, 402, 425, 426–427, 429–430, 442

Each Orange Had 8 Slices (Giganti), 162
Early number concepts, 120–124
counting, 122, 172–173
counting on and counting back, 123–124
numeral writing and recognition, 122–123
relationships of *more*, *less*, and *same*, 121–122, 136
technology and, 123
Early number sense, 124–141
anchors or "benchmarks" of 5 and 10, 125, 127–129
children's literature and, 138–139
defined, 124
extensions to early mental mathematics, 140–141
one and two more, one and two less, 125, 126–127, 168–169
part-part-whole relationships, 125, 129–134
real world and, 137–140
relationships among numbers 1 through 10, 124–135
relationships among numbers 10 to 20, 135–137
spatial relationships, 125–126
technology and, 132–133
Economopoulos, K., 21, 60
Edwards, L. D., 76
Edwards, T. G., 491
EdWeb Home Page, 118
Effective teaching
nature of, 34
strategies for, 34
8,000 Stones (Wolkstein), 405
Eisenhower National Clearinghouse, 118
Elapsed time, 392
Ellett, K., 215
Elliott, P. C., 117
Empson, S., 163, 186
Empty number line, 221–222
Engaging students, in problem solving, 47
English language learners (ELL), 100–102
electronic manipulatives and, 112
planning considerations for, 67
strategies for teaching mathematics to, 101–102

Enrichment, for mathematically promising students, 104
Environment
creating mathematical, 34
for doing mathematics, 14, 20
shifts in classroom, 5–6
Equal-group problems, 152–153
EQUALS and Family Math, 118
Equal sign, meaning of, 260–262
Equations
equal sign, meaning of, 260–262
linear, 288–289, 290
to represent functions, 278–280
variables in solving, 263–265
Equity
cultural and linguistic, 96, 99–102
gender, 102–103
teaching for, 65–66
Equity Principle (NCTM), 2–3, 51, 66
Equity Standard (NCTM), 79
Equivalent fractions, 305–306, 308–313, 370–371
Equivalent ratios, 358–359
e-Standards (NCTM), 64, 113, 119, 203–204, 419, 429, 434–435, 438
Estimation, 44, 137
with decimals, 256–257, 346–349
with fractions, 256–257, 306–308, 321–322, 326
large number, 213
in measurement process, 246, 378, 397–398
with percents, 256–257, 345–346
tips for teaching, 398
with whole numbers. *See* Computational estimation
Ethnomathematics, 100
eTools, 132–133, 192, 236
Evaluation
defined, 79
of programs, 80
of student achievement, 79
Events, 483–485, 489
Everybody Counts (MSEB), 13
Expectations, of teachers, 42–43, 56–57, 66
Experimental probability, 480–481, 489
Experiments, with functions, 286
Explanations, student, in problem solving, 47, 56
Exponents, 492–497
children's literature and, 507–508
negative, 495–496
in scientific notation, 494–495
in very large numbers, 494–495
in very small numbers, 497
Extensions, in problem solving, 46

Factor-of-change method of solving proportions, 367
Factors, 152, 155, 325–326
Fair-sharing problems, 152–153
Fennema, E., 60, 163, 186
Ferrini-Mundy, J., 9

Figure This!, 158
Findell, C. R., 292, 450
Fitzgerald, W., 508
Five-frames, 127–129
Fives facts, 178
Fizz & Martina series (Tom Snyder Productions), 114, 150, 158, 256
Flexible strategies, 226, 247
Flips, 431–432
Flores, A., 314
Foletta, G. M., 451
Formulas, 398–404, 404
for area of parallelograms triangles, and trapezoids, 399–402
for circles, 402
difficulties of, 399
functions from, 282–284
for volume, 402–404
Fosnot, C. T., 21, 141, 163–164, 243
Four-point rubric, 82–83
Fraction computation, 316–331
addition, 317–322
approximation, 340–341
connections with decimals, 333–343
division, 326–331, 504
estimation, 256–257, 306–308, 321–322, 326
multiplication, 312, 322–326
number sense and, 303–308, 316–317
subtraction, 317–322
technology and, 301, 302–303, 312–313, 331, 337
traditional algorithms in, 311–313, 316–317, 319–321, 324–326, 329–331
Fraction Operations (Tenth Planet), 331
Fractions, 293–313. *See also* Fraction computation
addition of, 317–322
children's literature and, 313
division of, 326–331
equivalent fractions, 305–306, 308–313, 370–371
improper, 300–301
as indicated division, 504
language of, 295, 297–298
mixed numbers, 300–301, 321
models for, 295–297, 311–313
number sense and, 303–308, 316–317
percents and, 344
as rational numbers, 504–505
sharing tasks and, 294–295, 297–298
symbols for, 298–303
technology and, 301, 302–303, 312–313, 331, 337
Franke, M. L., 163, 186, 291
Franklin, K., 164
Friel, S., 292
Frog and Toad Are Friends (Lobal), 472
Front-end methods, for computational estimation, 251
Frykholm, J., 450
Fulton, B. S., 292
Function graphers, 114

Functions and functional
relationships, 271–289, 471
contextual representations of,
277, 280
equations to represent, 278–280
experiments with, 286
functions, defined, 275
generalizations about, 287–289
graphical representations of,
278, 280, 287–289
language expressions for,
277–278
maximum/minimum problem,
284–285
measurement and, 284
proportional situations,
282–284
in real-world situations,
281–282
from scatter plot data,
285–286
table representations of, 277,
280
technology and, 280–281, 282
Fuson, K. C., 60, 141

Games, 63–64, 122–124
Gardella, T., 508–509
Gates, J., 94
Gator Pie (Mathews), 313
Gavin, M. K., 450
Gender equity
causes of inequity, 102–103
possible causes of inequity,
102–103
remedies for inequity, 103
Generalizations
in algebraic reasoning,
260–265
about functions, 287–289
in problem solving, 45
Geometer's Sketchpad, The (Key
Curriculum Press), 365, 402,
425, 426, 429–430, 442
Geometry, 407–450
analysis in, 410–411, 413–414,
420–427, 433–435, 440–442,
445–447
assessment in, 449–450
classroom strategies for,
413–414
content of, 408
development of thinking in,
408–414
goals of, 408
location in, 408, 437–443
measurement and, 399–404
proportional reasoning and, 355
spatial sense, 408, 449
task selection in, 413
technology in, 419, 438–440,
442, 445–446
tool software for, 114, 419, 425,
426–427, 429–430
transformations in, 408,
431–437
van Hiele levels of thought,
409–450
Geometry Inventor (Riverdeep
Interactive Learning), 402,
426
Geometry standard, 4, 446
Giant journal, 88
Glanfield, F., 94
Glass, B., 450

Grading, 82, 92–93
alignment in, 93
multidimensional reporting
system, 93
myth of, 92
values in, 92–93
Graeber, A. O., 508
Grandau, L., 141
Graph Club, The (Tom Snyder
Productions), 459, 471
Graphical representations, 138,
364–365, 458–464
bar graphs, 459–460
circle graphs, 463–464
cluster graphs, 459
continuous data graphs,
461–463
of functions, 278, 280, 287–289
of patterns, 274–275
stem-and-leaf plots, 460–461
tally charts, 459–460
Graphing calculators, 109–111,
114, 472
advantages of using, 109–110
electronic data collection with,
110–111
Gravemeijer, K., 474
Greenes, C. E., 292, 450
Grids, 19, 386
Griffin, S., 141
Griffith, L. K., 117
Group discussion, engaging all
class members in, 47
Groupings in mathematics, place-
value development, 188–197
Groupings of students
heterogeneous, 65
homogeneous, 96
GUESS boxes, 254
Guessing, 57, 246

Harper, S. R., 474
Hartman, C., 292
Height, measurement of, 399
Hensien, S. M., 491
Heterogeneous groupings, 65
Hexahedron, 448
Hiebert, J., 9–10, 60
High-stakes testing, 90–92
improving performance in,
90–92
teaching state-mandated
standards, 90–92
Hill, K. M., 215
Hillman, S. L., 117
Hints, in problem solving, 45
Hispanics. *See* Cultural and
linguistic diversity
Histograms, 462
Hitchings, 94
Holtzman, C., 258
Home Page for New Math
Teachers, 118
Homework, 70
drill as, 70
practice as, 70
Homogeneous grouping, 96
Hope, J., 351
How Big Is a Foot? (Myller), 404
How Many Snails? (Giganti), 162
How to Count Like a Martian (St.
John), 213
Huinker, D., 332
Human, P., 60
Humphreys, C., 59

Hundreds chart, 201–204,
207–208, 270
Hypotheses, in problem solving,
48

Icosahedron, 448
If You Hopped Like a Frog
(Schwartz), 371–372
Illuminations web site (NCTM),
10, 111, 113, 115, 118, 119,
446–447
Improper fractions, 300–301
Inchworm and a Half (Pinczes), 405
Incredible Comparisons (Ash),
472–473
Independent events, 484–485, 489
Inferences Standard (NCTM), 79
Informal deduction, in geometry,
411, 414, 427–431, 435–437,
442–443, 447–449
Informal units, 377
Instructional scaffolding, 30, 65
Instructional software, 114–116,
132–133
concept instruction, 114
drill, 115, 254, 256
problem solving, 114
selecting and using, 115–116
Instructional strategies
for effective teaching, 34
in geometry, 413
modifications for intellectual
disabilities, 98–99
problem-analysis skills, 57
problem solving. *See* Problem
solving
for teaching mathematics to
English language learners,
101–102
Instrumental understanding, 25
Integers, 497–504
children's literature and,
507–508
operations with, 498–499
problem-solving approach for,
499–504
Integrative deficits, adaptations
for, 98
Intellectual disabilities, 98–99
modifications in curriculum, 99
modifications in instruction,
98–99
Internalization, 29–30
International standards, 7
Internet resources
applets, 111, 116, 119, 204, 236,
282, 419, 439–440
professional information, 116,
118–119
for selecting software, 115
for teachers, 118–119
Interviews. *See* Diagnostic
interviews
In the Next Three Seconds
(Morgan), 507–508
Invented strategies
activities for flexible thinking,
226
for addition, 222–223, 224
benefits of, 219
contextual problems and, 221
for division, 236–238
estimations for, 248–249
mental computation strategy,
219–220

for multiplication, 228–234
nature of, 218
recording student processes,
221–222, 227–228, 234–235,
239
for subtraction, 222–226
three-part lesson format and,
221
traditional algorithms versus,
218–219
in whole-number computation,
218–226, 228–234, 236–238
*Investigations in Number, Data, and
Space*, 8, 51, 204, 349
Grade 1: Number Games and
Story Problems, 194–195,
196
Grade 1: Quilt Squares and
Block Towns, 417
Grade 2: Coins, Coupons, and
Combinations, 150, 151
Grade 3: From Paces to Feet,
382, 383
Grade 3: Things That Come in
Groups, 182
Grade 4: Different Shapes,
Equal Pieces, 307
Grade 4: Packages and Groups,
231–233
Grade 5: Building on Numbers
You Know, 249–250
Grade 5: Data, 454, 455
Grade 5: Patterns of Change,
275, 276
Irrational numbers, 505, 506
Irwin, K. C., 351
*Is a Blue Whale the Biggest Thing
There Is?* (Wells), 242

Jim and the Beanstalk (Briggs), 404
Johnson, A., 450
Johnson, M. L., 243
Join problems, 144
Jones, G. A., 215, 491
Joram, E., 292
Journals, 87–89
for early learners, 88–89
nature of, 87
Jung, W. S., 105

Kamii, C., 186, 332
Kari, A. R., 215
Kehle, P. E., 94
Kelly, C., 508–509
Key word strategy, 160
Kid Pix (Riverdeep Interactive
Learning), 150
Kieren, T., 332
Kim, O., 314
King's Commissioners, The
(Friedman), 213
Kitchen, R., 94
Klabunde, D. A., 406
Klein, E., 314
Koester, B. A., 450
Kouba, V. L., 164

Lambdin, D. V., 94
Lamon, S. J., 373
Lampert, M., 21, 35
Landmark numbers, 204–205
Langrall, C. W., 373, 491
Language
base-ten, 198–199
of doing mathematics, 13–14

English language learners
(ELL), 67, 100–102, 112
of estimation, 246
of fractions, 295, 297–298
for functions, 277–278
names for numbers, 198–201
native, in teaching English
language learners (ELL), 101
Lappan, G., 508
Large numbers
conceptualizing, 212–213
estimating, 213
law of, 481–483, 489
place-value development for,
211–213
whole-number computation
with, 223, 224, 226
Latinos. *See* Cultural and
linguistic diversity
Law of large numbers, 481–483
Lawrence, A., 451, 491
Lawrence, K., 94
Learning classification schemes,
456
Learning disabilities. *See* Specific
learning disabilities
Learning Principle (NCTM), 3,
28
Learning Standard (NCTM),
78–79
Least-squares regression line,
470–471
Leatham, K. R., 94
Lee, H., 105
Lehrer, R., 406
Leinwand, S., 94
Length
fractions and, 295–297,
380–381
measuring, 378–382
units of, 379–380
Lesson format
for problem solving, 41–48,
61–64, 72–75
textbook, 71
Lester, F. K., 60
Leutzinger, L. P., 186
Levi, L., 163, 186, 291
Linear equations, 288–289, 290
Linear functions, 288–289
Line graphs, 462–463
Line plots, 461–462
Line symmetry, 432–433
Listening
diversity of students and, 66–67
in problem solving, 45, 47–48,
58–59
Lists, in problem solving, 58
Literature. *See* Children's
literature
Litton, N., 76
Litwiller, B., 373
Lo, J., 373
Location, in geometry, 408,
437–443
Logic problems, 114
Logo, 439–440
Lombard, B., 292
Long-term memory deficits,
adaptations for, 97–98
Lotteries (Weiss), 490

Majka, M., 94
Make-ten facts, 170–172
Making Sense (Hiebert et al.), 30

Malloy, C. E., 21, 450
Malotka, C. M., 117
Manchester, P., 474
Manipulatives
electronic, 111–112, 119, 123,
156, 192, 203–204, 236,
312–313, 331, 419
tests and, 90
Mann, R. L., 292
Man Who Counted, The (Tahan),
313
Martinie, S. L., 351
Masalski, W. J., 117
Mason, R., 332
Mass
measuring, 389–390
units of, 390
Mastery of basic facts, 165–185
addition facts, 168–174
approaches to, 165–168
division facts, 181–183
drill in, 183–184
multiplication facts, 177–181
reasoning skills and, 185
remediation with upper-grade
students, 184–185
subtraction facts, 174–177
timed tests in, 184
Materials, attribute, 454–457
Math Archives: K-12 Internet
sites, 118
Math Blaster (Knowledge
Adventure), 183, 256
Math Curse (Scieska and Smith),
508
Mathematical conventions, in
problem solving, 55
Mathematically promising
students, 46, 103–104. *See*
Mathematically promising
students
depth for, 104
identifying, 103–104
Mathematically Sane, 118
Mathematical power, 39
Mathematician's rule, 263
Mathematics Standard (NCTM),
78
*Mathematics Teaching in the Middle
School* (journal), 52
Math Forum, The (web site), 118
MathKeys, 114
Math Munchers Deluxe (Riverdeep
Interactive Learning), 183,
342
Maximum/minimum problem,
284–285
McClain, K., 474
McGehee, J., 117
McIntosh, A., 351
Mean, 464–467
balance point concept of,
466–467
changes in, 467–469
leveling concept of, 465–466
Measurement, 137, 328–329,
374–405
of angles, 392–394
approximation in, 378
of area, 382–387, 399–402
assessment of, 380, 391
of capacity, 387–389,
402–404
children's literature and,
404–405

comparisons in, 376, 378–379,
382–384, 387–388, 389–390,
392
decimal with, 337
developing concepts and skills
in, 376–378
estimation in, 246, 378,
397–398
formulas for, 399–404
functions and, 284
informal units in, 377
instruments in, 377, 381–382,
389, 390–391, 392–394
of length, 378–382
of mass, 389–390
meaning and process of, 375–376
models for fractions, 295–297
proportional reasoning and,
363–365
standard units in, 377–378,
394–397, 404
technology and, 402
of time, 390–392
of volume, 387–389, 402–404
of weight, 389–390
Measurement problems, 152, 153
Measurement standard, 4, 378
Measures of central tendency,
464–467
Measuring cups, 389
Median, 464, 468
Median-median lines, 470–471
Median point, 470–471
MegaMath!, 118
Memory, relational understanding
and, 26–27
Memory deficits, adaptations for,
97–98
Mental computation, 44, 140–141,
219–220. *See also*
Computational estimation
Merk, M., 94
Metacognition
developing habit of, 58
nature of, 58
Metric system, 396
Mewborn, D., 94
Mighty Math (Riverdeep
Interactive Learning), 419
Million Fish . . . More or Less, A
(McKissack), 213–214
Minilessons, 63
Missing-factor strategies, in
division, 237–238
Missing-part activities, 131–133,
176–177
Mixed numbers, 300–301, 321
Mode, 464
Model-based problems. *See also*
Direct modeling
in addition, 147–148, 226
in algebra, 290
in division, 155, 238–239
for fractions, 295–297, 311–313
models, defined, 290
in multiplication, 155, 161,
233–234
for percents, 344
for place value, 191–192
in subtraction, 148, 227
Models, 17, 30–34
classroom use of, 32–33
examples of, 31–32
expanding idea of, 33
for fractions, 295–297, 311–313

incorrect use of, 33–34
instructional software and, 113
of integer operations, 498–499
for logico-mathematical
concepts, 30–31, 34
for mathematical concepts, 31
for measurement, 376–377
for place-value development,
191–192
in problem solving, 57
of signed quantities, 497–498
Modifications, for diversity, 65–66
Mogill, A. T., 215
Moira's Birthday (Munsch), 213
Mokros, J., 21, 60
Money, 209–211
coin recognition and values,
209–210
decimal with, 337
making change, 210–211
More Than One (Hoban), 162
Morrow, L., 243
Multicultural mathematics, 100
Multiple entry points, 39, 40–41,
51, 64
Multiplicand, 152
Multiplication, 152–162
computational estimation in,
251, 252–253
contextual problems, 154,
158–160
of decimals, 348
distributive property, 158
of fractions, 312, 322–326
invented strategies for, 228–234
model-based problems, 155,
161, 233–234
multiplicative identity, 312
order property, 157
in problem-solving approach
with integers, 502–503
problem structures, 152–153
proportional reasoning and,
355–358
by single-digit multiplier,
230–231, 234–235
strategies for mastery of facts,
177–181
symbolism in, 154
traditional algorithms for,
234–236, 324–326
by two-digit multiplier,
231–234, 235–236
using multiples of 10 and 100,
231
zero and one in, 157–158, 178
Multiplicative comparison
problems, 152, 153
Multipliers, 152
single-digit, 230–231, 234–235
two-digit, 231–234, 235–236
Murray, H., 60
My Little Sister Ate One Hare
(Grossman), 490

Names for numbers
in place-value development,
198–201
three-digit, 199
two-digit, 198–199
National Assessment of
Educational Progress
(NAEP), 6–7, 11, 27, 102,
108, 293, 304, 306, 340, 343,
377, 408

National Council of Teachers of
    Mathematics (NCTM), 1–9,
    243, 406
  *Assessment Standards for School
    Mathematics*, 2, 6, 78–80
  *Curriculum and Evaluation
    Standards for School
    Mathematics*, 2, 78
  e-Standards, 64, 113, 119,
    203–204, 419, 429, 434–435,
    438
  "Every Child" statement, 95
  growth and, 8–9
  Illuminations web site, 10, 111,
    113, 115, 118, 119, 446–447
  journals, 52
  Navigations series, 52, 111, 292
  News Bulletin, 116
  other influences and pressures
    on reform, 6–8
  *Principles and Standards for
    School Mathematics*, 1–5, 13,
    37, 39, 78, 99–100, 107, 111,
    245, 449–450
  *Professional Standards for
    Teaching Mathematics*, 2, 5–6
  Task Force on the
    Mathematically Promising,
    103–104
  web site, 5, 11, 118, 312
National Library of Virtual
    Manipulatives (NLVM), 119,
    156, 236, 312–313, 331, 419
National Research Council, 10
National Science Foundation
    (NSF), 8, 91–92
Native Americans. *See* Cultural
    and linguistic diversity
Native language, in teaching
    English language learners
    (ELL), 101
Navigations series (NCTM), 52,
    111, 292
Near-double relationships,
    136–137, 170
Negative exponents, 495–496
Negative numbers, 495–496, 498
Nelson, L. T., 351
New Standards Project, 82–83
Nines in multiplication, 178–179
Nitabach, E., 406
NLVM (National Library of
    Virtual Manipulatives), 119,
    156, 236, 312–313, 331, 449
No Child Left Behind Act (2001),
    1, 7, 90–92
Nohda, N., 258
Notation
    calculators and, 493–494
    place-value, 190, 199
    scientific, 494–495
Number and operations standard,
    4, 124, 226
Number concepts
    early, 26
    in mastery of basic facts, 166
    models for, 30–34
    problem solving examples,
      39–40
    relational understanding and,
      27
Number Devil, The
    (Enzensberger), 507
Number relationships, 124–137
    for addition, 206–209

anchoring numbers to 5 and 10,
    125, 127–129
double and near-double
    relationships, 136–137,
    169–170, 172, 177, 180
extending *more* and *less*
    relationships, 136
multidigit numbers, 201–209
one and two more, one and two
    less, 125, 126–127
part-part-whole relationships,
    125, 129–134
pre-place-value relationship
    with 10, 136
searching for, 272–273
spatial, 125–126
for subtraction, 206–209
technology and, 132–133
Number sense
    decimal, 338–343
    early. *See* Early number sense
    fraction, 303–308, 316–317
    real-world ideas and, 137–140
    rounding, 251–253
Number system, 266–270
Numerals, recognition and
    writing of, 122–123
Numerators, 299–300

Observation, 84–86, 241
    anecdotal notes in, 85
    checklists for, 85–86
    rubrics in, 85
Octahedron, 448
Odd-even relationships, 267–268
Olivier, A., 60
One and two more, one and two
    less, 125, 126–127
One-more-than and two-more-
    than facts, 168–169
Open-ended problem solving,
    104
Openness Standard (NCTM), 79
Open sentences, in algebraic
    reasoning, 261
Operations in mathematics,
    143–162
    addition. *See* Addition
    children's literature and, 162
    division. *See* Division
    with integers, 498–499
    in mastery of basic facts,
      165–166
    multiplication. *See*
      Multiplication
    subtraction. *See* Subtraction
Order property
    in addition, 149–150
    in multiplication, 157
Owens, D. T., 352

Parallel lines, 290
Parallelograms
    area of, 399–401
    nature of, 404
Partial product, 234–235
Partition concept, 326–328
Partitioning strategies, 230–231
Partition problems, 152–153, 153
Part-part-whole relationships,
    125, 129–134
    activities, 130–131
    basic ingredients, 130
    problems in, 145
    technology and, 132–133

Parts of numbers
    activities for flexible thinking,
      226
    parts-and-whole-tasks, 301–303
Part-to-part ratios, 354
Part-to-whole ratios, 354
Patterned set recognition,
    125–126
Pattern (Pluckrose), 289
Patterns
    graphing, 274–275
    multidigit numbers and,
      201–209
    in problem solving, 57
    relationships in, 270–275
    repeating, 268–270
    sequences, 271–275
Percents, 343–346
    children's literature and,
      349–350
    computational estimation with,
      256–257, 345–346
    fractions and, 344
    hundredths in, 343
    proportional reasoning and,
      370–371
    realistic problems with, 344–346
Perceptual deficits, adaptations
    for, 97
Performance assessment, 80–81.
    See also Assessment
Performance indicators, 83–84
Perimeter, 386–387
Perlwitz, M. D., 332
Perpendicular lines, 290
Personal digital assistants (PDAs),
    110–111
Phantom Tollbooth, The (Juster),
    350, 472, 507
Phillips, E., 508–509
Physical models, 17
Piaget, Jean, 2, 22, 23, 29, 30
Pie charts, 464
Place-value development,
    187–214. *See also* Whole-
    number computation
    activities for flexible thinking,
      226
    assessment in, 193–194, 209
    base-ten fraction models,
      334–335
    base-ten groupings, 188–197
    basic ideas in, 188–190
    children's literature and,
      213–214
    counting in, 188–189
    extension to decimals, 335–337
    grouping in, 188–197
    hundreds chart, 201–204,
      207–208, 270
    integrating computation with,
      221
    integration of groupings in,
      189–190
    models for place value, 191–192
    numbers beyond 1000, 211–213
    oral names for numbers in,
      198–201
    place-value notation in, 190,
      199
    pre-base-10 concepts, 136, 188
    symbols in, 199–201, 207
    technology in, 192, 203–204,
      215
    thousands chart, 203

Planning
    for all students, 68
    for English language learners
      (ELL), 67
    three-part lesson format, 61–64
Platonic solids, 448–449
Point symmetry, 433
Polyhedron, 448
Practice. *See* Drill and practice
Practice tests, 91–92
Praise, in problem solving, 47–48,
    58
Preston, R. V., 94, 450
Prime Time Math, 114
*Principles and Standards for School
    Mathematics* (NCTM), 1–5,
    37, 39, 78, 99–100, 107, 111,
    245, 449–450
    content standards in, 4, 124
    drills and, 13
    principles in, 2–3, 28, 78–80
    process standards in, 5–6
Prisms, 403
Probability, 475–490. *See also* Data
    analysis and probability
    standard
    assessment issues, 489
    children's literature and,
      472–473, 489–490
    continuum for, 476–479
    developing concepts of,
      476–479
    law of large numbers, 481–483
    simulations and, 486–489
    technology and, 113, 483,
      488–489
    theoretical versus experimental,
      479–483, 489
Probability software, 113, 483,
    488–489
Problem Centered Mathematics
    Project (PCMP), 218n
Problem solving, 37–59, 61–75
    addition and, 144–146, 499–502
    analytic scale for, 82–83
    assessment of, 80
    calculators in. *See* Calculators
    children's literature and, 51–52
    description of tasks or
      problems, 37–38
    designing and selecting tasks
      for, 48–53
    differentiated tasks in, 65
    examples of problem-based
      tasks, 39–41
    fractions and, 317
    frequently asked questions and,
      56–57
    goals of, 57–59
    instructional software and, 114
    listening in, 45, 47–48, 58–59
    multiple entry points for, 39,
      40–41, 51, 64
    open-ended, 104
    operations in, 499–504. *See also*
      Addition; Division;
      Multiplication; Subtraction
    as principal instructional
      strategy, 37–39
    problem, defined, 37
    relational understanding and,
      27
    shift in thinking about, 38–39
    task selection guide, 52–53
    teaching about, 57–59

teaching tips and questions for, 53–57
three-part lesson format, 41–48, 61–64, 72–75
value of teaching with problems, 39
worthwhile tasks and, 37–38, 48–53
Problem solving standard, 4, 5, 80
Procedural mathematics, 27
assessment of, 80, 93
defined, 28
examples of problem-based tasks in, 40–41
interaction with conceptual mathematics, 28
Process standards (NCTM), 5–6
Product, 152
Product-of-measures problems, 161–162
Professional Standards for Teaching Mathematics (NCTM), 2
shifts in classroom environment, 5–6
teaching standards, 6
Proportional models, 191
Proportional reasoning, 353–372, 435
activities to develop, 357–366, 369–370
additive, 355–357
characteristics of, 355
children and, 355
children's literature and, 371–372
functions in, 282–284
multiplicative, 355–358
percent problems in, 370–371
proportions in, 355, 366–370
ratios in, 355, 358–359, 366–367
solving proportions, 366–370
Protractor, 393–394
Pugalee, D. K., 450
Pumala, V. A., 406
Putt, I. J., 215
Pyramids, volume of, 403–404
Pythagorean relationship, 429, 442–443, 448

Quantity estimation, 246
Quartiles, 468

Rachlin, S., 292
Range, 468
Rate of change, 287–288
Rate problems, 152–153
Rates, as ratios, 354
Rathnell, E. C., 186
Rational numbers, 504–505, 506–507
Ratios, 26, 27
within and between, 366–367
comparing, 359–361, 366
defined, 354
equivalent, 358–359
ratio tables, 361–363
types of, 354
Real numbers, 505–508
Real-world situations
computational estimation in, 246
functions in, 281–282
number sense and, 137–140
percents in, 344–346
place value in, 209–211

Reasoning and proof standard, 4, 5, 80
Rectangles, area of, 399–401
Recursive relationships, 272
Reeves, C. A., 76, 509
Reeves, R., 76
Reflective thinking, 23, 29, 32, 34
Region models, for fractions, 295
Reinhart, S. C., 60
Relational understanding, 25, 26–28, 261–262
Remainders, in division, 154–155
Renne, C. G., 451
Repeated-addition problems, 152–153
Repeated-subtraction problems, 152–153
Repeating patterns, 268–270
Representations
equivalent, in place-value development, 197
useful, in invented strategies for multiplication, 229–230
Representation standard, 4, 5
Representing Fractions (Sunburst), 302–303
Reys, B. J., 258, 314, 351
Reys, R. E., 258, 351
Rich, B. S., 215
Richardson, K., 141–142, 215
Richardson, M. G., 491
Rigor, in geometry, 412
Robert, M., 106
Roots, 505–507
Rotational symmetry, 432–433
Rotations, 432–433
Rote learning, 24
Rounding, 251–253
Rowan, T. E., 60
Rubrics, 82–84
analytic scale, 82–83
four-point scale, 82–83
nature of, 82
observation, 85
performance indicators, 83–84
simple, 82–83
student involvement with, 84
Rulers, 381–382
Russell, S. J., 21, 60, 164, 215, 243

St. Marie, J., 450
Sample space, 483–484, 489
Scaffolding, 30, 65
Scales, 390
Scaling, with ratio tables, 361–363, 366
Scatter plots, 469–471
best-fit lines, 470
functions from, 285–286
Schaeffer, R., 473–474
Schifter, D., 21, 35, 164, 215, 292
Scientific concepts, 29–30
Scientific notation, 494–495
Secada, W. G., 106
Second language learners, 67, 100–102
Self-assessment, 89–90
attitude inventories in, 89–90
nature of, 89–90
Self-generativity, relational understanding and, 27
Semantic forms of equations, 145–146
Separate problems, 144–145
Sequences, 271–275

Set models, for fractions, 297
Shape of data, 458
Shapes. *See also names of specific shapes*
constructing and dissecting, 416–420, 425–426
definitions and proofs, 427–429
Pythagorean relationship, 429, 442–443, 448
sorting and classifying, 414–416, 423–425
three-dimensional, 419–420, 422–423
two-dimensional, 421–422
Shape Up (Sunburst), 446
Sharing tasks, fractions and, 294–295, 297–298
Shaughnessy, J. M., 491
Sheffield, L. J., 106, 450
Shodor Interactive, 119
Short-term memory deficits, adaptations for, 97–98
Silbey, R., 76
Simulations, 486–489
Sinelli, A. M., 450
Skip counting, 202
Slides, 431–432
Slope, 288–289, 443
Slovin, H., 450
Small, M., 292, 450
Sociocultural theory of learning, 29–30, 34
Software, 111–114
instructional, 114–116, 132–133, 254, 256
probability, 113, 483, 488–489
selecting and using, 115–116
tool, 111–114
Spatial relationships, 125–126
Spatial sense, 408, 449
Special children, problem solving and, 59
Specific learning disabilities, 96–98
adaptations for, 97–98
perspective on, 97
Spontaneous concepts, 29–30
Spreadsheets, 113–114, 364
Sproule, S., 117–118
Standard units, 377–378, 394–397, 404
choosing appropriate, 396
familiarity with, 395–396
important, 396–397
State-mandated standards, 90–91
State standards, 7–8
Stem-and-leaf plots, 460–461
Stenmark, J. K., 94
Stewart, J., 508–509
Story problems. *See* Contextual problems
Strategies for computational estimation, 250–254
compatible numbers, 253–254
front-end methods, 251
rounding methods, 251–253
Strategies for mastery of basic facts, 165–185
addition, 168–174
development of, 166–167
division, 181–183
drill-based, 165–166, 167–168, 183–184
fact remediation with upper-grade students, 184–185

multiplication, 177–181
selection or retrieval of, 165–166, 166–167, 183–184
subtraction, 174–177
timed tests, 184
Strategies for problem solving, 57–58
Structural set, 454
Stump, S., 314
Subdivisions, 397
Subitizing, 125–126
Subtraction, 144–151
comparison models, 149
computational estimation in, 251, 252
contextual problems, 146–147
of decimals, 347–348
of fractions, 317–322
invented strategies for, 222–226
model-based problems, 148, 227
number relationships for, 206–209
in problem-solving approach with integers, 499–502
problem structures, 144–146
strategies for mastery of basic facts, 174–177
symbolism in, 147
take-away, 225–226
technology and, 150
as think-addition, 148–149, 174, 233
traditional algorithms for, 227–228, 319–321
zero property, 150, 227
Success
building on, 184–185
in problem solving, 59
Suggestions, in problem solving, 46, 55
Sugiyama, P. A., 141
Summarizing, in problem solving, 38
Sums greater than 10, 174–177
Sums to 10, 174
Super, D. B., 352
Supporting Ten-Structured Thinking (STST), 218n
Swafford, J., 373
Symbolism
in addition, 147
calculators and notation, 493–494
in division, 154, 241
electronic manipulatives and, 112
for fractions, 298–303
models and, 33
in multiplication, 154
in place-value development, 199–201, 207
in subtraction, 147
Symmetry
axis of, 433
line, 432–433
point, 433
rotational, 432–433

Tables
in problem solving, 57
representations of functions, 277, 280
Tabletop, Jr. (Sunburst), 457
Take-away subtraction, 225–226

Tally charts, 459–460
Tangrams, 384
Tape measures, 381–382
Tarr, J. E., 491
Tasks
  for appropriate assessment, 81–82
  for problem solving, 39–41, 48–53, 62, 65
  selection of geometry, 413
Teachers
  expectations for students, 42–43, 56–57, 66
  gender issues and, 102–103
  Internet resources for. *See* Internet resources
  role in problem solving, 41–48
Teacher's editions, 71
Teachers of English to Speakers of Other Languages (TESOL), 100
Teaching Children Mathematics (journal), 52
Teaching Principle (NCTM), 3, 51
Teaching standards, 6
Technology in mathematics, 107–116
  addition and subtraction problems, 150
  calculators. *See* Calculators
  computational estimation and, 254, 256
  computers and software, 111–114
  data analysis and probability standard, 457, 458–459, 471–472
  decimals and, 342
  drill and practice, 183
  early number concepts, 123
  early number sense, 132–133
  fractions and, 301, 302–303, 312–313, 331, 337
  functions and, 280–281, 282
  geometry and, 419, 438–440, 442, 445–446
  Internet resources. *See* Internet resources
  measurement and, 402
  multiplication and division problems, 158
  place-value development, 192, 203–204, 215
  whole-number computation, 236
Technology Principle (NCTM), 3
Ten-frames, 127–129, 173–174
Teppo, A. R., 10
Tessellations, in geometry, 420, 435
Testing of ideas, in problem solving, 45–46
Tests, 90–92
  test-taking strategies, 92
  timed, 184
Tetrahedron, 448
Textbooks
  adapting, 48–51
  development of, 70–71

in problem-based classroom, 48–51, 70–71
  standards-based, 51
  suggestions for using, 71
  in task design and selection, 48–53
  teacher's editions, 71
  traditional, 48–51
  two-page lesson format, 71
Theoretical probability, 480, 489
Think-addition, subtraction as, 148–149, 174, 223
Thinking with Numbers (Rathmell et al.), 167
Think-pair-share approach, 42–43, 66
Third International Mathematics and Science Study (TIMSS/TIMSS-R), 7, 11, 70
Thompson, T., 117–118
Thornton, C. A., 215, 491
Thousands chart, 203
3D Geoshapes, 419–420
329th Friend, The (Sharmat), 257
Three-dimensional shapes, 419–420, 422–423
Three-part lesson format, 41–48, 61–64
  after phase, 41, 46–48, 63
  before phase, 41–44, 62
  during phase, 41, 44–46, 63
  to encourage invented strategy use, 221
  planning, 61–64, 67, 68
  sample lesson plans, 63, 72–75
  variations on, 63–64
Time
  elapsed, 392
  measurement of, 390–392
Timed tests, 184
Tomback, J., 292
Tool software, 111–114
  electronic manipulatives, 111–112, 123
  function graphers, 114
  geometry, 114, 419, 425, 426–427, 429–430
  probability and data analysis, 113–114, 483, 488–489
  selecting and using, 115–116
Tracking
  expectations and, 96
  negative effects of, 96
Traditional algorithms
  for addition, 226–228, 319–321
  for division, 238–241, 329–331
  for fractions, 311–313, 316–317, 319–321, 324–326, 329–331
  invented strategies versus, 218–219
  for multiplication, 234–236, 324–326
  for proportions, 368–369
  for subtraction, 227–228, 319–321
  timing of use, 220, 317
Trafton, P. R., 292
Transformations, in geometry, 408, 431–437

Trapezoids
  area of, 401
  nature of, 404
Tree diagrams, 18–19
Triangles
  area of, 401
  nature of, 404
Trubow, G., 94
True/false sentences, in algebraic reasoning, 261
Turns, 431–432
Turtle Math (Clements & Meredith), 439–440
Twelve Circus Rings, The (Chwast), 257
Two-dimensional shapes, 421–422
Two Ways to Count to Ten (Dee), 139
Tzur, R., 314

Understanding in mathematics, 22–34
  checking for, 42
  computational estimation, 246
  constructivism in, 24–28
  defined, 25
  developmental approach to, 29–30, 34
  examples of, 25–26
  instrumental, 25
  relational, 25, 26–28, 261–262
  role of models in developing, 30–34
  types of mathematical knowledge, 28
Unifix cubes, electronic, 111
Unifix Software (Hickey), 123
U.S. Census Data, 119
U.S. customary system, 396
Unit fractions, 301–302
Unit perspective, 48
Unit-rate method of solving proportions, 367
University of North Carolina Mathematics and Science Education Network, 474

Values, grading and, 92–93
Van Dyke, F., 292
van Hiele levels of thought, 409–450
  characteristics of, 412–413
  Level 0: Visualization, 409–410, 413, 414–420, 431–433, 437–440, 443–449
  Level 1: Analysis, 410–411, 413–414, 420–427, 433–435, 440–442, 445–447
  Level 2: Informal deduction, 411, 414, 427–431, 435–437, 442–443, 447–449
  Level 3: Deduction, 411–412
  Level 4: Rigor, 412
  task selection and, 414
Van Zoest, L. R., 215
Variables, 262–265
  as quantities that vary, 263
  in solving equations or equalities, 263–265
  as unknowns, 263

Verbs, of doing mathematics, 13–14
Very Hungry Caterpillar, The (Carle), 139
Very large numbers, 494–495
Very small numbers, 497
Visualization, in geometry, 408, 409–410, 413, 414–420, 431–433, 437–440, 443–449
Vocabulary, for English language learners (ELL), 102
Volume
  of cylinders, 403–404
  measurement of, 387–389, 402–404
  units of, 388–389
Vygotsky, Lev, 29–30

Warrington, M. A., 332
Watanabe, T., 314, 373
Wearne, D., 60
Webb, D., 509
Weight
  measuring, 389–390
  units of, 390
Whole-number computation, 216–242. *See also* Place-value development
  assessment and, 222–223, 241
  children's literature and, 241–242
  direct modeling in, 217–218
  estimation in. *See* Computational estimation
  invented strategies in, 218–226, 228–234, 236–238
  place values in. *See* Place-value development
  technology in, 236
  traditional algorithms in, 218–219, 220, 226–228, 234–236, 238–241
Whole-number divisors, 327
Whole-number exponents, 493
Winter, M. J., 508
Workstations, 63–64
World Fact Book, The, 118
Writing, 86–90
  importance of, 53
  of journals, 87–89
  prompts and ideas for, 87–88, 89
  student self-assessment of, 89–90
  in teaching English language learners (ELL), 101
  value of, 86–87
Wyat, K. W., 451

Yeatts, K., 292

Zero property
  in addition, 150, 169
  in division, 158
  fraction number sense and, 303–304
  in multiplication, 157–158, 178
  in subtraction, 150, 227
Zome System, 419
Zone of proximal development (ZPD), 29–30